The
Radio 5 Live
Sports Yearbook
1996

Published in Great Britain by Oddball Publishing Ltd, 38 Lincoln Street, Brighton, East Sussex BN2 2UH
01273 677761

Cover design by Rob Kelland
Cover pictures by Allsport
Text design and layout by Oddball Publishing Ltd, Brighton
using QuarkXpress on Apple Mac computers
Repro by Image Setting, Brighton
Printed and bound in Great Britain by Redwood Books, Trowbridge, Wilts

A catalogue record for this book is available from the British Library

ISBN 0-9524044-1-9

Foreword

Speak to George Graham, Jeff Tarango, Chris Boardman or Eric Cantona and they'll probably tell you that 1995 is a year they want to forget.

Dominic Cork, Jonathan Edwards, Philip Walton and Frank Bruno wouldn't agree. It was a fabulous year for all four of them.

But then that's sport for you, providing another non-stop, all-action year of success and failure, adulation and disgrace.

It was a year too in which sport and politics mixed for once with heart-warming effect when president Nelson Mandela handed over the Rugby World Cup to his captain Francois Pienaar after the final against the seemingly unstoppable All Blacks.

The Radio 5 Live Sports team were in Johannesburg to describe that special moment in history and they brought you all the other major sporting events from around the world during the year (free of charge, of course).

We are delighted to bring the best of the world's sport into your home and that is why we are pleased to be associated once again with this fascinating, invaluable Yearbook.

I hope that thumbing through the pages will bring the memories - good and bad - flooding back.

Mike Lewis
Deputy Controller, Radio 5 Live

Introduction

We had hoped to make huge additions to this year's book and make is so heavy that you'd need a truss just to get it off the bookshelf. That we haven't done so is due to the continuing escalation of paper prices which would have meant a small mortgage to buy the book as well as the truss to help you carry it. Altogether, a prospect hardly likely to encourage you, our readers. So we've kept our ambition in bounds and satisfied ourselves with just an extra 48 pages, a small price increase (£1) and a certain amount of tailoring of the content. For this year's book, a few sports have moved into the 'Extras' section or fallen off all together. This is to allow us to include historical records and to concentrate more on Olympic sports as 1996 is an Olympic year. We have included as many records of major events as we could but, with the limited extra space, there are still some more records we would like to include. That must wait till next year. As ever, if you do find any mistakes, please let us know. If we don't immediately reply, don't think we've forgotten you. It's just that when we are buried in the book, we don't notice much else happening.

Our thanks begin with **Hugh Wallace**, **Anna Wallace**, **Iain Smith**, **David Smith**, **Brian Smith**, **Chris Sainty**, **Rob Partos**, **Pat Molyneux**, **Betty Maitland**, **Andy Edwards** and **Penny Dain** who have continued to support this venture in the most productive of fashions. We are pleased to see that **BBC Radio 5 Live** goes deservedly from strength to strength and we are delighted to be associated with them again.

The federations, national and international, have again poured information in our direction. We could have done a whole book on power-lifting had we been so inclined such was the detail they supplied. Mind, it compensated for our failure to catch Wally Holland in the weightlifting office. Where are you, Wally?

The Guardian, **The Daily Telegraph**, **The Times**, **L'Equipe** and **The Sun** newpapers supply us with a wealth of information and we are grateful for that. Thanks also to **Ray Spiller** and the **Association of Football Statisticians**, **Mel Watman and Peter Matthew's Athletics International**, **Baseball Briefing**, **Claude Abrahams at Boxing News**, **Richard Lockwood at the Press Association**, **The Cricketer**, **John Ward**, **Cycle Sport**, **Mark Popham at Racenews**, **Raceform**, **Regatta**, **Chantal Geoffroy at the FIM**, **Mick Cleary**, **The Canadian Ski Federation**, **WTN Sport**, **Bernard at The Geese** and everyone else who helped along the way.

Finally, my thanks to **Tom Pinfield**, who wheedled out the calendar information from the federations and **Stuart Duff**, who picked holes in everything we thought was finished - next year we'll pay you lads. To **David Luckes**, my assistant editor, as assiduous as ever, and **Rose and Will**, who tolerated the padded cell we call home for the three months it took.

Peter Nichols

Contents

To Bob and David Smith
In a perfect world, they would middle every fairway,
chip on to every green and read every borrow.
We've got a pretty good idea that's exactly what
they'll be doing now.

Review

There were moments in the sporting calendar of 1995 when money did not seem to be an issue; that wonderful Ryder Cup victory at Oakhill or the stirring Rugby World Cup Final in Johannesburg. Somehow they seem almost isolated incidents in a year when the clinking, clanking sound just got louder and louder. Rugby Union is now in the process of reinventing itself as money is paid in the hand rather than the boot. Rugby League has become a summer sport with Rupert Murdoch calling the tune. Football spent the year fending off one money-related crisis after another, the word allegation appearing almost weekly in the football writers' columns. Grobbelaar, Fashanu and Segers currently fighting allegations (that word again) that they took bribes, George Graham out of a job because Norwegian agent Rune Hauge's money found its way into his account (and back out again) and the Bosman case threatening to impoverish every club outside the Premiership.

British Athletics spent the summer bedevilled by athletes asking for more (although the athletes in question were not the poorest in the sport, but the richest) and cricket had its own bribery scandal, with players swearing on the Koran that they wouldn't do such a thing.

Snooker found itself under investigation when betting patterns suggested that rather a lot of people thought Jimmy White would beat Peter Francisco by 10-2 in the World Championship at Sheffield. Lo and behold, he did. And there were similar concerns from the bookmakers when Declan Murphy trotted up on Geoff Lewis' Jibereen on his first mount back after the serious injuries incurred in 1994.

The Football Association had the worst of times. When the *Mail on Sunday* named Graham it seemed unlikely the buck would stop there. The FA avowed to fully expose the issue of transfer bungs, but it hasn't happened. For those in charge of the sport, it's the sort of information you could do without. The European Championships arrives in June, after the 12 months just gone, they could be forgiven for wanting to concentrate on the good news.

Even if the bungs issue is only aired with further help from the media, the Bosman case will surely demand attention. The idea that the wealth of football should be redistributed in favour of the Premiership clubs is an alarming proposition. Portsmouth have already taken steps to increase their income should this come about. As well as a possible ground-share with Brighton, the Fratton Park ground has now become the first English football ground licensed to perform marriage ceremonies. We think this could have been inspired by the communal wedding ceremony of followers of the Unification Church (Moonies, if you'd rather) in the Seoul Olympic Stadium. Three thousand couples pledged their troth in the stadium, which was linked by satellite to 160 countries where more than 330,000 couples were simultaneously married.

It should be noted that newly weds of the Unification Church do not consummate their marriages for 40 days, which wouldn't do for Portsmouth supporters who are miserable enough anyway, but it would be no good at all for US Baseball fan Tim Beggy. In July, Pittsburgh Pirates baseball team announced the suspension of Beggy, their team's buchaneer mascot. Beggy had been chosen for the illustrious role of club swashbuckler following a pre-season audition, but the 23-year-old was obviously ill-equipped to handle the fame that came with it. On July 12, Beggy, from Mount Lebanon, was charged with having sex with a woman in a public swimming pool. The police, checking the South Side pool at three in the morning, ordered Beggy to buckle his swash and come quietly.

Football's problems, we should add, were not entirely due to money. Eric Cantona, we feel sure, had no financial incentive for jumping into the crowd at Palace. Though, had he known how Nike would market his misdemeanour, he might have felt inclined to premeditate it. Cantona escaped a prison sentence, but Duncan Ferguson did not. Quite what the legal difference is between a head butt and a two-footed leap into someone's chest is a matter for debate. You could argue, perhaps, that a two-footed leap is closer to the spirit of football. Anyway Cantona's sentence was commuted to training kids and Ferguson's wasn't.

Ferguson would have been a lot better off if he'd seen the report of the Psychological Association of America before launching his cranium in the direction of the Raith Rovers fullback John McStay. The PAA's scientific survey suggested that footballers who head the ball more than ten times a game had a lower IQ than other players. The report concludes that the best way to limit potential brain damage is to use the flattest part of the head and keep the neck rigid. Actually, looking at that film again, maybe Ferguson did read the report.

England lost the World Cup in 1995. Thanks to the computer analysts of Oxford University's department of engineering science we now know that, in the 1966 Final, the ball didn't cross the line when Hurst's shot in the 102nd minute bounced off the bar, and that the lovely little Azerbayan linesman, Tofik Bakhramov, got it all wrong and the Germans were right after all. Thanks, Oxford.

Back in the financial world, Football's worries with Bosman should offer a warning to Rugby Union as it stumbles into professionalism. Rugby, incidentally, has spent years trying to persuade the Inland Revenue that it should qualify for charitable status. In the brave new world, Mike Catt might have pronounced himself the first player to go pro after the IRFB pronouncement in Paris in August, but it is Rob Andrew who exemplified the change. Andrew went from "golden bollocks", as he was affectionately known, to villain in the space of a few weeks. Yet Andrew was only taking the IRFB at its word. His conscription of fellow Wasps players was inevitable given that the 120-day transfer rule (which flies in the face of a free and open sport) meant that he couldn't go straight off and play for his new club.

What Rugby Union has in its favour is a product that is thrilling, at its best, and eminently marketable. The World Cup may only involve a handful of countries - 16 nations played out the championship, but the key teams came from only six countries - yet the contest was compelling viewing and the television audience included lots of those viewers, in the higher socio-economic ratings, that advertisers so love. The victory of South Africa also added an emotional component, the rainbow nation finding a unifying force in the success of its rugby team. Nelson Mandela, incarcerated for 26 years by the very people who would have been the Springbok's fiercest supporters in years past, led the support for the national team and, as he presented the trophy, wore a number six jersey, to let everyone know exactly where his heart lay. The extraordinary magnanimity of the man had cut no ice with the students of Warwick University who, earlier in the year, had changed the name of their bar from the Nelson Mandela Bar to the Des Lynam Bar. A new ideology? Well, who knows?

The change in status of Rugby Union has given Rugby League almost too much to think about. It's hard enough when a sport has spent a hundred years espousing the nature of its traditional base only to throw everything to the winds when News International pipe their seductive tune. It harder still when the media war in Australia denudes the sport's best team in its most prestigious event (The World Cup), but then to realise that there is an open gangway to Rugby Union as well and that the traffic is no longer one-way is almost too much to handle. Jonathan Davies may well be the first to walk the open gangway in the direction of Union, but with League active in the summer and Union in the winter, it could even be a ring road with players moving back and forth with the seasons.

Horse racing never had to come to terms with the professional transition, having been all about money for the past three hundred years. Bookmakers have been part of the infrastructure for about that long, although they only came out of the closet in the sixties when betting shops were allowed in the high street. This year the law finally allowed for the fact that punters were not all sad, shadowy characters who should be hidden from the public gaze by permitting clear windows in the bookies. You still can't see anything, of course, because every betting shop in Britain is just a fug of tobacco smoke and you can't legislate against that.

Nor would Bookmakers dare to because it would lose them the few punters they have left. This year Ladbrokes announced a £12m drop in profits (£49m to £37m) largely ascribed to the effect of the National Lottery. Bookmakers, though, will always find ways of getting it back - after all, they live in the real world. Instead of investigating unusual betting patterns when Jibereen won with Declan Murphy aboard, they should have investigated the bookmaking patterns a few weeks earlier when Jibereen was backed down to 9/2 favourite in a 30-runner Newmarket handicap and finished a well-beaten 19th. The book for that race was 151.7%, which means layers would take in 51.7% more than they would pay out. At the Britannia Stakes at Royal Ascot that percentage climbed to 156.7 Such high percentages in favour of the bookies is almost indefensible, except for one thing. The National Lottery constructs a "book" of around 400%, which makes bookmakers vie with Getty in the philanthropy stakes.

For all the money in horse racing, few of the sporting practitioners (the jockeys) now make it into the country's top sporting earners. A few years back, when the major owners paid retainers to the top jockeys, the money was handsome. Eddery, retained by Khaled Abdullah, was the last of those to keep a retainer, but he falls off our list as that contract has ended. Dettori will be comfortably the highest earner in Britain with prize money (in Europe) in excess off £2.5m.

WILLIAM HILLS TOP TEN BETTING TURNOVER	
1 FA Cup	£11m
2 Rugby World Cup	£2.5m
3 England v W Indies	£1.75m
4 British Open Golf	£1.5m
5 Wimbledon	£1.3m
6 Rugby 5 Nations	£1m
7 World Snooker Ch	£1m
8 Ryder Cup	£0.9m
9 World Athletics Chs	£0.75m
10 US Masters	£0.7m
US Open	£0.7m

Even allowing for an arrangement with the Sheikhs, it's hard to see Dettori topping the million. Gary Lineker drops off of last year's list, but only through his retirement. Mind, all that media work and those adverts, would keep him right up there if he was still kicking the occasional ball. Linford Christie comes off too. A year ago, the Olympic champion had deals with Puma, Lucozade, High and Mighty and the Banana Group, only Puma and Mercedes Trucks were on board this year. They might earn him £300,000 and a fairly prolific racing schedule could net £500,000, but that still falls some way short of the million mark.

No one player has cornered the financial market this year, as Nigel Mansell and Lennox Lewis did in the past two years. The money is spread more evenly. The real shift has been the growth in earning power of British footballers based in Britain. Paul Ince has followed the path trodden by Gascoigne and Platt in recent seasons and made a small fortune by travelling to Italy, but Shearer (with a renegotiated contract), Cole and Collymore have all benefited from the money that has flowed into the Premiership clubs. As well as the now-traditional boot contracts, footballers have lots of little add-ons these days. Shearer and Platt both have books coming out soon and Platt has a queue of sponsors capitalising on the fresh-faced England captain's image.

Sam Torrance is another newcomer to the list, proving that age is no handicap. Torrance, who hit 42 in August, has hardly taken the wrong line all summer and continued to sparkle, as we went to press, with a Dunhill Cup winning performance for Scotland - and another £100,000. Hendry remains the highest paid Scot, though this year sharing the honours with Colin Montgomerie. Hendry was given a Bentley by his sponsors, Sweater Shop, when he won the world title in 1994 and that car now sits in Lord Murray's Motor Museum at Doune. This year Sweater Shop presented him with a Ferrari, but Hendry has found using it a problem. The insurance company, conscious that Snooker's boy wonder is still only 26, has set a limit on how many miles he can drive it.

If Damon Hill didn't fancy a drive in a Ferrari at the beginning of the season, he surely did when he heard how much Ferrari decided to offer Michael Schumacher for next season's contract. Hill hasn't yet climbed into the nether regions of finance and earned anything remotely close to the $25 that Schumacher will earn in 1996. The Englishman has, at least, earned more than any other Briton in 1995 with a pay cheque of around £3m. Motor racing drivers and boxers are the two categories of sportsmen who earn every penny they get; nobody risks as much.

Boxing has supplied six millionaire earners with the retiring Eubank at the head of the list. The Brighton-based boxer was bemoaning a £2.2m debt to the taxman at the beginning of 1995, but the remainder of his Sky contract could settle that. Since his retirement, Eubank seems to be spending most of his time driving around his hometown in a huge, custom-built truck signing autographs and waving to all-comers. The ring he might have retired from, the limelight we fear not. Eubank found endorsements hard to come by - as boxers often do - but the latest ring star, Naseem Hamed, has already negotiated deals with Sony Playstation, Joe Bloggs, Audi and Reebok. Only Bruno has previously had that kind of advertiser appeal.

Bruno had a good year for earnings, but that will all be eclipsed in 1996 when he puts his title on the line for whatever sum you care to dream up. If it's against Tyson, you probably couldn't even dream up the noughts.

Britain's Millionaire Sports Stars in 1995

1 Damon Hill   Motor Racing   £3m
A salary of around £2.5m for driving Formula One boosts the Hill pay cheque.
Sponsorship deals with Harrods and Cellnet.

2 Chris Eubank   Boxing   £2.75m
Schommer, Wharton and two Collins fight come into the equation. £750,000
apiece for the first three, less when the title went.

3 Nick Faldo   Golf   £2.65m
Sun City $1m from last year, add £500,000 on course in 1995,
while Pringle, Mizuno, Bridgestone and Audemars Piguet top it up.

4 Frank Bruno   Boxing   £2.45m
A million pound earner from the McCall fight and decent pay cheques from
a couple of minutes with Evans and Marin. *The Sun* and Top Rank head a
healthy queue of endorsements, but next year this will look like small change.

5 David Platt   Footballer   £2.4m
Platt has cost clubs more money than any other player - a total of £22m.
Has lucrative deals with Mizuno, Ferraro, McDonalds and Parker Pens.

6 Nigel Benn   Boxing   £2.25m
£850,000 for the McClellan fight and around £650k each for Perez and
Nardiello account for most of Benn's money. Endorsement from No Fear.

7 Herbie Hide   Boxing   £2m
One fight, one payday. Riddick Bowe took the title, Hide took £2m.

8 Lennox Lewis   Boxing   £1.9m
The Morrison fight pulled in over a million for Lewis.

=9 Colin Montgomerie Golf   £1.75m
Best part of £1m on course earnings, augmented by deals with Pringle,
Calloway and Titlelist. Needs to win a major to move up alongside Faldo.

=9 Steve Hendry   Snooker   £1.75m
Best year yet for Hendry. Another world crown with the added bonus of a
147 and healthy contracts with Sweater Shop and E J Riley.

=11 Paul Ince   Football   £1.6m
The gravy train hasn't quite dried up in Italy. Ince would have earned a very
healthy signing-on fee and is on a salary not unadjacent to £1.5 a year.

=11 Paul Gascoigne Football   £1.6m
Moved from £1m+ at Lazio to £750k salary at Rangers. Fee for moving
and new Adidas contract help pay the bills.

13	Alan Shearer	Football	£1.4m
14	Nigel Mansell	Motor Racing	£1.3m
15	Andy Cole	Football	£1.25m
16	Naseem Hamed	Boxing	£1.2m
17	Stan Collymore	Football	£1.1m
17	Sam Torrance	Golf	£1.1m
18	Ian Woosnam	Golf	£1m

All figures estimated and for a period from October 1994-October 1995.

For all its earning potential, boxing has had a nightmare year. Gerald McClellan's injuries were inflicted in a fight against Nigel Benn that was watched by over 13 million viewers. Seven months later, James Murray died in a Glasgow ring. The fitter boxers get and the stronger boxers get, the more dangerous the sport becomes. It will not need too many more deaths before the cries to ban the sport become an irresistible clamour.

Having concentrated rather too much on the money in sport, we should point out that the embers of Corinthianism have not been completely doused. Down in East Sussex, officials from the Rother Youth League decided that enough professionalism is enough and suggested to teams that if a match was too one-sided they should swap their striker and keeper over in order to even things up. Mr Clarke, the league secretary, denied that the letter was directed at the Little Common club, whose under-15 side regularly defeated rival teams by a cricket score (it won one game 31-0). All this went down like a wet rag with Ken Cherry, who manages the Little Common side. "It is not fair on the boys to change the way we play," he said. "Some sides get well beaten, but that is football, that is life." Noises of the last embers dying.

We have had no reports of 14-year-old footballers on drugs, although the total number of positives from the sport reached a highpoint of 13. Eight of those were for cannabis. This was the year, though, when a 14-year-old South African athlete from Johannesburg was found positive. Liza de Villiers' urine sample revealed traces of Nandrolone, a steroid originally developed for vets. "Give two of these to your cow," Mrs De Villiers, "And one to your daughter."

Colin Welland was absolutely sure there were no drug-takers in Rugby League. "The whole idea of the Big League bristling with bulbous junkies is too ridiculous even to contemplate," said our Colin in *The Observer*, after Jamie Bloem, the South African import at Doncaster had tested positive. Well, not only were there more positives, but there was even the suggestion that up to 150 bulbous junkies could be operating in the League. Big boys do need a fix, Colin, that's the trouble.

As well as South African rugby players, Cuban boxers and Chinese swimmers found the wrongside of the testers and three New Zealand cricketers, Stephen Fleming, Dion Nash and Matthew Hart, tested positive for cannabis. There were flaws in the system, though. Diane Modahl, after a second hearing, was cleared of taking testosterone by the British Athletic Federation (but not yet the IAAF) and Katrin Krabbe won her case against the German Federation, which had banned her for two years for taking Clenbuterol.

It was the year that Lester Piggott retired because of his age and Juan Antonio Samaranch didn't. Well, he did and then he didn't. No sooner had the rule been brought in, at the International Olympic Committee meeting in Budapest - that members had to be under 75 - than it was lifted to 80, in order that the 74-year-old president could stand for another term as president. Two months later, the US TV deal was done for Sydney, with NBC paying a $705 (about £440m and a record for any sporting event) for the contract. Even the Atlanta Games only cost $465m. NBC also agreed a deal for the 2002 Winter Olympics, allocated to Salt Lake City at that Budapest conference, worth $545 (£340m). We can only think that these vast sums are a direct response to the IOC's decision to grant provisional recognition to ballroom dancing.

BEST-SELLING
SPORTS BOOKS

Oct 1, 1994 to Oct 1 1995
All editions are paperback, except where stated

1 **Football Against the Enemy***** £6.99
   by Simon Kruper (Orion Phoenix)
2 **United We Stood - The Unofficial History of
   the Ferguson Years** £6.95
   by Richard Kurt (Sigma)
3 **Rothmans Football Yearb'k 1994-95** £16.99
   Edited by Jack Rollin (Headline)
4 **Are You Watching, Liverpool?** £5.99
   by Jim White (Mandarin)
5 **One Hump or Two** £9.99
   by Frank Worthington (Polar Pblg)
6 **Physical Education and the
   Study of Sport** £16.95
   by Davis, Bull, Roscoe & Roscoe (Mosby)
7 **Playfair Cricket Annual** £4.50
   Edited by Bill Frindall (Headline)
8 **European Football Yearbook** £21.95
   by Mike Hammond (Sports Projects)
9 **Grand Prix Year - The Inside Story of a
   Formula One Season** £20.00
   by Damon Hill (McMillan)
10 **Wisden Cricketers' Almanack*** £23.50
   Edited by Matthew Engel (Wisden)
11 **McIlvanney on Football** £14.99
   by Hugh McIlvanney (Mainstream)
12 **Gladys Protheroe...Football Genius** £5.95
   by Simon Cheetham (Juma)
13 **The Far Corner - A Mazy Dribble Through
   North-East Football** £5.99
   by Harry Pearson (Warner)
14 **Fever Pitch** £5.99
   by Nick Hornby (Gollancz)
15 **XIII Winters - Reflections on Rugby League**
   by Dave Hadfield (Mainstream) £12.99
16 **Athletics 1995 - The International Track
   and Field Annual** £13.95
   Edited by Peter Matthews (SportsBooks)
17 **Anyone but England - Cricket and the
   National Malaise** £9.95
   by Mike Marqusee (Verso)
18 **The National Hockey League Official
   Guide and Record Book** £9.99
   (National Hockey League)
19 **The Official National Football League 1995
   Record and Fact Book** £14.99
   (National Football League)
20 **International Tennis Federation World of
   Tennis** £9.99
   Edited by John Barrett Collins Willow)

* Also sold in hardback at £23.50
*** Winner of the William Hill Sports Book of the
Year Award, 1994*

*List Provided by :Sportspages Bookshops 94-96
Charing Cross Road, London, 0171-240-9604 & St
Ann's Square, Manchester, 0161 832 8530*

We can report that the largest man in sport this year is a 7ft 7in American WWF wrestler who weighs in at 471lbs - WWF presumably standing for World Wildlife Fund in this instance. Lee Chin Yong, a South Korean estate agent broke his world record for chin-ups, completing 612 before collapsing and Bruce Bursford broke the cycling world record by travelling at 207mph at Brooklands race track. Bursford didn't go on the track. In fact, he didn't travel either. Rigged on a treadmill, the Norfolk designer pedalled his £1m bike at a standstill. Made from titanium and aluminium, with ceramic bearings and helium-filled tyres, and weighing just 11lbs - you can already see Obree on it at Atlanta.

It was the year in which Jimmy White and Graham Gooch both rejuvenated their barnets and the marbles went missing at the British Marbles Championship. Speaking of marbles, Joe Bugner proved that none of his had returned by making a comeback to the ring at the ripe of age of 45. It wasn't just like the good old days because Bugner won, defeating Vince Cervi to become the new Australian heavyweight champion. Bugner is now aiming for a fight against Foreman, but it'll have to happen quickly.

Finally, a word for the sports headline writers. Here at Oddball, we think they had a vintage year. ***ANNO DOMINIC*** in the *Telegraph*, when Cork was on song, ***SUMMERTIME AND THE LIVINGSTON'S EASY*** in *Scotland on Sunday*, when the new Livingston team won, and ***GOUGH DROP*** in the *Guardian*, were all fine examples of the art. The ultimate accolade, though, goes to the *Daily Mirror* with ***DECIDER WITH ROSIE***, when Ronnie Rosenthal settled the Spurs v Southampton Cup replay. It was a masterpiece, nothing less.

October

1   **Halling** won the Cambridgeshire; within a year he would be one of the highest rated horses in British racing.

   Clem O'Brien, former employee, was arrested for the murder of racehorse trainer Alex Scott.

2   **Steve Robinson** retained his WBO featherweight title, stopping Duke McKenzie in the ninth round.

   Carnegie, trained by André Fabre, won the Prix de l'Arc de Triomphe

4   **Vodafone** announced a three-year £3.5m sponsorship of the Epsom Derby meeting.

5   **Vincent O'Brien**, the greatest racehorse trainer of the modern era, stated he would retire at the end of the flat season.

8   **Unfancied Canada** upset the favourites, United States, in golf's Dunhill Cup.

   Manchester's new Velodrome was opened. Chris Boardman was among the stars racing at the £9m venue.

   Celtic Swing established himself as 1995 Derby favourite after winning at Ascot.

9   **Michelle Martin** won her second consecutive world squash title. The Australian defeated England's Cassie Jackman.

10 **Nigel Mansell** finished eighth in his final race for the Newman/Haas IndyCar team at Laguna Seca raceway.

12 **England's** footballers drew with Romania. Newcastle's Robert Lee scored on his debut.

   Neil Jenkins became the highest points scorer in the history of Welsh international rugby when he kicked 24 points in the 29-19 victory over Italy.

15 **Jeremy Guscott** returned to club rugby, having missed a year through injury.

   Chris Eubank retained his WBO world super-middleweight title, defeating Dan Schommer in Sun City with a lack-lustre display.

16 **Michael Schumacher** finished 25 seconds ahead of Damon Hill in the European Grand Prix at Jerez and established a five-point lead in the championship.

   Ernie Els beat Colin Montgomerie 4 & 2 to claim the World Matchplay title.

18 **England's** cricketers set off on their tour of Australia.

   Everton admitted that it was costing them £35,000 a week to have Duncan Ferguson on loan from Glasgow Rangers.

19 **Manchester United** drew 2-2 with Barcelona at Old Trafford, their first match in the Champions' League.

   Mike Atherton got embroiled in a row when the England team arrived in Perth. Atherton claimed Steve Waugh "was wetting himself against genuine quick bowlers".

21 **David Houghton** scored 266 for Zimbabwe against Sri Lanka. The innings took 11 and a quarter hours 541 deliveries, three more than Lara faced for his record-breaking 375 against England.

22 **England** scored an 8-4 victory over Australia in the rugby league Test at Wembley, but victory was marred by the sending-off of England captain Shaun Edwards.

Celtic Swing won the Racing Post Trophy and his odds shortened to 7/2 for the Epsom Derby, still eight months away.

Tony Rominger broke the world one-hour cycling record. The Swiss rider bettered the record of Miguel Induráin, covering 53.832km of the Bordeaux track.

23   **United States'** women golfers won eight of the ten final day singles to regain the Solheim Cup 13-7.

Herbie Hide and Billy Schwer lost the chance to bid for world titles when John Daly and Bob Arum's Hong Kong promotion was cancelled. Frank Bruno, also due for a non-title fight on the Hong Kong bill, got adequate compensation. Don King offered him a title chance against Oliver McCall.

27   **Brian Lara** was banned for dissent. Playing for West Indies against New Zealand in Goa, Lara motioned for the 3rd umpire after he was given out stumped, and was banned for one match.

30   **Carl Fogarty** clinched the World Superbike title, winning the first race at Phillip Island, Australia.

31   **Terry Venables'** finances probed by BBC *Panorama* programme.

November

1   **Osvaldo Ardilles** sacked as manager of Tottenham, after 16 months at White Hart Lane.

Newcastle and Aston Villa were eliminated from the UEFA Cup, respectively by Athletic Bilbao and Trabzonspor.

2   **Manchester United** defeated 4-0 by Barcelona at the Nou Camp Stadium, virtually ending hopes of success in the Champions' League.

Kapil Dev, the greatest wicket-taker in Test history, announced his retirement.

3   **Norman Hadley**, 6ft 9in and 19 stones rugby player for Wasps and Canada, punched a drunk on the London Underground and became a folk hero.

5   **Australia** defeated England 38-8 in the second rugby league Test at Old Trafford to square the series at one game apiece.

Barathea, trained by Luca Cumani and ridden by Frankie Dettori, won the Breeders' Cup Mile at Churchill Downs, Kentucky.

6   **George Foreman**, 46, regained the world heavyweight title 20 years after he lost it to Muhammad Ali. Foreman knocked out reigning WBA & IBF champion Michael Moorer in the 10th round, with Moorer having the fight all but won.

Damon Hill closed the world championship gap to one point when he won the Japanese Grand Prix at Suzuka.

8   **Mike Walker** sacked as Everton manager after just six victories in 35 matches.

9   **Bruce Grobbelaar** was accused by *The Sun* newspaper of accepting bribes to fix football matches. *The Sun* filmed Grobbelaar apparently accepting money.

Scotland 'A' defeated the South African rugby tourists 17-15, the tourists' first loss on the 13-match tour.

10 **Ron Atkinson** sacked as manager of Aston Villa, after four wins in 23 matches.
Joe Royle returned to Goodison to take over as Everton manager.

12 **England's** rugby union team beat Romania 54-3.
Jonah Barrington, six-time winner of the British Open, was elected president of the Squash Rackets Association.

13 **Michael Schumacher** caused a collision in the Australian Grand Prix that eliminated both his own and Damon Hill's cars. The crash determined the title, which went to Schumacher by a single point. Nigel Mansell won the race.

14 **Bruce Grobbelaar** charged by the Football Association on two counts of match-fixing.

16 **Wales** defeated 5-0 by Georgia in Tbilisi, ending their hopes of qualification for the 1996 European Championship.
Martina Navratilova bowed out of competitive singles at the Virginia Slims tournament at Madison Square Garden.

18 **Greg Norman** proposed a World Tour of golf, in association with Rupert Murdoch's Fox TV.

19 **Scotland** lost 34-10 to the South African rugby union tourists at Murrayfield.
Gary Lineker played his final game for Grampus Eight, but was substituted 10 minutes into the second half. It marked the end of Lineker's 18-year playing career.

20 **Australia** wrapped up the three-Test rubgy league series with a 23-4 victory at Elland Road. The match was the last international of celebrated Australian centre and captain Mal Meninga.

22 **Devon Malcolm** was diagnosed as having chicken pox and was ruled out of the first Test against Australia.
Wimbledon profits for the 1994 tournament were revealed. They shot up from £16.4m in 1993 to £27.9m in 1994, a 70% increase.
Alex Dampier quit as Britain's ice hockey coach. Dampier had taken Britain from Pool D to Pool A in World Championship ice hockey.

23 **Gothenburg** beat Manchester United 3-1 in the Champions' League.
Colin McRae won the RAC Rally, the first Briton to be succesful in the event since Roger Clark in 1976.

24 **John Toshack**, who resigned as manager of Wales in 1993 after only one match, was sacked as manager of Spanish club Real Sociedad.

25 **Paul Merson** 'confessed' in *The Daily Mirror* that he was a cocaine addict. Merson also admitted to excessive gambling and drinking.

26 **South Africa** defeated Wales 26-10 at Cardiff in the penultimate match of their Tour.

27 **Spencer Smith**, from Slough, retained the world Olympic-distance triathlon title in Wellington, New Zealand.

29 **Shane Warne** captured eight English second innings wickets for just 71 runs to lead Australia to a 184-run victory in the first Test at the 'Gabba, Brisbane.

December

1   **Viv Richards** forgot to attend his OBE investiture at Buckingham Palace.
    Paul Merson escaped a ban from the FA, despite admitting addictions to drink, cocaine and gambling.
4   **Pakistan** won hockey's World Cup in Sydney, beating Holland on penalties.
7   **Manchester United** were eliminated from the Champions' League despite a 4-0 victory over Turkish side Galatasaray.
    Angus Fraser was drafted into the England tour party, when Martin McCague joined the growing injury list.
8   **Team Lotus**, seven times winners of the constructors championship in F1, shut down because of financial problems.
    Vyv Simpson and Andrew Jennings, British authors of the book *Lords of the Rings*, were given suspended 5-day jail sentences after a court in Lausanne upheld a libel charge filed by Juan Antonio Samaranch, president of the IOC.
9   **Tottenham Hotspur** were reinstated in the FA Cup and had a six-point League penalty withdrawn when the FA backed down after independent arbitrators had backed the London club. The £1.5m fine was still imposed.
10 **Rob Andrew** equalled the world points scoring record of Frenchman Didier Camberabero. Andrew scored 30 points in England's 60-19 trouncing of Canada.
    Chris Eubank outpointed Henry Wharton to retain his WBO title.
11 **The Australian Cricket Academy**, whose oldest player was 22, completed a double victory over England, winning on successive days at Sydney.
    Damon Hill was voted Sports Personality of the Year by viewers of BBC television.
14 **Diane Modahl** was banned for four years for drug-taking by a five-strong British Athletic Federation disciplinary panel.
15 **The Aga Khan** announced that he would be ending his four-year boycott of British racing. The leading owner withdrew from events in Britain after his 1989 Oaks winner Aliysa was banned for testing positive. The Aga Khan disputed the test results.
18 **Sean Kelly** retired from international cycling. Kelly was officially the world's leading road racer from 1984 to 1989, although the Irishman never won a major tour. However, only three riders had won more classics than Kelly.
    Ernie Els won the Johnny Walker World Championship in Jamaica by six shots.
20 **Milton**, Britain's best show-jumper, retired. Milton won a total of over £1.25m prize money.
    Ivan Lendl also retired. Lendl won more than £14m in his career.
21 **Sri Lanka** confirmed they were seeking the services of Ian Botham as their national team manager. Botham was starring in the pantomime *Cinderella* at Wimbledon Theatre at the time.
27 **Peter May**, former captain of England, died. May played 66 Tests, making 4,537 runs at an average of 46.77. He captained the side in a record 41 Tests.
    Shane Warne took 6-64 as Australia moved into a commanding position in the second Test.

29 **England were** bowled out for 92 in the second innings and lost the second Test. Shane Warne took a hattrick.

31 **The Year ended** with Blackburn Rovers leading the Premiership by three points from Manchester United.

January ────────────────────────────────

3 **David Coulthard** was confirmed as second driver for the Williams Renault team for the 1995 F1 World championship. Coulthard's elevation meant that Nigel Mansell was left without a drive.

4 **Graeme Hick** was left two short of a Test century when captain Mike Atherton declared the England innings in the third Test with Hick on 98 not out.
Graeme Obree was sacked from his Le Groupement cycling team for failing to turn up at a pre-season training camp.

5 **England** drew the third Test in Sydney, but remained two down in the series.

7 **Graham Thorpe** collapsed after scoring 89 in England's World Series Cup victory over Zimbabwe. Thorpe suffered from heat exhaustion.

10 **Andy Cole** moved from Newcastle United to Manchester United after the League Champions paid a record fee of £7m for his services.

12 **England's** cricketers lost to Australia and failed to make the final of the World Series Cup. The final thus became Australia against Australia 'A'.

16 **Jannie Engelbrecht** was sacked as manager of the South African rugby union team.

18 **Richard Dunwoody**, champion jump jockey , was suspended for 30 days for intentional interference in a race at Uttoxeter.

19 **New Zealand** cricketers Matthew Hart, Stephen Fleming and Dion Nash were dropped from the one-day matches against the West Indies for having smoked cannabis on the recent tour of South Africa.

21 **England** defeated Ireland and France beat Wales in the first round of the Five Nations Championship.

22 **Alberto Tomba** equalled the record of seven World Cup slalom wins in the same season. Tomba matched Stenmark and Girardelli's record when he won at Wengen.

25 **Eric Cantona** attacked a spectator at Selhurst Park during the match between Manchester United and Crystal Palace. Cantona, leaving the pitch having been sent off, made a karate-style kick at the spectator.

26 **The World Skiing Championships,** scheduled to begin in Sierra Nevada at the end of the month were cancelled due to lack of snow. The organisers resorted to using more than a hundred snow machines but could still not save the event.

27 **Eric Cantona** is banned by Manchester United for the remainder of the season.

28 **Mary Pierce** won her first Grand Slam title in Melbourne. The Frenchwoman defeated Arantxa Sanchez Vicario in the Australian Open final 6-3 6-2.

29 **San Francisco 49ers** earned an unprecedented fifth Super Bowl title in Miami. They beat San Diego Chargers 49-26.

Andre Agassi beat Pete Sampras 4-6 6-1 7-6 6-4 in the final of the Australian Open.

Wigan romped home in the Regal Trophy final against Warrington, 40-10.

30 **England** won the fourth Test in Australia, Australia crashed to 156 all out in their second innings.

Nigel Mansell signed for McLaren for the 1995 F1 season.

Graham Gooch, the leading run-scorer in English Test history, announced his retirement from Test cricket at the end of the series against Australia.

February

1   **Sir Stanley Matthews** celebrated his 80th birthday.

2   **Fred Perry,** the last British player to win the men's singles at Wimbledon, died aged 85. He was Wimbledon champion from 1934-36 and was the first player to win all the Grand Slam tournaments.

Henry Olonga, the Zimbabwean cricketer, became only the sixth player in Test history to be no-balled for throwing, and the first for 32 years. Zimbabwe go on to record their first Test victory with an emphatic innings and 64 run defeat of Pakistan.

4   **Mike Gatting** joined Gooch in announcing his retirement from Test cricket.

England beat France 31-10, and Scotland defeated Ireland 26-13 in the Five Nations Championship.

7   **Dennis Wise** was withdrawn from the England football squad to face Ireland after being found guilty of attacking a taxi driver.

Australia clinch victory in the fifth Test at Perth to take the series 3-1, Craig McDermott taking 6-38 to leave England 123 all out in the second innings.

8   **Riots** erupted at Millwall at the fourth round FA Cup replay against Chelsea. Eleven policemen were injured and 38 arrests made. Millwall won after a penalty shoot-out.

11 **Mark Foster** broke his own world short course record for the 50m butterfly when he clocked 23.55 seconds in the World Cup meet in Sheffield.

13 **The International Cricket Council** launched an inquiry into allegations that Australian captain Allan Border was offered bribes to lose the fifth Test versus England in 1993.

15 **England** football fans rioted and forced the England-Ireland friendly in Dublin to be abandoned. Ireland led the game 1-0.

Salim Malik, the Pakistan cricket captain, denied claims in Australian newspapers that he had tried to bribe two Australian cricketers in September 1994.

18 **Scotland** shocked France with a 23-21 victory in Paris in the Five Nations rugby. England beat Wales 23-9 in Cardiff.

Frank Bruno enjoyed a 65 second victory over Rodolfo Marin in Shepton Mallet to set up a world title shot against Oliver McCall.

19 **Linford Christie** broke the world 200m indoor record in Lievin, France. Christie ran 20.25 to better the Frenchman Bruno Marie-Rose time of 20.36.

20 **Daily Telegraph** headline read "FOOTBALL BACK ON IT'S FEET"

21 **George Graham** sacked by Arsenal over transfer 'bung'.
Eric Cantona charged with common assault over the Selhurst Park incident.
23 **Premier League** pledged to expand it's inquiries into transfer payments.
24 **Eric Cantona's** ban from football was extended by the FA to October and the Frenchman was fined £10,000
25 **Gerald McClellan** was left in a coma after the WBC title fight against Nigel Benn. The fight was stopped in the 10th round, when the American was counted out. He returned to his corner and subsequently collapsed. McClellan was rushed to the London Hospital where they operated on a blood clot on the brain.
27 **One hundred and forty** Chelsea fans were expelled from Belgium prior to their European Cup Winners' Cup tie with Bruges.

March

3 **Chris Armstrong**, Crystal Palace striker, tested positive for cannabis.
4 **Manchester United** beat Ipswich Town 9-0 with Andy Cole scoring five. It was United's biggest victory for 103 years.
Scotland defeated Wales 26-13 to set up a Grand Slam decider against England at Twickenham. France toppled Ireland 25-7 in Dublin.
Wales won the European Rugby League Championship, beating France 22-10.
6 **OneAustralia** sank during the Americas Cup race off San Diego. The yacht, which cost £1.2m, was the first sinking in competition in the event's 144-year history.
Linford Christie pulled out of the British team for the World Indoor championships in Barcelona. Although pressured by IAAF chief Primo Nebiolo, Christie could not be persuaded to run.
8 **Keith Fletcher** dismissed as England team manager. In 26 Tests under his stewardship, England registered just five victories.
9 **Elvis Stojko** retained his world figure skating title at Birmingham.
11 **Wales** won the right to stage the 1999 rugby union World Cup.
Riddick Bowe stopped Herbie Hide to win the WBO World championship. Hide failed to beat the count in the sixth round and lost the title he won against Michael Bentt a year earlier.
13 **Dennis Wise**, the 28-year-old Chelsea captain, was given a three-month jail sentence for assaulting a taxi-driver (and his taxi). Wise was freed pending an appeal. Wise later won the appeal.
Adrian Maguire, the leading jump jockey, withdrew from the Cheltenham festival, remaining in Ireland following the death of his mother.
14 **Bruce Grobbelaar**, Hans Segers and John Fashanu arrested in dawn raids. They were released a day later without being charged.
Alderbrook won the Champion Hurdle, only his third race over jumps.
15 **Alberto Tomba** clinched the overall World Cup skiing title. It was the Italian's first overall title, he had previously been second three times.

16   **Master Oats** completed a big-race double for trainer Kim Bailey, winning the
Gold Cup, two days after the trainer's Adlerbrook had won the Champion Hurdle.
DeCarlo Deveaux, London Leopards' American basketball player received the
stiffest penalty in the sport's history , banned for two years for head-butting Derby's
Andy Gardiner and chasing his teammate Tim Lascelles brandishing a pole.

17   **Nigel Mansell** withdrew from the opening two races of the F1 world championship,
His cockpit in the McLaren-Mercedes having proved too small, Mansell was
replaced by Mark Blundell, who did fit the cockpit.

18   **England** won the Grand Slam, defeating Scotland 24-12. Ireland beat Wales,
consigning the 1994 champions to the wooden spoon position.
Chris Eubank lost his WBO super-middleweight title, outfought by Steve Collins in
Dublin. The Irishman won on points.
Michael Jordan announced his return to NBA basketball with Chicago Bulls.

21   **The Tote Jackpot** broke the £1m barrier for the first time. Stratford jumps meeting
was the unlikely occasion for this milestone.

23   **Eric Cantona** sentenced to two-weeks in jail by Croydon magistrate Mrs Jean
Pearch. Cantona, refused bail by the magistrates' court, was given bail following an
appeal to the adjacent crown court.
Davie Cooper, 39-year-old Clydebank winger, died. Cooper represented his country
22 times and won three championship medals with Rangers.

25   **Mike Tyson**, former world heavyweight champion and converted Muslim, was
released from Indiana Youth Centre, after serving three years of a ten-year
sentence for rape.
Kenya won all four team titles, but only one individual crown at the World Cross-
country Championships at Durham.

26   **Michael Schumacher** and David Coulthard finished first and second in the Brazilian
GP. They were disqualified post-race for fuel irregularities, but were later reinstated.

27   **Alan Davies** resigned as Welsh rugby union coach.

30   **Tony Lock**, former Surrey and England left-arm spinner, died in Australia aged 65.

31   **Eric Cantona** had his two-week sentence for assault commuted to 120 hours of
community service.
The Baseball Strike in America, which lasted 232 days ended.

April

1   **Cambridge** beat Oxford by four lengths in the Beefeater Boat Race.

2   **Liverpool** carried off the Coca-Cola Cup with a 2-1 victory over Bolton. McManaman
scored twice for the Merseysiders' first trophy for three years. How times change.
The London Marathon was won by the favourite, Mexico's Dionicio Ceron. The
women's race provided a surprise when Malgorzata Sobanska finished ahead of
Manuela Machado.
Australia defeated the West Indies by 10 wickets at Bridgetown, Barbados.

3 **Ballroom Dancing** gained provisional recognition as a major sport from the International Olympic Committee.

The Football Association completed a £5m sponsorship deal with Carling.

Jeremy Bates acheived a career-best world ranking of 62.

Monica Seles failed in her attempt to have her attacker Günther Parsche jailed. Judge Goering upheld the original verdict of a two-year suspended sentence.

6 **Ieuan Evans** replaced as Welsh rugby union captain by Mike Hall.

8 **Royal Athlete**, the 40/1 outsider, won the Grand National. Trained by Jenny Pitman, it was some compensation for the trainer who, two years earlier, had won the National that never was with Esha Ness.

Rugby League chairmen accept a £75m offer from Rupert Murdoch's News Corporation to set up a summer Super League. The controversial new deal involved the merger of a number of clubs.

9 **Damon Hill** won the Argentinian Grand Prix.

Ben Crenshaw earned a second Masters victory, winning by a single shot from Davis Love III.

10 **Crystal Palace fan** Paul Nixon was stabbed to death during a fight between Palace and Manchester United supporters outside a Walsall pub.

13 **Roy Keane** and Darren Patterson charged with bringing the game into disrepute following their sendings-off in the FA Cup semi-final replay on February 12.

14 **Wigan** beat St Helens 34-18 to clinch the rugby league championship for the sixth successive season.

15 **Rangers** claimed the Scottish League title for the 45th time when Celtic, the only team that could have caught them, were beaten 2-0 by Aberdeen.

16 **Sheffield Steelers** completed the domestic ice hockey double, when the beat Edinburgh Racers 7-2. Victory earned the Steelers the British Championship to add to the Premier Division title they had already won.

Match-fixing allegations surfaced at the World Snooker Championships in Sheffield, following unusual betting patterns on the Jimmy White-Peter Francisco match.

17 **Adrian Maguire** broke his arm and was ruled out for the remainder of the season.

18 **Eric Cantona** began his community service, working with under-11s at The Cliff, United's training ground.

British Steel withdrew its £10,000 a season sponsorship of Middlesborough football club, after discovering that the club's new Riverside Stadium was being constructed using (cheaper) German steel.

Andy Hicks, ranked 33 in the world, knocked number two seed and six-time winner Steve Davis out of the World Championships at Sheffield.

19 **Rob Jones**, a 19-year-old off-spinner, conceded 48 runs in a single over. Jones, playing against a Surrey XI at The Oval was hit for 6 6 4 4 6 6 6 6 by David Ward. As the over contained 2 no-balls, there was a further four-run penalty.

20 **David Seaman** saved three penalties in a shoot-out to put Arsenal in the final of the European Cup Winners' Cup. Arsenal won the shoot-out 3-2 after a 2-2 draw against Sampdoria to face Real Zaragoza, who beat Chelsea, in that final.

22 **Gavin Hastings** played his last international on home soil, captaining Scotland to a 49-16 win over Romania. Hastings scored 19 points.

George Foreman successfully defended his IBF world heavyweight title when he was given the verdict over Germany's Axel Schulz. Few (if any) onlookers agreed with the judges' decision.

Celtic Swing won the Tripleprint Greenham Stakes at Newbury and moved to 4/7 favourite for The Derby.

West Indies levelled the series 1-1 with Australia when they won the third Test at Port of Spain by nine wickets.

Graham Taylor performed a citizen's arrest on a Sheffield United supporter who spat in his face at Bramall Lane.

24 **Keighley Cougars** issued a writ against the Rugby Football League over the club's exclusion from the new Super League.

27 **Stephen Hendry** scored only the third maximum break of 147 in world championship history. Hendry earned £163,000 for the feat with took 11 minutes and 48 seconds.

28 **Eric Cantona** signed a new three-year contract with Manchester United.

29 **Wigan** beat Leeds 30-10 to win the Silk Cut Challenge Cup for the 8th year in a row.

Leicester rugby union club became Courage League champions for the first time since 1988.

30 **Damon Hill** took over the lead in the world championship after winning at Imola.

Stephen Hendry trounced Nigel Bond 18-9 to record his fourth world title in succession. The Scotsman took his career earnings to £4,156,975, making him the top earner in snooker history.

Mike Atherton confirmed as England captain for the Tests against West Indies.

Rugby League executives back-tracked on the original Super League deal, stating that no club would be forced to lose its identity.

May

3 **Australia** beat West Indies in the fourth and deciding Test at Kingston, Jamaica. The West Indies lost by an innings and 53 runs, their biggest defeat in 10 years, and the series defeat was the first they had suffered at home in 22 years.

6 **Will Carling** stripped of the captaincy of the England team, following his comments about the game's administrators on a Channel Four programme. Carling referred to the RFU as "57 old farts".

Bath won the Pilkington Cup final, beating Wasps 36-16.

Celtic Swing didn't win the 2000 Guineas. The widely touted "wonder horse" finished second to French horse Pennekamp, though beaten by only a head.

7 **Harayir** won the 1000 Guineas at Newmarket.

8 **Will Carling** was reinstated as England captain after apologising.

Peter Francisco was banned for five years by the World Professional Billiards and Snooker Association. Though cleared of match-rigging, Francisco was found guilty of unprofessional conduct.

10 **Real Zaragoza** beat Arsenal in the final of the European Cup Winners' Cup. Nayim scored the winning goal in extra time, lobbing the Arsenal 'keeper Seaman from 50 yards out.

11 **Jürgen Klinsmann** announced his departure from Tottenham Hotspur after one year of a two-year contract. Klinsmann stated his intention to return to Germany and play for Bayern Munich.

12 **Imran Khan** announced his impending marriage to Jemima Goldsmith.

13 **Frank Bruno** made it three victories in less than eight minutes when 19-stone American Mike Evans was stopped at the end of two rounds at the Kelvin Hall in Glasgow. Evans at least did better than Bruno's previous two opponents, who lasted a total of 107 seconds between them.

New Zealand overwhelmed United States in the America's Cup, Peter Blake's Team New Zealand completing a 5-0 whitewash over Dennis Connor's Young America.

14 **Blackburn** lost 2-1 at Liverpool, but claimed the Premiership title as Manchester United were held to a 1-1 draw at West Ham. For manager Kenny Dalglish it completed an extraordinary set of 14 championships; five Scottish titles while playing for Celtic, eight English titles with Liverpool and one as manager of Blackburn.

Godolphin, the Dubai-based racing operation of Sheikh Mohammed, won Group One races in France, Italy and Japan, netting over £750,000.

Michael Schumacher won the Spanish Grand Prix. Damon Hill dropped out on the final lap with a hydraulics failure. Nigel Mansell left the race on lap 18, claiming his McLaren Mercedes was "impossible to drive". Mansell didn't drive it again.

17 **Katrin Krabbe**, the former German sprinter, won her legal action against the two-year ban imposed for testing positive for Clenbuterol.

18 **The Rugby Football Union** announced the creation of a European Cup.

20 **Everton** upset the favourites Manchester United to win the FA Cup. Joe Royle's team won 1-0 from a 30th minute goal from Paul Rideout.

21 **Wigan** beat Leeds 69-12 to win the Premiership and complete the Grand Slam of rugby league trophies, the Championship, the Challenge Cup and the Regal Trophy.

22 **Greg Rusedski**, Canadian born tennis player, was cleared to play for Britain. Rusedski, who qualified because his mother came from Dewsbury, Yorkshire, immediately became the British number one.

23 **Nigel Mansell** confirmed his withdrawal from the McLaren-Mercedes team.

Chris Brasher and John Disley, founders of the London Marathon, won a £1m libel action against Channel 4 and *The New Statesman*.

24 **Ajax** defeated AC Milan 1-0 to win the European Cup, 22 years after the club last lifted the trophy.

Paul Ince, the Manchester United footballer, was cleared of assaulting a fan during the match against Crystal Palace.

25 **Rugby's World Cup** opened in Cape Town with the host nation South Africa defeating Australia 27-18.

26 **Scotland** overran Ivory Coast 89-0 in the World Cup. Gavin Hastings scored 44 pts.

27 **Celtic** beat Airdrie 1-0 in the Scottish Cup final, to end a six-year trophy drought.

England scraped a 24-18 victory against Argentina, while New Zealand overran Ireland 43-19 in rugby's World Cup.

28 **England** won the third one-day international against the West Indies at Lord's by 73 runs. Victory gave England a 2-1 one-day series win.

Michael Schumacher enjoyed an easy win at Monaco to go five points ahead in the drivers' championship.

29 **Bolton Wanderers** qualified to play in the leading division for the first time in 16 years when they defeated Reading 4-3 in the Wembley play-off.

30 **Richard Dunwoody** confirmed his split with leading NH trainer Martin Pipe.

31 **Ruud Gullit** signed for Chelsea.

England defeated Italy to qualify for the quarter-finals of rugby's World Cup.

June

1 **Celtic Swing** was withdrawn from the Derby, owner Peter Savill being unhappy with the firm going.

3 **Scotland** went down to a narrow defeat against France, the loss determining their next opponents as New Zealand. Three players sent off as the South Africa-Canada match erupted in violence. Max Brito, Ivory Coast winger, incurred a spinal injury in the Tonga match. It was later confirmed that he would be permanently paralysed.

4 **Celtic Swing** held off Poliglote by half a length to win the French Derby.

England defeated Western Samoa 44-22 in their final World Cup group match.

5 **Haile Gebresilasie** smashed the world 10,000m record in Hengelo, Holland by almost nine seconds.

6 **Monica Seles'** comeback was announced, though no date was given.

7 **Newcastle** signed Les Ferdinand from Queens Park Rangers for £6 million.

8 **Bruce Rioch** appointed Arsenal manager.

10 **Lammtarra** won the Epsom Derby and broke the course record in the process.

Steffi Graf beat Arantxa Sanchez Vicario to become French Open champion.

11 **Rob Andrew** dropped a goal in extra time to earn England victory over Australia and a place in the World Cup semi-finals.

West Indies comfortably won the first Test at Headingly, by nine wickets.

England's football team lost for the first time under Venables' stewardship when Brazil outclassed them in the Umbro Cup at Wembley.

Thomas Muster won the French Open, the first Austrian ever to win a grand slam title. Victory took Muster's winning streak on clay to five titles and 35 matches.

12 **Linford Christie**, in an emotional TV appearance, declared that he would not defend his Olympic title in Atlanta.

13 **Greg Rusedski** made his debut as an British player, at the Stella Artois, and lost, beaten by Mark Petchey.

Mark Ilott recorded the best bowling figures for the season with 9-19 against Northamptonshire, including a hattrick of lbws.

16 **IOC members** in Budapest voted that the 2002 Winter Olympics should go to Salt Lake City in America.

17 **South Africa** qualified for the World Cup final by defeating France 19-15.

18 **England** suffered a crushing defeat by New Zealand 45-29 in the World Cup semi-final. Jonah Lomu, 6ft 5in and over 18 stones, scored four tries.
Corey Pavin won his first major with a two-shot victory in the US Open.

19 **Play at the Direct Line** tournament at Eastbourne was interrupted when sunlight reflected off a 25ft red telephone blinded the players.
After an absence of almost five years, the Aga Khan's horses returned to British racetracks.

20 **Denis Bergkamp** signed for Arsenal from Inter Milan for a fee of £7.5 million.

22 **England** found France too strong in the third place play-off at the World Cup, losing 19-9 and thus having to qualify for the 1999 event.

23 **Paul Ince's** £6 million move to Inter Milan was confirmed.

24 **South Africa** won the World Cup, beating New Zealand 15-12 in extra time.
New Zealand rugby players walked out of the official World Cup banquet after Louis Luyt, president of the South African RFU, claimed that his team would have won both previous World Cups if they had been present.

25 **Jonathan Edwards** twice broke the world triple jump record at the European Cup in Lille, but both marks were ruled out because of the strength of the wind. His longest mark, of 18.43m, was almost half a metre ahead of the existing record.

26 **England** won the second Test at Lords by 72 runs.

29 **Jo Durie** played her last match at Wimbledon, defeated 6-2 6-2 by Jana Novotna.

30 **Temperature** on the centre court at Wimbledon climbed to 110°F, breaking all records since the championships began.

July

1 **Jeff Tarango** was defaulted in his third round match against Germany's Alexander Mronz. The American accused the umpire, Bruno Rebeuh, of being the most corrupt official in the game. Tarango's French wife, Benedicte later slapped Rebeuh.

2 **Chris Boardman** crashed out of the Tour de France, just two miles into the Prologue time trial. Boardman, travelling at 48 miles an hour, skidded into the barriers in torrential rain and broke his ankle and wrist.
Celtic Swing didn't win the Irish Derby. "It was too bad to be true," said his owner Peter Savill, whose horse finished eighth.
Jonathan Edwards broke the world triple jump record for the third time in a month, at Gateshead, but for the third time in a month found the wind just too strong.
Steve Redgrave made it 15 Henley medals when he won the Silver Goblets with his Olympic winning partner Matthew Pinsent.
Michael Schumacher won the French Grand Prix, taking his lead in the world championship to 11 points over Damon Hill.

3   **Stan Collymore**, after some delay, finally signed for Liverpool, who paid Nottingham Forest a British record of £8.5 million for the pleasure.

Nourredine Morceli broke the world 2000m record in Paris, running the distance in 4:47.88 to take almost three seconds from Said Aouita's old record.

Greg Rusedski lost to Pete Sampras and therefore did not become the first Briton for 20 years to reach a Wimbledon quarter-final.

West Indies suffered their worst defeat by an English county in 56 years when they lost by an innings and 121 runs to Sussex.

5   **Roberto Baggio** joined AC Milan from Juventus in a £12.9 million deal.

6   **The Emirate Racing Association** confirmed that the Nad al Sheba racecourse in Dubai will next March host the richest race in the world, the Dubai World Cup. It will be worth £2.5 million with £1.5 million of that going to the winner. However, on current evidence, the money won't be going very far as the winner is almost certain to come from the nearby Godolphin stables.

8   **Steffi Graf** won her sixth Wimbledon title, beating Arantxa Sanchez Vicario 4-6 6-1 7-5, to claim her 17th grand slam victory.

England are routed by the West Indians, the third Test at Edgbaston ending just 77 minutes into the third day. Scoring only 89 runs in their second innings, England were beaten by an innings and 64 runs. The erratic Egbaston wicket, which manager Ray Illingworth had requested be "shaven at both ends", was blamed.

9   **Pete Sampras** completed an easy victory over Boris Becker, 6-7 6-2 6-4 6-2, for a hattrick of Wimbledon wins.

Martina Navratilova won her 19th Wimbledon title, just one away from Billie Jean King's record, when she took the mixed doubles title with Jonathan Stark.

Miguel Induráin took the leader's yellow jersey after the seventh stage of the Tour de France. He kept the jersey till the race finish two weeks later.

10 **David Platt** joined Arsenal from Sampdoria in a £4.75 million deal. Paul Gascoigne completed his £4.3 million move from Lazio to Glasgow Rangers.

11 **Chris Brasher** retired as chairman of the London Marathon, the race he co-founded in 1981 with John Disley.

12 **George Graham** was found guilty of misconduct after accepting £425,500 as part of the transfer of two players. The FA later announced a 12-month ban from football.

Devon Malcom and Phillip DeFreitas issued writs for defamation over an article that appeared in *Wisden Cricket Monthly*.

Nourredine Morceli broke his own world record at Nice when he ran the 1500m in 3:27.37. It was the Algerian's second world record in nine days.

15 **Aravinda de Silva** played a brilliant innings for Kent, but could not prevent the Benson & Hedges Cup going Lancashire's way.

16 **Damon Hill** drove his car into Michael Schumacher's Benetton, as he attempted to overtake on the 46th lap of the British Grand Prix. With both cars eliminated, Johnny Herbert took the opportunity to win his first Grand Prix.

17 **Juan Fangio** died, aged 84. Fangio was world champion five times and won 24 of his 51 grands prix.

18   **Fabio Casartelli,** the Olympic road race champion, died on the 15th stage of the Tour de France when he crashed on the descent of the Col de Portet d'Aspet.
     Jonathan Edwards finally claimed the world triple jump record leaping 17.98 metres in Salamanca to better Willie Banks' record by just one centimetre.

20   **Jack Nicklaus,** playing in his 34th Open Championship, took a 10 at the 14th after needing four shots to get out of 'Hell Bunker'.

22   **Harold Larwood** died in Australia, aged 90.
     Nigel Benn returned to the London Arena, scene of the fateful fight against Gerald McClellan, to defeat the Italian Vincenzo Nardiello.
     Lammtarra won the King George VI and Queen Elizabeth Stakes at Ascot.

23   **John Daly** won the Open Championship after a play-off with Costantino Rocca.
     John Emburey, almost 43 years old, was recalled to the England squad for the fourth Test.

24   **Bruce Grobbelaar,** John Fashanu and Hans Segers were charged with taking money to fix football matches.

26   **Diane Modahl** won her appeal against a four-year ban from athletics for drug-taking. The decision of the appeals panel of the BAF "delighted and thrilled" Modahl, but didn't have the same effect on the IAAF, clearly unhappy with the verdict.

27   **The Fourth Test** at Old Trafford was interrupted when sunlight was reflected from a greenhouse in a local DIY store into the eyes of the West Indian batsmen. It must have worked; West Indies were all out for 216.

29   **Monica Seles** beat Martina Navratilova in an exhibition match at Atlantic City.

30   **England** beat West Indies by six wickets to square to series at 2-2. Dominic Cork broke the back of the West Indian batting with a hattrick, the first by an English bowler in a Test since Peter Loader in 1957.

31   **The IAAF** announced that it would be referring the Modahl case to its arbitration committee as it found the decision of the BAF to accept Modahl's appeal "surprising".
     The London Marathon announced a new three-year £6m sponsorship deal with Flora Margarine.

August ▬▬▬▬▬▬▬▬▬▬▬▬▬▬▬▬▬▬▬▬▬▬▬

2   **John Fashanu,** the Aston Villa striker charged with match-fixing, announced his retirement from football because of injury.

5   **Nick Barmby** agreed to join Middlesbrough from Tottenham, the fee £5.25m.

6   **Donovan Bailey,** of Canada, won the 100m title at the World Athletics Championships in Gothenburg. Christie, carrying an injury, finished sixth.

7   **Jonathan Edwards** broke the world triple jump record with his first two jumps at Gothenburg. Edwards jumped 18.16m and 18.29m to add over a foot to his record.

8   **Eric Cantona** requested a transfer from Manchester United. Cantona played in a training-ground game with Rochdale and the ensuing fuss over whether he broke his ban was thought to be the cause.

10 **The Admiral's Cup** was won by Italy, the first defat for America since 1969.

11 **Kim Batten** capitalised on Sally Gunnell's absence from the World Championships, taking both her title and world record for the 400m hurdles. Michael Johnson became the first athlete in the history to complete the 200m/400m double.

13 **Damon Hill** won the Hungarian GP to revive his flagging championship hopes.
Steve Elkington edged out Scotland's Colin Montgomerie to win the US PGA title. Montgomerie and Elkington tied scores after the final round, but the Australian won on the first play-off hole. It was the 2nd time the Scot had lost a 'major' in a play-off.

14 **England** drew the fifth Test against the West Indies at Trent Bridge. The series stayed at 2-2 with one Test remaining.

15 **Monica Seles** played her first tournament match for 28 months in the Canadian Open. Seles, in an explosive return, went on to win the tournament.
Halling won the Juddmonte International at York, easily beating Bahri.

16 **Ferrari** signed up Michael Schumacher for the 1996 season at a reputed £39m for the two-year deal.
Moses Kiptanui and Haile Gebresilasie broke world records in the steeplechase and the 5000m respectively at the Zürich meeting.
Ally McCoist scored with his first touch after coming on a s a substitute against Greece in the European Championship qualifier. Scotland's 1-0 win and Finland's 6-0 defeat by Russia made Scotland hot favourites to be the second qualifier in Group 8.

19 **Mike Tyson** won his comeback fight against Peter McNeeley. The fight was stopped after 89 seconds of the first round. Thus Tyson, reputed to be paid $25m for the fight, earned at the rate of $281,000 per second for his time in the ring.
Karrie Webb, a 20-year-old Australian rookie, won the Weetabix British Women's Golf Championship. Webb earned £60,000.
Monica Seles won the Canadian Open in Toronto.

22 **Mike Atherton** was confirmed as England's captain for the tour of South Africa.

25 **Andrew Symonds**, Gloucestershire's 20-year-old batsman, wrote his name in the record books with 16 sixes in an innings of 254 not out against Glamorgan.
Peter Haining made it a hattrick of world titles when he won the lightweight single sculls at the World championships in Tampere, Finland.
Will Carling announced his reappointment as England's captain for the forthcoming season. It was later unclear who would be captain.

26 **Steven Redgrave** and Matthew Pinsent made it four titles in succession when they won the coxless pairs in Tampere.

27 **The International Rugby Board**, following its meeting in Paris, scrapped the amateur rules of the sport and declared rugby union an open game.
Schumacher won the Belgian GP and stretched his lead over Hill to 16 points.

28 **England** drew the sixth Test against the West Indies and tied the series 2-2 with two games drawn. Brian Lara was named as West Indies' man of the series. Atherton won the award for England.
Nick Faldo and José Marie Olazábal were awarded the wild card places for the European Ryder Cup team by captain Bernard Gallacher.

September ————————————————————————

2   **Frank Bruno** landed a world title on his fourth attempt, beating Oliver McCall on points in front of 30,000 spectators at Wembley for the WBC heavyweight crown. Bruno had previously fought Tim Witherspoon, Mike Tyson and Lennox Lewis for a world title, but lost each time. On the same bill, Nigel Benn defeated Danny Ray Perez in defence of his WBC super-middleweight title.
Bobby Gould was appointed manager of Wales' football team.
South Africa, world champions, defeated Wales 40-11. Garin Jenkins, who came on as a sub for Wales, was sent off for fighting.

3   **Warwickshire** won the NatWest final over Northamptonshire by four wickets. The final was extended to a second day because of the weather.

6   **England** drew 0-0 with Colombia and Rene Higuita enhanced his reputation for eccentricity with a 'scorpion' kick clearance.
Scotland beat Finland 1-0 to make qualification for the European Championships almost certain, but Ireland fell again to Austria, putting their finals' place under threat.

7   **Cal Ripken jnr** established the longest uninterrupted run in baseball history when he completed his 2,131st consecutive game for the Baltimore Orioles.

9   **Steffi Graf** halted Monica Seles' all-conquering return to top-class tennis in the US Open. Graf won 7-6 0-6 6-3 for her 18th grand slam title.
Chris Eubank lost to Steve Collins on points in an attempt to regain his WBO super-middleweight title.
Classic Cliché won the St Leger to continue the outrageously successful run of trainer Saeed Bin Suroor and the Godolphin team.

10 **Pete Sampras** won the US Open for the third time in six years. The 24-year-old beat Andre Agassi 6-4 6-3 4-6 7-5.
Johnny Herbert, little more than a week after being sacked by Benetton for the 1996 season, won his second GP of the season at Monza.
Great Britain and Ireland surprised the Americans to win the Walker Cup 14-10. It was only the fourth time in the event's 73-year history that the Americans had lost.
Lester Piggott, for the second time in his career, announced his retirement.

11 **Middlesex** beat Leicester by one run, ensuring that the county championship would go to the final matches.

14 **Alan Sugar** lifted his White Hart Lane ban on Terry Venables.

16 **Warwickshire** retained the Britannic County Championship. They beat Kent emphatically in their final match, while their nearest challengers, Middlesex, could only draw with Somerset.

17 **Kent** celebrated victory in the AXA Equity Sunday League. Though they lost to Warwickshire in their final match, Worcestershire's rained-off game ensured the trophy was Kent-bound.

18   **Eric Cantona** and Diego Maradona establish the International Association of Professional Footballers

20   **Carl Otto Lenz**, advocate-general to the European Court of Justice, recommended to the court that, as Belgian footballer Jean-Marc Bosman was arguing, the current system of European football transfers was illegal.

21   **Rob Andrew** joined Newcastle Sporting Club as rugby development officer. Andrew's contract was believed to be worth £750,000 over five years.

22   **The Ryder Cup** began at Oak Hill Golf Club. After the first day's matches, Europe were 5-3 down to the American team.

23   **Costantino Rocca** holed-in-one at the Ryder Cup, but Europe still went into the final-day singles two matches down.

24   **David Couthard** won the European Grand Prix at Estoril in Portugal, his 21st Formula One drive and his first victory. The Scot chose a bad day to do it though as the spotlight is eslewhere. Across the Atlantic.......
     The Ryder Cup was won by the European team after a nail-biting final day. Irishman Philip Walton's victory against Jay Haas ensured the trophy came back to Europe. The final score was 14.5-13.5 to Europe.

26   **Manchester United** were knocked out of the UEFA Cup by the Russian team Volvograd. The Russians, who drew 0-0 at home in the first leg, drew 2-2 at Old Trafford to win on away goals.

27   **Graeme Obree**, banned in last year's world track championships, returned to take gold in the 4000m pursuit at the 1995 championships in Bogotá, regaining the title he won in 1993.

29   **Naseem Hamed** won the WBO featherweight title, stopping the holder Steve Robinson in the eighth round. It was Robinson's eighth title defence, but the Welshman was completely outclassed.

The Sports

Abbreviations

Where a time is shown, the hours minutes and seconds are separated by a colon. A full point is used only as a decimal point for parts of a second. eg 3 hours 23 minutes and 7.5 seconds is shown as 3:23:7.5

WR	World Record
ER	European Record
NR	National Record
BR	British Record
CR	Championship Record
J	Junior

COUNTRIES

ALB	Albania
ALG	Algeria
ANG	Anguilla
ANO	Angola
ANT	Antigua
ARG	Argentina
ARM	Armenia
AUS	Australia
AUT	Austria
AZE	Azerbaijan
BAH	Bahamas
BAR	Barbados
BEL	Belgium
BER	Bermuda
BHR	Bahrain
BLR/BLS	Belarus
BOS	Bosnia-Herzegovina
BRA	Brazil
BUL	Bulgaria
BUR	Burundi
CAN	Canada
CAY	Cayman Islands
CGO	Congo
CHI	Chile
CHN	People's Rep of China
CIV	Ivory Coast
CMR	Cameroon
COL	Colombia
CRC	Costa Rica
CRO	Croatia
CUB	Cuba
CYP	Cyprus
CZE/TCH	The Czech Republic
DEN	Denmark
DJI	Djibouti
DMN	Dominica
DOM	Dominican Republic
ECU	Equador
EGY	Egypt
ENG	England
ESA	El Salvador

ESP	Spain
EST	Estonia
ETH	Ethiopia
FIJ	Fiji
FIN	Finland
FRA	France
GAB	Gabon
GAM	The Gambia
GBR	Great Britain and NI
GEO	Georgia
GER	Germany
GHA	Ghana
GRE	Greece
GRN	Grenada
GUA	Guatemala
GUY	Guyana
HAW	Hawaii
HKG	Hong Kong
HON	Honduras
HUN	Hungary
INA	Indonesia
IND	India
IRL	Ireland
IRN	Iran
IRQ	Iraq
ISL	Iceland
ISR	Israel
ISV	US Virgin Islands
ITA	Italy
IVC	Ivory Coast
JAM	Jamaica
JOR	Jordan
JPN	Japan
KEN	Kenya
KGZ	Kyrgyzstan
KOR	Korea
KUW	Kuwait
KZK	Kazakhstan
LAT	Latvia
LES	Lesotho
LIE	Liechenstein
LTU	Lithuania
LUX	Luxembourg
MAC	Macedonia
MAD	Madagascar
MAL	Malaysia
MAR	Morocco
MEX	Mexico
MLD	Moldova
MON	Monaco
MOZ	Mozambique
MRI	Mauritius
MYA	Myanmar
NAM	Namibia
NAU	Nauru
NCA	Nicaragua
NED	Netherlands
NGR	Nigeria
NIR	Northern Ireland

NOR	Norway
NZL	New Zealand
OMA	Oman
PAK	Pakistan
PAN	Panama
PAR	Paraguay
PER	Peru
PHI	Philippines
PNG	Papua New Guinea
POL	Poland
POR	Portugal
PRK	North Korea
PUR	Puerto Rico
QUT	Qatar
ROM	Romania
RSA	South Africa
RUS	Russia
RWA	Rwanda
SAU	Saudi Arabia
SCO	Scotland
SEN	Senegal
SEY	Seychelles
SIN	Singapore
SLE	Sierra Leone
SLO	Slovenia
SNM	San Marino
SOM	Somalia
SRI	Sri Lanka
STL	St Lucia
SUD	Sudan
SUI	Switzerland
SUR	Surinam
SVK	Slovakia
SWE	Sweden
SYR	Syria
TAN	Tanzania
THA	Thailand
TJK	Tadjikistan
TKM	Turkmenistan
TON	Tonga
TPE	Taiwan (Chinese Taipeh)
TRI	Trinidad & Tobago
TUN	Tunisia
TUR	Turkey
UAE	United Arab Emirates
UGA	Uganda
UKR	Ukraine
URU	Uruguay
USA	United States
UZB	Uzbekistan
VAN	Vanuatu
VEN	Venezuela
WAL	Wales
WSA	Western Samoa
YUG	Yugoslavia
ZAI	Zaire
ZAM	Zambia
ZIM	Zimbabwe

American Football

The Super Bowl wasn't so super after all; the San Francisco 49ers so superior to the San Diego Chargers that it became a demonstration. San Francisco scored after just 1 minute 24 seconds, the quickest touchdown in a Super Bowl and by the third quarter, had extended their lead to 42-10. A second Super Bowl record seemed to be in prospect - the 45 point winning margin set by San Francisco when they defeated Denver in 1990 - until San Diego injected some late spirit into their play. Two touchdowns retrieved some self-respect for the Chargers, in their first Super Bowl, but San Francisco got a record anyway - the first team to win five Super Bowls and they achieved it in just 14 years. They had all the heroes; quarterback Steve Young (six touchdowns, no interceptions) was an easy choice for Most Valuable Player; wide receiver Jerry Rice (three touchdowns), playing most of the game with a dislocated shoulder, would have taken it in most years.

The reality was that the real Super Bowl had already taken place; when San Francisco met Dallas in the NFC Championship game. Those two teams have now won five of the last seven Super Bowls and are currently a distance ahead of the pack. Worse still, San Francisco's win was the 11th in succession by teams from the National Football Conference. Talk of change was in the wind, but it didn't happen. "The media were saying we should change," said a spokeman at the NFL, "But we never were." So they didn't. The net result will surely mean another championship where the best two teams meet before the final.

Steve Young's coronation came not before time; for four years he had understudied the best quarterback in the business, Joe Montana. The laconic Montana had won four Super Bowls with the 49ers and been named Most Valuable Player in three of them. As Young slipped on the crown, Montana bowed out, retiring two thirds of the way through his three year contract with Kansas City Chiefs. Montana had 16 seasons in the NFL and bade farewell at 38. Although his contract with Chiefs was only worth $3.3 million a year, Montana was football's biggest earner with endorsements bringing in another $12m. Young has not only inherited the mantle of football's best, but he'll also now be the sports biggest earner.

American football came back to Europe after a two-year absence when the World League was reconstituted. Rupert Murdoch's Fox Sports and the NFL combined to fund and organise the new six-team league. London, Amsterdam, Edinburgh, Frankfurt, Düsseldorf and Barcelona were the teams and everybody played everybody, leading to a modestly-titled World Bowl in June. Frankfurt Galaxy ran out champions, which was just reward for their fans who had turned out in considerable numbers to support them - over 33,000 for the German derby against Düsseldorf's Rhein Fire. More worrying for the World League was the lack of interest in Britain, where the London Monarchs could only entice 8,763 to their opening match at White Hart Lane and averaged about that for the season. In Edinburgh crowds dipped to just over 6,000 to watch the Scottish Claymores. Geoff Capes' son Lewis, who's almost as big as his dad, played for the Monarchs and generated some publicity, but little else did. Three years ago, American Football had the British media on-side and attendances for the Monarchs' games averaged 45,000. The crowds have gone, the media has lost interest, and the World League may find it difficult to recapture its brief golden days.

Super Bowl XXIX

San Francisco 49ers 49
San Diego Chargers 26

Joe Robbie Stadium, Miami Jan 29   74,107

TEAMS

San Francisco	Offense	San Diego
John Taylor	WR	Shawn Jefferson
Steve Wallace	LT	Harry Swane
Jesse Sapolu	LG	Isaac Davis
Bart Oates	C	Courtney Hall
Derrick Daese	RG	Joe Cocozzo
Harris Barton	RT	Stan Brock
Brent Jones	TE	Duane Young
Jerry Rice	WR	Mark Seay
Steve Young	QB	Stan Humphries
Ricky Watters	RB	Natrone Means
William Floyd	TE-RB	Alfred Pupunu
	Defense	
Dennis Brown	LE	Chris Mims
Bryant Young	LT	Shawn Lee
Dana Stubblefield	RT	Reuben Davis
Ricky Jackson	RE	Leslie O'Neal
Lee Woodall	LLB-OLB	David Griggs
Gary Plummer	MLB-ILB	Dennis Gibson
Ken Norton	RLB-ILB	Junior Seau
Eric Davis	LCB	Darrien Gordon
Deion Sanders	RCB	Dwayne Harper
Tim McDonald	SS	Darren Carrington
Merton Hanks	FS	Stanley Richard

SUBSTITUTIONS

San Francisco Offense: K-Doug Brien; P-Klaus Wilmsmeyer; QB-Elvis Grbac, Bill Musgrave; RB-Marc Logan, Derek Loville, Adam Walker; WR-Ed McCaffrey, Nate Singleton; TE-Ted Popson; T-Frank Pollack; G-Ralph Tamm; C-Chris Dalman; KR-Dexter Carter. Defense: DE-Tim Harris, Charles Mann, Troy Wilson; DT-Rhett Hall; LB-Antonio Goss, Darin Jordan, Kevin Mitchell; CB-Toi Cook, Tyronno Drakeford; S-Dana Hall. DNP-none

San Diego Offense: K-John Carney; P-Bryan Wagner; QB-Gale Gilbert; RB-Eric Bleniemy, Rodney Culver, Ronnie Harman; WR-Tony Martin; TE-David Binn, Shannon Mitchell; T-Eric Jonassen, Vaughn Parker; KR-Andre Coleman. Defense: DE-Raylee Johnson; DT-Les Miller, John Parrella; LB-Lewis Bush, Steve Hendrickson, Doug Miller; CB-Willie Clark, Sean Vanhorse; S-Eric Castle, Rodney Harrison. DNP: C-Curtis Whitley

SCORING

San Francisco (NFC)	14	14	14	7	49
San Diego (AFC)	7	3	8	8	26

SF Rice 44 pass from S Young (Brien kick)
SF Watters 51 pass from S Young (Brien kick)
SD Means 1 run (Carney kick)
SF Floyd 5 Pass from S Young (Brien kick)
SF Watters 8 pass from S Young (Brien kick)
SD FG Carney 31
SF Watters 9 run (Brien kick)
SF Rice 15 pass from S Young (Brien kick)
SD Coleman 98 kickoff retn (Seay pass from Humphries)
SF Rice 7 pass from S Young (Brien kick)
SD Martin 30 pass from Humphries (Pupunu pass from Humphries)

TEAM STATISTICS

	San Francisco	San Diego
Total First Downs	28	20
Total Net Yardage	455	354
Rushing Yards (Net)	139	67
Passing Yards (Net)	316	287
Total Return Yardage	76	243
Punts/Average	5/39.8	4/48.8
Third Downs	7/13	6/16
Fourth Downs	0/0	0/4
Time of Possession	31:31	28:29

INDIVIDUAL STATISTICS

RUSHING

San Francisco	No	Yds	LG	TD
Steve Young	5	49	21	0
Ricky Watters	15	47	13	1
William Floyd	9	32	6	0
Jerry Rice	1	10	10	0
San Diego				
Natrone Means	13	33	11	1
Shawn Jefferson	1	10	10	0
Ronnie Harman	2	10	10	0
Gale Gilbert	1	8	8	0

PASSING

San Francisco	Att	Comp	Yds	TD	Int
Steve Young	30	24	325	6	0
San Diego					
Stan Humphries	49	24	275	1	2

RECEIVING

San Francisco	No	Yds	LG	TD
Jerry Rice	10	149	44 t	3
John Taylor	4	43	10	0
William Floyd	4	26	9	1
Ricky Watters	3	61	51 t	2
San Diego				
Ronnie Harman	8	68	20	0
Mark Seay	7	75	22	0
Alfred Pupunu	4	48	23	0
Tony Martin	3	59	30 t	0

NFL Play-off Games

NATIONAL FOOTBALL CONFERENCE
Wild Card Play-off Games

Green Bay 16	Detroit 12
Chicago 35	Minnesota 18

Divisional Play-off Games

San Francisco 44	Chicago 15
Dallas 35	Green Bay 9

NFC Championship Game

San Francisco 38	Dallas 28

AMERICAN FOOTBALL CONFERENCE
Wild Card Play-off Games

Miami 27	Kansas 17
Cleveland 20	New England 13

Divisional Play-off Games

Pittsburgh 29	Cleveland 9
San Diego 22	Miami 21

AFC Championship Game

San Diego 17	Pittsburgh 13

NFL Final League Standings - 1994

NATIONAL FOOTBALL CONFERENCE

Eastern Division

	W	L	T	Pct	PF	PA
Dallas	12	4	0	.750	414	248
N Y Giants	9	7	0	.563	279	305
Arizona	8	8	0	.500	235	267
Philadelphia	7	9	0	.438	308	308
Washington	3	13	0	.188	320	412

Central Division

	W	L	T	Pct	PF	PA
Minnesota	10	6	0	.625	356	314
Green Bay*	9	7	0	.563	382	287
Detroit*	9	7	0	.563	357	342
Chicago*	9	7	0	.563	271	307
Tampa Bay	6	10	0	.375	251	351

Western Division

	W	L	T	Pct	PF	PA
San Francisco	13	3	0	.813	505	296
New Orleans	7	9	0	.438	348	407
Atlanta	7	9	0	.438	317	385
L A Rams	4	12	0	.250	286	365

AMERICAN FOOTBALL CONFERENCE

Eastern Division

	W	L	T	Pct	PF	PA
Miami	10	6	0	.625	389	327
New England	10	6	0	.625	351	312
Indianapolis	8	8	0	.500	307	320
Buffalo	7	9	0	.438	340	356
NY Jets	6	10	0	.375	264	320

Central Division

	W	L	T	Pct	PF	PA
Pittsburgh	12	4	0	.750	316	234
Cleveland*	11	5	0	.688	340	204
Cincinatti	3	13	0	.188	276	406
Houston	2	14	0	.125	226	352

Western Division

	W	L	T	Pct	PF	PA
San Diego	11	5	0	.688	381	306
Kansas City*	9	7	0	.563	319	298
LA Raiders	9	7	0	.563	347	396
Denver	7	9	0	.438	303	327
Seattle	6	10	0	.375	287	323

Wild cards

*Q*uotes

"Nobody is going to come out and walk through us. We're a professional team and you don't get to this level by being a pansy" - **Natrone Means, San Diego running-back.**

"We knew we were gonna kick their butts, but we couldn't say that. The real Superbowl was against the Cowboys. We just knew we'd beat the hell out of this team" - **Deion Sanders, 49ers cornerback, telling it like it was after the Super Bowl.**

"When he came out of the room with the papers smoking and that Albert Einstein look, I knew we had a game-plan" - **Steve Young, 49ers quarterback, on his team's offensive co-ordinator Mike Shanahan.**

"What we were doing out there today was like a symphony with Steve Young conducting" - **Jesse Sapolu, 49ers left-guard.**

"They've separated themselves from everyone else, from the Steelers, the Cowboys and anyone else. They're all a half-step back now. The 49ers are just superior in organization, in philosophy, in system, in playmakers" - **Jamie Williams, 49ers former tight-end.**

"I don't need anymore exposure, I'm household" - **Deion Sanders.**

"Bigger than Buddha, bigger than Godzilla" - **Kansas City Chief's president Carl Peterson describing the retiring Joe Montana.**

NFC Statistics

SCORING

	Td	Tdr	Tdp	Tdm	Xkg	X2g	Fg	Saf	Pts
San Francisco	66	23	37	6	60	2	15	0	505
Dallas	50	26	19	5	48	0	22	0	414
Green Bay	47	11	33	3	41	1	19	0	382
Detroit	43	12	24	7	39	2	18	1	357
Minnesota	36	11	18	7	30	4	34	0	356
New Orleans	38	11	22	5	32	2	28	0	348
Washington	37	5	25	7	30	3	20	1	320
Atlanta	36	8	25	3	32	3	21	0	317
Philadelphia	35	14	18	3	33	0	21	1	308
LA Rams	33	6	23	4	28	2	18	1	286
NY Giants	30	12	16	2	27	1	22	2	279
Chicago	30	10	19	1	24	2	21	0	271
Tampa Bay	26	8	17	1	20	3	23	0	251
Arizona	24	12	11	1	21	1	22	1	235

SCORERS

Records: Points 176-Paul Hornung, Green Bay 1960
Touchdowns 24-John Riggins, Washington 1983
Field Goals 35-Ali Haji-Sheikh, New York 1983
Extra points 62-Mark Moseley, Washington 1983

Kickers

	Xp	Xpa	FgFga		Pts
Fuad Reveiz (Minnesota)	30	30	34	39	132
Morten Anderson (New Orleans)	32	32	28	39	116
Chris Boniol (Dallas)	48	48	22	29	114
Doug Brien (San Francisco)	60	62	15	20	105
Chris Jacke (Green Bay)	41	43	19	26	98

Non-kickers

	Td	Tdr	TdpTdm		X2G	Pts
Emmitt Smith (Dallas)	22	21	1	0	0	132
Sterling Sharpe (Green Bay)	18	0	18	0	0	108
Jerry Rice (San Francisco)	15	2	13	0	1	92
Terance Mathis (Atlanta)	11	0	11	0	2	70
Herman Moore (Detroit)	11	0	11	0	0	66

PASSING

Records Completions: 363-Brett Favre, GB, 1994
Touchdowns: 36-Y A Tittle, NY 1963
Yards: 4,614-Neil Lomax, St L 1984
Longest for Td: 99yds-Frank Filchock, Was
1939; George Izo, Was 1963; Karl Sweetan, Det
1966; Sonny Jurgensen, Was 1968; Ron
Jaworski, Phi 1985

	Att	Com	Pct	Yds	Ave	Td	Rating
Steve Young (SF)	461	324	70.3	3969	8.61	35	112.8
Brett Favre (GB)	582	363	62.4	3882	6.67	33	90.7
Jim Everett (NO)	540	346	64.5	3855	7.14	22	84.9
Troy Aikman (Dallas)	361	233	64.5	2676	7.41	13	84.9
Jeff George (Atlanta)	524	322	61.5	3734	7.13	23	83.3

PUNTING

Records Number: 114-Bob Parsons, Chicago 1981
Average: 51.4yds-Sammy Baugh, Washington
1940; Longest: 94yds-Joe Lintzenich, Chicago
1931

	No	Yds	Lg	Ave	Ret yds	Net Ave
Sean Landeta (Rams)	78	3494	62	44.8	637	34.3
Reggie Roby (Wash)	82	3639	65	44.4	441	36.1
Greg Montgomery (Dt)	63	2782	64	44.2	431	34.2
Tom Barnhardt (NO)	67	2920	57	43.6	495	33.5
Mike Saxon (Min)	77	3301	67	42.9	410	36.2

RUSHING

Records Carries: 407-James Wilder, Tampa Bay 1984
Yards: 2,105-Eric Dickerson, Los Angeles 1984
TDs: 24-John Riggins, Washington 1983

	Att	Yds	Avg	Long	TD
Barry Sanders (Det)	331	1883	5.7	85	7
Emmitt Smith (Dallas)	368	1484	4.0	46	21
Rodney Hampton (Gia)	327	1075	3.3	27 t	6
Terry Allen (Min)	255	1031	4.0	45	8
Jerome Bettis (Rams)	319	1025	3.2	19	3

PASS RECEIVING

Records Receptions 122-Cris Carter, Min
1994; Yards 1570-Jerry Rice, San Francisco
1986; TDs 22-Jerry Rice, San Francisco 1987

	No	Yds	Avg	Long	TD
Cris Carter (Min)	122	1256	10.3	65 t	7
Jerry Rice (SF)	112	1499	13.4	69 t	13
Terance Mathis (Atl)	111	1342	12.1	81	11
Sterling Sharpe (GB)	94	1119	11.9	49	18
Jake Reed (Min)	85	1175	13.8	59	4

INTERCEPTIONS

Records Number: 14-Dick Lane, LA 1952
Yards: 304-Deion Sanders, SF, 1994
Longest Return: 102yds - Bob Smith, Detroit
1949; Erich Barnes, NY 1961
TDs: 3-Dick Lynch, NY 1963; Herb Adderley, GB
1965; Monte Jackson, LA 1976; Rod Perry, LA
1976; Ronnie Lott, SF 1981; Wayne Haddix,
TB,1990; Robert Massey, Pho 1992; Deion
Sanders, SF, 1994

	No	Yds	Avg	Long	TD
Aeneas Williams (Ariz)	9	89	9.9	43	0
Merton Hanks (SF)	7	93	13.3	38	0
Deion Sanders (SF)	6	303	50.5	93 t	3
Greg Jackson (Phi)	6	86	14.3	55 t	1
Vinnie Clark (Atl-NO)	5	149	29.8	74	0

PUNT RETURNS

Records Number: 70-Danny Reece, Tampa Bay 1979
Yards: 646-Eddie Brown, Washington 1976
Longest for TD: 103yds-Robert Bailey, Rams,
1994

	No	FC	Yds	Avg	Long	TD
Brian Mitchell (Wash)	32	14	452	14.1	78 t	2
David Meggett (Gia)	26	14	323	12.4	68 t	2
Mel Gray (Detroit)	21	12	233	11.1	24	0
Vernon Turner (TB)	21	4	218	10.4	80 t	1
Jeff Sydner (Phi)	40	17	381	9.5	49	0

KICKOFF RETURNS

Records Number: 63-Tyrone Hughes, NO, 1994
Yards: 1,556-Tyrone Hughes, NO, 1994
Longest: 106yds-Al Carmichael, GB 1956;Roy
Green, St L 1979 TDs: 4-Travis Williams, GB
1967; Cecil Turner, Chi, 1970

	No	Yds	Avg	Long	TD
Mel Gray (Detroi)	45	1276	28.4	102 t	3
Herschel Walker (Phi)	21	581	27.7	94 t	1
Kevin Williams (Dallas)	43	1148	26.7	87 t	1
Brian Mitchell (Wash)	58	1478	25.5	86	0
Nate Lewis (Chi)	35	874	25.0	55	0

AFC Statistics

SCORING

	Td	Tdr	Tdp	Tdm	Xkg	X2g	Fg	Saf	Pts
Miami	45	13	31	1	35	6	24	0	389
San Diego	40	13	20	7	33	3	34	0	381
New England	39	12	25	2	36	0	27	0	351
Denver	37	19	18	0	29	3	30	0	347
Cleveland	37	12	20	5	32	4	26	0	340
Buffalo	38	14	23	1	38	0	24	1	340
Kansas City	34	12	20	2	30	3	25	2	319
Pittsburgh	35	15	17	3	32	1	24	0	316
Indianapolis	37	15	15	7	37	0	16	0	307
LA Raiders	34	7	22	5	31	1	22	0	303
Seattle	32	16	13	3	25	4	20	1	287
Cincinatti	27	5	21	1	24	2	28	1	276
NY Jets	29	8	18	3	26	2	20	0	264
Houston	25	10	13	2	18	4	16	1	226

SCORERS

Records: Points 155-Gino Cappelleti, Bos 1964
Touchdowns 23-O J Simpson, Buf ,1975
Field Goals 34-Jim Turner, New York 1968
34-Nick Lowery, Kansas City 1990
34-John Carney, SD, 1994
Extra points 66-Uwe von Schamann, Mia, 1984

Kickers

	Xp	Xpa	FgFga		Pts
John Carney (San Diego)	33	33	34	38	135
Jason Elam (Denver)	29	29	30	37	119
Matt Bahr (New England)	36	36	27	34	117
Steve Christie (Buffalo)	38	38	24	28	110
Matt Stover (Cleveland)	32	32	26	28	110

Non-kickers

	Td	Tdr	TdpTdm		X2G	Pts
Marshall Faulk (Ind'polis)	12	11	1	0	0	72
Natrone Means (San Diego)	12	12	0	0	0	72
Chris Warren (Seattle)	11	9	2	0	1	68
Carl Pickens (Cincinatti)	11	0	11	0	0	66

PASSING

Records Completions: 404-Warren Moon, Houston 1991
Touchdowns: 48-Dan Marino, Miami 1984
Yards: 5,084-Dan Marino, Miami 1984
Longest for TD: 99yds-Jim Plunkett, LA 1983
99yds-Stan Humphries, SD, 1994

	Att	Com	Pct	Yds	Ave	Td	Rating
Dan Marino (Miami)	615	385	62.6	4453	7.24	30	89.2
John Elway (Denver)	494	307	62.1	3490	7.06	16	85.7
Jim Kelly (Buffalo)	448	285	63.6	3114	6.95	22	84.6
Joe Montana (KC)	493	299	60.6	3283	6.66	16	83.6
Stan Humphries (SD)	453	264	58.3	3209	7.08	17	81.6

PUNTING

Records Number: 105-Bob Scarpitto, Denver 1967
Average: 46.9-Greg Montgomery, Houston 1992
Longest: 98yds-Steve O'Neal, New York 1969

	No	Yds	Lg	Ave	Ret yds	Net Ave
Jeff Gossett (Raiders)	77	3377	65	43.9	366	35.2
Lee Johnson (Cin)	79	3461	64	43.8	459	35.3
Rick Tuten (Seattle)	91	3905	64	42.9	426	36.7
Tom Rouen (Denver)	76	3258	59	42.9	275	37.1
Rich Camarillo (Ho)	96	4115	58	42.9	438	36.4

RUSHING

Records Carries: 390-Barry Foster, Pit,1992
Yards: 2,003-O J Simpson, Buf 1973
TDs: 19-Earl Campbell, Hou 1979
Chuck Muncie, SD 1981

	Att	Yds	Avg	Long	TD
Chris Warren (Seattle)	333	1545	4.6	41	9
Natrone Means (SD)	343	1350	3.9	25	12
Marshall Faulk (Ind)	314	1282	4.1	52	11
Thurman Thomas (Bu)	287	1093	3.8	29	7
Harvey Williams (Rai)	282	983	3.5	28	4

PASS RECEIVING

Records Receptions 101-Charlie Hennigan, H'ston 1964
Yards 1,746-Charlie Hennigan, Houston 1961
TDs 18-Mark Clayton, Miami 1984

	No	Yds	Avg	Long	TD
Ben Coates (NE)	96	1174	12.2	62 t	7
Andre Reed (Buf)	90	1303	14.5	83 t	8
Tim Brown (Raiders)	89	1309	14.7	77 t	9
Shannon Sharpe (Den)	87	1010	11.6	44	4
Brian Blades (Seattle)	81	1086	13.4	45	4

INTERCEPTIONS

RecordsNumber: 13-Lester Hayes, Oak 1980
Yards: 349-Charlie McNeil, SD 1961
Longest Return: 103yds-Venice Glenn, SD 1987
Louis Oliver, Mia 1992
TDs: 4-Ken Houston, Hou 1971; JimKearney,KC 1972

	No	Yds	Avg	Long	TD
Eric Turner (Cleveland)	9	199	22.1	93 t	1
Ray Buchanan (Ind)	8	221	27.6	90 t	3
Darren Perry (Pittsb)	7	112	16.0	24	0
Terry McDaniel (Raidrs)	7	103	14.7	35	2
Maurice Hurst (NE)	7	68	9.7	24	0

PUNT RETURNS

Records Number: 62-Fulton Walker, LA1985
Yards: 692-Fulton Walker, Los Angeles 1985
Longest for TD: 98yds-Terance Mathis, NY 1990

	No	FC	Yds	Avg	Long	TD
Darrien Gordon (SD)	36	19	475	13.2	90 t	2
Tim Brown (Rai)	40	14	487	12.2	48	0
Corey Sawyer (Cin)	26	16	307	11.8	82 t	1
Jeff Burris (Buf)	32	6	332	10.4	57	0
Eric Metcalf (Cle)	35	6	348	9.9	92 t	2

KICKOFF RETURNS

Records Number: 55-Bruce Harper, NY 1978-9
David Turner, Cin 1979
Yards: 1,317-Bobby Jancik, Hou 1963
Longest: 106yds-Nolan Smith, KC 1967
TDs: 3-Ray Clayborn, NE 1977

	No	Yds	Avg	Long	TD
Randy Baldwin (Cle)	28	753	26.9	85 t	1
Andre Coleman (SD)	49	1293	26.4	90 t	2
Jon Vaughn (Sea-KC)	33	829	25.1	93 t	2
Butler By'Not'e (Den)	24	545	22.7	41	0
Ron Dickerson (KC)	21	472	22.5	62	0

World League ━━━━━━━

Week One
Olympic Stadium   Apr 8
Amsterdam Admirals 17
Barcelona Dragons 13
Waldstadion   Apr 8
Frankfurt Galaxy 45
London Monarchs 22
Murrayfield   Apr 9
Scottish Claymores 17
Rhein Fire 19
Week Two
De Meer Stadium   Apr 15
Amsterdam Admirals 14
Frankfurt Galaxy 12
Rheinstadion, Düsseldorf   Apr 15
Rhein Fire 7
London Monarchs 23
Montjuic Stadium   Apr 17
Barcelona Dragons 10
Scottish Claymores 7
Week Three
Montjuic Stadium   Apr 23
Barcelona Dragons 32
Rhein Fire 30
Waldstadion   Apr 22
Frankfurt Galaxy 14
Scottish Claymores 20
White Hart Lane   Apr 23
London Monarchs 10
Amsterdam Admirals 17
Week Four
Murrayfield   Apr 30
Scottish Claymores 0
Amsterdam Admirals 31
White Hart Lane   Apr 30
London Monarchs 24
Barcelona Dragons 39
Rheinstadion   Apr 30
Rhein Fire 21
Frankfurt Galaxy 20
Week Five
Olympic Stadium   May 6
Amsterdam Admirals 30
Rhein Fire 10
Waldstadion   May 6
Frankfurt Galaxy 24
Barcelona Dragons 20
Murrayfield   May 7
Scottish Claymores 10
London Monarchs 11
Week Six
Montjuic Stadium   May 15
Barcelona Dragons 34
Amsterdam Admirals 40
White Hart Lane   May 14
London Monarchs 7
Frankfurt Galaxy 27
Rheinstadion   May 13
Rhein Fire 33
Scottish Claymores 27

Week Seven
Olympic Stadium   May 20
Amsterdam Admirals 30
Scottish Claymores 13
Montjuic Stadium   May 20
Barcelona Dragons 22
London Monarchs 27
Waldstadion   May 20
Frankfurt Galaxy 28
Rhein Fire 41
Week Eight
Murrayfield   May 27
Scottish Claymores 13
Barcelona Dragons 16
Waldstadion   May 27
Frankfurt Galaxy 28
Amsterdam Admirals 13
White Hart Lane   May 29
London Monarchs 34
Rhein Fire 14
Week Nine
De Meer Stadium   June 3
Amsterdam Admirals 17
London Monarchs 7
Rheinstadion   June 3
Rhein Fire 21
Barcelona Dragons 31
Murrayfield   June 4
Scottish Claymores 24
Frankfurt Galaxy 37
Week Ten
Montjuic Stadium   June10
Barcelona Dragons 20
Frankfurt Galaxy 44
White Hart Lane   June 10
London Monarchs 9
Scottish Claymores 22
Rheinstadion   June 10
Rhein Fire 25
Amsterdam Admirals 37

Overall Table

Amsterdam	9	1	0 .800	246	152
Frankfurt	6	4	0 .600	285	196
Barcelona	5	5	0 .500	237	247
London	4	6	0 .400	174	220
Rhein	4	6	0 .400	221	279
Scotland	2	8	0 .200	153	210

World Bowl

Olympic Stadium
Amsterdam,   June 17
Amsterdam Admirals 22
Frankfurt Galaxy 26

Eurobowl IX

Qualification Round 1
Malmo   Apr 9
Limhamn Griffins SWE 45
Copenhagen Towers DEN 14
Birmingham Apr 9
Birmingham Bulls GBR 40
Rotterdam Trojans HOL 12
Brussels   Apr 9
Brussels Raiders BEL 8
Paris Castors/Sphinx FRA 51
Basel   Apr 2
Basilisk Mean Machine SUI 7
Vienna Vikings AUT 35
Quarter-finals
Helsinki   May 7
Limhamn Griffins 12
East City Giants FIN 15
Birmingham Apr 30
Birmingham Bulls 13
London Olympians GBR 14
Paris   Apr 30
Paris Castor/Sphinx 32
Legnano Frogs ITA 33
Vienna   May 7
Vienna Vikings 0
Düsseldorf Panthers GER 15
Semi-finals
London   June 4
London Olympians 14
East City Giants 13
Düsseldorf May 28
Düsseldorf Panthers 35
Legnano Frogs 31

Final
Stuttgart   July 7
Attendance 20,500
Düsseldorf Panthers 21
London Olympians 14
MVP: Estrus Crayton (DP-RB)

━━━━━━━

Baseball might have suffered a downturn in popularity following the strike, but the Superbowl still makes the cash registers ring. Such was the pull of the 1995 event that advertisers paid $800,000 for a 30-second spot during the game. Translated into sterling, it is over a million pounds a minute.

American Football History

Super Bowl

Season		Winner	Loser	Score	Venue	Attendance	MVP Team-Pos
I	15.1.67	Green Bay	Kansas City	35-10	Los Angeles	61,946	Bart Starr (GB-QB)
II	14.1.68	Green Bay	Oakland	33-14	Miami	75,546	Bart Starr (GB-QB)
III	12.1.69	New York Jets	Baltimore	16-7	Miami	75,389	Joe Namath (NY-QB)
IV	11.1.70	Kansas City	Minnesota	23-7	New Orleans	80,582	Len Dawson (KC-QB)
V	17.1.71	Baltimore	Dallas	16-13	Miami	79,204	Chuck Howley (D-LB)
VI	16.1.72	Dallas	Miami	24-3	New Orleans	81,023	Roger Staubach (D-QB)
VII	14.1.73	Miami	Washington	14-7	Los Angeles	90,182	Jake Scott (M-S)
VIII	31.1.74	Miami	Minnesota	24-7	Houston	71,882	Larry Csonka (M-RB)
IX	12.1.75	Pittsburgh	Minnesota	16-6	New Orleans	80,997	Franco Harris (P-RB)
X	18.1.76	Pittsburgh	Dallas	21-7	Miami	80,187	Lynn Swann (P-WR)
XI	9.1.77	Oakland	Minnesota	32-14	Pasadena	103,438	Fred Biletnikoff (O-WR)
XII	15.1.78	Dallas	Denver	27-10	New Orleans	75,583	White & Martin (D-DT/DE)
XIII	21.1.79	Pittsburgh	Dallas	35-31	Miami	79,484	Terry Bradshaw (P-QB)
XIV	20.1.80	Pittsburgh	Los Angeles	31-19	Pasadena	103,985	Terry Bradshaw (P-QB)
XV	25.1.81	Oakland	Philadelphia	27-10	New Orleans	76,135	Jim Plunkett (O-QB)
XVI	24.1.82	San Francisco	Cincinnati	26-21	Pontiac	81,270	Joe Montana (SF-QB)
XVII	30.1.83	Washington	Miami	27-17	Pasadena	103,667	John Riggins (W-RB)
XVIII	22.1.84	LA Raiders	Washington	38-9	Tampa	72,920	Marcus Allen (LA-RB)
XIX	20.1.85	San Francisco	Miami	38-16	Stanford	84,059	Joe Montana (SF-QB)
XX	26.1.86	Chicago	New England	46-10	New Orleans	73,818	Richard Dent (CH-DE)
XXI	25.1.87	New York Gts	Denver	39-20	Pasadena	101,063	Phil Simms (NY-QB)
XXII	13.1.88	Washington	Denver	42-10	San Diego	73,302	Doug Williams (W-QB)
XXIII	22.1.89	San Francisco	Cincinnati	20-16	Miami	75,129	Jerry Rice (SF-WR)
XXIV	28.1.90	San Francisco	Denver	55-10	New Orleans	72,919	Joe Montana (SF-QB)
XXV	27.1.91	New York Gts	Buffalo	20-19	Tampa	73,813	Ottis Anderson (NY-RB)
XXVI	26.1.92	Washington	Buffalo	37-24	Minneapolis	63,130	Mark Rypien (W-QB)
XXVII	31.1.93	Dallas	Buffalo	52-17	Pasadena	98,374	Troy Aikman (D-QB)
XXVIII	30.1.94	Dallas	Buffalo	30-13	Atlanta	72,817	Emmitt Smith (D-RB)
XXIX	29.1.95	San Francisco	San Diego	49-28	Miami	74,107	Steve Young (S-QB)

World Bowl

1991	London Monarchs 21	Barcelona Dragons 0	Wembley
1995	Frankfurt Galaxy 26	Amsterdam Admirals 22	Amsterdam

Eurobowl

1986	Eurobowl I	Taft Vantaa	Finland
1988	Eurobowl II	Helsinki Roosters	Finland
1989	Eurobowl III	Legnano Frogs	Italy
1990	Eurobowl IV	Manchester Spartans	Gt Britain
1991	Eurobowl V	Amsterdam Crusaders	Netherlands
1992	Eurobowl VI	Amsterdam Crusaders	Netherlands
1993	Eurobowl VII	London Olympians	Gt Britain
1994	Eurobowl VIII	London Olympians	Gt Britain
1995	Eurobowl IX	Düsseldorf Panther	Germany

Angling ━━━━━━━━━━━━

Fly Fishing
World Championship

Loughs Connemara and Corrib, Ireland Sep 3-7
Aggreggate placings after six periods of fishing determine
the final order. The lowest total wins.
Individual

1	**Jeremy Hermann**	**ENG**	**50**
2	Alain Gigot	FRA	51
3	Owen Nuttridge	AUS	57
4	Hywel Morgan	WAL	66
5	Chris Ogborne	ENG	68
6	George Barron	WAL	70

Team
1. England 423; 2. Wales 424;
3. Belgium 461; 4. Ireland 480;
5. Australia 490; 6. New Zealand 498

Coarse Angling
World Championship

Saimaa Canal, Lappeenranta, Finland   Aug 12-13
Individual

1	**Paul Jean**	**FRA**
2	J Wilmart	BEL
3	J Desque	FRA
4	J Fougeat	FRA
5	G Sorti	ITA
6	K Milson	ENG
Also		
11	A Scotthorne	ENG
21	M Addy	ENG
39	S Gardener	ENG
63	B Nudd	ENG

Team
1. France; 2 Belgium; 3. Italy; 4. England; 11. Wales;
14. Ireland; 22. Scotland

National Championship

Gloucester Canal   *July 1*

	Club	Pts	Peg
1	**Barnsley & District**	**807**	**85**
2	Leicester AS	778	79
3	Daiwa Goldthorpe	761	83
4	Nottingham & District	721	48
5	Tek Neek Niddmen	711	82
6	Essex Van Den Eynde	709	61
7	Dorking	676	57
8	Starlets	665	65
9	Bourne	657	84
10	Tri Cast Highfield	657	71
11	Daiwa Gordon League	654	2
12	Liverpool & District	652	51

Anglers' tales are the stuff of legend, so it should come as no surprise that *Anglers' Mail* launched their Fantasy Fishing League in 1995. Entrants to the competition 'buy' a five-strong team from a list of Britain's top 300 anglers and score from the weekend matches held throughout the nine-month coarse fishing season, which started in June. The prize is a £2,000 Drennan Polemaster, which extends to 14 metres.

One person who presumably won't be entering is Alex White, who lodged a claim for a British record carp, which weighed in at 55lbs 6ozs. This season the goalposts changed for coarse angling; on enclosed waters (not canals or rivers) you can now fish through the spring season and White's carp was, almost certainly, heavy with spawn. We don't know whether Mr White used the Drennan Polemaster, we think its more likely that, with a fish the weight of a Romanian gymnast, he used a small crane.

G O Edwards features in our new records section and, yes, it is *that* Gareth Edwards. He caught his mighty pike in Llandegledd Reservoir, Pontypool in 1990 and he thought the record had been broken - though it's still on the official list. The suggestion was someone else had caught his pike, too: that's the problem with angling, if somebody catches your fish and it's had a bigger lunch than when you caught it, you lose your record.

Chris Ogborne retired from the fly fishing scene this year. Ogborne's record, of qualifying for the England team for each of the past 15 years, is without parallel. Ogborne retired on a perfect note, England winning both the individual and team prizes in the World Championships in Ireland.

World Champions

WORLD COARSE ANGLING CHAMPIONS

Year	Individual	Team
1957	Mandelli ITA	Italy
1958	Garroit BEL	Belgium
1959	Robert Tesse FRA	France
1960	Robert Tesse FRA	Belgium
1961	Ramon Legogue FRA	East Germany
1962	Raimondo Tedasco ITA	Italy
1963	William Lane ENG	France
1964	Joseph Fontanet FRA	France
1965	Robert Tesse FRA	Romania
1966	Henri Guiheneuf FRA	France
1967	Jacques Isenbaert BEL	Belgium
1968	Gunter Grebenstein FRG	France
1969	Robin Harris ENG	Netherlands
1970	Marcel Van den Eynde BEL	Belgium
1971	Dino Bassi ITA	Italy
1972	Hubert Levels HOL	France
1973	Pierre Michiels BEL	Belgium
1974	Aribert Richter FRG	France
1975	Ian Heaps ENG	France
1976	Dino Bassi ITA	Italy
1977	Jean Mainil BEL	Luxembourg
1978	Jean-Pierre Fourgeat FRA	France
1979	Gerard Heulard FRA	France
1980	Wolf-Rudiger Kremkus FRG	West Germany
1981	Dave Thomas ENG	France
1982	Kevin Ashurst ENG	Netherlands
1983	Wolf-Rudiger Kremkus FRG	Belgium
1984	Bobby Smithers IRE	Luxembourg
1985	Dave Roper ENG	England
1986	Lud Wever HOL	Italy
1987	Clive Branson WAL	England
1988	Jean-Pierre Fougeat FRA	England
1989	Tom Pickering ENG	Wales
1990	Bob Nudd ENG	France
1991	Bob Nudd ENG	England
1992	David Wesson AUS	Italy
1993	Mario Barros POR	Italy
1994	Bob Nudd ENG	England
1995	Paul Jean FRA	France

WORLD FLY FISHING CHAMPIONS

1981	C Wittkamp HOL	Netherlands
1982	Viktor Diez ESP	Italy
1983	Segismondo Fernandez ESP	Italy
1984	Tony Pawson ENG	Italy
1985	Leslaw Frasik POL	Poland
1986	Slivoj Svoboda TCH	Italy
1987	Brian Leadbetter ENG	England
1988	John Pawson ENG	England
1989	Wladislaw Trzebuinia POL	Poland
1990	Franciszek Szajnik POL	Czechoslovakia
1991	Brian Leadbetter ENG	New Zealand
1992	Perluigi Cocito ITA	Italy
1993	Russell Owen WAL	England
1994	P Coquard FRA	Czech Republic
1995	Jeremy Herman ENG	England

NATIONAL LEAGUE, DIVISION CHAMPIONS

The National League began in 1906, results from 1960

Year	Individual	Team
1960	K Smith	King's Lynn
1961	J Blakey	Coventry
1962	V Baker	Lincoln
1963	R Sims	Northampton N
1964	C Burch	Kidderminster
1965	D Burr	Rugby
1966	R jarvis	Boston
1967	E Townsin	Derby Railway
1968	D Groom	Leighton Buzz
1969	R Else	Stoke
1970	B Lakey	Cambridge
1971	R Harris	Leicester
1972	P Coles	Birmingham
1973	A Wright	Grimsby
1974	P Anderson	Leicester
1975	M Hoad-Reddick	Birmingham
1976	N Wells	Birmingham
1977	R Foster	Coventry
1978	D Harris	Coleshill
1979	M Cullen	Barnsley
1980	P Burrell	Notts
1981	D Steer	Essex
1982	A Mayer	Rotherham
1983	D Howl	Notts
1984	C Gregg	Coleshill
1985	B Oliver	ABC
1986	M Stabler	I Walton, Staffs
1987	J Robinson	Nottingham
1988	S Hall	Redditch
1989	B Wickens	Reading
1990	S Cheetham	Trevs
1991	P Hargreaves	I Walton, Preston
1992	K Gregory	Nottingham
1993	S Canty	Liverpool
1994	S Ellis	Highfield
1995	S Tyler	Barnsley

BRITISH FRESHWATER RECORDS

Fish	Weight (lbs & ozs)		Fisher
Barbel	14	6	The Hon Aylmer D Tyron
Bream	16	6	A Bromley
Carp	51	8	C Yates
Catfish	43	8	R J Bray
Chub	8	4	G F Smith
Eel	11	2	S Terry
Grayling	4	3	Sean Lanigan
Gudgeon	0	5	D H Hull
Golden Orfe	5	15	G Sherwin
Perch	5	9	J Shayner
Pike	45	6	G O Edwards
Roach	4	3	R N Clarke
Rudd	4	8	Rev E C Alston
Salmon	64	0	Miss G W Ballatine
Tench	14	3	P A Gooriah
Trout, Brown	20	3	J Gardner
Trout, R'bow	24	2	J Moore
Trout, Sea	22	8	S Burgoyne

Archery

World Championships

Jakarta, Indonesia   *Aug 1-6*
MEN'S OLYMPIC
1. Lee Kyung-Chul KOR; 2. Wu Tsung Yi TPE;
3. Oh Kyo-Moon KOR; 77. Jonathan Shales GBR;
97. Dale Hughes GBR; 101. Roger Furness GBR.
Team 1. Korea; 2. Italy; 3. United States; 25. Great
Britain
MEN'S COMPOUND
1. Gary Broadhead USA; 2. John Vozzy USA; 3. Phillip
Tremelling AUS; 5. Simon Tarplee GBR; 15. Neil
Wakelin GBR
Team 1. France; 2. United States; 3. Australia
Neil Wakelin shot a personal best FITA of 1315 for his
15th placing
WOMEN'S OLYMPIC
1. Natayla Valeeva MLD; 2. Barbara Mensing GER;
3. Youm Young-Ja KOR ; 37. Alison Williamson GBR
Team 1. Korea; 2. Turkey; 3. Indonesia
Alison Williamson, by finishing in the top 46, earned
Britain a women's Olympic place in the Atlanta Games
WOMEN'S COMPOUND
1. Angela Moscarelli USA; 2. Petra Eriksson SWE;
3. Inga Low USA; 10. Nichola Simpson GBR
Team 1. United States; 2. Sweden; 3. Italy

British Target Championships

Lichfield, Staffs Aug 12-13
Men's Olympic
1. Steve Hallard (Dunlop); 2. Gary Hardinges (Ellswood);
3. Richard Priestman (Nethermoss)
Men's Compound
1. Stephen Gooden (Llantarnam)
Women's Olympic
1. Alison Williamson (Long Mynd); 2. Sue Wooff (Dunlop)
3. J Williams (Redruth)
Women's Compound
1. G Buckman (County Oak)

All British and Open Field Championships

Glycornel AC, Rhondda   *May 27-28*
Men's Olympic
1. Jonathan Shales (VAC); 2. Paul Kelly (Gawthorpe);
3. Gary Kinghorn (Worthing)
Men's Compound
1. Dave Jones (GNAS); 2. Simon Tarplee (Evesham);
3. Ben Jones (Merlin)
Women's Olympic
1. Pauline Edwards (Atkins); 2. Jackie Wilkinson
(Maryport); 3. Danielle Van Buren (GNAS)
Women's Compound
1. Carys Jones (GNAS); 2. Maggie Squires (Carlton
Hayes); 3. Jean Howells (Pentref)

UK Masters

Lilleshall, Shropshire   *June 10-11*
Men's Olympic (The Petty Trophy)
1. John Low; 2. Simon Needham; 3. John McIlroy
Men's Compound (The Red Rose Salver)
1. Simon Tarplee; 2. Jan Lesinski; 3. Neil Wakelin
Women's Olympic (The Ogden Trophy)
1. Alison Williamson; 2. Sue Wooff; 3. Sandy Snowden
Women's Compound (The White Rose Salver)
1. Nichola Simpson; 2. Wendy Lesinski

Grand National Meeting

Lilleshall, Shropshire   *June 28-30*
Double York (men) 1. Tony Nilsen 2181; 2. Michael
Holden 2165; 3. Dave Winfield 2154
Men's Best Double Distances 100yds: Nigel Thompson
947; 80yds: Ian Pugh 732; 60yds: Chris Marsh 395
Double Hereford (women) 1. Sandy Snowden 2197;
2. Jill Newland 2169; 3. Brenda Thomas 2149
Women's Best Double distances 80yds: Carol Shaw 926;
60yds: Margaret Osmond 704; 50yds: Sheila Wright 390

World Indoor Championships

NIA, Birmingham   *Mar 23-26*
Men's Olympic 1. Magnus Pettersson SWE; 2.
Sebastien Flute FRA; 3. Fred Van Zutphen HOL
Team 1. United States; 2. France; 3. Italy
Men's Compound 1. Michael Hendrikse USA; 2. Niels
Baldur DEN; 3. Dee Wilde USA
Team 1. United States; 2. Denmark; 3. Italy
Women's Olympic 1. Natalya Valeeva MLD; 2 Patricia
Michal FRA; 3. Natalya Nasaridze TUR
Team 1. Ukraine; 2. Russia; 3. Italy
Women's Compound 1. Glenda Penaz USA; 2. Petra
Eriksson SWE; 3. Nichola Simpson GBR
Team 1. United States; 2. Sweden; 3. Italy

National Indoor Championships

NIA, Birmingham   *Mar 19*
Men's Olympic 1. Dave Hodges (Harrow); 2. Bob Powell
(Evesham); 3. John Sansom (Gren Dragon)
Men's Compound 1. Andy Yardy (Oxford); 2. Neil
Wakelin (Stortford); 3. Pete Howlett (Buckland)
Women's Olympic 1. Josie Chandler (FOBB); 2. Susan
McGrath (Dunlop); 3. Alison Williamson (Long Mynd)
Women's Compound 1. Alex Tarasek (GNAS);
2.Nichola Simpson (Oxford); 3. Maryann Richardson
(Llandaff City)
Easton Cup (Home International)
1. England; 2. Scotland; 3. Northern Ireland; 4. Wales

World Champions

OUTDOOR WORLD CHAMPIONS (OLYMPIC)

Year	Men's Individual	Women's Individual	Men's Team	Women's Team
1931	Michal Sawicki POL	Janina Kurkowska POL	France	-
1932	Laurent Reith BEL	Janina Kurkowska POL	Poland	-
1933	Don Mackenzie USA	Janina Kurkowska POL	Belgium	Poland
1934	Henry Kjellson SWE	Janina Kurkowska POL	Sweden	Poland
1935	Adriaan van Kohlen BEL	Ina Catani SWE	Belgium	Great Britain
1936	Emil Heilborn SWE	Janina Kurkowska POL	Czechoslovakia	Poland
1937	George De Rons BEL	Ingo Simon GBR	Poland	Great Britain
1938	Frantisek Hadas TCH	Nora Weston Martyr GBR	Czechoslavakia	Poland
1939	Roger Beday FRA	Janina Kurkowska POL	France	Poland
1946	Einar Tang Holbek DEN	Nilla de Wharton Burr GBR	Denmark	Great Britain
1947	Hans Deutgen SWE	Janina Kurkowska POL	Czecholslovakia	Denmark
1948	Hans Deutgen SWE	Nilla de Wharton Burr GBR	Sweden	Czechoslovakia
1949	Hans Deutgen SWE	Barbara Waterhouse GBR	Czechoslovakia	Great Britain
1950	Hans Deutgen SWE	Jean Lee USA	Denmark	Finland
1952	Stellan Andersson SWE	Jean Lee USA	Sweden	United States
1953	Bror Lundgren SWE	Jean Richards USA	Sweden	Finland
1955	Nils Andersson SWE	Katarzyna Wisniowska POL	Sweden	Great Britain
1957	Oziek Smathers USA	Carole Meinhart USA	United States	United States
1958	Stig Thysell SWE	Sigrid Johansson SWE	Finland	United States
1959	James Caspers USA	Ann Corby USA	United States	United States
1961	Joe Thornton USA	Nancy Vanderheide USA	United States	United States
1963	Charles Sandlin USA	Victoria Cook USA	United States	United States
1965	Matti Haikonen FIN	Maire Lindholm FIN	United States	United States
1967	Ray Rogers USA	Maria Maczynska POL	United States	Poland
1969	Hardy Ward USA	Dorothy Lidstone CAN	United States	Soviet Union
1971	John Williams USA	Emma Gapchenko URS	United States	Poland
1973	Viktor Sidoruk URS	Linda Myers USA	United States	Soviet Uniion
1975	Darrell Pace USA	Zebiniso Rustamova URS	United States	Soviet Union
1977	Richard McKinney USA	Luann Ryon USA	United States	United States
1979	Darrell Pace USA	Kim Jin-ho KOR	United States	Korea
1981	Kyosti Laasonen FIN	Natalya Butuzova URS	United States	Soviet Union
1983	Richard McKinney USA	Kim Jin-ho KOR	United States	Korea
1985	Richard McKinney USA	Irina Soldatova URS	Korea	Soviet Union
1987	Vladimir Yesheyev URS	Ma Xiaojun CHN	West Germany	Soviet Union
1989	Stanislaw Zabrodskiy URS	Kim Soo-nyung KOR	Soviet Union	Korea
1991	Simon Fairweather AUS	Kim Soo-nyung KOR	Korea	Korea
1993	K Park KOR	K Hyo-Jung KOR	France	Korea
1995	Lee Kyung-Chul KOR	Natalya Valeeva MLD	Korea	Korea

INDOOR WORLD CHAMPIONS

Year	Men's Olympic Team	Men's Compound Team	Women's Olympic Team	Women's Compound Team
1991	Sebastian Flute FRA	Joe Asay USA	Natalya Valeyeva	Lucia Panico ITA
	-	-	-	-
1993	Gennady Metrofanov RUS	Kirk Ethridge USA	Jennifer O'Donnell USA	Inga Low USA
	-	-	-	-
1995	Magnus Pettersson SWE	M Hendrikse USA	Natalya Valeeva MOL	G Penaz USA
	United States	United States	Ukraine	United States

Association Football ▬▬▬▬

It's been the kind of year when you just didn't know where to look; one minute Eric Cantona was clearing out the front row at Crystal Palace, the next minute the Hampshire police were swooping in dawn raids on the homes of Grobbelaar and friends, implicating a Mr Big, or Mr Small or Mr Very Rich in Malaysia. George Graham, for so long a pillar of the Arsenal establishment, was sacked for accepting a bung (though he did give it back) and the Bosman case threatened (and still does) to pull the rug out from underneath the Endsleigh League. As if that was not enough, over a 12-month period almost half the managers in the Football League were sacked, Liverpool paid a stunning £8.5m for Stan Collymore and Raith Rovers won the Scottish League Cup. It's been that sort of year. Which makes it all the more remarkable that eight footballers tested positive for cannabis. If that's reality, you wouldn't have thought they needed a trip.

At least the new season started more hopefully. The influx of overseas internationals looks set to make the Premiership one of the great showcases of football. David Ginola, at Newcastle, and Ruud Gullitt, at Chelsea had immediate impact and Middlesbrough's signing of Juninho, shows just how ambitious British clubs have become.

However, more pressing than the state of the Premiership, is the state of the nation. If you are a Scot at this point, you can smile and pour yourself a celebratory pint of Belhaven because the FIFA rankings show that, with European Championship qualifying wins against Greece and Finland (narrow as they were) taken into account, Scotland hop above England, who now languish in 26th position.

"We're on target for where we are," said Terry Venables, after the game against Colombia, which clarified the position for everyone. The problem with Venables, though, is not his language, but his demeanour. Venables is perennially gloomy. Long gone are the days of the chirpy half-back who did Tony Bennett impersonations back in the sixties, this is the Venables of the nineties, carrying the world on his shoulders ....and England's hopes for the European Championship, too, as it happens. Maybe if he got rid of all those long, dark Sicilian overcoats it would help.

Anyway, he'll need to be on form if the European Championship has any chance of going to the home nation. Brazil, with alarming facility, took England apart in the Umbro Cup. Barmby looks thoroughly promising, but playing Gascoigne these days is a bit like bringing out the best china. He impresses guests,

FIFA RANKINGS
As at September 1995
Figures in brackets show placings as at Dec 31, 1994

1	(1)	Brazil	68.42
2	(2)	Spain	59.69
3	(5)	Germany	59.28
4	(8)	Norway	58.86
5	(4)	Italy	58.10
6	(10)	Argentina	57.80
7	(14)	Denmark	57.51
8	(13)	Russia	56.75
9	(15)	Mexico	54.93
10	(7)	Switzerland	54.41
11	(16)	Bulgaria	54.40
12	(20)	Portugal	54.17
13	(17)	Colombia	53.53
14	(11)	Romania	53.14
15	(3)	Sweden	52.84
16	(19)	France	52.83
17	(6)	Netherlands	51.25
18	(23)	United States	50.09
19	(34)	Czech Republic	49.32
20	(9)	Republic of Ireland	49.26
21	(22)	Egypt	48.97
22	(37)	Uruguay	48.68
23	(21)	Zambia	47.57
24	(32)	Scotland	47.56
25	(26)	Ghana	47.53
26	(18)	England	47.04
27	(30)	Tunisia	46.83
28	(29)	Poland	46.75
29	(48)	Turkey	46.43
30	(28)	Greece	46.30
56	(45)	Northern Ireland	35.15
61	(41)	Wales	33.78

but is very fragile. Venables continued to ignore the talents of Le Tissier who, for a brief period, appeared to be toying with the idea of playing for one of the other home countries, as his Jersey birthplace allows him to do. Le Tissier eventually confirmed his affiliations for England; it certainly wouldn't have taken him long to rule out Wales. Defeat by Georgia at home in June was the low point, a match that involved the sending off of Vinny Jones for trampling on an opponent. Wales' manager, Mike Smith was reported as being "absolutely ecstatic" in January when it was confirmed that Jones' grandfather had been born in Ruthin (not Watford where he lived most of his life) and the Wimbledon player was therefore elligible. Jones managed three matches without getting into trouble, but his sending-off (his ninth in football) may have signalled the end of his international career. It was certainly the end of Smith's. Bobby Gould came in and Wales won a game - 1-0 against Moldova. "We're on the first rung of the ladder," said scorer Gary Speed. Big ladder, though.

Northern Ireland beat Austria and drew away to Portugal, but kissed goodbye to any chance of qualifying when they lost at home to Latvia. "They sliced through us like butter, " said manager Brian Hamilton. Jack Charlton could say the same of Austria, who sliced through the Republic twice. To make matters worse, Ireland were held to a draw - hold your breath - by Liechtenstein. It's difficult to describe the tiny principality as even lowly. Only 27,000 people live there, which means you could pack the entire population into Barnsley's Oakwell ground and still leave a few seats for season ticket holders. Their European Championship qualifying record reads (as we go to press): played nine, drawn one; goals for, one; goals against, 36. Luxembourg usually measure their success against teams like Liechtenstein. However, in the biggest shock of the tournament so far, they defeated the Czech Repulic 1-0. The Luxembourgians, all 1,500 watching, were delirious. It was their best victory ever.

*E*ric Idol

"It's in my nature to react the way that I do. It's an instinct and to hell with people who are not happy about it" **- Eric Cantona, six months before Kung-Fuing Matthew Simonds at Crystal Palace.**

"Eric is an idol
Eric is a star
If my mother had her way
He'd also be my pa"
Sebastian Pennells, 13-year-old Cantona fan waiting outside court.

"Going down, going down, going down..." **- Crystal Palace fans also outside the court where Cantona was sentenced to two weeks in prison.**

"I don't think anyone in the history of football will get the sentence he got unless they had killed Bert Millichip's dog" **- United manager Alex Ferguson following Cantona's decision to stay at the club.**

"When seagulls follow the trawler, it is because they think that sardines will be thrown into the sea" **- Cantona.**

"If a Frenchman goes on about seagulls, sardines and trawlers he's called a philosopher. I'd just be called a short Scottish bum talking crap" **- Gordon Strachan speaking at the PFA awards.**

Blackburn won the League after 81 years proving that money can buy you happiness. If you're a Blackburn supporter, anyway. Jack Walker (estimated wealth £345m) lavished something like £55m in total and around £25m on players. Given that the club's total turnover in 1993-4 was less than £7m, it was clearly not an investment guided by business sense. The extra money from the television deal has helped to inflate the transfer market, but so too has the willingness of the wealthy to pour their money into the game. Only Manchester United could justify such an investment; from a turnover over £60.6m in the 1994-5 season, they made a profit of £20m. A fair few pounds came from the sale of Kanchelskis, Ince and Hughes (which more than balanced the outlay on Cole), but an awful lot came from the selling all those kits. If you could work out how much money was made by selling Cantona strip alone, you might also be able to calculate how much money that karate kick at Matthew Simmonds actually made, rather than lost. It certainly covered the meal and the tip at the Paris restaurant, Chez L'Ami Louis, in August when Ferguson persuaded Cantona that his future still lay with United.

Everton won the Cup Final leaving United without a trophy and they hardly started the new season auspiciously when they were knocked out of the UEFA Cup. Still, they could always check on the early-season form of the League champions, if they wanted to feel better. Blackburn had a horrible start to the season and new manager Ray Harford must be dreading the 'full support' speech from Walker.

In the 1994-5 season, the steady flow of managers shown the door in previous seasons turned into a deluge. It's hard to think of anybody with less job security; illegal immigrants, perhaps. The only compensation is that the merry-go-round does tend to drop managers off at another post and out-of-work Premiership managers have always got a media job to fall back on. With a few exceptions, though, they did manage to stay out of the courts, which is more than can be said for the players.

Football journalists had second jobs as court reporters, although most of those involved - including Wise, Ince and Collymore - were acquitted. On the pitch, there were some notable landmarks (or should it be studmarks) when Chic Charley, latterly of Partick Thistle, was sent off for the 13th time in his career, just two short of Willie Johnson's all-time record of 15 early-baths. Not one to be outdone, Terry Hurlock, now with Fulham, registered 61 points in April to become top-scorer in the 21-year history of the disciplinary points system. Julian Dicks began the new season as if he was chasing Hurlock's tally.

Clubs went into the transfer market with a vengeance. In a table in last year's book, we listed three British players in 12 months who were involved in transfers of over £3m. In this year's book *(see over)* 17 players are listed above that mark with Collymore fetching an astounding £8.6m (even higher than his Fantasy Football fee) when he went from Forest to Liverpool. An uncapped 27-year-old like Craig Short was valued at £2.7m and when the 16-year-old son of former Chelsea player Stan Wicks signed for Manchester United rather than stay with Arsenal, the London club were asking for £1.5m compensation.

All this flies in the face of the Jean Marc Bosman case still grinding through the European Court of Justice as we go to press. Should Bosman win, and the suggestion of the court lawyer is that he may well do so, then the transfer market will be thrown into turmoil. If Collymore isn't already on a ten-year contract, then you can bet Liverpool are now drawing it up. In the real world, employees sign a contract, the price of which is determined by the market place. When the contract expires, the employee is free. In every other way, football benefits by the competition of the marketplace. The £301m realised by the TV contract is a prime example. If the Bosman argument is accepted, the effect on British football could be considerable.

Even without Bosman, the rich have got richer and the poor poorer. Brighton have survived, though they've sold their ground to Woolworths and are threatening to play at Fratton Park next year. You can just imagine how many Brighton supporters will make that two-hour car trip every other Saturday. Gillingham are bumping along on their financial bottom and Scarborough have an annual turnover (1993-4) of just £408,000, or exactly 4.8 per cent of Collymore and less than George Graham lost his job for.

Graham's demise did not stop Arsenal reaching the final of the Cup Winners' Cup, where they lost to the goal of the season. Any season. In truth, they have only themselves to blame for Nayim's wondrous 50-yarder that looped over Seaman's head. When your goalkeeper has spent so long playing sweeper to a defence on the halfway line, that's exactly the shot that every attacker is looking for.

All this was as nothing, though, to the final day of the football season in Georgia. The two candidates vying for the title of the League's leading goal scorer were both on great form. Georgy Daraselia scored nine goals as Kolkheti-1913 beat Samgurali 10-5 and Mamuka Khundadze scored nine as Torpedo Kutaisi thrashed Sapovnela 11-4. It was all too much for the League officials who declared both games void. Corruption? Well, it couldn't possibly happen here.

THE MULTI-MILLION POUND MEN
Transfers at over £2m from Oct 1 to Sep 30

£8,500,000			
Stan Collymore	N Forest	Liverpool	Jul
£7,500,000			
Dennis Bergkamp	Inter Milan	Arsenal	Jun
£7,000,000			
Andy Cole	Newcastle	Man Utd	Jan
£6,000,000			
Les Ferdinand	QPR	Newcastle	Jun
Paul Ince	Man Utd	Inter Milan	Jun
£5,250,000			
Nick Barmby	Tottenham	Middlesbro	Aug
£5,500,000			
Andrei Kanchelskis	Man Utd	Everton	Aug
£4,750,000			
David Platt	Sampdoria	Arsenal	Jul
£4,500,000			
Chris Armstrong	Crystal P	Tottenham	Jun
Jason McAteer	Bolton W	Liverpool	Sep
£4,300,000			
Paul Gascoigne	Lazio	Rangers	Jul
£4,000,000			
Warren Barton	Wimbledon	Newcastle	Jun
Duncan Ferguson	Rangers	Everton	Dec
£3,500,000			
Savo Milosevic	P Belgrade	Aston Villa	Jun
£3,400,000			
Tony Yeboah	E Frankfurt	Leeds	Jan
£3,250,000			
Mark Draper	Leicester	Aston Villa	Jul
£3,000,000			
Kevin Campbell*	Arsenal	N Forest	Jun
£2,700,000			
Craig Short	Derby	Everton	Jul
£2,500,000			
Julian Dicks	Liverpool	West Ham	Oct
John Hartson	Luton	Arsenal	Jan
Chris Bart-Williams	Sheff Wed	N Forest	Jun
David Ginola	Paris S G	Newcastle	Jul
Gareth Southgate	C Palace	Aston Villa	Jun
£2,300,000			
Andy Roberts	Millwall	C Palace	Jun
Mark Kennedy	Millwall	Liverpool	Mar
Glenn Helder	V Arnhem	Arsenal	Feb
£2,000,000			
Georgi Kinkladze	D Tbilisi	Man City	Jun
John Salako*	C Palace	Coventry	Aug

* Initial fee £500,000 less, but rises to this.

Thank You and Goodnight

Managers who collected their P45s during the 1994-5 season are listed below
Note: In the close season Stewart Houston (Arsenal), Trevor Francis (Sheff Wed) and Alan Ball (Southampton) also left their posts to take the total number of premiership changes in a 10-month period to 14.

PREMIERSHIP

George Graham (Arsenal)
Sacked: Feb (8yrs 9mths)
Pos when left: 12th P28 W8 (29%)

Ron Atkinson (Aston Villa)
Sacked: Nov (3y 5m)
Pos: 14th P14 W2 (14%)

Phil Neal (Coventry City)
By mutual agreement: Feb (1y 3m)
Pos: 16th P28 W7 (25%)

Alan Smith (Crystal Palace)
By mutual agreement: May (2y)
Pos: 19th P42 W11 (26%)

Mike Walker (Everton)
Sacked: Nov (10m)
Pos: 22nd P14 W1 (7%)

John Lyall (Ipswich Town)
Resigned: Dec (4y 7m)
Pos: 22nd P17 W3 (18%)

Brian Little (Leicester City)
Resigned: Nov (3y 6m)
Pos: 21st P14 W2 (14%)

Brian Horton (Manchester City)
Sacked: May (1y 8m)
Pos: 17th P42 W12 (29%)

John Deehan (Norwich City)
Resigned: April (1y 3m)
Pos: 14th P37 W10 (27%)

Gerry Francis (QPR)
Resigned: Nov (3y 5m)
Pos: 17th P14 W3 (21%)

Osvaldo Ardiles (Tottenham H)
Sacked: Nov (1y 5m)
Pos: 11th P12 W5 (42%)

FIRST DIVISION

Russell Osman (Bristol City)
Sacked: Nov (1y 10m)
Pos: 22nd P16 W4 (25%)

Roy McFarland (Derby County)
Sacked: April (1y 6m)
Pos: 7th P45 W18 (40%)

Alan Buckley (Grimsby Town)
Resigned: Oct (6y 4m)
Pos: 17th P12 W3 (25%)

Mick Walker (Notts County)
Sacked: Sept (1y 8m)
Pos: 20th P7 W1 (14%)

Russell Slade (Notts County)
Sacked: Jan (5m)
Pos: 24th P18 W3 (17%)

Howard Kendall (Notts County)
Sacked: April (4m)
Pos: 24th P14 W4 (29%)

Joe Royle (Oldham Athletic)
Resigned: Nov (12y 4m)
Pos: 19th P16 W5 (31%)

Jim Smith (Portsmouth)
Sacked: Feb (3y 8m)
Pos: 19th P28 W7 (25%)

Mark McGhee (Reading)
Resigned: Dec (3y 7m)
Pos:6th P21 W9 (43%)

Peter Taylor (Southend Utd)
Resigned: Feb (1y 2m)
Pos: 19th P32 W10 (31%)

Joe Jordan (Stoke City)
By mutual agreement: Sept (10m)
Pos: 22nd P5 W1 (20%)

Mick Buxton (Sunderland)
Sacked: Mar (11m)
Pos: 20th P39 W9 (23%)

John Gorman (Swindon Town)
Sacked: Nov (1y 5m)
Pos: 16th P17 W6 (35%)

Keith Burkinshaw (West Brom)
Sacked: Oct (1y 4m)
Pos: 24th P11 W1 (9%)

SECOND DIVISION

Gary Johnson (Cambridge Utd)
Sacked: April (1y 11m)
Pos: 19th P40 W8 (20%)

Eddie May (Cardiff City)
Sacked: Nov (3y 4m)
Pos: 20th P18 W4 (22%)

Terry Yorath (Cardiff City)
Resigned: Mar (4m)
Pos: 22nd P20 W3 (15%)

Mike Pejic (Chester City)
Sacked: Jan (6m)
Pos: 24th P23 W3 (13%)

Derek Mann (Chester City)
Resigned April (1m)
Pos: 24th P10 W0 (0%)

John Sitton & Chris Turner (LO)
Sacked: April (11m)
Pos: 23rd P43 W6 (14%)

Peter Shilton (Plymouth Argyle)
Resigned: Jan (2y 10m)
Pos: 20th P22 W6 (27%)

Steve McCall (Plymouth Argyle)
Resigned: Mar (2m)
Pos: 21st P15 W3 (20%)

Danny Bergara (Stockport County)
Sacked: Mar (5y 11m)
Pos: 14th P39 W16 (41%)

THIRD DIVISION

George Burley (Colchester Utd)
Resigned: Dec (6m)
Pos: 6th P19 W9 (47%)

Alan Murray (Darlington)
Sacked: Mar (1y 5m)
Pos: 16th P29 W10 (34%)

Paul Futcher (Darlington)
Sacked: April (1m)
Pos: 18th P10 W0 (0%)

Mike Flanaghan (Gillingham)
Sacked: Feb (1y 7m)
Pos: 20th P29 W7 (24%)

John McPhail (Hartlepool Utd)
Sacked: Sept (10m)
Pos: 18th P5 W1 (20%)

David McCreery (Hartlepool Utd)
Sacked: April (7m)
Pos: 20th P30 W7 (23%)

Greg Downs (Hereford Utd)
Sacked: Sept (2y 4m)
Pos: 20th P8 W1 (13%)

John Barnwell (Northampton T)
Sacked: Dec (1y 3m)
Pos: 19th P30 W6 (20%)

John Beck (Preston North End)
Resigned: Dec (3y)
Pos: 15th P17 W6 (35%)

Dave Sutton (Rochdale)
Resigned: Nov (3y 9m)
Pos: 12th P17 W6 (35%)

Billy Ayre (Scarborough)
Resigned: Dec (4m)
Pos: 22nd P19 W3 (16%)

Kenny Hibbitt (Walsall)
Sacked: Sept (4y 4m)
Pos: 11th P8 W2 (25%)

Kenny Swain (Wigan Athletic)
Sacked: Sept (1y 4m)
Pos: 21st P5 W0 (0%)

*Q*uotes

"Even before the national anthem, he (Alex Ferguson) was glancing across at the United fans, marvelling at them. They knew he was looking at them and shouted all the louder: let our sound be your strength, forget your fear, find courage in our hope; we are here, we are with you, we are among you, of you we are you, and you are us" **- Kate Battersby in *The Sunday Telegraph* (originally) and *Private Eye's Pseuds Corner* (latterly).**

"All I know is that I'll never be able to achieve what Tommy did, and that is to take Aston Villa into the Third Division, and better than that, take Manchester United into the Second Division" **- Sacked Villa manager Ron Atkinson on remarks made by Tommy Docherty criticising his record.**

"I don't suppose that many would have taken the odds on us coming back from 2-0 down to win 6-2. Not unless you're that fellow who's lost all that money in Singapore" **- Gerry Francis after Spurs' FA Cup recovery against Southampton.**

"I don't think playing for Middlesbrough qualifies as staying in the game" **- Gordon Strachan on a £100 bet he has with 'Boro player-manager Bryan Robson as to who will retire first.**

"Seven games we've lost 1-0. Another seven we've drawn 0-0. If we had drawn the 1-0 games we'd lost we would have another seven points; if the seven goal-less draws had been 1-0 to us we would have 28 points more and we would be third in the Premier League" **- Alan Smith, Fantasy football manager of Crystal Palace.**

"I got the signal from Paul that he'd be okay in a few seconds, but Daniel misinterpreted and wandered onto the pitch. I think it was a good mistake to make" **- Everton manager, Joe Royle, on the unintentional substitution of Daniel Amokachi for Paul Rideout in the FA Cup semi final against Spurs. Amokachi scored twice as Everton won 4-1.**

"Go back to the golf course, breed horses, sail around the world, book a trip to the moon, but leave the rule book of our sport to us" **- FIFA spokesman Guido Tognoni in an open letter to Franz Beckenbauer after the German had had the temerity to criticise football's laws.**

"The Italian game is too slow...I've watched the Italian games on a Sunday afternoon and they're boring" **- Paul Ince prior to his departure from Manchester Utd to join Internazionale.**

"He signed it 'To Alan with a very special thank you'. I'm the blooming mug that relaunched his career. I wouldn't wash my car with that shirt now. You can auction it among your viewers for charity" **- Spurs' chairman Alan Sugar brandishing Jürgen Klinsmann's shirt at BBC presenter Ray Stubbs.**

"To take the pressure off myself I phoned Paul Merson last night. He sounded fantastic. I thought I might go down and join him for a couple of days" **- Arsenal manager, George Graham, putting his troubles into perspective following 'bung' allegations.**

"Rumours of my impending resignation have proved somewhat premature" **- George Graham's programme notes for the match v Nottingham Forest on the day he was sacked by Arsenal.**

"I can't take Cruyff any more. When we win, he wins and when we lose Stoichkov loses" **- Bulgarian star Hristo Stoichkov, on the ill feeling between himself and the Barcelona manager.**

European Championships

Qualifying Matches

GROUP 1

Israel 2	Poland 1
Slovakia 0	France 0
Romania 3	Azerbaijan 0
France 0	Romania 0
Israel 2	Slovakia 2
Poland 1	Azerbaijan 0
Romania 3	Slovakia 2
Poland 0	France 0
Azerbaijan 0	Israel 2
Israel 1	Romania 1
Azerbaijan 0	France 2
Romania 2	Poland 1
Slovakia 4	Azerbaijan 1
Israel 0	France 0
Poland 4	Israel 3
Azerbaijan 1	Romania 4
France 4	Slovakia 0
Poland 5	Slovakia 0
Romania 2	Israel 1
France 1	Poland 1
Azerbaijan 0	Slovakia 1
France 10	Azerbaijan 0
Slovakia 1	Israel 0
Poland 0	Romania 0

Group 1 Table
As at Sep 30

	P	W	D	L	F	A	Pts
Romania	8	5	3	0	15	6	18
France	8	3	5	0	17	1	14
Poland	8	3	3	2	13	8	12
Slovakia	8	3	2	3	10	15	11
Israel	8	2	3	3	11	11	9
Azerbaijan	8	0	0	8	2	27	0

GROUP 2

Belgium 2	Armenia 0
Cyprus 1	Spain 2
Macedonia 1	Denmark 1
Armenia 0	Cyprus 0
Denmark 3	Belgium 1
Macedonia 1	Spain 2
Belgium 1	Macedonia 1
Cyprus 2	Armenia 0
Spain 3	Denmark 0
Macedonia 3	Cyprus 0
Belgium 1	Spain 4
Spain 1	Belgium 1
Cyprus 1	Denmark 1
Armenia 0	Spain 2
Denmark 1	Macedonia 0
Belgium 2	Cyprus 0
Armenia 2	Macedonia 2
Denmark 4	Cyprus 0
Spain 1	Armenia 0
Macedonia 0	Belgium 5
Armenia 0	Denmark 2
Belgium 1	Denmark 3

Spain 6   Cyprus 0
Macedonia 1   Armenia 2

Group 2 Table
As at Sep 30

	P	W	D	L	F	A	Pts
Spain	8	7	1	0	21	3	22
Denmark	8	5	2	1	15	7	17
Belgium	8	3	2	3	14	12	11
Macedonia	8	1	3	4	8	14	6
Armenia	8	1	2	5	4	12	5
Cyprus	8	1	2	5	4	18	5

GROUP 3

Iceland 0	Sweden 1
Hungary 2	Turkey 2
Turkey 5	Iceland 0
Switzerland 4	Sweden 2
Sweden 2	Hungary 0
Switzerland 1	Iceland 0
Turkey 1	Switzerland 2
Hungary 2	Switzerland 2
Turkey 2	Sweden 1
Hungary 1	Sweden 0
Switzerland 1	Turkey 2
Sweden 1	Iceland 1
Iceland 2	Hungary 1
Iceland 0	Switzerland 2
Sweden 0	Switzerland 0
Turkey 2	Hungary 0

Group 3 Table
As at Sep 30

	P	W	D	L	F	A	Pts
Switzerland	7	4	2	1	12	7	14
Turkey	6	4	1	1	14	6	13
Sweden	7	2	2	3	7	8	8
Hungary	6	1	2	3	6	10	5
Iceland	6	1	1	4	3	11	4

GROUP 4

Estonia 0	Croatia 2
Slovenia 1	Italy 1
Ukraine 0	Lithuania 2
Estonia 0	Italy 2
Croatia 2	Lithuania 0
Ukraine 0	Slovenia 0
Ukraine 3	Estonia 0
Italy 1	Croatia 2
Slovenia 1	Lithuania 2
Croatia 4	Ukraine 0
Italy 4	Estonia 1
Lithuania 0	Croatia 0
Ukraine 0	Italy 2
Slovenia 3	Estonia 0
Estonia 0	Ukraine 1
Lithuania 0	Italy 1
Croatia 2	Slovenia 0
Lithuania 2	Slovenia 1
Estonia 1	Slovenia 3
Ukraine 1	Croatia 0
Estonia 0	Lithuania 1
Croatia 7	Estonia 1
Italy 1	Slovenia 0
Lithuania 1	Ukraine 3

Group 4 Table
As at Sep 30

	P	W	D	L	F	A	Pts
Croatia	8	6	1	1	19	3	19
Italy	7	5	1	1	12	4	16
Lithuania	8	4	1	3	8	8	13
Ukraine	8	4	1	3	8	9	13
Slovenia	8	2	2	4	9	9	8
Estonia	9	0	0	9	3	26	0

GROUP 5

Czech Rep 6	Malta 1
Luxembourg 0	Netherlands 4
Norway 1	Belarus 0
Malta 0	Czech Rep 0
Norway 1	Netherlands 1
Belarus 2	Luxembourg 0
Belarus 0	Norway 4
Netherlands 0	Czech Rep 0
Netherlands 5	Luxembourg 0
Malta 0	Norway 1
Malta 0	Luxembourg 1
Luxembourg 0	Norway 2
Netherlands 4	Malta 0
Czech Rep 4	Belarus 2
Belarus 1	Malta 1
Czech Rep 3	Netherlands 1
Norway 5	Luxembourg 0
Luxembourg 1	Czech Rep 0
Norway 2	Malta 0
Belarus 1	Netherlands 0
Norway 1	Czech Rep 1
Czech Rep 2	Norway 0
Luxembourg 1	Malta 0
Netherlands 1	Belarus 0

Group 5 Table
As at Sep 30

	P	W	D	L	F	A	Pts
Norway	9	6	2	1	17	4	20
Czech Rep	8	4	3	1	16	6	15
Netherlands	8	4	2	2	16	5	14
Luxembourg	8	3	0	5	3	18	9
Belarus	7	2	1	4	6	11	7
Malta	8	0	2	6	2	16	2

GROUP 6

N Ireland 4	Liechtenstein 1
Latvia 0	Ireland 3
Liechtenstein 0	Austria 4
N Ireland 1	Portugal 2
Latvia 1	Portugal 3
Austria 1	N Ireland 2
Ireland 4	Liechtenstein 0
Portugal 1	Austria 0
Liechtenstein 0	Latvia 1
N Ireland 0	Ireland 4
Portugal 8	Liechtenstein 0
Ireland 1	N Ireland 1
Austria 5	Latvia 0
Latvia 0	N Ireland 1
Austria 7	Liechtenstein 0
Ireland 1	Portugal 1
Portugal 3	Latvia 2
Liechtenstein 0	Ireland 0

N Ireland 1	Latvia 2
Ireland 1	Austria 3
Liechtenstein 0	Portugal 7
Latvia 3	Austria 2
Portugal 1	N Ireland 1
Austria 3	Ireland 1
Latvia 1	Liechtenstein 0

Group 6 Table
As at Sep 30

	P	W	D	L	F	A	Pts
Portugal	8	6	1	1	25	6	19
Austria	8	5	0	3	25	8	15
Ireland	8	4	2	2	15	7	14
Latvia	9	4	0	5	10	18	12
N Ireland	8	3	2	3	11	12	11
Liechtenstein	9	0	1	8	36	1	1

GROUP 7

Georgia 0	Moldova 1
Wales 2	Albania 0
Moldova 3	Wales 2
Bulgaria 2	Georgia 0
Albania 3	Germany 2
Bulgaria 4	Moldova 1
Georgia 5	Wales 0
Moldova 0	Germany 3
Wales 0	Bulgaria 3
Albania 0	Georgia 1
Germany 2	Albania 1

Georgia 0	Germany 2
Bulgaria 3	Wales 1
Albania 3	Moldova 0
Georgia 2	Albania 0
Moldova 0	Bulgaria 3
Germany 1	Wales 1
Bulgaria 3	Germany 2
Wales 0	Georgia 1
Moldova 2	Albania 3
Germany 4	Georgia 1
Wales 1	Moldova 0
Albania 1	Bulgaria 1

Group 7 Table
As at Sep 30

	P	W	D	L	F	A	Pts
Bulgaria	7	6	1	0	19	5	19
Germany	7	5	1	1	16	7	16
Georgia	8	4	0	4	10	9	12
Albania	8	2	1	5	9	12	7
Wales	8	2	1	5	7	16	7
Moldova	8	2	0	6	7	19	6

GROUP 8

Faeroes 1	Greece 5
Finland 0	Scotland 2
Scotland 5	Faeroes 1
Greece 4	Finland 0
Russia 4	San Marino 0
Finland 5	Faeroes 0

Greece 2	San Marino 0
Scotland 1	Russia 1
Finland 4	San Marino 1
Greece 1	Scotland 0
Russia 0	Scotland 0
San Marino 0	Finland 2
San Marino 0	Scotland 2
Greece 0	Russia 3
Faeroes 0	Finland 4
Russia 3	Faeroes 0
Faeroes 3	San Marino 0
San Marino 0	Russia 7
Faeroes 0	Scotland 2
Finland 2	Greece 1
Scotland 1	Greece 0
Finland 0	Russia 6
Scotland 1	Finland 0
Faeroes 2	Russia 5
San Marino 0	Greece 4

Group 8 Table
As at Sep 30

	P	W	D	L	F	A	Pts
Russia	8	6	2	0	29	3	20
Scotland	9	6	2	1	14	3	20
Greece	8	5	0	3	17	7	15
Finland	9	5	0	4	17	15	15
Faeroes	8	1	0	7	7	29	3
San Marino	8	0	0	8	1	28	0

British non-championship matches

Friendly matches

Wembley	Oct 12, 1994
England 1	Romania 1
(Lee)	(Dumitrescu)

Wembley	Nov 16, 1994
England 1	Nigeria 0
(Platt)	

Dublin	Feb 15
Ireland 1	England 0
(D Kelly)	

Match abandoned after 27 minutes because of crowd trouble

Wembley	Mar 29
England 0	Uruguay 0

Wembley	Sep 6
England 0	Colombia 0

Umbro Cup

Wembley	June 3
England 2	Japan 1
(Anderton, Platt-pen)	(Ihara)

Villa Park	June 4
Brazil 1	Sweden 0
(Edmundo)	

Goodison Pk	June 6
Japan 0	Brazil 3
	(Roberto Carlos, Zinho 2)

Elland Rd	June 8
England 3	Sweden 3
(Sheringham, Platt, Anderton)	(Mild 2, K Andersson)

City Gd, Nottm	June 10
Sweden 2	Japan 2
(K Andersson 2)	(Fujita, Kurosaki)

Wembley	June 11
England 1	Brazil 3
(Le Saux)	(Juninho, Ronaldo, Edmundo)

Final Table

	P	W	D	L	F	A	Pts
Brazil	3	3	0	0	7	1	9
England	3	1	1	1	6	7	4
Sweden	3	0	2	1	5	6	2
Japan	3	0	1	2	3	7	1

Kirin Cup

Scottish matches only

Hiroshima	May 21
Japan 0	Scotland 0

Toyama	May 24
Ecuador 1	Scotland 2
(Hurtado I-pen)	(Robertson, Crawford)

Canada Cup

Northern Ireland matches only

Edmonton	May 22
Canada 2	N Ireland 0
(Peschisolido 2)	

Edmonton	May 26
Chile 2	N Ireland 1
(Valencia, Mardones)	(Dowie)

English Football ▬▬▬▬▬▬

FA Carling Premiership 1994-95

		P	W	D	L	GF	GA	W	D	L	GF	GA	GD	Pts
1	Blackburn Rovers	42	17	2	2	54	21	10	6	5	26	18	+41	89
2	Manchester United	42	16	4	1	42	4	10	6	5	35	24	+49	88
3	Nottingham Forest	42	12	6	3	36	18	10	5	6	36	25	+29	77
4	Liverpool	42	13	5	3	38	13	8	6	7	27	24	+28	74
5	Leeds United	42	13	5	3	35	15	7	8	6	24	23	+21	73
6	Newcastle United	42	14	6	1	46	20	6	6	9	21	27	+20	72
7	Tottenham Hotspur	42	10	5	6	32	25	6	9	6	34	33	+8	62
8	Queens Park Rangers	42	11	3	7	36	26	6	6	9	25	33	+2	60
9	Wimbledon	42	9	5	7	26	26	6	6	9	22	39	-17	56
10	Southampton	42	8	9	4	33	27	4	9	8	28	36	-2	54
11	Chelsea	42	7	7	7	25	22	6	8	7	25	33	-5	54
12	Arsenal	42	6	9	6	27	21	7	3	11	25	28	+3	51
13	Sheffield Wednesday	42	7	7	7	26	26	6	5	10	23	31	-8	51
14	West Ham United	42	9	6	6	28	19	4	5	12	16	29	-4	50
15	Everton	42	8	9	4	31	23	3	8	10	13	28	-7	50
16	Coventry City	42	7	7	7	23	25	5	7	9	21	37	-18	50
17	Manchester City	42	8	7	6	37	28	4	6	11	16	36	-11	49
18	Aston Villa	42	6	9	6	27	24	5	6	10	24	32	-5	48
19	Crystal Palace	42	6	6	9	16	23	5	6	10	18	26	-15	45
20	Norwich City	42	8	8	5	27	21	2	5	14	10	33	-17	43
21	Leicester City	42	5	6	10	28	37	1	5	15	17	43	-35	29
22	Ipswich Town	42	5	3	13	24	34	2	3	16	12	59	-57	27

Prize Money

1	Blackburn Rovers	£897,820
2	Manchester United	£857,010
3	Nottingham Forest	£816,200
4	Liverpool	£775,390
5	Leeds United	£734,580
6	Newcastle United	£693,770
7	Tottenham Hotspur	£652,960
8	Queens Park Rangers	£612,150
9	Wimbledon	£571,340
10	Southampton	£530,530
11	Chelsea	£489,720
12	Arsenal	£448,720
13	Sheffield Wednesday	£408,100
14	West Ham United	£367,290
15	Everton	£326,480
16	Coventry City	£285,670
17	Manchester City	£244,860
18	Aston Villa	£204,050
19	Crystal Palace	£163,240
20	Norwich City	£122,430
21	Leicester City	£81,620
22	Ipswich Town	£40,810

Goalscorers

	Lg	Cp	CC	Other	Total
Alan Shearer (Blackburn)	34	0	2	1	37
Robbie Fowler (Liverpool)	25	2	4	0	31
Les Ferdinand (QPR)	24	1	1	0	26
Stan Collymore (Nottm F)	22	1	2	0	25
Andy Cole (Man Utd/Newc)	21	0	2	0	23
Jürgen Klinsmann (Spurs)	20	5	4	0	29
Matt Le Tissier (Soton)	19	5	5	0	29
Ian Wright (Arsenal)	18	0	3	9	30
Teddy Sheringham (Spurs)	18	4	1	0	23
Ashley Ward (N'ch/Crewe)	16	4	1	0	21
Uwe Rösler (Man City)	15	5	2	0	22
Chris Sutton (Blackburn)	15	2	3	1	21
Dean Saunders (Villa)	15	1	1	0	17
Paul Rideout (Everton)	14	2	0	0	16
Andrei Kanchelskis (Man U)	14	0	0	0	14

Results grid — home teams across the top, away teams down the side (home score shown first).

(Away \ Home)	Arsenal	Aston Villa	Blackburn	Chelsea	Coventry	Crystal Palace	Everton	Ipswich Town	Leeds United	Leicester City	Liverpool	Man City	Man United	Newcastle	Norwich	Nottm Forest	QPR	Sheff Weds	Southampton	Tottenham	West Ham	Wimbledon
Arsenal	****	0-4	3-1	2-1	0-1	0-1	1-1	4-1	1-3	1-1	2-1	3-0	0-0	2-3	5-1	0-2	1-3	0-0	1-3	1-1	0-2	0-0
Aston Villa	0-0	****	3-1	1-0	0-1	0-1	1-0	4-1	1-3	4-4	2-0	3-0	0-0	0-2	5-1	2-4	0-2	3-2	1-1	4-3	0-2	7-1
Blackburn	0-0	0-1	****	3-1	1-2	1-1	3-0	0-1	2-0	1-0	2-1	1-0	1-0	0-0	0-0	3-3	1-4	4-1	3-0	2-1	2-0	0-0
Chelsea	0-1	3-0	3-1	****	1-0	2-2	3-0	1-1	0-1	2-2	2-1	1-3	0-0	1-0	2-1	1-1	0-2	2-2	1-3	1-2	2-0	1-1
Coventry	1-2	0-0	4-0	2-1	****	2-2	4-0	1-2	2-0	0-1	2-3	0-0	5-0	1-0	1-1	0-0	0-0	1-2	2-0	0-1	1-3	2-0
Crystal P	1-1	1-1	2-1	0-1	2-2	****	1-4	0-0	3-1	0-0	1-1	0-0	3-0	2-0	1-0	1-7	0-2	3-2	2-1	1-0	0-4	2-0
Everton	1-1	1-0	3-0	3-0	2-0	2-1	****	4-1	3-0	2-0	1-6	1-1	4-0	0-2	4-0	0-2	3-2	4-1	3-0	2-1	0-0	0-0
Ipswich	4-1	4-1	0-1	1-1	0-2	0-0	1-0	****	0-1	2-0	1-3	2-1	0-0	0-1	1-0	1-2	1-1	4-1	2-1	1-1	2-1	1-1
Leeds Utd	1-3	1-3	2-0	0-1	3-1	3-1	2-2	4-0	****	1-3	2-0	2-0	0-0	0-0	2-1	1-3	0-0	2-0	0-0	0-0	0-1	0-0
Leicester	1-1	4-4	1-0	2-2	0-1	0-0	2-2	0-1	1-3	****	2-0	0-1	0-0	1-3	1-0	2-4	0-1	1-1	0-1	0-0	0-2	2-1
Liverpool	2-1	2-0	3-2	2-1	2-3	0-1	0-1	4-1	0-1	2-0	****	1-2	2-0	2-0	4-0	3-3	2-3	4-1	3-2	5-2	3-0	2-0
Man City	3-0	3-0	2-3	1-3	0-0	0-0	1-1	9-0	0-1	0-1	2-1	****	5-0	0-0	1-0	1-2	2-3	4-1	3-1	1-1	3-0	3-0
Man Utd	0-0	0-0	4-0	0-0	2-3	3-0	0-0	2-0	0-0	0-1	2-1	0-0	****	0-3	3-0	0-4	0-3	1-0	1-1	0-0	2-0	0-1
Newcastle	2-3	0-2	1-0	1-0	1-0	1-1	3-2	1-1	2-1	1-2	2-1	1-1	0-3	****	0-0	0-2	0-1	0-2	0-1	2-3	2-0	2-3
Norwich C	5-1	5-1	0-0	2-1	1-1	0-0	2-1	1-1	0-0	0-1	1-1	0-0	2-0	0-0	****	1-1	1-2	0-0	0-0	5-1	1-0	5-1
Nottm Forest	0-2	2-4	3-3	1-1	0-0	1-7	0-2	1-2	1-3	2-4	3-3	1-2	0-4	0-2	1-1	****	1-1	0-1	0-2	3-1	0-2	2-2
QPR	1-3	0-2	1-4	0-2	0-0	0-2	3-2	1-1	0-0	0-1	2-3	2-3	0-3	0-1	1-2	1-1	****	3-2	4-2	1-1	0-1	1-3
Sheff Wed	0-0	3-2	4-1	2-2	1-2	3-2	4-1	4-1	2-0	1-1	4-1	4-1	1-0	0-2	0-0	2-1	3-2	****	0-0	3-1	0-2	0-1
Southampt'n	1-3	1-1	3-0	1-3	2-0	2-2	3-0	2-1	0-0	0-1	3-3	3-1	1-1	0-1	0-0	1-2	2-2	1-1	****	4-3	1-2	0-2
Tottenham	1-1	4-3	2-1	1-2	0-1	2-1	2-1	1-1	0-0	0-0	5-2	1-1	0-0	2-3	5-1	2-2	0-0	4-3	4-3	****	3-1	1-2
West Ham	0-2	0-2	2-0	2-0	1-3	0-4	1-0	2-0	1-0	2-2	3-0	3-0	2-0	2-0	1-0	1-0	1-0	0-0	2-0	3-1	****	1-0
Wimbledon	0-0	7-1	0-0	0-3	2-0	1-1	0-0	0-0	3-1	3-0	2-0	3-0	1-2	3-0	3-0	3-0	3-1	0-1	1-2	2-3	3-0	****

Endsleigh Insurance League 1994-95

Division One

		P	W	D	L	GF	GA	W	D	L	GF	GA	GS	PTS
1	Middlesbrough	46	15	4	4	41	19	8	9	6	26	21	67	**82**
2	Reading	46	12	7	4	34	21	11	3	9	24	23	58	**79**
3	Bolton Wanderers	46	16	6	1	43	13	5	8	10	24	32	67	**77**
4	Wolverhampton Wand'rs	46	15	5	3	39	18	6	8	9	38	43	77	**76**
5	Tranmere Rovers	46	17	4	2	51	23	5	6	12	16	35	67	**76**
6	Barnsley	46	15	6	2	42	19	5	6	12	21	33	63	**72**
7	Watford	46	14	6	3	33	17	5	7	11	19	29	52	**70**
8	Sheffield United	46	12	9	2	41	21	5	8	10	33	34	74	**68**
9	Derby County	46	12	6	5	44	23	6	6	11	22	28	66	**66**
10	Grimsby Town	46	12	7	4	36	19	5	7	11	26	37	62	**65**
11	Stoke City	46	10	7	6	31	21	6	8	9	19	32	50	**63**
12	Millwall	46	11	8	4	36	22	5	6	12	24	38	60	**62**
13	Southend United	46	13	2	8	33	25	5	6	12	21	48	54	**62**
14	Oldham Athletic	46	12	7	4	34	21	4	6	13	26	39	60	**61**
15	Charlton Athletic	46	11	6	6	33	25	5	5	13	25	41	58	**59**
16	Luton Town	46	8	6	9	35	30	7	7	9	26	34	61	**58**
17	Port Vale	46	11	5	7	30	24	4	8	11	28	40	58	**58**
18	Portsmouth	46	9	8	6	31	28	6	5	12	22	35	53	**58**
19	West Bromwich Albion	46	13	3	7	33	24	3	7	13	18	33	51	**58**
20	Sunderland	46	5	12	6	22	22	7	6	10	19	23	41	**54**
21	Swindon Town	46	9	6	8	28	27	3	6	14	26	46	54	**48**
22	Burnley	46	8	7	8	36	33	3	6	14	13	41	49	**46**
23	Bristol City	46	8	8	7	26	28	3	4	16	16	35	42	**45**
24	Notts County	46	7	8	8	26	28	2	5	16	19	38	45	**40**

Play-offs

Semi-finals *(over 2 legs)*

Tranmere Rovers 1   Reading 3
(Malkin)   *(Lovell 2, Nogan)*

Reading 0   Tranmere Rovers 0
Reading won 3-1 on aggregate

Wolverhampton W 2   Bolton W 1
(Bull, Venus)   *(McAteer)*

Bolton W 2   Wolverhampton W 0
(McGinlay 2)
aet, Bolton won 3-2 on aggregate

FINAL

Wembley   *May 29*
Bolton W 4   **Reading 3**
(Coyle, De Freitas 2   *(Nogan, Williams, Quinn)*
Paatelainen)
aet
Bolton: Branagan, Green, Phillips, McAteer,
Bergsson, Stubbs, McDonald (De Freitas), Coyle,
Paatelainen, McGinlay, Thompson
Reading: Hislop, Bernal (Hopkins), Osborn,
Wdowczyk, Williams, McPherson, Gilkes, Goodwin,
Nogan (Quinn), Lovell, Taylor

Goalscorers

	Lg	Cp	CC	Other	Total
John Aldridge (Tranmere)	24	0	1	1	26
J-A Fjortoft (M'boro/Swin)	19	1	9	0	29
David Whyte (Charlton)	19	0	2	0	21
Gerry Creaney (Portsm'th)	18	1	3	0	22
Sean McCarthy (Oldham)	18	0	0	0	18
Nathan Blake (Sheff U)	17	0	1	0	18
John McGinlay (Bolton)	16	0	4	2	22
Martin Foyle (P Vale)	16	3	1	0	20
Chris Malkin (Tranmere)	16	1	0	2	19
Steve Bull (Wolves)	16	0	2	1	19
David Kelly (Wolves)	15	4	2	1	22
John Hendrie (M'boro)	15	1	1	0	17
Neil Woods (Grimsby)	14	0	0	0	14

	Barnsley	Bolton W	Bristol City	Burnley	Charlton	Derby Cty	Grimsby	Luton T	Middlesbro	Millwall	Notts County	Oldham	Port Vale	Portsmouth	Reading	Sheff Utd	Southend	Stoke C	Sunderland	Swindon T	Tranmere	Watford	West Brom	Wolves
Barnsley	***	3-0	2-1	2-0	2-1	2-1	4-1	3-1	1-1	4-1	1-1	2-1	1-0	3-0	0-3	0-0	3-1	0-0	2-0	0-0	6-1	3-2	2-1	0-0
Bolton W	2-1	****	0-2	1-1	5-1	1-0	3-3	1-0	1-0	1-0	3-1	3-1	1-1	1-1	2-1	3-1	2-1	3-1	1-1	0-1	1-0	0-0	1-0	3-1
Bristol City	3-2	0-1	****	1-1	0-2	2-1	1-0	2-1	1-0	3-0	0-1	1-0	2-0	1-0	0-0	3-0	2-1	2-1	2-1	0-3	2-0	1-0	1-0	2-0
Burnley	0-1	2-2	1-1	****	1-1	1-0	4-0	2-2	0-1	0-1	2-2	3-0	2-3	2-0	1-0	2-0	2-1	2-1	2-0	1-1	4-1	2-0	1-0	2-0
Charlton	2-2	1-2	3-2	2-0	****	2-0	0-2	0-0	0-3	0-1	0-1	1-0	0-1	3-2	2-1	2-1	2-1	2-1	3-2	0-1	1-1	3-1	2-0	2-0
Derby Cty	1-0	2-1	3-1	0-2	3-1	****	1-2	3-1	0-2	1-0	1-0	1-0	4-3	1-0	1-0	2-1	1-0	2-1	4-3	1-1	0-1	2-4	3-2	0-2
Grimsby	1-0	3-3	1-0	4-0	0-2	3-4	****	4-1	2-1	1-0	2-0	1-0	1-1	2-1	1-1	1-3	0-0	3-1	0-0	3-2	2-0	0-0	0-0	2-1
Luton T	0-1	1-0	2-2	2-2	2-0	0-1	2-1	****	1-1	0-1	2-1	1-3	1-2	2-0	4-1	1-1	2-0	0-1	1-0	2-0	4-2	1-1	1-3	1-1
Middlesbro	1-1	1-0	1-0	0-1	3-1	3-1	2-1	2-1	****	3-0	2-0	1-0	2-1	0-1	0-1	0-2	0-2	1-1	3-2	0-2	3-2	1-1	1-3	0-2
Millwall	0-1	1-0	3-0	0-1	2-1	0-1	0-2	0-1	5-1	****	2-1	2-1	1-0	3-2	0-1	0-1	4-3	0-1	0-0	3-3	0-1	1-0	2-0	3-3
Notts County	1-3	3-1	0-1	2-2	2-1	1-0	1-0	0-0	2-1	1-1	****	1-1	1-1	0-1	3-1	2-0	1-0	1-3	2-0	3-0	3-1	3-1	3-2	1-0
Oldham	1-0	3-1	1-0	3-0	1-0	1-0	1-0	0-1	0-1	1-0	1-1	****	3-1	2-1	1-1	1-3	2-0	1-0	3-0	3-1	3-2	3-1	3-0	2-1
Port Vale	2-1	1-1	2-0	1-0	0-2	1-0	1-0	0-0	2-1	3-2	2-0	1-3	****	1-1	1-1	3-3	0-0	1-1	2-0	3-1	3-0	1-2	1-1	2-1
Portsmouth	3-0	1-1	1-0	2-1	2-1	0-0	3-0	2-1	1-0	0-1	1-3	3-1	3-2	****	0-0	1-0	4-0	0-1	1-0	2-2	4-2	2-0	2-2	2-3
Reading	0-3	2-1	0-0	1-0	1-0	1-0	1-0	0-1	1-1	1-1	2-0	2-0	0-1	1-0	****	1-0	1-1	3-1	1-0	2-2	0-1	2-0	2-2	1-0
Sheff Utd	0-0	3-1	3-0	2-0	2-1	2-1	1-2	1-3	0-2	0-0	1-3	0-0	3-0	0-2	1-1	****	2-0	2-3	1-0	2-1	4-2	1-0	0-0	2-2
Southend	3-1	2-1	2-1	2-1	2-1	1-0	0-0	0-0	1-1	4-3	1-0	0-1	0-0	2-2	0-2	1-0	****	4-2	1-0	0-2	0-2	2-0	3-0	2-0
Stoke C	0-0	3-1	2-1	2-1	2-1	2-1	3-1	2-0	0-1	0-1	2-1	1-0	1-1	0-1	1-2	1-0	4-2	****	1-0	2-2	1-0	0-0	1-3	2-0
Sunderland	2-0	1-1	2-1	2-0	3-2	4-3	0-0	1-2	1-1	1-1	2-1	1-0	0-1	1-1	1-3	0-2	0-1	0-1	****	3-0	0-1	1-0	0-4	2-1
Swindon T	0-0	0-1	0-3	1-1	0-1	1-1	2-0	2-0	1-3	0-0	3-0	2-0	1-2	0-0	0-1	3-3	2-0	1-3	0-1	****	3-2	1-0	1-0	3-2
Tranmere	6-1	1-0	2-0	4-1	1-1	2-0	2-2	4-2	1-1	3-1	3-2	3-1	3-1	4-2	4-2	2-1	5-0	2-0	1-0	2-2	****	2-0	1-0	1-1
Watford	3-2	0-0	1-0	2-0	0-1	0-0	0-0	2-4	2-1	1-0	3-1	1-2	3-2	2-0	2-2	0-0	1-0	0-0	1-0	3-2	2-0	****	0-1	2-0
West Brom	2-1	1-0	1-0	1-0	0-1	0-0	0-0	2-0	1-3	3-1	3-2	3-1	1-1	3-2	2-0	0-0	0-2	3-0	0-4	3-1	2-0	2-1	****	2-1
Wolves	0-0	3-1	2-0	2-0	2-0	0-2	2-1	2-3	0-2	3-3	1-0	2-1	2-1	1-2	1-0	2-2	5-1	2-0	1-0	3-2	1-1	0-0	2-0	***

Endsleigh Insurance League 1994-95
Division Two

		P	W	D	L	GF	GA	W	D	L	GF	GA	GS	PTS
1	**Birmingham City**	46	15	6	2	53	18	10	8	5	31	19	84	**89**
2	**Brentford**	46	14	4	5	44	15	11	6	6	37	24	81	**85**
3	**Crewe Alexandra**	46	14	3	6	46	33	11	5	7	34	35	80	**83**
4	**Bristol Rovers**	46	15	7	1	48	20	7	9	7	22	20	70	**82**
5	**Huddersfield Town**	46	14	5	4	45	21	8	10	5	34	28	79	**81**
6	**Wycombe Wanderers**	46	13	7	3	36	19	8	8	7	24	27	60	**78**
7	**Oxford United**	46	13	6	4	30	18	8	6	9	36	24	66	**75**
8	**Hull City**	46	13	6	4	40	18	8	5	10	30	39	70	**74**
9	**York City**	46	13	4	6	37	21	8	5	10	30	30	67	**72**
10	**Swansea City**	46	10	8	5	23	13	9	6	8	34	32	57	**71**
11	**Stockport County**	46	12	3	8	40	29	7	5	11	23	31	63	**65**
12	**Blackpool**	46	11	4	8	40	36	7	6	10	24	34	64	**64**
13	**Wrexham**	46	10	7	6	38	27	6	8	9	27	37	65	**63**
14	**Bradford City**	46	8	6	9	29	32	8	6	9	28	32	57	**60**
15	**Peterborough United**	46	7	11	5	26	29	7	7	9	28	40	54	**60**
16	**Brighton & Hove Albion**	46	9	10	4	25	15	5	7	11	29	38	54	**59**
17	**Rotherham United**	46	12	6	5	36	26	2	8	13	21	35	57	**56**
18	**Shrewsbury Town**	46	9	9	5	34	27	4	5	14	20	35	54	**53**
19	**Bournemouth**	46	9	4	10	30	34	4	7	12	19	35	49	**50**
20	**Cambridge United**	46	8	9	6	33	28	3	6	14	19	41	52	**48**
21	**Plymouth Argyle**	46	7	6	10	22	36	5	4	14	23	47	45	**46**
22	**Cardiff City**	46	5	6	12	25	31	4	5	14	21	43	46	**38**
23	**Chester City**	46	5	6	12	23	42	1	5	17	14	42	37	**29**
24	**Leyton Orient**	46	6	6	11	21	29	0	2	21	9	46	30	**26**

Play-offs

Semi-finals *(over 2 legs)*
Bristol Rovers 0   Crewe Alexandra 0

Crewe Alexandra 1   Bristol Rovers 1
(Rowbotham)   *(Miller)*
aet, Bristol Rovers won on away goals

Huddersfield T 1   Brentford 1
(Billy)   *(Forster)*

Brentford 1   Huddersfield T 1
(Grainger-pen)   *(Booth)*
aet, Huddersfield won 4-3 on penalties

FINAL
Wembley   *May 28*
Bristol Rovers 1   Huddersfield Town 2
(Stewart)   *(Booth, Billy)*
Bristol Rovers: Parkin, Pritchard, Gurney, Stewart, Clark, Tillson, Sterling, Miller, Taylor (Browning), Skinner, Channing (Archer)
Huddersfield: Francis, Trevitt (Dyson), Cowan, Bullock, Scully, Sinnott, Billy, Duxbury, Booth, Jepson, Crosby (Dunn)

Goalscorers

	Lg	Cp	CC	Other	Total
Gary Bennett (Wrexham)	29	2	2	6	39
Andy Booth (Huddersf)	26	1	0	3	30
Nicky Forster (Brentford)	24	0	0	2	26
Robert Taylor (Brentford)	23	1	1	0	25
Steve Claridge (B'ham)	20	0	1	4	25
Paul Moody (Oxford)	20	0	1	2	23
Kevin Francis (B'ham/Stkpt)	20	0	1	1	22
Shaun Goater (R'ham)	19	3	0	3	25
Ronnie Jepson (Hudds)	19	1	2	1	23
Carlo Corazzin (Cambs)	19	0	0	2	21
Tony Ellis (Blackpool)	17	0	1	0	18
Paul Miller (Bris R)	16	4	0	2	22
Dean Windass (Hull)	16	2	0	0	18
Ken Charley (P'boro)	16	2	0	0	18
Paul Barnes (York)	16	0	0	1	17

	Birmingham	Blackpool	Bournem'th	Bradford C	Brentford	Brighton	Bristol R	Cambridge	Cardiff City	Chester C	Crewe Alex	Huddersfield	Hull City	Leyton O	Oxford Utd	Peterboro'	Plymouth	Rotherham	Shrewsbury	Stockport	Swansea	Wrexham	Wycombe	York City
Birmingham	****	7-1	0-0	0-0	2-0	0-0	1-1	1-0	2-1	1-0	5-0	2-2	2-0	2-1	3-0	2-1	4-2	1-0	2-0	1-0	0-1	5-2	0-1	4-2
Blackpool	1-1	****	3-1	2-0	2-1	3-3	1-2	2-3	3-1	1-0	1-1	2-2	2-3	2-2	2-0	2-1	4-0	0-3	2-2	1-2	0-1	2-1	0-1	0-5
Bournemouth	2-1	1-2	****	2-3	0-1	0-2	0-2	2-3	0-1	1-4	0-0	1-2	3-1	2-3	2-1	3-1	4-0	1-1	2-1	1-2	1-3	2-1	2-0	1-4
Bradford	1-1	0-1	1-2	****	1-0	0-1	2-0	1-1	1-2	1-4	2-0	3-4	2-2	2-0	2-0	2-0	2-0	0-1	1-0	0-2	1-2	4-0	2-0	0-0
Brentford	1-2	3-2	1-2	4-3	****	1-0	2-1	2-1	3-1	2-1	1-1	0-2	3-1	2-1	2-1	0-2	0-0	0-3	2-2	0-0	0-1	0-2	2-0	3-0
Brighton	0-1	2-2	0-0	1-0	1-0	****	3-0	2-0	2-0	2-0	2-0	3-0	2-1	3-0	2-0	1-0	3-0	1-0	1-0	2-0	1-3	0-2	2-0	3-0
Bristol Rovers	1-1	0-1	0-0	0-0	2-2	1-1	****	1-2	3-0	1-0	0-1	2-2	0-0	0-1	2-3	1-0	0-0	1-0	0-1	1-2	1-3	4-0	1-1	1-4
Cambridge	1-0	0-0	2-2	4-1	0-0	0-2	1-1	****	2-1	2-0	1-2	1-0	1-1	1-0	1-0	3-2	1-1	1-0	2-2	0-0	0-1	2-2	0-0	3-1
Cardiff City	0-1	0-1	0-1	0-0	0-1	3-0	1-2	2-0	****	2-1	1-2	1-1	2-2	2-0	1-0	3-1	2-0	0-2	2-1	2-1	0-2	3-4	0-1	1-2
Chester	0-4	2-0	1-1	0-1	1-4	0-1	1-2	2-2	2-1	****	0-1	1-2	2-0	2-1	1-3	1-1	4-4	1-1	1-2	1-3	1-1	1-2	2-0	0-4
Crewe Alex	2-1	4-3	2-0	2-4	1-4	2-1	0-0	3-0	0-2	2-1	****	3-3	3-2	3-0	1-0	2-0	1-3	1-0	1-3	1-0	1-3	1-0	1-2	2-1
Huddersfield	1-2	1-1	0-1	0-0	1-0	3-0	1-1	3-1	5-1	5-1	1-2	****	1-1	1-2	1-0	1-4	1-2	3-1	1-0	0-0	1-2	1-3	0-2	3-0
Hull City	0-0	1-0	3-1	2-0	0-0	4-0	4-0	1-0	4-0	2-0	7-1	3-3	****	2-1	3-0	3-3	2-2	3-1	2-0	2-1	0-1	4-0	0-0	3-1
Leyton O	2-1	0-1	3-2	0-3	0-2	0-3	1-1	1-0	5-1	5-1	1-4	1-2	1-1	****	2-0	3-2	1-0	1-0	2-0	4-0	1-2	4-2	2-0	1-0
Oxford Utd	1-1	3-2	0-3	1-2	1-1	1-2	2-0	1-0	0-2	2-1	7-1	1-0	4-0	3-2	****	1-1	1-0	4-1	3-0	2-0	1-0	4-0	1-1	0-2
Peterborough	1-1	1-0	0-0	0-0	2-2	2-1	2-2	2-2	1-0	1-0	1-5	0-3	0-0	1-0	1-4	****	1-0	2-2	1-1	4-0	1-1	2-2	2-0	3-0
Plymouth A	1-3	0-2	0-1	1-5	1-5	0-3	0-3	3-2	1-0	2-0	3-2	0-3	0-1	0-0	1-1	0-1	****	0-0	3-1	1-0	1-2	2-0	2-2	1-1
Rotherham	1-1	0-2	4-0	3-1	0-2	4-3	0-3	1-0	0-2	1-0	2-2	2-2	4-4	1-0	3-3	0-0	3-1	****	0-0	1-0	2-2	4-1	2-0	0-0
Shrewsbury	0-2	3-0	3-0	1-2	2-1	1-0	1-2	2-0	2-0	1-0	1-4	1-3	1-2	2-1	3-2	0-1	3-2	0-4	****	1-0	3-3	2-2	2-2	0-0
Stockport C	0-1	3-2	1-0	0-2	0-1	2-0	0-0	1-0	3-4	2-0	1-3	2-1	3-1	4-1	2-1	0-2	2-4	1-0	0-1	****	0-1	0-2	4-0	2-3
Swansea	0-2	1-0	1-0	1-2	0-2	1-1	0-0	2-1	4-1	2-2	1-0	1-0	2-0	2-0	1-0	1-3	2-0	0-2	3-0	2-0	****	0-1	1-1	1-0
Wrexham	1-1	0-1	2-0	0-1	0-0	2-1	2-1	1-0	0-3	2-2	1-2	2-2	2-2	4-1	3-2	2-0	3-1	2-1	0-1	0-1	4-1	****	0-0	0-0
Wycombe W	0-3	1-1	1-1	3-1	4-3	1-1	0-0	3-1	3-1	3-1	0-0	1-2	2-2	2-1	2-1	1-0	3-1	1-0	0-1	1-0	1-0	3-0	****	0-0
York City	2-0	4-0	1-0	0-0	0-1	1-0	0-3	2-0	1-1	3-1	1-2	3-0	3-1	2-1	4-1	0-2	1-0	1-1	3-0	2-4	2-4	0-1	4-1	****

Endsleigh Insurance League 1994-95

Division Three

		P	W	D	L	GF	GA	W	D	L	GF	GA	GS	PTS
1	Carlisle United	42	14	5	2	34	14	13	5	3	33	17	67	91
2	Walsall	42	15	3	3	42	18	9	8	4	33	22	75	83
3	Chesterfield	42	11	7	3	26	10	12	5	4	36	27	62	81
4	Bury	42	13	7	1	39	13	10	4	7	34	23	73	80
5	Preston North End	42	13	3	5	37	17	6	7	8	21	24	58	67
6	Mansfield Town	42	10	5	6	45	27	8	6	7	39	32	84	65
7	Scunthorpe United	42	12	2	7	40	30	6	6	9	28	33	68	62
8	Fulham	42	11	5	5	39	22	5	9	7	21	32	60	62
9	Doncaster Rovers	42	9	5	7	28	20	8	5	8	30	23	58	61
10	Colchester United	42	8	5	8	29	30	8	5	8	27	34	56	58
11	Barnet	42	8	7	6	37	27	7	4	10	19	36	56	56
12	Lincoln City	42	10	7	4	34	22	5	4	12	20	33	54	56
13	Torquay United	42	10	8	3	35	25	4	5	12	19	32	54	55
14	Wigan Athletic	42	7	6	8	28	30	7	4	10	25	30	53	52
15	Rochdale	42	8	6	7	25	23	4	8	9	19	44	44	50
16	Hereford United	42	9	6	6	22	19	3	7	11	23	43	45	49
17	Northampton Town	42	8	5	8	25	29	2	9	10	20	38	45	44
18	Hartlepool United	42	9	5	7	33	32	2	5	14	10	37	43	43
19	Gillingham	42	8	7	6	31	25	2	4	15	15	39	46	41
20	Darlington	42	7	5	9	25	24	4	3	14	18	33	43	41
21	Scarborough	42	4	7	10	26	31	4	3	14	23	39	49	34
22	Exeter City*	42	5	5	11	25	36	3	5	13	11	34	36	34

Exeter City not relegated as Macclesfield Town's ground did not meet Endsleigh League specifications.

Play-offs

Semi-finals *(over 2 legs)*

Mansfield Town 1	Chesterfield 1
(Hadley)	*(Robinson)*

Chesterfield 5	Mansfield Town 2
(Lormor, Robinson	*(Holland, Wilkinson)*
Law 2 (1 pen), Howard)	
aet, Chesterfield won 6-3 on aggregate

Preston North End 0	Bury 1
	(Pugh)

Bury 1	Preston North End 0
(Rigby)	
Bury won 2-0 on aggregate

FINAL
Wembley   *May 27*

Bury 0	Chesterfield 2
	(Lormor, Robinson)

Bury: G Kelly, Woodward, Stanilaus, Daws, Lucketti, Jackson, Mulligan (Hughes), Carter (Paskin), Stant, Rigby, Pugh
Chesterfield: Stewart, Hewitt, Rogers, Curtis, Carr, Law, Robinson, Hazel, Lormor (Davies), Morris, Howard (Perkins)

Goalscorers

	Lg	Cp	CC	Other	Total
Phil Stant (Bury/Cardiff)	26	0	2	0	28
Doug Freedman (Barnet)	24	0	5	0	29
Kyle Lightbourne (Wal)	23	3	1	0	27
Steve Wilkinson (Mansfield)	22	0	3	1	26
David Reeves (Carlisle)	21	2	2	0	25
Kevin Wilson (Walsall)	16	2	3	0	21
David Pugh (Bury)	16	0	0	1	17
Steve White (Hereford)	15	1	2	1	19
Andy Lyons (Wigan)	15	0	0	0	15
Mark Carter (Bury)	14	0	1	0	15
Chris Pike (Gillingham)	13	4	0	1	18
Keith Houchen (Hartlepool)	13	0	1	0	14
Graeme Jones (Doncaster)	12	1	1	1	15

	Barnet	Bury	Carlisle Utd	Chesterfield	Colchester Utd	Darlington	Doncaster Rov	Exeter City	Fulham	Gillingham	Hartlepool	Hereford Utd	Lincoln City	Mansfield T	Northampton	Preston NE	Rochdale	Scarborough	Scunthorpe	Torquay Utd	Walsall	Wigan Ath
Barnet	****	1-1	0-2	4-1	0-1	2-3	0-0	1-1	4-0	2-1	0-1	2-2	2-1	2-2	2-3	1-0	6-2	3-1	1-2	2-0	1-3	1-1
Bury	3-0	****	2-0	2-1	4-1	0-1	2-0	2-0	1-0	1-1	3-1	2-0	2-0	2-2	5-0	0-0	0-1	1-0	4-2	3-1	2-2	3-3
Carlisle Utd	4-0	3-0	****	2-0	2-0	2-1	2-0	1-1	0-0	0-1	1-5	2-1	1-3	2-0	2-1	3-1	0-1	2-0	3-1	3-1	0-0	2-1
Chesterfield	2-0	0-0	1-1	****	2-2	4-1	2-0	2-1	0-0	1-1	1-3	0-1	0-1	0-1	4-0	2-3	4-1	1-0	2-1	2-1	2-2	0-1
Colchester	1-1	1-0	0-1	1-1	****	0-1	3-0	0-1	0-1	1-0	3-1	2-0	2-0	2-0	1-0	1-1	0-0	1-0	2-0	0-1	0-2	2-4
Darlington	0-1	0-2	0-2	0-3	2-3	****	1-0	2-0	1-1	2-1	1-0	3-0	3-1	0-2	4-1	0-0	0-1	2-0	1-3	3-0	1-3	0-1
Doncaster R	1-1	1-2	0-0	0-1	1-2	1-0	****	0-2	1-1	1-3	2-1	1-2	1-0	2-5	0-1	2-1	4-0	2-1	0-2	3-0	5-3	1-3
Exeter City	1-2	0-4	1-1	1-2	0-0	3-1	0-2	****	5-2	3-0	3-1	3-0	1-3	3-3	1-0	0-1	2-2	0-2	1-1	2-1	1-1	0-1
Fulham	4-0	1-0	1-3	3-1	0-2	1-0	0-3	1-0	****	4-1	1-2	0-0	0-1	2-1	3-1	3-1	0-1	1-0	1-0	2-0	0-0	0-0
Gillingham	2-1	1-1	0-1	1-1	1-0	2-1	2-0	1-2	4-1	****	0-0	1-2	3-0	0-1	4-1	2-3	4-0	0-3	1-1	2-1	1-3	0-1
Hartlepool	0-1	3-1	1-5	1-1	3-1	1-0	2-1	3-0	1-2	0-0	****	2-1	4-0	3-2	2-1	3-1	1-1	1-0	2-1	1-1	0-1	1-2
Hereford Utd	3-2	1-0	0-1	0-2	3-0	0-0	0-1	0-1	2-0	0-0	2-1	****	2-0	0-0	0-0	2-1	1-0	2-1	1-4	1-1	1-3	0-1
Lincoln City	1-2	0-3	1-1	0-1	2-0	3-1	1-0	1-0	4-0	1-1	3-0	3-0	****	3-2	4-1	0-1	2-2	2-0	2-2	3-0	1-1	1-0
Mansfield T	3-0	0-2	1-2	4-2	2-0	0-1	2-2	2-0	4-2	0-0	3-2	0-0	0-3	****	4-4	0-1	0-0	1-2	3-0	2-1	1-1	0-1
Northampton	1-1	0-5	2-1	0-1	1-1	2-1	2-2	1-0	4-4	1-1	1-1	0-0	4-1	2-3	****	2-0	1-1	2-1	0-0	1-1	2-0	1-0
Preston NE	1-0	5-0	1-0	2-3	1-1	1-3	3-0	0-2	1-2	2-1	2-3	3-1	1-1	0-1	2-1	****	3-0	1-0	3-1	2-0	2-2	1-0
Rochdale	2-2	0-3	1-1	4-1	0-0	2-0	2-0	2-2	5-0	1-0	0-1	1-0	2-2	2-4	0-0	3-0	****	4-0	1-0	2-0	2-2	1-0
Scarborough	0-1	1-2	1-2	0-1	0-1	3-1	2-2	0-1	5-2	1-2	3-3	2-1	5-2	3-3	0-2	1-0	1-2	****	3-1	2-0	1-3	0-1
Scunthorpe	1-0	3-2	2-3	0-1	3-4	2-1	0-0	0-5	1-0	1-0	1-4	1-4	1-3	2-1	0-1	0-0	2-1	1-2	****	3-2	1-1	1-0
Torquay Utd	1-2	2-2	1-1	3-3	3-3	2-0	2-0	0-1	2-1	2-1	1-1	1-1	3-0	1-0	2-1	0-1	2-1	2-1	1-1	****	0-1	3-1
Walsall	4-0	0-1	1-2	1-3	2-0	1-0	2-0	0-2	5-1	2-1	2-2	4-3	2-1	1-0	2-1	2-2	0-0	4-1	2-1	1-0	****	2-0
Wigan Ath	1-2	0-3	0-2	2-3	1-2	4-1	3-2	1-5	1-1	2-0	2-0	1-1	1-1	0-4	2-1	1-1	4-0	1-1	1-1	0-0	1-0	****

English Non-League Football 1994-5 ■━━

GM Vauxhall Conference

	P	W	D	L	GF	GA	PTS
Macclesfield	42	24	8	10	70	40	80
Woking	42	21	12	9	76	54	75
Southport	42	21	9	12	68	50	72
Altrincham	42	20	8	14	77	60	68
Stevenage Borough	42	20	7	15	68	49	67
Kettering Town	42	19	10	13	73	56	67
Gateshead	42	19	10	13	61	53	67
Halifax Town	42	17	12	13	68	54	63
Runcorn	42	16	10	16	59	71	58
Northwich Victoria	42	14	15	13	77	66	57
Kidderminster Harriers	42	16	9	17	63	61	57
Bath City	42	15	12	15	55	56	57
Bromsgrove Rovers	42	14	13	15	66	69	55
Farnborough Town	42	15	10	17	45	64	55
Dagenham & Redbridge	42	13	13	16	56	69	52
Dover Athletic	42	11	16	15	48	55	49
Welling United	42	13	10	19	57	74	49
Stalybridge Celtic	42	11	14	17	52	72	47
Telford United	42	10	16	16	53	62	46
Merthyr Tydfil	42	11	11	20	53	63	44
Stafford Rangers	42	9	11	22	53	79	38
Yeovil Town	42	8	14	20	50	71	*37

* Yeovil deducted 1 pt for fielding an ineligible player

Leading Scorers

	Lge	Other
Paul Dobson (Gateshead)	25	7
Carl Alford (Kettering)	23	4

Unibond League
PREMIER DIVISION

	P	W	D	L	GF	GA	PTS
Marine	42	29	11	2	83	27	98
Morecambe	42	28	10	4	99	34	94
Guiseley	42	28	9	5	96	50	93
Hyde United	42	22	10	10	89	59	76
Boston United	42	20	11	11	80	43	71
Spennymoor United	42	20	11	11	66	52	71
Buxton	42	18	9	15	65	62	63
Gainsborough Trinity	42	16	13	13	69	61	61
Bishop Auckland*	42	16	12	14	68	55	57
Witton Albion	42	14	14	14	54	56	56
Barrow	42	17	5	20	68	71	56
Colwyn Bay	42	16	8	18	71	80	56
Emley	42	14	13	15	62	68	55
Matlock Town	42	15	5	22	62	72	50
Accrington Stanley	42	12	13	17	55	77	49
Knowsley United	42	11	14	17	64	83	47
Winsford United	42	10	11	21	56	75	41
Chorley	42	11	7	24	64	87	40
Frickley Athletic	42	10	10	22	53	79	40
Droylsden	42	10	8	24	56	93	38
Whitley Bay	42	8	8	26	46	97	32
Horwich RMI	42	9	4	29	49	94	31

* Bishop Auckland deducted 3 points for breach of rules

Leading Scorers

	Lge	Other
John Coleman (Morecambe)	31	15
Andy Whittaker (Barrow)	31	5

Beazer Homes League
PREMIER DIVISION

	P	W	D	L	GF	GA	PTS
Hednesford Town	42	28	9	5	99	49	93
Cheltenham Town	42	25	11	6	87	39	86
Burton Albion	42	20	15	7	55	39	75
Gloucester City	42	22	8	12	76	48	74
Rushden & Diamonds	42	19	11	12	99	65	68
Dorchester Town	42	19	10	13	84	61	67
Leek Town	42	19	10	13	72	60	67
Gresley Rovers	42	17	12	13	70	63	63
Cambridge City	42	18	8	16	60	55	62
Worcester City	42	14	15	13	46	34	57
Crawley Town	42	15	10	17	64	71	55
Hastings Town	42	13	14	15	55	57	53
Halesowen Town	42	14	10	18	81	80	52
Gravesend & Northft	42	13	13	16	38	55	52
Chelmsford City	42	14	6	22	56	60	48
Atherstone United	42	12	12	18	51	67	48
VS Rugby	42	11	14	17	49	61	47
Sudbury Town	42	12	10	20	50	77	46
Solihull Borough	42	10	15	17	39	65	45
Sittingbourne	42	11	10	21	51	73	43
Trowbridge Town	42	9	13	20	43	69	40
Corby Town	42	4	10	28	36	113	*21

* Corby Town deducted 1 point for fielding ineligible player

Leading Scorers

	Total
J O'Connor (Hednesford)	35
O Pickard (Dorchester)	29

Diadora League
PREMIER DIVISION

	P	W	D	L	GF	GA	PTS
Enfield	42	28	9	5	106	43	93
Slough Town	42	22	13	7	82	56	79
Hayes	42	20	14	8	66	47	74
Aylesbury United	42	21	6	15	86	59	69
Hitchin Town	42	18	12	12	68	59	66
Bromley	42	18	11	13	76	67	65
St Albans City	42	17	13	12	96	81	64
Molesey	42	18	8	16	65	61	62
Yeading	42	14	15	13	60	59	57
Harrow Borough	42	17	6	19	64	67	57
Dulwich Hamlet	42	16	9	17	70	82	57
Carshalton Athletic	42	16	9	17	69	84	57
Kingstonian	42	16	8	18	62	57	56
Walton & Hersham	42	14	11	17	75	73	53
Sutton United	42	13	12	17	74	69	51
Purfleet	42	13	12	17	76	90	51
Hendon	42	12	14	16	57	65	50
Grays Athletic	42	11	16	15	57	61	49
Bishop's Stortford	42	12	11	19	53	76	47
Chesham United	42	12	9	21	60	87	45
Marlow	42	10	9	23	52	84	39
Wokingham Town	42	6	9	27	39	86	27

Leading Scorers

	Lge	Other
Gary Abbott (Enfield)	34	0
Steve Clark (St Albans)	28	2
David Crown (Purfleet)	28	1

More Quotes

"No more nicey-nicey stuff...I don't mind if we pick up a few yellow cards...I'm looking for a team which fights" - **Steve McMahon on being appointed Swindon manager. In his first match McMahon picked up two yellow cards and was sent off.**

"I've seen some crap refereeing decisions, but that's the worst" - **Swindon Town announcer airing his views over the PA at half time. He was later sacked and escorted from the ground.**

"It may have looked as if I kissed the linesman when I walked across to him immediately after my caution, but in fact I was whispering what I thought of him in his ear. When I got up close he wasn't that pretty to kiss anyway" - **Jimmy Case, the evergreen Brighton midfielder, on the romantic encounter that led to his booking.**

"Dad, what are they doing? It's only a game" - **Seven-year-old James Eager commenting on the rioting that erupted at Lansdowne Road during the England-Ireland fixture.**

"I must have broken a job lot of mirrors and run over a few black cats" - **Everton boss Mike Walker on his team's dismal start to the season.**

"The first day I came to the club, David sent me a fax with a little motto of his about perseverance.. I've taken him at his word and I keep persevering about players I want. In the end to shut me up he finds the money, God bless him" - **Birmingham manager, Barry Fry, after club owner David Sullivan made available £800,000 to buy striker Kevin Francis.**

"It's the first time they've closed the gates here since shinguards were invented" - **Former Carlisle player Ivor Broadis on the Boxing Day full house for the game against Bury.**

"I thought they had slipped Steve McQueen on" - **Dave Bassett, the Sheffield United manager, after watching Wolves score twice in the last minute to 'escape' with a draw.**

"Our manager doesn't like losing and there's the old cliché about us having nothing to lose. But I'm sure we're going to" - **Cliff Hercules of non-League Aylesbury correctly predicting his team's FA Cup Third Round defeat.**

"I don't even know where Portsmouth is. All I know is there are a lot of sailors who live there" - **Boxing promoter Frank Maloney on rumours that he is about to take over the First Division Club.**

"I asked the players who wanted to take a penalty and there was an awful smell coming from a few of them" - **Millwall boss Mick McCarthy after his side beat Chelsea in an FA Cup penalty shoot-out.**

"As we have seen in Boulogne's harbour recently, French strikers can be a volatile bunch" - **Pat Nevin, the PFA chairman, on the strike at the channel ports.**

"Mr Whelan is a god and our father in England. He is a very good person and with him, Wigan will be in the First Division in two years" - **An optimistic Roberto Martinez, one of three Spanish players brought to the Third Division side by owner Dave Whelan.**

"I know Vinny Jones has learned to sing 'Land of my Fathers' in Welsh but if I could lead Wales to the 1998 World Cup Finals I'd even learn the French anthem" - **Wales' manager Bobby Gould.**

English Cup Competitions ▬▬▬

FA Challenge Cup

First Round

Altrincham 3 *(Green, Morton, France)*
Southport 2 *(Cunningham, McDonald)*

Ashford T 2 *(Arter, Dent)*
Fulham 2 *(Adams 2 (2 pens))*
Fulham 5 *(Morgan, Adams 2, Blake, Cork)*
Ashford Town 3 *(Stanton 2, Dent) aet*

Barnet 4 *(McMahon, Cooper 2, Hodges)*
Woking 4 *(Fielder, Dennis, Walker, Steele)*

Woking 1 *(Tucker)*
Barnet 0

Bath City 0
Bristol Rovers 5 *(Stewart, Miller 4)*

Bishop Auckland 0
Bury 0

Bury 1 *(Paskin)*
Bishop Auckland 1 *(Todd)*
Bury won 4-2 on penalties

Bournemouth 3 *(Morris, Russell, McElhatton)*
Worthing 1 *(Mintram)*

Bradford City 1 *(Tolson)*
Scunthorpe Utd 1 *(Hope)*

Scunthorpe Utd 3 *(Carmichael, Alexander, Thompstone)*
Bradford City 2 *(Power, Richards) aet*

Burnley 2 *(Heath, Dreary)*
Shrewsbury Town 1 *(Spink)*

Cambridge Utd 2 *(Lillis, Butler)*
Brentford 2 *(Annon, Taylor)*

Brentford 1 *(Grainger)*
Cambridge Utd 2 *(Lillis, Butler (pen))*

Chesham Utd 0
Bashley 1 *(Paskins)*

Chester City 2 *(Page, Alsford)*
Witton Albion 0

Chesterfield 0
Scarborough 0

Scarborough 2 *(Toman, White)*
Chesterfield 0

Crewe Alexandra 7 *(Rowbotham 2, Smith, Garvey, Ward 3)*
Gresley Rovers 1 *(Devaney)*

Doncaster Rovers 1 *(Jones)*
Huddersfield 4 *(Bullock, Booth, Jepson, Dunn)*

Enfield 1 *(Abbott)*
Cardiff City 0

Exeter City 1 *(Cecere)*
Crawley Town 0

Halifax Town 1 *(Kiwomya)*
Runcorn 1 *(Thomas (pen))*

Runcorn 1 *(Pugh)*
Halifax Town 3 *(Lancaster 2, Lambert) aet*

Hereford Utd 2 *(Lyne 2)*
Hitchin Town 2 *(Marshall 2)*

Hitchin Town 4 *(Bone, Williams, Wilson, Marshall)*
Hereford Utd 2 *(White, Pick)*

Hull City 0
Lincoln City 1 *(Bannister)*

Hyde Utd 1 *(Kimmins)*
Darlington 3 *(Slaven, Worboys 2)*

Kidderminster Harriers 1 *(Humphreys)*
Torquay Utd 1 *(Hathaway)*

Torquay Utd 1 *(Hancox)*
Kidderminster Harriers 0

Kingstonian 2 *(J Ndah 2)*
Brighton & Hove Albion 1 *(Codner)*

Mansfield Town 3 *(Hadley, Holland 2)*
Northwich Victoria 1 *(Oghani)*

Newport IoW 2 *(Soares 2)*
Aylebury Utd 3 *(Hercules 2, Pluckrose (pen))*

Peterborough Utd 4 *(Charlery 2 (1 pen), Williams, Henry)*
Northampton Town 0

Port Vale 6 *(Griffiths, Allon, Foyle 3, D Glover)*

Hartlepool 0

Slough Town 0
Birmingham City 4 *(Shearer 2, McGavin 2)*

Tiverton Town 1 *(Smith)*
Leyton Orient 3 *(Gray, Carter, West)*

Walsall 3 *(Lightbourne, Butler 2)*
Rochdale 0

Wigan Athletic 4 *(Leonard, Carragher 2, Kilford)*
Spennymoor Utd 0

Wrexham 1 *(Watkin)*
Stockport County 0

Wycombe Wanderers 4 *(Stapleton 2, Bell, Ryan)*
Chelmsford 0

Yeading 2 *(Hippolyte, Graham)*
Colchester Utd 2 *(Kinsella, Abrahams)*

Colchester Utd 7 *(Abrahams 2, Whitton 2, Brown 2, Kinsella)*
Yeading 1 *(McKinnon (pen))*

York City 3 *(Naylor 2, McCarthy)*
Rotherham Utd 3 *(Goater 2, Helliwell)*

Rotherham Utd 3 *(Davison 2, Goater)*
York City 0

Guiseley 1 *(Brockie)*
Carlisle Utd 4 *(Reeves 2, Conway, Mountfield)*

Preston North End 1 *(Conroy)*
Blackpool 0

Marlow 2 *(Caesar 2)*
Oxford Utd 0

Walton & Hersham 0
Swansea City 2 *(Ford, Ampadu)*

Kettering Town 0
Plymouth Argyle 1 *(Skinner)*

Heybridge Swifts 0
Gillingham 2 *(Reinelt, Pike)*

Second Round

Altrincham 1 *(Sharratt)*
Wigan Athletic 0

Crewe Alexandra 1 *(Ward)*
Bury 2 *(Johnrose, Rigby)*

Enfield 1 *(Abbott)*
Torquay Utd 1 *(Okorie)*

Torquay Utd 0
Enfield 1 *(Kerr)*

Exeter City 1 *(Morgan)*
Colchester Utd 2 *(Whitton, English)*

Gillingham 1 *(Pike)*
Fulham 1 *(Hamill)*

Fulham 1 *(Hamill)*
Gillingham 2 *(Pike, Reinelt) aet*

Halifax Town 0
Mansfield Town 0

Mansfield Town 2 *(Aspinall,
    Holland)*
Halifax Town 1 *(Lancaster)*

Hitchin Town 0
Wycombe Wanderers 5 *(Garner 3,
    Ryan, Bell)*

Kingstonian 1 *(Akuamoah (pen))*
Aylesbury Utd 4 *(Hercules, Bashir,
    Pluckrose (pen),
    Blencowe)*

Leyton Orient 0
Bristol Rovers 2 *(Stewart 2)*

Lincoln City 1 *(D Johnson)*
Huddersfield Town 0

Peterborough Utd 0
Cambridge Utd 2 *(Barrick, Hay)*

Plymouth Argyle 2 *(Ross 2)*
Bournemouth 1 *(Jones)*

Preston North End 1 *(Smart)*
Walsall 1 *(Wilson)*

Walsall 4 *(Houghton, Wilson,
    Lightbourne 2)*
Preson North End 0

Scarborough 1 *(Swann)*
Port Vale 0

Wrexham 5 *(Connolly 2, Bennett,
    Hughes, Watkin)*
Rotherham 2 *(Davison, Hurst)*

Carlisle Utd 2 *(Conway, Currie)*
Darlington 0

Chester City 1 *(Milner)*
Burnley 2 *(Eyres (pen), Heath)*

Birmingham City 0
Scunthorpe Utd 0

Scunthorpe Utd 1 *(Bullimore)*
Birmingham 2 *(McGavin, Cooper)*

Bashley 0
Swansea City 1 *(Torpey)*

Marlow 2 *(R Evans, C Evans)*
Woking 1 *(Tucker)*

Third Round

Aylesbury Utd 0
QPR 4 *(Maddix, Ferdinand, Gallen,
    Meaker)*

Barnsley 0
Aston Villa 2 *(Yorke, Saunders)*

Birmingham City 0
Liverpool 0

Liverpool 1 *(Redknapp)*
Birmingham City 1 *(Otto)*
aet Liverpool won 2-0 on penalties

Bristol City 0
Stoke City 0

Stoke City 1 *(Scott)   aet*
Bristol City 3 *(Baird, Tinnion, Bent)*

Bury 2 *(Lucketti, Stanislaus)*
Tranmere Rovers 2 *(Muir 2)*

Tranmere Rovers 3 *(O'Brien, Muir,
    Malkin)*
Bury 0

Cambridge Utd 2 *(Butler 2 (1 pen))*
Burnley 4 *(Eyres (pen), Robinson,
    Randall, Gayle)*

Chelsea 3 *(Peacock, Sinclair,
    Spencer)*
Charlton Athletic 0

Coventry City 1 *(Wegerle (pen))*
West Bromwich Albion 1 *(Ashcroft
    (pen))*

West Bromwich Albion 1 *(Raven)*
Coventry City 2 *(Dublin, Ndlovu)*

Everton 1 *(Hinchcliffe)*
Derby 0

Gillingham 1 *(Pike (pen))*
Sheffield Wednesday 2 *(Waddle,
    Bright)*

Grimsby Town 0
Norwich City 1 *(Crook)*

Leicester City 2 *(Oldfield, Roberts)*
Enfield 0

Luton Town 1 *(Hartson)*
Bristol Rovers 1 *(Stewart)*

Bristol Rovers 0
Luton Town 1 *(Marshall)*

Mansfield Town 2 *(Donaldson,
    Ireland)*
Wolverhampton Wdrs 3 *(Kelly,
    Dennison, Mills)*

Millwall 0
Arsenal 0

Arsenal 0
Millwall 2 *(Beard, Kennedy)*

Nottingham Forest 2 *(Collymore,
    Gemmill)*
Plymouth Argyle 0

Portsmouth 3 *(Creaney, Preki 2)*
Bolton Wanderers 1 *(Sneekes)*

Reading 1 *(Taylor)*
Oldham Athletic 3 *(Sharp,
    Richardson, Halle)*

Scarborough 0
Watford 0

Watford 2 *(Hessenthaler,
    Holdsworth)*
Scarborough 0

Southampton 2 *(Heaney, Le Tissier)*
Southend Utd 0

Sunderland 1 *(Russell)*
Carlisle Utd 1 *(Davey)*

Carlisle Utd 1 *(Walling)*
Sunderland 3 *(Armstrong 2, Gray)*

Swansea City 1 *(Ford)*
Middlesbrough 1 *(Moore)*

Middlesbrough 1 *(Hendrie)*
Swansea City 2 *(Torpey, Penney)*

Swindon Town 2 *(Fjortoft, Nijholt)*
Marlow 0

Tottenham Hotspur 3 *(Sheringham,
    Rosenthal, Nethercott)*
Altrincham 0

Walsall 1 *(Marsh)*
Leeds Utd 1 *(Wetherall)*

Leeds Utd 5 *(Deane, Wetherall,
    Masinga 3)*
Walsall 2 *(O'Connor (pen),
    Wetherall (og))aet*

Wimbledon 1 *(Harford)*
Colchester Utd 0

Wrexham 2 *(Durkan, Bennett (pen))*
Ipswich Town 1 *(Linighan)*

Wycombe Wanderers 0
West Ham Utd 2 *(Cottee, Brown)*

Crystal Palace 5 *(Coleman, Salako 2, Armstrong, Gordon (pen))*
Lincoln City 1 *(Greenall)*

Newcastle Utd 1 *(Lee)*
Blackburn Rovers 1 *(Sutton)*

Blackburn Rovers 1 *(Sutton)*
Newcastle Utd 2 *(Hottiger, Clark)*

Notts County 2 *(Matthews, White)*
Manchester City 2 *(Beagrie, D Brightwell)*

Manchester City 5 *(Rosler 4, Gaudino)*
Notts County 2 *(McSwegan, Matthews)*

Sheffield United 0
Manchester United 2 *(Hughes, Cantona)*

Fourth Round
Burnley 0
Liverpool 0

Liverpool 1 *(Barnes)*
Burnley 0

Coventry City 0
Norwich City 0

Norwich City 3 *(Sheron 2, Eadie)*
Coventry City 1 *(Ndlovu) aet*

Leeds Utd 3 *(White, Palmer, Masinga)*
Oldham Athletic 2 *(Halle, Palmer (og))*

Luton Town 1 *(Biggins)*
Southampton 1 *(Shipperley)*

Southampton 6 *(Le Tissier 2 (1 pen) Magilton, Heaney, Monkou, Hughes)*
Luton Town 0

Manchester City 1 *(Walsh)*
Aston Villa 0

Manchester Utd 5 *(Irwin 2 (1 pen), Giggs, McClair, Humes (og))*
Wrexham 2 *(Durkan, Cross)*

Millwall 0
Chelsea 0

Chelsea 1 *(Stein)*
Millwall 1 *(Savage)*
aet Millwall won 5-4 on penalties

Newcastle Utd 3 *(Kitson 3)*
Swansea City 0

Nottingham Forest 1 *(Bohinen)*
Crystal Palace 2 *(Armstrong, Dowie)*

Portsmouth 0
Leicester City 1 *(Roberts)*

QPR 1 *(Impey)*
West Ham Utd 0

Watford 1 *(Hessenthaler)*
Swindon Town 0

Bristol City 0
Everton 1 *(Jackson)*

Sunderland 1 *(Gray)*
Tottenham Hotspur 4 *(Sheringham, Klinsmann 2 (1 pen), Melville (og))*

Tranmere Rovers 0
Wimbledon 2 *(Leonhardsen, Earle)*

Sheffield Wednesday 0
Wolverhampton Wdrs 0

Wolverhampton Wdrs 1 *(Kelly)*
Sheffield Wednesday 1 *(Bright)*
aet Wolves won 4-3 on penalties

Fifth Round
Everton 5 *(Limpar, Parkinson, Stuart, Rideout, Ferguson)*
Norwich 0

QPR 1 *(Wilson (pen))*
Millwall 0

Tottenham Hotspur 1 *(Klinsmann)*
Southampton 1 *(Le Tissier (pen))*

Southampton 2 *(Shipperley, Le Tissier (pen))*
Tottenham Hotspur 6 *(Rosenthal 3, Sheringham, Barmby, Anderton) aet*

Watford 0
Crystal Palace 0

Crystal Palace 1 *(Ndah)*
Watford 0 *aet*

Wolverhampton Wdrs 1 *(Kelly)*
Leicester City 0

Liverpool 1 *(Fowler)*
Wimbledon 1 *(Clarke)*

Wimbledon 0
Liverpool 2 *(Barnes, Rush)*

Manchester Utd 3 *(Bruce, McClair, Hughes)*
Leeds Utd 1 *(Yeboah)*

Newcastle Utd 3 *(Gillespie 2, Beresford)*
Manchester City 1 *(Rösler)*

Sixth Round
Crystal Palace 1 *(Dowie)*
Wolverhampton Wdrs 1 *(Cowans)*

Wolverhampton Wdrs 1 *(Kelly)*
Crystal Palace 4 *(Armstrong 2, Dowie, Pitcher)*

Liverpool 1 *(Fowler)*
Tottenham Hotspur 2 *(Sheringham, Klinsmann)*

Everton 1 *(Watson)*
Newcastle Utd 0

Manchester Utd 2 *(Sharpe, Irwin)*
QPR 0

Semi Finals
Manchester Utd 2 *(Irwin, Pallister)*
Crystal Palace 2 *(Dowie, Armstrong)*
aet

Crystal Palace 0
Manchester Utd 2 *(Bruce, Pallister)*

Tottenham Hotspur 1 *(Klinsmann (pen))*
Everton 4 *(Jackson, Stuart, Amokachi 2)*

FA CUP FINAL
Wembley   May 20
Everton 1 *(Rideout)*
Manchester Utd 0

Everton: Southall, Jackson, Watson, Unsworth, Ablett, Limpar (Amokachi), Horne, Parkinson, Hinchcliffe, Stuart, Rideout (Ferguson)
Manchester Utd: Schmeichel, Neville, Bruce (Giggs), Pallister, Irwin, Butt, Keane, Ince, Sharpe (Scholes), McClair, Hughes
Referee: G Ashby (Worcester)

Coca-Cola Cup

First Round *(over 2 legs)*
Doncaster Rvrs 2 *(Jones, Torfason)*
Wrexham 4 *(Bennett, Connolly,*
Humes, Watkin)

Wrexham 1 *(Watkin)*
Doncaster Rvrs 1 *(Swailes)*
Wrexham won 5-3 on aggregate
....
Barnet 4 *(Freedman 2, Cooper 2)*
Leyton Orient 0

Leyton Orient 1 *(Cockerill)*
Barnet 1 *(Freedman)*
Barnet won 5-1 on aggregate
....
Blackpool 1 *(Quinn)*
Chesterfield 2 *(Perkins, Cheetham)*

Chesterfield 4 *(Norris-pen, Davies,*
Morris, Curtis)
Blackpool 2 *(Ellis, Brown)*
Chesterfield won 6-3 on aggregate
....
Bournemouth 2 *(Russell, Cotterill)*
Northampton Town 0

Northampton Town 0
Bournemouth 1 *(Cotterill)*
Bournemouth won 3-0 on aggregate
....
Bradford City 2 *(Taylor, Duxbury)*
Grimsby Town 1 *(Gilbert)*

Grimsby Town 1 *(Groves)*
Bradford City 2 *(Murray, Richards)*
Bradford City won 4-2 on aggregate
....
Brighton 2 *(McDougald, Nogan)*
Wycombe W 1 *(Regis)*

Wycombe W 1 *(Turnbull)*
Brighton 3 *(Nogan 2, McDougald)*
Brighton won 5-2 on aggregate
....
Bristol Rovers 1 *(Tillson)*
Port Vale 3 *(Foyle, Naylor, L Glover)*

Port Vale 1 *(L Glover)*
Bristol Rovers 1 *(Stewart)*
Port Vale won 4-2 on aggregate
....
Burnley 1 *(Joyce)*
York City 0

York City 2 *(Pepper, Cooper)*
Burnley 2 *(Robinson, Gayle)*
Burnley won 3-2 on aggregate
....
Bury 2 *(Carter-pen, Lynch-og)*
Hartlepool 0

Hartlepool 5 *(Houchen, Southall 2,*
Jackson-og, Thompson)
Bury 1 *(Rigby)* aet
Hartlepool won 5-3 on aggregate
....

Cardiff City 1 *(Oatway)*
Torquay 0

Torquay 4 *(Goodridge, Hancox 3)*
Cardiff City 2 *(Stant 2)*
Torquay won 4-3 on aggregate
....
Colchester 0
Brentford 2 *(Stephenson, Taylor)*

Brentford 2 *(Parris, Smith)*
Colchester 0
Brentford won 4-0 on aggregate
....
Crewe Alexandra 2 *(Garvey, Ward)*
Wigan 1 *(Gavin)*

Wigan 3 *(Gavin, Rennie, Carragher)*
Crewe Alexandra 0
Wigan won 4-2 on aggregate
....
Darlington 2 *(Cross, Slaven)*
Barnsley 2 *(Taggart, Redfearn)*

Barnsley 0
Darlington 0
aet, 2-2 on aggregate
Barnsley won on away goals
....
Gillingham 0
Reading 1 *(Williams)*

Reading 3 *(Quinn 2, Lovell)*
Gillingham 0
Reading won 4-0 on aggregate
....
Hereford U 0
West Brom 0

West Brom 0
Hereford U 1 *(White)*
Hereford won 1-0 on aggregate
....
Hull City 2 *(Peacock, Lee)*
Scarborough 1 *(Young)*

Scarborough 2 *(Blackstone 2)*
Hull City 0
Scarboro' won 3-2 on aggregate
....
Lincoln C 2 *(Carbon, Schofield)*
Chester City 0

Chester C 2 *(Whelan, Chambers)*
Lincoln C 3 *(Schofield, West,*
D Johnson-pen)
Lincoln won 5-2 on aggregate
....
Luton Town 1 *(Oakes)*
Fulham 1 *(Moore)*

Fulham 1 *(Haworth)*
Luton Town 1 *(Marshall)*
aet, 2-2 on aggregate
Fulham won 4-3 on penalties
....

Oxford Utd 3 *(Moody-pen, Massey*
Robinson)
Peterborough 1 *(Morrison)*

Peterborough 0
Oxford 1 *(Dyer)*
Oxford won 4-1 on aggregate
....
Rochdale 1 *(Whitehall)*
Mansfield Town 2 *(Wilkinson 2)*

Mansfield Town 1 *(Wilkinson)*
Rochdale 0
Mansfield won 3-1 on aggregate
....
Rotherham 1 *(Varadi)*
Carlisle Utd 0

Carlisle U 3 *(Reeves 2, Walling)*
Rotherham 1 *(Hayward)*
Carlisle won 3-2 on aggregate
....
Scunthorpe 2 *(Henderson,*
Bullimore)
Huddersfield Town 1 *(Scully)*

Huddersfield 3 *(Jepson 2, Reid)*
Scunthorpe 0
Huddersfield won 4-2 on aggregate
....
Shrewsbury 2 *(W Clarke, Spink)*
Birmingham City 1 *(Daish)*

Birmingham 2 *(Saville,Claridge-pen)*
Shrewsbury 0
Birmingham won 3-2 on aggregate
....
Southend United 0
Watford 0

Watford 1 *(Ramage)*
Southend United 0
Watford won 1-0 on aggregate
....
Walsall 4 *(Wilson 2, Lightbourne,*
O'Connor)
Plymouth Argyle 0

Plymouth A 2 *(Swan, Castle)*
Walsall 1 *(Wilson)*
Walsall won 5-2 on aggregate
....
Exeter City 2 *(Turner, Cecere)*
Swansea City 2 *(Harris, Hodge)*

Swansea City 2 *(Penney 2-1 pen)*
Exeter City 0
Swansea won 4-2 on aggregate
....
Portsmouth 2 *(Stimson, Powell)*
Cambridge Utd 0

Cambridge Utd 2 *(Craddock,*
Barrick)
Portsmouth 3 *(Creaney, Powell 2)*
Portsmouth won 5-2 on aggregate
....

Preston NE 1 *(Fensome-pen)*
Stockport Co 1 *(Chalk)*

Stockport Co 4 *(Emerson, Ward,*
Armstrong,Beaumont)
Preston NE 1 *(Moyes)*
Stockport won 5-2 on aggregate

Second Round *(over two legs)*
Barnet 1 *(Freedman)*
Man City 0

Man City 4 *(Quinn 2, Walsh,*
Summerbee)
Barnet 1 *(Freedman)*
Man City won 4-2 on aggregate

Blackburn R 2 *(Wilcox, Sutton)*
Birmingham City 0

Birmingham City 1 *(McGavin)*
Blackburn R 1 *(Sutton)*
Blackburn won 3-1 on aggregate

Bristol City 0
Notts County 1 *(Devlin)*

Notts County 3 *(Jemson, Lund 2)*
Bristol City 0
Notts County won 4-0 on aggregate

Carlisle Utd 0
QPR 1 *(Ferdinand)*

QPR 2 *(Allen, Wilson-pen)*
Carlisle Utd 0
QPR won 3-0 on aggregate

Chesterfield 1 *(Moss)*
Wolverhampton W 3 *(Bull 2, Kelly)*

Wolverhampton W 1 *(Froggatt)*
Chesterfield 1 *(Jules)*
Wolves won 4-2 on aggregate)

Everton 2 *(Samways, Stuart-pen)*
Portsmouth 3 *(Creaney 2,*
Kristensen)

Portsmouth 1 *(Hall)*
Everton 1 *(Watson)*
Portsmouth won 4-3 on aggregate

Fulham 3 *(Moore, Haworth, Blake)*
Stoke C 2 *(Orlygsson-pen,*
Gleghorn)

Stoke C 1 *(Peschisolido)*
Fulham 0
aet, 3-3 on aggregate
Stoke won on away goals

Huddersfield T 0
Southampton 1 *(Le Tissier)*

Southampton 4 *(Le Tissier 4-1 pen)*
Huddersfield 0
Southampton won 5-0 on aggregate

Lincoln City 1 *(Johnson)*
Crystal Palace 0

Crystal Palace 3 *(Gordon,*
Armstrong, Dyer)
Licoln City 0
Crystal Palace won 3-1 on agg.

Oxford Utd 1 *(Ford)*
Oldham Ath 1 *(Ritchie)*

Oldham Ath 1 *(Richardson)*
Oxford Utd 0
Oldham won 2-1 on aggregate

Reading 3 *(Quinn 2, Holsgrove)*
Derby Co 1 *(Gabbiadini)*

Derby Co 2 *(Gabbiadini, Williams)*
Reading 0
aet, 3-3 on aggregate
Derby Co won on away goals

Scarborough 1 *(Rowe)*
Middlesbrough 4 *(Hendrie, Pollock,*
Moore, Mustoe)

Middlesbrough 4 *(Wilkinson 3,*
Hignett)
Scarborough 1 *(Charles-pen)*
Middlesbrough won 8-2 on agg.

Stockport Co 1 *(Francis)*
Sheffield Utd 5 *(Whitehouse 3-1 pen*
Flo 2)

Sheffield Utd 1 *(Scott)*
Stockport Co 0
Shefield Utd won 6-1 on agg.

Tranmere R 1 *(Brannan)*
Brentford 0

Brentford 0
Tranmere R 0
Tranmere won 1-0 on aggregate

Walsall 2 *(Watkiss, Potts-og)*
West Ham Utd 1 *(Ntamark-og)*

West Ham Utd 2 *(Hutchison,*
Moncur)
Walsall 0   *aet*
West Ham Utd won 3-2 on agg.

Wimbledon 2 *(Gayle, Harford)*
Torquay Utd 0

Torquay Utd 0
Wimbledon 1 *(Holdsworth)*
Wimbledon won 3-0 on aggregate

Wrexham 1 *(Jones)*
Coventry 2 *(Darby, Flynn)*

Coventry 3 *(Dublin 2, Wegerle)*
Wrexham 2 *(Cross, Bennett -pen)*
Coventry won 5-3 on aggregate

Aston Villa 5 *(Yorke, Atkinson 2,*
Saunders, Lamptey)
Wigan Ath 0

Wigan Ath 0
Aston Villa 3 *(Lamptey 2,*
Whittingham)
Aston Villa won 8-0 on aggregate

Brighton 1 *(Nogan)*
Leicester C 0

Leicester C 0
Brighton 2 *(Munday, Nogan)*
Brighton won 3-0 on aggregate

Chelsea 1 *(Rocastle)*
Bournemouth 0

Bournemouth 0
Chelsea 1 *(Peacock)*
Chelsea won 2-0 on aggregate

Hartlepool 0
Arsenal 5 *(Adams, Smith, Wright 2,*
Merson)

Arsenal 2 *(Campbell, Dickov)*
Hartlepool 0
Arsenal won 7-0 on aggregate

Ipswich T 0
Bolton W 3 *(McAteer, McGinlay,*
Thompson)

Bolton W 1 *(Sneekes)*
Ipswich T 0
Bolton won 4-0 on aggregate

Leeds Utd 0
Mansfield 1 *(Ireland)*

Mansfield 0
Leeds Utd 0
Mansfield won 1-0 on aggregate

Liverpool 2 *(Scales, Fowler)*
Burnley 0

Burnley 1 *(Robinson)*
Liverpool 4 *(Redknapp 2, Fowler,*
Clough)
Liverpool won 6-1 on aggregate

Millwall 2 *(Goodman, Kennedy)*
Sunderland 1 *(Russell)*

Sunderland 1 *(P Gray)*
Millwall 1 *(Goodman)*
Millwall won 3-2 on aggregate

Newcastle Utd 2 *(Cole, Fox)*
Barnsley 1 *(Redfearn)*

Barnsley 0
Newcastle Utd 1 *(Cole)*
Newcastle won 3-1 on aggregate

Norwich C 3 *(Sheron, Bradshaw-pen, Adams)*
Swansea C 0

Swansea C 1 *(Pascoe)*
Norwich C 0
Norwich won 3-1 on aggregate

Nottingham F 2 *(Collymore 2)*
Hereford Utd 1 *(White)*

Hereford Utd 0
Nottingham F 0
Nottingham F won 2-1 on aggregate

Port Vale 1 *(Glover)*
Man Utd 2 *(Scholes 2)*

Man Utd 2 *(McClair, May)*
Port Vale 0
Manchester U won 4-1 on aggreg.

Sheffield Wed 2 *(Taylor, Hyde)*
Bradford City 1 *(Shutt)*

Bradford City1 *(Taylor)*
Sheffield Wed 1 *(Bart-Williams)*
Sheffield Wed won 3-2 on aggreg.

Swindon T 1 *(Scott)*
Charlton Ath 3 *(Nelson 2, Whyte)*

Charlton Ath 1 *(Whyte)*
Swindon T 4 *(Fjortoft 3, Petterson-og)* aet
Swindon T won 5-4 on aggregate

Watford 3 *(Ramage, Mooney, Mabbutt-og)*
Tottenham H 6 *(Anderton, Klinsmann 3, Sheringham, Dumitrescu)*

Tottenham H 2 *(Barmby, Klinsmann)*
Watford 3 *(Foster, Nogan 2)*
Tottenham won 8-6 on aggregate

Third Round
Aston Villa 1 *(Townsend)*
Middlesbrough 0

Blackburn R 2 *(Shearer 2)*
Coventry City 0

Brighton & HA 1 *(McCarthy)*
Swindon 1 *(Thomson)*

Liverpool 2 *(Rush 2)*
Stoke City 1 *(Peschisolido)*

Mansfield Town 0
Millwall 2 *(Cadette, Kennedy)*

Newcastle 2 *(Albert, Kitson)*
Manchester Utd 0

Notts Co 3 *(Agana, McSwegan 2)*
Tottenham H 0

Oldham Athletic 0
Arsenal 0

QPR 3 *(Gallen, Sinclair, Penrice)*
Manchester City 4 *(Summerbee, Curle-pen, Beagrie, Lomas)*

Portsmouth 0
Derby Co 1 *(Simpson)*

Sheffield Weds 1 *(Bart-Williams)*
Southampton 0

Sheffield Utd 1 *(Blake)*
Bolton W 2 *(Paatalainen,A Scott-og)*

Tranmere R 1 *(Aldridge)*
Norwich City 1 *(Polston)*

West Ham 1 *(Hutchison)*
Chelsea 0

Wimbledon 0
Crystal Palace 1 *(Armstrong)*

Wolves 2 *(Birch, D Kelly)*
Nottm F 3 *(Pearce, Roy 2)*

Thrid Round Replays

Arsenal 2 *(Dickov 2)*
Oldham Athletic 0

Norwich 4 *(Prior, McGreal-og, Polston, Newman)*
Tranmere 2 *(Irons, Nevin)*

Swindon 4 *(Scott 2, Fjortoft 2)*
Brighton & HA 1 *(Chamberlain)*

Fourth Round
Arsenal 2 *(Morrow, Wright)*
Sheffield Wednesday 0

Blackburn R 1 *(Sutton)*
Liverpool 3 *(Rush 3)*

Crystal Palace 4 *(Armstrong 2, Southgate 2)*
Aston Villa 1 *(Atkinson)*

Manchester City 1 *(Rösler)*
Newcastle United 1 *(Jeffrey)*

Norwich City 1 *(Eadie)*
Notts County 0

Nottm Forest 0
Millwall 2 *(Berry 2)*

Swindon 2 *(Fjortoft 2)*
Derby Co 1 *(Stallard)*

West Ham 1 *(Cottee)*
Bolton W 3 *(McGinlay 2, Lee)*

Fourth Round Replays
Newcastle United 0
Manchester C 2 *(Rösler, Walsh)*

Fifth Round
Bolton W 1 *(Lee)*
Norwich City 0

Crystal P 4 *(Pitcher, Salako, Armstrong, Preece)*
Manchester City 0

Liverpool 1 *(Rush)*
Arsenal 0

Swindon Town 3 *(Mutch 2, Fjortoft)*
Millwall 1 *(Mitchell)*

Semi-finals *(over 2 legs)*
Swindon Town 2 *(Thorne 2)*
Bolton W 1 *(Stubbs)*

Bolton W 3 *(McAteer, Paatelainen, McGinlay*
Swindon T 1 *(Fjortoft)*
Bolton won 4-3 on aggregate

Liverpool 1 *(Fowler)*
Crystal Palace 0

Crystal Palace 0
Liverpool 1 *(Fowler)*
Liverpool won 2-0 on aggregate

COCA COLA CUP FINAL
Wembley   Apr 2
Bolton Wanderers 1 *(Thompson)*
Liverpool 2 *(McManaman 2)*
Bolton: Branagan, Green (Bergsson), Phillips, McAteer, Seagraves, Stubbs, Lee, Sneekes, Paatelainen, McGinlay, Thompson
Liverpool: James, R Jones, Bjornebye, Scales, Babb, Ruddock, McManaman, Redknapp, Rush, Barnes, Fowler

Auto Windscreens Shield

Clubs from Divisions 2 and 3

North Area Quarter-finals
Bury 2 *(T Kelly 2)*
Huddersfield 1 *(Clayton)*

Carlisle 2 *(Thomas, Hunter-og)*
Wrexham 1 *(Bennett)*

Rochdale 2 *(Whitehall 2)*
Stockport County 1 i(Wallace)

Wigan 1 *(Farrell)*
Crewe Alex 3 *(Whalley, Macauley, Adebola)*

South Area Quarter-finals
B'ham 3 *(Claridge, Ward-pen, Otto)*
Hereford Utd 1 *(Lyne)*

Leyton Orient 0
Bristol Rovers 0
aet, Leyton O won 4-3 on penalties

Oxford Utd 1 *(R Ford)*
Swansea City 2 *(Torpey, Hayes)*

Shrewsbury T 3 *(Spink, Stevens 2)*
Exeter City *(Richardson)*

North Area Semi-final
Bury 1 *(Paskin)*
Rochdale 2 *(Sharpe, Reid)*

Crewe Alex 0
Carlisle Utd 1 *(Thomas)*

South Area Semi-final
Birmingham 3 *(Claridge, Francis, Tait)*
Swansea C 2 *(Pascoe, Lowe-og)*
asdet

Leyton Orient 2 *(Warren, Brooks)*
Shrewsbury 1 *(Stevens)*

Northern Final *(over 2 legs)*
Carlisle 4 *(Currie, Thomas 2, Conway)*
Rochdale 1 *(Whitehall-pen)*

Rochdale 2 *(Whitehall, Reid)*
Carlisle U 1 *(Mountfield)*
Carlisle won 5-3 on aggregate

Southern Final *(over 2 legs)*
Birmingham City 1 *(Shearer)*
Leyton Orient 0

Leyton Orient 2 *(Purse, McGleish)*
Birmingham 3 *(Claridge 2, Williams)*
Birmingham won 4-2 on aggregate

AUTO WINDSCREENS SHIELD FINAL
Wembley   Apr 23
Birmingham City 1 *(Tait)*
Carlisle United 0
Birmingham: Bennett, Poole, Cooper, Ward, Barnett, Daish, Hunt, Claridge, Francis (Donowa), Otto, Shearer (Tait)
Carlisle: Caig, Edmondson, Gallimore, Walling, Mountfield (Robinson), Hayward, Thomas, Currie, Reeves, Conway, Prokas (Thorpe)
asdet

Anglo-Italian Cup

Clubs from Division 1 in England and Serie B in Italy

Semi-finals *(over 2 legs)*
Ancona 1 *(Centofanti)*
Ascoli 2 *(Incocciati 2)*

Ascoli 0
Ancona 1 *(Cornacchia)*
Ascoli won on away goals
....
Notts County 0
Stoke City 0

Stoke City 0
Notts County 0
aet, Notts County won 3-2 on pens

FINAL
Wembley   Mar 19
Notts County 2 *(Agana, White)*
Ascoli 1 *(Mirabelli)*
Notts County: Cherry (Reece), Mills, Legg, Turner, Murphy, Johnson (Emenalo), Devlin, Simpson, White, Short, Agana (Gallagher)
Ascoli: Bizzarri, Benetti, Mancuso (Milana), Marcato, Pascucci, Zanoncelli, Binotto (Menolascina), Bosi, Favo, Mirabelli, Bierhoff

---

Inter-Toto Cup

Qualification for the UEFA Cup
Results only for British teams
Group 1
Sheffield Weds 0
Basle 1

Sheffield Weds* 3
Gornik Zabrze 2

Karlsruhe 1
Sheffield Weds 1

Sheffield Weds* 3
Arhus 1

Group 2
Tottenham H** 0
Lucerne 2

Rudar 1
Tottenham H 2

Tottenham H** 1
Oysters 2

Cologne 8
Tottenham H 0

Group 4
Ton Pentre 0
Heerenveen 7

Bekescsaba 4
Ton Pentre 0

Ton Pentre 0
Uniao Leiria 3

Nasteved 2
Ton Pentre 0

Group 6
Linz 2
Partick Thistle 2

Partick Thistle 3
Keflavik 1

Metz 1
Partick Thistle 0

Partick Thistle 1
Zagreb 2

Group 10
Wimbledon** 0
Bursaspor 4

Kosice 1
Wimbledon 1

Wimbledon** 0
Beitar 0

Charleroi 3
Wimbledon 0

* Played at Rotherham
** Played at Brighton

Scottish Football

Dancing started in the streets of Raith (Kirkcaldy, to you) after the Coca-Cola Cup Final and is probably still going on. A gloriously romantic double by the other Rovers was by far the highlight of an otherwise forgettable Scottish season. Rangers won the title for a seventh successive time without ever looking as if they had a squad capable of success at a higher level. Only the skills of Brian Laudrup, who had swept up most of the player of the year awards by Christmas, stood out amidst the general mediocrity on show. The major talking point in the Premier League was the demise of the 'New Firm' - Aberdeen and Dundee United - who found themselves facing relegation. Both acquired new managers, but only Roy Aitken's team scrambled to survival, beating the luckless Dunfermline in a play-off to secure their place in the top flight for another year. United, Cup winners in 1994, dropped out of the Premier League for the first time. They will not find the First Division easy to escape from.

At Celtic, the signs were encouraging, their hard-fought 1-0 victory in the Scottish Cup the first time a trophy had graced the club cabinet for six years. A successful share issue led to the construction of a magnificent new stand at Celtic Park and the club returned home after playing a season at Hampden. After narrowly failing to sign Ginola (though, didn't everyone?), Andreas Thom was brought to the club; showing their supporters that financial firepower wasn't exclusive to Ibrox. Even Thom, though, could hardly match the celebrity status of Gazza who was lured to Rangers in June after a fairly dismal spell at Lazio.

Rangers had missed out on the big money last season when another preliminary round failure saw them out of the Champions' League. Already this year, however, two workmanlike performances have seen them past the first hurdle and with glimpses of class from Gascoigne, Rangers may yet make an impact in Europe. The 1994/5 season was one of abject failure for Scottish clubs in Europe, so its a welcome change that the club sides are proving, like the national team, difficult to beat.....if uninspiring.

Scotland lost just one of their first nine games in the European Championship and can surely not fail to qualify. Craig Brown's team is built around a secure defence (three goals conceded in nine games) with Jim Leighton and Andy Goram defying even Jimmy Greaves to slag off Scottish 'keepers. The midfield is established and only the partnership up-front needs to be settled. Duncan Ferguson is a must in most people's eyes and Scott Booth seems to flourish on the international stage. If all else fails, Brown can summon Ally McCoist from the treatment room, hospital bed or TV studio, put him on with 15 minutes to go and sit back while Super Ally performs a miracle or two. Doesn't happen? Ask anyone at Hampden in August. Especially a Greek.

Back on the domestic front, Forfar and Greenock Morton enjoyed the champagne, while the south-west struggled as both Ayr and Stranraer were relegated. Meadowbank went down from the Second Division, moved to Livingston, adopted the new town name, and started the new season with sufficient flourish to earn the headline in *Scotland on Sunday*, 'Summertime and the Livingston's Easy'.

The saddest event of the year was the sudden death of Davie Cooper. 'Coop' was loved by supporters of the clubs he played for and admired and respected by all. His magical skills were reminiscent of Scottish football at its height.

Scottish Leagues 1994-5 ▬▬▬

PREMIER DIVISION

		P	W	D	L	GF	GA	W	D	L	GF	GA	GD	PTS
1	**Rangers**	36	11	5	2	31	14	9	4	5	29	21	+25	**69**
2	**Motherwell**	36	8	6	4	29	23	6	6	6	21	27	0	**54**
3	**Hibernian**	36	9	7	2	37	19	3	10	5	12	18	+12	**53**
4	**Celtic**	36	6	8	4	23	19	5	10	3	16	14	+6	**51**
5	**Falkirk**	36	8	3	7	26	24	4	9	5	22	23	+1	**48**
6	**Heart of Midlothian**	36	9	4	5	26	14	3	3	12	18	37	-7	**43**
7	**Kilmarnock**	36	8	4	6	22	16	3	6	9	18	32	-8	**43**
8	**Partick Thistle**	36	4	9	5	23	23	6	4	8	17	27	-10	**43**
9	**Aberdeen**	36	7	7	4	24	16	3	4	11	19	30	-3	**41**
10	**Dundee United**	36	6	6	6	24	20	3	3	12	16	36	-16	**36**

Goalscorers

	Lg	Cups	Total		Lg	Cups	Total
Tommy Coyne (Motherwell)	16	2	18	Darren Jackson (Hibernian)	10	1	11
Billy Dodds (Aberdeen)	15	2	17	Keith Wright (Hibernian)	10	1	11
Mark Hateley (Rangers)	13	2	15	Dougie Arnott (Motherwell)	10	0	10
John Robertson (Hearts)	10	4	14	C McDonald (Falkirk)	9	1	10
Michael O'Neill (Hibernian)	10	4	14	John Collins (Celtic)	8	4	12
Brian Laudrup (Rangers)	10	3	13	Craig Brewster (Dundee United)	8	1	9

	Aberdeen	Celtic	Dundee Utd	Falkirk	Hearts	Hibernian	Kilmarnock	Motherwell	Partick T	Rangers
Aberdeen	**** ****	0-0 2-0	3-0 2-1	2-2 0-0	3-1 3-1	0-0 0-0	0-1 0-1	1-3 0-2	1-1 3-1	2-2 2-0
Celtic	0-0 2-0	**** ****	2-1 1-1	0-2 2-0	1-1 0-1	2-0 2-2	1-1 2-1	2-2 1-1	0-0 1-3	1-3 3-0
Dundee Utd	2-1 0-0	2-2 0-1	**** ****	1-0 1-0	5-2 1-1	0-0 0-1	2-2 1-2	1-1 6-1	0-1 2-0	0-3 0-2
Falkirk	2-1 0-2	1-1 1-2	1-3 3-1	**** ****	2-1 2-0	0-0 1-0	3-3 2-0	0-1 3-0	2-1 1-3	0-2 2-3
Hearts	2-0 1-2	1-0 1-1	2-1 2-0	1-1 0-1	**** ****	0-1 2-0	3-0 2-2	1-2 2-0	3-0 0-1	1-1 2-1
Hibernian	2-2 4-2	1-1 1-1	5-0 4-0	2-2 0-2	2-1 3-1	**** ****	0-0 2-1	2-2 2-0	3-0 1-2	2-1 1-1
Kilmarnock	2-1 3-1	0-0 0-1	0-2 2-0	1-1 2-1	3-1 3-2	0-0 1-2	**** ****	0-1 2-0	2-0 0-0	1-2 0-1
Motherwell	0-1 2-1	1-1 1-0	1-1 2-1	5-3 2-2	1-1 1-2	1-1 0-0	3-2 2-0	**** ****	3-1 1-2	2-1 1-3
Partick T	2-1 2-2	1-2 0-0	2-0 1-3	1-2 3-1	0-1 3-1	2-2 2-2	2-0 2-2	2-2 0-0	**** ****	0-2 1-1
Rangers	1-0 3-3	0-2 1-1	2-0 1-1	1-1 2-2	3-0 1-0	2-0 3-1	2-0 3-0	2-1 0-2	3-0 1-1	**** ****

FIRST DIVISION

		P	W	D	L	GF	GA	W	D	L	GF	GA	GD	PTS
1	Raith Rovers	36	8	8	2	27	18	11	4	3	27	14	+22	69
2	Dunfermline Athletic	36	11	5	2	35	11	7	9	2	28	21	+31	68
3	Dundee	36	11	4	3	34	18	9	4	5	31	18	+29	68
4	Aidrieonians	36	7	6	5	22	14	10	4	4	28	19	+17	61
5	St Johnstone	36	10	6	2	36	15	4	8	6	23	24	+20	56
6	Hamilton Academicals	36	9	3	6	23	22	5	4	9	19	26	-6	49
7	St Mirren	36	7	5	6	20	18	1	7	10	14	32	-16	36
8	Clydebank	36	4	6	8	20	25	4	5	9	13	22	-14	35
9	Ayr United	36	6	5	7	22	24	0	6	12	9	34	-27	29
10	Stranraer	36	3	4	11	15	37	1	1	16	10	44	-56	17

PREMIER/FIRST DIVISION PLAY-OFF

First Leg
Aberdeen 3 *(Glass, Shearer 2)* Dunfermline Athletic 1 *(Robertson)*
Second Leg
Dunfermline Athletic 1 *(Smith)* Aberdeen 3 *(Dodds, Miller, Glass)*

SECOND DIVISION

		P	W	D	L	GF	GA	W	D	L	GF	GA	GD	PTS
1	Greenock Morton	36	12	5	1	33	11	6	5	7	22	22	+22	64
2	Dumbarton	36	12	4	2	43	16	5	5	8	14	19	+22	60
3	Stirling Albion	36	9	3	6	28	20	8	4	6	26	23	+11	58
4	Stenhousemuir	36	7	10	1	24	14	7	4	7	22	25	+7	56
5	Berwick Rangers	36	10	6	2	23	13	5	4	9	29	33	+6	55
6	Clyde	36	8	5	5	33	25	6	5	7	20	23	+5	52
7	Queen of the South	36	6	3	9	25	26	5	8	5	21	25	-5	44
8	East Fife	36	7	3	8	31	27	4	7	7	17	29	-8	43
9	Meadowbank Thistle	36	7	2	9	16	21	4	3	11	16	33	-22	35 *
10	Brechin City	36	4	5	9	15	26	2	1	15	7	34	-38	24

* Meadowbank deducted 3 pts for fielding an ineligible player

THIRD DIVISION

		P	W	D	L	GF	GA	W	D	L	GF	GA	GD	PTS
1	Forfar Athletic	36	14	3	1	42	16	11	2	5	25	17	+34	80
2	Montrose	36	9	4	5	33	17	11	3	4	36	15	+37	67
3	Ross County	36	9	1	8	35	26	9	5	4	24	18	+15	60
4	East Stirling	36	10	2	6	28	20	8	3	7	33	30	+11	59
5	Alloa	36	7	4	7	23	20	8	5	5	27	25	+5	54
6	Caledonian Thistle	36	5	7	6	27	33	7	2	9	21	28	-13	45
7	Arbroath	36	6	3	9	21	23	7	2	9	30	39	-11	44
8	Queen's Park	36	7	2	9	21	27	5	4	9	25	30	-11	42
9	Cowdenbeath	36	4	5	9	23	36	7	2	9	25	24	-12	40
10	Albion Rovers	36	3	0	15	16	39	2	3	13	11	43	-55	18

Goalscorers

DIVISION 1	Lg	Cp	Ttl
Duffield (Hamilton)	20	3	23
O'Boyle (St Johnstone)	19	7	26
Shaw (Dundee)	16	4	20
Petrie (Dunfermline)	14	7	21
Dalziel (Raith)	14	3	17
Andy Smith (Airdrie)	12	7	19
Britton (Dundee)	12	6	18
French (Dunfermline)	12	2	14
Hamilton (Dundee)	12	1	13

DIVISION 2	Lg	Cp	Ttl
Mooney (Dumbarton)	17	0	17
Lilley (G Morton)	16	4	20
Hawke (Berwick)	16	2	18
Watters (Stirling)	15	2	17
Rajamaki (G Morton)	14	1	15
Scott (East Fife)	14	1	15
Ward (Dumbarton)	12	2	14
Irvine (Berwick)	11	1	12
Dickson (Clyde)	10	1	11

DIVISION 3	Lg	Cp	Ttl
Yardley (Cowdenb'th)	23	4	27
Bingham (Forfar)	21	0	21
McGlashan (Montrose)	20	5	25
Kennedy (Montrose)	18	5	23
Gerraghty (E Stirling)	16	0	16
Ross (Forfar)	14	0	14
Moffatt (Alloa)	13	1	14
Grant (Ross Co)	12	2	14
Tosh (Arbroath)	12	0	12

Scottish Cup Competitions

Scottish Cup

First Round
Caledonian 1 *(McAllister)*
Queen of the South 2 *(Bell, Bryce)*

Dumbarton 3 *(Ward 2, McKinnon)*
Stirling 3 *(Watters,Mitchell-pen,Tait)*

Stenhousemuir 3 *(Mathieson,*
Sprott-pen, Christie)
East Stirling 0

Albion Rovers 2 *(McBride, Doherty)*
Montrose 5 *(MacRonald 2, Milne,*
Kennedy-pen, McGlashan)

First Round Replays
Stirling A 3 *(Taggart 2, McInnes)*
Dumbarton 0

Second Round
Alloa 2 *(Lamont, Diver)*
Ross Co 3 *(Connelly 2, McPherson)*

Brechin City 2 *(McNeill, Brand)*
Stirling A 3 *(McInnes 2,Taggart)*

Buckie T 1 *(Robertson)*
Berwick R 4 *(Hawke, Graham,*
Mann-og, Valentine)

Burntisland Shipyards 6 *(Matthew 3,*
Taylor, Paton, Drummond)
St Cuthbert W 2 *(Tweedie, Baker)*

Cove 2 *(Caldwell 2)*
Cowdenbeath 1 *(Conn)*

Forfar 0
Meadowbank 1 *(Sinclair)*

Gala F'dean 2 *(Cockburn,Hunter)*
East Fife 6 *(Burns-pen, Hutcheon 3,*
Allan, Donaghy)

Keith 2 *(Rougvie-og, Thomson)*
Huntley 2 *(Whyte, Thomson)*

Queen of the South 0
Clyde 2 *(Dickson, O'Neill)*

Sten'muir 4 *(Fisher, Mathieson 2,*
Steel)
Arbroath 0

Whitehill Welfare 0
Montrose 0

Queen's Park 2 *(G Orr, Rodden)*
Greenock 2 *(Alexander, Anderson)*

Second Round Replays
Huntley 3 *(Rougvie, Stewart,Whyte)*
Keith 1 *(Lavelle)*

Montrose 5 *(Kennedy 2, Masson,*
McGlashan, Stephen)
Whitehill Welfare 2 *(Millar, Steel)*

Greenock M 2 *(Rajamaki, Lilley)*
Queen's Park 1 *(Caven) aet*

Third Round
Aberdeen 1 *(Jess)*
Stranraer 0

Celtic 2 *(Falconer, Van Hooijdonk)*
St Mirren 0

Cove R 0
Dunf'line 4 *(Petrie 2,Smith,Hawkins)*

Dundee United 0
Clyde 0

Huntley 7 *(Stewart 3, Whyte,*
Lawrie-og, Thornton, De Barros)
Burntislands Shipyards 0

Kilmarnock 0
Greenock Morton 0

Montrose 0
Hibernian 2 *(McGinlay, D Jackson)*

Raith Rovers 1 (Crawford)
Ayr United 0

Dundee 2 *(Shaw, Hamilton)*
Partick 1 *(Craig)*

St Johnstone 1 *(McNiven-og)*
Stenhousemuir 1 *(Sprott)*

Clydebank 1 *(Eadie)*
Hearts 1 *(Robertson)*

East Fife 1 *(Allan)*
Ross County 0

Stirling Albion 1 *(McQuilter)*
Airdrie 2 *(Andrew Smith 2)*

Falkirk 0
Motherwell 2 *(Burns 2)*

Hamilton 1 *(Lorimer)*
Rangers 3 *(Steven, Boli, Laudrup)*

Meadowbank 1 *(Cowan-og)*
Berwick Rangers 1 *(Fraser)*

Third Round Replays
Greenock Morton 1 *(Anderson)*
Kilmarnock 2 *(Maskrey 2) aet*

Berwick 3 *(Irvine, Neil, Clegg)*
M'bank 3 *(Graham, Bailey, Wilson)*
aet M'bank won 7-6 on penalties

Clyde 1 *(Angus)*
Dundee United 5 *(McKinlay, Craig,*
Hannah, Bowman, Nixon)

Hearts 2 *(Robertson, Thomas)*
Clydebank 1 *(Eadie)*

Sten' 4 *(Sprott 2,Clarke,Donaldson)*
St Johnstone 0

Fourth Round
Airdrie 2 *(Cooper , Andrew Smith)*
Dunfermline 0

Celtic 3 *(Van Hooijdonk 2, Falconer)*
Meadowbank 0

Dundee 1 *(Shaw)*
Raith R 2 *(Graham, Rowbotham)*

Hibernian 2 *(Harper, McGinlay)*
Motherwell 0

Huntley 1 *(Stewart)*
Dundee U 3 *(Brewster, Malpas,*
Hannah)

Kilmarnock 4 *(Maskrey 2, Reilly,*
Black)
East Fife 0

Stenhousemuir 2 *(Steel 2)*
Aberdeen 0

Hearts 4 *(C Miller, McPherson,*
Robertson, Thomas)
Rangers 2 *(Laudrup, Durie)*

Quarter-finals
Celtic 1 *(Collins)*
Kilmarnock 0

Raith 1 *(Cameron)*
Airdrie 4 *(Harvey 2, Davies, Black)*

Stenhousemuir 0
Hibs 4 *(Harper 2, Tortolano, O'Neill)*

Hearts 2 *(J Millar 2)*
Dundee United 1 *(Gomes)*

Semi-finals
Celtic 0
Hibernian 0

Airdrie 1 *(Cooper)*
Hearts 0

Semi-final Replay
Celtic 3 *(Falconer, Collins,*
O'Donnell)
Hibernian 1 *(Wright)*

FINAL
Hampden Park   May 27
Celtic 1 *(Van Hooijdonk)*
Airdrieonians 0
Celtic: Bonner, Boyd, McKinlay,
Vata, McNally, Grant, McLaughlin,
McStay, Van Hooijdonk (Falconer),
Donnelly (O'Donnell), Collins
Airdrie: Martin, Stewart, Jack,
Sandison, Hay (J McIntyre), Black,
Boyle, Andrew Smith, Cooper,
Harvey (Tony Smith), Lawrence

Coca-Cola Cup (Scottish League Cup)

First Round
Berwick Rangers 0
Montrose 0 *aet*
Montrose won 3-2 on penalties

East Fife 1 *(Allan)*
Forfar Athletic 0

East Stirling 0
Caledonian 2 *(Robertson, I Lee-og)*

Stenhousemuir 0
Meadowbank T 4 *(Bailey, McLeod, Hutchison, Little)*

Arbroath 1 *(Reilly)*
Alloa 1 *(Morrison) aet*
Arbroath won 5-4 on penalties

Queen of the S 2 *(McLaren, Bryce)*
Albion Rovers 0

Ross Co 3 *(Grant 2,MacPherson)*
Queen's Park 2 *(G Orr, Maxwell)*

Stranraer 2 *(Cody, Ferguson)*
Cowdenbeath 2 *(Black, Soutar) aet*
Stranraer won 4-2 on penalties

Second Round
Ayr 0
Celtic 1 *(Grant)*

Dumbarton 0
Hearts 4 *(Millar, Robertson, A Johnston 2)*

Falkirk 1 *(Cadette)*
Montrose 1 *(Kennedy) aet*
Falkirk won 5-4 on penalties

Greenock Morton 1 *(Lilley)*
Airdrie 1 *(Andrew Smith) aet*
Airdire won 5-3 on penalties

Motherwell 3 *(Burns, Coyne-pen, Kirk)*
Clydebank 1 *(Grady)*

Partick T 5 *(Taylor, Jamieson, Charnley 3-1 pen)*
Brechin City 0

St Mirren 0
Dundee United 1 *(Ristic) aet*

Aberdeen 1 *(Shearer)*
Stranraer 0

Arbroath 1 *(McKinnon)*
Rangers 6 *(Hately 2, D Ferguson 3, McCall)*

Dundee 3 *(Shaw, Tosh 2)*
Caledonian 0

Dunfermline 4 *(McCathie, Den*

Bieman, Petrie, Ward)
Meadowbank *(Sorbie)*

Hamilton 5 *(McEntegart, Baptie, McLean, Campbell, Sherry)*
Clyde 0

Kilmarnock 4 *(Henry, McCluskey, Maskrey 2)*
East Fife 1 *(Hope)*

Queen of the South 0
Hibernian 3 *(Evans, Tweed, O'Neill)*

Ross County 0
Raith Rvrs 5 *(Cameron, Graham 3, Dalziel)*

Stirling Albion 0
St Johnstone 2 *(O'Boyle, Scott)*

Third Round
Hibernian 2 *(O'Neill 2)*
Dunfermline Athletic 0

Partick Thistle 0
Aberdeen 5 *(Shearer 3-1pen, Kane, Dodds)*

Dundee 1 *(Farningham)*
Celtic 2 *(Collins, Walker)*

Hamilton A 2 *(Cleland -og, Duffield)*
Dundee United 2 *(Hannah 2) aet*
Dundee Utd won 5-3 on penalties

Hearts 2 *(Locke, Colquhoun)*
St Johnstone 4 *(O'Neil, Miller, O'Boyle, Irons)*

Motherwell 1 *(McCart)*
Airdrie 2 *(Boyle 2) aet*

Raith Rovers 3 *(Cameron 3)*
Kilmarnock 2 *(Montgomerie, Williamson)*

Rangers 1 *(Laudrup)*
Falkirk 2 *(Cadette 2)*

Quarter Finals
St Johnstone 1 *(O'Neil)*
Raith Rovers 3 *(Dennis, Graham, Lennon)*

Celtic 1 *(Collins)*
Dundee United 0

Falkirk 1 *(McDonald)*
Aberdeen 4 *(Booth 3, Rice-og)*

Hibernian 1 *(Evans)*
Airdrie 2 *(Andrew Smith, Lawrence)*

Semi Finals
Airdrie 1 *(Cooper)*
Raith Rovers 1 *(Graham) aet*
Raith won 5-4 on penalties

Celtic 1 *(O'Neil)*
Aberdeen 0

SCOTTISH LEAGUE CUP FINAL
Ibrox Stadium   Nov 27
Raith Rovers 2 *(Crawford, Dalziel)*
Celtic 2 *(Walker, Nicholas) aet*
Raith won 6-5 on penalties
Raith: Thompson, McAnespie,
Broddle (Rowbotham), Narey,
Dennis, Sinclair, Crawford, Dalziel
(Redford), Graham, Cameron, Dair
Celtic: Marshall, Galloway, Boyd,
McNally, Mowbray, O'Neil,
Donnelly, (Falconer), McStay,
Nicholas (Byrne), Walker, Collins

B & Q Cup
From quarter-finals
Quarter-finals
Airdrie 2 *(Cooper, Davies)*
Ayr United 0

Cowdenbeath 1 *(Yardley)*
Dunfermline 3 *(Smith, French, Petrie)*

Dundee 2 *(Britton, Wieghorst)*
Greenock Morton 1 *(Anderson)*

Montrose 1 *(Kennedy-pen)*
Clydebank 2 *(Flannigan, Cooper) aet*

Semi-finals
Airdrie 3 *(Boyle, Stewart, Cooper)*
Clydebank 1 *(Cooper)*

Dunfermline 1 *(Tod)*
Dundee 2 *(Bain-pen, McCann)*

FINAL
McDiarmid Park   Nov 6
Airdrieonians 3 *(Harvey, Boyle-pen, Andrew Smith)*
Dundee 2 *(Hay-og, Britton) aet*
Airdrie: Martin, Stewart (Tony
Smith), Jack, Sandison, Hay, Black,
Boyle, Davies, Cooper, Harvey,
Lawrence (Andrew Smith)
Dundee: Pageaud, McQuillan, Bain,
Farningham, J Duffy, Wieghorst,
Shaw, Vrto, Tosh (Hamilton),
Britton, McCann

Welsh Football 1994-5
Konica League of Wales

	P	W	D	L	GF	GA	Pts
Bangor City	**38**	**27**	**7**	**4**	**96**	**26**	**88**
Afan Lido	38	24	7	7	60	36	79
Ton Pentre	38	23	8	7	84	50	77
Newtown	38	20	8	10	78	47	68
Cwmbran Town	38	20	7	11	69	49	67
Flint Town United	38	20	3	15	77	60	63
Barry Town	38	16	11	11	71	57	59
Holywell United	38	16	10	12	62	55	58
Llansantffriad	38	15	10	13	57	57	55
Inter Cardiff	38	14	11	13	58	43	53
Rhyl	38	16	5	17	74	69	53
Conwy United	38	14	7	17	60	65	49
Ebbw Vale	38	12	9	17	51	57	45
Caersws	38	11	11	16	57	64	44
Connah's Quay Nmds	38	12	7	19	57	79	43
Porthmadog	38	11	7	20	57	73	40
Aberystwyth Town	38	9	12	17	57	75	39
Llanelli	38	10	6	22	64	104	36
Mold Alexandra	38	10	4	24	57	90	34
Maesteg Park Athletic	38	2	6	30	23	113	12

Welsh Cup Final: Wrexham 2 Cardiff City 1

Northern Irish Football
Smirnoff Irish League

	P	W	D	L	GF	GA	Pts
Crusaders	**30**	**20**	**7**	**3**	**58**	**25**	**67**
Glanavon	30	18	6	6	76	40	60
Portadown	30	15	5	10	59	41	50
Ards	30	15	5	10	55	42	50
Glentoran	30	14	8	8	53	41	50
Cliftonville	30	13	11	6	44	32	50
Coleraine	30	12	13	5	52	39	49
Linfield	30	11	11	8	48	34	44
Omagh Town	30	10	12	8	42	38	42
Distillery	30	12	6	12	45	47	42
Bangor	30	8	14	8	42	38	38
Ballymena United	30	7	8	15	43	53	29
Carrick Rangers	30	7	7	16	46	75	28
Ballyclare Comrades	30	5	6	19	39	66	21
Newry Town	30	4	9	17	34	74	21
Larne	30	3	4	23	18	69	13

Ulster Cup Final: Bangor 2 Linfield 1
Irish Cup Final: Carrick Rangers 1 Linfield 3

European Leagues 1994-5

Final League Tables, the teams below the line are those relegated

BELGIUM

	P	W	D	L	GF	GA	PTS
Anderlecht	**34**	**23**	**6**	**5**	**80**	**31**	**52**
Standard Liege	34	21	9	4	53	23	51
FC Brugge	34	21	7	6	68	32	49
Aalst	34	14	11	9	58	56	39
Ekeren	34	12	13	9	57	39	37
Lierse	34	14	9	11	52	52	37
Lommel	34	13	9	12	44	40	35
St Truiden	34	11	13	10	34	35	35
Seraing	34	12	10	12	53	45	34
Beveren	34	10	12	12	40	46	32
RWD Molenbeek	34	10	11	13	34	41	31
Charleroi	34	10	11	13	33	43	31
Gent	34	11	8	15	41	53	30
Mechelen	34	10	9	15	40	47	29
CS Brugge	34	9	10	15	43	52	28
Antwerp	34	8	8	18	40	56	24
Liege	34	6	7	21	36	71	19
Ostend	34	5	9	20	32	76	19

FC Brugge won the Cup Final beating Ekeren 3-1
Top Scorer: Vidmar (Standard) 22

FRANCE

	P	W	D	L	GF	GA	PTS
Nantes	**38**	**21**	**16**	**1**	**71**	**34**	**79**
Lyon	38	19	12	7	56	38	69
Paris St Germain	38	20	7	11	58	41	67
Auxerre	38	15	17	6	59	34	62
Lens	38	15	14	9	48	44	59
Monaco	38	15	12	11	60	39	57
Bordeaux	38	16	9	13	52	47	57
Metz	38	16	8	14	50	44	56
Cannes	38	15	8	15	56	48	53
Strasbourg	38	13	12	13	43	43	51
Martigues	38	13	12	13	37	49	51
Le Havre	38	12	13	13	46	49	49
Rennes	38	12	12	14	53	55	48
Lille	38	13	9	16	29	44	48
Bastia	38	11	11	16	44	56	44
Nice	38	11	10	17	39	52	43
Montpellier	38	9	14	15	38	53	41
St Etienne	38	9	11	18	45	55	38
Caen	38	10	6	22	38	58	36
Sochaux	38	6	5	27	29	68	23

Cup Final: Paris St Germain 1 Strasbourg 0
Top scorer: Loko (Nantes) 22

GERMANY

	P	W	D	L	GF	GA	PTS
Borussia Dortmund	**34**	**20**	**9**	**5**	**67**	**33**	**49**
Werder Bremen	34	20	8	6	70	39	48
Freiburg	34	20	6	8	66	44	46
Kaiserslautern	34	17	12	5	58	41	46
Mönchengladbach	34	17	9	8	66	41	43
Bayern Munich	34	15	13	6	55	41	43
Leverkusen	34	13	10	11	62	51	36
Karlsruhe	34	11	14	9	51	47	36
Eintracht Frankfurt	34	12	9	13	41	49	33
Cologne	34	11	10	13	54	54	32
Schalke	34	10	11	13	48	54	31
Stuttgart	34	10	10	14	52	66	30
Hamburg	34	10	9	15	43	50	29
Munich 1860	34	8	11	15	41	57	27
Uerdingen	34	7	11	16	37	52	25
Bochum	34	9	4	21	43	67	22
Duisberg	34	6	8	20	31	64	20
Dynamo Dresden	34	4	8	22	33	68	16

Cup Final: Mönchengladbach 3 Wolfsburg 0
Top scorer: Basler (W Bremen), Herrlich (Gladbach) 20

IRELAND

	P	W	D	L	GF	GA	PTS
Dundalk	**33**	**17**	**8**	**8**	**41**	**25**	**51**
Shelbourne	33	16	9	8	45	32	49
Derry City	33	16	10	7	45	30	46
Bohemians	33	14	11	8	48	31	45
St Patricks Athletic	33	13	14	6	53	36	41
Cork City	33	15	4	14	54	42	39
Shamrock Rovers	33	14	9	10	46	36	39
Sligo Rovers	33	12	7	14	43	41	35
Galway United	33	10	9	14	39	53	31
Athlone Town	33	6	14	13	31	44	30
Cobh Ramblers	33	5	11	17	29	51	26
Monaghan United	33	5	4	24	22	75	25

Cup Final: Derry City 2 Shelbourne 1
Top scorer: Caufield (Cork City) 16

ITALY

	P	W	D	L	GF	GA	PTS
Juventus	**34**	**23**	**4**	**7**	**59**	**32**	**73**
Lazio	34	19	6	9	69	34	63
Parma	34	18	9	7	51	30	63
AC Milan	34	17	9	8	53	32	60
Roma	34	16	11	7	46	25	59
Internazionale	34	14	10	10	39	34	52
Napoli	34	13	12	9	40	45	51
Sampdoria	34	13	11	10	51	37	50
Cagliari	34	13	10	11	40	39	49
Fiorentina	34	12	11	11	61	57	47
Torino	34	12	9	13	44	48	45
Bari	34	12	8	14	40	43	44
Cremonese	34	11	8	15	35	38	41
Genova	34	10	10	14	34	49	40
Padova	34	12	4	18	32	58	40
Foggia	34	8	10	16	32	50	34
Reggiana	34	4	6	24	23	56	18
Brescia	34	2	6	26	18	65	12

Juventus defeated Parma 3-0 after a two-leg Cup final.
Top scorer: Batistuta (Fiorentina) 26

NETHERLANDS

	P	W	D	L	GF	GA	PTS
Ajax	**34**	**27**	**7**	**0**	**106**	**28**	**61**
Roda	34	22	10	2	70	28	54
PSV Eindhoven	34	20	7	7	85	46	47
Feyenoord	34	19	5	10	66	56	43
Twente	34	17	8	9	66	50	42
Vitesse	34	14	12	8	53	44	40
Willem II	34	13	8	13	44	48	34
RKC Waalwijk	34	11	11	12	46	49	33
Heerenveen	34	12	6	16	48	60	30
NAC Breda	34	11	7	16	54	60	29
Volendam	34	8	13	13	37	55	29
Utrecht	34	8	11	15	43	60	27
Groningen	34	8	10	16	47	63	26
Sparta	34	8	10	16	42	58	26
NEC Nijmegen	34	9	7	18	48	60	25
Maastricht*	34	7	9	18	41	71	23
Go Ahead	34	7	9	18	41	74	23
Dordrecht	34	5	10	19	40	67	20

Feyenoord beat Volendam 2-1 in the Cup final
Top scorer: Ronaldo (PSV) 30
* Also relegated after play-off with Go Ahead

PORTUGAL

	P	W	D	L	GF	GA	PTS
Porto	**34**	**29**	**4**	**1**	**73**	**15**	**62**
Sporting Lisbon	34	22	9	3	57	22	53
Benfica	34	22	5	7	61	28	49
Guimaraes	34	16	10	8	54	43	42
Farense	34	16	5	13	44	38	37
Leiria	34	13	10	11	41	44	36
Maritimo	34	12	11	11	41	45	35
Tirsense	34	14	6	14	35	34	34
Braga	34	11	10	13	34	42	32
Boavista	34	12	8	14	40	49	32
Salgueiros	34	11	7	16	43	50	29
Belenenses	34	10	7	17	30	39	27
Gil Vicente	34	7	13	14	30	40	27
Chaves	34	10	7	17	33	49	27
Amadora	34	6	14	14	27	40	26
Madeira	34	7	10	17	30	54	24
Beira Mar	34	8	5	21	33	54	21
Setubal	34	3	13	18	25	45	19

Cup Final: Sporting Lisbon 2 Maritimo 0
Top scorer: Hassan Nader (Farense) 21

RUSSIA

	P	W	D	L	GF	GA	PTS
Spartak Moscow	**30**	**21**	**8**	**1**	**73**	**21**	**50**
Dynamo Moscow	30	13	13	4	55	35	39
Lokomotiv Moscow	30	12	12	6	49	28	36
Rotor Volgograd	30	10	16	4	39	23	36
Vladikavkaz	30	11	11	8	32	34	33
Novgorod	30	11	9	10	36	34	31
Kamaz	30	11	9	10	38	37	31
Tekstilchik Kamychin	30	11	7	12	30	37	29
Sotchi	30	8	11	11	44	48	27
CSKA Moscow	30	8	10	12	30	32	25
Torpedo Moscow	30	7	12	11	28	37	25

Krylia Sovekov	30	6	12	12	30	51	24
Toumen	30	7	10	13	24	49	24
Ekaterinbourg	30	7	9	14	33	49	23
Stavropol	30	6	11	13	25	34	23
Lada	30	6	10	14	24	41	22

Cup Final: Dynamo Moscow 0 Volvograd 0
Dynamo won 8-7 on penalties
Top scorer: Simoutenkov (Dynamo Moscow) 21

SPAIN

	P	W	D	L	GF	GA	PTS
Real Madrid	**38**	**23**	**9**	**6**	**76**	**29**	**55**
La Coruña	38	20	11	7	68	32	51
Betis	38	15	16	7	46	25	46
Barcelona	38	18	10	10	60	45	46
Español	38	14	15	9	51	35	43
Sevilla	38	16	11	11	55	41	43
Zaragoza	38	18	7	13	56	51	43
Athletic Bilbao	38	16	10	12	39	42	42
Oviedo	38	13	13	12	45	42	39
Real Sociedad	38	12	14	12	56	44	38
Valencia	38	13	12	13	53	48	38
Santander	38	13	10	15	42	47	36
Celta	38	11	14	13	36	48	36
Atletico Madrid	38	13	9	16	56	54	35
Tenerife	38	13	9	16	57	57	35
Compostela	38	11	12	15	44	56	34
Albercete*	38	10	14	14	44	61	34
Sporting Gijon	38	8	12	18	42	67	28
Valladolid	38	8	9	21	25	63	25
Logrones	38	2	9	27	15	79	13

* Relegated after play-offs
Cup Final: La Coruña 2 Valencia 1 . Match abandoned after 79 minutes with the score at 1-1. The last 11 minutes were replayed.
Top scorer: Zamorano (Real Madrid) 28

SWEDEN

	P	W	D	L	GF	GA	PTS
IFK Gothenburg	**26**	**16**	**6**	**4**	**54**	**28**	**54**
Orebro	26	15	7	4	61	30	52
Malmo	26	14	7	5	51	33	49
Norrkoping	26	13	8	5	52	21	47
Osters	26	13	6	7	48	30	45
AIK	26	11	6	9	42	41	39
Halmstad	26	10	8	8	41	39	38
Degerfors	26	8	8	10	28	37	32
Helsingborg	26	9	5	12	30	46	32
Trelleborg	26	7	9	10	25	40	30
Frolunda	26	7	6	13	30	33	27
Hammarby	26	4	8	14	25	44	20
Landskrona	26	4	6	14	22	56	18
Hacken	26	2	8	16	27	58	14

Cup Final: Halmstad 3 AIK 1
Top scorer: Kindvall (Norrkoping) 23

European Cup Competitions

European Cup

Preliminary Round
(over 2 legs)
AEK Athens 2 *(Saravakos 2)*
Rangers 0

Rangers 0
AEK Athens 1 *(Savevski)*
....

Avenir Beggen 1 *(Zaritski)*
Galatasaray 5 *(Turkyilmaz, Saffet,*
Hakan, Arif 2)
Galatasaray 4 *(Hakan Sukur 3-1*
pen, Saffet)
Avenir Beggen 0
....

Legia Warsaw 0
Hajduk Split I *(Rapajic)*

Hajduk Split 4 *(Asanovic, Vulic,*
Rapajic, Erceg)
Legia Warsaw 0
....

Maccabi Haifa 1 *(Revivo-pen)*
Salzburg 2 *(Hutter, Mladenovic-pen)*

Salzburg 3 *(Mladenovic 2, Jurcevic)*
Maccabi Haifa 1 *(Hazan)*
....

Paris St Germain 3 *(Ricardo, Weah,*
Roche 82)
Vac 0

Vac 1 *(Fule)*
Paris St Germain 2 *(Mboma 2)*
....

Silkeborg 0
Dynamo Kiev 0

Dynamo Kiev 3 *(Skatchenko,*
Kovalets, Kossovski)
Silkeborg 1 *(Fernandez)*
....

Sparta Prague 1 *(Budka)*
IFK Gothenburg 0

IFK Gothenburg 2 *(Blomqvist,*
Lindqvist)
Sparta Prague 0
....

Steaua Bucharest 4 *(Ilie, Stan-pen,*
Parvu, Lacatus)
Servette 1 *(Neuville)*

Servette 1 *(Schepull)*
Steaua 1 *(Parvu)*
....

Champions' League
Group A
Manchester Utd 4 *(Giggs 2,*
Kanchelskis, Sharpe)
IFK Gothenburg 2 *(Petterson, Rehn)*

Barcelona 2 *(Koeman, Amor)*
Galatasaray 1 *(Turkyilmaz)*

IFK Gothnburg 2 *(Erlingmark,*
Blomqvist)
Barcelona 1 *(Stoichkov)*

Galatasaray 0
Manchester Utd 0

Manchester U 2 *(Hughes, Sharpe)*
Barcelona 2 *(Romario, Bakero)*

IFK Gothenburg 1 *(Erlingmark)*
Galatasaray 0

Barcelona 4 *(Pallister-og, Romario*
Stoichkov, Ferrer)
Manchester Utd 0

Galatasaray 0
IFK Gothenburg 1 *(Nilsson)*

IFK Gothenburg 3 *(Blomqvist,*
Erlingmark, Kamark-pen)
Manchester U 1 *(Hughes)*

Galatasaray 2 *(Hakan-pen, Arif)*
Barcelona 1 *(Romario)*

Manchester U 4 *(Davies, Beckham,*
Keane, Bulent-og)
Galatasaray 0

Barcelona 1 *(Bakero)*
IFK Gothenburg 1 *(Rehn)*

Final Table

	P	W	D	L	F	A	Pt
Gothenburg	6	4	1	1	10	7	9
Barcelona	6	2	2	2	11	8	6
Man Utd	6	2	2	2	11	11	6
Galatasaray	6	1	1	4	3	9	3

Group B
Dynamo Kiev 3 *(Leonenko 2,*
Rebrov)
Spartak Moscow 2 *(Pisarev,*
Tichonov)

Paris SG 2 *(Weah, Bravo)*
Bayern Munich 0

Spartak Moscow 1 *(Rachimov)*
Paris SG 2 *(Le Guen, Valdo)*

Bayern Munich 1 *(Scholl)*
Dynamo Kiev 0

Spartak Moscow 1 *(Pisarev)*
Bayern Munich 1 *(Babbel)*

Dynamo Kiev 1 *(Leonenko-pen)*
Paris SG 2 *(Guerin, Weah)*

Bayern Munich 2 *(Nerlinger,*
Kuffour)
Spartak Moscow 2 *(Tikhonov,*
Alenichev)

Paris SG 1 *(Weah)*
Dynamo Kiev 0

Spartak Moscow 1 *(Mukhamadiyev)*
Dynamo Kiev 0

Bayern Munich 0
Parsi SG 1 *(Weah)*

Dynamo Kiev 1 *(Shevchenko)*
Bayern Munich 4 *(Nerlinger,*
Papin 2, Scholl)

Paris SG 4 *(Weah 2, Ginola, Rai)*
Spartak Moscow 1 *(Rodionov)*

Final Table

	P	W	D	L	F	A	Pt
Paris S-G	6	6	0	0	12	3	12
Bayern M	6	2	2	2	8	7	6
Spartak M	6	1	2	3	8	12	4
Dynamo K	6	1	0	5	5	11	2

Group C
Hajduk Split 0
Benfica 0

Anderlecht 0
Steaua 0

Steaua 0
Hajduk Split 1 *(Asanovic)*

Benfica 3 *(Caniggia 2, Tavares)*
Anderlecht 1 *(Madeira-og)*

Benfica 2 *(Caniggia-pen,*
Joao Pinto II)
Steaua 1 *(Militaru)*

Hajduk Split 2 *(Pralija, Butorovic)*
Anderlecht 1 *(Weber)*

Steaua 1 *(Panduru)*
Benfica 1 *(Helder)*

Anderlecht 0
Hajduk Split 0

Benfica 2 *(Isaias, Joao Pinto)*
Hajduk Split 1 *(Andrijasevic)*

Steaua 1 *(Dobos)*
Anderlecht 0 *(Bosman)*

Hajduk Split 1 *(Andrijasevic)*
Steaua 4 *(Ilie 2, Lacatus, Galca)*

Anderlecht 1 *(Rutjes)*
Benfica 1 *(Edilson)*

Final Table

	P	W	D	L	F	A	Pt
Benfica	6	3	3	0	9	5	9
Hajduk Split	6	2	2	2	5	7	6
Steaua B	6	1	3	2	7	6	5
Anderlecht	6	0	4	2	4	7	4

Group D

Salzburg 0
AEK Athens 0

Ajax 2 *(R de Boer, Litmanen)*
AC Milan 0

AC Milan 3 *(Stroppa, Simone 2)*
Salzburg 0

AEK Athens 1 *(Savevski)*
Ajax 2 *(Litmanen, Kluivert)*

AEK Athens 0
AC Milan 0

Salzburg 0
Ajax 0

AC Milan 2 *(Panucci 2)*
AEK Athens 1 *(Savevski)*

Ajax 1 *(Litmanen)*
Salzburg 1 *(Kocljan)*

AEK Athens 1 *(Vlachos)*
Salzburg 3 *(Pfeifenberger 2, Hasenhuttl)*

AC Milan 0
Ajax 2 *(Litmanen, Baresi-og)*

Salzburg 0
AC Milan 1 *(Massaro)*

Ajax 2 *(Oulida 2)*
AEK Athens 0

Final Table

	P	W	D	L	F	A	Pt
Ajax	6	4	2	0	9	2	10
AC Milan	6	3	1	2	6	5	5
Salzburg	6	1	3	2	4	6	5
AEK Athens	6	0	2	4	3	9	2

AC Milan deducted 2 pts for crowd trouble

Quarter Finals *(over 2 legs)*
Bayern Munich 0
IFK Gothenburg 0

IFK Gothenburg 2 *(Lilienberg, Martinsson)*
Bayern Munich 2 *(Zickler, Nerlinger)*
Bayern Munich won on away goals

Hajduk Split 0
Ajax 0

Ajax 3 *(Kanu, F de Boer 2)*
Hajduk Split 0
Ajax won 3-0 on aggregate

AC Milan 2 *(Simone 2)*
Benfica 0

Benfica 0
AC Milan 0
AC Milan won 2-0 on aggregate

Barcelona 1 *(Korneev)*
Paris SG 1 *(Weah)*

Paris SG 2 *(Rai, Guerin)*
Barcelona 1 *(Bakero)*
Paris SG won 3-2 on aggregate

Semi Finals *(Over 2 legs)*
Bayern Munich 0
Ajax 0

Ajax 5 *(Litmanen 2, George, R de Boer, Overmars)*
Bayern Munich 2 *(Witeczek, Scholl)*
Ajax won 5-2 on aggregate

Paris SG 0
AC Milan 1 *(Boban)*

AC Milan 2 *(Savicevic) 2*
Paris SG 0
AC Milan won 3-0 on aggregate

EUROPEAN CUP FINAL
Vienna   May 24
Ajax 1 *(Kluivert)*
AC Milan 0
Ajax: Van der Sar, Reiziger, Blind, F de Boer, Rijkaard, Seedorf (Kanu), Davids, Litmanen (Kluivert), George, R de Boer, Overmars
AC Milan: Rossi, Panucci, Baresi, Costacurta, Maldini, Desailly, Donadoni, Albertini, Boban (Lentini), Massaro (Eranio), Simone

European Cup Winners' Cup

Preliminary Round *(over 2 legs)*
British and Irish clubs only
Floriana 2 *(Stefanovic 2)*
Sligo Rovers 2 *(Moran, Reid)*

Sligo Rovers 1 *(Brennan)*
Floriana 0
Sligo won 3-2 on aggregate

Barry Town 0
Zalgiris Vilnius 1 *(Vencevicius)*

Zalgiris Vilnius 6 *(Karvelis 2, Baltusnikas, Poderis, Maciulevicius, Jankauskas)*
Barry Town 0
Vilnius won 7-0 on aggregate

Bangor 0
Tatran Presov 1 *(Nenadic)*

Tatran Presov 4 *(Kocis 2, Matta, Hoger)*
Bangor 0
Presov won 5-0 on aggregate

First Round *(over 2 legs)*
Besiktas 2 *(Oktay, Ertugrul)*
HJK Helsinki 0

HJK Helsinki 1 *(Rantanen)*
Besiktas 1 *(Derelioglu)*
Besiktas won 3-1 on aggregate

Bodo Glimt 3 *(Staurvik, Johnsen 2)*
Sampdoria 2 *(Bertarelli, Platt)*

Sampdoria 2 *(Platt, Lombardo)*
Bodo Glimt 0
Sampdoria won 4-3 on aggregate

Branik Maribor 1 *(Bozgo-pen)*
FK Austria 1 *(Prosenik)*

FK Austria 3 *(Flogel, Kubica 2)*
Branik Maribor 0
FK Austria won 4-1 on aggregate

Brondby 3 *(Jensen-pen, Hansen, Bjur)*
SK Tirana 0

SK Tirana 0
Brondby 1 *(Strudal)*
Brondby won 4-0 on aggregate

Chelsea 4 *(Furlong, Sinclair, Rocastle, Wise)*
Viktoria Zizkov 2 *(Majoros 2)*

Viktoria Zizkov 0
Chelsea 0
Chelsea won 4-2 on aggregate

Croatia Z 3 *(Jelicic, Soldo,Pamic)*
Auxerre 1 *(Diomede)*

Auxerre 3 *(Diomede, Mahe,
    Lamouchi)*
Croatia Zagreb 0
Auxerre won 4-3 on aggregate
....

CSKA Moscow 2 *(Mamchur,
    Sergeyev)*
Ferencvaros 1 *(Christiansen)*

Ferencvaros 2 *(Sinov-og, Neagoe)*
CSKA Moscow 1 *(Radimov)*
Ferencvaros won 7-6 on penalties
....

Dundee Utd 3 *(Petric, Nixon,
    Hannah)*
Tatran Presov 2 *(Skalka, Zvara-pen)*

Tatran Presov 3 *(Zvara 2, Kocis)*
Dundee Utd 1 *(Nixon)*
Presov won 5-4 on aggregate
....

Gloria Bistrita 2 *(Raduta, Lungu)*
Zaragoza 1 *(Esnaider)*

Zaragoza 4 *(Pardeza, Aguado,
    Poyet 2)*
Gloria Bistrita 0
Zaragoza won 5-2 on aggregate
....

Grasshoppers 3 *(Bickel, Koller,
    Subiat)*
Odessa 0

Odessa 1 *(Guseyov)*
Grasshoppers 0
Grasshoppers won 3-1 on aggreg.
....

Maccabi Tel Aviv 0
Werder Bremen 0

Werder Bremen 2 *(Bode, Basler)*
Maccabi Tel Aviv 0
Werder Bremen won 2-0 on agg
....

Omonia 1 *(Malekos)*
Arsenal 3 *(Merson 2, Wright)*

Arsenal 3 *(Wright 2, Schwarz)*
Omonia 0
Arsenal won 6-1on aggregate
....

Pirin 0
Panathinaikos 2*(Nioblias,Alexoudis)*

Panathinaikos 6 *(Warzycha 3,
    Alexoudis 2, Borelli)*
Pirin 1 *(Orachev)*
*Panathinaikos won 8-1 on
aggregate*
....

Porto 2 *(Domingos, Rui Barros)*
LKS Lodz 0

LKS Lodz 0
Porto 1 *(Drulovic)*
Porto won 3-0 on aggregate
....

Sligo Rovers 1 *(Kenny)*
FC Brugge 2 *(Vermant, Verheyen)*

FC Brugge 3 *(Staelens 2-1 pen,
    Eykelkamp)*
Sligo Rovers 1 *(Rooney)*
FC Brugge won 5-2 on aggregate
....

Zalgiris Vilnius 1 *(Tereskinas-pen)*
Feyenoord 1 *(Larsson)*

Feyenoord 2 *(Larsson, Heus)-pen*
Zalgiris Vilnius 1 *(Vencevicius)*
Feyenoord won 3-2 on aggregate

Second Round *(over 2 legs)*
Besiktas 2 *(Mehmet, Ertugrul)*
Auxerre 2 *(Saib, Martins)*

Auxerre 2 *(Lamouchi 2)*
Besiktas 0
Auxerre won 4-2 on aggregate
....

Brondby 1 *(Strudal)*
Arsenal 2 *(Wright, Smith)*

Arsenal 2 *(Wright-pen, Selley)*
Brondby 2 *(B Hansen, Eggen)*
Arsenal won 4-3 on aggregate
....

FC Brugge 1 *(Staelens-pen)*
Panathinaikos 0

Panathinaikos 0
FC Brugge 0
FC Brugge won 1-0 on aggregate
....

Chelsea 0
FK Austria 0

FK Austria 1 *(Narbekovas)*
Chelsea 1 *(Spencer)*
Chelsea won on away goals
....

Feyenoord 1 *(Larsson)*
Werder Bremen 0

Werder Bremen 3 *(Bestchastnich 2,
    Basler)*
Feyenoord 4 *(Larsson 3-1 pen,
    Heus-pen)*
Feyenoord won 5-3 on aggregate
....

Porto 6 *(Jorge Costa, Rui Barros,
    Drulovic 2, Domingos, Aloisio)*
Ferencvaros 0

Ferencvaros 2 *(Zavatsky, Neagoe)*
Porto 0
Porto won 6-2 on aggregate
....

Sampdoria 3 *(Melli, Mihailovic,
    Maspero)*
Grasshoppers 0

Grasshoppers 3 *(Willems, Bickel,
    Koller)*
Sampdoria 2 *(Melli, Lombardo)*
Sampdoria won 5-3 on aggregate

Tatran Presov 0
Zaragoza 4 *(Poyet, Varga-og,
    Esnaider 2)*

Zaragoza 2 *(Esnaider, Celada)*
Tatran Presov 1 *(Kocis)*
Zaragoza won 6-1 on aggregate

Quarter Finals *(over 2 legs)*
FC Brugge 1 *(Verheyen)*
Chelsea 0

Chelsea 2 *(Stein, Furlong)*
FC Brugge 0
Chelsea won 2-1 on aggregate
....

Arsenal 1 *(Wright-pen)*
Auxerre 1 *(Verlaat)*

Auxerre 0
Arsenal 1 *(Wright)*
Arsenal won 2-1 on aggregate
....

Feyenoord 1 *(Larsson)*
Zaragoza 0

Zaragoza 2 *(Pardeza, Esnaider)*
Feyenoord 0
Zaragoza won 2-1 on aggregate
....

Sampdoria 0
Porto 1 *(Yuran)*

Porto 0
Sampdoria 1 *(Mancini)*
Sampdoria won 5-3 on penalties

Semi Finals *(over 2 legs)*
Arsenal 3 *(Bould 2, Wright)*
Sampdoria 2 *(Jugovic 2)*

Sampdoria 3 *(Mancini, Bellucci 2)*
Arsenal 2 *(Wright, Schwarz)*
Arsenal won 3-2 on penalties
....

Zaragoza 3 *(Pardeza, Esnaider 2)*
Chelsea 0

Chelsea 3 *(Furlong, Sinclair, Stein)*
Zaragoza 1 *(Aragon)*
Zaragoza won 4-3 on aggregate

CUP WINNERS CUP FINAL
Paris   May 10
Arsenal 1 *(Hartson)*
Zaragoza 2 *(Esnaider, Nayim)*
aet
Arsenal: Seaman, Dixon,
Winterburn (Morrow), Schwarz,
Linighan, Adams, Keown (Hillier),
Wright, Hartson, Merson, Parlour
Zaragoza: Cedrun, Belsue, Aguado,
Caceres, Solana, Poyet, Aragon,
Nayim, Higuera (Sanjuan/Geli),
Pardeza, Esnaider

UEFA Cup

Quarter-finals *(over two legs)*
Eintracht Frankfurt 1 *(Furtok)*
Juventus 1 *(Marocchi)*

Juventus 3 *(Conte, Ravanelli, Del Piero)*
Eintracht Frankfurt 0
Juventus won 4-1 on aggregate
....

Bayer Leverkusen 5 *(Lehnhoff, Kirsten 2, Sergio 2)*
Nantes 1 *(Ouedec-pen)*

Nantes 0
Bayer Leverkusen 0
Leverkusen won 5-1 on aggregate
....

Lazio 1 *(Freund-og)*
Borussia Dortmund 0

B Dortmund 2 *(Chapuisat-pen, Riedle)*
Lazio 0
Dortmund won 2-1 on aggregate
....

Parma 1 *(Zola-pen)*
Odense 0

Odense 0
Parma 0
Parma won 1-0 on aggregate
....

Semi-finals *(over two legs)*
Bayer Leverkusen 1 *(Sergio)*
Parma 2 *(D Baggio, Asprilla)*

Parma 3 *(Aspilla 2, Zola)*
Bayer Leverkusen 0
Parma won 5-1 on aggregate
....

Juventus 2 *(R Baggio-pen, Kohler)*
B Dortmund 2 *(Reuter, Möller)*

B Dortmund 1 *(Cesar)*
Juventus 2 *(Porrini, R Baggio)*
Juventus won 4-3 on aggregate
....

FINAL *(over two legs)*
Parma 1 *(D Baggio)*
Juventus 0
Parma: Bucci, Benarrivo (Mussi), Minotti, Apolloni, Fernando Couto, Di Chiara, Pin, D Baggio, Sensini, Zola (Fiore), Asprilla
Juventus: Rampulla, Fusi (Del Piero), Tacchinardi, Carrera (Marocchi), Jarni, Paulo Sousa, Di Livio, Deschamps, Vialli, R Baggio, Ravanelli

Juventus 1 *(Vialli)*
Parma 1 *(D Baggio)*
Juventus: Peruzzi, Ferrara, Torricelli, Porrini, Jarni, Paulo Sousa, Di Livio (Carrera), Marocchi (Del Piero), R Baggio, Vialli, Ravanelli,
Parma: Bucci, Benarrivo (Mussi), Minotti, Susic, Fernando Couto, Di Chiara (Castellini), D Baggio, Fiore, Crippa, Zola, Asprilla
Parma won 2-1 on aggregate

Other Competitions

World Club Championship
Played annually between the winners of the European Cup and the winners of the South American Champions Cup (Copa Libertadores).

Tokyo   Dec 1   *(55,860)*
AC Milan 0   Velez Sarsfield 2
                        Trotta-pen, Asad
AC Milan: Rossi, Tassotti, Maldini, Albertini, Costacurta, Baresi, Donadoni, Desailly, Boban, Massaro (Panucci), Savicevic (Simone)
Velez Sarsfield: Chilavert, Trotta, Cardozo, Almandoz, Gomez, Sotomayor, Bassedas, Basualdo, Asad, Pompei, Flores

European Super Cup
Played annually between the winners of the Champions Cup and the Cup-Winners' Cup.
First Leg
Highbury   Feb 1   *(38,044)*
Arsenal 0   AC Milan 0

Second Leg
Milan   Feb 8   *(23,953)*
AC Milan 2   Arsenal 0
Boban, Massaro

Copa America
Quarter-finals
Paraguay 1 Colombia 1
Colombia won 5-4 on penalties
Uruguay 2 Bolivia 1
USA 0 Mexico 0
USA won 4-1 on penalties
Brazil 2 Argentina 2
Brazil won 4-2 on penalties

Semi-finals
Uruguay 2 Colombia 0
USA 0 Brazil 1

Third Place Play-off
Colombia 4 USA 1

FINAL
Uruguay 1 *(Bengoechea)*
Brazil 1 *(Tulio)*
Uruguay won 5-3 on penalties

South American Super Cup
Final *(over 2 legs)*
Boca Juniors 1 Independiente 1
Independiente 1 Boca Juniors 0
Independiente won 2-1 on aggregate

Panamerican Games
Final
Argentina 0   Mexico 0
Argentina won 5-4 on penalties

FIFA U-17 World Championship
Ecuador   Aug 3-20
Quarter-finals
Ghana 2 Portugal 0
Oman 2 Nigeria 1
Brazil 3 Australia 1
Argentina 3 Ecuador 1

Semi-finals
Ghana 3 Oman 1
Brazil 3 Argentina 0

FINAL
Ghana 3 Brazil 2

Asian Games
Final
Uzbekistan 4   China 2

Women's Football

World Championship

Sweden   June 5-18

Qualifying Rounds
Sweden 0 Brazil 1
Germany 1 Japan 0
Norway 8 Nigeria 0
England 3 Canada 2
United States 3 China 3
Denmark 5 Australia 0
Sweden 3 Germany 2
Brazil 1 Japan 2
Norway 2 England 0
Nigeria 3 Canada 3
United States 2 Denmark 0
China 4 Australia 2
Sweden 2 Japan 0
Brazil 1 Germany 6
Norway 7 Canada 0
Nigeria 2 England 3
United States 4 Australia 1
China 3 Denmark 1

Quarter-finals
Vasteras   June 13
Germany 3 England 0

Helsingborg June 13
China 1 Sweden 1
China won 4-3 on penalties

Gavle   June 13
United States 4 Japan 0

Karlstad   June 13
Norway 3 Denmark 1

Semi-finals
Helsingborg June 15
Germany 1 China 0

Vasteras   June 15
United States 0 Norway 1

Third Place Play-off
Gavle   June 17
China 0 United States 2

FINALS
Stockholm June 18
Norway 2 Germany 0

National League

Premier Division

	P	W	D	L	GF	GA	Pts
Arsenal	18	17	1	0	60	8	52
Liverpool	18	12	3	3	58	17	39
Doncaster Belles	18	12	2	4	56	24	38
Croydon	18	9	2	7	42	24	29
Wembley	18	8	3	7	34	17	27
Leasowe Pacific	18	5	3	10	36	47	18
Ilkeston Town Rangers	18	4	3	11	20	49	15
Millwall Lionesses	18	4	3	11	25	60	15
Wolverhampton Wdrs	18	4	1	13	23	66	13
Red Star Southampton	18	3	3	12	23	65	12

Division One North

Villa Aztecs	18	11	4	3	59	22	37
Cowgate Kestrels	18	11	3	4	63	30	36
St Helens/Garswood	18	11	3	4	44	26	36
Sheffield Wednesday	18	9	4	5	38	27	31
Ipswich Town	18	8	4	6	33	29	28
Bronte	18	8	3	7	42	28	27
Langford	18	8	0	10	30	40	24
Kidderminster Harriers	18	4	2	12	24	57	14
Nottingham Argyle	18	3	2	13	22	66	11
Solihull Borough	18	4	1	13	22	52	10*

* 3 points deducted

Division One South

Maidstone Tigresses	14	10	2	2	34	10	32
Berkhamsted & Hemel	14	8	4	2	28	13	28
Oxford United	14	7	3	4	28	28	24
Wimbledon	14	6	2	6	28	20	20
Brighton & Hove Albion	14	6	1	7	20	30	19
Town & Country	14	5	3	6	22	25	18
Brentford	14	3	4	7	29	41	13
Horsham	14	0	3	11	16	38	3

FA Women's Challenge Cup

Sixth Round
Liverpool 3 Croydon 0
Leyton Orient 1 Arsenal 8
Bristol City 4 Huddersfield 3
Doncaster Belles 4 St Helens/Garwood 0

Semi-finals
Doncaster Belles 1 Arsenal 3
Bristol City 0 Liverpool 5

Final
Tranmere Rovers FC
Arsenal 3 *(Lonergan 2, Spacey)*
Liverpool 2 *(Burke 2)*

World Cup & European Championship Winners

WORLD CUP FINALS

Year	Winners	Runners-up	Venue	Attendance
1930	**Uruguay** 4	Argentina 2	Montevideo, Uruguay	90,000
	Dorado, Cea, Iriarte, Castro	*Peucelle, Stabile*		
1934	**Italy** 2	Czechoslovakia 1 *	Rome, Italy	55,000
	Orsi, Schiavio	*Puc*		
1938	**Italy** 4	Hungary 2	Paris, France	50,000
	Colaussi (2), Piola (2)	*Titkos, Sarosi*		
1950	**Uruguay** 2	Brazil 1 **	Rio de Janeiro, Brazil	199,854
	Schiaffino, Ghiggia	*Friaca*		
1954	**West Germany** 3	Hungary 2	Berne, Switzerland	55,000
	Morlock, Rahn (2)	*Puskas, Czibor*		
1958	**Brazil** 5	Sweden 2	Stockholm, Sweden	49,737
	Vava (2), Pele (2), Zagalo	*Liedholm, Simonsson*		
1962	**Brazil** 3	Czechoslovakia 1	Santiago, Chile	69,068
	Amarildo, Zito, Vava	*Masopust*		
1966	**England** 4	West Germany 2 *	London, England	93,000
	Hurst (3), Peters	*Haller, Weber*		
1970	**Brazil** 4	Italy 1	Mexico City, Mexico	110,000
	Pele, Gerson,	*Boninsegna*		
	Jairzinho, Carlos Alberto			
1974	**West Germany** 2	Holland 1	Munich, West Germany	77,833
	Breitner (pen), Müller	*Neeskens (pen)*		
1978	**Argentina** 3	Holland 1 *	Buenos Aires, Argentina	77,000
	Kempes (2), Bertoni	*Nanninga*		
1982	**Italy** 3	West Germany 1	Madrid, Spain	92,000
	Rossi, Tardelli, Altobelli	*Breitner*		
1986	**Argentina** 3	West Germany 2	Mexico City, Mexico	114,580
	Brown, Valdano,	*Rummenigge, Völler*		
	Burruchaga			
1990	**West Germany** 1	Argentina 0	Rome, Italy	73,603
	Brehme (pen)			
1994	**Brazil** 0	Italy 0 *	Los Angeles, USA	94,194
	Brazil won 3-2 on penalties			

* after extra time ** deciding match of final pool

EUROPEAN CHAMPIONSHIP FINALS

Year	Winners	Runners-up	Venue	Attendance
1960	**Soviet Union** 2	Yugoslavia 1 *	Paris, France	17,966
	Metreveli, Ponedelnik	*Galic*		
1964	**Spain** 2	Soviet Union 1	Madrid, Spain	105,000
	Pereda, Marcellino	*Khusainov*		
1968	**Italy** 1	Yugoslavia 1 *	Rome, Italy	85,000
	Domenghini	*Dzajic*		
Replay	**Italy** 2	Yugoslavia 0	Rome, Italy	50,000
	Riva, Anastasi			
1972	**West Germany** 3	Soviet Union 0	Brussels, Belgium	43,437
	G Müller (2), Wimmer			
1976	**Czechoslovakia** 2	West Germany 2 *	Belgrade, Yugoslavia	45,000
	Svehlik, Dobias	*D Muller, Holzenbein*		
	(Czechoslovakia won 5-4 on penalties)			
1980	**West Germany** 2	Belgium 1	Rome, Italy	47,864
	Hrubesch (2)	*Van der Eycken*		
1984	**France** 2	Spain 0	Paris, France	47,000
	Platini, Bellone			
1988	**Holland** 2	Soviet Union 0	Munich, Germany	72,308
	Gullit, Van Basten			
1992	**Denmark** 2	Germany 0	Gothenburg, Sweden	37,800
	Jensen, Vilfort			

* after extra time

European Cup Competitions

EUROPEAN CHAMPIONS CUP

Year	Winner	Runner-up
1956	**Real Madrid** 4	Relms 3
1957	**Real Madrid** 2	Florentina 0
1958	**Real Madrid** 3	AC Milan 2 *(aet)*
1959	**Real Madrid** 2	Reims 0
1960	**Real Madrid** 7	Eintracht Frankfurt 3
1961	**Benfica** 3	Barcelona 2
1962	**Benfica** S	Real Madrid 3
1963	**AC Milan** 2	Benfica 1
1964	**Internazionale** 3	Real Madrid 1
1965	**Internazionale** 1	Benfica 0
1966	**Real Madrid** 2	Partizan Belgrade 1
1967	**Celtic** 2	Internazionale 1
1968	**Manchester Utd** 4	Benfica 1 *(aet)*
1969	**AC Milan** 4	Ajax 1
1970	**Feyenoord** 2	Celtic 1 *(aet)*
1971	**Ajax** 2	Panathinaikos 0
1972	**Ajax** 2	Internazionale 0
1973	**Ajax** l	Juventus 0
1974	**Bayern Munich** 1	Atletico Madrid l
Rply	**Bayern Munich** 4	Atletico Madrid 0
1975	**Bayern Munich** 2	Leeds Utd 0
1976	**Bayern Munich** l	St Etienne 0
1977	**Liverpool** 3	B Moenchengladbach 1
1978	**Liverpool** l	FC Brugge 0
1979	**Nottingham Forest** 1	Malmo 0
1980	**Nottingham Forest** 1	Hamburg 0
1981	**Liverpool** 1	Real Madrid 0
1982	**Aston Villa** 1	Bayern Munich 0
1983	**Hamburg** 1	Juventus 0
1984	**Liverpool** 1	Roma 1
	(aet: Liverpool won 4-2 on penalties)	
1985	**Juventus** 1	Liverpool 0
1986	**Steaua Bucharest** 0	Barcelona 0
	(aet: Steaua won 2-0 on penalties)	
1987	**Porto** 2	Bayern Munich 1
1988	**PSV Eindhoven** 0	Benfica 0
	(aet: PSV won 6-5 on penalties)	
1989	**AC Milan** 4	Steaua Bucharest 0
1990	**AC Milan** 1	Benfica 0
1991	**Red Star Belgrade** 0	Marseille 0
	(aet: Red Star won 5-3 on penalties)	
1992	**Barcelona** 1	Sampdoria 0 *(aet)*
1993	**Marseille*** 1	**AC Milan** 0
1994	**AC Milan** 4	Barcelona 0
1995	**Ajax** 1	AC Milan 0

* subsequently stripped of title

EUROPEAN CUP WINNER'S CUP

Year	Winners	Runner-up
1961	**Fiorentina** 2	Rangers 0 *(1st Leg)*
	Fiorentina 2	Rangers 1 *(2nd Leg)*
1962	**Atletico Madrid** 1	Fiorentina 1
Rply	**Atletico Madrid** 3	Fiorentina 0
1963	**Tottenham H** 5	Atletico Madrid l
1964	**Sporting Lisbon** 3	MTK Budapest 3 *(aet)*
Rply	**Sporting Lisbon** 1	MTK Budapest 0
1965	**West Ham Utd** 2	Munich 1860 0
1966	**B Dortmund** 2	Liverpool 1 *(aet)*

Year	Winner	Runner-up
1967	**Bayern Munich** 1	Rangers 0 *(aet)*
1968	**AC Milan** 2	Hamburg 0
1969	**Slovan Bratislava** 3	Barcelona 2
1970	**Manchester City** 2	Gornik Zabrze 1
1971	**Chelsea** 1	Real Madrid 1 (aet)
Rply	**Chelsea** 2	Real Madrid 1 (aet)
1972	**Rangers** 3	Dynamo Moscow 2
1973	**AC Milan** 1	Leeds Utd 0
1974	**Magdeburg** 2	AC Milan 0
1975	**Dynamo Kiev** 3	Ferencvaros 0
1976	**Anderlecht** 4	West Ham U 2
1977	**Hamburg** 2	Anderlecht 0
1978	**Anderlecht** 4	Austria/WAC 0
1979	**Barcelona** 4	Fort. Dusseldorf 3 *(aet)*
1980	**Valencia** 0	Arsenal 0
	(aet: Valencia won 5-4 on penalties)	
1981	**Dynamo Tblisi** 2	Carl Zeiss Jena 1
1982	**Barcelona** 2	Standard Liege 1
1983	**Aberdeen** 2	Real Madnd 1 *(aet)*
1984	**Juventus** 2	Porto 1
1985	**Everton** 3	Rapid Vienna 1
1986	**Dynamo Kiev** 3	Atletico Madrid 0
1987	**Ajax** 1	Lokomotiv Leipzig 0
1988	**Mechelen** 1	Ajax 0
1989	**Barcelona** 2	Sampdoria 0
1990	**Sampdoria** 2	Anderlecht 0
1991	**Manchester Utd** 2	Barcelona 1
1992	**Werder Bremen** 2	Monaco 0
1993	**Parma** 3	Antwerp 1
1994	**Arsenal** 1	Parma 0
1995	**Real Zaragoza** 2	Arsenal 1

UEFA CUP *(from 1971)*

Year	Winners	Score	Runners-up
1972	**Tottenham H**	2-1 1-1	Wolverhampton W
1973	**Liverpool**	3-0 0-2	B M'chengladbach
1974	**Feyenoord**	2-0 2-2	Tottenham H
1975	**B M'chengladbach**	1-0 1-1	Twente Enschede
1976	**Liverpool**	3-2 1-1	F C Bruges
1977	**Juventus**	1-0 1-2*	Athletic Bilbao
1978	**PSV Eindhoven**	3-0 0-0	Bastia
1979	**B M'chengladbach**	1-0 1-1	Red Star Belgrade
1980	**E'tracht Frankfurt**	1-0 2-3*	B M'chengladbach
1981	**Ipswich Town**	3-0 2-4	AZ 67 Alkmaar
1982	**IFK Gothenburg**	1-0 3-0	SV Hamburg
1983	**Anderlecht**	1-0 1-1	Benfica
1984	**Tottenham H**	1-1 1-1**	Anderlecht
1985	**Real Madrid**	3-0 0-1	Videoton
1986	**Real Madrid**	5-1 0-2	Cologne
1987	**IFK Gothenburg**	1-0 1-1	Dundee Utd
1988	**Bayer Leverkusen**	0-3 3-0**	Espanol
1989	**Napoli**	2-1 3-3	VFB Stuttgart
1990	**Juventus**	3-1 0-0	Fiorentina
1991	**Internazionale**	2-0 0-1	AS Roma
1992	**Ajax**	2-2 0-0*	Torino
1993	**Juventus**	3-1 3-0	Borussia Dortmund
1994	**Internazionale**	1-0 1-0	Salzburg
1995	**Parma**	1-0 1-1	Juventus

* won on away goals   ** won on penalties

English League Champions

ENGLISH FOOTBALL LEAGUE

	Winners	Pts	Runners-up	Pts
1895-96	Aston Villa	45	Derby County	41
1896-97	Aston Villa	47	Sheffield Utd	36
1897-98	Sheffield Utd	42	Sunderland	37
I 898 99	Aston Villa	45	Liverpool	43
1899-00	Aston Villa	50	Sheffield Utd	48
1900-01	Liverpool	45	Sunderland	43
1901-02	Sunderland	44	Everton	41
1902-03	Sheffield Wed	42	Aston Villa	41
1903-04	Sheffield Wed	47	Man City	44
1904-05	Newcastle Utd	48	Everton	47
1905-06	Liverpool	51	Preston NE	47
1906-07	Newcastle Utd	51	Bristol City	48
1907-08	Man Utd	52	Aston Villa	43
1908-09	Newcastle Utd	53	Everton	46
1909-10	Aston Villa	53	Liverpool	48
1910-11	Man Utd	52	AstonVilla	51
1911-12	Blackburn Rvrs	49	Everton	46
1912-13	Sunderland	54	Aston Villa	50
1913.14	Blackburn Rvrs	51	AstonVilla	44
1914-15	Everton	46	Oldham Ath	45
1919-20	West Brom Alb	60	Burnley	51
1920-21	Burnley	59	Man City	54
1921-22	Liverpool	57	Tottenham	51
1922-23	Liverpool	60	Sunderland	54
1923-24	Huddersfield T	57	Cardiff City	57
1924-25	Huddersfield T	58	West Brom Alb	56
1925-26	Huddersfield T	57	Arsenal	52
1926-27	Newcastle Utd	56	Huddersfield T	51
1927-28	Everton	53	Huddersfield T	51
1928-29	Sheffield Wed	52	Leicester City	51
1929-30	Sheffield Wed	60	Derby County	50
1930-31	Arsenal	66	Aston Villa	59
1931-32	Everton	56	Arsenal	54
1932 33	Arsenal	58	Aston Villa	54
1933-34	Arsenal	59	Huddersfield T	56
1934-35	Arsenal	58	Sunderland	54
1935-36	Sunderland	56	Derby County	48
1936-37	Man City	57	Charlton Ath	54
1937-38	Arsenal	52	W'olv'hampton	51
1938-39	Everton	59	W'olv'hampton	55
1946-47	Liverpool	57	Man Utd	56
1947-48	Arsenal	59	Man Utd	52
1948-49	Portsmouth	58	Man Utd	53
1949-50	Portsmouth	53	Wolv'hampton	53
1950-51	Tottenham H	60	Man Utd	56
1951-52	Man Utd	57	Tottenham H	53
1952-53	Arsenal	54	Preston NE	54
1953 54	Wolv'hampton	57	West Brom Alb	53
1954-55	Chelsea	52	Wolv'hampton	48
1955-56	Man Utd	60	Blackpool	49
1956-57	Man Utd	64	Tottenham	56
1957-58	Wolv'hampton	64	Preston NE	59
1958-59	Wolv'hampton	61	Man Utd	55
1959-60	Burnley	55	Wolv'hampton	54
1960-61	Tottenham H	66	Sheffield Wed	58
1961-62	Ipswich Town	56	Burnley	53
1962-63	Everton	61	Tottenham	55
1963-64	Liverpool	57	Man Utd	53
1964-65	Man Utd	61	Leeds United	61
1965-66	Liverpool	61	Leeds United	55
1966-67	Man Utd	60	Nottingham F	56
1967-68	Man City	58	Man Utd	56
1968 69	Leeds Utd	67	Liverpool	61
1969-70	Everton	66	Leeds Utd	57
1970-71	Arsenal	65	Leeds Utd	64
1971-72	Derby County	58	Leeds Utd	57
1972-73	Liverpool	60	Arsenal	57
1973-74	Leeds Utd	62	Liverpool	57
1974-75	Derby County	53	Liverpool	51
1975-76	Liverpool	60	QPR	59
1976-77	Liverpool	57	Man City	56
1977-78	Nottingham F	64	Liverpool	57
1978-79	Liverpool	68	Nottingham F	60
1979-80	l.iverpool	60	Man Utd	58
1980-81	Aston Villa	60	Ipswich Town	56
1981-82	Liverpool	87	Ipswich Town	83
1982-83	Liverpool	82	Watford	71
1983-84	Liverpool	80	Southampton	77
1984-85	Everton	90	Liverpool	77
1985-86	Liverpool	88	Everton	86
1986-87	Everton	86	Liverpool	77
1987-88	Liverpool	90	Man Utd	81
1988-89	Arsenal	76	Liverpool	76
1989-90	Liverpool	79	Aston Villa	70
1990-91	Arsenal	83	Liverpool	76
1991-92	Leeds Utd	82	Man Utd	78
1992-93	Man Utd	84	Aston Villa	74
1993-94	Man Utd	92	Blackburn Rvrs	84

FA Cup Winners

Scorers from first Wembley final (1923) onwards

Year	Winners	Runners-up
1872	**Wanderers** 1	Royal Engineers 0
1873	**Wanderers** 2	Royal Engineers 0
1874	**Oxford University** 2	Royal Engineers 0
1875	**Royal Engineers** 1	Old Etonians 1*
Rply	**Royal Engineers** 2	Old Etonians 0
1876	**Wanderers** 1	Old Etonians 1
Rply	**Wanderers** 3	Old Etonians 0
1877	**Wanderers** 2	Oxford University 1*
1878	**Wanderers** 3	Royal Engineers 1
1879	**Old Etonians** 1	Clapham Rovers 0
1880	**Clapham Rovers** 1	Oxford University 0
1881	**Old Carthusians** 3	Old Etonians 0
1882	**Old Etonians** 1	Blackburn Rovers 0
1883	**Blackburn Olympic** 2	Old Etonians 1*
1884	**Blackburn Rovers** 2	Queen's Park 1
1885	**Blackburn Rovers** 2	Queen's Park 0
1886	**Blackburn Rovers** 0	West Bromich Alb 0
Rply	**Blackburn Rovers** 2	West Bromich Alb 0
1887	**Aston Villa** 2	West Bromich Alb 0
1888	**West Bromich Alb** 2	Preston North End 1
1889	**Preston North End** 3	Wolv'hampton Wdrs 0
1890	**Blackburn Rovers** 6	Sheffield Wednesday 1
1891	**Blackburn Rovers** 3	Notts County 1
1892	**West Bromich Alb** 3	Aston Villa 0
1893	**Wolv'hampton W** 1	Everton 0
1894	**Notts County** 4	Bolton Wanderers 1
1895	**Aston Villa** 1	West Bromich Alb 0
1896	**Sheffield Wed** 2	Wolv'hampton Wdrs 1
1897	**Aston Villa** 3	Everton 2
1898	**Nottingham Forest** 3	Derby County 1
1899	**Sheffield United** 4	Derby County 1
1900	**Bury** 4	Southampton 0
1901	**Tottenham Hotspur** 2	Sheffield United 2
Rply	**Tottenham Hotspur** 3	Sheffield United 1
1902	**Sheffield United** 1	Southampton 1
Rply	**Sheffield United** 2	Southampton 1
1903	**Bury** 6	Derby County 0
1904	**Manchester City** 1	Bolton Wanderers 0
1905	**Aston Villa** 2	Newcastle United 0
1906	**Everton** 1	Newcastle United 0
1907	**Sheffield Wed** 2	Everton 1
1908	**Wolv'hampton W** 3	Newcastle United 1
1909	**Manchester United** 1	Bristol City 0
1910	**Newcastle United** 1	Barnsley 1
Rply	**Newcastle United** 2	Barnsley 0
1911	**Bradford City** 0	Newcastle United 0
Rply	**Bradford City** 1	Newcastle United 0
1912	**Barnsley** 0	West Bromich Alb 0
Rply	**Barnsley** 1	West BromichAlb 0*
1913	**Aston Villa** 1	Sunderland 0
1914	**Burnley** 1	Liverpool 0
1915	**Sheffield United** 3	Chelsea 0
1920	**Aston Villa** 1	Huddersfield Town 0*
1921	**Tottenham Hotspur** 1	Wolv'hampton Wdrs 0
1922	**Huddersfield Town** 1	Preston North End 0
1923	**Bolton Wanderers** 2	West Ham United 0
	Jack, JR Smith	
1924	**Newcastle United** 2	Aston Villa 0
	Harris, Seymour	
1925	**Sheffield United** 1	Cardiff City 0
	Tunstall	
1926	**Bolton Wanderers** 1	Manchester City 0
	Jack	
1927	**Cardiff City** 1	Arsenal 0
	Ferguson	
1928	**Blackburn Rovers** 3	Huddersfield Town 1
	Roscamp (2), McLean	*Jackson*
1929	**Bolton Wanderers** 2	Portsmouth 0
	Butler, Blackmore	
1930	**Arsenal** 2	Huddersfield Town 0
	James, Lambert	
1931	**West Bromich Alb** 2	Birmingham City 1
	WG Richardson (2)	*Bradford*
1932	**Newcastle United** 2	Arsenal 1
	Allen (2)	*John*
1933	**Everton** 3	Manchester City 0
	Stein, Dean, Dunn	
1934	**Manchester City** 2	Portsmouth 1
	Tilson (2)	*Rutherford*
1935	**Sheffield Wed** 4	West Bromich Alb 2
	Rimmer (2), Hooper,	*Boyes, Sandford*
	Palethorpe	
1936	**Arsenal** 1	Sheffield United 0
	Drake	
1937	**Sunderland** 3	Preston North End 1
	Gurney, Carter, Burbanks	*F O'Donnell*
1938	**Preston North End** 1	Huddersfield Town 0*
	Mutch (pen)	
1939	**Portsmouth** 4	Wolv'hampton Wdrs 1
	Parker (2), Barlow,	*Dorsett*
	Anderson	
1946	**Derby County** 4	Charlton Athletic 1*
	Stamps (2), Doherty,	*H Turner*
	H Turner (og)	
1947	**Charlton Athletic** 1	Burnley 0*
	Duffy	
1948	**Manchester United** 4	Blackpool 2
	Rowley (2), Pearson,	*Shimwell (pen),*
Mortensen		
	Anderson,	
1949	**Wolv'hampton Wdrs** 3	Leicester City 1
	Pye (2), Smyth	*Grifflths*
1950	**Arsenal** 2	Liverpool 0
	Lewis (2)	
1951	**Newcastle United** 2	Blackpool 0
	Milburn (2)	
1952	**Newcastle United** 1	Arsenal 0
	G Robledo	
1953	**Blackpool** 4	Bolton Wanderers 3
	Mortensen (3), Perry	*Lofthouse, Moir, Bell*
1954	**West Bromich Alb** 3	Preston North End 2
	Allen (2,1 pen), Griffin	*Morrison, Wayman*
1955	**Newcastle United** 3	Manchester City 1
	Milburn, Mitchell,	*Johnstone*
	Hannah	
1956	**Manchester City** 3	Birmingham City 1
	Hayes, Dyson, Johnstone	*Kinsey*

FA Cup Winners

1957 **Aston Villa** 2 Manchester United 1
McParland (2) *Taylor*
1958 **Bolton Wanderers** 2 Manchester United 0
Lofthouse (2)
1959 **Nottingham Forest** 2 Luton Town 1
Dwight, Wilson *Pacey*
1960 **Wolv'hampton Wdrs** 3 Blackburn Rovers 0
McGrath (og), Deeley (2)
1961 **Tottenham Hotspur** 2 Leicester City 0
Smith, Dyson
1962 **Tottenham Hotspur** 3 Burnley 1
Greaves, Smith, *Robson*
Blanchflower (pen)
1963 **Manchester United** 3 Leicester City 1
Herd (2), Law *Keyworth*
1964 **West Ham United** 3 Preston North End 2
Sissons, Hurst, Boyce Holden, Dawson
1965 **Liverpool** 2 Leeds United 1*
Hunt, St John *Bremner*
1966 **Everton** 3 Sheffield Wednesday 2
Trebilcock (2), Temple McCalliog, Ford
1967 **Tottenham Hotspur** 2 Chelsea 1
Robertson, Saul *Tambling*
1968 **West Bromich Alb** 1 Everton 0*
Astle
1969 **Manchester City** 1 Leicester City 0
Young
1970 **Chelsea** 2 Leeds United 2*
Houseman, Hutchinson Charlton, Jones
Rply **Chelsea** 2 Leeds United 1*
Osgood, Webb *Jones*
1971 **Arsenal** 2 Liverpool 1*
Kelly, George *Heighway*
1972 **Leeds United** 1 Arsenal 0
Clarke
1973 **Sunderland** 1 Leeds United 0
Porterfield
1974 **Liverpool** 3 Newcastle United 0
Keegan (2), Heighway
1975 **West Ham United** 2 Fulham 0
A Taylor (2)
1976 **Southampton** 1 Manchester United 0
Stokes
1977 **Manchester United** 2 Liverpool 1
Pearson, J Greenhoff Case
1978 **Ipswich Town** 1 Arsenal 0
Osborne
1979 **Arsenal** 3 Manchester United 2
Talbot, Stapleton, *McQueen, McIlroy*
Sunderland
1980 **West Ham United** 1 Arsenal 0
Brooking
1981 **Tottenham Hotspur** 1 Manchester City 1*
Hutchison (og) *Hutchison*
Rply **Tottenham Hotspur** 3 Manchester City 2
Villa (2), Crooks *Mackenzie, Reeves (pen)*
1982 **Tottenham Hotspur** 1 Queens Park Rangers 1*
Hoddle *Fenwick*
Rply **Tottenham Hotspur** 1 Queens Park Rangers 0
Hoddle (pen)

1983 **Manchester United** 2 Brighton & Hove Alb 2*
Stapleton, Wilkins *Smith, Stevens*
Rply **Manchester United** 4 Brighton & Hove Alb 0
Robson (2), Whiteside,
Muhren (pen)
1984 **Everton** 2 Watford 0
Sharp, Gray
1985 **Manchester United** 1 Everton 0*
Whiteside
1986 **Liverpool** 3 Everton 1
Rush (2), Johnston *Lineker*
1987 **Coventry City** 3 Tottenham Hotspur 2*
Bennett, Houchen, *C Allen, Mabbutt*
Mabbutt (og)
1988 **Wimbledon** 1 Liverpool 0
Sanchez
1989 **Liverpool** 3 Everton 2*
Aldridge, Rush (2) *McCall (2)*
1990 **Manchester United** 3 Crystal Palace 3*
Pemberton (og), *O'Reilly, I Wright (2)*
Hughes (2)
Rply **Manchester United** 1 Crystal Palace 0
Martin
1991 **Tottenham Hotspur** 2 Nottingham Forest 1*
Stewart, Walker (og) *Pearce*
1992 **Liverpool** 2 Sunderland 0
Thomas, Rush
1993 **Arsenal** 1 Sheffield Wednesday 1*
Wright *Hirst*
Rply **Arsenal** 2 Sheffield Wednesday 1*
Wright, Linighan *Waddle*
1994 **Manchester United** 4 Chelsea 0
Cantona 2 (2 pens)
Hughes, McClair
1995 **Everton** 1 Manchester United 0
Rideout
* after extra time

Scottish League Champions & Cup Winners

Season	LEAGUE Winners	Runner-up	CUP Winners
	Winners	*Runner-up*	*Winners*
1873-74	-	-	Queen 's Park
1874-75	-	-	Queen 's Park
1875-76	-	-	Queen 's Park
1876-77	-	-	Vale of Leven
1877-78	-	-	Vale of Leven
1878-79	-	-	Vale of Leven
1879-80	-	-	Queen's Park
1880-81	-	-	Queen's Park
1881-82	-	-	Queen's Park
1882-83	-	-	Dumbarton
1883-84	-	-	Queen's Park
1884-85	-	-	Renton
1885-86	-	-	Queen's Park
1886-87	-	-	Hibernian
1887-88	-	-	Renton
1888-89	-	-	Third Lanark
1889-90	-	-	Queen's Park
1890-91	Dumbarton/Rangers		Hearts
1891-92	Dumbarton	Celtic	Celtic
1892-93	Celtic	Rangers	Queen's Park
1893-94	Celtic	Hearts	Rangers
1894-95	Hearts	Celtic	St. Bernard's
1895-96	Celtic	Rangers	Hearts
1896-97	Hearts	Hibernian	Rangers
1897-98	Celtic	Rangers	Rangers
1898-99	Rangers	Hearts	Celtic
1899-00	Rangers	Celtic	Celtic
1900-01	Rangers	Celtic	Hearts
1901-02	Rangers	Celtic	Hibernian
1902-03	Hibernian	Dundee	Rangers
1903-04	Third Lanark		Hearts Celtic
1904-05	Celtic	Rangers	Third Lanark
1905-06	Celtic	Hearts	Hearts
1906-07	Celtic	Dundee	Celtic
1907-08	Celtic	Falkirk	Celtic
1908-09	Celtic	Dundee	*
1909-10	Celtic	Falkirk	Dundee
1910-11	Rangers	Aberdeen	Celtic
1911-12	Rangers	Celtic	Celtic
1912-13	Rangers	Celtic	Falkirk
1913-14	Celtic	Rangers	Celtic
1914-15	Celtic	Hearts	-
1915-16	Celtic	Rangers	-
1917-18	Rangers	Celtic	-
1919-20	Rangers	Celtic	Kilmarnock
1920-21	Rangers	Celtic	Partick Thistle
1921-22	Celtic	Rangers	Morton
1922-23	Rangers	Aidrieonians	Celtic
1923-24	Rangers	Aidrieonians	Airdrieonians
1924-25	Rangers	Aidrieonians	Celtic
1925-26	Celtic	Aidrieonians	St. Mirren
1926-27	Rangers	Motherwell	Celtic
1927-28	Rangers	Celtic	Rangers
1928-29	Rangers	Celtic	Kilmarnock
1929-30	Rangers	Motherwell	Rangers
1930-31	Rangers	Celtic	Celtic
1931-32	Motherwell	Rangers	Rangers
1932-33	Rangers	Motherwell	Celtic
1933-34	Rangers	Motherwell	Rangers

Season	LEAGUE Winners	Runner-up	CUP Winners
1934-35	Rangers	Celtic	Rangers
1935-36	Celtic	Rangers	Rangers
1936-37	Rangers	Aberdeen	Celtic
1937-38	Celtic	Hearts	East Fife
1938-39	Rangers	Celtic	Clyde
1946-47	Rangers	Hibernian	Aberdeen
1947-48	Hibernian	Rangers	Rangers
1948-49	Rangers	Dundee	Rangers
1949-50	Rangers	Hibernian	Rangers
1950-51	Hibernian	Rangers	Celtic
1951-52	Hibernian	Rangers	Motherwell
1952-53	Rangers	Hibernian	Rangers
1953-54	Celtic	Hearts	Celtic
1954-55	Aberdeen	Celtic	Clyde
1955-56	Rangers	Aberdeen	Hearts
1956-57	Rangers	Hearts	Falkirk
1957-58	Hearts	Rangers	Clyde
1958-59	Rangers	Hearts	St. Mirren
1959-60	Hearts	Kilmarnock	Rangers
1960-61	Rangers	Kilmarnock	Dunfermline
1961-62	Dundee	Rangers	Rangers
1962-63	Rangers	Kilmarnock	Rangers
1963-64	Rangers	Kilmarnock	Rangers
1964-65	Kilmarnock	Hearts	Celtic
1965-66	Celtic	Rangers	Rangers
1966-67	Celtic	Rangers	Celtic
1967-68	Celtic	Rangers	Dunfermline
1968-69	Celtic	Rangers	Celtic
1969-70	Celtic	Rangers	Aberdeen
1970-71	Celtic	Aberdeen	Celtic
1971-72	Celtic	Aberdeen	Celtic
1972-73	Celtic	Rangers	Rangers
1973-74	Celtic	Hibernian	Celtic
1974-75	Rangers	Hibernian	Celtic
1975-76	Rangers	Celtic	Rangers
1976-77	Celtic	Rangers	Celtic
1977-78	Rangers	Aberdeen	Rangers
1978-79	Celtic	Rangers	Rangers
1979-80	Aberdeen	Celtic	Celtic
1980-81	Celtic	Aberdeen	Rangers
1981-82	Celtic	Aberdeen	Aberdeen
1982-83	Dundee Utd	Celtic	Aberdeen
1983-84	Aberdeen	Celtic	Aberdeen
1984-85	Aberdeen	Celtic	Celtic
1985-86	Celtic	Hearts	Aberdeen
1986-87	Rangers	Celtic	St. Mirren
1987-88	Celtic	Hearts	Celtic
1988-89	Rangers	Aberdeen	Celtic
1989-90	Rangers	Aberdeen	Aberdeen
1990-91	Rangers	Aberdeen	Motherwell
1991-92	Rangers	Hearts	Rangers
1992-93	Rangers	Aberdeen	Rangers
1993-94	Rangers	Aberdeen	Dundee Utd
1994-95	Rangers	Motherwell	Celtic

*After 2 drawn games between Celtic & Rangers, the Cup was withdrawn following a riot

Scottish League Cup

Year	Winners	Runners-up
1946-47	Rangers 4	Aberdeen 0
1947-48	East Fife 1	Falkirk 1 *
Replay	East Fife 4	Falkirk 1
1948-49	Rangers 2	Raith Rovers 0
1949-50	East Fife 3	Dunfermline A 0
1950-51	Motherwell 3	Hibernian 0
1951-52	Dundee 3	Rangers 2
1952-53	Dundee 2	Kilmarnock 0
1953-54	East Fife 3	Partick Thistle 2
1954-55	Hearts 4	Motherwell 2
1955-56	Aberdeen 2	St Mirren 1
1956-57	Celtic O	Partick Thistle 0 *
Replay	Celtic 3	Partick Thistle 0
1957-58	Celtic 7	Rangers 1
1958-59	Hearts 5	Partick Thistle 1
1969-60	Hearts 2	Third Lanark 1
1960-61	Rangers 2	Kilmarnock 0
1961-62	Rangers 1	Hearts 1 *
Replay	Rangers 3	Hearts 1
1962-63	Hearts 1	Kilmarnock 0
1963-64	Rangers 5	Morton 0
1966-45	Rangers 2	Celtic 1
1965-66	Celtic 2	Rangers 1
1966-67	Celtic 1	Rangers 0
1967-68	Celtic 5	Dundee 3
1968-69	Celtic 6	Hibernian 2
1969-70	Celtic 1	St.Johnstone 0
1970-71	Rangers 1	Celtic 0
1971-72	Partick Thistle 4	Celtic 1
1972-73	Hibernian 2	Celtic 1
1973-74	Dundee 1	Celtic 0
1974-75	Celtic 6	Hibernian 3
1975-76	Rangers 1	Celtic 0
1976-77	Aberdeen 2	Celtic 1
1977-78	Rangers 2	Celtic 1
1978-79	Rangers 2	Aberdeen 1
1979-80	Dundee United O	Aberdeen 0
Replay	Dundee United 3	Aberdeen 0 **
1980-81	Dundee United 3	Dundee 0 **
1981-82	Rangers 2	Dundee United 1
1982-83	Celtic 2	Rangers 1
1983-84	Rangers 3	Celtic 2 *
1984-85	Rangers 1	Dundee United 0
1985-86	Aberdeen 3	Hibernian 0
1986-87	Rangers 2	Celtic 1
1987-88	Rangers 3	Aberdeen 3 *
	Rangers won 5-3 on penalties	
1988-89	Rangers 3	Aberdeen 2
1989-90	Aberdeen 2	Rangers 1 *
1990-91	Rangers 2	Celtic 1 *
1991-92	Hibernian 2	Dunfermline 0
1992-93	Rangers 2	Aberdeen 1
1993-94	Rangers 2	Hibernian 1
1994-95	Raith Rovers 2	Celtic 2
	Raith won 6-5 on penalties	

* after extra time
** Played at Dens Park, Dundee

Athletics

Jonathan Edwards wasn't exactly a nobody before the year began. He was a very likeable, very approachable and quite talented athlete. He had won a World Cup event and finished third in a World Championship. He was expected to perform at the highest level, but not to win. A sort of male Yvonne Murray. Then, at the beginning of June, Mel Watman and Peter Matthews in their invaluable *Athletics International* warned us that the world triple jump record was under threat. It had trickled out (the triple jump wasn't news then) that the Commonwealth record had been broken with a leap of 17.92m in Odessa, Texas in May, just five centimetres short of the world record. The athlete in question was Jamaica's James Beckford. James, who? The editorial did not mention Jonathan Edwards. Why should it?

Edwards' season started well enough a few weeks later with a British record at Loughborough in June. The Gateshead athlete jumped 17.58m to better Keith Connor's record by a single centimetre. Connor's record had been set at altitude and stood far too long (13 years), so Edward's feat still did not set the wires buzzing. Six days later, at Villeneuve D'Ascq near Lille, he won a strong triple jump competition with 17.46m. Over half a metre back was James Beckford. Still no buzzing.

In the same triple jump pit eight days later, Edward's world turned upside down. A committed Christian, it wasn't until 1993 that Edwards would even compete on a Sunday. On the second day of the European Cup, a Sunday, Edwards achieved the longest jump in history by miles. He leapt 18.43 metres; measure it out in your living room. If you can, you're extremely rich or you live in a nissan hut. It was the first leap in history over 60 feet, almost half a metre further than the world record and fully 23cms longer than Willie Banks' 18.20m in 1988 when he had a small gale at his back. God, obviously, had decided it was all right to compete on Sunday. There was only one snag. The wind reading was 2.4 metres a second: just 0.4 above the legal limit. Maybe God wasn't quite sure.

It took fully three weeks before Edwards could register a legal world record and with a Bubkaesque margin; in Salamanca he took just one centimetre out of the record with a 17.98m jump. Edwards, though, was saving it for a more worthy stage. In Gothenburg, when British athletics was bemoaning the triple catastrophe of Gunnell, Jackson and Christie all succumbing to injury, Edwards turned it on. In successive jumps he reconstructed the world record. It put Sergey Bubka (and Daniela Bartová) to shame. While they nudge the bar up a centimetre at a time, to gain the maximum number of world records, Edwards added 31 centimetres in one stroke. There were no world record bonuses on offer in Gothenburg, although Edwards did get a Mercedes for winning. Does God like Mercedes, we wonder?

Kelly Holmes was Britain's other success story in Gothenburg. She turned her back on the sport after a promising junior career and only returned in 1993. A silver and a bronze was a magnificent return and, if Holmes was not too enamoured of the colour of either medal, it says much for her competitive instincts. If she can channel those into her Olympic preparations, Holmes could do very well indeed in Atlanta.

There were silvers for Steve Backley and Tony Jarrett amidst noises of disappointment that Britain could only take home five medals. However, the absence of Gunnell and Jackson counted for much and besides these are transitional times for British athletics. The sprint results (men's anyway) from the European Junior Championships showed there is much promise in that direction and the attitude of marathon runner Peter Whitehead in coming fourth in the marathon at Gothenburg, showed that we don't always have to finish in the pack in distance events.

Christie is still there, but only just. You have to hand it to Christie. He's his own man. Anyone else aproaching the twilight zone of their career would make subtle preparations for the future. It is a well-known athletic fact this usually involves conversions that would make St Paul blush. Steve Ovett, an athlete who refused to speak to the media, is now a media man. Daley Thompson, who actively deplored those who work in the same sphere. Is now a media man. Linford Christie would be an obvious candidate to travel down the same path. Yet, if anything, his aversion to the media is growing as his career is diminishing.

To add to his arguments Christie, through his agency Nuff Respect, spent most of the summer in dispute with the British Athletic Federation. It was not the sprinter's finest hour. Having initially determined that the dispute was over money, Christie then decided it was over principles instead. In the end, it just looked like Christie was holding the sport to

---

WORLD OUTDOOR RECORDS 1995

Men

1500m	3:27.37	**Noureddine Morceli**	ALG	Nice	July 12
2000m	4:47.88	**Noureddine Morceli**	ALG	Paris	July 3
5000m	12:55.30	**Moses Kiptanui**	KEN	Rome	June 8
	12:44.39	**Haile Gebresilasie**	ETH	Zürich	July 16
10,000m	26:43.53	**Haile Gebresilasie**	ETH	Hengelo, Ned	June 5
3000msc	7:59.18	**Moses Kiptanui**	KEN	Zürich	Aug 16
Triple Jump	17.98m	**Jonathan Edwards**	GBR	Salamanca, Esp	July 18
	18.16m	**Jonathan Edwards**	GBR	Gothenburg	Aug 7
	18.29m	**Jonathan Edwards**	GBR	Gothenburg	Aug 7

Edwards broke the record with his first and second round jumps at the World Championships

Women

1000m	2:29.34	**Maria Mutola**	MOZ	Brussels	Aug 25
5000m	14:36.45	**Fernanda Ribeiro**	POR	Hechtel, Bel	July 22
400mh	52.61	**Kim Batten**	USA	Gothenburg	Aug 11
Pole Vault	4.06m	**Sun Caiyun**	CHN	Guangzhou, Chn	Mar 25
	4.08m	**Sun Caiyun**	CHN	Tiayuan, Chn	May 18
	4.08m	**Zhong Guiging**	CHN	Tiayuan	May 18
	4.10m*	**Daniela Bartová**	CZE	Ljubljana, Slo	May 21
	4.12m*	**Daniela Bartová**	CZE	Duisburg, Ger	June 18
	4.13m*	**Daniela Bartová**	CZE	Wesel, Ger	June 24
	4.14m	**Daniela Bartová**	CZE	Gateshead	July 2
	4.15m	**Daniela Bartová**	CZE	Ostrava, Svk	July 5
	4.16m*	**Daniela Bartová**	CZE	Feldkirch, Aut	July 14
	4.17m*	**Daniela Bartová**	CZE	Gisingen	July 15
	4.18m*	**Andrea Müller**	GER	Zittau, Ger	Aug 5
	4.20m*	**Daniela Bartová**	CZE	Cologne	Aug 18
	4.21m*	**Daniela Bartová**	CZE	Linz	Aug 22
	4.22m*	**Daniela Bartová**	CZE	Salgótarján, Hun	Sep 11
Triple Jump	15.50m	**Inessa Kravets**	UKR	Gothenburg	Aug 10
Hammer	66.86m*	**Mihaela Melinte**	ROM	Bucharest	Mar 4
	68.14m	**Olga Kuzenkova**	RUS	Moscow	June 5
	68.16m	**Olga Kuzenkova**	RUS	Moscow	June 18

* awaiting ratification

ransom. It was, after all, just three years earlier that the clubs, at the AGM, had voted in Radford, among others, on a ticket that would give less, not more, of the sport's money to the elite athletes and more to the clubs.

Christie's second mistake was to rule out the Olympics. He may not be the force he was in 1993, but he remains a superb athlete. The Olympic champion may believe that running 'for himself' in 1996 will keep the spotlight on him. But it won't. He may believe that by refusing to run for his country at the Games he will undermine the British Athletics Federation. But he won't. The sport and the Games are far bigger than Christie was, is, or ever will be. Jackson, of course, is his own man too and, by coincidence, was also at loggerheads with the BAF.

If the flood of money that poured into the sport in the mid-eighties has dried up, it was nevertheless encouraging that TSB had enough faith to invest £4 million over the next couple of years. If they are happy with the sport, though, they can't possibly be happy with their rankings system, which was launched this year.

Whoever dreamt up the formula is not the Einstein of sports statistics. Sally Gunnell, without a significant race during the year and having lost both her world title and her world record, is comfortably clear at the top of the women's rankings. Did she earn points for her post-race interview with Kim Batten? And Jonathan Edwards, a world title and three world records, ranking *below* Tony Jarrett, who calls himself (with commendable modesty) the Merlene Ottey of men's track because he doesn't win anything (as Ottey never used to).

Ottey did win a title (by default), but was not one of the stars of the summer. Morceli, Kiptanui and Gebresilasie (who breaks world records as frequently as the spelling of his name changes) takes the honours alongside Edwards. Gebresilasie's 5000m run was incredible. And Bartová made Bubka look like an amateur. The Czech vaulter recording 10 world records; only twice did she slip up and take the record up by two centimetres.

Diane Modahl continued to confuse the BAF. Having decided she was a sinner in December, they conferred sainthood on her in July. Unravelling the truth of the Modahl affair seems impossible. The salient fact might simply be that no court would uphold a suspension when the samples were not properly stored for two days.

There are some of us that might wonder if Chris Chataway is on a wonder drug. Now chairman of the Civil Aviation Authority the former world 5000m record holder turned out for the 100th anniversary of the Oxford and Cambridge match against Harvard and Yale at Oxford's Iffley Road in June. According to our correspondent, Chataway, on the track where he paced Bannister to a world record in 1954, ran the mile in 5 minutes and 48 seconds. Chataway is now 64. I wonder what Linford will be doing when he's 64?

Michael Johnson's win in Berlin took his sequence of 400m wins (straight finals only) to 49. Of those wins, 30 were sub-45 second runs and nine sub-44. The last time that Johnson was beaten over the distance was in 1989 at the US Indoor Championships at New York's Madison Square Garden. Johnson has won the last two world 400m titles, but has also managed a couple of world titles at 200m just to rub in his superiority.

*Q*uotes *(world champs)*

"They're going to have to do 9.79 to beat me" - **Linford Christie before the 100m final.**

"10.12 on one leg, it's still world class" - **Linford Christie after the 100m final.**

"I feel I have let a lot of people down. I did the injury a week ago, but I'm the captain and I wanted to go down with the ship" - **Christie again.**

"No more questions about Ben Johnson" - **Donovan Baily, Canadian winner of the 100m.**

"Don't talk about his style. Look, if that guy ran with his fingers up his bum he could still run 42 seconds" - **Roger Black on Michael Johnson.**

"A person can't enjoy winning that way. I clearly beat them. I know it in my heart" - **Gwen Torrence, disqualified for running out of her lane after winning the 200m final.**

"She cheated. she ran about two metres shorter than everybody else and she ran in somebody else's lane" - **Merlene Ottey on Gwen Torrence's disqualification.**

"I'm very very disturbed that Merlene would make such a comment. Not as a competitor, but as a mother, I've always tried to instil in my little boy that you don't have to cheat to get anything" - **Torrence again.**

"I could probably drink two cups of tea before he says 'set' " - **Merlene Ottey, one of many who complained about the starter's delay.**

"I don't ever wish Colin Jackson any harm. If he wasn't around, I'd win more often...." - **Tony Jarrett before the World Indoor Championship. Jackson wasn't there, but Jarrett still finished third.**

I'm going to be the Merlene Ottey of men's track and field" - **Tony Jarrett after finishing second in the World Championships. Jackson wasn't there either.**

"When I'm here, I'm representing my country, not a tribe. On the track, I'm not a Hutu, not a Tutsi. I am a Burundian" - **Arthemon Hatungimana, when asked about his tribal roots after finishing second in the 800m.**

"I still cannot drive. but if I won one more, I would try a little harder. If I had just one and I had an accident, learning to drive would be quite difficult" - **Haile Gebresilasie, before he retained his world 10,000m title in Gothenburg and so earned a second Mercedes.**

"If someone said to me, 'You can be Olympic champion, but the price you pay is you will be dead the next day', I would say 'I will take it'. That's how much being Olympic champion means to me" - **Peter Whitehead, who finished fourth in the World Championship marathon.**

"As organisers, the Greeks have shown in the past that they are horrible" - **José Maria Odrizola, president of the Spanish Federation, after Athens had been awarded the 1997 World Championships following the withdrawal of Mexico. Odrizola's outburst had nothing to do with the fact that Madrid also bid for the championships. He says.**

World Championships

Gothenburg   Aug 4-13

100m	1	**Donovan Bailey**	**CAN**	**9.97**	
	2	Bruny Surin	CAN	10.03	
	3	Ato Boldon	TRI	10.03	
	6	Linford Christie	GBR	10.12	
		Darren Braithwaite elim sf 10.28			
		Jason John elim 2nd rd 10.39			
200m	1	**Michael Johnson**	**USA**	**19.79**	
	2	Frank Fredericks	NAM	20.12	
	3	Jeff Williams	USA	20.18	
	7	John Regis	GBR	20.67	
		Solomon Wariso elim sf 20.58			
400m	1	**Michael Johnson**	**USA**	**43.39**	
	2	Butch Reynolds	USA	44.22	
	3	Greg Haughton	JAM	44.56	
	5	Mark Richardson	GBR	44.81	
	7	Roger Black	GBR	45.28	
		Adrian Patrick elim 2nd rd 46.27			
800m	1	**Wilson Kipketer**	**DEN**	**1:45.08**	
	2	Arthémon Hatungimana	BUR	1:45.64	
	3	Vebjørn Rodal	NOR	1:45.68	
		Curtis Robb elim sf 1:50.12			
		David Strang elim ht 1:48.76			
1500m	1	**Noureddine Morceli**	**ALG**	**3:33.73**	
	2	Hicham El Guerrouj	MAR	3:35.28	
	3	Venusté Niyongabo	BUR	3:35.56	
	9	Gary Lough	GBR	3:37.59	
		John Mayock elim sf 3:40.20			
		Kevin McKay elim ht 3:43.87			
5000m	1	**Ismael Kirui**	**KEN**	**13:16.77**	
	2	Khalid Boulami	MAR	13:17.15	
	3	Shem Kororia	KEN	13:17.59	
	14	John Nuttal	GBR	13:49.25	
		Rob Denmark elim 13:37.14			
10,000m	1	**Haile Gebresilasie**	**ETH**	**27:12.95**	
	2	Khalid Skah	MAR	27:14.53	
	3	Paul Tergat	KEN	27:14.70	
		Paul Evan elim 28:14.76			
Mar	1	**Martin Fiz**	**ESP**	**2:11:41**	
	2	Dionicio Ceron	MEX	2:12:13	
	3	Luiz dos Santos	BRA	2:12:49	
	4	Peter Whitehead	GBR	2:14:08	
	7	Richard Nerurkar	GBR	2:15:47	
3000msc	1	**Moses Kiptanui**	**KEN**	**8:04.16**	
	2	Christopher Koskei	KEN	8:09.30	
	3	S Shaddad Al-Asmari	SAU	8:12.95	
		Justin Chaston elim sf 8:38.90			
110mh	1	**Allen Johnson**	**USA**	**13.00**	
	2	Tony Jarrett	GBR	13.04	
	3	Roger Kingdom	USA	13.19	
		Andy Tulloch 13.62 & Neil Owen 13.92			
		both elim sf			
400mh	1	**Derrick Adkins**	**USA**	**47.98**	
	2	Samuel Matete	ZAM	48.03	
	3	Stéphane Diagana	FRA	48.14	
		Jennings & Cadogan elim hts, both dq			
HJ	1	**Troy Kemp**	**BAH**	**2.37m**	
	2	Javier Sotomayor	CUB	2.37m	
	3	Artur Partyka	POL	2.35m	
	=4	Steve Smith	GBR	2.35m	
		Dalton Grant 2.27m & Brendan Reilly			
		2.24m both elim			

PV	1	**Sergey Bubka**	**UKR**	**5.92m**	
	2	Maksim Tarasov	RUS	5.86m	
	3	Jean Galfione	FRA	5.86m	
		Neil Buckfield elim 5.55m			
LJ	1	**Ivan Pedroso**	**CUB**	**8.70m**	
	2	James Beckford	JAM	8.30m	
	3	Mike Powell	USA	8.29m	
		Fred Salle elim nj			
TJ	1	**Jonathan Edwards**	**GBR**	**18.29m**	*WR*
	2	Brian Wellman	BER	17.62m	
	3	Jerome Romain	DMN	17.59m	
		Francis Agyepong elim 16.58m			
Shot	1	**John Godina**	**USA**	**21.47m**	
	2	Mika Halvari	FIN	20.93m	
	3	Randy Barnes	USA	20.41m	
		Mike Proctor elim 18.08m			
Discus	1	**Lars Riedel**	**GER**	**68.76m**	
	2	Vladimir Dubrovshchik	BLS	65.98m	
	3	Vasily Kaptyukh	BLS	65.88m	
	9	Robert Weir	GBR	63.14m	
HT	1	**Andrey Abduvaliev**	**TJK**	**81.56m**	
	2	Igor Astapkovich	BLS	81.10m	
	3	Tibor Gecsek	HUN	80.98m	
		Peter Vivian elim 67.28m			
JT	1	**Jan Zelezny**	**CZE**	**89.58m**	
	2	Steve Backley	GBR	86.30m	
	3	Boris Henry	GER	86.08m	
	6	Mick Hill	GBR	81.06m	
Dec	1	**Dan O'Brien**	**USA**	**8695**	
	2	Eduard Hämäläinen	BLS	8489	
	3	Mike Smith	CAN	8419	
	12	Alex Kruger	GBR	7993	
20kmw	1	**Michele Didoni**	**ITA**	**1:19:59**	
	2	Valentin Massana	ESP	1:20:23	
	3	Yevgeny Misyulya	BLS	1:20:48	
	25	Stone	GBR	1:28:48	
50kmw	1	**Valentin Kononen**	**FIN**	**3:43:42**	
	2	Giovanni Perricelli	ITA	3:45:11	
	3	Robert Korzeniowski	POL	3:45:57	
		Les Morton disq			
4x100m	1	**Canada**		**38.31**	
	2	Australia		38.50	
	3	Italy		39.07	
		Great Britain elim sf 38.75			
4x400m	1	**United States**		**2:57.32**	
	2	Jamaica		2:59.88	
	3	Nigeria		3:03.18	
	5	Great Britain		3:03.75	
		(McKenzie, Hylton, Patrick, Black)			
Women					
100m	1	**Gwen Torrence**	**USA**	**10.85**	
	2	Merlene Ottey	JAM	10.94	
	3	Irina Privalova	RUS	10.96	
		Paula Thomas elim hts 11.33			
200m	1	**Merlene Ottey**	**JAM**	**22.12**	
	2	Irina Privalova	RUS	22.12	
	3	Galina Malchugina	RUS	22.37	
		Paula Thomas elim sf 23.03			
400m	1	**Marie-José Pérec**	**FRA**	**49.28**	
	2	Pauline Davis	BAH	49.96	
	3	Jearl Miles	USA	50.00	
		Melanie Neef elim sf 51.18			

800m	1	**Ana Quirot**	**CUB**	**1:56.11**
	2	Letitia Vriesde	SUR	1:56.68
	3	Kelly Holmes	GBR	1:56.95
1500m	1	**Hassiba Boulmerka**	**ALG**	**4:02.42**
	2	Kelly Holmes	GBR	4:03.04
	3	Carla Sacramento	POR	4:03.79
5000m	1	**Sonia O'Sullivan**	**IRL**	**14:46.47**
	2	Fernanda Ribeiro	POR	14:48.54
	3	Zohra Ouaziz	MAR	14:53.77
	5	Paula Radcliffe	GBR	14:57.02
		Alison Wyeth elim dnf		
10,000m	1	**Fernanda Ribeiro**	**POR**	**31:04.99**
	2	Derartu Tulu	ETH	31:08.10
	3	Tecla Lorupe	KEN	31:17.66
	6	Liz McColgan	GBR	31:40.14
	15	Jill Hunter	GBR	32:24.93
Mar	1	**Manuela Machado**	**POR**	**2:25:39**
	2	Anuta Catuna	ROM	2:26:25
	3	Ornella Ferrara	ITA	2:30:11
	22	Trudi Thompson	GBR	2:41:42
	28	Alison Rose	GBR	2:45:52
100mh	1	**Gail Devers**	**USA**	**12.68**
	2	Olga Shishigina	KZK	12.80
	3	Yulya Graudyn	RUS	12.85
		Jackie Agyepong elim sf 13.14		
400mh	1	**Kim Batten**	**USA**	**52.61** *WR*
	2	Tonja Buford	USA	52.62
	3	Deon Hemmings	JAM	53.48
		Louise Frase elim hts 57.99		
HJ	1	**Stefka Kostadinova**	**BUL**	**2:01m**
	2	Alina Astafei	GER	1.99m
	3	Inga Babakova	UKR	1.99m
		Lea Haggett elim 1.75m		
LJ	1	**Fiona May**	**ITA**	**6.98m**
	2	Niurka Montalvo	CUB	6.86m
	3	Irina Mushayilova	RUS	6.83m
TJ	1	**Inessa Kravets**	**UKR**	**15.50m** *WR*
	2	Iva Prandzheva	BUL	15.18m
	3	Anna Biryukova	RUS	15.08m
	12	Michelle Griffith	GBR	13.59m
		Ashia Hansen elim 13.61m		
SP	1	**Astrid Kumbernuss**	**GER**	**21.22m**
	2	Huang Zhihong	CHN	20.04m
	3	Svetla Mitkova	BUL	19.56m
		Judy Oakes elim 17.87m		
DT	1	**Ellina Svereva**	**BLR**	**68.64m**
	2	Ilka Wyludda	GER	67.20m
	3	Olga Chernyavskaya	RUS	66.86m
		Jackie McKernan elim 54.78m		
JT	1	**Natalya Shikolenko**	**BLR**	**67.56m**
	2	Felicea Tilea	ROM	65.22m
	3	Mikaela Ingberg	FIN	56.16m
Hep	1	**Ghada Shouaa**	**SYR**	**6651**
	2	Svetlana Moskalets	RUS	6575
	3	Rita Inancsi	HUN	6522
	7	Denise Lewis	GBR	6299
10kmw	1	**Irini Stankina**	**RUS**	**42:13**
	2	Elisabetta Perrone	ITA	42:16
	3	Yelena Nikolayeva	RUS	42:20
	35	Lisa Langford	GBR	46:06
4x100m	1	**United States**		**42.12**
	2	Jamaica		42.25
	3	Germany		43.01
4x400m	1	**United States**		**3:22.39**
	2	Russia		3:23.98
	3	Australia		3:25.88
	5	Great Britain		3:26.89

Final Medal Table

	G	S	B
United States	**12**	**2**	**5**
Belarus	2	3	2
Italy	2	2	2
Germany	2	2	2
Cuba	2	2	0
Kenya	2	1	3
Portugal	2	1	1
Canada	2	1	1
Ukraine	2	0	1
Algeria	2	0	0
Russia	1	4	7
Jamaica	1	4	2
Great Britain	1	3	1
Finland	1	1	1
Bugaria	1	1	1
Ethiopia	1	1	0
Spain	1	1	0
Bahamas	1	1	0
France	1	0	2
Tadjikistan	1	0	0
Czech Republic	1	0	0
Syria	1	0	0
Ireland	1	0	0
Denmark	1	0	0
Morocco	0	3	1
Romania	0	2	0
Burundi	0	1	1
Australia	0	1	1
Zambia	0	1	0
Surinam	0	1	0
Namibia	0	1	0
Mexico	0	1	0
Kazakhstan	0	1	0
China	0	1	0
Bermuda	0	1	0
Hungary	0	0	2
Poland	0	0	2
Brazil	0	0	1
Dominica	0	0	1
Nigeria	0	0	1
Norway	0	0	1
Trinidad	0	0	1
Saudi Arabia	0	0	1

European Cup Super League

Lille   June 24-25

100m	1 L Christie GBR	**10.05**
(+2.0)	2 A Grigoryev RUS	10.27
	3 E Madonia ITA	10.32
	3 Ghansah SWE	10.32
200m	1 L Christie GBR	**20.11**
	2 V Dologodin UKR	20.35
	3 Sokolov RUS	20.64
400m	1 M Richardson GBR	**45.43**
	2 A Nuti ITA	46.40
	3 K Just GER	46.42
800m	1 Motchebon GER	**1:46.75**
	2 A Jakubiec POL	1:47.15
	3 A Giocondi ITA	1:47.33
	8 C Winrow GBR	1:48.84
1500m	1 R Stenzel GER	**3:42.58**
	2 V Shabunin RUS	3:42.59
	3 F Cacho ESP	3:44.20
	4 G Lough GBR	3:45.11
5000m	1 G Di Napoli ITA	**13:45.57**
	2 J Nuttall GBR	13:46.82
	3 M Pancorbo ESP	13:48.93
10km	1 S Baldini ITA	**28:45.77**
	2 S Freigang GER	28:46.34
	3 A Goméz ESP	28:46.76
	6 J Hobbs GBR	29:25.92
3ksc	1 Lambruschini ITA	**8:21.94**
	2 S Brand GER	8:24.00
	3 J Rodriguez ESP	8:25.03
	5 J Chastin GBR	8:26.82
110mh	1 F Schwarthoff GER	**13.28**
(+1.0)	2 A Tulloch GBR	13.64
	3 Kolesnichenko UKR	13.67
400mh	1 L Ottoz ITA	**49.30**
	2 R Mashchenko RUS	49.49
	3 S Nylander SWE	49.64
	4 G Jennings GBR	50.43
HJ	1 S Smith GBR	**2.31m**
	2 P Sjöberg SWE	2.31m
	3 A Partyka POL	2.25m
PV	1 I Tradenkov RUS	**5.80m**
	2 P Stenlund SWE	5.60m
	3 J Garcia ESP	5.50m
	6 N Buckfield GBR	5.20m
LJ	1 S Tarasenko RUS	**8.32m**
	2 K Krause GER	8.11m
	3 V Kirilenko UKR	8.11m
	8 J Monroe GBR	7.64m
TJ	1 J Edwards GBR	**18.43m**
(w)	2 J Butkiewicz POL	17.14m
	3 A Holm SWE	16.70m

Jonathan Edward's jump was the longest in history, beating Willie Banks' 18.20m. Neither mark was legal, but Banks was aided by a +5.2 wind, Edwards by a mere +2.4 wind. Banks' record, 17.97m, later fell to Edwards at the Salamanca meeting in July

Shot	1 A Bagach UKR	**20.65m**
	2 S Buder GER	20.28m
	3 P Dal Soglio ITA	19.80m
	8 M Simson GBR	17.72m

DT	1 Lars Riedel GER	**68.76m**
	2 S Lyachov RUS	63.82m
	3 R Weir GBR	62.94m
HT	1 I Konovalov RUS	**79.66m**
	2 V Kolesnik BLS	77.00m
	3 K Kobs GER	76.32m
	7 P Vivian GBR	71.28m
JT	1 R Hecht GER	**87.24m**
	2 A Moruyev RUS	82.80m
	3 S Backley GBR	81.96m
4x100	1 Great Britain	**38.73**

(Gardener, Jarrett, Braithwaite, Christie)

	2 Germany	39.12
	3 Italy	39.19
4x400	1 Great Britain	**3:00.34**

(Thomas, Patrick, Richardson, Black)

	2 Italy	3:04.27
	3 Germany	3:04.28

FINAL POSITIONS:
1. Germany 118pts; 2. Great Britain 107; 3. Russia 105; 4. Italy 96.5; 5. Ukraine 82; 6. Sweden 78.5; 7. Spain 67; 8. Poland 66.

Women

100m	1 M Paschke GER	**11.08**
(+2.0)	2 Y Leshchova RUS	11.16
	3 D Combe FRA	11.30
	4 S Douglas GBR	11.30
200m	1 S Knoll GER	**22.45**
(+0.8)	2 M Trandenkova RUS	22.67
	3 V Fomenko UKR	22.75
	4 P Thomas GBR	22.89
400m	1 M Neef GBR	**51.35**
	2 Y Sotnikova RUS	51.81
	3 Y Rurak UKR	52.92
800m	1 Afanasyeva RUS	**1:59.26**
	2 P Djaté FRA	1:59.73
	3 N Dukhnova BLS	2:00.07
	4 S Bowyer GBR	2:01.67
1500m	1 K Holmes GBR	**4:07.02**
	2 Y Podkopayeva	4:07.88
	3 S Miroschnik UKR	4:07.94
5000m	1 Nenasheva RUS	**15:16.06**
	2 A Wyeth GBR	15:19.44
	3 T Koba UKR	15:20.97
10km	1 M Guida ITA	**32:01.75**
	2 U Pippig GER	32:14.66
	3 A Zhilyayeva RUS	32:17.62
	4 L McColgan GBR	32:22.09
100mh	1 Y Graudyn RUS	**12.86**
	2 Y Ovcharova UKR	12.88
	3 J Agyepong GBR	12.90
400mh	1 M-J Pérec FRA	**54.51**
	2 T Kurochkina BLS	55.59
	3 T Tereschchuk UKR	56.05
	7 L Fraser GBR	57.91
HJ	1 A Astafei GER	**2.00m**
	2 T Motkova RUS	1.98m
	3 T Shevchik BLS	1.96m
	6 L Haggett GBR	1.86m

LJ	1 H Drechsler GER	**7.04m**
	2 F May ITA	6.98m
	3 N Caster FRA	6.94m
	8 D Lewis	6.51m
TJ	1 A Hansen GBR	**14.37m**
	2 Y Sinchukova RUS	14.30m
	3 Z Gureyeva BLS	14.25m
SP	1 Kumbernuss GER	**20.00m**
	2 Korzhanenko RUS	18.32m
	3 J Oakes GBR	18.17m
DT	1 N Sadova RUS	**66.86m**
	2 I Wyludda GER	66.04m
	3 I Yatchenko BLS	64.46m
	5 J McKernan GBR	59.06m
JT	1 S Nerius GER	**68.42m**
	2 N Shikolenko BLS	63.42m
	3 Y Ivakina RUS	61.36m
	7 S Gibson GBR	54.38m
4x100	1 Russia	**42.74**
	2 Germany	43.15
	3 France	43.63
	4 Great Britain	44.10

(Douglas, Murphy, Jacobs, Thomas)

4x400	1 Russia	**3:24.69**
	2 Germany	3:26.23
	3 Ukraine	3:27.33
	4 Great Britain	3:28.34

(Neef, Hansen, Tunaley, Oladapo)

FINAL POSITIONS:
1. Russia 117; 2. Germany 100; 3. Great Britain 85; 4. France 75; 5. Ukraine 75; 6. Belarus 71; 7. Italy 52; 8. Poland 37.
Poland and Italy relegated to the 1st League.

European Cup

1st League

GROUP 1

Basel, Switzerland   June 10-11
Men 100m(+0.4): Sebastien Carrat FRA 10.34; 200m(+1.1): Geir Moen NOR 20.44; 400m: Matthias Rusterholz SUI 45.74; 800m: Wilson Kipketer DEN 1:46.61; 1500m: José Jesus POR 3:39.70; 5000m: Walem BEL 13:47.72; 10,000m: José Ramos POR 29:07.24; 3000msc: Marcel Laros NED 8:29.53; 110mh(-0.2): Dan Philibert FRA 13.54; 400mh: Stéphane Diagana FRA 49.02; PV: Nuño Fernandes POR 5.30m; HJ: Steinar Hoen NOR 2.25m; LJ: Gombala CZE 7.74m; TJ: Serge Hélan FRA 16.60m; SP: Anderson NOR 18.59m; DT: van Daele BEL 60.42m; HT: Christophe Epalle FRA 78.72m; JT: Robert Srovnal CZE 77.90m; 4x100m: France 39.49; 4x400m: Sui 3:05.79.

Final Positions 1. France 122.5 pts, 2. Norway 101, 3. Czech Republic 98.5, 4. Portugal 88, 5. Switzerland 84, 6. Denmark 80.5, 7. Netherlands 73.5, 8. Belgium 70 *France promoted to Super League* **Women** 100m(+0.4): Sandra Myers ESP 11.36; 200m(+1.8): Myers ESP 23.06; 400m: Myers ESP 51.75; 800m: Carla Sacramento POR 2:04.14; 1500m: Sacramento POR 4:14.32; 5000m: Fernanda Ribeiro POR 15:24.48; 10,000m: Albertina Dias POR 31:46.31; 100mh(-0.5): Abrantes POR 13.38; 400m: Mercken BEL 56.90; HJ: H Haugland NOR 1.94m; LJ: L Ninova AUT 6.38m; TJ:N Kasparkova CZE 14.12m; SP: Jacqueline Goormachtigh NED 16.78m;DT: Mette Bergmann NOR 62.78m; JT: Trine Hattestad NOR 66.18m; 4x100m: Cze 44.19; 4x400m: Cze 3:39.29. **Final Positions** 1. Spain 94; 2. Portugal 88; 3. Czech Republic 85.5; 4. Norway 82; 5. Netherlands 78; 6. Switzerland 74; 7. Belgium 56; 8. Austria 53.5. *Spain promoted to Super League.*

GROUP 2
Turku, Finland   June 10-11
Men 100m: Cojocaru ROM 10.48; 200m: Sbokos GRE 21.00; 800m: Komar BLS 1:48.36; 1500m: Oltenau ROM 3:41.75; 5000m: Papoulias GRE 13:28.59; 3000msc: Ionescu ROM 8:26.08; 110mh: Haapakoski FIN 13.54; 400mh: Kucej SVK 49.80; HJ: Isolehto FIN 2.30m; PV: Bagyula HUN 5.60m; LJ: Mladenov BUL 8.12m; TJ: Bruziks LAT 17.30m; SP: Halvari FIN 20.48; DT: Baraznovsky BLS 57.84m; HT: Kiss HUN 80.04m; JT: Räty 82.68m; 4x100m: Greece 39.55; 4x400m: Finland 3:08.60. **Final Table** 1. Finland 122; 2. Belarus 102; 3. Romania 101.5; 4. Greece 100; 5. Hungary 90.5; 6. Latvia 83.5; 7. Bulgaria 60.5; 8. Slovakia 59. *Finland promoted to the Super League.* **Women** 100m: Thanou GRE 11.42; 200m: Z Georgieva BUL 23.47; 400m: D Georgieva BUL 51.69; 800m: Strashilova BUL 2:05.91; 1500m: Strashilova BUL 4:14.64; 5000m: Szabo ROM 15:15.45; 10,000m: Sandell FIN 32:10.19; 100mh: Donkova BUL 13.45; 400mh: Tirlea ROM 56.34; HJ: Iagar ROM 1.92m; LJ: Prandzheva BUL 6.84m; TJ: Prandzheva 14.37m; SP:

Mitkova BUL 18.44m; DT: Grasu ROM 61.96m; JT: Uppa FIN 61.56; 4x100m: Bulgaria 44.42; 4x400m: Romania 3:32.80. **Final Table** 1. Bulgaria 117; 2. Romania 100; 3. Finland 98; 4. Hungary 72; 5. Greece 68; 6. Sweden 65; 7. Lithuania 46; 8. Turkey 39. *Bulgaria promoted to the Super League.*

European Cup
2nd League

Group 1
Tallin, Estonia   June 11-12
Men's Final Positions 1. AUT 109; 2. IRL 100; 3. YUG 99; 4. EST 82; 5. ISL 72; 6. LIT 50; 7. Small Nat'ns 43.

Women's Final P's 1. DEN 97; 2. ISL 81; 3. IRL 74; 4. EST 72; 5. LAT 69; 6. YUG 47; 7. Small Nations 35.

Group 2
Velenje, Slovenia   June 11-12
Men's Final Positions 1. SLO 101; 2. TUR 95; 3. CRO 94; 4. CYP 91; 5. MOL 73; 6. ISR 71; 7. ALB 30. **Women's Final P's** 1. SLO 106; 2. CRO 88; 3. SVK 79; 4. CYP 64; 5. MOL 49; 6. ALB 42; 7. ISR 41.

European Cup
Combined Events
SUPER LEAGUE
Decathlon
Valladolid, Spain   July 1-2
1. Tomás Dvorák CZE 8347 (10.74/7.73m/15.40m/2.01m/48.34/ 14.39/42.26m/4.60m/61.32m /4:31.96); 2. Alex Kruger GBR 8131; 3. Henrik Dagard SWE 8114 Teams 1. Czech Republic 23,826; 2. France 23,462; 3. Sweden 23,408.
Heptathlon
Helmond, Netherlands   July 1-2
1. Denise Lewis GBR 6299 (13.66/1.78m/13.19m/25.13 /6.52m/49.34m/2:18.54); 2. Sharon Jaklofsky NED 6197; 3. Anzela Atroschenko BLS 6186; Teams 1. Belarus 18,150; 2. Germany 17,755; 3. Russia 17,705.

DIVISION 1
Decathlon
Helmond   July 1-2
1. Paul Meier GER 8199 (11.00/7.27m/15.41m/2.13m/50.34 /15.08/46.64m/4.60m/63.54m /4:36.98); 2. Indrek Kaseorg EST 8131; 3. Valery Belusov RUS 8099; Teams 1. Germany 24,087; 2.

Switzerl'd 23,106; 3. Estonia 22,802.
Heptathlon
Valladolid   July 1-2
1. Rita Ináncsi HUN 6435 (13.76/1.87m/14.47m/24.48/6.56m /43.02m/2:18.55); 2. Karin Periginelli ITA 6047; 3. Tiia Hautala FIN 5809. Teams 1. Hungary 17,544; 2. Finland 16,979; 3. Italy 16,931.

European Junior Championships
Nyiregyhaza, Hungary   July 27-30
Men 100m: Chambers GBR 10.41; 200m: Devonish GBR 21.04; 400m: Hylton GBR 45.97; 800m: Parra ESP 1:45.90; 1500m: Estevez ESP 3:45.74; 5000m/10,000m: Zwierzchiewski FRA 13:55.75/29:46.42; 3000msc Alvarez ESP 8:50.75; 110mh: Pieters BEL 14.06; 400mh: Hechler GER 50.42; HJ: Frosen FIN 2.19m; PV: Smiryagin RUS 5:50m; LJ: Schurenko UKR 7.78m; TJ: Servius FRA 15.71m: SP: Reinikainen FIN 17.20m; DT: Krawczyk POL 58.22m; HT: Ziolkowski POL 75.24m; JT: Nicolay GER 76.88; Dec: Lindqvist FIN 7363; 10kW: Erm GER 40:51.38; 4x100: GBR 39.43; 4x400: GBR 3:07.09. **Women** 100m: Bangue FRA 11.48; 200m: Ivanova BUL 23.44; 400m: Kotlyarova RUS 52.03; 800m: Cosoleanu ROM 2:04.15; 1500m: Chojecka POL 4:17.29; 3000m: Costescu ROM 9:13.14; 100mh: Ovcharova UKR 13.09; 400mh: Tilea ROM 56.04; HJ: Styopina UKR 1.91m; LJ: Ferga FRA 6.56m; TJ: Marinova BUL 13.90m; SP/DT: de Bruin NED 17.76m/57.46m; JT: Uppa FIN 60.72m; Hep: Monteil FIN 5546; 5kW: Avoila POR 22:13.23; 4x100: GER 44.77; 4x400: FRA 3:32.79.

IAAF Grand Prix I

Sao Paulo International

Sao Paulo, Brazil   May 14

Men 100m(-0.6): Michael Green JAM 10.13; 200m(-2.4): Michael Johnson USA 20.22; 400m: Inaldo Sena BRA 45.58; 800m: Jose Parrilla USA 1:45.15; 1500m: Joaquim Cruz BRA 3:40.49; 3000: Simon Chemoiywo KEN 7:43.15; 110mh(-0.8): Jack Pierce USA 13.30; 400mh: Araujo BRA 49.06; PV: Igor Trandenkov RUS 5.85m; LJ: Ivan Pedroso CUB 8.54w; JT: Jan Zelezny CZE 88.20m. **Women** 100m(+1.1): Mary Onyali NGR 11.23; 200m(-2.0): Gwen Torrence USA 22.43; 400m: Ximena Restrepo COL 52.25; 800m: Maria Mutola MOZ 1:58.79; 3000m: Olga Churbanova RUS 9:02.19; 400mh: Kim Batten USA 53.86; HJ: Yelena Gulyayeva RUS 1.99m; TJ: Anna Biryukova RUS 14.73; SP: Astrid Kumbernuss GER 19.96m.

New York Games

New York   May 21

Men 100m(+2.2): Bruny Surin CAN 9.92; 200m(+1.9): Carl Lewis USA 20.28; 400m: Derek Mills USA 44.86; 800m: Wilson Kipketer DEN 1:47.51; 3000m: Shaun Creighton AUS 7:46.02; 110mh(+2.1): Roger Kingdom USA 13.18; PV: Igor Potapovich KZK 5.78m; LJ: Kareem Streete-Thompson USA 8.56m; DT: Nick Sweeney IRL 59.88m. **Women** 200m(+0.6): Gwen Torrence USA 22.04; 400m: Cathy Freeman AUS 51.52; 3000m: Olga Churbanova RUS 9:03.14; 400mh: Deon Hemmings JAM 54.15; HJ: Tisha Waller USA 1.94m; Astrid Kumbernuss GER 19.97m.

Bruce Jenner Classic

San Jose   May 27

Men 100m(-0.6): Ray Stewart JAM 10.23; 200m(+2.5): Michael Johnson 19.99; 800m: Sammy Langat KEN 1:45.34; 110mh(0.0): Derek Knight USA 13.42; PV: Nick Hysong USA 5.65m; LJ: Erick Waldner USA 8.18m; DT: John Godina USA 64.92m; JT: Tom Pukstys USA 80.28m. **Women** 200m(+1.7): Cathy Freeman AUS 22.50; 800m: Meredith Rainey USA 2:00.91; 3000m: Mykytok USA 8:52.54; 100mh(+2.0): Doris Williams USA 13.02; 400mh: Tonja Buford USA 55.28; HJ: Tisha Waller USA 1.98m; SP: Connie Price-Smith USA 19.58m.

Golden Gala

Rome   June 8

Men 100m(+0.8): Davidson Ezinwa NGR 10.10; 200m: Frankie Fredericks NAM 20.42; 800m: Andrea Giocondi ITA 1:44.85; 2000m: Venuste Niyongabo BUR 4:54.02; 5000m: Moses Kiptanui KEN 12:55.30 *WR*, 2nd Daniel Komen KEN 12:56.15; 3000msc: Richard Kosgei KEN 8:07.47; 110mh(+0.7): Colin Jackson GBR 13.18; 400mh: Samuel Matete ZAM 48.40; PV: Sergey Bubka UKR 5.90m; SP: Aleksandr Klimenko UKR 20.06m; JT: Raymond Hecht GER 85.26m. **Women** 200m(+2.1): Merlene Ottey JAM 22.29; 3000m: Olga Churbanova RUS 8:41.42; 400m: Deon Hemmings JAM 54.20; HJ: Alina Astafei GER 2.00m; LJ: Fiona May ITA 6.74m; TJ: Iva Prandzheva BUL 14.51m; SP: Astrid Kumbernuss GER 20.08m.

Meeting BNP de Paris

Paris   July 3

Men 100m(+0.8): Linford Christie GBR 10.06; 200m(+3.7): Michael Johnson USA 19.92; 800m: Bruno Konczylo FRA 1:46.12; 2000m: Noureddine Morceli ALG 4:47.88 *WR*; 5000m: Haile Gebresilasie ETH 13:07.81; 3000msc: Mark Croghan USA 8:16.72; 110mh(+3.0): Mark Crear USA 13.08; 400mh: Derrick Adkins USA 47.87; PV: Sergey Bubka UKR 5.90m; LJ: Ivan Pedroso CUB 8.52; JT: Raymond Hecht GER 85.64. **Women** 100m(+0.8): Merlene Ottey JAM 11.00; 200m(+0.1): Mary Onyali NGR 22.53; 800m: Meredith Rainey USA 1:59.12; 100mh(+1.0): Olga Shishigina KZK 12.52; 400mh: Marie-J Pérec FRA 54.48; HJ: Alina Astafei GER 2.01m; TJ: Iva Prandzheva BUL 14.71m; JT: N Shikolenko BLR 65.90m.

Athletissima '95

Lausanne   July 5

Men 100m(+2.3): Mike Marsh USA 9.96; 200m(+2.3): Michael Johnson USA 19.96; 400m: Darnell Hall USA 44.34; 800m: Kibitok KEN 1:46.09; 1500m: Vénuste Niyongabo BUR 3:32.37; 5000m: Ismael Kirui KEN 13:07.80; 110mh(+1.5): Roger Kingdom USA 13.11; 400mh: Stéphane Diagana FRA 47.37 *ER*; PV: Maksim Tarasov RUS 5.80m; LJ: Ivan Pedroso CUB 8.56; HT: Baláks Kiss HUN 79.00m. **Women** 100m(+1.9): Merlene Ottey JAM 10.92; 200m(+1.6): Merlene Ottey JAM 22.07; 3000m: Fernanda Ribeiro POR 8:41.99; 100mh(+2.2): Olga Shishigina KZK 12.41; 400mh: Tonja Buford USA 53.63; HJ: Irina Babakova UKR 2.02m; TJ: Iva Prandzheva BUL 14.97m; DT: M Bergmann NOR 66.58m.

KP Games

London   July 7

Men 100m(-0.3): Donovan Bailey CAN 10.16; 200m(-0.5): Jeff Williams USA 20.47; 400m: Darnell Hall USA 44.94; 800m: Brandon Rock USA 1:44.97; 1500m: Vénuste Niyongabo BUR 3:33.30; 10,000m: Aloÿs Nizigama BUR 27:20.38; 3000msc: Patrick Sang KEN 8:08.11; 110mh (-0.3): Tony Jarrett GBR 13.20; 400mh: Derrick Adkins USA 47.74; HJ: Troy Kemp BAH 2.31m; PV: Okkert Brits RSA 5.85m; TJ: Jonathan Edwards GBR 17.69; JT: Steve Backley GBR 88.54. **Women** 100m(+0.7): Simmone Jacobs GBR 11.34; 200m(-0.5): M Ottey JAM 22.32; 800m: Kelly Holmes GBR 1:58.77; 5000m: Sonia O'Sullivan IRL 14:47.64; 100mh(-0.5): Olga Shishigina KZK 12.89; 400mh: Tonja Buford USA 54.07; TJ: Anna Biryukova RUS 14.81m; SP: A Kumbernuss GER 20.79m.

DN Galan

Stockholm   July 10

Men 100m(-0.5): Dennis Mitchell USA 10.21; 200m(-0.1): Michael Johnson USA 20.15; 800m: Jose Parilla USA 1:45.48; 5000m: Shem Kororia KEN 13:02.80; 3000msc: Christopher Koskei KEN 8:06.86; 110mh(+0.8): Mark Crear USA 13.20; 400mh: Danny Harris USA 48.46; HJ: Steinar Hoen NOR 2.29m; LJ: Kareem Streete-Thompson USA 8.16m; SP: Andrey Nemchaninov UKR 19.86m; JT: Jan Zelezny CZE 87.78m. **Women** 200m(-0.1): Gwen Torrence USA 22.24; 1000m: Maria Mutola MOZ 2:30.72; 5000m: Tecla Lorupe KEN 15:08.86; 100mh(+0.2): Olga Shishigina KZK 12.57; HJ: Irina Babakova UKR 1.99m; TJ: I Kravets UKR 14.65m; JT: T Hattestad NOR 64.20m.

Nikaïa Meeting
Nice   July 12
Men 200m(-0.7): John Regis GBR 20.26; 1000m:
Mahjoub Haida MAR 2:14.69; 1500m: Noureddine
Morceli ALG 3:27.37 *WR*; 2000m: Vénuste Niyongabo
BUR 4:48.69; 3000m: Salah Hissou MAR 7:35.66;
3000msc: Eliud Barngetuny KEN 8:09.24; 110mh(-1.0):
Florian Schwarthoff GER 13.29; 400mh: Danny Harris
USA 47.98; HJ: Troy Kemp BAH 2.38m; PV: Okkert Brits
RSA 5.85m; JT: Jan Zelezny CZE 87.10m.
Women 200m(+0.6): Melinda Gainsford AUS 22.63;
400m: Marie-José Pérec FRA 50.20; 800m: Letitia
Vriesde SUR 1:58.68; Mile: Sonia O'Sullivan IRL 4:23.61;
3000m: Elena Fidatov ROM 8:45.71; 100mh(-0.8): Brigita
Bukovec SLO 12.89; 400mh: Ionela Tirlea ROM 55.26;
TJ: Anna Biryukova RUS 14.91m; SP: Astrid
Kumbernuss GER 20.64.

Mobil Bislett Games
Oslo   July 21
Men 100m(-0.8): Linford Christie GBR 10.12;
200m(+2.2): Geir Moen NOR 20.40; 400m: Michael
Johnson USA 43.86; 800m: Wilson Kipketer DEN
1:43.98; 1500m: Vénuste Niyongabo BUR 3:30.79;
3000m: Dieter Baumann GER 7:33.56; 5000m: Shem
Kororia KEN 13:05.72; 3000msc: Moses Kiptanui KEN
8:03.36; 110mh(-0.6): Tony Jarrett GBR 13.31; HJ: Javier
Sotomayor CUB 2.31m; JT: Raymond Hecht GER
92.60m. Women 200m(-1.7): Gwen Torrence USA 22.36;
3000m: Sonia O'Sullivan IRL 8:34.31; 5000m: Lynn
Jennings USA 15: 18.20; 100mh(+2.9): Solli NOR 13.17;
400mh: Marie-José Pérec FRA 53.92; HJ: Alina Astafei
GER 1.96m; TJ: Anna Biryukova RUS 14.38m; DT: Ilka
Wyludda GER 68.54m; JT: N Shikolenko BLR 68.36.

Herculis Vittel
Monte Carlo   July 25
Men 100m(-0.1): Donovan Bailey CAN 10.05;
200m(+0.2): Frankie Fredericks NAM 20.23; 400m: Greg
Haughton JAM 44.61; 800m: Wilson Kipketer DEN
1:42.87; 1500m: Noureddine Morceli ALG 3:27.52;
3000m: Moses Kiptanui KEN 7:27.18; 3000msc: Eliud
Barngetuny KEN 8:05.01; 110mh(+0.4): Mark Crear USA
13.15; 400mh: Derrick Adkins USA 47.79; HJ: Steinar
Hoen NOR 2.32m; PV: Dean Starkey USA 5.80m; LJ:
Ivan Pedroso CUB 8.58m; DT: Lars Riedel GER 69.08m.
Women 200m(0.0): Gwen Torrence USA 21.81; 400m:
Cathy Freeman AUS 50.34; 800m: Maria Mutola MOZ
1:57.40; 1500m: Sonia O'Sullivan 3:58.85; 100mh(+0.9):
Olga Shishigina KZK 12.61; 400mh: Kim Batten USA
53.85; TJ: Galina Chistyakova RUS 14.34m; JT: Tanja
Damaske GER 63.90m.

Weltklasse
Zürich   Aug 16
Men 100m(-1.0): Linford Christie GBR 10.03; 400m:
Michael Johnson USA 43.88; 800m: Wilson Kipketer
DEN 1:42.87; 1500m: Azzeddine Seddiki MAR 3:34.09;
1 Mile: Noureddine Morceli ALG 3:45.19; 5000m: Haile
Gebresilasie ETH 12:44.39 *WR*; 3000msc: Moses
Kiptanui KEN 7:59.18 *WR*; 110h(+1.5): Mark Crear USA
13.18; 400mh: Derrick Adkins USA 47.65; HJ: Troy Kemp
BAH 2.30m; PV: Sergey Bubka UKR 5.90m; LJ: Ivan
Pedroso CUB 8.60m; DT: Lars Riedel GER 67.36m; JT:
Raymond Hecht GER 87.30m.

Women 200m(-0.7): Gwen Torrence USA 21.98; 800m:
Maria Mutola MOZ 1:55.93; 3000m: Sonia O'Sullivan IRL
8:27.57; 100mh(-2.0): Gail Devers USA 12.75; 400m:
Tonja Buford USA 52.90; TJ: Anna Biryukova RUS
15.03m; JT: Natalya Shikolenko BLR 71.18.

Weltklasse
Cologne   Aug 18
Men 100m(+0.2): Donovan Bailey CAN 10.11; 800m:
Wilson Kipketer DEN 1:44.09; 1500m: Hicham El
Guerrouj MAR 3:31.16; 3000m: Moses Kiptanui KEN
7:28.04; 110mh(+0.2): Allen Johnson USA 12.98; 400mh:
Danny Harris USA 47.63; PV: Okkert Brits RSA 6.03m;
DT: Dmitry Shevchenko RUS 68.04m. Women 200m:
Gwen Torrence USA 21.77; 800m: Ana Quirot CUB
1:58.21; 1 Mile: Sonia O'Sullivan IRL 4:24.13; 5000m:
Gabriela Szabo ROM 14:53.91; 100mh(-0.1): Olga
Shishigina KZK 12.80; 400mh: Kim Batten USA 53.29;
HJ: Irina Babakova UKR 2.02m; PV: Daniela Bartová
CZE 4.20 *WR*; SP: Astrid Kumbernuss GER 20.66m.

Memorial Ivo Van Damme
Brussels   Aug 25
Men 100m(-0.4): Linford Christie GBR 10.08;
200m(0.0): Frank Fredericks; 400m: Michael Johnson
USA 44.63; 800m: Sammy Langat KEN 1:45.08; 1500m:
Venusté Niyongabo BUR 3:31.68; 3000m: Noureddine
Morceli ALG 7:27.50; 10,000m: Worku Bikila ETH
27:06.44; 3000msc: Moses Kiptanui 7:59.52; 400m:
Samuel Mataete ZAM 47.52; HJ: Javier Sotomayor CUB
2.33m; LJ: Ivan Pedroso CUB 8.36m; TJ: Jonathan
Edwards GBR 17.60m; JT: Jan Zelezney CZE 90.50m.
Women 200m(+1.0): Gwen Torrence USA 21.86; 400m:
Cathy Freeman AUS 50.21; 1000m: Maria Mutola MOZ
2:29.34 *WR*; 5000m: S O'Sullivan IRL 14.50.69; 400mh:
Kim Batten USA 54.03; TJ: Inessa Kravets UKR 14.65m;
JT: Natalya Shikolenko BLR 68.42m

ISTAF '95
Berlin   Sep 1
Men 100m(0.0): Donovan Bailey CAN 10.10; 400m:
Michael Johnson USA 44.56; 800m: Atle Douglas NOR
1:44.95; 1 Mile: Nourredine Morceli ALG 3:48.26; 5000m:
Haile Gebresilasie ETH 12:53.19; 3000msc: Johnstone
Kipkoech 8:16.51; 110mh(-0.3): Mark Crear USA 13.28;
HJ: Jaroslaw Kotewicz POL 2.30m; PV: Okkert Brits RSA
5.59m; TJ: Jonathan Edwards GBR 17.35m; JT: Jan
Zelezney CZE 91.30m. Women 200m(+0.9): Gwen
Torrence USA 21.98; 400m: Cathy Freeman AUS 50.98;
800m: Maria Mutola MOZ 1:57.61; 5000m: S O'Sullivan
IRL 14.41.40; 400mh: Deon Hemmings JAM 54.40; HJ:
Irina Babakova UKR 2.01m; JT: Natalya Shikolenko BLR
67.72m

Quotes

"Athletes everywhere must know that the war against drugs is the one that we will never abandon. We may lose some battles, but we will fight on and fight on. And if we lose, we will fight again. This is a war which, for their sakes, *must* be won" - **Peter Radford, chief executive of the British Athletic Federation, in an impassioned speech to the IAAF Congress at Gothenburg, arguing that the four-year drugs ban should not be reduced to a two-year ban. It was not. The vote going 137-49 in favour of Radford's argument.**

"I was incredibly shocked. I've worked for 23 years as a foreign correspondent, interviewed dictators and other nuts, but I've never met anyone who behaves like Nebiolo" - **Britt-Maria Matteson, interviewer on Swedish television. Nebiolo stopped an interview with Matteson, when he didn't like the line of questioning, and asked her what she would think if he asked her how many men she had slept with.**

"Primo Nebiolo Go Home" - *Goteborg-Posten* **headline prior to the World Championships in Gothenburg.**

"He's such a nice guy, that's the problem. I can't get any energy from him, any rage. I can't go grrrrr" - **Mike Powell on Ivan Pedroso. The Cuban exceeded Powell's world long jump record at altitude in Sestriere, but the distance did not forward for ratification following reports that a man in a blue jacket had stood in front of the wind gauge. Italy and long jumps; it's a perpetual problem.**

"I've heard you can't be a world-class sprinter coming from a cold, northern country and being white. But as everyone on the track, I have two arms and two legs so on that we're equal. I don't think I have a handicap" - **Geir Moen, the Norwegian sprinter, after winning the world indoor title.**

"I'm at the stage where I'm so fed up with it all that I could walk out of the sport any day" - **Linford Christie, announcing his decision not to compete in the 1996 Olympics.**

"IS LINFORD JUST A BIG GIRL'S BLOUSE?" - July front cover headline from *The Voice.*

"I believe the world is consumed by Satan and it is important to shine forth with the light" - **Jonathan Edwards.**

"We simply couldn't take it anymore. We had absolutely no freedom and were on the brink of going crazy" - **Wang Junxia, world 10,000m record holder, explaining the break-up of coach Ma Junren's 'army'.**

"I know Diane is innocent. If she was found guilty by another five hearings, I would know she's innocent" - **Kevin McKay, clubmate of Diane Modahl after the first BAF hearing in December 1994 found her guilty. The second BAF hearing, seven months later, found her not guilty.**

"I need an intravenous drip. I need one every time I run here" - **Athol Rand, a systems manager from Durban, after finishing his 16th Comrades Marathon in South Africa.**

Grand Prix Final

Monaco   Sep 9

Men 100m(+0.1): Damien Marsh AUS 10.13; 200m(-0.3): Michael Johnson USA 19.93; 800m: Benson Koech KEN 1:45.27; 1500m: Nourredine Morceli ALG 3:28.37; 3000m: Haile Gebresilasie ETH 7:35.90; 3000msc: Moses Kiptanui KEN 8:02.45; 110mh(+0.6): Mark Crear USA 13.07; PV: Okkert Brits RSA 5.95m; LJ: Ivan Pedroso CUB 8.49m; DT: Dmitry Shevchenko RUS 67.94m; JT: Jan Zelezny CZE 92.28m. **Women** 200m(+0.1): Gwen Torrence USA 22.20; 800m: Maria Mutola MOZ 1:55.72; 3000m: Sonia O'Sullivan IRL 8:39.94; 400mh: Kim Batten USA 53.49; HJ: Irina Babakova UKR 2.03m; TJ: Anna Biryukova RUS 14.99m; SP: Astrid Kumbernuss GER 20.20m

Grand Prix - Final Placings

MEN 1. Moses Kiptanui KEN 84pts $100,000; 2. Jan Zelezny CZE 72 $50,000; 3. Mark Crear USA 72 $30,000; 4. Michael Johnson USA $20,000; 5. Ivan Pedroso CUB $15,000; 6. Haile Gebresilasie ETH $13,000; 7. Okkert Brits RSA $12,000; 8. Lars Riedel GER $10,000

WOMEN 1. Maria Mutola MOZ 78pts $100,000; 2. Anna Biryukova RUS 72 $50,000; 3. Gwen Torrence USA 72 $30,000; 4. Sonia O'Sullivan IRL 72 $20,000; 5. Astrid Kumbernuss GER 72 $15,000; 6. Irina Babakova UKR 70 $13,000; 7. Kim Batten USA 69 $12,000; 8. Tonja Buford USA 64 $10,000

IAAF Grand Prix II

Slovnaft '95

Bratislava   May 30

Men 100m(+0.8): Marcus Green USA 10.19; 200m(+0.9): Andrew Tynes BAH 20.50; 800m: Kipkemboi Langat KEN 1:45.93; 300m: Venuste Niyongabo BUR 7:39.19; 110mh(+0.6): Roger Kingdom USA 13.35; 400mh Oleg Tverdokhleb UKR 48.64; PV: Tim Lobinger GER 5.70m; TJ: James Beckford JAM 17.23m; DT: Lars Riedel GER 64.34m; JT: Jan Zelezny CZE 90.80m. **Women** 100m(+0.2): Juliet Cuthbert JAM 11.17; 3000m: Sonia O'Sullivan IRL 8:45.50; 400mh: Tatyana Kurochkina BLR 54.69; HJ: Irina Babakova UKR 2.03m; TJ: Galina Chistyakova RUS 14.42; SP: Viktoria Pavlysh UKR 18.86m.

St Denis - L'Humanité

June 1

Men 100m(+0.3): Glenroy Gilbert CAN 10.19; 200m(+0.9): Frankie Fredericks NAM 20.41; 1500m: Vyacheslav Shabunin RUS 3:36.66; 5000m: Sghir MAR 13:16.80; 3000msc: Matthew Birir KEN 8:12.95; 110mh(+1.7): Antti Haapakoski FIN 13.47; 400mh: Derrick Adkins USA 48.11; HJ: Artur Partyka POL 2.30m; JT: Andrey Moruyev RUS 83.18m. **Women** 100m(+0.3): Zhanna Petusevich UKR 11.10; 200m(+0.9): Zhanna Petusevich UKR 22.79; 800m: Luciana Mendes BRA 2:00.64; 5000m: Fernanda Ribeiro POR 14:55.02; 100mh(+0.9): Brigita Bukovec SLO 12.89; 400mh: Deon Hemmings JAM 55.14; LJ: Heike Drechsler GER 6.80m; JT: Natalya Shikolenko BLR 68.22m.

Gran Premio Diputacion Provincial

Seville   June 3

Men 200m: Jeff Williams USA 20.59; 1500m: Noureddine Morceli ALG 3:32.99; 5000m: Paul Tergat KEN 13:22.12; 3000msc: Matthew Birir KEN 8:14.59; 110mh(-1.9): Courtney Hawkins USA 13.46; LJ: Ivan Pedroso CUB 8.49w; HT: Igor Astapkovich BLR 81.62. **Women** 100m(-2.1): Ogunkoya NGR 11.47; 800m: Lyudmila Rogachova RUS 2:00.64; 5000m: Derartu Tulu ETH 15:40.03; 400mh: Dion Hemmings JAM 54.97; HJ: Yelena Topchina RUS 1.93m; TJ: Inna Lasovskaya RUS 15.05w; SP: Valentina Fedyushina UKR 19.42.

Znamensky Memorial

Moscow   June 5

100m(+0.7): Michael Green JAM 10.19; 1500m: N Morceli ALG 3:33.25; 5000m: P Tergat KEN 13:24.55; 3000msc: M Kiptanui KEN 8:18.46; 110mh(+0.6): Igor Kovac SVK 13.40; 400m: Derrick Adkins USA 48.08; PV: M Tarasov RUS 5.80m; TJ: D Kapustin RUS 17.42w; DT: Lars Riedel GER 68.06m; HT: Igor Astapkovich BLR 78.90m; JT: A Moruyev RUS 81.08m. **Women** 100m(+1.6): Z Pintusevich UKR 11.14; 400m: T Zakharova RUS 51.12; 800m: Y Afanasyeva RUS 1:59.20; 1500m: Sonia O'Sullivan IRL 4:17.38; 5000m: V Nenasheva RUS 15:16.29; 100mh(+2.0): L Yurkova BLR 13.10; 400mh: T Kurochkina BLR 55.14; HJ: T Motkova RUS 1.98m; LJ: Inessa Kravets UKR 6.97m; TJ: Inna Lasovskaya RUS 14.89m; SP: Irina Khudoroshkina RUS 19.12m; HT: Olga Kuzenkova RUS 68.14m *WR*.

Adriaan Paulen Memorial

Hengleo   June 5

Men 100m(+0.6): Davidson Ezinwa HGR 10.22; 800m: Mahjoub MAR 1:45.73; 1500m: Hlcham El Guerrouj MAR 3:34.28; 10,000m: Haile Gebresilasie ETH 26:43.53; 3000msc: Larbi El Khattabi MAR 8:12.02; 110mh(+0.6): Mark McKoy AUT 13.32; PV: Riaan Botha RSA 5.65m. **Women** 100m(+1.5): Merlene Ottey JAM 11.00; 800m: M Rainey USA 1:58.65; 5000m: Paula Radcliffe GBR 15:02.87; 100mh(+1.3): Jackie Adyepong GBR 130.06; 400mh: S Rieger GER 55.71; HJ: S Kirchmann AUT/Y Zhdanova RUS 1.94m; SP: A Kumbernuss GER 20.48.

World Games

Helsinki   June 28

Men 100m(+1.4): Frankie Fredericks NAM 10.10; 200m(+1.1): Geir Moen NOR 20.40; 400m: Darnell Hall USA 45.32; 800m: Vebjörn Rodal NOR 1:46.36; 1500m: Jones NZL 3:40.65; 5000m: Zeroual MAR 13:20.20; 110mh(+0.6): Tony Jarrett GBR 13.13; 400m: Maurice Mitchell USA 49.29; PV: Viktor Chistyakov RUS 5.85m; SP: Mika Halvari FIN 20.71m; JT: S Räty FIN 83.94m. **Women** 200m(+1.2): Galina Malchugina RUS 22.84; 400m: Naylor AUS 52.59; 800m: Kelly Holmes GBR 2:00.43; 5000m: Gabriela Szabo ROM 15:08.64; LJ: V Vershinina UKR 6.64m; JT: N Shikolenko BLR 66.22m.

BUPA Games
Gateshead   July 2
Men 100m(+1.2): Michael Green JAM 10.19; 200m(+2.2): Jeff Williams USA 20.58; 400m: Darnell Hall USA 45.14; 800m: Vebjörn Rodal NOR 1:45.55; 1500m: John Mayock GBR 3:40.09; 5000m: Shadrack Hoff RSA 13:14.16; 110mh(+3.0): Allen Johnson USA 13.15; 400mh: Igor Tverdokhleb UKR 49.74; HJ: Mark Mandy IRL 2.25m; PV: Neil Winter GBR 5.20m; TJ: J Edwards GBR 18.03m; JT: Vladimir Sasimovich BLR 83.26m. **Women** 100m(+0.9): Savathea Fynes BAH 11.31; 200m(+0.9): Cathy Freeman AUS 23.10; 1500m: Kelly Holmes GBR 4:04.20; 100mh(+2.0): Gillian Russell JAM 12.93;400mh: Deon Hemmings JAM 54.68; PV: Daniela Bártová CZE 4.14m WR; TJ: Maria Sokova RUS 14.21m; SP: Irina Khudoroshkina RUS 18.86m.

Zipfer Grand Prix
Linz   Aug 22
Men 100m(-0.7): Bruny Surin CAN 10.09; 200m(-0.2): Damien Marsh AUS 20.32; 800m: Johnny Gray USA 1:45.07; 3000msc: Patrick Sang KEN 8:20.28; 110mh (-0.7): Allen Johnson USA 13.10; 400mh: Winthrop

Graham JAM 48.33; LJ: Ivan Pedroso CUB 8.66m; DT: Lars Riedel GER 67.16m. **Women** 100m(-0.2): Merlene Ottey JAM 11.00; 1500m: Margarita Maruseva RUS 4:08.13; 3000m: Yvonne Graham JAM 8:48.43; 100mh(+0.2): Olga Shishgina KZK 12.78; 400mh: Kim Batten USA 54.46; HJ: Yelena Gulyayeva RUS 1.96m; PV: Daniela Bartová CZE 4.21m WR; LJ: Heike Drechsler GER 7.07m; SP: Huang Zhihong CHN 20.07m; JT: Natalya Shikolenko BLR 66.74.

Rieti '95
Rieti   Sep 5
Men 100m(+0.8): Linford Christie GBR 10.20; 400m: Samson Kitur KEN 44.93; 800m: Atle Douglas NOR 1:43.69; 1500m: Venusté Niyongabo BUR 3:32.57; 3000m: Nourredine Morceli ALG 7:29.36; 2 Miles: Moses Kiptanui KEN 8:13.40; 400mh: Winthrop Graham JAM 48.50; TJ: Jonathan Edwards GBR 17.29; SP: Corrado Fantini ITA 18.75m. **Women** 200m(-1.2): Irina Privalova RUS 22.84; 800m: Jearl Miles USA 2:00.86; Mile: Sonia O'Sullivan IRL 4:29.82; 400mh: T Kurochkina BLR 55.12; HJ: Stefka Kostadinova BUL 2.00m; LJ: Heike Drechsler GER 6.81m; SP: Irina Khudorozhkina RUS 18.59m

Other Meetings

Asian Games
Hiroshima   Oct 9-16, 1994
100m: T Mansoor QAT 10.18; 200m: Mansoor 20.41; 400m: I Ismail QAT 45.48; 800m: Lee Jin-il KOR 1:45.72; 1500m: M Suleiman QAT 3:40.00; 5000m: Toshinari Takaoka JPN 13:38.37; 10,000m: Takaoka 28:15.48; Mar: Hwang Young-cho KOR 2:11:13; 3000msc: Sun Riping CHN 8:31.73; 110mh: Li Tong CHN 13.30; 400mh: S Karube JPN 49.13; HJ: T Yoshida JPN 2.27m; PV: I Potapovich KZK 5.65m; LJ: Huang Geng CHN 8.34mw; TJ: O Sakirkin KZK 17.21m; SP: Liu Hao CHN 19.26m; DT: Zhang Cunbiao CHN 58.78m; HT: Bi Zhong CHN 72.24m; JT: Zhang Lianbiao CHN 83.38m; Dec: R Ganiyev UZB 8005; 20kw: Chen Shaoguo CHN 1:21:15; 50kw: Korepanov KZK 3:54.37; 4x100: Japan 39.37; 4x400: Korea 3:10.19 **Women** 100m: Liu Xiaomei CHN 11.27; 200m: Wang Huei-chen TPE 23.34; 400m: Ma Yuqin CHN 51.17; 800m: Qu Yunxia CHN 1:59.85; 1500m: Qu Yunxia 4:12.48; 3000m: Zhang Linli CHN 8:52.97; 10,000m: Wang Junxia CHN 30:50.34; Mar: Zhong Huandi CHN 2:29:32; 100mh: O Shishigina KZK 12.80; 400mh: Han Qing CHN 54.74; HJ: S Mounkova UZB 1.92m; LJ: Yao Weili CHN 6.91m; SP: Sui Xinmei CHN 20.45m; DT: Chunfeng CHN 62.52m; JT: O Yarygina UZB 64.62m; Hep: G Shouaa SYR 6360; 10kw: Hongmiao CHN 44.11; 4x100m:China 43.85; 4x400m: China 3:29.11

US Championships
Sacramento   June 14-18
Men 100m(-1.2): Mike Marsh 10.23; 200m((+3.5): Michael Johnson 19.83; 400m: Johnson 43.66; 800m: B Rock 1:46.50; 1500m: McMullen 3:43.90; 5000m: Rob Kennedy 13:19.99; 10,000m: Williams 28:01.84; 3000msc: Mark Croghan 8:17.54; 110mh(+4.2): Roger Kingdon 13.09; 400mh: Derrick Adkins 48.44; HJ: Charles Austin 2.30m; PV: Scott Huffman 5.80m; LJ: Mike Powell 8.55w; TJ: Mike Conley 17.18; SP: Brent Noon 21.08m; DT: Mike

Buncic 64.82; HT: Lance Deal 77.68m; JT: Tom Pukstys 81.48m; Dec: Dan O'Brien 8682. **Women** 100m(0.0): Gwen Torrence 11.04; 200m(+2.3): Torrence 22.03; 400m: Jearl Miles 50.90; 800m: Meredith Rainey 2:00.07; 1500m: Regina Jacobs 4:05.18; 5000m: Gina Procaccio 15:26.34; 10,000m: Lynn Jennings 31:57.19; 110mh(+1.6): Gail Devers 12.77; 400mh: Kim Batten 54.74; HJ: Amy Acuff 1.95m; LJ: J Joyner-Kersee 6.88w; TJ: Strudwick-Hudson 14.66w; SP: Connie Price-Smith 19.05m; DT: E Boyer 62.58m; HT: Ellerbe 55.38m; JT: D Mayhew 59.16m; Hep: J Joyner-Kersee 6375

Salamanca Meeting
July 18
Men 200m(+2.1): Ivan Garcia CUB 20.50; 400m: Butch Reynolds USA 44.70; 800m: José Arconada ESP 1:46.34; 1000m: Venusté Niyongabo BUR 2:15.63; 100mh(+1.1): Antti Haapakoski FIN 13.59; 400mh: Samuel Matete ZAM 47.85; HJ: Sotomayor CUB 2.37m; LJ: Ivan Pedroso CUB 8.71m; TJ: Jonathan Edwards GBR 17.98m WR; SP: J-L Martinez ESP 19.31m; DT: Alexis Elizalde CUB 60.52m. **Women** 100m(+2.4): B McDonald JAM 11.17; 400m: Sandra Myers ESP 51.05; 800m: A Paulino MOZ 2:01.31; 400mh: A Alonso ESP 58.02; DT: M Martén CUB 61.30m.

7th International Meeting
Sestriere, Italy   July 29
Men 100m(+2.8): Olapade Adeniken NGR 9.92; 200m(+3.9): Jeff Williams USA 20.08; 400m: Samson Kitur KEN 45.26; 3000m: Philip Mosima KEN 8:05.10; 110mh(+3.1): Mark Crear USA 13.03; 400mh: Danny Harris USA 48.58; PV: Sergey Bubka UKR 6.00m; LJ: Ivan Pedroso CUB 8.96m WR distance, but not ratified; TJ: Jonathan Edwards GBR 17.58; SP: Sven Buder GER 19.62. **Women** 100m(+5.1): Gwen Torrence 10.83; 400m: Pauline Davis BAH 51.04; 100mh(+3.8): Aliuska López CUB 12.77; 400mh: Rosey Edeh CAN 56.27; LJ: Fiona May ITA 7.23m; SP: Kathrin Neimke GER 20.20m.

Domestic Events ▬▬▬▬▬▬

KP National Championships

Birmingham   July 15-16

MEN

100m	1	Linford Christie	TVH	10.18
(-1.2)	2	Darren Braithwaite	Haringey	10.33
	3	Jason John	Birchfield	10.34

Christie was eliminated in the heats when he slowed rapidly in the last 20m and placed only fourth. Christie was offered a place in the final and, though he won, Braithwaite became the AAA champion.

200m	1	John Regis	Belgrave	20.37
(+0.5)	2	Solomon Wariso	Haringey	20.53
	3	Darren Braithwaite	Haringey	20.64
400m	1	Mark Richardson	Windsor	44.94
	2	Mark Hylton	Windsor	45.83
	3	Adrian Patrick	Windsor	46.11
800m	1	Curtis Robb	Liverpool	1:46.78
	2	David Strang	Haringey	1:47.06
	3	Gary Lough	Annadale	1:48.03
1500m	1	John Mayock	Cannock	3:40.55
	2	Kevin McKay	Sale	3:40.83
	3	Bruno Witchalls	Dorking	3:41.51
5000m	1	Rob Denmark	Basildon	13:37.57
	2	Jon Brown	Sheffield	13:37.83
	3	P Ndrango	Kenya	13:39.57
10,000m	1	Gary Staines	Belgrave	28:49.29
	2	Jon Solly	Bingley	28:58.29

Held at Loughborough on June 11

3000msc	1	Spencer Duval	Cannock	8:24.64
	2	G Siamusiye	Zambia	8:25.49
	3	Keith Cullen	Chelmsford	8:29.64
110mh	1	Neil Owen	Belgrave	13.63
(-0.3)	2	Andy Tulloch	W & B	13.76
	3	Lloyd Cowan	Haringey	13.97
400mh	1	Rohan Robinson	AUS	49.21
	2	Gary Cadogan	Haringey	49.70
	3	Gary Jennings	Newham	50.34
PV	1	Neil Buckfield	Crawley	5.50m
	2	Andy Ashurst	Sale	5.10m
	3	Mike Edwards	Belgrave	5.10m
HJ	1	Steve Smith	Liverpool	2.35m
	2	Chris Anderson	Australia	2.22m
	3	Dalton Grant	Haringey	2.17m
LJ	1	Fred Salle	Belgrave	7.66m
	2	Jai Taurima	Australia	7.63m
	3	Barrington Williams	W & B	7.50m
TJ	1	Francis Agyepong	Shaftesbury	17.13m
	2	Tayo Erogbogbo	Birchfield	15.83m
	3	Tosi Fasinro	Haringey	15.65m
SP	1	M Proctor	RAF	18.81m
	2	Matt Simson	Thurrock	18.27m
	3	Sean Pickering	Haringey	17.71m
DT	1	Nick Sweeney	IRL	60.34m
	2	Robert Weir	Birchfield	60.18m
	3	Simon Williams	Enfield	58.20m
HT	1	Sean Carlin	Blackheath	73.40m
	2	Mike Jones	Shaftesbury	69.44m
	3	Jason Byrne	Berry Hill	69.44m
JT	1	Mick Hill	Leeds	80.54m
	2	Colin McKenzie	Newham	77.50m
	3	Nigel Bevan	Belgrade	76.58m
10kW	1	Darrell Stone	Steyning	41:10.11
	2	Stephen Partington	Isle of Man	41:14.61
	3	Martin Bell	Splott	41:16.13

WOMEN

100m	1	Paula Thomas	Trafford	11.48
(+1.5)	2	Simmone Jacobs	Shaftesbury	11.50
	3	Stephanie Douglas	Sale	11.53
200m	1	Catherine Murphy	Shaftesbury	23.40
(+0.1)	2	Simmone Jacobs	Shaftesbury	23.48
	3	Joyce Maduaka	Bromley	23.95
400m	1	Melanie Neef	Glasgow	51.63
	2	Lorraine Hanson	Birchfield	52.68
	3	Georgina Oladapo	Hounslow	52.71
800m	1	Kelly Holmes	Ealing	1:57.56
	2	J Stamison	USA	2:02.27
	3	Abigail Hunte	Unattached	2:02.47
1500m	1	Yvonne Murray	Motherwell	4:11.47
	2	Debbie Gunning	Andover	4:14.42
	3	Una English	Havering	4:16.37
5000m	1	Alison Wyeth	Parkside	15:39.14
	2	N Lynch	Footlocker	16:10.69
	3	Lesley Watson	GECAvionics	16:11.23
110mh	1	Melanie Wilkins	Aldershot	13.34
(+1.6)	2	M Campbell	Essex Ladies	13.36
	3	Kerry Maddox	Cannock	13.40
400mh	1	Gowry Retchakan	Thurrock	57.18
	2	Stephanie McCann	Lisburn	58.21
	3	Louise Brunning	Sutton	58.58
HJ	1	Lea Haggett	Croydon	1.85m
	2	Di Davies	Leicester	1.85m
	3	Debbie Marti	Bromley	1.85m
PV	1	Price	USA	3.70m
	2	Kate Staples	Essex Ladies	3.50m
	3	ClaireMorrison		3.30m
LJ	1	Nicole Boegman	Hounslow	6.50m
	2	Denise Lewis	Birchfield	6.42m
	3	Yinka Idowu	Essex Ladies	6.35m
TJ	1	Michelle Griffith	Windsor	13.43m
	2	Rachel Kirby	Blackheath	12.96m
	3	Karen Skeggs	Ashford	12.11m
SP	1	Judy Oakes	Croydon	17.75m
	2	Maggie Lynes	Essex Ladies	15.47m
	3	Carol Cooksley	Coventry	14.07m
DT	1	Lisa Vizaniari	Australia	61.98m
	2	Jackie McKernan	Lisburn	58.88m
	3	Shelley Drew	Sutton	53.74m
HT	1	Debbie Sosimenko	Australia	65.24m
	2	B MacNaughton	Australia	56.62m
	3	Lorraine Shaw	Gloucester	56.26m
JT	1	Lorna Jackson	Edinburgh	55.48m
	2	Sharon Gibson	Notts	55.14m
	3	Karen Martin	Derby	54.96m
5000mW	1	Lisa Langford	W & B	22:20.03
	2	Vicki Lupton	Sheffield	22:23.80
	3	Carolyn Partington	Isle of Man	22:40.19

BUPA International
Sheffield   *July 23*

Men 150m(+3.9): Linford Christie 14.74; 400m: Sunday Bada NGR 45.08; 800m: Curtis Robb GBR 1:47.14; 3000m: John Mayock GBR 7:47.28; 3000msc: Robert Hough GBR 8:36.18; 110mh(+2.5): Allen Johnson USA 13.17; 400mh: Samuel Matete ZAM 49.38; HJ: Charles Austin USA 2.28m; PV: Andrej Tiwontschik GER 5.85m; TJ: Jonathan Edwards GBR 18.08w; JT: Steve Backley GBR 86.30m.

Women 100m: Sophia Smith GBR 11.50; 400m: Sandie Richards JAM 51.64; 1000m: Kelly Holmes 2:32.82; 100mh(+1.2): Gillian Russell JAM 13.03; PV: Andrea Müller GER 4.02m; TJ: Hudson-Strudwick USA 14.41m.

BUPA Challenge - GBR v USA
Gateshead   *Aug 21*

Men 100m(-0.4): Tony McCall USA 10.26; 200m(+0.2): John Regis GBR 20.63; 400m: Marlon Ramsey USA 44.96; 800m: Terrance Herrington USA 1:46.52; 1500m: McMullen USA 3:46.87; 3000m: Rob Denmark GBR 8:02.16; 3000msc: Tom Hanlon GBR 8:24.37; 110mh(+0.2): Colin Jackson GBR 13.18; 400mh: Danny Harris USA 48.70; HJ: Charles Austin USA 2.31m; PV: Scott Huffman USA 5.70m; LJ: Percy Knox USA 7.90m; TJ: Jonathan Edwards GBR 17.49m; SP: Kevin Toth USA 20.57m; DT: Robert Weir GBR 62.54m; HT:Glen Smith GBR 69.20m; JT: Steve Backley GBR 83.00m; 4x100m: USA 38.55; 4x400m: GBR 3:03.16
Men's Result: GBR 203   USA 182

Women 100m(-0.5): Paula Thomas GBR 11.62; 200m(+0.2): Celena Mondie-Milner USA 22.99; 400m: Kim Graham USA 51.15; 800m: Amy Wickus USA 2:00.58; 1500m: Ruth Wysocki USA 4:05.03; 3000m: Yvonne Murray GBR 8:59.80; 100mh(+0.5): Jackie Agyepong GBR 13.09; 400mh: Trevaia Williams USA 56.48; HJ: Lea Haggett GBR 1.88m; PV: Price USA 3.80m; LJ: Denise Lewis GBR 6.56m; TJ: Ashia Hansen GBR 14.66 *NR*; SP: Connie Price-Smith USA 19.52m; DT: Pam Dukes USA 56.50m; JT: Sharon Gibson GBR 58.10m; 4x100m: USA 43.10; 4x400m: USA 3:28.22
Women's Result: USA 210.5   GBR 156.5

McDonald's Games
Crystal Palace   *Aug 27*

Men 100m(+2.2): Christie/Drummond GBR/USA d-ht 10.00; 400m: Derek Mills USA 44.75; 800m: Benson Koech KEN 1:44.36; Mile: Venusté Niyongabo BUR 3:49.80; 3000m: Paul Bitok KEN 7:44.36; 110mh(-0.6): Allen Johnson USA 13.05; 400mh: Danny Harris USA 48.79; HJ: Dalton Grant GBR 2.30m; PV: Pat Manson USA 5.70m; TJ: Jonathan Edwards GBR 18.00m; JT: Jan Zelezny CZE 92.12m

Women 200m(-1.6): Beverly McDonald JAM 22.85; 400m: Cathy Freeman AUS 50.43; 800m: Kelly Holmes GBR 2:00.78; 3000m: Sonia O'Sullivan IRL 8:40.22; 100mh: Monique Tourret FRA 12.90; TJ: Rodica Petrescu ROM 14.45m; SP: Sui Xinmei CHN 19.27m

Listen to this from Richard Brown on his last run from Land's End to John O'Groats:

"When I was in Perth last time we had a tea break and I suddenly jumped out of the van and started running along the road. I had done a mental calculation and thought I would not make it in time unless I started to run. There was an imbalance in salts which confused my mind. We will get to the stage where we will be entirely in the hands of our support crews brecause we will not be conscious enough to decide what we need to eat"

What fun, eh? On that occasion, Richard set the record for the trip taking 10 days 18 hours and 21 minutes, but a year later Don Ritchie had broken it.

Brown set out in June to beat Richie's record. Difficult, or what? On the first eight nights, the 48-year-old slept for only four hours and covered around 80 miles a day. On the penultimate night he slept for only 30 minutes and the last night on the road was spent without sleep altogether.

Brown, blistered and bruised arrived in John O'Groats after 10 days 2 hours and 25 minutes to break the record by 13 hours. Three days later, his wife Sandra reached John O'Groats too. She had walked the distance in 13 days 10 hours and 1 minute, seven hours quicker than the previous women's record.

Indoor Athletics

World Indoor Championships

Barcelona   Mar 10-12

Men

60m	1	**Bruny Surin**	CAN	**6.46**
	2	Darren Braithwaite	GBR	6.51
	3	Robert Esmie	CAN	6.55
200m	1	**Geir Moen**	NOR	**20.58**
	2	Troy Douglas	BER	20.94
	3	Sebastian Keitel	CHI	20.98
400m	1	**Darnell Hall**	USA	**46.17**
	2	Sunday Bada	NGR	46.38
	3	Mikhail Vdovin	RUS	46.65
800m	1	**Clive Terrelonge**	JAM	**1:47.30**
	2	Benson Koech	KEN	1:47.51
	3	Pavel Soukup	CZE	1:47.74
1500m	1	**Hicham El Guerrouj**	MAR	**3:44.54**
	2	Mateo Cañellas	ESP	3:44.85
	3	Eric Nedeau	USA	3:44.91
3000m	1	**Gennaro Di Napoli**	ITA	**7:50.89**
	2	Anacleto Jimenez	ESP	7:50.98
	3	Brahim Jabbour	MAR	7:51.42
110mh	1	**Allen Johnson**	USA	**7.39**
	2	Courtney Hawkins	USA	7.41
	3	Tony Jarrett	GBR	7.42
HJ	1	**Javier Sotomayor**	CUB	**2.38m**
	2	Lambros Papakostas	GRE	2.35m
	3	Tony Barton	USA	2.32m
PV	1	**Sergey Bubka**	UKR	**5.90m**
	2	Igor Potapovich	KZK	5.80m
	=3	Okkert Brits	RSA	5.75m
	=3	Andrej Tiwontschik	GER	5.75m
LJ	1	**Ivan Pedroso**	CUB	**8 51m**
	2	Mattias Sunneborn	SWE	8.20m
	3	Erick Walder	USA	8.14m
TJ	1	**Brian Wellman**	BER	**17.72m**
	2	Yoelvis Quesada	CUB	17.62m
	3	Serge Hélan	FRA	17.06m
SP	1	**Mika Halvari**	FIN	**20.74m**
	2	C J Hunter	USA	20.58m
	3	Dragan Peric	YUG	20.36m
Hept	1	**Christian Plaziat**	FRA	**6246pts**
	2	Tomas Dvorak	CZE	6169pts
	3	Henrik Dagard	SWE	6142pts
4x400m	1	**United States**	USA	**3:07.37**
	2	Italy	ITA	3:09.12
	3	Japan	JPN	3:09.73

Women

60m	1	**Merlene Ottey**	JAM	**6.97**
	2	Melanie Paschke	GER	7.10
	3	Carlette Guidry	USA	7.11
200m	1	**Melinda Gainsford**	AUS	**22.64**
	2	Pauline Davis	BAH	22.68
	3	NatalyaVoronova	RUS	23.01
400m	1	**Irina Privalova**	RUS	**50.23**
	2	Sandie Richards	JAM	51.38
	3	Daniela Georgieva	BUL	51.78
800m	1	**Maria Mutola**	MOZ	**1:57.62**
	2	Yelena Afanasyeva	RUS	1:59.79
	3	Letitia Vriesde	SUR	2:00.36
1500m	1	**Regina Jacobs**	USA	**4:12.61**
	2	Carla Sacramento	POR	4:13.02
	3	Lyubov Kremylova	RUS	4:13.19
3000m	1	**Gabriela Szabo**	ROM	**8:54.50**
	2	Lynn Jennings	USA	8:55.23
	3	Joan Nesbit	USA	8:56.08
60mh	1	**Aliuska Lopez**	CUB	**7.92**
	2	Olga Shishiginia	KZK	7.92
	3	Brigita Bukovec	SLO	7.93
HJ	1	**Alina Astafei**	GER	**2.01m**
	2	Britta Bilac	SLO	1.99m
	3	Heike Henkel	GER	1.99m
LJ	1	**Lyudmila Galkina**	RUS	**6.95m**
	2	Irina Mushayilova	RUS	6.90
	3	Susan Tietdke-Greene	GER	6.90
TJ	1	**Yolanda Chen**	RUS	**15.03** WR
	2	Iva Prandzheva	BUL	14.71
	3	Ren Ruiping	CHN	14.37
SP	1	**Larisa Peleshenko**	RUS	**19.93**
	2	Kathrin Neimke	GER	19.40
	3	Connie Price-Smith	USA	19.12
Pent	1	**Svetlana Moskalets**	RUS	**4834**
	2	Kym Carter	USA	4632
	3	Irina Tyukhay	RUS	4622
4x400m	1	**Russia**		**3:29.29**
	2	Czech Republic		3:30.27
	3	United States		3:31.43

Medal Table

	G	S	B	Total
Russia	6	2	3	11
United States	4	4	7	15
Cuba	3	1	-	4
Jamaica	2	1	-	3
Germany	1	2	3	6
Bermuda	1	1	-	2
Italy	1	1	-	2
Canada	1	-	1	2
France	1	-	1	2
Morocco	1	-	1	2
Australia	1	-	-	1
Finland	1	-	-	1
Mozambique	1	-	-	1
Norway	1	-	-	1
Romania	1	-	-	1
Ukraine	1	-	-	1
Czech Republic	-	2	1	3
Spain	-	2	1	3
Kazakhstan	-	2	-	2
Bulgaria	-	1	1	2
Great Britain	-	1	1	2
Slovenia	-	1	1	2
Sweden	-	1	1	2
Bahamas	-	1	-	1
Greece	-	1	-	1
Kenya	-	1	-	1
Nigeria	-	1	-	1
Portugal	-	1	-	1

Chile, China, Japan, South Africa, Surinam, Yugoslavia, 1 bronze apiece.

McDonalds International
Birmingham   Jan 28
Men 60m: Jackson GBR 6.58; 200m: Regis GBR 20.65; 400m: Golovastov RUS 47.09; 800m: McKean GBR 1:50.04; 1500m: Grime GBR 3:52.02; 3000m: Shabunin RUS 8:14.49; 60mh: Jackson GBR 7.43; HJ: Reilly GBR 2.26m; PV: Strogalyov RUS 5.20m; LJ: Williams GBR 7.54m; TJ: Markov RUS 17.00m; SP: Smirnov RUS 18.71m; 4x400m: GBR 3:09.22. Teams GBR 72pts; RUS 64pts
Women 60m: Thomas GBR 7.29; 200m: Thomas GBR 23.61; 400m: Andreyeva RUS 52.57; 800m: Afanasyeva RUS 2:05.14; 1500m: Griffiths GBR 4:14.74; 3000m: Kashapova RUS 9:15.45; 60mh: Agyepong GBR 8.05; HJ: Motkova RUS 1.98m; PV: Staples GBR 3.75m; LJ: Galkina RUS 6.58m; TJ: Hansen GBR 14.17m; SP: Peleshenko RUS 19.57m; 4x400m: RUS 3:32.26. Teams RUS 78; GBR 62

The Samsung Cup
Budapest   Jan 29
Men 800m: B Koech KEN 1:46.67; 3000m: Di Napoli ITA 7:43.48; PV: Tarasov RUS 5.60m **Women** 60m: Cuthbert JAM 7.22; 200m: Cuthbert 22.85; 800m: Rogachova RUS 2:00.44; 60mh: Shishigina KZK 7.98; HJ: Babakova UKR 1.95m; TJ: Prandzheva BUL 14.39m

Chemical Bank Millrose Games
New York   Feb 3
Men 60m: Neal USA 6.59; 400m: Valmon USA 48.36; 500m: Adkins USA 61.70; 800m: M Everett USA 1:50.90; Mile: Hood CAN 3:57.08; 60mh: Johnson 7.54; HJ: Austin 2.27m; PV: Trandenkov RUS 5.80m; LJ: McGhee USA 8.28m; SP: Toth USA 20.79m **Women** 60m: Torrence USA 7.09; 400m: Miles USA 54.35; 800m: Mutola MOZ 2:02.00; Mile: Chalmers USA 4:31.66; 60mh: Joyner-Kersee USA 7.96; HJ: Bradburn USA 1.95m; LJ: Drechsler GER 6.96m; SP: Price-Smith USA 17.99m

Ricoh Meeting
Stuttgart   Feb 5
Men 60m: Surin CAN 6.61; 200m: Regis GBR 20.47; 400m: Hall USA 45.82; 800m: Motchebon GER 1:44.88 *ER;* 1500m: El Guerrouj MAR 3:35.70; 3000m: Baumann GER 7:42.56; 60mh: Jackson GBR 7.44; PV: Chistyakov UKR 5.60m; TJ: Wellman BER 17.05m **Women** 60m: Nuneva BUL 7.16; 200m: Voronova RUS 22.80; 400m: Andreyeva RUS 51.64; 800m: Kremlyova RUS 2:03.87; 60mh: Girard FRA 8.05; HJ: Astafei GER 2.03m; LJ: Drechsler GER 6.94m

GBR v France
Glasgow   Feb 11
Men 60m: Christie GBR 6.56; 200m: Regis GBR 20.67; 400m: Hylton GBR 47.06; 800m: McKean GBR 1:48.72; 1500m: Dubus FRA 3:41.66; 3000m: Carlier FRA 7:58.03; 60mh: Jackson GBR 7.39; HJ: Detchenique FRA 2.23m; PV: Andji FRA 5.30m; LJ: Klouchi FRA 7.65m; TJ: Herbert GBR 16.50m; SP: Proctor GBR 18.39m; 4x400m: GBR 3:09.28 **Women** 60m: Douglas GBR 7.21; 400m: Neef GBR 53.67; 800m: Djaté-Taillard FRA 2:02.99; 1500m: Quentin FRA 4:18.04; 3000m: Duquenoy FRA 9:20.49; 60mh: Agyepong GBR 8.08; HJ: Courgeon FRA 1.86m; PV: Staples GBR 3.60m; LJ: Lewis GBR 6.35m; TJ: Griffith GBR 13.76m; SP: Oakes GBR 17.15m;

4x400m: GBR 3:37.60. Teams: GBR 155 FRA 122.

Sunkist International
Los Angeles   Feb 11
Men 50m: Marsh USA 5.73; 500y: D Harris USA 56.58; 880y: Gray USA 1:52.94; Mile: Bruton IRL 3:58.30; 50mh: Crear USA 6.50; PV: Hysong USA 5.65m **Women** 500y: Richards CAN 62.64; 800m: Mutola MOZ 2:01.05; 50mh: Joyner-Kersee USA 6.82

Vittel du Pas de Calais
Lievin   Feb 19
Men 60m: Christie GBR 6.47 *EIR*; 200m: Christie GBR 20.25 *WIR*; 400m: Hall USA 45.76; 3000m: Kiptanui KEN 7:37.14; 60mh: Johnson USA 7.40; HJ: Sotomayor CUB 2.38m; PV: Bubka UKR 6.00m; TJ: Quesada CUB 17.18m **Women** 60m: Privalova RUS 6.94; 200m: Privalova RUS 22.10; 800m: Van Langen NED 2:00.36; 60mh: Shishigina KZK 7.85; LJ: Drechsler GER 7.09m

Mobil 1 Invitational
Fairfax, USA   Feb 25
Men 60m: Neal 6.56; 400m: Johnson 45.55; 800m: Tengelei KEN 1:47.57; Mile: O'Sullivan IRL 3:56.48; 3000m: Kennedy USA 7:45.34; 60mh: Johnson USA 7.44; HJ: Barton USA 2.31m; PV: Manson USA 5.70m **Women** 60m: Torrence USA 7.10; 200m: Davis BAH 23.20; 400m: Miles USA 51.92; 800m: Mutola MOZ 1:59.41; Mile: Jacobs USA 4:31.94; HJ: Waller USA 1.95m

TSB International
Birmingham   Feb 25
Men 60m: Braithwaite GBR 6.54; 200m: Fredericks NAM 20.65; 400m: Hall USA 45.78; 800m: Komar BLS 1:46.79; 1500m: El Guerrouj MAR 3:36.22; 3000m: Niyongabo BUR 7:37.82; 60mh: Jarrett GBR 7.44; HJ: Ruffini SVK 2.26m; PV: Gataullin RUS 5.60m; TJ: Quesada CUB 17.22m **Women** 60m: Privalova RUS 7.07; 200m: McDonald JAM 23.19; 400m: Richards JAM 52.38; 800m: van Langen NED 2:01.79; 60mh: Shishigina KZK 7.88; TJ: Biryukova RUS 14.35

DN Games
Stockholm   Feb 27
Men 60m: Bailey CAN 6.57; 200m: Moen NOR 20.72; 400m: Hall USA 46.71; 800m: Loginov RUS 1:46.61; 1000m: Niyongabo BUR 2:15.62; 1500m: Vroemen NED 3:42.91; 3000m: Kiptanui KEN 7:39.36; 60mh: Jarrett GBR 7.57; PV: Trandenkov RUS 5.80m; TJ: Quesada CUB 17.03m; SP: Kleiza LIT 19.62m **Women** 60m: Privalova RUS 7.07; 800m: van Langen NED 2:00.44; 60mh: Shishigina KZK 7.94; HJ: Haugland NOR 1.96m

IHS Meeting
Sindelfingen   Mar 4
Men 60m: Christie GBR 6.49; 200m: Bailey CAN 20.82; 400m: Bada NGR 47.00; 800m: B Koech KEN 1:46.99; 1500m: Niyongabo BUR 3:36.33; 5000m: Franke GER 13:30.15; 60mh: Fenner GER 7.57; PV: Lobinger GER 5.70m; LJ: Tretyak RUS 8.03m **Women** 60m: Privalova RUS 7.00; 200m: Privalova RUS 22.32; 400m: Andreyeva RUS 52.62; 800m: Samorokova RUS 2:00.92; 1500m: Quentin FRA 4:15.01; 60mh: Grefstad Nor 8.11; HJ: Henkel GER 1.96m; LJ: Drechsler GER 7.09m

Cross-country

IAAF/Snickers World Cross Country Championships

Durham   Mar 25

Senior Men (12,020 metres)

1	Paul Tergat	KEN	34:05
2	Ismael Kirui	KEN	34:13
3	Salah Hissou	MAR	34:14
4	Haile Gebreselasie	ETH	34:26
5	Brahim Lahlafi	MAR	34:34
6	Paulo Guerra	POR	34:38
7	James Songok	KEN	34:41
8	Simon Chemoiywo	KEN	34:46
9	Todd Williams	USA	34:47
10	Martin Fiz	ESP	34:50
11	Larbi El Khattabi	MAR	34:55
12	Abdelaziz Sahere	MAR	35:00
13	Jose Garcia	ESP	35:01
14	Bob Kennedy	USA	35:02
15	Julius Ondieki	KEN	35:02
16	Mustapha Essaid	FRA	35:03
17	Abdellah Behar	FRA	35:03
18	Jose Carlos Adan	ESP	35:05
19	Antonio Serrano	ESP	35:07
20	Andrew Pearson	GBR	35:07

Also GBR

55. Keith Cullen 36:00; 59. Martin Jones 36:02; 71. Adrian Passey 36:14;72. Christian Stephenson 36:14;77. Dave Clarke 36:17; 81. Tommy Murray 36:20; 100. Robert Quinn 36:36; 121. Spencer Duval 37:03.

Teams 1. Kenya 62; 2. Morocco 111; 3. Spain 120; 9. Great Britain 354.

Junior Men (8470m)

1	Assefa Mezgebu	ETH	24:12
2	Dejene Lidetu	ETH	24:14
3	David Chelule	KEN	24:16
4	Andrew Panga	TAN	24:19
5	Philip Mosima	KEN	24:23
6	Abreham Tsige	ETH	24:40
7	Hezron Otwori	KEN	24:43
8	Mark Bett	KEN	24:48
9	Sammy Kipruto	KEN	24:58
10	Christopher Kelong	KEN	25:02

Also GBR

67. Allen Graffin 26:46; 76. Tony Forrest 26:54; 85 Matthew O'Dowd 27:04; 92. Ben Reese 27:10; 107. Robert Brown 27:36; 128. Nathanial Lane 28:46.

Teams 1. Kenya 23 pts; 2. Ethiopia 25; 3. Morocco 72; 15. Britain 320.

Senior Women (6470 metres)

1	Derartu Tulu	ETH	20:21
2	Catherina McKiernan	IRL	20:29
3	Sally Barsosio	KEN	20:39
4	Margaret Ngotho	KEN	20:40
5	Gete Wami	ETH	20:49
6	Joan Nesbit	USA	20:50
7	Merima Denboba	ETH	20:53
8	Rose Cheruiyot	KEN	20:54
9	Albertina Dias	POR	20:56
10	Gabriela Szabo	ROM	20:57
11	Catherine Kirui	KEN	20:58
12	Zahra Ouaziz	MAR	21:06
13	Olga Bondarenko	RUS	21:06
14	Olga Appell	USA	21:07
15	Yukiko Okamoto	JPN	21:07
16	Julia Vaquero	ESP	21:12
17	Helen Kimaiyo	KEN	21:13
18	Paula Radcliffe	GBR	21:14
19	Annette Palluy	FRA	21:15
20	Kanako Haginaga	JPN	21:17

Also GBR

24. Bev Hartigan 21:21; 44. Alison Wyeth 21:38; 78. Angie Hulley 22.07; 83. Lucy Elliott 22:09; 102. Andrea Duke 22:31.

Teams 1. Kenya 26 pts; 2. Ethiopia 38; 3. Romania 84; 9. Great Britain 164

Junior Women (4470 metres)

1	Annemari Sandell	FIN	14:04
2	Jebiwot Keitany	KEN	14:09
3	Nancy Kipron	KEN	14:17
4	Jepkorir Aiyabei	KEN	14:21
5	Berhane Dagne	ETH	14:25
6	Anita Weyermann	SUI	14:25
7	Alemitu Bekele	ETH	14:26
8	Yimenashu Taye	ETH	14:27
9	Eliz. Cheptanui	KEN	14:28
10	Pam Chepchumba	KEN	14:31

Also GBR

20. Alice Braham 14:58; 27. Nicola Slater 15:08; 30. Beverley Gray 15:15; 56. Heidi Moulder 15:41; 58. Alison Outram 15:44; 78. Michelle Mann 16:10.

Teams 1. Kenya 18 pts; 2. Ethiopia 31; 3. Japan 56; 6. Great Britain 133

European Cross-country Championships

Alnwick   Dec 10, 1994

Men (9km)

1	Paulo Guerra	POR	27:43
2	Domingos Castro	POR	27:59
3	Antonio Serrano	ESP	28 03
4	Carlos Adan	ESP	28:06
5	Abdellah Behar	FRA	28:08
6	Luca Barzaghi	ITA	28:10
7	Jose Manuel Garcia	ESP	28:11
8	Antonio Pinto	POR	28:12
9	Alberto Maravilha	POR	28:13
10	Mustapha Essaid	FRA	28:19
11	Andrew Pearson	GBR	28:20
12	Joao Junqueira	POR	28:21
13	Alejandro Gomez	ESP	28:22
14	Barry Royden	GBR	28:23
15	Carsten Jorgensen	DEN	28:24

Also GBR

25.Richard Nerurkar 28:41; 27.Dave Lewis GBR 28:46; 29.Adrian Passey GBR 28:52; 47.Steffan White GBR 29:16

Teams

1.Portugal 20; 2.Spain 27; 3.France 50; 4.Great Britain 77

Women (4.5km)

1	Catherina McKiernan	IRL	14:29
2	Julia Vaquero	ESP	40:30
3	Elena Fidatof	ROM	14:36
4	Alla Zjiliayeva	RUS	14:45
5	Maria Rebelo	FRA	14:46
6	Fernanda Ribeiro	POR	14:47
7	M Chirila Stanescu	ROM	14:48
8	Lieve Slegers	BEL	14:49
9	B Bitzner-Ducret	FRA	14:50
10	Tamara Koba	UKR	14:51
11	Carla Sacramento	POR	14:52
12	Ana Dias	POR	14:54
13	Flavia Gaviglo	ITA	14:54
14	Farida Fates	FRA	14:55
15	Nina Belikova	RUS	14:55

Also GBR

26. Andrea Wallace 15:10; 27.Laura Adam GBR 15:11; 31.Bev Hartigan GBR 15:13; 57. Andrea Duke GBR 15:47

Teams

1.Romania 26; 2.France 28; 3. Portugal 29; 9.Great Britain 84

IAAF World Cross Challenge

Date	Venue (Distance M/W)	Men's Winner	Time	Women's Winner	Time
Nov 27	Bolbec (9420m/6500m)	Shem Kororia KEN	27:48	Fernanda Ribeiro POR	16:05
Dec 4	Algiers (9450m/4350m)	Eliud Barngetuny KEN	26:33	Rose Cheruiyot KEN	14:00
Dec 18	Brussels (10,500m/6k)	Fita Bayesa ETH	31:25	Derartu Tulu ETH	19:52
Dec 31	Durham (9200m/6200m)	Ismael Kirui KEN	30:03	Rose Cheruiyot KEN	22:37
Jan 7	Mallusk (8k/4800m)	Ismael Kirui KEN	23:21	Rose Cheruiyot KEN	15:57
Jan 15	Amorebieta (11,500m/6000m)	Paulo Guerra POR	31:22	Rose Cheruiyot KEN	18:28
Jan 22	Seville (10k/5600m)	Paulo Guerra POR	28:49	Catherine McKiernan IRL	17:43
Jan 29	San Sebastian (10k/5624m)	Paulo Guerra POR	32:13	Elena Fidatov ROM	19:50
Feb 4	Tourcoing (10,300m/5300m)	Laban Chege KEN	29:28	Gabriela Szabo ROM	16:26
Feb 12	Acoteias (10k/6k))	Paulo Guerra POR	29:21	Gabriela Szabo ROM	19:31
Feb 19	Chiba (12k/6k)	Daniel Njenga KEN	35:32	Tudorita Chidu ROM	19:17
Feb 19	Diekirch (10,200m/4800m)	Dave Lewis GBR	33:09	Gabriela Szabo ROM	16:53
Feb 25	Nairobi (12k/6k)	Paul Tergat KEN	35:30	Rose Cheruiyot KEN	20:33
Mar 4	San Vittore Olana (10k/5k)	Fita Bayesa ETH	34:26	Albertina Dias POR	20:15

FINAL STANDINGS - MEN

			Score	Award	1994
1	Ismael Kirui	KEN	135	$10,000	3rd
2	Paulo Guerra	POR	130	$8000	4th
3	Salah Hissou	MAR	117	$6000	45th
4	Paul Tergat	KEN	97	$5000	22nd
5	James Kariuki	KEN	72	$4000	=39th
6	Martfn Fiz	ESP	63	$3500	=115th
7	Umberto Pusterla ITA		60	$3000	=71st
8	Domingos Castro	POR	57	$2500	=54th
9	Shem Kororia	KEN	56	$2000	=35th
10.	Haile Gebresilasie ETH		53	$1500	1 st
11	Ondoro Osoro	KEN	52	$1000	=15th
12	Fita Bayesa	ETH	50	$250	19th
	Paul Evans	GBR	50	$250	=123rd

FINAL STANDINGS - WOMEN

			Score	Award	1994
1	Catherina McKiernan IRL		135	$10,000	1st
2	Rose Cheruiyot	KEN	126	$8000	
3	Catherine Kirui	KEN	100	$6000	
4	Gabriela Szabo	ROM	97	$5000	=20th
5	Derartu Tulu	ETH	92	$4000	
6	Albertina Dias	POR	88	$3500	2nd
7	Elena Fidatov	ROM	77	$3000	
8	Helen Kimaiyo	KEN	75	$2500	=20th
9	Sally Barsosio	KEN	74	$2000	
10	Fernanda Ribeiro POR		69	$1500	28th
11	Joyce Koech	KEN	69	$1000	=94th
12	Martha Erntsdottir ISL		63	$500	19th

Road Racing

IAAF/RICOH WORLD MARATHON CUP
Athens   Apr 9

Men

1 Douglas Wakiihuri KEN 2:12:01
2 Takahiro Sunada JPN 2:13:16
3 Davide Milesi ITA 2:13:23
4 Juan Torres ESP 2:14:48
5 Moges Taye ETH 2:14:53
6 Marco Gozzano ITA 2:14:58

Also GBR

18.Bill Foster 2:18:45; 34.Daniel
Rathbone 2:22:48; 40.Trevor Clark
2:24:10; 50.Robin Nash 2:26:31
Teams 1.Italy 6:43:42; 2.France
6:48:47; 3.Spain 6:51:05; 9.Great
Britain 7:05:43

Women

1 Anuta Catuna ROM 2:31:10
2 Lidia Simon ROM 2:31:46
3 Cristina Pomacu ROM 2:32:09
4 Ornella Ferrara ITA 2:32:56
5 Maria Munoz ESP 2:34:35
6 Larisa Zyusko RUS 2:34:43

Also GBR

24.Alison Rose 2:42.42; 25.Trudi
Thompson 2:42.44; 27.Caroline
Horne 2:43.19; 33.Lesley Turner
2:46.46; Dnf.Zina Marchant
Teams 1.Romania 7:35:05;
2.Russia 7:47:39; 3.Italy 7:50:46;
7.Great Britain 8:08:45

IAAF/RICOH WORLD HALF MARATHON CHAMPIONSHIPS
Oslo   Sep 24, 1994

Women

1 Elana Meyer RSA 68:36
2 Iulia Negura ROM 69:15
3 Anuta Catuna ROM 69:35
4 Albertina Dias POR 69:57

Also GBR

29.Danielle Sanderson 73:13;
31.Angie Hulley 73:19; 46.Heather
Heaseman 74:06; 47.Cath Mijovic
74:15; 72.Marion Sutton 76:15
Teams 1. Romania 3:29:03;
2.Norway 3:33:36; 3.Japan 3:35:39;
9.Great Britain 3:40:38

Men

1 Khalid Skah MAR 60:27
2 German Silva MEX 60:28
3 Ronaldo da Costa BRA 60:54
4 Godfrey Kiprotich KEN 61:01

Also GBR

29.Martin McLoughlin 62:45; 47.Carl
Udall 63:36; 60.Andrew Pearson
64.30; 61.Mark Croasdale 64:4
Teams 1. Kenya 3:03:36; 2. Mexico
3:03:47; 3. Morocco 3:05:58; 12.
Great Britain 3:10:51

Berlin Marathon
Sep 25, 1994

Men

1 Antonio Pinto POR 2:08:31
2 Sam Nyangincha KEN 2:08:50
3 Antonio Serrano ESP 2:09:13

Women

1 Katrin Dörre GER 2:25:15
2 Rocio Rios ESP 2:29:00
3 Malgor. Sobanska POL 2:30:00

Frankfurt Marathon
Oct 23, 1994

Men

1 Terje Naess NOR 2:13:19

Women

1 Franziska Moser SUI 2:27:44

Beijing Marathon
Oct 30, 1994

Men

1 Hu Gangjun CHN 2:10:56

Women

1 Wang Junxia CHN 2:31:11

Chicago Marathon
Oct 30, 1994

Men

1 Luis dos Santos BRA 2:11:16

Women

1 Kristy Johnson USA 2:31:34

New York Marathon
Nov 6, 1994

Men

1 German Silva MEX 2:11:21
2 Benjamin Paredes MEX 2:11:23
3 Arturo Barrios MEX 2:11:43

Women

1 Tecla Lorupe KEN 2:27:37
2 Madina Biktagorova BLS 2:30:00
3 Anne-Marie Letko USA 2:30:19

Tokyo Women's Marathon
Nov 20, 1994

1 Val'tina Yegorova RUS 2:30:09
2 Sachiyo Seiyama JPN 2:30:30
3 Lisa Ondieki AUS 2:31:01

Fukuoka Men's Marathon
Dec 4, 1994

1 Boay Akonay TAN 2:09:45
2 Mañuel Matias POR 2:09:50
3 Vald'r dos Santos BRA 2:10:25

Sao Silvestre 15k
Sao Paulo   Dec 31

Men

1 Ronaldo da Costa BRA 44:11

Women

1 Derartu Tulu ETH 51:17

Marrakesh Road Races
Jan 15

Men's Marathon

1 Abdulilah Zerdal 2:11:50

Men's Half-Marathon

1 Paul Evans GBR 60:09

Women's Half-Marathon

1 Ferrara ITA 71:30

Beppu/Oita Men's Marathon
Feb 5

1 Pat Carroll AUS 2:09:39
2 Stephan Freigang GER 2:10:12
3 Vald'r dos Santos BRA 2:11:14

Gasparilla 15k
Tampa   Feb 18

Men

1 Josephat Machuka KEN 42:37

Women

1 Delilah Asiago KEN 48:38
3 Liz McColgan GBR 48:59

Lake Biwa Men's Marathon
Mar 19

1 Yuji Nakamura JPN 2:10:49

London Marathon
Blackheath-The Mall, April 2

Men

1 Dionicio Ceron MEX 2:08:30
2 Steve Moneghetti AUS 2:08:33
3 Antonio Pinto POR 2:08:48
4 Xolile Yawa RSA 2:10:22
5 Paul Evans GBR 2:10:31
6 Joaquim Pinheiro POR 2:10:35
7 Willie Mtolo RSA 2:11:35
8 Luigi Di Lello ITA 2:11:36
9 Johannes Mabitle RSA 2:11:39
10 Zach'h Nyambaso KEN 2:11:56

Women

1 Malgorzata Sobanska
POL 2:27:43
2 Manuela Machado POR 2:27:53
3 Ritva Lemettinen FIN 2:28:00
4 Renata Kokowska POL 2:30:35
5 Liz McColgan GBR 2:31:14
6 Kim Jones USA 2:31:35
7 Katrin Dörre GER 2:32:16
8 Nyla Carroll NZL 2:33:19
9 Kerrin McCann AUS 2:33:23
10 Anita Haakenstad NOR 2:33:56

Wheelchair

1 Heinz Frei SUI 1:39:14
2 David Holding GBR 1:47:36
3 G Shattenecker AUT 1:47:41
22 Rose Hill GBR 2:17:02

Total Finishers: 25,326

Korean Marathon
Gyeongju   Mar 19
Men
1 Lee Bong-ju   KOR 2:10:58
2 Richard Nerurkar   GBR 2:11:03
3 Andres Espinosa   MEX 2:11:08
Women
1 Lee Mi-kyung   KOR 2:38:08

Boston Marathon
Apr 17
Men
1 Cosmas Ndeti   KEN 2:09:22
2 Moses Tanui   KEN 2:10:22
3 A Dos Santos   BRA 2:11:02
Women
1 Uta Pippig   GER 2:25:11
2 Elana Meyer   RSA 2:26:51
3 Madina Biktagirova   BLS 2:29:00

Rotterdam Marathon
Apr 23
Men
1 Martin Fiz   ESP 2:08:56
2 B Van Vlaanderen   NED 2:10:34
3 I Garcia   MEX 2:10:53
Women
1 Monica Pont   ESP 2:30:35
2 Carmen de Fuentes   ESP 2:31:21
3 Carla Beurskens   NED 2:32:40

Hamburg Marathon
Apr 30
Men
1 Antonio Silio   ARG 2:09:57
2 Carlos Monteiro   POR 2:11:34
3 E Tukhbatullin   RUS 2:12:29
Women
1 Angelina Kanana   KEN 2:27:24
Kanana won by almost 10 minutes

Comrades Marathon (91km)
Pietermaritzburg to Durban   May 20
Men
1 Shaun Meikeljohn   RSA 5:34:02
Women
1 Maria Bak   GER 6:22:46

Great North Run (Half-marathon)
Newcastle-South Shields   Sep 17
Men
1 Moses Tanui   KEN   60:39
2 Benson Masya   KEN   61:59
3 James Kariuki   KEN   62:29
4 Paul Evans   GBR   62:30
Women
1 Liz McColgan   GBR   71:42
2 Fatuma Roba   ETH   72:05
3 Manuela Machado   POR   73:22

Great North Run (Half-marathon)
Newcastle-South Shields   Sep 17
Men
1 Sammy Lelei   KEN 2:07:03
2 Vincent Rousseau   BEL 2:07:19
3 Antonio Pinto   POR 2:08:56
Women
1 Uta Pippig   GER 2:25:36
2 Kanana   KEN 2:27:40
3 Maraoui   MAR 2:28:26

Berlin Marathon
Sep 24
Men
1 Sammy Lelei   KEN 2:07:02
2 Vincent Rousseau   BEL 2:07:19
3 Antonio Pinto   POR 2:08:56
Women
1 Uta Pippig   GER 2:25:36
2 Angelina Kanana   KEN 2:27:40
3 M Maraoui   MAR 2:28:18

Walking

IAAF/REEBOK WORLD RACE WALKING CUP
Beijing   Apr 29-30
Men's 20k
1 Li Zewen   CHN 1:19:44
2 Mikhail Schennikov   RUS 1:19:58
3 Bernardo Segura   MEX 1:20:32
Also GBR
29. Darrell Stone 1:24:49; 58. Steve Partington 1:30:02; 70. Andrew Penn 1:31:46; 80. Chris Cheeseman 1:34:23
Teams 1. China 436; 2. Italy 422; 3. Mexico 420; 13. Great Britain 314
Men's 50k
1 Zhao Yongshen   CHN 3:41:20
2 Jesus Garcia   ESP 3:41:54
3 Valentin Kononen   FIN 3:42:50
Also GBR
42. Mark Easton 4:06:01; 44. Les Morton 4:08:52; 71. Graham White 4:29.41
Teams 1. Mexico 426; 2. Russia 419; 3. Spain 413; 16. Great Britain 312
Women's 10k
1 Gao Hongmiao   CHN   42:19
2 Yelena Nikolayeva   RUS   42:32
3 Liu Hongyu   CHN   42:49
Also GBR
36. Lisa Langford 46:00; 51. Vicky Lupton 47:04; 60. Carolyn Partington 48:17; 69. Verity Snook 48:42; 82. Melanie Wright 50:50;
Teams 1. China 443; 2. Italy 427; 3. Russia 422; 16. Great Britain 323

World Records

MEN

100m	9.85 (+1.2)	Leroy Burrell	USA	Lausanne	1994
200m	19.72 (+1.8)	Pietro Mennea	ITA	Mexico City	1972
400m	43.29	Butch Reynolds	USA	Zürich	1988
800m	1:41.73	Sebastian Coe	GBR	Florence	1981
1500m	3:27.37	Noureddine Morceli	ALG	Nice	1995
1 Mile	3:44.39	Noureddine Morceli	ALG	Rieti	1993
2000m	4:47.88	Noureddine Morceli	ALG	Paris	1995
3000m	7:25.11	Noureddine Morceli	ALG	Monte Carlo	1994
5000m	12:44.39	Haile Gebresilasie	ETH	Zürich	1995
10,000m	26:43.53	Haile Gebresilasie	ETH	Hengelo	1995
20,000m	56:55.6	Arturo Barrios	MEX	La Fleche	1991
1 Hour	21,101m	Arturo Barrios	MEX	La Fleche	1991
25,000m	1:13:55.8	Toshihiko Seko	JPN	Christchurch	1981
30,000m	1:29:18.8	Toshihiko Seko	JPN	Christchurch	1981
Marathon	2:06:50	Belayneh Dinsamo	ETH	Rotterdam	1988
3000msc	7:59.18	Moses Kiptanui	KEN	Zürich	1992
110mh	12.91 (+0.5)	Colin Jackson	GBR	Stuttgart	1993
400mh	46.78	Kevin Young	USA	Barcelona	1992
High Jump	2.45m	Javier Sotomayor	CUB	Salamanca	1993
Pole Vault	6.14m	Sergey Bubka	UKR	Sestriere	1994
Long Jump	8.95m (+0.3)	Mike Powell	USA	Tokyo	1991
Triple Jump	18.29m (+1.3)	Jonathan Edwards	GBR	Gothenburg	1995
Shot	23.12m	Randy Barnes	USA	Los Angeles	1990
Discus	74.08m	Jürgen Schult	GER	Neubrandenburg	1986
Hammer	86.74m	Yury Sedykh	URS	Stuttgart	1986
Javelin	95.66m	Jan Zelezny	CZE	Sheffield	1993
Decathlon	8891	Dan O'Brien	USA	Talence	1992
4x100m	37.40	United States		Barcelona/Stuttgart	1992/1993
4x200m	1:18.68	Santa Monica Track Club	USA	Walnut	1994
4x400m	2:54.29	United States		Stuttgart	1993
4x800m	7:03.89	Great Britain (Elliott, Cook, Cram, Coe)		London	1982
4x1500m	14:38.8	West Germany		Cologne	1977

WOMEN

100m	10.49 (0.0)	Florence Griffith-Joyner	USA	Seoul	1988
200m	21.34 (+1.3)	Florence Griffith-Joyner	USA	Seoul	1988
400m	47.60	Marita Koch	GDR	Canberra	1985
800m	1:53.28	Jarmila Kratochvilova	TCH	Munich	1983
1000m	2:29.34	Maria Mutola	MOZ	Brussels	1995
1500m	3:50.46	Qu Yunxia	CHN	Beijing	1993
1 Mile	4:15.61	Paula Ivan	ROM	Nice	1989
3000m	8:06.11	Wang Junxia	CHN	Beijing	1993
5000m	14:36.45	Fernanda Ribeiro	POR	Hechtel	1995
10,000m	29:31.78	Wang Junxia	CHN	Beijing	1993
1 Hour	18,084m	Silvana Cruciata	ITA	Rome	1981
20,000m	1:06:48.8	Izumi Maki	JPN	Amagasaki	1993
Marathon	2:21:06	Ingrid Kristiansen	NOR	London	1985
100mh	12.21 (+0.7)	Yordanka Donkova	BUL	Stara Zagora	1988
400mh	52.61	Kim Batten	USA	Gothenburg	1995
High Jump	2.09m	Stefka Kostadinova	BUL	Rome	1987
Pole Vault	4.22m	Daniela Bártová	CZE	Salgotarjan	1995
Long Jump	7.52m (+1.4)	Galina Chistyakova	URS	Leningrad	1988
Triple Jump	15.50m	Inessa Kravets	UKR	Gothenburg	1994
Shot	22.63m	Natalya Lisovskaya	URS	Moscow	1987
Discus	76.80m	Gabriele Reinsch	GER	Neubrandenburg	1988
Hammer	68.16m	Olga Kuzenkova	RUS	Moscow	1995
Javelin	80.00m	Petra Felke	GDR	Potsdam	1988
Heptathlon	7291	Jackie Joyner-Kersee	USA	Seoul	1988
4x100m	41.37	East Germany		Canberra	1985
4x200m	1:28.15	East Germany		Jena	1980
4x400m	3:15.17	Soviet Union		Seoul	1988

World Champions

WC venues: 1983 Helsinki;
1987 Rome; 1991 Tokyo; 1993
Stuttgart; 1995 Gothenburg

MEN

100m
1983 Carl Lewis USA
1987 Carl Lewis USA*
1991 Carl Lewis USA
1993 Linford Christie GBR
1995 Donovan Bailey CAN
*Won by Ben Johnson, later
stripped of title for drug-taking*

200m
1983 Calvin Smith USA
1987 Calvin Smith USA
1991 Michael Johnson USA
1993 Frank Fredericks NAM
1995 Michael Johnson USA

400m
1983 Bert Cameron JAM
1987 Thomas Schonlebe GDR
1991 Antonio Pettigrew USA
1993 Michael Johnson USA
1995 Michael Johnson USA

800m
1983 Willi Wulbeck FRG
1987 Billy Konchellah KEN
1991 Billy Konchellah KEN
1993 Paul Ruto KEN
1995 Wilson Kipketer DEN

1500m
1983 Steve Cram GBR
1987 Abdi Bile SOM
1991 Noureddine Morceli ALG
1993 Noureddine Morceli ALG
1995 Noureddine Morceli ALG

5000m
1983 Eamonn Coghlan IRE
1987 Said Aouita MOR
1991 Yobes Ondieki KEN
1993 Ismael Kirui KEN
1995 Ismael Kirui KEN

10,000m
1983 Alberto Cova ITA
1987 Paul Kipkoech KEN
1991 Moses Tanui KEN
1993 Haile Gebresilasie ETH
1995 Haile Gebresilasie ETH

Marathon
1983 Rob de Castella AUS
1987 Douglas Wakiihuri KEN
1991 Hiromi Taniguchi JPN
1993 Mark Plaatjes USA
1995 Martin Fiz ESP

3000m Steeplechase
1983 Patriz Ilg FRG
1987 Francesco Panetta ITA
1991 Moses Kiptanui KEN
1993 Moses Kiptanui KEN
1995 Moses Kiptanui KEN

110m Hurdles
1983 Greg Foster USA
1987 Greg Foster USA
1991 Greg Foster USA
1993 Colin Jackson GBR
1995 Allen Johnson USA

400m Hurdles
1983 Edwin Moses USA
1987 Edwin Moses USA
1991 Samuel Matete ZAM
1993 Kevin Young USA
1995 Derrick Adkins USA

High Jump
1983 Genn. Avdeyenko URS
1987 Patrik Sjoberg SWE
1991 Charles Austin USA
1993 Javier Sotomayor CUB
1995 Troy Kemp BAH

Pole Vault
1983 Sergey Bubka URS
1987 Sergey Bubka URS
1991 Sergey Bubka URS
1993 Sergey Bubka UKR
1995 Sergey Bubka UKR

Long Jump
1983 Carl Lewis USA
1987 Carl Lewis USA
1991 Mike Powell USA
1993 Mike Powell USA
1995 Ivan Pedroso CUB

Triple Jump
1983 Zdzislaw Hoffmann POL
1987 Khristo Markov BUL
1991 Kenny Harrison USA
1993 Mike Conley USA
1995 Jonathan Edwards GBR

Shot
1983 Edward Sarul POL
1987 Werner Günthör SUI
1991 Werner Günthör SUI
1993 Werner Günthör SUI
1995 John Godina USA

Discus
1983 Imrich Bugar TCH
1987 Jorgen Schult GDR
1991 Lars Riedel GER
1993 Lars Reidel GER
1995 Lars Reidel GER

Hammer
1983 Sergey Litvinov URS
1987 Sergey Litvinov URS
1991 Yuriy Sedykh URS
1993 Andrey Abduvalyev TJK
1995 Andrey Abduvalyev TJK

Javelin
1983 Detlef Michel GDR
1987 Seppo Räty FIN
1991 Kimmo Kinnunen FIN
1993 Jan Zelezny CZE
1995 Jan Zelezny CZE

Decathlon
1983 Daley Thompson GBR
1987 Torsten Voss GDR
1991 Dan O Brien USA
1993 Dan O'Brien USA
1995 Dan O'Brien USA

4x100m Relay
1983 United States
1987 United States
1991 United States
1993 United States
1995 Canada

4x400m Relay
1983 Soviet Union
1987 United States
1991 Great Britain
1993 United States
1995 United States

20km Walk
1983 Ernesto Canto MEX
1987 Maurizio Damilano ITA
1991 Maurizio Damilano ITA
1993 Valentin Massana ITA
1995 Michele Didoni ITA

50km Walk
1983 Ronald Weigel GDR
1987 Hartwig Gauder GDR
1991 Alek. Potashov URS
1993 Jesús Angel Garcia ESP
1995 Valentin Kononen FIN

WOMEN

100m
1983 Marlies Gohr GDR
1987 Silke Gladisch GDR
1991 Katrin Krabbe GER
1993 Gail Devers USA
1995 Gwen Torrence USA

200m
1983 Marita Koth GDR
1987 Silke Gladisch GDR
1991 Katrin Krabbe GER
1993 Merlene Ottey JAM
1995 Merlene Ottey* JAM
*Gwen Torrence crossed the
line first, but was disqualified for
running outside her lane around
the bend*

World Champions

400m
1983 Jarm. Kratochvilova TCH
1987 Olga Bryzgina URS
1991 Marie-José Pérec FRA
1993 Jearl Miles USA
1995 Marie-José Pérec FRA

800m
1983 Jarm. Kratochvilova TCH
1987 Sigrun Wodars GDR
1991 Lilia Nurutdinova URS
1993 Maria Mutola MOZ
1995 Anna Quirot CUB

1500m
1983 Mary Decker USA
1987 Tatyana Samolenko URS
1991 Hassiba Boulmerka ALG
1993 Liu Dong CHN
1995 Hassiba Boulmerka ALG

3000m*
1983 Mary Decker USA
1987 Tatyana Samolenko URS
1991 Taty. Dorovskikh** URS
1993 Qu Yunxia CHN
Superceded by the 5000m in 1995
** *Née Samolenko*

5000m
1995 Sonia O'Sullivan IRL

10,000m
1983 No event
1987 Ingrid Kristiansen NOR
1991 Liz McColgan GBR
1993 Wang Junxia CHN
1995 Fernanda Ribeiro

Marathon
1983 Grete Waitz NOR
1987 Rosa Mota POR
1991 Wanda Panfil POL
1993 Junko Asari JPN
1995 Manuela Machado POR

100m Hurdles
1983 Bettine Jahn GDR
1987 Ginka Zagorcheva BUL
1991 Lyud. Narozhilenko URS
1993 Gail Devers USA
1995 Gail Devers USA

400m hurdles
1983 Yekaterina Fesenko URS
1987 Sabine Busch GDR
1991 Tatya. Ledovskaya URS
1993 Sally Gunnell GBR
1995 Kim Batten USA

High Jump
1983 Tamara Bykova URS
1987 Stefka Kostadinova BUL
1991 Heike Henkel GER
1993 Iomnet Quitero CUB
1995 Stefka Kostadinova BUL

Long Jump
1983 Heike Daute GDR
1987 J Joyner-Kersee USA
1991 J Joyner-Kersee USA
1993 Heike Drechsler GER
1995 Fiona May ITA

Triple Jump
1993 Ana Biryukova RUS
1995 Inessa Kravets UKR

Shot
1983 Helena Fibingerova TCH
1987 Natalya Lisovskaya URS
1991 Zhihong Huang CHN
1993 Zhihong Huang CHN
1995 Astrid Kumbernuss GER

Discus
1983 Martina Opitz GDR
1987 Martina Hellmann* GDR
1991 Tsvet. Khristova BUL
1993 Olga Burova RUS
1995 Ellina Svereva BLR
* *Née Opitz*

Javelin
1983 Tiina Lillak FIN
1987 Fatima Whitbread GBR
1991 Xu Demei CHN
1993 Trine Hattestad NOR
1995 Natalya Shikolenko BLR

Heptathlon
1983 Ramona Neubert GDR
1987 J Joyner-Kersee USA
1991 Sabine Braun GER
1993 J Joyner-Kersee USA
1995 Ghada Shouaa SYR

10km walk
1983 No event
1987 Irina Strakhova URS
1991 Alina Ivanova URS
1993 Sari Essayah FIN
1995 Irina Stankina RUS

4x100m Relay
1983 East Germany
1987 United States
1991 Jamaica
1993 Russia
1995 United States

4x400m Relay
1983 East Germany
1987 East Germany
1991 Soviet Union
1993 United States
1993 United States

World Cross-country & Major Marathons

World Cross-country Championships

Year	Men	Women
1973	Pekka Paivarinto FIN	Paolo Cacchi ITA
1974	Eric de Beck BEL	Paolo Cacchi ITA
1975	Ian Stewart SCO	Julie Brown USA
1976	Carlos Lopes POR	Carmen Valero ES
1977	Leon Schots BEL	Carmen Valero ESP
1978	John Treacy IRL	Grete Waitz NOR
1979	John Treacy IRL	Grete Waitz NOR
1980	Craig Virgin USA	Grete Waitz NOR
1981	Craig Virgin USA	Grete Waitz NOR
1982	Mohamed Kedir ETH	Maricica Puica ROM
1983	Bekele Debele ETH	Grete Waitz NOR
1984	Carlos Lopes POR	Maricica Puica ROM
1985	Carlos Lopes POR	Zola Budd ENG
1986	John Ngugi KEN	Zola Budd ENG
1987	John Ngugi KEN	Annette Sergent FRA
1988	John Ngugi KEN	Ingrid Kristiansen NOR
1989	John Ngugi KEN	Annette Sergent FRA
1990	Khalid Skah MAR	Lynn Jennings USA
1991	Khalid Skah MAR	Lynn Jennings USA
1992	John Ngugi KEN	Lynn Jennings USA
1993	William Sigei KEN	Albertina Dias POR
1994	William Sigei KEN	Helen Chepngeno KEN
1995	Paul Tergat KEN	Derartu Tulu ETH

Boston Marathon

The oldest of the major marathons, Boston was first run in 1897 although not over a distance of just under 40km. It was run over the full distance for the first time in 1927

1975	Bill Rogers USA	Liane Winger FRG
1976	Jack Fultz USA	Kim Merritt USA
1977	Jerome Drayton CAN	Miki Gorman USA
1978	Bill Rogers USA	Gayle Barron USA
1979	Bill Rogers USA	Joan Benoit USA
1980	Bill Rogers USA	Jacqui Gareau CAN
1981	Toshihiko Seko JPN	Allison Roe NZL
1982	Alberto Salazar USA	Charlotte Teske FRG
1983	Greg Meyer USA	Joan Benoit USA
1984	Geoff Smith GBR	Lorraine Moller NZL
1985	Geoff Smith GBR	Lisa Weidenbach USA
1986	Rob de Castella AUS	Ingrid Kristiansen NOR
1987	Toshihiko Seko JPN	Rosa Mota POR
1988	Ibrahim Hussein KEN	Rosa Mota POR
1989	Abebe Mekonnen ETH	Ingrid Kristiansen NOR
1990	Gelindo Bordin ITA	Rosa Mota POR
1991	Ibrahim Hussain KEN	Wanda Panfil POL
1992	Ibrahim Hussain KEN	Olga Markova RUS
1993	Cosmas N'Deti KEN	Olga Markova RUS
1994	Cosmas N'Deti KEN	Uta Pippig GER
1995	Cosams N'Deti KEN	Uta Pippig GER

London Marathon

Year	Men	Women
1981	Dick Beardsley USA & Inge Simonsen NOR	Joyce Smith GBR
1982	Hugh Jones GBR	Joyce Smith GBR
1983	Mike Gratton GBR	Grete Waitz NOR
1984	Charlie Spedding GBR	Ingrid Kristiansen NOR
1985	Steve Jones GBR	Ingrid Kristiansen NOR
1986	Toshihiko Seko JPN	Grete Waitz NOR
1987	Hiromi Taniguchi JPN	Ingrid Kristiansen NOR
1988	H Jorgensen DEN	Ingrid Kristiansen NOR
1989	Doug. Wakiihuri KEN	Veronique Marot GBR
1990	Allister Hutton GBR	Wanda Panfil POL
1991	Yakov Tolstikov URS	Rosa Mota POR
1992	Antonio Pinto POR	Katrin Dörre GER
1993	Eamonn Martin GBR	Katrin Dörre GER
1994	Dionicio Ceron MEX	Katrin Dörre GER
1995	Dionicio Ceron MEX	Malgorzata Sobanska POL

New York Marathon

Year	Men	Women
1976	Bill Rodgers USA	Miki Gorman USA
1977	Bill Rodgers USA	Miki Gorman USA
1978	Bill Rodgers USA	Grete Waitz NOR
1979	Bill Rodgers USA	Grete Waitz NOR
1980	Alberto Salazar USA	Grete Waitz NOR
1981	Alberto Salazar USA	Allison Roe NZL*
1982	Alberto Salazar USA	Grete Waitz NOR
1983	Rod Dixon NZL	Grete Waitz NOR
1984	Orlando Pizolato ITA	Grete Waitz NOR
1985	Orlando Pizolato ITA	Grete Waitz NOR
1986	Gianni Poli ITA	Grete Waitz NOR
1987	Ibrahim Hussein KEN	Priscilla Welch GBR
1988	Steve Jones GBR	Grete Waitz NOR
1989	Juma Ikangaa TAN	Ingrid Kristiansen NOR
1990	Doug Wakiihuri KEN	Wanda Panfil POL
1991	Salvador Garcia MEX	Liz McColgan GBR
1992	Willie Mtolo RSA	Lisa Ondieki AUS
1993	Andres Espinoza MEX	Uta Pippig GER
1994	German Silva MEX	Tecla Lorupe KEN

* The course used in 1981-1983 was found to be 155m short and the world bests of Salazar and Roe were invalidated

Badminton

Just as England were settling into a gentle decline, with only Archer and Bradbury reaching the quarter-final stage at the World Championships and not a single finallist at the All England, a team blended from age and youth beat China in a six-match series. "This may not have been the best China side," said manager Ciro Ciniglio, "But they never bring a bad one." When the England team took a 4-1 winning lead at Salisbury in October, it secured their first-ever series win against the Sudirman Cup holders.

England had done well to finish fifth themselves in the Sudirman, but there was not too much else to write home about in the year and, for Ciro Ciniglia, who makes way for the former European champion Steve Baddeley next year, the win over China was a decent swansong.

Earlier in the year, Ciniglio had made the decision not to even book flights for singles players on the trip to the Malaysian, Singapore and Indonesian Opens. The money saved allocated to the development programme (rewards from that policy coming quicker than expected with the China win). Bradbury and Wright, at least, justified their tickets with a straight sets doubles victory in Kuala Lumpur over the world champions and world top-ranked Gil Young Ah and Jang Hye Ock.

Indonesian, Chinese, Korean and Malaysian players continued to sew up the major events, although Lund and Thompsen, of Denmark, won the mixed doubles title in Lausanne and there was another Danish success when Poul-Erik Hoyer, inflicted a rare defeat on world singles champion, Heryanto Arbi, in the All England final at Birmingham in March.

IBF WORLD RANKINGS
As at Sept 1
Men's Singles

1	**Heryanto Arbi**	**INA**	**318.04**
2	Hermawan Susanto	INA	288.37
3	Ardy Wiranata	INA	272.88
4	Allan Budi Kusuma	INA	267.48
5	Joko Suprianto	INA	263.24
6	P-E Hoyer-Larsen	DEN	258.84
7	Park Sung Woo	KOR	250.24
8	Rashid Sidek	MAL	223.67
9	Lee Kwang Jin	KOR	211.26
10	H Hendrawan	INA	199.67
28	Darren Hall	ENG	113.51
41	Anders Nielsen	ENG	86.97
46	Bruce Flockhart	SCO	83.53

Women's Singles

1	**Susi Susanti**	**INA**	**330.83**
2	Bang Soo Hyun	KOR	324.64
3	Ye Zhaoying	CHN	318.89
4	Lim Xiao Qing	SWE	282.10
5	Mia Audina	INA	232.85
6	Ra Kyung Min	KOR	231.65
7	Camilla Martin	DEN	202.28
8	Kim Ji Hyun	KOR	201.34
9	Han Jingna	CHN	189.93
10	Wang Chen	CHN	184.16
39	Joanne Muggeridge	ENG	94.20
46	Julia Mann	ENG	86.49

Men's Doubles

1	**Subagja/Mainaky**	**INA**	**353.00**
2	Cheah/Yap	MAL	336.21
3	Gunawan/Suprianto	INA	314.28
4	Yoo/Kim	KOR	283.46
5	Kantono/Antonius	INA	275.12
14	Hunt/Archer	ENG	178.07

Women's Doubles

1	**Gil Young Ah/ Jang Hye Ock**	**KOR**	**396.23**
2	Ge/Gu	CHN	321.02
3	Kim/Kim	KOR	257.35
4	Stuer-Lauridsen/ Thomsen	DEN	245.14
5	Qin/Tang	CHN	240.75
10	Bradbury/Wright	ENG	216.68

Mixed Doubles

1	**Kim Dong Moon/ Gil Young Ah**	**KOR**	**378.27**
2	Heryanto/Timur	INA	325.97
3	Lund/Thomsen	DEN	321.53
4	Ponting/Wright	ENG	211.90
5	Holst-Christiansen/ Olsen	DEN	210.99

World Championships

Lausanne, Switzerland   May 17-21

Heryanto Arbi INA
Lee Kwang Jin KOR
Joko Suprianto INA
Dong Jiong CHN
Poul-Erik Hoyer Larsen DEN
Chen Gang CHN
Hermawan Susanto INA
Robert Liljequist FIN
Peter Rasmussen DEN
Park Sung Woo KOR
Jens Olsson SWE
Allan Budi Kusuma INA
Ahn Jae Chang KOR
Thomas Stuer-Lauridsen DEN
Rashid Sidek MAL
Ardy Wiranata INA

Men's Singles

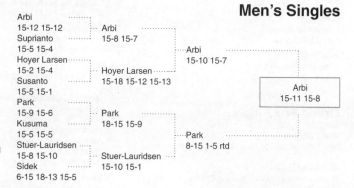

Arbi
15-12 15-12   Arbi
Suprianto   15-8 15-7
15-5 15-4   Arbi
Hoyer Larsen   15-10 15-7
15-2 15-4   Hoyer Larsen
Susanto   15-18 15-12 15-13   Arbi
15-5 15-1   15-11 15-8
Park
15-9 15-6   Park
Kusuma   18-15 15-9
15-5 15-5   Park
Stuer-Lauridsen   8-15 1-5 rtd
15-8 15-10   Stuer-Lauridsen
Sidek   15-10 15-1
6-15 18-13 15-5

Susi Susanti INA
Yao Yan CHN
Ra Kyung Min KOR
Zhang Ning CHN
Camilla Martin DEN
Yasuko Mizui JPN
Ye Zhaoying CHN
Yuni Kartika INA
Yuliana Sentosa INA
Han Jingna CHN
Hu Ning CHN
Lim Xiao Qing SWE
Chung Jae Hee KOR
Mia Audina INA
Denyse Julien CAN
Bang Soo Hyun KOR

Women's Singles

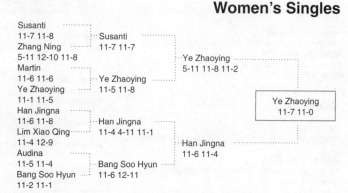

Susanti
11-7 11-8   Susanti
Zhang Ning   11-7 11-7
5-11 12-10 11-8   Ye Zhaoying
Martin   5-11 11-8 11-2
11-6 11-6   Ye Zhaoying
Ye Zhaoying   11-5 11-8   Ye Zhaoying
11-1 11-5   11-7 11-0
Han Jingna
11-6 11-8   Han Jingna
Lim Xiao Qing   11-4 4-11 11-1
11-4 12-9   Han Jingna
Audina   11-6 11-4
11-5 11-4   Bang Soo Hyun
Bang Soo Hyun   11-6 12-11
11-2 11-1

Men's Doubles
Quarter-finals
Mainaky/Subagja INA bt Jonsson/Axelsson SWE 18-16 15-8
Cheah/Yap MAL bt Antonius/Kantono INA 15-12 15-6
Kim/Yoo KOR bt Suprianto/Gunawan INA 15-9 15-6
Holst-Christiansen/Lund DEN bt Huang/Jiang CHN 17-14 15-11

Semi-finals
Mainaky/Subagja bt Cheah/Yap 15-8 15-6
Holst-Christiansen/Lund bt Kim/Yoo 15-12 15-2

FINAL
Mainaky/Subagja bt Holst-Christiansen 15-5 15-2

Women's Doubles
Quarter-finals
Gil/Jang KOR bt Ge/Gu CHN 15-12 11-15 15-11
Qin/Tang CHN bt Stuer-Lauridsen/Thomsen 15-12 18-16
Finarsih/Tampi INA bt Peng/Zhang CHN 15-12 15-6
Kirkegaard/Olsen DEN bt Schmidt/Ubben GER 15-11 15-5

Semi-finals
Gil/Jang bt Qin/Tang 15-8 15-6
Finarsih/Tampi bt Kirkegaard/Olsen 15-8 17-16

FINAL
Gil Young Ah/Jang Hye Ock bt Finarsih/Tampi 3-15 15-11 15-10

Mixed Doubles
Quarter Finals
Lund/Thomsen DEN bt Kim/Gil KOR 15-10 15-7
Antonsson/Crabo SWE bt Archer/Bradbury ENG 17-15 15-4
Eriksen/Kirkegaard DEN bt Holst-Christiansen/Olsen DEN 13-18 15-9 15-11
Liu/Ge CHN bt Heryanto/Timur INA 15-8 15-6

Semi Finals
Lund/Thomsen bt Antonsson/Crabo 12-15 17-14 15-9
Eriksen/Kirkegaard bt Liu/Ge 15-5 15-3

FINAL
Lund/Thomsen bt Eriksen/Kirkegaard 15-2 15-6

Sudirman Cup
Lausanne, Switzerland   May 17-28
5th/6th Position
England 3 Thailand 2

Semi-finals
Indonesia 4 Korea 1
China 4 Denmark 1

Final
China 3 Indonesia 1
(Last match not played)

Grand Prix Finals
Bangkok, Thailand   Dec 11, 1994
Men's Singles
Ardy Wiranata INA bt Allan Budi Kusuma INA 9-15 15-7 15-5
Women's Singles
Susi Susanti INA bt Ye Zhaoying CHN 4-11 12-10 11-4
Men's Doubles
Subagja/Mainaky INA bt Gunawan/Suprianto INA 15-10 15-7
Women's Doubles
Ge/Gu CHN bt Finarsih/Tampi INA 13-15 15-12 15-5
Mixed Doubles
Lund/Thomsen DEN bt Antonsson/Crabo SWE 12-15 15-4 15-9

World Cup
Jakarta   Sep 13-17
Men's Singles
Joko Suprianto INA bt Allan Budi Kusuma INA 15-7 11-15 15-8
Women's Singles
Ye Zhaoying CHN bt Susi Susanti INA 12-9 2-11 12-9
Men's Doubles
Heryanto/Timur INA bt Kim/Kim KOR 15-9 13-18 15-12
Women's Doubles
Eliza/Zelin INA bt Tampi/Finarsih INA bt 10-15 15-11 10-11 *Tampi/Finarsih rtd*
Mixed Doubles
Subagja/Mainaky INA bt Thongsari/Teerawiwatana THA 15-4 15-9

All England Championships
Birmingham   Mar 14-18
MEN'S SINGLES
Quarter-finals
Heryanto Arbi INA bt Soren Nielsen DEN 15-3 15-6
Loh Ah Meng MAL bt Andreij Antropov RUS 18-17 15-10
Poul-Erik Hoyer Larsen DEN bt Ahn Jae Chang KOR 9-15 15-7 15-12
Hermawan Susanto INA bt Ardy Wiranata INA 15-12 15-7

Semi-finals
Arbi bt Loh 17-15 15-0
Hoyer-Larsen bt Susanto 15-8 12-15 18-16

Final
Hoyer-Larsen bt Arbi 17-16 15-6

WOMEN'S SINGLES
Quarter-finals
Susi Susanti INA bt Ra Kyung Min KOR 11-3 11-0
Lim Xiao Qing SWE bt Han Jingna CHN 11-0 11-8
Camilla Martin DEN bt Kim Ji Hyun KOR 11-8 11-6
Mia Audina INA bt Wang Chen CHN 10-12 12-11 12-10

Semi-finals
Lim bt Susanti 12-11 11-7
Martin bt Audina 11-6 12-10

Final
Lim bt Martin 11-9 10-12 11-7

MEN'S DOUBLES
Quarter-finals
Mainaky/Subagja INA bt Soo/Tan MAL 15-4 15-2
Yap/Cheah MAL bt Razak/Santosa INA 15-7 18-14
Antonius/Kantono INA bt Archer/Hunt ENG 15-12 7-15 15-9
Gunawan/Suprianto INA bt Yap/Yap MAL 15-9 15-2

Semi-finals
Mainaky/Subagja bt Yap/Cheah 15-3 17-15
Antonius/Kantono bt Gunawan/Suprianto 5-15 15-9 15-11

Final
Mainaky/Subagja bt Antonius/Kantono 15-12 15-18 15-8

LADIES DOUBLES
Quarter-finals
Kirkegaard/Olsen DEN bt Wang/Ye CHN 15-9 15-12
Eliza/Zelin INA bt Kim/Kim KOR 10-15 15-2 15-9
Bradbury/Wright ENG bt Jorgensen/Olsen DEN 15-0 7-15 15-12
Gil/Jang KOR bt Stuer-Lauridsen/Thomsen DEN 15-13 15-9

Semi-finals
Eliza/Zelin bt Kirkegaard/Olsen 15-10 15-12
Gil/Jang bt Bradbury/Wright 15-10 15-3

Final
Gil/Jang bt Eliza/Zelin 15-6 15-3

MIXED DOUBLES
Quarter-finals
Lund/Thomsen DEN bt Ha/Kim KOR 15-7 18-17
Archer/Bradbury ENG bt Antonsson/Crabo SWE 15-9 7-15 15-12
Heryanto/Timur INA bt Ponting/Wright ENG 6-15 15-7 15-4
Holst-Christiansen/Olsen DEN bt Kim/Gil KOR 15-9 15-5

Semi-finals
Lund/Thomsen bt Archer/Bradbury 18-14 15-4
Holst-Christiansen/Olsen bt Timur/Heryanto 15-10 15-8

Final
Thomsen/Lund bt Holst-Christiansen/Olsen 15-7 15-7

England v China
Series of six international matches during September and early October

Final Result: England 4 China 2

DANISH OPEN
Esbjerg   Oct 12 1994
Men's Singles
Poul-Erik Hoyer Larsen DEN bt Allan Budi Kusuma INA
17-18 15-4 15-10
Women's Singles
Camilla Martin DEN bt Lim Xiao Qing SWE 11-5 5-11
12-11
Men's Doubles
Kantono/Antonius INA bt Lund/Holst-Christiansen DEN
15-8 5-15 15-9
Women's Doubles
Lim/Magnusson SWE bt Thomsen/Bille DEN 15-12 7-15
15-2
Mixed Doubles
Thomsen/Lund DEN bt Archer/Bradbury ENG 15-8 15-3

THAILAND OPEN
Bangkok   Oct 31-Nov 6, 1994
Men's Singles
Joko Suprianto INA bt Sun Jun CHN 10-15 15-11 15-5
Women's Singles
Susi Susanti INA bt Lim Xiao Qing SWE 11-5 12-10
Men's Doubles
Kantono/Antonius INA bt Thongsari/Teerawiwatana THA
12-15 15-12 17-10
Women's Doubles
Ge/Gu CHN bt Bradbury/Wright ENG 15-12 15-4
Mixed Doubles
Heryanto/Timur INA Ponting/Wright ENG 15-10 15-12

HONG KONG OPEN
Hong Kong   Nov 8-13, 1994
Men's Singles
Heryanto Arbi INA bt Ardy Wiranata INA 15-9 15-11
Women's Singles
Bang Soo Hyun KOR bt Lim Xiao Qing SWE 11-7 11-6
Men's Doubles
Subagja/Mainaky INA bt Gunawan/Suprianto INA 15-12
14-17 15-7
Women's Doubles
Shim/Jang KOR bt Ge/Gu CHN 15-11 18-14
Mixed Doubles
Lund/Thomsen DEN bt Ha/Shim KOR 17-14 15-12

CHINESE OPEN
Dalian   Nov 1994
Men's Singles
Allan Kusuma INA bt Ardy Wiranata INA 15-10 15-12
Women's Singles
Bang Soo Hyun KOR bt Ye Zhaoying CHN 11-8 11-6
Men's Doubles
Jiang/Huang CHN bt Yap/Tan MAL 15-10 15-8
Women's Doubles
Ge/Gu CHN bt Bang/Jang KOR 15-8 15-2
Mixed Doubles
Lund/Thomsen DEN bt Sogaard/Gowers DEN/ENG 15-3
15-6

KOREAN OPEN
Seoul   Jan 17-22
Men's Singles
Heryanto Arbi INA bt Permadi Fung TPE 15-10 15-6
Women's Singles
Susi Susanti INA bt Bang Soo Hyun KOR 3-11 11-7 11-9
Men's Doubles
Mainaky/Subagja INA bt Holst/Lund DEN15-6 11-15 15-7

Women's Doubles
Gil/Jang bt Gu/Ge CHN 15-13 1-15 15-11
Mixed Doubles
Thomsen/Lund DEN bt Liu/Ge CHN 15-4 18-15

JAPANESE OPEN
Tokyo   Jan 24-29
Men's Singles
Heryanto Arbi INA bt Joko Suprianto INA 15-8 15-8
Women's Singles
Susi Susanti INA bt Bang Soo Hyun KOR 11-7 12-11
Men's Doubles
Mainaky/Subagja INA bt Gunawan/Suprianto INA 15-8
15-9
Women's Doubles
Gu/Ge CHN bt Tampi/Finarsih INA 15-11 15-8
Mixed Doubles
Thomsen/Lund DEN bt Heryanto/Timur INA 15-4 14-17
15-10

MALAYSIAN OPEN
Kuala Lumpur   July 4-9
Men's Singles
Allan Budi Kusuma INA bt Ardy Wiranata INA 15-5 15-8
Women's Singles
Susi Susanti INA bt Bang Soo Hyun KOR 11-1 11-6
Men's Doubles
Thongsari/Teerawiwatana THA bt Cheah/Yap MAL 5-15
15-12 15-5
Women's Doubles
Bradbury/Wright ENG bt Gil/Jang KOR 15-10 15-11
Mixed Doubles
Kim/Gil KOR bt Tao/Wang CHN 15-7 15-9

INDONESIAN OPEN
Jakarta   July 10-16
Men's Singles
Ardy Wiranata INA bt Joko Suprianto INA 15-9 14-17
15-9
Women's Singles
Susi Susanti INA bt Bang Soo Hyun KOR 11-6 11-7
Men's Doubles
Gunawan/Suprianto INA bt Antonius/Kantono INA 15-12
15-9
Women's Doubles
Ge/Gu CHN bt Qin/Tang CHN 15-6 15-5
Mixed Doubles
Heryanto/Timur INA bt Limpele/Rosalina INA 15-10
15-5

SINGAPORE OPEN
July 17-23
Men's Singles
Joko Suprianto INA bt Hermawan Susanto INA 15-11
3-15 15-10
Women's Singles
Lim Xiao Qing SWE bt Bang Soo Hyun KOR 11-7 6-11
11-8
Men's Doubles
Subagja/Mainaky INA bt Antonius/Kantono INA 15-7
18-16
Women's Doubles
Gu/Ge CHN bt Gil/Jang KOR 15-12 15-7
Mixed Doubles
Heryanto/Timur INA bt Kim/Gil KOR 15-12 9-15 15-10

World Champions & European Champions

World Champions

MEN'S SINGLES
1977	Flemming Delfs	DEN
1980	Rudy Hartono	INA
1983	Icuk Sugiarto	INA
1985	Hang Jian	CHN
1987	Yang Yang	CHN
1989	Yang Yang	CHN
1991	Zhao Jianhua	CHN
1993	Joko Suprianto	INA
1995	Heryanto Arbi	INA

WOMEN'S SINGLES
1977	Lene Köppen	DEN
1980	Wiharjo Verawaty	INA
1983	Li Lingwei	CHN
1985	Han Aiping	CHN
1987	Han Aiping	CHN
1989	Li Lingwei	CHN
1991	Tang Jiuhong	CHN
1993	Susi Susanti	INA
1995	Ye Zhaoying	CHN

MEN'S DOUBLES
1977	Wahjudi/Tjun	INA
1980	Chandra/Christian	INA
1983	Fladberg/Hellerdie	DEN
1985	Park Joo-bong/Kim Moon-soo	KOR
1987	Li Yongbo/Tian Bingye	CHN
1989	Li Yongbo/Tian Bingye	CHN
1991	Park Joo-bong/Kim Moon-soo	KOR
1993	Subagja/Gunawam	INA
1995	Mainaky/Subagja	INA

WOMEN'S DOUBLES
1977	Tuganoo/Vero	JPN
1980	Perry/Webster	GBR
1983	Lin Ying/Wu Dixie	CHN
1985	Han Aiping/Li Lingwei	CHN
1987	Lin Ying/Guan Weizhen	CHN
1989	Lin Ying/Guan Weizhen	CHN
1991	Gan Weizhen/Nong Qunha	CHN
1993	Nong Qunha/Zhou Lei	CHN
1995	Gil/Jang	KOR

MIXED DOUBLES
1977	Stovgaard/Köppen	DEN
1980	Christian/Wogoeno	INA
1983	Kihlström/Perry	SWE/GBR
1985	Park Joo-bong/Yoo Sang-hee	KOR
1987	Wang Pengrin/Shi Fagying	CHN
1989	Park Joo-bong/Chung Myung-hee	KOR
1991	Park Joo-bong/Chung Myung-hee	KOR
1993	Subagja/Gunawam	INA
1995	Lund/Thomsen	DEN

SUDIRMAN TROPHY (TEAM)
1989	Indonesia
1991	Korea
1993	Korea
1995	China

Thomas Cup (Men's Team)
1949	Malaya
1952	Malaya
1955	Malaya
1958	Indonesia
1961	Indonesia
1964	Indonesia
1967	Malaysia
1970	Indonesia
1973	Indonesia
1976	Indonesia
1979	Indonesia
1982	China
1984	Indonesia
1986	China
1988	China
1990	China
1992	Malaysia
1994	Indonesia

Uber Cup (Women's Team)
1957	United States
1959	United States
1963	United States
1966	Japan
1969	Japan
1972	Japan
1975	Indonesia
1978	Japan
1981	Japan
1984	China
1986	China
1988	China
1990	China
1992	China
1994	Indonesia

European Champions

MEN'S SINGLES
1976	Flemming Delfs	DEN
1978	Flemming Delfs	DEN
1980	Flemming Delfs	DEN
1982	Jens Peter Nierhoff	DEN
1984	Morten Frost	DEN
1986	Morten Frost	DEN
1988	Darren Hall	ENG
1990	Steve Baddeley	ENG
1992	Paul-Eric Høyer-Larsen	DEN
1994	Paul-Eric Høyer-Larsen	DEN

WOMEN'S SINGLES
1978	Lene Köppen	DEN
1980	Liselotte Blumer	SWE
1982	Lene Köppen	DEN
1984	Helen Troke	ENG
1986	Helen Troke	ENG
1988	Kirsten Larsen	DEN
1990	Pernille Nedergaard	DEN
1992	Pernille Nedergaard	DEN
1994	Lim Xiaoqing	SWE

Baseball

It began on August 12, 1994 and finally ended on March 31, 1995, 232 days later. In between almost everyone tried to make some sense of it. The president got involved in February; the benefits were obvious to the man in The White House, whose own popularity did not rate much higher than a baseball club owner at this point. Clinton talked forcefully about the strike not being settled without an umpire, but appointing the 71-year-old Bill Usery was not the answer. When one of the players' representatives called him "senile" to his face, it seemed reasonable to assume that things weren't going well. Clinton tossed the ball to Congress, before going back in the dug-out. But Congress didn't want to impose a settlement and the strike continued.

With replacement players lining up to start the season, the National Labor Relations Board, arguing that the owners were not negotiating in good faith, applied for an injunction to reinstate the salary arbitration system and the US District Court in New York granted it. On Friday, March 31, the players made an unconditional offer to return to work and the strike was effectively over. The replacement players were paid off just 24 hours before their big day. Some did well; the Florida Marlins were awarded a $25,000 bonus as well as the $5,000 signing on fee. At Cincinatti, the Reds gave Dan Rohrmeier, a would-be infielder, just $19 for some petrol. "I asked for it in nickels, to make it look more," he said.

The season's schedule was rejigged; it was reduced to 144-games down from the regular 162-game season, but it wasn't quite all settled. The umpires wanted a piece of the action and so decided to have their own strike. The season started without replacement players, but with replacement umpires instead. Their dispute only lasted a week. They settled for a deal that offered a minumum salary of $75,000 for rookie umpires increasing to $225,000 for veterans. The sort of numbers that would have David Shepherd hopping about.

It surprised nobody that when the season began the reception for the teams was cool, to say the least. If they had abandoned the fans, the fans now abandoned them. In a Harris Poll carried out in July, only 33 percent of adults said they followed Major League baseball. The figure was down from 45 percent two years earlier. In the search to accentuate the positive in the game, attention lighted on Hideo Nomo, the first Japanese-born player in 30 years to play for a Major League club. Nomo did the business; the right-handed Los Angeles pitcher bemusing hitters with his exaggerated wind-up and wildy dipping ball, and earning a place in the All Star Game.

The best news for baseball, though, wasn't Nomo. It was Cal Ripken. The Baltimore Oriole's shortstop played his 2,131st straight game on September 6th, 1995 against California Angels to break the record of baseball legend Lou Gehrig. The mid-game celebration lasted 22 minutes and included a firework display. It had taken

A 1934 baseball, signed by Babe Ruth and Lou Gehrig, disappeared from the Babe Ruth Museum in Baltimore. Three days later the ball just as mysteriously returned to the Museum. The ultimate curve ball, perhaps.

Ripken 13 years to break the record, the streak beginning on May 30th 1982. To put the achievement into some kind of perspective, when Ripken broke the record, the next longest streak was that of Chicago White Sox's Frank Thomas, who had played just 226 straight games. Only another 12 years to go, Frank.

Mickey Mantle died on August 13th of cancer. The 63-year-old had been given a kidney transplant two months earlier, but the years of alcohol abuse eventually took their toll. New York Yankee Mantle was described as the most exciting player since Joe DiMaggio. At the All-Star game in July, DiMaggio, 80 this year, was the guest of honour. It was also the year that Bo Jackson retired; for four years in the late eighties, Jackson was that rare breed who excelled in both football and baseball. So Bo Goes.

Quotes

"A few hundred folks trying to figure out how to divide nearly $2 billion" - **President Bill Clinton, on what the strike really came down to.**

"We didn't really accomplish anything, except the damage we did to baseball. Baseball will pay a price for what happened this year" - **David Glass, chairman of Kansas City Royals.**

"This strike may be solved by the wives" - **Bill Giles, chairman of the Phillies, noting that one agent reckoned that average player was losing about $7,000 a day.**

"What would you want from me? Everything I have is worn out. I've had a lot of people say they would like to have my heart because it's never been used" - **Micky Mantle, when asked if he would fill out a donor card.**

"I have been offered as high as $2,500 for the ball, but it's not for sale, for no price" - **Mike Stirn, a 32-year-old from Maryland who retrieved the home run hit by Cal Ripken in his record-tying 2,130th game. Stirn left the stadium under police escort.**

"You are sending the worst possible message to the youth of America that if you use drugs you can be rewarded with big money in big-time sports" - **National Drug Policy Director Lee Brown, on the signing of Darryl Strawberry for the Yankees. Strawberry, who signed for $675,000 with an further $1.8m for next season, has previously been suspended after testing positive for cocaine. Strawberry was also sentenced to three years probation for failing to reveal over $300,000 earnings that came from signing autographs.**

Baseball Briefing

Subscriptions: Trevor Kendall, 2 Drury Close, Waltham, Grimsby DN37 0XP

World Series

	Winners	Losers	Score
1903	Boston Red Sox (AL)	Pittsburgh Pirates (NL)	5-3
1904	*No Series*		
1905	New York Giants (NL)	Philadelphia Athletics (AL)	4-1
1906	Chicago White Sox (AL)	Chicago Cubs (NL)	4-2
1907	Chicago Cubs (NL)	Detroit Tigers (AL)	4-0 with 1 tie
1908	Chicago Cubs (NL)	Detroit Tigers (AL)	4-1
1909	Pittsburgh Pirates (NL)	Detroit Tigers (AL)	4-3
1910	Philadelphia Athletics (AL)	Chicago Cubs (NL)	4-1
1911	Philadelphia Athletics (AL)	New York Giants (NL)	4-2
1912	Boston Red Sox (AL)	New York Giants (NL)	4-3 with 1 tie
1913	Philadelphia Athletics	New York Giants (NL)	4-1
1914	Boston Braves (NL)	Philadelphia Athletics (AL)	4-0
1915	Boston Red Sox (AL)	Philadelphia Phillies (NL)	4-1
1916	Boston Red Sox (AL)	Brooklyn Dodgers (NL)	4-1
1917	Chicago White Sox (AL)	New York Giants (NL)	4-2
1918	Boston Red Sox (AL)	Chicago Cubs (NL)	4-2
1919	Cincinnati Reds (NL)	Chicago White Sox (AL)	5-3
1920	Cleveland Indians (AL)	Brooklyn Dodgers (AL)	5-2
1921	New York Giants (NL)	New York Yankees (AL)	5-3
1922	New York Giants (NL)	New York Yankees (AL)	4-0 with 1 tie
1923	New York Yankees (AL)	New York Giants (NL)	4-2
1924	Washington Senators (AL)	New York Giants (NL)	4-3
1925	Pittsburgh Pirates (NL)	Washington Senators (AL)	4-3
1926	St Louis Cardinals (NL)	New York Yankees (AL)	4-3
1927	New York Yankees (AL)	Pittsburgh Pirates (NL)	4-0
1928	New York Yankees (AL)	St Louis Cardinals (NL)	4-0
1929	Philadelphia Athletics (AL)	Chicago Cubs (NL)	4-1
1930	Philadelphia Athletics (AL)	St Louis Cardinals (NL)	4-2
1931	St Louis Cardinals (NL)	Philadelphia Athletics (AL)	4-3
1932	New York Yankees (AL)	Chicago Cubs (NL)	4-0
1933	New York Giants (NL)	Washington Senators (AL)	4-1
1934	St Louis Cardinals (NL)	Detroit Tigers (AL)	4-3
1935	Detroit Tigers (AL)	Chicago Cubs (NL)	4-2
1936	New York Yankees (AL)	New York Giants (NL)	4-2
1937	New York Yankees (AL)	New York Giants (NL)	4-1
1938	New York Yankees (AL)	Chicago Cubs (NL)	4-0
1939	New York Yankees (AL)	Cincinnati Reds (NL)	4-0
1940	Cincinnati Reds (NL)	Detroit Tigers (AL)	4-3
1941	New York Yankees (AL)	Brooklyn Dodgers (NL)	4-1
1942	St Louis Cardinals (NL)	New York Yankees (AL)	4-1
1943	New York Yankees (AL)	St Louis Cardinals (NL)	4-1
1944	St Louis Cardinals (NL)	St Louis Browns (AL)	4-2
1945	Detroit Tigers (AL)	Chicago Cubs (NL)	4-3
1946	St Louis Cardinals (NL)	Boston Red Sox (AL)	4-3
1947	New York Yankees (AL)	Brooklyn Dodgers (NL)	4-3
1948	Cleveland Indians (AL)	Boston Braves (NL)	4-2
1949	New York Yankees (AL)	Brooklyn Dodgers (NL)	4-1
1950	New York Yankees (AL)	Philadelphia Phillies (NL)	4-0
1951	New York Yankees (AL)	New York Giants (NL)	4-2
1952	New York Yankees (AL)	Brooklyn Dodgers (NL)	4-3
1953	New York Yankees (AL)	Brooklyn Dodgers (NL)	4-2
1954	New York Giants (NL)	Cleveland Indians (AL)	4-0
1955	Brooklyn Dodgers (NL)	New York Yankees (AL)	4-3
1956	New York Yankees (AL)	Brooklyn Dodgers (NL)	4-3
1957	Milwaukee Braves (NL)	New York Yankees (AL)	4-3
1958	New York Yankees (AL)	Milwaukee Braves (NL)	4-3
1959	Los Angeles Dodgers (NL)	Chicago White Sox (ZAL)	4-2
1960	Pittsburgh Pirates (NL)	New York Yankees (AL)	4-3
1961	New York Yankees (AL)	Cincinnati Reds (NL)	4-1

World Series

	Winners	Losers	Score
1962	New York Yankees (AL)	San Francisco Giants (NL)	4-3
1963	Los Angeles Dodgers (NL)	New York Yankees (AL)	4-0
1964	St Louis Cardinals (NL)	New York Yankees (AL)	4-3
1965	Los Angeles Dodgers (NL)	Minnesota Twins (AL)	4-3
1966	Baltimore Orioles (AL)	Los Angeles Dodgers (NL)	4-0
1967	St Louis Cardinals (NL)	Boston Red Sox (AL)	4-3
1968	Detroit Tigers (AL)	St Louis Cardinals (NL)	4-3
1969	New York Mets (NL)	Baltimore Orioles (AL)	4-1
1970	Baltimore Orioles (AL)	Cincinnati Reds (NL)	4-1
1971	Pittsburgh Pirates (NL)	Baltimore Orioles (AL)	4-3
1972	Oakland Athletics (AL)	Cincinnati Reds (NL)	4-3
1973	Oakland Athletics (AL)	New York Mets (NL)	4-3
1974	Oakland Athletics (AL)	Los Angeles Dodgers (NL)	4-1
1975	Cincinnati Reds (NL)	Boston Red Sox (AL)	4-3
1976	Cincinnati Reds (NL)	New York Yankees (AL)	4-0
1977	New York Yankees (AL)	Los Angeles Dodgers (NL)	4-2
1978	New York Yankees (AL)	Los Angeles Dodgers (NL)	4-2
1979	Pittsburgh Pirates (NL)	Baltimore Orioles (AL)	4-3
1980	Philadelphia Phillies (NL)	Kansas City Royals (AL)	4-2
1981	Los Angeles Dodgers (NL)	New York Yankees (AL)	4-2
1982	St Louis Cardinals (NL)	Milwaukee Brewers (AL)	4-3
1983	Baltimore Orioles (AL)	Philadelphia Phillies (NL)	4-1
1984	Detroit Tigers (AL)	San Diego Padres (NL)	4-1
1985	Kansas City Royals (AL)	St Louis Cardinals (NL)	4-3
1986	New York Mets (NL)	Boston Red Sox (AL)	4-3
1987	Minnesota Twins (AL)	St Louis Cardinals (NL)	4-3
1988	Los Angeles Dodgers (NL)	Oakland Athletics (AL)	4-1
1989	Oakland Athletics (AL)	San Francisco Giants (NL)	4-0
1990	Cincinnati Reds (NL)	Oakland Athletics (AL)	4-0
1991	Minnesota Twins (AL)	Atlanta Braves (NL)	4-3
1992	Toronto Blue Jays (AL)	Atlanta Braves (NL)	4-2
1993	Toronto Blue Jays (AL)	Philadelphia Phillies	4-2
1994	No Series		

Basketball ━━━━━━━━━━━━━━━━━━

Yugoslavia wins the European Championships and the final ends in uproar. Michael Jordan returns from his self-imposed exile in baseball's Minor Leagues. England's team qualify for the semi-final rounds of the 1997 European Championship. The domestic season is dominated by a team that didn't even exist 12 months earlier. And DeCarlo Deveaux earns the longest ever suspension, two years, in the English game. If any sport courted the headlines this year, it was basketball.

Yugoslavia have been treated as the pariahs of the sporting world since conflict erupted in their region in 1991. Banned for three years from basketball (through the UN Security Council sanctions) they came back for the European Championship in Athens. It offered a rare opportunity for the national team and they took the chance with both hands, winning the final against Lithuania 96-90, but not before the Lithuanian coach, Vladas Garastas, had marched his players off the court with 2 minutes and 15 seconds of the match left. Garastas claimed that the refereeing favoured the Yugoslavs; the Greek crowd jeered because they didn't like the Yugoslavs either; and when it was all settled (the Lithuanians returned to play out the game), the Croatians left the podium early refusing to stay while the Yugoslav national anthem was being played. And, just in case anyone didn't realise this was all about sport *and* politics; around Sarajevo, the skies were lit by tracer bullets as the Bosnian Serbs celebrated the Yugoslav victory.

England had their little bit of European Championship glory when they qualified for the next round of the 1997 championship. It may be a little hasty to say too much here as the first three matches of the semi-finals take place just after our deadline. The England coach, Dr Laszlo Nemeth typed out his resignation prior to the earlier qualifying round, insisting that it would be with the EBA if England failed to reach the next stage. It is less likely that he will stake his job on success in the semi-final round; Latvia, Germany and Russia await.

Sheffield Sharks had their way in the domestic season, securing the Budweiser League with a victory over Doncaster at the beginning of April and the Chrysalis Cup with a win over Thames Valley. It was the Sharks first season. They were established by Chris Wright, who founded Chrysalis Records. This year, Chrysalis was bought out by EMI, which leaves Wright with even more money to plough into the sport. Worthing won the finals - Sainsbury came on board to sponsor those and a series of schools road shows - and Thames Valley won the League Cup.

Michael Jordan, having quit basketball in October 1993, found the allure of Minor League baseball waning, and returned to the Chicago Bulls in March. Maybe he was worried that they would try to draught him in as a replacement during the baseball strike or perhaps he was anxious about his income which slipped to under $35m a year. You have to take drastic action when that happens. Anyway, there was no fairy story as the Bulls didn't win the championship for a fourth time with Jordan, though the man himself, now wearing 45 instead of 23, did sell a lot of new shirts and push the income back up. The title went instead to Houston Rockets who beat Orlando in the final. Houston make much of the fact that they are a born-again team. It was, you could say, four games to religion, none to Magic.

European Championship 1995 ▬▬▬▬

Athens   *June 21-July 2*

GROUP A
Lithuania 96 Germany 82; Italy 73 Israel 71;
Yugoslavia 84 Greece 80; Italy 68 Germany 67;
Lithuania 89 Greece 73; Israel 87 Sweden 62;
Yugoslavia 70 Lithuania 61; Germany 81 Sweden 71;
Greece 67 Italy 61; Yugoslavia 87 Italy 74;
Israel 78 Germany 60; Greece 86 Sweden 68;
Yugoslavia 85 Sweden 58; Greece 59 Israel 49;
Lithuania 80 Italy 69; Yugoslavia 72 Israel 59;
Lithuania 96 Sweden 73; Greece 83 Germany 79;
Italy 93 Sweden 61; Yugoslavia 92 Germany 79;
Lithuania 91 Israel 75

Final Table

	P	W	L	PF	PA	Pt
1 Yugoslavia	6	6	0	490	411	12
2 Lithuania	6	5	1	513	442	11
3 Greece	6	4	2	448	430	10
4 Italy	6	3	3	438	433	9
5 Israel	6	2	4	419	417	8
6 Germany	6	1	5	448	488	7
7 Sweden	6	0	6	393	528	6

GROUP B
Russia 126 Finland 74; France 89 Slovenia 68;
Spain 85 Turkey 70; Croatia 91 Slovenia 83;
Russia 85 France 65; Spain 87 Finland 74
Turkey 81 Finland 79; France 86 Spain 75;
Croatia 100 Russia 94; France 90 Turkey 76;
Russia 92 Slovenia 82; Croatia 80 Spain 70;
Croatia 90 Turkey 68; France 94 Finland 81;
Spain 88 Slovenia 85; Slovenia 93 Turkey 74;
Croatia 92 Finland 77; Spain 94 Russia 78
Slovenia 94 Finland 72; Russia 102 Turkey 93;
Croatia 81 France 72

Final Table

	P	W	L	PF	PA	Pt
1 Croatia	6	6	0	534	464	12
2 Spain	6	4	2	499	473	10
3 Russia	6	4	2	577	508	10
4 France	6	4	2	496	466	10
5 Slovenia	6	2	4	505	506	8
6 Turkey	6	1	5	462	539	7
7 Finland	6	0	6	457	574	6

Quarter-finals
Lithuania 82 Russia 71
Croatia 71 Italy 61
Yugoslavia 104 France 86
Greece 66 Spain 64
Semi-finals
Yugoslavia 60 Greece 52
Lithuania 80 Croatia 70

FINAL
Yugoslavia 96 Lithuania 90

Final Rankings: 1. Yugoslavia; 2. Lithuania; 3. Croatia;
4. Greece; 5. Italy; 6. Spain; 7. Russia; 8. France
The first four teams qualify for the Atlanta Olympics

Quotes ▬▬▬▬

"I think our decision to leave the court was the right one, but they told us we had to pay a $50,000 penalty if we did (not return) and we were not brave enough to do it, although Sabonis offered to pay" - **Vladas Garastas, coach of the Lithuanian team, which walked off the court with two minutes of the final remaining.**

"An interview is like a box of chocolates. You never know what you are going to get" - **Jack Haley, of the San Antonio Spurs, on his teammate Dennis Rodman.**

"One day, Dennis Rodman will need to ask somebody to tell him about the nineties" - **Bernie Lincicome in the Chicago Tribune.**

"The path of desire without spirit is where the losers stumble. All the Rockets hear it. Stay hungry, but be humble" - **Sign at the entrance to the Houston Rockets' locker-room.**

"They should give him a one-way ticket back to America. You don't go around attacking peole with a wooden stake, especially in front of three or four hundred children" - **Andy Maher, Derby player, after Leopard's DeCarlo Deveaux flipped and chased Tim Lascelles around the court brandishing a wooden post.**

European Championship 1997

Qualifying Round

Birmingham NEC   May 24-28
Denmanrk 95 Luxembourg 75; Georgia 68 Poland 91;
England 96 Wales 57; Georgia 97 Denmark 86;
Wales 71 Poland 111; England 102 Luxembourg 72;
Denmark 65 Poland 75; Wales 73 Luxembourg 76;
England 84 Georgia 74; Poland 122 Luxembourg 76;
Georgia 101 Wales 73; England 88 Denmark 70;
Georgia 81 Luxembourg 64; Denmark 105 Wales 57;
England 71 Poland 88

Final Table

		P	W	L	PF	PA	Pt
1	Poland	5	5	0	487	351	10
2	England	5	4	1	441	361	9
3	Georgia	5	3	2	421	398	8
4	Denmark	5	2	3	421	392	7
5	Luxembourg	5	1	4	363	473	6
6	Wales	5	0	5	331	489	5

Poland, England and Georgia qualify for the semi-final rounds. England are in Group B , which consists of: Estonia, Latvia, Germany, Russia, England, Portugal. Wales did not qualify.

Domestic Results

Budweiser League
MEN

	Premier Division	P	W	L	PF	PA	Pt
1	Sheffield Sharks	36	29	7	2842	2444	58
2	Thames Valley Tigers	36	28	8	3348	2975	56
3	London Towers	36	28	8	3215	2842	56
4	Manchester Giants	36	26	10	3200	2817	52
5	Doncaster Panthers	36	25	11	3198	3008	50
6	Leopards	36	23	13	3184	2940	46
7	Worthing Bears	36	20	16	3211	3110	40
8	Birmingham Bullets	36	18	18	3116	2974	36
9	Derby Bucks	36	10	26	2986	3207	20
10	H Hempstead Royals	36	9	27	2913	3441	18
11	Leicester Riders	36	8	28	2721	2993	16
12	Chester Jets	36	6	30	2946	3289	12
13	Sunderland Scorpions	36	4	32	2830	3670	8

	Division One	P	W	L	PF	PA	Pt
1	Crystal Palace	22	21	1	1883	1467	42
2	Coventry Crusaders	22	18	4	1799	1572	36
3	Ware Rebels	22	17	5	1969	1643	34
4	Oldham Celtics	22	14	8	1800	1731	28
5	Brixton Topcats	22	13	9	1905	1830	26
6	Stockton Mohawks	22	10	12	1848	1873	20
7	Bury Wildcats	22	9	13	1801	1852	18
8	Nottingham Cobras	22	9	13	1549	1638	18
9	Plymouth Raiders	22	7	15	1725	1855	14
10	Solent Stars	22	7	15	1624	1785	14
11	Slough Waterside	22	6	16	1477	1695	12
12	Swindon Sonics	22	1	21	1562	2001	2

	Division Two	P	W	L	PF	PA	Pt
1	Cardiff Phoenix	20	18	2	1753	1439	36
2	Mid Sussex Magic	20	15	5	1710	1513	30
3	Worcester City Chiefs	20	12	8	1607	1684	24
4	Liverpool Atac	20	12	8	1566	1468	24
5	Oxford Dons	20	12	8	1585	1533	24
6	South Bank	20	10	10	1458	1443	20
7	Westminster Warriors	20	9	11	1460	1421	18
8	Sheffield Forgers	20	8	12	1367	1473	16
9	Northampton 89'ers	20	7	13	1523	1575	14
10	Stevenage Phoenix	20	5	15	1518	1658	10
11	Greenwich Admirals	20	2	18	1359	1699	4

PREMIER DIVISION
Play-off Final: Worthing Bears 77 Manchester Giants 73

DIVISION ONE
Play-off Final: Crystal Palace 69 Coventry 62

DIVISION TWO
Play-off Final: Cardiff 74 South Bank 64

NATIONAL MEN'S CUP
Final: Sheffield Sharks 89 Thames Valley Tigers 66

BASKETBALL LEAGUE CUP
Final: Thames Valley Tigers 74 Sheffield Sharks 69

NATIONAL MEN'S TROPHY
Final: Crystal Palace 57 Ware Rebels 47

NBL Women's League

	Division One	P	W	L	PF	PA	Pt
1	Sheffield Hatters	20	18	2	1396	1035	36
2	Barking & D Bobcats	20	14	6	1313	1227	28
3	Rhondda Rebels	20	13	7	1269	1156	26
4	Thames Valley Ladies	20	13	7	1189	1085	26
5	Northampton 76'ers	20	11	9	1406	1266	22
6	London Heat	20	9	9	1056	1052	21
7	Birmingham Q'ty Cats	20	10	10	1235	1212	20
8	Ipswich	20	9	11	1215	1131	18
9	Nottingham Wildcats	20	6	13	960	1145	13
10	Cardiff Flyers	20	4	16	935	1412	8
11	Liverpool	20	1	19	1098	1351	2

	Division Two	P	W	L	PF	PA	Pt
1	Tyne & Wear	18	17	1	1311	951	34
2	Spelthorne Acers	18	14	4	1225	960	28
3	Plymouth City Racers	18	12	6	1112	1019	24
4	Doncaster Free Press	18	12	6	1175	1106	24
5	Leicester Ladies	18	7	10	903	979	15
6	Manchester Flames	18	7	11	955	995	14
7	Brixton Lady Topcats	18	7	11	1002	1088	13
8	Luton Fliers	18	6	12	952	1066	12
9	Harlesden Amazons	18	5	13	925	1105	10
10	Shropshire	18	2	15	989	1280	5

National Basketball Association

EASTERN CONFERENCE
Atlantic Division

	W	L	Pct	GB	Home	Road
Orlando	57	25	.695	-	39-2	18-23
New York	55	27	.671	2	29-12	26-15
Boston	53	47	.427	22	20-21	15-26
Miami	32	50	.390	25	22-19	10-31
New Jersey	30	52	.366	27	20-21	10-31
Philadelphia	24	58	.293	33	14-27	10-31
Washington	21	61	.256	36	13-28	8-33

Central Division

	W	L	Pct	GB	Home	Road
Indiana	52	30	.634	-	33-8	19-22
Charlotte	50	32	.610	2	29-12	21-20
Chicago	47	35	.573	5	28-13	19-22
Cleveland	43	39	.524	9	26-15	17-24
Atlanta	42	40	.512	10	24-17	18-23
Milwaukee	34	48	.415	18	22-19	12-29
Detroit	28	54	.341	24	22-19	6-35

WESTERN CONFERENCE
Midwest Division

	W	L	Pct	GB	Home	Road
San Antonio	62	20	.756	-	33-8	29-12
Utah	60	22	.732	2	33-8	27-14
Houston	47	35	.573	15	25-16	22-19
Denver	41	41	.500	21	23-18	18-23
Dallas	36	46	.439	26	19-22	17-24
Minnesota	21	61	.256	41	13-28	8-33

Pacific Division

	W	L	Pct	GB	Home	Road
Phoenix	59	23	.720	-	32-9	27-14
Seattle	57	25	.695	2	32-9	25-16
LA Lakers	48	34	.585	11	29-12	19-22
Portland	44	38	.537	15	26-15	18-23
Sacramento	39	43	.476	20	27-14	12-29
Golden State	26	56	.317	33	15-26	11-30
LA Clippers	17	65	.207	42	13-28	4-37

Play-offs

EASTERN CONFERENCE
Orlando v Boston
Orlando 124 Boston 77; Orlando 92 Boston 99;
Boston 77 Orlando 82; Boston 92 Orlando 95
Orlando Magic win series 3-1
Indiana v Atlanta
Indiana 90 Atlanta 82; Indiana 105 Atlanta 97;
Atlanta 89 Indiana 105
Indiana Pacers win series 3-0
New York v Cleveland
New York 103 Cleveland 79; New York 84 Cleveland 90;
Cleveland 81 New York 83; Cleveland 80 New York 93
New York Knicks win series 3-1
Charlotte v Chicago
Charlotte 100 Chicago 108; Charlotte 106 Chicago 89;
Chicago 103 Charlotte 80; Chicago 85 Charlotte 84
Chicago Bulls win series 3-1

WESTERN CONFERENCE
San Antonio v Denver
San Antonio 104 Denver 88; San Antonio 122 Denver 96;
Denver 95 San Antonio 99 *San Antonio win series 3-0*
Phoenix v Portland
Phoenix 129 Portland 102; Phoenix 103 Portland 94;
Portland 109 Phoenix 117 *Phoenix win series 3-0*
Utah v Houston
Utah 102 Houston 100; Utah 126 Houston 140;
Houston 82 Utah 95; Houston 123 Utah 106;
Utah 91 Houston 95 *Houston win series 3-2*
Seattle v LA Lakers
Seattle 96 LA Lakers 71; Seattle 82 LA Lakers 84;
LA Lakers 105 Seattle 101; LA Lakers 114 Seattle 110
LA Lakers win series 3-1

Conference Semi-finals
EASTERN CONFERENCE
Indiana v New York
New York 105 Indiana 107; New York 96 Indiana 77;
Indiana 97 New York 95; Indiana 98 New York 84;
New York 96 Indiana 95; Indiana 82 New York 92;
New York 95 Indiana 97 *Indiana win series 4-3*
Orlando v Chicago
Orlando 94 Chicago 91; Orlando 94 Chicago 104;
Chicago 101 Orlando 110; Chicago 106 Orlando 95;
Orlando 103 Chicago 95; Chicago 102 Orlando 108
Orlando Magic win series 4-2
Phoenix v Houston
Phoenix 130 Houston 108; Phoenix 118 Houston 94;
Houston 118 Phoenix 85; Houston 110 Phoenix 114;
Phoenix 97 Houston 103; Houston 116 Phoenix 103;
Phoenix 114 Houston 115 *Houston win series 4-3*
San Antonio v LA Lakers
San Antonio 110 Lakers 94; San Antonio 97 Lakers 90;
Lakers 92 San Antonio 85; Lakers 71 San Antonio 80;
San Antonio 96 Lakers 98; Lakers 88 San Antonio 100
San Antonio win series 4-2

Conference Finals
EASTERN CONFERENCE
Orlando v Indiana
Orlando 105 Indiana 101; Orlando 119 Indiana 114;
Indiana 105 Orlando 100; Indiana 94 Orlando 93;
Orlando 108 Indiana 106; Indiana 123 Orlando 96;
Orlando 105 Indiana 81
Orlando Magic win series 4-3
WESTERN CONFERENCE
San Antonio v Houston
S Antonio 93 Houston 94; S Antonio 96 Houston 106;
Houston 103 S Antonio 107; Houston 81 S Antonio 103;
S Antonio 90 Houston 111; Houston 100 S Antonio 95
Houston Rockets win series 4-2

NBA Finals
Orlando v Houston
June 7-14
Orlando 118 Houston 120; Orlando 106 Houston 117;
Houston 106 Orlando 103; Houston 113 Orlando 101
Houston Rockets win series 4-0

English National Cup & League Winners

NATIONAL CUP WINNERS

Year	Winners	Runner-up	Score
1936	**Hoylake YMCA**	London Polytechnic	32-21
1937	**Hoylake YMCA**	Laner Day Saints	23-17
1938	**Catford Saints**	Rochdale Greys	61-47
1939	**Catford Saints**	Rochdale Greys	53-41
1940	**Birmingham Inst.**	Central YMCA	35-30
1947	**Carpathians**	Birmingham D'bran	48-25
1948	**Latter Day Saints**	Latvian Society	*N/A*
1949	**Latter Day Saints**	Birmingham D'bran	*N/A*
1950	**Latter Day Saints**	USAF Burtonwood	*N/A*
1951	**BirminghamD'bran**	London Polytechnic	34-33
1952	**London Poly**	Birmingham D'bran	40-29
1953	**London Poly**	Birmingham D'bran	55-46
1954	**London Poly**	Nottingham YMCA	98-53
1955	**London Poly**	Birmingham D'bran	58-54
1956	*No competition*		
1957	**Central YMCA**	London Polytechnic	63-51
1958	**Central YMCA**	East Ham	48-40
1959	**Aspley O.B.**	Birmingham D'bran	58-39
1960	**Central YMCA**	London Polytechnic	95-62
1961	**London University**	Central YMCA	68-59
1962	**Central YMCA**	RAE Eagles	87-47
1963	**Central YMCA**	London University	70-69
1964	**Central YMCA**	London University	78-56
1965	**Aldershot Warriors**	Oxford University	79-63
1966	**Oxford University**	Aldershot War's	91-70
1967	**Central YMCA**	Vauxhall Motors	64-62
1968	**Oxford Univeristy**	Aldershot War's	61-59
1969	**Central YMCA**	Aldershot War's	70-62
1970	**Liverpool Police**	Oxford University	73-67
1971	**Manchester Univ.**	Sutton	88-81
1972	**Avenue** (Leyton)	Cambridge	58-66
1973	**London Latvian SK**	Sutton	70-69
1974	**Sutton & C. Palace**	Embassy All Stars	120-100
1975	**Embassy All Stars**	Sutton & C Palace	82-81
1976	**Crystal Palace**	Embassy All Stars	108-88
1977	**Crystal Palace**	Embassy All Stars	91-90
1978	**Crystal Palace**	Coventry	89-87
1979	**Doncaster**	Crystal Palace	73-71
1980	**Crystal Palace**	Doncaster	97-67
1981	**Crystal Palace**	Doncaster	91-74
1982	**Solent**	Doncaster	127-91
1983	**Solent**	Birmingham	98-97
1984	**Solent**	Leicester	86-67
1985	**Kingston**	Manchester United	103-98
1986	**Kingston**	Solent	113-82
1987	**Kingston**	Portsmouth	95-87
1988	**Kingston**	Portsmouth	90-84
1989	**Bracknell**	Manchester	87-75
1990	**Kingston**	Sunderland	103-78
1991	**Sunderland**	Leicester	88-81
1992	**Kingston**	Thames Valley	90-71
1993	**Guildford**	Worthing	82-72
1994	**Worthing**	Thames Valley	92-83
1995	**Sheffield Sharks**	Thames Valley	89-66

NATIONAL LEAGUE CHAMPIONS - MEN

Year	Winners	Runners-up
1972/73	**Avenue** (Leyton)	Liverpool
1973/74	**Crystal Palace**	Islington
1974/75	**Islington**	Crystal Palace
1975/76	**Crystal Palace**	Islington
1976/77	**Crystal Palace**	Manchester
1977/78	**Crystal Palace**	Milton Keynes
1978/79	**Doncaster**	Crystal Palace
1979/80	**Crystal Palace**	Doncaster
1980/81	**Birmingham**	Crystal Palace
1981/82	**Crystal Palace**	Solent
1982/83	**Crystal Palace**	Sunderland
1983/84	**Solent**	Crystal Palace
1984/85	**Kingston**	Manchester United
1985/86	**Manchester United**	Kingston
1986/87	**Portsmouth**	Kingston
1987/88	**Portsmouth**	Kingston
1988/89	**Glasgow**	Livingston
1989/90	**Kingston**	Sunderland
1990/91	**Kingston**	Sunderland
1991/92	**Kingston**	Thames Valley
1992/93	**Worthing**	Thames Valley
1993/94	**Thames Valley**	Worthing
1994/95	**Sheffield Sharks**	Thames Valley

NATIONAL LEAGUE CHAMPIONS - WOMEN

Year	Winners	Runners-up
1975/76	**Tigers** (Herts)	Cleveland E.
1976/77	**Tigers** (Herts)	Southgate
1977/78	**Cleveland E.**	Tigers (Herts)
1978/79	**Cleveland E.**	Tigers (Herts)
1979/80	**Tigers** (Herts)	Cleveland E.
1980/81	**Southgate**	Crysal Palace
1981/82	**Southgate**	Northampton
1982/83	**Southgate**	Northampton
1983/84	**Northampton**	Nottingham
1984/85	**Northampton**	Crystal Palace
1985/86	**Crystal Palace**	Northampton
1986/87	**Northampton**	Crystal Palace
1987/88	**Northampton**	Stockport
1988/89	**Northampton**	Stockport
1989/90	**Northampton**	Sheffield
1990/91	**Sheffield**	London YMCA
1991/92	**Sheffield**	Thames Valley
1992/93	**Sheffield**	Northampton
1993/94	**Sheffield**	Northampton
1994/95	**Sheffield**	Barking & Dagenham

National League & NBA Champions

National League

1938 Goodyears
1939 Firestones
1940 Firestones
1941 Oshkosh
1942 Oshkosh
1943 Fort Wayne Pistons
1944 Fort Wayne Pistons
1945 Fort Wayne Pistons
1946 Rochester Royals
1947 Chicago Stags
1948 Minneapolis Lakers
1949 Anderson Packers

NBA

1947 Philadelphia Warriors
1948 Baltimore Bullets
1949 Minneapolis Lakers
1950 Minneapolis Lakers
1951 Rochester Royals
1952 Minneapolis Lakers
1953 Minneapolis Lakers
1954 Minneapolis Lakers
1955 Syracuse Nationals
1956 Philadelphia Warriors
1957 Boston Celtics
1958 St Louis Hawks
1959 Boston Celtics
1960 Boston Celtics
1961 Boston Celtics
1962 Boston Celtics
1963 Boston Celtics
1964 Boston Celtics
1965 Boston Celtics
1966 Boston Celtics
1967 Philadelphia 76ers
1968 Boston Celtics
1969 Boston Celtics
1970 New York Knicks
1971 Milwaukee Bucks
1972 Los Angeles Lakers
1973 New York Knicks
1974 Boston Celtics
1975 Golden State Warriors
1976 Boston Celtics
1977 Portland Trail Blazers
1978 Washington Bullets
1979 Seattle Supersonics
1980 Los Angeles Lakers
1981 Boston Celtics
1982 Los Angeles Lakers
1983 Philadelphis 76ers
1984 Boston Celtics
1985 Los Angeles Lakers
1986 Boston Celtics
1987 Los Angeles Lakers
1988 Los Angeles Lakers
1989 Detroit Pistons
1990 Detroit Pistons
1991 Chicago Bulls

1992 Chicago Bulls
1993 Chicago Bulls
1994 Houston Rockets
1995 Orlando Magic

NBA leading scorers

Year	Name	Pts
1950	George Mikan (Mn)	1865
1951	George Mikan (Mn)	1932
1952	Paul Arizin (Ph)	1674
1953	Neil Johnston (Ph)	1564
1954	Neil Johnston (Ph)	1759
1955	Neil Johnston (Ph)	1631
1956	Bob Pettit (St L)	1849
1957	Paul Arizin (Ph)	1817
1958	George Yardley (Dt)	2001
1959	Bob Pettit (St L)	2105
1960	Wilt Chamberlain (Ph)	2707
1961	Wilt Chamberlain (Ph)	3033
1962	Wilt Chamberlain (Ph)	4029
1963	Wilt Chamberlain (SF)	3586
1964	Wilt Chamberlain (SF)	2948
1965	Wilt Chamberlain (SF/Ph)	2534
1966	Wilt Chamberlain (Ph)	2649
1967	Rick Barry (SF)	2775
1968	Dave Bing (Dt)	2142
1969	Elvin Hayes (SD)	2327
1970	Jerry West (LA)	2309
1971	Lew Alcindor* (Ml)	2596

took name of Kareem Abdul-Jabbar

1972	K Abdul-Jabbar (Ml)	2822
1973	Nate Archibald (KC/Om)	2719
1974	Bob McAdoo (Bf)	2261
1975	Bob McAdoo (Bf)	2831
1976	Bob McAdoo (Bf)	2427
1977	Pete Maravich (NO)	2273
1978	George Gervin (SA)	2232
1979	George Gervin (SA)	2365
1980	George Gervin (SA)	2585
1981	Adrian Dantley (Ut)	2452
1982	George Gervin (SA)	2551
1983	Alex English (Dn)	2326
1984	Adrian Dantley (Ut)	2418
1985	Bernard King (NY)	1809
1986	Dom'que Wilkins (At)	2366
1987	Michael Jordan (Ch)	3041
1988	Michael Jordan (Ch)	2868
1989	Michael Jordan (Ch)	2633
1990	Michael Jordan (Ch)	2753
1991	Michael Jordan (Ch)	2580
1992	Michael Jordan (Ch)	2404
1993	Michael Jordan (Ch)	2541
1994	David Robinson (SA)	2383
1995	Shaquille O'Neal (orl)	2315

1996 US OLYMPIC TEAM ROSTER

Anfernee Hardaway (Orlando)
Grant Hill (Detroit)
Karl Malone (Utah)
Reggie Miller (Indiana)
Hakeem Olajuwon (Houston)
Shaquille O'Neal (Orlando)
Scottie Pippen (Chicago)
David Robinson (San Antonio)
Glenn Robinson (Milwaukee)
John Stockton (Utah)

Billiards

1994 World Championships

Bombay, India   Sep 27-Oct 2, 1994

ROUND 1	ROUND 2	QUARTER-FINAL	SEMI-FINAL	FINAL
Nalin Patel IND 1420 / David Edwards WAL 839				
Michael Ferreira IND 1755 / Des Heald ENG 799	Geet Sethi IND 1823 / Nalin Patel 849	Geet Sethi 1716	Geet Sethi 916	
Clive Everton ENG 707 / Eugene Hughes 641	Michael Ferreira 717 / Clive Everton 798	Clive Everton 724		
Mark Wildman ENG 1034 / Manoj Kothari IND 1109	Norman Dagley ENG 1263 / Manoj Kothari IND 1225	Norman Dagley 795	Peter Gilchrist 1312	Peter Gilchrist 1539
Roxton Chapman ENG 1171 / Ashok Shandilya 569	Peter Gilchrist ENG 790 / Roxton Chapman 758	Peter Gilchrist 1687		**Peter Gilchrist**
Rex Williams ENG 1190 / Steve Hardcastle 718	Robbie Foldvari AUS 882 / Rex Williams 533	Robbie Foldvari 504	Ian Williamson 806	
John Murphy ENG 1357 / Howard Griffiths WAL 876	Ian Williamson ENG 1253 / John Murphy 265	Ian Williamson 682		Mike Russell 645
Bob Close ENG 1093 / John Caven 890	Bob Close 1062 / Derendra Joshi 1211	Devendra Joshi 678	Mike Russell 1556	
Derendra Joshi IND 1971 / M Spoormans 775	Mike Russell ENG 2159 / Subhash Agarwal 787	Mike Russell 2188		
Subhash Agarwal IND 1471 / David Rees 771				

1995 World Championships

Bombay, India   Sep 25-30

PRELIMINARY ROUND	ROUND 2	QUARTER-FINAL	SEMI-FINAL	FINAL
P Gilchrist bt D Causier				
C Everton bt J Bodle				
D Joshi bt H Griffiths	Peter Gilchrist ENG / Clive Everton ENG	Peter Gilchrist	Devendra Joshi	
I Williamson bt B Bhaskar	Devendra Joshi IND / Ian Williamson ENG	Devendra Joshi		Devendra Joshi
B Close bt R Shah	Bob Close ENG / Michael Ferreira IND	Bob Close	Robbie Foldvari	
M Ferreira bt D Heald	Nalin Patel IND / Robbie Foldvari AUS	Robbie Foldvari		**Geet Sethi**
N Patel bt E Hughes	Geet Sethi IND / Mark Wildman ENG	Geet Sethi	Geet Sethi	
R Foldvari bt J Caven	Ashok Shandilya / Norman Dagley ENG	Ashok Shandilya		Geet Sethi
G Sethi bt A Savur	Roxton Chapman ENG / Subhash Agarwal IND	Roxton Chapman	Roxton Chapman	
M Wildman bt G Jayaram	Rex Williams ENG / Mike Russell ENG	Mike Russell		
A Shandilya bt J Murphy				
N Dagley bt A Kumar				
R Chapman bt A Potikyan				
S Agarwal bt M Spoormans				
R Williams bt S Hardcastle				
M Russell bt M Rehani				

World Champions

World Professional Champions
England unless otherwise stated

1870	William Cook	1926	Tom Newman
1870	John Roberts jnr	1927	Tom Newman
1870	Joseph Bennett	1928	Joe Davis
1871	John Roberts jnr	1929	Joe Davis
1871	William Cook	1930	Joe Davis
1875	John Roberts jnr	1931	*No event*
1880	Joseph Bennett	1932	Joe Davis
1885	John Roberts jnr	1933	Walter Lindrum AUS
1889	Chrles Dawson	1934	Walter Lindrum AUS
1901	H W Stevenson	1951	Clark McConachy NZL
1901	Charles Dawson	1968	Rex Williams
1901	H W Stevenson	1971	Leslie Driffield
1903	Charles Dawson	1971	Rex Williams
1908	Melbourne Inman	1980	Fred Davis
1909	H W Stevenson	1982	Rex Williams
1910	H W Stevenson	1983	Rex Williams
1911	H W Stevenson	1984	Mark Wildman
1912	Melbourne Inman	1985	Ray Edmonds
1913	Melbourne Inman	1986	Robbie Foldvari AUS
1914	Melbourne Inman	1987	Norman Dagley
1919	Melbourne Inman	1988	Norman Dagley
1920	Willie Smith	1989	Mike Russell
1921	Tom Newman	1990	*No Event*
1922	Tom Newman	1991	Mike Russell
1923	Willie Smith	1992	Geet Sethi IND
1924	Tom Newman	1993	Geet Sethi IND
1925	Tom Newman	1994	Peter Gilchrist
		1995	Geet Sethi IND

Bobsleigh/Luge

Bobsleigh

World Championships
Winterberg, Germany Feb 6-19
Two Man

1	Christoph Langan/Olaf Hampel	GER I	3:46.91
2	Pierre Lueders/Jack Pyc	CAN I	3:48.68
3	Eric Alard/Eric Le Chanony	FRA I	3:48.72
dnf	Mark Tout/Lennox Paul	GBR I	

Four Man

1	Wolfgang Hoppe	GER II	3:43.20
2	Hubert Schoesser	AUT II	3:44.22
3	Harald Czudaj	GER I	3:44.28
4	Mark Tout	GBR I	3:44.48

World Cup
Calgary, Canada Nov 16-19
Two Man (Round 1)

1	Pierre Lueders/Jack Pyc	CAN I	1:53.80
2	Gunther Huber/A Tartaglia	ITA I	1:53.97
3	Christoph Langen/K-U Kohlert	GER I	1:54.08
9	Mark Tout/Lennox Paul	GBR I	1:54.73
17	Sean Olsson/Chris Symonds	GBR II	1:55.27

Four Man (Round 1)

1	Dirk Wiese	GER I	1:49.35
2	Pierre Lueders	CAN II	1:49.46
3	Mark Tout	GBR I	1:49.58
15	Sean Olsson	GBR II	1:50.87

Kunsteisbahn am Königssee, Germany Nov 28-Dec 3
Two Man (Round 2)

1	Christoph Langan/Peer Joechel	GER I	1:37.98
2	Gunther Huber/A Tartaglia	ITA I	1:38.16
3	Brian Shimer/Jeff Woodward	USA I	1:38.40

Four Man (Round 2)

1	Harald Czudaj	GER I	1:35.70
2	Matthias Benesch	GER III	1:35.92
3	Stephan Bosch	GER II	1:36.12

Winterberg, Germany Dec 5-10
Two Man (Round 3)

1	Sandis Prusis/Adris Pluksna	LAT I	1:53.13
2	Pierre Lueders/Jack Pyc	CAN I	1:53.16
3	Reto Götschi/Guido Acklin	SUI I	1:53.24
10	Mark Tout/Lennox Paul	GBR I	1:53.42
13	Sean Olsson/Chris Symonds	GBR II	1:53.95

Four Man (Round 3)

1	Wolfgang Hoppe	GER II	1:49.99
2	Dirk Wiese	GER I	1:50.53
3	Chris Lori	CAN I	1:50.71
10	Mark Tout	GBR I	1:51.24
17	Sean Olsson	GBR II	1:52.13

Altenberg, Germany Dec 11-18
Two Man (Round 4)

1	Pierre Lueders/Jack Pyc	CAN I	1:56.51
2	Christoph Langan/K-U Kohlert	GER I	1:56.59
3	Rene Spies/Sven Peter	GER II	1:56.96
8	Mark Tout/Lennox Paul	GBR I	1:57.89
15	Sean Olsson/Chris Symonds	GBR II	1:58.80

Four Man (Round 4)

1	Wolfgang Hoppe	GER I	1:51.26
2	Mark Tout	GBR I	1:51.64
3	Brian Shimer	USA I	1:51.68
16	Sean Olsson	GBR II	1:53.13

St Moritz, Switzerland Jan 29-Feb 1
Two Man (Round 5)

1	Reto Götschi/Guido Acklin	SUI I	2:09.78
2	Dirk Wiese/Christoph Bartsch	GER I	2:10.12
3	Chri Lori/Sheridon Baptiste	CAN II	2:10.17
12	Mark Tout/Lennox Paul	GBR I	2:11.16
16	Sean Olsson/Chris Symonds	GBR II	2:11.81

Four Man (Round 5)

1	Dirk Wiese	GER I	2:05.66
2	Reto Götschi	SUI I	2:06.04
3	Pierre Lueders	CAN II	2:06.07
4	Mark Tout	GBR I	2:06.09
20	Sean Olsson	GBR II	2:07.74

FINAL STANDINGS
Two Man
1. Pierre Lueders CAN 127; 2. Reto Götschi SUI 126;
3. Günther Huber ITA 122; 9. Mark Tout GBR 85;
17. Sean Olsson GBR 63.
Four Man
1. Pierre Lueders CAN 116; 2. Mark Tout GBR 111;
3. Dirk Wiese GER 103; 18. Sean Olsson GBR 51.

Luge

World Championships
Lillehammer Jan 31-Feb 5
Men

1	Armin Zöggeler	ITA
2	Georg Hackl	GER
3	Markus Prock	AUT

Women

1	Gabi Kohlisch	GER
2	Susi Erdmann	GER
3	Gerda Weissensteiner	GER

Doubles

1	Krausse/Behrendt	GER
2	Thorpe/Sheer	USA

World Cup Final Standings
Men

1	Markus Prock	AUT	292
2	Armin Zöggeler	ITA	281
3	Jens Müller	GER	262

Women

1	Sylke Otto	GER	164
2	Gabi Kohlisch	GER	145
3	Jana Bode	GER	135

Doubles

1	Krausse/Behrendt	GER	165
2	Brugger/Huber	ITA	151
3	Thorpe/Sheer	USA	150

World Champions

BOBSLEIGH

Year	Two-man	Four-man
1930	*No event*	Italy
1931	Killian/Huber GER	Germany
1933	Papana/Hubert ROM	*No event*
1934	Frim/Dumitrescu ROM	Germany
1935	Capadrutt/Diener SUI	Germany
1937	McEnvoy/Black GBR	Great Britain
1938	Fischer/Thielacke GER	Great Britain
1939	Lundnen/Kuffer BEL	Switzerland
1947	Feierabend/Waser SUI	Switzerland
1949	Endrich/Waller SUI	USA
1950	Feierabend/Waser SUI	USA
1951	Osterl/Nieberl FRG	W Germany
1953	Endrich/Stoeckli SUI	USA
1954	Scheibmeier/Zambelli ITA	Switzerland
1955	Feierabend/Warburton SUI	Switzerland
1957	Monti/Alvera ITA	Switzerland
1958	Monti/Alvera ITA	W Germany
1959	Monti/Alvera ITA	USA
1961	Monti/Siorpaes ITA	Italy
1962	Ruatti/De Lorenzo ITA	W Germany
1963	Monti/Siorpaes ITA	Italy
1965	Nash/Dixon GBR	Canada
1966	Monti/Siorpaes ITA	*
1967	Thaler/Durnthaler AUT	**
1969	de Zordo/Frassinelli ITA	W Germany
1970	Floth/Bader FRG	Italy
1971	Gaspari/Armano ITA	Switzerland
1973	Zimmerer/Utzshneider FRG	Switzerland
1974	Zimmerer/Utzshneider FRG	W Germany
1975	Alvera/Perruquet ITA	Switzerland
1977	Hiltebrand/Meier SUI	E Germany
1978	Schärer/Benz SUI	E Germany
1979	Schärer/Benz SUI	W Germany
1981	Germeshausen/Gerhardt GDR	E Germany
1982	Shärer/Benz SUI	Switzerland
1983	Pichler/Leuthold SUI	Switzerland
1985	Hoppe/Schauerhammer GDR	E Germany
1986	Hoppe/Schauerhammer GDR	Switzerland
1987	Pichler/Poltera SUI	Switzerland
1989	Hoppe/Musiol GDR	Switzerland
1990	Weder/Gerber SUI	Switzerland
1991	Lochner/Zimmermann GER	Germany
1993	Langan/Joechel GER	Switzerland
1995	Langan/Hampel GER	Germany

* Not decided due to fatal accident
** Not decided due to thaw

1959	Herbert Thaler AUT	Elly Lieber AUT
1960	Helmuth Berndt FRG	Maria Isser AUT
1961	Jerzy Wojnar POL	Elisab. Nagele SUI
1962	Thomas Kohler GDR	Ilse Geisler GDR
1963	Fritz Nachmann FRG	Ilse Geisler GDR
1965	Hans Plenk FRG	O Enderlein GDR
1967	Thomas Kohler GDR	O Enderlein GDR
1969	Josef Feistmantl AUT	Petra Tierlich GDR
1970	Josef Fendt FRG	Barbara Piecha POL
1971	Karl Brunner ITA	E Demleitner FRG
1973	Hans Rinn GDR	M Schumann GDR
1974	Josef Fendt FRG	M Schumann GDR
1975	Wolfram Fiedler GDR	M Schumann GDR
1977	Hans Rinn GDR	M Schumann GDR
1978	Paul Hildgartner ITA	Vera Sosulya URS
1979	Detlef Gunther GDR	Mel Sollmann GDR
1981	Sergey Danilin URS	Mel Sollmann GDR
1983	Miroslav Zajonc CAN	Steffi Martin GDR
1985	Michael Walter GDR	Steffi Martin GDR
1987	Markus Prock AUT	C Schmidt GDR
1989	Georg Hackl FRG	Susi Erdmann GDR
1990	Georg Hackl FRG	G Kohlisch GDR
1991	Arnold Huber ITA	Susi Erdmann GDR
1993	Wendel Suckow USA	G Weissensteiner ITA
1995	Armin Zöggeler ITA	Gabi Kohlisch GER

Men's two-seater

1955	Hans Krausner & Herbert Thaler AUT
1957	Josef Strillinger & Fritz Nachmann FRG
1958	Josef Strillinger & Fritz Nachmann FRG
1960	Reinhold Frosch & Ewald Walch AUT
1961	Roman Pichler & Raimondo Prinoth ITA
1962	Giovanni Graber & Gianp'lo Ambrosi ITA
1963	Ryszard Pedrak & Lucjan Kudzia POL
1965	Wolfgang Scheidel & Thomas Kohler GDR
1967	Klaus Bonsack & Thomas Kohler GDR
1969	Manfred Schmid & Ewald Walch AUT
1970	Manfred Schmid & Ewald Walch AUT
1971	Paul Hildgartner & Walter Plaikner ITA
1973	Horst Hornlein & Reinhard Bredow GDR
1974	Bernd Hann & Ulrich Hann GDR
1975	Bernd Hann & Ulrich Hann GDR
1977	Hans Rinn & Norbert Hahn GDR
1978	Dainis Bremse & Aigars Krikis URS
1979	Hans Brandner & Balthasar Schwarm FRG
1981	Bernd Hann & Ulrich Hann GDR
1983	Jorg Hoffmann & Jochen Pietzsch GDR
1985	Jorg Hoffmann & Jochen Pietzsch GDR
1987	Jorg Hoffmann & Jochen Pietzsch GDR
1989	Stefan Krausse & Jan Behrendt GDR
1990	Hansjorg Raffl & Norbert Huber ITA
1991	Stefan Krausse & Jan Behrendt GER
1993	Stefan Krausse & Jan Behrendt GER
1995	Stefan Krausse & Jan Behrendt GER

LUGE
Single seater

	Men	Women
1955	Anton Salvesen NOR	Karla Kienzl AUT
1956	-	Maria Isser AUT
1957	Hans Schaller FRG	M Semczyszak POL
1958	Jerzy Wojnar POL	-

Bowls

Men

British Championships
Llanelli   July 3-7
Singles
K B Morley (England) 21 A McCarley (Wales) 5
Pairs
England 16 Scotland 15
Triples
Wales 24 Ireland 13
Fours
England 21 Scotland 11
International Series - Final Table

	W	D	L	For	Ag	Pts
Wales	3	0	1	517	420	6
England	3	0	1	504	439	6
Scotland	3	0	1	485	433	6
Ireland	1	0	3	415	509	2
Channel Is	0	0	4	410	530	0

Sanatogen Champion of Champions Singles
Worthing   Aug 20
Semi-finals
H Whitehead 21 bt M Bantock 20
C W Wright 21 bt D Vaux 19
Final
C W Wright 21 H Whitehead 7

EBA National Championships
Worthing   Aug 20-Sep 1
SINGLES
Semi-finals
J Leeman (Durham) 21 bt P J Butcher (Kent) 12
L J Gillett (Gloucs) 21 bt D G Hobbis (Warwicks) 17
Final
J Leeman 21 bt L J Gillett 13

DOUBLES
Semi-finals
Biggs/Warren (Wiltshire) 21 bt
Robinson/Brittan (Warwicks) 11

Donnelly/Farrant (Essex) 25 bt
Shaw/Wilkinson (Derby) 15
Final
Biggs/Warren 21 bt Donnelly/Farrant 20

TRIPLES
Semi-finals
Sampson/D Taylor/T Taylor (Cumbria) 22 bt
Farrinton/Napthen/Topham (Cambs) 17

Wills/Jones/Allcock (Gloucs) 18 bt
Robinson/Thomas/Brittan (Warwicks) 10
Final
Wills/Jones/Allcock 16 bt Sampson/D Taylor/T Taylor 14

FOURS
Semi-finals
Barker/Clarke/Mulligan.Stockley (Middx) 21 bt
Hooper/Price/Hill/Adams (Gloucs) 16

Pannett/Rampley/Morley/Prince (Sussex) 23 bt
Cracknell/Nicholl/Gaskins/Hanger (Bucks) 22
Final
Pannett/Rapley/Morley/Prince 18 bt
Barker/Clarke/Mulligan/Stockley 17

Middleton Cup
(INTER-COUNTY CHAMPIONSHIP)
Worthing   Sep 2
Final
Cumbria 119 Suffolk 107

Churchill World Indoor Championships
Guild Hall, Preston   Feb 26
Singles Final
Andy Thomson (England) bt Richard Corsie (Scotland)
7-2 7-6 7-3
Doubles Final
A Marshall/R Corsie (Scotland) bt D Bryant/A Allcock
(England) 6-7 7-4 7-3 1-7 7-4

Women

British Isles Championships
Portrush, N Ireland   June 23-27
Singles
Winner: England; Runner-up: Scotland
Pairs
Winner: Wales; Runner-up: Ireland
Triples
Winner: England; Runner-up: Scotland
Fours
Winner: Ireland; Runner-up: England

British Championships
Portrush, N Ireland   June 23-27
Singles final
B Morgan WAL 25 N Johnston IRL 23

EWBA Championships
Leamington Spa   Aug 2-12
Singles final
V Wade (Northants) 21 S Thomas (Warwicks) 14
Pairs final
Beales/Prince (Bucks) 28 Moore/Barnard (Devon) 13
Triples final
Cambridge Chesterton 22 Northfleet 12
Fours final
Marlow, Bucks 23 Blackwell, Derbyshire 16

World & EBA Champions

WORLD OUTDOOR CHAMPIONSHIPS - MEN

	Singles	Pairs	Triples	Fours	Team
1966	David Bryant ENG	Kelly/Palm AUS	Australia	New Zealand	Australia
1972	Malwyn Evans WAL	Delgado/Liddell HKG	United States	England	Scotland
1976	Doug Watson RSA	Watson/Moseley RSA	South Africa	South Africa	South Africa
1980	David Bryant ENG	Sandercock/Reuben RSA	England	Hong Kong	England
1984	Peter Belliss NZL	Adrain/Arculli SCO/USA	Ireland	England	Scotland
1988	David Bryant ENG	Brassey/Belliss NZL	New Zealand	Ireland	England
1992	Tony Allcock ENG	Corsie/Marshall SCO	Israel	Scotland	Scotland

WORLD OUTDOOR CHAMPIONSHIPS - WOMEN

	Singles	Pairs	Triples	Fours	Team
1969	Gladys Doyle PNG	McDonald/Cridlan RSA	South Africa	South Africa	South Africa
1973	Elsie Wilkie NZL	Lucas/Jenkinson AUS	New Zealand	New Zealand	New Zealand
1977	Elsie Wilke NZL	Wong/Chok HKG	Wales	Australia	Australia
1981	Norma Shaw ENG	Bell/Allely IRE	Hong Kong	England	England
1985	Merle Richardson AUS	Richardson/Craig AUS	Australia	Scotland	Australia
1988	Janet Ackland WAL	Johnston/Nolan IRE	Australia	Australia	England
1992	Margaret Johnston IRE	Johnston/Nolan IRE	Scotland	Scotland	Scotland

WORLD INDOOR CHAMPIONSHIPS - MEN

	Singles	Pairs
1979	David Bryant ENG	No event
1980	David Bryant ENG	No event
1981	David Bryant ENG	No event
1982	John Watson SCO	No event
1983	Bob Sutherland SCO	No event
1984	Jim Baker IRE	No event
1985	Terry Sullivan WAL	No event
1986	Tony Allcock ENG	Bryant/Allcock ENG
1987	Tony Allcock ENG	Bryant/Allcock ENG
1988	Hugh Duff SCO	Schuback/Yates AUS
1989	Richard Corsie SCO	Bryant/Allcock ENG
1990	John Price WAL	Bryant/Allcock ENG
1991	Richard Corsie SCO	Bryant/Allcock ENG
1992	Ian Schuback AUS	Bryant/Allcock ENG
1993	Richard Corsie SCO	Smith/Thomson ENG
1994	Andy Thomson ENG	Curtis/Schuback AUS
1995	Andy Thomson ENG	Marshall/Corsie SCO

WORLD INDOOR CHAMPS - WOMEN

Singles only

1988	Margaret Johnston IRE
1989	Margaret Johnston IRE
1990	Fleur Bougourd ENG
1991	Mary Price ENG
1992	Sarah Gourlay SCO
1993	Kate Adams SCO
1994	Jan Woodley SCO

ENGLISH BOWLING ASSOCIATION CHAMPIONSHIPS

First competition 1905 - results from 1982 only

	Singles	Pairs	Triples	Fours
1982	Chris Ward, Norfolk	Bedford Borough	Lenham, Kent	Castle, Notts
1983	John Bell, Cumbria	Eldon Grove, Durham	Marlborough, Suffolk	Bolton, Lancs
1984	Wynne Richards, Surrey	Lenham, Kent	Clevedon, Somerset	Boscombe Cliff, Hants
1985	Roy Keating, Devon	Haxby Road, Yorks	Clevedon, Somerset	Aldershot, Essex
1986	Wynne Richards, Surrey	Owton Lodge, Durham	Poole Park, Dorset	Stony Stratford, Bucks
1987	David Holt, Lancs	Bolton, Lancs	Worcester County	Aylesbury Tn, Bucks
1988	Richard Bray, Cornwall	Leicester	Belgrave, Leics	Summertown, Oxon
1989	John Ottaway, Norfolk	Essex County	Southbourne, Sussex	Blackheath & G, Kent
1990	Tony Allcock, Gloucs	Wymondham D, Norfolk	Cheltenham, Gloucs	Bath, Avon
1991	Tony Allcock, Gloucs	Wigton, Cumbria	Wigton, Cumbria	Wokingham, Berks
1992	Stephen Farish, Cumbria	Blackheath & G, Kent	Chandos Pk, Bucks	Bournemouth, Hants
1993	John Wickham, Devon	Erdington Ct, Warwicks	Preston, Sussex	Reading, Berks
1994	Kevin Morley, Notts	Pontelan, North'berland	Torquay, Devon	Cheltenham, Gloucs
1995	John Leeman, Durham	Swindon W, Wiltshire	Cheltenham, Gloucs	Hollingbury Pk, Sussex

Boxing

In every sense, it was a timely win. Just as the sun was setting on his career, Frank Bruno became a world heavyweight champion. Indeed, the first British-born champion this century. This statistic is a little harsh on Herbie Hide, who not only won a world title in 1994, but had the nerve to defend it against Riddick Bowe and the temerity to think he could outpunch him too. But Herbie, he's bigger than you, dance a little. Sadly, no. Riddick saw the target and duly hit it. The fight over in the sixth.

Bruno against McCall was a very different affair. McCall won the title when he clocked Lennox Lewis in the second round of their Wembley fight a year earlier. On that occasion McCall chose to look at the target before he threw the punch. You would have thought he might have learned something from the experience, but apparently he didn't. Against Bruno, he threw almost every punch while staring at his feet. Was something wrong with his boots? We can only guess, but Bruno must have been grateful for blows that brushed his shoulders rather than his chin. As the fight progressed it was apparent that the Briton, at his fourth attempt (Witherspoon, Tyson and Lewis were the others), would win a world title.

Having berated Bruno for the quality of his three previous fights - lasting in total less than eight minutes and the last against the whale-like 19-stoner Mike Evans - Britain now heralded his triumph. American fight fans were not greatly moved. Having watched McCall labour against 45-year-old Larry Holmes at Las Vegas in the first defence of his title, they were probably just pleased that he'd left the country for his second.

For Bruno, the obvious swansong to his career awaits. Mike Tyson, released from jail on March 25th, reopened his boxing account with an 89-second win over Peter McNeeley, the fight stopped when McNeeley's manager Vinny Vecchione stepped between the boxers. Tyson earned $25m for that brief workout and the lure for whoever offers Tyson a chance at their title is the millions they will earn: that offsets the obvious risk. Bruno could earn more in a single fight than he has earned in the rest of his career. Negotiations starting at £10m plus.

Nigel Benn took the role of cheerleader at the Bruno title fight. Had any other spectator behaved in the same fashion, they would have been quietly assisted from the arena. But Benn was just returning the compliment; at all his fights Bruno now supplies the sideshow.

Benn didn't need one at the McClellan fight; the action was extraordinary. If McClellan had not been crippled by the punches of Benn, it would have rated as one of the best bouts in history. Yet never has the paradox of boxing been made more cruelly apparent. With few exceptions, the quality of a fight directly relates to the danger it presents. McClellan is now wheelchair-bound, blind and deaf. Jimmy Garcia, too, is dead.

Benn returned to the ring to defeat Vincent Nardiello and Danny Ray Perez in defence of his super-middleweight title and to relish even more the failure of Chris Eubank to defend his. Eubank fell for Steve Collins' line about hypnotism and failed to beat him twice. Eubank's star may have set, but Naseem Hamed's is on a vertical path upward. Steve Robinson, in his eighth title defence, had no chance. He should have gone fishing instead. Hamed might even be as good as he says he is. If he isn't, there's no sport that will bring him back down to earth as quickly as this one.

PROFESSIONAL BOXING ▬▬▬

World Title Fights

HEAVYWEIGHT
WBA/IBF
Las Vegas   Nov 5, 1994
George Foreman USA bt
Michael Moorer USA
ko, round 10
Foreman stripped of WBA title in March 1995

WBA
Las Vegas   Apr 8
Bruce Seldon USA bt
Tony Tucker USA
retired, round 7
Seldon took vacant title

WBA
Las Vegas   Aug 19
Bruce Seldon USA bt
Joe Hipp USA
rsf, round 10

IBF
Las Vegas   Apr 22
George Foreman USA bt
Axel Schulz
pts, 12 rounds
Foreman vacated title in July

WBC
Las Vegas   Apr 8
Oliver McCall USA bt
Larry Holmes USA
pts, 12 rounds

Wembley   Sep 2
Frank Bruno GBR bt
Oliver McCall USA
pts, 12 rounds

WBO
Las Vegas   Mar 11
Riddick Bowe USA bt
Herbie Hyde GBR
ko, round 6

Las Vegas   June 17
Riddick Bowe USA bt
Jorge Luis Gonzalez CUB
ko, round 6
Bowe vacated title in July

CRUISERWEIGHT
WBA
Mexico City   Nov 12, 1994
Orlin Norris USA bt
James Heath USA
ko, round 2

WBA
Worcester, USA   Mar 17
Orlin Norris USA bt
Adolpho Washington USA
pts, 12 rounds

Wembley   July 22
Nate Miller USA bt
Orlin Morris USA
ko, round 8

IBF
Atlantic City   June 24
Alfred Cole USA bt
Uriah Grant JAM
pts, 12 rounds

WBC
Salta   Dec 3, 1994
Anaclet Wamba FRA bt
Marcelo Dominguez ARG
pts, 12 rounds

Gualeguaychu, Arg   Sep 4
Marcel Dominguez ARG bt
Reynaldo Giminez ARG
rsf, round 12

WBO
Buenos Aires   Oct 1, 1994
Nestor Giovannini ARG bt
Larry Carlisle USA
retired, round 6

Hamburg   Dec 17
Dariusz Michalczewski GER bt
Nestor Giovannini ARG
rsf, round 10
Michalczewski vacated title

Manchester   June 10
Ralf Rocchigiani GER bt
Carl Thompson GBR
rsf, round 11

LIGHT-HEAVYWEIGHT
WBA
Stateline, Miss   Apr 1
Virgil Hill USA bt
Crawford Ashley GBR
pts, 12 rounds

Wembley   Sep 2
Virgil Hill USA bt
Drake Thadzi MAL
pts, 12 rounds

IBF
Halle, Germany   Oct 8, 1994
Henry Maske GER bt
Iran Barkley USA
retired, round 9

Frankfurt   Feb 11
Henry Maske GER bt
Egerton Marcus CAN
pts, 12 rounds

Dortmund   May 27
Henry Maske GER bt
Graciano Rocchigiani GER
pts, 12 rounds

WBC
London Arena   Feb 25
Mike McCallum JAM bt
Carl Jones USA
rsf, round 7

Lyon, France   June 16
Fabrice Tiozzo FRA bt
Mike McCallum USA
pts, 12 rounds

WBO
Cologne   Mar 11
Dariusz Michalczewski GER bt
Roberto Dominguez ESP
rsf, round 2

Hamburg   May 20
Dariusz Michalczewski GER bt
Paul Carlo USA
ko, round 4

Düsseldorf   Aug 19
Dariusz Michalczewski GER bt
Everardo Armenta MEX
ko, round 5

SUPER-MIDDLEWEIGHT
WBA
Quito, Ecuador   Dec 16
Frank Liles USA bt
Michael Nunn USA
pts, 12 rounds

Fort Lauderdale, Fla   May 27
Frank Liles USA bt
Frederic Seillier FRA
rsf, round 6

WBC
London Arena   Feb 25
Nigel Benn GBR bt
Gerald McClellan USA
ko, round 10

London Arena   July 22
Nigel Benn GBR bt
Vincenzo Nardiello ITA
rsf, round 8

Wembley   Sep 2
Nigel Benn GBR bt
Danny Ray Perez USA
ko, round 7

IBF
Las Vegas   Nov 18, 1994
Roy Jones USA bt
James Toney USA
pts, 12 rounds

Pensacola, Fla   Mar 18
Roy Jones USA bt
Antoine Byrd USA
rsf, round 1

Atlantic City   June 24
Roy Jones USA bt
Vinny Pazienza USA
rsf, round 6

WBO
Sun City   Oct 15, 1994
Chris Eubank GBR bt
Dan Schommer USA
pts, 12 rounds

Manchester   Dec 10, 1994
Chris Eubank GBR bt
Henry Wharton GBR
pts, 12 rounds

Millstreet, Ireland   Mar 18
Steve Collins IRL bt
Chris Eubank GBR
pts, 12 rounds

Cork   Sep 9
Steve Collins IRL bt
Chris Eubank GBR
pts, 12 rounds

MIDDLEWEIGHT
WBA
Caleta Olivia, Arg   Nov 5, 1994
Jorge Castro ARG bt
Alex Ramos USA

ko, round 2
Monterrey, Mex   Dec 10, 1994
Jorge Castro ARG bt
John David Jackson USA
rsf, round 9

Fort Lauderdale, Fla   May 27
Jorge Castro ARG bt
Anthony Andrews GUY
rsf, round 12

IBF
Quito, Ecuador   Dec 16, 1994
Bernard Hopkins USA bt
Segundo Mercado ECU
drew, 12 rounds
For vacant title

Landover   Apr 29
Bernard Hopkins USA bt
Segundo Mercado ECU
rsf, round 9

WBC
Worcester, USA   Mar 17
Julian Jackson ISV bt
Agostino Cardamone ITA
rsf, round 2
Jackson took vacant title

Las Vegas   Aug 19
Quincy Taylor USA bt
Julian Jackson ISV
rsf, round 6

WBO
Jean, USA   May 19
Lonnie Bradley USA bt
David Mendez MEX
rsf, round 12

Inglewood, Cal   July 15
Lonnie Bradley USA bt
Dario Galindez ARG
rsf, round 1

LIGHT-MIDDLEWEIGHT
WBA
Tucuman, Arg   Nov 11, 1994
Julio Cesar Vasquez ARG bt
Tony Marshall USA
pts, 12 rounds

Atlantic City   Mar 4
Pernell Whitaker USA bt
Julio Cesar Vasquez ARG
pts, 12 rounds
Whitaker relinquished title in March

Lyon, France   June 16
Carl Daniels USA bt
Julio Cesar Green USA
pts, 12 rounds

IBF
Las Vegas   Sep 17, 1994
Vincent Pettway USA bt
Gianfranco Rosi ITA
ko, round 4

Landover   Apr 29
Vincent Pettway USA bt
Simon Brown JAM
ko, round 6

WBC
Mexico City   Nov 12, 1994
Luis Santana DOM bt
Terry Norris USA
disq, round 5

Las Vegas   Apr 8
Luis Santana DOM bt
Terry Norris USA
disq, round 3

Las Vegas   Aug 19
Terry Norris USA bt
Luis Santana DOM
rsf, round 2

WBO
New Orleans   Nov 9, 1994
Verno Phillips USA bt
Santos Cardona PUR

pts, 12 rounds
Bushkill, Penn   Feb 3
Verno Phillips USA bt
Santos Cardona PUR
pts, 12 rounds

Perugia, Italy   May 17
Gianfranco Rosi ITA bt
Verno Phillips USA
pts, 12 rounds
Rosi failed post-match dope test and was stripped of title

WELTERWEIGHT
WBA
Carpentras, France   Oct 1, 1994
Ike Quartey GHA bt
Alberto Cortes ARG
ko, round 5

Atlantic City   Mar 4
Ike Quartey GHA bt
Jung-Oh Park KOR
rsf, round 4

Le Cannet, France   Aug 23
Ike Quartey GHA bt
Andrew Murray GUY
rsf, round 4

IBF
Monterrey   Dec 10, 1994
Felix Trinidad PUR bt
Oba Carr USA
rsf, round 8

Las Vegas   Apr 8
Felix Trinidad PUR bt
Roger Turner USA
rsf, round 2

WBC
Norfolk, USA   Oct 1, 1994
Pernell Whitaker USA bt
Buddy McGirt USA
pts, 12 rounds

Atlantic City   Aug 26
Pernell Whitaker USA bt
Gary Jacobs GBR
pts, 12 rounds

WBO
Manchester   Dec 10,1994
Eamonn Loughran IRL bt
Manning Galloway USA
tech dec, round 5

*Q*uotes

"You have to go to war and in war you have to be prepared to die. That's what boxing is" - **Gerald McClellan, two days before his fight against Nigel Benn.**

"It was brutal, brutal. This is the best fight I have seen in a British ring in all my time in boxing" - **Frank Warren, immediately after the Benn-McClellan fight.**

"I made a judgment. My job is the safety of the fighter. I thought he was wobbled bad" - **Vinny Vecchione, manager of Peter McNeeley, who stepped into the ring and forced the end of McNeeley's fight against Mike Tyson, after just 89 seconds of round one.**

"All men must suffer defeat, it is the way they get stronger. When they raised his hand I thought of Kipling's poem 'If' and said, 'Here I am, a mortal man at last' " - **Chris Eubank, after losing to Irishman Steve Collins.**

"Collins can have the devil on his side, but it won't count. His hypnotherapist will be out of a job on September 10th" - **Chris Eubank, on his rematch with Collins. The Irishman claimed a hypnotist helped him win the first fight.**

"I kept telling him, 'Chris, you can't hypnotise a chin' " - **Barry Hearn, on his efforts to convince Eubank that Collins 'hypnotism' was nonsense. Eubank lost the rematch.**

"A rematch with Eubank is not on.....he's got nothing I want except a Harley-Davidson motorbike" - **Nigel Benn.**

"It doesn't matter to me if it's my brother or my father that I'm fighting. Anyone who gets in the ring with me will have to be ready to rumble" - **Dennies Andries, 48.**

"He just wants to get in there and mash them. If you broke his arm, he'd kick you. If you broke his leg, he'd bite you. And if you took out his teeth, he'd nut you. This boy wants to fight" - **Brendan Ingle, on Naseem Hamed, whom he manages.**

"I'll take him out and try to do to him what he (Benn) did to my friend Gerald....This isn't a sporting event. I'm going in with bad intentions" - **Oliver McCall, before the Bruno fight.**

"I can't wait to fight. I can't wait to put my fist in his face and shove all those words down his throat" - **Frank Bruno, responding to McCall's taunts.**

"The Empire has struck back. I've been trying for 14 years to be the first British-born champion for 75 years. Now I'm going to enjoy it. If I were to get shot, run over or never walk again, it wouldn't matter to me. I've done what I've always wanted" - **Frank Bruno.**

"Is Frank taking it to bed with him? Yes, but he's taking me as well" - **Laura Bruno, talking about the WBC belt.**

"For many years people have regarded Frank as the 'Eddie the Eagle' of boxing. Now all of a sudden he is 'Roy of the Rovers' " - **Steve Davis, on Bruno.**

"It's my aim to get into the ring with Foreman. I was supposed to fight him in 1977, but the bout fell through. If people think I'm crazy, so be it" - **Joe Bugner, before his winning comeback at the age of 45.**

Belfast   May 27
**Eamonn Loughran IRL bt
Angel Beltre DOM**
nc, round 3

Belfast   Aug 26
**Eamonn Loughran IRL bt
Tony Ganarelli USA**
rsf, round 6

LIGHT-WELTERWEIGHT
WBA
Monterrey   Dec 10, 1994
**Frankie Randall USA bt
Rodney Moore USA**
rsf, round 7

Lyon, France   June 16
**Frankie Randall USA bt
Jose Barboza VEN**
pts, 12 rounds

IBF
Las Vegas   Jan 28
**Konstantin Tszyu RUS bt
Jake Rodriguez USA**
rsf, round 6

Newcastle   June 25
**Konstantin Tszyu RUS bt
Roger Mayweather USA**
pts, 12 rounds

WBC
Monterrey   Dec 10, 1994
**Julio Cesar Chavez MEX bt
Tony Lopez USA**
rsf, round 10

Las Vegas   Apr 8
**Julio Cesar Chavez MEX bt
Giovanni Parisi ITA**
pts, 12 rounds

Las Vegas   Sep 17
**Julio Cesar Chavez MEX bt
David Kaman KEN**
pts, 12 rounds

WBO
Inglewood, California   Feb 20
**Sammy Fuentes PUR bt
Fidel Avendano MEX**
rsf, round 2

Las Vegas   June 10
**Sammy Fuentes PUR bt
Hector Lopez USA**
pts, 12 rounds

LIGHTWEIGHT
WBA
Portland, Ore   Dec 10, 1994
**Orzoubek Nazarov KGZ bt
Joey Gamache USA**
ko, round 2

Tokyo   May 15
**Orzoubek Nazarov KGZ bt
Won Park KOR**
ko, round 2

IBF
Las Vegas   Jan 28
**Rafael Ruelas USA bt
Billy Schwer GBR**
rsf, round 8

Sun City   Aug 19
**Phillip Holiday RSA bt
Miguel Julio COL**
retired, round 11
Holiday took vacant title

WBC
Albuquerque, NMex   Dec 13, 1994
**Miguel Angel Gonzalez MEX bt
Calvin Grove USA**
retired, round 5

South Padre Island   Apr 25
**Miguel Angel Gonzalez MEX bt
Ricardo Silva ARG**
pts, 12 rounds

Ledyard   June 2
**Miguel Angel Gonzalez MEX bt
Marty Jakubowski USA**
pts, 12 rounds

Las Vegas   Aug 19
**Miguel Angel Gonzalez MEX bt
Lamar Murphy USA**
pts, 12 rounds

WBO
Las Vegas   Nov 18, 1994
**Oscar De La Hoya USA bt
Carl Griffith USA**
rsf, round 3

Los Angeles Dec 10, 1994
**Oscar De La Hoya USA bt
Johnny Avila USA**
rsf, round 9

Las Vegas   Feb 18
**Oscar De La Hoya USA bt
John-John Molina PUR**
pts, 12 rounds

Las Vegas   Sep 9
**Oscar De La Hoya USA bt
Gennaro Hernandez USA**
rtd, round 6

WBO/IBF
Las Vegas
**Oscar De La Hoya USA bt
Rafael Ruelas USA**
rsf, round 2
De La Hoya vacated IBF title in July

SUPER-FEATHERWEIGHT
WBA
Mexico City   Nov 12, 1994
**Genaro Hernandez USA bt
Jimmy Garcia COL**
pts, 12 rounds

IBF
Bayamon, Pur Nov 26, 1994
**John-John Molina PUR bt
Wilson Rodriguez DOM**
ko, round 10

Atlantic City   Apr 22
**Eddie Hopson USA bt
Moises Pedroza COL**
ko, round 7
Hopson took vacant title

Reno, Nevada   July 9
**Tracy Patterson USA bt
Eddie Hopson USA**
rsf, round 2

WBC
Las Vegas   Sep 17, 1994
**Gabe Ruelas USA bt
Jesse James Leija MEX**
pts, 12 rounds

Las Vegas   Jan 28
**Gabe Ruelas USA bt
Freddie Liberatore USA**
retired, round 2

Las Vegas   May 6
**Gabe Ruelas USA bt
Jimmy Garcia COL**
rsf, round 11

WBO
Rotterdam   Sep 24, 1994
**Regilio Tuur NED bt
Eugene Speed USA**
pts, 12 rounds
Tuur took vacant title

Groningen, Ned   Mar 9
**Regilio Tuur NED bt
Tony Pep CAN**
pts, 12 rounds

New Orleans June 17
**Regilio Tuur NED bt
Pete Taliefero USA**
rsf, round 5

The Hague   Sep 17
**Regilio Tuur NED bt
Luis Mendozo COL**
rtd, round 10

FEATHERWEIGHT
WBA
Trang, Tha   Sep 11, 1994
Eloy Rojas VEN bt
Samart Payakaroon THA
rsf, round 8

Bogota, Col   Dec 3, 1994
Eloy Rojas VEN bt
Luis Mendoza COL
pts, 12 rounds

Tagawa   Aug 13
Eloy Rojas VEN bt
Nobutoshi Hiranaka JPN
pts, 12 rounds

IBF
Atlantic City   Oct 22, 1994
Tom Johnson USA bt
Francisco Segura USA
pts, 12 rounds

Atlantic City   Jan 28
Tom Johnson USA bt
Manuel Medina MEX
pts, 12 rounds

South Padre Island   May 28
Tom Johnson USA bt
Eddie Croft USA
pts, 12 rounds

WBC
San Antonio, Tex   Jan 7
Alejandro Gonzalez MEX bt
Kevin Kelley USA
retired, round 11

Anaheim, Cal   Mar 31
Alejandro Gonzalez MEX bt
Louie Espinoza USA

pts, 12 rounds

Ledyard   June 2
Alejandro Gonzalez MEX bt
Tony Green USA
rsf, round 9

WBO
Cardiff   Oct 1, 1994
Steve Robinson GBR bt
Duke McKenzie GBR
ko, round 9

Cardiff   Feb 4
Steve Robinson GBR bt
Domingo Damigella ARG
pts, 12 rounds

Cardiff   July 7
Steve Robinson GBR bt
Pedro Ferradas ESP
rsf, round 7

Cardiff   Sep 30
Naseem Hamed GBR bt
Steve Robinson GBR
rsf, round 6

SUPER-BANTAMWEIGHT
WBA
Levallois Perret   Oct 13, 1994
Wilfredo Vasquez COL bt
Juan Polo Perez COL
pts, 12 rounds

San Antonio, Tex   Jan 7
Wilfredo Vasquez COL bt
Orlando Canizales USA
pts, 12 rounds

Bayamon, Pur   May 13
Antonio Cermeno VEN bt
Wilfredo Vasquez COL
pts, 12 rounds

IBF
Hammanskraal, Rsa   Nov 19, 1994
Vuyani Bungu RSA bt
Felix Camacho PUR
pts, 12 rounds

Hammanskraal, Rsa   Mar 4
Vuyani Bungu RSA bt
Mohammed Al Haji Nurhuda IND
pts, 12 rounds

Johannesburg   Apr 29
Vuyani Bungo RSA bt
Victor Llerena COL
pts, 12 rounds

WBC
Atlantic City   Mar 11
Hector Acero Sanchez DOM bt
Julio Gervacio PUR
pts, 12 rounds

Ledyard   June 2
Hector Acero Sanchez DOM bt
Daniel Zaragoza MEX
drew, 12 rounds

WBO
Anaheim, Cal   Mar 31
Marco Antonio Barrera MEX bt
Daniel Jimenez PUR
pts, 12 rounds

Ledyard   June 2
Marco Antonio Barrera MEX bt
Frankie Toledo USA
rsf, round 2

Inglewood, Cal   July 15
Marco Antonio Barrera MEX bt
Maui Diaz USA
rsf, round 1

South Padre Island   Aug 22
Marco Antonio Barrera MEX bt
Agapito Sanchez DOM
pts, 12 rounds

BANTAMWEIGHT
WBA
Bangkok   Nov 20, 1994
Daorung MP Petroleum THA bt
Koh In Sik KOR
rsf, round 5

Bangkok   May 27
Daorung MP Petroleum THA and
Lakhin CP Gym THA
drew, 12 rounds

IBF
Laredo, Tex   Oct 15, 1994
Orlando Canizales USA bt
Sergio Reyes USA
pts, 12 rounds
Canizales vacated title

Cartagena, Col   Jan 21
Harold Mestre COL bt
Juvenal Berrio COL
rsf, round 8
Mestre took vacant title

Johannesburg   Apr 29
Mbulelo Botile RSA bt
Harold Mestre COL
ko, round 2

Hammanskraal, Rsa   July 4
Mbulelo Botile RSA bt
Sam Stewart LIB
pts, 12 rounds

WBC
Nagoya, Jpn   Dec 4, 1994
Yasuei Yakushiji JPN bt
Joichiro Tatsuyoshi JPN
pts, 12 rounds

Nagoya   Apr 2
Yasuei Yakushiji JPN bt
Cuauhtemoc Gomez MEX
pts, 12 rounds

Nagoya   July 30
Wayne McCullough IRL bt
Yasuei Yakushiji JPN bt
pts, 12 rounds

WBO
Middlesbrough   Oct 25, 1994
Alfred Kotey GHA bt
Armando Castro MEX
pts, 12 rounds

Cumbernauld   Feb 17
Alfred Kotey GHA bt
Drew Docherty GBR
rsf, round 4

SUPER-FLYWEIGHT
WBA
Tokyo   Sep 18, 1994
Hyung Chul Lee KOR bt
Katsuya Onizuka JPN
rsf, round 9

Pusan, Kor   Feb 25
Hyung Chul Lee KOR bt
Tamonori Tamura JPN
ko, round 12

Seoul, Kor   July 22
Alimi Goitia VEN bt
Hyung Chul Lee KOR
ko, round 4

IBF
Cagliari, Sardinia   Dec 17, 1994
Harold Grey COL bt
Vincenzo Belcastro ITA
pts, round 12

Cartegena, Col   Mar 18
Harold Grey COL bt
Orlando Tobon COL
pts, round 12

Cartagena, Col   June 24
Harold Grey COL bt
Julio Cesar Borboa MEX
pts, round 12

WBC
Yokohama, Jpn   Jan 18
Hiroshi Kawashima JPN bt
Jose Luis Bueno MEX
pts, 12 rounds

WBO
Albuquerque Oct 12, 1994
Johnny Tapia USA bt
Henry Martinez USA
rsf, round 11 *Tapia took vacant title*

Albuquerque   Feb 10
Johnny Tapia USA bt
Jose Rafael Sosa ARG
pts, 12 rounds

Las Vegas   May 6
Johnny Tapia USA bt
Ricardo Vargas MEX
tech draw, round 8

Albuquerque   July 2
Johnny Tapia USA bt
Arthur Johnson USA
pts, 12 rounds

FLYWEIGHT
WBA
Kanchanaburi   Sep 25, 1994
Saensor Ploenchit THA bt
Yong-Kang Kim KOR
pts, 12 rounds

Rayong   Dec 26
Saensor Ploenchit THA bt
Danny Nunez DOM
ko, round 11

Songkhia   May 7
Saensor Ploenchit THA bt
Evangelio Perez PAN
pts, 12 rounds

IBF
Cartagena, Colombia   Feb 18
Francisco Tejedor COL bt
Jose Luis Zepeda MEX
rsf, round 7

Las Vegas   Apr 22
Danny Romero USA bt
Francisco Tejedor COL
pts, 12 rounds

San Antonio, Texas   July 29
Danny Romero USA bt
Miguel Martinez MEX
ko, round 6

WBC
Sapporo, Jpn   Jan 30
Yuri Arbachakov RUS bt
Oscar Arciniega MEX
pts, 12 rounds

Tokyo   Sep 25
Yuri Arbachakov RUS bt
Chatchai Sasakul THA
pts, 12 rounds

WBO
Sun City, Rsa   Oct 15, 1994
Jake Matlala RSA bt
Domingo Lucas PHI
pts, 12 rounds

Hammanskraal   Feb 11
Alberto Jimenez MEX bt
Jake Matlala RSA
rsf, round 8

Cardiff   June 17
Alberto Jimenez MEX bt
Robbie Regan WAL
retired, round 9

LIGHT-FLYWEIGHT
WBA
Bangkok   Oct 9, 1994
Leo Gamez VEN bt
Pichitnoi Sithbangprachan THA
rsf, round 6

Ulsan, Kor   Feb 4
Hiyong Choi KOR bt
Leo Gamez VEN
pts, 12 rounds

Osaka   Sep 5
Hiyong Choi KOR bt
Keiji Yamaguchi JPN
pts, 12 rounds

WBC/IBF
Lake Tahoe   Sep 10, 1994
Humberto Gonzalez MEX bt
Juan Domingo Cordoba ARG
retired, round 7

Mexico City   Nov 12, 1994
Humberto Gonzalez MEX bt
Michael Carbajal USA
pts, 12 rounds

Anaheim, Cal   Mar 31
Humberto Gonzalez MEX bt
Jesus Zuniga COL
ko, round 5

Inglewood, Cal   July 15
Saman Sorjaturong THA bt
Humberto Gonzalez MEX
rsf, round 7

WBO
Irvine, Sco   Nov 23, 1994
Paul Weir GBR bt
Paul Oulden RSA
pts, 12 rounds
Weir took vacant title

Irvine, Sco   Apr 5
Paul Weir GBR bt
Ric Magramo PHI
pts, 12 rounds

STRAWWEIGHT
WBA
Hatya   Nov 5, 1994
Chana Porpaoin THA bt
Manuel Herrera DOM
pts, 12 rounds

Bangkok   Aug 5
Chana Porpaoin THA bt
Ernesto Rubillar jnr PHI
ko, round 6

IBF
Khon Kaen, Tha   Nov 12, 1994
Ratanapol Sorvorapin THA bt
Carlos Rodriguez VEN
ko, round 3

Bangkok   Feb 25
Ratanapol Sorvorapin THA bt
Jerry Pahayahay PHI
rsf, round 3

Chiang Mai, Tha   May 20
Ratanapol Sorvorapin THA bt
Oscar Flores COL
rsf, round 2

WBC
Mexico City   Nov 12, 1994
Ricardo Lopez MEX bt
Javier Varguez MEX
rsf, round 8

Monterrey, Mex   Dec 10, 1994
Ricardo Lopez MEX bt
Yamil Caraballo COL
ko, round 1

Stateline, Miss   Apr 1
Ricardo Lopez MEX bt
Andy Tabanas PHI
rsf, round 12

WBO
Hamburg   Sep 10, 1994
Alex Sanchez PUR bt
Oscar Andrade MEX
ko, round 4

Las Vegas   Jan 28
Alex Sanchez PUR bt
Rafael Orozco MEX
pts, 12 rounds

San Antonio, Tex   July 29
Alex Sanchez PUR bt
Tomas Rivera MEX
pts, 12 rounds

British Champions
As at September 30, 1995
Heavyweight
James Oyebola
Cruiserweight
Terry Dunstan
Light-heavyweight
Crawford Ashley
Super-middleweight
Sam Storey
Middleweight
Neville Brown
Light-middleweight
Robert McCracken
Welterweight
Del Bryan
Light-welterweight
Ross Hale
Lightweight
Michael Ayers
Super-featherweight
Floyd Havard
Featherweight
Jonjo Irvin
Super-bantamweight
Richie Wenton
Bantamweight
Drew Docherty
Flyweight
Francis Ampofo

Amateur Boxing
Berlin   May 3-14

WORLD CHAMPIONSHIPS
Super-heavyweight (+91kg)
1	**Alexei Lezin**	**RUS**
2	Vitaly Klitschko	UKR
3	Rene Monse	GER
3	Lawrence Clay-Bey	USA

Heavyweight (91kg)
1	**Felix Savon**	**CUB**
2	Luan Krasniqi	GER
3	Christophe Mendy	FRA
3	Sinan Samilsam	TUR

Light-heavyweight (81kg)
1	**Antonio Tarver**	**USA**
2	Diosvani Vega	CUB
3	Thomas Ulrich	GER
3	Vasily Shirow	KZK

Middleweight (75kg)
1	**Ariel Hernandez**	**CUB**
2	Tomasz Borowski	POL
3	Dilschod Jarbekow	UZB
3	Mohamed Mesbahi	MAR

Light-middleweight (71kg)
1	**Franciso Vastag**	**ROM**
2	Alfredo Duvergel	CUB
3	Markus Beyer	GER
3	Slavisa Popovic	YUG

Welterweight (67kg)
1	**Juan Hernandez**	**CUB**
2	Oleg Saitov	RUS
3	Andreas Otto	GER
3	V Karpaciauskas	LIT

Light-welterweight (63.5kg)
1	**Hector Vinent**	**CUB**
2	Nurhan Suleymanoglu	TUR
3	Oktay Urkal	GER
3	Radoslaw Suslekow	BUL

Lightweight (60kg)
1	**Leonard Doroftei**	**ROM**
2	Bruno Wartelle	FRA
3	Marco Rudolph	GER
3	Pablo Rojas	CUB

Featherweight (57kg)
1	**Serafim Todorow**	**BUL**
2	Noureddine Medjihoud	ALG
3	Falk Huste	GER
3	Vidas Biciulaitis	LIT

Bantamweight (54kg)
1	**Raimkul Malachbekow**	**RUS**
2	Robert Ciba	POL
3	Dirk Krüger	GER
3	Artur Mikaelian	ARM

Flyweight (51kg)
1	**Zoltan Lunka**	**GER**
2	Bolat Jumadilow	KZK
3	Raul Gonzalez	CUB
3	Joni Turunen	FIN

Light-flyweight (48kg)
1	**Daniel Petrov**	**BUL**
2	Bernard Inom	FRA
3	Juan Ramirez	CUB
3	Hamid Berhili	MAR

ABA CHAMPIONS
Super-heavyweight
Rod Allen
Heavyweight
Matthew Ellis
Light-heavyweight
Kelly Oliver
Middleweight
Jason Matthews
Light-middleweight
Chris Bessey
Welterweight
Mike Hall
Light-welterweight
Alan Vaughan
Lightweight
Roy Rutherford
Featherweight
David Burrows
Bantamweight
Noel Wilders
Flyweight
Danny Costello
Light-flyweight
Darren Fox

Try this quiz question for starters. What do Francisco Damiani, Jimmy Thunder, Johnny Nelson, Tim Puller, Bruce Seldon and Frank Bruno have in common? The answer is that, in the past five years, they have all held a world heavyweight title. There are currently eight organisations that lay claim to governing world pro-boxing. They are the WBA, WBC, WBF, WBO, WBU, IBC, IBF and the IBO. It seems reasonable to assume that the IBA and the IBU won't be long coming either.

World Champions (Undisputed)

HEAVYWEIGHT
Over 86.2kg (190lb)
1882 John L Sullivan USA
1892 James J Corbett USA
1897 Bob Fitzsimmons GBR
1899 James J Jeffries USA
1905 Marvin Hart USA
1906 Tommy Burns CAN
1908 Jack Johnson USA
1915 Jess Willard USA
1919 Jack Dempsey USA
1926 Gene Tunney USA
1930 Max Schmeling GER
1932 Jack Sharkey USA
1933 Primo Carnera ITA
1934 Max Baer USA
1935 James J Braddock USA
1937 Joe Louis USA
1949 Ezzard Charles USA
1951 Jersey Joe Walcott USA
1952 Rocky Marciano USA
1956 Floyd Patterson USA
1959 Ingemar Johansson SWE
1960 Floyd Patterson USA
1962 Sonny Liston USA
1964 Cassius Clay USA
1970 Joe Frazier USA
1973 George Foreman USA
1974 Muhammed Ali USA
1978 Leon Spinks USA
1987 Mike Tyson USA

CRUISERWEIGHT
Under 86.2kg (190lb)
1988 Evander Holyfield USA

LIGHTT HEAVYWEIGHT
Under 79.4kg (175lb)
1903 Jack Root AUT
1903 George Gardner IRL
1903 Bob Fitzsimmons GBR
1905 Jack O'Brien USA
1912 Jack Dillon USA
1916 Battling Levinsky USA
1920 Georges Carpentier FRA
1922 Battling Siki SEN
1923 Mike McTigue IRL
1925 Paul Berlenbach USA
1926 Jack Delaney CAN
1927 Jim Slattery USA
1927 Tommy Loughran USA
1930 Jim Slattery USA
1930 Maxie Rosenbloom USA
1934 Bob Olin USA
1935 John Henry Lewis USA
1939 Melio Bettina USA
1939 Billy Conn USA
1941 Anton Christoforidis GRE
1941 Gus Lesnevich USA
1948 Freddie Mills GBR
1950 Joey Maxim USA

1952 Archie Moore USA
1962 Harold Johnson USA
1963 Willie Pastrano USA
1965 José Torres PUR
1966 Dick Tiger NGR
1968 Bob Foster USA
1983 Michael Spinks USA

MIDDLEWEIGHT
Under 72.6kg (160lb)
1891 Jack 'Nonpareil'
    Dempsey IRL
1891 Bob Fitzsimmons GBR
1898 Tommy Ryan USA
1907 Stanley Ketchel USA
1908 Billy Papke USA
1908 Stanley Ketchel USA
1910 Billy Papke USA
1911 Cyclone Thompson USA
1913 Frank Klaus USA
1913 George Chip USA
1914 Al McCoy USA
1917 Mike O'Dowd USA
1920 Johnny Wilson USA
1923 Harry Greb USA
1926 Tiger Flowers USA
1926 Mickey Walker USA
1931 Gorilla Jones USA
1932 Marcel Thil FRA
1941 Tony Zale USA
1947 Rocky Graziano USA
1948 Tony Zale USA
1948 Marcel Cerdan ALG
1949 Jake la Motta USA
1951 Sugar Ray Robinson USA
1951 Randolph Turpin GBR
1951 Sugar Ray Robinson USA
1953 Carl 'Bobo' Olsen HAW
1955 Sugar Ray Robinson USA
1957 Gene Fullmer USA
1957 Sugar Ray Robinson USA
1957 Carmen Basilio USA
1958 Sugar Ray Robinson USA
1960 Paul Pender USA
1961 Terry Downes GBR
1962 Paul Pender USA
1963 Dick Tiger NGR
1963 Joey Giardello USA
1965 Dick Tiger NGR
1966 Emile Griffith USA
1968 Nino Benvenuti ITA
1970 Carlos Monzon ARG
1976 Carlos Monzon ARG
1977 Rodrigo Valdez COL
1978 Hugo Corro ARG
1979 Vito Antuofermo ITA
1980 Alan Minter GBR
1980 Marvin Hagler USA

JUNIOR MIDDLEWEIGHT
Under 69.9kg (154lb)
1962 Denny Moyer USA
1963 Ralph Dupas USA
1963 Sandro Massinghi ITA
1965 Nino Benvenuti ITA
1966 Kim Ki-soo KOR
1968 Sandro Massinghi ITA
1969 Freddie Little USA
1970 Carmelo Bossi ITA
1971 Koichi Wajima JPN
1974 Oscar Albarado USA
1975 Koichi Wajima JPN

WELTERWEIGHT
Under 66.7kg (147lb)
1892 Mysterious Billy Smith
    CAN
1894 Tommy Ryan USA
1896 Charles 'Kid' McCoy USA
1898 Mysterious Billy Smith
1900 Rube Ferns USA
1900 Matty Matthews USA
1901 Rube Ferns USA
1901 Joe Walcott BAR
1904 Dixie Kid USA
1905 Joe Walcott BAR
1906 Honey Mellody USA
1907 Mike 'Twin' Sullivan USA
1915 Ted Kid Lewis GBR
1916 Jack Britton USA
1917 Ted Kid Lewis GBR
1919 Jack Britton USA
1922 Micky Walker USA
1926 Pete Latzo USA
1927 Joe Dundee ITA
1929 Jackie Fields USA
1930 Jack Thompson USA
1930 Tommy Freeman USA
1931 Jack Thompson USA
1931 Lou Broulliard CAN
1932 Jackie Fields USA
1933 Young Corbett III ITA
1933 Jimmy McLarnin IRL
1934 Barney Ross USA
1934 Jimmy McLarnin IRL
1935 Barney Ross USA
1938 Henry Armstrong USA
1940 Fritzie Zivic USA
1941 Freddie Cochrane USA
1946 Marty Servo USA
1946 Sugar Ray Robinson USA
1951 Johnny Bratton USA
1951 Kid Gavilan CUB
1954 Johnny Saxton USA
1955 Tony de Marco USA
1955 Carmen Basilio USA
1956 Johnny Saxton USA
1956 Carmen Basilio USA
1958 Virgil Atkins USA
1958 Don Jordon DOM

World Champions (Undisputed)

1960 Benny Kid Paret CUB	
1961 Emile Griffth USA	
1961 Benny Kid Paret CUB	
1962 Emile Griffith USA	
1963 Louis Rodriguez CUB	
1963 Emile Griffith USA	
1966 Curtis Cokes USA	
1969 Jose Napoles CUB	
1970 Billy Backus USA	
1971 Jose Napoles CUB	
1981 Sugar Ray Leonard USA	
1985 Don Curry USA	
1986 Lloyd Honeyghan GBR	

JUNIOR WELTERWEIGHT
Under 63.5kg (140lb)
1922 Pinky Mitchell USA
1926 Mushy Callahan USA
1930 Jackie Kid Berg GBR
1931 Tony Canzoneri USA
1932 Johnny Jaddick USA
1933 Battling Shaw MEX
1933 Tony Canzoneri USA
1933 Barney Ross USA
1946 Tippy Larkin USA
1959 Carlos Ortiz PUR
1960 Duilio Loi ITA
1962 Eddie Perkins USA
1962 Duilio Loi ITA
1963 Roberto Cruz PHI
1963 Eddie Perkins USA
1965 Carlos Hernandez VEN
1966 Sandro Lopopolo ITA
1967 Paul Fujii USA

LIGHTWEIGHT
Under 61.2kg (135lb)
1896 George Lavigne USA
1899 Frank Erne SUI
1902 Joe Gans USA
1908 Battling Nelson DEN
1910 Ad Wolgast USA
1912 Willie Ritchie USA
1914 Freddie Welsh GBR
1917 Benny Leonard USA
1925 Jimmy Goodrich USA
1925 Rocky Kansas USA
1926 Sammy Mandell USA
1930 Al Singer USA
1930 Tony Canzoneri USA
1933 Barney Ross USA
1935 Tony Canzoneri USA
1936 Lou Ambers USA
1938 Henry Armstrong USA
1939 Lou Ambers USA
1940 Lew Jenkins USA
1941 Sammy Angott USA
1942 Beau Jack USA
1943 Bob Montgomery USA
1943 Sammy Angott USA
1944 Juan Zurita MEX

1945 Ike Williams USA
1951 Jimmy Carter USA
1952 Lauro Salas MEX
1952 Jimmy Carter USA
1954 Paddy de Marco USA
1954 Jimmy Carter USA
1955 Wallace Bud Smith USA
1956 Joe Brown USA
1962 Carlos Ortiz PUR
1965 Ismael Laguna PAN
1965 Carlos Ortiz PUR
1968 Carlos Teo Cruz DOM
1969 Mando Ramos USA
1970 Ismael Laguna PAN
1978 Roberto Duran PAN

JUNIOR LIGHTWEIGHT
Under 59kg (130lb)
1921 Johnny Dundee ITA
1923 Jack Bernstein USA
1923 Johnny Dundee ITA
1924 Kid Sullivan USA
1925 Mike Ballerino USA
1925 Tod Morgan USA
1929 Benny Bass USA
1931 Kid Chocolate CUB
1933 Frankie Klick USA
1959 Harold Gomes USA
1960 Flash Elorde PHI
1967 Yoshiaki Numata JPN
1967 Hiroshi Kobayashi JPN

FEATHERWEIGHT
Under 57.2kg (126lb)
1892 George Dixon CAN
1897 Solly Smith USA
1898 Dave Sullivan IRL
1898 George Dixon CAN
1900 Terry McGovern USA
1901 Young Corbett USA
1904 Abe Attell USA
1912 Johnny Kilbane USA
1923 Eugene Criqui FRA
1923 Johnny Dundee ITA
1925 Louis Kid Kaplan USA
1927 Benny Bass USA
1928 Tony Canzoneri USA
1928 Andre Routis FRA
1929 Battling Battalino USA
1933 Freddie Miller USA
1936 Petey Sarron USA
1937 Henry Armstrong USA
1938 Joey Archibald USA
1946 Willie Pep USA
1948 Sandy Saddler USA
1949 Willie Pep USA
1950 Sandy Saddler USA
1957 Hogan Kid Bassey NGR
1959 Davey Moore USA
1963 Sugar Ramos CUB
1964 Vicente Saldivar MEX

JUNIOR FEATHERWEIGHT
Under 55.3kg (122lb)
1922 Jack Kid Wolfe USA
1923 Carl Duane USA

BANTAMWEIGHT
Under 53.5kg (118lb)
1890 George Dixon CAN
1899 Terry McGovern USA
1901 Harry Forbes USA
1903 Frankie Neil USA
1904 Joe Bowker GBR
1905 Jimmy Walsh USA
1910 Johnny Coulon CAN
1914 Kid Williams DEN
1917 Pete Herman USA
1920 Joe Lynch USA
1921 Pete Herman USA
1921 Johnny Buff USA
1922 Joe Lynch USA
1924 Abe Goldstein USA
1924 Eddie Martin USA
1925 Charley Rosenberg USA
1929 Al Brown PAN
1936 Tony Marino USA
1936 Sixto Escobar PUR
1937 Harry Jeffra USA
1938 Sixto Escobar PUR
1940 Lou Salica USA
1942 Manuel Ortiz USA
1947 Harold Dade USA
1947 Manuel Ortiz USA
1950 Vic Toweel RSA
1952 Jimmy Carruthers AUS
1954 Robert Cohen ALG
1956 Mario D'Agata ITA
1957 Alphonse Halimi ALG
1959 Joe Becerra MEX
1962 Eder Jofre BRA
1965 Fighting Harada JPN
1968 Lionel Rose AUS
1969 Ruben Olivares MEX
1970 Chucho Castillo MEX
1971 Ruben Olivares MEX
1972 Rafael Herrera MEX
1972 Enrique Pinder PAN

World Champions (undisputed/disputed)

FLYWEIGHT
Under 50.8kg (112lb)
1916 Jimmy Wilde GBR
1923 Pancho Villa PHI
1925 Fidel La Barba USA
1937 Benny Lynch GBR
1938 Peter Kane GBR
1943 Jackie Paterson GBR
1948 Rinty Monaghan GBR
1950 Terry Allen GBR
1950 Dado Marino HAW
1952 Yoshio Shirai JPN
1954 Pascual Perez ARG
1960 Pone Kingpetch THA
1962 Fighting Harada JPN
1963 Pone Kingpetch THA
1963 Hiroyuki Ebihara JPN
1964 Pone Kingpetch THA
1965 Salvatore Burruni ITA

Disputed Titles

HEAVYWEIGHT
WBA
1958 Virgil Atkins USA
1965 Ernie Terrell USA
1968 Jimmy Ellis USA
1978 Muhammad Ali USA
1979 John Tate USA
1980 Mike Weaver USA
1982 Mike Dokes USA
1983 Gerrie Coetzee RSA
1984 Greg Page USA
1985 Tony Tubbs USA
1986 Tim Witherspoon USA
1986 James Smith USA
1987 Mike Tyson USA
1990 J 'Buster' Douglas USA
1990 Evander Holyfield USA
1992 Riddick Bowe USA
1993 Evander Holyfield USA
1994 Michael Moorer USA
1994 George Foreman USA
1995 Bruce Seldon USA

WBC
1978 Ken Norton USA
1978 Larry Holmes USA
1984 Tim Witherspoon USA
1984 Pinklon Thomas USA
1986 Trevor Berbick JAM
1989 Mike Tyson USA
1990 J 'Buster' Douglas USA
1990 Evander Holyfield USA
1992 Riddick Bowe USA
1992 Lennox Lewis GBR
1994 Oliver McCall USA
1995 Frank Bruno GBR

IBF
1984 Larry Holmes USA

1985 Michael Spinks USA
1987 Tony Tucker USA
1989 J 'Buster' Douglas USA
1990 Evander Holyfield USA
1992 Riddick Bowe USA
1993 Evander Holyfield USA
1994 Michael Moorer USA
1994 George Foreman USA

WBO
1989 Francesco Damiani ITA
1991 Ray Mercer USA
1992 Michael Moorer USA
1993 Tommy Morrison USA
1993 Michael Bentt USA
1994 Herbie Hide GBR
1995 Riddick Bowe USA

CRUISERWEIGHT
WBA
1982 Ossie Ocasio PUR
1984 Piet Crous RSA
1985 Dwight Muh'd Qawi USA
1986 Evander Holyfield USA
1989 Taoufik Belbouli FRA
1989 Robert Daniels USA
1991 Bobby Cruz USA
1993 Orlin Norris USA
1995 Nate Miller USA

WBC
1979 Marvin Camel USA
1980 Carlos de Leon PUR
1982 S T Gordon USA
1983 Carlos de Leon PUR
1985 Alfonso Ratliff USA
1985 Bernard Benton USA
1986 Carlos de Leon PUR
1988 Evander Holyfield USA
1989 Carlos de Leon PUR
1990 Massimiliano Duran ITA
1991 Anaclet Wamba FRA
IBF
1983 Marvin Camel USA
1984 Lee Roy Murphy USA
1986 Rickey Parkey USA
1987 Evander Holyfield USA
1989 Glenn McCrory GBR
1990 Jeff Lampkin USA
1991 James Warring USA
1992 Alfred Cole USA

WBO
1989 Richard Pultz USA
1990 Magne Havna NOR
1992 Tyrone Booze USA
1993 Markus Bott GER
1993 Nestor Giovannini ITA
1995 Dariusz Michalczewski
GER
1995 Ralf Rocchigiani GER

LIGHT-HEAVYWEIGHT
WBA
1971 Vicente Rondon VEN
1974 Victor Galindez ARG
1978 Mike Rossman USA
1979 Victor Galindez ARG
1979 Marvin Johnson USA
1980 Eddie Mustafa Mh'd USA
1981 Michael Spinks USA
1986 Marvin Johnson USA
1987 Leslie Stewart JAM
1987 Virgil Hill USA
1991 Thomas Hearns USA
1992 Iran Barkley USA
1992 Virgil Hill USA

WBC
1974 John Conteh GBR
1977 Miguel Cuello ARG
1978 Mate Parlov YUG
1978 Marvin Johnson USA
1979 Matthew Saad Mh'd USA
1981 Dwight Muh'd Qawi USA
1985 JB Williamson USA
1986 Dennis Andries GBR
1987 Thomas Hearns USA
1988 Donny Lalonde CAN
1988 Sugar Ray Leonard USA
1989 Dennis Andries GBR
1989 Jeff Harding AUS
1990 Dennis Andries GBR
1991 Jeff Harding AUS
1994 Mike McCallum JAM
1995 Fabrice Tiozzo FRA

IBF
1985 Slobodan Kacar YUG
1986 Bobby Czyz USA
1987 P Charles Williams USA
1993 Henry Maske GER

WBO
1988 Michael Moorer USA
1991 Leeonzer Barber USA
1995 D Michalczewski GER

SUPER-MIDDLEWEIGHT
WBA
1984 Park Chong-pal KOR
1988 Fulgen. Obelmejias VEN
1989 Baek In-chul KOR
1990 Christophe Tiozo FRA
1991 Victor Cordoba PAN
1992 Michael Nunn USA
1994 Steve Little USA
1994 Frank Liles USA

WBC
1988 Sugar Ray Leonard USA
1990 Mauro Galvano ITA
1992 Nigel Benn GBR

World Champions (disputed)

IBF
1984 Murray Sutherland CAN
1988 Grac. Rocchigiani FRG
1990 Lindell Holmes USA
1991 Darrin van Horn USA
1992 Iran Barkley USA
1993 James Toney USA
1994 Roy Jones USA

WBO
1988 Thomas Hearns USA
1991 Chris Eubank GBR
1995 Steve Collins IRL

MIDDLEWEIGHT
WBA
1987 Sambu Kalambay ZAI
1989 Mike McCallum USA
1992 Reggie Johnson USA
1994 John D Jackson USA
1994 Jorge Castro ARG

WBC
1974 Rodrigo Valdez COL
1987 Sugar Ray Leonard USA
1987 Thomas Hearns USA
1988 Iran Barkley USA
1989 Roberto Duran PAN
1990 Julian Jackson USA
1993 Gerald McClellan USA
1995 Julian Jackson USA
1995 Quincy Taylor USA

IBF
1987 Frank Tate USA
1988 Michael Nunn USA
1991 James Toney USA
1993 Roy Jones USA
1994 Bernard Hopkins USA

WBO
1989 Doug De Witt USA
1990 Nigel Benn GBR
1990 Chris Eubank GBR
1991 Gerald McClellan USA
1993 Chris Pyatt GBR
1994 Steve Collins IRL
1995 Lonnie Bradley USA

LIGHT-MIDDLEWEIGHT
WBA
1975 Yuh Jae-do KOR
1976 Koichi Wajima JPN
1976 Jose Duran ESP
1976 Angel Castellini ARG
1977 Eddie Gazo NCA
1978 Masashi Kudo JPN
1979 Ayube Kalule UGA
1981 Sugar Ray Leonard USA
1981 Tadashi Mihara JPN

1982 Davey Moore USA
1983 Roberto Duran PAN
1984 Mike McCallum JAM
1988 Julian Jackson USA
1991 Gilbert Dele FRA
1991 Vinny Pazienza USA
1992 Cesar Vasquez ARG
1992 Vinny Pazienza USA
1992 Julio Cesar Vasquez ARG
1995 Pernell Whitaker USA
1995 Carl Daniels USA

WBC
1975 Miguel de Oliviera BRA
1975 Elisha Obed BAH
1976 Eckhard Dagge FRG
1977 Rocky Mattioli ITA
1979 Maurice Hope GBR
1981 Wilfred Benitez USA
1982 Thomas Hearns USA
1986 Duane Thomas USA
1987 Lupe Aquino MEX
1988 Gianfranco Rosi ITA
1988 Don Curry USA
1989 Rene Jacquot FRA
1989 John Mugabi UGA
1990 Terry Norris USA
1993 Simon Brown JAM
1994 Terry Norris USA
1995 Luis Santana DOM
1995 Terry Norris USA

IBF
1984 Mark Medal USA
1984 Carlos Santos PUR
1986 Buster Drayton USA
1987 Matthew Hilton CAN
1988 Robert Hines USA
1989 Darrin Van Horn USA
1989 Gianfranco Rosi ITA
1994 Vincent Pettway USA

WBO
1988 John David Jackson USA
1993 Verno Phillips USA
1995 Gianfranco Rosi ITA

WELTERWEIGHT
WBA
1975 Angel Espada PUR
1976 Pipino Cuevas MEX
1980 Thomas Hearns USA
1983 Don Curry USA
1987 Mark Breland USA
1987 Marlon Starling USA
1988 Tomas Molinares COL
1989 Mark Breland USA
1990 Aaron Davis USA
1991 Meldrick Taylor USA
1992 Crisanto Espana VEN
1994 Ike Quartey GHA

WBC

1975 John H Stracey GBR
1976 Carlos Palomino MEX
1979 Wilfred Benitez USA
1979 Sugar Ray Leonard USA
1980 Roberto Duran PAN
1980 Sugar Ray Leonard USA
1983 Milton McCrory USA
1987 Lloyd Honeyghan GBR
1987 Jorge Vaca MEX
1988 Lloyd Honeyghan GBR
1989 Marlon Starling USA
1990 Maurice Blocker USA
1991 Simon Brown JAM
1991 Buddy McGirt USA
1993 Pernell Whitaker USA

IBF
1984 Don Curry USA
1987 Lloyd Honeyghan GBR
1988 Simon Brown JAM
1991 Buddy McGirt USA
1992 Felix Trinidad PUR

WBO
1989 Genaro Leon MEX
1989 Manning Galloway USA
1993 Gert Bo Jacobsen DEN
1993 Eamonn Loughran IRL

LIGHT-WELTERWEIGHT
WBA
1968 Nicolino Loche ARG
1972 Alfonso Frazer PAN
1972 Antonio Cervantes COL
1976 Wilfred Benitez USA
1977 Antonio Cervantes COL
1980 Aaron Pryor USA
1984 Johnny Bumphus USA
1984 Gene Hatcher USA
1985 Ubaldo Sacco ARG
1986 Patrizio Oliva ITA
1987 Juan Martin Coggi ARG
1990 Loreto Garza USA
1991 Edwin Rosario PUR
1992 Morris East PHI
1993 Juan Martin Coggi ARG
1994 Frankie Randall USA

WBC
1968 Pedro Adigue PHI
1970 Bruno Acari ITA
1974 Perico Fernandez ESP
1975 Saensak Muangsurin THA
1976 Miguel Velasquez ESP
1976 Saensak Muangsurin THA
1978 Kim Sang-hyun KOR
1980 Saoul Mamby USA
1982 Leroy Haley USA
1983 Bruce Curry USA
1984 Billy Costello USA
1985 Lonnie Smith USA
1986 Tsuyoshi Hamada JAP

World Champions (disputed)

1986 **Rene Arredondo** MEX
1987 **Rene Arredondo** MEX
1988 **Roger Mayweather** USA
1989 **Julio Cesar Chavez** MEX
1994 **Frankie Randall** USA
1994 **Julio Cesar Chavez** MEX

IBF
1983 **Aaron Pryor** USA
1986 **Gary Hinton** USA
1986 **Joe Louis Manley** USA
1987 **Terry Marsh** GBR
1988 **James Buddy McGirt** USA
1988 **Meldrick Taylor** USA
1990 **Julio Cesar Chavez** MEX
1991 **Rafael Pineda** COL
1992 **Pernell Whitaker** USA
1993 **Charles Murray** USA
1994 **Jake Rodriguez** USA
1995 **Konstantin Tszyu** RUS

WBO
1989 **Hector Camacho** PUR
1991 **Greg Haugen** USA
1991 **Hector Camacho** PUR
1992 **Carlos Gonzalez** MEX
1993 **Zack Padilla** USA
1994 **Sammy Fuentes** PUR

LIGHTWEIGHT
WBA
1970 **Ken Buchanan** GBR
1972 **Roberto Duran** PAN
1979 **Ernesto Espana** VEN
1980 **Hilmer Kenty** USA
1981 **Sean O'Grady** USA
1981 **Claude Noel** TRI
1981 **Arturo Frias** USA
1982 **Ray Mancini** USA
1984 **Livingstone Bramble** USA
1986 **Edwin Rosario** PUR
1987 **Julio Cesar Chavez** MEX
1989 **Edwin Rosario** USA
1990 **Juan Nazario** PUR
1990 **Pernell Whitaker** USA
1992 **Joey Gamache** USA
1992 **Tony Lopez** USA
1993 **Dingaan Thobela** RSA
1993 **Orzoubek Nararov** KGZ

WBC
1971 **Pedro Carrasco** ESP
1972 **Mando Ramos** USA
1972 **Chango Carmona** MEX
1972 **Rodolfo Gonzalez** MEX
1974 **Guts Ishimatsu** JPN
1976 **Esteban de Jesus** PUR
1979 **Jim Watt** GBR
1981 **Alexis Arguello** NCA
1983 **Edwin Rosario** PUR
1984 **Jose Luis Ramirez** MEX
1985 **Hector Camacho** PUR

1987 **Jose Luis Ramirez** MEX
1988 **Julio Cesar Chavez** MEX
1989 **Pernell Whitaker** USA
1992 **Miguel Angel Gonzalez**
     MEX

IBF
1984 **Charlie Brown** USA
1984 **Harry Arroyo** USA
1985 **Jimmy Paul** USA
1986 **Greg Haugen** USA
1987 **Vinny Pazienza** USA
1988 **Greg Haugen** USA
1989 **Pernell Whitaker** USA
1992 **Tracy Spann** USA
1993 **Freddie Pendleton** USA
1994 **Rafael Ruelas** USA
1995 **Phillip Holliday** RSA

WBO
1989 **Amancio Castro** COL
1989 **Mauricio Aceves** MEX
1990 **Dingaan Thobela** RSA
1992 **Giovanni Parisi** ITA
1994 **Oscar De La Hoya** USA

SUPER-FEATHERWEIGHT
WBA
1971 **Alfredo Marcano** VEN
1972 **Ben Villaflor** PHI
1973 **Kuniaki Shibata** JPN
1973 **Ben Villaflor** PHI
1976 **Sam Serrano** PUR
1980 **Yasutsune Uehara** JPN
1981 **Sam Serrano** PUR
1983 **Roger Mayweather** USA
1984 **Rocky Lockridge** USA
1985 **Wilfredo Gomez** PUR
1986 **Alfredo Layne** PAN
1986 **Brian Mitchell** RSA
1991 **Joey Gamache** USA
1991 **Genaro Hernandez** USA

WBC
1969 **Rene Barrientos** PHI
1970 **Yoshiaki Numata** JPN
1971 **Ricardo Arredondo** MEX
1974 **Kuniaki Shibata** JPN
1975 **Alfredo Escalera** PUR
1978 **Alexis Arguello** NCA
1980 **Rafael Limon** MEX
1981 **Cornelius Boza Edwards**
     UGA
1981 **Rolando Navarette** PHI
1982 **Rafael Limon** MEX
1982 **Bobby Chacon** USA
1983 **Hector Camacho** PUR
1984 **Julio Cesar Chavez** MEX
1988 **Azumah Nelson** GHA
1994 **Jesse James Leija** MEX
1995 **Gabe Ruelas** USA

IBF

1984 **Yuh Hwan-kil** KOR
1985 **Lester Ellis** AUS
1985 **Barry Michael** AUS
1987 **Rocky Lockridge** USA
1988 **Tony Lopez** USA
1989 **Juan Molina** PUR
1990 **Tony Lopez** USA
1991 **Brian Mitchell** RSA
1993 **John John Molina** PUR
1995 **Eddie Hopson** USA
1995 **Tracy Patterson** USA

WBO
1989 **Juan Molina** PUR
1989 **Kamel Bou Ali** TUN
1992 **Jimmy Bredhal** DEN
1994 **Oscar De La Hoya** USA
1994 **Regilio Tuur** NED

FEATHERWEIGHT
WBA
1968 **Raul Rojas** USA
1968 **Shozo Saijyo** JPN
1971 **Antonio Gomez** VEN
1972 **Ernesto Marcel** PAN
1974 **Ruben Olivares** MEX
1974 **Alexis Arguello** NCA
1977 **Rafael Ortega** PAN
1977 **Cecilio Lastra** ESP
1978 **Eusebio Pedroza** PAN
1985 **Barry McGuigan** IRL
1986 **Steve Cruz** USA
1987 **Toni Esparragoza** VEN
1991 **ParkYoung-kyun** KOR
1992 **Wilfredo Vazquez** PUR
1992 **Park Young-kyun** KOR
1993 **Eloy Rojas** VEN

WBC
1968 **Howard Winstone** GBR
1968 **Jose Legra** CUB
1969 **Johnny Famechon** FRA
1970 **Vicente Saldivar** MEX
1970 **Kuniaki Shibata** JPN
1972 **Clemente Sanchez** MEX
1972 **Jose Legra** CUB
1973 **Eder Jofre** BRA
1974 **Bobby Chacon** USA
1975 **Ruben Olivares** MEX
1975 **David Kotey** GHA
1976 **Danny Lopez** USA
1980 **Salvador Sanchez** MEX
1982 **Juan Laporte** PUR
1984 **Wilfredo Gomez** PUR
1984 **Azumah Nelson** GHA
1988 **Jeff Fenech** AUS
1990 **Marcos Villasana** MEX
1991 **Paul Hodkinson** GBR
1993 **Gregorio Vargas** MEX
1993 **Kevin Kelley** USA
1995 **Alejandro Gonzalez** MEX

World Champions (disputed)

IBF
1984 **Oh Min-keum** KOR
1985 **Chung Ki-young** KOR
1986 **Antonio Rivera** PUR
1988 **Calvin Grove** USA
1988 **Jorge Paez** MEX
1991 **Troy Dorsey** USA
1991 **Manuel Medina** MEX
1993 **Tom Johnson** USA

WBO
1989 **Maurizio Stecca** ITA
1989 **Louie Espinoza** USA
1990 **Jorge Paez** MEX
1991 **Maurizio Stecca** ITA
1992 **Colin McMillan** GBR
1992 **Ruben Palacio** COL
1993 **Steve Robinson** GBR

SUPER BANTAMWEIGHT
WBA
1977 **Hong Soo-hwan** KOR
1978 **Ricardo Cardona** COL
1980 **Leo Randolph** USA
1980 **Sergio Palma** ARG
1982 **Leo Cruz** DOM
1984 **Loris Stecca** ITA
1984 **Victor Callejas** PUR
1987 **Louis Espinoza** USA
1987 **Julio Gervacio** DOM
1988 **Bernardo Pinango** VEN
1988 **Juan Jose Estrada** MEX
1989 **Jesus Salud** USA
1990 **Luis Mendoza** COL
1991 **Raul Perez** MEX
1992 **Wilfredo Vasquez** PUR
1995 **Antonio Cermeno** VEN

WBC
1976 **Rigoberto Riasco** PAN
1976 **Royal Kobayashi** JPN
1976 **Yum Dong-kyun** KOR
1977 **Wilfredo Gomez** PUR
1983 **Jaime Garza** USA
1984 **Juan Meza** MEX
1985 **Lupe Pintor** MEX
1986 **Samart Payakarun** THA
1987 **Jeff Fenech** AUS
1988 **Daniel Zaragoza** MEX
1990 **Paul Banke** USA
1990 **Pedro Decima** ARG
1991 **Kiyoshi Hatanaka** JPN
1991 **Daniel Zaragoza** MEX
1992 **Thierry Jacob** FRA
1992 **Tracy Patterson** USA
1994 **Hector Acero Sanchez** DOM

IBF
1983 **Bobby Berna** PHI
1984 **Suh Seung-il** KOR

1985 **Kim Ji-won** KOR
1987 **Lee Seung-hoon** KOR
1988 **Jose Sanabria** VEN
1989 **Fabrice Benichou** FRA
1990 **Welcome Ncita** RSA
1992 **Kennedy McKinney** USA
1994 **Vuyani Bungu** RSA

WBO
1989 **Kenny Mitchell** USA
1989 **Valerio Nati** ITA
1990 **Orlando Fernandez** PUR
1991 **Jesse Benevides** USA
1992 **Duke McKenzie** GBR
1993 **Daniel Jimenez** PUR
1995 **Marco Antonio Barrera** MEX

BANTAMWEIGHT
WBA
1973 **Romeo Anaya** MEX
1973 **Arnold Taylor** RSA
1974 **Hong Soo-hwan** KOR
1975 **Alfonso Zamora** MEX
1977 **Jorge Lujan** PAN
1980 **Julian Solis** PUR
1980 **Jeff Chandler** USA
1984 **Richard Sandoval** USA
1986 **Gaby Canizales** USA
1986 **Bernardo Pinango** VEN
1987 **Takuya Muguruma** JPN
1987 **Park Chang-young** KOR
1987 **Wilfredo Vasquez** PUR
1988 **Khaokor Galaxy** THA
1988 **Moon Sung-kil** KOR
1989 **Khaokor Galaxy** THA
1989 **Luisito Espinosa** PHI
1991 **Israel Contreras** VEN
1992 **Eddie Cook** USA
1992 **Jorge Julio** COL
1993 **Junior Jones** USA
1994 **John M Johnson** USA
1994 **Doarung MP Petroleum** THA

WBC
1973 **Rafael Herrera** MEX
1974 **Rodolfo Martinez** MEX
1976 **Carlos Zarate** MEX
1979 **Lupe Pintor** MEX
1983 **Alberto Davila** USA
1985 **Daniel Zaragoza** MEX
1985 **Miguel Lora** COL
1988 **Raul Perez** MEX
1991 **Greg Richardson** USA
1991 **Joichiro Tatsuyoshi** JPN
1992 **Victor Rabanales** MEX
1993 **Byun Jong-il** KOR
1993 **Yasuei Yakushiji** JPN
1995 **Wayne McCullough** IRL

IBF
1984 **Satoshi Shingaki** JPN
1985 **Jeff Fenech** AUS
1987 **Kelvin Seabrooks** USA
1988 **Orlando Canizales** USA
1995 **Harold Maestre** COL
1995 **Mbulelo Botile** RSA

WBO
1989 **Israel Contreras** VEN
1991 **Gaby Canizales** USA
1991 **Duke McKenzie** GBR
1992 **Rafael Del Valle** PUR
1994 **Alfred Kotey** GHA

SUPER FLYWEIGHT
WBA
1981 **Gustavo Ballas** ARG
1981 **Rafael Pedroza** PAN
1982 **Jiro Watanabe** JPN
1984 **Khaosai Galaxy** THA
1992 **Katsuya Onizuka** GBR
1994 **Hyung Chui-lee** KOR
1995 **Alimi Goitea** VEN

WBC
1980 **Rafael Orono** VEN
1981 **Kim Chul-ho** KOR
1982 **Rafael Orono** VEN
1983 **Payao Poontarat** THA
1984 **Jiro Watanabe** JPN
1986 **Gilberto Roman** MEX
1987 **Santos Laciar** ARG
1987 **Jesus Rojas** COL
1988 **Gilberto Roman** MEX
1989 **Nana Yaw Konadu** GHA
1990 **Moon Sung-kil** KOR
1993 **Jose Luis Bueno** MEX
1994 **Hiroshi Kawashima** JPN

IBF
1983 **Chun Joo-do** KOR
1985 **Ellyas Pical** INA
1986 **Cesar Polanco** DOM
1986 **Chang Tae-il** KOR
1987 **Ellyas Pical** INA
1989 **Juan Polo Perez** COL
1990 **Robert Quiroga** USA
1993 **Julio Cesar Borboa** MEX
1994 **Harold Grey** USA

WBO
1989 **Jose Ruiz** PUR
1992 **Johnny Bredhal** DEN
1994 **Johnny Tapia** USA

FLYWEIGHT
WBA
1966 **Horacio Accavallo** ARG
1969 **Hiroyuki Ebihara** JPN
1969 **Bernabe Villacampo** PHI

World Champions (disputed)

1970 Berkrerk Chartvanchai THA
1970 Masao Ohba JPN
1973 Chartchai Chionoi THA
1974 Susumu Hanagata JPN
1975 Erbito Salavarria PHI
1976 Alfonso Lopez PAN
1976 Guty Espadas MEX
1978 Betulio Gonzalez VEN
1979 Luis Ibarra PAN
1980 Kim Tae-shik KOR
1980 Shoji Oguma JPN
1980 Peter Mathebula RSA
1981 Santos Laciar ARG
1981 Luis Ibarra PAN
1981 Juan Herrera MEX
1982 Santos Laciar ARG
1985 Hilario Zapata PAN
1987 Fidel Bassa COL
1989 Jesus Rojas VEN
1990 Lee Yul-woo KOR
1990 Yukihito Tamakama JPN
1991 Elvis Alvarez COL
1991 Kim Yong-kang KOR
1992 Aqueles Guzman VEN
1992 David Griman VEN
1994 Saensor Ploenchit THA

WBC

1966 Walter McGowan GBR
1966 Chartchai Chionoi THA
1969 Efren Torres MEX
1970 Chartchai Chionoi THA
1970 Erbito Salavarria PHI
1972 Venice Borkorsor THA
1973 Betulio Gonzalez VEN
1974 Shoji Oguma JPN
1975 Miguel Canto MEX
1979 Park Chan-hee KOR
1981 Antonio Avelar MEX
1982 Prudencio Cardona COL
1982 Freddie Castillo MEX
1982 Eleoncio Mercedes DOM
1983 Charlie Magri GBR
1983 Frank Cedeno PHI
1984 Koji Kobayashi JPN
1984 Gabriel Bernal MEX
1984 Sot Chitalada THA
1988 Kim Yong-kang KOR
1989 Sot Chitalda THA
1991 Muangchai Kittikasem THA
1992 Yuri Arbachakov RUS

IBF

1983 Kwon Soon-chun KOR
1985 Chung Chong-kwan KOR
1986 Chung Bi-won KOR
1986 Shin Hi-sup KOR
1987 Dodie Penalosa PHI
1987 Choi Chang-ho KOR

1988 Rolando Bohol PHI
1988 Duke McKenzie GBR
1989 Dave McAuley GBR
1992 Rodolfo Blanco COL
1992 Pichit Sitbangprachan THA
1994 Francisco Tejedor COL
1995 Danny Romero USA

WBO

1989 Elvis Alvarez COL
1990 Isidro Perez MEX
1992 Pat Clinton GBR
1993 Jake Matlala RSA
1995 Alberto Jimenez MEX

LIGHT FLYWEIGHT
WBA

1975 Jaime Rios PAN
1976 Juan Jose Guzman DOM
1976 Yoko Gushiken JPN
1981 Pedro Flores MEX
1981 Kim Hwan-jin KOR
1981 Katsuo Takashiki JPN
1983 Lupe Madera MEX
1984 Francisco Quiroz DOM
1985 Joey Olivo USA
1985 Yuh Myung-woo KOR
1992 Hiroki Ioka JPN
1992 Yuh Myung-woo KOR
1993 Leo Gamez VEN
1995 Hiyong Choi KOR

WBC

1975 Franco Udella ITA
1975 Luis Estaba VEN
1978 Freddie Castillo MEX
1978 Netrnoi Vorasingh THA
1978 Kim Sung-jun KOR
1980 Shigeo Nakajima JPN
1980 Hilario Zapata PAN
1982 Amado Ursua MEX
1982 Tadashi Tomori JPN
1982 Hilario Zapata PAN
1983 Chang Jung-koo KOR
1988 German Torres MEX
1989 Lee Yul-woo KOR
1989 Humberto Gonzalez MEX
1990 Rolando Pascua PHI
1991 Melchor Cob Castro MEX
1991 Humberto Gonzalez MEX
1993 Michael Carbajal USA
1994 Humberto Gonzalez MEX

IBF

1983 Dodie Penalosa PHI
1986 Choi Chong-hwan KOR
1988 Tacy Macalos PHI
1989 Muancgchai Kittikasem THA
1990 Michael Carbajal USA

1991 Welcome Ncita RSA
1992 Michael Carbajal USA
1994 Humberto Gonzalez MEX

WBO

1989 Jose de Jesus PUR
1993 Josue Camacho PUR
1994 Michael Carbajal USA
1994 Paul Weir GBR

STRAWWEIGHT
WBA

1988 Leo Gamez DOM
1989 Kim Bong-jun KOR
1991 Choi Hi-yong KOR
1992 Hideyuki Ohashi JPN
1993 Chana Porpaoin THA

WBC

1987 Lee Kyung-yung KOR
1988 Hiroki Ioka JPN
1988 Napa Kiatwanchai THA
1989 Choi Jeum-hwan KOR
1990 Hideyuki Ohashi JPN
1990 Ricardo Lopez MEX

IBF

1988 Sam Sithnaruepol THA
1989 Nico Thomas INA
1989 Eric Chavez PHI
1990 Fahlan Lookmingkwan THA
1992 Manuel Melchor PHI
1992 Ratan. Sorvorapin THA

WBO

1989 Rafael Torres DOM
1993 Paul Weir GBR
1993 Alex Sanchez PUR

Canoeing

Slalom Racing

World Championship

Nottingham   Aug 29-Sep 3
*In all events, competitors take two runs down the course
and the better time (including any penalties) counts.*

MEN

K1 (Kayak Singles)

1	**Oliver Fix**	**GER**	**125.72**
2	Scott Shipley	USA	127.09
3	Jiri Prskavec	CZE	127.47
5	Paul Ratcliffe	GBR	127.81
8	Andrew Raspin	GBR	129.14
10	Shaun Pearce	GBR	129.42
27	Ian Raspin	GBR	138.21

K1 Team

1	**Fix/Letimann/Becker**	**GER**	**145.27**
2	Vehouar/Strukels/Marusic	SLO	152.31
3	Raspin/Pearse/Raspin	GBR	153.41

C1 (Canadian Singles)

1	**David Hearn**	**USA**	**134.86**
2	Sören Kaufmann	GER	135.72
3	Michal Martikan	SVK	135.97
15	Gareth Marriott	GBR	140.56

C1 Team

1	**Lang/Husek/Kaufmann**	**GER**	**166.05**
2	Herceg/Perestegi/Sedlar	CRO	171.25
3	Martikan/Ontko/Mincik	SVK	173.23
11	Marriott/Delaney/Morgan	GBR	185.62

C2 (Canadian Doubles)

1	**Kolomanski/Staniszewski**	**POL**	**138.61**
2	Adisson/Forgues	FRA	139.09
3	Biau/Daille	FRA	140.25

C2 Team

1	**Czech Republic**		**178.87**
	(Simek/Rohan, Stercl/Stercl, Pospisil/Pollert)		
2	France		186.05
	(Saidi/Del Rey, Adisson/Forgues, Biau/Daille)		
3	Germany		187.85
	(Trummer/Berro, Hübbers/Raumann, Ehrenberg/Senft)		

WOMEN

K1

1	**Lynn Simpson**	**GBR**	**140.81**
2	Anne Boixel	FRA	142.32
3	Kordula Striepecke	GER	143.61
4	Rachel Crosbee	GBR	143.72
14	Heather Corrie	GBR	155.19

K1 Team

1	**Boixel/Depres/Fox**	**FRA**	**175.82**
2	Corrie/Crosbee/Simpson	GBR	180.64
3	Striepecke/Huss/Micheler	GER	182.33

Wild Water Racing

World Championship

Bala   Aug 26

MEN

K1

1	**Markus Gickler**	**GER**	**21:00.76**
2	Robert Pantarollo	ITA	21:01.25
3	Thomas Koelman	GER	21:06.92
15	Ian Tordoff	GBR	21:28.90
17	Alan Tordoff	GBR	21:36.15
25	Michael Mason	GBR	22:04.21
34	David Taylor	GBR	22:23.35

K1 Team

1	**New Zealand**	**21:25.98**
2	France	21:28.39
3	Germany	21:32.92
6	Great Britain	22:12.85

C1

1	**Vladi Carlo Panato**	**ITA**	**23:56.78**
2	Stefan Stiefenhofer	GER	24:00.53
3	Jerome Bonnardel	FRA	24:06.68
16	Rob Pumphrey	GBR	25:18.42
20	John Willacy	GBR	25:35.79
23	Mark de Freitas	GBR	26:20.86
24	James Lee	GBR	26:25.08

C1 Team

1	**Germany**	**24:07.43**
2	France	24;17.54
3	Slovenia	25:07.86
5	Great Britain	26:06.02

C2

1	**Vala/Slucik**	**SVK**	**22:49.27**
2	Faysse/Roos	FRA	22:50.41
3	Dajek/Knittel	GER	22:52.52
10	Belbin/Caunt	GBR	23:51.98
12	Guest/Lyons	GBR	24:16.14
13	Blackman/Blackman	GBR	24:19.30
14	Clough/Clough	GBR	24:37.42

C2 Team

1	**France**	**23:14.32**
2	Germany	23:14.63
3	Great Britain	24:30.73

WOMEN

K1

1	**Ursula Profanter**	**AUT**	**22:56.68**
2	Laurence Castet	FRA	23:07.17
3	Aurore Brigard	FRA	23:13.11
9	Cynthia Berry	GBR	23:44.08
11	Tina Parsons	GBR	23:45.12
12	Andrea Tordoff	GBR	23:47.59

K1 Team

1	**France**	**23:35.84**
2	Germany	23:47.67
3	Great Britain	23:49.64

Sprint Racing

World Championship

Duisburg   *Aug 15-20*
Winners over 200m were as follows:
Men *K1: Piotr Markiewicz POL; K2: Jorgensen/Mooney*
USA; K4: Hungary; C1: Nikolai Buhalov BUL;
C2: Horvath/Kolonics HUN; C4: Hungary
Women *K1: Rita Koban HUN; K2: Kennedy/Gibeau*
CAN; K4: Canada
The detailed results below are for Olympic events.

MEN

K1 500m

1	**Piotr Markiewicz**	**POL**
2	Knut Holmann	NOR
3	Geza Magyar	ROM

K2 500m

1	**Bonomi/Scarpa**	**ITA**
2	Gyulay/Bartfai	HUN
3	Freimuth/Wysocki	GER

K4 500m
1. Russia; 2. Germany; 3. Poland

C1 500m

1	**Nikolai Buhalov**	**BUL**
2	Martin Doktor	CZE
3	Imre Pulai	HUN

C2 500m

1	**Horvath/Kolonics**	**HUN**
2	Yourravsky/Reneysky	MLD
3	Dittmer/Kirchbach	GER

C4 500m
1. Hungary; 2. Romania; 3. Bulgaria

K1 1000m

1	**Knut Holmann**	**NOR**
2	Clint Robinson	AUS
3	Lutz Liwowski	GER

K2 1000m

1	**Rossi/Scarpa**	**ITA**
2	Bluhm/Gutsche	GER
3	Kotowicz/Bialkowski	POL

K4 1000m
1. Germany; 2. Hungary; 3. Poland

C1 1000m

1	**Imre Pulai**	**HUN**
2	Martin Doktor	CZE
3	Ivan Klementjev	LAT

C2 1000m

1	**Kolonics/Horváth**	**HUN**
2	Borsan/Glavan	ROM
3	Dittmer/Kirchbach	GER

C4 1000m
1. Romania; 2. Hungary; 3. Germany

WOMEN

K1 500m

1	**Rita Koban**	**HUN**
2	Caroline Brunet	CAN
3	Susanna Gunnarsson	SWE

K2 500m

1	**Portwich/Schuck**	**GER**
2	Urbanczyk/Dylewska	POL
3	Rosenqvist/Gunnarsson	SWE

K4 500m
1. Germany; 2. China; 3. Hungary

Marathon Racing

World Cup

Unquera, Spain   *Aug 26-27*

MEN

K1

1	Rui Cancio	POR	2:10:46
6	Gregg Slater	GBR	2:12:38
11	Neal Coleman	GBR	2:18:08

K2

1	Lawler/Harris	GBR	2:03:10

C1

1	Frank Balciero	CUB	1:59:53
12	Derek Hall	GBR	2:12:02

C2

1	A Train/S Train	GBR	1:44:47

WOMEN

1	Nicole Bulk	NED	1:52:21
2	Anna Hemmings	GBR	1:52:22
3	Sonja Bapty	GBR	1:57:08

K2

1	Schuck/Portwich	GER	1:50:11
4	Davey/Dawe	GBR	1:53:27

National Championships

Sprint Racing

Nottingham   June

MEN
200m K1: Mark Train (Fladbury); K2: Dorrell/Clark
(Royal); K4: Royal Canoe Club; C1: Tom Love (Lmgtn)
500m K1: Duncan Roeser (Wey); K2: Block/Tordoff
(Notts & Chester); K4: Royal Canoe Club; C1: Tom Love
(Leamington); C2: Yurkwich/Lane (Leamington)
1000m K1: David Smith (Elmbridge);
K2: Brabants/Darby-Dowman (Elmbridge);
K4: Elmbridge/Wey; C1: Eric Jamieson (Wey);
C2: Yurkwich/Lane (Leamington)

WOMEN
200m K1: Becky Train (Fladbury); K2: Train/McGee
(Fladbury)
500m K1: Becky Train (Fladbury); K2: B Train/R Train
(Fladbury); K4: Fladbury/Chelmsford/Leighton Buzzard

It's difficult to log up a world record if
you're a slalom canoeist, but Helen
Barnes managed it at the International
Canoe Exhibition in February. Barnes
attempted to break the world record for
100 eskimo rolls, which stood at 4m 30s.
The Nottingham paddler made the
Guinness Book of Records with some
ease, completing her spin cycle in just
3m 47s. Not after lunch, we hope.

World Champions

Sprint (or Flatwater)
Every year except Olympic years.

MEN 200m
K1
1994 Sergey Kalesnik BLR
1995 Piotr Markiewicz POL
K2
1994 Friemuth/Wysocki GER
1995 Bonomi/Scarpa ITA
K4
1994 Russia
1995 Hungary
C1
1994 Nikolay Buhalov BUL
1995 Nikolay Buhalov BUL
C2
1994 Masojkov/DovgalionokBLR
1995 Kolonics/Horváth HUN
C4
1994 Russia
1995 Hungary

MEN 500m
K1
1989 Martin Hunter AUS
1990 Sergey Kalesnik URS
1991 Renn Crichlow CAN
1993 Mikko Kolehmainen FIN
1994 Zsombor Borhi HUN
1995 Piotr Markiewicz POL
K2
1989 Bluhm/Gutsche GDR
1990 Kalesnik/Tishchenko URS
1991 Roman/Sánchez ESP
1993 Bluhm/Gutsche GER
1994 Bluhm/Gutsche GER
1995 Bonomi/Scarpa ITA
K4
1989 Soviet Union
1990 Soviet Union
1991 Germany
1993 Russia
1994 Russia
1995 Russia
C1
1989 Mikhail Slivinsky URS
1990 Mikhail Slivinsky URS
1991 Mikhail Slivinsky RUS
1993 Nikolay Buhalov BUL
1994 Nikolay Buhalov BUL
1995 Nikolay Buhalov BUL
C2
1989 Zhuravsky/Reneysky URS
1990 Zhuravsky/Reneysky URS
1991 Paliza/Szabó HUN
1993 Kolonics/Horváth HUN
1994 Andreiev/Obreja ROM
1995 Kolonics/Horváth HUN
C4
1989 Soviet Union
1990 Soviet Union

1991 Soviet Union
1993 Hungary
1994 Hungary
1995 Hungary

MEN 1000m
K1
1989 Zsolt Gyulay HUN
1990 Knut Holmann NOR
1991 Knut Holmann NOR
1993 Knut Holmann NOR
1994 Clint Robinson AUS
1995 Knut Holmann NOR
K2
1989 Bluhm/Gutsche GDR
1990 Bluhm/Gutsche GDR
1991 Bluhm/Gutsche GER
1993 Bluhm/Gutsche GER
1994 Staal/Nielsen DEN
1995 Rossi/Scarpa ITA
K4
1989 Hungary
1990 Hungary
1991 Hungary
1993 Germany
1994 Russia
1995 Germany
C1
1989 Ivan Klementyev URS
1990 Ivan Klementyev URS
1991 Ivan Klementyev LAT
1993 Ivan Klementyev LAT
1994 Ivan Klementyev LAT
1995 Imre Pulai HUN
C2
1989 Fredriksen/Nielsson DEN
1990 Papke/Spelly GDR
1991 Papke/Spelly GER
1993 Nielsson/FredericksenDEN
1994 Dittmer/Kirchbach GER
1995 Kolonics/Horváth HUN
C4
1989 Soviet Union
1990 Soviet Union
1991 Soviet Union
1993 Hungary
1994 Hungary
1995 Romania

WOMEN 200m
K1
1994 Rita Koban HUN
1995 Rita Koban HUN
K2
1994 Koban/Laky HUN
1995 Kennedy/Gibeau CAN
K4
1994 Hungary
1995 Canada

WOMEN 500m
K1
1989 Katrin Borchert GDR

1990 Josefa Idem FRG
1991 Katrin Borchert GER
1993 Birgit Schmidt GER
1994 Birgit Schmidt GER
1995 Rita Koban HUN
K2
1989 Nothnagel/Singer GDR
1990 Portwich/Von Seck GDR
1991 Portwich/Von Seck GER
1993 Olsson/Andersson SWE
1994 Urbanczyk/Hajcel POL
1995 Portwich/Schuck GER
K4
1989 East Germany
1990 East Germany
1991 Germany
1993 Germany
1994 Germany
1995 Germany

Slalom
(Held since 1949, selected only)
MEN
K1
1981 Richard Fox GBR
1983 Richard Fox GBR
1985 Richard Fox GBR
1987 Tony Prijon GER
1989 Richard Fox GBR
1991 Shaun Pearce GBR
1993 Richard Fox GBR
1995 Oliver Fix GER

K1 Team
1981 Great Britain
1983 Great Britain
1985 Great Britain
1987 Great Britain
1989 Yugoslavia
1991 France
1993 Great Britain
1995 Germany

C1
1991 Martin Lang GER
1993 Martin Lang GER
1995 David Hearn USA

C1 Team
1991 United States
1993 Slovakia
1995 Czech Republic

C2
1991 Hemmer/Loose FRG
1993 Simek/Rohan CZE
1995 Kolomanski/Staniszewski
     POL

C2 Team
1991 France
1993 Czech Republic
1995 Czech Republic

Cricket

The English season began amidst demands for the complete overhaul of the domestic game. The results of the Ashes series in Australia the catalyst for those who saw the present county structure as an anachronism. The tour results added weight to the argument that a lot of the cricket being played in this country is sub-standard. When the national team gets beaten twice in succession by the Australian Cricket Academy, the average age of which was about half that of Graham Gooch, it's hard to believe you're doing much right. There was a call for a two-division championship and the abolition of the Sunday League; others demanded the scrapping of the National Cricket Association. From the TCCB's point of view the Test series with the West Indies provided a welcome respite *(see in section for an analysis of the series)*. Packed houses and a closely fought series of Tests made everyone briefly forget about the cracks.

Raymond Illingworth was appointed as head, indeed sole paperer. Keith Fletcher dispensed with to make way for the Yorkshireman after a run of only five wins in 26 Tests under his stewardship. Fletcher was relieved of the England captaincy in 1982 after the players apparently no longer looked to him for advice and motivation. This obviously made him a natural for the role of England Team manager. Paying him off cost the TCCB £100,000 for the remaining half of his contract.

The summer gave us a second helping of Brian Lara in all his glory, although none of his three Test hundreds led to a victory for the tourists. The world's best batsman did suffer the ignominy of collecting the first pair of his career in the tour match against Kent. To add to his embarassment the bowler, both times, was Dr Julian Thompson who is usually to be found at the Royal Berkshire Hospital working as a house surgeon. Dr Thompson obviously has an affinity for the great man as he played his one and only championship match against Lara's Warwickshire last season, though with less success. "He seemed to like my bowling in the Sunday League," he confessed.

Warwickshire proved that last season's exploits were not the product of a one-man band. In lifting the Championship and the Natwest Trophy 'The Bears' have established themselves as the premier county; Lancashire and Kent collected the other one-day silverware. With the glut of records last year, the championship looked as if it had settled down to a more cosy tempo. Enter Andrew Symonds, Queensland and Gloucestershire, who blasted a world record 16 sixes in his 254 not out against Glamorgan at Abergavenny. Symonds was seemingly out to make his mark in his first season of county cricket, as he proceeded to be selected for the England A team by dint of having been born in Birmingham. Unfortunately, although he had signed a form stating his desire to represent England, he decided that he didn't want to

INTERNATIONAL RATINGS
As at September 1, 1995

Test Matches		One Day	
Australia	74	India	64
West Indies	62	England	62
Pakistan	60	West Indies	58
India	54	South Africa	53
South Africa	52	Australia	51
England	42	Pakistan	44
Sri Lanka	29	Sri Lanka	44
Zimbabwe	23	New Zealand	32
New Zealand	22	Zimbabwe	25
		Bangladesh	10

after all. He prefers the idea of playing for Australia, which is not much of a surprise.

The other record to go was claimed by Essex's Mark Ilott against title challengers Northants. The Essex left-armer's first innings statistics included a spell of nine wickets for 11 runs in 36 balls which is the fewest number of deliveries it has taken to claim nine wickets in the history of the game. The hattrick with which he finished off the innings was the first all-lbw hattrick since Mike Procter achieved it in 1979. Alas for Ilott, although Northants could only muster 46 in their first innings, they proceeded to win the match comfortably.

Ilott might well have asked for some divine guidance before his remarkable feat, but at Lytham St Annes it was rather more forthcoming. During the Sussex innings, play was held up after the voice of the Reverend Leslie Smethurst was heard over the public address system. Unknown to the priest, who was conducting a funeral at the next door church, the signal from the wireless microphone that he was wearing underneath his cassock was being picked up by the PA system at the next door venue. Mike Atherton said of the live link-up "we heard the words 'rest in peace' and I thought they were laying Sussex to rest".

Others to find a spiritual awakening included Jemima Goldsmith, daughter of billionaire Sir James Goldsmith, who converted to Islam in order to marry Pakistan's Imran Khan. The one-time playboy, who started last year's furore with confessions of ball tampering, finally tied the knot to put an end to his 'eligible bachelor' tag. He is currently considering entering the maelstrom that is Pakistani politics. It seems that the Indian sub-continent is suddenly becoming the resting ground for old all-rounders. Kapil Dev decided that after 434 Test wickets it was time to retire to the rarefied world of Indian television punditry. Not to be left out Ian Botham announced that he had been approached as a potential manager for the Sri Lankan team. "Let's face it, if I can't do a better job for Sri Lanka than Ray Illingworth is doing for England then something is very wrong," boomed Beefy.

Botham's old mate and sparring partner Viv Richards must have had other things on his mind when he failed to show up at Buckingham Palace to collect his OBE. The West Indian great was said to be "very embarrassed" at having stood up the Prince of Wales and was in trouble with his mother Gretel, 70, who chided "How could he forget such an appointment?"

Other batting greats have been doing similarly curious things. Graham Gooch

---

Peter May's Career Highlights

Test Career: **1951-1961**

Matches: **106**

Captain for 41 matches

W 20, D 11, L 10

Runs: **4537**

Highest Score: **285***

v West Indies at Edgbaston 1957.
He shared a record fourth wicket
partnership of 411 with Colin Cowdrey

Average: **46.77**

Hundreds: **13**   Fifties: **22**

First Class Career: **1951-1962**

Cambridge Univ & Surrey

Captained Surrey to the last two of their
seven successive championship wins in
1957 & 1958

Runs: **27,592**

Average: **51**

Hundreds: **85**

celebrated his retirement from the international scene by having his balding pate re-thatched after consulting Greg Matthews, a fellow follically challenged cricketer. With a new head of hair, the record breaking England opener decided that the growth under his nose was now surplus to requirements so off it came. The famous top lip accompaniment which had led to the nickname of 'Zap', after the moustachioed Mexican bandit Zapata, was auctioned off for £500 on Channel 4's *The Big Breakfast*.

The portrait of another cricketer famed for his facial hair was dicovered by workmen in a South London pub. The drawing of the Victorian colossus W G Grace, found in the Hanover Arms in Kennington, was set to open up a whole new area of Van Gogh scholarship. Experts claimed that the young Vincent had became a regular visitor to the Oval during a stay in London in 1874. It made such sense, after all the Dutch have been playing some decent cricket lately (Holland are in England's group for the World Cup, don't forget). Anyway, before we could start compiling our top-ten left-handed, one-eared openers, we noticed the date on *The Independent* newspaper, in which the article appeared. It was April 1st.

Had Vincent played, it is quite likely (given his fragile state of mind) that he would have been given out "huffed". This mode of dismissal was officially recognised by the MCC custodians as a legitimate way of losing one's wicket. The man responsible was Robin Wightman of Whiteleas CC who was recorded as "R Wightman, absent huffed, 0" on the local scorecard against local rivals East Rainton. Mr Wightman had taken 7-58 in a Northeast Durham League match when he stepped up to bowl the last over of the innings. However the captain decided that he would be taking over instead, "I don't believe it" muttered Mr Wightman and departed the ground....well, in a "huff". His side, now comprised of 10 men, were skittled out for 100. Said Mr Wightman on the incident "I told a couple of lads I was going home, but didn't tell the captain. I have heard he submitted the scorecard after a pint too many in the club". Other unusual dismissals recorded by the MCC include "sick on wicket", "ran away scared by bowler", "dropped spectacles on wicket", "shamefully refused to go in", "remembered a previous engagement" and "left to catch train to Continent".

GRAHAM GOOCH'S
TEST RECORD

Breakdown by Country

	M	I	No	Runs	HS	Ave	100	50
Australia	42	79	0	2632	196	33.32	4	16
West Indies	26	51	2	2197	154*	44.83	5	13
New Zealand	15	24	2	1148	210	52.18	4	3
India	19	33	2	1725	333	55.64	5	8
Pakistan	10	16	0	683	135	42.68	1	5
South Africa	3	6	0	139	33	23.16	-	-
Sri Lanka	3	6	0	376	174	62.66	1	1

Essex Man in History

	M	I	No	Runs	HS	Ave	100	50
A R Border	156	265	44	11,174	205	50.56	27	63
S M Gavaskar	125	214	16	10,122	236*	51.12	34	45
G A Gooch	**118**	**214**	**6**	**8900**	**333**	**42.58**	**20**	**46**
Javed Miandad	124	189	21	8832	280*	52.57	23	43
I V A Richards	121	182	12	8540	291	50.23	24	45

Another notable occurrence in the lower reaches of English cricket, occurred in Division 3 of the Thames Valley League. Johan van Niekerk, who had played in more exalted company for Western Province under-19s, scored an undefeated century and took all ten opposition wickets including a hat-trick. He steered Marlow Park to victory by scoring 102 of his team's 237-3 and taking 10-46 in Stoke Green's total of 94. The 'innings double' has been achieved by four first class cricketers, but what makes Niekerk's effort special was that he captured his final three wickets in successive balls.

Apparently a shower between innings had changed the placid nature of the pitch. "It was lethal", admitted Mr Niekerk.

Other scoring excesses included 48 off one over by West Indian Steve Dublin in the Bolton League. Dublin who comes from Montserrat, and was once hailed as the hardest hitter in the game by none other than Viv Richards (almost OBE), clouted eight sixes. The unfortunate bowler, Rob Slater, who

ENGLAND TESTS UNDER FLETCHER

Opponents	Date	Venue	P	W	L	D
India	1992-3	away	3	0	3	0
Sri Lanka	1992-3	away	1	0	1	0
Australia	1993	home	6	1	4	1
West Indies	1993-4	away	5	1	3	1
New Zealand	1994	home	3	1	0	2
South Africa	1994	home	3	1	1	1
Australia	1994-5	away	5	1	3	1
Totals			**26**	**5**	**15**	**6**

"didn't think I bowled badly" admitted to sitting in front of the television wondering 'why me' for the remainder of the week. "People were running out into their gardens hoping that they might be able to guard their property" the club secretary was reported as saying. Slater should take heart, though. It also happened in a friendly game at The Oval, when the Rob Jones was the bowler. Jones and Slater should get together and organise cricket's first victim support system; they might even make Martin McCague feel better.

Looking forward to the next season, the World Cup will lighten up the dark February mornings with England hoping to go one better on the Indian sub-continent than they did eight years ago. Lancashire will have to come through a tough pool if they are to have any hope of holding onto the Benson & Hedges Cup, whilst Warwickshire begin their defence of the NatWest Trophy with a journey down the M5, and then some, to visit Cornwall.

NATWEST TROPHY DRAW 1996

First Round (to be played on June 25)
Cambridgeshire v Kent....Cornwall v Warwickshire....Cumberland v Middlesex....Durham v Scotland....Essex v Devon....Glamorgan v Worcestershire....Hampshire v Norfolk....Ireland v Sussex....Leicestershire v Berkshire....Lincolnshire v Gloucestershire....Northamptonshire v Cheshire....Oxfordshire v Lancashire....Somerset v Suffolk....Staffordshire v Derbyshire....Surrey v Holland....Yorkshire v Nottinghamshire

BENSON & HEDGES CUP GROUP DRAW 1996
(competition begins Sunday April 26)

Group A	Group B	Group C	Group D
Derbyshire	Northamptonshire	British Univs.	Gloucestershire
Durham	Nottinghamshire	Essex	Hampshire
Lancashire	Scotland	Glamorgan	Ireland
Leicestershire	Worcestershire	Kent	Surrey
Minor Counties	Yorkshire	Middlesex	Sussex
Warwickshire		Somerset	

Quotes

"One began to feel that the right adjective was the one never atttached to him in his playing days: amateurish" **- Matt Engel, editor of Wisden, on Illingworth.**

"You might as well call him Raymond 'Pontius Pilate' Illingworth. The man's a fool. I think he should be out." **- Ian Botham offering his opinions on Illingworth.**

"I have a lot I could say about Mr Illingworth. If I had my way, I would take him to the Traitor's Gate and personally hang, draw and quarter him" **- Ian Botham again**

"Some might say Ian is just a talented thug, but I believe there is far more to him than that" **- Dennis Silk, chairman of the TCCB. Who need enemies when you've got supporters like Dennis.**

"He is just the man who hits all the catches" **- Ray Illingworth on Keith Fletcher's highly paid job as England Team Manager**

"I don't think he could motivate a stuffed mullet at the moment" **- Northants captain Allan Lamb on Fletcher**

"Doug Insole asked me during the interview whether I would be prepared to lend a hand with the baggage. The attitude of people at Lord's has amazed me for years" **- Ray Illingworth, explaining why he turned down the team manager's job in 1986.**

"Young Gough took the trouble to come and see me, I can't believe people want to meet me after all these years. It brings tears to my eyes, it really does" **- Harold Larwood.**

"Not many people had heard of him, but I had. I was his first Test victim at Old Trafford" **- Allan Lamb on Indian leg-spinner Anil Kumble who went on to bag 105 wickets for Northants in the County Championship.**

"I'm no Pom, mate" **- Andrew Symonds in December, after scoring a century for Queensland against the touring England side.**

"Bring back Dion Hash" **- New Zealand cricket fans' banner. Dion Nash was one of three New Zealand cricketers suspended after admitting smoking cannabis.**

"He should stay a doctor. It's a tough life you know - a real hard, hard life. You are on the road and away from your family for months at a time, playing everyday in hot, hot sunshine"

- Brian Lara on asked whether Dr Julian Thompson should give up his day job and turn pro. Thompson had just bowled the West Indian out twice for nought.

"Being the manager of a touring team is rather like being in charge of a cemetary. Lots of people underneath you - but no one listening" **- Wes Hall, manager of the West Indian touring team.**

"I hadn't had much bowling pre-season and I didn't really know my run-up, so I just thought I'd turn my arm over and he hit it out of the ground. After that, I froze and the rest is history" **- Rob Jones, one of two bowlers in 1995 to be hit for 48 runs in an over. Jones, playing against Surrey in a friendly went for 6,6,4,4,6,6,6,6, plus two each for the no-balls.**

England v West Indies ━━━━━━━━━━━

The seemingly endless cycle of international cricket was again exposed as the West Indians embarked on their demanding tour of England only days after their series defeat by Australia. No player in the touring party had ever had to deal with the aftermath of losing a series, their last defeat having been 15 years earlier to New Zealand. Having lost the unofficial title of world champions, the talk was of a side out of sorts with itself, of internal feuds and of the erratic form of its talisman Brian Lara. For England this was the time to eradicate the poor performances of the winter. Kick them while they're down.

The Texaco one-day series has never shown itself to be an accurate yardstick for gauging Test performances, England have made a habit of winning the prelims only to falter when the real event started. Nevertheless, in light of the tourists recent demises, the clinching of the Texaco trophy had pundits reaching for their keys as they saw cracks opening up in the West Indian batting. Atherton's century in the deciding encounter had hogged the limelight but it was the 3-27 from Derbyshire's Dominic Cork that proved the most useful pointer to the Test series to come.

Cork was not party to the opening encounter at Headingley which saw England slump to a 9 wicket defeat. Much of the cause of England's discomfort, rested in the hands of Ian Bishop, playing in his first Test in over two years. His 5-32 in the first innings effectively sealed the outcome and secured him a well deserved man-of-the-match award.

There was few grounds for optimism as the second Test began at Lord's. In the 14 Tests played there since 1983, England had won only three: two against Sri Lanka and one against India. Ramprakash failed again, bagging a pair on his home ground, but Smith proved all his doubters wrong with two blazing innings. The match, though, belonged to Cork. His second innings analysis of 19.3-5-43-7 was the best performance by an England debutant this century and was at the heart of England's first victory over the West Indies at Lord's since 1957.

With this unscheduled setback, the tourists hit a crisis patch with the expulsion of Winston Benjamin for off-field misdemeanours and a severe thrashing by lowly Sussex. The innings and 121 run loss was the heaviest defeat ever inflicted on the West Indies by a county. Down but not yet out. The pitch at Edgbaston, supposedly tailored for England's seamers, provided a lifeline for the West Indian pace attack who ripped apart England's batting and ended the match before lunch on the third day. The 1034 balls bowled in the game was the lowest number in a Test for 50 years.

It was left to Cork to claim back the headlines at Manchester, as he followed his 56 not out with only the 22nd hat-trick in Test history. It was the first such feat by an Englishman since Peter Loader's hattrick at Headingley in 1957 and, despite Lara's match aggregate of 232 runs, set up the series levelling victory.

With the fate of the Wisden trophy left hanging in the balance, the two remaining Tests proved to be anti-climaxes. On perfect pitches, batsmen dominated, Jack Russell resurrected his Test career and Lara showed his class with two more large centuries. Even Graeme Hick made runs. Lara's tally of 765 runs in the summer led to his nomination as the West Indies man-of-the-series and confirmed that Caribbean flair is alive and well after all.

*Q*uotes

"Cricket is 50 per cent in the head, 50 per cent in the heart and bugger technique" - **Ray Illingworth.**

"The team says a prayer every day before play and it is an intense bonding experience. If anyone did not join in there would be great concern' - **Wes Hall, former West Indies paceman (opening partner Charlie Griffith) and manager of the 1995 tourists.**

"Rhodes will definitely play" - **Supremo Ray Illingworth announcing the return of wicket-keeper Steve Rhodes before the Second Test. Rhodes did not play either in the Test or in the remainder of the series.**

"He had a fantastic day that he will never forget. But after the hattrick, he bowled like a pillock" - **Peter Lever, England's bowling coach, on Dominic Cork's performance in the second Test.**

"My mum's at home looking after my nine-month old son. She said if I took a wicket, she would throw him up in the air. He's probably been sick by now" - **Dominic Cork.**

"Curtly has copped some stick so far this tour but I promise you, from 22 yards away he's bowling as well as ever" - **Alec Stewart.**

"If even the Poms can beat them it takes a bit of the gloss off our win" - **Sydney Morning Herald.**

"I thought they were only allowed two bouncers in one over" - **Bill Frindall, after streaker Madeleine Perry ran onto the pitch at Lord's.**

"There's no-one sulking in our dressing room. We'll have a good talk and I'm sure we'll bounce back in the Edgbaston Test' - **Richie Richardson, West Indies captain, after being thrashed by Sussex, their first loss to a county in 19 years. The last time they were made to follow on in a county tour match was against Kent in 1933. He was right about Edgbaston though.**

"A diabolical pitch to play Test cricket on...." - **Mike Atherton, on the Edgbaston pitch which was supposedly prepared to suit England's bowlers.**

"We'll play them anywhere. We'll play them in the car park" - **Wes Hall.**

"There were a couple of times out there when I wondered if I had enough life assurance" - **Robin Smith, the only England batsmen to reach double figures in both innings.**

"It's up to each individual what he wears. He'll probably use a grille from now on. Most people do after being hit in the face" - **Illingworth on Smith, after the England batsman had his cheekbone fractured by a Bishop bouncer in the Fourth Test.**

"He looks as if he wants a throat spray, but he's limping. There must be a connection somewhere, but I hate to think what it is" - **Richie Benaud on Dominic Cork's discomfort while batting in the final Test.**

1ST TEST ━━━━━━━━━━━━━━━━━━━━

Headingley   June 8-12

ENGLAND - First Innings

				Min	Bls
R A Smith	c Richardson	b Benjamin	16	67	48
M A Atherton*	c Murray	b Bishop	81	212	145
G A Hick	c Campbell	b Benjamin	18	35	24
G P Thorpe	lbw	b Bishop	20	98	68
A J Stewart†	c Hooper	b Bishop	2	27	17
M Ramprakash	c Campbell	b Bishop	4	12	10
P A J DeFreitas	c Murray	b Benjamin	23	53	27
D Gough	c Ambrose	b Bishop	0	1	1
P J Martin	c Murray	b Ambrose	2	6	5
R K Illingworth	not out		17	41	28
D E Malcolm		b Benjamin	0	3	4
Extras (B1, NB15)			16		
Total (59.5 overs, 286 mins)			**199**		

Fall of wickets: 52 (Smith), 91 (Hick), 142 (Thorpe), 148 (Atherton), 153 (Ramprakash), 154 (Stewart), 154 (Gough), 157 (Martin), 199 (DeFreitas), 199 (Malcolm)

Bowling: Ambrose 17-4-56-1, **Walsh** 13-2-50-0, **Bishop** 16-2-32-5, **Benjamin** 13.5-2-60-4

ENGLAND - Second Innings

				Min	Bls
R A Smith	c Arthurton	b Ambrose	6	10	10
M A Atherton*	c Murray	b Walsh	17	67	42
G A Hick	c Walsh	b Bishop	27	61	47
G P Thorpe	c Campbell	b Walsh	61	160	119
A J Stewart†	c Murray	b Benjamin	4	36	11
M Ramprakash		b Walsh	18	88	55
P A J DeFreitas	c sub*	b Walsh	1	8	5
D Gough	c sub**	b Ambrose	29	73	50
P J Martin	c Lara	b Bishop	19	57	39
R K Illingworth	not out		10	27	27
D E Malcolm		b Ambrose	5	22	7
Extras (B1, LB3, NB7)			11		
Total (67.2 overs, 311 mins)			**208**		

Fall of wickets: 6 (Smith), 55 (Atherton), 55 (Hick), 82 (Stewart), 130 (Ramprakash), 136 (DeFreitas), 152 (Thorpe), 193 (Gough), 193 (Martin), 208 (Malcolm)

Bowling: Ambrose 20.2-6-44-3, **Walsh** 22-4-60-4, **Bishop** 19-3-81-2, **Benjamin** 6-1-19-1

*sub: Chanderpaul   **sub: Williams

WEST INDIES - First Innings

				Min	Bls
C L Hooper	c Thorpe	b Malcolm	0	1	1
S L Campbell	run out (DeFreitas)		69	132	101
B C Lara	c Hick	b Illingworth	53	71	55
J A Adams	c Martin	b Hick	58	154	109
K L Arthurton	c Stewart	b DeFreitas	42	196	153
R Richardson*	lbw	b Martin	0	11	7
J R Murray†	c Illingworth	b DeFreitas	20	59	50
I R Bishop	run out (Malcolm/Stewart)		5	32	19
C E L Ambrose	c Gough	b Malcolm	15	48	31
C A Walsh	c Stewart	b Gough	4	25	13
K C Benjamin	not out		0	14	5
Extras (B4, LB11, NB1)			16		
Total (90.3 overs, 380 mins)			**282**		

Fall of wickets: 0 (Hooper), 95 (Lara), 141 (Campbell), 216 (Adams), 219 (Richardson), 243 (Murray), 254 (Atherton), 254 (Bishop), 275 (Walsh), 282 (Ambrose)

Bowling: Malcolm 7.3-0-48-2, **Gough** 5-1-24-1, **DeFreitas** 23-3-82-2, **Martin** 27-9-48-1, **Illingworth** 24-9-50-1, **Hick** 4-0-15-1

Toss: West Indies   Man of the Match: **I R Bishop**
Umpires: **H D Bird & S Venkataraghavan** (TV) **P Willey**

WEST INDIES - Second Innings

				Min	Bls
C L Hooper	not out		74	83	72
S L Campbell	c Atherton	b Martin	2	9	5
B C Lara	not out		48	73	40
J C Adams					
K L Arthurton					
R Richardson*					
J R Murray†					
I R Bishop					
C E L Ambrose					
C A Walsh					
K C Benjamin					
Extras (B1, LB2, NB 2)			5		
Total (1 wkt, 19 overs, 83 mins)			**129**		

Fall of wickets: 11 (Campbell)

Bowling: Martin 8-1-49-1, **DeFreitas** 4-0-33-0, **Illingworth** 3-0-31-0, **Malcolm** 4-0-13-0

WEST INDIES WON BY 9 WICKETS

2ND TEST

Lord's June 22-26

ENGLAND - First Innings

			Min	Bls
M A Atherton*		b Ambrose	21	*54 41*
A J Stewart†	c Arthurton	b Gibson	34	*124 85*
G A Hick	c Lara	b Bishop	13	*64 44*
G P Thorpe	c Lara	b Ambrose	52	*154 108*
R A Smith		b Hooper	61	*126 107*
M Ramprakash	c Campbell	b Hooper	0	*12 14*
D G Cork		b Walsh	30	*105 77*
D Gough	c Campbell	b Gibson	11	*29 19*
P J Martin		b Walsh	29	*99 63*
R K Illingworth	not out		16	*43 39*
A R C Fraser	lbw	b Walsh	1	*8 6*
Extras (B1, LB10, NB4)			15	
Total (99.4 overs, 416 mins)			283	

Fall of wickets: 29 (Atherton), 70 (Hick), 74 (Stewart), 185 (Smith), 187 (Ramprakash), 191 (Thorpe), 205 (Gough), 255 (Cork), 281 (Martin), 283 (Fraser)

Bowling: Ambrose 26-6-72-2, **Walsh** 22.4-6-50-3, **Gibson** 20-2-81-2, **Bishop** 17-4-33-1, **Hooper** 14-3-36-2

WEST INDIES - First Innings

			Min	Bls
S L Campbell	c Stewart	b Gough	5	*4 5*
C L Hooper		b Martin	40	*151 107*
B C Lara	lbw	b Fraser	6	*46 31*
J C Adams	lbw	b Fraser	54	*220 165*
R Richardson*	c Stewart	b Fraser	49	*109 71*
K L Arthurton	c Gough	b Fraser	75	*223 169*
J R Murray†		c & b Martin	16	*41 22*
O D Gibson	lbw	b Gough	29	*55 40*
I R Bishop		b Cork	8	*26 15*
C E L Ambrose	c Ramp'kash	b Fraser	12	*57 38*
C A Walsh	not out		11	*26 10*
Extras (B8, LB11)			19	
Total (112 overs, 489 mins)			324	

Fall of wickets: 6 (Campbell), 23 (Lara), 88 (Hooper), 166 (Richardson), 169 (Adams), 197 (Murray), 246 (Gibson), 272 (Bishop), 305 (Ambrose), 324 (Arthurton)

Bowling: Gough 27-2-84-2, **Fraser** 33-13-66-5, **Cork** 22-4-72-1, **Martin** 23-5-65-2, **Illingworth** 7-2-18-0

Toss: **England**   Man of the Match: **D G Cork**
Umpires: **D R Shepherd & S Venkataraghavan**
(TV) **A G T Whitehead**

ENGLAND - Second Innings

			Min	Bls
M A Atherton*	c Murray	b Walsh	9	*33 26*
A J Stewart†	c Murray	b Walsh	36	*50 37*
G A Hick		b Bishop	67	*124 92*
G P Thorpe	c Richardson	b Ambrose	42	*143 99*
R A Smith	lbw	b Ambrose	90	*364 227*
M Ramprakash	c sub*	b Bishop	0	*13 10*
D G Cork	c Murray	b Bishop	23	*67 50*
D Gough		b Ambrose	20	*47 44*
P J Martin	c Arthurton	b Ambrose	1	*17 6*
R K Illingworth	lbw	b Walsh	4	*15 10*
A R C Fraser	not out		2	*4 4*
Extras (B6, LB27, W2, NB7)			42	
Total (99.1 overs, 447 mins)			336	

Fall of wickets: 32 (Atherton), 51 (Stewart), 150 (Hick), 155 (Ramprakash), 240 (Thorpe), 290 (Cork), 320 (Smith), 329 (Gough), 334 (Martin), 336 (Illingworth)

Bowling: Ambrose 24-5-70-4, **Walsh** 28.1-10-91-3, **Gibson** 14-1-51-0, **Bishop** 22.5-5-56-3, **Hooper** 9-1-31-0, **Adams** 2-0-4-0   *sub: S C Williams

WEST INDIES - Second Innings

			Min	Bls
C L Hooper	c Martin	b Gough	14	*23 18*
S L Campbell	c Stewart	b Cork	93	*310 222*
B C Lara	c Stewart	b Gough	54	*86 62*
J C Adams	c Hick	b Cork	13	*38 21*
R Richardson*	lbw	b Cork	0	*9 9*
K L Arthurton	c sub*	b Cork	0	*49 40*
J R Murray†	c sub*	b Gough	9	*37 26*
O D Gibson	lbw	b Cork	14	*44 22*
I R Bishop	not out		10	*46 19*
C E L Ambrose	c Illingworth	b Cork	11	*30 30*
C A Walsh	c Stewart	b Cork	0	*1 2*
Extras (LB5)			5	
Total (78.3 overs, 346 mins)			223	

Fall of wickets: 15 (Hooper), 99 (Lara), 124 (Adams), 130 (Richardson), 138 (Arthurton), 177 (Murray), 198 (Gibson), 201 (Campbell), 223 (Ambrose), 223 (Walsh)

Bowling: Fraser 25-9-57-0, **Gough** 20-0-79-3, **Illingworth** 7-4-9-0, **Martin** 7-0-30-0, **Cork** 19.3-5-43-7

* sub: P N Weekes

ENGLAND WON BY 72 RUNS

3RD TEST

Edgbaston   July 6-10

ENGLAND - First Innings

				Min	Bls
M A Atherton*	c Murray	b Ambrose	0	2	3
A J Stewart†	lbw	b Benjamin	37	114	70
G A Hick	c Richardson	b Walsh	3	12	5
G P Thorpe	c Campbell	b Ambrose	30	46	33
R A Smith	c Arthurton	b Bishop	46	144	92
J E R Gallian		b Benjamin	7	27	20
D G Cork	lbw	b Walsh	4	16	18
D Gough	c Arthurton	b Bishop	1	28	17
P J Martin	c sub*	b Walsh	1	25	12
R K Illingworth		b Bishop	0	11	7
A R C Fraser	not out		0	2	2
Extras (LB4, W4, NB10)			18		
Total (44.2 overs, 222 mins)			147		

Fall of wickets: 4 (Atherton), 9 (Hick), 53 (Thorpe), 84 (Stewart), 100 (Gallian), 109 (Cork), 124 (Gough), 141 (Smith), 147 (Martin), 147 (Illingworth)

Bowling: Ambrose 7.5-1-26-2, Walsh 17.1-4-54-3, Bishop 6.2-0-18-3, Benjamin 13-4-45-2

ENGLAND - Second Innings

				Min	Bls
M A Atherton*		b Walsh	4	32	21
R A Smith		b Bishop	41	156	84
G A Hick	c Hooper	b Bishop	3	2	2
G P Thorpe	c Murray	b Bishop	0	9	6
D G Cork	c sub*	b Walsh	16	43	33
P J Martin	lbw	b Walsh	0	9	5
J E R Gallian	c Murray	b Walsh	0	1	2
D Gough	c Campbell	b Walsh	12	42	30
R K Illingworth	c Hooper	b Bishop	0	12	8
A R C Fraser	not out		1	4	1
A J Stewart†	absent		0		
Extras (NB12)			12		
Total (30 overs, 162 mins)			89		

Fall of wickets: 17 (Atherton), 20 (Hick), 26 (Thorpe), 61 (Cork), 62 (Martin), 63 (Gallian), 88 (Gough), 88 (Smith), 89 (Illingworth)

Bowling: Walsh 15-2-45-5, Bishop 13-3-29-4, Benjamin 2-0-15-0
* sub: S C Williams

WEST INDIES - First Innings

				Min	Bls
C L Hooper	c Stewart	b Cork	40	94	71
S L Campbell		b Cork	79	203	140
B C Lara	lbw	b Cork	21	52	42
J C Adams	lbw	b Cork	10	36	25
R Richardson*		b Fraser	69	241	174
K L Arthurton	lbw	b Fraser	8	35	21
J R Murray†	c Stewart	b Martin	26	33	24
I R Bishop	c Martin	b Illingworth	16	79	59
K C Benjamin	run out		11	53	34
C A Walsh	run out		0	1	0
C E L Ambrose	not out		4	10	6
Extras (B5, LB5, NB6)			16		
Total (98 overs, 427 mins)			300		

Fall of wickets: 73 (Hooper), 105 (Lara), 141 (Adams), 156 (Campbell), 171 (Arthurton), 198 (Murray), 260 (Bishop), 292 (Benjamin), 292 (Walsh), 300 (Richardson)

Bowling: Fraser 31-7-93-2, Gough 18-3-68-0, Cork 22-5-69-4, Martin 19-5-49-1, Illingworth 8-4-11-1

Toss: England   Man of the Match: S L Campbell
Umpires: M J Kitchen & I D Robinson (Zim)
(TV) J W Holder

WEST INDIES WON BY AN INNINGS AND 64 RUNS

4TH TEST

Old Trafford   July 27-31

WEST INDIES - First Innings

				Min	Bls
C L Hooper	c Crawley	b Cork	16	57	50
S L Campbell	c Russell	b Fraser	10	36	23
B C Lara	lbw	b Cork	87	153	118
J C Adams	c Knight	b Fraser	24	50	39
R Richardson*	c Thorpe	b Fraser	2	8	7
K L Arthurton	c Cork	b Watkinson	17	55	48
J R Murray†	c Emburey	b Watkinson	13	38	21
I R Bishop	c Russell	b Cork	9	33	18
C E L Ambrose	not out		7	42	18
K C Benjamin		b Cork	14	15	11
C A Walsh	c Knight	b Fraser	11	12	14
Extras (LB1, NB5)			6		
Total (60.2 overs, 257 mins)			216		

Fall of wickets: 21 (Campbell), 35 (Hooper), 86 (Adams), 94 (Richardson), 150 (Lara), 166 (Lara), 184 (Murray), 185 (Bishop), 205 (Benjamin), 216 (Walsh)
Bowling: Fraser 16.2-5-45-4, **Cork** 20-1-86-4, **White** 5-0-23-0, **Emburey** 10-2-33-0, **Watkinson** 9-2-28-2

WEST INDIES - Second Innings

				Min	Bls
S L Campbell	c Russell	b Watkinson	44	137	102
K L Arthurton	run out		17	86	74
B C Lara	c Knight	b Fraser	145	281	226
J C Adams		c & b Watkinson	1	6	3
R Richardson*		b Cork	22	84	57
J R Murray†	lbw	b Cork	0	1	1
C L Hooper	lbw	b Cork	0	1	1
I R Bishop	c Crawley	b Watkinson	9	37	23
K C Benjamin	c Knight	b Fraser	15	37	23
C E L Ambrose	not out		23	82	43
C A Walsh		b Cork	16	24	18
Extras (B5, LB9, NB8)			22		
Total (91.5 overs, 396 mins)			314		

Fall of wickets: 36 (Arthurton), 93 (Campbell), 97 (Adams), 161 (Richardson), 161 (Murray), 161 (Hooper), 191 (Bishop), 234 (Benjamin), 283 (Lara), 314 (Walsh)
Bowling: Fraser 19-5-53-2, **Cork** 23.5-2-111-4, **Emburey** 20-5-49-0, **White** 6-0-23-0, **Watkinson** 23-4-64-3

ENGLAND - First Innings

				Min	Bls
N V Knight		b Walsh	17	76	45
M A Atherton*	c Murray	b Ambrose	47	172	130
J P Crawley		b Walsh	8	33	26
G P Thorpe	c Murray	b Bishop	94	258	147
R A Smith	c sub*	b Ambrose	44	146	106
C White	c Murray	b Benjamin	23	83	52
R C Russell†	run out		35	102	86
M Watkinson	c sub*	b Walsh	37	116	107
D G Cork	not out		56	140	91
J E Emburey		b Bishop	8	51	43
A R C Fraser	c Adams	b Walsh	4	36	23
Extras (B18, LB11, W1, NB34)			64		
Total (136 overs,616 mins)			437		

Fall of wickets: 45 (Knight), 65 (Crawley), 122 (Atherton), 226 (Smith), 264 (Thorpe), 293 (White), 337 (Russell), 378 (Watkinson), 418 (Emburey), 437 (Fraser)

Bowling: Ambrose 24-2-91-2, **Walsh** 38-5-92-4, **Bishop** 29-3-103-2, **Benjamin** 28-4-83-1, **Adams** 8-1-21-0, **Arthurton** 9-2-18-0   *sub: S C Williams

ENGLAND - Second Innings

				Min	Bls
N V Knight	c sub**	b Bishop	13	81	64
M A Atherton*	run out		22	59	40
J P Crawley	not out		15	59	40
G P Thorpe	c Ambrose	b Benjamin	0	6	6
R A Smith	retired hurt		1	13	8
C White	c sub**	b Benjamin	1	9	5
R C Russell†	not out		31	54	39
M Watkinson					
D G Cork					
J E Emburey					
A R C Fraser					
Extras (LB2, W1, NB8)			11		
Total (4 wkts, 35.5 overs, 171 mins)			94		

Fall of wickets: 39 (Atherton), 41 (Knight), 45 (Thorpe), 48 (White)
Bowling: Ambrose 5-1-16-0, **Walsh** 5-0-17-0, **Bishop** 12-6-18-1, **Benjamin** 9-1-29-2, **Arthurton** 2.5-1-5-0, **Adams** 2-0-7-0
**sub: S Chanderpaul

Toss: West Indies   Man of the Match: **D G Cork**
Umpires: **H D Bird & C Mitchley** (TV) **J C Balderstone**

ENGLAND WON BY 6 WICKETS

5TH TEST ━━━━━━━━━━━━━━━━━━━━━━━━━

Trent Bridge   *Aug 10-14*

ENGLAND - First Innings

				Min	Bls
N V Knight	lbw	b Benjamin	57	254	191
M A Atherton*	run out		113	337	247
J P Crawley	c Williams	b Benjamin	14	42	32
G P Thorpe	c Browne	b Bishop	19	51	36
R K Illingworth	retired hurt		8	41	28
G A Hick	not out		118	304	213
C White	c Browne	b Bishop	1	28	13
R C Russell†	c Browne	b Bishop	35	114	76
M Watkinson	lbw	b Benjamin	24	65	40
D G Cork	c Browne	b Benjamin	31	61	48
A R C Fraser		b Benjamin	0	1	1
Extras (B4, LB8, NB8)			20		
Total (152.4 overs,654 mins)			440		

Fall of wickets: 148 (Knight), 179 (Crawley), 206 (Atherton), 211 (Thorpe), 239 (White), 323 (Russell), 380 (Watkinson), 440 (Cork), 440 (Fraser)
Bowling: Walsh 39-5-93-0, **Bishop** 30.1-6-62-3, **Benjamin** 34.3-7-105-5, **Dhanraj** 40-7-137-0, **Arthurton** 9-0-31-0

ENGLAND - Second Innings

				Min	Bls
M A Atherton*	c Browne	b Bishop	43	218	152
J P Crawley		b Walsh	11	30	18
G A Hick		b Benjamin	7	32	25
G P Thorpe	c Browne	b Walsh	76	268	183
C White	c Campbell	b Bishop	1	27	17
R C Russell†	c Browne	b Benjamin	7	29	16
N V Knight	c Browne	b Benjamin	2	21	13
M Watkinson	not out		82	165	137
D G Cork	c Browne	b Benjamin	4	7	6
A R C Fraser	c Arthurton	b Benjamin	4	29	22
R K Illingworth	not out		14	91	52
Extras (LB4, NB14)			18		
Total (9 wkts dec, 104 overs, 465 mins)			269		

Fall of wickets: 17 (Crawley), 36 (Hick), 117 (Atherton), 125 (White), 139 (Russell), 148 (Knight), 171 (Thorpe), 176 (Cork), 189 (Fraser)
Bowling: Walsh 30-6-70-2, **Bishop** 21-8-50-2, **Benjamin** 25-8-69-5, **Dhanraj** 15-1-54-0, **Arthurton** 13-3-22-0

WEST INDIES - First Innings

				Min	Bls
S C Williams	c Atherton	b Illingworth	62	165	143
S L Campbell	c Crawley	b Watkinson	47	307	225
B C Lara	c Russell	b Cork	152	255	182
R Richardson*	c Hick	b Illingworth	40	53	45
K L Arthurton		b Illingworth	13	52	28
R Dhanraj	c Knight	b Cork	3	60	46
S Chanderpaul	c Crawley	b Watkinson	18	124	101
C O Browne†	st Russell	b Illingworth	34	101	67
I R Bishop	c Hick	b Watkinson	4	14	11
K C Benjamin	not out		14	52	21
C A Walsh		b Fraser	19	33	24
Extras (B2, LB7, NB2)			11		
Total (148.3 overs, 613 mins)			417		

Fall of wickets: 77 (Williams), 217 (Campbell), 273 (Richardson), 319 (Arthurton), 323 (Lara), 338 (Dhanraj), 366 (Chanderpaul), 374 (Bishop), 384 (Browne), 417 (Walsh)
Bowling: Fraser 17.3-6-77-1, **Cork** 36-9-110-2 ,**Watkinson** 35-12-84-3, **Illingworth** 51-21-96-4, **Hick** 4-1-11-0, **White** 5-0-30-0

WEST INDIES - Second Innings

				Min	Bls
B C Lara	c Russell	b Fraser	20	33	30
S L Campbell	c Russell	b Cork	16	40	22
S Chanderpaul	not out		5	15	8
C O Browne†	not out		1	8	6
S C Williams					
R Richardson*					
K L Arthurton					
R Dhanraj					
I R Bishop					
K C Benjamin					
C A Walsh					
Extras			0		
Total (2 wkts, 11 overs, 49 mins)			42		

Fall of wickets: 36 (Lara), 36 (Campbell)
Bowling: Fraser 6-1-17-1, **Cork** 5-1-25-1

Toss: England   Man of the Match: **K C G Benjamin**
Umpires: **N T Plews, C J Mitchley & G Sharp (TV)**

MATCH DRAWN

6TH TEST

The Oval   *Aug 24-28*

ENGLAND - First Innings

				Min	*Bls*
M A Atherton*	c Williams	b Benjamin	36	*107*	*85*
J E Gallian	c Hooper	b Ambrose	0	*12*	*8*
J P Crawley	c Richardson	b Hooper	50	*230*	*159*
G P Thorpe	c Browne	b Ambrose	74	*215*	*177*
G A Hick	c Williams	b Benjamin	96	*248*	*164*
A P Wells	c Campbell	b Ambrose	0	*1*	*1*
R C Russell†		b Ambrose	91	*292*	*221*
M Watkinson	c Browne	b Walsh	13	*63*	*55*
D G Cork		b Ambrose	33	*107*	*63*
A R C Fraser	not out		10	*55*	*35*
D E Malcolm	c Lara	b Benjamin	10	*7*	*7*
Extras (B15, LB11, NB15)			41		
Total (159 overs, 675 mins)			454		

Fall of wickets: 9 (Gallian), 60 (Atherton), 149 (Crawley), 192 (Thorpe), 192 (Wells), 336 (Hick), 372 (Watkinson), 419 (Russell), 443 (Cork), 454 (Malcolm)
Bowling: Ambrose 42-10-96-5, Walsh 32-6-84-1, Benjamin 27-6-81-3, Bishop 35-5-111-0, Hooper 23-7-56-1

ENGLAND - Second Innings

				Min	*Bls*
J E Gallian	c Williams	b Ambrose	25	*115*	*97*
M A Atherton*	c Browne	b Bishop	95	*356*	*269*
J P Crawley	c Browne	b Ambrose	2	*16*	*11*
G P Thorpe	c Williams	b Walsh	38	*93*	*67*
G A Hick	not out		51	*172*	*114*
A P Wells	not out		3	*42*	*39*
R C Russell†					
M Watkinson					
D G Cork					
A R C Fraser					
D E Malcolm					
Extras (LB4, NB5)			9		
Total (4 wkts, 98 overs, 399 mins)			223		

Fall of wickets: 60 (Gallian), 64 (Crawley), 132 (Thorpe), 212 (Atherton)
Bowling: Walsh 28-7-80-1, Ambrose 19-8-35-2, Hooper 22-11-26-0, Chanderpaul 6-0-22-0, Bishop 22-4-56-1, Lara 1-1-0-0

WEST INDIES - First Innings

				Min	*Bls*
S C Williams	c Russell	b Malcolm	30	*47*	*40*
S L Campbell	c Russell	b Fraser	89	*219*	*152*
K C Benjamin	c Atherton	b Cork	20	*79*	*44*
B C Lara	c Fraser	b Malcolm	179	*267*	*206*
R Richardson*	c Hick	b Cork	93	*232*	*156*
C L Hooper	c Russell	b Malcolm	127	*285*	*180*
S Chanderpaul	c Gallian	b Cork	80	*208*	*146*
C O Browne†	not out		27	*58*	*32*
I R Bishop	run out		10	*29*	*18*
C E L Ambrose	not out		5	*7*	*8*
C A Walsh					
Extras (B5, LB20, W5, NB2)			32		
Total (8 wkts dec, 163 overs, 720 mins)			692		

Fall of wickets: 40 (Williams), 94 (Benjamin), 202 (Campbell), 390 (Lara), 435 (Richardson), 631 (Chanderpaul), 653 (Hooper), 686 (Bishop)
Bowling: Malcolm 39-7-160-3, Fraser 40-6-155-1, Watkinson 26-3-113-0, Cork 36-3-145-3, Gallian 12-1-56-0, Hick 10-3-38-0

Toss: England   Man of the Match: B C Lara
Umpires: V K Ramaswamy, D R Shepherd & J H Hampshire (TV)

MATCH DRAWN
Series Result: England 2   West Indies 2 (2 Drawn)
Series Awards: M A Atherton (for England)
               B C Lara (for West Indies)

Test Series Averages

Batting

ENGLAND	M	In	NO	Rns	HS	Avge	100s	50s
M Watkinson	3	4	1	156	82*	52.00	-	1
G A Hick	5	10	2	403	118*	50.37	1	3
R C Russell	3	5	1	199	91	49.75	-	1
R A Smith	4	8	1	305	90	43.57	-	2
G P Thorpe	6	12	0	506	94	42.16	-	5
M A Atherton	6	12	0	488	113	40.66	1	2
D G Cork	5	8	1	197	56*	28.14	-	1
R K Illingworth	4	8	5	69	17*	23.00	-	-
A J Stewart	3	5	0	113	37	22.60	-	-
N V Knight	2	4	0	89	57	22.25	-	1
J P Crawley	3	6	1	100	50	20.00	-	1
D Gough	3	6	0	73	29	12.16	-	-
P A J DeFreitas	1	2	0	24	23	12.00	-	-
P J Martin	3	6	0	52	29	8.66	-	-
J E Emburey	1	1	0	8	8	8.00	-	-
J E R Gallian	2	4	0	32	25	8.00	-	-
C White	2	4	0	26	23	6.50	-	-
A R C Fraser	5	8	4	22	10*	5.50	-	-
M R Ramprakash	2	4	0	22	18	5.50	-	-
D E Malcolm	2	3	0	15	10	5.00	-	-
A P Wells	1	2	1	3	3*	3.00	-	-

WEST INDIES	M	In	NO	Rns	HS	Avge	100s	50s
B C Lara	6	10	1	765	179	85.00	3	3
C O Browne	2	3	2	62	34	62.00	-	-
S Chanderpaul	2	3	1	103	80	51.50	-	1
S C Williams	2	2	0	92	62	46.00	-	1
S L Campbell	6	10	0	454	93	45.40	-	4
C L Hooper	5	8	1	310	127	44.28	1	1
R B Richardson	6	8	0	275	93	34.37	-	2
J C Adams	4	6	0	160	58	26.66	-	2
C E L Ambrose	5	7	4	77	23*	25.66	-	-
K L T Arthurton	5	7	0	172	75	24.57	-	1
O D Gibson	1	2	0	43	29	21.50	-	-
K C G Benjamin	5	6	2	74	20	18.50	-	-
J R Murray	4	6	0	84	26	14.00	-	-
C A Walsh	6	7	1	61	19	10.16	-	-
I R Bishop	6	8	1	71	16	10.14	-	-
R Dhanraj	1	1	0	3	3	3.00	-	-

Bowling

ENGLAND	O	M	R	W	Avge	Best	S/Rate
D G Cork	184.2	30	661	26	25.42	7-43	42.54
A R C Fraser	187.5	52	563	16	35.18	5-66	70.44
R K Illingworth	100	40	215	6	35.83	4-96	100.0
M Watkinson	93	21	289	8	36.12	3-64	69.75
D Gough	70	6	255	6	42.50	3-79	70.00
D E Malcolm	50.3	7	220	5	44.00	3-160	60.60
P J Martin	84	21	241	5	48.20	2-65	100.8
P A J DeFreitas	27	3	115	2	57.50	2-82	81.00
G A Hick	18	4	64	1	64.00	1-15	108.0
J E R Gallian	12	1	56	0	-	-	-
C White	16	0	76	0	-	-	-
J E Emburey	30	7	82	0	-	-	-

WEST INDIES	O	M	R	W	Avge	Best	S/Rate
K C Benjamin	158.2	33	506	23	22.00	5-69	41.30
I R Bishop	242.3	49	649	27	24.03	5-32	53.89
C E L Ambrose	185.1	43	506	21	24.09	5-96	52.90
C A Walsh	290	57	786	26	30.23	5-45	66.92
C L Hooper	68	22	149	3	49.66	2-36	136.0
O D Gibson	34	3	132	2	66.00	2-81	102.0
B C Lara	1	1	0	0	-	-	-
S Chanderpaul	6	0	22	0	-	-	-
J C Adams	12	1	32	0	-	-	-
K L T Arthurton	33.5	6	76	0	-	-	-
R Dhanraj	55	8	191	0	-	-	-

Tetley Bitter Tour Matches

WEST INDIES XI V WORCESTERSHIRE
New Road   May 16-18
W Indies XI   241-9 dec (B Lara 78, P Thomas 5-70)
Worcs   86-5
Match drawn

WEST INDIES XI V SOMERSET
Taunton   May 19-21
W Indies XI   449-8 dec (C Hoooper 176, S Campbell 93,
J Adams 91)
176-3 dec (S Campbell 80)
Somerset   301-9 dec (P Bowler 84)
159-2   (M Lathwell 76)
Match drawn

WEST INDIES XI V LEICESTERSHIRE
Grace Road   May 30-June 1
W Indies XI   468-7 dec (K Arthurton 146,
S Chanderpaul 140*)
143-4 dec
Leics   194 (J Whitaker 75, R Dhanraj 6-50)
130
West Indies won by 287 runs

WEST INDIES XI V NORTHAMPTONSHIRE
Northampton   June 3-5
Northants   281 (A Penberthy 73, I Bishop 4-64)
W Indies XI   268-5 dec (K Arthurton 121*, J Adams 93)
Match drawn

WEST INDIES XI V DURHAM
Chester-le-Street   June 17-19
Durham   364-8 dec (M Roseberry 79, J Morris 75)
259
W Indies XI   462-5 dec (S Campbell 113, C Browne
102*, R Richardson 101*, B Lara 91)
16-1
Match drawn

Continued on page 162

1st One Day International

Trent Bridge   May 24-25

ENGLAND

				Min	Bls
M A Atherton*	c Lara	b Walsh	8	35	33
A J Stewart†		b Hooper	74	157	127
G A Hick	c Murray	b Benjamin	8	51	27
G P Thorpe	c Murray	b Walsh	7	25	10
N H Fairbrother		b Bishop	12	30	23
M Ramprakash		b Walsh	32	51	36
P A J DeFreitas	run out (Ambrose/Murray)		15	23	29
D G Cork		b Arthurton	14	21	27
D Gough	run out (Hooper)		3	5	4
S D Udal	not out		5	9	7
A R C Fraser	not out		4	7	8
Extras	(LB11, W5, NB1)		17		
Total	(55 overs) (9 wkts)		**199**		

Fall of wickets: 25 (Atherton), 60 (Hick), 85 (Thorpe), 121 (Fairbrother), 125 (Stewart), 157 (DeFreitas), 186 (Ramprakash), 190 (Cork), 191 (Gough)

Bowling: Ambrose 8-1-33-0, **Walsh** 10-1-28-3, **Bishop** 11-2-30-1, **Benjamin** 8-1-22-1, **Hooper** 10-0-45-1, **Arthurton** 8-0-30-1

Umpires: **D R Shepherd & N T Plews**
Man of the Match: **C A Walsh**

WEST INDIES

				Min	Bls
C L Hooper		b Cork	34	62	57
S L Campbell	run out (Udal/Stewart)		80	193	137
B C Lara	c Atherton	b Gough	70	100	95
R Richardson*	c DeFreitas	b Gough	1	7	7
J C Adams	lbw	b Cork	2	12	12
K L Arthurton	not out		1	10	3
J R Murray†	not out		7	4	6
I R Bishop					
W K Benjamin					
C A Walsh					
C E L Ambrose					
Extras	(LB1, W4, NB1)		6		
Total	(52.4 overs) (5 wkts)		**201**		

Fall of wickets: 66 (Hooper), 180 (Lara), 183 (Richardson), 191 (Adams), 194 (Campbell)

Bowling: DeFreitas 10.4-1-44-0, Fraser 10-2-29-0, Gough 11-1-30-2, Cork 11-0-48-2, Udal 8-0-37-0, Hick 2-0-12-0

Toss: **West Indies**
WEST INDIES WON BY 5 WICKETS

2nd One Day International

The Oval   May 26

ENGLAND

				Min	Bls
M A Atherton*		b Benjamin	92	161	118
A J Stewart†	c Murray	b Bishop	16	38	37
G A Hick	run out (Hooper)		66	112	81
G P Thorpe	run out (Lara)		26	38	28
N H Fairbrother	not out		61	67	52
M Ramprakash	c Adams	b Hooper	16	29	16
D Gough	not out		8	5	6
D G Cork					
P A J DeFreitas					
S D Udal					
P J Martin					
Extras	(B6, LB5, W7, NB3)		21		
Total	(55 overs) (5 wkts)		**306**		

Fall of wickets: 33 (Stewart), 177 (Hick), 188 (Atherton), 243 (Thorpe), 296 (Ramprakash)

Bowling: Ambrose 10-1-47-0, Walsh 5.2-0-17-0, Bishop 11-0-60-1, Benjamin 10.4-0-55-1, Arthurton 8-0-48-0, Hooper 10-0-68-1

Umpires: **H D Bird & R Palmer**
Man of the Match: **P J Martin** Toss: **West Indies**
Text

WEST INDIES

				Min	Bls
C L Hooper	c Atherton	b Gough	17	19	21
S L Campbell	c Thorpe	b Martin	20	52	35
B C Lara		b Martin	39	51	36
J C Adams	lbw	b Martin	2	6	8
R Richardson*		c & b Cork	15	40	28
K L Arthurton	run out (Cork)		39	67	65
J R Murray†	run out (Fairbrother)		86	109	77
W K Benjamin	c Ramp'kash	b DeFreitas	17	25	15
I R Bishop	run out (Udal/Gough)		18	25	16
C E L Ambrose		b Martin	10	10	13
C A Walsh	not out		5	6	4
Extras	(LB6, W7)		13		
Total	(53 overs)		**281**		

Fall of wickets: 25 (Hooper), 69 (Campbell), 77 (Adams), 88 (Lara), 114 (Richardson), 166 (Arthurton), 213 (Benjamin), 261 (Bishop), 275 (Ambrose), 281 (Murray)

Bowling: Gough 11-0-62-1, DeFreitas 10-0-73-1, Cork 11-0-56-1, Udal 11-0-40-0, Martin 10-1-44-4

ENGLAND WON BY 25 RUNS

3rd One Day International
Lord's   May 28
ENGLAND

			Min	Bls	
M A Atherton*	c Adams	b Gibson	127	202	160
A J Stewart†	c Lara	b Bishop	8	24	16
G A Hick		b Hooper	24	75	55
G P Thorpe	c Hooper	b Gibson	28	47	49
M Ramprakash	not out		29	73	43
A P Wells		b Gibson	15	9	10
D Gough		b Benjamin	8	5	5
D G Cork	lbw	b Benjamin	0	1	1
P J Martin	not out		4	1	1
S D Udal					
A R C Fraser					
Extras (B4, LB13, W9, NB7)			33		
Total (55 overs) (7 wkts)			276		

Fall of wickets: 12 (Stewart), 79 (Hick), 152 (Thorpe), 244 (Atherton), 263 (Wells), 272 (Gough), 272 (Cork)
Bowling: Ambrose 11-1-45-0, Bishop 11-2-53-1, Benjamin 10-0-61-2, Gibson 11-0-51-3, Hooper 11-0-38-1, Arthurton 1-0-11-0

Umpires: **J H Hampshire & M J Kitchen**
TV umpire: **J C Balderstone**
Man of the Match: **M A Atherton** Toss: **West Indies**

WEST INDIES

			Min	Bls	
S C Williams	c Atherton	b Cork	21	38	30
C L Hooper	c Gough	b Cork	40	132	89
B C Lara	c Stewart	b Cork	11	15	10
J C Adams	c Stewart	b Martin	29	47	46
K L Arthurton	c Stewart	b Gough	35	56	49
R Richardson*	lbw	b Gough	23	38	33
J R Murray†		b Fraser	5	16	7
O D Gibson	c Atherton	b Fraser	7	14	8
W K Benjamin		b Fraser	6	11	9
I R Bishop	not out		1	11	5
C E L Ambrose		b Martin	1	6	4
Extras (LB13, W11)			24		
Total (48.2 overs)			203		

Fall of wickets: 29 (Williams), 44 (Lara), 94 (Adams), 128 (Hooper), 171 (Arthurton), 184 (Richardson), 190 (Murray), 198 (Gibson), 201 (Benjamin), 203 (Ambrose)
Bowling: Fraser 11-3-34-3, Martin 9.2-1-36-2, Cork 9-2-27-3, Gough 10-0-31-2, Udal 8-0-52-0, Hick 1-0-10-0

ENGLAND WON BY 73 RUNS

Tetley Bitter Tour Matches
Continued from page 160

WEST INDIES XI V COMBINED UNIVERSITIES
The Parks, Oxford   June 28-30
W Indies XI	637-5 dec (C Hooper 118, S Williams 114, J Adams 114, K Arthurton 102*)
	216-6 dec (J Murray 100, S Ellis 5-59)
Comb Unis	310 (G Macmillan 71, R Dhanraj 5-87)
	136-1 (I Sutcliffe 63*)

Match drawn

WEST INDIES XI V SUSSEX
Hove   July 1-3
Sussex	446-9 dec (K Newell 135, N Lenham 128, R Dhanraj 6-144)
W Indies XI	186 (K Arthurton 75)
	139 (E Hemmings 4-33, J Lewry 4-38)

Sussex won by an innings and 121 runs

WEST INDIES XI V KENT
Canterbury   July 19-21
W Indies XI	337 (S Williams 137, J Adams 77)
	92-4
Kent	95 (V Drakes 5-20)
	331 (P de Silva 102, D Fulton 89)

West Indies won by 6 wickets

WEST INDIES XI V MIDDLESEX
Lord's   July 22-24
W Indies XI	456 (S Campbell 102, K Arthurton 83, P Tufnell 6-111)
	213-9 dec (M Feltham 6-41)
Middx	237 (J Carr 115)
	52-0

Match drawn

WEST INDIES XI V SOMERSET
Taunton   Aug 2-4
W Indies XI	230 (S Chanderpaul 100, J Kerr 5-82)
	386 (S Williams 119, O Gibson 101*)
Somerset	374 (J Kerr 80, R Turner 72)
	87 (O Gibson 4-32)

West Indies won by 155 runs

WEST INDIES XI V GLOUCESTERSHIRE
Bristol   Aug 5-7
W Indies XI	242 (K Sheeraz 6-67)
	193 (K Sheeraz 5-44)
Gloucs	239 (A Wright 78)
	122 (K Benjamin 5-52)

West Indies won by 74 runs

WEST INDIES XI V HAMPSHIRE
Southampton   Aug 16-18
Hampshire	192 (A Cummins 5-60)
	302-5
W Indies XI	696-6 dec (C Hooper 195, Campbell 172)

Match drawn

WEST INDIES XI V ESSEX
Chelmsford   Aug 19-21
W Indies XI	366 (P Simmons 112)
	260-0 dec (Simmons 139*, Ch'paul 103*)
Essex	300-4 dec (G Gooch 109)
	202-6

Match drawn

WEST INDIES XI V YORKSHIRE
Scarborough   Aug 30-Sep 1
W Indies XI	426 (C Browne 102, K Arthurton 94)
	356-4 dec (Chand'paul 132*, Hooper 105)
Yorkshire	297 (M Bevan 105, A Metcalfe 100)
	143-3

Match drawn

England v Australia

They had hardly started playing Test cricket before Robert Louis Stevenson died. Still, he must have known something about it for it was Stevenson who wrote that it was a better thing to travel hopefully than arrive. Which meant, surely, that he knew all about Test tours to Australia. If only it was 1890 (when Stevenson was still penning his tales) and if only England had gone by boat as they did then and for many a year after, at least then they would have missed the first two Tests and been in with a shout. They didn't though. The plane landed on the day it was supposed to and Slater and Waugh put the English bowlers to the sword on schedule at Brisbane.

When they had finished, taking particular delight in savaging McCague for over five an over, McDermott and Warne took up arms and England were all out for 167. It wasn't even the total, but the brevity of the England innings that so demeaned. They stayed at the wicket for just 67.2 overs; it was like a World Series match (but let's not talk about that either, eh?). Warne cleaned up in the second innings, when England saved some face, but it was still the 12th loss in 18 Tests against the Australians. The number of victories during that seven-year period, just one. Yes, better to travel hopefully than arrive.

The second Test was no better. Worse, is the word that springs to mind. When Warne took a hattrick in England's second innings, the first in Ashes Tests since Hugh Trumble in 1904, it was of no real significance to the match. Warne's wickets were the seventh, eighth and ninth of an innings that had crumbled much earlier. England were all out for 92 and at the crease for just 42 overs. Oh, for the heady days when an England innings lasted over 60 overs. "It's hard to see us coming back from here," said Atherton. Was he talking about the series or the flight home? Did anyone want him back home? Well, apparently Illingworth, who spent a lunch with journalists griping about Atherton and then, a week later, spent a day with another journalist griping about journalists.

Meanwhile, if Atherton had no plans to return home, it seemed that almost every other player did. The injury list grew to epidemic proportions and included, of all things, chicken pox. When the England physio, Dave Roberts, broke a finger during fielding practice, it may well have been felt that unseen forces were at work. Then Ray Illingworth arrived in Australia and it all changed. No, only joking, but England did draw a Test match and Darren Gough and Graham Thorpe did thump the ball about a bit and Fraser (who wasn't even selected) did take 5-75 in the Australians' second innings.

Australia 'A' knocked England out of World Series Cup and Darren Gough went home with a stress fracture just to make sure their was no complacency in the England camp. And then England won a Test and Chris Lewis (who took 4-24) was fined for pointing to the pavilion when he dismissed Craig McDermott. Referee John Reid called it a "cowardly act", though he could have been referring to the English win or the fact that Lewis, with a Test average approaching 38, had actually returned decent figures.

Anyway, it was back to normal at Perth where England were thumped. Only Thorpe and Ramprakash came away with much credit in the final game. In all, it was an unhappy tour and manager Keith Fletcher was washed away in a tide of defeat. I suppose Stevenson would have loved it. He was a Scot, after ail.

Quotes

"I've not heard from him so I can only assume there are no problems. but I would have though he would have given me a tinkle" **- Ray Illingworth at a Sportswriters' lunch in London in November. Illlingworth, then only in the part-time job as chairman of selectors, did not travel out to Australia until December 21.**

"There are some people trying to drive a wedge between me and Athers and I won't have it. The fact is we get on bloody well" **- Illingworth, a week later.**

"My contract with the Test and County Cricket Board stipulates that I work for 110 days a year and I have already gone over that" **- Illingworth.**

"Man for man, on paper, the Australian side stand out like dogs' balls" **- Greg Chappell, former Australian captain, offering expert opinion on the outcome of the series.**

"Who knows? Maybe I might bowl one that will spin right back down the wicket" **- Shane Warne, on the eve of the first Test.**

"My tactic would have been to have taken a single as soon as possible and observe him from the other end" **- Geoff Boycott's tactics on playing Warne.**

"Shane Warne is the best young leg-spinner I've ever seen. I'm assuming he's going to be the best old leg-spinner. He's streets ahead of where I was at that stage" **- Richie Benaud, singing Warne's praises.**

"He didn't look like he was going to get a wicket every ball, so maybe the English are improving" **- Mark Waugh, after two days of the second Test at Melbourne. Warne took 9-80 in the match, which included a hattrick in the second innings.**

"I suppose I'll wake up now" **- Warne after the second Test.**

"Australia's getting carried away with Warne, with one man. Without him it would be an even contest" **- Illingworth.**

"He's from Barnsley and in the republic of South Yorkshire you don't get carried away by your own importance" **- Chris Hassell, Yorkshire chief executive, on Darren Gough, who took 6-49 in the Australian's first innings in the third Test.**

"I don't care who it is, everybody has a sell-by date" **- Greg Chappell on Graham Gooch.**

"Zimbabwe has only three professional cricketers, we have 400" **- Bob Willis, berating England after their loss in the World Series.**

"Australia plays with itself and enjoys it" **- Banner at the final of the World Series, contested by Australia and Australia 'A'.**

"We came here with a short-term ambition which failed and I don't think we have made any progress at all in Australia" **- Mike Atherton, at the end of the series.**

"I can't recall a game against Australia without coming in for personal abuse, but in terms of discipline and aggression, I'm a great believer in the way they play" **- Atherton.**

1ST TEST

The 'Gabba, Brisbane Nov 25-29

AUSTRALIA - First Innings

M J Slater	c Gatting	b Gooch	176
M A Taylor*	run out		59
D C Boon		b Gough	3
M E Waugh	c Stewart	b Gough	140
M G Bevan	c Hick	b Gough	7
S K Warne	c Rhodes	b Gough	2
S R Waugh	c Hick	b DeFreitas	19
I A Healy†	c Hick	b DeFreitas	7
C J McDermott	c Gough	b McCague	2
T B A May	not out		3
G D McGrath	c Gough	b McCague	0
Extras (B5, LB2, NB1)			8
Total (120.2 overs, 506 min)			426

Fall of wickets: 1-99, 2-126, 3-308, 4-326, 5-352, 6-379, 7-407, 8-419, 9-425, 10-426

Bowling: DeFreitas 31-8-102-2, McCague 19.2-4-96-2, **Gough** 32-7-107-4, **Tufnell** 25-3-72-0, **Hick** 4-0-22-0, **Gooch** 9-0-20-1

AUSTRALIA - Second Innings

M A Taylor*	c Stewart	b Tufnell	58
M J Slater	lbw	b Gough	45
D C Boon		b Tufnell	28
M E Waugh		b Tufnell	15
M G Bevan	c Rhodes	b DeFreitas	21
S R Waugh	c sub*	b Tufnell	7
I A Healy†	not out		45
S K Warne	c sub*	b DeFreitas	0
C J McDermott	c Rhodes	b Gough	6
T B A May	not out		9
G D McGrath			
Extras (B2, LB9, W2, NB1)			14
Total (8 wkts dec)			248

Fall of wickets: 1-109, 2-117, 3-139, 4-174, 5-183, 6-190, 7-191, 8-201

Bowling: DeFreitas 22-1-74-2, **Gough** 23-3-78-2, **Tufnell** 38-10-79-4, **Hick** 2-1-1-0, **Gooch** 3-2-5-0
*sub: C White

ENGLAND - First Innings

M A Atherton*	c Healy	b McDermott	54
A J Stewart	c Healy	b McDermott	16
G A Hick	c Healy	b McDermott	3
G P Thorpe		c & b Warne	28
G A Gooch	c Healy	b May	20
M W Gatting	lbw	b McDermott	10
M J McCague		b McDermott	1
S J Rhodes†	lbw	b McDermott	4
P A J DeFreitas	c Healy	b Warne	7
D Gough	not out		17
P C R Tufnell	c Taylor	b Warne	0
Extras (LB1, NB6)			7
Total (67.2 overs)			167

Fall of wickets: 1-22, 2-35, 3-82, 4-105, 5-131, 6-133, 7-140, 8-147, 9-151, 10-167

Bowling: McDermott 19-3-53-6, McGrath 10-2-40-0, **May** 17-3-34-1, **Warne** 21.2-7-39-3

Umpires: **C J Mitchley & S G Randell**
Man of the Match: **S K Warne**   Toss: **Australia**

ENGLAND - Second Innings

M A Atherton*	lbw	b Warne	23
A J Stewart		b Warne	33
G A Hick	c Healy	b Warne	80
G P Thorpe		b Warne	67
G A Gooch	c Healy	b Warne	56
M W Gatting	c Healy	b McDermott	13
S J Rhodes†	c Healy	b McDermott	2
P A J DeFreitas		b Warne	11
D Gough	c M Waugh	b Warne	10
M J McCague	lbw	b Warne	0
P C R Tufnell	not out		2
Extras (B9, LB5, NB12)			26
Total (137.2 overs)			323

Fall of wickets: 1-50, 2-59, 3-219, 4-220, 5-250, 6-280, 7-309, 8-310, 9-310, 10-323

Bowling: McDermott 23-4-90-2, McGrath 19-4-61-0, **Warne** 50.2-22-71-8, **May** 35-16-59-0, **M Waugh** 7-1-17-0, **Bevan** 3-0-11-0

AUSTRALIA WON BY 184 RUNS

2ND TEST

Melbourne Cricket Ground   Dec 24-29

AUSTRALIA - First Innings

				Min	Bls
M J Slater	run out		3	*26*	*19*
M A Taylor*	lbw	b DeFreitas	9	*73*	*41*
D C Boon	c Hick	b Tufnell	41	*148*	*100*
M E Waugh	c Thorpe	b DeFreitas	71	*219*	*155*
M G Bevan	c Atherton	b Gough	3	*28*	*23*
S R Waugh	not out		94	*266*	*191*
I A Healy†	c Rhodes	b Tufnell	17	*59*	*42*
S K Warne	c Hick	b Gough	6	*27*	*25*
T B A May	lbw	b Gough	9	*51*	*31*
C J McDermott		b Gough	0	*2*	*3*
D W Fleming	c Hick	b Malcolm	16	*33*	*19*
Extras (LB7, NB3)			10		
Total (107.3 overs, 471 min)			279		

Fall of wickets: 1-10, 2-39, 3-91, 4-100, 5-171, 6-208, 7-220, 8-242, 9-242, 10-279

Bowling: Malcolm 28.3-4-78-1, **DeFreitas** 23-4-66-2, **Gough** 26-9-60-4, **Tufnell** 28-7-59-2, **Hick** 2-0-9-0

AUSTRALIA - Second Innings

				Min	Bls
M A Taylor*	lbw	b Gough	19	*81*	*64*
M J Slater	st Rhodes	b Tufnell	44	*121*	*74*
D C Boon	lbw	b DeFreitas	131	*378*	*277*
M E Waugh		c & b Gough	29	*128*	*82*
M G Bevan	c sub**	b Tufnell	35	*189*	*134*
S R Waugh	not out		26	*93*	*73*
I A Healy†	c Thorpe	b Tufnell	17	*62*	*38*
S K Warne	c DeFreitas	b Gough	0	*3*	*2*
C J McDermott	not out		2	*6*	*7*
T B A May					
D W Fleming					
Extras (B1, LB9, W1, NB6)			17		
Total (7 wkts dec, 124 overs, 533 min)			320		

Fall of wickets: 1-61, 2-81, 3-157, 4-269, 5-275, 6-316, 7-317

Bowling: Malcolm 22-3-86-0, **DeFreitas** 26-2-70-1, **Tufnell** 48-8-90-3, **Gough** 25-6-59-3, **Hick** 3-2-5-0
** sub: J P Crawley

ENGLAND - First Innings

				Min	Bls
M A Atherton*	lbw	b Warne	44	*200*	*156*
A J Stewart		c & b Warne	16	*52*	*26*
G A Hick	c Healy	b McDermott	23	*44*	*34*
G P Thorpe	c M Waugh	b Warne	51	*150*	*117*
G A Gooch		c & b McDermott	15	*67*	*52*
M W Gatting	c S Waugh	b Warne	9	*23*	*24*
D Gough	c Healy	b McDermott	20	*66*	*51*
S J Rhodes†	c M Waugh	b Warne	0	*13*	*11*
P A J DeFreitas	st Healy	b Warne	14	*24*	*19*
D E Malcolm	not out		11	*25*	*13*
P C R Tufnell	run out		0	*7*	*4*
Extras (LB7, NB2)			9		
Total (83.4 overs, 340 mins)			212		

Fall of wickets: 1-40, 2-119, 3-124, 4-140, 5-148, 6-151, 7-185, 8-189, 9-207, 10-212

Bowling: McDermott 24-6-72-3, **Fleming** 11-5-30-0, **M Waugh** 3-1-11-0, **Warne** 27.4-8-64-6, **May** 18-5-28-0

Toss: **England**   Man of the Match: **C J McDermott**
Umpires: **S A Bucknor & S G Randell**

ENGLAND - Second Innings

				Min	Bls
G A Gooch	c Healy	b Fleming	2	*9*	*8*
M A Atherton*	c Healy	b McDermott	25	*73*	*43*
G A Hick		b Fleming	2	*9*	*6*
G P Thorpe	c Healy	b McDermott	9	*22*	*20*
M W Gatting	c Taylor	b McDermott	25	*86*	*72*
S J Rhodes†	c M Waugh	b McDermott	16	*93*	*72*
A J Stewart	not out		8	*54*	*29*
P A J DeFreitas	lbw	b Warne	0	*4*	*4*
D Gough	c Healy	b Warne	0	*1*	*1*
D E Malcolm	c Boon	b Warne	0	*2*	*1*
P C R Tufnell	c Healy	b McDermott	0	*4*	*4*
Extras (LB2, NB3)			5		
Total (42.5 overs, 184 mins)			92		

Fall of wickets: 1-3, 2-10, 3-23, 4-43, 5-81, 6-88, 7-91, 8-91, 9-91, 10-92

Bowling: McDermott 16.5-5-42-5, **Fleming** 9-1-24-2, **Warne** 13-6-16-3, **May** 4-1-8-0

AUSTRALIA WON BY 295 RUNS

3RD TEST

Sydney Cricket Ground   Jan 1-5

ENGLAND - First Innings

				Min	Bls
G A Gooch	c Healy	b Fleming	1	7	9
M A Atherton*		b McDermott	88	331	267
G A Hick		b McDermott	2	21	13
G P Thorpe	lbw	b McDermott	10	27	17
J P Crawley	c M Waugh	b Fleming	72	291	226
M W Gatting	c Healy	b McDermott	0	3	4
A R C Fraser	c Healy	b Fleming	27	141	96
S J Rhodes†	run out		1	3	2
D Gough	c Fleming	b McDermott	51	72	56
D E Malcolm		b Warne	29	23	18
P C R Tufnell	not out		4	26	17
Extras (B8, LB7, NB9)			24		
Total (119.2 overs, 478 min)			309		

Fall of wickets: 1-1, 2-10, 3-20, 4-194, 5-194, 6-196, 7-197, 8-255, 9-295, 10-309

Bowling: McDermott 30-7-101-5, Fleming 26.2-12-52-3, Warne 36-10-88-1, May 17-4-35-0, M Waugh 6-1-10-0, Bevan 4-1-8-0

ENGLAND - Second Innings

				Min	Bls
G A Gooch	lbw	b Fleming	29	61	37
M A Atherton*	c Taylor	b Fleming	67	220	165
G A Hick	not out		98	255	166
G P Thorpe	not out		47	97	71
J P Crawley					
M W Gatting					
S J Rhodes†					
D Gough					
A R C Fraser					
D E Malcolm					
P C R Tufnell					
Extras (LB6, W1, NB7)			14		
Total (2 wkts dec, 72 overs, 317 min)			255		

Fall of wickets 1-54, 2-158

Bowling: McDermott 24-2-76-0, Fleming 20-3-66-2, M Waugh 2-1-4-0, Warne 16-2-48-0, May 10-1-55-0

AUSTRALIA - First Innings

				Min	Bls
M J Slater		b Malcolm	11	36	24
M A Taylor*	c &	b Gough	49	209	131
D C Boon		b Gough	3	5	5
M E Waugh	c Rhodes	b Malcolm	3	4	4
M G Bevan	c Thorpe	b Fraser	8	55	31
S R Waugh		b Gough	1	13	8
I A Healy†	c Hick	b Gough	10	19	19
S K Warne	c Gatting	b Fraser	0	4	5
T B A May	c Hick	b Gough	0	7	2
C J McDermott	not out		21	61	30
D W Fleming		b Gough	0	1	1
Extras (B6, LB1, NB3)			10		
Total (42.5 overs, 211 min)			116		

Fall of wickets: 1-12, 2-15, 3-18, 4-38, 5-39, 6-57, 7-62, 8-65, 9-116, 10-116

Bowling: Malcolm 13-4-34-2, Gough 18.5-4-49-6, Fraser 11-1-26-2

Toss: England   Man of the Match: **D Gough**
Umpires: **S Bucknor & D B Hair** (TV) **W A Cameron**

AUSTRALIA - Second Innings

				Min	Bls
M A Taylor*		b Malcolm	113	364	248
M J Slater	c Tufnell	b Fraser	103	283	237
D C Boon	c Hick	b Gough	17	107	68
M E Waugh	lbw	b Fraser	25	61	34
M G Bevan	c Rhodes	b Fraser	7	21	14
S R Waugh	c Rhodes	b Fraser	0	7	8
I A Healy†	c Rhodes	b Fraser	5	13	11
S K Warne	not out		36	87	59
T B A May	not out		10	77	64
C J McDermott					
D W Fleming					
Extras (B12, LB3, W1, NB12)			21		
Total (7 wkts, 121.4 overs, 514 min)			344		

Fall of wickets: 1-208, 2-239, 3-265, 4-282, 5-286, 6-289, 7-292

Bowling: Malcolm 21-4-75-1, Gough 28-4-72-1, Fraser 25-3-75- 5, Tufnell 35.4-9-61-0, Hick 5-0-21-0, Gooch 7-1-27-0

MATCH DRAWN

4TH TEST ━━━━━━━━━━━━━━━━━

Adelaide Oval   Jan 26-30

ENGLAND - First Innings

				Min	Bls
G A Gooch	c M Waugh	b Fleming	47	147	105
M A Atherton*	c M Waugh	b Fleming	80	273	215
M W Gatting	c S Waugh	b McIntyre	117	411	286
G P Thorpe	c Taylor	b Warne	26	20	19
J P Crawley		b Warne	28	121	110
S J Rhodes†	c Taylor	b McDermott	6	27	20
C C Lewis	c Blewett	b McDermott	10	33	20
P A J DeFreitas	c Blewett	b McIntyre	21	28	32
A R C Fraser	run out		7	24	22
D E Malcolm		b McDermott	0	3	1
P C R Tufnell	not out		0	6	5
Extras (B2, LB5, W2, NB2)			11		
Total (141.3 overs, 559 min)			353		

Fall of wickets: 1-93, 2-175, 3-211, 4-286, 5-293, 6-307, 7-334, 8-353, 9-353, 10-353
Bowling: McDermott 41-15-66-3, **Fleming** 25-6-65-2, **Blewett** 16-4-59-0, **Warne** 31-9-72-2, **McIntyre** 19.3-3-51-2, **M Waugh** 9-1-33-0

ENGLAND - Second Innings

				Min	Bls
G A Gooch	c Healy	b McDermott	34	132	101
M A Atherton*	lbw	b M Waugh	14	61	55
M W Gatting		b M Waugh	0	6	5
G P Thorpe	c Warne	b McDermott	83	140	117
J P Crawley	c & b M Waugh		71	212	152
S J Rhodes†	c Fleming	b Warne	2	20	8
C C Lewis		b Fleming	7	23	19
P A J DeFreitas	c Healy	b M Waugh	88	120	95
A R C Fraser	c McDermott	b M Waugh	5	27	11
D E Malcolm	not out		10	7	4
P C R Tufnell	lbw	b Warne	0	4	3
Extras (B6, LB8)			14		
Total (94.5 overs, 382 min)			328		

Fall of wickets: 1-26, 2-30, 3-83, 4-154, 5-169, 6-181, 7-270, 8-317, 9-317, 10-328
Bowling: McDermott 27-5-96-2, **Fleming** 11-3-37-1, **Warne** 30.5-9-82-2, **M Waugh** 14-4-40-5, **McIntyre** 8-0-36-0, **Blewett** 4-0-23-0

AUSTRALIA - First Innings

				Min	Bls
M J Slater	c Atherton	b DeFreitas	67	152	113
M A Taylor*	lbw	b Lewis	90	267	200
D C Boon	c Rhodes	b DeFreitas	0	9	5
M E Waugh	c Rhodes	b Fraser	39	110	64
S R Waugh	c Atherton	b Lewis	19	45	33
G S Blewett	not out		102	261	180
I A Healy†	c Rhodes	b Malcolm	74	173	121
S K Warne	c Thorpe	b Fraser	7	16	12
D W Fleming	c Rhodes	b Malcolm	0	4	4
P E McIntyre		b Malcolm	0	17	6
C J McDermott	c Crawley	b Fraser	5	6	7
Extras (B2, LB7, NB7)			16		
Total (121.5 overs, 535 min)			419		

Fall of wickets: 1-128, 2-130, 3-202, 4-207, 5-232, 6-396, 7-405, 8-406, 9-414, 10-419
Bowling: Malcolm 26-5-78-3, **Fraser** 28.5-6-95-3, **Tufnell** 24-5-64-0, **DeFreitas** 20-3-70-2, **Lewis** 18-1-81-2, **Gooch** 5-0-22-0

Toss: **England**   Man of the Match: **P A J DeFreitas**
Umpires: **P D Parker & S Venkataraghavan**
(TV) **S J Davis**

AUSTRALIA - Second Innings

				Min	Bls
M A Taylor*	c Thorpe	b Malcolm	13	37	32
M J Slater	c Tufnell	b Malcolm	5	51	29
D C Boon	c Rhodes	b Fraser	4	8	7
M E Waugh	c Gatting	b Tufnell	24	58	33
S R Waugh		b Malcolm	0	2	1
G S Blewett	c Rhodes	b Lewis	12	74	54
I A Healy†	not out		51	168	136
S K Warne	lbw	b Lewis	2	18	20
C J McDermott	c Rhodes	b Lewis	0	2	4
D W Fleming	lbw	b Lewis	24	112	66
P E McIntyre	lbw	b Malcolm	0	10	4
Extras (B3, LB5, NB13)			21		
Total (61.1 overs, 274 min)			156		

Fall of wickets 1-17, 2-22, 3-22, 4-23, 5-64, 6-75, 7-83, 8-83, 9-152, 10-156
Bowling: Malcolm 16.1-3-39-4, **Fraser** 12-1-37-1, **DeFreitas** 11-3-31-0, **Lewis** 13-4-24-4, **Tufnell** 9-3-17-1

ENGLAND WON BY 106 RUNS

5TH TEST

WACA Ground, Perth   Feb 3-7

AUSTRALIA - First Innings

				Min	Bls
M J Slater	c Lewis	b DeFreitas	124	297	231
M A Taylor*	c Rhodes	b Lewis	9	58	36
D C Boon	c Ramp'kash	b Lewis	1	10	8
M E Waugh	c DeFreitas	b Lewis	88	243	177
S R Waugh	not out		99	292	183
G S Blewett	c Rhodes	b Fraser	20	73	67
I A Healy†	c Lewis	b DeFreitas	12	59	38
S K Warne	c Rhodes	b DeFreitas	1	27	17
J Angel	run out		11	67	43
G D McGrath	run out		0	18	10
C J McDermott	run out		6	27	15
Extras (B14, LB4, W4, NB9)			31		
Total (135.5 overs, 590 min)			402		

Fall of wickets: 1-47, 2-55, 3-238, 4-247, 5-287, 6-320, 7-328, 8-386, 9-388, 10-402
Bowling: Malcolm 31-6-93-0, DeFreitas 29-8-91-3, Fraser 32-11-84-1, Lewis 31.5-8-73-3, Gooch 1-1-0-0, Ramprakash 11-0-43-0

AUSTRALIA - Second Innings

				Min	Bls
M A Taylor*		b Fraser	52	185	122
M J Slater	c Atherton	b Fraser	45	82	55
J Angel	run out		0	7	5
D C Boon	c Rhodes	b Malcolm	18	44	31
M E Waugh	c Rhodes	b DeFreitas	1	21	14
S R Waugh	c Ramp'kash	b Lewis	80	215	141
G S Blewett	c Malcolm	b Lewis	115	202	158
I A Healy†	not out		11	27	14
S K Warne	c Lewis	b Malcolm	6	15	12
G D McGrath					
C J McDermott					
Extras (B1, LB9, NB7)			17		
Total (8 wkts dec, 90.3 overs, 404 min)			345		

Fall of wickets: 1-75, 2-79, 3-102, 4-115, 5-123, 6-326, 7-333, 8-345
Bowling: Malcolm 23.3-3-105-2, Fraser 21-3-74-2, Lewis 16-1-71-2, DeFreitas 22-10-54-1, Ramprakash 8-1-31-0

ENGLAND - First Innings

				Min	Bls
G A Gooch	lbw	b M Waugh	37	101	76
M A Atherton*	c Healy	b McGrath	4	7	3
M W Gatting		b McGrath	0	1	1
G P Thorpe	st Healy	b Warne	123	301	218
J P Crawley	c Warne	b M Waugh	0	2	3
M Ramprakash		b Warne	72	240	178
S J Rhodes†		b Angel	2	22	16
C C Lewis	c Blewett	b McGrath	40	60	62
P A J DeFreitas		b Angel	0	7	6
A R C Fraser	c Warne	b Angel	9	48	18
D E Malcolm	not out		0	4	1
Extras (B4, LB1, NB3)			8		
Total (96.3 overs, 402 min)			295		

Fall of wickets: 1-5, 2-5, 3-77, 4-77, 5-235, 6-246, 7-246, 8-247, 9-293, 10-295
Bowling: Angel 22.3-7-65-3, McGrath 25-6-88-3, Blewett 4-1-9-0, M Waugh 9-2-29-2, Warne 23-8-58-2, McDermott 13-5-41-0

Toss: **Australia** Man of the Match: **S R Waugh**
Umpires: **K E Liebenberg & S G Randell** (TV) **T A Prue**
Man of the Series: **C J McDermott**

ENGLAND - Second Innings

				Min	Bls
G A Gooch	c &	b McDermott	4	11	12
M A Atherton*	c Healy	b McGrath	8	73	43
M W Gatting		b McDermott	8	16	14
A R C Fraser	lbw	b McGrath	5	21	13
G P Thorpe	c Taylor	b McGrath	0	1	1
J P Crawley	c M Waugh	b McDermott	0	5	4
M Ramprakash	c S Waugh	b M Waugh	42	70	57
S J Rhodes†	not out		39	105	73
C C Lewis	lbw	b McDermott	11	36	26
P A J DeFreitas	c Taylor	b McDermott	0	9	5
D E Malcolm		b McDermott	0	2	3
Extras (LB1, W1, NB4)			6		
Total (41 overs, 179 min)			123		

Fall of wickets: 1-4, 2-17, 3-26, 4-26, 5-27, 6-27, 7-95, 8-121, 9-123, 10-123
Bowling: McDermott 15-4-38-6, McGrath 13-4-40-3, Angel 3-0-20-0, Warne 7-3-11-0, M Waugh 3-0-13-1

AUSTRALIA WON BY 329 RUNS
AUSTRALIA WON SERIES 3-1

ENGLAND AVERAGES

BATTING

	M	In	NO	Rns	HS	Avge	100s	50s
G P Thorpe	5	10	1	444	123	49.33	1	3
G A Hick	3	6	1	208	98*	41.60	-	2
M A Atherton	5	10	0	407	88	40.70	-	4
J P Crawley	3	5	0	171	72	34.20	-	2
G A Gooch	5	10	0	245	56	24.50	-	1
D Gough	3	5	1	98	51	24.50	-	1
A J Stewart	2	4	1	73	33	24.33	-	-
M W Gatting	5	9	0	182	117	20.22	1	-
P A J DeFreitas	4	8	0	141	88	17.62	-	1
C C Lewis	2	4	0	68	40	17.00	-	-
D E Malcolm	4	7	3	50	29	12.50	-	-
A R C Fraser	3	5	0	53	27	10.60	-	-
S J Rhodes	5	9	1	72	39*	9.00	-	-
P C R Tufnell	4	7	3	6	4*	1.50	-	-

Also M R Ramprakash 72 & 42, M J McCague 1 & 0

BOWLING

	O	M	R	W	Avge	Best	S/Rate
D Gough	152.5	33	425	20	21.25	6-49	45.85
C C Lewis	78.5	13	249	11	22.63	4-24	43.00
A R C Fraser	129.5	25	389	14	27.78	5-73	55.64
P A J DeFreitas	184	39	558	13	42.92	3-91	84.92
P C R Tufnell	207.4	45	442	10	44.20	4-79	124.60
D E Malcolm	181.1	32	588	13	45.23	4-39	83.62
M J McCague	19.2	4	96	2	48.00	2-96	58.00
G A Gooch	25	6	74	1	74.00	1-20	150.00

Also G A Hick 16-3-58-0, M R Ramprakash 19-1-74-0

AUSTRALIA AVERAGES

BATTING

	M	In	NO	Rns	HS	Avge	100s	50s
G S Blewett	2	4	1	249	115	83.00	2	-
M J Slater	5	10	0	623	176	62.30	3	1
S R Waugh	5	10	3	345	99*	49.28	-	3
M A Taylor	5	10	0	471	113	47.10	1	4
M E Waugh	5	10	0	435	140	43.50	1	2
I A Healy	5	10	3	249	74	35.57	-	2
D C Boon	5	10	0	246	131	24.60	1	-
T B A May	3	5	3	31	10*	15.50	-	-
M G Bevan	3	6	0	81	35	13.50	-	-
D W Fleming	3	4	0	40	24	10.00	-	-
C J McDermott	5	8	2	42	21*	7.00	-	-
S K Warne	5	10	1	60	36*	6.66	-	-
G D McGrath	2	2	0	0	0	0.00	-	-

Also J Angel 11 & 0, P E McIntyre 0 & 0

BOWLING

	O	M	R	W	Avge	Best	S/Rate
M E Waugh	53	11	157	8	19.62	5-40	39.75
S K Warne	256.1	84	549	27	20.33	8-71	56.93
C J McDermott	232.5	56	675	32	21.09	6-38	43.66
D W Fleming	102.2	30	274	10	27.40	3-52	61.40
J Angel	25.3	7	85	3	28.33	3-65	51.00
G D McGrath	67	16	229	6	38.16	3-40	67.00
P E McIntyre	27.3	3	87	2	43.50	2-51	82.50
T B A May	101	30	219	1	219.00	1-34	606.00

Also M G Bevan 7-1-19-0, G S Blewett 24-5-91-0

England v Australia

(World Series Cup - 3rd match)
Sydney Cricket Ground   Dec 6

AUSTRALIA

				Min	Bls
M A Taylor*		c & b Hick	57	126	96
M J Slater	c Hick	b Udal	50	93	66
M E Waugh		b Udal	4	14	15
D C Boon	not out		64	88	64
M G Bevan	c Gooch	b Gough	46	66	59
S G Law	not out		0	3	0
I A Healy†					
S K Warne					
C J McDermott					
T B A May					
G D McGrath					
Extras (LB2, W1)			3		
Total (4 wkts, 50 overs)			224		

Fall of wickets: 1-96, 2-106, 3-126, 4-218
Bowling: Benjamin 6-0-25-0, DeFreitas 9-1-43-0, Gough 10-0-51-1, White 5-0-22-0, Udal 10-1-37-2, Hick 10-0-44-1

Toss: **Australia** Man of the Match: **D C Boon**
Umpires: **D B Hair & P D Parker**

ENGLAND

				Min	Bls
M A Atherton*	lbw	b Law	60	138	101
A J Stewart	c Law	b May	48	98	73
G A Hick	c Boon	b May	6	13	16
G P Thorpe	c Bevan	b McDermott	21	42	34
G A Gooch	c McDermott	b Warne	21	48	23
C White		b McDermott	0	3	1
S J Rhodes†	c Warne	b Law	8	12	12
P A J DeFreitas	run out		6	8	6
D Gough	not out		8	22	10
S D Udal		b McGrath	4	11	10
J E Benjamin		b McDermott	0	4	6
Extras (LB7, W6, NB1)			14		
Total (48.3 overs)			196		

Fall of wickets: 1-100, 2-112, 3-133, 4-147, 5-149, 6-164, 7-180, 8-187, 9-195, 10-196
Bowling: McDermott 9.3-0-34-3, McGrath 9-4-22-1, Warne 10-0-46-1, Law 10-0-52-2, May 10-1-35-2

AUSTRALIA WON BY 28 RUNS

England v Australia A
(World Series Cup - 7th match)
Sydney Cricket Ground   Dec 13
ENGLAND

G A Gooch	c Emery	b Hughes	6
A J Stewart*	c Emery	b Reiffel	5
G A Hick	c Emery	b Moody	32
G P Thorpe	run out		29
M W Gatting	st Emery	b Robertson	23
C White	run out		43
S J Rhodes†	run out		21
P A J DeFreitas	c Hayden	b Hughes	11
S D Udal	run out		9
P C R Tufnell	not out		0
A R C Fraser			
Extras (LB7, W2)			9
Total (9 wkts, 50 overs)			188

Fall of wickets: 1-9, 2-23, 3-55, 4-95, 5-97, 6-137, 7-170, 8-187, 9-188
Bowling: Hughes 10-3-22-2, **Reiffel** 10-0-45-1, **Moody** 10-0-33-1, **Angel** 9-1-45-0, **Robertson** 10-0-31-1, **Martyn** 1-0-5-0

Toss: **England**   Man of the Match: **C White**
Umpires: **A J McQuillan & S G Randell**

AUSTRALIA A

D S Lehmann	c Rhodes	b Fraser	3
M L Hayden	c Rhodes	b Fraser	12
D R Martyn*	c Gooch	b Tufnell	40
J L Langer	run out		55
R T Ponting		b White	31
T M Moody		b White	2
P A Emery†	c Rhodes	b DeFreitas	2
G R Robertson	run out		2
P R Reiffel	c Rhodes	b DeFreitas	1
M G Hughes		b White	2
J Angel	not out		3
Extras (LB2, W1, NB1)			4
Total (45.5 overs)			157

Fall of wickets: 1-7, 2-20, 3-79, 4-138, 5-142, 6-145, 7-151, 8-152, 9-153, 10-157
Bowling: DeFreitas 10-2-24-2, **Fraser** 9-1-31-2, **White** 8.5-1-35-3, **Udal** 8-0-33-0, **Tufnell** 10-0-32-1

ENGLAND WON BY 31 RUNS

England v Zimbabwe
(World Series Cup - 8th match)
Sydney Cricket Ground   Dec 15
ZIMBABWE

				Min	Bls
A Flower*†	c Stewart	b Fraser	12	22	15
G W Flower	not out		84	198	143
A D Campbell		b Gough	23	43	30
G J Whittal	c Stewart	b Gough	0	2	2
D L Houghton	c Stewart	b Gough	57	83	74
M H Dekker	c DeFreitas	b Fraser	5	11	8
G C Martin		b DeFreitas	7	15	11
P A Strang	run out		0	1	2
H H Streak	run out		1	5	3
S G Peall	c Stewart	b Gough	0	2	2
D H Brain		b Gough	7	3	8
Extras (LB7, W1, NB1)			9		
Total (49.3 overs)			205		

Fall of wickets: 1-24, 2-61, 3-61, 4-171, 5-179, 6-192, 7-192, 8-197, 9-198, 10-205
Bowling: DeFreitas 10-2-27-1, **Fraser** 10-0-45-2, **Gough** 9.3-0-44-5, **Tufnell** 10-0-43-0, **Udal** 8-0-31-0, **Hick** 2-0-8-0

Toss: **Zimbabwe**   Man of the Match: **G W Flower**
Umpires: **D B Hair & C D Timmins**

ENGLAND

				Min	Bls
G A Gooch		c & b Strang	38	69	54
M A Atherton*	c A Flower	b Whittal	14	55	38
G A Hick	run out		64	130	88
G P Thorpe	lbw	b Strang	0	4	3
J P Crawley	lbw	b Dekker	18	50	55
A J Stewart†		b Streak	29	59	38
P A J DeFreitas	run out		5	6	3
D Gough		b Streak	2	7	4
S D Udal	run out		10	11	9
A R C Fraser		b Dekker	2	4	3
P C R Tufnell	not out		0	1	0
Extras (L5, W5)			10		
Total (49.1 overs)			192		

Fall of wickets: 1-49, 2-60, 3-60, 4-105, 5-169, 6-178, 7-179, 8-181, 9-192, 10-192
Bowling: Brain 8-1-27-0, **Streak** 8.1-1-36-2, **Whittal** 4-1-21-1, **Strang** 10-2-30-2, **Peall** 10-2-29-0, **Dekker** 9-0-44-2

ZIMBABWE WON BY 13 RUNS

England v Zimbabwe

(World Series Cup - 9th match)
The 'Gabba, Brisbane   Jan 7

ENGLAND

				Min	Bls
G A Gooch		b Brain	0	2	4
M A Atherton*	lbw	b Martin	26	96	64
G A Hick	c A Flower	b Streak	8	32	19
G P Thorpe	c Brain	b Strang	89	155	119
N Fairbrother	run out		7	9	8
J P Crawley	lbw	b G Flower	14	22	22
S J Rhodes†	st A Flower	b Dekker	20	44	28
D Gough	c Campbell	b Dekker	4	6	6
P A J DeFreitas	not out		12	21	17
S D Udal	not out		11	11	13
J E Benjamin					
Extras (B4, LB2,W3)			9		
Total (8 wkts, 50 overs)			200		

Fall of wickets: 1-0, 2-20, 3-72, 4-82, 5-107, 6-164, 7-170, 8-182

Bowling: Brain 8-0-27-1, **Sreak** 7-1-26-1, **Whittal** 5-0-19-0, **Martin** 5-1-15-1, **Peall** 5-0-19-0, **Strang** 10-0-42-1, **G Flower** 3-0-16-1, **Dekker** 7-0-32-2

Toss: **England**   Man of the Match: **G P Thorpe**
Umpires: **A J McQuillan & C D Timmins**

ZIMBABWE

				Min	Bls
G W Flower	c Rhodes	b Udal	19	74	48
A D Campbell	c Fairbrother	b DeFreitas	3	28	23
M H Dekker		b Benjamin	5	13	12
A Flower*†	c Rhodes	b Gough	52	83	60
G J Whittal	c Rhodes	b DeFreitas	53	97	74
I P Butchart	run out		2	20	12
G C Martin	st Rhodes	b Hick	1	5	10
P A Strang		b Gough	16	37	29
D H Brain	c Hick	b Udal	2	6	4
H H Streak	not out		9	19	12
S G Peall	run out		3	8	5
Extras (LB7, W2)			9		
Total (48.1 overs)			174		

Fall of wickets: 1-8, 2-16, 3-56, 4-103, 5-123, 6-124, 7-149, 8-156, 9-169, 10-174

Bowling: Gough 9.1-3-17-2, **DeFreitas** 10-0-28-2, **Benjamin** 6-0-22-1, **Udal** 8-0-41-2, **Hick** 7-1-29-1, **Gooch** 8-0-30-0

ENGLAND WON BY 26 RUNS

England v Australia

(World Series Cup - 11th match)
Melbourne Cricket Ground   Jan 10

ENGLAND

				Min	Bls
G A Gooch	c Taylor	b McGrath	2	16	14
M A Atherton*	c S Waugh	b M Waugh	14	47	30
G A Hick	c Fleming	b Warne	91	178	120
G P Thorpe	c Healy	b M Waugh	8	10	14
N Fairbrother	c Healy	b Warne	35	65	58
J P Crawley	c Healy	b McGrath	2	6	7
S J Rhodes†	lbw	b McGrath	2	7	5
D Gough		b McGrath	45	62	49
P A J DeFreitas	not out		2	8	4
S D Udal	not out		2	1	1
A R C Fraser					
Extras (B4, LB10, W6, NB2)			22		
Total (8 wkts, 50 overs)			225		

Fall of wickets: 1-11, 2-31, 3-44, 4-133, 5-136, 6-142, 7-216, 8-223

Bowling: Fleming 10-1-36-0, **McGrath** 10-1-25-4, **M Waugh** 10-1-43-2, **Warne** 10-0-37-2, **Robertson** 5-0-38-0, **Law** 5-0-32-0

Toss: **England**   Man of the Match: **G A Hick**
Umpires: **P D Parker & S G Randell**

AUSTRALIA

				Min	Bls
M A Taylor*	c Rhodes	b Fraser	6	33	13
M J Slater		b Fraser	2	13	12
M E Waugh		b Hick	41	90	66
S R Waugh	c Rhodes	b Fraser	0	7	3
S G Law		c & b Udal	17	50	28
D C Boon		b Hick	26	53	47
I A Healy†	c Atherton	b Hick	56	78	63
G R Robertson	run out		1	6	7
S K Warne		b Fraser	21	33	25
D W Fleming	not out		5	19	12
G D McGrath		b DeFreitas	10	15	12
Extras (W3)			3		
Total (48 overs)			188		

Fall of wickets: 1-3, 2-16, 3-19, 4-62, 5-76, 6-125, 7-131, 8-173, 9-173, 10-188

Bowling: Fraser 10-2-22-4, **DeFreitas** 9-0-32-1, **Gooch** 10-0-50-0, **Udal** 9-1-43-1, **Hick** 10-1-41-3

ENGLAND WON BY 37 RUNS

England v Australia A
(World Seies Cup - 12th match)
Sydney Cricket Ground   Jan 12

AUSTRALIA A

				Min	Bls
M L Hayden	c Gooch	b DeFreitas	4	30	21
G S Blewett	c Thorpe	b Lewis	113	174	133
D R Martyn*	c Thorpe	b Lewis	13	32	24
M G Bevan		c & b Udal	105	145	102
J L Langer	c Gooch	b Udal	16	21	12
R T Ponting	not out		6	13	7
P A Emery†	not out		0	1	1
P E McIntyre					
M G Hughes					
P R Reiffel					
S P George					
Extras (LB7)			7		
Total (5 wkts, 50 overs)			264		

Fall of wickets: 1-11, 2-46, 3-207, 4-245, 5-262
Bowling: Fraser 10-1-36-0, **DeFreitas** 10-2-43-1, **Lewis** 6-0-48-2, **Udal** 10-0-56-2, **Hick** 8-0-40-0, **Gooch** 6-0-34-0

Toss: Australia A   Man of the Match: G S Blewett
Umpires: **D B Hair & T A Prue**

ENGLAND

				Min	Bls
G A Gooch	c Emery	b Hughes	17	57	36
M A Atherton*	c Emery	b Reiffel	20	32	21
G A Hick		b McIntyre	35	71	47
G P Thorpe	c Reiffel	b McIntyre	24	54	44
J P Crawley	c Emery	b George	37	67	47
M W Gatting	lbw	b Hughes	15	28	25
S J Rhodes†	c George	b McIntyre	23	34	29
C C Lewis	not out		22	49	25
P A J DeFreitas		b Blewett	12	23	14
S D Udal	lbw	b Reiffel	9	14	11
A R C Fraser	not out		1	4	2
Extras (LB13, W7)			20		
Total (9 wkts, 50 overs)			235		

Fall of wickets: 1-40, 2-55, 3-100, 4-105, 5-143, 6-179, 7-187, 8-215, 9-232
Bowling: Hughes 8-0-43-2, **Reiffel** 10-2-42-2, **Blewett** 8-0-44-1, **George** 10-1-33-1, **McIntyre** 10-0-45-3, **Martyn** 4-0-15-0

AUSTRALIA A WON BY 29 RUNS

World Series Cup
Excluding matches involving England

AUSTRALIA v ZIMBABWE (1st match)
Perth   Dec 2, 1994
Zimbabwe   166-9 (50 overs)
Australia   167-8 (47.2 overs)
(G W Flower 3-15)
Australia won by 2 wickets   Award: S K Warne

AUSTRALIA A v ZIMBABWE (2nd match)
Perth   Dec 4, 1994
Zimbabwe   166-9 (50 overs)
(T M Moody 3-16)
Australia A 167-5 (35.1 overs)
(D S Lehmann 85)
Australia A won by 5 wickets   Award: T M Moody

AUSTRALIA v ZIMBABWE (4th match)
Hobart   Dec 8, 1994
Australia   254-3 (50 overs)
(S G Law 110, D C Boon 98*)
Zimbabwe   170-8 (50 overs)
Australia won by 84 runs   Award: S G Law

AUSTRALIA A v ZIMBABWE (5th match)
Adelaide   Dec 10, 1994
Zimbabwe   201-8 (50 overs)
(G J Whittal 59*, A D R Campbell 54)
Australia A 202-3 (48.5 overs)
(M L Hayden 100*, D R Martyn 70)
Australia A won by 7 wickets   Award: M L Hayden

AUSTRALIA v AUSTRALIA A (6th match)
Adelaide   Dec 11, 1994
Australia   202 (48.3 overs)
(M J Slater 64, M G Hughes 3-33)
Australia A 196 (47.4 overs)
(G D McGrath 4-43, S K Warne 3-40)
Australia won by 6 runs   Award: G D McGrath

AUSTRALIA v AUSTRALIA A (10th match)
Brisbane   Jan 8
Australia   252-5 (50 overs)
(M E Waugh 93, D C Boon 86*)
Australia A 218 (47.5 overs)
(G S Blewett 63, S G Law 3-46)
Australia won by 34 runs   Award: M E Waugh

AUSTRALIA v AUSTRALIA A (1st final)
Sydney   Jan 15
Australia A 209-8 (50 overs)
(M G Bevan 73, M L Hayden 50, C J McDermott 4-25)
Australia   213-5 (50 overs)
(M J Slater 92)
Australia won by 5 wickets

AUSTRALIA v AUSTRALIA A (2nd final)
Melbourne   Jan 17
Australia A 226 (49.4 overs)
(G S Blewett 64, D R Martyn 58, D W Fleming 4-28, G D McGrath 3-41)
Australia   229-4 (49 overs)
(M J Slater 56, S R Waugh 56)
Australia won by 6 wickets to win the WSC 2-0

Other Tour Matches

ENGLAND XI v ACB CHAIRMAN'S XI
Lilac Hill   Oct 25
ACB XI   232 (49.2 overs, R T Ponting 82)
England XI   236-3 (47.2 overs, G A Gooch 129)
England XI won by 7 wickets

ENGLAND XI v WESTERN AUSTRALIA
Perth   Oct 27
W Australia   248-5 (50 overs)
England XI   197 (45.5 overs)
Western Australia won by 51 runs

ENGLAND XI v WESTERN AUSTRALIA
Perth   Oct 29-Nov 1
England XI   245 (M A Atherton 68, B A Reid 4-71)
                  393-6 dec (G A Hick 172, G A Gooch 68)
W Australia   238 (M Goodwin 91, D E Malcolm 6-70)
                  272-5 (M Goodwin 77, M P Lavender 51)
Match drawn

ENGLAND XI v SOUTH AUSTRALIA
Adelaide   Nov 4-7
S Australia   102 (M J McCague 5-31)
                  480 (J D Siddons 121, J A Brayshaw 101)
England XI   323 (G A Hick 101, G P Thorpe 80)
                  262-6 (G A Gooch 101, M W Gatting 56)
England XI won by 4 wickets

ENGLAND XI v PRIME MINISTER'S XI
Canberra   Nov 9
England XI   143 (46.3 overs)
P M's XI   144-8 (47.4 overs)
Prime Minister's XI won by 2 wickets

ENGLAND XI v NEW SOUTH WALES
Newcastle   Nov 12-15
England XI   328 (G A Hick 73, J P Crawley 71)
                  244
NSW   365 (M A Taylor 150, M E Waugh 80)
                  211-6 (M J Slater 94)
New South Wales won by 4 wickets

ENGLAND XI v AUSTRALIAN XI
Hobart   Nov 18-21
Australian XI 385-7 dec (D R Martyn 103)
England XI   209 (G A Gooch 50, S J Rhodes 50)
                  207-1 (A J Stewart 101*)
Match drawn

ENGLAND XI v BRADMAN XI
Bowral   Dec 2
Bradman XI   205-4 (50 overs)
England XI   208-6 (48.5 overs, J P Crawley 91*)
England XI won by 4 wickets

ENGLAND XI v AUSTRALIAN CAPITAL TERRITORY
Canberra   Dec 4
England XI   253-5 (50 overs)
ACT   153 (42.2 overs)
England XI won by 100 runs

ENGLAND XI v AUSTRALIAN ACADEMY
North Sydney Oval   Dec 10
England XI   231-4 (50 overs, G A Hick 118)
Academy   234-5 (48.2 overs, I J Harvey 80)
Australian Academy won by 5 wickets

ENGLAND XI v AUSTRALIAN ACADEMY
North Sydney Oval   Dec 11
England XI   245-7 (50 overs)
                  (M A Atherton 95, M W Gatting 62)
Academy   249-4 (43.1 overs)
                  (B J Hodge 96*, R M Campbell 57)
Australian Academy won by 6 wickets

ENGLAND XI v QUEENSLAND
Toowomba   Dec 17-20
England XI   507-6 dec (M W Gatting 203*)
                  236-8 dec (J P Crawley 63)
Queensland   392-4 dec (A Symonds 108*)
                  314 (M L Hayden 119)
England XI won by 37 runs

ENGLAND XI v VICTORIA
Bendigo   Jan 20-23
Victoria   246
                  334-8 dec (B J Hodge 104, M T Elliott 73)
England XI   329 (G A Hick 143, P R Reiffel 4-63)
                  139-1 (M A Atherton 59*)
Match drawn

FIRST CLASS TOUR AVERAGES 1994-95

BATTING	M	In	NO	Rns	HS	Avge	100s	50s
G A Hick	8	15	1	877	172	62.64	3	3
A J Stewart	5	9	4	291	101*	58.20	1	1
G P Thorpe	10	20	3	756	123	44.47	1	5
J P Crawley	9	15	2	563	91	43.30	-	6
M A Atherton	10	20	1	755	88	39.73	-	6
G A Gooch	10	19	0	685	101	36.05	1	5
M W Gatting	9	16	1	532	203*	35.46	2	1
C White	3	5	1	125	46	25.00	-	-
D Gough	5	8	2	114	51	19.00	-	1
C C Lewis	2	4	0	68	40	17.00	-	-
P A J DeFreitas	7	13	1	190	88	15.83	-	1
S J Rhodes	11	19	2	240	50	14.11	-	1
A R C Fraser	4	6	1	60	27	12.00	-	-
D E Malcolm	8	12	4	91	29	11.37	-	-
S D Udal	2	4	0	30	16	7.50	-	-
M J McCague	4	5	1	29	16	7.25	-	-
J E Benjamin	4	4	0	11	7	2.75	-	-
P C R Tufnell	9	13	7	12	4*	2.00	-	-

Also batted: M R Ramprakash 72 & 42

BOWLING	O	M	R	W	Avge	Best
C C Lewis	78.5		249	11	22.63	4-24
D Gough	222.5	44	688	26	26.46	6-49
C White	60.5	10	195	7	27.85	3-13
D E Malcolm	340.3	55	1133	34	33.32	6-70
M J McCague	125.2	21	487	14	34.78	5-31
P A J DeFreitas	299.1	67	852	24	35.50	4-60
A R C Fraser	157.5	30	504	14	36.00	5-73
P C R Tufnell	384.2	70	1018	27	37.70	5-71
G A Gooch	27	7	79	2	39.50	1-5
J E Benjamin	105.5	23	341	6	56.83	2-36
S D Udal	81.5	4	345	5	69.00	2-95
G A Hick	61	8	224	2	112.00	1-11

Also bowled: M A Atherton 2-0-6-0, G P Thorpe 2-1-6-0, M R Ramprakash 19-1-74-0

England A in India 1994-95

ENGLAND A v INDIA A (1st unofficial Test)
Bangalore Jan 14-17
India A   **300** (V Rathore 90, R D Stemp 6-83)
             104 (G Chapple 5-32)
England A **289** (M R Ramprakash 99)
             117-6
England A won by 4 wickets

ENGLAND A v INDIA A (2nd unofficial Test)
Calcutta Jan 27-31
India A   **216** (U Chatterjee 72*)
             353 (V Rathore 127, R S Dravid 52)
England A **316** (A P Wells 93, J E R Gallian 77)
             254-5 (D L Hemp 99*, A P Wells 65)
England A won by 5 wickets

ENGLAND A v INDIA A (3rd unofficial Test)
Chandiagarh Feb 4-8
India A   **229** (R S Dravid 59, G Chapple 4-60)
             156 (A A Mazumdar 55, G Chapple 5-38)
England A **209** (P L Mhambrey 4-63)
             179-9
England A won by 1 wicket

ENGLAND A v INDIAN YOUTH
Bombay Jan 3-6
England A **283** (D G Cork 69, M R Ramprakash 59)
             204 (B Rao 5-56)
Indian Youth 199 (A A Mazumdar 68, I Salisbury 6-48)
             192 (Jatinder Singh 63, D G Cork 4-46)
England A won by 96 runs

ENGLAND A v PRESIDENT'S XI
Madras Jan 8-11
President's XI 333-6 dec (R S Dravid 84)
             204-4 dec (Saurav Ganguly 65)
England A **247** (J E R Gallian 79)
             168-9 (Kanwaljit Singh 4-67)
Match drawn

ENGLAND A v COMBINED UNIVERSITIES
Delhi Jan 21-24
England A **553** (M R Ramprakash 124,
             J E R Gallian 100*, P N Weekes 93)
             214-5 dec (M P Vaughan 87, M Patel 56)
Comb Univs 165
             163 (P Partak 58, M M Patel 6-35)
England A won by 439 runs

ENGLAND A v BANGLADESH
Dhaka Feb 24-26
Bangladesh 365-6 dec (Amin-ul-Islam 121,
             Minhazal Abedin 81)
England A **421-7** (D L Hemp 190, N V Knight 150)
Match drawn

ENGLAND A v INDIA A (one day)
Indore Feb 12
India A   **201-7** (50 overs)
             (A A Mazumdar 79)
England A **195** (49 overs)
             (U Chatterjee 4-32)
India A won by 6 runs

ENGLAND A v INDIA A (one day)
Ahmedabad Feb 14
India A   **207-8** (50 overs)
             (A A Mazumdar 69, R S Dravid 57)
England A **208-7** (48.4 overs)
             (M R Ramprakash 70)
England A won by 3 wickets

ENGLAND A v INDIA A (one day)
Hyderabad Feb 16
England A **254-6** (50 overs)
             (N V Knight 114*, M R Ramprakash 57)
India A   **156** (46 overs)
England A won by 98 runs

ENGLAND A v BANGLADESH (one day)
Dhaka Feb 20
England A **203-8** (50 overs)
             (J E R Gallian 58)
Bangladesh 145-8 (50 overs)
England A won by 58 runs

ENGLAND A v BANGLADESH (one day)
Dhaka Feb 22
England A **235-8** (50 overs)
             (N V Knight 117, D L Hemp 52)
Bangladesh 215 (48.3 overs)
             (Amin-ul-Islam 52)
England A won by 20 runs

FIRST CLASS TOUR AVERAGES 1995

(India only)

BATTING	M	In	NO	Rns	HS	Avge	100s	50s
M R Ramprakash	2	4	1	210	99	70.00	-	2
A P Wells	5	10	0	363	93	36.30	-	2
J E R Gallian	5	10	0	327	79	32.70	-	3
D L Hemp	4	8	1	208	99*	29.71	-	1
N V Knight	5	10	0	286	50	28.60	-	1
M M Patel	3	6	2	86	35	21.50	-	-
R L Johnson	2	4	1	64	33*	21.33	-	-
P N Weekes	3	6	0	114	38	19.00	-	-
D G Cork	5	10	1	154	69	17.11	-	1
R D Stemp	4	6	4	32	11*	16.00	-	-
P A Nixon	3	5	1	60	23	15.00	-	-
I D K Salisbury	4	6	1	62	21	12.40	-	-
G Chapple	4	6	1	60	26	12.00	-	-
K J Piper	2	4	0	40	30	10.00	-	-
M P Vaughan	3	6	0	50	17	8.33	-	-
M C Ilott	1	2	1	2	2	2.00	-	-

BOWLING	O	M	R	W	Avge	Best
G Chapple	155.2	48	337	20	16.85	5-32
D G Cork	175.3	46	406	19	21.36	4-46
R D Stemp	198.5	58	384	17	22.58	6-83
M C Ilott	12	3	27	1	27.00	1-27
M P Vaughan	8	2	27	1	27.00	1-20
I D K Salisbury	119	18	421	15	28.06	6-48
M M Patel	152.3	50	297	10	29.70	3-43
P N Weekes	48	6	131	2	65.50	1-2
R L Johnson	40.3	4	110	1	110.00	1-29
J E R Gallian	12	1	61	0	-	-

Pakistan v Australia 1994

FIRST TEST
Karachi   Sep 28-Oct 2, 1994
Australia   337(M G Bevan 82, S R Waugh 73)
232(D C Boon 114*, M E Waugh 61, Wasim
Akram 5-64, Waqar Younis 4-69)
Pakistan   256(Saeed Anwar 85)
315-9 (Saeed Anwar 77,
Inzamam-ul-Haq 58*, S K Warne 5-89)
Pakistan won by 1 wicket

SECOND TEST
Rawalpindi   Oct 5-9, 1994
Australia   521-9 dec (M J Slater 110, S R Waugh 98,
M G Bevan 70, M A Taylor 69,
M E Waugh 68, I A Healy 58)
14-1
Pakistan   260(Aamir Sohail 80, C J McDermott 4-74)
537(Salim Malik 237, Saeed Anwar 75,
Aamir Sohail 72, Aamer Malik 65)
Match drawn

THIRD TEST
Lahore   Nov 1-5, 1994
Pakistan   373(Moin Khan 115*, Salim Malik 75,
Inzamam-ul-Haq 66, S K Warne 6-136)
404(Salim Malik 143, Aamir Sohail 105,
G D McGrath 4-92)
Australia   455(M G Bevan 91, M J Slater 74,
M E Waugh 71, J L Langer 69, Mohsin
Kamal 4-116, Mushtaq Ahmed 4-121)
Match drawn

TEST AVERAGES

BATTING

Pakistan	M	In	NO	Rns	HS	Avge	100s	50s
Moin Khan	1	2	1	131	115*	131.00	1	-
Salim Malik	3	6	0	557	237	92.83	2	1
Aamir Sohail	3	6	0	328	105	54.66	1	2
Saeed Anwar	3	6	0	314	85	52.33	-	3
Aamer Malik	1	2	0	76	65	38.00	-	1

Australia	M	In	NO	Rns	HS	Avge	100s	50s
J L Langer	1	1	0	69	69	69.00	-	1
M G Bevan	3	4	0	243	91	60.75	-	3
S R Waugh	2	3	0	171	98	57.00	-	2
M E Waugh	3	4	0	220	71	55.00	-	3
D C Boon	3	5	2	149	114*	49.66	1	-

BOWLING

Pakistan	O	M	R	W	Avge	Best
Wasim Akram	70.5	9	201	9	22.33	5-64
Waqar Younis	74.2	13	258	10	25.80	4-69
Mohsin Kamal	54	6	225	7	32.14	4-116
Aamir Sohail	33	3	105	3	35.00	2-67
Mushtaq Ahmed	127.1	13	415	9	46.11	4-121

Australia	O	M	R	W	Avge	Best
M J Slater	1.1	0	4	1	4.00	1-4
M A Taylor	3	1	11	1	11.00	1-11
D W Fleming	48	5	161	7	23.00	4-75
S K Warne	181.4	50	504	18	28.00	6-136
G D McGrath	80.1	15	245	7	35.00	4-92

India v West Indies 1994

FIRST TEST
Bombay   Nov 18-22, 1994
India   272(N R Mongia 80, S V Manjrekar 51,
C A Walsh 6-79)
333(S R Tendulkar 85, S V Manjrekar 66,
J Srinath 60, K C G Benjamin 4-82)
W Indies   243(Venkatapathy Raju 5-60)
266(J R Murray 85, J C Adams 81,
J Srinath 4-48)
India won by 96 runs

SECOND TEST
Nagpur   Dec 1-5, 1994
India   546-9 dec (S R Tendulkar 179, N Sidhu 107,
M Azharuddin 97, A R Kumble 52*,
C L Hooper 5-116)
208-7 dec (N S Sidhu 76, S R Tendulkar 54)
W Indies   428(J C Adams 125*, C L Hooper 81,
J R Murray 54, P V Simmons 50,
B C Lara 50, Venkatapathy Raju 5-127)
132-5 (C L Hooper 67)
Match drawn

THIRD TEST
Chandigarh   Dec 10-14, 1994
W Indies   443(J C Adams 174*, A C Cummins 50,
A R Kumble 4-90)
301-3 dec (B C Lara 91, J C Adams 78*,
K L T Arthurton 70*)
India   387(M Prabhakar 120, J Srinath 52*)
114(K C G Benjamin 5-65)
West Indies won by 243 runs

TEST AVERAGES

BATTING

India	M	In	NO	Rns	HS	Avge	100s	50s
S R Tendulkar	3	6	0	402	179	67.00	1	2
J Srinath	3	6	3	136	60	45.33	-	2
N S Sidhu	3	6	0	224	107	37.33	1	1
M Azharuddin	3	6	1	178	97	35.60	-	1
N R Mongia	3	6	0	183	80	30.50	-	1

West Indies	M	In	NO	Rns	HS	Avge	100s	50s
J C Adams	3	6	3	520	174*	173.33	2	2
J R Murray	3	4	0	193	85	48.25	-	2
C L Hooper	3	6	0	262	81	43.66	-	2
K L T Arthurton	3	6	2	164	70*	41.00	-	1
A C Cummins	2	2	0	67	50	33.50	-	1

BOWLING

India	O	M	R	W	Avge	Best
Venkatapathy	172.5	33	463	20	23.15	5-60
A R Kumble	145.5	33	409	13	31.46	4-90
J Srinath	106	19	337	8	42.12	4-48
R K Chauhan	75	22	214	3	71.33	1-45
M Prabhakar	38	5	149	2	74.50	2-17

West Indies	O	M	R	W	Avge	Best
C A Walsh	140.5	31	361	17	21.23	6-79
K C G Benjamin	137.4	27	490	17	28.82	5-65
C L Hooper	115.1	19	320	9	35.55	5-116
C E Cuffy	52.2	10	190	5	38.00	3-80
R Dhanraj	25.1	1	93	2	46.50	1-46

1ST ONE DAY INTERNATIONAL
Faridabad   Oct 17, 1994
W Indies   **273-5** (50 overs)
                (P V Simmons 76, C L Hooper 61*,
                S C Williams 61)
India   **177**(45 overs)
                (N S Sidhu 52, A C Bedade 51)
W Indies won by 96 runs   Award: P V Simmons

2ND ONE DAY INTERNATIONAL
Bombay   Oct 20, 1994
W Indies   **192-9** (50 overs)
                (C L Hooper 70)
India   **135-4** (33.1 overs)
                (N S Sidhu 65*)
India won a faster scoring rate   Award: N S Sidhu

3RD ONE DAY INTERNATIONAL
Visakhapatnam   Nov 7, 1994
India   **260-4** (44 overs)
                (N S Sidhu 115*, S R Tendulkar 53)
W Indies   **256-7** (43 overs)
                (C L Hooper 74*, P V Simmons 51)
India won by 4 runs   Award: N S Sidhu

4TH ONE DAY INTERNATIONAL
Cuttack   Nov 9, 1994
W Indies   **251-9** (50 overs)
                (B C Lara 89)
India   **256-2** (49.2 overs)
                (A Jadeja 104, S R Tendulkar 88)
India won by 8 wickets   Award: A Jadeja

5TH ONE DAY INTERNATIONAL
Jaipur   Nov 11, 1994
India   **259-5** (50 overs)
                (S R Tendulkar 105, V G Kambli 66)
W Indies   **254**(49 overs)
                (C L Hooper 84, J C Adams 51)
India won by 5 runs   Award: C L Hooper

COOPERS & LYBRAND RATINGS
For Test matches up to September 27th

Batsmen

1	Steve Waugh (Australia)	907
2	Brian Lara (West Indies)	888
3	Inzamam-ul-Haq (Pakistan)	813
4	Graham Thorpe (England)	783
5	Jimmy Adams (West Indies)	781
6	Sachin Tendulkar (India)	774
7	Graeme Hick (England)	705
8	Hashan Tillekeratne (Sri Lanka)	703
9	Mike Atherton (England)	698
10	Michael Slater (Australia)	690
11	Mark Waugh (Australia)	676
12	Hansie Cronje (South Africa)	667
13	Gary Kirsten (South Africa)	647
14	Robin Smith (England)	637
15	Richie Richardson (West Indies)	634
16	David Boon (Australia)	632
17	Alec Stewart (England)	622
18	Mohammed Azharuddin (India)	618
19	Mark Taylor (Australia)	610
20	Navjot Sidhu (India)	603
21	Saeed Anwar (Pakistan)	581
22	Andy Flower (Zimbabwe)	572
23	Martin Crowe (New Zealand)	562
24	Carl Hooper (West Indies)	556
25	Brian McMillan (South Africa)	551

Bowlers

1	Curtly Ambrose (West Indies)	862
2	Waqar Younis (Pakistan)	815
3	Fanie de Villiers (South Africa)	814
4	Shane Warne (Australia)	807
5	Anil Kumble (India)	797
6	Ian Bishop (West Indies)	781
7	Wasim Akram (Pakistan)	769
8	Heath Streak (Zimbabwe)	762
9	Chaminda Vaas (Sri Lanka)	761
10	Courtney Walsh (West Indies)	725
	Kenny Benjamin (West Indies)	725
12	Venkat Raju (India)	705
13	Craig McDermott (Australia)	691
14	Allan Donald (South Africa)	676
15	Paul Reiffel (Australia)	647
16	Angus Fraser (England)	634
17	Brian McMillan (South Africa)	599
18	Mutt. Muralitharan (Sri Lanka)	572
19	Dominic Cork (England)	554
20	Danny Morrison (New Zealand)	545
21	Craig Matthews (South Africa)	531
22	Manoj Prabhakar (India)	523
23	Glenn McGrath (Australia)	517
24	Philip DeFreitas (England)	505
25	Aqib Javed (Pakistan)	484
	Darren Gough (England)	484

For Coopers & Lybrand Ratings Information:
call the Ratings Hotline on 0891 501501

South Africa v New Zealand

FIRST TEST
Johannesburg   Nov 25-29, 1994
N Zealand   411 (S A Thomson 84, M D Crowe 83,
                    K R Rutherford 68)
                194 (C R Matthews 5-42, P S de Villiers 4-
                    52)
S Africa   279 (D J Richardson 93, D J Cullinan 58)
                189 (W J Cronje 62, M N Hart 5-77,
                    S B Doull 4-33)
New Zealand won by 137 runs

SECOND TEST
Durban   Dec 26-30, 1994
N Zealand   185 (S A Thomson 82, P S de Villiers 5-64)
                192 (B A Young 51)
S Africa   226 (S B Doull 5-73, D K Morrison 4-70)
                153-2 (G Kirsten 66*)
South Africa won by 8 wickets

THIRD TEST
Cape Town   Jan 2-6
N Zealand   288 (S P Fleming 79, K R Rutherford 56,
                    B M McMillan 4-65, S D Jack 4-69)
                239 (S P Fleming 53, B A Young 51,
                    P S de Villiers 5-61)
S Africa   440 (W J Cronje 112, D J Richardson 109,
                    G Kirsten 64)
                89-3
South Africa won by 7 wickets

BATTING

South Africa	M	In	NO	Rns	HS	Avge	100s	50s
D J Richardson	3	4	1	247	109	82.33	1	1
W J Cronje	3	5	1	227	112	56.75	1	1
G Kirsten	3	6	1	226	66*	45.20	-	2
J B Commins	2	4	1	112	45	37.33	-	-
P S de Villiers	3	4	3	36	28	36.00	-	-

New Zealand	M	In	NO	Rns	HS	Avge	100s	50s
S A Thomson	3	6	0	246	84	41.00	-	2
S P Fleming	3	6	0	230	79	38.33	-	2
B A Young	3	6	0	174	51	29.00	-	2
K R Rutherford	3	6	0	156	68	26.00	-	2
S B Doull	3	6	2	95	31*	23.75	-	-

BOWLING

South Africa	O	M	R	W	Avge	Best
G Kirsten	5	2	11	1	11.00	1-0
P S de Villiers	169.2	50	401	20	20.05	5-61
B M McMillan	126	39	267	13	20.53	4-65
C R Matthews	78	26	194	8	24.25	5-42
S D Jack	77	24	196	8	24.50	4-69

New Zealand	O	M	R	W	Avge	Best
S B Doull	115.1	37	257	14	18.35	5-73
R P de Groen	33	5	80	3	26.66	2-59
M N Hart	158.4	28	432	15	28.80	5-77
S A Thomson	56	17	126	4	31.50	3-65
D J Nash	32	8	98	3	32.66	3-81

South Africa v Pakistan

ONLY TEST
Johannesburg   Jan 19-23
S Africa   460 (B M McMillan 113, J N Rhodes 72,
                   P S de Villiers 66*, G Kirsten 62)
               259-7 dec (D J Cullinan 69*)
Pakistan   230 (Salim Malik 99, P S de Villiers 6-81)
               165 (Inzamam-ul-Haq 95, P de Villiers 4-27)
South Africa won by 324 runs

Zimbabwe v Pakistan

FIRST TEST
Harare   Jan 31-Feb 4
Zimbabwe   544-4 dec (G W Flower 201*, A Flower 156,
                   G J Whittal 113*)
Pakistan   322 (Inzamam-ul-Haq 71, H H Streak 6-90)
               158 (Inzamam-ul-Haq 65)
Zimbabwe won by an innings and 64 runs

SECOND TEST
Bulawayo   Feb 7-9
Zimbabwe   174 (A D R Campbell 60)
               146 (Wasim Akram 5-43)
Pakistan   260 (Ijaz Ahmed 76, H H Streak 5-70)
               61-2
Pakistan won by 8 wickets

THIRD TEST
Harare   Feb 15-19
Pakistan   231 (Inzamam-ul-Haq 101, H H Streak 4-53)
               250 (Inzamam-ul-Haq 83, H H Streak 4-52)
Zimbabwe   243 (Aqib Javed 4-64)
               139 (Aamir Nazir 5-46)
Pakistan won by 99 runs

BATTING

Zimbabwe	M	In	NO	Rns	HS	Avge	100s	50s
G W Flower	3	5	1	237	201*	59.25	1	-
A Flower	3	5	0	250	156	50.00	1	-
G J Whittal	3	5	1	161	113*	40.25	1	-
S V Carlisle	3	4	1	78	46*	26.00	-	-
A D R Campbell	3	5	0	93	60	18.60	-	1

Pakistan	M	In	NO	Rns	HS	Avge	100s	50s
Inzamam-ul-Haq	3	5	0	367	101	73.40	1	3
Ijaz Ahmed	3	5	0	239	76	47.80	-	3
Aamir Sohail	3	6	0	178	61	29.66	-	1
Salim Malik	3	5	0	107	44	21.40	-	-
Akram Raza	1	2	1	21	19	21.00	-	-

BOWLING

Zimbabwe	O	M	R	W	Avge	Best
B Strang	84.4	43	120	9	13.33	3-43
H H Streak	118	30	298	22	13.54	6-90
H R Olonga	10	0	27	1	27.00	1-27
G J Whittal	100	22	288	10	28.80	3-58
D H Brain	88.4	15	337	8	42.12	3-50

Pakistan	O	M	R	W	Avge	Best
Aamir Nazir	61	11	171	11	15.54	5-46
Aamir Sohail	10.1	2	39	2	19.50	2-5
Aqib Javed	76.5	16	163	8	20.37	4-64
Manzoor Elahi	48	17	110	5	22.00	2-38
Wasim Akram	132.2	31	313	13	24.07	5-43

New Zealand v West Indies

FIRST TEST
Christchurch   Feb 3-7
N Zealand   341-8 dec (A C Parore 100*, S P Fleming 56)
**   61-2**
W Indies   312 (W K M Benjamin 85, S Chanderpaul 69,
            S L Campbell 51, D K Morrison 6-69)

Match drawn

SECOND TEST
Wellington   Feb 10-13
W Indies   660-5 dec (J C Adams 151, B C Lara 147,
            J R Murray 101*, S L Campbell 88, K L
            T Arthurton 70, S Chanderpaul 61*)
N Zealand   216 (D J Murray 52, C A Walsh 7-37)
**   122** (C A Walsh 6-18)

West Indies won by an innings and 322 runs

BATTING

New Zealand	M	In	NO	Rns	HS	Avge	100s	50s
A C Parore	2	3	2	137	100*	137.00	1	-
S P Fleming	2	3	0	133	56	44.33	-	1
D J Murray	2	4	0	146	52	36.50	-	1

West Indies	M	In	NO	Rns	HS	Avge	100s	50s
S Chanderpaul	2	2	1	130	69	130.00	-	2
J R Murray	2	2	1	129	101*	129.00	1	-
W K M Benjamin	1	1	0	85	85	85.00	-	1

BOWLING

New Zealand	O	M	R	W	Avge	Best
D K Morrison	55.2	14	151	8	18.87	6-69
S A Thomson	18	3	61	2	30.50	2-61
S B Doull	59.2	10	247	3	82.33	2-162

West Indies	O	M	R	W	Avge	Best
C A Walsh	70	21	132	16	8.25	7-37
C E L Ambrose	58.1	22	113	5	22.60	3-57
R Dhanraj	45	8	146	4	36.50	2-49

New Zealand v South Africa

ONLY TEST
Auckland   Mar 4-8
S Africa   294 (D J Cullinan 96, D J Nash 4-72)
**   308-6** dec (W J Cronje 101, G Kirsten 76,
            A C Hudson 64)
N Zealand   328 (A C Parore 89, B A Young 74,
            A A Donald 4-88)
**   181** (K R Rutherford 56, P S de Villiers 4-42)
South Africa won by 93 runs

New Zealand v Sri Lanka

FIRST TEST
Napier   Mar 11-15
Sri Lanka   183 (A Ranatunga 55)
**   352** (C I Dunusinghe 91, H P Tillekeratne
            74, P A de Silva 62, D K Morrison 4-61)
N Zealand   109 (U C J Vaas 5-47)
**   185** (U C J Vaas 5-43, M Muralitharan 5-64)
Sri Lanka won by 241 runs

SECOND TEST
Dunedin   Mar 18-22
Sri Lanka   233 (U C J Vaas 51)
**   411** (A P Gurusinha 127, H P Tillekeratne
            108, A Ranatunga 90, D N Patel 4-96)
N Zealand   307 (B A Young 84, S P Fleming 66,
            D N Patel 52, U C J Vaas 6-87)
**   0-0**
Match drawn

BATTING

New Zealand	M	In	NO	Rns	HS	Avge	100s	50s
D N Patel	1	1	0	52	52	52.00	-	1
S P Fleming	2	3	0	101	66	33.66	-	1
B A Young	2	4	1	100	84	33.33	-	1

Sri Lanka	M	In	NO	Rns	HS	Avge	100s	50s
H P Tillekeratne	2	4	0	227	108	56.75	1	1
A Ranatunga	2	4	0	173	90	43.25	-	2
A P Gurusinha	2	4	0	165	127	41.25	1	-

BOWLING

New Zealand	O	M	R	W	Avge	Best
D K Morrison	44.3	10	101	7	14.42	4-61
D N Patel	78	23	158	7	22.57	4-96
G R Larsen	94.4	35	173	7	24.71	3-73

Sri Lanka	O	M	R	W	Avge	Best
U C J Vaas	85.4	22	177	16	11.06	6-87
M Muralitharan	86	35	141	7	20.14	5-64
G Wickremasinghe	58	15	124	3	41.33	3-33

West Indies v Australia

FIRST TEST
Bridgetown   Mar 31-Apr 2
W Indies   195 (B C Lara 65, C L Hooper 60,
            B P Julian 4-36)
**   189** (G D McGrath 5-68)
Australia   346 (I A Healy 74*, S R Waugh 65,
            M A Taylor 55)
**   39-0**
Australia won by 10 wickets

SECOND TEST
St John's   Apr 8-13
Australia   216 (C A Walsh 6-54)
**   300-7** dec (D C Boon 67, S R Waugh 65*,
            M E Waugh 61)
W Indies   260 (B C Lara 88)
**   80-2**
Match drawn

THIRD TEST
Port of Spain   Apr 21-23
Australia   128 (S R Waugh 63*, C E L Ambrose 5-45)
**   105** (C E L Ambrose 4-20)
W Indies   136 (G D McGrath 6-47)
**   98-1**
West Indies won by 9 wickets

FOURTH TEST

Kingston   Apr 29-May 3
W Indies   265 (R B Richardson 100, B C Lara 65)
              213 (W K M Benjamin 51)
Australia   531 (S R Waugh 200, M E Waugh 126,
              G S Blewett 69)
Australia won by an innings and 53 runs

TEST AVERAGES

BATTING

West Indies	M	In	NO	Rns	HS	Avge	100s	50s
B C Lara	4	8	1	308	88	44.00	-	3
R B Richardson	4	8	1	229	100	32.71	1	-
J C Adams	4	7	2	160	42	32.00	-	-
C O Browne	1	2	1	32	31*	32.00	-	-
C L Hooper	4	6	0	144	60	24.00	-	1

Australia	M	In	NO	Rns	HS	Avge	100s	50s
S R Waugh	4	6	2	429	200	107.25	1	3
M E Waugh	4	6	0	240	126	40.00	1	1
I A Healy	4	6	1	128	74*	25.60	-	1
M A Taylor	4	7	1	153	55	25.50	-	1
D C Boon	4	6	0	152	67	25.33	-	1

BOWLING

West Indies	O	M	R	W	Avge	Best
K L T Arthurton	6	1	18	1	18.00	1-17
C E L Ambrose	100.1	25	258	13	19.84	5-45
C A Walsh	148.3	33	431	20	21.55	6-54
W K M Benjamin	97.2	16	291	9	32.33	3-71
K C G Benjamin	93.4	9	359	10	35.90	3-32

Australia	O	M	R	W	Avge	Best
S R Waugh	24	7	62	5	12.40	2-14
P R Reiffel	98.4	31	263	15	17.53	4-47
G D McGrath	121.1	32	369	17	21.70	6-47
B P Julian	71	15	236	9	26.22	4-36
S K Warne	138	35	406	15	27.06	4-70

1ST ONE DAY INTERNATIONAL

Bridgetown   Mar 8
W Indies   257 (49.4 overs)
              (C L Hooper 84, B C Lara 55)
Australia   251-6 (50 overs)
              (D C Boon 85*)
West Indies won by 6 runs

2ND ONE DAY INTERNATIONAL

Port of Spain   Mar 11
Australia   260-8 (50 overs)
              (S R Waugh 58, M J Slater 55)
W Indies   234 (47.5 overs)
              (B C Lara 62)
Australia won by 26 runs

3RD ONE DAY INTERNATIONAL

Port of Spain   Mar 12
W Indies   282-5 (50 overs)
              (B C Lara 139, J C Adams 51*)
Australia   149 (34.5 overs)
              (P V Simmons 4-18)
West Indies won by 133 runs

4TH ONE DAY INTERNATIONAL

Arnos Vale   Mar 15
Australia   210-9 (48 overs)
              (M J Slater 68)
W Indies   208-3 (43.1 overs)
              (P V Simmons 86, C L Hooper 60)
West Indies won on a faster scoring rate

5TH ONE DAY INTERNATIONAL

Georgetown   Mar 18
Australia   286-9 (50 overs)
              (M E Waugh 70, M A Taylor 66)
W Indies   287-5 (47.2 overs)
              (P V Simmons 70, J C Adams 60*)
West Indies won by 5 wickets

Pakistan v Sri Lanka

FIRST TEST

Peshawar   *Sep 8-11*
Pakistan   459 (Inzamam-ul-Haq 95, Ramiz Raja 78)
Sri Lanka   186 (Wasim Akram 5-55)
              233 (A Ranatunga 76)
Pakistan won by an innings and 40 runs

SECOND TEST

Faisalabad   *Sep 15-19*
Sri Lanka   223 (H P Tillekeratne 115)
              361 (P A de Silva 105, C Hathurusinghe 83,
              Aqib Javed 5-84)
Pakistan   333 (Ramiz Raja 75, M Muralitharan 5-68)
              209
Sri Lanka won by 42 runs

THIRD TEST

Sialkot   *Sep 22-26*
Sri Lanka   232 (H P D K Dharmasena 62*)
              338-9 dec (A Ranatunga 87,
              U Hathurusinghe 73)
Pakistan   214 (M Muralitharan 4-72)
              212 (Moin Khan 117*, U C J Vaas 4-37)
Sri Lanka won by 144 runs

Domestic Competitions ▬▬▬▬▬▬▬

"On the basis that lightning doesn't strike twice, the Bears are sensibly restricting their ambitions to no more than one trophy", wrote *The Independent* in their season's preview. It made sense, after all Warwickshire had lost two of the key ingredients in their recipe for success. Brian Lara had been called up for national service on the West Indies tour and Bob Woolmer had gone off to take up office as coach to the South African team. To a lesser team, it could have meant the difference between success and failure. To Warwickshire, it appeared to mean nothing.

Not only did they win both the Championship and the NatWest Trophy, but took the former by winning 14 out of their 17 matches, the highest proportion since the war. Warwickshire like to play down the importance of individuals, but two contributions were vital. Dermot Reeve is not lacking in self-belief and has become adept at infusing this confidence into the team. Allan Donald is quick. Very quick. The South African took 88 wickts at 15 runs apiece and his 3-33 in the NatWest final left Northants with their backs to the wall. Whether the overseas player is Donald or Lara or whoever, it is doubtful if *The Independent* or anyone will be quite so conservative in their estimates for the 1996 season.

Mark Ramprakash had a point to prove after his pair in the Lord's Test. Few cricketers can ever have proved it so emphatically. His championship record of 10 centuries and 2147 runs took him past the run aggregate of Lara in 1994. Of those runs, 1628 came after the Lord's Test and that total included nine centuries, three of them doubles. He was instrumental in Middlesex's push for the title that failed by a whisker. It was John Emburey's last chance of a title with Middlesex, too. In the year that he received the England call once again, Emburey announced his departure from the county that he had served for 499 matches, taking 1577 wickets and scoring 11,779 runs. Emburey, manager of the 'A' team, is likely to move on a player/coach position at another county.

Northants and Lancashire were also title contenders; Lamb's bullish leadership (and batting) did much for the East Midlanders, but it was the redoubtable Anil Kumble, with 105 championship wickets, who was the key component. Lancashire faded on the run-in, but could claim they were weakened by Test call-ups. After all, at The Oval they had four players in the England team for the first time since the Test against India in Kampur in 1951-2.

Kent had a muddled existence in 1995. They finished rooted to the bottom of the table in the championship, but prospered in the one-day competitions. Again, though, they stuttered their lines when thrust in the limelight. In the Benson & Hedges final, Aravinda de Silva played a jewell of an innings, 112 runs from 95 balls as Kent chased the 274 total that Lancashire had amassed. Yet it was to no avail, as his colleagues came and went with monotonous regularity. De Silva departed for Test duty to Pakistan before the season ended and so missed out when Kent finally did win a trophy.

Even then, victory was in someone else's hands. Kent had to beat Warwickshire on the final Sunday to win the trophy so, being Kent, they lost. For their supporters, it was out with the calculators, to work out the run-rates, and out with the prayer mats, to pray for a thunderstorm at New Road. For once their prayers were answered. Kent took the AXA Equity & Law title for their first trophy since 1978.

Britannic Assurance County Championship

FINAL TABLE
Last year's position in brackets

		P	W	L	D	Bt	Bl	Pts
1	**Warwickshire (1)**	17	14	2	1	49	64	**337**
2	Middlesex (4)	17	12	2	3	51	62	305
3	Northants (5)	17	12	2	3	41	57	290
4	Lancashire (10)	17	10	4	3	48	61	269
5	Essex (6)	17	8	9	0	42	58	228
6	Gloucestershire (12)	17	8	4	5	45	50	223
7	Leicestershire (2)	17	7	8	2	41	61	214
8	Yorkshire (14)	17	7	8	2	39	55	206
9	Somerset (11)	17	7	5	5	40	49	201
10	Worcestershire (15)	17	6	7	4	29	57	182
11	Nottinghamshire (3)	17	5	9	3	41	54	175
12	Surrey (7)	17	5	8	4	34	55	169
13	Hampshire (13)	17	5	8	4	32	56	168
14	Derbyshire (17)	17	4	10	3	39	64	167
15	Sussex (8)	17	4	7	6	37	51	152
16	Glamorgan (18)	17	3	8	6	40	57	145
17	Durham (16)	17	4	13	0	20	53	137
18	Kent (9)	17	3	10	4	40	44	132

WHYTE & MACKAY RANKINGS
(England qualified players only)

Batting

1	M R Ramprakash (Middlesex)	710	£10,000
2	N Hussain (Essex)	673	£7,000
3	G A Hick (Worcestershire)	626	£5,000
4	M A Atherton (Lancashire)	594	£2,750
	G P Thorpe (Surrey)	594	£2,750
6	D Byas (Yorkshire)	584	
7	A J Wright (Gloucestershire)	583	
8	G A Gooch (Essex)	582	
9	R T Robinson (Nottinghamshire)	567	
10	M P Maynard (Glamorgan)	537	
11	J P Crawley (Lancashire)	529	
12	P D Bowler (Somerset)	528	
13	H Morris (Glamorgan)	524	
14	A Symonds (Gloucestershire)	518	
15	R J Harden (Somerset)	511	
	A P Wells (Sussex)	511	

Bowling

1	D G Cork (Derbyshire)	637	£10,000
2	A R C Fraser (Middlesex)	604	£7,000
3	P J Newport (Worcestershire)	554	£5,000
4	M C Ilott (Essex)	537	£3,000
5	P J Hartley (Yorkshire)	525	£2,500
6	S L Watkin (Glamorgan)	523	
7	J E Emburey (Middlesex)	517	
8	P A J DeFreitas (Derbyshire)	509	
9	P M Such (Essex)	503	
10	R D B Croft (Glamorgan)	499	
11	E S H Giddins (Sussex)	480	
12	A D Mullally (Leicestershire)	463	
13	M Watkinson (Lancashire)	462	
14	P C R Tufnell (Middlesex)	458	
	J P Taylor (Northamptonshire)	458	

SEASON'S STATISTICS
Top Individual Scores

255	P A de Silva (Kent v Derby)
254*	A Symonds (Gloucs v Glamorgan)
235	M R Ramprakash (Middx v Yorks)
230*	S James (Glamorgan v Leics)
228*	D J Bicknell (Surrey v Notts)
225	P A de Silva (Kent v Notts)
216	C J Adams (Derby v Kent)
214	M R Ramprakash (Middx v Surrey)
213	D Byas (Yorks v Worcs)
213	W J Cronje (Leics v Somerset)

Leading Run Scorers

2258	M R Ramprakash (Middlesex)
1913	D Byas (Yorkshire)
1854	N Hussain (Essex)
1781	P A de Silva (Kent)

First (and only) to 2000 Runs
M R Ramprakash (Middlesex)

Leading Wicket Takers

105	A Kumble (Northants)
95	Mushtaq Ahmed (Somerset)
90	D G Cork (Derbyshire)
89	A A Donald (Warwickshire)

Best Bowling (Match)

15-83	C L Cairns (Notts v Sussex)
14-105	M C Ilott (Essex v Northants)
14-177	A Walker (Durham v Essex)
13-93	D G Cork (Derbyshire v Northants)
13-150	J Srinath (Gloucs v Glamorgan)
13-192	A Kumble (Northants v Hampshire)

Best Bowling (Innings)

9-19	M C Ilott (Essex v Northants)
9-41	P J Hartley (Yorkshire v Derbyshire)
9-43	D G Cork (Derbyshire v Northants)
9-76	J Srinath (Gloucs v Glamorgan)
8-47	C L Cairns (Notts v Sussex)
8-69	A R Caddick (Somerset v Durham)

Highest Team Scores

781-7	Northants v Notts
696-6	West Indies v Hampshire
692-8	West Indies v England

Lowest Team Scores

46	Northants v Notts
59	Northants v Surrey
67	Leicestershire v Warwickshire

Leading Catcher

42	D Byas (Yorkshire)

Leading Wicketkeeper

65	G J Kersey (Surrey) (60 ct, 5 st)

1995 Final Averages - All First-Class Matches

BATTING
Qualification: 6 Innings

	M	In	NO	Rns	HS	Avge	100s	50s
M Ramprakash(M)	20	32	3	2258	235	77.86	10	7
M D Moxon (Yk)	13	23	8	1145	203*	76.33	3	8
A C Gilchrist (YA)	8	11	3	495	122	61.87	2	2
P A de Silva (K)	16	30	0	1781	255	59.36	7	7
B C Lara (WI)	13	20	1	1126	179	59.26	3	7
S Chanderp'l(WI)	15	25	8	1003	140*	59.00	4	5
J L Langer (YAus)	7	12	3	516	149	57.33	2	2
K L Athurton(WI)	15	23	4	1077	146	56.68	3	6
D Byas (Yk)	20	37	3	1913	213	56.26	4	10
A J Lamb (Nr)	16	26	4	1237	166	56.22	3	6
A Symonds (Gc)	18	31	5	1438	254*	55.30	4	9
T M Moody (Wc)	18	31	2	1600	168	55.17	5	7
M G Bevan (Yk)	20	34	5	1598	153*	55.10	6	7
N Hussain (Ex)	19	35	1	1854	186	54.52	6	10
A P Wells (Sx)	18	30	2	1524	178	54.42	7	4
M W Gatting (Mx)	16	22	1	1139	148	54.23	5	3
R T Robinson(Nt)	18	32	0	1728	209	54.00	7	5
P D Bowler (So)	19	33	3	1619	196	53.96	6	5
P Holloway (So)	12	22	6	863	129*	53.93	2	6
R A Smith (Ha)	12	23	2	1117	172	53.19	3	4
H Morris (Gm)	18	33	3	1574	166*	52.46	6	8
M E Waugh (Ex)	16	29	2	1392	173	51.55	5	6
J C Pooley (Mx)	18	30	4	1335	136	51.34	5	6
G A Gooch (Ex)	18	34	1	1669	165	50.57	7	6
W J Cronje (Le)	16	28	1	1362	213	50.44	4	7
T L Penney (Wk)	19	27	3	1198	144	49.91	4	4
W G Khan (Wk)	13	23	6	847	181	49.82	1	6
G A Hick (Wo)	16	27	3	1193	152	49.70	4	5
N V Knight (Wk)	13	23	5	887	174	49.27	1	7
R J Harden (So)	19	35	6	1429	129*	49.27	5	6
P A Cottey (Gm)	19	33	3	1465	130	48.83	5	7
J D Carr (Mx)	20	29	6	1098	129	47.73	4	3
J P Crawley (La)	18	31	2	1377	182	47.48	3	10
S Ecclestone (So)	7	12	2	472	81	47.20	-	3
S L Campbell (WI)	16	26	0	1225	172	47.11	3	6
A J Wright (Gc)	18	34	4	1401	193	46.70	4	5
R Q Cake (CU)	7	14	3	511	101	46.45	1	2
M L Love (Y Aus)	7	13	2	510	181	46.36	2	1
C L Hooper (WI)	15	25	2	1063	195	46.21	5	2
R T Ponting (YA)	7	12	2	460	103*	46.00	1	4
M L Hayden (YA)	7	14	2	551	178	45.91	2	1
R G Twose (Wk)	19	30	4	1186	191	45.61	4	3
D J Cullinan (De)	14	26	4	1003	161	45.59	5	1
M Maynard (Gm)	20	36	1	1590	164	45.42	3	12
C O Browne (Wc)	12	16	5	498	102*	45.27	2	1
K J Barnett (De)	17	31	3	1251	169	44.67	2	7
R C Russell (Gc)	17	26	4	977	91	44.40	-	8
A J Moles (Wk)	9	16	0	710	131	44.37	1	6
G R Cowdrey (Kt)	13	22	1	930	137	44.28	2	6
S G Law (Y Aus)	7	11	2	397	134	44.11	1	1

BOWLING
Qualification: 10 wickets

	O	M	R	W	Avge	Best
A A Donald (Wk)	535.3	136	1431	89	16.07	6-56
D A Reeve (Wk)	312	118	661	38	17.39	5-30
J Lewis (Gc)	67.4	12	209	12	17.41	4-34
K E Cooper (Gc)	103	32	228	13	17.53	4-34
J Srinath (Gc)	568.4	147	1661	87	19.09	9-76
Wasim Akram (La)	518.1	108	1598	81	19.72	7-52
T A Munton (Wk)	373.5	119	952	48	19.83	5-37
C L Cairns (Nt)	375.5	89	1035	52	19.90	8-47
D G Cork (De)	586.5	111	1800	90	20.00	9-43
R L Johnson (Mx)	301.4	79	812	40	20.30	5-48
S M Milburn (Yk)	69	15	204	10	20.40	4-68
A Kumble (Nr)	899.4	265	2143	105	20.40	7-82
K C G Benjamin (WI)	284.1	71	923	43	21.46	5-52
A M Smith (Gc)	415.3	104	1275	59	21.61	7-70
J Wood (Du)	97.4	25	303	14	21.64	4-54
P C R Tufnell (Mx)	678.1	207	1634	74	22.08	6-111
A F Giles (Wk)	146.5	46	354	16	22.12	5-23
M S Kaprowicz (YA)	175.1	42	599	27	22.18	5-19
S Young (Y Aus)	128	36	359	16	22.43	3-23
P J Newport (Wo)	548	148	1551	69	22.47	5-45
A J Tudor (Sy)	83.3	7	320	14	22.85	5-32
P J Hartley (Yk)	549	120	1861	81	22.97	9-41
J E Emburey (Mx)	708.4	198	1701	74	22.98	7-82
V J Wells (Le)	139.3	33	438	19	23.05	3-28
D J Capel (Nr)	358.2	70	1206	51	23.64	7-44
M P Bicknell (Sy)	285	65	978	41	23.85	5-61
M C Ilott (Ex)	582.4	126	1897	78	24.32	9-19
P Aldred (De)	108.2	23	375	15	25.00	3-47
V C Drakes (WI)	106	17	400	16	25.00	5-20
J E Benjamin (sy)	420.4	85	1326	53	25.01	5-37
N A Mallender (Nr)	142.2	32	427	17	25.11	4-49
A J Harris (De)	85.5	16	354	14	25.28	4-84
I D Austin (La)	363.4	111	889	35	25.40	4-50
A R Caddick (So)	183.1	34	613	24	25.54	8-69
M T Brimson (Le)	110	24	310	12	25.83	2-11
J H Childs (Ex)	678.2	183	1757	68	25.83	6-36
I R Bishop (WI)	334.1	69	983	38	25.86	5-32
D E Malcolm (De)	461.4	82	1692	65	26.03	6-61
R Dhanraj (WI)	475.3	79	1596	61	26.16	6-50
J Angel (Y Aus)	179.4	38	709	27	26.25	4-31
P J Martin (La)	349.5	96	922	35	26.34	4-51
J D Lewry (Sx)	350.1	62	1247	47	26.53	6-43
D Gough (Yk)	414.5	89	1365	51	26.76	7-28
P M Such (Ex)	748.4	174	2064	77	26.80	8-93
A P Igglesden (Kt)	171.2	37	563	21	26.80	5-92
A E Warner (De)	375.1	90	1050	39	26.92	6-21
R K Illingworth (Wo)	524	172	1212	45	26.93	4-30
M A Feltham (Mx)	273.1	72	783	29	27.00	6-41
S L Watkin (Gm)	590.4	144	1755	65	27.00	7-49
J N B Bovill (Ha)	251.3	62	814	30	27.13	6-29

CATCHES
D Byas (Yorks) 42
J D Carr (Middx) 39
N Hussain (Essex) 34
T M Moody (Worcs) 31
V P Terry (Hants) 30
N V Knight (Warwicks) 26
J C Pooley (Middx) & M A Lynch (Gloucs) 25

WICKET-KEEPING
G J Kersey (Surrey) 60c 5st
R J Turner (Somerset) 54c 10st
R J Blakey (Yorks) 59c 4st
W K Hegg (Lancs) 53c 9st
R J Rollins (Essex) 53c 9st
K J Piper (Warwicks) 59c 2st
S J Rhodes (Worcs) 51c 7st

Benson and Hedges Cup

(All Matches over 55 overs)
* Denotes team batting first

First Round

GROUP A

Durham* 165 (54.2 overs) bt **Leics** 115 (44.4 overs)
Notts* 230-6 (55 overs) bt **Warwicks** 224 (54.5 overs)
Lancs 71-1 (24.1 overs) bt **Minor Co's*** 70 (35.5 overs)
Lancs 318-5 (54.3 overs) bt **Leics*** 312-5 (55 overs)
Notts 115-1 (38.5 overs) bt **Minor Co's*** 114 (53.2 overs)
Warwicks* 285-7 (55 overs) bt **Durham** 194 (47.3 overs)
Notts 271-5 (53.5 overs) bt **Durham*** 268 (55 overs)
Minor Co's* 224 (54.4 overs) bt **Leics** 198 (50.3 overs)
Lancs* 305-2 (55 overs) bt **Warwicks** 265 (51.1 overs)
Lancs* 353-7 (55 overs) bt **Notts** 276-7 (55 overs)
Warwicks 227-2 (52 overs) bt **Leics*** 224-8 (55 overs)
Durham* 250-9 (55 overs) bt **Minor Co's** 243-9 (55 overs)
Durham* 57-2 (18 overs) v **Lancs** *No result*
Leics* 211-6 (49.3 overs) v **Notts** *No result*
Warwicks* 100-1 (23 overs) v **Minor Co's** *No result*

Final Standings	*P*	*W*	*L*	*N/R*	*Pts*	*R/Rate*
Lancashire	5	4	-	1	9	22.56
Nottinghamshire	5	3	1	1	7	0.70
Warwickshire	5	2	2	1	5	4.69
Durham	5	2	2	1	5	-3.18
Minor Counties	5	1	3	1	3	-11.76
Leicestershire	5	-	4	1	1	-7.58

GROUP B

Worcs 119-0 (27.1 overs) bt **Scotland*** 118 (53.1 overs)
Derbys 180-2 (39.5 overs) bt **Northants*** 179 (53.1 overs)
Derbys* 220-6 (55 overs) bt **Scotland** 174 (53 overs)
Yorkshire 212-4 (51.4 overs) bt **Worcs*** 208-6 (55 overs)
Worcs* 240-7 (55 overs) bt **Northants** 137 (46.5 overs)
Yorkshire 130-0 (22.3 overs) bt **Scotland*** 129 (51.1 overs)
Worcs* 267-7 (55 overs) bt **Derbys** 135 (41 overs)
Yorkshire* 223 (53.4 overs) bt **Northants** 213 (54.4 overs)
Derbys v **Yorkshire** *No result*
Northants* 304-6 (55 overs) bt **Scotland** 151-5 (55 overs)

Final Standings	*P*	*W*	*L*	*N/R*	*Pts*	*R/Rate*
Yorkshire	4	3	-	1	7	17.34
Worcestershire	4	3	1	-	6	26.02
Derbyshire	4	2	1	1	5	-3.11
Northamptonshire	4	1	3	-	2	-1.49
Scotland	4	-	4	-	0	-37.35

GROUP C

Glamorgan* 277-7 (55 overs) bt **Essex** 249 (52.2 overs)
Middlesex 212-4 (51.3 overs) bt **Hants*** 208-8 (55 overs)
Gloucs* 259-9 (55 overs) bt **Comb. U** 133 (43.3 overs)
Middlesex 228-3 (50.1 overs) bt **Essex*** 225-8 (55 overs)
Glamorgan* 318-3 (55 overs) bt **Comb. U** 101 (34.2 overs)
Gloucs 166-6 (50.1 overs) bt **Hants*** 162 (55 overs)
Essex 213-2 (50.4 overs) bt **Comb. U*** 209-7 (55 overs)
Gloucs* 186-8 (55 overs) bt **Middlesex** 181 (54.4 overs)
Glamorgan 227-3 (46.1 overs) bt **Hants*** 225-6 (55 overs)
Hants 228-8 (55 overs) bt **Comb. U*** 228-9 (55 overs)
Gloucs 211-8 (55 overs) bt **Essex*** 208-8 (55 overs)
Middx 210-5 (53.3 overs) bt **Glamorgan*** 209-9 (55 overs)
Gloucs* 176-8 (55 overs) bt **Glamorgan** 167 (53.1 overs)
Essex* 211-4 (49 overs) v **Hants** *No result*
Middx* 276-8 (55 overs) bt **Comb. U** 135-4 (38.4 overs)

Final Standings	*P*	*W*	*L*	*N/R*	*Pts*	*R/Rate*
Gloucestershire	5	5	-	-	10	9.99
Middlesex	5	4	1	-	8	7.70
Glamorgan	5	3	2	-	6	16.45
Essex	5	1	3	1	3	-2.48
Hampshire	5	1	3	1	3	-6.10
Combined Univs	5	-	5	-	0	-28.04

GROUP D

Somerset* 241-7 (55 overs) bt **Sussex** 187 (46 overs)
Surrey 81-2 (17.1 overs) bt **Ireland*** 80 (32 overs)
Kent* 318-8 (55 overs) bt **Surrey** 225-7 (55 overs)
Sussex* 261-8 (55 overs) bt **Ireland** 198-9 (55 overs)
Kent 280-6 (55 overs) bt **Somerset** 161 (52.5 overs)
Sussex 240-2 (52.1 overs) bt **Surrey*** 239-7 (55 overs)
Kent 149-0 (32.1 overs) bt **Ireland*** 146 (54 overs)
Surrey 203-3 (53.1 overs) bt **Somerset*** 202 (54 overs)
Somerset* 316-5 (55 overs) bt **Ireland** 83 (39.2 overs)
Kent 307-2 (52.1 overs) bt **Sussex*** 303-6 (55 overs)

Final Standings	*P*	*W*	*L*	*N/R*	*Pts*	*R/Rate*
Kent	4	4	-	-	8	27.14
Somerset	4	2	2	-	4	12.17
Surrey	4	2	2	-	4	4.67
Sussex	4	2	2	-	4	0.46
Ireland	4	-	4	-	0	-46.00

Quarter Finals

Somerset v Gloucestershire
Bristol   May 30-31
Gloucs 113 (49.4 overs)
(R I Dawson 38, Mushtaq 10.4-4-23-3)
Somerset 114-4 (35.1 overs)
(M E Trescothick 52, J Srinath 10.1-3-35-2)
Somerset won by 6 wickets   Award: J D Batty

Kent v Middlesex
Canterbury   May 30
Kent 250-9 (55 overs)
(T R Ward 64, M A Ealham 30)
Middlesex 224 (54.4 overs)
(J C Pooley 47, M V Fleming 10.4-1-41-3)
Kent won by 26 runs   Award: M A Ealham

Lancashire v Nottinghamshire
Old Trafford   May 30
Notts 201-8 (55 overs)
(C C Lewis 48, I D Austin 11-0-45-3)
Lancashire 205-4 (49.4 overs)
(G D Lloyd 72*, K P Evans 9-2-28-2)
Lancashire won by 6 wickets   Award: G D Lloyd

Yorkshire v Worcestershire
Headingley   May 30
Yorkshire 88 (48.5 overs)
(D Byas 47, S R Lampitt 7.5-2-16-4)
Worcs 89-3 (22.5 overs)
(T M Moody 32*, G A Hick 27)
Worcestershire won by 7 wickets   Award: S R Lampitt

Semi Finals

Worcesteshire v Lancashire
Worcester   June 13
Worcs 261-5 (55 overs)
(G A Hick 109, T Moody 75*, T S Curtis 50,
Wasim Akram 11-1-59-3)
Lancashire 264-8 (54.2 overs)
(Wasim Akram 64, W K Hegg 31*)
Lancashire won by 2 wickets   Award: Wasim Akram

Kent v Somerset
Canterbury   June 13-14
Kent 250-9 (55 overs)
(M A Ealham 52, P A de Silva 39)
Somerset 219-8 (55 overs)
(A N Hayhurst 69*, P D Bowler 53,
T N Wren 11-1-34-3, M Fleming 11-0-51-3)
Kent won by 31 runs   Award: M A Ealham

THE FINAL
LANCASHIRE v KENT
Lord's   July 15

LANCASHIRE

			Min	Bls
M A Atherton	c Fulton	b Headley	93	162 141
J E R Gallian		b Ealham	36	76 64
J P Crawley	c Taylor	b McCague	83	114 90
N H Fairbrother	c McCague	b Headley	16	17 13
G D Lloyd	run out (McCague)		12	14 12
Wasim Akram	run out (Ward/Wren)		10	12 7
M Watkinson*	c McCague	b Fleming	0	4 1
I D Austin	not out		5	6 6
W K Hegg†				
G Chapple				
G Yates				
Extras (LB2, W10, NB7)			19	
Total (7 wickets, 55 overs, 206 min)			274	

Fall of wickets: 1-80 (Gallian), 2-201 (Atherton), 3-236 (Fairbrother), 4-258 (Crawley), 5-259 (Lloyd), 6-266 (Watkinson), 7-274 (Wasim Akram)

Bowling: Wren 5-0-21-0, **Headley** 11-0-57-2, **McCague** 11-0-65-1, **Ealham** 11-0-33-1, de Silva 8-0-36-0, **Fleming** 9-0-60-1

Progressive scores: 10 overs: **38-0**, 20: **80-1**, 30: **121-1**, 40: **164-1**, 50: **241-3**

Toss: **Kent**   Gold Award: **P A de Silva**
Umpires: **N T Plews & D R Shepherd** (TV) **J Hampshire**

KENT

			Min	Bls
D P Fulton	lbw	b Chapple	25	42 49
T R Ward	c Hegg	b Chapple	7	26 11
N R Taylor		b Yates	14	47 38
P A de Silva	c Lloyd	b Austin	112	139 95
G R Cowdrey	lbw	b Yates	25	50 48
M V Fleming		b Yates	11	22 24
M A Ealham	lbw	b Watkinson	3	12 11
S A Marsh*†	c Crawley	b Austin	4	19 16
M J McCague	not out		11	19 10
D W Headley	c Chapple	b Watkinson	5	4 6
T N Wren	c Austin	b Watkinson	7	12 8
Extras (LB7, W2, NB6)			15	
Total (52.1 overs, 205 min)			239	

Fall of wickets: 1-28 (Ward), 2-37 (Fulton), 3-81 (Taylor), 4-142 (Cowdrey), 5-162 (Fleming), 6-180 (Ealham), 7-214 (de Silva), 8-214 (Marsh), 9-219 (Headley), 10-239 (Wren)

Bowling: Wasim 10-0-57-0, **Chapple** 10-2-56-2, **Austin** 11-4-36-2, **Watkinson** 10.1-0-42-3, **Yates** 11-0-42-3

Progressive scores: 10 overs: **30-1**, 20: **77-2**, 30: **119-3**, 40: **162-4**, 50: **224-8**

LANCASHIRE WON BY 35 RUNS

NatWest Trophy
(All matches played over 60 overs)

FIRST ROUND   June 27-28

Cambridgeshire v Derbyshire at March
Derby 289-3 (60 overs) D J Cullinan 119*
Cambs 132 (49.2) P A J DeFreitas 5-28
Derby won by 157 runs
Match Award: D J Cullinan

Cheshire v Essex at Chester
Essex 265-8 (60) P J Prichard 81
Cheshire 201 (57.4) G A Gooch 5-8
Essex won by 64 runs
Match Award: P J Prichard

Cornwall v Middlesex at St Austell
Middlesex 304-8 (60) P N Weekes 143*
Cornwall 200 (59.2)
Middlesex won by 104
Match Award: P N Weekes

Durham v Herefordshire at Chester-le-Street
Durham 326-4 (60) S Hutton 125, M A Roseberry 121
Hereford 119 (45.4) J Boiling 4-22
Durham won by 207 runs
Match Award: M A Roseberry

Glamorgan v Dorset at Cardiff
Dorset 191-4 (60) J J E Hardy 89*
Glamorgan 192-0 (40.5) H Morris 105*
Glamorgan won by 10 wickets
Match Award: H Morris

Gloucestershire v Suffolk at Bristol
Gloucs 301-5 (60) A J Wright 142*
Suffolk 177 (58.4) D J P Boden 5-26
Gloucs won by 124 runs
Match Award: A J Wright

Lancashire v Norfolk at Manchester
Norfolk 188 (59.2)
Lancashire 190-2 (40.4) J E R Gallian 101*
Lancs won by 8 wickets
Match Award: J E R Gallian

Leicestershire v Hampshire at Leicester
Hampshire 204-9 (60)
Leics 204-9 (60) C A Connor 4-41
Hants won on higher run rate after 30 overs
Match Award: A R K Pierson

Northamptonshire v Holland at Northampton
Holland 267-9 (60) N E Clarke 86, A Kumble 4-50
Northants 269-3 (56.5) A Fordham 99
Northants won by 7 wickets
Match Award: N E Clarke

Nottinghamshire v Scotland at Nottingham
Scotland 171-9 (60) R A Pick 5-23
Notts 172-2 (36.3) P R Pollard 83*
Notts won by 8 wickets
Match Award: R A Pick

Staffordshire v Kent at Stone
Kent 349-8 (60) N R Taylor 86
Staffs 258-6 (60) L Potter 105*
Kent won by 91 runs
Match Award: L Potter

Surrey v Berkshire at The Oval
Berkshire 148 (51.1) J E Benjamin 4-20
Surrey 151-1 (24.2) M A Butcher 79*
Surrey won by 9 wickets
Match Award: J E Benjamin

Sussex v Devon at Hove
Devon 267-4 (60) N A Folland 104
Sussex 271-3 (55.2) N J Lenham 129*
Sussex won by 7 wickets
Match Award: N J Lenham

Warwickshire v Somerset at Edgbaston
Warwicks 357-3 (60) N V Knight 151, A J Moles 90
Somerset 339-9 (60) R J Harden 104, D A Reeve 4-54
Warwicks won by 18 runs
Match Award: N V Knight

Worcestershire v Cumberland at New Road
Worcs 257-8 (60) G R Haynes 116*
Cumberland 192-9 (59) P J Berry 81
Worcs won by 65 runs
Match Award: G R Haynes

Yorkshire v Ireland at Headingley
Yorks 299-6 (60) C White 113, S A Kellett 107
Ireland 228-7 (60) S J S Warke 82
Yorks won by 71 runs
Match Award: S A Kellett

SECOND ROUND   July 12-13

Durham v Gloucestershire at Chester-le-Street
Gloucs 276-6 (60) A J Wright 84
Durham 117 (42)
Gloucs won by 159 runs
Match Award: A J Wright

Essex v Yorkshire at Chelmsford
Yorks 307-3 (60) S A Kellett 92, M G Bevan 91*
Essex 210 (48.2)
Yorks won by 97 runs
Match Award: M G Bevan

Lancashire v Worcestershire at Old Trafford
Worcs 271-6 (60) T S Curtis 106*, G A Hick 87
Lancs 275-6 (59) S P Titchard 92, M A Atherton 70
Lancs won by 4 wickets
Match Award: S P Titchard

Leicester v Glamorgan at Grace Road
Leics 197-7 (60)
Glamorgan 198-4 (54.2) D L Hemp 78
Glamorgan won by 6 wickets
Match Award: D L Hemp

Nottinghamshire v Northamptonshire at Trent Bridge
Northants 352-8 (60) A Fordham 132, R Montgomerie 109
Notts 314-8 (60) P R Pollard 96
Northants won by 38 runs
Match Award: R J Bailey

Surrey v Middlesex at The Oval
Middlesex 304-7 (60) T A Radford 82, A J Hollioake 4-53
Surrey 225 (55.5)
Middlesex won by 79 runs
Match Award: J E Emburey

Sussex v Derbyshire at Hove
Sussex 222-8 (60) D G Cork 4-50
Derby 225-2 (53.5) C J Adams 109*
Derby won by 8 wickets
Match Award: C J Adams

Warwickshire v Kent at Edgbaston
Warwicks 262-7 (60) R G Twose 93*
Kent 252-9 (60)
Warwicks won by 10 runs
Match Award: R G Twose

QUARTER-FINALS *Aug 1-2*
Glamorgan v Middlesex at Sophia Gardens
Glamorgan 242-9 (60)
Middlesex 176 (51.5) H Anthony 4-25, S L Watkin 4-26
Glamorgan won by 66 runs
Match Award: C P Metson

Gloucestershire v Northamptonshire at Bristol
Northants 226 (58.2) R J Bailey 52, J Srinath 4-38
Gloucs 203 (57.4) J P Taylor 4-34
Northants won by 23 runs
Match Award: R J Bailey

Derbyshire v Warwickshire at Derby
Warwicks 290-6 (60) N V Knight 71
Derby 174 (46.5) A Donald 5-41
Warwicks won by 116 runs
Match Award: T A Munton

Yorkshire v Lancashire at Headingley
Lancs 169 (53.3) M Watkinson 55
Yorks 170-8 (59.3) M G Bevan 60*
Yorks won by 2 wickets
Match Award: M G Bevan

SEMI-FINALS *Aug 15*
Glamorgan v Warwickshire at Sophia Gardens
Glamorgan 86 (47) A F Giles 3-14
Warwicks 88-2 (24.1)
Warwicks won by 8 wickets
Match Award: T A Munton

Yorkshire v Northamptonshire at Headingley
Northants 296-5 (60) R J Bailey 93*
Yorks 199 (54.3)
Northants won by 87 runs
Match Award: R J Bailey

THE FINAL
NORTHAMPTONSHIRE V WARWICKSHIRE
Lord's   Sept 2

NORTHAMPTONSHIRE

R R Montgomerie		b Donald	1	19	17
A Fordham		b Brown	20	49	30
R J Bailey		b N Smith	44	95	90
A J Lamb*	c Ostler	b Brown	0	2	3
K M Curran		b Donald	30	107	80
D J Capel	c Piper	b Reeve	12	19	28
R J Warren†		b Bell	41	93	66
A L Penberthy	run out		5	26	12
J N Snape	c Piper	b Donald	21	32	28
A Kumble	c Twose	b Bell	2	5	5
J P Taylor	not out		0	1	0
Extras (B4, LB9, W11)			24		
Total (59.5 overs)			200		

Fall of wickets: 1-4 (Montgomerie), 2-39 (Fordham), 3-39(Lamb), 4-89 (Bailey), 5-110 (Capel), 6-128 (Curran), 7-158 (Penberthy), 8-197 (Snape), 9-200 (Kumble), 10-200 (Warren)
Bowling: Donald 12-1-33-3, **Brown** 10-2-35-2, **Bell** 8.5-1-41-2, **N M K Smith** 12-1-23-1, **Reeve** 12-1-31-1, **P A Smith** 5-0-24-0

WARWICKSHIRE

N V Knight	c Bailey	b Taylor	2	41	34
N M K Smith	c Warren	b Taylor	2	20	13
D P Ostler		b Kumble	45	110	77
D R Brown	c Warren	b Pemberthy	8	27	18
R G Twose	run out		68	170	127
T L Penney	c Montgomery b Pemberthy		20	52	35
D A Reeve*	not out		37	71	47
P A Smith	not out		4	12	2
K J Piper†					
A A Donald					
M A V Bell					
Extras (B2, LB14, W1)			17		
Total (6 wickets, 58.5 overs)			203		

Fall of wickets: 1-5 (N Smith), 2-14 (Knight), 3-28 (Brown), 4-74 (Ostler), 5-122 (Penney), 6-176 (Twose)
Bowling: Taylor 11.5-4-37-2, **Curran** 11-3-31-0, **Penberthy** 11-1-44-2, **Kumble** 12-0-29-1, **Capel** 12-0-40-0, **Snape** 1-0-6-0

Toss: **Northamptonshire**
Umpires: **H D Bird** & **M J Kitchen** (TV replay: **R Palmer**)
Match Award: **D A Reeve** (Adjudicator: R Benaud)

WARWICKSHIRE WON BY 4 WICKETS

AXA Equity & Law League

Played on Sundays over 40 overs

FINAL TABLE

Last year's position in brackets

		P	W	L	T	NR	Pts
1	Kent (3)	17	12	4	0	1	50
2	Warwickshire (1)	17	12	4	0	1	50
3	Worcestershire (2)	17	11	3	1	2	50
4	Lancashire (4)	17	11	5	0	1	46
5	Essex (17)	17	10	6	1	0	42
6	Glamorgan (7)	17	8	6	0	3	38
7	Leicestershire (10)	17	8	7	0	2	36
8	Derbyshire (8)	17	7	6	1	3	36
9	Surrey (6)	17	7	8	0	2	32
10	Sussex (15)	17	7	8	0	2	32
11	Nottinghamshire (11)	17	7	9	0	1	30
12	Yorkshire (5)	17	7	9	0	1	30
13	Northants (13)	17	6	8	1	2	30
14	Somerset (16)	17	5	9	0	3	26
15	Gloucestershire (18)	17	5	10	0	2	24
16	Durham (9)	17	4	9	1	3	24
17	Middlesex (14)	17	4	11	0	2	20
18	Hampshire (12)	17	3	12	1	1	16

SEASON'S STATISTICS

Top Batsmen

1	S P James (Glamorgan)	815

James wins £3,000 award

2	T M Moody (Worcs)	797
3	M G Bevan (Yorkshire)	704
4	N Hussain (Essex)	634
5	P Johnson (Notts)	617
6	C L Cairns (Notts)	615
7	M E Waugh (Essex)	608
8	G R Cowdrey (Kent)	593
9	P R Pollard (Notts)	577
10	G A Hick (Worcs)	551

Top Bowlers

1	S L Watkin (Glamorgan)	32

Watkin wins £3,000 award

2	S R Barwick (Glamorgan)	30
3	Wasim Akram (Lancs)	29
4	D W Headley (Kent)	24
5	R C Irani (Essex)	22
	M C Ilott (Essex)	22
	H H Streak (Hants)	22
8	S R Lampitt (Worcs)	21
	M McCague (Kent)	21

Best Bowling

6-15 A A Donald Warwicks v Yorks
6-29 P W Jarvis Sussex v Northants
6-39 N M K Smith Warwicks v Sussex

Top Wicketkeeper

Colin Metson, Glamorgan 27 dismissals
Metson wins £1,500 award

Women's Cricket

EUROPEAN CUP

Dublin

Ireland	150-8	(M Grealy 46, E Owens 37)
England	153-3	(B Daniels 47, J Smit 40*)

England won by 7 wickets

AREA CHAMPIONSHIP

Division 1

Final Placings

1. Yorkshire 91.5; 2. East Midlands 85.5; 3. Surrey I 72;
4. West Midlands 52.5; 5. East Anglia 31; 6. Kent 30.5
Kent relegated

Division 2

Final Placings

1. The West 100.5; 2. Middlesex 72.5; 3. Surrey II 70.5;
4. Thames Valley 57; 5. Sussex 47; 6. Lancs and
Cheshire 46.5
The West are promoted

NATIONAL CLUB KNOCK-OUT

Final

Invicta	61	(K Smithies 5-6)
Newark & Sherwood	61-1	(J Smit 31)

NATIONAL CLUB LEAGUE

Northern Premier League
Winners: Wakefield WCC
Southern Premier League
Winners: Redoubtables WCC

PREMIER LEAGUE FINAL

*Final rained off: Wakefield and Redoutables
share the trophy*

Australia 1994-5
Sheffield Shield Final

The 'Gabba, Brisbane   Mar 24-28

S Australia	214	(J Brayshaw 53, T Nielsen 53)
	349	
Queensland	664	(T J Barsby 151, M L Love 146,
		A R Border 98)

Queensland won by an innings and 101 runs

*Only needing a draw to secure their first victory in the
competition's 68 year history, Queensland (who have
come runners-up on 14 occasions) won by a record Final
margin of an innings and 101 runs.*

England's Test Record

v AUSTRALIA

	W	L	D
1876-77	1	1	0
1878-79	0	1	0
1880	1	0	0
1881-82	0	2	2
1882	0	1	0
1882-83	2	2	0
1884	1	0	2
1884-85	3	2	0
1886	3	0	0
1886-87	2	0	0
1887-88	1	0	0
1888	2	1	0
1890	2	0	0
1891-92	1	2	0
1893	1	0	2
1894-95	3	2	0
1896	2	1	0
1897-98	1	4	0
1899	0	1	4
1901-02	1	4	0
1902	1	2	2
1903-04	3	2	0
1905	2	0	3
1907-08	1	4	0
1909	1	2	2
1911-12	4	1	0
1912	1	0	2
1920-21	0	5	0
1921	0	3	2
1924-25	1	4	0
1926	1	0	4
1928-29	4	1	0
1930	1	2	2
1932-33	4	1	0
1934	1	2	2
1936-37	2	3	0
1938	1	1	2
1946-47	0	3	2
1948	0	4	1
1950-51	1	4	0
1953	1	0	4
1954-55	3	1	1
1956	2	1	2
1958-59	0	4	1
1961	1	2	2
1962-63	1	1	3
1964	0	1	4
1965-66	1	1	3
1968	1	1	3
1970-71	2	0	4
1972	2	2	1
1974-75	1	4	1
1975	0	1	3
1976-77	0	1	0
1977	3	0	2
1978-79	5	1	0
1979-80	0	3	0
1980	0	0	1
1981	3	1	2
1982-83	1	2	2
1985	3	1	2
1986-87	2	1	2
1987-88	0	0	1
1989	0	4	2
1990-91	0	3	2
1993	1	4	1
1994-5	1	3	1
Total	90	108	87

v SOUTH AFRICA

	W	L	D
1888-89	2	0	0
1891-92	1	0	0
1895-96	3	0	0
1898-99	2	0	0
1905-06	1	4	0
1907	1	0	2
1909-10	2	3	0
1912	3	0	0
1913-14	4	0	1
1922-23	2	1	2
1924	3	0	2
1927-28	2	2	1
1929	2	0	3
1930-31	0	1	4
1935	0	1	4
1938-39	1	0	4
1947	3	0	2
1948-49	2	0	3
1951	3	1	1
1955	3	2	0
1956-57	2	2	1
1960	3	0	2
1964-65	1	0	4
1965	0	1	2
1994	1	1	1
Total	46	18	38

v WEST INDIES

	W	L	D
1928	3	0	0
1929-30	1	1	2
1933	2	0	1
1934-35	1	2	1
1939	1	0	2
1947-48	0	2	2
1950	1	3	0
1953-54	2	2	1
1957	3	0	2
1959-60	1	0	4
1963	1	3	1
1966	1	3	1
1967-68	1	0	4
1969	2	0	1
1973	0	2	1
1973-74	1	1	3
1976	0	3	2
1980	0	1	4
1980-81	0	2	2
1984	0	5	0
1985-86	0	5	0
1988	0	4	1
1989-90	1	2	1
1991	2	2	1
1994	1	3	1
Total	25	46	38

v NEW ZEALAND

	W	L	D
1929-30	1	0	3
1931	1	0	2
1932-33	0	0	2
1937	1	0	2
1946-47	0	0	1
1949	0	0	4
1950-51	1	0	1
1954-55	2	0	0
1958	4	0	1
1958-59	1	0	1
1962-63	3	0	0
1965	3	0	0
1965-66	0	0	3
1969	2	0	1
1970-71	1	0	1
1973	2	0	1
1974-75	1	0	1
1977-78	1	1	1
1978	3	0	0
1983	3	1	0
1983-84	0	1	2
1986	0	1	2
1987-88	0	0	3
1990	1	0	2
1994	1	0	2
Total	31	4	34

v INDIA

	W	L	D
1932	1	0	0
1933-34	2	0	1
1936	2	0	1
1946	1	0	2
1951-52	1	1	3
1952	3	0	1
1959	5	0	0
1961-62	0	2	3
1963-64	0	0	5
1967	3	0	0
1971	0	1	2
1972-73	1	2	2
1974	3	0	0
1976-77	3	1	1
1979	1	0	3
1979-80	1	0	0
1981-82	0	1	5
1982	1	0	2
1984-85	2	1	2
1986	0	2	1

England's Test Record & County Champions

1990	1	0	2
1993	0	3	0
Total	31	14	36

v PAKISTAN

	W	L	D
1954	1	1	2
1961-62	1	0	2
1962	4	0	1
1967	2	0	1
1968-69	0	0	3
1971	1	0	2
1972-73	0	0	3
1974	0	0	3
1977-78	0	0	3
1978	2	0	1
1982	2	1	0
1983-84	0	1	2
1987	0	1	4
1987-88	0	1	2
1992	1	2	2
Total	14	7	31

v SRI LANKA

	W	L	D
1981-82	1	0	0
1984	0	0	1
1988	1	0	0
1991	1	0	0
1993	0	1	0
Total	3	1	1

COUNTY CHAMPIONSHIP

1864	Surrey
1865	Nottinghamshire
1866	Middlesex
1867	Yorkshire
1868	Nottinghamshire
1869	Notts & Yorks *(shared)*
1870	Yorkshire
1871	Nottinghamshire
1872	Nottinghamshire
1873	Gloucs & Notts *(shared)*
1874	Gloucestershire
1875	Nottinghamshire
1876	Gloucestershire
1877	Gloucestershire
1878	*Undecided*
1879	Lancs & Notts *(shared)*
1880	Nottinghamshire
1881	Lancashire
1882	Lancs & Notts *(shared)*
1883	Nottinghamshire
1884	Nottinghamshire
1885	Nottinghamshire
1886	Nottinghamshire
1887	Surrey
1888	Surrey
1889	Lancs, Notts & Surrey *(shared)*

1890	Surrey
1891	Surrey
1892	Surrey
1893	Yorkshire
1894	Surrey
1895	Surrey
1896	Yorkshire
1897	Lancashire
1898	Yorkshire
1899	Surrey
1900	Yorkshire
1901	Yorkshire
1902	Yorkshire
1903	Middlesex
1904	Lancashire
1905	Yorkshire
1906	Kent
1907	Nottinghamshire
1908	Yorkshire
1909	Kent
1910	Kent
1911	Warwickshire
1912	Yorkshire
1913	Kent
1914	Surrey
1915-1918	*Not held*
1919	Yorkshire
1920	Middlesex
1921	Middlesex
1922	Yorkshire
1923	Yorkshire
1924	Yorkshire
1925	Yorkshire
1926	Lancashire
1927	Lancashire
1928	Lancashire
1929	Nottinghamshire
1930	Lancashire
1931	Yorkshire
1932	Yorkshire
1933	Yorkshire
1934	Lancashire
1935	Yorkshire
1936	Derbyshire
1937	Yorkshire
1938	Yorkshire
1939	Yorkshire
1940-1945	*Not held*
1946	Yorkshire
1947	Middlesex
1948	Glamorgan
1949	Middx & Yorks *(shared)*
1950	Lancs & Surrey *(shared)*
1951	Warwickshire
1952	Surrey
1953	Surrey
1954	Surrey
1955	Surrey
1956	Surrey
1957	Surrey

1958	Surrey
1959	Yorkshire
1960	Yorkshire
1961	Hampshire
1962	Yorkshire
1963	Yorkshire
1964	Worcestershire
1965	Worcestershire
1966	Yorkshire
1967	Yorkshire
1968	Yorkshire
1969	Glamorgan
1970	Kent
1971	Surrey
1972	Warwickshire
1973	Hampshire
1974	Worcestershire
1975	Leicestershire
1976	Middlesex
1977	Kent & Middx *(shared)*
1978	Kent
1979	Essex
1980	Middlesex
1981	Nottinghamshire
1982	Middlesex
1983	Essex
1984	Essex
1985	Middlesex
1986	Essex
1987	Nottinghamshire
1988	Worcestershire
1989	Worcestershire
1990	Middlesex
1991	Essex
1992	Essex
1993	Middlesex
1994	Warwickshire
1995	Warwickshire

Knock-out Cups & Sunday League Winners

NATWEST TROPHY
(Gillette Cup 1963-80)
1963 **Sussex** beat Worcestershire by 14 runs
1964 **Sussex** beat Warwickshire by 8 wickets
1965 **Yorkshire** beat Surrey by 175 runs
1966 **Warwickshire** beat Worcs by 5 wickets
1967 **Kent** beat Somerset by 32 runs
1968 **Warwickshire** beat Sussex by 4 wickets
1969 **Yorkshire** beat Derbyshire by 69 runs
1970 **Lancashire** beat Sussex by 6 wickets
1971 **Lancashire** beat Kent by 24 runs
1972 **Lancashire** beat Warwickshire by 4 wickets
1973 **Gloucestershire** beat Sussex by 40 runs
1974 **Kent** beat Lancashire by 4 wickets
1975 **Lancashire** beat Middlesex by 7 wickets
1976 **Northants** beat Lancashire by 4 wickets
1977 **Middlesex** beat Glamorgan by 5 wickets
1978 **Sussex** beat Somerset by 5 wickets
1979 **Somerset** beat Northants by 45 runs
1980 **Middlesex** beat Surrey by 7 wickets
1981 **Derbyshire** beat Northants fewer wickets lost
(scores level)
1982 **Surrey** beat Warwickshire by 9 wickets
1983 **Somerset** beat Kent by 24 runs
1984 **Middlesex** beat Kent by 4 wickets
1985 **Essex** beat Nottinghamshire by I run
1986 **Sussex** beat Lancashire by 7 wickets
1987 **Nottinghamshire** beat Northants by 3 wickets
1988 **Middlesex** beat Worcestershire by 3 wickets
1989 **Warwickshire** beat Middlesex by 4 wickets
1990 **Lancashire** beat Northants by 7 wickets
1991 **Hampshire** beat Surrey by 4 wickets
1992 **Northants** beat Leicestershire by 8 wickets
1993 **Warwickshire** beat Sussex by 5 wickets
1994 **Worcestershire** beat Warwickshire by 8 wickets
1995 **Warwickshire** beat Northants by 4 wickets

BENSON & HEDGES CUP
1972 **Leicestershire** beat Yorkshire by 5 wickets
1973 **Kent** beat Worcestershire by 39 runs
1974 **Surrey** beat Leicestershire by 27 runs
1975 **Leicestershire** beat Middlesex by 5 wickets
1976 **Kent** beat Worcestershire by 43 runs
1977 **Gloucestershire** beat Kent by 64 runs
1978 **Kent** beat Derbyshire by 6 wickets
1979 **Essex** beat Surrey by 35 runs
1980 **Northants** beat Essex by 6 runs
1981 **Somerset** beat Surrey by 7 wickets
1982 **Somerset** beat Nottinghamshire by 9 wickets
1983 **Middlesex** beat Essex by 4 runs
1984 **Lancashire** beat Warwickshire by 6 wickets
1985 **Leicestershire** beat Essex by 5 wickets
1986 **Middlesex** beat Kent by 2 runs
1987 **Yorkshire** beat Northants fewer wickets lost
(scores level)
1988 **Hampshire** beat Derbyshire by 7 wickets
1989 **Nottinghamshire** beat Essex by 3 wickets
1990 **Lancashire** beat Worcestershire by 69 runs
1991 **Worcestershire** beat Lancashire by 65 runs
1992 **Hampshire** beat Kent by 41 runs

1993 **Derbyshire** beat Lancashire by 6 runs
1994 **Warwickshire** beat Worcestershire by 6 wickets
1995 **Lancashire** beat Kent by 35 runs

AXA EQUITY & LAW LEAGUE
(John Player League 1969-86,
Refuge Assurance League 1987-91,
no sponsor 1992)
1969 **Lancashire**
1970 **Lancashire**
1971 **Worcestershire**
1972 **Kent**
1973 **Kent**
1974 **Leicestershire**
1975 **Hampshire**
1976 **Kent**
1977 **Leicestershire**
1978 **Hampshire**
1979 **Somerset**
1980 **Warwickshire**
1981 **Essex**
1982 **Sussex**
1983 **Yorkshire**
1984 **Essex**
1985 **Essex**
1986 **Hampshire**
1987 **Worcestershire**
1988 **Worcestershire**
1989 **Lancashire**
1990 **Derbyshire**
1991 **Nottinghamshire**
1992 **Middlesex**
1993 **Glamorgan**
1994 **Warwickshire**
1995 **Kent**

Cycling ━━━━━━━━━━━━━━━━━━━━━━━

Sometime it seems that Chris Boardman and Graeme Obree take it in turns. An Olympic title in 1992 put Boardman in the spotlight. A world title and one-hour record for Obree in 1993 gave the Scot the edge. In 1994, Boardman's exploits in the Tour were hard to match. So the pendulum was due to swing back...but it hardly seemed that way in January. In September last year, Obree had signed a professional contract with Le Groupement. It was due to start at the beginning of January. It ended at the beginning of January too. If you want to cast it in the best light you could say that the contract lasted three days. Obree failed to turn up for training and was dismissed.

Boardman, on the other hand, the model-professional, had become the lynch-pin of the Gan team. Strong early season performances, including a second in the Dauphiné to Induráin, had hopes running high for the Tour. One week prior, Obree could afford a wry grin. The team that sacked him, collapsed. Le Groupement, a pyramid sales group from northern France which had spent an alarming one eighth of its turnover on the racing team, pulled out of the sport as the company veered towards bankruptcy. Yet, if Obree was grinning, Robert Millar wasn't. Five days before the Tour opened, he was left riderless.

Day one of the Tour and the pendulum swung from Boardman. Conditions were miserable, yet expectations were high. Boardman had taken the Prologue apart in 1994. This time he got barely two kilometres into the time trial before his machine slid away on a left-handed curve and the Gan support car almost ran him over. Good job it didn't, things were bad enough as it was; a broken wrist and ankle and the end of the Tour for Boardman. Within little more than a fortnight, though, Boardman could feel fortunate.

The Tour had developed into one of the best of recent years (meaning it had taken a few more stages than usual before it was certain Induráin would win) when it was all rendered meaningless. On July 18th, the 24-year-old Italian Fabio Casartelli, the Olympic road race champion, died after crashing on the descent of the Col de Portet d'Aspet. Casartelli was only the third rider in the Tour to die while racing. The following day's stage was a moving testament to the young rider as the peloton drifted back to allow Casartelli's Motorola teammates to finish together.

Induráin's fifth Tour victory in succession gave the Spaniard a unique position in the event's history. Neither Anquetil, nor Hinault, nor Merckx could achieve their five-timers in a row. Induráin skipped the Vuelta (where Jalabert won everything and established himself as world number one - though only the French believed it) but didn't end his season there, chosing to tackle the time trial in the World Championships at Bogotá. It almost goes without saying that Induráin won, but it does bring us neatly back to Obree who also found the thin air of Bogotá to his liking. Obree finished down the field in the time trial, but had already struck gold in the pursuit, to take Boardman's title. Obree himself had won the crown in 1993 and was prevented from defending last year in Sicily when the governing body outlawed his riding position. His chest wasn't on the handlebars this time; the secret instead a gear so high that you suspected he might be caught on the first couple of laps. He wasn't. The Scot had done his homework and in the final lap of the Final, flew home.

World Track Championships

Bogota, Colombia   Sep 26-30

<table>
<tr><td>

Men

KILOMETRE
1	Shane Kelly	AUS	1:00.613
2	Florian Rousseau	FRA	1:01.350
3	Erin Hartwell	USA	1:01.740

4000M PURSUIT
Semi-finals
Andrea Collinelli ITA 4:22.265 bt
Stuart O'Grady AUS 4:23.637

Graeme Obree GBR 4:22.917 bt
Philippe Ermenault FRA 4:25.634
O'Grady, as fastest loser, takes bronze

Final
Graeme Obree 4:24.182 bt
Andrea Collinelli ITA 4:25.677

SPRINT
Semi-finals
Darryn Hill AUS bt Gary Neiwand AUS 2-1
10.186 (Hill), 11.046 (Neiwand), 10.602 (Hill)

Curt Harnett CAN bt Frédéric Magne FRA 2-0
10.399, 10.807

3rd/4th place
F Magne FRA bt Gary Neiwand AUS
10.930, 11.437

Final
Darryn Hill bt Curt Harnett
10.540 (Harnett), 10.525 (Hill), 10.523 (Hill)

OLYMPIC SPRINT
Final
Germany (Fiedler/Van Eijden/Hübner) 58.089 bt
France (Vetu/Thuet/Rousseau) 58.335

3rd/4th place
United States 59.289 bt Spain 59.941

4000M TEAM PURSUIT
Semi-finals
Ukraine 4:12.460 bt Germany 4:13.537
Australia 4:08.987 bt United States 4:12.930
United States, as fastest losers, take the bronze
Final
Australia 4:05.010 bt Ukraine 4:07.906

POINTS RACE
1	Silvio Martinello	ITA	38
2	R Lupeikis	LAT	16
3	S Laurenenko	KZK	16

KEIRIN
1	Frédéric Magne	FRA	10.598
2	Michael Hübner	GER	
3	Federico Paris	ITA	

MADISON
1	Marinello/Villa	ITA	31pts
2	G Curuchet/J Curuchet	ARG	11pts
3	Betschart/Risi	SUI	at 1 lap

</td><td>

Women

3000M PURSUIT
Semi-finals
Antonella Bellutti ITA 3:37.361 bt
Marion Clignet FRA 3:38.420

Rebecca Twigg USA 3:36.338 bt
May-Britt Vaaland NOR 3:37.437
Vaaland, as fastest loser, takes bronze

Final
Rebecca Twigg 3:36.081 *WR* bt
Antonella Bellutti 3:46.610

SPRINT
Semi-finals
Félicia Ballanger FRA bt Galina Enioukhina RUS 2-1
11.796 (Enioukhina), 11.764, 11.624

Olga Slioussareva RUS bt Erika Salumae EST 2-0
11.680, 11.206

3rd/4th place
Erika Salumae bt Galina Enioukhina 2-0
12.564, 11.928

Final
Félicia Ballanger bt Olga Slioussareva 2-1
11.923 (Slioussareva), 11.491, 12.048

500M TIME TRIAL
1	Félicia Ballanger	FRA	34.017
2	Galina Enoukhina	RUS	34.962
3	Michelle Ferris	AUS	35.313

POINTS RACE
1	Svetlana Samokhvalova	RUS	25
2	Nada Christofoli	ITA	20
3	Natalie Lancien	FRA	18

Medal Table

	G	S	B
France	3	2	2
Australia	3	0	2
Italy	2	3	1
Russia	1	2	0
United States	1	0	3
Germany	1	1	0
Great Britain	1	0	0
Argentina	0	1	0
Canada	0	1	0
Latvia	0	1	0
Ukraine	0	1	0
Estonia	0	0	1
Kazakhstan	0	0	1
Norway	0	0	1
Switzerland	0	0	1

</td></tr>
</table>

Tour de France ▬▬▬▬▬▬▬▬▬▬▬▬

July 2-24

Date	Stage	Route (distance)	Winner(Team)		Race Leader
Jul 1	Prologue	St Brieuc* (7.3km)	**Jacky Durand (Castorama)**	FRA	Durand
Jul 2	1	Dinan-Lannion (233.5km)	**Fabio Baldato (MG-Technogym)**	ITA	Durand
Jul 3	2	Perros Guirec-Vitré (235.5km)	**Mario Cipollini (Mercatone Uno)**	ITA	Jalabert
Jul 4	3	Mayenne-Alençon (67km)**	**Gewiss-Ballan**		Jalabert
Jul 5	4	Alençon-Le Havre (162km)	**Mario Cipollini (Marcatone Uno)**	ITA	Gotti
Jul 6	5	Fécamp-Dunkirk (261km)	**Jeroen Blijlevens (TVM)**	NED	Gotti
Jul 7	6	Dunkirk-Charleroi (202km)	**Erik Zabel (Telecom-ZG)**	GER	Riis
Jul 8	7	Charleroi-Liège (203km)	**Johan Bruyneel (ONCE)**	BEL	Riis
Jul 9	8	Huy-Seraing (54km)*	**Miguel Induráin (Banesto)**	ESP	Induráin
Jul 11	9	Le Grand Bornand-La Plagne (160km)	**Alex Zülle (ONCE)**	SUI	Induráin
Jul 12	10	Aime la Plagne-Alpe d'Huez (162.5km)	**Marco Pantani (Carrera)**	ITA	Induráin
Jul 13	11	Bourg d'Oisans-St Etienne (199km)	**Max Sciandri (MG-Techogym)**	GBR	Induráin
Jul 14	12	Saint Etienne-Mendé (222.5km)	**Laurent Jalabert (ONCE)**	FRA	Induráin
Jul 15	13	Mendé-Revel (245km)	**Sergey Outschakov (Polti)**	RUS	Induráin
Jul 16	14	St Orens de Gameville-Guzet (164km)	**Marco Pantani (Carrera)**	ITA	Induráin
Jul 18	15	Saint Girons-Cauterets (206km)	**Richard Virenque (Festina)**	FRA	Induráin
Jul 19	16	Tarbes-Pau (237km)	*no classification for the stage*		
Jul 20	17	Pau-Bourdeaux (246km)	**Erik Zabel (Telecom-ZG)**	GER	Induráin
Jul 21	18	Montpon Menestrol-Limoges (166.5km)	**Lance Armstrong (Motorola)**	USA	Induráin
Jul 22	19	Lac de Vassivière (46.5km)*	**Miguel Induráin (Banesto)**	ESP	Induráin
Jul 23	20	St Guinevière des Bois-Paris (155km)	**Djamo. Abduzhaparov (Novell)**	UZB	Induráin

* Individual Time Trial ** Team Time Trial

FINAL CLASSIFICATION

Rider	Ctry	Time
1 Miguel Induráin (Banesto)	**ESP**	**92:54:49**
2 Alex Zülle (ONCE)	SUI	at 4:35
3 Bjarne Riis (Gweiss)	DEN	6:47
4 Laurent Jalabert (ONCE)	FRA	8:24
5 Ivan Gotti (Gweiss)	ITA	11:33
6 Melchior Mauri (ONCE)	ESP	15:20
7 Fernando Escarpin (Mapei-GB)	ESP	15:49
8 Tony Rominger (Mapei-GB)	SUI	16:46
9 Richard Virenque (Festina)	FRA	17:31
10 Hernan Buenahore (Kelme)	COL	18:50
11 Claudio Chiappucci (Carrera)	ITA	18:55
12 Laurent Madouas (Casto)	FRA	20:37
13 Marco Pantani (Carrera)	ITA	26:20
14 Paolo Lanfranchi (Brescialat)	ITA	29:41
15 Bruno Cenghialta (Gewiss)	ITA	29:55
16 Alvaro Mejia (Motorola)	COL	33:40
17 Bo Hamburger (TVM)	DEN	34:49
18 Viatchevslav Ekimov (Novell)	RUS	39:51
19 Laurent Dufaux (Festina)	FRA	45:55
20 Erik Breukink (ONCE)	NED	47:27
dnf: Chris Boardman GBR		
Sean Yates GBR		

Points (Green Jersey)

1 Laurent Jalabert (ONCE)	FRA	333
2 Djamo Abduzhaparov (Novell)	UZB	271
3 Miguel Induráin (Banesto)	ESP	180

King of the Mountains (Polka-dot Jersey)

1 Richard Virenque (Festina)	FRA	438
2 Claudio Chiappucci (Carrera)	ITA	214
3 Alex Zülle (ONCE)	SUI	205

Teams

1 ONCE	278:29:35
2 Gewiss	at 13:23
3 Mapei-GB	55:53

Quotes

"I just want to go to Paris. I am not interested in winning Saturday's time trial. What is victory after what has happened" - **Tony Rominger, after Fabio Casartelli died in the Tour.**

"It was a very quiet peloton, there wasn't much to say. At the end we made sure the Motorola team were at the front and then we all dropped back. It was our way of saying goodbye" - **Stephen Hodge, Australian Tour rider, on the day's racing after the tragedy.**

"Sur La Planète Indurain" - **Headline in French sportspaper L'Equipe, the day after the Tour finished.**

"Miguel Induráin has been lucky not to ride at the same time as me because it would have been relatively easy for me to set a trap for him" - **Bernard Hinault, who also won the Tour de France five times, but not in succession.**

"It was like riding behind a motorbike" - **Johan Bruyneel, who broke with Induráin on the Liège stage.**

"He's a great rider, but I don't ever see him getting over the big cols in the Tour de France" - **Richard Virenque on Boardman.**

"Great! Daddy's coming home" - **Eddie Boardman, on hearing his dad had crashed out of the Tour de France.**

"A lot of people were expecting more than I was ready for - all that talk of a top ten finish - I felt a little out of my depth" - **Boardman on the Tour.**

"It's grim when you're not very fit, because you suffer. It's very unpleasant" - **Chris Boardman, three weeks back into 'reasonable training' following his Tour crash.**

"Not so much George Michael as Compo from Last of the Summer Wine. It had to go" - **Boardman on his short-lived beard.**

"They say I don't have many friends in the bunch because I win everything" - **Tony Rominger, after winning the Giro.**

"It was harder pissing than it was winning the stage" - **Rominger, after stage four of the Giro. Maybe that's why he hasn't got many friends.**

"I'm not going to the Dauphiné to train, but to suffer" - **Induráin on his preparation for the Tour.**

"If I'm in the lead on the last lap with a Colombian, I would prefer to be bought off and avoid being shot" - **Maurizio Fondriest, taking a gloomy view of the world championships in Bogotá.**

"We exist and we will exist for a long time" - **Guy Mollet, manager of the Le Groupement team, back in January.**

"It was the most stupid thing I've ever done in my life" - **Luc Leblanc, world road race champion, on his decision to join Le Groupement. The team folded in June.**

Giro D'Italia
(Tour of Italy)
Perugia-Milano May 22-June 12

STAGE WINNERS

1 **Mario Cipollini (Mercatone) ITA 5:15:53**
  (Perugia-Terni 205km)
2 **Tony Rominger (Mapei-GB) SUI 25:05**
  (Spoleto-Assisi 19km time trial)
3 **Mario Cipollini (Mercatone) ITA 3:56:11**
  (Spoleto-Marotta 161km)
4 **Tony Rominger (Mapei-GB) SUI 5:30:53**
  (Mondolfo-Loreto 192km)
5 **Filippo Casagrande (Brescia.) ITA 4:39.02**
  (Porto Recanati-Tortoreto Lido 182km)
6 **Nicola Minali (Gewiss) ITA 4:11:15**
  (Trani-Taranto 165km)
7 **Maurizio Fondriest (Lampre) ITA 5:11:50**
  (Taranto-Terme Luigiane 216km)
8 **Laudelino Cubino (Kelme) ESP 5:52:03**
  (Acquappesa-Monte Sirino 206km)
9 **Rolf Sorensen (MG-Techn.) DEN 3:32:12**
  (Terme La Calde-Salerno 165km)
10 **Tony Rominger (Mapei-GB) SUI 51:54**
  (Telese Terme-Maddaloni 42km time trial)
11 **Enrico Zaina (Carrera) ITA 4:37:36**
  (Pietrasanta-Il Ciocco 175km)
12 **Jan Svorada (Lampre) SVK 5:04:50**
  (Borgo a Mozzano-Cento 201km)
13 **Pascal Richard (MG-Techn.)SUI 5:44:07**
  (Pieve di Cento-Rovereto 218km)
14 **Oliverio Rincon (ONCE) COL 7:32:07**
  (Trento-Val Senales 240km)
15 **Mariano Piccoli (Brescia.) ITA 4:42:09**
  (Val Senates-Lenzerheide 185km)
16 **Giuseppe Citterio (AKI) ITA 5:44:44**
  (Lenzerheide-Treviglio 234km)
17 **Tony Rominger (Mapei-GB) SUI 1:05:59**
  (Gewiss Cenate-Selvino 43km time trial)
18 **Denis Zanette (AKI) ITA 5:30:44**
  (Stradello-Vicoforte 221km)
19 **Pascal Richard (MG-Techn.) SUI 4:01:11**
  (Mondovi-Briançon 129km)
20 **Sergey Outschakov (Polti) RUS 4:59:58**
  (Briançon-Gressoney Saint Jean 208km)
21 **Evgeny Berzin (Gewiss) RUS 5:04:59**
  (Pont Saint Martin-Luino 190km)
22 **Giovanni Lombardi (Polti) ITA 3:32:53**
  (Luino-Milano 148km)

FINAL CLASSIFICATION

1	**Tony Rominger (Mapei-GB)**	**SUI**	**97:39:50**
2	Evgeny Berzin (Gewiss)	RUS	at 4:13
3	Piotr Ugroumov (Gewiss)	RUS	4:55
4	Claudio Chiappucci (Carrera)	ITA	9:23
5	Oliverio Rincon (ONCE)	COL	10:03
6	Pavel Tonkov (Lampre)	RUS	11:31
7	Enrico Zaina (Carrera)	ITA	13:40
8	Heinz Imboden (Refin)	SUI	16:23
9	Georg Totschnig (polti)	AUT	18:05
10	Filippo Casagrande (Brescialat)	ITA	18:50

King of the Mountains:
Mariano Piccoli (Brescialat) ITA
Points: Tony Rominger

Vuelta a España
(Tour of Spain)
Zaragoza-Madrid   Sep 2-24

STAGE WINNERS

Prologue
  Abraham Olano (Mapei-GB) ESP 7:51
  (Zaragoza time trial 7km)
1 **Nicola Minali (Gewiss-Ballan) ITA 5:42:45**
  (Zaragoza-Logrono 186.6km)
2 **Gianluca Pianegonda (Polti) ITA 6:12:34**
  (San Asensio-Santander 223km)
3 **Laurent Jalabert (ONCE) FRA 5:02:39**
  (Santander-Alto de Naranco 206km)
4 **Marcel Wust (Castellblanch) GER 2:15:52**
  (Tapia de Casriego-La Coruña 82.6km)
5 **Laurent Jalabert (ONCE) FRA 4:41:04**
  (La Coruña-Orense 179.8km)
6 **Nicola Minali (Gewiss) ITA 7:27:00**
  (Orense-Zamora 264km)
7 **Abraham Olano (Mapei-GB) ESP 47:37**
  (Salamanca time trial 41km)
8 **Laurent Jalabert (ONCE) FRA 6:05:12**
  (Salamanca-Avila 219.8km)
9 **Jesper Skibby (TVM) DEN 2:51:37**
  (AVila-DYC Segovia 122.5km)
10 **Jeroen Blijlevens (TVM) NED 4:21:26**
  (Cordoue-Seville 162.5km)
11 **Nicola Minali (Gewiss) ITA 4:18:12**
  (Seville-Marbella 187km)
12 **Bert Dietz (Telekom) GER 6:52:20**
  (Marbella-Sierra Nevada 238.5km)
13 **Christian Henn (Telekom) GER 4:01:07**
  (Olula Del Rio-Murcia 181km)
14 **Marcel Wust (Castellblanch) GER 5:31:00**
  (Elche-Valencia 207km)
15 **Laurent Jalabert (ONCE) FRA 3:59:50**
  (Barcelona 154km)
16 **Alex Zülle (ONCE) SUI 5:13:24**
  (Tarrega-Plade Beret 211km)
17 **Laurent Jalabert (ONCE) FRA 5:34:45**
  (Salardu-Luz Ardiden 179.2km)
18 **Asiate Saitov (Artiiach) RUS 4:05:46**
  (Luz St Sauveur-Sabin Anigo 156km)
19 **Adriano Baffi (Mapei-GB) ITA 5:55:26**
  (Sabin Anigo-Calatayud 243km)
20 **Abraham Olano (Mapei-GB) ESP 49:37**
  (Alcala de Henares 41.6km)
21 **Marcel Wust (Castellblanch) GER 4:14:59**
  (Alcala de Henares-Madrid 171.2km)

FINAL CLASSIFICATION

1	**Laurent Jalabert (ONCE)**	**FRA**	**95:30:33**
2	Abraham Olano (Mapei-GB)	ESP	at 4:22
3	Johan Bruyneel (ONCE)	BEL	6:48
4	Melchior Mauri (ONCE)	ESP	8:04
5	Richard Virenque (Festina)	FRA	11:38
6	Pistore (Polti)	ITA	11:54
7	David Garcia (Banesto)	ESP	13:50
8	DanielClavero (Artiach)	ESP	15:03
9	Michele Bartoli (Mercatone)	ITA	19:14
10	Stefano Della Santa (Mapei)	ITA	19:42

King of the Mountains: Laurent Jalabert
Points: Laurent Jalabert

World Cup Series

Milan-San Remo (294km)
Mar 18

1	Laurent Jalabert (ONCE)	FRA	6:45:20
2	Maurizio Fondriest (Lampre)	ITA	st
3	Stefano Zanini (Gewiss)	ITA	at 4

Tour of Flanders (261km)
Apr 2

1	Johan Museeuw (Mapei-GB)	BEL	6:36:24
2	Fabio Baldato (Mg-Technogym)	ITA	at 1:27
3	Andrey Tchmil (Lotto)	RUS	st

Paris-Roubaix (266.5km)
Apr 9

1	Franco Ballerini (Mapei-GB)	ITA	6:27:08
2	Andrey Tchmil (Lotto)	RUS	at 1:56
3	Johan Museeuw (Mapei-GB)	BEL	st

Liège-Bastogne-Liège (261km)
Apr 16

1	Mauro Gianetti (Polti)	ITA	6:38:25
2	Gianni Bugno (MG Boys)	ITA	at 15
3	Michele Bartoli (Mercatone)	ITA	st

Amstel Gold (256km)
Apr 22

1	Mauro Gianetti (Polti)	ITA	6:38:52
2	Davide Cassani (MG-Technogym)	ITA	st
3	Beat Zberg (Carrera)	SUI	at 27

Grand Prix of Frankfurt (252km)
Apr 22

1	Francesco Frattini (Gewiss)	ITA	6:25:05
2	Jens Heppner (Telekom)	GER	st
3	Massimo Podenzana (Bres)	ITA	at 3

Leeds International Classic (231km)
Aug 6

1	Max Sciandri (MG-Techno)	GBR	6:00:20
2	Roberto Caruso (ZG)	ITA	at 44
3	Alberto Elli (MG-Tehcno)	ITA	st

San Sebastian Classic (238km)
Aug 13

1	Lance Armstrong (Motorola)	USA	5:31:17
2	Stefano Della Santa (Mapei)	ITA	at 2
3	Johan Museeuw (Mapei)	BEL	at 27

Zurich Classic (235km)
Aug 20

1	Johan Museeuw (Mapei)	BEL	5:34:15
2	Gianni Bugno (Mg-Techno)	ITA	st
3	Giorgio Furlan (Gewiss)	ITA	st

WORLD CUP POINTS *(two events remaining)*

1	Johan Museeuw	BEL	199
2	Laurent Jalabert	FRA	111
3	Mauro Gianetti	SUI	100
4	Fabio Baldato	ITA	91
5	Gianni Bugno	ITA	88
6	Maurizio Fondriest	ITA	82
7	Max Sciandri	GBr	79
	Andrey Tchmil	RUS	79
9	Lance Armstrong	USA	74
10	Michele Bartoli	ITA	65

1994 World Cup

Paris-Tours (250km)
Oct 2, 1994

1	Erik Zabel (Telekom)	GER	6:15:37
2	Gianluca Bortolami (Mapei-Clas)	ITA	st
3	Zbigniew Spruch (Lampre)	POL	st

Tour of Lombardy (244km)
Oct 9, 1994

1	Vladislav Bobrik (Gewiss)	RUS	6:03:21
2	Claudio Chiappucci (Carrera)	ITA	at 2
3	Pascal Richard (GB-MG)	SUI	3

World Cup 1994 - Final Classification

1	Gianluca Bortolami (Mapei-Clas)	ITA	151
2	Johan Museeuw (GB-MG)	BEL	125
3	Andrey Tchmil (Lotto)	RUS	115
4	Claudio Chiappucci (Carrera)	ITA	89

Other Events

Mldi Libre (Beaucaire-Perpignan)
May 24-29

Stage 1(206km) Zbigniew Spruch (Lam)	POL	5:25:28
Stage 2/1(75km) Wilfried Nelissen (Lot)	BEL	1:50:09
Stage 2/2(90km)T Bourguignon (le G)	FRA	2:25:08
Stage 3(205km) Laurent Jalabert (ONCE)	FRA	5:07:51
Stage 4(191km) Jacky Durand (Cast)	FRA	4:53:40
Stage 5(183km) Johan Bruyneel (ONCE)	BEL	4:42:11
Stage 6(17.5*km) Chris Boardman (Gan)	GBR	20:03

* Time Trial

Final Overall
1. Miguel Induráin (Banesto) ESP 24:55:51
2. Richard Virenque (Festina) FRA at 1:35
3. T Laurent (Castorama) FRA at 2:00
10. Chris Boardman (Gan) GBR at 4:13

Dauphiné Libéré (Evian-Chambéry)
May 30-June 6

Prologue(6.7km) Chris Boardman (Gan)	GBR	8:20
Stage 1(225km) Andrey Tchmil (Lotto)	RUS	5:17:14
Stage 2(173km) Wieben Veenstra (Mot)	NED	4:12:26
Stage 3(36km*) Miguel Induráin (Ban)	ESP	44:41
Stage 4(205km) Richard Virenque (Fes)	FRA	5:07:44
Stage 5(198km) Gilles Talmant (Cast)	FRA	5:00:54
Stage 6(143km) Richard Virenque (Fes)	FRA	4:15:22
Stage 7(159km) Fabian Jeker (Festina)	SUI	4:03:31

Final Overall
1. Miguel Induráin (Banesto) ESP 28:51:32
2. Chris Boardman (Gan) GBR at 2:21
3. Vicente Aparicio (Banesto) ESP at 3:39

British Road Race Championship
June 25 - 113.25m

1	Robert Millar (Le Groupement)		4:32.53
2	C Walker (Cycles Peugeot)		at 2.06
3	P Painard (France)		2.50

One-hour
Manchester Velodrome   June 17

Yvonne McGregor GBR covered 47.112 km to break Catherine Marsal's world record.

Bordeaux   Oct 22, 1994

Tony Rominger SUI covered 53.832km to break Miguel Induráin's world record.

National Track Championships

Leicester   July 29th-Aug 5

MEN

4000m Pursuit
1 Graeme Obree
2 Bryan Steel
3 Rob Hayles

4000m Team Pursuit
1 North Wirral Velo
2 City of Ediburgh CC
3 De Laune CC

1000m Sprint
1 Steve Paulding
2 Neil Potter
3 Craig Percival

Kilometre Time Trial
1 Shaun Wallace
2 Rob Hayles
3 Anthony Stirrat

Olympic sprint
1 City of Edinburgh
2 CC Lancashire
3 TS Thameside

Open Omnium
1 Rob Hayles
2 Anthony Stirrat
3 Nicky Hall

40km Points Race
1 John Clay
2 Bryan Steel
3 Rob Hayles

Keirin
1 Steve Paulding
2 Chris Pyatt
3 Rob Jeffries

Madison
1 Hayles/Williams
2 Steel/Wingrave
3 Lillestone/Newton

WOMEN

500m TT
1 Wendy Everson
2 Megan Hughes
3 Sally Boyden

30km Points
1 Sally Boyden
2 Maria lawrence
3 Vicki Filsell

3000m Pursuit
1 Yvonne McGregor
2 Mxine Johnson
3 Vicki Filsell

1000m Sprint
1 Wendy Everson
2 Sally Boyden
3 Emma Davies

Cyclo-cross

World Championships

Eschenbach, Sui   Jan 29
1 Dieter Runkel   SUI   57:44
2 R Groenendaal   NED   at 37s
3 Beat Wabel   SUI   57
4 Adrie Van der Poel NED   1:18
5 Roger Honneger   SUI   1:26
6 Peter Van Santvliet BEL   1:43

World Cup Series

ROUND 1
Wangen, Sui   Oct 16,1994
1 Dom. Arnould   FRA   57:09
2 Pavel Camdra   CZE   at 5

3 Emmanuel Magnien FRA   12

ROUND 2
Corva, Ita   Nov 13, 1994
1 Daniele Pontoni   ITA 1:00:06
2 Paul Herijgers   BEL   at 26
3 Marc Janssens   NED   36

ROUND 3
Igorre, Esp   Dec 11, 1994
1 Daniele Pontoni   ITA   57:08
2 Jerome Chiotti   FRA   at 33
3 Paul Herijgers   BEL   1:09

ROUND 4
Loenhout, Bel   Dec 28, 1994
1 Radomir Simonek CZE 1:01:17
2 R Groenendaal   NED   at 7

3 Daniele Pontoni   ITA   24
ROUND 5 (FINAL)
Sable-sur-Sarthe, Fra   Jan 15
1 Dom. Arnould   FRA   58:27
2 Emmanuel Magnien FRA   at 3
3 Daniele Pontoni   ITA   6

FINAL PLACINGS
1. Daniele Pontoni 66pts; 2.
Dominique Arnould 54; 3. Radomir
Simonek 52; 4. Adrie Van der Poel
48; 5. Jerome Chiotti 40; 6.
Emmanuel Magnien 37

National Championships

Birmingham   Jan 8
Men
1 Barrie Clarke   58:52
2 Steve Douce   at 7
3 Nick Craig   7
Women
1 Caroline Alexander 39:23
2 Louise Robinson   at 2:36
3 Isla Rowntree   2:54

National Trophy

OVERALL
Men
1. Roger Hammond 120 pts;
2. Steve Douce 105; 3. Barrie
Clarke 96.
Women
1. Deb Murrel 86; 2. Louise
Robinson 75; 3. Caroline
Alexander 60.

World Champions

*For all track events, the men's
amateur categories ceased in
1991, the professional events in
1992. They were replaced by
Open events. We have listed the
Open events first, followed by the
amateur and professional records.*

SPRINT
1993 Gary Neiwand AUS
1994 Martin Nothstein USA
1995 Darryn Hill AUS

INDIVIDUAL PURSUIT
1993 Graeme Obree GBR
1994 Chris Boardman GBR
1995 Graeme Obree GBR

TEAM PURSUIT
1993 Australia
1994 Germany
1995 Australia

POINTS RACE
1993 Etienne de Wilde BEL
1994 Bruno Risi SUI
1995 Silvio Martinello ITA

KEIRIN
1993 Gary Neiwand AUS
1994 Mazartin Nothstein USA
1995 Frédéric Magne FRA

KILOMETRE TIME TRIAL
1993 Florain Rousseau FRA
1994 Florian Rousseau FRA
1995 Shane Kelly AUS

MADISON
1995 Marinello/Villa ITA

OLYMPIC SPRINT
1995 Germany

INDIVIDUAL TIME TRIAL
1994 Chris Boardman GBR
1995 Miguel Induráin ESP

MOTOR PACED
1993 Jens Veggerby DEN
1994 Carsten Podlesch GER

TANDEM
1993 Paris/Chiappa ITA
1994 Colas/Magné FRA

AMATEUR SPRINT
First held 1893
1970 Daniel Morelon FRA
1971 Daniel Morelon FRA
1973 Daniel Morelon FRA
1974 Anton Tkac TCH
1975 Daniel Morelon FRA
1977 Hans-Jorgen Geschke
     GDR
1978 Anton Tkac TCH
1979 Lutz Hesslich GDR
1981 Sergey Kopylov URS
1982 Sergey Kopylov URS
1983 Lutz Hesslich GDR
1985 Lutz Hesslich GDR
1986 Michael Hubner GDR
1987 Lutz Hesslich GDR
1989 Bill Huck GDR
1989 Bill Huck GDR
1991 Jens Fiedler GER

AMATEUR 1 KM TIME TRIAL
First held 1966
1970 Niels Fredborg DEN
1971 Eduard Rapp URS
1973 Janusz Kierzkowski POL
1974 Eduard Rapp URS
1975 Klaus Gronke GDR
1977 Lothar Thoms GDR
1978 Lothar Thoms GDR
1979 Lothar Thoms GDR
1981 Lothar Thoms GDR
1982 Fredy Schmidtke FRG
1983 Sergey Kopylov URS
1985 Jens Glucklich GDR
1986 Maik Malchow GDR
1987 Martin Vinnicombe AUS
1989 Jens Glucklich GDR
1990 Aleks. Kirichenko URS
1991 Jose Manuel Moreno ESP

AMATEUR 4KM PURSUIT
First held 1946
1970 Xavier Kurmann SUI
1971 Martin-E Rodriguez COL
1973 Knut Knudsen NOR
1974 Hans Lutz FRG
1975 Thomas Huschke GDR
1977 Norbert Durpisch GDR
1978 Detlef Macha GDR
1979 Nikolay Makarov URS
1981 Detlef Macha GDR
1982 Detlef Macha GDR
1983 Viktor Kupovets URS
1985 Vyacheslav Yekimov URS
1986 Vyacheslav Yekimov URS
1987 Gintautas Umaras URS
1989 Vyacheslav Yekimov URS
1990 Yevgeniy Berzhin URS
1991 Jens Lehmann GER

AMATEUR 4KM TEAM PURSUIT
First held 1962
1970 West Germany
1971 Italy
1973 West Germany
1974 West Germany
1975 West Germany
1977 East Germany
1978 East Germany
1979 East Germany
1981 East Germany
1982 Soviet Union
1983 West Germany
1985 Italy
1986 Czechoslovakia
1987 Soviet Union
1989 East Germany
1990 Soviet Union
1991 Germany

AMATEUR MOTOR-PACED
*Held at 100km 1893-1914; for 1
hour 1958-71; at50km from 1970*
1970 Cees Stam NED
1971 Horst Gnas FRG
1972 Horst Gnas FRG
1973 Horst Gnas FRG
1974 Jean Breuer FRG
1975 Gaby Minneboo NED
1976 Gaby Minneboo NED
1977 Gaby Minneboo NED
1978 Rainer Podlesch GDR
1979 Matthe Pronk NED
1980 Gaby Minneboo NED
1981 Matthe Pronk NED
1982 Gaby Minneboo NED
1983 Rainer Podlesch GDR
1984 Jan de Nijs NED
1985 Roberto Dotti ITA
1986 Mario Gentili ITA
1987 Mario Gentili ITA
1988 Vincenzo Colamartino ITA
1989 Roland Konigshofer AUT
1990 Roland Konigshofer AUT
1991 Roland Konigshofer AUT
1992 Carsten Podlesch GER

AMATEUR 50KM POINTS
First held 1976
1976 Walter Baumgartner SUI
1977 Constant Tourne BEL
1978 Noel de Jonckheere BEL
1979 Jiri Slama TCH
1980 Gary Sutton AUS
1981 Lutz Haueisen GDR
1982 Hans-Joachim Pohl GDR
1983 Michael Marcussen DEN
1985 Martin Penc TCH
1986 Dan Frost DEN
1987 Marat Ganeeyev URS

World Champions

1989	Marat Satybyidiev	URS
1990	Stephen McGlede	AUS
1991	Bruno Risi	SUI

AMATEUR TANDEM SPRINT
First held 1966

1970	Jorgen Barth	
	Rainer Muller	FRG
1971	Jurgen Geschke	
	Werner Otto	GDR
1973	Vladimir Vackar	
	Miroslav Vymazal	TCH
1974	Vladimir Vackar	
	Miroslav Vymazal	TCH
1976	Benedykt Kocot	
	Janusz Kotlinski	POL
1977	Vladimir Vackar	
	Miroslav Vymazal	TCH
1978	Vladimir Vackar	
	Miroslav Vymazal	TCH
1979	Yave Cahard	
	Frank Depine	FRA
1980	Van Kucirek	
	Pavel Martinek	TCH
1981	Van Kucirek	
	Pavel Martinek	TCH
1982	Van Kucirek	
	Pavel Martinek	TCH
1983	Philippe Vernet	
	Frank Depine	FRA
1984	Jorgen Greil	
	Frank Weber	FRG
1985	Vitezlav Voboril	
	Roman Rehousek	TCH
1986	Vitezlav Voboril	
	Roman Rehousek	TCH
1987	Fabrice Colas	
	Frederic Magne	FRA
1988	Fabrice Colas	
	Frederic Magne	FRA
1989	Fabrice Colas	
	Frederic Magne	FRA
1990	Gianiuca Capitano	
	Federico Paris	ITA
1991	Eyk Pokorny	
	Emanuel Raasch	GER
1992	Gianiuca Capitano	
	Federico Paris	ITA

AMATEUR ROAD RACE

1970	Jorgen Schmidt	DEN
1971	Regis Ovion	FRA
1973	Ryszard Szurkowski	POL
1974	Janusz Kowalski	POL
1975	Andre Gevers	NED
1977	Claudio Corti	ITA
1978	Gilbert Glaus	SUI
1979	Gianni Giacomini	ITA
1981	Andrey Vedernikov	URS
1982	Bernd Drogan	GDR
1983	Uwe Raab	GDR

1985	Lech Piasecki	POL
1986	Uwe Ampler	GDR
1987	Richard Vivien	FRA
1989	Joachim Halupczok	POL
1990	Mirko Gualdi	ITA
1991	Viktor Ryaksinskiy	URS
1993	Jan Ullrich	GER
1994	Alex Pederson	DEN
1995	D Nellison	HOL

AMATEUR TEAM TIME TRIAL

1962	Italy
1963	France
1964	Italy
1965	Italy
1966	Denmark
1967	Sweden
1968	Sweden
1969	Sweden
1970	Soviet Union
1971	Belgium
1973	Poland
1974	Sweden
1975	Poland
1977	Soviet Union
1978	Nedland
1979	East Germany
1981	East Germany
1982	Nedland
1983	Soviet Union
1985	Soviet Union
1986	Nedland
1987	Italy
1989	East Germany
1991	Italy
1993	Italy
1994	Italy

PROFESSIONAL SPRINT

1970	Gordon Johnson	AUS
1971	Leijin Loevesijn	NED
1972	Robert van Lancker	BEL
1973	Robert van Lancker	BEL
1974	Peder Pedersen	DEN
1975	John Nicnedson	AUS
1976	John Nicnedson	AUS
1977	Koichi Nakano	JPN
1978	Koichi Nakano	JPN
1979	Koichi Nakano	JPN
1980	Koichi Nakano	JPN
1981	Koichi Nakano	JPN
1982	Koichi Nakano	JPN
1983	Koichi Nakano	JPN
1984	Koichi Nakano	JPN
1985	Koichi Nakano	JPN
1986	Koichi Nakano	JPN
1987	Noboyuki Tawara	JPN
1988	Stephen Pate	AUS
1989	Claudio Golinelli	ITA

1990	Michael Hubner	GDR
1991	Carey Hall	AUS
	failed a drugs test	
	title left vacant	
1992	Michael Hubner	GER

PROFESSIONAL 5KM PURSUIT
First held in 1939

1970	Hugh Porter	GBR
1971	Dirk Baert	BEL
1972	Hugh Porter	GBR
1973	Hugh Porter	GBR
1974	Roy Schuiten	NED
1975	Roy Schuiten	NED
1976	Francesco Moser	ITA
1977	Gregor Braun	FRG
1978	Gregor Braun	FRG
1979	Bert Osterbosch	NED
1980	Tony Doyle	GBR
1981	Alain Bondue	FRA
1982	Alain Bondue	FRA
1983	Steele Bishop	AUS
1984	Hans-Henrik Oersted	DEN
1985	Hans-Henrik Oersted	DEN
1986	Tony Doyle	GBR
1987	Hans-Henrik Oersted	DEN
1988	Lech Piasecki	POL
1989	Colin Sturgess	GBR
1990	Vyacheslav Yekimov	URS
1991	Francis Moreau	FRA
1992	Mike McCarthy	USA

PROFESSIONAL POINTS PACE
First held 1980

1980	Stan Tourne	BEL
1981	Urs Freuler	SUI
1982	Urs Freuler	SUI
1983	Urs Freuler	SUI
1984	Urs Freuler	SUI
1985	Urs Freuler	SUI
1986	Urs Freuler	SUI
1987	Urs Freuler	SUI
1988	Daniel Wyder	SUI
1989	Urs Freuler	SUI
1990	Laurent Blondl	FRA
1991	Vyacheslav Yekimov	URS
1992	Bruno Risi	SUI

PROFESSIONAL KEIRIN
First held 1980

1980	Danny Clark	AUS
1981	Danny Clark	AUS
1982	Gordon Singleton	Can
1983	Urs Freuler	SUI
1984	Robert Dill-Bundi	SUI
1985	Urs Freuler	SUI
1986	Michel Vaarten	BEL
1987	Harurni Honda	Jap
1988	Claudio Golinelli	ITA
	failed drugs test	
	title left vacant	

World Champions

1989	Claudio Golinelli ITA
1990	Michael Hubner GDR
1991	Michael Hubner GER
1992	Michael Hubner GER

PROFESSIONAL MOTOR-PACED
First held 1895

1970	Ehrenfried Rudolph FRG
1971	Theo Verschueren BEL
1972	Theo Verschueren BEL
1973	Cees Stam NED
1974	Cees Stam NED
1975	Dieter Kemper FRG
1976	Wilfried Peffgen FRG
1977	Cees Stam NED
1978	Wilfried Peffgen FRG
1979	Martin Venix NED
1980	Wilfried Peffgen FRG
1981	Rene Kos NED
1982	Martin Venix NED
1983	Bruno Vicini ITA
1984	Horst Schotz FRG
1985	Bruno Vicini ITA
1986	Bruno Vicini ITA
1987	Max Hurtzler SUI
1988	Danny Clark AUS
1989	Giovanni Renosto ITA
1990	Walter Brugna ITA
1991	Danny Clark AUS
1992	Peter Steiger SUI

PROFESSIONAL ROAD RACE
First held 1927

1970	Jean-Pierre Monsere BEL
1971	Eddy Merckx BEL
1972	Marino Basso ITA
1973	Felice Gimondi ITA
1974	Eddy Merckx BEL
1975	Hennie Kuiper NED
1976	Freddy Maertens BEL
1977	Francesco Moser ITA
1978	Gerrie Knetemann NED
1979	Jan Raas NED
1980	Bernard Hinault FRA
1981	Freddy Maertens BEL
1982	Giuseppe Saronni ITA
1983	Greg LeMond USA
1984	Claude Criquielion BEL
1985	Joop Zoetemelk NED
1986	Moreno Argentin ITA
1987	Stephen Roche IRE
1988	Maurizio Fondriest ITA
1989	Greg LeMond USA
1990	Rudy Dhaenens BEL
1991	Gianni Bugno ITA
1992	Gianni Bugno ITA
1993	Lance Armstrong USA
1994	Luc Leblanc FRA
1995	Abraham Olano ESP

Women's Events

SPRINT
First held 1958

1969	Galina Tsareva URS
1970	Galina Tsareva URS
1971	Galina Tsareva URS
1972	Galina Yermolayeva URS
1973	Sheila Young USA
1974	Tamara Piltsikova URS
1975	Sue Novarra USA
1976	Sheila Young USA
1977	Galina Tsareva URS
1978	Galina Tsareva URS
1979	Galina Tsareva URS
1980	Sue Reber-Novarra USA
1981	Sheila Ochowitz-Young USA
1982	Connee Paraskevin USA
1983	Connee Paraskevin USA
1984	Connee Paraskevin USA
1985	Isabelle Nicoloso FRA
1986	Christa Rothenburger GDR
1987	Erika Salumyae URS
1989	Erika Salumyae URS
1990	C Young-Paraskevin USA
1991	Ingrid Haringa NED
1993	Tanya Dubnikoff CAN
1994	Galina Enioukina RUS
1995	Félicia Ballanger FRA

3KM PURSUIT

1970	Tamara Garkushina URS
1971	Tamara Garkushina URS
1972	Tamara Garkushina URS
1973	Tamara Garkushina URS
1974	Tamara Garkushina URS
1975	K van Oosten-Hage NED
1976	K van Oosten-Hage NED
1977	Vera Kuznetsova URS
1978	K van Oosten-Hage NED
1979	K van Oosten-Hage NED
1980	Nadezhda Kibardina URS
1981	Nadezhda Kibardina URS
1982	Rebecca Twigg USA
1983	Connie Carpenter USA
1984	Rebecca Twigg USA
1985	Rebecca Twigg USA
1986	Jeannie Longo FRA
1987	Rebecca Twigg USA
1988	Jeannie Longo FRA
1989	Jeannie Longo FRA
1990	L van Moorsel NED
1991	Petra Rossner GER
1993	Rebecca Twigg USA
1994	Marion Clignet FRA
1995	Rebecca Twigg USA

500M TIME TRIAL

1995	Félicia Ballanger FRA

30KM POINTS

1987	Sally Hodge GBR
	demonstration event
1989	Jeannie Longo FRA
1990	Karen Nedliday NZL
1991	Ingrid Haringa NED
1992	Ingrid Haringa NED
1993	Ingrid Haringa NED
1994	Ingrid Haringa NED
1995	Svetlana Samokhvalova RUS

ROAD RACE
First held 1958

1970	Anna Konkina URS
1971	Anna Konkina URS
1972	Genevieve Gambillon FRA
1973	Nicole Vandenbroeck BEL
1974	Genevieve Gambillon FRA
1975	Trijntje Fopma NED
1976	K van Oosten-Hage NED
1977	Josiane Bost FRA
1978	Beate Habetz FRG
1979	Petra de Bruin NED
1980	Beth Heiden USA
1981	Ute Enzenauer FRG
1982	Mandy Jones GBR
1983	Marianne Berglund SWE
1985	Jeannie Longo FRA
1986	Jeannie Longo FRA
1987	Jeannie Longo FRA
1989	Jeannie Longo FRA
1990	Catherine Marsal FRA
1991	L van Moorsel NED
1993	L Van Moorsel NED
1994	Monica Valvik NOR
1995	Jeannie Longo FRA

INDIVIDUAL TIME TRIAL
First held 1994

1994	Karen Kurreck USA
1995	Jeannie Longo FRA

WOMEN'S 50 KM TEAM TRIAL

1987	Soviet Union
1988	Italy
1989	Soviet Union
1990	Netherlands
1991	France
1992	USA
1993	Russia
1994	Russia

Grand Tours Winners

TOUR DE FRANCE
First held in 1903

1903	Maurice Garin FRA
1904	Henri Cornet FRA
1905	Louis Trousselier FRA
1906	Rene Pottier FRA
1907	Lucien Petit-Breton FRA
1908	Lucien Petit-Breton FRA
1909	Francois Faber LUX
1910	Octave Lapize FRA
1911	Gustave Garrigou FRA
1912	Odile Defraye BEL
1913	Philippe Thys BEL
1914	Philippe Thys BEL
1919	Firmin Lambot BEL
1920	Philippe Thys BEL
1921	Leon Scieur BEL
1922	Firmin Lambot BEL
1923	Henri Pelissier FRA
1924	Ottavio Bottecchia ITA
1925	Ottavio Bottecchia ITA
1926	Lucien Buysse BEL
1927	Nicholas Frantz LUX
1928	Nicholas Frantz LUX
1929	Maurice De Waele BEL
1930	Andre Leducq FRA
1931	Antonin Magne FRA
1932	Andre Leducq FRA
1933	Georges Speicher FRA
1934	Antonin Magne FRA
1935	Romain Maes BEL
1936	Sylvere Maes BEL
1937	Roger Lapebie FRA
1938	Gino Bartali ITA
1939	Sylvere Maes BEL
1947	Jean Robic FRA
1948	Gino Bartali ITA
1949	Fausto Coppi ITA
1950	Ferdinand Kubler SUI
1951	Hugo Koblet SUI
1952	Fausto Coppi ITA
1953	Louison Bobet FRA
1954	Louison Bobet FRA
1955	Louison Bobet FRA
1956	Roger Walkowiak FRA
1957	Jacques Anquetil FRA
1958	Charly Gaul LUX
1959	Federico Bahamontes ESP
1960	Gastone Nencini ITA
1961	Jacques Anquetil FRA
1962	Jacques Anquetil FRA
1963	Jacques Anquetil FRA
1964	Jacques Anquetil FRA
1965	Felice Gimondi ITA
1966	Lucien Aimar FRA
1967	Roger Pingeon FRA
1968	Jan Janssen HOL
1969	Eddy Merckx BEL
1970	Eddy Merckx BEL
1971	Eddy Merckx BEL
1972	Eddy Merckx BEL
1973	Luis Ocana ESP
1974	Eddy Merckx BEL
1975	Bernard Thevenet FRA
1976	Lucien van Impe BEL
1977	Bernard Thevenet FRA
1978	Bernard Hinault FRA
1979	Bernard Hinault FRA
1980	Joop Zoetemelk HOL
1981	Bernard Hinault FRA
1982	Bernard Hinault FRA
1983	Laurent Fignon FRA
1984	Laurent Fignon FRA
1985	Bernard Hinault FRA
1986	Greg LeMond USA
1987	Stephen Roche IRE
1988	Pedro Delgado ESP
1989	Greg LeMond USA
1989	Greg LeMond USA
1991	Miguel Induráin ESP
1992	Miguel Induráin ESP
1993	Miguel Induráin ESP
1994	Miguel Induráin ESP
1995	Miguel Induráin ESP
1989	Pedro Delgado ESP
1990	Marco Giovannetti ITA
1991	Melchior Mauri ESP
1992	Tony Rominger SUI
1993	Alex Zülle SUI
1994	Tony Rominger SUI
1995	Laurent Jalabert FRA

GIRO D'ITALIE (TOUR OF ITALY)
First held 1909

1980	Bernard Hinault FRA
1981	Giovani Battaglin ITA
1982	Bernard Hinault FRA
1983	Guiseppe Saronni ITA
1984	Francesco Moser ITA
1985	Bernard Hinault FRA
1986	Roberto Visentini ITA
1987	Stephen Roche IRE
1988	Amdy Hampsten USA
1989	Laurent Fignon FRA
1990	Gianni Bugno ITA
1991	Franco Chioccioli ITA
1992	Miguel Induráin ESP
1993	Miguel Induráin ESP
1994	Evgeny Berzin RUS
1995	Tony Rominger SUI

VUELTA A ESPAÑA (TOUR OF SPAIN)
First held 1909

1980	Fausino Ruperez ESP
1981	Giovani Battaglin ITA
1982	Marino Lejaretta ESP
1983	Bernard Hinault FRA
1984	Eric Caritoux FRA
1985	Pedro Delgado ESP
1986	Alvaro Pino ESP
1987	Luis Herrera COL
1988	Sean Kelly IRL

Darts

Embassy World Championship

Lakeside CC, Frimley Green Jan 1-8

First Round

Richie Burnett WAL bt Peter Wright ENG	3-1
Russell Stewart AUS bt Alan Brown SCO	3-2
Sean Palfrey WAL bt Andy Jenkins ENG	3-1
Paul Hogan ENG bt Per Skau DEN	3-1
Paul Williams ENG bt Bob Taylor SCO	3-0
John Part CAN bt Paul Knighton ENG	3-2
Ronnie Sharp SCO bt Bobby George ENG	3-0
Andy Fordham ENG bt Nicky Turner ENG	3-2
Ian Brand ENG bt Wayne Atkins AUS	3-0
Mike Gregory ENG bt Yves Chamberland CAN	3-2
Kevin Painter ENG bt Magnus Caris SWE	3-2
Martin Adams ENG bt Bruno Raes BEL	3-1
Peter Hunt NZL bt Stefan Eeckelaert BEL	3-0
Colin Monk ENG bt Roland Scholten HOL	3-1
Dave Askew ENG bt Steve Beaton ENG	3-2
Raymond Barneveld HOL bt Les Wallace SCO	3-2

Second Round

Richie Burnett bt Russell Stewart	3-2
Paul Hogan bt Sean Palfrey	3-0
Paul Williams bt John Part	3-2
Andy Fordham bt Ronnie Sharp	3-2
Mike Gregory bt Ian Brand	3-2
Martin Adams bt Kevin Painter	3-0
Colin Monk bt Peter Hunt	3-2
Raymond Barneveld bt Dave Askew	3-0

Quarter-finals

Richie Burnett bt Paul Hogan	4-2
Andy Fordham bt Paul Williams	4-2
Martin Adams bt Mike Gregory	4-3
Raymond Barneveld bt Colin Monk	4-2

Semi-finals

Richie Burnett bt Andy Fordham	5-2
Raymond Barneveld bt Martin Adams	5-4

FINAL

Richie Burnett bt Raymond Barneveld	**6-3**

Skol World Championship

Circus Tavern, Purfleet   Dec 27-Jan 2

Quarter-finals

Rod Harrington bt Jamie Harvey	4-1
Peter Evison bt Kevin Spiolek	4-1
Phil Taylor bt Bob Anderson	4-1
John Lowe bt Dennis Smith	4-0

Semi-finals

Phil Taylor bt John Lowe	5-4
Rod Harrington bt Peter Evison	5-1

3rd/4th Play-off

John Lowe bt Peter Evison	4-2

FINAL

Rod Taylor bt Rod Harrington	**6-2**

British Open 1994

Park Inn Hotel, London   Dec

MEN

Al Hedman bt Andy Fordham 2-1

WOMEN

Frances Hoenselaar bt Pauline Dyer 3-2

Tournament Records

WORLD PROFESSIONAL CHAMPIONSHIPS

Year	Winner	Runner-up	Score
1978	Leighton Rees	John Lowe	11-7
1979	John Lowe	Leighton Rees	5-0
1980	Eric Bristow	Bobby George	5-3
1981	Eric Bristow	John Lowe	5-3
1982	Jocky Wilson	John Lowe	5-3
1983	Keith Deller	Eric Bristow	6-5
1984	Eric Bristow	Dave Whitcombe	7-1
1985	Eric Bristow	John Lowe	6-2
1986	Eric Bristow	Dave Whitcombe	6-0
1987	John Lowe	Eric Bristow	6-4
1988	Bob Anderson	John Lowe	6-4
1989	Jocky Wilson	Eric Bristow	6-4
1990	Phil Taylor	Eric Bristow	6-1
1991	Dennis Priestley	Eric Bristow	6-0
1992	Phil Taylor	Mike Gregory	6-5
1993	John Lowe	Alan Warriner	6-3
1994*	John Part	Bobby George	6-0
	Dennis Priestley	Phil Taylor	6-1
1995	Richie Burnett	Raymond Barneveld	6-3
	Rod Taylor	Rod Harrington	6-2

BDO version is given first, WDC version second

WORLD MASTERS

1974 **Cliff Inglis** ENG
1975 **Alan Evans** WAL
1976 **John Lowe** ENG
1977 **Eric Bristow** ENG
1978 **Ronnie Davis** ENG
1979 **Eric Bristow** ENG
1980 **John Lowe** ENG
1981 **Eric Bristow** ENG
1982 **Dave Whitcombe** ENG
1983 **Eric Bristow** ENG
1984 **Eric Bristow** ENG
1985 **Dave Whitcombe** ENG
1986 **Bob Anderson** ENG
1987 **Bob Anderson** ENG
1988 **Bob Anderson** ENG
1989 **Peter Evison** ENG
1990 **Phil Taylor** ENG
1991 **Rod Harrington** ENG
1992 **Dennis Priestley** ENG
1993 **Steve Beaton** ENG
1994 **Richie Burnett** ENG

WORLD CUP

Year	Individual title	Team title
1977	Leighton Rees WAL	Wales
1979	Nicky Virachkul USA	England
1981	John Lowe ENG	England
1983	Eric Bristow ENG	England
1985	Eric Bristow ENG	England
1987	Eric Bristow ENG	England
1989	Eric Bristow ENG	England
1991	John Lowe ENG	England
1993	Roland Scholten HOL	Wales

NEWS OF THE WORLD CHAMPIONSHIP

Competition terminated when paper withdrew its support in 1991. (British unless stated)

1948 **Harry Leadbetter**
1949 **Jack Boyce**
1950 **Dixie Newberry**
1951 **Harry Perryman**
1952 **Tommy Gibbons**
1953 **Jimmy Carr**
1954 **Oliver James**
1955 **Tom Reddington**
1956 **Trevor Peachey**
1957 **Alwyn Mullins**
1958 **Tommy Gibbons**
1959 **Albert Welch**
1960 **Tom Reddington**
1961 **Alec Adamson**
1962 **Eddie Brown**
1963 **Robbie Rumney**
1964 **Tom Barrett**
1965 **Tom Barrett**
1966 **Wilf Ellis**
1967 **Wally Seaton**
1968 **Bill Duddy**
1969 **Barry Twomlow**
1970 **Henry Barney**
1971 **Dennis Filkins**
1972 **Brian Netherton**
1973 **Ivor Hodgkinson**
1974 **Peter Chapman**
1975 **Derek White**
1976 **Bill Lennard**
1977 **Mick Norris**
1978 **Stefan Lord** SWE
1979 **Bobby George**
1980 **Stefan Lord** SWE
1981 **John Lowe**
1982 **Roy Morgan**
1983 **Eric Bristow**
1984 **Eric Bristow**
1985 **Dave Lee**
1986 **Bobby George**
1987 **Mike Gregory**
1988 **Mike Gregory**
1989 **Dave Whitcombe**
1990 **Paul Cook**

Equestrianism ━━━━━━━

Britain's record in the European Championships is enviable; 16 times in 21 championships spread over 42 years has either the team or individual gold been won by domestic riders and their mounts. On ten occasions both titles have come home. It caused, therefore, few shock waves when Great Britain won the team title again, with some ease, from the French and Irish teams. Rather the surprise came in the condition of one of the riders. Mary King announced, after the victory, that she was five months pregnant. Well, Ingrid Kristiansen won the world cross-country title in Gateshead in 1983 when she was almost five months pregnant and, such was the success of athletic mothers at that time, that distance runners (though not Kristiansen, it should be said) were getting pregnant deliberately in the belief that it would subsequently improve their performance. As King also won a bronze in the individual event, on the notoriously shaky jumper King William, we can now watch to see if a similar trend starts in Eventing. Tough on William Fox-Pitt if it does. Even tougher if it works.

Britain could almost claim the individual title as well. Only a year earlier Lucy Thompson had been a British rider. She changed allegiance to Ireland, but just to rub it in at Rome took the title on Welton Romance, a horse that she had bought for her from three-time European champion Ginny Elliott. We might have felt more generous except that Ireland had already reclaimed another title.

In European show jumping our competition record is good, rather than auspicious. In 1989, John Whitaker (on Milton) and the team doubled up, but in the two championships since the golds have proved elusive. Michael Whitaker, who won a silver and a bronze at Gijon two years earlier, could have come no closer. Everest Two Step clattered the last in the jump-off and then watched Peter Charles, on the Belgian bred La Ina, equal his faults, but better his time. Charles was born in Liverpool and still lives in England and only chose to ride for Ireland four years ago. The change was obviously good for both of them; it was Charles' and Ireland's first major success. Of course, if you wanted to be paranoid, the Swiss team which took the team title, included Lesley McNaught-Mändli, who is also British and now rides for her husband's country.

Nick Skelton has been somewhat overhadowed by the Whitakers, but took his first major individual title when he won the Volvo World Cup in Gothenburg. Michael Whitaker was the overnight leader on Everest Two Step, crashed through the blue and white poles of Fence Seven and ruled himself out. "I think he thought they were water," said Whitaker. The 37-year-old Skelton guided Everest Dollar Girl through a clear round and duly collected the first prize of £55,000, plus a £17,000 Volvo.

Skelton almost didn't get the car; Volvo was on the verge of pulling out of the World cup, irate that the International Equestrian Federation (FEI) had sold the rights to the championships and that the final could not be shown on Swedish television. The FEI, which had done a deal with the German TV company DSF, then had to buy part of the rights back again. In Britain, there's no Volvo to put the financial backbone into the sport, but the banking and insurance group Frizzell did commit £250,000 to the sport this year. However, there's less money around generally as TV remains ambivalent.

European Three-day Championship

Rome   Sep 28-Oct 1
Team Championship
1 **Great Britain**   167.10
   Bathe (The Cool Customer), Fox-Pitt
   (Cosmopolitan II), Gifford (Midnight Blue II), King
   (King William)
2 France   231.45
   Bigot (Twist la Beige HN), Pons (Ramdame),
   Scherer (Urane des Pins),Willefert (Seducteur Biolay)
3 Ireland   238.60
   Smiley (Enterprise), Thompson (Welton Romance),
   McGrath (Yellow Earl), Barry (Vagabond Collongues)

Individual Championship
1 **Lucy Thompson**   IRL   41.55
   (Welton Romance)
2 Marie-Christine Duroy   FRA 45.30
   (Ut du Placineau BF)
3 Mary King   GBR 47.25
   (King William)

European Jumping Championship

St Gallen, Switzerland   Sep 20-24
Team Championship
1 **Switzerland**   8.00
   Melliger (Calvaro V), McNaight-Mändli (Doenhoff),
   Lauber (Bay Networks Escado), Fuchs (Major AC
   Folien)
2 Great Britain   12.00
   (Skelton (Everest Dollar Girl), M Whitaker (Everest
   Two Step), Bradley (Endeavour), J Whitaker
   (Welham)
3 France   16.00
   Godignon (Unic du Perchis), Bonneau (Urleven
   Pironniere), Ledermann (Rochet M), Bost (Souviens
   Toi III Equus)

Individual Championship
1 **Peter Charles***   IRL   8.00
   (La Ina)
2 Michael Whitaker*   GBR   8.00
   (Everest Twostep)
3 Willi Melliger   SUI 12.00
   (Calvaro V)
*After jump-off

Warsteiner Grand Prix   Time/Flts
1 **Michael Whitaker**   GBR   35.10/0.00
   (Everest Midnight Madness)
2 Roger-Yves Bost   FRA   36.17/0.00
   (Vondeen)
3 Herve Godignon   FRA   38.51/0.00
   (Twist du Valon)

European Dressage Championship

Mondorf-les-Bains, Luxembourg   Aug 30-Sep 3
Team Championship
1 Germany   5483
2 Netherlands   5374
3 France   4964
8 Great Britain   4699

Individual Championship
1 **Isabell Werth**   GER   236.29
   (Nobilis Gigolo)
2 Anky van Grunsven   NED   232.11
   (Cameleon Bonfire)
3 Sven Rothenberger   NED   221.87
   (Olympic Bo)

FEI-BCM WORLD JUMPING
RANKINGS
as at Sep 24

1 Ludger Beerbaum	GER	4362.5
2 Franke Sloothaak	GER	3977.9
3 Michael Whitaker	GBR	3852.7
4 Jan Tops	NED	3632.6
5 Roger-Yves Bost	FRA	2674.7
6 John Whitaker	GBR	2662.9
7 Hervé Godignon	FRA	2351.6
8 Nick Skelton	GBR	2226.0
9 Hugo Simon	AUT	2208.6
10 Jos Lansink	NED	2170.7
11 Thomas Fuchs	SUI	2009.5
12 Lesley McNaught-Mändli	SUI	1982.1
13 Markus Fuchs	SUI	1973.2
14 Peter Charles	IRL	1706.8
15 Michel Robert	FRA	1703.4
16 Leslie Burr-Lenehan	USA	1664.5
17 Ludo Philippaerts	BEL	1649.2
18 Eddie Macken	IRL	1594.3
19 Rodrigo Pessoa	BRA	1524.5
20 Lars Nieberg	GER	1468.2

Show Jumping

Volvo World Cup Final
Gothenburg   *Apr 13-17*
Final Placings

	Rider (Horse/s)	Cty	Pens
1	**Nick Skelton (Everest Dollar Girl)**	**GBR**	**7**
2	Lars Nieberg (For Pleasure)	GER	9
3	Lesley McNaught-Mändli	SUI	13
	(Barcelona SVH/Doenhoff)		
4	Ludger Beerbaum	GER	14.5
	(Gaylord/Sprehe Ratina Z)		
5	Michael Whitaker (Everest Two Step)	GBR	16.5
6	Peter Eriksson (Robin Z)	SWE	17
	Chris Kappler (Zanzibar)	USA	17
	Jan Tops	NED	17
	(Sonora La Silla/ Top Gun La Silla)		
9	Eddie Macken (Miss FAN)	IRL	17.5
10	McLain Ward (Orchestre)	USA	19

Nations Cup 1995
Standings after 21 events (5 remaining)

1	**France**	**30.00**
2	Germany	28.00
3	Great Britain	24.00
4	Ireland	23.00
5	Switzerland	22.50
6	Netherlands	21.50

Nations Cup 1994
Final Standings *(over 25 events, Apr 23-Nov 19)*

1	**Germany**	**34.00**
2	Switzerland	32.00
3	Italy	27.50
4	Netherlands	25.50
5	Great Britain	24.50
6	Sweden	23.50

Presidents Cup 1995
Standings after 25 events (7 remaining)

1	**France**	**33.00**
2	Switzerland	32.00
3	Germany	28.00
4	Great Britain	28.00
5	Ireland	27.00
6	United States	23.50

Presidents Cup 1994
Final Standings *(over 29 events, Jan 16-Nov 19)*

1	**Germany**	**40.00**
2	Switzerland	36.00
3	Italy	27.50
	Great Britain	27.50
5	Netherlands	25.50
6	United States	25.00

Horse of the Year Show
Wembley Arena   Sep 26-Oct 1
LEADING SHOWJUMPER

1	**Michael Whitaker (Everest Midnight Madness)**	
2	John Whitaker (Everest Gammon)	GBR
3	Paul Darragh (Ghandy)	IRL

TWIN TOWERS TROPHY

1	**Robert Smith (Tees Hanauer)**	**GBR**
2	Michael Whitaker (Everest Magic Carpet)	GBR
3	John Whitaker (Everest Randi)	GBR

SPEED HORSE OF THE YEAR

1	**Michael Whitaker (Everest My Mesieur)**	GBR
2	E Wauters (Isuara van de Helle)	BEL
3	Nick Skelton (Everest Limited Edition)	GBR

GOLDEN SADDLE GRAND PRIX

1	**Nick Skelton (Everest Showtime)**	**GBR**
2	Paul Darragh (Ghandy)	IRL
3	Robert Smith (Tees Hanauer)	GBR

WEMBLEY INTERNATIONAL CUP

1	**Matthew Lanni (Secret Pride)**	**GBR**
2	Zöe Bates (Floyd McBee)	GBR
3	James Fisher (Bowriver Queen)	GBR

Hickstead Derby Meeting
Hickstead, W Sussex   Aug 17-20
SILK CUT DERBY

1	**Capt John Ledingham (Kilbaha)**	**IRL**
2	John Whitaker (Everest Gammon)	GBR
=3	Geoff Luckett (Vantage)	GBR
	Gerry Mullins (Millstreet Ruby)	IRL
	John Whitaker (Welham)	GBR

SILK CUT SPEED DERBY

1	**Capt John Ledingham (Castlepollard)**	**IRL**
2	Capr John Ledingham (Garraun)	IRL
3	Francis Connors (Diamond Express)	IRL

SILK CUT TROPHY

1	**John Whitaker (Roddy's Revenge)**	**GBR**
2	John Renwick (Already)	GBR
3	Peter Murphy (Orthos)	GBR

OLYMPIC SHOWJUMPING QUALIFIERS

The 17 nations that qualify for the Olympic Games are: Netherlands (holders), United States (hosts), Germany, France, Switzerland, Brazil, Great Britain, Canada, Mexico, Colombia, Chile, New Zealand, Japan, Ireland, Belgium, Sweden, Austria

Royal International Horse Show
Hickstead   July 13-16

KING GEORGE V GOLD CUP
1 **Robert Splaine**   IRL   **0 Flts**
   (Heather Blaze)
2 Michael Whitaker   GBR   4 Flts
   (Everest Midnight Madness)
3 William Funnell   GBR   4 Flts
   (Comex)

QUEEN ELIZABETH II CUP
1 **Marion Hughes**   IRL   **0 Flts/42.32**
   (Flo Jo)
2 Di Lampard   GBR   0 Flts/45.01
   (Abbervail Dream)
3 Malin Baryard   SWE   0 Flts/45.02
   (Corrmint)

ROYAL INTERNATIONAL CLASSIC
1 **William Funnell**   GBR   **0 flts/50.99**
   (Comex)
2 Malin Baryard   SWE   4 Flts/49.50
   (Corrmint)
3 Robert Splaine   IRL   4 Flts/50.24
   (Heather Blaze)

WEST SANDS SPEED GRAND PRIX
1 **Geoffrey Glazzard**   GBR   **78.15**
   (Hello Feliz)
2 Geoff Luckett   GBR   78.40
   (Vantage)
3 William Funnell   GBR   78.60
   (Impressionist)

The Olympia International
The Grand Hall, Olympia   Dec 15-19, 1994

VOLVO WORLD CUP QUALIFIER
1 **Jan Tops (Sonora La Silla)   NED**
2 Ludger Beerbaum (Sprehe Gaylord) GER
3 Leslie McNaught-Mändli (Pirol IV) SUI

CHRISTMAS CAROL STAKES
1 **Michael Whitaker (Everest My Mesieur) GBR**
2 Marie Edgar (Everest Winstar)   GBR
3 Stefan Lauber (Saphir)   SUI

CHRISTMAS CAKE STAKES
1 **Nick Skelton (Everest Dollar Girl) GBR**
2 Roger-Yves Bost (President Papillon) FRA
3 Goeff Billington (It's Otto)   GBR

MINCE PIE PUISSANCE
1 **Robert Smith (Gold)   GBR**
2 Thomas Fruhmann (Bockmann's As)   AUT
3 Geoff Billington (Mancuso)   GBR

Horse of the Year Show
Wembley Arena   Sep 29-Oct 2, 1994

EVEREST NATIONAL CHAMPIONSHIP
All GBR
1 **John Whitaker (Everest Grannusch)**
2 Michael Whitaker (Everest Midnight Madness)
3 William Funnell (Comex)

SNOWFLAKE INTERNATIONAL CUP
1 **Marion Hughes (Flo Jo)   IRL**
2 Trevor Coyle (Cruising)   IRL
3 Nick Skelton (Everest Showtime)GBR

INTERNATIONAL TROPHY
1 **Eddie Macken (FAN Skyview)   IRL**
2 Philippe Lejeune (Hot Sport)   BEL
3 Peter Charles (La Ina)   IRL

MASTERLOCK DRESSAGE GRAND PRIX
1 **Sven Rothenberger (Bo)   NED**
2 Ferdi Eilberg (Arun Tor)   GBR
3 Emile Faurie (Virtu)   GBR

VOLVO WORLD CUP QUALIFIER - DRESSAGE
1 **Anky van Grunsven (Olympic Cocktail) NED**
2 Sven Rothenberger (Bo)   NED
3 Emile Faurie (Virtu)   GBR

LEADING SHOWJUMPER
1 **Michael Whitaker (Everest Midnight Madness)**

TOP 20 HORSES
January 1-July 31

1	**Everest Dollar Girl**	**£91,230**
2	**Everest Two Step**	**£60,691**
3	**It's Otto**	**£57,476**
4	**Everest Grannusch**	**£39,692**
5	**Everest Showtime**	**£31,841**
6	**Everest Midnight Madness**	**£31,819**
7	**Comex**	**£27,256**
8	**Bowriver Queen**	**£26,063**
9	**Everest Magic Carpet**	**£18,604**
10	**Sublime**	**£18,526**
11	**Itziweeni**	**£16,259**
12	**Orthos**	**£15,588**
13	**Everest Gammon**	**£14,504**
14	**Jolly Boy**	**£14,222**
15	**Everest Randi**	**£12,336**
16	**Hello Oscar**	**£11,112**
17	**Rose Princess**	**£10,924**
18	**Welham**	**£10,914**
19	**Suntory**	**£10,910**
20	**Ben Hur**	**£10,84**

Dressage

Volvo World Cup Final
Burbank, Los Angeles   Apr 20-23
Individual
1 Anky van Grunsven   NED   100
   (Cameleon Bonfire)
2 Monica Theodorescu   GER   95
   (Ganimedes Tecrent)
3 Sven Rothenberger   NED   90
   (Olympic Bo)

Three Day Eventing

Badminton
May 4-7
1 **Bruce Davidson (Eagle Lion)**   USA   46.60
2 Matt Ryan (Kibah Tic Toc)   AUS   48.30
3 Karen O'Connor (Biko)   USA   51.00

Punchestown
June 1-5
1 **Mary Thompson (Star Appeal)**   GBR   49.30
2 Matt Ryan (Alater Pedis)   AUS   51.20
3 Terry Boon (Vital Decision)   GBR   56.05

Bramham
June 8-11
1 **William Fox-Pitt (Cosmopolitan II)** GBR 42.40
2 Andrew Nicholson (Cartoon II)   NZL   49.20
3 Didier Seguret (Coeur de Rocker) FRA   58.40

Burghley
Aug 31-Sep 3
1 **Andrew Nicholson (Buckley Province)** NZL 50.00
2 Dag Albert (Nice 'n' Easy)   SWE   60.90
3 Justine Ward (The Bullett)   GBR   62.40

Blenheim
Sep 14-17
1 **Pippa Funnell (Bits and Pieces)** GBR 47.00
2 Paddy Muir (Maisy Brown)   GBR   54.40
3 Victoria Latta (Broadcast News)   NZL   59.00

Horse Trials

British Open Championship
Gatcombe Park   Aug 4-6
1 **William Fox-Pitt (Hackett's Chaka)** GBR 45.00
2 Mary King (Frizzell's Star Appeal) GBR   50.00
3 Kristina Gifford (Song & Dance Man) GBR   51.00

LAND ROVER THREE-DAY EVENT WORLD RANKINGS
as at August 23

1	Bruce Davidson	USA	311
2	Andrew Nicholson	NZL	226
3	Matt Ryan	AUS	181
4	Mary King	GBR	146
5	Mark Todd	NZL	145
6	Ian Stark	GBR	123
7	Didier Seguret	FRA	122
8	Kristina Gifford	GBR	120
9	Sam Lyle	AUS	118
10	Terry Boon	GBR	117

World Champions

SHOW JUMPING
World Championship - Men

Year	Rider	Horse
1953	Francisco Goyoago ESP	Quorum
1954	Hans Gunter Winkler FRG	Halla
1955	Hans Gunter Winkler FRG	Halla
1956	Raimondo d'Inzeo ITA	Merano
1960	Raimondo d'Inzeo ITA	Gowran Girl
1966	P Jonqueres d'Oriola FRA	Pomone B
1970	David Broome GBR	Beethoven
1974	Hartwig Steenken FRG	Simona
1978	Gerd Wilffang FRG	Roman
1982	Norbert Koof FRG	Fire II
1986	Gail Greenhough CAN	Mr T
1990	Eric Navet FRA	Quito de Baussy
1994	Franke Sloothaak GER	San Patrignano Weihaiwej

World Championship - Women

Year	Rider	Horse
1965	Marion Coakes GBR	Stroller
1970	Janou Lefebvre FRA	Rocket
1974	Janou Tissot (née Lefebvre)	Rocket

Volvo World Cup

Year	Rider	Horse
1979	Hugo Simon AUT	Gladstone
1980	Conrad Homfeld USA	Balbuco
1981	Michael Matz USA	Jet Run
1982	Melanie Smith USA	Calypso
1983	Norman Dello Joio USA	I Love You
1984	Mario Deslauriers CAN	Aramis
1985	Conrad Homfeld USA	Abdullah
1986	Leslie Burr-Lenehan USA	McLain
1987	Katharine Burdsall USA	The Natural
1988	Ian Millar CAN	Big Ben
1989	Ian Millar CAN	Big Ben
1990	John Whitaker GBR	Milton
1991	John Whitaker GBR	Milton
1992	Thomas Fruhmann AUT	Bockmann's Genius
1993	Ludger Beerbaum GER	Almox Ratina Z
1994	Jos Lansink HOL	Bollvorm's Libero H
1995	Nick Skelton GBR	Midnight Madness

THREE-DAY EVENTING
World Championships - Individual

Year	Rider	Horse
1966	Carlos Moratorio ARG	Chalon
1970	Mary Gordon-Watson GBR	Cornishman V
1974	Bruce Davidson USA	Irish Cap
1978	Bruce Davidson USA	Might Tango
1982	Lucinda Green GBR	Regal Realm
1986	Virginia Leng GBR	Priceless
1990	Blyth Tait NZL	Messiah
1994	Vaughan Jefferis NZL	Bounce

Badminton Horse Trials

Year	Rider	Horse
1949	John Shedden GBR	Golden Willow
1950	Tony Collings GBR	Remus

Year	Rider	Horse
1951	Hans Schwarzenbach SUI	Vae Victus
1952	Mark Darley IRE	Emily Little
1953	Lawrence Rook GBR	Starlight
1954	Margaret Hough GBR	Bambi
1955	Frank Weldon GBR *	Kilbarry
1956	Frank Weldon GBR	Kilbarry
1957	Sheila Willcox GBR	High and Mighty
1958	Sheila Willcox GBR	High and Mighty
1959	Sheila Waddington (née Willcox) GBR	Airs and Graces
1960	Bill Roycroft AUS	Our Solo
1961	Lawrence Morgan AUS	Salad Days
1962	A Drummond-Hay GBR	Merely-a-Monarch
1963	Susan Fleet GBR **	Gladiator
1964	James Templer GBR	M'Lord Connolly
1965	Eddie Boylan IRE	Durlas Eile
1966	*Not held*	
1967	Celia Ross-Taylor GBR	Jonathan
1968	Jane Bullen GBR	Our Nobby
1969	Richard Walker GBR	Pasha
1970	Richard Meade GBR	The Poacher
1971	Mark Phillips GBR	Great Ovation
1972	Mark Phillips GBR	Great Ovation
1973	Lucinda Prior-Palmer GBR	Be Fair
1974	Mark Phillips GBR	Columbus
1975	*Cancelled after dressage*	
1976	Lucinda Prior-Palmer GBR	Wideawake
1977	Lucinda Prior-Palmer GBR	George
1978	Jane Holderness-Roddam (née Bullen) GBR	Warrior
1979	Lucinda Prior-Palmer GBR	Killaire
1980	Mark Todd NZL	Southern Comfort
1981	Mark Phillips NZL	Lincoln
1982	Richard Meade GBR	Speculator lil
1983	Lucinda Green (née Prior-Palmer) GBR	Regal Realm
1984	Lucinda Green GBR	Beagle Bay
1985	Virginia Holgate GBR	Priceless
1986	Ian Stark GBR	Sir Wattie
1987	*Not held*	
1988	Ian Stark GBR	Sir Wattie
1989	Virginia Leng (née Holgate) GBR	Master Craftsman
1990	Nicola Mcirvine GBR	Middle Road
1991	Rodney Powell GBR	The Irishman
1992	Mary Thomson GBR	King William
1993	Virginia Leng GBR	Welton Houdini
1994	Mark Todd GBR	Horton Point

Fencing

World Championships

The Hague, Holland   July 18-23

Men's Foil

1	Dmitri Chevtchenko	RUS
2	Jose Guerra	ESP
3	Serg Goloubitski	UKR
3	Gil Gregory	CUB
50	Paul Walsh	GBR

Men's Team Foil

1	Hungary
2	France
3	Estonia
20	Great Britain

Women's Foil

1	Laura Badea	ROM
2	Giovanna Trillini	ITA
3	Valentin Vezzali	ITA
3	Dianna Bianchedi	ITA
47	Fiona McIntosh	GBR

Women's Team Foil

1	Italy
2	Romania
3	Germany
14	Great Britain

Men's Epee

1	Eric Srecki	FRA
2	Robert Leroux	FRA
3	Sandra Cuomo	ITA
3	Nieto Rivas	COL
90	Chris Howser	GBR

Men's Team Epee

1	Germany
2	France
3	Hungary
15	Great Britain

Women's Epee

1	Joanna Jakimiuk	POL
2	Gyongyi Szalay	HUN
3	Laura Flessel	FRA
3	Sophie Moresee	FRA
32	Penny Tomlinson	GBR

Women's Team Epee

1	Hungary
2	France
3	Estonia
20	Great Britain

Men's Sabre

1	Grigory Kirienko	RUS
2	Felix Becker	GER
3	Tohni Terenzi	ITA
3	Luigi Tarantino	ITA
41	Ian Williams	GBR

Men's Team Sabre

1	Italy
2	Russia
3	Hungary
12	Great Britain

British Senior Championships

London   May 12

Men's Foil

1	Paul Walsh	Sussex House
2	Khaled Beydoun	Sussex House
3	Nick Payne	Salle Paul
3	Kola Abidogun	Boston

Women's Foil

1	Linda Strachan	Salle Paul
2	Fiona McIntosh	Salle Paul
3	Lucy Harris	Salle Paul
4	Sarah Mawby	Salle Paul

Men's Epee

1	Quentin Berriman	*unattached*
2	Steven Paul	Poly
3	John Llewellyn	Reading
3	H West	LTFC

Women's Epee

1	Kate Houston	MPAGB
2	Carol Greenway	MPAGB
3	L Roy	Eclipse
3	M Young	*unattached*

Men's Sabre

1	Amin Zahir	Salle Frohlich
2	Steven Potts	Salle Frohlich
3	Paul Hoenigmann	Meadowbank
3	Ian Williams	Salle Frohlich

Women's Sabre

1	Sue Benny	Glastonbury
2	Lyn Bornemisza	Bath Swords

London International

London   Mar 4-5

Men's Epee

1	A Schmitt	GER
2	M Flegler	GER
3	S Resegotti	ITA
3	O Kayser	AUT
15	G Liston	GBR
40	R Davenport	GBR

Ipswich Cup

Ipswich   Apr 22-23

Women's Epee

1	C Bokel	GER
2	A Hormay	HUN
3	G Szalay	HUN
3	H Kiraly	HUN
64	V Cramb	GBR
66	C Read	GBR

Eden Cup

London   Nov 17-18

Men's Foil

1	S Sanzo	ITA
2	C Schlechtweg	GER
3	G Salbrechter	AUT
3	F Reichling	GER
11	K Beydoun	GBR
26	J Beevers	GBR

Corble Cup

Hendon   Jan 28

Men's Sabre

1	J Scheicher	AUT
2	I Williams	GBR
3	N Fletcher	GBR
3	S Potts	GBR

World Champions

	FOIL	EPEE	SABRE
1921	-	Lucien Gaudin FRA	-
1922	-	Raoul Herde NOR	Adrianus de Jong HOL
1923	-	Wouter Brouwer HOL	Adrianus de Jong HOL
1925		-	János Garay HUN
1926	Giorgio Chiavacci ITA	Georges Tainturier FRA	Sándor Gambos HUN
1927	Oreste Puliti ITA	Georges Buchard FRA	Sándor Gambos HUN
1929	Oreste Puliti ITA	Philippe Cattiau FRA	Gyula Glykais HUN
1930	Giulio Gaudini ITA	Philippe Cattiau FRA	György Piller HUN
1931	Rene Lemoine FRA	Georges Buchard FRA	György Piller HUN
1933	Gioacch'o Guaragna ITA	Georges Buchard FRA	Endre Kabos HUN
1934	Giulio Gaudini ITA	Pál Dunay HUN	Endre Kabos HUN
1935	*shared by four men*	Hans Drakenberg SWE	Aladár Gerevich HUN
1937	Gustavo Marzi ITA	Bernard Schmetz FRA	Pál Kovács HUN
1938	Gioacch'o Guaragna ITA	Michel Pécheux FRA	Aldo Montano ITA
1947	Christian d'Oriola FRA	Edouard Artigas FRA	Aldo Montano ITA
1949	Christian d'Oriola FRA	Dario Mangiarotti ITA	Gastone Daré FRA
1950	Renzo Nostino ITA	Mogens Luchow DEN	Jean Levavasseur FRA
1951	Manlio Di Rosa ITA	Edoardo Mangiarotti ITA	Aladar Gerevich HUN
1953	Christian d'Oriola FRA	Jozsef Sakovics HUN	Pál Kovács HUN
1954	Christian d'Oriola FRA	Edoardo Mangiarotti ITA	Rudolf Kárpáti HUN
1955	Jozsef Gyuricza HUN	Giorgio Anglesio ITA	Aladár Gerevich HUN
1957	Mihaly Fülöp HUN	Armand Mouyal FRA	Jerzy Pawlowski POL
1958	Giancarlo Bergamini ITA	Bill Hoskyns GBR	Yakov Rylsky URS
1959	Allan Jay GBR	Bruno Khabarov URS	Rudolf Kárpáti HUN
1961	Ryszard Parulski POL	Jack Guittet FRA	Yakov Rylsky URS
1962	German Sveshnikov URS	Istvan Kausz HUN	Zoltan Horvath HUN
1963	Jean-Cl'de Magnan FRA	Roland Losert AUT	Yakov Rylsky URS
1965	Jean-Cl'de Magnan FRA	Zoltan Nemere HUN	Jerzy Pawlowski POL
1966	German Sveshnikov URS	Aleksey Nikanchikov URS	Jerzy Pawlowski POL
1967	Viktor Putyatin USSR	Aleksey Nikanchikov URS	Mark Rakita URS
1969	Friedrich Wessel FRG	Bogdan Andrzejewski POL	Viktor Sidiak URS
1970	Friedrich Wessel FRG	Aleksey Nikanchikov URS	Tibor Pézsa HUN
1971	Vasiliy Stankovich URS	Grigoriy Kriss URS	Michele Maffei ITA
1973	Christian Noël FRA	Rolf Edling SWE	Mario Aldo Monttano ITA
1974	Aleks'dr Romankov URS	Rolf Edling SWE	Mario Aldo Monttano ITA
1975	Christian Noël FRA	Alexander Pusch FRG	Vladimir Nazlimov URS
1977	Aleks'dr Romankov URS	Johan Harmenberg SWE	Pál Gerevich HUN
1978	Didier Flament FRA	Alexander Pusch FRG	Viktor Krovopuskov URS
1979	Aleks'dr Romankov URS	Philippe Riboud FRA	Vladimir Nazlimov URS
1981	Vladimir Smirnov URS	Zoltan Szekely HUN	Mariusz Wodke POL
1982	Aleks'dr Romankov URS	Jenö Pap HUN	Viktor Krovopuskov URS
1983	Aleks'dr Romankov URS	Ellmar Bormann FRG	Vasiliy Etropolski BUL
1985	Mauro Numa ITA	Philippe Boisse FRA	Gyorgy Nebald HUN
1986	Andrea Borella ITA	Philippe Riboud FRA	Sergey Mindirgassov URS
1987	Mathias Gey FRG	Volker Fischer FRG	Jean François Lamour FRA
1989	Alexander Koch FRG	Manuel Pereira ESP	Grigoriy Kirienko URS
1990	Philippe Omnès FRA	Thomas Gerull FRG	György Nébald HUN
1991	Ingo Weissenborn GER	Andrey Shuvalov URS	Grigory Kirienko URS
1993	Alexander Koch GER	Pavel Kolobkov RUS	Grigory Kirienko RUS
1994	Rolando Tuckers CUB	Pavel Kolobkov RUS	Felix Becker GER
1995	Dmitri Chevtchenko RUS	Eric Srecki FRA	Grigory Kirienko RUS

Golf

The Americans stopped the rot in 1995; three out of the four majors fell to American golfers, three more than 1994 when three Africans and a Spaniard claimed the trophies. The Americans were obviously cock-a-hoop about this; until September at least. Would they have swapped those triumphs for a different set of figures from the third day at the Oak Hill Country Club? Looking at their faces as Bernard Gallacher made his acceptance (if that's the right word) speech, then the answer has to be that they would have exchanged every single Tour victory as well. The Ryder Cup, as it's inclined to do, dominated everything in golf this year. Europe won; America lost. Even in victory, the Europeans queued up to say how they had been shaking their way to victory, so great was the pressure. Walton made the crucial putt, to within a foot of the pin on the 18th. Yet he could so easily have gone the way of Rocca and Langer after an edgy putt on the 17th. Was he the hero of it all? Probably not. That honour surely goes to the madman who wore the 'Desert Storm' cap a few years back; Corey Pavin. Four wins out of five in the Ryder Cup, three times against Langer and twice against Faldo, and that sweet chip. It'll do.

In the Open at St Andrews, the final round was a gourmet's delight; the pasta-loving Rocca against the doughnut eating Daly. On the final round, Daly was spotted buying four doughnuts from a van by the eighth tee. At the eighteenth, he again got the munchies and devoured an unspecified number of chocolate muffins. This was all too much for Rocca (himself no sveldte) and though he holed that magnificent putt at the last to take it to a play-off, he could not compete with the American thereafter. Out-eaten and out-played.

Colin Montgomerie is the European golfer who could best match Daly in the weighing-room. At the season's beginning, David Leadbetter (Faldo's coaching guru) went so far as to suggest that the Scot might even be carrying a little *too* much weight. We have no evidence that Montgomerie has lost any weight, but even less that it has yet affected his game. He lost a majors' play-off for the second successive year and, as we went to press, led the European Tour ratings. he doesn't win much from February to July, we note, but can't yet advance a weight-related theory about that.

Greg Norman flew ahead in the Sony Rankings, but came to Earth with his suggestion for a World Tour. Norman wanted, among other things, to tap the vast potential of Asia. Presumably he'd got wind of the feats of the new North Korean leader, Kim Jong Il, who took over as head of state from the recently deceased and quite mad Kim Il Sung. Kim Jong Il had just negotiated Pyongyang's championship course in 38 shots. According to the government news agency the prodigious Kim hit no fewer than five holes-in-one (or is that hole-in-ones, we're new to the plural).

Madness, though, is not under copyright. Gary Dawson competes as a triathlete and has a golfing handicap of six. At the Northbridge course in Sydney's northern suburbs, Dawson broke the world record for marathon golfing by playing 1,180 holes in seven days. He beat the record by 52 holes. We presume he lives alone. You could hardly say to your wife or partner, "Won't be long, darling, just popping out for 1,180 holes or so". Could you?

Ryder Cup ▬▬▬▬▬▬▬▬▬▬

Oak Hill Country Club, Rochester, New York State   Sep 22-24

Friday
FOURSOMES

Jay Haas & Fred Couples lost to
Sam Torrance & Costantino Rocca 3 & 2

Davis Love III & Jeff Maggert beat
Howard Clark & Mark James 4 & 3

Corey Pavin & Tom Lehman beat
Nick Faldo & Colin Montgomerie 1 hole

Ben Crenshaw & Curtis Strange lost to
Bernhard Langer & P Johansson 1 hole
USA 2 EUR 2

FOURBALLS

Brad Faxon & Peter Jacobsen lost to
David Gilford & Seve Ballesteros 4 & 3

Jeff Maggert & Loren Roberts beat
Sam Torrance & Costantino Rocca 6 & 5

Fred Couples & Davis Love III beat
Nick Faldo & Colin Montgomerie 3 & 2

Corey Pavin & Phil Mickelson beat
Bernhard Langer & P Johansson 5 & 4
USA 5 EUR 3

Saturday
FOURSOMES

Curtis Strange & Jay Haas lost to
Nick Faldo & Colin Montgomerie 4 & 2

Davis Love III & Jeff Maggert lost to
Sam Torrance & Costantino Rocca 6 & 5

Loren Roberts & Peter Jacobsen beat
Ian Woosnam & Philip Walton 1 hole

Corey Pavin & Tom Lehman lost to
Bernhard Langer & David Gilford 3 & 2
USA 6 EUR 6

FOURBALLS

Brad Faxon & Fred Couples beat
Sam Torrance & Colin Montgomerie 4 & 2

Davis Love III & Ben Crenshaw lost to
Ian Woosnam & Costantino Rocca 3 & 2

Jay Haas & Phil Mickelson beat
Seve Ballesteros & David Gilford 3 & 2

Corey Pavin & Loren Roberts beat
Nick Faldo & Bernhard Langer 1 hole
USA 9 EUR 7

Sunday
SINGLES
Tom Lehman beat
Seve Ballesteros 4 & 3

Peter Jacobsen lost to
Howard Clark 1 hole

Jeff Maggert lost to
Mark James 4 & 3

Fred Couples halved with
Ian Woosnam

Davis Love III beat
Costantino Rocca 3 & 2

Brad Faxon lost to
David Gilford 1 hole

Ben Crenshaw lost to
Colin Montgomerie 3 & 1

Curtis Strange lost to
Nick Faldo 1 hole

Loren Roberts lost to
Sam Torrance 2 & 1

Corey Pavin beat
Bernhard Langer 3 & 2

Jay Haas lost to
Philip Walton 1 hole
Phil Mickelson beat
Per-Ulrik Johansson 2 & 1

EUROPE BEAT USA 14.5 - 13.5

The European Tour has had its fair share of detractors over the past year, many of them from across the Atlantic. Word had it that if the Europeans lost again then the event, as a contest, would be over. Have none of it. The victory, clinched by Philip Walton's 15 foot approach putt on the 18th hole at Oak Hill, showed that Europe's best can still show their trans-Atlantic cousins a thing or two in match-play. For the first time in history, Europe (with Britain & Ireland) are now in possession of the Ryder, Walker and Curtis Cups. Indeed it is only the sixth time in 31 attempts that the Ryder Cup has come to this side of the Atlantic.

As they boarded Concorde on the way out, the noise ringing in the Europeans' ear was that of controversy. Tony Jacklin had slated Bernard Gallacher's style of captaincy. Faldo's marriage had made front page news on the tabloids. The Americans might have been forgiven for thinking that the oppostion was in turmoil. Instead, the off-course distractions had the effect of pulling the disparate threads of the team together. The opening foursomes saw Ryder Cup legend Ballesteros left out, but Europe nevertheless went into lunch all-square. The 38 year old Spaniard, who has won 19 of his Ryder Cup matches, opened up the afternoon session with the David Gilford. "You are the best player here," said Ballesteros, zig-zagging from bush to bunker, Gilford believed him and won the match. Yet it was Europe's only win that afternoon and they ended day one 5-3 down.

Europe clawed back the deficit on Saturday's foursomes, Costantino Rocca's hole in one at the par 3 sixth hole finally burying the memory of The Belfry two years ago when one up with two to play on the final became one down with none to play. His was only the third ace in Ryder Cup history (Faldo hit one two years ago). Torrance and Rocca eventually completed a very comfortable 6 & 5 win over Love and Maggert. Yet whilst Europe seem to have mastered the art of the foursome, the fourball is still an enigma. The afternoon produced a spell of American dominance which culminated in one of the great matches; Pavin and Roberts against Faldo and Langer. As the shadows lengthened the match became a personal duel between US Open champion Pavin and Faldo, a Ryder Cup regular since 1977. With Faldo on the 18th green and close, Pavin smashed a four-iron from the rough and holed the chip to render Faldo speechless.

Going into the singles 9-7 down, history was not on Europe's side. Not since 1957 at Lindrick had the Americans lost after beginning the singles with a lead. To make matters worse Ballesteros missed every fairway going in the singles opener and capitulated to the Lehman. Yet it was England's quiet men who provided the impetus in the middle order. Mark James and David Gilford performed stoically to secure crucial victories, whilst Howard Clark brought off the performance of the day with his defeat of Jacobsen, including another hole-in-one at the sixth. As if to emphasise the quality of the European Tour, it's two leading 1995 money earners, Torrance and Montgomerie finished off their opponents to take it to the wire. Faldo, one-down with two to play to Strange, got up and down on the 17th green to take the match to the final hole. After three shots both were equi-distant, 12 feet or so away the hole. With 25,000 American supporters around the course holding their breath, Strange pushed his putt wide. Faldo bent over his putt and sunk it to the wild delight of team-mates and supporters alike. With Johansson down in the final game, it meant Walton had to win. Haas prolonged the agony to the 18th where Walton had to two-putt from 15 feet. He putted to within a foot. Haas conceded. Seve cried. And Europe cried with him.

Golf

The 124th Open Championship

Old Course, St Andrews, Scotland   July 20-23

282	**John Daly USA**	67 71 73 71
	(£125,000)	
	Costantino Rocca ITA	69 70 70 73
	(£100,000)	

Daly won following a four-hole play-off; at the 1st, 2nd, 17th & 18th holes.

283	Michael Campbell NZL	71 71 65 76
	Mark Brooks USA	70 69 73 71
	Steven Bottomley ENG	70 72 72 69
	(£65,666.67 each)	
284	Vijay Singh FIJ	68 72 73 71
	Steve Elkington AUS	72 69 69 74
	(£40,500 each)	
285	Corey Pavin USA	69 70 72 74
	Mark James ENG	72 75 68 70
	Bob Estes USA	72 70 71 72
	(£33,333.33 each)	
286	Brett Ogle AUS	73 69 71 73
	Sam Torrance SCO	71 70 71 74
	Payne Stewart USA	72 68 75 71
	Ernie Els RSA	71 68 72 75
	(£26,000 each)	
287	Greg Norman AUS	71 74 72 70
	Brad Faxon USA	71 67 75 74
	Ben Crenshaw USA	67 72 76 72
	Robert Allenby AUS	71 74 71 71
	Per-Ulrik Johansson SWE	69 78 68 72
	(£18,200 each)	
288	David Duval USA	71 75 70 72
	Barry Lane ENG	72 73 68 75
	Peter Mitchell ENG	73 74 71 70
	Andrew Coltart SCO	70 74 71 73
	(£13,500 each)	
289	Bernhard Langer GER	72 71 73 73
	Mark Calcavecchia USA	71 72 72 74
	Jesper Parnevik SWE	75 71 70 73
	Lee Janzen USA	73 73 71 72
	Katsuyoshi Tomori JPN	70 68 73 78
	Bill Glasson USA	68 74 72 75
	(£10,316.67 each)	
	Steve Webster* ENG	70 72 74 73
290	David Frost RSA	72 72 74 72
	David Feherty NIR	68 75 71 76
	Tom Watson USA	67 76 70 77
	Darren Clarke NIR	69 77 70 74
	Ross Drummond SCO	74 68 77 71
	José-Maria Olazábal ESP	72 72 74 72
	Hisayuki Sasaki JPN	74 71 72 73
	John Huston USA	71 74 72 73
	Peter Jacobsen USA	71 76 70 73
	(£8,122.22 each)	
291	Nick Price ZIM	70 74 70 77
	Mark McNulty ZIM	67 76 74 74
	Nick Faldo ENG	74 67 75 75
	Seve Ballesteros ESP	75 69 76 71
	Brian Watts USA	72 71 73 75
	John Cook USA	69 70 75 77
	Phil Mickelson USA	70 71 77 73
	Warren Bennett ENG	72 74 73 72
	(£7,050 each)	
291	Gordon Sherry* SCO	70 71 74 76
292	Mark O'Meara USA	72 72 75 73
	Ian Woosnam WAL	71 74 76 71
	Brian Claar USA	71 75 71 75
	Tommy Nakajima JPN	73 72 72 75
	Ken Green USA	71 72 73 76
	Anders Forsbrand SWE	70 74 75 73
	(£6,350 each)	
293	Russell Claydon ENG	70 74 71 78
	Jim Gallagher jr USA	69 76 75 73
	Peter O'Malley AUS	71 73 74 75
	(£5,900 each)	
294	Raymond Floyd USA	72 74 72 76
	Tom Kite USA	72 76 71 75
	Peter Senior AUS	71 75 78 70
	Paul Broadhurst ENG	73 72 76 73
	Paul Lawrie SCO	73 71 74 76
	David Gilford ENG	69 72 75 78
	Justin Leonard USA	73 67 77 77
	Martin Gates ENG	73 73 72 76
	Eduardo Herrera COL	74 72 73 75
	Derrick Cooper ENG	71 76 74 73
	(£5,475 each)	
295	Jonathan Lomas ENG	74 73 75 73
	Olle Karlsson SWE	71 76 73 75
	Gary Hallberg USA	72 74 72 77
	Gary Player RSA	71 73 77 74
	Peter Baker ENG	70 74 81 70
	Scott Hoch USA	74 72 73 76
	José Rivero ESP	70 72 75 78
	Jeff Maggert USA	75 70 78 72
	Frank Nobilo NZL	70 71 80 74
	Matts Hallberg SWE	68 76 75 76
	(£4,975 each)	
	Tiger Woods* USA	74 71 72 78
296	Patrick Burke AUS	75 72 78 71
	Jay Haas USA	76 72 70 78
	Ricky Kawagishi JPN	72 76 80 68
	Steve Lowery USA	69 74 76 77
	Bob Lohr USA	76 68 79 73
	Sandy Lyle SCO	71 71 79 75
	Jack Nicklaus USA	78 70 77 71
	Jarmo Sandelin SWE	75 71 77 73
	Dean Robertson SCO	71 73 74 78
	(£4,500 each)	

297: Miguel Angel Jiménez ESP 75 73 76 73; Mark Davis ENG 74 71 76 76; Eduardo Romero ARG 74 74 72 77; Jay Delsing USA 72 75 73 77; Gene Sauers USA 69 73 75 80; Wayne Riley AUS 70 72 75 80 (£4,125 each); 298: John Hawksworth ENG 73 74 75 76; Bill Longmuir SCO 72 76 72 78; 299: Lee Westwood ENG 71 72 82 74; José Coceres ARG 71 76 78 74; 300: Simon Burnell ENG 72 76 75 77; David Love III USA 70 78 74 78; 301: Gary Clark* ENG 71 75 80 74; 302: Mark Nichols ENG 75 68 78 81; 302: Don Pooley USA 76 71 80 75; 303 Pedro Linhart ESP 72 75 77 79 (scorers from 298-303 earn £4000 each).

Denotes Amateur

Final Scores (cont.)

The following did not make the cut:
149: Paul Azinger USA 74 75, Mike Springer USA 75 74, Masashi Ozaki JPN 70 79, Bob Charles NZL 73 76, Scott Simpson USA 72 77, Howard Clark ENG 76 73, John Morse USA 75 74, Curtis Strange USA 73 76, Peter Fowler AUS 74 75, Nigel Graves ENG 72 77, John Watson ENG 76 73, Bob Tway USA 71 78; **150**: Loren Roberts USA 76 74, Wayne Grady AUS 75 75, Tony Johnstone ZIM 75 75, Brandt Jobe USA 74 76, Colin Montgomerie SCO 75 75, Craig Stadler USA 74 76, Mark McCumber USA 73 77, Miguel Angel Martin ESP 73 77, Michel Besanceney FRA 73 77, Jamie Spence ENG 77 73, Mark Roe ENG 75 75, Stephen Leaney AUS 76 74; **151**: Mike Clayton AUS 74 77, Andrew Crerar SCO 77 74, Tom Wargo USA 72 79, Robert Karlsson SWE 77 74, Paul Carman ENG 72 79, John Bickerton ENG 71 80, Larry Mize USA 74 77, Steven Gallacher* SCO 72 79; **152**: Carl Mason ENG 75 77, Billy Andrade USA 76 76, Lee Trevino USA 75 77, Brad Bryant USA 78 74, Tom Weiskopf USA 76 76; **153**: Craig Parry AUS 76 77, Adam Tillman ENG 75 78, Neil Roderick WAL 74 79, John Wither ENG 75 78, Fredrik Andersson SWE 77 76, Mathias Grönberg SWE 81 72, Ian Baker-Finch AUS 77 76, Toru Suzuki JPN 80 73, Ronan Rafferty NIR 75 78, Kazuhiro Takami JPN 76 77, Russell Weir SCO 71 82, Richard Boxall ENG 72 81; **155**: Martyn Thompson ENG 76 79; **158**: Brandel Chamblee USA 80 78, Arnold Palmer USA 83 75; **159**: Paul Mayo WAL 77 82; **162**: Gary Stafford ENG 78 84.
Retirements after first round: Andrew Oldcorn ENG and Philip Walton IRL.

When John Daly lifted the Auld Claret Jug at St Andrews few could resist commenting on the irony; the reformed alcoholic holding an empty wine jug. This was Daly's first triumph in a major since his victory as a qualifier at the US PGA Championship at Crooked Stick in 1991. In those days, though, the Claret Jug would not have been empty, not ever, and Daly would admit that, like Joe Cocker and the sixties, he wouldn't remember much about it.

It might have just a little to do with those days that Daly is known as the 'Wild Thing'. At the Royal and Ancient he wasn't wild, just unstoppable. In the four-hole play-off, Daly trounced Costantino Rocca by four shots. Rocca, though, should not have even been in the play-off, he had performed his miracle by getting there. Needing a birdie three at the last to tie, Rocca hit a fine drive but proceded to duff his chip into the notorious Valley of Sin. As Daly embraced his wife Paulette (they think it's all over), the Italian lined up his 40- foot putt and ran it up the sharply-contoured sides of the green. The ball held its line and, to a roar of delight from the crowd, dropped in to level the contest. Rocca sank to his knees and banged the turf as tears of joy rolled down his cheeks.

The tears had hardly dried when the former worker in a polystyrene factory had to face the Wild Thing in a play-off. It was all too much for Rocca. He had sat atop Everest, but without being able to plant the flag. What could he do now but lose? In his head, he'd won it with a forty-footer half an hour ago. So, he lost. And Daly held an empty jug, but I bet it felt full enough.

There was a surprise package in the shape of Steve Bottomley who finished an inspired third. The 30-year-old from Bingley, whose caddie is a professional magician (which could only help) had a 69 to finish alongside Mark Brooks and overnight leader Michael Campbell on 283. Bottomley, who had made seven trips to the Tour qualifying school had a highest-ever finish on the European Tour of tenth before this. Campbell too is another coming man; the young New Zealander claiming the esoteric mix of Maori and Scot. Campbell also acquitted himself well at the US PGA, finishing equal seventeenth.

St Andrews bade farewell to Arnold Palmer, who won the Open twice in 1961 & 1962 when his 'army' were on the move. Palmer's 158 left him bottom of the field and out at the halfway stage. On his final round, he wore a Royal and Ancient sweater, "Since I played like a member," he said "I might as well act like one."

US Masters

Augusta National Course, Augusta, Georgia   *Apr 6-9*

274	**Ben Crenshaw USA**	70 67 69 68
	($396,000)	
275	Davis Love III USA	69 69 71 66
	($237,600)	
277	Jay Haas USA	71 64 72 70
	Greg Norman AUS	73 68 68 68
	($127,600 each)	
279	Steve Elkington AUS	73 67 67 72
	David Frost RSA	66 71 71 71
	($83,600 each)	
280	Scott Hoch USA	69 67 71 73
	Phil Mickelson USA	66 71 70 73
	($70,950 each)	
281	Curtis Strange USA	72 71 65 73
	($63,800)	
282	Fred Couples USA	71 69 67 75
	Brian Henninger USA	70 68 68 76
	($57,200 each)	
283	Lee Janzen USA	69 69 74 71
	Kenny Perry USA	73 70 71 69
	($48,400 each)	
284	Hale Irwin USA	69 72 71 72
	Tom Watson USA	73 70 69 72
	José Maria Olazábal ESP	66 74 72 72
	($39,600 each)	
285	Paul Azinger USA	70 72 73 70
	Brad Faxon (USA)	76 69 69 71
	Ray Floyd USA	71 70 70 74
	John Huston USA	70 66 72 77
	Colin Montgomerie SCO	71 69 76 69
	Corey Pavin USA	67 71 72 75
	Ian Woosnam WAL	69 72 71 73
	($28,786 each)	
286	David Edwards USA	69 73 73 71
	Nick Faldo ENG	70 70 71 75
	David Gilford ENG	67 73 75 71
	Loren Roberts USA	72 69 72 73
	Duffy Waldorf USA	74 69 67 76
	($18,260 each)	
287	Bob Estes USA	73 70 76 68
	Masashi Ozaki JPN	70 74 70 73
	($15,300 each)	
288	Peter Jacobsen USA	72 73 69 74
	Bernhard Langer GER	71 69 73 75
	Bruce Lietzke USA	72 71 71 74
	Mark O'Meara USA	68 72 71 77
	($13,325 each)	
290	Chip Beck USA	68 76 69 77
	Dan Forsman USA	71 74 74 71
	Wayne Grady AUS	69 73 74 74
	Mark McCumber USA	73 69 69 79
	Jack Nicklaus USA	67 78 70 75
	($10,840 each)	
292	Tom Lehman USA	71 72 74 75
	($9,500)	
293	Mark Calcavecchia USA	70 72 78 73
	Jeff Sluman USA	73 72 71 77
	Payne Stewart USA	71 72 72 78
	($8,567 each)	
	Tiger Woods* USA	72 72 77 72
295	Seve Ballesteros ESP	75 68 78 75
	John Daly USA	75 69 71 81
	($7,500 each)	
297	Rick Fehr USA	76 69 69 83
	($6,800)	

Did not make the cut: **146**: Hal Sutton USA 77 69, Sandy Lyle SCO 75 71, Clark Dennis USA 73 73, Tommy Nakajima JPN 72 74, Fuzzy Zoeller USA 72 74, Craig Stadler USA 70 76; **147**: Brad Bryant USA 77 70, Larry Mize USA 76 71, Tom Kite USA 74 73, Charles Coody USA 74 73, John Cook USA 73 74, Mike Heinen USA 73 74, Ernie Els RSA 72 75, Mike Sullivan USA 72 75; **148**: Jeff Maggert USA 78 70, Vijay Singh FIJ 77 71, Mark McNulty ZIM 75 73, Steve Lowery USA 75 73, John Morse USA 74 74; **149**: Gay Brewer USA 70 79, Nick Price ZIM 76 73, Gary Player RSA 76 73, Lanny Wadkins USA 74 75; **150**: Jim McGovern USA 77 73, Neal Lancaster USA 76 77, Bill Glasson USA 71 80; **152**: Arnold Palmer USA 79 73, Dicky Pride* USA 79 73; **153**: Mark Brooks USA 76 77; **154**: Frank Nobilo NZL 73 81; **155**: T Kuehne* USA 79 76, T Jackson* USA 79 76; **157**: Mike Springer USA 79 80, Lee James* ENG 77 80; **160**: Ian Baker-Finch AUS 79 81; **161**: G Yamamoto* USA 77 84.

"I had a fifteenth club in my bag this week, and that was Harvey," said Ben Crenshaw on his inspiration after winning the 59th Masters. Harvey Penick, Crenshaw's lifelong mentor, had died the previous Sunday and when gentle Ben strode of the 18th tee, there were tears in his eyes. Davis Love had gone shot for shot with Crenshaw until the Texan lofted a perfect six-iron over the water on the 16th to secure a birdie. The emotions that had been bubbling under the surface flooded out when Crenshaw sunk the 18 inch putt on the 18th green. He dropped the putter and buried his face in his hands, overcome. For the American audience, which had witnessed six European successes in seven years, Crenshaw's first major since 1984 was an occasion for celebration. The top European was the defending champion, José Maria Olazábal, but the Spaniard was back in equal fourteenth.

US Open

Shinnecock Hills, Long Island　　*June 15-18*

280	**Corey Pavin USA**	**72 69 71 68**
	($350,000)	
282	Greg Norman AUS	68 67 74 73
	($207,000)	
283	Tom Lehman USA	70 72 67 74
	($131,974)	
284	Neal Lancaster USA	70 72 77 65
	Jeff Maggert USA	69 72 77 66
	Bill Glasson USA	69 70 76 69
	Jay Haas USA	70 73 72 69
	Davis Love III USA	72 68 73 71
	Phil Mickelson USA	68 70 72 74
	($66,633.66 each)	
285	Frank Nobilo NZL	72 72 70 71
	Vijay Singh FIJ	70 71 72 72
	Bob Tway USA	69 69 72 75
	($44,184.33 each)	
286	Mark McCumber USA	70 71 77 68
	Duffy Waldorf USA	72 70 75 69
	Brad Bryant USA	75 71 70 70
	Jeff Sluman USA	72 69 74 71
	Mark Roe ENG	71 69 74 72
	Lee Janzen USA	70 72 72 72
	Nick Price ZIM	66 73 73 74
	Steve Stricker USA	71 70 71 74
	($30,934 each)	
287	Fuzzy Zoeller USA	69 74 76 68
	Payne Stewart USA	71 74 73 69
	Brett Ogle AUS	71 75 72 69
	Pete Jordan USA	74 71 71 71
	Billy Andrade USA	72 69 74 72
	Scott Verplank USA	72 69 71 75
	Ian Woosnam WAL	72 71 69 75
	($20,085.43 each)	
288	Colin Montgomerie SCO	71 74 75 68
	Miguel Angel Jiménez ESP	72 72 75 69
	Mike Holbert USA	74 72 72 70
	Masashi Ozaki JPN	69 68 80 71
	Scott Simpson USA	67 65 74 72
	David Duval USA	70 73 73 72
	José Maria Olazábal ESP	73 70 72 73
	Gary Hallberg USA	70 76 69 73
	($13,912.12 each)	
289	Bill Porter USA	73 70 79 67

	Ray Floyd USA	74 72 76 67
	Hal Sutton USA	71 74 76 68
	Curtis Strange USA	70 72 76 71
	Guy Boros USA	73 71 74 71
	Steve Elkington AUS	72 73 73 71
	Curt Byrum USA	70 70 76 73
	Bernhard Langer GER	74 67 74 74
	($9,812.37 each)	
290	Barry Lane ENG	74 72 71 73
	($8,147)	
291	Jim McGovern USA	73 69 81 68
	Christian Pena USA	74 71 76 70
	Omar Uresti USA	71 74 75 71
	John Daly USA	71 75 74 71
	Nick Faldo ENG	72 68 79 72
	Bradley Hughes AUS	72 71 75 73
	($7,146 each)	
292	Bob Burns USA	73 72 75 72
	Eduardo Romero ARG	71 73 75 73
	Ted Tryba USA	71 75 73 73
	Peter Jacobsen USA	72 72 74 74
	Matt Gogel USA	73 70 73 76
	($5,842.60 each)	
293	Brad Faxon USA	71 73 77 72
	Tom Watson USA	70 73 77 73
	Chris Perry USA	70 74 75 74
	Steve Lowery USA	69 72 75 79
	Scott Hoch USA	74 72 70 77
	Greg Bruckner USA	70 72 73 78
	($4,833.83 each)	

294: Jim Gallagher jr USA 71 75 77 71, John Cook USA 70 75 76 73, Brandt Jobe USA 71 72 76 75, David Edwards USA 72 74 72 76, Paul Goydos USA 73 73 70 78 ($3,969 each); **295**: Tom Kite USA 70 72 82 71, Tommy Armour III USA 77 69 74 75, Mike Brisky USA 71 72 77 75 ($3,349 each); **296**: John Connelly USA 75 71 74 76 ($3,039); **297**: Ben Crenshaw USA 72 71 79 75; John Maginnes USA 75 71 74 77 ($2,806.50 each); **301**: Joey Gullion USA 70 74 81 76 ($2,574).
Among those who did not make the cut: Seve Ballesteros ESP, Paul Azinger USA, Larry Mize USA, Fred Couples USA, David Gilford ENG, Ian Baker-Finch, Jack Nicklaus USA, Ernie Els RSA.

Pavin's 200 yard four wood into the final hole must surely rank as one of the greatest pressure shots in US Open history. The shot left him a five-foot putt to lift his first major title. Pavin is a man of 5ft 7in who weighs in at little more than 10 stones and is one of the shortest hitters on the Tour, so it was a tribute to the quality of his short play that he could even keep in touch with the leaders let alone overhaul them. That he did, was due to the magical touch of his putter. For 72 holes he had only 106 putts, fewer than any other competitior. The man who enraged Europeans with his antics at the 1991 Ryder Cup at Kiawah Island again showed his street fighting qualities to claim victory with a round of two-under for a level-par total of 280.

Quotes

"Never, never, never, never. I'll be glad to move out of the public light" - **Bernard Gallacher, being very sure about his Ryder Cup future.**

"I only played three matches here and hit only three fairways. My biggest contribution was to get the team colours for Sunday changed from green to my lucky blue" - **Seve Ballesteros at the Ryder Cup.**

"People who cheat in life may not necessarily cheat in golf, but people who cheat in golf always cheat in life" - **Rabbi Marc Gellman, quoted in** *Golf Digest.*

"It used to be called the Walkover Cup. We've guaranteed they don't call it that any more" - **Jody Fanaghan after Britain and Ireland's Walker Cup victory.**

"I've got a bad eye and almost had pheumonia and I've won the English Open. If I get healthy again I suppose I'll start missing cuts again" - **Philip Walton, after winning at Forest of Arden.**

"The game just embarrasses you until you feel inadequate and pathethic and you want to cry like a child" - **Ben Crenshaw, after the US Masters which he won.**

"At least he can watch this year's Masters with Bob Jones" - **Crenshaw, on his lifelong mentor Harvey Penick, who died just before the Masters.**

"It's bad enough being in the bunker, without the world watching you trying to get out" - **Walter Woods, St Andrews' head greenkeeper bemoaning the presence of the miniature camera set into the face of the treacherous Road Hole bunker on the 17th hole.**

"Not if I had to learn some rules and all that crap" - **Open champion John Daly when asked if he would become a member of the Royal and Ancient.**

"My wife laughed when I told her I was a skinhead. If she gives me any flak about it, I'll shave her head as well" - **John Daly.**

"There were no high-fives, we're not that Americanised up here. Anyway I do not think Jack and Tom could get up high enough" - **Gordon Sherry, after he holed-in-one at the 158-yard eighth, while practising for the Open with Nicklaus and Watson. Sherry is 6ft 8in.**

"I couldn't believe what I was hearing. They were pulling for Faldo and not for me. Whose country is this anyway" - **US golfer Mark O'Meara, after beating Faldo in the Honda Classic on the US Tour**

"On the course I would take out one of those water bottles that athletes use, except mine would be filled with vodka-orange with the emphasis firmly on vodka" - **Brian Barnes, now successful on the Seniors' Tour.**

"I wish my name was Tom Kite" - **Ian Baker-Finch, former Open champion, after an autograph signing session.**

US PGA

Riviera CC, Pacific Palisades, California   Aug 10-13

267	**Steve Elkington AUS**	**68 67 68 64**		Nick Faldo ENG	69 73 70 67
	Elkington won after a play-off			Gil Morgan USA	66 73 74 66
	($360,000)			José Maria Olazábal ESP	72 66 70 71
	Colin Montgomerie SCO	68 67 67 65		Job Ozaki JPN	71 70 65 73
	($216,000)			D A Weibring USA	74 68 69 68
269	Ernie Els RSA	66 65 66 72		($8,906 each)	
	Jeff Maggert USA	66 69 65 69	280	Lenny Clements USA	67 71 72 70
	($116,000 each)			Fred Funk USA	70 72 68 70
271	Brad Faxon USA	70 67 71 73		Sandy Lyle SCO	67 73 69 71
	($80,000)			Nick Price ZIM	71 71 70 68
273	Bob Estes USA	69 68 68 68		Philip Walton IRL	71 70 71 68
	Mark O'Meara USA	64 67 69 73		($6,750 each)	
	($68,500 each)		281	Chip Beck USA	66 74 73 68
274	Jay Has USA	69 71 64 70		Ben Crenshaw USA	68 73 73 67
	Justin Leonard USA	68 66 70 70		Jim Gallagher jnr USA	64 72 73 72
	Steve Lowery USA	69 68 68 69		Gene Sauers USA	69 71 68 73
	Jeff Sluman USA	69 67 68 70		Peter Senior AUS	68 71 74 68
	Craig Stadler USA	71 66 66 71		($5,600 each)	
	($50,000 each)		282	John Adams USA	65 76 71 70
275	Jim Furyk USA	68 70 69 68		Brian Claar USA	68 67 73 74
	Miguel Angel Jiménez ESP	69 69 67 70		Robin Freeman USA	71 69 70 72
	Payne Stewart USA	69 70 69 67		Jumbo Ozaki JPN	73 68 69 72
	Kirk Triplett USA	71 69 68 67		Kenny Perry USA	75 67 70 70
	($33,750 each)			($4,620 each)	
276	Michael Campbell NZL	71 65 71 69	283	Michael Bradley USA	63 73 73 74
	Costantino Rocca ITA	70 69 68 69		Hale Irwin USA	71 68 71 73
	Curtis Strange USA	72 68 68 68		Tom Kite USA	70 69 70 74
	($26,000 each)			Scott Simpson USA	71 67 71 74
277	Greg Norman AUS	66 69 70 72		($4,050 each)	
	Jesper Parnevik SWE	69 69 70 69			
	Duffy Waldorf USA	69 69 67 72			
	($21,000 each)				
278	Woody Austin USA	70 70 70 68			
	Nolan Henke USA	68 73 67 70			
	Peter Jacobsen USA	69 67 71 71			
	Lee Janzen USA	66 70 72 70			
	Bruce Lietzke USA	73 64 67 70			
	Billy Mayfair USA	68 68 72 70			
	Steve Stricker USA	75 64 69 70			
	Sam Torrance SCO	69 69 69 71			
	($15,500 each)				
279	Paul Azinger USA	70 70 72 67			
	Mark Brooks USA	67 74 69 69			
	Fred Couples USA	70 69 74 66			

284: Ed Dougherty USA 68 72 74 70, Per-Ulrik Johansson SWE 72 69 71 72, Steve Pate USA 71 71 71 71, Loren Roberts USA 74 68 71 71, Tom Watson USA 71 71 72 70 ($3,630 each); 285: Barry Lane EG 74 68 75 68, Mike Sullivan USA 72 69 71 73, Lanny Wadkins USA 73 69 71 72 ($3,400 each); 286: Dillard Pruitt USA 73 69 72 72 ($3,300); 287: David Frost RSA 69 73 72 73, Jack Nicklaus USA 69 71 71 76 ($3,262 each); 288: Fuzzy Zoeller USA 72 69 75 72 ($3,225); 289: Brian Kamm USA 71 66 74 78 ($3,200); 291: Curt Byrum USA 71 71 78 71, Wayne Defrancesco USA 69 73 74 75 ($3,162 each) *Those who missed the cut include:* 143: Ian Woosnam WAL 71 72

Colin Montgomerie lost a play-off in an American major for the second time in little more than a year, this time to Australian Steve Elkington. Having capitulated in the 18-hole play-off at last year's US Open, Monty again succumbed to a birdie on the first extra hole to keep the tag of the best player not to have won a major. Elkington must have thought he was home and dry with his final round 64 for a 17-under total of 267, equalling Greg Norman's major championship record achieved in the Open at St George's two years ago. However, the Scot responded by finishing with three consecutive birdies to take it to the extra hole. Elkington's victory was his sixth on the US Tour this year following a string of injuries last year. The Australian underwent surgery for sinus trouble, had a growth removed from his shoulder and overcame the most incovenient illness of all for a golfer - an allergy to grass.

Sony Rankings

as at September 17th

	Player	Ctry	Pts/Evts	Average			Player	Ctry	Pts/Evts	Average
1	Greg Norman	AUS	1475/67	**22.01**		51	John Daly	USA	394/81	**4.86**
2	Nick Price	ZIM	1211/75	**16.15**		52	Paul Azinger	USA	326/69	**4.72**
3	Ernie Els	RSA	1482/95	**15.60**		53	Robert Allenby	AUS	445/95	**4.68**
4	Nick Faldo	ENG	1111/74	**15.01**		54	Peter Senior	AUS	439/94	**4.67**
5	Bernhard Langer	GER	1120/76	**14.74**		55	Barry Lane	ENG	469/101	**4.64**
6	Colin Montgomerie	SCO	1332/94	**14.17**		56	Craig Parry	AUS	428/93	**4.60**
7	Corey Pavin	USA	986/80	**12.32**		57	Mark James	ENG	345/76	**4.54**
8	Fred Couples	USA	810/68	**11.91**		58	David Gilford	ENG	380/84	**4.52**
9	Masashi Ozaki	JPN	814/73	**11.15**		59	Tsun'ki Nakajima	JPN	374/85	**4.40**
10	José Maria Olazábal	ESP	783/75	**10.44**		60	Hale Irwin	USA	283/65	**4.35**
11	Steve Elkington	AUS	734/74	**9.92**		61	Curtis Strange	USA	324/77	**4.21**
12	Tom Lehman	USA	830/87	**9.54**		62	Bob Tway	USA	328/78	**4.21**
13	Vijay Singh	FIJ	1022/111	**9.21**		63	John Huston	USA	374/89	**4.20**
14	Mark McCumber	USA	543/62	**8.76**		64	Darren Clarke	NIR	367/88	**4.17**
15	Seve Ballesteros	ESP	641/75	**8.55**		65	Brett Ogle	AUS	307/77	**3.99**
16	David Frost	RSA	809/96	**8.43**		66	Billy Mayfair	USA	374/95	**3.94**
17	Sam Torrance	SCO	742/89	**8.34**		67	Gil Morgan	USA	269/69	**3.90**
18	Lee Janzen	USA	754/93	**8.11**		68	Steve Lowery	USA	349/90	**3.88**
19	Davis Love III	USA	694/86	**8.07**		69	Kirk Triplett	USA	320/84	**3.81**
20	Loren Roberts	USA	558/77	**7.25**		70	Per-Ulrik Johansson	SWE	292/77	**3.79**
21	Peter Jacobsen	USA	543/75	**7.24**		71	Jeff Sluman	USA	358/96	**3.73**
22	Fuzzy Zoeller	USA	434/60	**7.23**		72	David Edwards	USA	268/72	**3.72**
23	Scott Hoch	USA	614/85	**7.22**		73	Howard Clark	ENG	256/69	**3.71**
24	Phil Mickelson	USA	532/76	**7.00**		74	Steve Stricker	USA	257/70	**3.67**
25	Ben Crenshaw	USA	542/78	**6.95**		75	Woody Austin	USA	256/70	**3.66**
26	Ian Woosnam	WAL	547/79	**6.92**		76	Naomichi Ozaki	JPN	344/100	**3.44**
27	Jim Gallagher jnr	USA	566/85	**6.66**		77	D A Weibring	USA	229/67	**3.42**
28	Costantino Rocca	ITA	588/89	**6.61**		78	John Cook	USA	264/79	**3.34**
29	Jay Haas	USA	579/88	**6.58**		79	Rick Fehr	USA	253/76	**3.33**
30	Jeff Maggert	USA	545/86	**6.34**		80	Eduardo Romero	ARG	256/77	**3.32**
31	Brad Faxon	USA	562/89	**6.31**		81	Mark Roe	ENG	272/82	**3.32**
32	Mark McNulty	ZIM	456/74	**6.16**		82	Masahito Kuramoto	JPN	297/90	**3.30**
33	Tom Watson	USA	368/60	**6.13**		83	Duffy Waldorf	USA	283/86	**3.29**
34	Mark Calcavecchia	USA	603/100	**6.03**		84	Hal Sutton	USA	282/86	**3.28**
35	Payne Stewart	USA	502/84	**5.98**		85	Brandt Jobe	USA	198/61	**3.25**
36	Bob Estes	USA	495/86	**5.76**		86	Wayne Riley	AUS	284/89	**3.19**
37	Bill Glasson	USA	385/68	**5.66**		87	Robert Gamez	USA	262/83	**3.16**
38	Michael Campbell	NZL	394/71	**5.55**		88	Todd Hamilton	USA	304/97	**3.13**
39	David Duval	USA	355/64	**5.55**		89	Joakim Haeggman	SWE	249/80	**3.11**
40	Craig Stadler	USA	409/76	**5.38**		90	Greg Turner	AUS	245/79	**3.10**
41	Jesper Parnevik	SWE	424/79	**5.37**		91	Lennie Clements	USA	225/73	**3.08**
42	Scott Simpson	USA	427/80	**5.34**			José Rivero	ESP	225/73	**3.08**
43	Bruce Lietzke	USA	314/60	**5.23**		93	Justin Leonard	USA	220/72	**3.06**
44	Mark O'Meara	USA	450/87	**5.17**		94	Fred Funk	USA	299/99	**3.02**
45	Miguel A Jiménez	ESP	460/91	**5.05**		95	Nolan Henke	USA	247/83	**2.98**
46	Brian Watts	USA	361/72	**5.01**		96	Brad Bryant	USA	286/97	**2.95**
47	Tom Kite	USA	376/75	**5.01**		97	Peter O'Malley	AUS	255/89	**2.87**
48	Frank Nobilo	NZL	413/83	**4.98**		98	Peter Baker	ENG	255/91	**2.80**
49	Larry Mize	USA	380/77	**4.94**		99	Tony Johnstone	ZIM	248/90	**2.76**
50	Kenny Perry	USA	409/84	**4.87**		100	Mark Brooks	USA	289/106	**2.73**

Volvo European Tour ▬▬▬▬

Date	Tournament	Venue	Winner	Score	1st Prize	Runner(s)-up	Margin
Sep 30 Oct 3	Mercedes German Masters	Motzener See GC Berlin	**Seve Ballesteros** ESP	270 (-18)	£104,125	Ernie Els RSA	play-off
Oct 6 -9	Alfred Dunhill Cup	Old Course St Andrews	**Canada**	2-1	£300,000 (team)	USA	
Oct 13 -16	Toyota Match Play Championship	Wentworth Surrey	**Ernie Els** RSA	4 & 2	£160,000	Colin Montgomerie SCO	
Oct 20 -23	Czech Open	Marianské Lazne Czech Republic	**Per-Ulrik Johansson** SWE	237 (+1)	£83,330	Klas Eriksson SWE	3
Oct 27 -30	Volvo Masters	Valderrama Spain	**Bernhard Langer** GER	276 (-8)	£125,000	Vijay Singh FIJ	1
Nov 10 -13	World Cup Golf by Heineken	Dorada Beach GC Puerto Rico	**USA**	536	$150,000 (each)	Zimbabwe	14
Dec 15 -18	Johnnie Walker World Champ'ship	Tryall, Montego Bay Jamaica	**Ernie Els** RSA	268 (-16)	$550,000	Mark McCumber USA	6
Jan 19 -22	Dubai Desert Classic	Emirates GC Dubai	**Fred Couples** USA	268 (-20)	£75,000	Colin Montgomerie SCO	3
Jan 26 -29	Johnnie Walker Classic	Orchard G & CC Manila	**Fred Couples** USA	277 (-11)	£100,000	Nick Price ZIM	2
Feb 2 -5	Madeira Island Open	Campo de Golfe da Madeira	**Santiago Luna** ESP	272 (-16)	£41,660	Christian Cevaer FRA	4
Feb 9 -12	Turespaña Open de Canarias	Masplomas GC Gran Canaria	**Jarmo Sandelin** SWE	282 (-6)	£40,719	Paul Eales ENG Seve Ballesteros ESP	1
Feb 16 -19	Lexington SA PGA Championship	Wanderers Club Johannesburg	**Ernie Els** RSA	271 (-9)	£39,478	Roger Wessels RSA	2
Feb 23 -26	Turespaña Open Mediterrania	Escorpion Valencia	**Robert Karlsson** SWE	276 (-12)	£50,000	Jiménez/Forsbrand Sandelin/Torrance	3
Mar 2 -5	Turespaña Open de Andalucia	Islantilla GC Spain	**Alexander Cejka** GER	278 (-6)	£49,344	Costantino Rocca ITA	3
Mar 9 -12	Moroccan Open	Royal Golf Links Agadir	**Mark James** ENG	275 (-13)	£58,330	David Gilford ENG	1
Mar16 -19	Portuguese Open	Penha Longa GC Lisbon	**Adam Hunter** SCO	277 (-11)	£50,000	Darren Clarke NIR	play-off
Mar 23 -26	Turespaña Open Baleares	Santa Ponsa II Majorca	**Greg Turner** NZL	274 (-14)	£40,478	Costantino Rocca ITA	2
Apr 14 -17	Open Catalonia Turespaña Series	Peralada Girona	**Philip Walton** IRL	281 (-7)	£50,000	Andrew Coltart SCO	3
Apr 20 -23	Air France Cannes Open	Royal Mougins	**André Bossert** SUI	132 (-10)	£37,500	O Rojhan NOR J van de Velde FRA	2
Apr 27 -30	Tournoi Perrier de Paris	Golf de Saint-Cloud	**Seve Ballesteros/ José Maria Olazábal**	256 (-24)	£70,000 (pair)	Mike Clayton/ Peter O'Malley AUS	3
May 4 -7	Conte of Florence Italian Open	Le Rovedine GC Milan	**Sam Torrance** SCO	269 (-19)	£61,716	José Rivero ESP	2
May 11 -14	Benson & Hedges International Open	St Melion Plymouth	**Peter O'Malley** AUS	280 (-8)	£108,330	Mark James ENG Costantino Rocca ITA	1
May 18 -21	Peugeot Open de España	Club de Campo Madrid	**Seve Ballesteros** ESP	274 (-14)	£91,660	José Rivero ESP Ignacio Garrido ESP	2

Date	Tournament	Venue	Winner	Score	Prize	Runner(s)-up
May 26 -29	Volva PGA Championship	Wentworth Surrey	**Bernhard Langer** GER	279 (-9)	£150,000	M Campbell NZL 1 P-Ulrik Johansson SWE
June 1 -4	Murphy's English Open	Forest of Arden Warwickshire	**Philip Walton** IRL	274 (-14)	£108,330	Colin Montgomerie SCO play-off
June 8 -11	Deutsche Bank Open	Gut Kaden Hamburg	**Bernhard Langer** GER	270 (-18)	£108,330	Jamie Spence 6 ENG
June 15 -18	DHL Jersey Open	La Moye GC St Brelade	**Andrew Oldcorn** ENG	273 (-15)	£50,000	Dean Robertson 3 SCO
June 22 -25	Peugeot Open de France	National GC Paris	**Paul Broadhurst** ENG	274 (-14)	£91,660	Neal Briggs 8 ENG
June 29 July 2	BMW International Open	St Eurach GC Munich	**Frank Nobilo** NZL	272 (-16)	£91,660	Bernhard Langer 2 GER
July 6 --9	Murphy's Irish Open	Mount Juliet GC Co Kilkenny	**Sam Torrance** SCO	277 (-11)	£111,107	S Cage ENG play-off Howard Clark ENG
July 12 -15	Scottish Open	Carnoustie Angus	**Wayne Riley** AUS	276 (-12)	£108,330	Nick Faldo 2 ENG
July 20 -23	The Open	Old Course St Andrews	**John Daly** USA	282 (-6)	£125,000	Costantino Rocca ITA play-off
July 27 -30	Heineken Dutch Open	Hilversum GC Utrecht	**Scott Hoch** USA	269 (-15)	£108,330	Sam Torrance 2 SCO
Aug 3 -6	Volvo Scandinavian Masters	Barsebäck Sweden	**Jesper Parnevik** SWE	270 (-18)	£108,330	Colin Montgomerie 5 SCO
Aug 10 13	Hohe Brücke Open	GC Waldviertel Litschau, Austria	**Alexander Cejka** GER	267 (-21)	£41,660	Muntz, Rafferty 4 Garrido
Aug 17 -20	Chemapol Trophy Czech Open	Mariánské Lázne GC, Czech Rep	**Peter Teravainen** USA	268 (-16)	£125,000	Howard Clark ENG 1
Aug 24 -27	Volvo German Open	Nippenburg GC Stuttgart	**Colin Montgomerie** SCO	268 (-16)	£108,330	Sam Torrance SCO 1 Niclas Fasth SWE
Aug 31 Sep 3	Canon European Masters	Crans-sur Sierre Switzerland	**Mathias Grönberg** SWE	270 (-18)	£116,660	Barry Lane ENG 2 Costantino Rocca ITA
Sep 7 Sep 10	Trophé Lancôme Paris	St Nom la Bretéche Paris	**Colin Montgomerie** SCO	269 (-11)	£100,000	Sam Torrance SCO 1
Sep 14 -17	British Masters	Collingtree Pk Northampton	**Sam Torrance** SCO	270 (-18)	£108,330	Michael Campbell 1 NZL
Sep 28 Oct 1	Smurfit European Open	The K Club County Kildare	**Bernhard Langer** GER	280 (-8)	£108,330	Barry Lane play-off ENG

EUROPEAN MONEY LIST 1994
as at December 31st, 1994

1	**Colin Montgomerie**	**SCO**	**£762,719**
2	Bernhard Langer	GER	£635,483
3	Seve Ballesteros	ESP	£590,101
4	José Maria Olazábal	ESP	£516,107
5	Miguel Angel Jiménez	ESP	£437,403
6	Vijay Singh	FIJ	£364,313
7	David Gilford	ENG	£326,629
8	Nick Faldo	ENG	£321,256
9	Mark Roe	ENG	£312,539
10	Ernie Els	RSA	£311,849
11	Barry Lane	ENG	£277,362
12	Ian Woosnam	WAL	£273,264
13	Mark McNulty	ZIM	£270,349
14	Eduardo Romero	ARG	£269,422
15	Per-Ulrik Johansson	SWE	£259,952

EUROPEAN MONEY LIST 1995
as at October 1st

1	**Colin Montgomerie**	**SCO**	**£626,651**
2	Sam Torrance	SCO	£625,671
3	Bernhard Langer	GER	£497,964
4	Costantino Rocca	ITA	£459,945
5	Michael Campbell	NZL	£359,239
6	Mark James	ENG	£265,827
7	Barry Lane	ENG	£259,196
8	Wayne Riley	AUS	£237,432
9	Peter O'Malley	AUS	£234,376
10	Philip Walton	IRL	£218,056
11	Howard Clark	ENG	£215,168
12	Darren Clarke	NIR	£208,675
13	Paul Broadhurst	ENG	£191,887
14	José Riveiro	ESP	£179,903
15	Frank Nobilo	NZL	£173,456

PGA European Seniors Tour

Date	Tournament	Venue	Winner	Score	Prize Money	1st Prize
Feb 22 24	PGA European Seniors Qualifying	Hyatt La Manga Spain	**Walter Sauer** USA	216 (par)	£4,500	£1,000
Mar 30 Apr 1	Windsor Senior Masters	Windsor G & CC Nairobi, Kenya	**Brian Huggett** WAL	209 (-7)	£54,000	£8,887
Jul 14 16	German PGA Seniors Championship	Idstein GC Frankfurt, Germany	**Renato Campagnoli** ITA	208 (-8)	£80,000	£13,350
Jul 27 29	Senior British Open	Royal Portrush GC Northern Ireland	**Brian Barnes** SCO	281 (-7)	£350,000	£58,330
Aug 2 Aug 4	Lawrence Batley Seniors	Fixby GC Huddersfield, Yorks	**Alberto Croce** ITA	209 (-3)	£70,000	£11,000
Aug 11 13	Forte PGA Seniors Championship	Sunningdale GC Berks	**John Morgan** ENG	204 (-6)	£90,000	£15,000
Aug 18 20	Northern Electric Seniors	Slaley Hall GC Northumberland	**Brian Waites** ENG	215 (-1)	£60,000	£9,700
Aug 24 26	Collingtree Seniors	Collingtree Park GC Northampton	**Neil Coles** ENG	211 (-5)	£52,000	£8,085
Sep 1 3	Shell Scottish Seniors Open	Royal Aberdeen GC Scotland	**Brian Huggett** WAL	200 (-10)	£100,000	£16,660
Sep 8 10	De Vere Hotels Seniors Classic	Belton Woods GC Grantham	**Tommy Horton** ENG	213 (-3)	£60,000	£9,380
Sep 29 Oct 1	London Masters	The London GC	**John Bland** RSA	210 (-6)	£80,000	£13,350

Walker Cup
Porthcawl   Sep 9-10

Saturday
FOURSOMES
British & Irish names first

Gordon Sherry & Stephen Gallacher lost to
John Harris & Tiger Woods 4& 3

Mark Foster & David Howell halved with
Alan Bratton & Chris Riley

Graham Rankin & Barclay Howard lost to
Notah Begay & Tim Jackson 4 & 3

Padraig Harrington & Jody Fanaghan bt
Kris Cox & Trip Kuehne 5 & 3

SINGLES
Gordon Sherry bt Notah Begay 3 & 2
Lee James lost to **Kris Cox** 1 hole
Mark Foster bt Buddy Marucci 4 & 3
Stephen Gallacher bt Tim Jackson 4 & 3
Padraig Harrington bt Jerry Courville 2 holes
Barclay Howard halved with Alan Bratton
Graham Rankin lost to **John Harris** 1 hole
Gary Wolstenholme bt Tiger Woods 1 hole

Sunday
FOURSOMES
Gordon Sherry & Stephen Gallacher lost to
Alan Bratton & Chris Riley 4 & 2

Mark Foster & David Howell bt
Kris Cox & Trip Kuenhe 3 & 2

Gary Wolstenholme & Lee James lost to
Buddy Marucci & Jerry Courville 6 & 5

Padraig Harrington & Jody Fanaghan bt
John Harris & Tiger Woods 2 & 1

SINGLES
Gordon Sherry bt Chris Riley 2 holes
David Howell bt Notah Begley 2 & 1
Stephen Gallacher bt Trip Kuenhe 3 & 2
Jody Fanaghan bt Jerry Courville 3 & 2
Barclay Howard halved with Tim Jackson
Mark Foster halved with Buddy Marucci
Padraig Harrington lost to **John Harris** 3 & 2
Gary Wolstenhome lost to **Tiger Woods** 4 & 3

MATCH RESULT:
GREAT BRITAIN & IRELAND 14   USA 10

The Amateur Championship

Royal Liverpool & Wallasey   June 5-10
FINAL
Gordon Sherry (Kilmarnock Barassie) bt
Michael Reynard (Moseley) 7 & 6

USPGA Money List 1995
as at Sep 24

	Player	Ctry	Evts	Money $
1	**Greg Norman**	**AUS**	**14**	**1,555,709**
2	Lee Janzen	USA	26	1,311,561
3	Corey Pavin	USA	20	1,071,793
4	Peter Jacobsen	USA	23	1,014,157
5	Davis Love III	USA	22	1,004,349
6	Jim Gallagher jnr	USA	24	991,805
7	Steve Elkington	AUS	19	988,852
8	Vijay Singh	FIJ	21	910,713
9	Billy Mayfair	USA	25	839,032
10	David Duval	USA	23	791,158
11	Mark Calcavecchio	USA	27	788,202
12	Ernie Els	RSA	17	781,690
17	Nick Faldo	ENG	18	719,561
39	Bernhard Langer	GER	7	394,877
47	Colin Montgomerie	SCO	8	335,617
91	Costantino Rocca	ITA	2	185,500
97	Ian Woosnam	WAL	8	74,464

USPGA Money List 1994
as at Dec 31, 1994

	Player	Ctry	Evts	Money $
1	**Nick Price**	**ZIM**	**19**	**1,499,927**
2	Greg Norman	AUS	16	1,330,307
3	Mark McCumber	USA	20	1,208,209
4	Tom Lehman	USA	23	1,031,144
5	Fuzzy Zoeller	USA	19	1,016,804
6	Loren Roberts	USA	22	1,015,671
7	José Maria Olazábal	ESP	8	969,900
8	Corey Pavin	USA	20	906,305
9	Jeff Maggert	USA	26	814,475
10	Hale Irwin	USA	22	814,436
11	Scott Hoch	USA	28	804,559
12	Steve Lowery	USA	30	794,048
83	Nick Faldo	ENG	9	221,146
87	Colin Montgomerie	SCO	5	213,828
136	Sam Torrance	SCO	5	123,492

USPGA Seniors Money List 1995
as at Sep 24

	Player	Ctry	Evnts	Money $
1	**Dave Stockton**	**USA**	**27**	**1,041,564**
2	Jim Colbert	USA	27	1,036,735
3	Bob Murphy	USA	21	1,032,741
4	Ray Floyd	USA	18	1,010,545
5	Isao Aoki	JPN	20	900,033
13	Jack Nicklaus	USA	7	538,800
30	Tony Jacklin	ENG	28	341,832
80	Brian Barnes	SCO	4	56,717

USPGA Seniors Money List 1994
as at Dec 31st, 1994

	Player	Ctry	Evnts	Money $
1	**Dave Stockton**	**USA**	**32**	**1,402,519**
2	Ray Floyd	USA	20	1,382,762
3	Jim Albus	USA	35	1,237,128
4	Lee Trevino	USA	23	1,202,369
5	Jim Colbert	USA	33	1,012,115
34	Jack Nicklaus	USA	6	239,278
98	Tommy Horton	ENG	7	18,119

US PGA Tour

Date	Tournament	Venue	Winner	Score	1st Prize	Runner(s)-up	Margin
Sep 29 Oct 2	Buick Southern Open	Calloway Gardens Pine Mountain, GA	**Steve Elkington** AUS	200 (-16)	$144,000	Steve Rintoul	5
Oct 6 -9	Walt Disney World Oldsmobile Classic	Eagle Pines Orlando, Fla	**Rich Fehr** USA	269 (-19)	$198,000	Craig Stadler Fuzzy Zoeller	2
Oct 13 -16	H-E-B Texas Open	Oak Hills GC San Antonio, TX	**Bob Estes** USA	265 (-19)	$180,000	Gil Morgan	1
Oct 19 -23	Las Vegas Invitational	Sahara CC Las Vegas	**Bruce Lietzke** USA	332 (-27)	$270,000	Robert Gamez	1
Oct 27 -30	THE TOUR Championship	The Olympic Club San Francisco	**Mark McCumber** USA	274 (-10)	$540,000	Fuzzy Zoeller	play-off
Nov 3 -6	Lincoln Mercury Kapalua Interntl	Kapalua Resort Maui, HI	**Fred Couples** USA	279 (-11)	$180,000	B Gilder	2
Nov 10 -13	World Cup of Golf	Hyatt Dorado Beach Peurta Rico	**United States** Couples & Love	536	$150,000 each	Zimbabwe McNulty & Johnstone	14
Nov 17 -20	Franklin Funds Shark Shootout	Sherwood CC Thousand Oaks, CA	**Fred Couples** USA		$150,000		
Nov 26 -27	The Skins Game	Bighorn GC Palm Desert, CA	**Tom Watson** USA		$210,000		play-off
Dec 1 -4	JCPenney Mixed Classic	Innisbrook Resort Tarpon Springs, FL	**Dotti/Bryant** ESP/USA	262	$150,000	Alfredsson/ Gamez	play-off
Dec 8 -11	Diners Club Matches	PGA West La Quinta, CA	**Jeff Maggert** USA		$125,000		play-off
Jan 5 -8	Mercedes Championship	La Costa Carlsbad, CA	**Steve Elkington** AUS	278 (-10)	$180,000	Bruce Lietzke	play-off
Jan 12 -15	United Airlines Hawaiian Open	Waialae CC Honolulu, HI	**John Morse** USA	269 (-19)	$216,000	Tom Lehman Duffy Waldrof	3
Jan 19 -22	Northern Telecom Open	Tucson National Starr Pass, AZ	**Phil Mickelson** USA	269 (-18)	$225,000	Jim Gallagher jnr Scott Simpson	1
Jan 26 -29	Phoenix Open Scottsdale, AZ	TPC of Scottsdale	**Vijay Singh** FIJ	269 (-15)	$234,000	Billy Mayfair	play-off
Feb 2 -5	AT & T Pebble Beach Pro-Am	Pebble Bch, Poppy Hills & Spyglass	**Peter Jacobsen** USA	271 (-17)	$252,000	David Duval	2
Feb 9 -12	Buick Invitational	Torrey Pines GC La Jolla, CA	**Peter Jacobsen** USA	269 (-19)	$216,000	Sutton/Calcavecchia Hulbert/Triplett	4
Feb 15 -19	Bob Hope Chrysler Classic	Bermuda Dunes & Indian Wells, CA	**Kenny Perry** USA	335 (-25)	$216,000	David Duval	1
Feb 23 -26	Nissan Los Angeles Open	Riviera CC Pacific Palisds, CA	**Corey Pavin** USA	268 (-16)	$216,000	Jay Don Blake Kenny Perry	3
Mar 2 -5	Doral-Ryder Open	Doral Resort & CC Miami, FL	**Nick Faldo** ENG	273 (-15)	$270,000	Greg Norman Peter Jacobsen	1
Mar 9 -12	Honda Classic	Weston Hills CC Ft Lauderdale, FL	**Mark O'Meara** USA	275 (-9)	$216,000	Nick Faldo	1
Mar 16 -19	Bay Hills Invitational	Bay Hill Club Orlando, FL	**Loren Roberts** USA	272 (-16)	$216,000	Brad Faxon	2
Mar 23 -26	THE PLAYERS Championship	TPC at Sawgrass Ponte Vedre, FL	**Lee Janzen** USA	283 (-5)	$540,000	Bernhard Langer	1
Mar 30 Apr 2	Freeport-McMoRan Classic	English Turn G&CC New Orleans, LA	**Davis Love III** USA	274 (-14)	$216,000	Mike Heinen	play-off

Date	Tournament	Venue	Winner	Score	1st Prize	Runner(s)-up	Margin
Apr 6 -9	The Masters	Augusta National Augusta, GA	**Ben Crenshaw** USA	274 (-14)	$396,000	Davis Love III	1
Apr 13 -16	MCI Heritage Classic	Harbour Town GL Hilton Head, SC	**Bob Tway** USA	275 (-9)	$234,000	Nolan Henke David Frost	play-off
Apr 20 -23	Kmart Greater Greensboro Open	Forest Oaks CC Greensboro, NC	**Jim Gallagher jnr** USA	274 (-14)	$270,000	Jeff Sluman Peter Jacobsen	1
Apr 27 -30	Shell Houston Open	TPC at Woodlands The Woodlands, TX	**Payne Stewart** USA	276 (-12)	$252,000	Scott Hoch	play-off
May 4 -7	BellSouth Classic	Atlanta CC Marietta, GA	**Mark Calcavecchia** USA	271 (-17)	$234,000	Jim Gallagher jnr	2
May 11 -14	GTE Byron Nelson Classic	TPC at Las Colinas Irving, TX	**Ernie Els** RSA	263 (-17)	$234,000	Robin Freeman Mike Neinan	3
May 18 -21	Buick Classic	Westchester CC Rye, NY	**Vijay Singh** FIJ	278 (-6)	$216,000	Doug Martin	play-off
May 25 -28	Colonial National	Colonial CC Fort Worth, TX	**Tom Lehman** USA	271 (-9)	$252,000	Craig Parry	1
June 1 -4	Memorial Tournament	Muirfield Village Dublin, OH	**Greg Norman** AUS	269 (19)	$306,000	Elkington, Duval Calcavecchia	4
June 8 -11	Kemper Open	TPC at Avenel Potomac, MD	**Lee Janzen** USA	272 (-1)	$252,000	Corey Pavin	play-off
June 15 -18	US Open	Shinnecock Hills New York State	**Corey Pavin** USA	280 (par)	$350,000	Greg Norman	2
June 22 -25	Canon Greater Hartford Open	TPC at R. Highlands Cromwell, CT	**Greg Norman** AUS	267 (-13)	$216,000	Dave Stockton jnr	2
June 29 -31	Federal Express St Jude Classic	TPC at Southwind Memphis, TN	**Jim Gallagher jnr** USA	267 (-17)	$225,000	Ken Green Jay Delsing	1
July 6 July 9	Motorola Western Open	Cog Hill G & CC Lemont, IL	**Billy Mayfair** USA	279 (-9)	$360,000	Haas, Maggert, Leonard	1
July 13 -16	Anheuser Busch Golf Classic	Kinsmill GC Williamsburg, VA	**Ted Tryba** USA	272 (-12)	$198,000	Scott Simpson	1
July 20 -23	Deposit Guaranty	Annandale GC Madison, MS	**Ed Dougherty** USA	272 (-16)	$126,000	Gil Morgan	2
July 27 -30	Ideon Classic	Pleasant Valley CC Sutton, MA	**Fred Funk** USA	268 (-16)	$180,000	Jim McGovern	1
Aug 3 -6	Buick Open	Warwick Hills CC Grand Blanc, MI	**Woody Austin** USA	270 (-18)	£216,000	Mike Brisky	play-off
Aug 10 -13	PGA Championship	Riviera CC Pacific Palisades	**Steve Elkington** AUS	267 (-17)	$310,000	C Montgomerie	play-off
Aug 17 -20	The Sprint International	Castle Pines GC Castle Rock, CO	**Lee Janzen** USA	34pts	$270,000	Ernie Els	1 point
Aug 24 -27	NEC World Series of Golf	Firestone CC Akron, OH	**Greg Norman** AUS	278 (-2)	$360,000	Nick Price Billy Mayfair	play-off
Aug 31 Sep 3	Greater Milwaukee Open	Brown Deer Pk GC Milwaukee, WI	**Scott Hoch** USA	269 (-15)	$180,000	Marco Dawson	3
Sep 7 -10	Bell Canadian	Glen Abbey GC Oakville, Ontario	**Mark O'Meara** USA	274 (-14)	$234,000	Bob Lohr	play-off
Sep 14 -17	BC Open	En-Joie GC Endicott, NY	**Hal Sutton** USA	269 (-15)	$180,000	Jim McGovern	1
Sep 21 -24	The Quad City Classic	Oakwood CC Coal Valley, IL	**D A Weibring** USA	197 (-13)	$180,000	Jonathan Kaye	1

Women's Golf

Solheim Cup (USA v Europe)

The Greenbrier, West Virginia, USA   Oct 21-23

FIRST DAY - FOURSOMES
USA names first
Dottie Mochrie & Brandie Burton bt
Liselotte Neumann & Helen Alfredsson 3 & 2

Beth Daniel & Meg Mallon lost to
Annika Sorenstam & Catrin Nilsmark 1 hole

Tammie Green & Kelly Robbins lost to
Dale Reid & Lora Fairclough 2 & 1

Donna Andrews & Betsy King lost to
Laura Davies & Alison Nicholas 2 & 1

Patty Sheehan & Sherri Steinhauer bt
Pam Wright & Trish Johnson 2 holes

End of 1st day: United States 2 **Europe 3**

SECOND DAY - FOURBALLS
Dotty Mochrie & Brandie Buton bt
Laura Davies & Alison Nicholas 2 & 1

Beth Daniel & Meg Mallon bt
Catrin Nilsmark & Annika Sorenstam 6 & 5

Tammie Green & Kelly Robbins lost to
Dale Reid & Lora Fairclough 4 & 3

Donna Andrews & Betsy King bt
Trish Johnson & Pam Wright 3 & 2

Patty Sheehan & Sherri Steinhauer lost to
Liselotte Neumann & Helen Alfredsson 1 hole

End of 2nd day: United States 5 Europe 5

THIRD DAY - SINGLES

Dottie Mochrie bt Catrin Nilsmark 6 & 5
Betsy King lost to **Helen Alfresson** 2 & 1
Kelly Robbins bt Lora Fairclough 4 & 2
Beth Daniel bt Trish Johnson 2 holes
Pattie Sheehan lost to **Alison Nicholas** 3 & 2
Meg Mallon bt Pam Wright 1 hole
Brandie Burton bt Laura Davies 2 holes
Sherri Steinhauer bt Dale Reid 2 holes
Donna Andrews bt Liselotte Neumann 3 & 2

Final Result: United States 13 Europe 7

The second Solheim Cup, at Dalmahoy in 1992, had been a revelation. Europe spurred on by a scornful comment from American Beth Daniel had come home 11.5 to 6.5 victors. With the third Solheim, at the Greenbrier, came realisation. Even motivation is not always enough. For Daniel's scorn at Dalmahoy, substitute Dottie Mochrie's contempt at The Greenbrier. The fiery Mochrie, having rejected a handshake from Laura Davies on the first day, cheered a missed putt by Davies on the second, when she was in opposition to the West Byfleet golfer in the fourballs. That might have rated as the perfect motivation for the women who is arguably the world's best, but Mochrie and her partner, Brandie Burton, won that match. Their victory helped to balance out the advantage that Europe had taken into the second day's competition. The 3-2 lead from day one was cancelled out and the scores were all square going into the final day's singles.

Europe had expected to do well at the foursomes; the partnerships were canny, with Dale Reid's experience weighing against Lora Fairclough's innocence (her only previous golf in the US had been on a holiday in Florida), Davies and Nicholas a powerful double act, and the Swedish pairing of Sorenstam and Nilsmark apparently annoying the Americans because they chattered away in Swedish. What language, you may ask, did the Americans expect them to speak? Narrow leads, though, are quickly eaten away and the final day was little short of a rout. Mochrie, as her opponent Nilsmark pointed out, had no need to resort to anything other than fine play to canter home a 6 & 5 winner. Alfredsson pulled it back to level, but Fairclough and Johnson both drew blanks and the only further victory of the day came from Nicholas - the last four matches all going America's way.

Date	Tournament	Venue	Winner	Score	1st Prize	Runner(s)-up	Margin
May 11 -13	Costa Azul Open	Montado GC Lisbon	**M-L De Lorenzi** FRA	205 (-4)	£8,250	Evelyn Orley	2
May 18 -21	Ford Golf Classic	Chart Hills GC	**Lora Fairclough** ENG	277 (-11)	£16,500	Florence Descamp	1
Jun 7 -10	Evian Masters	Royal GC Evian	**Laura Davies** ENG	271 (-17)	£40,630	Annika Sorenstam	5
Jun 15 Jun 18	OVB Open	Zell am See Austria	**Annika Sorenstam** SWE	270 (-22)	£15,000	Laura Davies	3
Jun 23 -25	European Masters	Cleydael GC Antwerpen,Belgium	**Lora Fairclough** ENG	206 (-10)	£22,500	Frederica Dassu	2
Jun 29 Jul 2	Hennessy Cup	Cologne GC Germany	**Annika Sorenstam** SWE	271 (-17)	£45,000	Trish Johnson Liselotte Neumann	1
Jul 27 -30	Guardian Irish Holidays Open	St Margaret's CC Dublin	**Laura Davies** ENG	267 (-25)	£15,000	Asa Gottmo	16
Aug 3 -6	Payne & Gunter Scottish Open	Dalmahoy G & CC Kirknewton	**Alison Nicholas** ENG	272 (-16)	£11,250	Patricia Meunier	1
Aug 10 -13	Woodpecker Welsh Open	St Pierre Hotel CC Chepstow, Gwent	**Laura Davies** ENG	278 (-14)	£9,000	Wendy Doolan	3
Aug 25 -27	Ford-Stimorol Danish Open	Vejle GC Vejle, Denmark	**Caroline Hall** ENG	201 (-15)	£9,000	Corinne Dibnah	8
Aug 31 Sep-3	Wilkinson Sword English Open	Oxfordshire GC Thame	**Laura Davies** ENG	279 (-9)	£13,500	Karina Orum	1
Sep 7 -10	Trygg Hansa Open	Haninge GC Stockholm	**Liselotte Neumann** SWE	281 (-11)	£17,250	Annika Sorenstam	1
Sep 15 -17	Staatsloterij Dutch Open	Rijk van Nijmegan	**M-L De Lorenzi** FRA	201 (-18)	£10,500	Lora Fairclough	9
Sep 21 -24	Maredo Open	Treudelberg GC Hamburg	**Rachel Hetherington** AUS	275 (-17)	£11,250	Caroline Hall	2
Sep 28 Oct 1	Italian Open de Sicilia	Il Picciolo GC Castiglione Sicilia	**Denise Booker** AUS	284 (-8)	£15,000	Amaia Arruti	1
Final Events 1994 Tour							
Sep 29 Oct 2	La Manga Spanish Open	Hyatt La Manga Murcia	**M-L de Lorenzi** FRA	282 (-6)	£9,000	S Gronberg-Whitmore	play-off
Oct 13 15	Var Open de France	Saint Endréol	**Julie Forbes** ENG	213 (-3)	£8,250	Dale Reid S Strudwick	3-way play-off

USA LPGA MONEY LIST
1994 (final)

	Player	Ctry	Evnts	Money $
1	**Laura Davies**	ENG	22	687,201
2	Beth Daniel	USA	25	659,426
3	Liselotte Neumann	SWE	21	505,701
4	Dottie Mochrie	USA	27	472,728
5	Donna Andrews	USA	23	429,015

USA LPGA MONEY LIST
1995 (at 25th Sep)

	Player	Ctry	Evnts	Money $
1	**Annika Sorenstam**	SWE	17	542,724
2	Kelly Robbins	USA	23	527,655
3	Dottie Mochrie	USA	22	481,000
4	Betsy King	USA	24	464,149
5	Laura Davies	ENG	15	462,995

Weetabix British Open

Woburn G & CC, Beds   *Aug 17-20*
Yardage: 6258   Par: 73

278	**Karrie Webb AUS**	**69 70 69 70**
	(£60,000)	
284	Annika Sorenstam SWE	70 72 71 71
	Jill McGill USA	71 73 71 69
	(£30,000 each)	
285	Val Skinner USA	74 68 67 76
	Caroline Pierce ENG	70 70 72 73
	Michelle Berteotti USA	73 71 71 70
	(£14,333 each)	
286	Suzanne Strudwick ENG	73 68 71 74
	(£9,500)	
288	Marie Laure de Lorenzi FRA	68 74 73 73
	Liselotte Neumann SWE	67 74 71 76
	Wendy Doolan AUS	73 71 70 74
	Nancy Lopez USA	71 73 70 74
	(£6,937 each)	
289	Patricia Meunier FRA	73 71 71 74
	Vicki Goetze USA	73 72 71 73
	Catriona Matthew SCO	74 71 73 71
	Kris Tschetter USA	73 7574 7674 67
	(£4,957 each)	
290	Sally Prosser ENG	70 74 74 72
	Julie Forbes SCO	69 73 77 71
	Hiromi Kobayashi JPN	72 70 74 74
	(£4,430 each)	
291	Karen Pearce AUS	74 71 72 74
	Asa Gottmo SWE	70 73 72 74
	Brandie Burton USA	72 70 74 75
	Lynette Brooky NZL	69 74 76 72
	(£4,032 each)	

292	Rachel Hetherington AUS	74 76 76 66
	Joanne Morley ENG	72 72 74 74
	Evelyn Orley SUI	71 73 74 74
	(£4,100 each)	
293	Alison Nicholas ENG	73 72 76 72
	Mardi Lunn AUS	73 67 73 80
	Stephanie Dallongeville FRA	76 72 72 73
	Tina Fischer GER	76 66 77 74
	Lora Fairclough ENG	76 68 72 77
	Valerie Michaud FRA	76 73 75 69
	Lisa Hackney ENG	74 74 70 75
	Marnie McGuire NZL	68 78 73 74
	(£3,215 each)	

294 Trish Johnson ENG, Melissa McNamara USA, Li Wen-Lin TPE, Stefania Croce ITA,Shani Waugh AUS, Lori West USA; 295 Diane Barnard ENG, Caroline Hall ENG; 296 Carin Hjalmarsson SWE, Tracy Hanson USA, Penny Hammel USA; 297 Laura Davies ENG, Leigh Ann Mills USA, Wendy Dicks ENG, Pamela Wright SCO, Sarah Burnell ENG, Katie Peterson-Parker USA, Emilee Klein USA; 298 Claire Duffy ENG, Jane Geddes USA, Estefania Knuth ESP, Karina Orum DEN, Alison Brighouse ENG; 299 Sofia Gronberg SWE, Liz Weima NED, Aideen Rogers IRL, Kathryn Marshall SCO, Charlotta Eliasson Wharton SWE; 300 Karen Davies USA, Allison Shapcott ENG, Amaia Arruti ESP, Tina Barrett USA; 301 Gillian Stewart SCO, Lisa Dermott* WAL; 302 Susan Moon USA, Dale Reid SCO; 303 Janet Soulsby ENG, Pernilla Sterner SWE; 304 Helen Hopkins AUS, Caryn Louw RSA; 305 Karen Stupples* ENG

EUROPEAN TOUR
FORD ORDER OF MERIT
1994 *(final)*

	Player	Ctry	Evnts	Money £
1	**Liselotte Neumann**	**SWE**	**4**	**102,750**
2	Helen Alfredsson	SWE	5	63,315
3	Laura Davies	ENG	7	59,384
4	Annika Sorenstam	SWE	5	58,360
5	Corinne Dibnah	AUS	15	57,040
6	Lora Fairclough	ENG	13	44,585
7	Tracy Hanson	USA	5	44,205
8	Helen Wadsworth	WAL	11	41,979
9	Alison Nicholas	ENG	11	38,550
10	Karina Orum	DEN	15	34,613
11	Sarah Gautrey	AUS	12	34,547
12	Florence Descampe	BEL	6	31,862
13	Dale Reid	SCO	14	31,792
14	Marie-Laure de Lorenzi	FRA	14	31,593
15	Trish Johnson	ENG	9	31,309

EUROPEAN TOUR
FORD ORDER OF MERIT
1995 *(as at Oct 1)*

	Player	Ctry	Evnts	Money £
1	**Annika Sorenstam**	**SWE**	**6**	**130,324**
2	Laura Davies	ENG	9	100,697
3	Karrie Webb	AUS	12	90,556
4	Lora Fairclough	ENG	13	80,647
5	Marie Laure de Lorenzi	FRA	12	69,852
6	Alison Nicholas	ENG	7	53,076
7	Corinne Dibnah	AUS	14	51,244
8	Trish Johnson	ENG	10	51,042
9	Liselotte Neumann	SWE	3	49,887
10	Jill McGill	USA	7	41,226
11	Frederica Dassu	ITA	15	38,031
12	Rachel Hetherington	AUS	16	36,943
13	Karina Orum	DEN	16	35,301
14	Caroline Hall	ENG	16	33,694
15	Evelyn Orley	SUI	12	31,368

Open Champions

Year	Champion	Score	Venue		Year	Champion	Score	Venue
1860	Willie Park Snr GBR	174	Prestwick		1929	Walter Hagen USA	292	Muirfield
1861 & 62	Tom Morris Snr GBR	163	Prestwick		1930	Bobby Jones (am) USA	291	Hoylake
1862	Tom Morris Snr GBR	163	Prestwick		1931	Tommy Armour USA	296	Carnoustie
1863	Willie Park Snr GBR	168	Prestwick		1932	Gene Sarazen USA	283	Prince's
1864	Tom Morris Snr GBR	167	Prestwick		1933	Densmore Shute USA	292*	St Andrews
1865	Andrew Strath GBR	162	Prestwick		1934	Henry Cotton GBR	283	Sandwich
1866	Willie Park Snr GBR	169	Prestwick		1935	Alfred Perry GBR	283	Muirfield
1867	Tom Morris Snr GBR	170	Prestwick		1936	Alfred Padgham GBR	287	Hoylake
1868, 1869, 1870 & 1872	all at Prestwick				1937	Henry Cotton GBR	290	Carnoustie
	Tom Morris Jnr GBR	157, 154, 149, 166			1938	Reg Whitcombe GBR	295	Sandwich
1873	Tom Kidd GBR	179	St Andrews		1939	Dick Burton GBR	290	St Andrews
1874	Mungo Park GBR	159	Musselburgh		1946	Sam Snead USA	290	St Andrews
1875	Willie Park Snr GBR	166	Prestwick		1947	Fred Daly GBR	293	Hoylake
1876	Bob Martin GBR	176	St Andrews		1948	Henry Cotton GBR	284	Muirfield
1877	Jamie Anderson GBR	160	Musselburgh		1949	Bobby Locke RSA	283*	Sandwich
1878	Jamie Anderson GBR	157	Prestwick		1950	Bobby Locke RSA	279	Troon
1879	Jamie Anderson GBR	169	St Andrews		1951	Max Faulkner GBR	285	Portrush
1880	Robert Ferguson GBR	162	Musselburgh		1952	Bobby Locke RSA	287	Royal Lytham
1881	Robert Ferguson GBR	170	Prestwick		1953	Ben Hogan USA	282	Carnoustie
1882	Robert Ferguson GBR	171	St Andrews		1954	Peter Thomson AUS	283	Royal Birkdale
1883	Willie Fernie GBR	158*	Musselburgh		1955	Peter Thomson AUS	281	St Andrews
1884	Jack Simpson GBR	160	Prestwick		1956	Peter Thomson AUS	286	Hoylake
1885	Bob Martin GBR	171	St Andrews		1957	Bobby Locke RSA	279	St Andrews
1886	David Brown GBR	157	Musselburgh		1958	Peter Thomson AUS	278*	Royal Lytham
1887	Willie Park Jnr GBR	161	Prestwick		1959	Gary Player RSA	284	Muirfield
1888	Jack Burns GBR	171	St Andrews		1960	Kel Nagle AUS	278	St.Andrews
1889	Willie Park Jnr GBR	155*	Musselburgh		1961	Arnold Palmer USA	284	Royal Birkdale
1890	John Ball (am) GBR	164	Prestwick		1962	Arnold Palmer USA	276	Troon
1891	Hugh Kirkaldy GBR	166	St Andrews		1963	Bob Charles NZL	277*	Royal Lytham
1892	Harold Hilton (am)GBR	305	Muirfield		1964	Tony Lema USA	279	St Andrews
1893	Will Auchterlonie GBR	322	Prestwick		1965	Peter Thomson AUS	285	Royal Birkdale
1894	John H Taylor GBR	326	Sandwich		1966	Jack Nicklaus USA	282	Muirfield
1895	John H Taylor GBR	322	St Andrews		1967	Rob. de Vicenzo ARG	278	Hoylake
1896	Harry Vardon GBR	316*	Muirfield		1968	Gary Player RSA	289	Carnoustie
1897	Harold Hilton (am)GBR	314	Hoylake		1969	Tony Jacklin GBR	280	Royal Lytham
1898	Harry Vardon GBR	307	Prestwick		1970	Jack Nicklaus USA	283*	St Andrews
1899	Harry Vardon GBR	310	Sandwich		1971	Lee Trevino USA	278	Royal Birkdale
1900	John H Taylor GBR	309	St Andrews		1972	Lee Trevino USA	278	Muirfield
1901	James Braid GBR	309	Muirfield		1973	Tom Weiskopf USA	276	Troon
1902	Sandy Herd GBR	307	Hoylake		1974	Gary Player RSA	282	Royal Lytham
1903	Harry Vardon GBR	300	Prestwick		1975	Tom Watson USA	279*	Carnoustie
1904	Jack White GBR	296	Sandwich		1976	Johnny Miller USA	279	Royal Birkdale
1905	James Braid GBR	318	St Andrews		1977	Tom Watson USA	268	Turnberry
1906	James Braid GBR	300	Muirfield		1978	Jack Nicklaus USA	281	St Andrews
1907	Arnaud Massy FRA	312	Hoylake		1979	Seve Ballesteros ESP	283	Royal Lytham
1908	James Braid GBR	291	Prestwick		1980	Tom Watson USA	271	Muirfield
1909	John H Taylor GBR	295	Deal		1981	Bill Rogers USA	276	Sandwich
1910	James Braid GBR	299	St Andrews		1982	Tom Watson USA	284	Troon
1911	Harry Vardon GBR	303	Sandwich		1983	Tom Watson USA	275	Royal Birkdale
1912	Edward Ray GBR	295	Muirfield		1984	Seve Ballesteros ESP	276	St Andrews
1913	John H Taylor GBR	304	Hoylake		1985	Sandy Lyle GBR	282	Sandwich
1914	Harry Vardon GBR	306	Prestwick		1986	Greg Norman AUS	280	Turnberry
1920	George Duncan GBR	303	Deal		1987	Nick Faldo GBR	279	Muirfield
1921	Jock Hutchinson USA	296*	St Andrews		1988	Seve Ballesteros ESP	273	Royal Lytham
1922	Walter Hagen USA	300	Sandwich		1989	Mark Calcavecchia USA	275*	Troon
1923	Arthur Havers GBR	295	Troon		1990	Nick Faldo GBR	270	St Andrews
1924	Walter Hagen USA	301	Hoylake		1991	Ian Baker-Finch AUS	272	Royal Birkdale
1925	Jim Barnes USA	300	Prestwick		1992	Nick Faldo GBR	272	Muirfield
1926	Bobby Jones (am) USA	291	Royal Lytham		1993	Greg Norman AUS	267	Sandwich
1927	Bobby Jones (am) USA	285	St Andrews		1994	Nick Price ZIM	268	Turnberry
1928	Walter Hagen USA	292	Sandwich		1995	John Daly USA	282	St Andrews

US Open Champions

Year	Winner (USA unless stated)	Score	Venue
1895	Horace Rawlins	173	Newport
1896	James Foulis	152	Shinnecock Hs
1897	Joe Lloyd	162	Chicago
1898	Willie Smith	315	Baltimore
1900	Harry Vardon GBR	313	Chicago
1901	Willie Anderson	331*	Myopia Hunt
1902	Laurie Auchterlonie	307	Garden City
1903	Willie Anderson	307*	Baltusrol
1904	Willie Anderson	303	Glen View
1905	Willie Anderson	314	Myopia Hunt
1906	Alex Smith	295	Onwentsia
1907	Alex Ross	302	Philadelphia
1908	Fred McLeod	322*	Myopia Hunt
1909	George Sargent	290	Englewood
1910	Alex Smith	298*	Philadelphia
1911	John McDermott	307*	Chicago
1912	John McDermott	294	Buffalo
1913	Francis Ouimet (am)	304*	Brookline
1914	Walter Hagen	290	Midlothian
1915	JeromeTravers (am)	297	Baltusrol
1916	Charles Evans Jnr (am)	286	Minikahda
1919	Walter Hagen	301*	Brae Burn
1920	Edward Ray GBR	295	Inverness
1921	Jim Barnes	289	Columbia
1922	Gene Sarazen	288	Skokie
1923	Bobby Jones (am)	296*	Inwood
1924	Cyril Walker	297	Oakland Hills
1925	Willie Macfarlane	291*	Worcester
1926	Bobby Jones (am)	293	Scioto
1927	Tommy Armour	301 *	Oakmont
1928	Johnny Farrell	294*	Olympia Flds
1929	Bobby Jones (am)	294*	Winged Foot
1930	Bobby Jones (am)	287	Interlachen
1931	Billy Burke	292*	Inverness
1932	Gene Sarazen	286	Fresh Meadow
1933	Johnny Goodman (am)	287	North Shore
1934	Olin Dutra	293	Merion
1935	Sam Parks Jnr	299	Oakmont
1936	Tony Manero	282	Baltusrol
1937	Ralph Guldahl	281	Oakland Hills
1938	Ralph Guldahl	284	Cherry Hills
1939	Byron Nelson	284*	Philadelphia
1940	Lawson Little	287*	Canterbury
1941	Craig Wood	284	Colonial
1946	Lloyd Mangrum	284*	Canterbury
1947	Lew Worsham	282*	St Louis
1948	Ben Hogan	276	Riviera
1949	Cary Middlecoff	286	Medinah
1950	Ben Hogan	287*	Merion
1951	Ben Hogan	287	Oakland Hills
1952	Julius Boros	281	Northwood
1953	Ben Hogan	283	Oakmont
1954	Ed Furgol	284	Baltusrol
1955	Jack Fleck	287*	Olympic
1956	Cary Middlecoff	281	Oak Hill
1957	Dick Mayer	282*	Inverness
1958	Tommy Bolt	283	Southern Hills
1959	Billy Casper	282	Winged Foot
1960	Arnold Palmer	280	Cherry Hills
1961	Gene Littler	281	Oakland Hills
1962	Jack Nicklaus	283*	Oakmont
1963	Julius Boros	293*	Brookline
1964	Ken Venturi	278	Congressional
1965	Gary Player RSA	282*	Bellerive
1966	Billy Casper	278*	Olympic
1967	Jack Nicklaus	275	Baltusrol
1968	Lee Trevino	275	Oak Hill
1969	Orville Moody	281	Champions
1970	Tony Jacklin GBR	281	Hazeltine
1971	Lee Trevino	280*	Merion
1972	Jack Nicklaus	290	Pebble Beach
1973	Johnny Miller	279	Oakmont
1974	Hale Irwin	287*	Winged Foot
1975	Lou Graham	287	Medinah
1976	Jerry Pate	277	Atlanta
1977	Hubert Green	278	Southern Hills
1978	Andy North	285	Cherry Hills
1979	Hale Irwin	284	Inverness
1980	Jack Nicklaus	272	Baltusrol
1981	David Graham AUS	273	Merion
1982	Tom Watson	282	Pebble Beach
1983	Larry Nelson	280	Oakmont
1984	Fuzzy Zoeller	276*	Winged Foot
1985	Andy North	279	Oakland Hills
1986	Raymond Floyd	279	Shinnecock Hls
1987	Scott Simpson	277	Olympic Club
1988	Curtis Strange	278	Brookline
1989	Curtis Strange	278	Oak Hill
1990	Hale Irwin	280*	Medinah
1991	Payne Stewart	282*	Hazeltine
1992	Tom Kite	285	Monterey
1993	Lee Janzen	272	Baltusrol
1994	Ernie Els RSA	279	Oakmont
1995	Corey Pavin	280	Shinnecock Hls

after play off

US Masters & US PGA Champions

US MASTERS *(US unless stated)*

Year	Winners	Score
1934	Horton Smith	284
1935	Gene Sarazen	282*
1936	Horton Smith	285
1937	Byron Nelson	283
1938	Henry Picard	285
1939	Ralph Guldahl	279
1940	Jimmy Demaret	280
1941	Craig Wood	280
1942	Byron Nelson	280*
1946	Herman Keiser	282
1947	Jimmy Demaret	281
1948	Claude Harmon	279
1949	Sam Snead	282
1950	Jimmy Demaret	283
1951	Ben Hogan	280
1952	Sam Snead	286
1953	Ben Hogan	274
1954	Sam Snead	289*
1955	Cary Middlecoff	279
1956	Jack Burke Jnr	289
1957	Doug Ford	282
1958	Arnold Palmer	284
1959	Art Wall Jnr	284
1960	Arnold Palmer	282*
1961	Gary Player RSA	280
1962	Arnold Palmer	280*
1963	Jack Nicklaus	286
1964	Arnold Palmer	276
1965	Jack Nicklaus	271
1966	Jack Nicklaus	288*
1967	Gay Brewer	280
1968	Bob Goalby	277
1969	George Archer	281
1970	Billy Casper	279*
1971	Charles Coody	279
1972	Jack Nicklaus	286
1973	Tommy Aaron	283
1974	Gary Player RSA	278
1975	Jack Nicklaus	276
1976	Raymond Floyd	271
1977	Tom Watson	276
1978	Gary Player RSA	277
1979	Fuzzy Zoeller	280*
1980	S Ballesteros ESP	275
1981	Tom Watson	280
1982	Craig Stadler	284*
1983	S Ballesteros ESP	280
1984	Ben Crenshaw	277
1985	Bernh. Langer FRG	282
1986	Jack Nicklaus	279
1987	Larry Mize	285*
1988	Sandy Lyle GBR	281
1989	Nick Faldo GBR	283*
1990	Nick Faldo GBR	278*
1991	Ian Woosnam GBR	277
1992	Fred Couples	275
1993	Bernh. Langer GER	277
1994	J-M Olazábal ESP	279
1995	Ben Crenshaw	274

US PGA CHAMPIONSHIP

Year	Winner	Score
1916	Jim Barnes	1 up
1919	Jim Barnes	6 & 5
1920	Jock Hutchison	1 up
1921	Walter Hagen	3 & 2
1922	Gene Sarazen	4 & 3
1923	Gene Sarazen	38th
1924	Walter Hagen	2 up
1925	Walter Hagen	6 & 5
1926	Walter Hagen	5 & 3
1927	Walter Hagen	1 up
1928	Leo Diegel	6 & 5
1929	Leo Diegel	6 & 4
1930	Tommy Armour	1 up
1931	Tom Creavy	2 & 1
1932	Olin Dutra	4 & 3
1933	Gene Sarazen	5 & 4
1934	Paul Runyan	38th
1935	Johnny Revolta	5 & 4
1936	Densmore Shute	3 & 2
1937	Densmore Shute	37th
1938	Paul Runyan	8 & 7
1939	Henry Picard	37th
1940	Byron Nelson	1 up
1941	Vic Ghezi	38th
1942	Sam Snead	2 & 1
1944	Bob Hamilton	1 up
1945	Byron Nelson	4 & 3
1946	Ben Hogan	6 & 4
1947	Jim Ferrier	2 & 1
1948	Ben Hogan	7 & 6
1949	Sam Snead	3 & 2
1950	Chandler Harper	4 & 3
1951	Sam Snead	7 & 6
1952	Jim Turnesa	1 up
1953	Walter Burkemo	2 & 1
1954	Chick Harbert	4 & 3
1955	Doug Ford	4 & 3
1956	Jack Burke	3 & 2
1957	Lionel Hebert	2 & 1
1958	Dow Finsterwald	276
1959	Bob Rosburg	277
1960	Jay Hebert	281
1961	Jerry Barber	277*
1962	Gary Player RSA	278
1963	Jack Nicklaus	279
1964	Bobby Nichols	271
1965	Dave Marr	280
1966	Al Geiberger	280
1967	Don January	281*
1968	Julius Boros	281
1969	Raymond Floyd	276
1970	Dave Stockton	279
1971	Jack Nicklaus	281
1972	Gary Player RSA	281
1973	Jack Nicklaus	277
1974	Lee Trevino	276

Year	Winner	Score
1975	Jack Nicklaus	276
1976	Dave Stockton	281
1977	Lanny Wadkins	282*
1978	John Mahaffey	276*
1979	David Graham AUS	272*
1980	Jack Nicklaus	274
1981	Larry Nelson	273
1982	Raymond Floyd	272
1983	Hal Sutton	274
1984	Lee Trevino	273
1985	Hubert Green	278
1986	Bob Tway	276
1987	Larry Nelson	287*
1988	Jeff Sluman	272
1989	Payne Stewart	276
1990	Wayne Grady AUS	282
1991	John Daly	276
1992	Nick Price ZIM	278
1993	Paul Azinger	272
1994	Nick Price	269
1995	Steve Elkington	267

* after play off

World Tournaments & Ryder Cup History

WORLD MATCHPLAY

Year	Winner	Runner-up	Score
1964	**Arnold Palmer** USA	Neil Coles GBR	2&1
1965	**Gary Player** RSA	Peter Thomson AUS	3&2
1966	**Gary Player** RSA	Jack Nicklaus USA	6&4
1967	**Arnold Palmer** USA	Peter Thomson AUS	1 up
1968	**Gary Player** RSA	Bob Charles NZ	1 up
1969	**Bob Charles** NZL	Gene Littler USA	37th
1970	**Jack Nicklaus** USA	Lee Trevino USA	2&1
1971	**Gary Player** RSA	Jack Nicklaus USA	5&4
1972	**Tom Weiskopf** USA	Lee Trevino USA	4&3
1973	**Gary Player** RSA	G Marsh AUS	40th
1974	**Hale Irwin** USA	Gary Player RSA	3&1
1975	**Hale Irwin** USA	Al Geiberger USA	4&2
1976	**David Graham** AUS	Hale Irwin USA	38th
1977	**Graham Marsh** AUS	Ray Floyd USA	5&3
1978	**Isao Aoki** JPN	Simon Owen NZL	3&2
1979	**Bill Rogers** USA	Isao Aoki JPN	1 up
1980	**Greg Norman** AUS	Sandy Lyle GBR	1 up
1981	**S Ballesteros** ESP	Ben Crenshaw USA	1 up
1982	**S Ballesteros** ESP	Sandy Lyle GBR	37th
1983	**Greg Norman** AUS	Nick Faldo GBR	3&2
1984	**S Ballesteros** ESP	B Langer FRG	2&1
1985	**S Ballesteros** ESP	B Langer FRG	6&5
1986	**Greg Norman** AUS	Sandy Lyle GBR	2&1
1987	**Ian Woosnam** GBR	Sandy Lyle GBR	1 up
1988	**Sandy Lyle** GBR	Nick Faldo GBR	2&1
1989	**Nick Faldo** GBR	Ian Woosnam GBR	1 up
1990	**Ian Woosnam** GBR	Mark McNulty ZIM	4&2
1991	**S Ballesteros** ESP	Nick Price ZIM	3&2
1992	**Nick Faldo** GBR	Jeff Sluman USA	8&7
1993	**Corey Pavin** USA	Nick Faldo GBR	1 up
1994	**Ernie Els** RSA	C Montgomerie GBR	4&2

WORLD CUP

Year	Winning team	Score
1953	**Argentina** (de Vicenzo & Cerda)	*287
1954	**Australia** (Thomson & Nagle)	556
1955	**USA** (Furgol & Harbert)	560
1956	**USA** (Hogan & Snead)	567
1957	**Japan** (Nakamura & Ono)	557
1958	**Ireland** (Bradshaw & O'Connor)	579
1959	**Australia** (Nagle & Thomson)	563
1960	**USA** (Palmer & Snead)	565
1961	**USA** (Demaret & Snead)	560
1962	**USA** (Palmer & Snead)	557
1963	**USA** (Nicklaus & Palmer)	*482
1964	**USA** (Nicklaus & Palmer)	554
1965	**South Africa** (Henning & Player)	571
1966	**USA** (Nicklaus & Palmer)	548
1967	**USA** (Nicklaus & Palmer)	557
1968	**Canada** (Balding & Knudson)	569
1969	**USA** (Moody & Trevino)	552
1970	**Australia** (Devlin & Graham)	544
1971	**USA** (Nicklaus & Trevino)	555
1972	**Taiwan** (Hsieh & Lu)	*438
1973	**USA** (Miller & Nicklaus)	558
1974	**South Africa** (Cole & Hayes)	554
1975	**USA** (Graham & Miller)	554
1976	**Spain** (Ballesteros & Pinero)	574
1977	**Spain** (Ballesteros & Garrido)	591
1978	**USA** (Mahaffey & North)	564
1979	**USA** (Mahaffey & Irwin)	575
1980	**Canada** (Halidorson & Nelford)	572
1982	**Spain** (Canizares & Pinero)	563
1983	**USA** (Caldwell & Cook)	565
1984	**Spain** (Canizares & Rivero)	*414
1985	**Canada** (Halidorson & Barr)	559
1987	**Wales** (Woosnam & Llewellyn)	574
1988	**USA** (Crenshaw & McCumber)	560
1989	**Australia** (Fowler & Grady)	*278
1990	**Germany** (Langer & Giedeon)	556
1991	**Sweden** (Forsbrand & Johansson)	563
1992	**USA** (Couples & Love III)	548
1993	**USA**	556
1994	**USA**	536

played over 36 holes in 1953, 63 holes in 1963, 54 holes in 1972 & 1984. Rain reduced play to 36 holes in 1989.

RYDER CUP

Year	Venue	Winner	Score
1927	Worcester, Massachusetts	USA	9.5-2.5
1929	Moortown, Yorkshire	GBR	7-5
1931	Scioto, Ohio	USA	9-3
1933	Southport & Ainsdale, Lancs	GBR	6.5-5.5
1935	Ridgewood, New Jersey	USA	9-3
1937	Southport & Ainsdale, Lancs	USA	8-4
1947	Portland, Oregon	USA	11-1
1949	Ganton, Yorkshire	USA	7-5
1951	Pinehurst, North Carolina	USA	9.5-2.5
1953	Wentworth, Surrey	USA	6.5-5.5
1955	Thunderbird G&CC, C'fornia	USA	8-4
1957	Lindrick, Yorkshire	GBR	7.5-4.5
1959	Eldorado CC, California	USA	8.5-3.5
1961	Royal Lytham, Lancs	USA	14.5-9.5
1963	Atlanta, Georgia	USA	23-9
1965	Royal Birkdale, Lancs	USA	19.5-12.5
1967	Houston, Texas	USA	23.5-8.5
1969	Royal Birkdale, Lancs	Drawn	16-16
1971	St Louis, Missouri	USA	18.5-13.5
1973	Muirfield, Scotland	USA	19-13
1975	Laurel Valley, Pennsylvania	USA	21-11
1977	Royal Lytham, Lancs	USA	12.5-7.5
1979	Greenbrier, West Virginia	USA	17-11
1981	Walton Heath, Surrey	USA	I8.5-9.5
1983	PGA National, Florida	USA	14.5-13.5
1985	The Belfry, Sutton Coldfield	Europe	16.5-11.5
1987	MuirfieldVillage, Ohio	Europe	15-13
1989	The Belfry, Sutton Coldfield	Drawn	14-14
1991	Kiawah Island, S Carolina	USA	14.5-13.5
1993	The Belfry, Sutton Coldfield	USA	15-13
1995	Oak Hill CC, Rochester, NY	Europe	14-5-13.5

Gymnastics ▬▬▬▬▬

Artistic Gymnastics

World Team Championships
Dortmund, Germany   Nov 15-20, 1994

MEN
1	China	283.333

*(Floor: 46.837, P Horse 48.149, Rings: 46.537
Vault: 47.598, P Bars: 47.598, H Bar: 47.112)*

2	Russia	282.158
3	Ukraine	281.086

WOMEN
1	Romania	195.847

*(Vault: 49.050, A Bars: 48.374,
Beam: 49.049, Floor: 49.374)*

2	United States	194.645
3	Russia	194.546

European Cup
Rome   June 16-18

WOMEN
All Round
1	Svetlana Khorkina	RUS	39.311
2	Simona Amanar	ROM	39.187
3	Yelena Piskoun	BLR	39.099

Vault
1	Simon Amanar	ROM	9.787

Asymmetric Bars
1	Lilia Podkopayeva	UKR	9.862

Beam
1	Lilia Podkopayeva	UKR	9.737

Floor
1	Simone Amanar	ROM	9.825

British Team Championships
Liverpool   Feb 18-19
1	City of Liverpool	210.00
2	Nottingham Gym. School	196.45
3	City of Leeds	184.40

British Women's Championships
Guildford   June 30-July 2
All Around
1	Annika Reeder (South Essex)	73.737
2	Zita Lusack (Heathrow)	73.462
3	Sonia Lawrence (Spelthorne)	73.087

Vault
1	Annika Reeder (South Essex)	9.575

Bars
1	Gemma Cuff (Heathrow)	9.425

Beam
1	Zita Lusack (Heathrow)	9.325

Floor
1	Annika Reeder (South Essex)	9.675

Rhythmic Gymnastics

World Championships
Paris, France   Oct 6-9, 1994

TEAM
All Around *(4 Hoop + 2 Club, 6 Rope)*
1	Russia	38.925

(Hoop+Club: 19.500, Rope: 19.425)

2	Spain	38.700
3	Bulgaria	38.675

Hoop & Club *(4 Hoop + 2 Club)*
1	Bulgaria	19.550
2	Russia	19.400
3	Spain	19.325

Rope *(6 Rope)*
1	Russia	19.587
2	Bulgaria	19.537
3	Spain	19.400

INDIVIDUAL
All Around
1	Maria Petrova	BUL	38.900

(Hoop: 9.750, Ball: 9.700, Clubs: 9.700, Ribbon: 9.750)

2	Amina Zaripova	RUS	38.850
2	Larissa Lukyanenko	BLS	38.850

Hoop
1	Larissa Lukyanenko	BLS	9.875
1	Ekaterina Serebrianskaya	UKR	9.875
1	Maria Petrova	BUL	9.875

Ball
1	Ekaterina Serebrianskaya	UKR	9.875
1	Elena Vitrichenko	UKR	9.875
3	Maria Petrova	BUL	9.825

Clubs
1	Ekaterina Serebrianskaya	UKR	9.900
2	Maria Petrova	BUL	9.825
3	Amina Zaripova	RUS	9.800

Ribbon
1	Ekaterina Serebrianskaya	UKR	9.900
2	Amina Zaripova	RUS	9.850
3	Maria Petrova	BUL	9.850

European Championships
Prague, Czech Republic   July 2-10

TEAM
All Around *(3 Ball + 2 Ribbon, 5 Hoop)*
1	Russia	38.875
2	Bulgaria	38.825
3	Spain	38.625

Ball & Ribbon *(3 Ball + 2 Ribbon)*
1	Bulgaria	19.550
2	Spain	19.543
3	France	18.775

Hoop *(5 Hoop)*
1	Russia	19.800
2	Bulgaria	19.700
3	Spain	19.512

European Cup Final
Telford, England   June 24-25

INDIVIDUAL
All Around
1 Ekaterina Serebrianskaya UKR   39.700
Rope
1 Larissa Lukyanenko   BLS   9.925
1 Ekaterina Serebrianskaya UKR   9.925
Ball
1 Larissa Lukyanenko   BLS   9.950
1 Olgar Gontar   BLS   9.950
Club
1 Ekaterina Serebrianskaya UKR   9.950
Ribbon
1 Amina Zaripova   RUS   9.950
1 Yana Batyrchina   RUS   9.950

British Championships
Bletchley   Mar 25

INDIVIDUAL
All Around
1 Jennifer McGuire (unattached)   34.35
Rope
1 Jennifer McGuire (unattached)   9.10
Ball
1 Jennifer McGuire (unattached)   8.80
Clubs
1 Aicha McKenzie (Westminster)   9.075
Ribbon
1 Aicha McKenzie (Westminster)   9.075

Sports Acrobatics
British Championships
Kings Lynn   Mar 18-19

Women's Tumbling
1 Kathryn Peberdy (West Kirby)   26.16
2 Melanie Thompson (West Kirby)   24.93
3 Leanne Esdaile (South Tyneside)   24.38

Men's Tumbling
1 Craig Smith (West Bromwich)   25.93
2 Craig Filmer (Salto)   25.13
3 Andrew Griffiths (Spelthorne)   24.95

Mixed Pair
1 Wharton/Grimes (Deerness Valley) 29.72
2 Griffiths/Crocker (Spelthorne)   29.66

Men's Pair
1 Martin/Hopkins (Heathrow)   29.22
2 Reddy/Green (Wakefield)   28.04

Women's Pair
1 Yellop/Ellison (South Tyneside)   28.72
1 Greggs/Kaye (South Tyneside)   28.72

Women's Groups
1 Arnold/Kirkham/Hope (Deerness Valley)   29.52
2 Brelsford/Lawton/Wass (Deerness Valley)   29.06

Men's Groups
1 Smailes/Moore/Bryan/Newton (King Edmund) 25.08

World Artistic Championships

MEN

Year	Venue	All-round Champion	Team
	Floor Exercises	*Pommel Horse*	*Rings*
	Vault	*Parallel Bars*	*High Bar*
1983	**Budapest**	Dmitry Bilozerchev URS	China
	Tong Fei CHN	Dmitry Bilozerchev URS	Bilozerchev URS/Koji Gushiken JPN
	Artur Akopian URS	V Artemov URS/Lou Yun CHN	Dmitriy Bilozerchev URS
1985	**Montreal**	Yury Korolev URS	Soviet Union
	Tong Fei CHN	Valentin Mogilnyi URS	Li Ning CHN/Yury Korolev URS
	Yuri Korolev URS	S Kroll GDR/V Mogilnyi URS	Tong Fei CHN
1987	**Rotterdam**	Dmitry Bilozerchev URS	Soviet Union
	Lou Yun CHN	Bilozerchev URS/Z Borkai HUN	Yury Korolev URS
	S Kroll GDR/Lou Yun CHN	Vladimir Artemov URS	Dmitriy Bilozerchev URS
1989	**Stuttgart**	Igor Korobchinsky URS	Soviet Union
	Igor Korobchinsky URS	Valentin Mogilnyi URS	Andreas Aguilar FRG
	Jörg Behrendt GDR	Li Jing CHN/V Artemov URS	Li Chunyang CHN
1991	**Indianapolis**	Grigory Misutin URS	Soviet Union
	Igor Korobchinsky URS	Valery Belenky URS	Grigory Misutin URS
	Yu Ok-yul KOR	Li Jing CHN	Li Chunyang CHN/Ralf Büchner GER
1993	**Birmingham**	Vitaly Scherbo BLR	
	Grigory Misutin UKR	Gil Su Pae KOR	Yuri Cechi ITA
	Vitaly Scherbo BLS	Vitaly Scherbo BLR	Sergei Charkov RUS
1994	**Brisbane**	Ivan Ivankov BLS	
	Vitaly Scherbo BLS	Marius Urzica ROM	Yuri Chechi ITA
	Vitaly Scherbo BLS	Liping Huang CHN	Vitaly Scherbo BLS

WOMEN

Year	Venue	All-round Champion	Team
		Beam	*Floor Exercises*
		Asymmetric Bars	*Vault*
1983	**Budapest**	Natalya Yurchenko URS	Soviet Union
		Olga Mostepanova URS	Ekaterina Szabo ROM
		Maxi Gnauck GDR	Boriana Stoyanova BUL
1985	**Montreal**	Omelianchik URS/Shushnova URS	Soviet Union
		Daniela Silivas ROM	Oksana Omelianchik URS
		Gabriela Fahnrich GDR	Yelena Shushnova URS
1987	**Rotterdam**	Aurelia Dobre ROM	Romania
		Aurelia Dobre ROM	Y Shushnova URS/D Silivas ROM
		D Silivas ROM/D Thümmler GDR	Yelena Shushnova URS
1989	**Stuttgart**	Svetlana Boginskaya URS	Soviet Union
		Daniela Silivas ROM	D Silivas ROM/S Boginskaya URS
		Fan Di CHN/D Silivas ROM	Olessia Dudnik URS
1991	**Indianapolis**	Kim Zmeskal USA	Soviet Union
		Svetlana Boginskaya URS	C Bontas ROM/O Chusovitina URS
		Kim Gwang-suk KOR	Lavinia Milosovici ROM
1993	**Birmingham**	Shannon Miller USA	
		Lavinia Milosovici ROM	Shannon Miller USA
		Shannon Miller USA	Yelena Piskoun BLS
1994	**Brisbane**	Shannon Miller USA	
		Shannon Miller USA	Dina Kochetkova RUS
		Li Luo CHN	Gina Gogean ROM

Handball ████████████████

Men's World Championship

Iceland   *May 7-21*

Group A

Final Table	P	W	D	L	PF	PA	Pts
Switzerland	5	5	0	0	133	103	10
Korea	5	4	0	1	140	112	8
Iceland	5	3	0	2	119	107	6
Tunisia	5	2	0	3	110	125	4
Hungary	5	1	0	4	119	121	2
United States	5	0	0	5	82	135	0

Group B

Final Table	P	W	D	L	PF	PA	Pts
Croatia	5	4	0	1	140	119	8
Russia	5	4	0	1	112	96	8
Czech Rep	5	4	0	1	121	111	8
Cuba	5	2	0	3	136	132	4
Slovenia	5	1	0	4	131	126	2
Morocco	5	0	0	5	93	149	0

Group C

Final Table	P	W	D	L	PF	PA	Pts
Germany	5	5	0	0	128	93	10
Romania	5	3	0	2	121	121	6
France	5	3	0	2	122	108	6
Algeria	5	2	0	3	103	113	4
Denmark	5	2	0	3	126	117	4
Japan	5	0	0	5	101	149	0

Group D

Final Table	P	W	D	L	PF	PA	Pts
Sweden	5	5	0	0	151	114	10
Spain	5	4	0	1	123	104	8
Egypt	5	3	0	2	111	106	6
Belarus	5	2	0	3	154	125	4
Kuwait	5	1	0	4	85	131	2
Brazil	5	0	0	5	96	140	0

Quarter-finals

Switzerland 18	France 28
Russia 17	Germany 20
Croatia 30	Egypt 16
Sweden 21	Czech Rep 17

Semi-finals

Germany 20	France 22
Croatia 28	Sweden 25

3rd-4th Place Play-off

Sweden 26	Germany 20

FINAL

France 23   Croatia 19

Men's European Cup

Group A

	P	W	D	L	PF	PA	Pts
Badel Zagreb	6	4	1	1	156	147	9
TEKA Santander	6	3	1	2	155	125	7
Fotex Veszprem	6	2	2	2	131	147	6
Kolding IF	6	1	0	5	140	163	2

Group B

	P	W	D	L	PF	PA	Pts
Elgorriaga Bidasoa	6	4	0	2	137	126	8
THW Kiel	6	3	0	3	137	136	6
OM Vitrolles	6	3	0	3	133	133	6
Dukla Prague	6	2	0	4	139	151	4

Final

Elgorriaga Bidasoa ESP 56 Badel Zagreb CRO 47

Women's European Cup

Group A

	P	W	D	L	PF	PA	Pts
Niederösterreich	6	6	0	0	162	111	12
Mar Valencia	6	3	1	2	144	138	7
Larvik HK	6	2	1	3	141	144	5
Olimpija Ljubljana	6	0	0	6	115	169	0

Group B

	P	W	D	L	PF	PA	Pts
Pod'ka Koprivnica	6	3	2	1	147	127	8
Walle Bremen	6	3	2	1	141	138	8
Ferenc. Budapest	6	3	1	2	135	129	7
Swift Roermond	6	0	1	5	124	153	1

Final

Hypo Niederösterreich 40 Podravka Koprivnica 36

World Champions

Men *(Indoors)*		Women *(Indoors)*	
1938	**Germany**	1957	**Czechoslovakia**
1954	**Sweden**	1962	**Romania**
1958	**Sweden**	1965	**Hungary**
1961	**Romania**	1971	**East Germany**
1964	**Romania**	1973	**Yugoslavia**
1967	**Czechoslovakia**	1975	**East Germany**
1970	**Romania**	1979	**East Germany**
1978	**West Germany**	1982	**Soviet Union**
1982	**Soviet Union**	1986	**Soviet Union**
1986	**Yugoslavia**	1990	**Soviet Union**
1990	**Sweden**	1994	**Germany**
1995	**France**		

Hockey ━━━━━━━━━━━━━━━━━━━━━━━━

Pakistan's victory in the men's World Cup in Sydney saw them return to the top of world hockey after a break of 10 years. Their penalty shoot-out victory was just revenge for the 1990 Final defeat at the hands of the Dutch, even if they did have to suffer the ignominy of losing to the English in the pool matches. Their inspirational captain, Shabhaz, again announced his international retirement, only to return at the Champion's Trophy.

Whilst England hacked about in the World Cup to reach a creditable sixth and qualify for the 1998 event in Holland, the European Cup provided them with a rare glimpse of a medal. England showed their capabilities by defeating Olympic champions Germany. Then, with an inviting semi-final against Belgium beckoning, drew with Switzerland. The dropped point put Germany top of Pool B and left England needing to overcome the Netherlands to reach the final. Their narrow defeat (the only one of the championship) left them with a play-off against Belgium, which they won 2-1, to take the bronze medal.

Much of the credit for England's performance must lay at the stick of Calum Giles, who only appeared on the pitch whenever a corner was awarded. On the occasions when he was roused from his slumberings on the bench, Giles clocked up nine goals which gave him the prestigious top goalscorer trophy. Wales and Scotland filled 8th & 10th places respectively, but Scotland did at least have something to crow about. They beat Switzerland.

India provided the setting for another of the professional versus amateur confrontations that seem to be *en vogue*. At the Indira Ghandi Gold Cup in February, the organisers had already handed out a couple of televisions and had a fleet of shiny new locally produced cars in the wings, when the FIH representative, Phil Appleyard, interceded. He stated that the cars, worth 450,000 rupees (£9,000), and the TVs must be converted into cash prizes and the money sent to the national federations. Well, you can imagine how keen everyone was to abide by that rule. The cars were driven away, the televisions carried off and the International Hockey Federation buffed up its halo. Rugby Union, this isn't.

On the women's scene, Amstelveen played host to the European Cup. England, the holders, managed the feat of not conceding a goal in their five pool matches, which was a far cry from their disastrous World Cup campaign the previous year. However, successive defeats in the final stage meant they came away empty-handed.

Domestically, Slough claimed their first title for three years and produced a prolonged European campaign which saw them edged out by German team Rüsselheim in both the Cup Winners' Cup and the Indoor European Cup. Their ever-present stalwart, Karen Brown, was named as player of the year for 1994 and was persuaded out of retirement to return to the England fold.

In the men's National League, Teddington finally shrugged off their tag of 'nearly men' and clinched their first title in the closest finish to any season. Reading went to Stourport for the final game with their goal difference five goals inferior to Teddington's. The West Londoners beat East Grinstead 4-2 and then had heart failure when they heard that Reading were 4-0 up at half time. In the second half, though, the challenge petered out. Reading won just 5-1 and the Bushy Park clubhouse had a noisy night. Teddington's at last.

Men's Hockey

World Cup

Sydney, Australia   Nov 23-Dec 4, 1994

Pool A

Results	Arg	Aus	Bls	Eng	Pak	Esp
Argentina	-	-	-	-	-	-
Australia	2-1	-	-	-	-	-
Belarus	1-4	0-2	-	-	-	-
England	1-1	0-2	1-0	-	-	-
Pakistan	3-0	2-1	2-0	0-2	-	-
Spain	1-2	1-2	4-1	0-0	1-3	-

Final Table	P	W	D	L	GF	GA	Pts
1 Pakistan	5	4	0	1	10	4	8
2 Australia	5	4	0	1	9	4	8
3 England	5	2	2	1	4	3	6
4 Argentina	5	2	1	2	8	8	5
5 Spain	5	1	1	3	7	8	3
6 Belarus	5	0	0	5	2	13	0

Pool B

Results	Bel	Ger	Ned	Ind	Rsa	Kor
Belgium	-	-	-	-	-	-
Germany	6-0	-	-	-	-	-
Netherlands	8-1	0-0	-	-	-	-
India	4-2	1-2	2-4	-	-	-
South Africa	1-1	1-1	1-5	1-1	-	-
South Korea	7-2	1-1	2-4	0-2	0-0	-

Final Table	P	W	D	L	GF	GA	Pts
1 Netherlands	5	4	1	0	21	6	9
2 Germany	5	2	3	0	10	3	7
3 India	5	2	1	2	11	10	5
4 South Korea	5	1	2	2	10	9	4
5 South Africa	5	0	4	1	5	9	4
6 Belgium	5	0	1	4	6	26	1

Classification Matches

9th-12th places
Spain 1 Belgium 1 *(Spain won 8-7 after pens)*
Belarus 2 South Africa 3
11-12th places
Belgium 1 Belarus 0
9th-10th places
Spain 2 South Africa 0
5th-8th places
England 3 South Korea 1
Argentina 2 India 2 *(India won 6-3 after pens)*
7th-8th places
South Korea 3 Argentina 3 *(Argentina won 5-3 after pens)*
5th-6th places
England 0 India 1

Semi-finals
Australia 1 Netherlands 3
Pakistan 1 Germany 1 *(Pakistan won 5-3 after pens)*

3rd-4th places
Australia 5 Germany 2

WORLD CUP FINAL
Pakistan 1 Netherlands 1 *(Pakistan won 4-3 on pens)*

European Cup

Dublin, Ireland   Aug 16-27

Pool A

Results	Bel	Fra	Ned	Sco	Esp	Wal
Belgium	-	-	-	-	-	-
France	1-2	-	-	-	-	-
Netherlands	1-1	6-1	-	-	-	-
Scotland	1-3	1-1	1-4	-	-	-
Spain	2-2	3-1	1-3	3-0	-	-
Wales	1-3	1-1	0-3	2-0	0-2	-

Final Table	P	W	D	L	GF	GA	Pts
1 Netherlands	5	4	1	0	17	4	9
2 Belgium	5	3	2	0	11	8	8
3 Spain	5	3	1	1	11	6	7
4 Wales	5	1	1	3	4	9	3
5 France	5	0	2	3	5	13	2
6 Scotland	5	0	1	4	3	13	1

Pool B

Results	Bls	Eng	Ger	Ire	Pol	Sui
Belarus	-	-	-	-	-	-
England	4-0	-	-	-	-	-
Germany	9-0	2-3	-	-	-	-
Ireland	2-1	1-1	0-2	-	-	-
Poland	3-2	1-3	0-3	1-1	-	-
Switzerland	0-4	4-4	0-7	2-1	2-3	-

Final Table	P	W	D	L	GF	GA	Pts
1 Germany	5	4	0	1	23	2	8
2 England	5	3	2	0	15	8	8
3 Poland	5	2	1	2	8	11	5
4 Ireland	5	1	2	2	5	7	4
5 Switzerland	5	1	1	3	8	19	3
6 Belarus	5	1	0	4	7	18	2

Classification Matches

9th-12th places
France 2 Belarus 4
Switzerland 2 Scotland 3
11-12th places
France 2 Switzerland 2
9th-10th places
Belarus 4 Scotland 2
5th-8th places
Spain 1 Ireland 3
Poland 3 Wales 1
7th-8th places
Spain 1 Wales 2
5th-6th places
Ireland 4 Poland 3

Semi-finals
Netherlands 2 England 1
Germany 4 Belgium 0

3rd-4th places
England 2 Belgium 1

EUROPEAN CUP FINAL
Germany 2 Netherlands 2 *(Germany won 9-8 on pens)*

Champion's Trophy

Berlin, Germany   Sep 23-Oct 1
Final Play-offs
5th-6th place
India 2 England 2 *(India won 6-5 after pens)*

3rd-4th place
Pakistan 2 Netherlands 1

Final
Germany 2 Australia 2 *(Germany won 4-2 after pens)*

Other England Internationals

Moenchengladbach, Germany   Oct 14-16, 1994

Results	Ned	Esp	Ger	Eng
Netherlands	-	-	-	-
Spain	2-3	-	-	-
Germany	1-1	0-1	-	-
England	2-2	2-1	0-1	-

Brussels, Belgium   Nov 4-6, 1994

Results	Ned	Esp	Bel	Eng
Netherlands	-	-	-	-
Spain	0-2	-	-	-
Belgium	1-8	1-4	-	-
England	1-4	2-1	4-0	-

Test series v Australia   May
1st Test *(Perth-11th)*   Australia 4 England 1
2nd Test *(Adelaide-13th)* Australia 3 England 1
3rd Test *(Adelaide-15th)* Australia 4 England 0
4th Test *(Hobart-17th)*   Australia 3 England 3
5th Test *(Melbourne-19th)*Australia 3 England 1
6th Test *(Brisbane-21st)* Australia 5 England 0

Brussels, Belgium   July 15-16
Belgium 1 England 2
Belgium 0 England 8

Netherlands   Aug 6-7
Netherlands 5 England 1
Netherlands 5 England 2

European Club Championship (Div A)

Terrassa, Spain   June 2-5
5th-8th Play-off
Havant ENG 3 Royal Baudouin BEL 3
(Royal Baudouin won 4-2 after pens; Havant finished joint 7th, relegating this season's champions to the B Division)
Final
Uhlenhorst GER 1 Amsterdam NED 0

European Club Cup Winners' Cup (Div A)

Cagliari, Italy   Apr 14-17
3rd/4th Place Play-off
Teddington ENG 2 Royal Club de Barcelona ESP 3
Final
HDM NED 0 Harvestehuder GER 0
(Harvestehuder won 4-1 after pens)

HA Cup

6th Round
Formby 1 Richmond 0
Guildford 4 Barford Tigers 1
Isca 2 Cannock 1
Southgate 0 Teddington 1

Semi-finals
Formby 1 Teddington 4
Guildford 5 Isca 1

FINAL
Canterbury May 28
Guildford 4 (Hall, Jennings 2, Markham)
Teddington 1 *(Billson)*

National Hockey League

Division 1	P	W	D	L	GF	GA	Pts
1 Teddington	17	13	1	3	50	25	40
2 Reading	17	13	1	3	45	22	40
3 Cannock	17	11	5	1	57	19	38
4 Guildford	17	11	1	5	54	30	34
5 Southgate	17	9	5	3	45	25	32
6 Hounslow	17	9	4	4	33	21	31
7 Old Loughtonians	17	8	2	7	45	34	26
8 Surbiton	17	7	5	5	30	22	26
9 East Grinstead	17	8	2	7	32	27	26
10 Havant	17	6	5	6	34	32	23
11 Bournville	17	5	4	8	33	42	19
12 Canterbury	17	4	6	7	29	33	18
13 Trojans	17	5	3	9	27	42	18
14 Indian Gymkhana	17	5	2	10	23	39	17
15 Stourport	17	3	6	8	25	37	15
16 Hull	17	4	1	12	20	59	13
17 Firebrands	17	2	2	13	15	44	8
18 Slough	17	1	3	13	17	61	6

Division 2	P	W	D	L	GF	GA	Pts
1 St Albans	17	11	3	3	40	24	36
2 Barford Tigers	17	9	4	4	33	21	31
3 Brooklands	17	9	3	5	32	25	30
4 Doncaster	17	8	5	4	29	16	29
5 Edgbaston	17	7	6	4	18	18	27
6 Isca	17	7	5	5	32	22	26
7 Harleston Magpies	17	8	2	7	25	20	26
8 Richmond	17	7	5	5	27	24	26
9 Hampstead & W	17	7	5	5	25	26	26
10 Oxford University	17	7	4	6	31	31	25
11 Beeston	17	7	4	6	28	30	25
12 Bromley	17	6	5	6	25	23	23
13 Sheffield	17	6	4	7	35	33	22
14 Gloucester City	17	6	3	8	35	36	21
15 Whitchurch	17	5	4	8	23	30	19
16 Crostyx	17	5	4	8	22	31	19
17 Neston	17	1	4	12	12	32	7
18 Cambridge City	17	1	2	14	16	46	5

Following inter-league play-offs, Crostyx retained place in League and were joined by Portsmouth, Olton & West Warwicks and Blueharts.

NORWICH UNION COUNTY CHAMPIONSHIP
Final
Portsmouth   May 21
Kent 2 Yorkshire 3

HA INDOOR CLUB CHAMPIONSHIP
Final
Crystal Palace NSC   Jan 21
Old Loughtonians 6 Barford Tigers 5

Women's Hockey

European Cup
Amstelveen, Holland   June 14-25
Pool A

Results	Bel	Eng	Fra	Ire	Ita	Ger
Belgium	-	-	-	-	-	-
England	9-0	-	-	-	-	-
France	5-2	0-4	-	-	-	-
Ireland	2-1	0-2	2-1	-	-	-
Italy	1-1	0-3	0-4	0-1	-	-
Germany	15-0	0-1	3-1	4-0	3-0	-

Final Table		P	W	D	L	GF	GA	Pts
1	**England**	5	5	0	0	19	0	10
2	Germany	5	4	0	1	25	2	8
3	Ireland	5	3	0	2	5	8	6
4	France	5	2	0	3	11	11	4
5	Italy	5	0	1	4	1	12	1
6	Belgium	5	0	1	4	4	32	1

Pool B

Results	Cze	Ned	Rus	Sco	Esp	Swe
Czech Rep.	-	-	-	-	-	-
Netherlands	8-0	-	-	-	-	-
Russia	5-0	0-3	-	-	-	-
Scotland	3-1	0-1	2-2	-	-	-
Spain	7-0	0-2	3-0	1-0	-	-
Sweden	0-1	0-10	0-6	0-9	0-4	-

Final Table		P	W	D	L	GF	GA	Pts
1	**Holland**	5	5	0	0	24	0	10
2	Spain	5	4	0	1	15	2	8
3	Scotland	5	2	1	2	14	5	5
4	Russia	5	2	1	2	13	8	5
5	Czech Republic	5	1	0	4	2	23	2
6	Sweden	5	0	0	5	0	30	0

Classification Matches
9th-12th places
Italy 4 Sweden 0
Belgium 0 Czech Republic 0 *(Czech R won 2-1 after pens)*
11-12th places
Belgium 6 Sweden 0
9th-10th places
Italy 1 Czech Republic 0

5th-8th places
Ireland 0 Russia 4
France 0 Scotland 3
7th-8th places
Ireland 1 France 1 *(France won 4-3 after pens)*
5th-6th places
Russia 2 Scotland 2 *(Russia won 6-5 after pens)*

Semi-finals
England 1 Spain 3
Germany 1 Netherlands 2

3rd-4th places
England 0 Germany 1

EUROPEAN CUP FINAL
Netherlands 2 Spain 2 *(Netherlands won 4-1 on pens)*

Champion's Trophy
Mar del Plata, Argentina   Sep 9-19
Final Play-offs
5th-6th place
Spain 2 Argentina 1

3rd-4th place
USA 0 Germany 0 *(USA won 4-1 after pens)*

Final
Australia 1 South Korea 1 *(Australia won 4-3 after pens)*

Other Internationals

Test series v USA (San Diego   January)
1st Test *(28th)* USA 0 Great Britain 2
2nd Test *(29th)* USA 2 Great Britain 0
3rd Test *(31st)* USA 3 Great Britain 1

Bisham Abbey   Jan 28-29
England 1 Russia 0
England 1 Russia 2

Lilleshall   Feb 25-26
England 1 Scotland 0
England 3 Scotland 1

Test series v Netherlands
Amstelveen Apr 28
Netherlands 3 England 3

Hertogenbosch Apr 29
Netherlands 5 England 2

Vlissingen Apr 30
Netherlands 0 England 0

Centenary International   Sheffield   May 13
England 1 Germany 1

Madrid   May 26-28
Spain 2 England 1
Spain 1 England 1

Lilleshall   June 3-4
England 1 Scotland 0
England 5 Scotland 1

Sydney, Australia   Aug 31-Sep 3
Australia 4 Great Britain 1
Australia 2 Great Britain 1
Australia 3 Great Britain 2

European Indoor Club Championships

Russelsheim, Germany   Feb 17-19
A Division
Final Standings: **1 Russelsheim GER,** 2 Slough ENG, 3 Aldeasa Valdeluz ESP, 4 Inter Eurovil Siaulia LIT

European Cup for Club Champions

Utrecht, Holland   June 2-5
A Division
Final Standings: **1 S V Kampong NED,** 2 Berliner HC GER, 3 HC Siauliai LIT, 4 Glasgow Western SCO

European Clubs Cup Winners Cup

Groningen, Holland   Apr 14-17
A Division
Final Standings: **1 Russelsheim GER,** 2 Slough ENG, 3 Groningen NED, 4 Muckross IRE

National League

Premier League

		P	W	D	L	GF	GA	Pts
1	Slough	14	12	1	1	41	9	37
2	Hightown	14	8	4	2	32	10	28
3	Ipswich	14	9	1	4	22	15	28
4	FP Sutton Coldfield	14	5	4	5	19	18	19
5	Balsam Leicester	14	4	5	5	14	16	17
6	Clifton	14	4	2	8	14	24	14
7	Bracknell	14	2	3	9	8	29	9
8	Chelmsford	14	1	2	11	11	40	5

First Division

		P	W	D	L	GF	GA	Pts
1	Doncaster	14	12	0	2	29	8	36
2	Trojans	14	8	1	5	25	12	25
3	Wimbledon	14	6	5	3	20	15	23
4	Exmouth	14	6	3	5	16	17	21
5	Canterbury	14	5	4	5	13	17	19
6	Bradford S'bank	14	4	3	7	20	27	15
7	Blueharts	14	2	4	8	10	22	10
8	Ealing	14	2	2	10	11	26	8

Second Division

		P	W	D	L	GF	GA	Pts
1	Sunderland Bedans	14	8	4	2	28	16	28
2	Loughborough Stdts	14	7	5	2	25	15	26
3	Olton	14	8	1	5	29	12	25
4	Woking	14	6	4	4	25	18	22
5	Sherwood	14	5	4	5	16	22	19
6	St Albans	14	5	3	6	15	18	18
7	Blackburn & Gt H	14	2	5	7	20	36	11
8	Pickwick	14	1	2	11	11	32	5

AEWHA Cup

Quarter-finals
Balsam Leicester 7 Winchester 0
Ealing 0 Exmouth 4
Harleston Magpies 0 Trojans 2
Hightown 2 Chelmsford 0

Semi-finals
Exmouth 1 Hightown 3
Trojans 0 Balsam Leicester 0 *(Trojans won 4-3 after pens)*

Final
Milton Keynes   May 21
Hightown 5 Trojans 0

AEWHA PLATE
Final
Milton Keynes   May 21
Liverpool 1 Crimson Ramblers 0

Scottish National League

First Division

		P	W	D	L	GF	GA	Pts
1	Western Klick P	16	13	1	2	79	4	40
2	Bonagrass Grove	16	13	1	2	50	10	40
3	Edinburgh Ladies*	16	11	3	2	47	9	36
4	Hyndland	16	9	4	3	33	17	31
5	Royal High Gym	16	5	5	6	25	21	20
6	Heriot-Watt Uni*	16	5	2	9	16	23	17
7	Boroughmuir	16	3	2	11	7	52	11
8	Western Klick 'A'	16	3	1	12	9	48	10
9	Grange	16	1	1	14	8	87	4

* Incomplete GF & GA Tallies

Second Division

		P	W	D	L	GF	GA	Pts
1	Menzieshill	16	15	1	0	43	4	46
2	C Bryson Melrose	16	7	5	4	21	16	26
3	Edinburgh University	16	7	4	5	15	13	25
4	Aberdeen B Accord	16	7	3	6	17	15	24
5	Eglinton	16	8	0	8	16	15	24
6	Stepps	16	6	6	4	16	15	24
7	Kelburne	16	4	2	10	17	30	14
8	Hutcheson's FP	16	4	2	10	10	25	14
9	Hyndland A	16	2	1	13	5	27	7

Teams for the 1996 Men's Olympic Qualifying Tournament

To be played at Terrassa, Spain Jan 19-28

England, Netherlands, India, Spain, Belarus, Belgium, Canada, Malaysia

To be played on a round-robin basis, the top five ranked teams will qualify for the Atlanta Olympics

International & Domestic Records

WORLD CUP WINNERS

	Men		Women
1971	Pakistan	1974	Netherlands
1973	Netherlands	1976	West Germany
1975	India	1978	Netherlands
1978	Pakistan	1981	West Germany
1982	Pakistan	1983	Netherlands
1986	Australia	1986	Netherlands
1990	Netherlands	1990	Netherlands
1994	Pakistan	1994	Australia

EUROPEAN CUP WINNERS

	Men	Women
1970	West Germany	-
1974	Spain	-
1978	West Germany	-
1983	Netherlands	Netherlands (1984)
1987	Netherlands	Netherlands
1991	Germany	England
1995	Germany	Netherlands

EUROPEAN CLUB CHAMPIONS CUP

Men

1969	Club Egara de Terrasa ESP
1970	Club Egara de Terrasa ESP
1971	Frankfurt 1880 FRG
1972	Frankfurt 1880 FRG
1973	Frankfurt 1880 FRG
1974	Frankfurt 1880 FRG
1975	Frankfurt 1880 FRG
1976	Southgate ENG
1977	Southgate ENG
1978	Southgate ENG
1979	Klein Zwitserland NED
1980	Slough ENG
1981	Klein Zwitserland NED
1982	Dynamo Alma-Ata URS
1983	Dynamo Alma-Ata URS
1984	TG 1846 Frankental FRG
1985	Atletico Terrasa ESP
1986	Kampong, Utrecht NED
1987	Bloemendaal NED
1988	Uhlenhorst Mülheim FRG
1989	Uhlenhorst Mülheim FRG
1990	Uhlenhorst Mülheim FRG
1991	Uhlenhorst Mülheim GER
1992	Uhlenhorst Mülheim GER
1993	Uhlenhorst Mülheim GER
1994	Uhlenhorst Mülheim GER
1995	Uhlenhorst Mülheim GER

Women

1974	Harvestehuder, Hamburg FRG
1976	Amsterdam NED
1977	Amsterdam NED
1978	Amsterdam NED
1979	Amsterdam NED
1980	Amsterdam NED
1981	Amsterdam NED
1982	Amsterdam NED
1983	HGC Wassenaar NED
1984	HGC Wassenaar NED
1985	HGC Wassenaar NED
1986	HGC Wassenaar NED
1987	HGC Wassenaar NED
1988	Amsterdam NED
1989	Amsterdam NED
1990	Amsterdam NED
1991	HGC Wassenaar NED
1992	Amsterdam NED
1993	Russulheim GER
1994	HGC Wassenaar NED
1995	S V Kampong NED

NATIONAL LEAGUE WINNERS

	Men	Women
1989	Southgate	-
1990	Hounslow	Slough
1991	Havant	Slough
1992	Havant	Slough
1993	Hounslow	Ipswich
1994	Havant	Leicester
1995	Teddington	Slough

NATIONAL CUP CHAMPIONS

	Men	Women
1972	Hounslow	-
1973	Hounslow	-
1974	Southgate	-
1975	Southgate	-
1976	Nottingham	-
1977	Slough	-
1978	Guildford	-
1979	Slough	Chelmsford
1980	Slough	Norton
1981	Slough	Sutton Coldfield
1982	Southgate	Slough
1983	Neston	Slough
1984	East Grinstead	Sheffield
1985	Southgate	Ipswich
1986	Southgate	Slough
1987	Southgate	Ealing
1988	Southgate	Ealing
1989	Hounslow	Ealing
1990	Havant	Sutton Coldfield
1991	Hounslow	Sutton Coldfield
1992	Hounslow	Hightown
1993	Hounslow	Leicester
1994	Teddington	Slough
1995	Guildford	Hightown

Horse Racing

Nigel Gray, the British Horseracing Board's handicapper, must be sick to the teeth of Lammtarra. The Godolphin horse wins the Derby and earns from Gray a rating of 123, which is about a furlong behind Dancing Brave and even three pounds behind the 1994 Derby winner, Erhaab. Lammtarra wins the King George and Gray sneaks him up about a half a length, playing down the quality of the opposition. So, Lammtarra wins the Arc and finally Gray has to place him in the bigtime with a rating of 130. Gray could argue, though, that Lammtarra could never have won a race in England in the same way he won the Arc. Out on his hooves at the three furlong mark, Dettori hit the colt 16 times in the final three furlongs. It was a brave horse, said everyone afterwards, ignoring the fact that being belted about the neck and rump is a great assistance to "bravery". In England, Dettori would have been stood down for the rest of the season. In France, they are less sensitive about horseflesh. They eat it, after all.

Lammtarra continued the extraordinary run of success of the Godolphin operation. As well as the Derby, they won the Oaks and the St Leger and Saeed Bin Suroor, the ex-policeman from Dubai sits atop the trainers' earning table with £1,691,704 from just 14 victories, an average of £120,856 a victory. Sheikh Mohammed also announced that Dubai would be staging the world's richest event in March 1996, the Dubai World Cup worth £2.5m. Currently, the Japan Cup is the world's most valuable event, worth about £100,000 less. In all, the Sheikh had a wildly successful year so it was a shame the season ended with a bit of a spat as he removed all his horses from Henry Cecil's stable. That he did so may not have been totally unconnected with criticism that he received from Cecil's wife; Sheikhs from Dubai, after all, do not often have to put up with criticism from women. Cecil, incidentally, had just one Group One winner all year, Bosra Sham, the 530,000 guineas yearling who does look a bit special.

The Aga Khan returned to racing in Britain after a four-year boycott in protest at the disqualification of Aliysa from first place in the 1989 Oaks. The Aga Khan disputed the testing procedures involved when his horse was found positive for the banned substance camphor. The procedures have since been updated, so it looks like the Aga Khan has won his argument.

Celtic Swing started the season as the wonder horse in waiting. His two-year-old rating of 130 from an international panel of handicappers - based on his 12 length victory in the Racing Post Stakes - was the best turf rating since modern records began. As a soft-ground specialist, Celtic Swing was unfortunate to be a three-year-old in one of the driest summers this century. On a bog, he may still have been a wonder horse. On decent ground, though, he wasn't.

Lester Piggott finally retired and the man who was once hailed as the "new Piggott", Paul Cook received £352,000 damages against Doncaster Racecourse. Cook fell at the course in 1989 and the injuries ended his career. Jenny Pitman gained compensation for Esha Ness's worthless win in 1993, by winning the Grand National with Royal Athlete and Kim Baily doubled the Gold Cup and the Champion Hurdle.

*Q*uotes

"When he came to me, I gave him one out of ten for trying and I didn't think he had a prayer" - **Kim Bailey, on his horse Alderbrook, who won the Champion Hurdle eight weeks after Bailey first trained him over obstacles.**

"Have I won the Cheltenham Gold Cup? Dear, oh dear. I don't know why I won or how I won. I really don't know what I'm doing here. I thought I'd go on driving a bus. I can't think of anything to compare with this unless the wife produces quins" - **Paul Matthew, former milkman, bus driver and bank clerk, who owns Master Oats.**

"Everything went wrong in the first two furlongs, so as we went down the hill and up the straight I was saying, 'help me, Alex, help me'. I know he was helping me from above" - **Walter Swinburn, jockey of Lammtara, as they won the Derby. Lammtara was formerly trained by Alex Scott, who was murdered at his yard.**

"He scared us all to death and over the years he has cost us millions. He was always the housewifes' choice. It was simple, when Piggott won, we lost" - **Mike Dillon of Ladbrokes.**

"There will never be another jockey like him. I learned from his great discipline. He would lock away his Yorkie bars and cigars and when he unlocked the cupboard he would take out one piece of Yorkie at a time" - **Walter Swinburn paying a sort of tribute to Piggott.**

"I work hard for my money. I wouldn't put it on a racehorse' - **Frankie Dettori.**

"I am aware of the problems. I am not trying to bully anybody. My trainers must remember I am the owner. These are my horses and when you own something and see it every day, you always appreciate it more" - **Sheikh Mohammed responding to trainers complaining about losing horses in the winter to the Godolphin operation in Dubai.**

"It was a great race to watch and a wonderful spectacle for the crowd, but my interpretation of it, with the first five so close together, is that it is unlikely they are all superstars" - **Nigel Gray, the BHB handicapper's modest assessment of Lammtarra's performance in winning the King George VI and Queen Elizabeth Diamond Stakes.**

"Swing Hits Rhythm" - **Tasteful headline in *The Independent* following Celtic Swing's opening victory of the summer at Newbury.**

"I see they've got him as low as 8-1 for the Derby, but he is only that price to run in the race" - **Dick Hern, trainer of the latest wonder horse, Alhaarth, after the horse won the Solario Stakes at Sandown in August.**

"Wear the Fox Hat" - **Julian Wilson's choice of name for his horse. The name was barred and Wilson, a Suffolk farmer, suggested he might change it to his second choice, "Hoof Hearted".**

"I have been approached several times over the past year, but this offer seems genuine and serious. Of course, I am operating on a no foal-no fee basis" - **Stan Cosgrove, an Irish vet, who was offered Shergar's bones for £20,000.**

C=colt, f=filly, the weight carried is in brackets after the horse's name, the starting price follows the jockey's name, the prize money is after the trainer

THE CLASSICS ▬

MADAGANS 2000 GUINEAS
Newmarket, May 6   3y c&f (1m)
PENNEKAMP (3-9-0)
Thierry Jarnet   **9/2**
A Fabre (France)   £117,912

MADAGANS 1000 GUINEAS
Newmarket, May 7   3y f (1m)
HARAYIR (3-9-0)
Richard Hills   **5/1**
Major W R Hern   £110,791

VODAFONE OAKS STAKES
Epsom, June 9   3y f (1m4f 10y)
MOONSHELL (3-9-0)
Frankie Dettori   **3/1**
Saeed Bin Suroor (Dubai) £147,800

VODAFONE DERBY STAKES
Epsom, June 10 3y c&f (1m 4f 10y)
LAMMTARRA (3-9-0)
Walter Swinburn   **14/1**
Saeed Bin Suroor   £504,500

PERTEMPS ST LEGER STAKES
Doncaster, Sep 9
3y c&f (1m 6f 132y)
CLASSIC CLICHE (3-9-0)
Frankie Dettori   **100/30F**
Saeed Bin Suroor   £166,802

GROUP 1 ▬

JUDDMONTE LOCKINGE STAKES
Newbury, May 21   4y+ (1m)
SOVIET LINE (5-9-0)
Walter Swinburn   **2/1F**
M R Stoute   £70,210

VODAFONE CORONATION CUP
Epsom, June 10   4y+ (1m 4f 10y)
SUNSHACK (4-9-0)
Pat Eddery   **10/1**
A Fabre (France)   £92,520

CORAL-ECLIPSE STAKES
Sandown, July 8
3y+ (1m 2f 7y)
HALLING (4-9-7)
Walter Swinburn   **7/1**
Saeed Bin Suroor (Dubai) £154,560

JULY CUP STAKES
Newmarket, July 13   3y+ (6f)
LAKE CONISTON (4-9-6)
Pat Eddery   **13/8F**
G Lewis   £85,774

KING GEORGE VI & QUEEN
ELIZABETH DIAMOND STAKES
Ascot, July 22   3y+ (1m 4f)
LAMMTARRA (3-8-9)
Frankie Dettori   **9/4F**
Saeed Bin Suroor(Dubai) £278,760

SUSSEX STAKES
Goodwood, July 26   3y+ (1m)
SAYYEDATI (5-9-4)
Brett Doyle   **11/2**
C E Brittain   £111,220

JUDDMONTE INTERNATIONAL
STAKES
York, Aug 15   3y+ (1m 2f 85y)
HALLING (4-9-6)
Walter Swinburn   **9/4F**
Saeed Bin Suroor   £161,720

ASTON UPTHORPE YORKSHIRE
OAKS
York, Aug 16
3y+ f&m   (1m 3f 195y)
PURE GRAIN (3-8-8)
John Reid   **11/10F**
M Stoute   £82,730

NUNTHORPE STAKES
York, Aug 17   All (5f)
SO FACTUAL (5-9-6)
Frankie Dettori   **9/2**
Saeed Bin Suroor   £72,029

HAYDOCK PARK SPRINT CUP
Haydock, Sep 2   3y+ (6f)
CHEROKEE ROSE (4-8-11)
Cash Asmussen   **5/1**
J E Hammond (France) £72,160

QUEEN ELIZABETH STAKES
Ascot Sep 23 3y+ (1m)
BAHRI (3-8-11)
Willie Carson   **5/2**
J L Dunlop   £194,760

FILLIES' MILE STAKES
Ascot Sep 24 2y f (1m)
BOSRA SHAM (2-8-10)
Pat Eddery   **10/11F**
H R A Cecil   £90,495

MIDDLE PARK STAKES
Newmarket, Sep 28 2y c (6f)
ROYAL APPLAUSE (2-8-11)
Walter Swinburn   **3/1**
B W Hills   £72,928

1994 Group 1

GENEROUS DEWHURST STAKES
Newmarket, Oct 14 2y c&f (7f)
PENNEKAMP (2-9-0)
Thierry Jarnet   **5/2F**
A Fabre (France)   £96,585

CHAMPION STAKES
Newmarket, Oct 15 3y+ (1m 2f)
DERNIER EMPEREUR (4-9-4)
Sylvain Guillot   **8-1**
A Fabre (France)   £165,948

RACING POST TROPHY
Doncaster, Oct 22 2y c&f (1m)
CELTIC SWING (2-9-0)
Kevin Darley   **EvsF**
Lady Herries   £90,758

GROUP 2 ▬

SANDOWN MILE STAKES
Sandown, Apr 28   4y+ (1m 14y)
MISSED FLIGHT (5-9-4)
George Duffield   **7/4F**
C F Wall   £34,250

MADAGANS JOCKEY CLUB STKS
Newmarket, May 5   4y+ (1m 4f)
ONLY ROYALE (6-8-11)
Frankie Dettori   **4/1**
L M Cumani   £32,589

HOMEOWNERS DANTE STAKES
York, May 17   3y (1m 2f 85y)
CLASSIC CLICHE (3-8-11)
Walter Swinburn   **9/1**
Saeed Bin Suroor (Dubai) £63,931

YORKSHIRE CUP STAKES
York, May 18   4y+ (1m 5f 194y)
MOONAX (4-9-0)
Pat Eddery   **11/4F**
Saeed Bin Suroor (Dubai)
£51,963

TRIPLEPRINT TEMPLE STAKES
Sandown, May 29   3y+ (5f 6y)
MIND GAMES (3-8-8)
John Carroll   **10/11F**
J Berry   £38,075

PRINCESS OF WALES' STAKES
Newmarket, July 11   3y+ (1m 4f)
BEAUCHAMP HERO (5-9-5)
John Reid   **8/1**
J L Dunlop   £35,576

FALMOUTH STAKES
Newmarket, July 12 3y+ f&m (1m)
CARAMBA (3-8-6)
Michael Roberts   **5/2**
R Hannon   £34,099

TIFFANY GOODWOOD CUP
Goodwood, July 27   3y+ (2m)
DOUBLE TRIGGER (4-9-5)
Jason Weaver   **2/1F**
M Johnston   £36,080

Royal Ascot

TUES, JUNE 20TH

QUEEN ANNE STAKES (Group 2)
3y+ (1m)
NICOLETTE (4-9-2)
Michael Hills   16/1
G Wragg   £51,030

PRINCE OF WALES' STAKES
(Group 2)
3y+ (1m 2f)
MUHTARRAM (6-9-8)
Willie Carson   5/1
J H M Gosden   £57,852

ST JAMES' PALACE STAKES
(Group 1)
3y c&f (1m)
BAHRI (3-9-0)
Willie Carson   11/4F
J L Dunlop   £124,056

COVENTRY STAKES (Group 3)
2y (6f)
ROYAL APPLAUSE (2-8-12)
Walter Swinburn   13/2
B W Hills   £26,080

BRITANNIA HANDICAP (Class B)
3y c&g (1m)
MEDAILLE MILITAIRE (3-8-3)
Richard Quinn   4/1F
J L Dunlop   £27,352

ASCOT STAKES HANDICAP
(Class C)
4y+ (2m 4f)
HARLESTONE BROOK (5-9-8)
Michael Kinane   6/1
J L Dunlop   £26,328

WEDS, JUNE 21ST

JERSEY STAKES (Group 3)
3y (7f)
SERGEYEV (3-8-10)
Richard Hughes   5/1F
R Hannon   £33,950

QUEEN MARY STAKES (Group 3)
2y f (5f)
BLUE DUSTER (2-8-8)
Michael Kinane   7/4F
D R Loder   £25,840

CORONATION STAKES (Group 1)
3y f (1m)
RIDGEWOOD PEARL (3-9-0)
J Murtagh   9/2
J Oxx (Ireland)   £119,133

ROYAL HUNT CUP HANDICAP
(Class B)
3y+ (1m)
REALITIES (5-9-0)
Michael Kinane   11/1
G Harwood   £49,322

QUEEN'S VASE STAKES (Group
3)
3y (2m 45y)
STELVIO (3-8-11)
Michael Kinane   7/4F
H R A Cecil   £32,150

BESSBOROUGH HANDICAP
(Class B)
3y+ (1m 4f)
SON OF SHARP SHOT (5-8-13)
Pat Eddery   5/1
J L Dunlop   £26,556

THURS, JUNE 22ND

RIBBLESDALE STAKES (Group 2)
3y f (1m 4f)
PHANTOM GOLD (3-8-8)
Frankie Dettori   5/1
Lord Huntingdon   £55,332

NORFOLK STAKES (Group 3)
2y (5f)
LUCKY LIONEL (2-8-12)
Frankie Dettori   11/1
R Hannon   £25,360

GOLD CUP STAKES (Group 1)
4y+ (2m 4f)
DOUBLE TRIGGER (4-9-0)
Jason Weaver   9/4
M Johnston   £111,750

CORK AND ORRERY STAKES
(Group 3)
3y+ (6f)
SO FACTUAL (5-8-13)
Frankie Dettori   9/2
S Bin Suroor   £33,350

CHESHAM STAKES (Listed)
2y (6f)
WORLD PREMIER (2-9-2)
Brett Doyle   6/1
C E Brittain   £21,888

KING GEORGE V HANDICAP
(Class B)
3y (1m 4f)
DIAGHILEF (3-9-7)
Darryl Holland   40/1
M Johnston   £26,328

FRI, JUNE 23RD

WINDSOR CASTLE STAKES
(Class B)
2y (5f)
KUANTAN (2-8-11)
Richard Quinn   11/1
P F I Cole   £17,325

HARDWICKE STAKES (Group 2)
4y+ (1m 4f)
BEAUCHAMP HERO (5-8-9)
John Reid   11/2
J L Dunlop   £64,063

WOKINGHAM HANDICAP
(Class B)
3y+ (6f)
ASTRAC (4-8-7)
Seb Sanders   14/1
R Akehurst   £50,118

KING'S STAND STAKES (Group 2)
3y+ (5f)
PICCOLO (4-9-6)
Richard Hughes   20/1
M Channon   £61,354

KING EDWARD VII STAKES
(Group 2)
3y c&g (1m 4f)
PENTIRE (3-8-8)
Michael Hills   4/1
G Wragg   £62,832

QUEEN ALEXANDRA STAKES
(Class B)
4y+ (2m 6f 34y)
CUFF LINK (5-9-4)
Paul Eddery   EvsF
Major W R Hern   £19,845

LEADING JOCKEYS

Michael Kinane	4 wins
Frankie Dettori	3
Michael Hills	2
Richard Hughes	2
Richard Quinn	2
Willie Carson	2

RICHMOND STAKES
Goodwood, July 27   2y c&g (6f)
POLARIS FLIGHT (2-8-11)
John Reid   9/4
P W Chapple-Hyam   £31,325

VODAFONE NASSAU STAKES
Goodwood, July 29
3y+ f&m (1m 2f)
CARAMBA (3-8-9)
Michael Roberts
R Hannon   £46,300

GEOFFREY FREER STAKES
Newbury, Aug 12   3y+ (1m 5f 61y)
PRESENTING (3-8-5)
John Reid   10/11F
J H M Gosden   £43,970

GREAT VOLTIGEUR STAKES
York, Aug 15   3y c&g
(1m 3f 195y)
PENTIRE (3-8-12)
Michael Hills   4/5F
G Wragg   £49,736

SCOTTISH EQUITABLE
GIMCRACK STAKES
York, Aug 16   2y c&g (6f)
ROYAL APPLAUSE (2-9-0)
Walter Swinburn   4/6F
B W Hills   £70,143

LOWTHER STAKES
York, Aug 17   2y f (6f)
DANCE SEQUENCE (2-8-11)
Walter Swinburn   5/4F
M R Stoute   £40,521

TRIPLEPRINT CELEBRATION
MILE STAKES
Goodwood, Aug 26   3y+ (1m)
HARAYIR (3-8-12)
Willie Carson   5/4F
Major W R Hern   £35,387

LAURENT PERRIER CHAMPAGNE
STAKES
Doncaster, Sep 8   2y c&g (7f)
ALHAARTH (2-9-0)
Willie Carson   2/5F
Major W R Hern   £45,621

TRIPLEPRINT FLYING CHILDERS
STAKES
Doncaster, Sep 9   2y (5f)
CAYMAN KAI (2-8-12)
Pat Eddery   7/1
R Hannon   £29,007

BONUSPRINT MILL REEF STKS
Newbury   Sep 16   2y (6f 8y)
KAHIR ALMAYDAN (2-8-12)
Willie Carson   2/1F
J L Dunlop   £32,018

ROYAL LODGE STAKES
Ascot Sep 23   2y c&g (1m)
MONS (2-8-11)
Frankie Dettori   7/2
L M Cumani   63,730

SUN CHARIOT STAKES
Newmarket, Sep 30
3y+ f&m (1m 2f)
WARNING SHADOWS (3-8-8)
Kevin Darley   6/1
C E Brittain   £33,691

1994 Group 2

CHALLENGE STAKES
Newmarket, Oct 13   3y+ (7f)
ZIETEN (4-9-0)
Frankie Dettori   13/2
J M Gosden   £33,459

GROUP 3

SHADWELL STUD NELL GWYN
STAKES (Class A)
Newmarket, Apr 18   3y f (7f)
MYSELF (3-8-9)
John Reid   5/1
P W Chapple-Hyam   £22,589

EARL OF SEFTON STAKES
Newmarket, Apr 19   4y+ (1m 1f)
DESERT SHOT (5-8-10)
Walter Swinburn   5/2
M R Stoute   £21,574

CRAVEN STAKES
Newmarket, Apr 20   3y c&g (1m)
PAINTER'S ROW (3-8-12)
John Reid   5/1
P W Chapple-Hyam   £22,141

GAINSBOROUGH STUD FRED
DARLING STAKES
Newbury, Apr 21   3y f (7f 64y)
AQAARID (3-9-0)
Willie Carson   9/4JF
J L Dunlop   £22,740

LANES END JOHN PORTER
STAKES
*Newbury, Apr 22   4y+ (1m 4f
5y)*
STRATEGIC CHOICE (4-8-11)
Richard Quinn   12/1
P F I Cole   £22,020

TRIPLEPRINT GREENHAM
STAKES
Newbury, Apr 22   3y c&g (7f)
CELTIC SWING (3-9-0)
Kevin Darley   4/9F
Lady Herries   £21,840

THRESHER CLASSIC TRIAL
Sandown, Apr 29   3 (1m 2f 7y)
PENTIRE (3-8-10)
Michael Hills   25/1
G Wragg   £42,636

T G I FRIDAY'S GORDON
RICHARD STAKES
Sandown, Apr 29   4y+ (1m 2f 7y)
PRINCE OF ANDROS (5-8-10)
Jason Weaver   6/1
D R Loder   £22,020

INSULPAK SAGARO STAKES
Ascot, May 3   4y+ (2m 45y)
DOUBLE TRIGGER (4-8-12)
Jason Weaver   9/2JF
M Johnston   £25,480

DUBAI RACING CLUB PALACE
HOUSE STAKES
Newmarket, May 6   3y+ (5f)
MIND GAMES (3-8-5)
John Carroll   4/1
J Berry   £23,807

DALHAM CHESTER VASE
*Chester, May 9   3y (1m 4f
66y)*
LUSO (3-8-10)
Michael Kinane   11/1
C E Brittain   £29,250

ORMONDE STAKES
Chester, May 11   4y+ (1m 5f 89y)
ZILZAL ZAMAAN (4-8-11)
Walter Swinburn   9/2
M R Stoute   £28,170

TRIPLEPRINT DERBY TRIAL
STAKES
Lingfield, May 13   3y (1m 3f 106y)
MUNWAR (3-8-7)
Willie Carson   5/6F
P T Walwyn   £30,820

TATTERSALLS MUSIDORA
STAKES
York, May 16   3y f (1m 2f 85y)
PURE GRAIN (3-8-10)
John Reid   EvsF
M R Stoute   £22,141

DUKE OF YORK STAKES
York, May 18   3y+ (6f)
LAKE CONISTON (4-9-4)
Pat Eddery   8/11F
G Lewis   £22,242

BONUSPRINT HENRY II STAKES
Sandown, May 29   4y+ (2m 78y)
DOUBLE TRIGGER (4-8-13)
Jason Weaver   5/4F
M Johnston   £25,500

SPILLERS BRIGADIER GERARD
STAKES
Sandown, May 30   4y+ (1m 2f 7y)
ALRIFFA (4-8-10)
Pat Eddery   11/2
R Hannon   £21,840

VODAFONE DIOMED STAKES
Epsom, June 9   3y+ (1m 114y)
MR MARTINI (5-9-4)
Michael Roberts   25/1
C E Brittain   £28,400

VAN GEEST CRITERION STAKES
Newmarket, July 1   3y+ (7f)
PIPE MAJOR (3-8-8)
Jason Weaver   5/2F
P C Haslam   £23,807

LANCASHIRE OAKS STAKES
Haydock, July 8 3y+ f&m (1m 3f 200y)
FANJICA (3-8-4)
G Carter   6/1
J L Dunlop   £21,400

HILLSDOWN CHERRY HINTON
STAKES
Newmarket, July 11   2y f (6f)
APPLAUD (2-8-9)
Pat Eddery   11/2
D R Loder   £18,360

SBJ GROUP JULY STAKES
Newmarket, July 12 2y c&g (6f)
TAGULA (2-8-10)
Walter Swinburn   7/2
I A Balding   £18,476

TENNENTS SCOTTISH CLASSIC
STAKES
Ayr, July 17   3y+ (1m 2f)
BARON FERDINAND (5-9-2)
Kevin Darley   100/30F
R Charlton   £19,984

PRINCESS MARGARET STAKES
Ascot, July 22   2y f (6f)
BLUE DUSTER (2-9-0)
Michael Kinane   30/100F
D R Loder   £21,770

BEESWING STAKES
Newcastle, July 24   3y+ (7f)
SHAHID (3-8-7)
Willie Carson   3/1
J L Dunlop   £21,450

WESTMINSTER TAXI INSURANCE
GORDON STAKES
Goodwood, July 25   3y (1m 4f)
PRESENTING (3-8-10)
Frankie Dettori   7/4F
J M H Gosden   £22,183

KING GEORGE STAKES
Goodwood, July 25   3y+ (5f)
HEVER GOLF ROSE (4-9-5)
Jason Weaver   10/1
T J Naughton   £27,920

LANSON CHAMPAGNE VINTAGE
STAKES
Goodwood, July 26   2y (7f)
ALHAARTH (2-8-11)
Willie Carson   5/6F
Major W R Hern   £22,540

ROSE OF LANCASTER STAKES
Haydock, Aug 5 3y+ (1m 2f 120y)
FAHAL (3-8-7)
Richard Hills   3/1
D Morley   £21,760

HUNGERFORD STAKES
Newbury, Aug 11   3y+ (7f 64y)
HARAYIR (3-8-13)
Willie Carson   9/4F
Major W R Hern   £23,100

SOLARIO STAKES
Sandown, Aug 18   2y (7f 16y)
ALHAARTH (2-9-2)
Willie Carson   30/100F
Major W R Hern   £21,480

WINTER HILL STAKES
Windsor, Aug 26   3y+ (1m 2f 7y)
DESERT SHOT (5-9-4)
Walter Swinburn   12/1
M R Stoute   £23,460

CROWSON PRESTIGE STAKES
Goodwood, Aug 27   2y f (7f)
BINT SHADAYID (2-8-9)
Willie Carson   EvsF
J L Dunlop   £18,700

BONUSPRINT SEPTEMBER
STAKES
Kempton, Sep 2   3y+ (1m 3f 30y)
BUROOJ (5-9-0)
Brent Thompson   8/1
D Morley   £22,280

STONES BITTER PARK HILL
STAKES
Doncaster, Sep 6
3y+ f&m (1m 6f 123y)
NOBLE ROSE (4-9-3)
Frankie Dettori   11/4F
L M Cumani   £22,748

MAY HILL STAKES
Doncaster, Sep 7   2y f (1m)
SOLAR CRYSTAL (2-8-9)
Willie Ryan   15/2
H R A Cecil   £18,052

KIVETON PARK STAKES
Doncaster, Sep 7   3y+ (1m)
BISHOP OF CASHEL (3-8-9)
Walter Swinburn   9/2
J R Fanshawe   £23,020

EAST COAST DONCASTER CUP
Doncaster, Sep 7   3y+ (2m 2f)
DOUBLE TRIGGER (4-9-7)
Jason Weaver   4/11F
M Johnston   £21,019

WESTMINSTER TAXI INSURANCE
SELECT STAKES
Goodwood, Sep 9   3y+ (1m 2f)
TRIARIUS (5-9-0)
G Carter   7/4F
Saeed Bin Suroor   £22,242

CUMBERLAND LODGE STAKES
Ascot Sep 23 3y+ (1m 4f)
RIYADIAN (3-8-6)
Richard Quinn   2/1F
P F I Cole   £31,550

DIADEM STAKES
Ascot Sep 24 3y+ (6f)
COOL JAZZ (4-9-0)
Cory Nakatani   33/1
C E Brittain   £40,560

CHARLTON HUNT SUPREME
STAKES
Goodwood, Sep 30   3y+ (7f)
INZAR (3-8-8)
Richard Quinn   3/1
P F I Cole   £23,232

JOCKEY CLUB STAKES
Newmarket, Sep 30 3y+ (2m)
FURTHER FLIGHT (9-9-3)
Michael Hills   5/2
B W Hills   £22,995

MAJOR HANDICAPS

WILLIAM HILL LINCOLN H'CAP
Doncaster, Mar 25   1m
ROVING MINSTREL (4-8-3)
Kevin Darley   33/1
B A McMahon   £46,332

LADBROKES CHESTER CUP
HANDICAP
Chester, May 10   4y+ (2m 2f 147y)
TOP CEES (5-8-8)
Kieran Fallon   8/1
Mrs J R Ramsden   £29,325

WILLIAM HILL TROPHY H'CAP
York, June 17   3y (6f)
BOLD EFFORT (3-8-8)
Tony Ives   10/1
K O Cunningham-Brown £38,958

'NEWCASTLE BROWN ALE'
NORTHUMBERLAND PLATE
HANDICAP
Newcastle, July 1   3y+ (2m 19y)
BOLD GAIT (4-9-10)
David Harrison   12/1
J R Fanshawe   £50,071

ROYAL HONG KONG JOCKEY
CLUB TROPHY HANDICAP
Sandown, July 7
3y+ (1m 2f 7y)
YOUSH (3-8-1)
Brett Doyle   6/1F
M A Jarvis   £45,950

WEATHERBYS SUPER SPRINT
STAKES
Newbury, July 15   2y (5f 34y)
BLUE IRIS (2-8-1)
Willie Carson   13/2
M A Jarvis   £71,214

JOHN SMITH'S MAGNET CUP
York, July 15   3y+ (1m 2f 85y)
NAKED WELCOME (3-8-4)
Darryl Holland   6/1
M J Fetherston-Godley £56,730

WILLIAM HILL CUP HANDICAP
Goodwood, July 25   4y+ (1m 2f)
SILVER GROOM (5-7-6)
Matthew Henry   6/1
R Akehurst   £35,337

TOTE GOLD TROPHY
Goodwood, July 26   3y (1m 4f)
PILSUDSKI (3-8-12)
Walter Swinburn   11/2
M R Stoute   £37,270

SCHWEPPES GOLDEN MILE
Goodwood, July 27   3y+ (1m)
KHAYRAPOUR (5-7-13)
Brett Doyle   15/2
B J Meehan   £48,250

VODAC STEWARDS' CUP
Goodwood, July 29   3y+ (6f)
SHIKARI'S SON (8-8-13)
Richard Hughes   40/1
J White   £50,525

TOTE EBOR HANDICAP
York, Aug 16   3y+ (1m 5f 194y)
SANMARTINO (3-7-11)
Willie Carson   8/1
B W Hills   £98,255

LADBROKE (AYR) GOLD CUP
Ayr Sep 16   3y+ (6f)
ROYALE FIGURINE (4-8-9)
Darryl Holland   8/1
M J Featherston-Godley £51,792

TOTE FESTIVAL HANDICAP
Ascot   Sep 23 3y+ (7f)
NIGHT DANCE (3-7-10)
A Whelan   20/1
G Lewis   £52,913

WILLIAM HILL CAMBRIDGESHIRE
Newmarket, Sep 30
3y+ (1m 1f)
CAP JULUCA (3-9-10)
Richard Hughes   11/1
R Charlton   £55,716

1994 Major Handicap

TOTE CESAREWITCH H'CAP
Newmarket, Oct 15
3y+ (2m 2f)
CAPTAIN'S GUEST (4-9-9)
Tony Clark   25/1
G Harwood   63,730

AUSTRALIA

1994 Race

FOSTERS MELBOURNE CUP
Flemington, Nov 2   (2m)
JEUNE
Wayne Harris   16/1
David Hayes

FRANCE

PRIX GANAY
Longchamp, Apr 30
4y+ c&f (1m 2f 110y)
PELDER (5-9-2)
Frankie Dettori   13.90F
P A Kelleway   £59,880

PRIX LUPIN
Longchamp, May 14
3y c&f (1m 2f 110y)
FLEMENSFIRTH (3-9-2)
Frankie Dettori   2.70FF
J H M Gosden   £57,401

DUBAI POULE D'ESSAI DES
POULICHES
Longchamp, May 14   3y f (1m)
MATIARA (3-9-2)
Freddie Head   3.60FF
Mme C Head (France)£119,760

DUBAI POULE D'ESSAI DES
POULAINS
Longchamp, May 14   3y c (1m)
VETTORI (3-9-2)
Frankie Dettori   5.50FF
Saeed Bin Suroor (Dubai)
£119,760

PRIX SAINT-ALARY STAKES
Longchamp, May 21   3y f (1m 2f)
MUNCIE (3-9-2)
O Peslier   1.30FF
A Fabre (France)   £61,449

PRIX D'ISPAHAN (Group 1)
Longchamp, May 28
4y+ c&f (1m 1f)
GREEN TUNE (4-9-2)
Olivier Doleuze   2.60FF
Mme C Head (France)£59,880

LES EMIRATES ARABES UNIS
PRIX DU JOCKEY-CLUB (Group 1)
Chantilly, June 4 3y c&f (1m 4f)
CELTIC SWING (3-9-2)
Kevin Darley   2.00FF
Lady Herries   £299,401

PRIX JEAN PRAT (Group 1)
Chantilly, June 4
3y c&f (1m 1f)
TORRENTIAL (3-9-2)
Frankie Dettori   3.60FF
J H M Gosden   £47,904

PRIX DE DIANE HERMES
Chantilly, June 11
3y f (1m 2f 110y)
CARLING (3-9-2)
T Thulliez   4.50FF
Mme P Barbe (France) £167,665

GRAND PRIX DE PARIS
Longchamp, June 25
3y c&f (1m 2f)
VALANOUR (3-9-2)
Gerald Mosse   7.30FF
A Royer Dupre (France) £143,713

GRAND PRIX DE SAINT-CLOUD
Saint-Cloud, July 2   3y+ (1m 4f)
CARNEGIE (4-9-8)
Thierry Jarnet   2.90FF
A Fabre (France)   £143,713

PRIX MAURICE DE GHEEST
Deauville, Aug 6   3y+ (6f 110y)
CHEROKEE ROSE (4-8-12)
Cash Asmussen   1.80FF
J Hammond (France) £59,880

PRIX DU HARAS DE FRESNAY-LE
BUFFARD JACQUES LE MAROIS
Deauville, Aug 13   3y+ c&f (1m)
MISS SATAMIXA (3-8-8)
S Guillot   22.70FF
A Fabre (France)   £119,760

PRIX MORNY PIAGET
Deauville, Aug 20   2y c&f (6f)
TAGULA (2-9-0)
Walter Swinburn   9.70FF
I Balding   £95,808

EMIRATES PRIX DU MOULIN DE LONGCHAMP
Longchamp, Sep 3   3y+ c&f (1m)
RIDGEWOOD PEARL (3-8-8)
J P Murtagh   2.30FF
J Oxx (Ireland)   £107,784

PRIX VERMEILLE
Longchamp Sep 10
3y f (1m 4f)
CARLING (3-9-2)
Thierry Thulliez   7.60FF
Mme P Barbe (France)   £95,808

PRIX DE LA SALAMANDRE
Longchamp Sep 17 2y c&f (7f)
LORD OF MEN (2-8-11)
Frankie Dettori   7.00FF
J H M Gosden   £47,904

PRIX DU CADRAN
Longchamp, Sep 30
3y+ (2m 4f)
ALWAYS ERNEST (7-9-2)
A Badel
Mme C Bourg (France)   £59,880

PRIX DE L'ABBAYE DE L'CHAMP
Longchamp, Oct 1   3y+ (5f)
HEVER GOLF ROSE (4-9-8)
Jason Weaver   4.10FF
T J Naughton   £59,880

PRIX MARCEL BOUSSAC
Longchamp, Oct 1 2y f (1m)
MISS TAHITI (2-8-11)
O Peslier   11.60FF
A Fabre   £95,808

FORTE PRIX DE L'ARC DE TRIOMPHE
Longchamp, Oct 1   3y+ (1m 4f)
LAMMTARRA (3-8-11)
Frankie Dettori   3.10FF
Saeed Bin Suroor   £479,042

1994 Race

PRIX ROYAL-OAK
Longchamp, Oct 23   3y+ (1m 6f)
MOONAX
Pat Eddery
B W Hills

GERMANY ▬▬▬

BMW DEUTSCHES DERBY
Hamburg, July 2
3y c&f (1m 4f)
ALL MY DREAMS (3-9-2)
K Woodburn   35DM
H Remmert (Germany)   £202,469

PREIS DER PRIVATBANKIERS MERCK FINCK & CO
Düsseldorf, July 23   3y+ (1m 4f)
LANDO (5-9-7)
P Schiergen   16DM
H Jentzsch (Germany) £98,765

DR POTH-BAYERISCHES ZUCHTRENNEN
Munich, July 30   3y+ (1m 2f)
GERMANY (4-9-6)
Frankie Dettori   51DM
B Schutz (Germany)   £90,535

ARAL POKAL
Gelsenkirchen-Horst, Aug 6
3y+ (1m 4f)
WIND IN HER HAIR (4-9-2)
Richard Hills   138DM
J W Hills   £86,420

GROSSER PREIS VON BADEN
Baden-Baden, Sep 3   3y+ (1m 4f)
GERMANY (4-9-6)
Frankie Dettori   47DM
B Schutz (Germany)   £133,745

HONG KONG ▬▬▬

QUEEN ELIZABETH II CUP STAKES (Class A)
Sha Tin, Apr 1   1m 3f
RED BISHOP (7-9-0)
Michael Kinane
H Ibrahim (Dubai)   £191,736

IRELAND ▬▬▬

FIRST NATIONAL BUILDING SOCIETY IRISH 2000 GUINEAS
Curragh, May 21   3y c&f (1m)
SPECTRUM (3-9-0)
John Reid   £4.20
P W Chapple-Hyam   £130,700

AIRLIE/COOLMORE IRISH 1000 GUINEAS
Curragh, May 27   3y f (1m)
RIDGEWOOD PEARL (3-9-0)
Christy Roche   9/4
J Oxx (Ireland)   £84,250

BUDWEISER IRISH DERBY
Curragh, July 2
3y c&f (1m 4f)
WINGED LOVE (3-9-0)
O Peslier   5/1
A Fabre (France)   £338,350

KILDANGAN STUD IRISH OAKS
Curragh, July 16   3y f (1m 4f)
PURE GRAIN (3-9-0)
John Reid   £4.50
M R Stoute   £112,700

HEINZ 57 PHOENIX STAKES
Leopardstown, Aug 13
2y c&f (6f)
DANEHILL DANCER (2-9-0)
Pat Eddery   2/1F
N A Callaghan   £98,000

GUINNESS CHAMPION STAKES
Leopardstown, Sep 9
3y c&f (1m 2f)
PENTIRE (3-8-11)
Michael Hills   9/4F
G Wragg   £87,300

MOYGLARE STUD STAKES
Curragh Sep 10 2y f (7f)
PRIORY BELLE (2-8-11)
P V Gilson   16/1
J S Bolger (Ireland)   £56,100

NATIONAL STAKES
Curragh Sep 16 3y+ (7f)
DANEHILL DANCER (2-9-0)
Pat Eddery   4/5F
N A Callaghan   £58,515

JEFFERSON SMURFIT MEMORIAL IRISH ST LEGER
Curragh Sep 16 3y+ (1m 6f)
STRATEGIC CHOICE (4-9-8)
Richard Quinn   6/1
P F I Cole   £87,921

ITALY ▬▬▬

PREMIO PARIOLI
Capannelle, Apr 30   3y c&f (1m)
PRINCE ARTHUR (3-9-2)
John Reid   32L
P W Chapple-Hyam   £59,024

PREMIO PRESIDENTE DELLA REPUBBLICA
Capanelle, May 14   4y+ (1m 2f)
FLAGBIRD (4-8-13)
Kevin Darley   94L
Saeed Bin Suroor   £52,722

OAKS D'ITALIA STAKES
San Siro, May 21   3y f (1m 3f)
VALLEY OF GOLD (3-8-11)
S Guillot   24L
A Fabre (France)   £86,112

DERBY ITALIANO
Capannelle, May 28   3y c&f (1m 4f)
LUSO (3-9-2)
Michael Kinane   57L
C E Brittain   £234,439

GRAN PREMIO DI MILANO
San Siro, June 18   3y c&f (1m 4f)
LANDO (5-9-7)
Michael Roberts   16L
H Jentzch (Germany)   £130,023

GRAN PREMIO D'ITALIA
San Siro   Sep 16   3y (1m 4f)
POSIDONAS (3-9-2)
Richard Hughes   45L
P F I Cole   £88,751

JAPAN

KEIO HAI CUP STAKES (Group 2)
Fuchu, Apr 22   4y+ (7f)
DUMAANI (4-8-12)
Richard Hills
K McLaughlin (Dubai)   £392,466

YASUDA KINEN
Fuchu, May 14   4y+ (1m)
HEART LAKE (4-9-0)
Y Take   1030Y
Saeed Bin Suroor (Dubai) £670,840

UNITED STATES

KENTUCKY DERBY
Churchill Downs, May 6
3y c&f (1m 2f)
THUNDER GULCH (3-9-0)
G Stevens $12.20
D W Lukas (USA)   £453,461

PREAKNESS STAKES
Pimlico, May 20   3y (1m 1f 110y)
TIMBER COUNTRY (3-9-0)
P Day $5.80?
D W Lukas (USA)   £286,417

BELMONT STAKES
Belmont Park, June 10   3y (1m 4f)
THUNDER GULCH (3-9-0)
G Stevens   £5.00
D W Lukas (USA)   £268,205

ARLINGTON MILLION
Arlington Park   3y+ (1m 2f)
AWAD (5-9-0)
E Maple   £13.80
D Donk (USA)   £384,61

FLOWER BOWL INVITATIONAL
Belmont Pk, Sep 23   3y f&m (1m 2f)
NORTHERN EMERALD (5-8-1)
R Perez   £17.20
W Mott (USA)   £76,923

Breeders' Cup races held at
Churchill Downs on Nov 5, 1994
BREEDERS' CUP SPRINT
6f dirt
CHEROKEE RUN
M Smith $7.60/$2
F Alexander (USA)

BRDRS' CUP JUVENILE FILLIES
1m 110y dirt
FLANDERS
P Day $2.80
D W Lukas (USA)

BREEDERS' CUP DISTAFF
1m 1f dirt
ONE DREAMER
G Stevens $96.20
T Procter (USA)

BREEDERS' CUP MILE
1 mile turf
BARATHEA
Frankie Dettori $22.80
L Cumani   £351,351

BREEDERS' CUP JUVENILE
1m 110y dirt
TIMBER COUNTRY
P Day $6.80
D W Lukas (USA)

BREEDERS' CUP TURF
1m 4f turf
TIKKANEN
M Smith $35.20
J Pease (France)

BREEDERS' CUP CLASSIC
1m 2f dirt
CONCERN
J Bailey $17.00
R Small

Final Figures for 1994

Top Trainers (Turf only) - by money

		Wins	£
1	M R Stoute	107	1,382,783
2	J L Dunlop	82	1,309,842
3	H R A Cecil	76	1,046,640
4	J H M Gosden	90	763,878
5	R Hannon	108	629,489
6	M Johnston	81	549,194
7	P F I Cole	67	481,860
8	L Cumani	47	456,724
9	J Berry	102	417,299
10	G Wragg	28	415,118

Top Jockeys (Turf only) - by wins

		Wins	Total Rides	%
1	Frankie Dettori	179	1069	16.7
2	Pat Eddery	154	800	19.3
3	Jason Weaver	143	831	17.2
4	Kevin Darley	132	848	15.6
5	Richard Quinn	102	835	12.2
6	John Reid	97	690	14.1
7	Willie Carson	87	650	13.4
8	Michael Hills	81	593	13.7
9	Michael Roberts	80	763	10.5
10	John Carroll	78	577	13.5

1995 - As at Oct 9th

Top Trainers (Turf only) - by money

		Wins	£
1	Saeed Bin Suroor	14	1,691,704
2	J L Dunlop	114	1,272,941
3	M R Stoute	68	710,387
4	M Johnston	84	696,538
5	B W Hills	67	667,637
6	R Hannon	97	646,756
7	J H M Gosden	75	514,960
8	H R A Cecil	67	495,926
9	P F I Cole	69	447,502
10	C E Brittain	35	423,700

Top Jockeys - by wins

		Wins	£	%
1	Frankie Dettori	154	1,827,400	22.0
2	Willie Carson	133	1,557,124	20.4
3	Kevin Darley	123	680,220	16.2
4	Pat Eddery	111	1,105,078	18.8
5	Richard Quinn	102	616,739	13.8
6	Jason Weaver	88	722,523	14.1
7	John Reid	87	821,389	14.5
8	Kieran Fallon	79	349,134	14.4
9	Willie Ryan	71	352,103	14.8
10	Darryl Holland	69	482,752	16.0

National Hunt ▬▬▬▬▬▬▬▬▬

All UK races valued at over £12,000 are listed

DESERT ORCHID SOUTH
WESTERN CHASE (Grade 2)
Wincanton, Oct 20 1994 2m 5f
GIVUS A BUCK (11-11-10)
Paul Holley   15/2
D R C Elsworth   £16,075

CHARLIE HALL CHASE (Grade 2)
Wetherby, Oct 29 1994   3m 110y
YOUNG HUSTLER (7-11-10)
Carl Llewellyn   8/1
N A Twiston-Davies   £18,930

UNITED HOUSE CONSTRUCTION
HANDICAP CHASE
Ascot, Oct 29 1994   2m
STORM ALERT (8-12-0)
Simon McNeill   11/4
A Turnell   £15,407

PLYMOUTH GIN HALDON GOLD
CHALLENGE CUP
(Grade 2)
Exeter, Nov 1 1994   2m 2f
TRAVADO (8-11-6)
Jamie Osborne   8/11F
N J Henderson   £15,475

TOTE SILVER TROPHY
(Handicap Hurdle)
Chepstow, Nov 5 1994   2m 4f 110y
HER HONOUR (5-10-11)
Richard Dunwoody   7/1
M Pipe   £15,534

STEEL PLATE AND SECTIONS
YOUNG CHASERS
CHAMPIONSHIP FINAL (Handicap
Chase)
Cheltenham, Nov 11 1994
3m 1f
EARTH SUMMIT (6-11-7)
David Bridgwater   11/2
N A Twiston-Davies   £13,550

MURPHY'S HANDICAP HURDLE
Cheltenham, Nov 12 1994
2m 110y
ATOURS (6-11-5)
Paul Holley   3/1F
D R C Elsworth   £28,010

MACKESON GOLD CUP
(Handicap Chase - Grade 3)
Cheltenham, Nov 12 1994
2m 4f 110y
BRADBURY STAR (9-11-11)
Philip Hide   5/1
J Gifford   £38,386

COOPERS & LYBRAND ASCOT
HURDLE (Grade 2)
Ascot, Nov 18 1994   2m 4f
OH SO RISKY (7-11-0)
Paul Holley   8/11F
D R C Elsworth   £12,810

FIRST NATIONAL BANK GOLD
CUP (Handicap Chase - Grade 2)
Ascot, Nov 19 1994   2m 3f 110y
RAYMYLETTE (7-11-10)
Mick Fitzgerald   10/1
N J Henderson   £26,056

CROWTHER HOMES BECHER
HANDICAP CHASE
Aintree, Nov 19 1994 3m 3f
INTO THE RED (10-10-4)
Richard Guest   13/2
J White   £18,903

PETERBORO' CHASE (Grade 2)
Hunt'don, Nov 22 1994 2m 4f 110y
MARTHA'S SON (7-11-1)
R Farrant   2/1
T A Forster   £16,823

HENNESSY COGNAC GOLD CUP
(Handicap Chase - Grade 3)
Newbury, Nov 26 1994   3m 2f 110y
ONE MAN (6-10-0)
Tony Dobbin   4/1
G Richards   £42,874

BELLWAY HOMES 'FIGHTING
FIFTH' HURDLE (Grade 2)
Newcastle, Nov 26 1994   2m 110y
BATANABOO (5-11-0)
Peter Niven   6/4F
Mrs M Reveley   £15,660

MASON CHAMPION CHASE
Kelso, Nov 28 1994   3m 4f
MORGANS HARBOUR (8-10-1)
Peter Niven   3/1
M Reveley   £12,104

WILLIAM HILL HANDICAP
HURDLE (Grade 3)
Sandown, Dec 3 1994 2m 110y
RELKEEL (5-10-2)
Adrian Maguire   4/5F
D Nicholson   £20,750

MITSUBISHI SHOGUN TINGLE
CREEK TROPHY (Chase-Grade 1)
Sandown, Dec 3 1994 2m
VIKING FLAGSHIP (7-11-7)
Adrian Maguire   9/2
D Nicholson   £31,330

REHEARSAL HANDICAP CHASE
(Grade 2)
Chepstow, Dec 3 1994   3m
MASTER OATS (8-11-4)
Norman Williamson   3/1
K C Bailey   £19,121

TOMMY WHITTLE CHASE
Haydock, Dec 7 1994 3m
CHATAM (10-11-2)
Richard Dunwoody   11/4
M C Pipe   £12,465

BONUSPHOTO BULA HURDLE
(Grade 2)
Cheltenham, Dec 10 1994 2m 1f
LARGE ACTION (6-11-4)
Jamie Osborne   8/11F
O Sherwood   £21,875

TRIPLEPRINT GOLD CUP
(Handicap Chase - Grade 3)
Cheltenham, Dec 10 1994
2m 5f
DUBLIN FLYER (8-10-2)
Brendan Powell   100/30
T A Forster   £38,386

LONG WALK HURDLE (Grade 1)
Ascot, Dec 17 1994   3m 1f 110y
HEBRIDEAN (7-11-7)
Adrian Maguire   100/30
D Nicholson   £25,384

BETTERWARE CUP (H'cap Chase)
Ascot, Dec 17 1994   3m 110y
RAYMYLETTE (7-10-9)
Mick Fitzgerald   3/1JF
N J Henderson   £21,036

TRIPLEPRINT FELTHAM
NOVICES' CHASE (Grade 1)
Kempton, Dec 26 1994 3m
BROWNHALL (6-11-7)
Adrian Maguire   5/1
D Nicholson   £21,399

KING GEORGE VI TRIPLEPRINT
CHASE (Grade 1)
Kempton, Dec 26 1994 3m
ALGAN (6-11-10)
Philippe Chevalier   16/1
F Doumen (France)   £58,500

BONUSPRINT CHRISTMAS
HURDLE (Grade 1)
Kempton, Dec 27 1994 2m
ABSALOM'S LADY (6-11-2)
Paul Holley   9/2
D R C Elsworth   £31,440

ROWLAND MEYRICK HANDICAP
CHASE
Wetherby, Dec 26 1994   3m 110y
COGENT (10-10-8)
Mr Chris Bonner   7/2
J A Glover   £16,380

CASTLEFORD CHASE
(Grade 2)
Wetherby, Dec 27 1994 2m
VIKING FLAGSHIP (7-11-10)
Adrian Maguire   2/5F
D Nicholson   £24,640

CHALLOW HURDLE
(Grade 1)
Newbury, Dec 31 1994   2m 5f
BERUDE NOT TO (5-11-7)
Jamie Osborne   8/11F
O Sherwood   £18,020

LADBROKE GOLD CUP
(Handicap Chase)
Newbury, Dec 31 1994   3m 2f 110y
LO STREGONE (8-10-8)
Jamie Osborne   4/1JF
T P Tate   £17,210

CORAL WELSH NATIONAL
HANDICAP CHASE
(Grade 3)
Newbury, Dec 31 1994   3m 6f
MASTER OATS (8-11-6)
Norman Williamson 5/2JF
K C Bailey   £25,106

NEWTON HANDICAP CHASE
(Grade 2)
Haydock, Jan 7   2m 4f
MIINNEHOMA (12-11-8)
Richard Dunwoody 5/2
M C Pipe   £17,211

BARING SECURITIES TOLWORTH
HURDLE
Sandown, Jan 7   2m 110y
SILVER WEDGE (4-10-9)
Norman Williamson 4/1
D Nicholson   £15,700

ANTHONY MILDMAY PETER
CAZALET MEMORIAL HANDICAP
CHASE
Sandown, Jan 7   3m 5f 110y
DEEP BRAMBLE (8-11-3)
Chris Maude   11/2
P Nicholls   £17,587

PML LIGHTNING NOVICES'
CHASE
Ascot, Jan 13   2m
GALES CAVALIER (7-11-12)
Mark Dwyer   13/8
D R Gandolfo   £13,760

VICTOR CHANDLER HANDICAP
CHASE (Grade 2)
Ascot, Jan 14   2m
MARTHA'S SON (8-10-9)
R Farrant   3/1
T A Forster   £25,420

PETER MARSH HANDICAP
CHASE (Grade 2)
Haydock, Jan 21   3m
EARTH SUMMIT (7-10-4)
T Jenks (3)   7/1
N A Twiston-Davies   £15,625

PILLAR PROPERTY
INVESTMENTS CHASE
Cheltenham, Jan 28
3m 1f 110y
MASTER OATS (9-11-6)
Norman Williamson 6/4F
K C Bailey   £13,615

CLEEVE HURDLE (Grade 1)
Cheltenham, Jan 28   2m 5f 110y
MUHADIM (9-11-8)
Norman Williamson 13/2
C D Broad   £25,120

SCILLY ISLES NOVICES' CHASE
(Grade 1)
Sandown, Feb 4   2m 4f 110y
BANJO (5-10-10)
Adrian Maguire   11/4
M C Pipe   £22,715

AGFA DIAMOND HANDICAP
CHASE
Sandown, Feb 4   3m 110y
DEEP BRAMBLE (8-11-10)
Chris Maude   6/1
P Nicholls   £19,560

NATIONAL HUNT 1994-5

Top Trainers

		Wins	£	%
1	D Nicholson	96	896,683	25
2	M C Pipe	137	846,077	23
3	K C Bailey	72	704,480	23
4	N A Twiston-Davies	81	525,999	16
5	Mrs M Reveley	100	475,435	27
6	O Sherwood	48	447,985	22
7	P J Hobbs	86	433,247	23
8	Mrs J Pitman	36	429,319	16
9	J T Gifford	47	413,264	17
10	N J Henderson	45	341,801	21
11	Capt T A Forster	32	279,360	18
12	G Richards	43	275,418	15
13	Miss H C Knight	44	221,299	20
14	M Hammond	42	211,843	15
15	J White	52	208,320	16
16	J H Johnson	32	203,972	13
17	D R C Elsworth	13	203,272	14
18	C P E Brooks	31	199,667	19
19	G B Balding	41	199,568	14
20	J G Fitzgerald	37	184,519	20

Top Jockeys

		1st	2nd	3rd	%
1	R Dunwoody	160	117	102	21
2	A Maguire	130	111	106	19
3	N Williamson	130	113	93	18
4	J Osborne	111	80	66	22
5	P Niven	106	74	50	27
6	D Bridgwater	78	53	48	17
7	A P McCoy	74	63	56	16
8	M A Fitzgerald	68	89	91	12
9	W Marston	66	36	46	17
10	M Dwyer	65	77	40	16
11	A Dobbin	57	40	43	16
12	Peter Hobbs	53	60	26	15
13	G McCourt	47	40	32	16
14	C Llewellyn	45	43	31	16
15	D Gallagher	42	36	27	12
16	G Bradley	41	33	27	15
17	S McNeill	40	37	34	12
18	Richard Guest	36	34	28	11
19	P Hide	34	36	24	16
20	L Wyer	32	42	29	12

SANDOWN HANDICAP HURDLE
(Grade 3)
Sandown, Feb 4   2m 6f
MIRACLE MAN (7-10-0)
Peter Hobbs   **3/1F**
C Weedon   £13,085

COMET CHASE (Grade 1)
Ascot, Feb 8   2m 3f 110y
MARTHA'S SON (8-11-7)
R Farrant   **EvsF**
T A Forster   £31,475

REYNOLDSTOWN NOVICES'
CHASE
Ascot, Feb 8   3m 110y
SWEET DUKE (8-11-9)
T Jenks   **100/30F**
N A Twiston-Davies   £14,858

MITSUBISHI SHOGUN GAME
SPIRIT CHASE (Grade 2)
Newbury, Feb 11   2m 1f
NAKIR (7-11-10)
Jamie Osborne   **5/2**
S Christian   £19,793

TOTE GOLD TROPHY
(Handicap Hurdle - Grade 3)
Newbury, Feb 11   2m 110y
MYSILV (5-10-8)
Jamie Osborne   **9/4F**
C R Egerton   £33,770

TOTE EIDER HANDICAP CHASE
(Class B)
Newcastle, Feb 18   4m 1f
WILLSFORD (12-10-6)
Peter Niven   **4/1**
Mrs J Pitman   £16,599

K J PIKE & SONS
KINGWELL HURDLE
(Grade 2)
Wincanton, Feb 23   2m
ALDERBROOK (6-11-2)
Norman Williamson **11/4**
K C Bailey   £15,625

GREENALLS GOLD CUP
HANDICAP CHASE
(Class B)
Haydock, Feb 25   3m 4f 110y
NUAFFE (10-11-0)
S O'Donovan   **4/1**
P A Fahy   £25,523

RACING POST HANDICAP CHASE
(Grade 3)
Kempton, Feb 25   3m
VAL D'ALENE (8-11-2)
Adam Kondrat   **11/2**
F Doumen (France)   £29,700

MARSTON MOOR HANDICAP
CHASE (Grade 2)
Wetherby, Mar 1   2m 4f 110y
GAELSTROM (8-10-11)
David Bridgwater   **15/8**
N A Twiston-Davies   £17,138

BEAUFORT NOVICES' HURDLE
Chepstow, Mar 11   2m 110y
CHALLENGER DU LUC (5-11-5)
Richard Dunwoody **4/1**
M C Pipe   £13,875

BET WITH THE TOTE NOVICES'
HANDICAP CHASE FINAL
Chepstow, Mar 11   3m
A N C EXPRESS (7-10-10)
T Jenks   **9/1**
J S King   £13,875

SUNDERLANDS IMPERIAL CUP
HANDICAP HURDLE
(Class B)
Sandown, Mar 11   2m 110y
COLLIER BAY (5-10-2)
T Grantham   **6/1**
J A B Old   £20,333
EUROPEAN BREEDERS FINAL
NOVICES' H'CAP HURDLE (Gr 3)
Cheltenham, Mar 17   2m 4f
BEAR CLAW (6-11-8)
Jamie Osborne   **3/1F**
O Sherwood   £22,665

PURE GENIUS HANDICAP CHASE
(Class D)
Cheltenham, Mar 17   3m 2f 110y
HILL TRIX (9-11-0)
Anthony Tory   **5/1**
K Bishop   £15,500

TETLEY MIDLANDS NATIONAL
HANDICAP CHASE (Grade 3)
Uttoxeter, Mar 18   4m 2f
LUCKY LANE (11-10-0)
Norman Williamson **12/1**
P J Hobbs   £32,623

DHL WORLDWIDE EXPRESS
HANDICAP CHASE (Class B)
Uttoxeter, Mar 18   3m 2f
A N C EXPRESS (7-10-11)
T Jenks   **7/2**
J S King   £14,785
LETHERBY & CHRISTOPHER
LONG DISTANCE HURDLE (Grade
2)
Ascot, Apr 1   3m
CAB ON TARGET (9-11-7)
Peter Niven   **11/8F**
Mrs M Reveley   £15,440

DAILY TELEGRAPH NOVICES'
HANDICAP CHASE (Class B)
Ascot, Apr 5   2m 3f 110y
POSTAGE STAMP (8-10-13)
Mark Dwyer   **5/2**
F Murphy   £14,265

MARTELL CUP CHASE
(Grade 2)
Aintree, Apr 6   3m 1f
MERRY GALE (7-11-9)
Graham Bradley   **5/2**
J T R Dreaper (Ireland) £31,558

SANDEMAN MAGHULL NOVICES'
CHASE (Grade 1)
Aintree, Apr 6   2m
MORCELI (7-11-3)
Norman Williamson **11/4F**
J H Johnson   £22,640

JOHN HUGHES MEMORIAL
TROPHY HANDICAP CHASE
(Class B)
Aintree, Apr 6   2m 6f
DUBLIN FLYER (9-12-0)
Brendan Powell   **11/2F**
Capt T A Forster   £24,955

GLENLIVET ANNIVERSARY
HURDLE (Grade 2)
Aintree, Apr 6   2m 110y
STOMPIN (4-11-0)
Jamie Osborne   **9/1**
Miss H C Knight   £25,460

MUMM MELLING CHASE
(Grade 1)
Aintree, Apr 7   2m 4f
VIKING FLAGSHIP (8-11-10)
Adrian Maguire   **5/2**
D Nicholson   £40,680

MUMM MILDMAY NOVICES'
CHASE (Grade 2)
Aintree, Apr 7   3m 1f
BANJO (5-11-0)
Richard Dunwoody **6/4F**
M C Pipe   £22,187

MARTELL FOXHUNTERS' CHASE
(Class B)
Aintree, Apr 7   2m 6f
SHEER JEST (10-12-0)
Mr A Hill   **5/1F**
W J Warner   £15,045

BELLE EPOQUE SEFTON
NOVICES' HURDLE (Grade 1)
Aintree, Apr 7   3m 110y
MORGANS HARBOUR (9-11-4)
Peter Niven   **6/1**
Mrs M Reveley   £19,624

Cheltenham Festival

CITROEN SUPREME NOVICES'
HURDLE (Grade 1)
Cheltenham, Mar 14 2m 110y
TOURIST ATTRACTION (6-11-3)
Mark Dwyer   25/1
W P Mullins (Ireland) £35,850

GUINNESS ARKLE CHALLENGE
TRPY NOVICES' CHASE (Grade 1)
Cheltenham, Mar 14 2m
KLAIRON DAVIS (6-11-8)
F Woods   7/2
A L T Moore (Ireland) £46,625

SMURFIT CHAMPION
CHALLENGE TROPHY HURDLE
(Grade 1)
Cheltenham, Mar 14 2m 110y
ALDERBROOK (6-12-0)
Norman Williamson 11/2
K C Bailey   £103,690

RITZ CLUB NATIONAL HUNT
HANDICAP CHASE (Class B)
Cheltenham, Mar 14 3m 1f
ROUGH QUEST (9-10-3)
Mick Fitzgerald   16/1
T Casey   £32,660

FULKE WALWYN KIM MUIR
CHALLENGE CUP AMATEUR
HANDICAP CHASE (Class B)
Cheltenham, Mar 14 3m 1f
FLYER'S NAP (9-9-10)
Mr P Henley   11/1
R H Alner   £17,779

ASTEC VODAFONE GOLD CARD
H'CAP HURDLE FINAL (Class B)
Cheltenham, Mar 14 3m 2f
MIRACLE MAN (7-10-11)
Peter Hobbs   9/2F
C Weedon   £22,906

SUN ALLIANCE NOVICES
HURDLE (Grade 1)
Cheltenham, Mar 15 2m 5f
PUTTY ROAD (5-11-7)
Norman Williamson 7/1
D Nicholson   £41,824

QUEEN MOTHER CHAMPION
CHASE (Grade 1)
Cheltenham, Mar 15 2m
VIKING FLAGSHIP (8-12-0)
Charlie Swan   5/2F
D Nicholson   £77,848

CORAL CUP HANDICAP HURDLE
(Class B)
Cheltenham, Mar 15 2m 5f
CHANCE COFFEY (10-10-0)
G M O'Neill   11/1
P F O'Donnell (Ireland) £39,822

SUN ALLIANCE NOVICES' CHASE
(Grade 1)
Cheltenham, Mar 15 3m 1f
BRIEF GALE (8-10-13)
Philip Hide   13/2
J Gifford   £49,162

NATIONAL HUNT CHALLENGE
CUP AMATEUR CHASE (Class C)
Cheltenham, Mar 15 4m
FRONT LINE (8-12-7)
Mr J Berry   7/1
J J O'Neill   £17,662

MILDMAY OF FLETE CHALLENGE
CUP HANDICAP CHASE
(Class B)
Cheltenham, Mar 15 2m 4f 110y
KADI (6-10-4)
Norman Williamson 11/2
D Nicholson   £25,927

PRESTIGE MEDICAL FESTIVAL
BUMPER STAKES OPEN NH FLAT
RACE
Cheltenham, Mar 15 2m 110y
DATO STAR (4-10-12)
Mark Dwyer   7/2
J M Jefferson   £15,844

DAILY EXPRESS TRIUMPH
HURDLE (Grade 1)
Cheltenham, Mar 16 2m 1f
KISSAIR (4-11-0)
John Lower   16/1
M C Pipe   £39,098

BONUSPRINT STAYERS' HURDLE
(Grade 1)
Cheltenham, Mar 16 3m 110y
DORANS PRIDE (6-11-10)
J P Broderick   11/4F
M Hourigan (Ireland)   £47,422

TOTE CHELTENHAM GOLD CUP
STEEPLECHASE (Grade 1)
Cheltenham, Mar 16 3m 2f 110y
MASTER OATS (9-12-0)
Norman Williamson 100/30F
K C Bailey   £122,540

CHRISTIES FOXHUNTER
CHALLENGE CUP HUNTERS'
CHASE (Class B)
Cheltenham, Mar 16 3m 2f 110y
FANTUS (8-12-0)
Miss P Curling   8/1
R Barber   £15,582

CHELTENHAM GRAND ANNUAL
CHALLENGE CUP HANDICAP
CHASE (Class B)
Cheltenham, Mar 16 2m 110y
SOUND REVEILLE (7-10-10)
Graham Bradley   7/1
C P E Brooks   £23,373

CATHCART CHALLENGE CUP
CHASE (Class B)
Cheltenham, Mar 16 2m 5f
COULTON (8-11-7)
Jamie Osborne   11/2
O Sherwood   £29,552

VINCENT O'BRIEN COUNTY
HANDICAP HURDLE (Grade 3)
Cheltenham, Mar 16 2m 1f
HOME COUNTIES (6-10-12)
D J Moffat   14/1
D Moffat   £23,000

ODDBINS HANDICAP HURDLE
(Class B)
Aintree, Apr 7   2m 4f
SQUIRE SILK (6-11-0)
Simon McNeil   16/1
A Turnell   £13,810

CORDON BLEU HANDICAP
HURDLE (Class B)
Aintree, Apr 8   2m 110y
THINKING TWICE (6-10-1)
Mick Fitzgerald   11/2
N J Henderson   £19,220

MARTELL AINTREE HANDICAP
CHASE (Grade 2)
Aintree, Apr 8   2m
COULTON (8-11-8)
Jamie Osborne   6/1
O Sherwood   £26,020

MARTELL AINTREE HURDLE
(Grade 1)
Aintree, Apr 8   2m 4f
DANOLI (7-11-7)
Charlie Swan   2/1JF
T Foley (Ireland)   £30,610

MARTELL GRAND NATIONAL
HANDICAP CHASE (Grade 3)
Aintree, Apr 8   4m 4f
ROYAL ATHLETE (12-10-6)
Jason Titley   40/1
Mrs J Pitman   £118,854

EDINBURGH WOOLLEN MILL'S
FUTURE CHAMPION NOVICES'
CHASE (Grade 2)
Ayr, Apr 22   2m
DANCING PADDY (7-11-7)
Richard Dunwoody   13/8
K O Cunningham-Brown £13,736

DAILY STAR SCOTTISH
CHAMPION HURDLE (Grade 2)
Ayr, Apr 22   2m
HOME COUNTIES (6-11-2)
D J Moffat   7/2
D Moffat   £12,660

STAKIS CASINOS SCOTTISH
GRAND NATIONAL HANDICAP
CHASE (Grade 3)
Ayr, Apr 22   4m 1f
WILLSFORD (12-10-12)
R Farrant   16/1
Mrs J Pitman   £35,650

BREWER'S FAYRE SILVER
TROPHY CHASE (Grade 2)
Sandown, Apr 29   2m 4f 110y
COULTON (8-11-7)
Jamie Osborne   11/10F
O Sherwood   £15,625

WHITBREAD GOLD CUP
HANDICAP CHASE (Grade 3)
Sandown, Apr 29   3m 5f 110y
CACHE FLEUR (9-10-1)
Richard Dunwoody   10/1
M C Pipe   £58,589

CROWTHER HOMES SWINTON
HANDICAP HURDLE (Grade 3)
Haydock, May 6   2m
CHIEF MINSTER (6-11-6)
Peter Hobbs   16/1
T Dyer   £23,555

Raceform
Top Rated Chasers
1994-5

1	**Master Oats**	**186**
2	The Fellow	174
	Merry Gale	174
	Bradbury Star	174
5	Viking Flagship	173
	Jodami	173
	Barton Bank	173
8	Flashing Steel	172
	Dubacilla	172
10	Val d'Alene	171
	Miinnehoma	171
12	Deep Sensation	169
	Coulton	169
14	Young Hustler	168
	Martha's Son	168
	Katabatic	168
17	Travado	167
	Royal Athlete	167
	Dockland's Express	167
20	Nakir	166
	Cogent	166
	Black Humour	166
	Algan	166
24	Zeta's Lad	165
	Southolt	165

Raceform
Top Rated Hurdlers
1994-5

1	**Alderbrook**	**165**
2	Fortune and Fame	162
3	Oh So Risky	161
	Danoli	161
5	Large Action	160
	Boro Eight	160
7	Halkopous	158
	Atours	158
9	Mole Board	157
	Flakey Dove	157
	Dorans Pride	157
	Destriero	157
13	Land Afar	156
	Jazilah	156
15	Sweet Glow	154
	Cyborgo	154
17	Moorish	153
18	Simpson	151
	Mysilv	151
	Derrymoyle	151
21	Hebridean	150
	Avro Anson	150
23	Granville Again	149
24	Cab on Target	147

OVERSEAS

VELKA PARDUBICE CHASE
Pardubice, CZE Oct 9 1994
4m 2f 110y
ERUDIT (8-11-1)
V Snitkovsky 79K
F Holcak (Czech Rep) £13,535

GRAND STEEPLECHASE
D'ENGHIEN
Enghien, France Oct 29, 1994 3m
1f
CHENE (5-10-6)
D Mescam 4.30F
J Gallorini (France) £57,208

MARION DUPONT SCOTT
COLONIAL CUP CHASE
Camden, USA Nov 13, 1994 2m 6f
LONESOME GLORY (6-11-8)
Blythe Miller
F Bruce Miller (USA) £40,541

ESB WINELECTRIC DRINMORE
NOVICES' CHASE
Fairyhouse, Dec 4 1994 2m 4f
SOUND MAN (6-11-7)
Charlie Swan 4/1
E J O'Grady (Ireland) £21,500

HATTONS GRACE HURDLE
Fairyhouse, Dec 4 1994 2m 4f
DANOLI (6-10-0)
Charlie Swan 4/6
T Foley (Ireland) £24,571

DENNYS GOLD MEDAL CHASE
Leopardstown, Dec 26 1994 2m 1f
KLAIRON DAVIS (5-11-6)
F Woods 100/30
A L T Moore (Ireland) £21,667

FINDUS HANDICAP CHASE
Leopardstown, Dec 27 1994 3m
BELMONT KING (6-10-10)
T P Treacy 10/1
S J Lambert (Ireland) £22,143

ERICSSON CHASE
Leopardstown, Dec 28 1994 3m
COMMERICAL ARTIST (8-12-0)
Graham Bradley 9/1
V Bowens (Ireland) £33,810

LADBROKE HANDICAP HURDLE
Leopardstown, Jan 14 2m
ANUSHA (5-10-2)
J P Broderick 25/1
M Hourigan (Ireland) £37,333

AIG CHAMPION HURDLE
Fairyhouse, Jan 29 2m
FORTUNE AND FAME (8-11-10)
Mark Dwyer 1/2F
D K Weld (Ireland) £32,381

HENNESSY COGNAC GOLD CUP
Leopardstown, Feb 5 3m
JODAMI (10-12-0)
Mark Dwyer 13/8
P Beaumont £46,429

JAMESON IRISH NATIONAL
HANDICAP CHASE (Grade 1)
Fairyhouse, Apr 17 3m 5f
FLASHING STEEL (10-12-0)
Jamie Osborne 9/1
J E Mulhern (Ireland) £62,700

POWER GOLD CUP NOVICES'
CHASE (Grade 1)
Fairyhouse, Apr 18 2m 4f
STRONG PLATINUM (7-11-7)
C O'Dwyer 7/2
P Burke (Ireland) £23,100

BMW DROGHEDA HANDICAP
CHASE (Grade 1)
Punchestown, Apr 25 2m
STRONG PLATINUM (7-11-1)
Connor O'Dwyer 3/1F
A P O'Brien (Ireland) £25,000

WOODCHESTER CREDIT
LYONNAIS DOWNSHIRE HURDLE
(Grade 2)
Punchestown, Apr 26 2m
FORTUNE AND FAME (8-11-8)
Richard Dunwoody 4/7F
D K Weld (Ireland) £26,000

HEINEKEN GOLD CUP NOVICES'
H 'CAP CHASE (Grade 1)
Punchestown, Apr 26 3m 1f
BUTCHES BOY (6-10-7)
F Woods 14/1
P A Fahy (Ireland) £37,200

MURPHY'S IRISH STOUT
CHAMPION 4-Y-O HURDLE (Grade
1)
Punchestown, Apr 27 2m
SHAIHAR (4-11-0)
Kevin F O'Brien 16/1
M J P O'Brien (Ireland) £31,000

DAVENPORT HOTEL
TIPPERKEVIN HURDLE (Grade 1)
Punchestown, Apr 27 3m
DERRMOYLE (6-11-11)
Mark Dwyer 8/1
M Cunningham (Ireland) £24,800

PRIX LEON RAMBAUD HURDLE
Auteuil, May 18 2m 4f 110y
POPLIFE (5-9-10)
M Maussion 7.70FF
H-A Pantall £47,904

Raceform

The Official Form Book, Compton, Newbury, Berkshire RG16 ONL

The Derby Winners

* filly

Year	Winner	Jockey
1780	Diomed	S Arnull
1781	Young Eclipse	C Hindley
1782	Assassin	S Arnull
1783	Saltram	C Hindley
1784	Sergeant	S Arnull
1785	Aimwell	C Hindley
1786	Noble	J White
1787	Sir Peter Teazle	S Arnull
1788	Sir Thomas	W South
1789	Skyscraper	S Chifney
1790	Rhadamanthus	J Arnull
1791	Eager	Stephenson
1792	John Bull	F Buckle
1793	Waxy	B Clift
1794	Daedalus	F Buckle
1795	Spread Eagle	Wheatley
1796	Didelot	J Arnull
1797	(unnamed colt)	J Singleton
1798	Sir Harry	S Arnull
1799	Archduke	J Arnull
1800	Champion	B Clift
1801	Eleanor*	J Saunders
1802	Tyrant	F Buckle
1803	Ditto	B Clift
1804	Hannibal	B Arnull
1805	Cardinal Beaufort	Fitzpatrick
1806	Paris	Shepherd
1807	Election	J Arnull
1808	Pan	Collinson
1809	Pope	Goodison
1810	Whalebone	B Clift
1811	Phantom	F Buckle
1812	Octavius	B Arnull
1813	Smolensko	Goodison
1814	Blucher	B Arnull
1815	Whisker	Goodison
1816	Prince Leopold	Wheatley
1817	Azor	J Robinson
1818	Sam	S Chifney
1819	Tiresias	B Clift
1820	Sailor	S Chifney
1821	Gustavus	S Day
1822	Moses	Goodison
1823	Emilius	F Buckle
1824	Cedric	J Robinson
1825	Middleton	J Robinson
1826	Lapdog	Dockeray
1827	Mameluke	J Robinson
1828	Cadland	J Robinson
1829	Frederick	J Forth
1830	Priam	S Day
1831	Spaniel	Wheatley
1832	St Giles	B Scott
1833	Dangerous	J Chapple
1834	Plenipotentiary	P Conolly
1835	Mundig	B Scott
1836	Bay Middleton	J Robinson
1837	Phosphorus	G Edwards
1838	Amato	J Chapple
1839	Bloomsbury	Temp'man
1840	Little Wonder	MacDonald
1841	Coronation	P Conolly
1842	Attila	B Scott
1843	Cotherstone	B Scott
1844	Orlando	N Flatman
1845	Merry Monarch	F Bell
1846	Pyrrhus the First	S Day
1847	Cossack	Temp'man
1848	Surplice	Temp'man
1849	The Flying Dutchman	C Marlow
1850	Voltigeur	J Marson
1851	Teddington	J Marson
1852	Daniel O'Rourke	F Butler
1853	West Australian	F Butler
1854	Andover	A Day
1855	Wild Dayrell	Sherwood
1856	Ellington	T Aldcroft
1857	Blink Bonny*	J Charlton
1858	Beadsman	J Wells
1859	Musjid	J Wells
1860	Thormanby	Custance
1861	Kettledrum	R Bullock
1862	Caractacus	J Parsons
1863	Macaroni	Challoner
1864	Blair Athol	J Snowden
1865	Gladiateur	Grimshaw
1866	Lord Lyon	Custance
1867	Hermit	J Daley
1868	Blue Gown	J Wells
1869	Pretender	J Osborne
1870	Kingcraft	T French
1871	Favonius	T French
1872	Cremorne	Maidment
1873	Doncaster	F Webb
1874	George Freder'k	Custance
1875	Galopin	J Morris
1876	Kisber	Maidment
1877	Silvio	F Archer
1878	Sefton	Constable
1879	Sir Bevys	Fordham
1880	Bend Or	F Archer
1881	Iroquois	F Archer
1882	Shotover*	T Cannon
1883	St Blaise	C Wood
1884	St Gatien	C Wood
	Harvester d/h	S Loates
1885	Melton	F Archer
1886	Ormonde	F Archer
1887	Merry Hampton	J Watts
1888	Ayrshire	F Barrett
1889	Donovan	T Loates
1890	Sainfoin	J Watts
1891	Common	G Barrett
1892	Sir Hugo	F Allsopp
1893	Isinglass	T Loates
1894	Ladas	J Watts
1895	Sir Visto	S Loates
1896	Persimmon	J Watts
1897	Galtee More	C Wood
1898	Jeddah	Madden
1899	Flying Fox	M Cannon
1900	Diamond Jubilee	H Jones
1901	Volodyovski	L Reiff
1902	Ard Patrick	S Martin
1903	Rock Sand	D Maher
1904	St Amant	K Cannon
1905	Cicero	D Maher
1906	Spearmint	D Maher
1907	Orby	J Reiff
1908	Signorinetta*	B Bullock
1909	Minoru	H Jones
1910	Lemberg	B Dillon
1911	Sunstar	G Stern
1912	Tagalie*	J Reiff
1913	Aboyeur	E Piper
1914	Durbar II	MacGee
1915	Pommern	Donoghue
1916	Fifinella*	J Childs
1917	Gay Crusader	Donaghue
1918	Gainsborough	J Childs
1919	Grand Parade	Temp'man
1920	Spion Kop	F O'Neill
1921	Humorist	Donoghue
1922	Captain Cuttle	Donoghue
1923	Papyrus	Donoghue
1924	Sansovino	T Weston
1925	Manna	Donoghue
1926	Coronach	J Childs
1927	Call Boy	C Elliott
1928	Fellstead	H Wragg
1929	Trigo	J Marshall
1930	Blenheim	H Wragg
1931	Cameronian	F Fox
1932	April the Fifth	F Lane
1933	Hyperion	T Weston
1934	Windsor Lad	C Smirke
1935	Bahram	F Fox
1936	Mahmoud	C Smirke
1937	Mid-day Sun	M Beary
1938	Bois Roussel	C Elliott
1939	Blue Peter	E Smith
1940	Pont l'Eveque	S Wragg
1941	Owen Tudor	B Nevett
1942	Watling Street	H Wragg
1943	Straight Deal	T Carey
1944	Ocean Swell	B Nevett
1945	Dante	B Nevett
1946	Airborne	T Lowrey
1947	Pearl Diver	Bridgland
1948	My Love	Johnstone
1949	Nimbus	C Elliott
1950	Galcador	Johnstone
1951	Arctic Prince	C Spares
1952	Tulyar	C Smirke
1953	Pinza	G Richards
1954	Never Say Die	L Piggott

The Derby & other English Classic Winners

1955 Phil Drake	F Palmer
1956 Lavandin	Johnstone
1957 Crepello	L Piggott
1958 Hard Ridden	C Smirke
1959 Parthia	H Carr
1960 St Paddy	L Piggott
1961 Psidium	Poincelet
1962 Larkspur	Sellwood
1963 Relko	St-Martin
1964 Santa Claus	S Breasley
1965 Sea Bird II	P Glennon
1966 Charlottown	S Breasley
1967 Royal Palace	G Moore
1968 Sir Ivor	L Piggott
1969 Blakeney	E Johnson
1970 Nijinsky	L Piggott
1971 Mill Reef	G Lewis
1972 Roberto	L Piggott
1973 Morston	E Hide
1974 Snow Knight	B Taylor
1975 Grundy	P Eddery
1976 Empery	L Piggott
1977 The Minstrel	L Piggott
1978 Shirley Heights	G Starkey
1979 Troy	W Carson
1980 Henbit	W Carson
1981 Shergar	Swinburn
1982 Golden Fleece	P Eddery
1983 Teenoso	L Piggott
1984 Secreto	C Roche
1985 Slip Anchor	S Cauthen
1986 Shahrastani	Swinburn
1987 Reference Point	S Cauthen
1988 Kahyasi	Cochrane
1989 Nashwan	W Carson
1990 Quest For Fame	P Eddery
1991 Generous	A Munro
1992 Dr Devious	J Reid
1993 Commander in Chief	M Kinane
1994 Erhaab	W Carson
1995 Lammtarra	Swinburn

1000 GUINEAS (since 1965)

Year Winner	Jockey
1965 Night Off	Will'mson
1966 Glad Rags	P Cook
1967 Fleet	G Moore
1968 Caergwrle	S Barclay
1969 Full Dress II	Hutchinson
1970 Humble Duty	L Piggott
1971 Altesse Royale	St-Martin
1972 Waterloo	E Hide
1973 Mysterious	G Lewis
1974 Highclere	J Mercer
1975 Nocturnal Spree	J Roe
1976 Flying Water	St-Martin
1977 Mrs McArdy	E Hide
1978 Enstone Spark	E Johnson
1979 One in a Million	J Mercer
1980 Quick As L'ning	B Rouse

1981 Fairy Footsteps	L Piggott
1982 On The House	J Reid
1983 Ma Biche	F Head
1984 Pebbles	Robinson
1985 Oh So Sharp	S Cauthen
1986 Midway Lady	Cochrane
1987 Miesque	F Head
1988 Ravinella	G Moore
1989 Musical Bliss	Swinburn
1990 Salsabil	W Carson
1991 Shadayid	W Carson
1992 Hatoof	Swinburn
1993 Sayyedati	Swinburn
1994 Las Meninas	J Reid
1995 Harayir	R Hills

2000 GUINEAS (since 1965)

Year Winner	Jockey
1965 Niksar	D Keith
1966 Kashmir II	J Lindley
1967 Royal Palace	G Moore
1968 Sir Ivor	L Piggott
1969 Right Tack	G Lewis
1970 Nijinsky	L Piggott
1971 Brigadier Gerard	J Mercer
1972 High Top	W Carson
1973 Mon Fils	F Durr
1974 Nonoalco	St-Martin
1975 Bolkonski	G Dettori
1976 Wollow	G Dettori
1977 Nebbiolo	G Curran
1978 Roland Gardens	F Durr
1979 Tap On Wood	S Cauthen
1980 Known Fact	W Carson
1981 To-Agori-Mou	G Starkey
1982 Zino	F Head
1983 Lomond	P Eddery
1984 El Gran Senor	P Eddery
1985 Shadeed	L Piggott
1986 Dancing Brave	G Starkey
1987 Don't Forget Me	W Carson
1988 Doyoun	Swinburn
1989 Nashwan	W Carson
1990 Tirol	M Kinane
1991 Mystiko	M Roberts
1992 Rodrigo de Triano	Piggott
1993 Zafonic	P Eddery
1994 Mister Baileys	J Weaver
1995 Pennekamp	T Jarnet

THE OAKS (Since 1965)

Year Winner	Jockey
1965 Long Look	J Purtell
1966 Valoris	L Piggott
1967 Pia	E Hide
1968 La Lagune	Thiboeuf
1969 Sleeping Partner	J Gorton
1970 Lupe	S Barclay
1971 Altesse Royale	G Lewis
1972 Ginevra	T Murray

1973 Mysterious	G Lewis
1974 Polygamy	P Eddery
1975 Juliette Marny	L Piggott
1976 Pawneese	St-Martin
1977 Dunfermline	W Carson
1978 Fair Salinia	G Starkey
1979 Scintillate	P Eddery
1980 Bireme	W Carson
1981 Blue Wind	L Piggott
1982 Time Charter	B Newnes
1983 Sun Princess	W Carson
1984 Circus Plume	L Piggott
1985 Oh So Sharp	S Cauthen
1986 Midway Lady	Cochrane
1987 Unite	Swinburn
1988 Diminuendo	S Cauthen
1989*Snow Bride	S Cauthen
1990 Salsabil	W Carson
1991 Jet Ski Lady	C Roche
1992 User Friendly	G Duffield
1993 Intrepidity	M Roberts
1994 Balanchine	F Dettori
1995 Moonshell	F Dettori

Aliysa (Walter Swinburn) won, but was disq after a drugs test

ST LEGER (since 1965)

Year Winner	Jockey
1965 Provoke	J Mercer
1966 Sodium	F Durr
1967 Ribocco	L Piggott
1968 Ribero	L Piggott
1969 Intermezo	Hutch'son
1970 Nijinsky	L Piggott
1971 Athens Wood	L Piggott
1972 Boucher	L Piggott
1973 Peleid	F Durr
1974 Bustino	J Mercer
1975 Bruni	T Murray
1976 Crow	St-Martin
1977 Dunfermline*	W Carson
1978 Julio Mariner	E Hide
1979 Son of Love	Lequeux
1980 Light Cavalry	J Mercer
1981 Cut Above	J Mercer
1982 Touching Wood	P Cook
1983 Sun Princess*	W Carson
1984 Commanche Run	L Piggott
1985 Oh So Sharp*	S Cauthen
1986 Moon Madness	P Eddery
1987 Reference Point	S Cauthen
1988 Minster Son	W Carson
1989 Michelozo	S Cauthen
1990 Snurge	R Quinn
1991 Toulon	P Eddery
1992 User Friendly*	G Duffield
1993 Bob's Return	Robinson
1994 Moonax	P Eddery
1995 Classic Cliché	F Dettori

Grand National Winners

Year	Winnner	Jockey	Year	Winner	Jockey	Year	Winner	Jockey
1836	The Duke	N/A	1895	Wild Man from Borneo	J Widger*	1958	Mr. What	Freeman
1837	The Duke	Mr Potts*	1896	The Soarer	Campbell*	1959	Oxo	Scudamore
1838	Sir William	T Oliver	1897	Manifesto	Kavanagh	1960	Merryman II	G Scott
1839	Lottery	J Mason	1898	Drogheda	J Gourley	1961	Nicolaus Silver	B Beasley
1840	Jerry	Bretherton*	1899	Manifesto	Will'mson	1962	Kilmore	F Winter
1841	Charity	H Powell	1900	Ambush II	Anthony	1963	Ayala	P Buckley
1842	Gay Lad	T Oliver	1901	Grudon	Night'gall	1964	Team Spirit	Robinson
1843	Vanguard	T Oliver	1902	Shannon Lass	D Read	1965	Jay Trump	T Smith*
1844	Discount	Crickmere	1903	Drumcree	Woodland	1966	Anglo	T Norman
1845	Cureall	B Loft	1904	Moifaa	A Birch	1967	Foinavon	Buck'ham
1846	Pioneer	W Taylor	1905	Kirkland	T Mason	1968	Red Alligator	B Fletcher
1847	Matthew	D Wynne	1906	Ascetic's Silver	Hastings*	1969	Highland Wedding	E Harty
1848	Chandler	J Little*	1907	Eremon	A Newey			
1849	Peter Simple	Cunn'ham	1908	Rubio	H Bletsoe	1970	Gay Trip	P Taaffe
1850	Abd-el-Kader	C Green	1909	Lutteurill	Parfrement	1971	Specify	J Cook
1851	Abd-el-Kader	T Abbott	1910	Jenkinstown	Chadwick	1972	Well To Do	G Thorner
1852	Miss Mowbray	Goodman*	1911	Glenside	Anthony*	1973	Red Rum	B Fletcher
1853	Peter Simple	T Oliver	1912	Jerry M	E Piggott	1974	Red Rum	B Fletcher
1854	Bourton	J Tasker	1913	Covertcoat	Woodland	1975	L'Escargot	Carberry
1855	Wanderer	J Hanlon	1914	Sunloch	W Smith	1976	Rag Trade	J Burke
1856	Freetrader	G Stevens	1915	Ally Sloper	J Anthony*	1977	Red Rum	T Stack
1857	Emigrant	C Boyce	1916	Vermouth	J Reardon	1978	Lucius	B Davies
1858	Little Charley	W Archer	1917	Ballymacad	T Driscoll	1979	Rubstic	M Barnes
1859	Half Caste	C Green	1918	Poethlyn	E Piggott	1980	Ben Nevis	Fenwick*
1860	Anatis	Pickernell*	1919	Poethlyn	E Piggott	1981	Aldaniti	Champion
1861	Jealousy	J Kendall	1920	Troytown	J Anthony*	1982	Grittar	Saunders*
1862	Huntsman	Lamplugh	1921	Shaun Spadah	D Rees	1983	Corbiere	B De Haan
1863	Emblem	G Stevens	1922	Music Hall	B Rees	1984	Hallo Dandy	Doughty
1864	Emblematic	G Stevens	1923	Sergeant Murphy	T Bennett*	1985	Last Suspect	H Davies
1865	Alcibiade	Coventry*				1986	West Tip	Dunwoody
1866	Salamander	Goodman*	1924	Master Robert	B Trudgill	1987	Maori Venture	S Knight
1867	Cortolvin	J Page	1925	Double Chance	J Wilson*	1988	Rhyme'N Reason	B Powell
1868	The Lamb	G Ede*	1926	Jack Horner	Watkinson			
1869	The Colonel	G Stevens	1927	Sprig	T Leader	1989	Little Polveir	J Frost
1870	The Colonel	G Stevens	1928	Tipperary Tim	B Dutton*	1990	Mr Frisk	Armytage*
1871	The Lamb	Pickernell*	1929	Gregalach	B Everett	1991	Seagram	N Hawke
1872	Casse Tete	J Page	1930	Shaun Goilin	Cullinan	1992	Party Politics	Llewellyn
1873	Disturbance	Rich'dson*	1931	Grakle	B Lyall	1993	Not Run	
1874	Reugny	Rich'dson*	1932	Forbra	J Hamey	1994	Miinnehoma	Dunwoody
1875	Pathfinder	Pickernell*	1933	Kellsboro' Jack	Williams	1995	Royal Athlete	J Titley
1876	Regal	J Cannon	1934	Golden Miller	G Wilson		*amateur jockey	
1877	Austerlitz	F Hobson*	1935	Reynoldstown	F Furlong*			
1878	Shifnal	J Jones	1936	Reynoldstown	F Walwyn*			
1879	The Liberator	G More*	1937	Royal Mail	Williams			
1880	Empress	T Beasley*	1938	Battleship	B Hobbs			
1881	Woodbrook	T Beasley*	1939	Workman	T Hyde			
1882	Seaman	Manners*	1940	Bogskar	M Jones			
1883	Zoedone	G Kinsky*	1946	Lovely Cottage	B Petre*			
1884	Voluptuary	T Wilson*	1947	Caughoo	Dempsey			
1885	Roquefort	T Wilson*	1948	Sheila's Cottage	Thompson			
1886	Old Joe	T Skelton	1949	Russian Hero	McMorrow			
1887	Gamecock	B Daniels	1950	Freebooter	J Power			
1888	Playfair	Mawson	1951	Nickel Coin	J Bullock			
1889	Frigate	T Beasley*	1952	Teal	Thompson			
1890	Ilex	Night'gall	1953	Early Mist	B Marshall			
1891	Come Away	H Beasley*	1954	Royal Tan	B Marshall			
1892	Father O'Flynn	R Owen*	1955	Quare Times	P Taaffe			
1893	Cloister	B Dollery	1956	E.S.B.	D Dick			
1894	Why Not	Night'gall	1957	Sundew	F Winter			

Ice Hockey ━━━━━━━━━━━━━━━━━━━━

There is a God; at least Alex Dampier must think so. Having guided Great Britain into the uncharted waters of World Championship Pool A and suffered five mighty blows below the water line there (12-3, 10-2, 10-0, 8-2 & 6-0 defeats for the short of memory), Dampier might have been forgiven for casting his eyes skyward in the search for some kinder reparation. It came. Bidding goodnight to the national side before the year (1994) was out, Dampier concentrated on his day job, coach to the Steelers of Sheffield and led them to victories in both the League and the British Championship. A commendable achievement for a club only formed four years earlier. Happier times for Dampier.

His national chalice was temporarily passed to George Peternousek, a Czech-born Dutchman, who took up hs appointment as GB coach on March 1, which left poor Peternousek with almost exactly six weeks to prepare his team for Pool B duty in this year's World Championship. That was only half the problem. In the middle of the pool games the British Championship final was played, which ruled out those players. When they crucially lost to Romania in their second game, Peternousek's team looked set for further demotion. But Romania proved even more fragile (they were routed by Latvia 18-1) and when Britain surprisingly overcame Poland in their final game, a Pool B future for 1996 was assured.

In the loftier realms of Pool A, Finland finally captured the world title. Canada had monopolised the early years, the Soviet Union had been pre-eminent more recently; poor Finland had never won it. Their potential had been apparent at the Lillehammer Olympics where, in the early rounds, they were the team everyone was talking about. On Sunday May 7th, an estimated 2.15 million people, from a population of just 5 million, watched on television as the "Lion Kings" took the crown. That they defeated their next-door neighbours, Sweden, made it all the more sweet. That they were coached by a Swede, Curre Lindstrom, made their neighbours even more sour.

In the European Cup, Cardiff Devils trod virgin ground for a British club when they reached the semi-finals. John Lawless, the Devils' manager and coach was in tears after his team's victory over Torpedo Ust-Kamengorsk in the Netherlands, which secured their place in the Minsk round. Lawless and his team had a crash landing in the Belarus capital, feeling much as the British team had a year earlier, but it was a fine achievement nevertheless.

In America, New Jersey Devils, like the Finns, broke their duck, winning a first-ever Stanley Cup with something approaching consummate ease. The New Jersey team, 13 years after gaining their franchise, defeated Detroit Red Wings in four straight games to romp the best-of-seven series. Yet all the odds were against them. They had finished the season with the ninth best record in the NHL and failed in all four post-season series to get home advantage. There were other landmarks: for coach Jacques Lemaire, who won eight Stanley Cups as a player, a first as a coach. Neal Broten, who scored twice in the final 5-2 win over the Red Wings, became only the second member of the legendary 1980 Olympic squad to win a Stanley Cup. And of course it nearly didn't happen. The players were locked out for 15 weeks until the middle of January when an agreement reached with the owners finally allowed for a reduced 48-game season.

World Championship

Pool A

Stockholm, Sweden Apr 23-May 7

GROUP A

Results	Can	Fra	Ger	Ita	Rus	Sui
Canada	-	-	-	-	-	-
France	4-1	-	-	-	-	-
Germany	2-5	0-4	-	-	-	-
Italy	2-2	5-2	2-1	-	-	-
Russia	5-4	3-1	6-3	4-2	-	-
Switzerland	3-5	2-3	3-5	2-3	0-8	-

League Standings		P	W	D	L	GF	GA	Pts
1	Russia	5	5	0	0	26	10	10
2	Italy	5	3	1	1	14	11	7
3	France	5	3	0	2	14	11	6
4	Canada	5	2	1	2	17	16	5
5	Germany	5	1	0	4	11	20	2
6	Switzerland	5	0	0	5	10	24	0

Top four qualify for quarter-finals

GROUP B

Results	Aut	Cze	Fin	Nor	Swe	USA
Austria	-	-	-	-	-	-
Czech Rep.	5-2	-	-	-	-	-
Finland	7-2	0-3	-	-	-	-
Norway	5-3	1-3	2-5	-	-	-
Sweden	5-0	2-1	3-6	5-0	-	-
USA	5-2	4-2	4-4	2-1	2-2	-

League Standings		P	W	D	L	GF	GA	Pts
1	USA	5	3	2	0	17	11	8
2	Finland	5	3	1	1	22	14	7
3	Sweden	5	3	1	1	17	9	7
4	Czech Republic	5	3	0	2	14	9	6
5	Norway	5	1	0	4	9	18	2
6	Austria	5	0	0	5	9	27	0

Top four qualify for quarter-finals

Quarter-finals

Italy	0	Sweden	7
Finland	5	France	0
Russia	0	Czech R.	2
USA	1	Canada	4

Relegation Games

Austria	4	Switzerland	0
Austria	4	Switzerland	4

(Switzerland are relegated to Pool B)

Semi-finals

Sweden	3	Canada	2
Czech R.	0	Finland	3

3rd/4th Play-off

Canada	4	Czech R.	1

FINAL   Finland 4 Sweden 1

Pool B

Bratislava, Slovakia Apr 12-21

Results	Den	Gbr	Jpn	Lat	Ned	Pol	Rom	Svk
Denmark	-	-	-	-	-	-	-	-
Gt Britain	2-9	-	-	-	-	-	-	-
Japan	1-5	4-3	-	-	-	-	-	-
Latvia	9-2	8-4	15-2	-	-	-	-	-
Netherl'ds	3-2	2-3	4-3	1-6	-	-	-	-
Poland	3-1	3-4	7-5	2-6	8-1	-	-	-
Romania	4-9	2-0	2-8	1-18	3-5	3-6	-	-
Slovakia	6-2	7-3	9-3	4-3	13-4	10-0	11-0	-

Final Standings		P	W	D	L	GF	GA	Pts
1	**Slovakia**	**7**	**7**	**0**	**0**	**60**	**15**	**14**
2	Latvia	7	6	0	1	65	16	12
3	Poland	7	4	0	3	29	30	8
4	Netherlands	7	3	0	4	20	38	6
5	Denmark	7	3	0	4	30	28	6
6	Japan	7	2	0	5	26	45	4
7	Great Britain	7	2	0	5	19	35	4
8	Romania	7	1	0	6	15	57	2

Slovakia promoted to Pool A, Romania relegated to Pool C

Pool C (Group 1)

Sofia, Bulgaria Mar 20-26

Group A (Top)

Final Standings		P	W	D	L	GF	GA	Pts
1	Belarus	2	2	0	0	5	2	4
2	Kazakhstan	2	0	1	1	3	4	1
3	Ukraine	2	0	1	1	3	5	1

Group B (Middle)

4	Estonia	2	2	0	0	15	7	4
5	China	2	1	0	1	9	12	2
6	Hungary	2	0	0	2	5	10	0

Group C (Bottom)

7	Slovenia	2	2	0	0	21	4	4
8	Yugoslavia	2	1	0	1	9	7	2
9	Bulgaria	2	0	0	2	1	20	0

Belarus are promoted to Pool B
Yugoslavia and Bulgaria are relegated to Pool D

Pool C (Group 2)

Johannesburg, South Africa Mar 21-30

Group A (Top)

Final Standings		P	W	D	L	GF	GA	Pts
1	Croatia	3	2	1	0	13	9	5
2	Lithuania	3	2	1	0	12	8	5
3	Spain	3	1	0	2	13	15	2
4	Korea	3	0	0	3	10	16	0

Group B (Middle)

5	Belgium	3	2	0	1	22	10	4
6	Israel	3	2	0	1	16	8	4
7	Australia	3	2	0	1	17	17	4
8	South Africa	3	0	0	3	8	28	0

Group C (Bottom)

9	Greece	1	1	0	0	10	7	2
10	New Zealand	1	0	0	1	7	10	0

European Cup

Quarter-finals

Pool A
Tilburg, Netherlands   Oct 7-9, 1994
Cardiff Devils & Ust-Kamengorsk KZK qualified
(Cardiff matches: Devils 6 Sokol Kiev 2; Tilburg Trappers 7 Devils 4; Devils 4 Ust-Kamengorsk 3)

Pool B
Budapest   Oct 7-9, 1994
HK Jesenice SLO & Steaua Bucharesti ROM qualified

Pool C
Riga, Latvia   Oct 7-9, 1994
Rouen FRA & HC Pardau Riga LAT qualified

Pool D
Nowy Targ, Poland   Oct 7-9, 1994
Dukla Trencin SVK & Pod. Nowy Targ POL qualified

Pool E
Feldkirch, Austria   Oct 7-9, 1994
EHC Kloten SUI & VEU-Feldkirch AUT qualified

Semi-finals

Pool F
Olomouc, Czech Republic   Nov 11-13, 1994
Lada Togliatti RUS & HC Olomouc CZE qualified

Pool G
Munich   Nov 11-13, 1994
EC Hedos München GER qualified

Pool H
Minsk, Belarus   Nov 11-13, 1994
Tivali Minsk BLS & Dukla Trencin SVK qualified
Cardiff Devils eliminated *(Matches: Trenchin 13 Devils 2; Tivali Minsk 14 Devils 0; VEU-Feldkirch 13 Devils 1)*

Pool J
Malmö   Nov 11-13, 1994
Malmö IF SWE qualified

Finals

Helsinki, Turku, Finland   Dec 26-30

Group A

	P	W	D	L	GF	GA	Pts
1 Lada Togliatti RUS	3	2	1	0	15	6	5
2 TPS Turku FIN	3	2	1	0	12	4	5
3 Malmö IF SWE	3	1	0	2	6	9	2
4 Dukla Trencin SVK	3	0	0	3	4	18	0

Group B

	P	W	D	L	GF	GA	Pts
1 Jokerit Helsinki FIN	3	3	0	0	18	6	6
2 HC Olomouc CZE	3	1	0	2	5	9	2
3 Pardaugava Riga LAT	3	1	0	2	9	14	2
4 Tivali Minsk BLS	3	1	0	2	6	9	2

3rd/4th Play-off
TPS Turku 8 HC Olomouc 1

FINAL   Jokerit Helsinki 4 Lada Togliatti 2

Women's European Championship

POOL A
Riga, Latvia   Mar 20-25
Final Standings: 1. Finland; 2. Sweden; 3. Switzerland; 4. Norway; 5. Germany; 6. Latvia

POOL B
Odense & Esbjerg, Denmark   Mar 27-31
Final Standings: 1. Russia; 2. Denmark; 3. Czech Republic; 4. Slovakia; 5. France; 6. Netherlands; 7. Great Britain; 8. Ukraine

Domestic Events

British National League

PREMIER DIVISION

Final Standings	P	W	L	D	GF	GA	Pts
1 Sheffield Steelers	44	35	5	4	334	183	74
2 Cardiff Devils	44	32	8	4	366	217	68
3 Nottingham P'thers	44	32	8	4	372	213	68
4 Edinburgh Racers	44	25	14	5	335	289	55
5 Durham Wasps	44	22	19	3	264	242	47
6 Fife Flyers	44	20	20	4	271	242	42
7 Basingstoke Beavers	44	20	22	2	271	279	42
8 Humberside Hawks	44	17	21	6	331	330	40
9 Peterborough Pirates	44	12	27	5	248	368	29
10 Whitley Warriors	44	10	30	4	242	372	24
11 Milton Keynes Kings	44	9	31	4	248	363	22
12 Bracknell Bees	44	6	35	3	189	373	15

Leading Scorers	P	Goals	Assists	Pts
Tony Hand (Edn)	42	70	137	207
Ivan Matulik (Edn)	44	87	80	167
Randy Smith (Pet)	44	83	84	167
Chris Palmer (Edn)	37	82	85	167

DIVISION ONE

Final Standings	P	W	L	D	GF	GA	Pts
1 Slough Jets	44	37	2	5	451	232	79
2 Telford Tigers	44	31	12	1	359	238	63
3 Paisley Pirates	44	29	11	4	394	302	62
4 Swindon Wildcats	44	29	15	0	431	271	58
5 Trafford Metros	44	22	14	8	325	283	52
6 Solihull Barons	44	19	19	6	328	315	44
7 Guildford Flames	44	19	20	5	317	273	43
8 Medway Bears	44	19	21	4	290	328	42
9 Blackburn Hawks	44	17	23	4	341	357	38
10 Chelmsford Ch'tains	44	10	30	4	274	404	24
11 Dumfries Vikings	44	5	37	2	253	455	12
12 Lee Valley Lions	44	5	38	1	191	498	11

British Championship

Wembley   Apr 14-16

Quarter-finals

Group A

	P	W	D	L	GF	GA	Pts
1 Sheffield Steelers	6	4	2	0	35	24	8
2 Nottingham P'thers	6	3	3	0	36	25	6
3 Fife Flyers	6	3	3	0	29	37	6
4 Humberside Hawks	6	2	4	0	28	42	4

Group B

	P	W	D	L	GF	GA	Pts
1 Edinburgh Racers	6	4	1	1	42	37	9
2 Cardiff Devils	6	3	1	2	46	30	8
3 Basingstoke Beavers	6	2	3	1	33	38	5
4 Durham Wasps	6	0	4	2	23	39	2

Semi-finals
Cardiff Devils 4 Sheffield Steelers 4
(Sheffield won 3-1 after pens)
Nottingham Panthers 7 Edinburgh Racers 11

FINAL   Sheffield Steelers 7 Edinburgh Racers 2

Benson & Hedges Cup

Sheffield   Dec 4, 1994
Nottingham Panthers 7 Cardiff Devils 2

National Hockey League

Eastern Conference
NORTHEAST DIVISION

	P	W	L	T	GF	GA	Pts
Québec Nordiques	48	30	13	5	185	134	65
Pittsburgh Penguins	48	29	16	3	181	158	61
Boston Bruins	48	27	18	3	150	127	57
Buffalo Sabres	48	22	19	7	130	119	51
Hartford Whalers	48	19	24	5	127	141	43
Montreal Canadiens	48	18	23	7	125	148	43
Ottawa Senators	48	9	34	5	117	174	23

ATLANTIC DIVISION

	P	W	L	T	GF	GA	Pts
Philadelphia Flyers	48	28	16	4	150	132	60
New Jersey Devils	48	22	18	8	136	121	52
Washington Capitals	48	22	18	8	136	120	52
New York Rangers	48	22	23	3	139	134	47
Florida Panthers	48	20	22	6	115	127	46
Tampa Bay Lightning	48	17	28	3	120	144	37
New York Islanders	48	15	28	5	126	158	35

Western Conference
CENTRAL DIVISION

	P	W	L	T	GF	GA	Pts
Detroit Red Wings	48	33	11	4	180	117	70
St Louis Blues	48	28	15	5	178	135	61
Chicago Blackhawks	48	24	19	5	156	115	53
Toronto Maple Leafs	48	21	19	8	135	146	50
Dallas Stars	48	17	23	8	136	135	42
Winnipeg Jets	48	16	25	7	157	177	39

PACIFIC DIVISION

	P	W	L	T	GF	GA	Pts
Calgary Flames	48	24	17	7	163	135	55
Vancouver Canucks	48	18	18	12	153	148	48
San Jose Sharks	48	19	25	4	129	161	42
Los Angeles Kings	48	16	23	9	142	174	41
Edmonton Oilers	48	17	27	4	136	183	38
Mighty Ducks of Anaheim	48	16	27	5	125	164	37

Conference Quarter Finals

EASTERN CONFERENCE *(Best of 7 Series)*
New York Rangers bt Québec Nordiques 4-2
Philadelphia Flyers bt Buffalo Sabres 4-1
Pittsburgh Penguins bt Washington Capitals 4-3
New Jersey Devils bt Boston Bruins 4-1

WESTERN CONFERENCE *(Best of 7 Series)*
Detroit Red Wings bt Dallas Stars 4-1
San Jose Sharks bt Calgary Flames 4-3
Vancouver Canucks bt St Louis Blues 4-3
Chicago Blackhawks bt Toronto Maple Leafs 4-3

Conference Semi Finals

EASTERN CONFERENCE *(Best of 7)*
Philadelphia Flyers bt New York Rangers 4-0
New Jersey Devils bt Pittsburgh Penguins 4-1

WESTERN CONFERENCE *(Best of 7)*
Detroit Red Wings bt San Jose Sharks 4-0
Chicago Blackhawks bt Vancouver Canucks 4-0

Conference Finals

EASTERN DIVISION *(Best of 7)*
New Jersey Devils bt Philadelphia Flyers 4-2
WESTERN DIVISION *(Best of 7)*
Detroit Red Wings bt Chicago Blackhawks 4-1

NHL Stanley Cup Championship
Best of 7 series - home team shown first
Game 1: Detroit Red Wings 1 New Jersey Devils 2
Game 2: New Jersey Devils 4 Detroit Red Wings 2
Game 3: Detroit Red Wings 2 New Jersey Devils 5
Game 4: New Jersey Devils 5 Detroit Red Wings 2

The defeat of Detroit in the Stanley Cup not only depressed their supporters, it really annoyed the local fishmongers. It has become a habit, at the Joe Louis Arena, to throw octopuses onto the ice. Anticipating four home games in the championship series, local fishmongers had ordered plenty of our eight-legged friends. As we know, however, the series only went to the second game at the Arena before it was all over. The Detroit crowd were left counting their sorrows, the fishmongers counting their octopuses. What else, pray, do you do with an octopus except throw it on an ice-rink?

Hard to believe, but a British duke has been charged with trying to swindle banks and NHL team-backers out of more than $25m. Angus Charles Drogo Montagu, the Duke of Manchester, is alleged to have promised to invest $50m in Tampa Bay Lightning, having told officials at the club he was worth $800m. Montagu lives at Kimbolton Castle in Cambridgeshire and has a net worth of about $5m. Still not bad, though.

World Champions & Stanley Cup Winners

WORLD CHAMPIONSHIPS

Year	Winner	Runner-up	Venue
1920	Canada	USA	Antwerp
1924	Canada	USA	Chamonix
1928	Canada	Sweden	St. Moritz
1930	Canada	Germany	Cham.-Berlin
1931	Canada	USA	Krynica
1932	Canada	USA	Lake Placid
1933	USA	Canada	Prague
1934	Canada	USA	Milan
1935	Canada	Switzerland	Davos
1936	Great Britain	Canada	Garmisch
1937	Canada	Great Britain	London
1938	Canada	Great Britain	Prague
1939	Canada	USA	Zurich-Basle
1947	Czechoslov'a	Sweden	Prague
1948	Canada	Czechoslovakia	St. Moritz
1949	Czechoslov'a	Canada	Stockholm
1950	Canada	USA	London
1951	Canada	Sweden	Paris
1952	Canada	USA	Oslo
1953	Sweden	West Germany	Zurich-Basle
1954	Soviet Union	Canada	Stockholm
1955	Canada	Soviet Union	W Germany
1956	Soviet Union	USA	Cortina
1957	Sweden	Soviet Union	Moscow
1958	Canada	Soviet Union	Oslo
1959	Canada	Soviet Union	Czechoslovakia
1960	USA	Canada	Squaw Valley
1961	Canada	Czechoslovakia	Geneva
1962	Sweden	Canada	Colorado Spr
1963	Soviet Union	Sweden	Stockholm
1964	Soviet Union	Sweden	Innsbruck
1965	Soviet Union	Czechoslovakia	Tampere
1966	Soviet Union	Czechoslovakia	Ljubljana
1967	Soviet Union	Sweden	Vienna
1968	Soviet Union	Czechoslovakia	Grenoble
1969	Soviet Union	Sweden	Stockholm
1970	Soviet Union	Sweden	Stockholm
1971	Soviet Union	Czechoslovakia	Berne-Geneva
1972	Czechoslov'a	Soviet Union	Prague
1973	Soviet Union	Sweden	Moscow
1974	Soviet Union	Czechoslovakia	Helsinki
1975	Soviet Union	Czechoslovakia	Munich
1976	Czechoslov'a	Soviet Union	Katowice
1977	Czechoslov'a	Sweden	Vienna
1978	Soviet Union	Czechoslovakia	Prague
1979	Soviet Union	Czechoslovakia	Moscow
1981	Soviet Union	Sweden	Gothenburg
1982	Soviet Union	Czechoslovakia	Helsinki
1983	Soviet Union	Czechoslovakia	Düsseldorf
1985	Czechoslov'a	Canada	Prague
1986	Soviet Union	Sweden	Moscow
1987	Sweden	Soviet Union	Vienna
1989	Soviet Union	Canada	Stockholm
1990	Soviet Union	Sweden	Berne
1991	Sweden	Canada	Turku
1992	Sweden	Finland	Bratislava
1993	Russia	Sweden	Dortmund
1994	Canada	Finland	Bozen-Milan
1995	Finland	Sweden	Stockholm

STANLEY CUP *(from 1937-38 season)*

Year	Winner
1937-38	Chicago Blackhawks
1938-39	Boston Bruins
1939-40	New York Rangers
1940-41	Boston Bruins
1941-42	Toronto Maple Leafs
1942-43	Detroit Red Wings
1943-44	Montreal Canadiens
1944-45	Toronto Maple Leafs
1945-46	Montreal Canadiens
1946-47	Toronto Maple Leafs
1947-48	Toronto Maple Leafs
1948-49	Toronto Maple Leafs
1949-50	Detroit Red Wings
1950-51	Toronto Maple Leafs
1951-52	Detroit Red Wings
1952-53	Montreal Canadiens
1953-54	Detroit Red Wings
1954-55	Detroit Red Wings
1955-56	Montreal Canadiens
1956-57	Montreal Canadiens
1957-58	Montreal Canadiens
1958-59	Montreal Canadiens
1959-60	Montreal Canadiens
1960-61	Chicago Blackhawks
1961-62	Toronto Maple Leafs
1962-63	Tomnto Maple Leafs
1963-64	Toronto Maple Leafs
1964-65	Montreal Canadiens
1965-66	Montreal Canadiens
1966-67	Toronto Maple Leafs
1967-68	Montreal Canadiens
1968-69	Montreal Canadiens
1969-70	Boston Bruins
1970-71	Montreal Canadiens
1971-72	Boston Bruins
1972-73	Montreal Canadiens
1973-74	Philadelphia Flyers
1974-75	Philadelphia Flyers
1975-76	Montreal Canadiens
1976-77	Montreal Canadiens
1977-78	Montreal Canadiens
1978-79	Montreal Canadiens
1979-80	New York Islanders
1980-81	New York Islanders
1981-82	New York Islanders
1982-83	New York Islanders
1983-84	Edmonton Oilers
1984-85	Edmonton Oilers
1985-86	Montreal Canadiens
1986-87	Edmonton Oilers
1987-88	Edmonton Oilers
1988-89	Calgary Flames
1989-90	Edmonton Oilers
1990-91	Pittsburgh Penguins
1991-92	Pittsburgh Penguins
1992-93	Montreal Canadiens
1993-94	New York Rangers
1994-95	New Jersey Devils

Ice Skating ━━━━━━━━━━━━━

A world without Tonya, who spent the first half of the year finishing her community service, was illuminated by the arrival of another scandal-wrapped American skater, Nicole Bobek. Bobek followed Harding as the American champion and, it transpired, had other similarities with the disgraced skater. Bobek had a criminal record. It wasn't much of a record, about as long as one of her bitten-back fingernails, but it got everybody excited. It was effectively a breaking and entering offence, without the breaking. To her credit, Bobek did not let the brouhaha get to her (which is where she and Harding part ways) and after the technical programme in the World Championships at Birmingham, she was even in the lead. She came back to earth with a literal bump in the free programme, but the impression that Bobek made on the ice was greatly to her credit. Lu Chen won the women's title, but in skating terms it was an undistinguished competition. Just a year earlier, Witt, Kerrigan, Harding and Baiul had competed at the Olympics and it wasn't community service that explained all their absences. Aware of the erosion of their ranks, the International Skating Union set up a Grand Prix circuit for the year ahead. Skate Canada, Trophée de France, the Nations Cup in Germany, NHK Skate in Japan and Skate America would be the five GP events, with the top skaters qualifying for a new event, the GP final. The prize money is designed to dissuade further defections, although Baiul for one may only be lured back by the Olympics.

The absence of Gordeeva and Grinkov from the pairs programme at Birmingham also detracted and, of course, there was no T & D in the ice dance (not even in spirit - they stayed well away). Gritschuk and Platov won that competition and then illustrated the ISU's problem by confirming their defection to the pro ranks. The men's competiton remained the beacon with Elvis Stojko, the reigning champion, Alexey Urmanov, the Olympic champion, Philippe Candeloro and Todd Eldredge giving it quality in depth. It was worth going to Birmingham for - and a lot of people did.

Quotes ━━━━━━━━━━━━━

"After seeing Tonya Harding dressed as Mrs Claus, it certainly is easier to understand why Santa stays out all night" - **Gary Shelton of the St Petersburg Times (Florida) after seeing Tonya Harding's Christmas skating exhibition**

"It was the public I got the flak from. You get the sturdy Friday night drinkers at chucking out time and they'd recognise the ice dancing policeman. I couldn't assert my authority. Everbody wanted to have a go" - **Christopher Dean recalling his days in the force**

"Let's say she's not playing with a full deck of cards" - **Dean on Tonya Harding**

"I believe the end of their career together could prove as psychologically traumatic as surgically serparating siamese twins" - **Dr David Lewis, on Torvill and Dean**

"On ice, Torvill and Dean become one, not only skating in unison but experiencing emotional and intellectual harmony. Almost literally, they are two souls with but a single thought - two hearts that beat as one" - **Dr David Lewis, again**

World Championships

Birmingham, England Mar 7-12

ICE DANCING

Four elements; 2 compulsory, original and free dances.

			C1	C2	OD	FD	Ttl
1	**Oksana Gritschuk**	**RUS**	**0.2**	**0.2**	**0.6**	**1.0**	**2.0**
	Evgeny Platov						
2	Susanna Rahkamo	FIN	0.4	0.4	1.2	2.0	4.0
	Petri Kokko						
2	Sophie Moniotte	FRA	0.6	0.6	1.8	3.0	6.0
	Pascal Lavanchy						
21	Michelle Fitzgerald	GBR	3.6	4.0	12	21	40.6
	Vincent Kyle						

PAIRS

Two elements: technical & free-skating.

			TP	FS	Ttl
1	**Radka Kovarikova**	**CZE**	**0.5**	**1.0**	**1.5**
	Rene Novotny				
2	Evgenya Shishkova	RUS	1.5	2.0	3.5
	Vadim Naumov				
3	Jenni Meno	USA	2.5	3.0	5.5
	Todd Sand				
17	Lesley Rogers	GBR	8.5	16.0	24.5
	Michael Aldred				

FIGURE SKATING

Men			TP	FS	Ttl
1	**Elvis Stojko**	**CAN**	**1.0**	**1.0**	**2.0**
2	Todd Eldredge	USA	0.5	2.0	2.5
3	Philippe Candeloro	FRA	2.5	3.0	5.5
8	Steven Cousins	GBR	3.0	9.0	12.0
19	Clive Shorten	GBR	11	18	29.0

Women			TP	FS	Ttl
1	**Lu Chen**	**CHN**	**1.5**	**1.0**	**2.5**
2	Surya Bonaly	FRA	2.0	2.0	4.0
3	Nicole Bobek	USA	0.5	4.0	4.5
24	Jenna Arrowsmith	GBR	14.5	24	38.5

European Championships

Dortmund, Germany Jan 29-Feb 5

ICE DANCING

			C1	C2	OD	FD	Ttl
1	**Susanna Rahkamo**	**FIN**	**0.4**	**0.4**	**0.6**	**1.0**	**2.4**
	Petri Kokko						
2	Sophie Moniotte	FRA	0.2	0.2	1.2	2.0	3.6
	Pascal Lavanchy						
3	Anjelika Krylova	RUS	0.6	0.6	1.8	3.0	6.0
	Oleg Ovsiannikov						
18	Michelle Fitzgerald	GBR	3.2	3.0	9.6	18.0	33.8
	Vincent Kyle						
19	Clair Wileman	GBR	3.6	3.6	11.4	19.0	37.6
	Andrew Place						
20	Lynn Burton	GBR	4.0	4.0	12.0	20.0	40.0
	Duncan Lenard						

FIGURE SKATING

Men			TP	FS	Ttl
1	**Ilya Kulik**	**RUS**	**0.5**	**2.0**	**2.5**
2	Alexey Urmanov	RUS	3.0	1.0	4.0
3	Viacheslav Zagorodniuk	UKR	1.0	3.0	4.0
8	Steven Cousins	GBR	5.0	6.0	11.0

Women			TP	FS	Ttl
1	**Surya Bonaly**	**FRA**	**1.0**	**1.0**	**2.0**
2	Olga Markova	RUS	0.5	2.0	2.5
3	Elena Liashenko	UKR	2.5	2.0	7.5
28	Jenna Arrowsmith	GBR	14.0	-	-

PAIRS			TP	FS	Ttl
1	**Mandy Wötzel**	**GER**	**1.0**	**1.0**	**2.0**
	Ingo Steuer				
2	Radka Kovarikova	CZE	0.5	2.0	2.5
	Rene Novotny				
3	Evgenya Shishkova	RUS	1.5	3.0	4.5
	Vadim Naumov				
12	Lesley Rogers	GBR	6.0	12.0	18.0
	Michael Aldred				

World Junior Championships

Budapest   Nov 21-27, 1994

ICE DANCING

1. **Olga Sharutenko/Dmitri Naumkin RUS**
2. Stephanie Guardia/Francke Laporte FRA
3. Iwona Filipowicz/Michal Szumski POL
16. Charlotte Clements/Gary Shortland GBR

FIGURE SKATING

Women
1. **Irina Slutskaya RUS**
2. Elena Ivanova RUS
3. Krisztina Czako HUN
26. Jenna Arrowsmith GBR

Men
1. **Ilya Kulik RUS**
2. Thierry Cerez FRA
3. Seiichi Suzuki JPN
12. Neil Wilson GBR

PAIRS

1. **Maria Petrova/Anton Sikharulidze RUS**
2. Danielle Hartsell/Steve Hartsell USA
3. Evgenya Filonenko/Igor Marchenko UKR

British Championships

Humberside   Nov 29-Dec 3, 1994

ICE DANCING

1. **Michelle Fitzgerald/Vincent Kyle Slough**
2. Clair Wileman/Andrew Place Notts/M Keynes
3. Lynn Burton/Duncan Lenard Slough

FIGURE SKATING

Men
1. **Steven Cousins** Deeside
2. Clive Shorten Stevenage
3. Stuart Bell Solihull

Women
1. **Jenna Arrowsmith** Swindon
2. Zoë Jones Swindon
3. Stephanie Main Murrayfield

PAIRS

1. **Lesley Rogers/Michael Aldred Solihull**
2. Jacqueline Soames/John Jenkins Queens
3. Nicola Thomas/Daniel Thomas Chelmsford

World Champions

Figure skating champs began in 1986 for men, 1906 women and 1908 pairs. First official ice dance champs 1952.

	Men	Women	Pairs	Ice Dancing
1986	G Fuchs GER	-		-
1987	G Hügel AUT	-	-	-
1898	H Grenander SWE	-		-
1899	G Hügel AUT	-	-	-
1900	G Hügel AUT	-		-
1901	U Salchow SWE	-		-
1902	U Salchow SWE	-	-	-
1903	U Salchow SWE	-		-
1904	U Salchow SWE	-		-
1905	U Salchow SWE	-		-
1906	G Fuchs GER	M Syers GBR	-	-
1907	U Salchow SWE	M Syers GBR	-	-
1908	U Salchow SWE	L Kronberger HUN	Hübler/Berger GER	-
1909	U Salchow SWE	L Kronberger HUN	Johnson/Johnson	-
1910	U Slachow SWE	L Kronberger HUN	Hübler/Burger GER	-
1911	U Salchow SWE	L Kronberger HUN	Eilers/Jakobsson FIN	-
1912	F Kachler AUT	O M Horvath HUN	Johnson/Johnson	-
1913	F Kachler AUT	O M Horvath HUN	Englemann/Mejstrick AUT	-
1914	G Sandahl SWE	O M Horvath HUN	Eilers/Jakobsson FIN	-
1922	G Grafstrom SWE	H Planck AUT	Engelmann/Berger AUT	-
1923	F Kachler AUT	H Planck AUT	Jakobsson/Jakobsson FIN	-
1924	G Grafstrom SWE	H Planck AUT	Englenmann/Berger AUT	-
1925	W Böckl AUT	H Jaross AUT	Jaross/Wrede AUT	-
1926	W Böckl AUT	H Jaross AUT	Joly/Brunet FRA	-
1927	W Böckl AUT	S Henie NOR	Jaross/Wrede AUT	-
1928	W Böckl AUT	S Henie NOR	Joly/Brunet FRA	-
1929	G Grafstrom SWE	S Henie NOR	Scholz/Kaiser AUT	-
1930	K Schäfer AUT	S Henie NOR	A Brunet/P Brunet FRA	-
1931	K Schäfer AUT	S Henie NOR	Rotter/Szollas HUN	-
1932	K Schäfer AUT	S Henie NOR	A Brunet/P Brunet FRA	-
1933	K Schäfer AUT	S Henie NOR	Rotter/Szollas HUN	-
1934	K Schäfer AUT	S Henie NOR	Rotter/Szollas HUN	-
1935	K Schäfer AUT	S Henie NOR	Rotter/Szollas HUN	-
1936	K Schäfer AUT	S Henie NOR	Herber/Baier GER	-
1937	F Kaspar AUT	C Colledge GBR	Herber/Baier GER	-
1938	F Kaspar AUT	M Taylor GBR	Herber/Baier GER	-
1939	G Sharp GBR	M Taylor GBR	Herber/Baier GER	-
1947	H Gerschwiler SUI	B Ann Scott CAN	Lannoy/Baugniet BEL	-
1948	R Button USA	B Ann Scott CAN	Lannoy/Baugniet BEL	-
1949	R Button USA	A Vrzanova TCH	Kekesy/Kiraly HUN	-
1950	R Button USA	A Vrzanova TCH	K Kennedy/P Kennedy USA	-
1951	R Button USA	J Altwegg GBR	R Falk/P Falk FRG	-
1952	R Button USA	J du Bief FRA	R Falk/P Falk FRG	Westwood/Demmy GBR
1953	H A Jenkins USA	T Albright USA	J Nicks/J Nicks GBR	Westwood/Demmy GBR
1954	H A Jenkins USA	G Busch FRG	Dafoe/Bowden CAN	Westwood/Demmy GBR
1955	H A Jenkins USA	T Albright USA	Dafoe/Bowden CAN	Westwood/Demmy GBR
1956	H A Jenkins USA	C Heiss USA	Schwarz/Oppelt AUT	Weight/Thomas GBR
1957	D Jenkins USA	C Heiss USA	Wagner/Paul CAN	Markham/Jones GBR
1958	D Jenkins USA	C Heiss USA	Wagner/Paul CAN	Markham/Jones GBR
1959	D Jenkins USA	C Heiss USA	Wagner/Paul CAN	Denny/Jones GBR
1960	A Giletti FRA	C Heiss USA	Wagner/Paul CAN	Denny/Jones GBR
1962	D Jackson CAN	S Dijkstra HOL	Jelinek/Jelinek CAN	Romanova/Roman TCH
1963	D McPherson CAN	S Dijkstra HOL	Kilius/Bäumler FRG	Romanova/Roman TCH
1964	Schnelidorfer FRG	S Dijkstra HOL	Kilius/Bäumler FRG	Romanova/Roman TCH
1965	A Calmat FRA	P Burka CAN	Belousova/Protopopov URS	Romanova/Roman TCH
1966	E Danzer AUT	P Fleming USA	Belousova/Protopopov URS	Towler/Ford GBR
1967	E Danzer AUT	P Fleming USA	Belousova/Protopopov URS	Towler/Ford GBR
1968	E Danzer AUT	P Fleming USA	Belousova/Protopopov URS	Towler/Ford GBR
1969	T Wood USA	G Seyfert GDR	Rodnina/Ulanov URS	Towler/Ford GBR

World Champions & British Champions

	Men	Women	Pairs	Ice Dancing
1970	T Wood USA	G Seyfert GDR	Rodnina/Ulanov URS	Pakhomova/Gorshkov URS
1971	O Nepela TCH	B Schuba AUT	Rodnina/Ulanov URS	Pakhomova/Gorshkov URS
1972	O Nepela TCH	B Schuba AUT	Rodnina/Ulanov URS	Pakhomova/Gorshkov URS
1973	O Nepela TCH	K Magnussen CAN	Rodnina/Zaitsev URS	Pakhomova/Gorshkov URS
1974	J Hoffmann GDR	C Errath GDR	Rodnina/Zaitsev URS	Pakhomova/Gorshkov URS
1975	S Volkov URS	D De Leeuw HOL	Rodnina/Zaitsev URS	Moiseyeva/Minenkov URS
1976	J Curry GBR	D Hamill USA	Rodnina/Zaitsev URS	Pakhomova/Gorshkov URS
1977	V Kovalyev URS	L Fratianne USA	Rodnina/Zaitsev URS	Moiseyeva/Minenkov URS
1978	C Tickner USA	A Potzsch GDR	Rodnina/Zaitsev URS	Linichuk/Karponosov URS
1979	V Kovalyev USSR	L Fratianne USA	Babilonia/Gardner USA	Linichuk/Karponosov URS
1980	J Hoffmann GDR	A Potzsch GDR	Tcherkasova/Shakrai URS	Regoczy/Sallay HUN
1981	S Hamilton USA	D Biellmann SUI	Vorobyeva/Lissovsky URS	Torvill/Dean GBR
1982	S Hamilton USA	E Zayak USA	Baess/Theirbach GDR	Torvill/Dean GBR
1983	S Hamilton USA	R Sumners USA	Valova/Vasilyev URS	Torvill/Dean GBR
1984	S Hamilton USA	K Witt GDR	Underhill/Martini CAN	Torvill/Dean GBR
1985	A Fadeyev URS	K Witt GDR	Valova/Vasilyev URS	Bestiaminova/Bukin URS
1986	B Boitano USA	D Thomas USA	Gordyeva/Grinkov URS	Bestiaminova/Bukin URS
1987	B Orser CAN	K Witt GDR	Gordyeva/Grinkov URS	Bestiaminova/Bukin URS
1988	B Boitano USA	K Witt GDR	Valova/Vasilyev URS	Bestiaminova/Bukin URS
1989	K Browning CAN	M Ito JPN	Gordyeva/Grinkov URS	Klimova/PonomarenkoURS
1990	K Browning CAN	J Trenary USA	Gordyeva/Grinkov URS	Klimova/Ponomar'ko URS
1991	K Browning CAN	K Yamaguchi JPN	Mishkutienok/Dmitryev CIS	I & P DuchesnayFRA
1992	V Petrenko UKR	K Yamaguchi JPN	Mishkutienok/Dmitryev CIS	Klimova/Ponomar'ko URS
1993	K Browning CAN	O Baiul UKR	Brasseur/Eisler CAN	Usova/Zhulin RUS
1994	E Stojko CAN	Y Sato JPN	Shishkova/Naumov RUS	Gritschuk/Platov RUS
1995	E Stojko CAN	Lu Chen CHN	Kovarikova/Novotny TCH	Gritschuk/Platov RUS

BRITISH CHAMPIONS

The British Championships are usually held in November or December, therefore the championships in 1993, for example, will be in the same season as the 1994 world championships. The championships was first held in 1903 at Henglers rink, which is now the London Palladium. It was won by Madge Syers

1966	M Williams	S Stapleford	Bernard/Wilson	Towler/Ford
1967	M Williams	S Stapleford	Bernard/Wilson	Towler/Ford
1968	H Oundjian	P Dodd	Bernard/Wilson	Towler/Ford
1969	H Oundjian	P Dodd	Connolly/Taylforth	Getty/Bradshaw
1970	J Curry	P Dodd	Connolly/Taylfroth	Getty/Bradshaw
1971	H Oundjian	J Scott	Torvill/Hutchinson	Sawbridge/Dalby
1972	J Curry	M McLean	McCafferty/Taylforth	Green/Watts
1973	J Curry	J Scott	Sessions/Harrison	Green/Watts
1974	J Curry	G Keddie	McCafferty/Taylforth	Green/Watts
1975	J Curry	K Richardson	Taylforth/Taylforth	Green/Watts
1976	R Cousins	K Richardson	Lindsey/Beckwith	Thompson/Maxwell
1977	R Cousins	K Richardson	Lindsey/Beckwith	Thompson/Maxwell
1978	R Cousins	D Cottrill	Garland/Daw	Torvill/Dean
1979	R Cousins	K Richardson	Garland/Daw	Torvill/Dean
1980	C Howarth	K Wood	Garland/Daw	Torvill/Dean
1981	M Pepperday	D Cottrill	Garland/Jenkins	Torvill/Dean
1982	M Pepperday	K Wood	Garland/Jenkins	Torvill/Dean
1983	M Pepperday	S A Jackson	Garland/Jenkins	Torvill/Dean
1984	S Pickavance	S A Jackson	Cushley/Cushley	Barber/Slater
1985	S Pickavance	J Conway	Peake/Naylor	Jones/Askham
1986	P Robinson	J Conway	Peake/Naylor	Jones/Askham
1987	P Robinson	J Conway	Peake/Naylor	Jones/Askham
1988	C Newberry	J Conway	Peake/Naylor	Jones/Askham
1989	S Cousins	E Murdoch	Peake/Naylor	Burton/Place
1990	S Cousins	J Conway	Peake/Naylor	Hall/Bloomfield
1991	S Cousins	J Conway	Pritchard/Briggs	Bruce/Place
1992	S Cousins	C von Saher	Pearce/Shorten	Humphries/Lanning
1993	S Cousins	S Main	Mednick/Briggs	Torvill/Dean
1994	S Cousins	J Arrowsmith	Rogers/Aldred	Fitzgerald/Kyle

Judo

You have to go an awful long way down the medal table of the World Championships before you come to Britain; it was our worst championships since the men's and women's were combined in 1987. The reports were depressing; nothing on Thursday, nothing on Friday, a bronze on Saturday and nothing on Sunday. In the litany of defeat, Sharon Rendle stood out. If you ever jumped a queue, you wouldn't want to step in front of Rendle. She is pugnacious and persistent. With two featherweight titles under her belt - the first as long ago as 1987 - you might have though that warm coals would be all that's left of Rendle's fire. Some chance; at 32, the oldest member of the women's team still burrows in like an angry mole. She threw and armlocked her first two opponents before losing to the Cuban Rodrig Verdecia. In the repechage, Rendle needed four victories before securing the medal, the last a penalty win against China's Jin Wang. At the European Championships, in Birmingham back in April, Rendle was drafted into the team at the last moment (when Debbie Allan withdrew) yet still made her mark. A bronze at those championships, another in Makuhari, with Olympic qualification as a bonus. Rendle enjoyed her year.

Nicola Fairbrother was the only British fighter defending a title in Japan. Looking strictly at the figures, Fairbrother was on a roll. The 25-year-old had gone through a sequence of Olympic, European, World & European competitions and rattled up silver, gold, gold & gold respectively. Yet Fairbrother's second European victory, in Birmingham, was gained on a hairline verdict and she had lost her first bout in the British Open in April to Severine Poret. Her ambitions for gold or silver at Makuhuri were blunted by the Korean Jung Sun Yong, but that was not an end to her troubles. In the repechage, the Surrey fighter went down to Russia's Zoulfia Garipova, that defeat placing her outside the first eight and Olympic qualification. Indeed, of the 15-strong team only five fighters secured that qualification: Rendle, Diane Bell, Kate Howey, Ray Stevens and Danny Kingston.

Kingston did well to place fifth. The 22-year-old from Wokingham only missed out on a medal when he was beaten by the American James Pedro. Kingston had one thing in his favour, Toshihiko Toga had moved out of the lightweight division. If Kingston was smiling because he didn't have to meet the double world champion, the light-middleweights weren't. Koga may only be just over 5ft 6in (a sprite in the under 78kg class), but he still flattened the opposition. The 27-year-old gave Japan their first gold of the championship on the second day (the Koreans were ruffling a lot of Japanese feathers) and was surely the fighter of the tournament in the men's divisions.

The French might disagree. "This David is Goliath" screamed the L'Equipe headline following David Douillet's victory in the Open class to add to his Heavyweight title. L'Equipe went on to call it an historic double, which seemed to conveniently forget that Yamashita and Ogawa had both doubled up in recent years, but maybe that's unfair. Just because their Monsieur Chirac has gone bananas in the south Pacific doesn't mean we can't acknowledge that their team is now (with three golds and three bronzes) comfortably the best in Europe.

Finally, a word about Ryoko Tamura. The bantamweight was fearsomely good in Makuhari. If she barges into the bus queue ahead of you, just let her in.

World Championships

Makuhari, Japan   Sep 28-Oct 1

MEN
-60kg
1	Nikolai Ojeguine	**RUS**
2	Georgi Vazagachvili	GEO
3	Natik Bagirov	BLR
3	Ryuji Sonoda	JPN

-65kg
1	Udo Quellmalz	**GER**
2	Yukimasa Nakamura	JPN
3	Bektas Demirel	TUR
3	Kim Due Ik	KOR

-71kg
1	Daisuke Hideshima	**JPN**
2	Kwak Dea Sung	KOR
3	James Pedro	USA
3	Diego Brambilla	ITA
5	*Danny Kingston*	*GBR*

-78kg
1	Toshihiko Koga	**JPN**
2	Oren Smagda	ISR
3	Patrick Reiter	AUT
3	Djamel Bouras	FRA

-86kg
1	Jeon Ki-Young	**KOR**
2	Hidehiko Yoshida	JPN
3	Oleg Maltsev	RUS
3	Nicolas Gill	CAN

-95kg
1	Pawel Nastula	**POL**
2	Dmitri Sergueev	RUS
3	Stephane Traineau	FRA
3	Shigeru Okaizumi	JPN
7	*Ray Stevens*	*GBR*

+95kg
1	David Douillet	**FRA**
2	Frank Moller	GER
3	Naoya Ogawa	JPN
3	Dav Khakhaleishvili	GEO

Open
1	David Douillet	**FRA**
2	Sergey Kossorotov	RUS
3	Shinichi Shinohara	JPN
3	Selim Tararoglu	TUR

WOMEN
-48kg
1	Ryoko Tamura	**JPN**
2	Li Aiyue	CHN
3	Carmenaty Amar Savon	CUB
3	Malgorzata Roszkowska	POL

-52kg
1	Claire Restoux	**FRA**
2	Carolina Mariani	ARG
3	Rodrig Legna Verdecia	CUB
3	Sharon Rendle	GBR

-56kg
1	Driulis Gonzalez	**CUB**
2	Jung Sun Yong	KOR
3	Danielle Zangrando	BRA
3	Filipa Cavalleri	POR

-61kg
1	Jung Sung-Sook	**KOR**
2	Jenny Gal	NED
3	Gella Vandecaveye	BEL
3	Catherine Fleury	FRA
7	*Diane Bell GBR*	

-66kg
1	Cho Min Sun	**KOR**
2	Odalis Jimenez Reve	CUB
3	Aneta Szczepanska	POL
3	Liliko Ogawasawara	USA

-72kg
1	Castellano Luna	**CUB**
2	Ulla Werbrouck	BEL
3	Yoko Tanaba	JPN
3	Tatyana Beliaeva	UKR
5	*Kate Howey*	*GBR*

+72kg
1	Angelique Seriese	**NED**
2	Zhang Ying	CHN
3	Daime Beltran	CUB
3	Shon Hyun-Me	KOR

Open
1	Monique Van Der Lee	**NED**
2	Sun Fuming	CHN
3	Lee Hyun Kyung	KOR
3	Estela Rodriguez	ESP

Medal Table

	G	S	B
Japan	3	2	5
South Korea	3	2	3
France	3	0	3
Cuba	2	1	4
Netherlands	2	1	0
Russia	1	2	1
Germany	1	1	0
Poland	1	0	2
China	0	3	0
Belgium	0	1	1
Georgia	0	1	1
Israel	0	1	0
Argentina	0	1	0
United States	0	0	2
Turkey	0	0	2
Austria	0	0	1
Belarus	0	0	1
Brazil	0	0	1
Canada	0	0	1
Great Britain	0	0	1
Italy	0	0	1
Portugal	0	0	1
Ukraine	0	0	1

European Championships

Birmingham NIA   May 11-14

MEN
-60kg
1	Nigel Donohue	**GBR**
2	Georgi Vazagachvili	GEO
3	Natik Bagirov	BLS
3	Girolamo Giovinazzo	ITA

-65kg
1	Peter Schlatter	**GER**
2	Vsevolod Zeleny	LAT
3	Philip Laats	BEL
3	Bektas Demirel	TUR
	Simon Moss GBR lost 1st round	

-71kg
1	Martin Schmidt	**GER**
2	Christophe Gagliano	FRA
3	Davor Vlaskovac	BOS
3	Thomas Schleicher	AUT
7	*Danny Kingston*	*GBR*

-78kg
1	Patrick Reiter	**AUT**
2	Djamel Bouras	FRA
3	Irfam Toker	TUR
3	Johan Laats	BEL
5	*Ryan Birch*	*GBR*

-86kg
1	Maartens Arens	**NED**
2	Iveri Djikovraouli	GEO
3	Ruslan Mahsurenko	UKR
3	Oleg Maltsev	RUS
	Wayne Lakin GBR lost 2nd rd	

-95kg
1	Pawel Nastula	**POL**
2	Dmitri Sergueev	RUS
3	Pedro Soares	POR
3	Stephane Traineau	FRA
5	*Raymond Stevens*	*GBR*

+95kg
1	Sergey Kossorotov	**RUS**
2	Franck Moller	GER
3	Danny Ebbers	NED
3	Rafael Kubacki	POL
	Danny Sargent GBR lost 2nd rd	

Open
1	Imre Csosz	**HUN**
2	Ralf Koser	GER
3	Harry Van Berneveld	BEL
3	Ben Sonnemans	NED
	Danny Sargent GBR lost 2nd rd	

WOMEN
-48kg
1	Yolande Soler	**ESP**
2	Sylvie Meloux	FRA
3	Joyce Heron	GBR
3	Tatiana Kouvchinova	RUS

-52kg
1	Alessandra Giungi	**ITA**
2	Heidi Goossens	BEL
3	Sharon Rendle	GBR
3	Larysa Krause	POL

British Open Championships
Birmingham NIA   Apr 8

-56kg
1 **Nicola Fairbrother** GBR
2 Isabel Fernandez ESP
3 Eimat Yaron ISR
3 Jessica Gal NED

-61kg
1 **Jenny Gal** NED
2 Diane Bell GBR
3 Gella Vandecaveye BEL
3 Catherine Fleury FRA

-66kg
1 **Alice Dubois** FRA
2 Emanuela Pierantozzi ITA
3 Rowena Sweatman GBR
3 Ute Burmeister GER

-72kg
1 **Ulla Werbrouck** BEL
2 Estha Essombe FRA
3 Kate Howey GBR
3 Doris Pollhuber AUT

+72kg
1 **Svetlana Goundarenko** RUS
2 Christine Cicot FRA
3 Beata Maksymov POL
4 Monique Van Der Lee NED
Josie Horton GBR lost 2nd rd

Open
1 **Angelique Seriese** NED
2 Richter ROM
3 Raquel Barrientos ESP
3 Tzwetana Bojilova BUL
Josie Horton GBR lost 1st rd

MEDAL TABLE

	G	S	B
Netherlands	**3**	-	**4**
Germany	2	2	1
Great Britain	2	1	4
Russia	2	1	2
France	1	5	2
Belgium	1	1	4
Italy	1	1	1
Spain	1	1	1
Poland	1	-	3
Austria	1	-	2
Hungary	1	-	-
Georgia	-	2	-
Latvia	-	1	-
Romania	-	1	-
Turkey	-	-	2
Belarus	-	-	1
Bosnia	-	-	1
Bulgaria	-	-	1
Israel	-	-	1
Portugal	-	-	1
Ukraine	-	-	1

MEN
-60kg
1 **Jamie Johnson** GBR
2 Nigel Donohue GBR
3 Amit Lang ISR
3 Sam Dunkley GBR

-65kg
1 **Ben Boudaouci** FRA
2 Simon Moss GBR
3 Ian Freeman GBR
3 Julian Davies GBR

-71kg
1 **Danny Kingston** GBR
2 Haike Seidlitz GER
3 David Gonzale FRA
3 Bronislaw Maunsky ISR

-78kg
1 **Francois Laurent** FRA
2 Alain Arnault FRA
3 Gabor Szabo AUS
3 Jean Baptiste Givord FRA

-86kg
1 **Nomis Stephans** FRA
2 Thomas Saakachvili FRA
3 Bertrand Amonsson FRA
3 Yam Bartoni FRA

-95kg
1 **Raymond Stevens** GBR
2 Pascal Legoux FRA
3 Egon Muller GER
3 Eric Fauroux FRA

+95kg
1 **Ernesto Perez** ESP
2 Eduard Grams GER
3 Fabrice Guenet FRA
3 Laurent Crost FRA

WOMEN
-48kg
1 **Birte Stemens** GER
2 Dorte Damman GER
3 Sarah Flynn GBR
3 Servare Bruneau FRA

-52kg
1 **Debbie Allan** GBR
2 Georgina Singleton GBR
3 Cathy Bain AUS
3 Elise Summers GBR

-56kg
1 **Yaron Einat** ISR
2 Karine Paillard FRA
3 Marisa Pedulla USA
3 Lynn Roethke USA

-61kg
1 **Miriam Blasco** ESP
2 Valerie Fizellier FRA
3 Agnes Phillipe FRA
3 Sandra Wurm GER

-66kg
1 **Karren Powell** GBR
2 Michelle Holt GBR
3 Rowena Sweatman GBR
3 Sabin Van Crombrugge BEL

-72kg
1 **Christine Curto** ESP
2 Sabine Tisserand FRA
3 Laurence Sionneau FRA
3 Carol Piccoli FRA

+72kg
1 **Monique Van Der Lee** NED
2 Josie Horton GBR
3 Raquel Barrientos ESP
3 Gaelle Potel FRA

World Champions

Men

Except Open, categories changed for 1979 championships.

-60kg
1979 Thierry Ray FRA
1981 Yasuhiko Moriwaki JPN
1983 Khazret Tletseri URS
1985 Shinji Hosokawa JPN
1987 Kim Jae-yup KOR
1989 Amiran Totikashvilli URS
1991 Tadanori Koshino JPN
1993 Ryuki Sonoda JPN
1995 Nikolai Ojeguine RUS

-65kg
1979 Nikolay Soludukhin URS
1981 Katsu. Kashiwazaki JPN
1983 Nikolay Soludukhin URS
1985 Yuri Sokolov URS
1987 Yosuke Yamamoto JPN
1989 Drago Becanovic YUG
1991 Udo Quellmalz GER
1993 Yukimasa Nakamura JPN
1995 Udo Quellmalz GER

-71kg
1979 Kyoto Katsuki JPN
1981 Park Chong-hak KOR
1983 Hidetoshi Nakanishi JPN
1985 Ahn Byeong-kuen KOR
1987 Mike Swain USA
1989 Toshihiko Koga JPN
1991 Toshihiko Koga JPN
1993 Hoon Chung KOR
1995 Daisuke Hideshima JPN

-78kg
1979 Shozo Fujii JPN
1981 Neil Adams GBR
1983 Nobutoshi Hikage JPN
1985 Nobutoshi Hikage JPN
1987 Hirotaka Okada JPN
1989 Kim Byung-ju KOR
1991 Daniel Lascau GER
1993 Ki-Young Chun KOR
1995 Toshihiko Toga JPN

-86kg
1979 Detlef Ultsch GDR
1981 Bern'd Tchoullouyan FRA
1983 Detlef Ultsch GDR
1985 Peter Seisenbacher AUT
1987 Fabien Canu FRA
1989 Fabien Canu FRA
1991 Hirotaka Okada JPN
1993 Yoshio Nakamura JPN
1995 Jeon Ki-Young KOR

-95kg
1979 Tengiz Khubuluri URS
1981 Tengiz Khubuluri URS
1983 Valeriy Divisenko URS
1985 Hitoshi Sugai JPN
1987 Hitoshi Sugai JPN
1989 Koba Kurtanidze URS
1991 Stephane Traineau FRA
1993 Antal Kovacs HUN
1995 Pawel Nastula POL

+95kg
1979 Yasuhiro Yamashita JPN
1981 Yasuhiro Yamashita JPN
1983 Yasuhiro Yamashita JPN
1985 Cho Yong-chul KOR
1987 Grigory Vertichev URS
1989 Naoya Ogawa JPN
1991 Sergey Kosorotov RUS
1993 David Douillet FRA
1995 David Douillet FRA

Open
1956 Shokichi Natsui JPN
1958 Koji Sone JPN
1961 Anton Geesink HOL
1965 Isao Inokuma JPN
1967 Matsuo Matsunaga JPN
1969 Masatoshi Shinomaki JPN
1971 Masatoshi Shinomaki JPN
1973 Kazuhiro Ninomiya JPN
1975 Haruki Uemura JPN
1979 Sumio Endo JPN
1981 Yasuhiro Yamashita JPN
1983 Hitoshi Saito JPN
1985 Yoshimi Masaki JPN
1987 Naoya Ogawa JPN
1989 Naoya Ogawa JPN
1991 Naoya Ogawa JPN
1993 Rafael Kubacki POL
1995 David Douillet FRA

Women

-48kg
1980 Jane Bridge GBR
1982 Karen Briggs GBR
1984 Karen Briggs GBR
1986 Karen Briggs GBR
1987 Zhangyun Li CHN
1989 Karen Briggs GBR
1991 Cécile Nowak FRA
1993 Ryoko Tamura JPN
1995 Ryoko Tamura JPN

-52kg
1980 Edith Hrovat AUT
1982 Loretta Doyle GBR
1984 Kaori Yamaguchi JPN
1986 Dominique Brun FRA
1987 Sharon Rendle GBR
1989 Sharon Rendle GBR
1991 Alessandra Giungi ITA
1993 Rodriguez Verdecia CUB

-56kg
1980 Gerda Winklbauer AUT
1982 Beatrice Rodriguez FRA

1984 Ann-Maria Burns USA
1986 Ann Hughes GBR
1987 Catherine Arnaud FRA
1989 Catherine Arnaud FRA
1991 Miriam Blasco ESP
1993 Nicola Fairbrother GBR
1995 Driulis Gonzalez CUB

-61 kg
1980 Anita Staps HOL
1982 Martine Rothier FRA
1984 Natasha Hernandez VEN
1986 Diane Bell GBR
1987 Diane Bell GBR
1989 Catherine Fleury FRA
1991 Fraucke Eickoff GER
1993 Gella Vandecaveye BEL
1995 Jung Sung-Sook KOR

-66kg
1980 Edith Simon AUT
1982 Brigitte Deydier FRA
1984 Brigitte Deydier FRA
1986 Brigitte Deydier FRA
1987 Alexandra Schreiber FRG
1989 Emanuela Pierantozi ITA
1991 Emanuela Pierantozi ITA
1993 Cho Min-Sun KOR
1995 Cho Min-Sun KOR

-72kg
1980 Jocelyne Triadou FRA
1982 Barbara Classen FRG
1984 Ingrid Berghmans BEL
1986 Irene de Kok HOL
1987 Irene de Kok HOL
1989 Ingrid Berghmans BEL
1991 Kim Mi-jung KOR
1993 Chunhui Leng CHN
1995 Castellana Luna CUB

+72kg
1980 Margarita de Cal ITA
1982 Natalina Lupino FRA
1984 Maria-Teresa Motta ITA
1986 Gao Fengliang CHN
1987 Gao Fengliang CHN
1989 Gao Fengliang CHN
1991 Moon Ji-yoon KOR
1993 Johanna Hagn GER
1995 Angelique Seriese BEL

Open
1980 Ingrid Berghmans BEL
1982 Ingrid Berghmans BEL
1984 Ingrid Berghmans BEL
1986 Ingrid Berghmans BEL
1987 Gao Fengliang CHN
1989 Estella Rodriguez CUB
1991 Zhuang Xiaoyan CHN
1993 Beata Maksymow POL
1995 M Van Der Lee NED

Modern Pentathlon ━━━━━

World Championships

Basle, Switzerland   July 25-30

MEN'S INDIVIDUAL		Shoot	Fence	Swim	Ride	Run	Total
1 Dmitriy Svatkovsky	**RUS**	**1024**	**1000**	**1252**	**980**	**1327**	**5583**
2 Akos Hanzély	HUN	1048	850	1220	1100	1330	5548
3 Cesare Toraldo	ITA	1096	910	1288	1010	1216	5520
4 Per-Olov Danielsson	SWE	1120	940	1240	1010	1201	5511
5 Fabio Nebuloni	ITA	1084	1000	1156	980	1273	5493
6 Maciej Czyzowicz	POL	1036	790	1288	1100	1273	5487
7 Viacheslav Duhanov	LAT	1072	850	1188	1070	1288	5468
8 Richard Phelps	GBR	1000	820	1284	1010	1345	5459
9 Péter Sarfálvi	HUN	1036	820	1250	1010	1324	5450
10 Alexander Parygin	KZK	1036	940	1200	950	1318	5444
25 Greg Whyte	GBR	964	940	1260	872	1144	5180

WOMEN'S INDIVIDUAL		Shoot	Fence	Swim	Ride	Run	Total
1 Kerstin Danielsson	**SWE**	**988**	**1030**	**1216**	**1070**	**1220**	**5524**
2 Janna Choubenok	BLS	988	1030	1172	922	1345	5457
3 Dorota Idzi	POL	976	1000	1264	1010	1170	5420
4 Eszter Hortobagyi	HUN	940	790	1204	1100	1330	5364
5 Iwona Kowalewska	POL	940	940	1200	1070	1175	5325
6 Kitty Chiller	AUS	1036	690	1208	1100	1280	5314
7 Emese Köblö	HUN	868	970	1228	1040	1200	5306
8 Eva Fjellerup	DEN	976	760	1212	1040	1285	5273
9 Lucie Grolichova	CZE	1000	820	1216	1100	1135	5271
10 Barbara Boccolari	ITA	1012	790	1220	1061	1175	5258
24 Kate Allenby	GBR	976	550	1216	978	1235	4955

MEN'S TEAM
1. Italy
2. Poland
3. Czech Republic
4. Great Britain

MEN'S RELAY
1. Poland
2. Switzerland
3. Mexico
9. Great Britain

WOMEN'S TEAM
1. Poland
2. Hungary
3. Denmark
No GBR team

WOMEN'S RELAY
1. Poland
2. Italy
3. Denmark
5. Great Britain

British Open Championships

Stowe and Milton Keynes   July 1-2

MEN'S FINAL STANDINGS

1 Richard Phelps	Spartan	5313
2 Greg Whyte	Lygea	5309
3 Simeon Robbie	SEALions	5174
4 James Greenwell	Ind	4862
5 David Storer	Evesham	4806
6 Ed Egan	SEALions	4682
7 Sean Kinsey	Spartan	4496
8 Paul James	Cambs Uni	4196
9 Craig Storey	TVT	4058
10 Alastair George	O & C	3993

WOMEN'S FINAL STANDINGS

1 Julia Allen	Cambs Uni	5280
2 Helen Griffiths	W & B	5218
3 Rachael Wilmot	East Mid	5198
4 Kate Housten	SEALions	5160
5 Helen Shearn	WW	4543
6 Waveney Gooding	Cambs Uni	4306
7 Louise Yarroll	A12	3654
8 Catherina Yarroll	A12	3010
9 Philippa Kershaw	Stan	2186

MEN'S TEAM

1 SEALions (Egan/Robbie/Smale)	13.523
2 Spartan (Collliver/Kinsey/Phelps)	12,983
3 Oxford & Cambridge (Crowdy/George/Robbie)	11,257

WOMEN'S TEAM
No team competed

Biathlon World Championship

Alto Adige, Italy   Feb 12-19

MEN
Individual 20km
1	Tomasz Sikora POL	1:01:36.0
2	Jon Age Tyldum NOR	1:02:10.6
3	Oleg Ryshenkov BLS	1:02:16.4
45	Michael Dixon GBR	1:07:37.3

Sprint 10km
1	Patrice Bailly-Salins FRA	29:23.8
2	Pavel Mouslimov RUS	29:25.7
3	Ricco Gross GER	29:29.0
41	Jason Sklenar GBR	31:51.7

Team 10km
1	Norway	30:17.7
2	Czech Republic	30:57.8
3	France	31:07.4
19	Great Britain	35:37.4

Relay 4x7.5km
1	Germany	1:23:29.9
2	France	1:23:41.9
3	Belarus	1:24:06.0
17	Great Britain	1:30:58.7

WOMEN
Individual 15km
1	Corinne Niogret FRA	51:16.3
2	Uschi Disl GER	51:28.7
3	Ekaterina Dafovska BUL	52:10.6

Sprint 7.5km
1	Anne Briand FRA	24:00.0
2	Uschi Disl GER	24:05.9
3	Corinne Niogret FRA	24:07.0

Team 7.5km
1	Norway	25:48.7
2	Germany	26:38.4
3	France	27:01.0

Relay 4x7.5km
1	Germany	1:37:05.0
2	France	1:37:38.4
3	Norway	1:39:31.3

Biathlon World Cup

Overall Men
1	Jon Age Tyldum NOR	195
2	Patrick Favre ITA	193
3	Wilfried Pallhuber ITA	178
4	Ole Einar Bjoerndalen NOR	178
5	Oleg Ryshenkov BLS	169

Overall Women
1	Anne Briand FRA	241
2	Svetlana Paramygina BLS	233
3	Uschi Disl GER	220
4	Corinne Niogret FRA	208
5	Magdalena Wallin SWE	178

Modern Pent. World Champions

MEN

	Individual	Team
1949	Tage Bjurefelt SWE	Sweden
1950/51	Lars Hall SWE	Sweden
1953	Gábor Benedek HUN	Sweden
1954	Björn Thofelt SWE	Hungary
1955	K Salnikov URS	Hungary
1957/61	Igor Novikov URS	Soviet Union
1962	E Dobnikov URS	Soviet Union
1963/67	András Balczó HUN	Hungary
1969	András Balczó HUN	Soviet Union
1970	Peter Kelemen HUN	Hungary
1971	B Onischenko URS	Soviet Union
1973	Pavel Lednev URS	Soviet Union
1974	Pavel Lednev URS	Soviet Union
1975	Pavel Lednev URS	Hungary
1977	J Pyciak-Peciak POL	Poland
1978	Pavel Lednev URS	Poland
1979	Robert Nieman USA	USA
1981	J Pyciak-Peciak POL	Poland
1982	Daniele Masala ITA	Soviet Union
1983	Anatoly Starostin URS	Soviet Union
1985	Attila Mizsér HUN	Soviet Union
1986	Carlo Massullo ITA	Italy
1987	Joël Bouzou FRA	Hungary
1989	László Fábián HUN	Hungary
1990	Gianluca Tiberti ITA	Soviet Union
1991	A Skrzypaszek POL	Unified Team
1993	Richard Phelps GBR	Hungary
1994	D Svatkovsky RUS	France
1995	D Svatkovsky RUS	Italy

WOMEN *(First held 1981)*

	Individual	Team
1987	Irina Kiselyeva URS	Soviet Union
1988	Dorata Idzi POL	Poland
1989	Lori Norwood USA	Poland
1990	Eva Fjellerup DEN	Poland
1991	Eva Fjellerup DEN	Poland
1993	Eva Fjellerup DEN	
1994	Eva Fjellerup DEN	Italy
1995	K Danielsson SWE	Hungary

Motor Cycling

If the rumours are right, then Mick Doohan will be the $6 million man in 1996. And who could argue? Doohan does, after all, hold all the aces. With the retirement of Kevin Schwantz, who said a tearful goodbye at Mugello in June, Doohan is the only major name in the sport. The only world 500cc champion still racing. In July, at Donington, he took great umbrage when he was quoted as saying the racing was getting boring. After all, the Australian didn't look like he was romping away with it in the middle of June. Two victories for starters suggested we might see a repeat of the six-timer he achieved in 1994, but in Jerez and at the Nurburgring, Doohan tumbled out. Worse, he admitted confusion about the causes of the second spill. When you don't know why it happens then you start to worry. But, he needn't have. By the time Donington came around (one of the few tracks he had never won on) the Repsol Honda team was back on course. You could never call it boring, but you might just have called it predictable.

Doohan won at Donington in clinical fashion. He allowed Beattie to take a three-second lead early on but, as the tyres warmed on the Repsol Honda, Doohan ate away the lead. He passed Beattie on lap ten of 20 and came home comfortably, just over four seconds clear. Second places followed at Brno and Rio before Doohan sealed his second successive championship with a win at Buenos Aires. At Barcelona, in the final GP, you felt that Doohan just sat off the pace to allow his Spanish teammate Alex Criville to win on his home track. While all this was going on, the contracts were being pencilled in for 1996. With everyone after Doohan, it's little wonder that the Australian negotiated a healthy pay-rise. The kid who grew up in a Queensland beach house, already has an exclusive apartment in Monte Carlo. But, you know what they say...you can always do with another million.

It hard to imagine Carl Fogarty living in a seafront apartment at Monte Carlo. However, that's not likely. The Lancastrian is far too settled in Blackburn for that to happen and, besides, Ducati don't pay him $6m to race Superbikes. That aside, there are similarities. In 1994, Fogarty won the world title. This year, the laconic Ducati rider won it again. By the time they got to Brands Hatch in August, with the title almost won, Fogarty's status in the sport in Britain was flying at such a height that over 40,000 people arrived at the Kent track to see him race. The days of Sheene, you could believe, had come again.

Fogarty, now approaching 30, will probably not get the chance to compete for a works team in the GPs. In September, Ducati were pressuring him to re-sign, and the God of Youth is what the top factory teams worship.

Neil Hodgson has that going for him - and a fair bit more. Riding a works Yamaha, the 21-year-old from Burnley became the first British rider for five years to earn a front-row place on the grid when he qualified in fourth place for the Buenos Aires GP. At Donington, in July, there was a small crowd queueing as Hodgson signed pictures. If he continues to progress at this rate, the queue will get a lot longer.

Max Biaggi, who claims a Doohan-like status in the 250cc, won his second straight title with ease and will go for a third with Aprilia next year. In the 125cc World Championship, Hirachika Aoki was a distance ahead, but Alzamora was always the one to watch.

Australian GP

Eastern Creek   Mar 26

500CC (30 laps - 117.900km)

1	Michael Doohan (Honda)	AUS	46:06.030	25
2	Daryl Beattie (Suzuki)	AUS	+13.446	20
3	Alex Criville (Honda)	ESP	+19.068	16
4	Luca Cadalora (Yamaha)	ITA	+33.753	13
5	Kevin Schwantz (Suzuki)	USA	+34.372	11
6	Alexandre Barros (Honda)	BRA	+36.000	10

Also

12	Sean Emmett (Yamaha)	GBR	1:27.290	4

250CC (28 laps - 110.040km)

1	Ralf Waldmann (Honda)	GER	43:52.872	25
2	Tetsuya Harada (Yamaha)	JPN	+0.113	20
3	Max Biaggi (Aprilia)	ITA	+0.146	16
4	Carlos Checa (Honda)	ESP	+37.974	13
5	Nobuatsu Aoki (Honda)	JPN	+38.091	11
6	Doriano Romboni (Honda)	ITA	+40.756	10

125CC (26 laps - 102.180km)

1	Hirachika Aoki (Honda)	JPN	42:52.040	25
2	Kazuto Sakata (Aprilia)	JPN	+15.641	20
3	Tomomi Manako (Honda)	JPN	+22.096	16
4	Elisio Alzamora (Honda)	ESP	+22.164	13
5	Noboru Ueda (Honda)	JPN	+24.928	11
6	Stefano Perugini (Aprilia)	ITA	+25.434	10

Malaysian GP

Shah Alam   April 2

500CC (33 laps - 115.665km)

1	Michael Doohan (Honda)	AUS	47:54.380	25
2	Daryl Beattie (Suzuki)	AUS	+6.799	20
3	Alex Criville (Honda)	ESP	+10.107	16
4	Kevin Schwantz (Suzuki)	USA	+14.144	13
5	Alberto Puig (Honda)	ESP	+15.238	11
6	Alexandre Barros (Honda)	BRA	+15.304	10

Also

14	Jeremy McWilliams (Yamaha)	GBR	1 lap	2

Points after 2 rounds: *Doohan 50, Beattie 40, Criville 32, Schwantz 24, Barros 20*

250CC (31 laps - 108.655km)

1	Max Biaggi (Aprilia)	ITA	45:27.292	25
2	Tetsuya Harada (Yamaha)	JPN	+5.084	20
3	Tadayuki Okada (Honda)	JPN	+5.821	16
4	Ralf Waldmann (Honda)	GER	+9.188	13
5	Jean Philippe Ruggia (Honda)	FRA	+9.374	11
6	J Bayle (Aprilia)	FRA	34.638	10

Points after 2 rounds: *Biaggi 41, Harada 40, Waldmann 38, N Aoki 20*

125CC (12 laps - 42.060km)

1	Gerry McCoy (Honda)	AUS	21:18.350	25
2	Stefano Perugini (Aprilia)	ITA	+0.427	20
3	Akira Saito (Honda)	JPN	+6.334	16
4	Herri Torrontegui (Honda)	ESP	+9.810	13
5	A Ballerini (Aprilia) ITA	ITA	+10.295	11
6	T Yamamoto (Honda)	JPN	+10.564	10

Points after 2 rounds: *H Aoki 25, Sakata 23, Perugini 20, Manako 16, Saito & Alzamora 13*

Japanese GP

Suzuka   April 23

500CC (18 laps - 105.552km)

1	Daryl Beattie (Suzuki)	AUS	44:02.298	25
2	Michael Doohan (Honda)	AUS	+9.582	20
3	T Aoki (Honda)	JPN	+9.708	16
4	Luca Cadalora (Yamaha)	ITA	+19.624	13
5	Alberto Puig (Honda)	ESP	+21.682	11
6	Kevin Schwantz (Suzuki)	USA	+24.522	10

Also

13	Sean Emmett (Yamaha)	GBR	+1:53.434	3
14	Neil Hodgson (Yamaha)	GBR	+1:58.610	2

Points after 3 rounds: *Doohan 70, Beattie 65, Schwantz 34, Criville 32, Puig 31, Cadalora 26, Barros 20*

250CC (12 laps - 70.368km)

1	Ralf Waldmann (Honda)	GER	30:46.248	25
2	Nobuatsu Aoki (Honda)	JPN	+31.590	20
3	Sadanori Hikita (Honda)	JPN	+53.232	16
4	Tetsuya Harada (Yamaha)	JPN	+54.746	13
5	Jean-Philippe Ruggia (Honda)	FRA	+59.198	11
6	O Miyazaki (Aprilia)	JPN	+1:01.465	10

Points after 3 rounds: *Waldmann 63, Harada 53, Biaggi 48, N Aoki 40*

125CC (18 laps - 105.553km)

1	Hirachika Aoki (Honda)	JPN	46:28.996	25
2	Akira Saito (Aprilia)	JPN	+1.796	20
3	Kazuto Sakata (Aprilia)	JPN	+1.903	16
4	Hideyuki Nakajoh (Honda)	JPN	+2.140	13
5	S Ibaraki (Yamaha)	JPN	+7.273	11
6	Yoshiaki Kato (Yamaha)	JPN	+7.694	10

Points after 3 rounds: *H Aoki 50, Sakata 39, Saito 33*

Spanish GP

Jerez   May 7

500CC (27 laps - 119.421km)

1	Alberto Puig (Honda)	ESP	47:45.728	25
2	Luca Cadalora (Yamaha)	ITA	+5.093	20
3	Alex Criville (Honda)	ESP	+14.031	16
4	Norifumi Abe (Yamaha)	JPN	+14.264	13
5	Alexandre Barros (Honda)	BRA	+22.141	11
6	Loris Capirossi (Honda)	ITA	+22.798	10

Also

11	Jeremy McWilliams (Yamaha)	GBR	+1:18.844	5
12	Neil Hodgson (Yamaha)	GBR	+1:24.628	4
14	Eugene McManus (Yamaha)	GBR	+1:31.947	2

Points after 4 rounds: *Beattie 74, Doohan 70, Puig 56, Crivllle 48, Cadalora 46, Schwantz 34, Barros 31, Abe 27, Itoh & Borja 23*

250CC (26 laps - 114.998km)

1	Tetsuya Harada (Yamaha)	JPN	46:25.162	25
2	Max Biaggi (Aprilia)	ITA	+9.746	20
3	Luis D'Antin (Honda)	ESP	+9.904	16
4	Doriano Romboni (Honda)	ITA	+9.924	13
5	Ralf Waldemann (Honda)	GER	+10.196	11
6	Tadayuki Okada (Honda)	JPN	+10.424	10

Also

11	Niall Mackenzie (Aprilia)	GBR	+50.820	5

Points after 4 rounds: *Harada 78, Waldmann 74, Biaggi 68, Aoki 48, Ruggia 31, Okada 26, D'Antin 24*

125CC (23 laps - 101.729km)

1	Haruchika Aoki (Honda)	JPN	43:01.696	25
2	Stefano Perugini (Aprillia)	ITA	+0.012	20
3	Dirk Raudies (Honda)	GER	+0.742	16
4	Peter Oettl (Aprilia)	GER	+3.262	13
5	Noburu Ueda (Honda)	JPN	+3.416	11
6	Kazuto Sakata (Aprilia)	JPN	+3.952	10

Points after 4 rounds: Aoki 75, Sakata 49, Saito 41, Perugini 40, Alzamora 31, Manako 29,

German GP
Nurburgring   May 21

500CC (27 laps - 122.932km)

1	Daryl Beattie (Suzuki)	AUS	46:01.392	25
2	Luca Cadalora (Yamaha)	ITA	+9.874	20
3	Shinichi Itoh (Honda)	JPN	+9.967	16
4	Alex Criville (Honda)	ESP	+11.706	13
5	Alberto Puig (Honda)	ESP	+12.399	11
6	Loris Capirossi (Honda)	ITA	+25.668	10

Also

14	Neil Hodgson (Yamaha)	GBR	+1:35.056	2

Points after 5 rounds: Beatie 99, Doohan 70, Puig 67, Cadalora 66, Criville 61, Barros 40, Itoh 39, Abe 35, Schwantz 34, Borja 29

250CC (25 laps - 113.824km)

1	Max Biaggi (Aprilia)	ITA	43:39.378	25
2	Tetsuya Harada (Yamaha)	JPN	+1.608	20
3	Tadayuki Okada (Honda)	JPN	+9.620	16
4	Kenny Roberts jnr (Yamaha)	USA	+9.870	13
5	Jean-Phillipe Ruggia (Honda)	FRA	+10.408	11
6	Jean-Michel Bayle (Aprilia)	FRA	+10.700	10

Points after 5 rounds: Harada 98, Biaggi 93, Waldemann 74, Aoki 56, Okada & Ruggia 42, D'Antin 31, Roberts jnr 29, Bayle 27, Romboni 23

125CC (23 laps - 104.715km)

1	Haruchika Aoki (Honda)	JPN	42:40.574	25
2	Noboru Ueda (Honda)	JPN	+0.671	20
3	Emilio Alzamora (Honda)	ESP	+2.057	16
4	Stefano Perugini (Aprilia)	ITA	+11.688	13
5	Dirk Raudies (Honda)	GER	+15.473	11
6	Hideyuki Nakajo (Honda)	JPN	+25.742	10

Points after 5 rounds: Aoki 100, Perugini 53, Sakata 49, Alzamore 47, Ueda 44, Saito 41, Manako 36, Nakajoh 34, Raudies 31.5, Scalvini 21.5

Italian GP
Mugello   June 11

500CC (23 laps - 120.635km)

1	Michael Doohan (Honda)	AUS	44:20.790	25
2	Daryl Beattie (Suzuki)	AUS	+3.728	20
3	Alberto Puig (Honda)	ESP	+8.922	16
4	Shinichi Itoh (Honda)	JPN	+14.435	13
5	Alex Criville (Honda)	ESP	+16.310	11
6	Norifumi Abe (Yamaha)	JPN	+16.370	10

Also

14	Neil Hodgson (Yamaha)	GBR	+1:26.947	2

Points after 6 rounds: Beattie 119, Doohan 95, Puig 83, Criville 72, Cadalora 70, Itoh 52, Barros 49, Abe 45, Capirossi 35, Schwatnz & Reggiani 34

250CC (21 laps - 110.145km)

1	Max Biaggi (Aprilia)	ITA	41:06.275	25
2	Tetsuya Harada (Yamaha)	JPN	+1.075	20
3	Marcellino Lucchi (Aprilia)	ITA	+4.491	16
4	Ralf Waldemann (Honda)	GER	+9.814	13
5	Tadayuki Okada (Honda)	JPN	+9.983	11
6	Kenny Roberts jnr (Yamaha)	USA	+32.357	10

Points after 6 rounds: Biaggi & Harada 118, Waldemann 87, Aoki 65, Okada 53, Ruggia 49, Roberts jnr 39, D'Antin 31, Checa & Bayle 27

125CC (20 laps - 104.900km)

1	Haruchika Aoki (Honda)	JPN	41:24.470	25
2	Stefano Perugini (Aprilia)	ITA	+0.004	20
3	Masaki Tokudome (Aprilia)	JPN	+0.171	16
4	Peter Oettl (Aprilia)	GER	+0.240	13
5	Kazuto Sakata (Aprilia)	JPN	+0.359	11
6	Tomomi Manako (Honda)	JPN	+7.345	10

Points after 6 rounds: H Aoki 125, Perugini 73, Sakata 60, Manako 46

Dutch GP
Assen   June 24

500CC (20 laps - 120.980km)

1	Michael Doohan (Honda)	AUS	41:27.422	25
2	Alex Criville (Honda)	ESP	+0.114	20
3	Alberto Puig (Honda)	ESP	+0.596	16
4	Loris Capirossi (Honda)	ITA	+5.618	13
5	Alexandre Barros (Honda)	BRA	+12.455	11
6	Norifumi Abe (Yamaha)	JPN	+15.300	10

Also

13	Neil Hodgson (Yamaha)	JPN	+1:17.812	3
14	James Haydon (Yamaha)	GBR	+1:18.396	2

Points after 7 rounds: Doohan 120, Beattie 119, Puig 99, Criville 92, Cadalora 79, Itoh & Barros 60, Abe 55, Capirossi 48, Reggiani 41

250CC (18 laps - 108.882km)

1	Max Biaggi (Aprilia)	ITA	38:24.532	25
2	Ralf Waldemann (Honda)	GER	+4.622	20
3	Tadayuki Okada (Honda)	JPN	+4.896	16
4	Jean-Philippe Ruggia (Honda)	FRA	+17.434	13
5	Kenny Roberts jnr (Yamaha)	USA	+27.654	11
6	Jurgen Van Den Goorberg (H)	NED	+28.495	10

Also

12	Niall Mackenzie (Aprilia)	GBR	+1:00.732	4

Points after 7 rounds: Biaggi 143, Harada 118, Waldemann 107, Aoki 74, Okada 69, Ruggia 62, Roberts jnr 50 D'Antin 38, Checa 32

125CC (17 laps - 102.833km)

1	Dirk Raudies (Honda)	GER	38:50.272	25
2	Peter Oettl (Aprilia)	GER	+4.878	20
3	Akiro Saito (Honda)	JPN	+5.010	16
4	Kazuto Sakata (Aprilia)	JPN	+5.398	13
5	Haruchika Aoki (Honda)	JPN	+5.536	11
6	Herri Torrontegui (Aprilia)	ESP	+6.604	10

Points after 7 rounds: Aoki 136, Perugini 82, Sakata 73, Saito 66, Raudies 56.5, Manako 53, Oettl 51, Alzamora & Nakajoh 47, Ueda 44

French GP
Le Mans   July 9

500CC (27 laps - 119.610km)
1	Michael Doohan (Honda)	AUS	46:10.991	25
2	Luca Cadalora (Yamaha)	ITA	+21.923	20
3	Daryl Beattie (Suzuki)	AUS	+23.607	16
4	Shinichi Itoh (Honda)	JPN	+39.623	13
5	Alexandre Barros (Honda)	BRA	+51.700	11
6	Scott Russell (Suzuki)	USA	+1:19.276	10

Also
7	Jeremy McWilliams (Yamaha)	GBR	+1:20.533	8
8	Neil Hodgson (Yamaha)	GBR	+1:32.235	7

Points after 8 rounds: *Doohan 145, Beattie 135, Puig & Cadalora 99, Criville 92, Itoh 73, Barros 71, Abe 55, Capirossi 48, Reggiani 41*

250CC (25 laps - 110.750km)
1	Ralf Waldemann (Honda)	GER	43:39.063	25
2	Max Biaggi (Aprilia)	ITA	+0.551	20
3	Tadayuki Okada (Honda)	JPN	+7.175	16
4	Carlos Checa (Honda)	ESP	+12.907	13
5	Tetsuya Harada (Yamaha)	JPN	+24.999	11
6	Kenny Roberts jnr (Yamaha)	USA	+28.457	10

Points after 8 rounds: *Biaggi 163, Waldemann 132, Harada 129, Okada 85, N Aoki 74, Ruggia 70, Roberts 60*

125CC (23 laps - 101.890km)
1	Haruchika Aoki (Honda)	JPN	42:52.844	25
2	Dirk Raudies (Honda)	GER	+1.045	20
3	Peter Oettl (Aprilia)	GER	+1.652	16
4	Akira Saito (Honda)	JPN	+7.504	13
5	Tomomi Manako (Honda)	JPN	+8.002	11
6	Stefano Perugini (Aprilia)	ITA	+9.559	10

Points after 8 rounds: *Aoki 161, Perugini 92, Saito 79, Sakata 77, Raudies 76.5, Oettl 67, Manako 64, Alzamora 56, Nakajoh 52*

British GP
Donington Park   July 23

500CC (30 laps - 120.690km)
1	Michael Doohan (Honda)	AUS	47:28.602	25
2	Daryl Beattie (Suzuki)	AUS	+4.286	20
3	Alex Criville (Honda)	ESP	+22.192	16
4	Loris Capirossi (Honda)	ITA	+37.296	13
5	Luca Cadalora (Yamaha)	ITA	+40.413	11
6	Shinichi Itoh (Honda)	JPN	+46.131	10

Also
13	Sean Emmett (Yamaha)	GBR	1:37.132	3
14	Eugene McManus (Yamaha)	GBR	1:37.636	2
15	Chris Walker (Yamaha)	GBR	1 lap	1

Points after 9 rounds: *Doohan 170, Beattie 155, Cadalora 110, Criville 108, Puig 99, Itoh 83, Barros 71, Capirossi 61, Abe 55, Borja 43*

250CC (27 laps - 108.621km)
1	Max Biaggi (Aprilia)	ITA	43:14.102	25
2	Tetsuya Harada (Yamaha)	JPN	+2.848	20
3	Ralf Waldemann (Honda)	GER	+2.920	16
4	Olivier Jacque (Honda)	FRA	+19.798	13
5	Jean-Philippe Ruggia (Aprilia)	FRA	+20.722	11
6	Niall Mackenzie (Aprilia)	GBR	+27.054	10

Points after 9 rounds: *Biaggi 188, Harada 149, Waldemann 148, Okada 93, Ruggia 81, N Aoki 80*

125CC (26 laps - 104.598km)
1	Kazuto Sakata (Aprilia)	JPN	44:06.180	25
2	Stefano Perugini (Aprilia)	ITA	+3.151	20
3	Emilio Alzamora (Honda)	ESP	+5.563	16
4	Dirk Raudies (Honda)	GER	+7.766	13
5	Hideyuki Nakajo (Honda)	JPN	+20.560	11
6	Masaki Tokudome (Aprilia)	JPN	+26.934	10

Also
9	Darren Barton (Yamaha)	GBR	+28.318	7

Points after 9 rounds: *Aoki 161, Perugini 112, Sakata 102, Raudies 89.5, Saito 79, Alzamore 72, Oettl 67*

Czech Republic GP
Brno   Aug 21

500CC (22 laps - 118.668km)
1	Luca Cadalora (Yamaha)	ITA	45:28.725	25
2	Michael Doohan (Honda)	AUS	+4.148	20
3	Daryl Beattie (Suzuki)	AUS	+9.399	16
4	Loris Capirossi (Honda)	ITA	+15.646	13
5	Shinichi Itoh (Honda)	JPN	+18.831	11
6	Alex Criville (Honda)	ESP	+21.952	10

Also
10	Neil Hodgson (Yamaha)	GBR	+31.840	6

Points after 10 rounds: *Doohan 190, Beattie 171, Cadalora 135, Criville 118, Puig 99, Itoh 94, Barros 78, Capirossi 74, Abe 55, Reggiani 50*

250CC (20 laps - 107.880km)
1	Max Biaggi (Aprilia)	ITA	41:56.604	25
2	Tetsuya Harada (Yamaha)	JPN	+0.156	20
3	Ralf Waldmann (Honda)	GER	+13.442	16
4	Luis D'Antin (Honda)	ESP	+40.632	13
5	Doriano Romboni (Honda)	ITA	+40.652	11
6	Jean-Philippe Ruggia (Honda)	FRA	+40.774	10

Points after 10 rounds: *Biaggi 213, Harada 169, Waldmann 164, Okada 102, Ruggia 99, N Aoki 87*

125CC (19 laps - 102.486km)
1	Kazuto Sakata (Aprilia)	JPN	42:08.715	25
2	Haruchika Aoki (Honda)	JPN	+7.496	20
3	Akira Saito (Honda)	JPN	+7.967	16
4	Masaki Tokudome (Aprilia)	JPN	+7.970	13
5	Hideyuki Nakajo (Honda)	JPN	+11.068	11
6	Gianluigi Scalvini (Aprilia)	ITA	+20.659	10

Points after 10 rounds: *Aoki 181, Sakata 127, Perugini 112, Saito 95, Raudies 89.5, Alzamora 78, Nakajo 74*

Brazilian GP
Rio   Sep 17

500CC (24 laps)
1	Luca Cadalora (Yamaha)	ITA	46:18.208	25
2	Michael Doohan (Honda)	AUS	+5.569	20
3	Norifumi Abe (Yamaha)	JPN	+12.282	16
4	Daryl Beattie (Suzuki)	AUS	+15.208	13
5	Scott Russell (Suzuki)	USA	+15.610	11
6	Alex Criville (Honda)	ESP	+24.036	10

Also
11	Neil Hodgson (Yamaha)	GBR		5
12	Jeremy McWilliams (Yamaha)	GBR		4
14	Sean Emmett (Yamaha)	GBR		2

Points after round 13: *Doohan 210, Beattie 184, Cadalora 160, Criville 128, Itoh 100 Puig 99, Barros 86, Capirossi 81, Abe 71, Reggiani 50*

*Q*uotes

"When we started racing, Wayne and I were the biggest enemies I've ever known. but we grew to be friends and, while the decision I've made was based on my situation, what happened to Wayne is always something that I am thinking about" **- Kevin Schwantz, announcing his retirement from Grand Prix racing at the Italian GP in June.**

"The only thing I enjoy about it is winning. I don't enjoy anything else" **- Carl Fogarty, who had plenty of enjoyment in 1995.**

"There are things I can't do anymore, like run.....my right ankle doesn't move and the toes don't move either. They kind of lock. If I trip over a penny or something not level on the ground, it nearly makes me jump through the roof. But the passion to get back to where I was before the accident makes me ignore the pain. All you can see is where you want to be" **- Mick Doohan, talking about the accident in 1992 which almost took his life.**

"If you've just got big balls and bravery, you're going to get yourself hurt. Perhaps because I've grown up with it, I don't see it as brave. It's all calculation out there." **- Doohan.**

"To be out there on a grid with the likes of Doohan is all I've ever wanted" **- Chris Walker, who scored a point in his Grand Prix debut at Donington.**

"I'm just making sure I don't mess up at the moment. Just riding around doing enough to win. I reckon it's as boring as shit out there right now" **- Doohan quoted in *Motor Cycle News* prior to the British GP. Doohan later claimed that the British press "sensationalise the dirt".**

"I so wanted to win the championship, but not like this..." **- Steve Hislop, whose main rival for the British Supercup Championship, Jamie Whitham, had to pull out when he was diagnosed as suffering from Hodgkin's disease, a form of cancer.**

"The treatment will last at least six months. My hair and my teeth will fall out and I will turn yellow and feel terrible, but I have a 90 per cent chance" **- Whitham.**

"Well... he got engaged this weekend, so he could well be tired" **- television commentator explaining the moderate performance of Mike Rutter at Donington in September.**

"They are involved in the real-life risks of racing, not the phony risks of the entertainment industry. 'Dying' on stage, after all, doesn't even hurt" **- Garry Taylor, Luck Strike Suzuki team manager, responding to a column in *Motor Cycle News* in which Andy Kershaw claimed that riders at the British Grand Prix were so wooden at press conferences that they would "fail an audition for *Thunderbirds*".**

"During the night the rain was horrible...I was aquaplaning at 120mph in the dark" **- Brian Morrison on the joys of the thrid round race of the World Endurance Championships at Spa.**

"The circuit agreed that the marshalls were agressive" **- statement put out by Salzburgring after 20 marshalls and Ducati team staff traded blows in a pit-lane brawl during the Superbike round in July.**

250CC (22 laps - 111.936km)
1	Doriano Romboni (Honda)	ITA	43:45.464	25
2	Max Biaggi (Aprilia)	ITA	+1.345	20
3	Tadayuki Okada (Honda)	JPN	+1.390	16
4	Ralf Waldmann (Honda)	GER	+1.702	13
5	Tetsuya Harada (Yamaha)	JPN	+1.834	11
6	Jean-Philippe Ruggia (Honda)	FRA	+2.148	10

Points after 11 rounds: Biaggi 233, Harada 180, Waldmann 177, Okada 118, Ruggia 101, N Aoki 95

125CC (20 laps - 101.760km)
1	Masaki Tokudome (Aprilia)	JPN	41:29.854	25
2	Gianluigi Scalvini (Aprilia)	ITA	+0.204	20
3	Haruchika Aoki (Honda)	JPN	+0.422	16
4	Herri Torrontegui (Honda)	ESP	+0.548	13
5	Noboru Ueda (Honda)	JPN	+8.834	11
6	Akira Saito (Honda)	JPN	+8.950	10

Also
7	Darren Barton (Yamaha)	GBR	+9.012	9

Points after 11 rounds: Aoki 197, Sakata 127, Perugini 112, Saito 105, Raudies 97.5, Alzamora 84, Manako 79

Argentinian GP

Buenos Aires   Sep 24

500CC (27 laps - 117.450km)
1	Michael Doohan (Honda)	AUS	47:30.236	25
2	Daryl Beattie (Suzuki)	AUS	+2.293	20
3	Luca Cadalora (Yamaha)	ITA	+9.034	16
4	Alex Criville (Honda)	ESP	+10.675	13
5	Loris Capirossi (Honda)	ITA	+21.588	11
6	Norifumi Abe (Yamaha)	JPN	+22.006	10

Also
10	Neil Hodgson (Yamaha)	GBR	+50.555	6
13	James Haydon (Yamaha)	GBR	+1:18.132	3
14	Sean Emmett (Yamaha)	GBR	1:18.340	2

Points after 12 rounds: Doohan 235, Beattie 204, Cadalora 176, Criville 141, Itoh 107.....Hodgson 47.

250CC (25 laps - 108.750km)
1	Max Biaggi (Aprilia)	ITA	44:48.735	25
2	Tetsuya Harada (Yamaha)	JPN	+0.204	20
3	Doriano Romboni (Honda)	ITA	+7.083	16
4	Olivier Jacque (Honda)	FRA	+7.680	13
5	Jena-Philippe Ruggia (Honda)	FRA	+7.866	11
6	Ralf Waldmann (Honda)	GER	+16.154	10

Also
11	Niall McKenzie (Aprilia)	GBR	+43.936	5

Points after 12 rounds: Biaggi 258, Harada 200, Waldmann 187, Okada 127, Ruggia 112, N Aoki 96

125CC (23 laps - 100.050km)
1	Emilio Alzamora (Honda)	ESP	43:03.230	25
2	Masaki Tokudome (Aprilia)	JPN	+12.520	20
3	Dirk Raudies (Honda)	GER	+12.714	16
4	Akira Saito (Honda)	JPN	+12.967	13
5	Oliver Koch (Aprilia)	GER	+13.518	11
6	Herri Torrontegui (Honda)	ESP	+13.812	10

Points after 12 rounds: Aoki 199, Sakta 127, Saito 118, Raudies 113.5, Perugini 112, Alzamora 109

Catalunyan GP

Barcelona   Oct 8
(Brief Results only)
500CC: 1. Alex Criville (Honda) ESP; 2. Shinichi Itoh (Honda) JPN; 3. Loris Capirossi (Honda) ITA; 4. Michael

Doohan (Honda) AUS
Final Championship Placings: Doohan 248, Beattie 215, Cadalora 176
250CC: 1. Max Biaggi (Aprilia) ITA; 2. Tetsuya Harada (Yamaha) JPN; 3. Ralf Waldemann (Honda) GER
Final Championship Placings: Biaggi 283, Harada 220, Waldemann 203
125CC: 1. Haruchika Aoki (Honda) JPN; 2. Emilio Alzamora (Honda) ESP; 3. Tomomi Manako (Honda) JPN
Final Championship Placings: Aoki 224, Sakata 140, Alzamora 129

Sidecar World Championship

Spanish GP
Jerez - 23 laps (104.720km)   May 20
1	D Dixon/A Hetherington (Windle) GBR			
			41:30.522	25
2	S Abbot/J Tailford (Windle)	GBR	+0.345	20
3	M Boesiger/J Egli (ADM)	SUI	+34.722	16

Italian GP
Mugello - 20 laps (104.827km)   June 10
1	P Guedal/C Guedal (LCR)	SUI	45:43.874	25
2	D Dixon/A Hetherington (Windle) GBR		+0.206	20
3	K Klaffenbock/C Parzer (Windle)	GER	+9.616	16

Points after 2 rounds: Dixon 45, Abbott 31, Guedal 25, B Brindley GBR 23, Boesiger 20

Dutch GP2
Assem - 17 laps (102.833km)   Sep 10-11
1	Dixon/Hetherington (Windle) GBR 37:08.358			25
2	Abbott/Tailford (Windle)	GBR	+5.222	20
3	D Brindley/P Hutchinson (Honda) GBR		+24.956	16

Points after 3 rounds: Dixon 70, Abbott 51, B Brindley 33, Boesiger 31, Klaffenboch & D Brindley 29

French GP
Le Mans - 23 laps (101.890km)   Jul 8
1	R Biland/K Waltisperg (LCR) GER		42:15.432	25
2	Dixon/Hetherington (Windle)	GBR	+11.306	20
3	R Bohnhorst/P Brown (LCR)	GBR	+24.745	16

Points after 4 rounds: Dixon 90, Abbott 61, Boesiger 44, B Brindley 41, D Brindley 40, Kumagaya 30

British GP
Donington - 26 laps (104.598km)   Jul 22
1	R Biland/K Waltisperg (LCR) SUI		42:51.654	25
2	Boesiger/Egli (LCR)	SUI	+10.638	20
3	Bohnhorst/Brown (LCR)	GBR	+13.486	16

Points after 5 rounds: Dixon 100, Abbott 72, Boesiger 64, B Brindley & Biland 50, D Brindley 40, Kumagaya 37

Czech GP
Brno - 19 laps (102.414km)   Aug 19
1	R Biland/K Waltisperg (LCR) SUI		40:26.544	25
2	Abbott/Tailford (Windle)	GBR	+2.600	20
3	Boesiger/Egli (LCR)	SUI	+41.085	16

Points after 6 rounds: Dixon 111, Abbott 92, Boesiger 80, Biland 75, B Brindley 60, D Brindley 53

Superbike World Championship

German WSB
Hockenheim - 14 laps , 94.63km   May 7
RACE 1

1	**Carl Fogarty (Ducati)**	GBR	28:48.48	25
2	Fabrizio Priovani (Ducati)	ITA	+9.59	20
3	Jochen Schmid (Kawasaki)	GER	+11.64	16

RACE 2

1	**Carl Fogarty (Ducati)**	GBR	28:52.16	25
2	Jochen Schmid (Kawasaki)	GER	+4.23	20
3	Aaron Slight (Honda)	NZL	+4.46	16

Points: *Fogarty 50, Schmid 36, Nagai & Slight 26, Pirovano 23, Edwards 20, Crafar 17*

Italian WSB
Misano - 25 laps (101.43km)   May 21
RACE 1

1	**Mauro Lucchiari (Ducati)**	ITA	39:58.269	25
2	Carl Fogarty (Ducati)	GBR	+2.862	20
3	Troy Corser (Ducati)	AUS	+11.172	16

RACE 2

1	**Mauro Lucchiari (Ducati)**	ITA	38:52.193	25
2	Carl Fogarty (Ducati)	GBR	+1.208	20
3	Troy Corser (Ducati)	AUS	+1.560	16

Points after 2 rounds: *Fogarty 90, Lucchiari 59, Corser 46, Pirovani 44, Schmid 41, Chili 34, Crafar 30, Slight 29, Nagai 29, Bontempi 26*

British WSB
Donington - 26 laps (104.60km)   May 28
RACE 1

1	**Carl Fogarty (Ducati)**	GBR	41:40.53	25
2	Troy Corser (Ducati)	AUS	+1.00	20
3	James Whitham (Ducati)	GBR	+12.58	16

RACE 2

1	**Carl Fogarty (Ducati)**	GBR	41:47.90	25
2	Pier-Francesco Chili (Ducati)	ITA	+10.80	20
3	Aaron Slight (Honda)	NZL	+11.60	16

Points after 3 rounds: *Fogarty 140, Lucchiari 72, Corser 66, Pirovani 60, Slight 58, Chili 54, Bontempi 50, Crafar 48, Schmid 44, Nagai 40*

San Marino WSB
Monza - 18 laps (104.33km)   June 18
RACE 1

1	**Carl Fogarty (Ducati)**	GBR	32:51.38	25
2	Aaron Slight (Honda)	NZL	+1.95	20
3	Colin Edwards (Yamaha)	USA	+7.97	16

RACE 2

1	**Pier-Francesco Chili (Ducati)**	ITA	32:58.15	25
2	Carl Fogarty (Ducati)	GBR	+0.61	20
3	Aaron Slight (Honda)	NZL	+4.875	16

Points after 4 rounds: *Fogarty 185, Slight 94, Lucchiari 92, Chili 79, Pirovani 76, Crafar 70, Corser 66, Nagaai 64, Bontempi 59, Edwards 51*

Spain WSB
Albacete - 28 laps (98.938km)   June 25
RACE 1

1	**Aaron Slight (Honda)**	NZL	44:10.059	25
2	Carl Fogarty (Ducati)	GBR	+0.437	20
3	Troy Corser (Ducati)	AUS	+0.678	16

RACE 2

1	**Carl Fogarty (Ducati)**	GBR	44:12.784	25
2	Pier-Francesco Chili (Ducati)	ITA	+4.759	20
3	Aaron Slight (Honda)	NZL	+6.370	16

Points after 5 rounds: *Fogarty 230, Slight 135, Chili 112, Priovano 99, Corser 93, Lucchiari 92*

Austrian WSB
Salzburgring - 22 laps (93.289km)
RACE 1

1	**Carl Fogarty (Ducati)**	GBR	29:43.368	25
2	Anthony Gobert (Kawasaki)	AUS	+5.624	20
3	Troy Corser (Ducati)	AUS	+5.885	16

RACE 2

1	**Troy Corser (Ducati)**	AUS	29:45.939	25
2	Carl Fogarty (Ducati)	GBR	+0.237	20
3	Anthony Gobert (Kawasaki)	AUS	+4.505	16

Points after 6 rounds: *Fogarty 275, Slight 168, Corser 134, Pirovano 118, Chili 117, Lucchiari 104, Nagai 102*

United States WSB
Laguna Seca   July 23
RACE 1

1	**Anthony Gobert (Kawasaki)**	AUS		25
2	Troy Corser (Ducati)	AUS		20
3	Miguel DuHamel			16

RACE 2

1	**Troy Corser (Ducati)**	AUS		25
2	Anthony Gobert (Kawasaki)	AUS		20
3	Mike Hale			16

Points after 7 rounds: *Fogarty 295, Corser 179, Slight 161, Pirovano 126, Nagai 119, Chili 117, Lucchiari 108*

European WSB
Brands Hatch - 25 laps (104.61km) Aug 6
RACE 1

1	**Carl Fogarty (Ducati)**	GBR	37:13.87	25
2	Troy Corser (Ducati)	AUS	+2.93	20
3	Anthony Gobert (Kawasaki)	AUS	+4.05	16

RACE 2

1	**Carl Fogarty (Ducati)**	GBR	37:15.44	25
2	Coiln Edwards (Yamaha)	USA	+1.15	20
3	Yasutomo Nagai (Yamaha)	JPN	+2.86	16

Points after 8 rounds: *Fogarty 345, Corser 209, Slight 183, Pirovano 144, Gobert 137, Nagai 135*

Japanese WSB
Sugo - 25 laps (93.438km)   Aug 27
RACE 1

1	**Troy Corser (Ducati)**	AUS	38:43.351	25
2	Aaron Slight (Honda)	NZL	+0.049	20
3	Yasutomo Nagai (Yamaha)	JPN	+0.449	16

RACE 2

1	**Carl Fogarty (Ducati)**	GBR	38:32.450	25
2	Yasutomo Nagai (Yamaha)	JPN	+5.474	20
3	Katsuaki Fujiwara (Kamasaki)	JPN	++12.989	16

Points after 9 rounds: *Fogarty 370, Corser 242, Slight 216, Nagai 171, Gobert 145*

Dutch WSB
Assem   Sep 10
RACE 1

1 **Carl Fogarty (Ducati)**	GBR	33:56.88	25
2 Simon Crafar (Honda)	NZL	+2.21	20
3 Troy corser (Ducati)	AUS	+3.55	16

RACE 2

1 **Carl Fogarty (Ducati)**	GBR	29:38.34	25
2 AaronSlight (Honda)	NZL	+7.41	20
3 John Reynolds (Kawasaki)	GBR	+7.64	16

Points after 10 rounds: *Fogarty 420*, Corser 258, Slight 249, Nagai 188, Gobert 171, Pirovano 153*
* Fogarty's total of 420 means that he cannot be caught in the remaining two races (Indonesia & Australia) and retains his World Superbike title.

International Superbike Championship

FINAL STANDINGS
1. Matt Llewellyn 58 pts; 2. Steve Hislop 49; 3. Jamie Whitham 45; 4. Mike Rutter; 5. Ray Stringer 31; 6. Aaron Slight 30; 7. Jim Moodie 25; 8. Simon Crafar 24

British Supercup
FINAL STANDINGS
Superbike: 1. Steve Hislop (Ducati) 177.5; 2. Matts Llewellyn (Ducati) 128; 3. Jamie Whitham (Ducati) 115.5; 4. Mike Rutter (Ducati) 83; 5. Ray Stringer ((Ducati) 55; 6. Iain Simpson (Honda) & Paul Brown (Honda) 41.
250CC: 1. Jamie Robinson (Aprilia) 155; 2. Chris Walker (Honda) 119; 3. Ian Newton (Aprilia) 117.
Supersport 600: 1. Mike Edwards (Honda) 89; 2. Dave Heal (Yamaha) 88; 3. Iain Duffus (Honda) 63.
125CC: 1. arren Barton ((Yamaha) 159; 2. S Patrickson (Honda) 114; 3. Mick Lofthouse (Yamaha) 99
Formula 2 Sidecars: 1. Nelson/Camp (Yamaha) 79; 2. Fisher/B Hutchinson (Yamaha) 76; 3. Boddice/Wells (Honda) 61

Isle of Man TT
June 9
Senior TT

1 **Joey Dunlop (Honda)**	**1:54:01.9**
2 Iain Duffus ((Ducati)	1:54:35.4
3 Steve Ward (Honda)	1:54:51.7

This was 43-year-old Dunlop's 19th victory at the Isle of Man TT races.

Motocross World Championships

FINAL STANDINGS
500CC: 11. Joel Smets (Husaberg) BEL 344; 2. rampas Parker (KTM) USA 302; 3. Darryll King (Kawasaki) NZL 261
250CC: 1. Stefan Everts (Kawasaki) BEL 423; 2. Marnicq Bervoets (Suzuki) BEL 380; 3. Tallon Vohland (Kawasaki) USA 338.
125CC: 1. Alessandro Puzar (Honda) ITA 340; 2. Alessio

Chiodi (Yamaha) ITA 337; 3. Sébastian Tortelli (Kawasaki) FRA 266
Sidecar: 1. Fuhrer/Kaeser 261; 2. K Weinmann/T Weinmann 233; 3. Goeltz/Stettler 175.

British Championship
Elsworth, Cambs   June 4
250CC

1 Paul Malin (Yamaha)	40
2 Paul Cooper (Honda)	34
3 Rob Herring(Honda)	30

125CC

1 Rikki Priest (Kawasaki)	35
2 Joakim Carlsson (Honda)	33
3 Jon Barffot (Yamaha)	32

World Champions

125cc		250cc	500cc
1949	Nello Pagani ITA	Bruno Ruffo ITA	Leslie Graham GBR
1950	Bruno Ruffo ITA	Dario Ambrosini ITA	Umberto Masetti ITA
1951	Carlo Ubbiali ITA	Bruno Ruffo ITA	Geoff Duke GBR
1952	Cecil Sandford GBR	Enrico Lorenzetti ITA	Umberto Masetti ITA
1953	Werner Haas FRG	Werner Haas FRG	Geoff Duke GBR
1954	Rupert Hollaus AUT	Werner Haas FRG	Geoff Duke GBR
1955	Carlo Ubbiali ITA	Herman Muller FRG	Geoff Duke GBR
1956	Carlo Ubbiali ITA	Carlo Ubbiali ITA	John Surtees GBR
1957	Tarquinio Provini ITA	Cecil Sandford GBR	Libero Liberati ITA
1958	Carlo Ubbiali ITA	Tarquinio Provini ITA	John Surtees GBR
1959	Carlo Ubbiali ITA	Carlo Ubbiali ITA	John Surtees GBR
1960	Carlo Ubbiali ITA	Carlo Ubbiali ITA	John Surtees GBR
1961	Tom Phillis AUS	Mike Hailwood GBR	Gary Hocking ZIM
1962	Luigi Taveri SUI	Jim Redman ZIM	Mike Hailwood GBR
1963	Hugh Anderson NZL	Jim Redman ZIM	Mike Hailwood GBR
1964	Luigi Taveri SUI	Phil Read GBR	Mike Hailwood GBR
1965	Hugh Anderson NZL	Phil Read GBR	Mike Hailwood GBR
1966	Luigi Taveri SUI	Mike Hailwood GBR	Giacomo Agostini ITA
1967	Bill Ivy GBR	Mike Hailwood GBR	Giacomo Agostini ITA
1968	Phil Read GBR	Phil Read GBR	Giacomo Agostini ITA
1969	Dave Simmonds GBR	Kel Caruthers AUS	Giacomo Agostini ITA
1970	Dieter Braun FRG	Rod Gould GBR	Giacomo Agostini ITA
1971	Angel Nieto ESP	Phil Read GBR	Giacomo Agostini ITA
1972	Angel Nieto ESP	Jarno Saarinen FIN	Giacomo Agostini ITA
1973	Kent Andersson SWE	Dieter Braun FRG	Phil Read GBR
1974	Kent Andersson SWE	Walter Villa ITA	Phil Read GBR
1975	Paolo Pileri ITA	Walter Villa ITA	Giacomo Agostini ITA
1976	Pier-Paolo Bianchi ITA	Walter Villa ITA	Barry Sheene GBR
1977	Pier-Paolo Bianchi ITA	Mario Lega ITA	Barry Sheene GBR
1978	Eugenio Lazzarini ITA	Kork Ballington RSA	Kenny Roberts USA
1979	Angel Nieto ESP	Kork Ballington RSA	Kenny Roberts USA
1980	Pir-Paolo Bianchi ITA	Anton Mang FRG	Kenny Roberts USA
1981	Angel Nieto ESP	Anton Mang FRG	Marco Lucchinelli ITA
1982	Angel Nieto ESP	Jean-Louis Tournadre FRA	Franco Uncini ITA
1983	Angel Nieto ESP	Carlos Lavado VEN	Freddie Spencer USA
1984	Angel Nieto ESP	Christian Sarron FRA	Eddie Lawson USA
1985	Fausto Gresini ITA	Freddie Spencer USA	Freddie Spencer USA
1986	Luca Cadalora ITA	Carlos Lavado VEN	Eddie Lawson USA
1987	Fausto Gresini ITA	Anton Mang FRG	Wayne Gardner AUS
1988	Jorge Martinez ESP	Sito Pons ESP	Eddie Lawson USA
1989	Alex Criville ESP	Sito Pons ESP	Eddie Lawson USA
1990	Loris Capirossi ITA	John Kocinski USA	Wayne Rainey USA
1991	Loris Capirossi ITA	Luca Cadalora ITA	Wayne Rainey USA
1992	Alessandro Gramigni ITA	Luca Cadalora ITA	Wayne Rainey USA
1993	Dirk Raudies GER	Loris Capirossi ITA	Kevin Schwantz USA
1994	Kazuto Sakata JPN	Massimiliano Biaggi ITA	Michael Doohan AUS
1995	Haruchika Aoki JPN	Massimiliano Biaggi ITA	Michael Doohan AUS

Motor Racing ━━━━━━━━━━━━━

"Modern sports promoters believe that what the public wants is a bit of a grudge match", said Bernie Ecclestone, President of the F1 Constructors Association. Hill and Schumacher seemed eager to please. When Schumacher wiped out the unfortunate Hill in Adelaide, the Wiiliams driver was magnanimous in defeat. Six months later and the traditional English reserve had gone out of the window. Taking a leaf out of the World Champion's manual, Damon employed the 'if you can't win, then knock 'em off the road' tactic on two occasions. 'Racing accidents' was the Williams line, though rumour had it that Frank Williams apologised to the German after the British Grand Prix and referred to his number one driver as 'a prat'. At the time of going to press, the German looks assured of collecting his second successive title with Hill struggling to maintain the second place slot.

Both drivers have had eventful lives off the track as well. Schumacher married Corinna Betsch only months after he thought he was about to die when diving in the shark infested waters eight miles off Brazil. The diving party lost contact with their boat when it drifted on the tide and Schumacher was forced to swim over an hour to try to raise help. "No accident on the track has ever made me feel like that", he said later. Hill took on the only slightly less dangerous terrain of the M40, but was again overtaken, this time by the boys in blue. Hill, who was clocked at 102 mph, was disqualified for all of a week. Last year whilst driving to Silverstone he was stopped by police after driving at 120 mph but was left off with a caution. Who says Damon never gets a lucky break.

Someone who was feeling sorry for himself was former IndyCar and F1 World Champion Nigel Mansell. Unable to squeeze into the McLaren chassis at the start of the season, Nigel missed the opening two races whilst a bigger version was created at a cost of £300,000. Unfortunately when it boiled down to it, the chassis wasn't the only problem and Mansell, who barely made an impact in his two races, decided to call it a day. His involvement with the team for the opening part of the season set back the Marlboro-McLaren team an estimated £1.2 million. Whilst Britain may have lost one motor sport hero, it had gained another in the form of Colin McRae. The Scotsman, driving a Subaru, came home ahead of Finland's Juha Kankkunen last November, to give homegrown rally enthusiasts their first RAC Rally victory since Roger Clark in 1976.

The death of Juan Fangio closed the door on an era. The Argentinian remains the only driver to have won the world championship five times. The year also saw the demise of one of Formula One's most well known racing teams. Lotus, which had entered F1 in 1952, was officially wound up ending a history that included six World Drivers Championships and seven constructors titles.

The merry-go-round of team alignments for next season has seen The Ferrari pairing of Berger and Alesi depart for Benetton, whilst Schumacher is to be joined by Ulsterman Eddie Irvine. David Coulthard, is highly regarded as a driver, but obviously not by Frank Williams. Williams has decided to let the Scotsman seek pastures new at McLaren, and has signed the new IndyCar champion Jacques Villeneuve. The Canadian is hoping to go one better than his father, Gilles, who was runner-up to Jody Scheckter in 1979.

Brazilian Grand Prix

Interlagos   March 26
Laps: 71 x 4.325km   Total distance: 307.075km

1	**Michael Schumacher GER (Benetton) 1:38:34.154**	
		(183.975kmh)
2	David Coulthard GBR (Williams-Renault)	at 8.060
3	Gerhard Berger AUT (Ferrari)	1 lap
4	Mika Hakkinen FIN (McLaren-Mercedes)	1 lap
5	Jean Alesi FRA (Ferrari)	1 lap
6	Mark Blundell GBR (McLaren-Mercedes)	1 lap
7	Mika Salo FIN (Tyrrel-Yamaha)	2 laps*
8	Aguri Suzuki JPN (Ligier-Mugen)	2 laps*
9	Andrea Montermini ITA (Pacific-Ford)	6 laps
10	Pedro Diniz BRA (Forti-Ford)	7 laps

Pole position: Damon Hill
Fastest lap: Damon Hill 1:20.982 (192.264kmh)

Damon Hill had a near perfect weekend until lap 31 of the actual race, when engine failure made all the ideal preparation meaningless. Hill's Williams-Renault succumbed while in the lead and the Briton had the galling experience of watching his arch-rival Schumacher sweep into the lead. Even the events of the race, though, paled in comparison with the post-race shenanigans. Fined $30,000 before the race for irregularities in the fuel samples from both Schumacher's and Coulthard's cars, the leading pair were disqualified after the race when further irregularities were found. The appeal tribunal of the FIA eventually rescinded the disqualifications, but increased the fine to $200,000. And then there was the question of Schumacher's weight. A mere 10st 12lb weakling last season, the German weighed in at Sao Paolo at 12st 2lb prior to the race. As the regulations now include weight minimums for car and driver combined, there were those who wondered if Benetton were seeking to gain an advantage. Surely not.

WORLD CHAMPIONSHIP STANDINGS
Drivers: *Schumacher 10, Coulthard 6, Berger 4, Hakkinen 3, Alesi 2, Blundell 1.*
Constructors: *Ferrari 6, McLaren-Mercedes 4.*
The points for Benetton and Williams were not credited because of fuel irregularities

Argentinian Grand Prix

Buenos Aires   Apr 9
Laps: 72 x 4.257km   Total distance: 306.482

1	**Damon Hill GBR (Williams-Renault)**	**1:53:14.532**
		(162.385kmh)
2	Jean Alesi FRA (Ferrari)	6.407
3	Michael Schumacher GER (Benetton-Ren)	33.376
4	Johnny Herbert GBR (Benetton-Renault)	1 lap
5	Heinz-Harald Frentzen GER (Sauber-Merc)	2 laps
6	Gerhard Berger AUT (Ferrari)	2 laps
7	Olivier Panis FRA (Ligier-Mugen)	2 laps
8	Ukyo Katayama JPN (Tyrrell-Yamaha)	3 laps
9	Domenico Schiattarella ITA (Simtek-Ford)	4 laps

Pole position: David Coulthard
Fastest lap: Schumacher 1:30.522 (169.377kmh)

Hill was a very contented driver after his 10th GP victory. Schumacher may have blamed his performance on poor tyres, but that did not diminish the satisfaction of the Briton who overtook Schumacher on the 11th lap, darting inside at the end of the pit straight. Coulthard had won

the early skirmishes, the young Scot leading until lap seven when throttle problems checked his progress. Coulthard fought back into contention only to suffer further mechanical troubles on lap 17. The biggest skirmish of all happened on lap one when the cars avoiding a shunt were probably in the minority. A dash for spare cars and off at the second time of asking saw Coulthard into the lead. But this was Hill's day."I must have done some psychological damage," said Hill, referring to the manner in which he overtook Schumacher. That remained to be seen.

WORLD CHAMPIONSHIP STANDINGS
Drivers: *Schumacher 14, Hill 10, Alesi 8, Coulthard 6, Berger 5, Hakkinen & Herbert 3, Frentzen 2, Blundell 1.*
Constructors: *Williams-Renault 10, Benetton-Williams7, Ferrari 13, McLaren-Mercedes 4, Sauber-Mercedes 2.*

San Marino Grand Prix

Imola   Apr 30
Laps: 63 x 4.895km   Total distance: 308.385km

1	**Damon Hill GBR (Williams-Renault)**	**1:41:42.552**
		(181.921 kmh)
2	Jean Alesi FRA (Ferrari)	18.510
3	Gerhard Berger AUT (Ferrari)	43.116
4	David Coulthard GBR (Williams-Renault)	51.890
5	Mika Hakkinen FIN (McLaren-Mercedes)	1 lap
6	Heinz-Harald Frentzen GER (Sauber-Ford)	1 lap
7	Johnny Herbert GBR (Benetton-Renault)	2 laps
8	Eddie Irvine GBR (Jordan-Peugeot)	2 laps
9	Olivier Panis FRA (Ligier-Mugen)	2 laps
10	Nigel Mansell GBR (McLaren-Mercedes)	2 laps
11	Aguri Suzuki JPN (Ligier-Mugen)	3 laps
12	Pierluigi Martini ITA (Minardi-Ford)	4 laps
13	Gianni Morbidelli ITA (Arrows-Hart)	4 laps
14	Luca Badoer ITA (Minardi-Ford)	4 laps
15	Pedro Diniz BRA (Forti-Ford)	7 laps
16	Roberto Moreno BRA (Forti-Ford)	7 laps

Pole position: Michael Schumacher
Fastest lap: Gerhard Berger 1:29.568 (196.744kmh)

Morning rain made the remodelled circuit treacherous during the warm-up. It was still damp when the race began and six of the top drivers, including both Hill and Schumacher opted to begin the race on wet tyres. As the sun dried the track, the timing of the change to slick tyres was crucial. Schumacher, the early leader, came in to change on lap 10. On new tyres, he immediately crashed and was out of the race. Berger was left in the lead, but suffered when he pitted for the second time on lap 22 and his engine stalled. Hill took over and drove an astute race to maintain his lead.Alesi and Coulthard were at loggerheads for much of the race, until the Scot had a stop-go penalty for speeding in the pit lane and Nigel Mansell on his debut for McLaren had a "misunderstanding" with Eddie Irvine. In all, an incident packed race that helped eclipse a few of the sadder memories of just a year ago.

WORLD CHAMPIONSHIP STANDINGS
Drivers: *Hill 20, Schumacher & Alesi 14, Coulthard & Berger 9, Hakkinen 5, Herbert & Frentzen 3, Blundell 1.*
Constructors: *Williams-Renault & Ferrari 23, Benetton-Renault 7, McLaren-Mercedes 6, Sauber-Ford 3.*

Spanish Grand Prix

Jarama   May 14
Laps: 65 x 4.747km   Total distance: 308.555km

1 **Michael Schumacher GER (Benetton) 1:34:20.507**
                                              (195.320kmh)
2 Johnny Herbert GBR (Benetton-Renault)   51.988
3 Gerhard Berger AUT (Ferrari)   1:05.237
4 Damon Hill GBR (Williams-Renault)   2:01.749
5 Eddie Irvine GBR (Jordan-Peugeot)   1 lap
6 Olivier Panis FRA (Ligier-Mugen)   1 lap
7 Rubens Barrichello BRA (Jordan-Peugeot)   1 lap
8 Heinz-Harald Frentzen GER (Sauber-Ford)   1 lap
9 Martin Brundle GBR (Ligier-Mugen)   1 lap
10 Mika Salo FIN (Tyrrell-Yamaha)   1 lap
11 Gianni Morbidelli ITA (Footwork-Hart)   2 laps
12 Jos Verstappen HOL (Simtek-Ford)   2 laps
13 Karl Wendlinger GER (Sauber-Ford)   2 laps
14 Pierluigi Martini ITA (Minardi-Ford)   3 laps
15 Domenico Schiattarella ITA (Simtek-Ford)   4 laps

Pole position: Michael Schumacher
Fastest lap:Hill 1:24.531 (201.313kmh)

Schumacher took pole position by more than half a second and that superiority was reflected in a race which the German led from start to finish. The transformation of the B195 Benetton-Renault was put down to adjustments to the car's suspension. Alesi engaged in a hopeless chase of Schumacher until his engine went up in a puff of black smoke on lap 26 - Ferrari's first retirement of the season. Hill took over the hunt and even pared down the lead from 12.3 to 9.8 seconds. Yet Schumacher was never seriously threatened and when the hydraulics went on Hill's FW17 on the final lap, the poor Briton had to concede second place as well, eventually finishing fourth. Mansell had another unhappy race. He described the McLaren MP4/10B as being "....virtually impossible to drive" and odds were already being laid as to how long his season would last.

WORLD CHAMPIONSHIP STANDINGS

Drivers: *Schumacher 24, Hill 23, Alesi 14, Berger 13, Coulthard & Herbert 9, Hakkinen 5, Frentzen 3, Irvine 2, Blundell & Panis 1.*

Constructors: *Ferrari 27, Williams-Renault 26, Benetton-Ford 23, McLaren-Mercedes 6, Sauber-Ford 3, Jordan-Peugeot 2, Ligier-Mugen 1.*

Monaco Grand Prix

Monte Carlo   May 28
Laps: 78 x 3.328km   Total distance: 259.584km

1 **Michael Schumacher GER (Benetton) 1:53:11.258**
                                              (137.603kmh)
2 Damon Hill GBR (Williams-Renault)   34.817
3 Gerhard Berger AUT (Ferrari)   1:11.447
4 Johnny Herbert GBR (Benetton-Renault)   1 lap
5 Mark Blundell GBR (McLaren-Mercedes)   1 lap
6 Heinz-Harald Frentzen GER (Sauber-Ford)   2 laps
7 Pierluigi Martini ITA (Minardi-Ford)   2 laps
8 Jean-Christophe Boullion FRA (Sauber-Ford) 3 laps*
9 Gianni Morbidelli ITA (Footwork-Hart)   4 laps
10 Pedro Diniz BRA (Forti-Ford)   6 laps

Pole position: Damon Hill
Fastest lap: Alesi 1:24.621   (141.581kmh)

Schumacher had an easy time of it at Monaco, his victory largely ascribed to a single-pit-stop policy that left Hill,

who opted for two pit-stops, always up against it. Hill, from pole, lead for the first 24 laps, but as soon as he pitted Schumacher inherited the lead. The Benetton stayed ahead, bustled up by Alesi's Ferrari, until Schumacher made his single stop on lap 35. Alesi briefly held the lead, till his pit-stop on the succeeding lap, and would almost certainly have taken the second place points ahead of Hill had Brundle not decided to make life difficult. Although a lap down, the Liger driver would not concede ground to Alesi. Driving close to the limit, Brundle spun the Ligier on lap 42 and Alesi simply couldn't avoid him - 90 Grands Prix and still the Frenchman waits for his first victory. Coulthard had a dreadful day, the meat in a Ferrari sandwich just after the start, he fared no better in the restarted race when his gearbox gave up the ghost on lap 16.

WORLD CHAMPIONSHIP STANDINGS

Drivers: *Schumacher 34, Hill 29, Berger 17, Alesi 14, Herbert 12, Coulthard 9, Hakkinen 5, Frentzen 4, Blundell 3, Irvine 2, Panis 1.*

Constructors: *Benetton-Renault 36, Williams-Renault 32, Ferrari 31, McLaren-Mercedes 8, Sauber-Ford 4, Jordan-Peugeot 2, Ligier-Mugen 1.*

Canadian Grand Prix

Circuit Gilles Villeneuve, Montreal   June 11
Laps: 69 x 4.430km   Total distance: 305.670km

1 **Jean Alesi FRA (Ferrari)   1:46:31.333**
                                               (172.172 kmh)
2 Rubens Barrichello BRA (Jordan-Peugeot)   31.687
3 Eddie Irvine IRL (Jordan-Peugeot)   33.270
4 Olivier Panis FRA (Ligier-Mugen)   36.506
5 Michael Schumacher GER (Benetton-Ren)   37.060
6 Gianni Morbidelli ITA (Footwork-Hart)   1 lap
7 Luca Badoer ITA (Minardi-Ford)   1 lap
8 Mika Salo FIN (Tyrrell-Yamaha)   1 lap
9 Taki Inoue JPN (Footwork-Hart)   2 laps

Pole position: Michael Schumacher
Fastest lap: Schumacher 1:29.174 (178.841kmh)

After his sad exit at Monaco, events at Montreal might have proved to Alesi that there was a God after all. Six years and 91 races into his GP career and the Frenchman finally won a race. For 58 laps, though, it was all Schumacher. The German, on pole, had led from the start. Behind him, the Williams-Renault team were having a miserable time. Coulthard spun off on lap 2 and the hydraulic pump on Hill's FW17 blew on lap 50, when in third. The assessment from both Hill and Coulthard was that their cars were "undriveable". For 40 laps, Alesi chased Schumacher, though never with the slightest likelihood of catching him until lap 57, when the gearbox in Schumacher's B195 decided that three was its favourite number and wouldn't be shifted from it. Alesi, on his 31st birthday, sped past and on to victory. "It's the best birthday present I could have given him," said Schumacher, not averse to a little patronage.

WORLD CHAMPIONSHIP STANDINGS

Drivers: *Schumacher 36, Hill 29, Alesi 24, Berger 17, Herbert 12, Coulthard 9, Barrichello & Irvine 6, Hakkinen 5, Frentzen & Panis 4, Blundell 3, Morbidelli 1.*

Constructors: *Ferrari 41, Benetton-Renault 38, Williams-Renault 32, Jordan-Peugeot 12, McLaren-Mercedes 8, Ligier-Mugen & Sauber-Ford 4, Footwork-Hart 1.*

*Q*uotes

"I want to apologise for what my driver did. he was a bit of a prat" - **Williams-Renault boss Frank Williams apologising for the crash between Damon Hill and Benetton's Michael Schumacher at the British Grand Prix.**

"I started to cry in the car and I couldn't see the road because when I braked for the corners the tears went onto my visor" - **Jean Alesi on his problems after taking the lead en route to his first Formula One grand prix win in Montreal.**

"Come on Michael let's forget all this bullshit." - **Hill on the increasing antagonism with Schumacher before the British Grand Prix.**

"Yes...after the Championship" - **Schumacher's reply.**

"Damon Hill World Champion 1995.......You must be MAD" - **T shirts worn by Schumacher's supporters at the German Grand Prix at Hockenheim.**

"After poor Ayrton Senna got killed, everyone said, 'That's it. F1's finished, forget it.' Remember that? 'Brazil,' they said, 'don't even have a race in Brazil.' This year we had the biggest crowd ever in Brazil. The TV ratings have been bigger than ever and at every circuit the crowd has been up. Now, don't ask me why...." - **Bernie Ecclestone.**

"Schumacher has never been put to the test but there ain't anyone who's good enough to give him trouble" - **Ecclestone again.**

"I don't think Damon will brake test me again, I will make sure of that and so will the FIA. In the race it made me more motivated - it made me furious" - **Schumacher after the French Grand Prix at Magny Cours.**

"It's not very nice to see people we work with leaping for joy and pleasure in our garage when our cars are parked by the side of the track and another team's cars win a race but that's what they decided to do and they didn't give us an option" - **Frank Williams bemoaning the situation where Renault supply engines to their main rivals, Benetton.**

"The last time I was this far back, I was in Formula 1 - every single Grand Prix" - **Last years British Touring Car champion Gabriele Tarquini on finishing 11th at Oulton Park.**

THE LOTUS POSITION

Company formed: 1952 (Entered F1 1958) **Founder:** Colin Chapman

First GP: Monaco 1958 (drivers Cliff Allison & Graham Hill)

First GP win: USA 1961 (driver Innes Ireland)

F1 World Driver's Championship titles: 1963 & 1965 (Jim Clark), 1968 (Graham Hill), 1970 (Jochen Rindt), 1972 (Emerson Fittipaldi), 1978 (Mario Andretti)

F1 World Constructor's Championship titles: 1963, 1965, 1968, 1970, 1972, 1973, 1978

Last GP win: USA (Detroit) 1987 (driver Ayrton Senna)

French Grand Prix

Magny Cours   July 2
Laps:72 x 4.247km   Total distance:305.814km

1	**Michael Schumacher GER (Benetton) 1:38:28.429**	
		(186.332 kmh)
2	Damon Hill GBR (Williams-Renault)	31.309
3	David Coulthard GBR (Williams-Renault)	1:02.826
4	Martin Brundle GBR (Ligier-Mugen)	1:03.293
5	Jean Alesi FRA (Ferrari)	1:17.869
6	Rubens Barrichello BRA (Jordan-Peugeot)	1 lap
7	Mika Hakkinen FIN (McLaren-Mercedes)	1 lap
8	Olivier Panis FRA (Ligier-Mugen)	1 lap
9	Eddie Irvine GBR (Jordan-Peugeot)	1 lap
10	Heinz-Harald Frentzen GER (Sauber-Ford)	1 lap
11	Mark Blundell GBR (McLaren-Mercedes)	2 laps
12	Gerhard Berger AUT (Ferrari)	2 laps
13	Luca Badoer ITA (Minardi-Ford)	3 laps
14	Gianni Morbichelli ITA (Footwork-Hart)	3 laps
15	Mika Salo FIN (Tyrrell-Yamaha)	3 laps
16	Roberto Moreno BRA (Forti-Ford)	6 laps

Pole position: Damon Hill
Fastest lap: Schumacher 1:20.218 (190.730kmh)

Hill proved yet again that he can get the rehearsal right, but he can't do it when the curtain goes up. Fastest in qualifying, Hill led for the first 21 laps until he pit-stopped. Then a combination of a slow stop and running into traffic was taken into account, the British driver lost over eight seconds to Schumacher in two laps. However, that was only part of the problem for Schumacher eventually won by over 30 seconds . "I just can't seem to break this rut I am in," bewailed Hill. Coulthard surprised by finishing a race, holding off Brundle's Ligier which lunged at him on the final corner. Herbert, in the second Benetton, was unfortunate, shunted out by Alesi's Ferrari. "He always criticises everyone else," said a disgruntled Herbert. He would be a lot happier in a fortnight, though.

WORLD CHAMPIONSHIP STANDINGS

Drivers: Schumacher 46, Hill 35, Alesi 26, Berger 17, Coulthard 13, Herbert 12, Barrichello 7, Irvine 6, Hakkinen 5, Frentzen & Panis 4, Blundell & Brundle 3, Morbidelli 1.

Constructors: Benetton-Renault 48, Ferrari 43, Williams-Renault 42, Jordan-Peugeot 13, McLaren-Mercedes 8, Ligier-Mugen 7, Sauber-Ford 4, Footwork-Hart 1.

British Grand Prix

Silverstone   July 16
Laps: 61 x 5.057km   Total distance: 308.477km

1	**Johnny Herbert GBR (Benetton-Ren) 1:34:36.093**	
		(195.682kmh)
2	Jean Alesi FRA (Ferrari)	16.479
3	David Coulthard GBR (Williams-Renault)	23.888
4	Olivier Panis FRA (Ligier-Mugen)	1:33.168
5	Mark Blundell GBR (McLaren-Mercedes)	1:48.172
6	Heinz-Harald Frentzen GER (Sauber-Ford)	1 lap
7	Pierluigi Martini ITA (Minardi-Ford)	1 lap
8	Mika Salo FIN (Tyrrell-Yamaha)	1 lap
9	Jean-Christophe Boullion FRA (Sauber-Ford)	1 lap
10	Luca Badoer ITA (Minardi-Ford)	1 lap
11	Rubens Barrichello BRA (Jordan-Peugeot)	2 laps*
12	Bertrand Gachot FRA (Pacific-Ford)	3 laps

Pole position: Damon Hill

Fastest lap: Hill 1:29.752 (202.838kmh)

Hill managed to get out of the rut all right. He took Schumacher out of the rut too, the winning rut. In a manoeuvre that could best be described as optimistic, Hill decided to take his FW17 through Priory Bend on the inside of Schumacher's B195. As Schumacher was leading at the time, all the optimism in the world was never going to get the Williams-Renault through. As Schumacher closed the gap, Hill drove straight into the side of the Benetton. "It was very stupid mistake," said Schumacher and all the patriotism in the world found it hard to disagree. With both the main protagonists out of the race, the door was open to the minor players. Herbert has been just that for a long time, back in 1988 breaking both legs in a crash at Brands Hatch. He inherited the lead on lap 46, lost it to Coulthard on lap 49 and was able to reclaim it when the Scot suffered a 10-second penalty for speeding in the pit-lane. For once, everything worked in Herbert's favour and the 25-1 outsider had 90,000 voices cheering him home. Hill, at least, could argue that for the first GP since Imola, he had been in with a winning chance.

WORLD CHAMPIONSHIP STANDINGS

Drivers: Schumacher 46, Hill 35, Alesi 32, Herbert 22, Berger & Coulthard 17, Barrichello & Panis 7, Irvine 6, Hakkinen, Frentzen & Blundell 5, Brundle 3, Morbidelli 1.

Constructors: Benetton-Renault 58, Ferrari 49, Williams-Renault 46, Jordan-Peugeot 13, Ligier-Mugen & McLaren-Mercedes 10, Sauber-Ford 5, Footwork-Hart 1.

German Grand Prix

Hockenheim   July 30
Laps: 45 x 6.823km   Total distance:307.022km

1	**Michael Schumacher GER (Benetton) 1:22:56.043**	
		(222.120kmh)
2	David Coulthard GBR (Williams-Renault)	at 5.988
3	Gerhard Berger AUT (Ferrari)	1:08.097
4	Johnny Herbert GBR (Benetton-Renault)	1:23.436
5	Jean-Christophe Boullion FRA (Sauber-Ford)	1 lap
6	Aguri Suzuki JPN (Ligier-Mugen)	1 lap
7	Ukyo Katayama JPN (Tyrrell-Yamaha)	1 lap
8	Andrea Montermini ITA (Pacific Ford)	3 laps
9	Eddie Irvine GBR (Jordan-Peugeot)	4 laps*

Pole position: Damon Hill

Fastest lap: Schumacher 1:48.824 (225.711kmh)

In 25 years, no German had ever won this race and Schumacher's delight was evident. A vast crowd, reckoned at 128,000, watched the German's comfortable victory. It included the one driver who might have pushed him. Hill continued his woeful run with elimination on the first lap. On the Nord Kurve, with oil on the track, Hill could not control his car and spun off. "I am just gutted, completely gutted," said Hill. Coulthard kept the Williams-Renault flag flying, finishing only six seconds adrift, but really it was a measured victory by Schumacher.

WORLD CHAMPIONSHIP STANDINGS

Drivers: Schumacher 56, Hill 35, Alesi 32, Herbert 25, Coulthard 23, Berger 21, Barrichello & Panis 7, Irvine 6, Hakkinen, Frentzen & Blundell 5, Brundle 3, Boullion 2, Morbidelli & Suzuki 1.

Constructors: Benetton-Renault 71, Ferrari 53, Williams-Renault 52, Jordan-Peugeot 13, Ligier-Mugen 11, McLaren-Mercedes 10, Sauber-Ford 7, Footwork-Hart 1.

Hungarian Grand Prix

Hungaroring, Budapest   *Aug 13*
Laps: 77 x 3.968km   *Total distance:305.536km*

1	**Damon Hill GBR (Williams-Renault)**	**1:46:25.721**
		(172.248kmh)
2	David Coulthard GBR (Williams-Renault)	at 33.398
3	Gerhard Berger AUT (Ferrari)	1 lap
4	Johnny Herbert GBR (Benetton-Renault)	1 lap
5	Heinz-Harald Frentzen GER (Sauber-Ford)	1 lap
6	Olivier Panis FRA (Ligier-Mugen)	1 lap
7	Rubens Barrichello BRA (Jordan-Peugeot)	1 lap
8	Luca Badoer ITA (Minardi-Ford)	2 laps
9	Pedro Lamy POR (Minardi-Ford)	3 laps
10	Jean-Christophe Boullion FRA (Sauber-Ford)	3 laps
11	Michael Schumacher GER (Benetton-Ren)	4 laps*
12	Andrea Montermini ITA (Pacific-Ford)	4 laps
13	Eddie Irvine GBR (Jordan-Peugeot)	7 laps*

Pole position: Damon Hill
Fastest lap: Hill 1:20.247 (178.010kmh)

Hill started the good time on this track, gaining his first F1 victory here two years previously. The Williams-Renault driver had to give best to Schumacher in 1994, but the happy days returned with this win. This time it was Schumacher who got the strategy wrong, having to pit early for fuel and, as a consequence, having worn tyres for his final laps before his retirement - on lap 74 of 77 - with engine trouble. This was a race, though, that Hill won rather than Schumacher lost. "My best race ever," said a jubilant Hill, whose driving was almost faultless. With Schumacher failing to finish, the result also re-opened the world championship, Hill now just 11 points adrift.

WORLD CHAMPIONSHIP STANDINGS
Drivers: *Schumacher 56, Hill 45, Alesi 32, Coulthard 29, Herbert 28, Berger 25, Panis 8, Barrichello & Frentzen 7, Irvine 6, Hakkinen & Blundell 5, Brundle 3, Boullion 2, Morbidelli & Suzuki 1.*
Constructors: *Benetton-Renault 74, Williams-Renault 68, Ferrari 57, Jordan-Peugeot 13, Ligier-Mugen 12, McLaren-Mercedes 10, Sauber-Ford 9, Footwork-Hart 1.*

Belgian Grand Prix

Spa Francorchamps   *Aug 27*
Laps: 44 x 6.96km   *Total distance:306.856*

1	**Michael Schumacher GER (Benetton)**	**1:36:47.875**
		(190.204kmh)
2	Damon Hill GBR (Williams-Renault)	at 19.493
3	Martin Brundle GBR (Ligier-Mugen)	24.998
4	Heinz-Harald Frentzen GER (Sauber-Ford)	26.972
5	Mark Blundell GBR (McLaren-Mercedes)	33.772
6	Rubens Barrichello BRA (Jordan-Peugeot)	39.674
7	Johnny Herbert GBR (Benetton-Renault)	54.048
8	Mika Salo FIN (Tyrrell-Yamaha)	54.548
9	Olivier Panis FRA (Ligier-Mugen)	1:06.170
10	Pedro Lamy POR (Minardi-Ford)	1:19.789
11	Jean-Christophe Boullion FRA (Sauber-Ford)	1 lap
12	Taki Inoue JPN (Footwork-Hart)	1 lap
13	Pedro Diniz BRA (Forti-Ford)	2 laps
14	Roberto Moreno BRA (Forti-Ford)	2 laps

Pole position: Gerhard Berger
Fastest lap: Coulthard 1:53.412 (221.373kmh)

The Belgian circuit holds happy memories for Schumacher. He made his F1 debut here and also won his first Grand Prix. In treacherous conditions the German carved through the field from his lowly position of 16th on the grid. With the lead changing 11 times, Schumacher was given a one race ban, suspended for 4 races, for illegally blocking Damon Hill's Williams-Renault. Hill claimed that the championship leader was weaving along the straight and had banged wheels at the Les Combes chicane. "I can cope with anything but if the rules say we can go out and smash into each other as many times as possible then it's my decision as to whether I want to carry on in a sport like that", said the Englishman afterwards.

WORLD CHAMPIONSHIP STANDINGS
Drivers: *Schumacher 66, Hill 51, Alesi 32, Coulthard 29, Herbert 28, Berger 25, Frentzen 10, Panis & Barrichello 8, Brundle & Blundell 7, Irvine 6, Hakkinen 5, Boullion 2, Morbidelli & Suzuki 1.*
Constructors: *Benetton-Renault 84, Williams-Renault 74, Ferrari 57, Ligier-Mugen 16, Jordan-Peugeot 14, McLaren-Mercedes & Sauber-Ford 12, Footwork-Hart 1.*

Italian Grand Prix

Monza   *Sep 10*
Laps: 53 x 5.769km   *Total distance:305.772km*

1	**Johnny Herbert GBR (Benetton-Ren)**	**1:18:27.916**
		(233.014kmh)
2	Mika Hakkinen FIN (McLaren-Mercedes)	at 17.779
3	Heinz-Harald Frentzen GER (Sauber-Ford)	24.321
4	Mark Blundell GBR (McLaren-Mercedes)	28.223
5	Mika Salo FIN (Tyrrell-Yamaha)	1 lap
6	Jean-Christophe Boullion FRA (Sauber-Ford)	1 lap
7	Max Papis ITA (Footwork-Hart)	1 lap
8	Taki Inoue JPN (Footwork-Hart)	1 lap
9	Pedro Diniz BRA (Forti-Ford)	3 laps
10	Ukyo Katayama JPN (Tyrrell-Yamaha)	6 laps

Pole Position: Michael Schumacher
Fastest Lap: Gerhard Berger 1:26.419 (240.363kmh)

Whilst Johnny Herbert picked up his second win of the season, the headlines belonged to the two championship contenders. Approaching the Curva della Roggia on lap 23 out of 53, Hill ploughed into the back of Schumacher to send the two spinning into retirement in the gravel pit. The German blamed Hill; Hill blamed the German and the clumsy driving of backmarker Taka Inoue for the incident. Clearly Hill was to blame and was subsequently awarded a one race ban, suspended for one race. The day will be one to forget for David Coulthard who began on pole. Having performed the unlikely feat of spinning off on the leisurely warm-up lap, the Scotsman earned a reprieve following a red flag after an opening lap pile-up. Coulthard made a better fist of it in the spare car before a loose wheel-bearing sent him into the tyre wall for a second time. Frentzen's third place earned the Sauber team their first podium finish. With Alesi forced to retire eight laps from the end, the door was open for Herbert to inherit another famous victory.

WORLD CHAMPIONSHIP STANDINGS
Drivers: *Schumacher 66, Hill 51, Herbert 38, Alesi 32, Coulthard 29, Berger 25, Frentzen 14, Hakkinen 11, Blundell 10, Panis & Barrichello 8, Brundle 7, Irvine 6, Boullion 3, Morbidelli & Suzuki 1.*
Constructors: *Benetton-Renault 94, Williams-Renault 74, Ferrari 57, McLaren-Mercedes 21, Sauber-Ford 17, Ligier-Mugen 16, Jordan-Peugeot 14, Footwork-Hart 1.*

Portuguese Grand Prix

Estoril   Sep 24
Laps: 71 x 4.350km   Total distance:308.850km
1 **David Coulthard GBR (Williams-Ren) 1:41:52.145**
                                    (182.319kmh)
2 Michael Schumacher GER (Benetton-Ren) at 7.248
3 Damon Hill GBR (Williams-Renault)   22.121
4 Gerhard Berger AUT (Ferrari)   1:24.879
5 Jean Alesi FRA (Ferrari)   1:25.428
6 Heinz-Harald Frentzen GER (Sauber-Ford)   1 lap
7 Johnny Herbert GBR (Benetton-Renault)   1 lap
8 Martin Brundle GBR (Ligier-Mugen)   1 lap
9 Mark Blundell GBR (McLaren-Mercedes)   1 lap
10 Eddie Irvine GBR (Jordan-Peugeot)   1 lap
11 Rubens Barrichello BRA (Jordan-Peugeot)   1 lap
12 Jean-Christophe Boullion FRA (Saiber-Ford) 1 lap
13 Mika Salo FIN (Tyrrell-Yamaha)   2 laps
14 Luca Badoer ITA (Minardi-Ford)   3 laps
15 Taki Inoue JPN (Footwork-Hart)   3 laps
16 Pedro Diniz BRA (Forti-Ford)   5 laps
17 Roberto Moreno BRA (Forti-Ford)   7 laps
Pole Position: Michael Schumacher
Fastest Lap: David Coulthard 1:23.220 (188.608kmh)
Coulthard's first F1 victory was also the first by a Scot since Jackie Stewart triumphed at the Nurburgring in 1973. However the battle for second place was of greater significance as Schumacher outbraked Hill at the new chicane on lap 62 to give him the vital edge over his rival. Once taken, Hill, on worn tyres, had no response. Yet another F1 race had to be red-flagged after the start with Japan's Ukyo Katayama spiralling down the track in his Tyrell after contact with Badoer's Minardi. The race was restarted 20 minutes later, and again Coulthard led into the first corner. Pit-stops not withstanding, the Scot controlled the race as Schumacher concentrated his efforts on denying Hill the opportunity to close the gap in the driver's championship. Coulthard's win proved a point to boss Frank Williams who has replaced him with Canadian IndyCar specialist, Jacques Villeneuve, for next season.
WORLD CHAMPIONSHIP STANDINGS
Drivers: Schumacher 72, Hill 55, Coulthard 39, Herbert 38, Alesi 34, Berger 28, Frentzen 15, Hakkinen 11, Blundell 10, Panis & Barrichello 8, Brundle 7, Irvine 6, Boullion 3, Morbidelli & Suzuki 1.
Constructors: Benetton-Renault 100, Williams-Renault 88, Ferrari 62, McLaren-Mercedes 21, Sauber-Ford 18, Ligier-Mugen 16, Jordan-Peugeot 14, Tyrell-Yamaha 2, Footwork-Hart 1.

European Grand Prix

Nurburgring   Oct 1
Laps: 67 x 4.54km   Total distance:304.265km
1 **Michael Schumacher GER (Benetton-R)1:39:59.04**
                                    (176.875kmh)
2 Jean Alesi FRA (Ferrari)   at 2.684
3 David Coulthard GBR (Williams-Renault) 35.382
4 Rubens Barrichello BRA (Jordan-Peugeot)   1 lap
5 Johnny Herbert GBR (Benetton-Renault)   1 lap
6 Eddie Irvine GBR (Jordan-Peugeot)   1 lap
7 Martin Brundle GBR (Ligier-Mugen)   1 lap
8 Mika Hakkinen FIN (McLaren-Mercedes)   2 laps
9 Pedro Lamy POR (Minardi-Ford)   3 laps

10 Mika Salo FIN (Tyrrell-Yamaha)   3 laps
11 Luca Badoer ITA (Minardi-Ford)   3 laps
12 Max Papis ITA (Footwork-Hart)   3 laps
13 Pedro Diniz BRA (Forti-Ford)   5 laps
14 Gabriele Tarquini ITA (Tyrrell-Yamaha)   6 laps
15 J-D Deletraz SUI (Pacific-Lotus-Ford)   7 laps
Pole Position: David Coulthard
Fastest lap: Michael Schumacher 1:21.180 (202.039kmh)
Schumacher's victory in front of 100,000 adoring spectators all but clinched the 1995 drivers' championship. The track which lies in the Eifel mountains, only 60 miles from the German's home, was shouded in mist for much of the weekend. Pit-stops and tyre changes again were crucial on a track that began wet but continually dried as the race progressed. Hill ruled himself out of contention after attempting an unecessary overtaking manouevre on leader Jean Alesi. Hill, who was due to pit the next lap, was forced onto the kerb losing his front wing and precious seconds. His valiant attempt to reel in the German resulted in a terminal spin on lap 59. However, the day belonged to Schumacher who emerged from his second pit-stop 22 seconds behind Alesi with 14 laps remaining. To the delight of the crowd he pulled back the deficit to score his 17th career F1 win. The sight of Hill standing trackside applauding the German's victory lap signalled an end to their feuding and the championship. "We may not be friends, but we respect each other and there is no war between us" confirmed Schumacher.
WORLD CHAMPIONSHIP STANDINGS
Drivers: Schumacher 82, Hill 55, Coulthard 43, Herbert & Alesi 40, Berger 28, Frentzen 15, Hakkinen & Barrichello 11, Blundell 10, Panis 8, Brundle & Irvine 7, Boullion 3, Salo 2, Morbidelli & Suzuki 1.
Constructors: Benetton-Renault 112, Williams-Renault 92, Ferrari 68, McLaren-Mercedes 21, Sauber-Ford & Jordan-Peugeot 18, Ligier-Mugen 16, Tyrell-Yamaha 2, Footwork-Hart 1.

1994 Season
European Grand Prix

Jerez   *Oct 16*
Laps: 69 x 4.428   *Total distance: 305.531km*

1   **Michael Schumacher GER (Benetton) 1:40:26.689**
                                   (182.507kmh)

2	Damon Hill GBR (Williams-Renault)	24.689
3	Mika Hakinnen FIN (McLaren-Peugeot)	1:09.648
4	Eddie Irvine GBR (Jordan-Hart)	1:18.446
5	Gerhard Berger AUT (Ferrari)	1 lap
6	Heinz-Harald Frentzen GER (Sauber-Merc)	1 lap
7	Ukyo Katayama JPN (Tyrrell-Yamaha)	1 lap
8	Johnny Herbert GBR (Ligier-Renault)	1 lap
9	Olivier Panis FRA (Ligier-Renault)	1 lap
10	Jean Alesi FRA (Ferrari)	1 lap
11	Gianni Morbidelli ITA (Footwork-Ford)	1 lap
12	Rubens Barrichello BRA (Jordan-Hart)	1 lap
13	Mark Blundell GBR (Tyrrell-Yamaha)	1 lap
14	Michele Alboreto ITA (Minardi-Ford)	2 laps
15	Pierluigi Martini ITA (Minardi-Ford)	2 laps
16	Alessandro Zanardi ITA (Lotus-Mugen)	2 laps
17	Christian Fittipaldi BRA (Footwowrk-Ford)	3 laps
18	Eric Bernard FRA (Lotus-Mugen)	3 laps
19	Domenico Schiatterella ITA (Simtek-Ford)	5 laps

Fastest lap: Schumacher 1:25.040 (187.450kmh)

Hill's William-Renault may have had a power advantage - able to generate an extra 10kmh in a straight line - but it couldn't win him this crucial race. The tyre strategy proved critical; Schumacher played a waiting game and it paid dividends.

World Championship Standings
Drivers: Schumacher 86, Hill 81, Berger 35, Hakkinen 26, Alesi 19, Barrichello 16, Coulthard 14, Brundle 12, Verstappen 10, Blundell 8, Panis 7, Larini, Fittipaldi & Frentzen 6, Katayama 5, Wendlinger, de Cesaris, Martini, Bernard & Irvine 4, Morbidelli 3, Comas 2, Alboreto & Lehto 1.

Constructors: Benetton-Ford 97, Williams-Renault 95, Ferrari 60, McLaren-Peugeot 38, Jordan-Hart 23, Tyrrell-Yamaha 13, Sauber-Mercedes & Ligier-Renault 11, Footwork-Ford 9, Minardi-Ford 5, Larrousse-Ford 2.

Japanese Grand Prix

Suzuka   *Nov 6*
Laps:50 x 5.864km   *Total distance: 293.199km*

1   **Damon Hill GBR (Williams-Renault)**   **1:55:53.532**
                                     (151.796kmh)

2	Michael Schumacher GER (Benetton-Ford)	3.365
3	Jean Alesi FRA (Ferrari)	52.045
4	Nigel Mansell GBR (Williams-Renault)	56.074
5	Eddie Irvine GBR (Jordan-Hart)	1:42.107
6	Heinz-Harald Frentzen GER (Sauber-Merc)	1:59.863
7	Mika Hakinnen FIN (McLaren-Peugeot)	2:02.985
8	Christian Fittipaldi BRA (Footwork-Ford)	1 lap
9	Erik Comas FRA (Larrouse-Ford)	1 lap
10	Mika Salo FIN (Lotus-Mugen)	1 lap
11	Olivier Panis FRA (Ligier Renault)	1 lap
12	David Brabham AUS (Simtek-Ford)	2 laps
13	Alessandro Zanardi ITA (Lotus Mugen)	2 laps

Fastest lap: Hill 1:56.597 (181.054kmh)

A rainstorm made conditions so treacherous that, at one point, there were seven successive spins down the home straight. The race was red-flagged and divided into two,

final placings decided by the aggregate times. Hill drove to a memorable victory, altough Schumacher cut down a 15 second lead to just 2.4 seconds on the penultimate lap. Hill's victory set up a final showdown at Adelaide.

World Championship Standings
Drivers: Schumacher 92, Hill 91, Berger 35, Hakkinen 26, Alesi 23, Barrichello 16, Coulthard 14, Brundle 12, Verstappen 10, Blundell 8, Panis & Frentzen 7, Irvine, Larini & Fittipaldi 6, Katayama 5, Wendlinger, de Cesaris, Martini & Bernard 4, Morbidelli & Mansell 3, Comas 2, Alboreto & Lehto 1.

Constructors: Williams-Renault 108, Benetton-Ford 103, Ferrari 64, McLaren-Peugeot 38, Jordan-Hart 25, Tyrrell-Yamaha 13, Sauber-Mercedes 12, Ligier-Renault 11, Footwork-Ford 9, Minardi-Ford 5, Larrousse-Ford 2.

Australian Grand Prix

Adelaide   *Nov 13*
Laps:81 x 3.780km   *Total distance: 306.180km*

1   **Nigel Mansell GBR (Williams-Renault)1:47:51.480**
                                     (170.323 kmh)

2	Gerhard Berger AUT (Ferrari)	2.511
3	Martin Brundle GBR (McLaren-Peugeot)	52.487
4	Rubens Barrichello BRA (Jordan-Hart)	1:10.530
5	Olivier Panis FRA (Ligier-Renault)	1 lap
6	Jean Alesi FRA (Ferrari)	1 lap
7	Heinz-Harald Frentzen GER (Sauber-Merc)	1 lap
8	Christian Fittipaldi BRA (Footwork-Ford)	1 lap
9	Pierluigi Martini ITA (Minardi-Ford)	2 laps
10	J J Lehto FIN (Sauber-Mercedes)	2 laps
11	F Lagorce FRA (Ligier-Renault)	2 laps
12	Mika Hakkinen FIN (McLaren-Peugeot)	5 laps

Fastest lap: Schumacher 1:17.140 (176.406kmh)

Hill only had to pass Schumacher to win the title; yet that was the one thing that the German ensured did not happen. When Hill attempted to overtake on lap 35, Schumacher didn't just close the door, he slammed it shut. Schumacher's Benetton flew into a wall of tyres, Hill's Williams-Renault limped away from the collision. As far as race strategies go, it was questionable to say the least. Yet it gave the German the title and left Hill to lament. The incident was to provoke something close to a storm of protest, though not from Hill. Nine days after the race, following an FIA report, was Schumacher assured that he would keep the title. Lest we forget, the race was won by Mansell, who went on to talk optimistically about the 1995 season. It was the 31st F1 victory for the former world champion who, at 41, was comfortably the oldest driver in the race.

WORLD CHAMPIONSHIP FINAL STANDINGS
Drivers: Schumacher 92, *Hill 91, Berger 41, Hakkinen 26, Alesi 24, Barrichello 19, Brunle 16, Coulthard 14, Mansell 13, Verstappen 10, Panis 9, Blundell 8, Frentzen 7, Larini, Fittipaldi & Irvine 6, Katayama 5, Bernard, Wendlinger, de Cesaris & Martini 4, Morbidelli 3, Comas 2, Alboreto & Lehto 1.*

Constructors: Williams-Renault 118, *Benetton-Ford 103, Ferrari 71, McLaren-Peugeot 42, Jordan-Hart 28, Ligier-Renault & Tyrrell-Yamaha 13, Sauber-Mercedes 12, Footwork-Ford 9, Minardi-Ford 5, Larrousse-Ford 2.*

Formula 3000 International Championship

ROUND 1
Silverstone   May 7
1 **Ricardo Rosset BRA (Super Nova Racing)**
2 Vincenzo Sospiri ITA (Super Nova Racing)
3 Allan McNish GBR (Paul Stewart Racing)

ROUND 2
Barcelona   May 13
1 **Vincenzo Sospiri ITA (Super Nova Racing)**
2 Ricardo Rosset BRA (Super Nova Racing)
3 Tarso Marques BRA (Vortex Motorsport)

ROUND 3
Pau, France   June 5
1 **Vincenzo Sospiri ITA (Super Nova Racing)**
2 Allan McNish GBR (Paul Stewart Racing)
3 Marc Goossens BEL (Nordic Racing)

ROUND 4
Enna-Pergusa, Italy   July 23
1 **Ricardo Rosset BRA (Super Nova Racing)**
2 Vincenzo Sospiri ITA (Super Nova Racing)
3 Christian Pescatori ITA (Durango Equipe SRL)

ROUND 5
Hockenheim   July 30
1 **Marc Goossens BEL (Nordic Racing)**
2 Kenny Brack SUI (Madgwick International)
3 Guillaume Gomez FRA (Dams)

ROUND 6
Spa-Francorchamps   Aug 27
1 **Vincenzo Sospiri ITA (Super Nova Racing)**
2 Christophe Bouchut FRA (Danielson)
3 Guillaume Gomez FRA (Dams)

ROUND 7
Estoril   Sep 24
1 **Tarso Marques BRA (Vortex Motorsport)**
2 Emmanuel Clerico FRA (Apomatox F3000)
3 Kenny Brack SUI (Madgwick International)

POINTS WITH ONE RACE REMAINING
Sospiri 39, Rosset 29, Goossens 18, Marques & Brack 15, Clerico 13, McNish 11

Sospiri is 1995 Formula 3000 champion

Formula 3000 - 1994
Final Race

ROUND 9
Magny-Cours, France
1 **Jean-C Boullion FRA (Reynard-Cos)**
2 Franck Lagorce FRA (Reynard-Cos)
3 Guillaume Gomez FRA (Reynard-Cos)

FINAL CHAMPIONSHIP STANDINGS
Jean-Christophe Boullion 36, Franck Lagorce 34, Gil De Ferran 28, Vincenzo Sospiri 24, Max Papis 13

Le Mans 24 Hours
Circuit de la Sarthe, Le Mans   June 17-18

#	Team (Car)	Drivers	Result
1	**Kokusai Kaihatsu UK (McLaren F1 GTR)**	Yannick Dalmas/J J Lehto/Masanori Sekiya	**298 laps**
			4,055.800km
2	Courage Competition (Courage-Porsche C34)	Bob Wollek/Mario Andretti/Eric Helary	at 9.461km
3	Dave Price Racing (McLaren F1 GTR)	Andy Wallace/Derek Bell/Justin Bell	1 lap
4	Gulf Racing (McLaren F1 GTR)	Mark Blundell/Ray Bellm/Maurizio Sandro Sala	5 laps
5	Giroix Racing (McLaren F1 GTR)	Fabien Giroix/Olivier Grouillard/Jean-D Deletraz	7 laps
6	Kremer Racing (Kremer-Porsche K8)	Thierry Boutsen/Hans Stuck/Christophe Bouchet	8 laps
7	DTR Mazdaspeed (Kudzu-Mazda DG3)	Yojiro Terada/Jim Downing/Franck Freon	15 laps
8	Team Kunimitsu Honda (Honda NSX GT)	Keiichi Tsuchiya/Kunimitsu Takahashi/Akira Iida	22 laps
9	Calloway Competition (C'y Corvette LM GT2)	Enrico Bertaggia/Johnny Unser/Frank Jelinski	25 laps
10	NISMO (Nissan Skyline GT-RLM)	H Fukuyama/Masahiko Kondo/Shunju Kasuya	26 laps

Winner's Average Speed: 168.992kmh
Fastest Lap: Gonin 3:51.41 (211.571kmh)

Indy Car World Series (PPG) ▬▬▬▬▬

Jacques Villeneuve clinched the Indy Car title in dramatic fashion following the last race in Laguna Seca. The Canadian, who went into the final round 16 points clear, suffered two punctures and rear wing trouble which meant that he could only finish 11th. This left defending champion Al Unser Jr pushing for the lead which would have retained him the title. However, Unser suffered problems and could only muster a sixth spot behind former Formula 3000 racer Gil de Ferran. Villeneuve, last season's rookie of the year, had earlier clinched the prestigious Indianapolis 500 in only his second start at the famous Speedway. Lying third behind the two Scotts, Goodyear and Pruett, in the closing laps, Villeneuve watched as first Pruett crashed out after hitting oil and then Goodyear was black-flagged for overtaking the pace car with 10 laps to go. "It's the greatest race in the world", said Villeneuve, "Indy is *the* race to win. If you had a choice of a race to win over and over again, this would be it". The Canadian now has the difficult task of adapting his driving to suit the rigours of Formula One when he joins Damon Hill in the Williams-Renault team for the 1996 season.

The Indy Car Series comprises 17 races. In the race charts below, the drivers are given in finish positions, the numbers in brackets refer to the start grid position. The Laps column gives the position of the driver when the winner crossed the line - if the car withdrew, then it will show on which lap. If the driver was also in the final lap, the Status column shows an average speed figure in miles per hour. Otherwise, the Status column shows Running if the car was still racing (but not on the final lap) or the reason for withdrawal. All points scorers in each race shown. NB: Pole-sitters also score. In some races the leader of the highest number of laps also scores.

Marlboro Grand Prix of Miami (Race 1)

Miami   Mar 5

	Driver	Ctry	Car	Laps	Status	Pts	Total
1 (8)	**Jacques Villeneuve**	**CAN**	**Player's Ltd R 95 Ford-Cosworth**	**90**	**82.801**	**20**	**20**
2 (2)	Mauricio Gugelmin	BRA	PacWest Racing R95 Ford-Cos	90	82.789	16	16
3 (11)	Bobby Rahal	USA	Miller Genuine Draft L95 MB	90	82.785	14	14
4 (10)	Scott Pruett	USA	Patrick Racing L95 Ford-Cos	90	82.778	12	12
5 (7)	Christian Fittipaldi	BRA	Marlboro-Chapeco R95 Ford -Cos	90	82.742	10	10
6 (3)	Raul Boesel	BRA	The Duracell Charger L95 MB	90	82.741	8	8
7 (21)	Christian Danner	GER	No Touch-Van Dyne-Marcelo I93 Ford C	90	82.620	6	6
8 (12)	Jimmy Vasser	USA	Target/STP R94 Ford-Cos	90	82.176	5	5
9 (6)	Danny Sullivan	USA	Bank of America R95 Ford-Cos	89	Running	4	4
10 (20)	Bryan Herta	USA	Target-Scotch Video R95 Ford-Cos	87	Running	3	3
11 (7)	Adrian Fernandez	MEX	Tecate Beer/Quaker State L95 MB	86	Running	2	2
12 (26)	Dean Hall	USA	Subway L95 Ford-Cos	86	Running	1	1
Also							
20 (1)	Michael Andretti	USA	Kmart-Texaco Havoline L95 Ford-Cos	49	Contact	2	2

Time of Race: 1:59:16.863 Margin of Victory: 1.002 secs. Lap Leaders: Michael Andretti 1-48, Gugelmin 49-55, Villeneuve 56-90.

IndyCar Australia (Race 2)

Surfers' Paradise, Queensland   Mar 19

	Driver	Ctry	Car	Laps	Status	Pts	Total
1 (9)	**Paul Tracy**	**USA**	**Kmart-Budweiser Lola L95 Ford-Cos**	**65**	**92.335**	**20**	**20**
2 (13)	Bobby Rahal	USA	Miller Genuine Draft L95 MB	65	92.244	16	30
3 (11)	Scott Pruett	USA	Patrick Racing L95 Ford-Cos	65	92.183	14	26
4 (10)	Mauricio Gugelmin	BRA	PacWest R95 Ford-Cosworth	65	92.159	12	28
5 (19)	Danny Sullivan	USA	Bank of America R95 Ford-Cos	65	92.087	10	14
6 (3)	Al Unser Jr	USA	Marlboro Penske Mercedes P95 MB	65	91.879	8	8
7 (17)	Eddie Cheever	USA	A J Foyt Copenhagen L95 Ford-Cos	65	91.879	6	6
8 (21)	Raul Boesel	BRA	The Duracell Charger L95 MB	65	91.760	5	13
9 (1)	Michael Andretti	USA	Kmart-Caltex Havoline Lola L95 Ford-C	64	Contact	6	8
10 (23)	Eliseo Salazar	CHI	Cristal-Mobil 1-Copec L95 Ford-Cos	64	Running	3	3
11 (26)	Hiro Matsushita	JPN	Panasonic-Duskin-Arciero Wines R94 F-C	62	Running	2	2
12 (25)	Dean Hall	USA	Subway L95 Ford-Cosworth	61	Running	1	2

Time of Race: 1:58:26.054 Margin of Victory: 6.983 secs. Lap Leaders: Andretti 1-41, Johansson 42-47, Andretti 48-57, Tracy 58-65.

Slick-50 200 (Race 3)

Phoenix, Arizona   *Apr 2*

	Driver	Ctry	Car	Laps	Status	Pts	Total
1 (9)	**Robby Gordon**	**USA**	**Valvoline-Cummins Special R95 F-C**	**200**	**133.980**	**20**	**20**
2 (5)	Michael Andretti	USA	Kmart-Texaco Havoline L95 Ford-C	200	133.960	16	24
3 (2)	Emerson Fittipaldi	BRA	Marlboro Penske Mercedes P95 MB	200	133.857	15	15
4 (4)	Paul Tracy	USA	Kmart-Budweiser L95 Ford-Cos	200	133.760	12	32
5 (3)	Jacques Villeneuve	CAN	Players Ltd R95 Ford-Cos	200	133.737	10	30
6 (8)	Raul Boesel	BRA	The Duracell Charger L95 MB	198	Running	8	21
7 (16)	Teo Fabi	ITA	Combustion Eng-Indeck R95 Ford-Cos	198	Running	6	6
8 (17)	Al Unser Jr	USA	Marlboro Penske Mercedes P95 MB	197	Running	5	13
9 (6)	Scott Pruett	USA	Patrick Racing L95 Ford-Cos	197	Running	4	30
10 (19)	Christian Fittipaldi	BRA	Malboro-Chapeco Special R95 Ford-Cos	195	Running	3	13
11 (10)	Gil de Ferran	BRA	Pennzoil Special R95 Mecedes-Benz	195	Running	2	2
12 (12)	Adrian Fernandez	MEX	Tecate Beer-Quaker State L95 MB	195	Running	1	3
Also							
20 (1)	Bryan Herta	USA	Target-Scotch Video R95 ford-Cos	170	Handling	1	4

Time of Race: 1:29:33.930 Margin of Victory: 0.788 sec Lap Leaders: Herta 1-27, Tracy 28, Herta 29-31, Andretti 32-56, Tracy 57-71, Andretti 72-104, Fittipaldi 105-113, Andretti 114-115, Fittipaldi 116-121, Tracy 122-131, Fittipaldi 132-194, Gordon 195-200.

Toyota Grand Prix of Long Beach (Race 4)

Long Beach, California   *Apr 9*

	Driver	Ctry	Car	Laps	Status	Pts	Total
1 (4)	**Al Unser Jr**	**USA**	**Marlboro Penske Mercedes P95 MB**	**105**	**91.442**	**21**	**34**
2 (10)	Scott Pruett	USA	Patrick Racing L95 Ford-Cos	105	91.122	14	20
3 (7)	Teo Fabi	ITA	Combustion Eng-Indeck R95 Ford-Cos	105	90.944	14	20
4 (18)	Eddie Cheever	USA	A J Foyt-Copenhagen L95 Ford-Cos	104	Stop on Course	12	18
5 (5)	Mauricio Gugelmin	BRA	Hollywood-PacWest R95 Ford-Cos	104	Running	10	38
6 (24)	Stefan Johansson	SWE	Team Alumax P94 MB	104	Running	8	8
7 (22)	Eric Bachelart	BEL	The AGFA Car L94 Ford-Cos	104	Running	6	6
8 (20)	Alessandro Zampedri	ITA	The MI-Jack Car L94 Ford-Cos	104	Running	5	5
9 (1)	Michael Andretti	USA	Kmart-Texaco Havolin Lola L95 Ford-Cos	104	Running	5	29
10 (17)	Danny Sullivan	USA	VISA-PacWest R95 Ford-Cos	104	Running	3	17
11 (19)	Carlos Guerrero	MEX	Herdez-Bufalo-McCormick L95 Ford-Cos	104	Running	2	2
12 (21)	Andre Ribeiro	BRA	LCI Reynard Honda R95 Honda	104	Running	1	1

Time of Race: 1:49:32.667 Margin of Victory: 23.125 secs Lap Leaders: Andretti 1-16, Fabi 17-29, Unser 30-63, Rahal 64, Andretti 65, Unser 66-105.

Bosch Spark Plug Grand Prix (Race 5)

Nazareth, Pennsylvania   *Apr 23*

	Driver	Ctry	Car	Laps	Status	Pts	Total
1 (4)	**Emerson Fittipaldi**	**BRA**	**Marlboro Penske Mercedes P95 MB**	**200**	**131.305**	**20**	**35**
2 (3)	Jacques Villeneuve	CAN	Players Ltd R95 Ford-Cos	200	131.298	17	47
3 (13)	Stefan Johansson	SWE	Team Alumax Penske P94 MB	200	131.050	14	22
4 (1)	Robby Gordon	USA	Valvoline-Cummins Special R95 Ford-C	200	130.929	13	33
5 (21)	Eddie Cheever	USA	A J Foyt Copenhagen L95 Ford-Cos	199	Fuel	10	28
6 (7)	Bobby Rahal	USA	Miller Genuine Draft L95 MB	199	Running	8	38
7 (16)	Teo Fabi	ITA	Combustion Eng-Indeck R95 Ford-Cos	199	Running	6	26
8 (10)	Scott Pruett	USA	Patrick Racing L95 Ford-Cos	199	Running	5	51
9 (9)	Adrian Fernandez	MEX	Tecate Beer-Quaker State L95 MB	199	Running	4	7
10 (8)	Raul Boesel	BRA	The Duracell Charger L95 MB	199	Running	3	24
11 (6)	Andre Ribeiro	BRA	LCI Reynard Honda R95 Honda	199	Running	2	3
12 (14)	Eliseo Salazar	CHI	Cristal-Mobil 1-Copec L95 Ford-Cos	198	Running	1	4

Time of Race: 1:31:23.410 Margin of Victory: 0.309 sec Lap Leaders: Gordon 1-19, Andretti 20-56, Villeneuve 57-93, Fabi 94-106, C Fittipaldi 107-116, E Fittipaldi 117-152, Villeneuve 153-160, Cheever 161-198, E Fittipaldi 199-200.

Indianapolis 500 (Race 6)

Indianapolis   May 28

	Driver	Ctry	Car	Laps	Status	Pts	Total
1 (5)	**Jacques Villeneuve**	CAN	**Players Ltd R95 Ford-Cos**	**200**	**153.616**	**20**	**67**
2 (27)	Christian Fittipaldi	BRA	Marlboro-Chapeco Special R95 Ford-Cos	200	153.383	16	29
3 (21)	Bobby Rahal	USA	Miller Genuiine Draft L95 MB	200	153.577	14	52
4 (24)	Eliseo Salazar	CHI	Cristal-Mobil 1-Copec L95 Ford-Cos	200	153.553	12	16
5 (7)	Robby Gordon	USA	Valvoline-Cummins Special R95 Ford-Cos	200	153.420	10	43
6 (6)	Mauricio Gugelmin	BRA	Hollywood-PacWest R95 Ford-Cos	200	153.392	9	47
7 (2)	Arie Luyendyk	NED	Glidden-Quaker State L95 Menard	200	153.067	6	6
8 (15)	Teo Fabi	ITA	Combustion Eng-Indeck R95 Ford-Cos	199	Running	5	31
9 18)	Danny Sullivan	USA	VISA-PacWest R95 Ford-Cos	199	Running	4	21
10 (10)	Hiro Matsushita	JPN	Panasonic-Duskin-YKK R95 Ford-Cos	199	Running	3	5
11 (17)	Alessandro Zampedri	ITA	The MI-JACK Car L94 Ford-Cos	198	Running	2	7
12 (13)	Roberto Guerrero	MEX	Upper Deck-General Comp'nts R94 MB	198	Running	1	1
Also							
17 (1)	Scott Brayton	USA	Quaker State-Glidden L95 Menard	190	Running	1	1
19 (8)	Scott Pruett	USA	Firestone-Patrick Racing L95 Ford-Cos	184	Contact	0	51

Time of Race: 3:15:17.561   Margin of Victory: 2.481 secs   Lap Leaders: Goodyear 1-9, Luyendyk 10-16, Andretti 17-32, Goodyear 33-35, Villeneuve 36-38, Andretti 39-66, Goodyear 67, Gugelmin 68-76, Andretti 77, Goodyear 78-81, Gugelmin 82-116, Goodyear 117-120, Rahal 121, Boesel 122-123, Gugelmin 124-138, Goodyear 139, Vasser 140-155, Villeneuve 156-162, Pruett 163-165, Gordon 166, Vasser 167-170, Pruett 171-175, Goodyear 176-195, Villeneuve 196-200

Miller Genuine Draft 200 (Race 7)

Milwaukee, Wisconsin   June 4

	Driver	Ctry	Car	Laps	Status	Pts	Total
1 (7)	**Paul Tracy**	CAN	**Kmart-Budweiser L95 Ford-Cos**	**200**	**137.304**	**20**	**52**
2 (3)	Al Unser Jr	USA	Marlboro Penske Mercedes P95 MB	200	137.281	17	51
3 (4)	Michael Andretti	USA	Kmart-Texaco Havoline L95 Ford-Cos	199	Running	14	43
4 (1)	Teo Fabi	ITA	Combustion Eng-Indeck R95 Ford-Cos	198	Running	13	44
5 (6)	Robby Gordon	USA	Valvoline Cummins Special R95 Ford-C	197	Running	10	53
6 (11)	Jacques Villeneuve	CAN	Players Ltd R95 Ford-Cos	197	Running	8	75
7 (13)	Christian Fittipaldi	BRA	Marlboro-Chapeco Special R95 Ford-C	196	Running	6	35
8 (18)	Gil de Ferran	BRA	Pennzoil Special R95 MB	195	Running	5	7
9 (14)	Jimmy Vasser	USA	Target-STP R94 Ford-Cos	195	Running	4	9
10 (9)	Adrian Fernandez	MEX	Tecate Beer-Quaker State L95 MB	195	Running	3	10
11 (8)	Raul Boesel	BRA	The Duracell Charger L95 MB	194	Running	2	26
12 (12)	Scott Pruett	USA	Patrick Racing L95 Ford-Cos	194	Running	1	52

Time of Race: 1:27:23.853 Margin of Victory: 0.846 sec Lap Leaders: Fabi 1-27, Unser 28-64, Tracy 65-75, Andretti 76, Unser 77-124, Tracy 125-143, Unser 144-178, Tracy 179-200.

ITT Automotive Detroit Grand Prix (Race 8)

Detroit, Michigan   June 11

	Driver	Ctry	Car	Laps	Status	Pts	Total
1 (1)	**Robby Gordon**	USA	**Valvoline-Cummins Spl R95 Ford-Cos**	**77**	**83.499**	**22**	**75**
2 (14)	Jimmy Vasser	USA	Target-STP R95 Ford-Cos	77	83.495	16	25
3 (5)	Scott Pruett	USA	Patrick Racing L95 Ford-Cos	77	83.489	14	66
4 (6)	Michael Andretti	USA	Kmart-Texaco Havoline L95 Ford-Cos	77	83.486	12	55
5 2)	Al Unser Jr	USA	Marlboro Penske Mercedes P95 MB	77	83.450	10	61
6 (7)	Adrian Fernandez	MEX	Tecate Beer-Quaker State L95 MB	77	83.412	8	18
7 (3)	Teo Fabi	ITA	Combustion Eng-Indeck R95 Ford-Cos	77	83.343	6	50
8 (4)	Paul Tracy	CAN	Kmart-Budweiser L95 Ford-Cos	77	83.340	5	57
9 (9)	Jacques Villeneuve	CAN	Players Ltd R95 Ford-Cos	77	83.015	4	79
10 17)	Emerson Fittipaldi	BRA	Marlboro Penske Mercedes P95 MB	77	83.006	3	38
11 (12)	Stefan Johansson	SWE	Team Alumax Penske 94 MB	77	83.005	2	24
12 (10)	Danny Sullivan	USA	VISA-PacWest R95 Ford-Cos	77	82.973	1	22

Time of Race: 1:56:11.607 Margin of Victory: 0.345 sec Lap Leaders: Gordon 1-8, Unser 9-40, Tracy 41-42, Gordon 43-77.

Budweiser/G I Joe's 200 (Race 9)

Portland, Oregon   *June 25*

	Driver	Ctry	Car	Laps	Status	Pts	Total
1 (2)	**Jimmy Vasser**	**USA**	**Target-STP R95 Ford-Cos**	**102**	**103.504**	**20**	**45**
2 (9)	Bobby Rahal	USA	Miller Genuine Draft L95 MB	102	103.486	16	68
3 (10)	Michael Andretti	USA	Kmart-Texaco Havoline L95 Ford-Cos	102	103.318	14	69
4 (11)	Raul Boesel	BRA	The Duracell Charger L95 MB	102	103.294	12	38
5 (12)	Stefan Johansson	SWE	Team Alumax Penske 94 MB	101	Fuel	10	34
6 (4)	Mauricio Gugelmin	BRA	Hollywood-PacWest R95 Ford-Cos	101	Running	8	55
7 (16)	Robby Gordon	USA	Valvoline-Cummins Spl R95 Ford-Cos	101	Running	6	81
8 (14)	Adrian Fernandez	MEX	Tecate Beer-Quaker State L95 MB	101	Running	5	23
9 (6)	Gil de Ferran	BRA	Pennzoil Special R95 MB	100	Running	4	11
10 (22)	Marco Greco	BRA	Brastemp Lola L95 Ford-Cos	100	Running	3	3
11 (5)	Christian Fittipaldi	BRA	Marlboro-Chapeco Special R95 Ford-Cos	100	Running	2	37
12 (17)	Scott Pruett	USA	Patrick Racing L95 Ford-Cos	99	Running	1	67
Also							
17 (7)	Paul Tracy	CAN	Kmart-Budweiser L95 Ford-Cos	95	Transmission	0	57
19 (1)	Jacques Villeneuve	CAN	Players Ltd R95 Ford-Cos	70	Suspension	2	81

Time of Race: 1:55:17.971   Margin of Victory: 1.257 secs   Lap Leaders: Villeneuve 1-50, Tracy 51-95, Vasser 96-102.

Texaco/Havoline 200 (Race 10)

Elkhart Lake, Wisconsin   *July 9*

	Driver	Ctry	Car	Laps	Status	Pts	Total
1 (1)	**Jacques Villeneuve**	**CAN**	**Players Ltd R95 Ford-Cos**	**50**	**103.901**	**22**	**103**
2 (11)	Paul Tracy	CAN	Kmart-Budweiser L95 Ford-Cos	50	103.887	16	73
3 (14)	Jimmy Vasser	USA	Target-STP R95 Ford-Cos	50	103.866	14	59
4 (12)	Andre Ribeiro	BRA	LCI Reynard R95 Honda	50	103.852	12	15
5 (6)	Bobby Rahal	USA	Miller Genuine Draft L95 MB	50	103.849	10	78
6 (15)	Adrian Fernandez	MEX	Tecate Beer-Quaker Street L95 MB	50	103.822	8	31
7 (7)	Scott Pruett	USA	Patrick Racing L95 Ford-Cos	50	103.815	6	73
8 (9)	Christian Fittipaldi	BRA	Marlboro-Chapeco Special R95 Ford-Cos	50	103.719	5	42
9 (8)	Teo Fabi	ITA	Combustion Eng-Indeck R95 Ford-Cos	50	103.701	4	54
10 (17)	Stefan Johansson	SWE	Team Alumax penske 94 MB	50	103.669	3	37
11 (25)	Eric Bachelart	BEL	The AGFA Car L94 Ford-Cos	50	103.585	2	8
12 (13)	Parker Johnstone	USA	Motorola Cellular Reynard R95 Honda	50	103.584	1	1
Also							
26 (16)	Robby Gordon	USA	Valvoline-Cummins Special R95 Ford-C	17	Transmission	0	81

Time of Race: 1:55:29.659   Margin of Victory: 0.965 sec   Lap Leaders: Villeneuve 1-29, de Ferran 30-33, Villeneuve 34-50.

Molson Indy Toronto (Race 11)

Toronto, Canada   *July 16*

	Driver	Ctry	Car	Laps	Status	Pts	Total
1 (6)	**Michael Andretti**	**USA**	**Kmart-Texaco Havoline L95 Ford-Cos**	**98**	**94.787**	**21**	**90**
2 (5)	Bobby Rahal	USA	Miller Genuine Draft L95 MB	98	94.781	16	94
3 (1)	Jacques Villeneuve	CAN	Players Ltd R95 Ford-Cos	98	94.320	15	118
4 (3)	Teo Fabi	ITA	Combustion Eng-Indeck R95 Ford-Cos	98	94.313	12	66
5 (7)	Robby Gordon	USA	Valvoline-Cummins Special R95 Ford-Cos	98	94.293	10	91
6 (16)	Raul Boesel	BRA	The Duracell Charger L95 MB	98	94.240	8	46
7 (15)	Adrian Fernandez	MEX	Tecate Beer-Quaker State L95 MB	98	94.181	6	37
8 (10)	Paul Tracy	CAN	Kmart-Budweiser L95 Ford-Cos	98	94.024	5	78
9 (12)	Christian Fittipaldi	BRA	Marlboro-Chapeco Special R95 Ford-Cos	98	93.981	4	46
10 (17)	Emerson Fittipaldi	BRA	Marlboro Penske Mercedes P95 MB	98	93.972	3	41
11 (20)	Eddie Cheever	USA	A J Foyt Copenhagen L95 Ford-Cos	97	Running	2	30
12 (14)	Mauricio Gugelmin	BRA	Hollywood-PacWest R95 Ford-Cos	96	Running	1	56

Time of Race: 1:50:25.202   Margin of Victory: 0.425 sec   Lap Leaders: Villeneuve 1-23, Andretti 24-62, Villeneuve 63, Andretti 64-98.

Medic Drug Grand Prix of Cleveland (Race 12)

Cleveland, Ohio   July 23

	Driver	Ctry	Car	Laps	Status	Pts	Total
1 (2)	**Jacques Villeneuve**	CAN	**Players Ltd R95 Ford-cos**	90	130.113	20	138
2 (3)	Bryan Herta	USA	Target-Scotch Video R95 Ford-Cos	90	130.087	16	20
3 (15)	Jimmy Vasser	USA	Target-STP R95 Ford-Cos	90	130.034	14	73
4 (11)	Boby Rahal	USA	Miller Genuine Draft L95 MB	90	Running	12	106
5 (14)	Danny Sullivan	USA	VISA-PacWest R95 Ford-Cos	90	Running	10	32
6 (8)	Robby Gordon	USA	Valvoline-Cummins Special R95 Ford-Cos	90	Running	8	99
7 (10)	Michael Andretti	USA	Kmart-Texaco Havoline L95 Ford-Cos	90	Running	6	96
8 (20)	Stefan Johansson	SWE	Team Alumax Penske 94 MB	89	Running	5	42
9 (24)	Alessandro Zampedri	ITA	The MI-JACK Car L94 Ford-Cos	89	Running	4	11
10 (27)	Eliseo Salazar	CHI	Cristal-Mobil 1-Copec L95 Ford-Cos	88	Running	3	19
11 (19)	Parker Johnstone	USA	Motorola Cellular Reynard R95 Honda	88	Running	2	3
12 (18)	Adrian Fernandez	MEX	Tecate Beer-Quaker State L95 MB	87	Engine	1	38
Also							
14 (1)	Gil de Ferran	BRA	Pennzoil Special R95 MB	85	Contact	2	13
26 (6)	Paul Tracy	CAN	Kmart-Budweiser L95 Ford-Cos	17	Handling	0	78

Time of Race: 1:38:19.151   margin of Victory: 1.157 secs   Lap Leaders: de Ferran 1-28, Villeneuve 29-31, Fabi 32, de Ferran 33-60, Fabi 61-66, de Ferran 67-77, Andretti 78-88, Villeneuve 89-90.

Marlboro 500 (Race 13)

Brooklyn, Michigan   July 30

	Driver	Ctry	Car	Laps	Status	Pts	Total
1 (12)	**Scott Pruett**	**USA**	**Firestone L95 Ford-Cos**	250	159.676	20	93
2 (13)	Al Unser Jr	USA	Marlboro Penske Mercedes P95 MB	250	159.675	16	77
3 (11)	Adrian Fernandez	MEX	Tecate Beer-Quaker State L95 MB	249	Running	14	52
4 (2)	Teo Fabi	ITA	Combustion Eng-Indeck R95 Ford-Cos	247	Running	12	78
5 (17)	Emerson Fittipaldi	BRA	Marlboro Penske Mercedes P95 MB	245	Running	10	51
6 (21)	Stefan Johansson	SWE	Team Alumax Penske 94 MB	244	Running	8	50
7 (5)	Jimmy Vasser	USA	Target-STP R95 Ford-Cos	241	Running	6	79
8 (16)	Bobby Rahal	USA	Miller Genuine Draft L95 MB	240	Running	5	111
9 (25)	Christian Fittipaldi	BRA	Marlboro-Chapeco Spl R95 Ford-Cos	239	Running	4	50
10 (4)	Jacques Villeneuve	CAN	Players Ltd R95 Ford-Cos	235	Running	4	141
11 (6)	Mauricio Gugelmin	BRA	Hollywood-PacWest R95 Ford-Cos	232	Running	2	58
12 (15)	Gil de Ferran	BRA	Pennzoil Special R95 MB	226	Debris	1	14
Also							
22 (1)	Parker Johnstone	USA	Motorola Cellular Reynard R95 Honda	100	Brakes	1	4
23 (8)	Paul Tracy	CAN	Kmart-Budweiser L95 Ford-Cos	91	Engine	0	78

Time of Race: 3:07:52.826   Margin of Victory: 0.056 sec . Lap Leaders: Johnstone 1-45, Ribeiro 46, Tracy 47, Fabi 48, Cheever 49-50, Johnstone 51-57, Ribeiro 58-88, Pruett 89-90, Gugelmin 91-92, Ribeiro 93-128, Pruett 129-131, Unser 132-152, Pruett 153-154, Unser 155-176, Pruett 177-188, Unser 189, Pruett 190-207, Unser 208-229, Pruett 230-250.

Miller Genuine Draft 200 (Race 14)

Lexington, Ohio   Aug 13

	Driver	Ctry	Car	Laps	Status	Pts	Total
1 (8)	**Al Unser Jr**	**USA**	**Marlboro Penske Mercedes P95 MB**	83	107.110	20	97
2 (7)	Paul Tracy	CAN	Kmart-Budweiser L95 Ford-Cos	83	107.075	16	94
3 (1)	Jacques Villeneuve	CAN	Players Ltd R95 Ford-Cos	83	106.947	15	156
4 (11)	Adrian Fernandez	MEX	Tecate Beer-Quaker State L95 MB	83	106.926	12	64
5 (2)	Bryan Herta	USA	Target-Scotch Video R95 Ford-Cos	83	106.873	10	30
6 (4)	Mauricio Gugelmin	BRA	Hollywood-PacWest R95 Ford-Cos	83	106.858	8	66
7 (14)	Juan Manuel Fangio II	ARG	VISA-PacWest R95 Ford-Cos	83	106.663	6	6
8 (5)	Robby Gordon	USA	Valvoline-Cummins Special R95 Ford-Cos	83	106.637	5	104
9 (10)	Jimmy Vasser	USA	Target-STP R95 Ford-Cos	83	106.407	4	83
10 (23)	Eddie Cheever	USA	A J Foyt Copenhagen L95 Ford-Cos	83	106.065	3	33
11 (21)	Scott Pruett	USA	Firestone L95 Ford-Cos	82	Running	2	95
12 (19)	Scott Goodyear	CAN	LCI-CNN-Motorola R95 Honda	82	Running	1	1
Also							
19 (3)	Michael Andretti	USA	Kmart-Texaco Havoline L95 Ford-Cos	79	Engine	1	97
26 (9)	Bobby Rahal	USA	Miller Genuine Draft L95 MB	38	Contact	0	111

Time of Race: 1:44:04.774   Lap Leaders: Villeneuve 1-29, de Ferran 30-31, Andretti 32-59, Villeneuve 60, Tracy 61-62, Unser 63-69, Andretti 70-79, Unser 80-83.

New England 200 (Race 15)

Loudon, New Hampshire   Aug 20

	Driver	Ctry	Car	Laps	Status	Pts	Total
1 (1)	**Andre Ribeiro**	**BRA**	**LCI Reynard R95 Honda**	**200**	**134.203**	**22**	**38**
2 (9)	Michael Andretti	USA	Kmart-Texaco Havoline L95 Ford-Cos	200	133.861	16	113
3 (17)	Al Unser Jr	USA	Marlboro Penske Mercedes P95 MB	199	Running	14	111
4 (15)	Jacques Villeneuve	CAN	Players Ltd R95 Ford-Cos	199	Running	12	168
5 (16)	Emerson Fittipaldi	BRA	Marlboro Penske Mercedes P95 MB	199	Running	10	61
6 (6)	Jimmy Vasser	USA	Target-STP R95 Ford-Cos	198	Running	8	91
7 (8)	Gil de Ferran	BRA	Pennzoil Special R95 MB	198	Running	6	20
8 (5)	Christian Fittipaldi	BRA	Marlboro-Chapeco Special R95 Ford-Cos	198	Running	5	55
9 (4)	Robby Gordon	USA	Valvoline-Cummins Spl R95 Ford-Cos	197	Running	4	108
10 (20)	Bobby Rahal	USA	Miller Genuine Draft L95 MB	197	Running	3	114
11 (7)	Mauricio Gugelmin	BRA	Hollywood-PacWest R95 Ford-Cos	196	Running	2	68
12 (2)	Teo Fabi	ITA	Combustion Eng-Indeck R95 Ford-Cos	196	Running	1	79
Also							
23 (14)	Paul Tracy	CAN	Kmart-Budweiser L95 Ford-Cos	101	Oil Leak	0	94
24 (3)	Scott Pruett	USA	Firestone-Patrick L95 Ford-Cos	40	Contact	0	95

Time of Race: 1:34:36.192   Margin of Victory: 14.482secs.   Lap Leaders: Fabi 1-42, Andretti 43-99, Ribeiro 100-122, Andretti 123-127, Ribeiro 128-200.

Molson Indy Vancouver (Race 16)

Vancouver   Sep 3

	Driver	Ctry	Car	Laps	Status	Pts	Total
1 (9)	Al Unser Jr	USA	Marlboro Penske Mercedes P95 MB	100	95.571	21	153
2 (8)	Gil de Ferran	BRA	Pennzoil Special R95 MB	100	95.348	16	35
3 (7)	Robby Gordon	USA	Valvoline-Cummins Spl R95 Ford-Cos	100	95.184	14	121
4 (17)	Stefan Johansson	SWE	Team Alumax Penske 94 MB	100	95.178	12	60
5 (3)	Bobby Rahal	USA	Miller Genuine Draft L95 MB	100	95.176	10	122
6 (10)	Scott Pruett	USA	Firestone-Patrick L95 Ford-Cos	100	95.134	8	102
7 (14)	Emerson Fittipaldi	BRA	Marlboro Penske Mercedes P95 MB	100	94.806	6	67
8 (12)	Paul Tracy	CAN	Kmart-Budweiser L95 Ford-Cos	99	Running	5	99
9 (18)	Alessandro Zampredi	ITA	The MI-JACK Car L94 Ford-Cos	99	Running	4	15
10 (20)	Raul Boesel	BRA	The Duracell Charger L95 MB	99	Running	3	47
11 (22)	Parker Johnstone	USA	Motorola Cellular Reynard R95 Honda	99	Running	2	6
12 (1)	Jacques Villeneuve	CAN	Players Ltd R95 Ford-Cos	98	Running	2	169
Also							
21 (5)	Michael Andretti	USA	Kmart-Texaco Havoline LT95 Ford-Cos	63	Transmission	-	111

Time of race: 1:46:54.900   Margin of victory: 15.013 sec   Lap leaders: Villeneuve 1-26, Andretti 27-60, Al Unser Jr 61-100

Toyota GP of Monterey (Race 17)

Laguna Seca   Sep 10

	Driver	Ctry	Car	Laps	Status	Pts	Total
1 (3)	Gil de Ferran	BRA	Pennzoil Special R95 MB	84	98.493	21	56
2 (8)	Paul Tracy	CAN	Kmart-Budweiser L95 Ford-Cos	84	98.378	16	115
3 (6)	Mauricio Gugelmin	BRA	Hollywood-PacWest R951 Ford Cos	84	98.372	14	80
4 (12)	Michael Andretti	USA	Kmart-Texaco Havoline LT95 Ford-Cos	84	98.362	12	123
5 (5)	Scott Pruett	USA	Firestone-Patrick L95 Ford-Cos	84	98.166	10	112
6 (14)	Al Unser Jr	USA	Marlboro Penske Mercedes P95 MB	84	98.147	8	161
7 (11)	Bobby Rahal	USA	Miller Genuine Draft L95 MB	84	98.140	6	128
8 (7)	Jimmy Vasser	USA	Target-STP R95 Ford-Cos	84	98.116	5	92
9 (4)	Teo Fabi	ITA	Firestone-Patrick L95 Ford-Cos	84	98.106	4	83
10 (15)	Adrian Fernandez	MEX	Tecate Beer-Quaker State L95 MB	84	97.544	3	66
11 (1)	Jacques Villeneuve	CAN	Players Ltd R95 Ford-Cos	83	Running	3	172
12 (13)	Raul Boesel	BRA	The Duracell Charger L95 MB	83	Running	1	48
Also							
15 (16)	Robby Gordon	USA	Valvoline-Cummins Spl R95 Ford-Cos	83	Running	-	121

Time of race: 1:53:17.579   Margin of victory: 7.959 sec   Lap leaders: Villeneuve 1-28, de Ferran 29-54, Gugelmin 55-56, de Ferran 57-84

INDYCAR FINAL STANDINGS

Villeneuve 172, Unser Jr 161, Rahal 128, Andretti 123, Gordon 121, Tracy 115, Pruett 112, Vasser 92, Fabi 83

Formula 1 World Champions

Year	Winning Driver	Car	Runner up	Winning Constructor
1950	Giuseppe Farina ITA	Alfa Romeo	Juan Manuel Fangio ARG	-
1951	Juan Manuel Fangio ARG	Alfa Romeo	Alberto Ascari ITA	-
1952	Alberto Ascari ITA	Ferrari	Giuseppe Farina ITA	-
1953	Alberto Ascari ITA	Ferrari	Juan Manuel Fangio ARG	-
1954	Juan Manuel Fangio ARG	Maserati/Mercedes	Jose Gonzalez ARG	-
1955	Juan Manuel Fangio ARG	Mercedes-Benz	Stirling Moss GBR	-
1956	Juan Manuel Fangio ARG	Lancia-Ferrari	Stirling Moss GBR	-
1957	Juan Manuel Fangio ARG	Maserati	Stirling Moss GBR	-
1958	Mike Hawthorn GBR	Ferrari	Stirling Moss GBR	Vanwall
1959	Jack Brabham AUS	Cooper-Climax	Tony Brooks GBR	Cooper-Climax
1960	Jack Brabham AUS	Cooper-Climax	Bruce McLaren NZL	Cooper-Climax
1961	Phil Hill USA	Ferrari	Wolfgang von Trips FRG	Ferrari
1962	Graham Hill GBR	BRM	Jim Clark GBR	BRM
1963	Jim Clark GBR	Lotus-Climax	Graham Hill GBR	Lotus-Climax
1964	John Surtees GBR	Ferrari	Graham Hill GBR	Ferrari
1965	Jim Clark GBR	Lotus-Climax	Graham Hill GBR	Lotus-Climax
1966	Jack Brabham AUS	Brabham-Repco	John Surtees GBR	Brabham-Repco
1967	Denny Hulme NZL	Brabham-Repco	Jack Brabham AUS	Brabham-Repco
1968	Graham Hill GBR	Lotus-Ford	Jackie Stewart GBR	Lotus-Ford
1969	Jackie Stewart GBR	Matra-Ford	Jacky Ickx BEL	Matra-Ford
1970	Jochen Rindt AUT	Lotus-Ford	Jacky Ickx BEL	Lotus-Ford
1971	Jackie Stewart GBR	Tyrrell-Ford	Ronnie Peterson SWE	Tyrrell-Ford
1972	Emerson Fittipaldi BRA	Lotus-Ford	Jackie Stewart GBR	Lotus-Ford
1973	Jackie Stewart GBR	Tyrrell-Ford	Emerson Fittipaldi BRA	Lotus-Ford
1974	Emerson Fittipaldi BRA	McLaren-Ford	Clay Regazzoni SUI	McLaren-Ford
1975	Niki Lauda AUT	Ferrari	Emerson Fittipaldi BRA	Ferrari
1976	James Hunt GBR	McLaren-Ford	Niki Lauda AUT	Ferrari
1977	Niki Lauda AUT	Ferrari	Jody Scheckter RSA	Ferrari
1978	Mario Andretti USA	Lotus-Ford	Ronnic Peterson SWE	Lotus-Ford
1979	Jody Scheckter RSA	Ferrari	Gilles Villeneuve CAN	Ferrari
1980	Alan Jones AUS	Williams-Ford	Nelson Piquet BRA	Williams-Ford
1981	Nelson Piquet BRA	Brabham-Ford	Carlos Reutemann ARG	Williams-Ford
1982	Keke Rosberg FIN	Williams-Ford	Pironi FRA and Watson GBR	Ferrari
1983	Nelson Piquet BRA	Brabham-BMW	Alain Prost FRA	Ferrari
1984	Niki Lauda AUT	McLaren-TAG	Alain Prost FRA	McLaren-TAG
1985	Alain Prost FRA	McLaren-TAG	Michele Alboreto ITA	McLaren-TAG
1986	Alain Prost FRA	McLaren-TAG	Nigel Mansell GBR	Williams-Honda
1987	Nelson Piquet BRA	Williams-Honda	Nigel Mansell GBR	Williams-Honda
1988	Ayrton Senna BRA	McLaren-Honda	Alain Prost FRA	McLaren-Honda
1989	Alain Prost FRA	McLaren-Honda	Ayrton Senna BRA	McLaren-Honda
1990	Ayrton Senna BRA	McLaren-Honda	Alain Prost FRA	McLaren-Honda
1991	Ayrton Senna BRA	McLaren-Honda	Nigel Mansell GBR	McLaren-Honda
1992	Nigel Mansell GBR	Williams-Renault	Ricardo Patrese ITA	Williams-Renault
1993	Alain Prost FRA	Williams-Renault	Ayrton Senna BRA	Williams-Renault
1994	Michael Schumacher GER	Benetton-Ford	Damon Hill GBR	Williams-Renault

Indianapolis 500 & Le Mans Winners

INDIANAPOLIS 500 (USA unless stated)		LE MANS	
Year Winner	Manufacturer	Year Drivers	Car
1950 Johnny Parsons	Kurtis Kraft-Offenhauser	1949 Chinetti ITA/Selsdon GBR	Ferrari
		1950 Rosier/Rosier FRA	Talbot-Lago
1951 Lee Wallard	Kurtis Kraft-Offenhauser	1951 Walker/Whitehead GBR	Jaguar
		1952 Lang/Riess FRG	Mercedes-Benz
1952 Troy Ruttmann	Kuzna-Offenhauser	1953 Rolt/Hamilton GBR	Jaguar
1953 Bill Vukovich	Kurtis Kraft 500A-Offenhauser	1954 Gonzalez ARG/Trintignant FRA	Ferrari
		1955 Hawthorn/Bueb GBR	Jaguar
1954 Bill Vukovich	Kurtis Kraft 500A-Offenhauser	1956 Flockhart/Sanderson GBR	Jaguar
		1957 Flockhart/Bueb GBR	Jaguar
1955 Bob Sweikert	Kurtis Kraft 500C-Offenhauser	1958 Gendebien BEL/Hill USA	Ferrari
		1959 Shelby/Salvadori GBR	Aston Martin
1956 Pat Flaherty	Watson-Offenhauser	1960 Gendebien/Frere BEL	Ferrari
1957 Sam Hanks	Epperly-Offenhauser	1961 Gendebien BEL/Hill USA	Ferrari
1958 Jimmy Bryan	Epperly-Offenhauser	1962 Gendebien/Hill	Ferrari
1959 Rodger Ward	Watson-Offenhauser	1963 Scarfiotti/Bandini ITA	Ferrari
1960 Jim Rathmann	Watson-Offenhauser	1964 Guichet FRA/Vaccarella ITA	Ferrari
1961 AJ Foyt	Watson-Offenhauser	1965 Rindt AUT/Gregory USA	Ferrari
1962 Rodger Ward	Watson-Offenhauser	1966 Amon/McLaren NZL	Ford
1963 Parnelli Jones	Watson-Offenhauser	1967 Gurney/Foyt USA	Ford
1964 AJ Foyt	Watson-Offenhauser	1968 Rodriguez MEX/Bianchi BEL	Ford
1965 Jim Clark GBR	Lotus-Ford	1969 Ickx BEL/Oliver GBR	Ford
1966 Graham Hill GBR	Lola-Ford	1970 Herrmann FRG/Attwood GBR	Porsche
1967 AJ Foyt	Coyote-Ford	1971 Marko AUT/van Lennep HOL	Porsche
1968 Bobby Unser	Eagle-Offenhauser	1972 Pescarolo FRA/Hill GBR	Matra-Simca
1969 Mario Andretti	Hawk-Ford	1973 Pescarolo/Larrousse FRA	Matra-Simca
1970 Al Unser	PJ Colt-Ford	1974 Pescarolo/Larrousse FRA	Matra-Simca
1971 Al Unser	PJ Colt-Ford	1975 Ickx BEL/Bell GBR	Mirage-Ford
1972 Mark Donohue	McLaren-Offenhauser	1976 Ickx BEL/van Lennep HOL	Porsche
		1977 Ickx BEL/Barth FRG/ Haywood USA	Porsche
1973 Gordon Johncock	Eagle-Offenhauser		
1974 Johnny Rutherford	McLaren-Offenhauser	1978 Jaussaud/Pironi FRA	Renault Alpine
		1979 Ludwig FRG/Whittington USA /Whittington USA	Porsche
1975 Bobby Unser	Eagle-Offenhauser		
1976 Johnny Rutherford	McLaren-Offenhauser	1980 Jaussaud/Rondeau FRA	Rondeau-Ford
		1981 Ickx BEL/Bell GBR	Porsche
1977 AJ Foyt	Coyote-Ford	1982 Ickx/Bell	Porsche
1978 Al Unser	Lola-Cosworth	1983 Schuppan AUT/Haywood USA /Holbert USA	Porsche
1979 Rick Mears	Penske-Cosworth		
1980 Johnny Rutherford	Chaparral-Cosworth	1984 Ludwig FRG/Pescarolo FRA	Porsche
1981 Bobby Unser	Penske-Cosworth	1985 Ludwig/Winter FRG/ Barillo ITA	Porsche
1982 Gordon Johncock	Wildcat-Cosworth		
1983 Tom Sneva	March-Cosworth	1986 Stuck FRG/Bell GBR/ Holbert USA	Porsche
1984 Rick Mears	March-Cosworth		
1985 Danny Sullivan	March-Cosworth	1987 Stuck/Bell/Holbert	Porsche
1986 Bobby Rahal	March-Cosworth	1988 Lammers HOL/Dumfries GBR Wallace GBR	Jaguar
1987 Al Unser	March-Cosworth		
1988 Rick Mears	Penske-Chevrolet	1989 Mass/Reuter FRG/ Dickens SWE	Mercedes
1989 Emerson Fittipaldi BRA	Penske-Chevrolet		
1990 Arie Luyendyk HOL	Lola-Chevrolet	1990 Nielsen DEN/Brundle GBR/ Cobb USA	Jaguar
1991 Rick Mears	Penske-Chevrolet		
1992 Al Unser Jr	Penske-Chevrolet	1991 Herbert GBR/Gachot BEL/ Wendler GER	Mazda
1993 Emerson Fittipaldi BRA	Penske-Chevrolet		
1994 Al Unser Jr	Penske-Mercedes	1992 Warwick/Blundell GBR/ Dalmas FRA	Peugeot
1995 Jacques Villeneuve	Players Ford Cos		
		1993 Bouchut/Helary FRA	Peugeot
		1994 Dalmas FRA/Haywood USA/ Baldi ITA	Porsche
		1995 Dalmas FRA/Lehto FIN	McLaren

Netball ▬▬▬▬▬▬▬▬▬▬▬▬▬▬▬▬▬▬▬▬▬▬

You can tell netball is still an amateur game; they only have a world championship every four years. This year was the year and Birmingham the venue. As a tournament, it had much going for it with the return to the international fold of both Trinidad and South Africa, the latter after an absence of 28 years. Unfortunately, it also had a competition constructed on the most arcane lines, so that the idle spectator would have been completely bemused.

Australia won, let's get that over to start with. It was hardly a surprise, they have only twice in the tournament's 32-year history not won the title. In the ultimate team game, they are the ultimate team. In their first match, against St Vincent, they arrived on court with every players' hair in a regulation pony tail. One for all and all for one. If that didn't win the psychological battle, their warm-up surely did. A display of such precise power-passing that you wondered if the opposition would bother to stay. They always did, but only twice in the tournament did Australia take much notice.

New Zealand should have met them in the final. It was almost the natural order of things, but the New Zealanders rather took it for granted. They came up against South Africa on only the fifth day of the two-week tournament in a match that would virtually decide who would face the reigning champions in the final. New Zealand play the team game in much the same way as Australia, except what they lack in power, they make up for in pace. South Africa, on the other hand, channel everything towards their shooter, Irene Van Dyk.

Van Dyk did not get her hands dirty on court. She kept so close to the net and was almost as tall (6ft 4in) that it was sometimes difficult to tell them apart. But she could jump and she could shoot, with unfailing accuracy. New Zealand failed to stem the flow of passes (or to outjump her) and paid the penalty, defeated 59-57 and left with the task of beating Australia to have any chance of the title. That match proved the best in the tournament, with New Zealand losing out by a single point 45-44. In the final against South Africa, Australia gave a tactical lesson to their Kiwi neighbours. They cut out the passes to Van Dyck and sauntered home 68-48.

There was a postscript for the South Africans, an all-white team in Birmingham. In August, four black players were drafted into the squad and most of the team from Birmingham, including the captain, Debbie Hammon, stepped down in protest at the 'affirmative' action.

England did as expected; fourth for the fourth succesive year. They couldn't live with South Africa or New Zealand, though the tactical decision not to start the South African match with the inspriational Kendra Slewinski on court hardly helped. They did enjoy a comprehensive win over Trinidad, however, and that gave them their best moment in the tournament. A day earlier, Trinidad had faced South Africa in what was the most physical encounter of the tournament. Trinidad lost 58-49 and against a certain amount of criticism the coach Genita Lewis justified their tactics. "Netball is a physical game. You don't play it in your bedroom," she said.

Scotland had a fine opportunity to reach the top half of the seedings, but lost a crucial game against Canada and it was Wales who finished second best of the Home Nations.

World Championship

The 27 teams were divided into 8 sections. The first 2 teams in each section qualified for Group Y or Z in the 2nd phase. The bottom 2 teams were placed in Groups W or X. For the final phase, the corresponding teams in Groups Y & Z played off for the top 14 rankings - Groups W and X for the bottom 13. They tell me it wasn't meant to be simple.

SECTION A

P New Guinea 58 Sri Lanka 45
Australia 90 St Vincent 23
Australia 84 Papua New Guinea 26
St Vincent 73 Sri Lanka 48
St Vincent 64 Papua N Guinea 58
Australia 82 Sri Lanka 19

	P	W	D	L	GF	GA	Pt
Australia	3	3	0	0	256	68	6
St Vincent	3	2	0	1	160	196	4
Papua NG	3	1	0	2	142	193	2
Sri Lanka	3	0	0	3	112	213	0

SECTION B

New Zealand 87 Namibia 22
Sout Africa 110 Cayman Islds 22
New Zealand 114 Cayman Islds 15
South Africa 71 Namibia 28
South Africa 59 New Zealand 57
Namibia 61 Cayman Islds 38

	P	W	D	L	GF	GA	Pt
S Africa	3	3	0	0	240	107	6
N Zealand	3	2	0	1	258	96	4
Namibia	3	1	0	2	111	196	2
Cayman I	3	0	0	3	75	285	0

SECTION C

Malawi 56 Hong Kong 39
Jamaica 80 Hong Kong 29
Jamaica 70 Malawi 52

	P	W	D	L	GF	GA	Pt
Jamaica	2	2	0	0	150	81	4
Malawi	2	1	0	1	108	109	2
Hong Kong	2	0	0	2	68	136	0

SECTION D

England 61 Barbados 29
Barbados 73 Singapore 31
England 56 N Ireland 27
England 95 Singapore 21
N Ireland 60 Singapore 45
Barbados 64 N Ireland 34

	P	W	D	L	GF	GA	Pt
England	3	3	0	0	212	77	6
Barbados	3	2	0	1	166	126	4
N Ireland	3	1	0	2	121	165	2
Singapore	3	0	0	3	97	228	0

SECTION E

United States 49 Malaysia 42
Cook Islands 95 Ireland 29
United States 51 Ireland 30
Cook Islands 96 Malaysia 32

Malaysia 36 Ireland 36
Cook Islands 83 United States 33

	P	W	D	L	GF	GA	Pt
Cook I	3	3	0	0	274	94	6
USA	3	2	0	1	133	155	4
Malaysia	3	1	0	2	110	181	2
Ireland	3	0	0	3	95	182	0

SECTION F

Trinidad & Tobago 72 Scotland 37
Canada 54 Scotland 43
Trinidad & Tobago 94 Malta 21
Canada 91 Malta 24
Scotland 75 Malta 44
Trinidad & Tobago 68 Canada 41

	P	W	D	L	GF	GA	Pt
Trinidad	3	3	0	0	234	99	6
Canada	3	2	0	1	186	135	4
Scotland	3	1	0	2	155	170	2
Malta	3	0	0	3	89	260	0

SECTION G

Wales 63 Bermuda 33
Auntigua 75 Bermuda 37
Western Samoa 69 Wales 33
Western Samoa 85 Bermuda 30
Antigua 55 Wales 48
Western Samoa 76 Antigua 56

	P	W	D	L	GF	GA	Pt
W Samoa	3	3	0	0	230	119	6
Antigua	3	2	0	1	186	161	4
Wales	3	1	0	2	144	157	2
Bermuda	3	0	0	3	100	223	0

....

GROUP W

Bermuda 50 Ireland 43
Scotland 46 Ireland 40
Sri Lanka 61 Bermuda 55
Scotland 63 Bermuda 45
N Ireland 66 Ireland 49
Namaibia 59 N Ireland 49
Sri Lanka 49 Scotland 45
N Ireland 59 Bermuda 48
Sri Lanka 59 Ireland 38
Namibia 49 Scotland 40
N Ireland 60 Scotland 37
Namibia 65 Bermuda 25
N Ireland 64 Sri Lanka 44
Namibia 52 Ireland 50
Sri Lanka 38 Namibia 48

	P	W	D	L	GF	GA	Pt
Namibia	5	5	0	0	273	202	10
N Ireland	5	4	0	1	298	237	8
Sri Lanka	5	3	0	2	251	250	6
Scotland	5	2	0	3	231	243	4
Bermuda	5	1	0	4	223	291	2
Ireland	5	0	0	5	220	273	0

GROUP X

Singapore 63 Cayman Islands 43
Malaysia 56 Singapore 54
Papua N Guinea 71 Malta 46

Wales 65 Singapore 28
Papua N Guinea 61 Malaysia 34
Hong Kong 61 Malta 28
Papua N Guinea 66 Singapore 42
Cayman Islands 63 Malta 53
Wales 47 Malaysia 36
Wales 63 Cayman Islands 42
Singapore 86 Malta 40
Hong Kong 50 Malaysia 40
Wales 48 Hong Kong 39
Cayman Islands 51 Malaysia 49
Papua N Guinea 75 Cayman 36
Papua N Guinea 59 Hong Kong 41
Cayman I 42 Hong Kong 41
Singapore 51 Hong Kong 47
Malaysia 54 Malta 42
Papua N Guinea 60 Wales 54
Wales 74 Malta 26

	P	W	D	L	GF	GA	Pt
PN Guinea	6	6	0	0	392	253	12
Wales	6	5	0	1	351	231	10
Singapore	6	3	0	3	324	317	6
Cayman I	6	3	0	3	277	344	6
Hong Kong	6	2	0	4	279	268	4
Malaysia	6	2	0	4	269	305	4
Malta	6	0	0	6	235	409	0

GROUP Y

South Africa 77 England 54
England 82 St Vincent 51
South Africa 76 United States 30
Trinidad 59 Malawi 42
England 71 Antigua 38
St Vincent 71 United States 59
South Africa 58 Trinidad 49
Antigua 63 United States 59
England 68 Malawi 45
England 60 Trinidad 35
Malawi 60 United States 50
South Africa 75 Antigua 45
Malawi 71 Antigua 50
Trinidad 75 St Vincent 46
South Africa 69 St Vincent 60
Malawi 65 St Vincent 58
South Africa 77 Malawi 53
England 85 United States 23
Trinidad 63 United States 25St
Vincent 78 Antigua 54
Trinidad 84 Antigua 36

	P	W	D	L	GF	GA	Pt
S Africa	6	6	0	0	432	291	12
England	6	5	0	1	420	269	10
Trinidad	6	4	0	2	365	267	8
Malawi	6	3	0	3	336	362	6
St Vincent	6	2	0	4	364	404	4
Antigua	6	1	0	5	286	438	2
USA	6	0	0	6	246	418	0

GROUP Z

Australia 60 Jamaica 51
N Zealand 77 Barbados 44
Jamaica 84 Canada 39

Australia 79 Cook Islands 45
Western Samoa 58 Barbados 52
Australia 69 Barbados 33
Cook Islands 74 W Samoa 67
N Zealand 78 Canada 37
N Zealand 76 Western Samoa 45
Australia 82 Canada 27
Jamaica 74 Cook Islands 61
N Zealand 81 Cook Islands 49
Barbados 51 Canada 40
Jamaica 81 Western Samoa 41
Australia 45 New Zealand 44
New Zealand 70 Jamaica 52
Jamaica 71 Barbados 46
Cook Islands 58 Barbados 41
Cook Islands 83 Canada 61
Western Samoa 60 Canada 47

	P	W	D	L	GF	GA	Pt
Australia	6	6	0	0	410	232	12
N Zealand	6	5	0	1	426	272	10
Jamaica	6	4	0	2	413	317	8
Cook I	6	3	0	3	370	413	6
W Samoa	6	2	0	4	303	405	4
Barbados	6	1	0	5	267	373	2
Canada	6	0	0	6	251	438	0

FINAL PLAY-OFFS
27th place Malta
25th/26th Ireland 48 Malaysia 39
23rd/24th H Kong 52 Bermuda 42
21st/22nd Cayman 48 Scotland 47
19th/20th S Lanka 63 Singapore 53
17th/18th Wales 59 N Ireland 50
15th/16th PNGuinea 69 Namibia 45
13th/14th Canada 62 USA 42
11th/12th Barbados 64 Antigua 45

9th/10th W Samoa 63 St Vincent 58
7th/8th Cook I 85 Malawi 60
5th/6th Jamaica 64 Trinidad 40
3rd/4th N Zealand 60 England 31
1st/2nd Australia 68 S Africa 48

FINAL POSITIONS
1. Australia, 2. S Africa, 3. New Zealand, 4. England, 5. Jamaica, 6. Trinidad, 7. Cook I, 8. Malawi, 9. W Samoa, 10. St Vincent, 11. Barbados, 12. Antigua, 13. Canada, 14. USA, 15. PN Guinea,16. Namibia, 17. Wales, 18. N Ireland, 19. Sri Lanka, 20. Singapoer, 21. Cayman I, 22. Scotland, 23. Hong Kong, 24. Bermuda, 25. Ireland, 26. Malaysia, 27. Malta

---

National League

DIVISION 1

	P	W	D	L	GF	GA	Ave	Pts
New Campbell	7	7	0	0	400	310	1.29	35
Linden	7	6	0	1	405	322	1.25	31
Hertford Hornets	7	5	0	2	369	356	1.03	28
Aquila	7	4	0	3	340	365	0.93	23
Hirondelles	7	3	0	4	412	386	1.06	22
Harborne	7	2	0	5	361	381	0.94	17
Vauxhall Gold	7	1	0	6	264	384	0.68	10
Tongham	7	0	0	7	343	390	0.87	9

DIVISION 2

	P	W	D	L	GF	GA	Ave	Pts
Wyvern	7	6	0	1	353	283	1.24	31
Kelmscott	7	5	0	2	327	268	1.22	27
OPA	7	4	1	2	328	311	1.05	26
Helsby	7	4	0	3	362	351	1.03	24
Weston Park	7	4	0	3	286	304	0.94	21
Academy	7	3	1	3	292	319	0.91	21
Toucans	7	2	0	5	308	353	0.87	16
Henley	7	0	0	7	304	371	0.81	10

DIVISION 3

	P	W	D	L	GF	GA	Ave	Pts
Oakwood	7	6	0	1	355	289	1.22	32
Hucclecote	7	5	1	1	400	297	1.34	29
Wirral	7	5	1	1	252	255	1.12	29
Leeds Athletic	7	4	1	2	242	267	0.90	25
Essex Wanderers	7	3	0	4	286	300	0.95	18
YWCA	7	2	0	5	357	357	1.00	17
Chevrons	7	1	1	5	309	371	0.83	13
Hornsey	7	0	0	7	212	307	0.69	5

DIVISION 4

	P	W	D	L	GF	GA	Ave	Pts
GPT	7	7	0	0	307	236	1.30	35
Oaksway	7	5	0	2	383	279	1.37	28
Ipswich Ladies	7	5	0	2	291	253	1.15	27
The Downs	7	4	0	3	292	282	1.03	24
Watford Premier	7	2	1	4	282	314	0.89	18
Dudley Leisure	7	2	0	5	282	359	0.78	17
Chester	7	1	1	5	272	311	0.87	15
Kelly	7	1	0	6	294	369	0.79	12

English Counties League

1ST SENIOR

	P	W	D	L	GF	GA	Ave	Pts
Essex Met	7	7	0	0	409	285	1.435	35
Surrey	7	4	2	1	422	339	1.245	27
Middlesex	7	4	1	2	349	319	1.094	26
Bedfordshire*	6	4	0	2	266	252	1.056	22
East Essex	7	3	0	4	320	408	0.784	18
Birmingham*	6	2	1	3	287	301	0.953	17
Derbyshire	7	1	0	6	307	359	0.855	12
Cheshire	7	0	0	7	288	385	0.748	7

NATIONAL CLUBS CUP
Semi-finals
Wallsend 49   Kent County NC 57
Bristol United 40   Astrosyn Arupians 57
Final
Kent County 42   Astrosyn Arupians 49

SOMERSET PLATE COMPETITION
Winners Falcons

World Champions

1963	**Australia**
1967	**Australia**
1971	**New Zealand**
1975	**Australia**
1979*	**Australia**
	New Zealand
	Trinidad
1983	**Australia**
1987	**New Zealand**
1991	**Australia**
1995	**Australia**

Title shared

Orienteering

World Championships
Lippe   Aug 12-20

Men's Classic
16.22 km   670m drop   30 controls
1 **Jorgen Mårtensson SWE**   **1:30:19**
2 Janne Salmi FIN   1:32:04
3 Carsten Jorgensen DEN   1:33:38
4 Timo Karppinen FIN   1:33:39
5 Tomás Prokes CZE   1:33:51
31 Steven Hale GBR   1:40:29
36 Stephen Palmer GBR   1:41:13
42 Andy Kitchin GBR   1:43:26
47 David Peel GBR   1:46:35

Women's Classic
9.66 km   445m drop   21 controls
1 **Katalin Oláh HUN**   **1:05:50**
2 Yvette Hague GBR   1:08:39
2 Eija Koskivaara FIN   1:08:39
4 Marlena Jansson SWE   1:08:44
5 Vroni König SUI   1:09:22
39 Heather Monro GBR   1:20:59

Men's Short Race
5.62 km   210m drop   18 Controls
1 **Yuri Omeitchenko UKR**   **30:25**
2 Jorgen Mårtensson SWE   31:31
3 Bjornar Valstad NOR   31:36
18 Steven Hale GBR   33:36
24 Jonathan Musgrave GBR   34:03
28 Stephen Palmer GBR   34:32
39 David Peel GBR   35:51

Women's Short Race
4.55 km   180m drop   14 Controls
1 **Marie-Luce Romanens SUI**   **28:55**
2 Yvette Hague GBR   29:16
3 Marlena Jansson SWE   29:29

Men's Relay
1 **Switzerland**   **3:34:21**
2 Finland   3:35:43
3 Sweden   3:35:51
6 Great Britain   3:43:33
(Musgrave/Kitchin/Palmer/Hale)

Women's Relay
1 **Finland**   **2:50:33**
2 Sweden   2:52:11
3 Czech Rep.   2:53:06
8 Great Britain   3:06:52
(James/Bedwell/Monro/Hague)

World Cup 1994

Final Standings
Men
1 **Petter Thoresen NOR**   **183**
2 Janne Salmi FIN   176
3 Mika Kuisma FIN   171
10 Steven Hale GBR   158
23 Stephen Palmer GBR   115

Women
1 **Marlena Jansson SWE**   **193**
2 Yvette Hague GBR   179
3 Hanne Staff NOR   173
33 Heather Monro GBR   74
39 Jenny James GBR   56

Men's Relay
1 **Norway**   **37**
2 Sweden   37
3 Denmark   31
6 Great Britain   24

Women's Relay
1 **Norway**   **34**
2 Switzerland   33
3 Sweden   33
4 Great Britain   32

British Championships
North Wales   Mar 18-19

MEN'S INDIVIDUAL
14.9km   33 controls
1 **Jonathan Musgrave MAROC**   **90.49**
2 David Peel FVO   91.03
3 Neil Conway EPOC   95.43

WOMEN'S INDIVIDUAL
9.6 km   21 controls
1 **Yvette Hague WAROC**   **70.17**
2 Jenny James SYO   86.41
3 Karen Dalton NOC   91.13

Jan Kjellstrom
Yorkshire   Apr 14-17

MEN'S INDIVIDUAL
1 **Alain Berger SUI**   169.02
2 Andrew Kitchin GBR   170.11
3 Neil Conway GBR   171.59

WOMEN'S INDIVIDUAL
1 **Yvette Hague GBR**   **111.07**
2 Jenny James GBR   124.51
3 Megan Smith GBR   125.21

Rackets/Real Tennis ▬▬▬

Rackets

Manchester Gold Racquet
Manchester Oct 7-9
SINGLES
Division 1
J Snow bt S Shenkman 15-10, 10-15, 15-2
Division 2
C Danby bt A McDonald 25-16
Division 3
O Bridgeman bt H Eddis 25-23

DOUBLES
Orchard/Shenkman bt Devereux/Worlidge 25-20

Pro-Am Trophy
Queen's Club   Nov 12-13
Professionals bt Amateurs 7-2

Amateur Championships
SINGLES
Queen's Club   Dec 1-11
Semi-finals
J Male bt T Cockroft 15-6, 13-15, 15-6, 15-8
W Boone bt R Owen-Browne 17-16, 15-2, 15-10
Final
Male bt Boone 13-16, 15-2, 15-8, 15-4

DOUBLES
Queen's Club   Mar 11-14
Final
Prenn/Male bt Boone/Cockroft 15-3, 13-16, 7-15, 15-6,
10-15, 15-3, 15-12

Professional Championships
Malvern   Jan 27-29
SINGLES
Semi Finals
N Smith bt N Cripps 15-6, 16-9, 15-4
P Brake bt D Makey 15-2, 15-12, 15-9
Final
Brake bt Smith 15-12, 15-6, 11-15, 12-15, 15-8

Open Championships
Queen's Club
SINGLES   *Feb 1-12*
Semi Finals
N Smith bt J Prenn 8-15, 13-15, 15-3, 15-11, 15-13, 15-3
W Boone bt P Brake 15-6, 15-9, 15-3, 15-11
Final
Boone bt Smith 17-14, 16-15, 15-3, 15-0

DOUBLES   *Apr 18-23*
Final
Boone/Cockroft bt Smith/Brake 15-5, 15-4, 6-15, 8-15,
18-16, 13-16, 15-11

Real Tennis

World Championship Challenge
Hobart, Australia   Apr 14-18
R Fahey bt W Davies 6-2 *(ret)*

Manchester Gold Racquet
Manchester   Oct 7-9
SINGLES -Division 1
J Snow bt N Pendrigh 6-0, 6-1

DOUBLES
McMurragh/Snow bt Acheson-Gray/Pendrigh 6-2, 6-2

Open Championships
Queen's Club   Nov 19-28
SINGLES
 J Snow bt L Deuchar 6-3, 6-5, 1-6, 6-4

DOUBLES
Bray/Gooding bt Davies/Deuchar 6-5, 6-4, 6-2

Professional Championships
SINGLES
Holyport   May 2-7
L Deuchar bt M Gooding 6-5, 6-1, 2-6, 1-6, 6-3

DOUBLES
Queen's Club   Jan 6-9
Deuchar/Howell bt Bray/Gooding 6-5, 6-4, 4-6, 2-6, 6-4

Amateur Championships
SINGLES
Queen's Club   Mar 11-19
J Snow bt N Pendrigh 6-1, 6-4, 6-0

DOUBLES
Hatfield   Apr 29-May 2
Snow/McMurragh bt Acheson-Gray/Pendrigh 6-0, 6-2,
6-4

European Open Doubles
Queen's Club   Mar 25
Final
Davies/Deuchar bt Devine/Sheldon 6-3, 6-5, 6-2

Ladies Open Championships
DOUBLES
Canford   Jan 13-15
Final
Jones/Haswell bt Deuchar/Wood 6-4, 6-3

Rowing

"How's it going, Superstar", said Haining to a man who almost lazily entered the press conference. Peter Haining is joking, but only just. He has won two world titles and is on his way to a third. The Scot really doesn't have to defer to anyone but, as everyone in rowing does, he defers to Redgrave. Steve Redgrave nodded to Haining. He's not a man of that many words, but when your actions speak as loudly as his do, you don't have to say a lot. Redgrave has won three Olympic titles, three Commonwealth titles and five world titles. It is the pre-world championship press conference, within a month Redgrave's world championship count will move on to six.

Redgrave put his first stamp on the season at the end of June, as he always does, at Henley. He logged up his 15th Henley success; winning the Prince Philip Cup, with Pinsent, Michels and Reed, and the Silver Goblet and Nickalls Challenge Cup, with Pinsent. It was Redgrave's seventh success in the latter event, beating the record set by the eponymous Guy Nickalls, who won it six times before they added his name to the trophy. They can hardly add Redgrave's name to it too. Perhaps they should just christen that stretch of the river Redgrave, much as they call the Thames at Oxford the Isis.

Anyway, Redgrave duly went off to Tampere, Finland and added a sixth world title to the trove. It was his fifth coxless pairs title (he won the coxed pairs in 1986 with Holmes) and his fourth in a row with Matthew Pinsent. They did it with clinical ease, bringing their winning sequence to 52 races. Redgrave estimates they could take it to 100 by Atlanta *(see Atlanta Olympics, Preview for more on this)*.

Haining won Britain's other world championship gold. The race was not without incident as the Scot misplaced his inhaler which is usually strapped to the boat. A reserve inhaler arrived in the nick of time and Haining, an asthmatic, wheezed his way to victory. He had not intended to compete in the singles as it does not figure on the Olympic timetable and had prepared for the double sculls, teamed with Carl Smith. That had not been a productive partnership and Haining had reverted to the singles boat only four weeks before the Tampere event. In the Olympics, he is likely to quit the lightweights and compete as a heavyweight sculler. If he manages that title, Redgrave might have to call him Superstar.

Britain also won four silvers at Tampere to take the team's tally to six, a British best for a world championship. The coxless four almost made it three golds, the quartet of Greg and Jonny Searle, Rupert Obholzer and Tim Foster failing by about five feet to catch the Italians after having beaten them in the semi-final round.

The Boat Race went Cambridge's way for the third time in three years. It took the tally to 72-68 in favour of the light blues. If Oxford made the eighties their own (Cambridge only won once in that decade), Cambridge look to be laying claim to the nineties. Dan Topolski, who had much to do with the success of Oxford-past, turned back the clock by accepting the post of director of coaching, but could not turn the tide as well as his team lost by four lengths. Still, losing becomes a little more bearable when the sponsor is a gin company, Beefeater, which has just chosen to put another £1.35m into the event over the next five years. You've still got to pay for the tonic, mind.

World Championships

Tampere, Finland   *Aug 20-27*

MEN

Single Sculls

1	**Iztok Cop**	**SLO**	**6:52.93**
2	Juri Jaanson	EST	6:53.48
3	Vaclav Chalupa	CZE	6:54.14

Double Sculls

1	**Christiansen/Hansen**	**DEN**	**6:17.01**
2	Volkert/Steiner	GER	6:19.42
3	Undset/Skar Störseth	NOR	6:21.84

Quads

1	**Italy**	**6:10.09**
2	Germany	6:11.62
3	Argentina	6:12.62

Coxless Pairs

1	**Redgrave/Pinsent**	**GBR**	**6:28.11**
2	Walker/Wearne	AUS	6:29.87
3	Andrieux/Rolland	FRA	6:30.63

Coxed Pairs

1	**Sartori/de Stabile** Cirillo (cox)	**ITA**	**7:35.11**
2	Beghin/Beghin Lattaignan	FRA	7:37.97
3	Verdeyen/Moortgat Denoit	BEL	7:41.21

Coxless Fours

1	**Italy**	**5:58.28**
2	Great Britain	5:58.89
	(Foster/G Searle/J Searle/Obholzer)	
3	Poland	6:02.13

Coxed Fours

1	**United States**	**6:37.50**
2	New Zealand	6:38.65
3	Italy	6:40.14

Eights

1	**Germany**	**5:53.40**
2	Netherlands	5:55.54
3	United States	5:57.46
6	Great Britain	6:04.49

MEN'S LIGHTWEIGHT

Single Sculls

1	**Peter Haining**	**GBR**	**7:29.78**
2	Tomas Kacovski	CZE	7:31.60
3	Anders Brehms	DEN	7:33.24

Double Sculls

1	**Gier/Gier**	**SUI**	**6:45.56**
2	Tichy/Christensson	SWE	6:46.83
3	Edwards/Hick	AUS	6:47.60

Quads

1	**Austria**	**6:09.32**
2	Germany	6:11.07
3	Italy	6:13.71

Coxless Pairs

1	**Grande/Marigliano**	**ITA**	**7:08.64**
2	Bel/Dorfmann	FRA	7:11.77
3	Svendsen/Ebert	DEN	7:13.96

Coxless Fours

1	**Italy**	**6:16.46**
2	Denmark	6:17.83
3	Germany	6:18.44
5	Great Britain	6:24.64

Eights

1	**Denmark**	**5:53.45**
2	Great Britain	5:55.70
3	Italy	5:58.77

WOMEN

Single Sculls

1	**Maria Brandin**	**SWE**	**7:26.00**
2	Silken Laumann	CAN	7:29.07
3	Annelise Bredael	BEL	7:34.29

Double Sculls

1	**McBean/Heddle**	**CAN**	**6:55.76**
2	Eys/van Nes	NED	6:55.84
3	Baker/Lawson	NZL	6:59.43

Quads

1	**Germany**	**6:40.80**
2	Canada	6:43.02
3	Netherlands	6:43.22

Coxless Pairs

1	**Still/Slatter**	**AUS**	**7:12.70**
2	Schwen/Kraft	USA	7:14.90
3	Gosse/Garcia	FRA	7:16.49

Coxless Fours

1	**United States**	**7:03.53**
2	Germany	7:05.13
3	Belarus	7:07.98
5	Great Britain	7:23.64

Eights

1	**United States**	**6:50.73**
2	Romania	6:52.76
3	Netherlands	6:54.25

WOMEN'S LIGHTWEIGHT

Single Sculls

1	**Rebecca Joyce**	**AUS**	**8:14.66**
2	Catherine Muller	FRA	8:16.31
3	Annette Bogtstra	NED	8:18.61
4	Sue Appeloom	GBR	8:22.08

Double Sculls

1	**Wiebe/Miller**	**CAN**	**7:26.45**
2	Christoffersen/Andersson	DEN	7:27.28
3	Darvill/Kaps	GER	7:29.60

Coxless Pairs

1	**Smith/Minzner**	**USA**	**7:55.99**
2	Brownless/Hall	GBR	7:59.17
3	Jorgensen/Thilgreen	DEN	8:02.58

Coxless Fours

1	**United States**	**7:08.48**
2	Great Britain	7:09.74
3	Germany	7:13.91

World Championships
Medal Table

1	United States	5	1	1
2	Italy	5	0	3
3	Germany	2	4	3
4	Great Britain	2	4	0
5	Denmark	2	2	3
6	Canada	2	2	0
7	Australia	2	1	1
8	Sweden	1	1	0
9	Austria	1	0	0
10	Slovenia	1	0	0
11	Switzerland	1	0	0
12	France	0	3	2
13	Netherlands	0	2	3
14	Czech Republic	0	1	1
15	New Zealand	0	1	1
16	Estonia	0	1	0
17	Romania	0	1	0
18	Belgium	0	0	2
19	Argentina	0	0	1
20	Belarus	0	0	1
21	Norway	0	0	1
22	Poland	0	0	1

Henley Regatta

June 28-July 2

TEMPLE CHALLENGE CUP
Eights
Final
Oxford Brookes University bt
Trinity College   6:14

WYFOLD CHALLENGE CUP
Coxless Fours
Final
Lea Rowing Club 'A' bt
University of London Tyrian   6:42

PRINCESS ELIZABETH CHALLENGE CUP
Eights
Final
Eton College bt
Hampton School 'A'   6:25

STEWARDS' CHALLENGE CUP
Coxless Fours
Final
Cambridge University & Croatian Academic 'Mladost' bt
College BC   6:31

DOUBLE SCULLS CHALLENGE CUP
Final
Free/Antonie bt
Jamieson/Gleeson   6:58

BRITANNIA CHALLENGE CUP
Coxed Fours
Final
Wallingford bt
University of London   6:54

VISITORS' CHALLENGE CUP
Coxless Fours
Final
Isis BC bt
University of London   6:46

DIAMOND CHALLENGE SCULLS
Final
Juri Jaanson EST bt
Xeno Müller SUI   7:24

GRAND CHALLENGE CUP
Eights
Final
San Diego TC USA bt
Leander & Molesey BC   5:59

SILVER GOBLETS & NICKALLS' CHALLENGE CUP
Coxless Pairs
Final
Redgrave/Pinsent bt
Everington/Partridge   7:18

LADIES' CHALLENGE PLATE
Eights
Final
Notts CRA bt
Princeton University   6:05

WOMEN'S SINGLE SCULLS
Final
Maria Brandin SWE bt
Silken Laumann CAN   8:06

FAWLEY CHALLENGE CUP
Coxless Fours
Final
Windsor & Poplar bt
Norwich & Durham   6:44

PRINCE PHILIP CHALLENGE CUP
Coxed Fours
Final
Leander Rowing Club 'A' bt
Leander Rowing Club 'B'   6:44

THAMES CHALLENGE CUP
Eights
Final
Imperial College bt
University of Washington   6:15

QUEEN MOTHER CHALLENGE CUP
Coxless Fours
Final
Augusta TC USA bt
Dinamo Moscow RUS   6:19

*Q*uotes

"I feel the stress. Steve Redgrave says 'Okay I trust you, tell me what to do' and I feel that is bloody hard. At the end of the day we have only to lose. We have nothing more to win" - **Jürgen Gröbler, on the strains of coaching Redgrave.**

"When Jürgen arrived in 1991, all fell into place. We were motivated by new ideas, new crew, confidence. Then he threw a spanner in the works by changing us round. I'm not sure why. Steve still maintains it would be quicker the other way round. Jürgen said we'll try it for three weeks and we haven't heard from him since" - **Matthew Pinsent on coach Jürgen Gröbler.**

"Last time someone won that many Goblets they named the trophy after him. They should add the Redgrave Ladle or something" - **Pinsent, on his partner. Redgrave bowed out of Henley this year with 15 wins under his belt, including seven Silver Goblets.**

"Every day sportsmen train to increase the chance of winning. True champions train to eliminate the chance of losing" - **Pinsent's motto.**

"I believe in Jesus Christ, yes, but I don't wear it on my sleeve.....I'm not saying that the path I've chosen is going to be the one that gets me to the Pearly Gates, but I can't see that it's a back path that I'm on. He only has to look at my hands at the end of the day to see how hard I've tried. But he'll have to have a really, really, really big heart to ignore all the bad things I've done" - **Peter Haining.**

"I was tasting blood in the last 200m and he was still coming" - **Haining, who just held off the challenge of Giovanni Calabrese in the Thames Sculling Challenge.**

"The singles is all about having a point to prove. Nobody is nice, there are no soft options. These are the sort of people you want to stand beside you in trouble" - **Haining again.**

"It was more like surfing than rowing.....the waves kept pushing me from one side to the next. I kept losing my blades the water was so rough" - **Candian sculler, Silken Laumann, on conditions at the Pan-Am Games at Mar del Plate, Argentina.**

Lucerne Regatta

July 15-17
MEN
Double Sculls
1 Stortset/Undset   NOR   6:14.53
Quad Sculls
1 Germany   5:42.51
Coxless Pairs
1 Redgrave/Pinsent   GBR   6:23.73
Coxed Pairs
1 Gordon/Burke   AUS   7:03.60
Coxless Fours
1 Italy   5:47.89 *WR*
Coxed Fours
1 Germany   6:15.59
4 Great Britain   6:23.97
  (Leander)
Eights
1 Russia   5:29.86
6 Great Britain   5:35.72

LIGHTWEIGHT MEN
Single Sculls
1 Niall O'Toole   IRL   7:05.73
Double Sculls
1 Hick/Edwards   AUS   6:15.58 *WR*
Quad Sculls
1 Germany   5:59.25
Coxless Pairs
1 Hasslebach/Bayne   RSA   6:47.24
Coxless Fours
1 Italy   5:52.34
4 Great Britain   5:57.78
Eight
1 Great Britain   5:41.99

WOMEN
Double Sculls
1 McBean/Heddle   CAN   6:47.84
Quad Sculls
1 Germany   6:19.20
Coxless Pairs
1 Still/Slatter   AUS   7:12.17
Coxless Fours
1 Netherlands   6:47.52
Eights
1 Netherlands   6:05.78
5 Great Britain   6:11.83

LIGHTWEIGHT WOMEN
Single Sculls
1 Annette Bogststra   NED   7:54.71
Double Sculls
1 Burns/Zarzeczny   USA   6:56.92
Coxless Pairs
1 Borg/Eichhorn   GER   7:36.34
2 Brownless/Hall   GBR   7:39.18
Coxless Fours
1 Germany   6:55.87
2 Great Britain   6:58.41

World Cup

Singles Sculling

Hazewinkel   June 3-4
Men
1 Juri Jaanson   EST   7:01.45
2 Iztok Cop   SLO   7:03.44
Women
1 Trine Hansen   DEN   7:34.86
2 Silken Laumann   CAN   7:34:76
Arne La Vallé, Paris   June 17-18
Men
1 Juri Jaanson   EST   6:42.69
2 Xeno Müller   SUI   6:44.87
Women
1 Maria Brandin   SWE   7:17.92
2 Trine Hansen   DEN   7:21.51
Henley   July 1-2
Men
1 Juri Jaanson   EST   7:24
2 Xeno Müller   SUI
Women
1 Maria Brandin   SWE   8:06
2 Silken Laumann   CAN
Lucerne   July 7-8
Men
1 Juri Jaanson   EST   6:37.03 *WR*
2 Xeno Müller   SUI   6:37.17
Women
1 Trine Hansen   DEN   7:20.01
2 Kathrin Boron   GER   7:22.54

OVERALL WORLD CUP STANDINGS
Men: 1. Juri Jaanson EST; 2. Xeno Müller SUI;
3. Iztok Cop SLO
Women: 1. Trine Hansen DEN; 2. Maria Brandin SWE;
3. Silken Laumann CAN

Done everything in life? Want a new challenge? Then why not row the Atlantic. Chay Blyth, who did it in 1966, is organising The Atlantic challenge, a race from Tenerife to Bardados for two-person boats. The race will take place in September 1997, cross 2,900 miles of ocean and take several months out of your lives. It costs £20,000 to enter and, this is the best bit, previous experience of rowing is "advised". Bit like advertising for climbers to go on an Everest expedition - "must recognise a crampon"

National Championships

Holme Pierrepont   July 14-16

MEN
Single Sculls
1 S Goodbrand   8:01
Double Sculls
1 Notts Co   7:12
Quad Sculls
1 Tideway Scullers 6:26
Coxless Pairs
1 Thames Tradesman 7:26
Coxed Pairs
1 Isis 'B'   8:18
Coxless Fours
1 Notts Co   6:54
Coxed Fours
1 Lea RC   7:00
Eights
1 Notts Co   6:09
MEN LIGHTWEIGHT
Single Sculls
1 S Hames   7:55
Double Sculls
1 Notts Co   7:03
Quad SCulls
1 Notts Co   7:01
Coxless Fours
1 London RC   6:42
Eights
1 London RC   6:47
WOMEN
Single Sculls
1 P Reid   8:41
Double Sculls
Henley/Tideway   8:07
Quad Sculls
Notts Co   7:15
Coxless Pairs
Thames RC   8:45
Coxed Fours
Thames RC   8:02
Coxless Fours
1 Bedford/Thames/Weybridge 8:32
Eights
1 Tideway Scullers 7:10
WOMEN LIGHTWEIGHT
Single Sculls
1 N Ashcroft   9:23
Double Sculls
1 Tideway/Twickenahm 8:02
Coxless Pairs
1 Kingston/Thames   9:02
Coxless Fours
1 Bedfrod/Thames/Weybridge 7:50

Thames Sculling Challenge

Mortlake to Putney   Nov 5, 1994
1 Peter Haining   GBR
2 Giovanni Calabrese ITA

Head of the River Races

Chiswick to Putney (Women) Mar 11
1 Kingston/Thames/TSS   18:14
2 Deutscher Ruderverband   18:40

Mortlake to Putney (Men)   Mar 25
1 Netherlands Rowing Fed   16:58
2 Leander   17:00

Scullers Head

Putney - Mortlake   Apr 8
Men
1 Niall O'Toole   IRL   21:16
2 Peter Haining   GBR   21:19
3 Guy Pooley   GBR   21:21
Women
1 Guin Batten   GBR   23:04

The Beefeater Boat Race

Putney to Mortlake   Apr 1
Senior Race
Cambridge beat Oxford bt 4 lengths
Cambridge: Taylor, Parish, Newton, Phelps, Bangert, Brownlee, Banovic, Barnett, Slatford
Oxford: Kawaya, Rosengren, Mavra, Reed, McLanahan, Corroon, Clegg, Throndsen, Chapman
Times (Cambridge first)
Mile: 3:50, 3:51
Hammersmith Bridge: 6:44, 6:48
Chiswick Steps: 10:55, 11:04
Barnes Bridge: 14:51, 15:04
Finish: 18:04, 18:16

Reserve Race
Goldie (Cambridge) beat Isis (Oxford) by 14 lengths
Times (Goldie first)
Mile: 3:53, 3:57
Hammersmith Bridge: 6:59, 7:12
Chiswick Steps: 11:12, 11:35
Barnes Bridge: 15:12, 15:46
Finish: 18:29, 19:13

British Indoor Championships

Bracknell   Nov 26, 1994
Men: 1. S Brownlee (Cambs Uni) 7:36.0; 2. M Banovic (CU) 7:38.5; 3. J Elliott (CU) 7:46.1
Women: 1. C Bishop (Marlow) 8:44.3; 2 S Springman (TT) 8:46.8; 3. K Templeton 8:49.0

World Champions

Men

	SINGLE SCULLS			DOUBLE SCULLS	
1962	Vyacheslav Ivanov	URS		René Duhamel/Bernard Monnereau	FRA
1966	Don Spero	USA		Melchior Borgin/Martin Studach	SUI
1970	Alberto Demiddi	ARG		Jorgen Engelbrech/Niels Secher	DEN
1974	Wolfgang Honig	GDR		Christof Kreuziger/Hans-Ulrich Schmied	GDR
1975	Peter-Michael.Kolbe	FRG		Alf Hansen/Frank Hansen	NOR
1977	Joachim Dreifke	GDR		Chris Baillieu/Michael Hart	GBR
1978	Peter-Michael Kolbe	FRG		Alf Hansen/Frank Hansen	NOR
1979	Pertti Karppinen	FIN		Alf Hansen/Frank Hansen	NOR
1981	Peter-Michael Kolbe	FRG		Klaus Kroppelien/Joachim Dreifke	GDR
1982	Rodiger Reiche	GDR		Alf Hansen/Rolf Thorsen	NOR
1983	Peter-Michael Kolbe	FRG		Thomas Lange/Uwe Heppner	GDR
1985	Pertti Karppinen	FIN		Thomas Lange/Uwe Heppner	GDR
1986	Peter-Michael Kolbe	FRG		Alberto Belgori/Igor Pescialli	ITA
1987	Thomas Lange	GDR		Vasil Radeyev/Danatyl Yordanov	BUL
1989	Thomas Lange	GDR		Lars Bjoness/Rol Bent Thorsen	NOR
1990	Juri Jaanson	URS		Christophe Zerbst/Arnold Jonke	AUT
1991	Thomas Lange	GER		Henk-Jan Zwolle/Nicolaas Rienks	NED
1993	Derek Porter	CAN		Yves Lamargue/Samuel Barathay	FRA
1994	Andre Willms	GER		Lars Bjoness/Rol Bent Thorsen	NOR
1995	Iztok Cop	SLO		Christiansen/Halabo-Hansen	DEN

	COXLESS PAIRS		COXED PAIRS	QUAD SCULLS
1962	Dieter Bender/Gunther Zumkeller	FRG	West Germany	-
1966	Peter Gorny/Werner Klatt	GDR	Netherlands	-
1970	Peter Gorny/Werner Klatt	GDR	Romania	-
1974	Bernd Landvoig/Jorg Landvoig	GDR	Soviet Union	East Germany
1975	Bernd Landvoig/Jorg Landvoigt	GDR	East Germany	East Germany
1977	Vitaliy Yeliseyev/Aleksandr Kulagin	URS	Bulgaria	East Germany
1978	Bernd Landvoig/Jörg Landvoigt	GDR	East Germany	East Germany
1979	Bernd Landvoig/Jörg Landvoigt	GDR	East Germany	East Germany
1981	Yuriy Pimenov/Nikolay Pimenov	URS	Italy	East Germany
1982	Magnus Grepperud/Sverre Loken	NOR	Italy	East Germany
1983	Carl Ertel/Ulf Sauerbrey	GDR	East Germany	West Germany
1985	Nikolay Pimenov/Yury Pimenov	URS	Italy	Canada
1986	Nikolay Pimenov/Yury Pimenov	URS	Great Britain	Soviet Union
1987	Andrew Holmes/Steven Redgrave	GBR	Italy	Soviet Union
1989	Thomas Jung/Uwe Kellner	GDR	Italy	Romania
1990	Thomas Jung/Uwe Kellner	GDR	Italy	Soviet Union
1991	Steven Redgrave/Matthew Pinsent	GBR	Italy	Soviet Union
1993	Steven Redgrave/Matthew Pinsent	GBR	Great Britain	Germany
1994	Steven Redgrave/Matthew Pinsent	GBR	Croatia	Italy
1995	Steven Redgrave/Matthew Pinsent	GBR	Italy	Italy

	COXLESS FOURS				COXED FOURS		
1962	West Germany	1987	East Germany	1962	West Germany	1987	East Germany
1966	East Germany	1989	East Germany	1966	East Germany	1989	Romania
1970	East Germany	1990	Australia	1970	West Germany	1990	East Germany
1974	East Germany	1991	Australia	1974	East Germany	1991	Germany
1975	East Germany	1993	France	1975	Soviet Union	1993	Romania
1977	East Germany	1994	Italy	1977	East Germany	1994	Romania
1978	Soviet Union	1995	Italy	1978	East Germany	1995	United States
1979	East Germany			1979	East Germany		
1981	Soviet Union			1981	East Germany		
1982	Switzerland			1982	East Germany		
1983	West Germany			1983	New Zealand		
1985	West German			1985	Soviet Union		
1986	United States			1986	East Germany		

World Champions

LIGHTWEIGHT SINGLE SCULLS			LIGHTWEIGHT DOUBLE SCULLS	
1974	William Belden	USA	-	
1975	Reto Wyss	SUI	-	
1976	Raimund Haberl	AUT	-	
1977	Reto Wyss	SUI	-	
1978	José Antonio Montosa	ESP	Pal Bornick/Arne Gilje	NOR
1979	William Belden	USA	Pal Bornick/Arne Gilje	NOR
1980	Christian Georg Wahrlich	FRG	Francesco Esposito/Ruggero Verroca	ITA
1981	Scott Roop	USA	Francesco Esposito/Ruggero Verroca	ITA
1982	Raimund Haberl	AUT	Francesco Esposito/Ruggero Verroca	ITA
1983	Bjarne Eltang	DEN	Francesco Esposito/Ruggero Verroca	ITA
1984	Bjarne Eltang	DEN	Francesco Esposito/Ruggero Verroca	ITA
1985	Ruggero Verroca	ITA	Luc Crispon/Thierry Renault	FRA
1986	Peter Antonie	AUS	Carl Smith/Allan Whitwell	GBR
1987	Willem Van Belleghem	BEL	Enrico Gandola/Giovanni Calabrese	ITA
1988	Alwin Otten	FRG	Enrico Gandola/Giovanni Calabrese	ITA
1989	Frans Goebel	NED	Christoph Schmölzer/Walter Rantasa	AUT
1990	Frans Goebel	NED	Steve Peterson/Robert Dreher	USA
1991	Niall O'Toole	IRL	Kai Von Warburg/Michael Buchheit	GER
1992	Jens Mohr Ernst	DEN	Gary Lynagh/Bruce Hick	AUS
1993	Peter Haining	GBR	Gary Lynagh/Bruce Hick	AUS
1994	Peter Haining	GBR	Esposito/Crispi	ITA
1995	Peter Haining	GBR	Geir/Geir	SUI

LTWT COXLESS FOURS		LTWT EIGHTS	LTWT QUAD SCULLS
1974	Australia	United States	-
1975	France	West Germany	-
1976	France	West Germany	-
1977	France	Great Britain	-
1978	Switzerland	Great Britain	-
1979	Great Britain	Spain	-
1980	Australia	Great Britain	-
1981	Australia	Denmark	-
1982	Italy	Italy	-
1983	Spain	Spain	-
1984	Spain	Denmark	-
1985	West Germany	Italy	-
1986	Italy	Italy	-
1987	West Germany	Italy	-
1988	Italy	Italy	-
1989	West Germany	Italy	West Germany
1990	West Germany	Italy	Italy
1991	Great Britain	Italy	Australia
1992	Great Britain	Denmark	Italy
1993	United States	Canada	
1994	Denmark	Great Britain	Austria

EIGHTS

1962	West Germany	1987	United States
1966	West Germany	1989	West Germany
1970	East Germany	1990	West Germany
1974	United States	1991	Germany
1975	East Germany	1993	Germany
1977	East Germany	1994	United States
1979	East Germany	1995	Germany
1981	Soviet Union		
1982	New Zealand		
1983	New Zealand		
1985	Soviet Union		
1986	Australia		

World Champions

Women

	SINGLE SCULLS	DOUBLE SCULLS
1974	Christine Scheiblich GDR	Yelena Antonova/Galina Yermoleyeva URS
1974	Christine Scheiblich GDR	Yelena Antonova/Galina Yermoleyeva URS
1977	Christine Scheiblich GDR	Anke Borchmann/Roswietha Zobelt GDR
1978	Christine Hann (Scheiblich) GDR	Svetla Otzetova/Zdravka Yordanova BUL
1979	Sandra Toma ROM	Cornelia Linse/Heidi Westphal GDR
1981	Sandra Toma ROM	Margarita Kokarevitha/Antonina Makhina URS
1982	Irina Fettisova URS	Yelena Braticko/Antonina Makhina URS
1983	Jutta Hampe GDR	Jutta Scheck/Martina Schroter GDR
1985	Cornelia Linse GDR	Sylvia Schurabe/Martina Schroter GDR
1986	Jutta Hampe GDR	Sylvia Schurabe/Beate Schramm GDR
1987	Magdalena Georgeyeva BUL	Steska Madina/Violeta Ninova BUL
1989	Elisabeta Lipa ROM	Jana Sorgers/Beate Schramm GDR
1990	Birgit Peter GDR	Kathrin Boron/Beate Schramm GDR
1991	Silken Laumann CAN	Kathrin Boron/Beate Schramm GER
1993	Jana Thieme GER	P Lawson/B Lawson NZL
1994	Trine Hansen DEN	P Lawson/B Lawson NZL
1995	Maria Brandin SWE	Marnie McBean/Kathleen Heddle CAN

	COXLESS PAIRS	COXED FOURS	QUAD SCULLS
1974	Marilena Ghita/Cornelia Neascu ROM	East Germany	East Germany
1975	Sabine Dahne/Angelika Noack GDR	East Germany	East Germany
1977	Sabine Dahne/Angelika Noack GDR	East Germany	East Germany
1978	Cornelia Bugel/Ute Steindorf GDR	East Germany	Bulgaria
1979	Cornelia Bugel/Ute Steindorf GDR	Soviet Union	East Germany
1981	Sigrid Anders/Iris Rudolph GDR	Soviet Union	Soviet Union
1982	Silvia Frohlich/Marita Sandig GDR	Soviet Union	Soviet Union
1983	Silvia Frohlich/Marita Sandig GDR	Soviet Union	East Germany
1985	Rodica Arba/Elena Florea ROM	East Germany	East Germany
1986	Rodica Arba/Olga Homeghi ROM	Romania	East Germany
1987	Rodica Arba/Olga Homeghi ROM	Romania	East Germany
1989	Kathrin Haaker/Judith Zeidler GDR	-	East Germany
1990	Stefanie Werremeier/Ingeburg Althoff FRG	-	East Germany
1991	Marnie McBean/Kathleen Heddle CAN	-	Germany
1993	Gosse/Cortin FRA	-	China
1994	Gosse/Cortin FRA	-	Germany
1995	Still/Slatter AUS	-	Germany

	EIGHTS	COXLESS FRS		LTWT SINGLE SCULLS	LTWT COXLESS FRS
1974	East Germany	-	1985	Adair Ferguson AUS	-
1975	East Germany	-	1986	Maria Sava ROM	-
1977	East Germany	-	1987	M Georgieva BUL	-
1978	Soviet Union	-	1988	Kris Karlson USA	China
1979	Soviet Union	-	1989	Kris Karlson USA	China
1981	Soviet Union	-	1990	Mette Jenson DEN	Canada
1983	Soviet Union	-	1991	Philippa Baker NZL	China
1985	Soviet Union	-	1992	Mette Jensen DEN	Australia
1986	Soviet Union	United States	1993	Michelle Darvill CAN	Great Britain
1987	Soviet Union	-	1994	Constanta Pipota ROM	United States
1989	Romania	East Germany	1995	Regina Joyce AUS	United States
1990	Romania	Romania			
1991	Canada	Canada		LTWT DOUBLE SCULLS	
1993	Romania	China	1985	Clark/Crockford GBR	1991 Weber/Waldi GER
1994	Germany	Netherlands	1986	Ernst/Sands USA	1992 Weber/Waldi GER
1995	United States	United States	1987	Madina/Ninova BUL	1993 Wiebe/Miller CAN
			1988	Vermuist/Meliesie NED	1994 Wiebe/Miller CAN
			1989	Sands/Karlson USA	1995 Wiebe/Miller CAN
			1990	Jensen/Siggaard DEN	

Rugby League ▬▬▬▬▬▬▬▬

It was all so simple then; back in October of 1994 England beat Australia in the first Test at Wembley (Davies' try was a delight) to set up a passionate winter series. Australia levelled the the games at Old Trafford and reasserted their superiority at Elland Road to settle the series 2-1. It wasn't the perfect ending for England, but it was traditional, gripping stuff. The Oz publicists even told us that the tourists had sunk 9,409 cans of Castlemaine during their UK tour and what could be more traditional than that? Since that winter series, time has rewritten every line. Of the 17 players who stepped on the field for Australia in that final Test, only four made an appearance in the Aussie team that England beat in the opening game of the World Cup. Everything had changed and the changemonger was Rupert Murdoch.

It was the first week in April when discussions took place between Maurice Lindsay, chief executive of the Rugby League, and the News Limited group, owned by Murdoch. After two days of negotiations, Murdoch's number two Ken Cowley announced in Australia that a deal had been done. It was two days before the rugby league chairman were due to discuss it. What the chairmen did, in the face of a £77m offer, was either very calculating or beyond belief (depending on the intellectual credit you give to the chairmen). The proposed Super League would be made up of 14 teams, of which 11 were to come from the current Division One teams. The answer to this apparent conundrum (remember there are 16 teams to please - and newly-promoted Keighley) was amalgamation. Hull to become one team; Warrington and Widnes to become Cheshire; Wakefield Trinity, Castleford and Featherstone to become Calder. Well, didn't everybody just love that idea?

Keighley, who have never won anything before, threaten to sue the league after their exclusion from the Super League. France decide they don't want a place for Paris *and* Toulouse and so both Widnes and Warrington could be given places (which took the pressure off for one merger) and Halifax chairman Tony Gartland resigned as fans reacted strongly against his plan to merger with Bradford Northern. It reached the point where the House of Commons debated the Super League chaos for 90 minutes on April 26. That important, eh?

Having driven a bus through the estate of rugby league on April 9th, the chairmen decided to hastily rebuild their former manor on April 30th. Following a six-hour meeting at the Hilton Hotel in Huddersfield, the merger proposals were completely withdrawn. A new, 12-club Super League was set up: Bradford Northern, Castleford, Halifax, Leeds, London Broncos, Oldham, Paris, St Helens, Sheffield, Warrington, Wigan and Workington Town.

The First Division became: Batley, Dewsbury, Featherstone Rovers, Huddersfield, Hull, Keighley Cougars, Rochdale Hornets, Salford, Wakefield Trinity, Whitehaven and Widnes. The Second Division: Barrow, Bramely, Carlisle, Chorley, Highfield, Hull Kingston Rovers, Hunslet, Leigh, Ryedale-York and Swinton.

Murdoch increased the money available for the five-year contract to £87m: each Super League club to receive £900,000 for five years; First Division clubs to receive between £700,000 and £200,000 depending on performance; and the Second Division teams to receive £150,000.

Keighley decided not to sue, Chorley had threatened to and Widnes did, but lost on May 26 when Mr Justice Jonathan Parker at the Manchester High Court said there was no serious issue to be tried. The April 30th vote in favour of the Super League, 32 votes to 1, had shown there was overwhelming support for the new set-up.

It had all been done with a huge amount of fuss and the minimum of change, except that Rugby League had become a summer sport. The hole that it left in the 1995 winter calendar was filled in part by the eleventh World Cup, which began on October 7th with the England victory over Australia (and finishes after these pages go to press). Within a week the sport, already in a defensive mood as coverage of the World Cup failed to come up to supporters' expectations, was confronting the worst type of publicity. South Africa's Pierre Grobbelaar (no relation to our Bruce) tested positive for Nandrolone.

Grobbelaar had earlier been recruited by Tony Fisher to play for Dewsbury after the World Cup. It was a double blow for Fisher who had been coach at Doncaster, in November 1994, when Jamie Bloem (another South African) had tested positive for the same drug. Bloem went onto the back pages claiming it was rife in the sport before later retracting all that and going away to serve his two-year ban quietly. Before the World Cup, tournament director Maurice Lindsay had voiced concern that testing procedures in South Africa were not tight enough. Given that no player with any sense would have taken drugs immediately prior to the sport's biggest competition, you have to wonder whether the testing Lindsay was talking about was for drugs or IQs.

Wigan won everything in the last traditional year. There's a surprise. Their victorious sequences reflect the monopoly; they won their sixth First Division Championship, their third Premiership, their fourth Regal Trophy, and made it eight Silk Cut Challenge Cups. They bulldozed through Warrington in the Regal 40-10, with Tuigamala the star of the show. In the Silk Cut final, Leeds at least staved off a battering, going down by 30-10, a relatively close game in Wigan's world. Over the season, Wigan lost just twice in the Championship, narrow defeats by Leeds and Wigan, and once to the touring Australians, by 10 points in front of 20,000 at Central Park. They didn't retain their World Club Champions crown, but that was only because it wasn't played, due to the political uncertainty. In any other sport, Wigan would be in danger of destroying the interest in the game. It will be intruiging to see if the Super League changes that. Now that Union has gone open, they will find it harder to attract the Tuigamalas to Central Park. They may even find it harder to keep them.

Leeds thought they'd made the swoop of the year when their chairman, Alf Davies, was convinced that he had lured Johan Lomu from the new professionals to the old. In the way these deals are done, it's quite likely that the Lomu camp were just pushing up the price. It's a shame Lomu didn't go to Headingley. It would have made it just that much harder for Wigan.

There was one unpredictable result during the season; Wales defeated England to become European champions. It was the first time the competition has been played since 1981and the first time that Wales had won it since 1938 and that's an awful long time ago.

Quotes

"Does anyone here think that Mr Murdoch woke up in the middle of the night and thought, 'Jeez, I like rugby league' ?" **- Ken Arthurson, executive chairman of Australian Rugby League.**

"Twenty-five clubs are technically insolvent. Things cannot go on as they are. There has been no expansion for years and there is no sign of expansion" **- Jim Quinn, Oldham chairman, before the chairmen's meeting at Wigan on April 8.**

"Gone down like a loaded gun here, it has" **- Len Casey, former Hull player on the city's response to amalgamation.**

"Everyone is saying that we're ripping out the roots of the game, but I don't agree. All the other teams are dead limbs, they're hanging off the tree - which is the game - and pulling it down. There are people out there who have been pinching a living off rugby league for a long time" **- Denis Betts, Man of Steel for 1995, arguing for the Super League.**

"Pay off your debts and die clause" **- How the one-off £100,000 payments were described as club amalgamation was put forward.**

"Only the British seem to have the ability to make unqualified good news sound like a disaster" **- Rodney Walker, chairman of the Sports Council adn the Rugby League.**

"It is typical of the nonsense that rugby league has had to put with for the last 100 years" - **Maurice Lindsay, on the adjustments to the laws of rugby union whereby returning league players should serve a three-year ban.**

"There is a gap opening up for good midfield players at Warrington and Guscott fits the bill. It is a question of whether or not Warrington can pay the bill" **- Mike Burton on the suggestion that Guscott had been offered £500,000 to join Warrington.**

"If the testing was done more frequently there'd be 20 to 30 per cent getting two-year bans. You can talk to the players and they'll say they know" **- John Allen, former Swinton player on the BBC TV programme *Look North.***

"It's not the losing that gets me. It's the way you lose. If I've played a game and lost because my side has given in, that's what really hurts. It really burns me. I lie awake for hours and it's as if I am watching a video - what I could have done and so on. If my team has caved in.....and hasn't felt *guilty* about it...that really upsets me" **- Ellery Hanley as he took over the post of England coach.**

"I'm devastated. At five minutes to six, with everybody on standby, I was convinced we had got our man. The bad news from Phil Kingsley (Lomu's agent) was a reall hammer blow" **- Alf Davies, chief executive of Leeds, on the moment he knew that Jonah Lomu wasn't coming to the club.**

International Results

Australian Tour

1ST TEST
Wembley   Oct 22, 1994
Great Britain 8   Australia 4
Try: Davies   Try: Renouf
Goals: Davies, Golding
Great Britain: Davies (Bateman), Robinson, Connolly, Hunte, Offiah, Powell (McDermott), Edwards*, Harrison (Cassidy), Jackson, Joynt, Betts, Farrell (Goulding), Clarke
Australia: Mullins, Ettingshausen, Meninga*, Renouf, Sailor, Daley (Stuart), Langer, Roberts, Walters, Harragon, Sironen (Pay), Clyde (Furner), Fittler
Attendance: 57,034
Receipts: £1,107,423

2ND TEST
Old Trafford   Nov 5, 1994
Great Britain 8   Australia 38
Try: Newlove   Tries: Mullins (2), Clyde,
Goals: Goulding (2)   Daley, Ettingshausen,
*   Renouf*
*   Goals: Wishart (7)*
Great Britain: Steadman, Robinson, Connolly, Hunte (Newlove), Offiah, Powell (Schofield), Goulding, Harrison (McDermott), Jackson, Joynt (Cassidy), Betts, Farrell, Clarke*
Australia: Mullins, Ettingshausen, Meninga*, Renouf, Wishart, Daley (Sironen), Stuart, Lazarus, Walters, Roberts (Florimo/Langer), Pay, Clyde, Fittler
Attendance: 43,930
Receipts: £634,467

3RD TEST
Elland Road   Nov 20, 1994
Great Britain 4   Australia 23
Goals: Farrell (2)   Tries: Daley, Pay, Walters
*   Wishart*
*   Goals: Wishart (3)*
*   DG: Stuart*
Great Britain: Connolly, Robinson, Hunte (Powell), Newlove, Offiah, Clarke (Schofield), Edwards*, Harrison, Jackson, McDermott (Nickle), Betts, Farrell, Joynt (Goulding)
Australia: Mullins, Ettingshausen (Brasher), Meninga*, Renouf, Wishart, Daley, Stuart, Lazarus, Walters (Langer), Roberts (Florimo), Pay, Clyde, Fittler
Attendance: 39,468
Receipts: £584,264

Tour Results
Excluding Test results v Great Britain

Workington   Oct 2, 1994
Cumbria 8   Australia 52

Headingley   Oct 5, 1994
Leeds 6   Australia 48

Central Park   Oct 8, 1994
Wigan 20   Australia 30

Wheldon Road   Oct 12, 1994
Castleford 12   Australia 38

Thrum Valley   Oct 16, 1994
Halifax 12   Australia 26

Don Valley Std. Oct 26, 1994
Sheffield 2   Australia 80

Ninian Park   Oct 30, 1994
Wales 4   Australia 46

Knowsley Rd   Nov 1, 1994
St Helens 14   Australia 32

Wilderspool   Nov 9, 1994
Warrington 0   Australia 24

Odsal Stadium Nov 13, 1994
Bradford N 0   Australia 40

Gateshead   Nov 15, 1994
GB U-21s 10   Australia 54

Australia in France

Evry   Nov 24, 1994
President's XIII 7   Australia 42

Perpignan   Nov 27, 1994
Roussillon-Catalan XIII 16   Australia 60

Avignon   Nov 30, 1994
France B 9   Australia 64

Bezier   Dec 4, 1994
France 0   Australia 74

European Championship

Ninian Park, Cardiff   Feb 1
Wales 18   England 16
Try: Ellis   Tries: Gay, Fox, Robinson
Goals: Davies (4)
DG: Davies (2)

Gateshead   Feb 15
England 19   France 16
Tries: Broadbent,   Tries: Banquet (2), Garcia,
Pinkney, Cummins   Goals: Millet (2)
Goals: Fox (3)
DG: Wright

Carcassonne   Mar 5
Wales 22   France 10
Tries: Bateman (2)   Tries: Llong, Garcia
Harris, Atcheson   Goal: Millett
Goals: Davies (3)

FINAL TABLE

	P	W	D	L	GF	GA	Pts
Wales	**2**	**2**	**0**	**0**	**40**	**26**	**4**
England	2	1	0	1	35	34	2
France	2	0	0	2	26	41	0

Domestic Results ▬▬▬▬▬▬

Stones Bitter Championship

DIVISION 1		P	W	D	L	PF	PA	Pts
1	Wigan	30	28	0	2	1148	386	56
2	Leeds	30	24	1	5	863	526	49
3	Castleford	30	20	2	8	872	564	42
4	St Helens	30	20	1	9	893	640	41
5	Halifax	30	18	2	10	782	566	38
6	Warrington	30	18	2	10	753	570	38
7	Bradford North.	30	17	1	12	811	650	35
8	Sheff'ld Eagles	30	15	0	15	646	699	30
9	Workington T.	30	12	1	17	538	743	25
10	Oldham	30	11	1	18	534	746	23
11	Featherstone R.	30	10	1	19	582	687	21
12	Salford	30	10	1	19	613	775	21
13	Wakefield Tr'ty	30	9	0	21	434	807	18
14	Widnes	30	8	1	21	481	767	17
15	Hull	30	7	1	22	594	880	15
16	Doncaster	30	5	1	24	469	1007	11

DIVISION 2		P	W	D	L	PF	PA	Pts
1	Keighley C	30	23	2	5	974	337	48
2	Batley	30	23	0	7	754	423	46
3	Huddersfield	30	19	3	8	870	539	41
4	London Broncos	30	20	1	9	732	480	41
5	Whitehaven	30	19	0	11	766	507	38
6	Rochdale H'nets	30	18	0	12	805	544	36
7	Dewsbury	30	17	1	12	744	538	35
8	Hull KR	30	16	1	13	824	516	33
9	Ryedale-York	30	15	2	13	720	602	32
10	Hunslet	30	16	0	14	611	783	32
11	Leigh	30	12	0	18	622	787	24
12	Swinton	30	12	0	18	576	768	24
13	Bramley	30	10	0	20	554	655	20
14	Carlisle	30	8	0	22	546	877	16
15	Barrow	30	6	0	24	449	811	12
16	Highfield	30	1	0	29	224	1604	2

Stones Bitter Premiership

First Round

Castleford 22	Warrington 30
Leeds 50	Bradford Northern 30
St Helens 32	Halifax 16
Wigan 48	Sheffield Eagles 16

Semi Finals

Leeds 30	St Helens 26
Wigan 50	Warrington 20

FINAL

Old, Trafford, Manchester   May 21

Wigan 69   Leeds 12

Tries: Radlinski (3)   Tries: Eyres, Innes
Connolly (3), Betts   Goals: Holroyd (2)
Skerrett, Edwards
Paul, Hall, Haughton
Goals: Botica (10)
DG: Farrell

Wigan: Paul, Robinson, Radlinski, Connolly, Offiah, Botica, Edwards*, Skerrett (Cassidy), Hall, Cowie, Betts, Farrell (Haughton), Clarke **Leeds:** Tait, Fallon, Iro*, Hassan (Vassilakopoulos), Cummins, Innes, Holroyd, Howard (Harmon), Lowes, Faimalo, Mann, Eyres, Mercer

Stones Bitter
2nd Division Premiership

First Round

Batley 20	Dewsbury 16
Huddersfield 36	Rochdale Hornets 10
Keighley C 42	Hull KR 16
London Broncos 28	Whitehaven 1

Semi Finals

Batley 6	Huddersfield 13
Keighley C 38	London Broncos 4

FINAL

Old Trafford, Manchester   May 21

Keighley Cougars 26   Huddersfield 6

Tries: Wood, Pinkney   Goals: Pearce (2)
Powell, Eyres   DG: Austin, Kerry
Goals: Irving (4)
DG: Ramshaw (2)

Keighley: Stoop, Eyres, Pinkney, Irving*, Dixon, Powell, Appleby, Hill (Tupaea/Larder), Ramshaw, Gately, Fleary, Cochrane, Wood
Huddersfield: Hellewell, Barton, Shelford, Austin*, Reynolds, Hanger, Kerry, King, St Hilaire, Pucill, Richards (Coulter), Senior (Taylor), Pearce

Silk Cut Challenge Cup

First Round

Askam 10	Moorends 15
Barrow Island 26	Norland 8
Beverley 8	Chequerfield 6
Blackbrook 26	West Bowling 14
Blackpool G 27	Fryston 14
Chorley B 12	Simms Cross 8
Dewsbury Celtic 6	Thatto Heath 22
Dudley Hill 54	Cardiff Institute 4
East Leeds 22	Wath Brown H 14
Eastmoor 23	Upton & Frickley 22
Egremont 34	New Earswick AB 6
Greetland AB 12	Crosfield 6
Hemel Hempstead 52	Leeds Met Univ 0
Heworth 32	Littleborough 10
Leigh East 10	Bisons 16
Leigh Miners 7	Wigan St Judes 10
Lock Lane 36	Orrell St James 8
Mayfield 32	Park Amateurs 6
Milford 12	Thornhill 20
Millom 62	Northampton K 4
Moldgreen 30	Embassy 14
Nottingham C 0	Normanton 36
Oldham St Annes 20	Kells 24
Oulton 12	Ovenden 8
Redhill 22	Ellenborough 28
Saddleworth R 30	Skirlaugh 12
Shaw Cross 46	Fulham Travellers 20
Walney Central 4	Hensingham 14
West Hull 48	South London 10
Wigan St Patricks 22	Worth Village 0
Woolston 26	Eccles 10
York Acorn 18	Crown Malet 25

Second Round

Barrow Island 19	West Hull 12
Beverley 14	Normanton 16**
Bisons 8	East Leeds 33
Blackbrook 0	Chorley 23
Blackpool G 0	Thornhill 28
Eastmoor 8	Dudley Hill 16
Ellenborough 23	Egremont 10
Hensingham 8	Heworth 14
Lock Lane 20	Mayfield 14
Millom 38	Saddleworth R 16
Moorends 12	Thatto Heath 10
Oulton 12	Kells 14
Shaw Cross 9	Moldgreen 4
Wigan St Judes 14	Hemel Hempstead 13
Wigan St Patricks 42	Crown Malet 6
Woolston 14	Greetland AR 4

Replay

Beverley 20	Normanton 10

Third Round

Barrow 56	East Leeds 0
Batley 32	Shaw Cross 4
Bramley 42	Woolston 2
Carlisle 34	Dudley Hill 4
Dewsbury 72	Kells 12
Highfield 4	Beverley 27
Huddersfield 44	Wigan St Judes 10
Hull KR 58	Thornhill 6
Hunslet 64	Wigan St Patricks 4
Keighley C 68	Chorley 0
Leigh 40	Heworth 28
London B 30	Ellenborough 10
Rochdale H 48	Lock Lane 16
Ryedale-York 50	Barrow Island 20
Swinton 30	Millom 10
Whitehaven 64	Moorends 12

Fourth Round

Beverley 20	Batley 30

(at Hull)

Carlisle 2	Widnes 40
Doncaster 12	Sheffield E 22
Featherstone R 50	Barrow 22
Huddersfield 36	Halifax 30
Hunslet 32	Salford 32
KeighleyC 24	Dewsbury 12
Leeds 31	Bradford N 14
London B 20	Hull KR 26
Oldham 70	Bramley 10
Ryedale-York 18	Rochdale H 12
Swinton 22	Leigh 34
Warrington 17	Castleford 2
Whitehaven 24	Wakefield T 12
Wigan 16	St Helens 16
Workington T 30	Hull 6

Replays

St Helens 24	Wigan 40
Salford 52	Hunslet 10

Fifth Round

Batley 4	Wigan 70
Hull KR 14	Whitehaven 18
Keighley C 0	Huddersfield 30
Leeds 44	Ryedale-York 14
Salford 10	Featherstone R 30
Sheffield E 7	Widnes 19
Warrington 6	Oldham 17

Workington T 94	Leigh 4

Quarter-final s

Leeds 50	Workington T 16
Oldham 23	Huddersfield 12
Whitehaven 14	Featherstone R 42
Widnes 12	Wigan 26

Semi-finals

Huddersfield

Wigan 48	Oldham 20

Elland Rd, Leeds

Leeds 39	Featherstone R 22

***Match void, Normanton fielded ineligible player*

SILK CUT CHALLENGE CUP FINAL

Wembley   Apr 29

Wigan 30   **Leeds 10**
Tries: Robinson (2)   Try: Lowes
Paul, Hall, Tuigamala   Goals: Holroyd (3)
Goals: Botica (5)

Wigan: Paul, Robinson, Tuigamala, Connolly, Offiah, Botica, Edwards*, Skerrett (Atcheson), Hall, Cowie, Betts, Cassidy (Farrell), Clarke

Leeds: Tait, Fallon, Iro, Innes, Cummins, Schofield, Holroyd, Howard (Mann), Lowes, Faimalo (Harmon), Mercer, Eyres, Hanley*

Attendance: 78,550
Receipts: £2,040,000

Leading Tryscorers 1994-95

1	Martin Offiah	Wigan	53
2	Greg Austin	Huddersfield	52
3	Nick Pinkney	Keighley	46
4	Ellery Hanley	Leeds	41
5	David Plange	Hull KR	35
6	Mike Pechey	Whitehaven	34
7	Gary Connolly	Wigan	30
8	John Bentley	Halifax	29
	Scott Limb	Hunslet	29
	Alan Hunte	St Helens	29

Leading Goalscorers 1994-95

1	Frano Botica	Wigan	186
2	Bobby Goulding	St Helens	158
3	Simon Irving	Keighley	152
4	Martin Strett	Rochdale	150
5	John Schuster	Halifax	144
6	Mike Fletcher	Hull KR	142
7	Graham Holroyd	Leeds	135
8	Deryck Fox	Bradford N	131
9	Simon Wilson	Batley	127
10	Jonathan Davies	Warrington	126

Regal Trophy

First Round

Barrow 138	Nottingham C 0
Batley 38	Queens 8
Bramley 40	Mysons 14
Carlisle 25	Dudley Hill 12
Dewsbury 22	XIII Catalan 4
Highfield 12	Ovenden 6
Huddersfield 142	Blackpool G 4
Hull KR 48	Hensingham 8
Hunslet 14	St Esteve 18
Keighley C 56	Chorley 0
Leigh 18	Leigh MW 12
London B 34	Hemel Hempstead 16
Rochdale H 34	Woolston R 10
Ryedale-York 26	West Hull 9
Swinton 32	Saddleworth R 26
Whitehaven 66	Thatto Heath 0

Second Round

Batley 36	Ryedale-York 8
Bradford N 32	St Esteve 6
Carlisle 16	Dewsbury 30
Castleford 32	Halifax 26
Highfield 2	Widnes 50
(at St Helens)	
Huddersfield 11	St Helens 52
Hull 26	Barrow 16
Keighley C 28	Bramley 4
Leeds 54	Swinton 24
Oldham 28	Hull KR 0
Salford 16	London B 14
Sheffield E 46	Leigh 10
Warrington 44	Doncaster 14
Whitehaven 18	Featherstone R 12
Wigan 34	Rochdale H 12
Workington T 24	Wakefield T 8

Third Round

Batley 22	St Helens 22
Dewsbury 2	Castleford 30
Hull 14	Wigan 38
Keighley C 26	Sheffield E 10
Salford 24	Warrington 31
Whitehaven 14	Bradford N 34
Widnes 20	Oldham 6
Workington T 14	Leeds 18
Replay	
St Helens 50	Batley 22

Fourth Round

Keighley C 18	Warrington 20
Leeds 14	Castleford 34
Widnes 23	Bradford N 10
Wigan 24	St Helens 22

Semi-finals

Widnes 4	Warrington 30
Wigan 34	Castleford 6

REGAL TROPHY FINAL

Huddersfield   *Jan 28*
Wigan 40   **Warrington 10**
Tries: Tuigamala (2)   *Tries: Forster (2)*
Botica, Connolly   *Goal: Davies*
McDermott, Offiah
Goals: Botica (8)

Wigan: Paul, Robinson, Tuigamala (Atcheson), Connolly, Offiah, Botica, Edwards*, Skerrett, Hall, Cowie (McDermott), Betts, Cassidy, Clarke
Warrington: Davies, Forster, Bateman, Harris, Myler, Maloney, Mackey*, Tees, Barlow (Bennett), McGuire, Cullen, Darbyshire (Sanderson), Shelford
Attendance: 19,636

1995 AWARDS

Man of Steel: Denis Betts (Wigan)

1st Division Player: Bobby Goulding (St Helens)

2nd Division Player: Nick Pinkney (Keighley C)

Young Player: Andrew Farrell (Wigan)

Coach: Graeme West (Wigan)

Referee: Russell Smith (Castleford)

World Cup & Domestic Records

WORLD CUP

	Winner	Venue
1954	Great Britain	France
1957	Australia	Australia
1960	Great Britain	England
1968	Australia	Aus/N Zld
1970	Australia	England
1972	Great Britain	France
1975*	Australia	Worldwide
1977	Australia	Aus/N Zld
1988	Australia	N Zealand
1992	Australia	England

World Chps played home & away

LEAGUE CHAMPIONSHIP
Division One
1973-74	Salford
1974-75	St. Helens
1975-76	Salford
1976-77	Featherstone Rovers
1977-78	Widnes
1978-79	Hull Kingston Rovers
1979-80	Bradford Northern
1980-81	Bradford Northern
1981-82	Leigh
1982-83	Hull
1983-84	Hull Kingston Rovers
1984-85	Hull Kingston Rovers
1985-86	Halifax
1986-87	Wigan
1987-88	Widnes
1988-89	Widnes
1989-90	Wigan
1990-91	Wigan
1991-92	Wigan
1992-93	Wigan
1993-94	Wigan
1994-95	Wigan

PREMIERSHIP TROPHY
1975	Leeds
1976	St. Helens
1977	St. Helens
1978	Bradford Northern
1979	Leeds
1980	Widnes
1981	Hull Kingston Rovers
1982	Widnes
1983	Widnes
1984	Hull Kingston Rovers
1985	St. Helens
1986	Warrington
1987	Wigan
1988	Widnes
1989	Widnes
1990	Widnes
1991	Hull
1992	Wigan
1993	St. Helens
1994	Wigan
1995	Wigan

CHALLENGE CUP
1897	Batley
1899	Oldham
1900	Swinton
1901	Batley
1902	Broughton Rangers
1903	Halifax
1904	Halifax
1905	Warrington
1906	Bradford
1907	Warrington
1908	Hunslet
1909	Wakefield Trinity
1910	Leeds
1911	Broughton Rangers
1912	Dewsbury
1913	Huddersfield
1914	Hull
1915	Huddersfield
1920	Huddersfield
1921	Leigh
1922	Rochdale Hornets
1923	Leeds
1924	Wigan
1925	Oldham
1926	Swinton
1927	Oldham
1928	Swinton
1929	Wigan
1930	Widnes
1931	Halifax
1932	Leeds
1933	Huddersfield
1934	Hunslet
1935	Castleford
1936	Leeds
1937	Widnes
1938	Salford
1939	Halifax
1941	Leeds
1942	Leeds
1943	Dewsbury
1944	Bradford Northern
1945	Huddersfield
1946	Wakefield Trinity
1947	Bradford Northern
1948	Wigan
1949	Bradford Northern
1950	Warrington
1951	Wigan
1952	Workington Town
1953	Huddersfield
1954	Warrington
1955	Barrow
1956	St. Helens
1957	Leeds
1958	Wigan
1959	Wigan
1960	Wakefield Trinity
1961	St. Helens
1962	Wakefield Trinity
1963	Wakefield Trinity
1964	Widnes
1965	Wigan
1966	St. Helens
1967	Featherstone Rovers
1968	Leeds
1969	Castleford
1970	Castleford
1971	Leigh
1972	St. Helens
1973	Featherstone Rovers
1974	Warrington
1975	Widnes
1976	St. Helens
1977	Leeds
1978	Leeds
1979	Widnes
1980	Hull Kingston Rovers
1981	Widnes
1982	Hull
1983	Featherstone Rovers
1984	Widnes
1985	Wigan
1986	Castleford
1987	Halifax
1988	Wigan
1989	Wigan
1990	Wigan
1991	Wigan
1992	Wigan
1993	Wigan
1994	Wigan
1995	Wigan

KNOCKOUT TROPHY
(Regal Trophy since 1989)
1972	Halifax
1973	Leeds
1974	Warrington
1975	Bradford Northern
1976	Widnes
1977	Castleford
1978	Warrington
1979	Widnes
1980	Bradford Northern
1981	Warrington
1982	Hull
1983	Wigan
1984	Leeds
1985	Hull Kingston Rovers
1986	Wigan
1987	Wigan
1988	St. Helens
1989	Wigan
1990	Wigan
1991	Warrington
1992	Widnes
1993	Wigan
1994	Wigan
1995	Wigan

Rugby Union ▬▬▬▬▬▬▬▬▬▬

In any other year, a Grand Slam would have been enough. Rowell's England played well, too. They proved that they could contain and control. There was no tactical revolution; they wore the same clothes as they had for six winters, they just seemed to fit better. Nobody quite realised then how rapidly the fashion was changing. They applauded Rowell the motivator; lauded the strength of players like Richards and Clarke (though he did pick up the first yellow card in the championship) and the winter season ended with England generally feeling optimistic, Scotland reassured, France uncertain, and Ireland and Wales desperate. The winter season, though, quickly became a footnote to the year.

It wasn't just the World Cup that eclipsed it, professionalism came in from the wings and stood centre-stage so it couldn't be ignored any longer and Will Carling made the princely mistake of messing with a princess.

The professional argument was won surprisingly easily. The explosion of money in the game was simply a force that could not be resisted. In the Five Nations, England's gate revenue from four games amounted to £4.8m. The people creating that wealth (according to the Laws) got nothing. With the new stand completed for the 1996 Five Nations' games, the revenue for *each* match is expected to exceed £2.1m. If you'd like to tell Brian Moore that he's not worth a penny of that, go ahead.

Add to that the value of the TV contract (£27m for three years) and the top-ups from advertising and endorsements and you have a very wealthy sport. Yet even in March, full-blown professionalism still appeared to be off the agenda. Immediately prior to the World Cup, Rupert Murdoch (the cat among the IRFB pigeons) concluded a £360m deal with the southern hemisphere teams; Australia, New Zealand and South Africa. The World Cup came and went (profit £22.1m) and the stage was set for the critical meeting of the International Rugby Football Board in Paris in August. On Sunday, 27th August, the IRFB issued a release, point three of which clearly stated, "there will be no prohibition on payment or the provision of other material benefit to any person involved in the game".

A new game was born. In March, the RFU had tried to restrain the free movement between Union and League, enforcing a three-year moratorium for people changing codes. It must have been the briefest Law in Union's statue book. In August, it was out of the window. Come September, the talk was all of Jonathan Davies' return to Union.

Will Carling will benefit as much as anyone from the revolution. Though his position with the England team became rather confusing. Having announced that he was to be captain for the winter, it subsequently appeared he may have appointed himself. Yet Carling's year has all been a bit of a muddle. He called the sports administrators "Old Farts", to Greg Dyke, posing as a journalist for a Channel Four programme. Carling, having been around for an awful long time, really should have known better. Dyke, at the end of the day, didn't give a monkey's about Carling. He just wanted to sell his programme.

Then our Will got a royal appointment. What can you say? Well, if things do go dreadfully wrong with Rowell and the England team and Philip de Glanville gets favoured, he could just end up being King. No, hang on a minute..it doesn't work like that, does it?

*Q*uotes

"We had nice expenses.......we were brought up that way" - **Mike Catt, the first rugby player to go professional, admitting he always was.**

"We may have to recognise amateurism has been abandoned and then do our best to ensure we supervise the consequent changes" - **Vernon Pugh, IRFB chairman, after Australia announced a deal in which their players would get £40,000 for a one-year contract.**

"There's no way now that we can avoid the full-time employemnt of guys to play rugby" - **Tony Hallet, secretary of the RFU, responding to the news that Murdoch had signed the southern hemisphere international teams up to a £360m ten-year contract.**

"I did not expect them to go that far.....I admire them for their honesty" - **Carling offering rare praise to the game's administrators after the IRFB voted to abandon amateurism at their meeting in August.**

"Rob Andrew is the Kevin Keegan of rugby" - **Sir John Hall, after signing Andrew up for Newcastle (formerly Gosforth) rugby club.**

"You would never allow an amateur to run your business. You must never allow an amateur to run rugby football" - **Sir John Hall.**

"Sir John Hall has barely watched a game of rugby in his life and we should not stand by and let him hijack the sport. He's on a big ego trip with no consideration for English rugby at all" - **Brian Hanlon, Bristol coaching director.**

"The FFR (French Rugby Federation) has no vision. It is totally opposed to progress, with ten years of failure" - **Laurent Cabannes, French flanker.**

"England have tremendous strength in depth and personally I think it is desperately unfair that they are now actually picking their best players" - **Iain Morrison, Scottish flanker.**

"If the game is run properly as a professional game, you do not need 57 old farts running rugby' - **Will Carling, in an off-the-record comment to Greg Dyke for his Channel Four sports programme.**

"Will Carling wishes to apologise to every member of the committee of the RFU for his inapproiate and gratuitously offensive comment at the end of a recent TV programme..." - **Carling, the opening sentence of his formal apology made to the media. Carling was duly reinstated as captain.**

"This has been so bizarre, I expected Brian Rix to appear at some point" - **Brian Moore, on the Carling 'Old Farts' affair.**

"Perhaps we should despair of beating England again" - **Pierre Berbizier, French coach, after England beat his side for the eighth consecutive time in the Five Nations.**

"It was flattering that the Princess was interested in me. That is probably where I made my mistake" - **Will Carling**

World Cup ━━━━━━━━━━━━━━━━━━━━━━━━━━━

If there were doubts about a World Cup being played in South Africa, many of them were dispelled in the first game, a wonderfully comitted encounter between Australia and the host nation. And if there were doubts that South Africa couldn't carry off the title, they were dispelled too as they out-ran and out-tackled an Australian team that had the lion's share from the set pieces. Victory for Pienaar's team effectively set up a quarter-final game against the Western Samoans. Australia drew the shorter straw; they would meet England.

Scotland started at a gallop, but the scores they rattled up against Ivory Coast and Tonga were put into perspective when New Zealand put 145 points on the board against Japan, including 21 tries. Any number of World Cup records were broken, but it was a futile exercise. The gap in ability rendered it an unsporting exercise. In the 1999 World Cup they plan to extend the number of teams and presumably the number of mismatches.

Everybody looked good against Japan, but New Zealand looked good against Wales and Ireland, too. Jonah Lomu made his presence felt on the All Blacks' wing. Geoghegan got a hand on him, but no-one else did. Against Wales, Lomu was at least shown to be human, leaving the field in the 72nd minute with a bruised shoulder. But the myth was growing. With each report he seemed to be a few centimtres taller and a couple of pounds heavier. If finally settled at 6ft 5in and 18 and a half stones, but they might as well have said 10ft and 50 stones for the impact he was having.

Scotland's narrow defeat against the French meant they had to face New Zealand. The All Blacks would once have rolled over them, this time they ran round them. It was exhilarating stuff and Scotland replied in kind. It wasn't enough, but it was more than England would do. England were occupied playing their own final - against Australia - and won it too, with an Andrew dropped goal two minutes into time added-on. England forgot, though, that it was only a quarter-final. In the other quarter-final games, South Africa defeated the bullish Western Samoans and France had an easy time with Ireland.

In the semi-final, Lomu got the credit for the All Black demolition of England. It was unfair to give it all to the man mountain. England should get their share. From the reverse kick-off, when Carling and Tony Underwood collided, it was evident that their minds were elsewhere. The preparation had been curiously complacent; cameras in team meetings, jokes about Lomu from the captain. Out on the field, there seemed to be an absence of strategy. If Lomu was so devastating, why was there no policy of containment? He's all yours, Tony. And so he was. Even when the game was irretrievably lost - 25-3 at half-time - vision did not leave the tunnel. In his first possession of the second half, Andrew kicked.

South Africa survived their semi-final by about six inches. That was how far from the line Frenchman Benazzi was. New Zealand were favourite for the Johannesburg final, but the passion held for the hosts. South Africa put two men on Lomu and tackled and tackled some more. After 80 minutes it was tied at 9-9. A penalty each in the first half of extra time kept it level, till Joel Stransky popped over a dropped goal with eight minutes left. Nelson Mandela, in a number six shirt, presented the trophy to Pienaar, in a number six shirt. Politics and sport in a happy conjuction. For once. Only the injury to the Ivory Coast winger, Max Brito, paralysed for life after an injury in the Tonga match, left a sad shadow on the Cup.

World Cup Results

POOL A

Newlands, Cape Town   May 25   Ref: D Bevan
Australia (13) 18   **South Africa (14) 27**
Tries: Lynagh (31 min)   Tries: Hendriks (36 min)
    Kearns (76 min)   Stransky (62 min)
Conv: Lynagh   Conv: Stransky
PG: Lynagh (2)   PG: Stransky (4)
                            DG: Stransky

Boet Erasmus, Port Elizabeth   May 26   Ref: C Hawke
Canada (11) 34   **Romania (3) 3**
Tries: Snow (20 min)   PG: Nichitean
    Charron (58 min)
    McKenzie (73 min)
Conv: Rees (2)
PG: Rees (4)
DG: Rees

Newlands, Cape Town   May 30   Ref: K McCartney
South Africa (8) 21   **Romania (0) 8**
Tries: Richter (10, 54 min)   Try: Guranescu (76 min)
Conv: Johnson   PG: Ivanciuc
PG: Johnson (3)

Boet Erasmus, Port Elizabeth   May 31   Ref: P Robin
Australia (20) 27   **Canada (6) 11**
Tries: Tabua (7 min)   Try: Charron (76 min)
    Roff (9 min)   PG: Rees (2)
    Lynagh (55 min)
Conv: Lynagh (3)
PG: Lynagh (2)

Boet Erasmus, Port Elizabeth   June 3   Ref: D McHugh
Canada (0) 0   **South Africa (17) 20**
                            Tries: Richter (24, 31 min)
                            Conv: Stransky (2)
                            PG: Stransky (2)
Sent off: J Dalton RSA, G Rees CAN, R Snow CAN

Danie Craven, Stellenbosch   June 3   Ref: N Saito
Australia (14) 42   **Romania (3) 3**
Tries: Foley (27 min)   DG: Ivanciuc
    Roff (36, 60 min)
    Burke (65 min)
    Smith (70 min)
    Wilson (81 min)
Conv: Burke (2) , Eales (4)

Final Table	P	W	D	L	PF	PA	Pts
South Africa	3	3	0	0	68	26	9
Australia	3	2	0	1	87	41	7
Canada	3	1	0	2	45	50	5
Romania	3	0	0	3	14	97	3

POOL B

Basil Kenyon, East London   May 27   Ref: J Dume
Western Samoa (12) 42   **Italy (11) 18**
Tries: Lima (9, 46 min)   Tries: Cuttitta (35 min)
    Harder (15, 78 min)   Vaccari (63 min)
    Tatupu (52 min)   Conv: Dominguez
    Kellett (77 min)   PG: Dominguez
Conv: Kellett (3)   DG: Dominguez
PG: Kellett (2)

King's Park, Durban   May 27   Ref: J Fleming
England (12) 24   **Argentina (0) 18**
PG: Andrew (6)   Tries: Noriega (53 min)
DG: Andrew (2)   Arbizu (79 min)
                            Conv: Arbizu
                            PG: Arbizu (2)

Basil Kenyon, East London   May 30   Ref: D Bishop
Western Samoa (10) 32   **Argentina (16) 26**
Tries: Harder (9 min)   Try: Crexell (43 min)
    Leaupepe (73 min)   Pen Try: (7 min)
    Lam (76 min)   Conv: Cilley (2)
Conv: Kellett   PG: Cilley (4)
PG: Kellett (5)

King's Park, Durban   May 31   Ref: S Hilditch
England (16) 27   **Italy (10) 20**
Tries: T Underwood (8 m)   Tries: Vaccari (39 min)
    R Underwood (48 m)   Cuttitta (81 min)
Conv: Andrew   Conv: Dominguez (2)
PG: Andrew (5)   PG: Dominguez (2)

King's Park, Durban   June 4   Ref: P Robin
England (21) 44   **Western Samoa (0) 22**
Tries: Back (1 min)   Tries: Sini (46, 51 min)
    R Underwood   Umaga (78 min)
    (36, 69 min)   Conv: Fa'amasino (2)
Pen Try: (58 min)   PG: Fa'amasino
Conv: Callard (3)
PG: Callard (5)
DG: Catt

Basil Kenyon, East London   June 4   Ref: C Thomas
Argentina (12) 25   **Italy (12) 31**
Tries: Martin (9 min)   Tries: Vaccari (50 min)
    Corral (68 min)   Gerosa (53 min)
    Cilley (73 min)   Dominguez (76 min)
Pen Try: (34 min)   Conv: Dominguez (2)
Conv: Cilley   PG: Dominguez (4)
PG: Cilley

Final Table	P	W	D	L	GF	GA	Pts
England	3	3	0	0	95	60	9
Western Samoa	3	2	0	1	96	88	7
Italy	3	1	0	2	69	94	5
Argentina	3	0	0	3	69	87	3

World Cup quotes

"Most people feel sorry for us and that is more painful than any other reaction" - **Vernon Pugh, Welsh RFU president.**

"It was like the Falklands. I was counting them out and counting them in" - **Jack Rowell, England manager, after the Western Samoa match.**

"It's a cultural problem. You just can't get into their heads. The players don't need a coach, they need a psychiatrist" - **Georges Costa, the French-born coach of the Italians, admitting problems with his team.**

"I know that 'Campo' will have a go at me and England whenever he is asked. After all, why not criticise the opposition after he has slagged off his own teammates and management in the past?" - **Will Carling, after David Campese likened the England captain to a castrated bull.**

"Beforehand, I thought they were there for the taking. Unfortunately, I was proved wrong" - **Mike Hall, sublimely optimistic captain of Wales, on the match with New Zealand.**

"Remember rugby is a team game. all 14 of you make sure you pass the ball to Jonah" - **Auckland schoolkids, in a fax to the New Zealand team before the England semi-final.**

"I am hoping not to come across him again. He's a freak and the sooner he goes away the better" - **Will Carling, failing to appreciate the talents of Jonah Lomu.**

"It's nice to score one or two and run past that thing out there....' - **Carling again, who scored twice against in the later stages of the NZ game.**

"Clearly England are not a side with great innovation or great lateral thinking. So I decided that the first thing we would do would be the thing they least expected. Teams are like robots these days...." - **Laurie Mains, on why New Zealand chose the reverse kick-off.**

"There's no doubt about it, he's a big bastard" - **Gavin Hastings on Jonah Lomu.**

"I don't know about us not having a plan B when things went wrong, we looked like we didn't have a plan A" - **Geoff Cooke, former England manager, after the defeat by New Zealand.**

"I'm sure our prime minister will put the crown jewels up for sake to keep him in the game" - **Laurie Mains, All Black coach.**

"I took precautions. We drank the champagne before the match" - **Pierre Berbizier, French coach, after the semi-final defeat by the Springboks.**

"It was a pleasure to shake Carling's hand with a smile on my face for a change while he looked at the grass" - **Philippe Saint-André, French captain, after the third-place play-off victory over England. France's first in nine matches.**

"Gavin Hastings heart and spirit may come from Scotland, but he has the soul of an All Black" - **Sean Fitzpatrick, New Zealand captain, paying the Scottish captain the ultimate compliment.**

POOL C

Free State Stadium, Bloemfontein May 27   Ref: E Sklar
Wales (36) 57　　　**Japan (0) 10**
Tries: Moore (25 min)　Tries: Oto (61, 83 min)
*　　　I Evans (28, 39 min)*
*　　　Thomas (40, 43, 73 min)*
*　　　Taylor (76 min)*
Conv: Jenkins (5)
PG: Jenkins (4)

Ellis Park, Johannesburg May 27   Ref: W Erickson
New Zealand (20) 43　　**Ireland (12) 19**
Tries: Lomu (29, 42 min)　Tries: Halpin (7 min)
*　　　Bunce (32 min)　　　McBride (39 min)*
*　　　Kronfeld (68 min)　　Corkery (76 min)*
*　　　Osborne (80 min)　Conv: Elwood (2)*
Conv: Mehrtens (3)
PG: Mehrtens (4)

Ellis Park, Johannesburg May 31   Ref: E Morrison
New Zealand (20) 34　　**Wales (6) 9**
Tries: Little (18 min)　PG: Jenkins (2)
*　　　Ellis (35 min)　　DG: Jenkins*
*　　　Kronfeld (69 min)*
Conv: Mehrtens (2)
PG: Mehrtens (4) DG: Mehrtens

Free State Stadium, B'fontein May 31 Ref: S Neethling
Ireland (19) 50　　　**Japan (14) 28**
Tries: Corkery (10 min)　Tries: Latu (34 min)
*　　　Francis (19 min)　　Izawa (38 min)*
*　　　Geoghegan (25 min)　Hirao (59 min)*
*　　　Halvey (66 min)　　Takura (72 min)*
*　　　Hogan (76 min)　Conv: Yoshida (4)*
Pen Tries: (42, 64 min)
Conv: Burke (6) PG: Burke

Free State Stadium, B'fontein June 4 Ref: G Gadjovich
New Zealand (84) 145　**Japan (3) 17**
Tries: Rush (1, 38, 73m)　Tries: Kajihara (47, 64 min)
*　　　Loe (5 min)　　　Conv: Hirose (2)*
*　　　Ellis (8, 11, 32,　　PG: Hirose*
*　　　43, 68, 71 min)*
*　　　R Brooke (15, 58 min)*
*　　　Osborne (19, 41 min)*
*　　　Ieremia (22 min)*
*　　　Culhane (27 min)*
*　　　Wilson (29, 36, 76 min)*
*　　　Dowd (50 min)*
*　　　Henderson (78 min)*
Conv: Culhane (20)

Ellis Park, Johannesburg June 4 Ref: I Rogers
Ireland (14) 24　　　**Wales (6) 23**
Tries: Popplewell (5 min)　Tries: Humphreys (72 min)
*　　　McBride (13 min)　　　Taylor (84 min)*
*　　　Halvey (69 min)　Conv: Jenkins (2)*
Conv: Elwood (3)　　PG: Jenkins (2)
PG: Elwood　　　DG: A Davies

Final Table	P	W	D	L	GF	GA	Pts
New Zealand	3	3	0	0	222	45	9
Ireland	3	2	0	1	93	94	7
Wales	3	1	0	2	89	68	5
Japan	3	0	0	3	55	252	3

POOL D

Loftus Versveld, Pretoria May 26   Ref: S Lander
France (6) 38　　　**Tonga (0) 10**
Tries: Lacroix (64, 76 min)　Try: Va'enuku
*　　　Hueber (68 min)　Conv: Tu'ipolotu*
*　　　Saint-André (72m)　PG: Tu'ipolotu*
Conv: Lacroix (3)
PG: Lacroix (3)
DG: Delaigue
Sent off: F Mahoni TON

Olympia Park, Rustenburg May 26   Ref: F Vito
Scotland (34) 89　　**Ivory Coast (0) 0**
Tries: G Hastings (9, 29,
*　　　35, 74 min)*
*　　　Walton (37, 69 min)*
*　　　Logan (47, 55 min)*
*　　　Chalmers (49 min)*
*　　　Stanger (59 min)*
*　　　Burnell (62 min)*
*　　　Wright (72 min)*
*　　　Joiner (81 min)*
Conv: G Hastings (9)
PG: G Hastings (2)

Loftus Versveld, Pretoria May 30   Ref: B Leask
Scotland (18) 41　　**Tonga (5) 5**
Tries: Peters (57 min)　Try: Fenukitau (13 min)
*　　　G Hastings (66 min)*
*　　　S Hastings (78 min)*
Conv: G Hastings
PG: G Hastings (8)

Olympia Park, Rustenburg May 30   Ref: H Moon Soo
France (28) 54　　　**Ivory Coast (3) 18**
Tries: Lacroix (1, 67 min)　Tries: Camara (64 min)
*　　　Benazzi (24 min)　　Soulama (75 min)*
*　　　Accoceberry (32m)　Conv: Kouassi*
*　　　Viars (40 min)　　PG: Kouassi (2)*
*　　　Techoueyres (41m)*
*　　　Costes (59 min)*
*　　　Saint-André (71 min)*
Conv: Lacroix (2), Deylaud (2)
PG: Lacroix (2)

Loftus Versveld, Pretoria June 3   Ref: W Erickson
Scotland (13) 19　　**France (3) 22**
Try: Wainwright (40 min)　Try: N'Tamack (79 min)
Conv: G Hastings　Conv: Lacroix
PG: G Hastings (4)　PG: Lacroix (5)

Olympia Park, Rustenburg June 3   Ref: D Reardon
Tonga (24) 29　　　**Ivory Coast (0) 11**
Tries: Latukefu (26 min)　Try: Okou (73 min)
*　　　Otai (37 min)　　PG: Dali (2)*
*　　　Tu'ipolotu (53 min)*
Pen Try: (21 min)
Conv: Tu'ipolotu (3)
PG: Tu'ipolotu

Final Table	P	W	D	L	GF	GA	Pts
France	3	3	0	0	114	47	9
Scotland	3	2	0	1	149	27	7
Tonga	3	1	0	2	44	90	5
Ivory Coast	3	0	0	3	29	172	3

QUARTER-FINALS

King's Park, Durban   June 10   Ref: E Morrison
France (12) 36   **Ireland (12) 12**
Tries: Saint-André (78m)   PG: Elwood (4)
*   N'Tamack (84 min)*
Conv: Lacroix PG: Lacroix (8)
France: J-L Sadourny; E N'Tamack, P Sella, T Lacroix, P
Saint-Andre (capt); C Deylaud, A Hueber; L Armary, J-M
Gonzalez, C Califano, O Merle, O Roumat, A Benazzi, M
Cecillon, L Cabannes
Ireland: C M P O'Shea; D O'Mahony, B J Mullin, J C Bell,
S P Geoghegan; E P Elwood, N A Hogan; N J
Popplewell, T J Kingston (capt), G F Halpin, G M Fulcher,
N P J Francis, D Corkery, P S Johns, W D McBride

Ellis Park, Johannesburg   June 10   Ref: J Fleming
South Africa (23) 42   **Western Samoa (0) 14**
Tries: Williams (16, 34   Tries: Nu'ualiitia (69 min)
*   45, 76 min)   Tatupu (72 min)*
*   Rossouw (40 min)   Conv: Fa'amasino (2)*
*   Andrews (49 min)*
Conv: Johnson (3) PG: Johnson (2)
South Africa: A J Joubert (B Venter); G K Johnson, C P
Scholtz, J C Mulder, C M Williams; H P le Roux, J H van
der Westhuizen; J P du Randt, C L C Rossouw, I S
Swart, J J Wiese (A E Drotske), M G Andrews (K Otto), J
F Pienaar (capt), R A W Straeuli, R J Kruger (A Richter)
Western Samoa: M T Umaga; B Lima, T Vaega, T
Fa'amasino, G Harder (F Tuilagi); F Sini, T Nu'ualiitia; M
A N Mika (B P Reidy), T Leiasamaivao, G Latu (P
Fatialofa), L Falaniko, S Lemanea, S J Tatupu (S L
Vaifale), P R Lam (capt), P J Paramor

Newlands, Cape Town   June 11   Ref: D Bishop
England (13) 25   **Australia (6) 22**
Try: T Underwood (20m)   Try: Smith (40 min)
Conv: Andrew   Conv; Lynagh
PG: Andrew (5)   PG: Lynagh (5)
DG: Andrew
England: M J Catt; T Underwood, W D C Carling (capt),
J C Guscott, R Underwood; C R Andrew, C D Morris; J
Leonard, B C Moore, V E Ubogu, M O Johnson, M C
Bayfield, T A K Rodber, D Richards, B B Clarke
Australia: M Burke; D I Campese, J S Little, T J Horan,
D P Smith; M P Lynagh (capt); G M Gregan; D J Crowley,
P N Kearns, E J A McKenzie, R J McCall, J A Eales, V
Ofahengaue, B T Gavin, D J Wilson

Loftus Versveld, Pretoria   June 11   Ref: D Bevan
New Zealand (17) 48   **Scotland (9) 30**
Tries: Little (4, 20 min)   Tries: Weir (45, 65 min)
*   Lomu (27 min)   S Hastings (74 min)*
*   Mehrtens (42 min)   Conv: G Hastings (3)*
*   Bunce (47 min)   PG: G Hastings (3)*
*   Fitzpatrick (61 min)*
Conv: Mehrtens (6) PG: Mehrtens (2)
New Zealand: J W Wilson; M C G Ellis, F E Bunce, W K
Little, J T Lomu; A P Mehrtens, G T M Bachop; R W Loe,
S B T Fitzpatrick (capt), O M Brown, I D Jones, R M
Brooke, J W Joseph, Z V Brooke, J A Kronfeld
Scotland: A G Hastings (capt); C A Joiner, S Hastings, A
G Shiel, K M Logan; C M Chalmers (I C Jardine), B W
Redpath; D I W Hilton, K S Milne, P H Wright, D F Cronin
(S J Campbell), G W Weir, R I Wainwright, E W Peters, I
R Morrison

SEMI-FINALS

King's Park, Durban   June 17   Ref: D Bevan
South Africa (10) 19   **France (6) 15**
Try: Kruger (25 min)   PG: Lacroix (5)
Conv: Stransky
PG: Stransky (4)
South Africa: A J Joubert; J T Small, H P le Roux, J C
Mulder, C M Williams; J T Stransky, J H van der
Westhuizen (J P Roux); J P du Randt, C L C Rossouw, I
S Swart, J J Wiese, M G Andrews, J F Pienaar (capt), J J
Strydom, R J Kruger
France: J-L Sadourny; E N'Tamack, P Sella, T Lacroix, P
Saint-André (capt); C Deylaud, Galthié; L Armary, J-M
Gonzalez, C Califano, O Merle, O Roumat, A Benazzi, M
Cecillon, L Cabannes

Newlands, Cape Town   June 18   Ref: S Hilditch
New Zealand (25) 45   **England (3) 29**
Tries: Lomu (2, 25,   Tries: R Underwood (58, 80m)
*   41, 70 min)   Carling (67, 72 min)*
*   Kronfeld   Conv: Andrew (3)*
*   Bachop   PG: Andrew*
Conv: Mehrtens
PG: Mehrtens, DG: Z Brooke
New Zealand: G M Osborne; J W Wilson, F E Bunce, W
K Little, J T Lomu; A P Mehrtens, G T M Bachop; C W
Dowd, S B T Fitzpatrick (capt), O M Brown, I D Jones, R
M Brooke, M R Brewer, Z V Brooke (B P Larsen), J A
Kronfeld
England: M J Catt; T Underwood, W D C Carling (capt),
J C Guscott, R Underwood; C R Andrew, C D Morris; J
Leonard, B C Moore, V E Ubogu, M O Johnson, M C
Bayfield, T A K Rodber, D Richards, B B Clarke

3RD PLACE PLAY OFF

Loftus Versfeld, Pretoria   June 22   Ref: D Bishop
France (3) 19   **England (3) 9**
Tries: Roumat (58 min)   PG: Andrew (3)
*   N'Tamack (79 min)*
PG: Lacroix (3)
France: J-L Sadourny; E N'Tamack, P Sella, T Lacroix, P
Saint-André (capt), F Mesnel, Galthié; L Benezech, J-M
Gonzalez, C Califano, O Merle (O Brouzet), O Roumat, A
Benazzi, A Cigagna, L Cabannes
England: M J Catt; I Hunter, W D C Carling (capt), J C
Guscott, R Underwood, C R Andrew, C D Morris; J
Leonard, B C Moore, V E Ubogu, M O Johnson, M C
Bayfield, T A K Rodber, S O Ojomoh, B B Clarke

WORLD CUP FINAL

Ellis Park, Johannesburg   June 24   Ref: E Morrison
South Africa (9) 15   New Zealand (6) 12   aet
PG: Stransky (3)   PG: Mehrtens (3)
DG: Stransky (2)   DG: Mehrtens
South Africa: A J Joubert; J T Small (B Venter), H P le
Roux, J C Mulder, C M Williams; J T Stransky, J H van
der Westhuizen; J P du Randt, C L C Rossouw, I S Swart
(G L Pagel), J J Wiese, M G Andrews (R A W Straeuli), J
F Pienaar (capt), J J Strydom, R J Kruger
New Zealand: G M Osborne; J W Wilson (M Ellis), F E
Bunce, W K Little, J T Lomu; A P Mehrtens, G T M
Bachop; C W Dowd (R Loe), S B T Fitzpatrick (capt), O M
Brown, I D Jones, R M Brooke, M R Brewer (J Joseph), Z
V Brooke (B P Larsen), J A Kronfeld

*M*ore *World Cup quotes*

"Imagine England and South Africa getting through to the final. Why would you go and watch rugby if those two were fighting it out to be world champions?" **- David Campese, proving that Aussies too can whinge.**

"Good Luck Bokke" **- Painted on the wings of a Boeing 747 which flew above the stadium just before the final.**

"There were not 63,000 cheering us on out there. There were 43 million" **- Francois Pienaar, after the final.**

You have been a shining example of dignity and fortitude" **- Nelson Madela to Francois Pienaar.**

"When he gave me the trophy he said, "Thank you for what you have done for South Africa" but I told him that nobody has done as much for our country as him" **- Pienaar, relating his conversation with Mandela when the South African president presented the trophy.**

"Unity in our coutry has been given a wonderful shot in the arm" **- Desmond Tutu, Archbishop opf Cape Town, who watched the game in an Irish pub in Los Angeles.**

"Upon reaching the summit of Everest, Edmund Hilary didn't feel like mountaineering again. Kitch reached his Everest yesterday and I respect him for that" **- Edward Griffiths, South African RFU official, on SA coach Christie's resignation after the World Cup.**

"I saw the World Cup in England and it was laughable" **- Louis Luyt, president ofthe South African Rugby Union, in October 1994.**

"I reject all charges of bringing the game into disrepute. I was expressing my sincere and honest views on the game of rugby union" **- Luyt, later that month.**

"I don't know why I am perceived to be this ogre..." **- Luyt in London in November, 1994.**

"We boasted in 1987 the the real World Cup could not be won in New Zealand because we were not there. It was the same in England in 1991. In 1995, we have proved that, if we were there, we could have won" **- Luyt, at the post World Cup final dinner, being graceless in victory.**

"Tired and emotional are the words that spring to mind" **- Morne Du Plessis, South African team manager, on the comments of Louis Luyt.**

Five Nations Championship

Parc des Princes, Paris   Jan 21
France 21   **Wales 9**
Tries: N'Tamack   *PG: N Jenkins (3)*
   Saint-André
Conv: Lacroix
PG: Lacroix (3)
France: Sadourny, N'Tamack, Sella, Lacroix, Saint-André*, Deylaud, Accoceberry, Benezech, Gonzalez, Califano, Benazzi, Merle, Roumat, Cabannes, Benetton
Wales: Clement, Hill (Back), Hall, Taylor, Walker, N Jenkins, R Jones, R Evans (Griffiths), G Jenkins, J Davies, S Davies, D Jones, Llewellyn*, Collins, P Davies

Lansdowne Road, Dublin   Jan 21
Ireland 8   **England 20**
Try: Foley   *Tries: Carling*
PG: Burke   *Clarke*
                                 T Underwood
                                Conv: Andrew
                                PG: Andrew
Ireland: O'Shea, Geoghegan, Mullin*, Danaher, Woods, Burke, Hogan, Popplewell, Wood, Clohessy, Foley, Galwey, Francis (Fulcher), Corkery, Johns
England: Catt, T Underwood, Carling*, Guscott, R Underwood, Andrew, Bracken, Leonard, Moore, Ubogu, Rodber, Johnson, Bayfield, Clarke, Richards

Twickenham, London   Feb 4
England 31   **France 10**
Tries: T Underwood (2)   *Try: Viars*
   Guscott   *Conv: Lacroix*
Conv: Andrew (2)   *PG: Lacroix*
PG: Andrew (4)
England: Catt, T Underwood, Carling*, Guscott, R Underwood, Andrew, Bracken, Leonard, Moore, Ubogu, Rodber, Johnson, Bayfield, Clarke, Richards
France: Sadourny (Viars), Bernat-Salles, Sella, Lacroix, Saint-André*, Deylaud, Accoceberry, Benezech (Seigne), Gonzalez, Califano, Benazzi, Brouzet, Roumat, Cabannes, Benetton

Murrayfield, Edinburgh   Feb 4
Scotland 26   **Ireland 13**
Tries: Joiner   *Tries: Mullin*
   Cronin   *Bell*
Conv: Hastings (2)   *PG: Burke*
PG: Hastings (4)
Scotland: Hastings*, Joiner, Townsend, Jardine, Logan, Chalmers, Redpath, Hilton, Milne, Wright, D Cronin, Campbell, Wainwright, Peters, Morrison
Ireland: O'Shea, Geoghegan, Mullin, Danaher, Bell, Burke, Bradley*, Popplewell, Wood, Clohessy, Johns, Fulcher, Foley, B Cronin, McBride

National Stadium, Cardiff   Feb 18
Wales 9   **England 23**
PG: N Jenkins (3)   *Tries: Ubogu*
                                   R Underwood (2)
                                Conv: Andrew
                                PG: Andrew (2)
Wales: Clement (Back), Evans*, M Taylor, N Davies, Walker (Moon), N Jenkins, R Jones, Griffiths, G Jenkins, J Davies, D Jones, Llewellyn, H Taylor (Williams-Jones), Lewis, Collins
England: Catt, T Underwood, Carling*, Guscott, R Underwood, Andrew, Bracken, Leonard, Moore, Ubogu, Rodber, Johnson, Bayfield, Clarke, Richards

Parc des Princes, Paris   Feb 18
France 21   **Scotland 23**
Tries: Saint-André (2)   *Tries: Townsend*
   Sadourny   *Hastings*
PG: Lacroix   *Conv: Hastings (2)*
DG: Deylaud   *PG: Hastings (3)*
France: Sadourny, Bernat-Salles, Sella, Lacroix, Saint-André*, Deylaud, Accoceberry, Seigne, Gonzalez, Califano, Benazzi, Brouzet, Roumat, Cabannes, Benetton
Scotland: Hastings*, Joiner, Townsend, Jardine, Logan, Chalmers, Redpath, Hilton, Milne, Wright, Cronin (Weir), Campbell, Wainwright, Peters, Morrison

Lansdowne Road, Dublin   Mar 4
Ireland 7   **France 25**
Try: Geoghegan   *Tries: Cecillon*
Conv: Elwood   *Delaigue*
                                   N'Tamack
                                   Saint-André
                                Conv: N'Tamack
                                PG: N'Tamack
Ireland: Staples, Geoghegan, Mullin (Field), Danaher, Woods, Elwood, Bradley*, Popplewell, Kingston, Clohessy, Tweed, Fulcher, Halvey, McBride, Foley
France: Sadourny, N'Tamack, Sella, Mesnel, Saint-André*, Delaigue, Accoceberry, Armary, Gonzalez, Califano, Merle, Brouzet, Benetton, Benazzi, Cecillon

Murrayfield, Edinburgh   Mar 4
Scotland 26   **Wales 13**
Tries: Peters   *Try: R Jones*
   Hilton   *Conv: N Jenkins*
Conv: G Hastings (2)   *PG: N Jenkins (2)*
PG: G Hastings (4)
Scotland: G Hastings*, Joiner, Townsend, S Hastings, Logan, Chalmers, Redpath, Hilton, Milne, Wright, Weir, Campbell, Wainwright, Peters, Morrison
Wales: Back, Evans*, Hall, N Davies, Proctor, N Jenkins, R Jones, Griffiths, G Jenkins, John, Taylor, D Jones, Llewellyn, Collins, Lewis

National Stadium, Cardiff   Mar 18
Wales 12   **Ireland 16**
PG: N Jenkins (4)   *Try: Mullin*
                                Conv: Burke
                                PG: Burke (2)
                                DG: Burke
Wales: Back, Evans*, Hall, N Davies, Proctor, N Jenkins, Jones, Griffiths, G Jenkins, John, P Davies, Llewellyn, Gibbs, Lewis, Collins
Ireland: Staples, Wallace, Mullin, Danaher, Geoghegan, Elwood (Burke), Hogan, Popplewell, Kingston*, Clohessy, Fulcher, Tweed, Foley, Johns, Halvey

Twickenham, London   Mar 18
England 24   **Scotland 12**
PG: Andrew (7)   PG: G Hastings (2)
DG: Andrew   DG: Chalmers (2)
England: Catt, T Underwood, Carling*, Guscott, R
Underwood, Andrew, Bracken, Leonard, Moore, Ubogu,
Rodber, Johnson, Bayfield, Clarke, Richards (Ojomoh)
Scotland: G Hastings*, Joiner, Townsend, S Hastings,
Logan, Chalmers, Redpath, Hilton (Manson), Milne,
Wright, Weir, Campbell, Wainwright, Peters, Morrison

FINAL 5 NATIONS TABLE

		P	W	D	L	PF	PA	Diff	Pts
1	England	4	4	0	0	98	39	+59	8
2	Scotland	4	3	0	1	87	71	+16	6
3	France	4	2	0	2	77	70	+7	4
4	Ireland	4	1	0	3	44	83	-39	2
5	Wales	4	0	0	4	43	86	-43	0

World Cup Qualifiers

EUROPEAN SEEDING MATCHES
Catania, Italy   Oct 1
Italy 24   **Romania 6**
(PG:8)   (PG:2)

Cardiff, Wales   Oct 12
Wales 29   **Italy 19**
(T:1, PG:7, DG:1)   (G:1, PG:4)

Final Table	P	W	D	L	PF	PA	Pts
1 Wales	2	2	0	0	45	28	6
2 Italy	2	1	0	1	43	35	4
3 Romania	2	0	0	2	15	40	2

Wales joined Pool C, Italy: Pool B, Romania: Pool A

ASIAN QUALIFYING TOURNAMENT
Kuala Lumpur, Malaysia   Oct 22-29
Group A
Malaysia 23   Sri Lanka 18
Japan 56   Chinese Taipei 5
Sri Lanka 3   Japan 67
Chinese Taipei 23   Malaysia 15
Malaysia 9   Japan 103
Chinese Taipei 25   Sri Lanka 9

Final Table	P	W	D	L	PF	PA	Pts
1 Japan	3	3	0	0	226	17	9
2 Chinese Taipei	3	2	0	1	53	80	7
3 Malaysia	3	1	0	2	47	144	5
4 Sri Lanka	3	0	0	3	30	115	3

Group B
Singapore 5   Thailand 69
Hong Kong 17   Korea 28
Thailand 0   Hong Kong 93
Korea 90   Singapore 3
Singapore 13   Hong Kong 164
Korea 65   Thailand 11

Final Table	P	W	D	L	PF	PA	Pts
1 Korea	3	3	0	0	183	31	9
2 Hong Kong	3	2	0	1	274	41	7
3 Thailand	3	1	0	2	80	163	5
4 Singapore	3	0	0	3	21	323	3

Third Place Play Off
Hong Kong 80   **Chinese Taipei 26**

Qualification Final
Japan 26   **Korea 11**
(G:2, PG:4)   (T:1, PG:2)
Japan joined Pool C

International Tours
Argentina to South Africa
1st Test
Boet Erasmus, Port Elizabeth   Oct 8
South Africa 42   **Argentina 22**
Tries: Roux (2),   Tries: Loffreda, Pfister, Teran
Stransky, Strauss   Conv: G del Castillo (2)
Williams   PG: G del Castillo
Conv: Stransky (4)
PG: Stransky (3)

2nd Test
Ellis Park, Johannesburg   Oct 15
South Africa 46   **Argentina 26**
Tries: Badenhorst (2)   Tries: Llanes, Cilley
Stransky, Andrews   Conv: Cilley (2)
Straeuli, Williams   PG: Cilley (4)
vd Westhuizen
Conv: Stransky (4)
PG: Stransky

Other Matches
Bosman Stadium, Brakpan   Oct 4
Argentina XV 12   South Africa A 56

North West Stadium, Welkom   Oct 11
Argentina XV 64   Northern Orange Free State 27

South Africa to Wales, Scotland, Ireland
1st Test
Murrayfield, Edinburgh   Nov 19
Scotland 10   **South Africa 34**
Try: Stanger   Tries: vd Westhuizen (2)
Conv: G Hastings   Williams, Straeuli, Mulder
PG: G Hastings   Conv: Joubert (3) PG: Joubert
Scotland: G Hastings*, Stanger, S Hastings, Shiel,
Logan, Chalmers, Patterson, Sharp, Milne, Burnell,
Richardson, Reed, McIvor, Weir, Morrison
South Africa: Joubert, Hendriks, P Müller, Mulder,
Williams, Le Roux, van der Westhuizen, Du Randt,
Schmidt, Laubscher, Andrews, Schutte, Pienaar*,
Straeuli, Kruger

2nd Test
National Stadium, Cardiff   Nov 26
Wales 12   **South Africa 20**
PG: N Jenkins (4)   Tries: Straeuli, Joubert, Williams
                         Conv: Le Roux   PG: Le Roux
Wales: Clement, Proctor, Hall, M Taylor, Hill, N Jenkins,
Moon, Evans, G Jenkins, J Davies, Jones, Llewellyn, H
Taylor, Lewis, Collins
South Africa: Joubert, Hendriks, P Müller, Mulder,
Williams, Le Roux, van der Westhuizen, Du Randt,
Schmidt, Laubscher, Andrews, Schutte, Pienaar*,
Straeuli, Kruger

TOUR MATCHES

Cardiff Arms Park   Oct 22, 1994
Cardiff 6   South African XV 11

Rodney Parade, Newport   Oct 26, 1994
Wales A 13   South African XV 25

Stradey Park, Llanelli   Oct 29, 1994
Llanelli 12   South African XV 30

The Gnoll, Neath   Nov 2, 1994
Neath 13   South African XV 16

St Helen's, Swansea   Nov 5, 1994
Swansea 7   South African XV 78

The Greenyards, Melrose   Nov 9, 1994
Scotland A 17   South African XV 15

Old Anniesland, Glasgow   Nov 12, 1994
Scottish C Districts 6   South African XV 33

Rubislaw Playing Fields, Aberdeen   Nov 15, 1994
Scottish Select 10   South African XV 35

Sardis Rd, Pontypridd   Nov 22,1994
Pontypridd 3   South African XV 9

Ravenhill, Belfast   Nov 29, 1994
Comb. Provinces 19   South African XV 54

Lansdowne Road, Dublin   Dec 3, 1994
Barbarians 23   South Africa 15
Tries: Saint-André,   Tries: Kruger, Müller, Johnson
Geoghegan
Conv: Callard (2)
PG: Callard (2) DG: Chalmers

Canada to Europe

1st Test
Twickenham, London   Dec 10, 1994
England 60   Canada 19
Tries: T Underwood   Tries: Lougheed (2), Evans
R Underwood (2)   Conv: Rees (2)
Bracken, Catt (2)
Conv: Andrew (6)
PG: Andrew (6)
England: Hull (Catt), T Underwood (de Glanville),
Carling*, Guscott, R Underwood, Andrew, Bracken,
Leonard, Moore, Ubogu, Johnson, Bayfield, Richards,
Clarke, Rodber
Canada: S Stewart, Toews, C Stewart, Stuart* (Gray),
Lougheed, Rees, Graf, Evans, Cardinal, Jackart, James,
Hadley, Gordon, McKenzie, MacKinnon

2nd Test
Stade Leo Lagrange, Besançon   Dec 17, 1994
France 28   Canada 9
Tries: Benetton,   PG: Rees (3)
Sadourny, Sella
Conv: Lacroix (2)
PG: Lacroix (2), DG: Delaigue

TOUR MATCHES
Rovigo, Italy   Nov 30, 1994
Italy A 18   Canada XV 11

Devonport   Dec 3, 1994
Combined Services 21 Canada XV 20

Recreation Grd, Bath   Dec 6, 1994
Emerging England XV 34 Canada XV 6

USA to Ireland
Test
Lansdowne Rd, Dublin   Nov 5, 1994
Ireland 26   USA 15
Tries: Geoghegan   Tries: Anitoni, Bachelet
Bradley   Conv: Williams
Conv: McGowan (2)   PG: Williams
PG: McGowan (3)
O'Shea

TOUR MATCHES
Sports Gd, Galway   Nov 1, 1994
Irish Development XV 13 USA XV 20

Cork   Nov 9, 1994
Irish Universities 11   USA XV 9

Donnybrook, Dublin   Nov 12, 1994
Leinster 9   USA XV 6

Romania to England
Test
Twickenham, London   Nov 12, 1994
England 54   Romania 3
Tries: T Underwood (2)   PG: Ivanciuc
Carling, Rodber,
R Underwood &
penalty try
Convs: Andrew (6)
PG: Andrew (4)
England: Hull, T Underwood, Carling*, Guscott, R
Underwood, Andrew, Morris, Leonard, Moore, Ubogu,
Johnson, Bayfield, Rodber, Clarke, Ojomoh
Romania: Brici, Solomie, Vioreanu, Tofan, Cioca,
Ivanciuc, Neaga, Costea (Marioara), Negreci (Gheorghe),
Vlad, Cojocariu, Branescu (Guranescu), Oroian
(Draguceanu), Brinza*, Gealapu

TOUR MATCHES
Iffley Rd, Oxford   Nov 5, 1994
Oxford Uni XV 26   Romania XV 16

Grange Rd, Cambridge   Nov 8, 1994
Cambridge Uni XV 18   Romania XV 27

Italy to England & Scotland
TOUR MATCHES
Stoop , Twickenham   Dec 29, 1994
Middlesex 3   Italy XV 50

McDiarmid Park, Perth   Jan 7
Scotland A 18   Italy 16

Other Internationals

Murrayfield, Edinburgh   Jan 21
Scotland 22   **Canada 6**
Try: Cronin   *PG: Rees (2)*
Conv: G Hastings
PG: G Hastings (5)
Scotland: G Hastings*, Joiner, Townsend, Jardine,
Logan, Chalmers, Redpath, Hilton, Milne, Wright, Cronin,
Campbell, Wainwright, Peters, Morrison
Canada: S Stewart, Stanley, C Stewart, Gray, Toews,
Rees (Hutchinson), Graf, Evans, Cardinal, Jackart,
James, Whitley, Gordon, McKenzie, MacKinnon

National Stadium, Bucharest   Apr 8
Romania 15   **France 24**
PG: Nichitean (2)   *Tries: Sadourny,*
DG: Nichitean (3)   *penalty try*
                               Conv: Lacroix
                               PG: Lacroix (4)

Ellis Park, Jo'burg   Apr 13
South Africa 60   **Western Samoa 8**
Tries: Johnson (3)   *Try: Lima*
Williams (2), Stransky   *PG: Umaga*
Small, Rossouw, Andrews
Conv: Johnson (5)
Stransky
PG: Johnson

Eden Park, Auckland   Apr 22
New Zealand 73   **Canada 7**
Tries: Osborne (2)   *Try: C Stewart*
Bunce (2), Ellis (2)   *Conv: Ross*
Brown, Mehrtens
Bachop, Wilson
Conv: Mehrtens (7)
PG: Mehrtens (3)

Murrayfield, Edinburgh   Apr 22
Scotland 49   **Romania 16**
Tries: Stanger (2)   *Try: Racean*
G Hastings, Shiel,   *Conv: Nichitean*
Peters, Joiner, Logan   *PG: Nichitean (3)*
Conv: G Hastings (4)
PG: G Hastings (2)

Ballymore, Brisbane   Apr 30
Australia 53   **Argentina 7**
Tries: Lynagh (2)   *Try: Pichot*
Eales, Ofahengaue   *Conv: Arbizu*
Pini, Smith, Campese
Conv: Lynagh (3)
PG: Lynagh (4)

Sydney Football Stadium   May 6
Australia 30   **Argentina 13**
Tries: Campese (2)   *Try: Arbizu*
Wilson   *Conv: Crexell*
PG: Lynagh (5)   *PG: Meson, Crexell*

Monigo Treviso   May 6
Italy 22   **Ireland 12**
Try: Vaccari   *PG: Burke (4)*
Conv: Dominguez
PG: Dominguez (4)
DG: Dominguez
Italy: Vaccari, Ravazzolo, Francescato, Bonomi
(Bordon), Marcello Cuttitta, Dominguez, Troncon,
Massimo Cuttitta*, Orlandi, Properzi Curti, Favaro,
Giacheri (Capuzzoni), Arancio, Pedroni, Gardner
Ireland: Staples (Field), Wallace, Mullin, Bell, Darragh
O'Mahony, Burke, David O'Mahony (Rolland),
Popplewell, Kingston*, Halpin, Fulcher, Tweed, Foley,
Johns, Halvey

HONG KONG SEVENS
Hong Kong   Mar 25-6
FINAL
New Zealand 35   **Fiji 17**

COURAGE CLUBS CHAMPIONSHIP
DIVISION 1

		P	W	D	L	PF	PA	Pts
1	Leicester	18	15	1	2	400	239	31
2	Bath	18	12	3	3	373	245	27
3	Wasps	18	13	0	5	470	313	26
4	Sale	18	7	2	9	327	343	16
5	Orrell	18	6	3	9	256	326	15
6	Bristol	18	7	0	11	301	353	14
7	Gloucester	18	6	1	11	269	336	13
8	Harlequins	18	6	1	11	275	348	13
9	West Hartlepool	18	6	1	11	312	412	13
10	Northampton	18	6	0	12	267	335	12

DIVISION 2

		P	W	D	L	PF	PA	Pts
1	Saracens	18	15	1	2	389	213	31
2	Wakefield	18	12	1	5	354	261	25
3	Newcastle Gos	18	8	2	8	373	281	18
4	London Scottish	18	9	0	9	351	321	18
5	London Irish	18	9	0	9	363	381	18
6	Moseley	18	8	1	9	299	303	17
7	Nottingham	18	8	1	9	299	322	17
8	Waterloo	18	8	0	10	287	331	16
9	Fylde	18	8	0	10	250	329	16
10	Coventry	18	2	0	16	213	436	4

DIVISION 3

		P	W	D	L	PF	PA	Pts
1	Bedford	18	13	1	4	421	238	27
2	Blackheath	18	12	2	4	299	190	26
3	Rugby	18	11	0	7	333	271	22
4	Rosslyn Park	18	10	0	8	313	280	20
5	Morley	18	9	2	7	277	326	20
6	Otley	18	9	0	9	278	248	18
7	Harrogate	18	7	2	9	275	404	16
8	Richmond	18	6	1	11	319	290	13
9	Clifton	18	5	1	12	242	344	11
10	Exeter	18	3	1	14	153	319	7

DIVISION 4

		P	W	D	L	PF	PA	Pts
1	Rotherham	18	17	0	1	576	267	34
2	Reading	18	14	1	3	435	319	29
3	Liverpool St H	18	10	3	5	374	243	23
4	Havant	18	10	2	6	390	330	22
5	Leeds	18	8	0	10	335	291	16
6	Aspatria	18	7	1	10	265	378	15
7	Redruth	18	6	2	10	309	387	14
8	Plymouth Albion	18	4	2	12	324	381	10
9	Askeans	18	4	1	13	257	451	9
10	Broughton Park	18	4	0	14	217	435	8

CIS INSURANCE DIVISIONAL CHAMPIONSHIP

Otley   Nov 19, 1994
Northern Division 10   Midlands Division 12
Bristol Nov 19, 1994
South & SW Division 18   London & SE Division 23
Wasps   Nov 26, 1994
London & SE Division 38   Northern Division 16
Leicester   Nov 26, 1994
Midlands Division 43   South & SW Division 23
Wasps   Dec 3, 1994
London & SE Division 15   Midlands Division 17
Sale   Dec 3, 1994
Northern Division 33   South & SW Division 26
Midlands are the Divisional Champions

CIS INSURANCE COUNTY CHAMPIONSHIP

NORTH DIVISION

Durham 5 Yorkshire 13; Cheshire 3 Lancs 16; Cumbria 15 North'land 10; Cheshire 10 Cumbria 6; Lancs 43 Durham 8; North'land 30 Yorks 14; Cumbria 6 Durham 5; Cheshire 17 North'land 19; Yorks 27 Lancs 27; Cumbria 24 Lancs 17; North'land 11 Durham 3; Yorks 49 Cheshire 19; Durham 5 Cheshire 6; Lancs 8 North'land 17; Yorks 25 Cumbria 18

		P	W	D	L	PF	PA	Pts
1	Northumberl'd	5	4	0	1	87	57	8
2	Yorkshire	5	3	1	1	128	99	7
3	Cumbria	5	3	0	2	69	67	6
4	Lancashire	5	2	1	2	111	79	5
5	Cheshire	5	2	0	3	55	95	4
6	Durham	5	0	0	5	26	79	0

MIDLAND DIVISION
Group A

Staffs 12 Leics 15; Leics 13 North Mids 14; North Mids 17 Staffs 25

		P	W	D	L	PF	PA	Pts
1	Staffordshire	2	1	0	1	37	32	2
2	Leicestershire	2	1	0	1	28	26	2
3	North Midlands	2	1	0	1	31	38	2

Group B

East Mids 29 N, L & D 31; N, L & D 8 Warwicks 42; Warwicks 70 East Mids 3

		P	W	D	L	PF	PA	Pts
1	Warwickshire	2	2	0	0	112	11	4
2	Notts, Lincs & D	2	1	0	1	39	71	2
3	East Midlands	2	0	0	2	32	101	0

MIDLAND DIVISION PLAY-OFFS

Semi-finals: Staffs 18 Notts, Lincs & D 8; Warwicks 21 Leics 8
Final: Warwicks 30 Staffs 3

LONDON & SOUTH-WEST
Group 1

Surrey 42 Herts 7; Herts 18 Somerset 14; Somerset 27 Surrey 20

		P	W	D	L	PF	PA	Pts
1	Surrey	2	1	0	1	62	34	2
2	Somerset	2	1	0	1	41	38	2
3	Hertfordshire	2	1	0	1	25	56	2

Group 2

Bucks 16 Sussex 18; Gloucs 25 Devon 12; Devon 16 Sussex 13; Gloucs 41 Bucks 13; Bucks 3 Devon 3; Sussex 19 Gloucs 42

		P	W	D	L	PF	PA	Pts
1	Gloucest'shire	3	3	0	0	108	44	6
2	Devon	3	1	1	1	31	41	3
3	Sussex	3	1	0	2	50	74	2
4	Buckingh'mshire	3	0	1	2	32	62	1

Group 3

Hants 40 Oxon 15; Kent 49 E Counties 32; Hants 20 Kent 24; Oxon 19 E Counties 37; E Counties 18 Hants 21; Kent 62 Oxon 0

		P	W	D	L	PF	PA	Pts
1	Kent	3	3	0	0	135	52	6
2	Hampshire	3	2	0	1	81	57	4
3	Eastern C'ties	3	1	0	2	87	89	2
4	Oxfordshire	3	0	0	3	34	134	0

Group 4

Cornwall 16 Mddx 17; Dorset & Wilts 13 Berks 28; Cornwall 39 Dorset & Wilts 15; Middx 13 Berks 18; Berks 22 Cornwall 11; Dorset & Wilts 6 Middx 58

		P	W	D	L	PF	PA	Pts
1	Berkshire	3	3	0	0	68	37	6
2	Middlesex	3	2	0	1	88	40	4
3	Cornwall	3	1	0	2	66	54	2
4	Dorset & Wilts	3	0	0	3	34	125	0

LONDON & SOUTH-WEST PLAY-OFFS

Gloucester 23 Surrey 6; Berkshire 25 Kent 12

SEMI-FINALS

Rugby Lions   Mar 11
Warwickshire 31   Berkshire 5

Tynedale   Mar 11
Northumberland 14   Gloucestershire 13

FINAL

Twickenham   Apr 22
Warwickshire 15   Northumberland 9

Middlesex Sevens

Twickenham   May 13
FINAL
Leicester 38   Ithuba (South Africa) 19

The Pilkington Cup

Fourth Round
Wakefield 19 Gloucester 9; Aspatria 32 Bedford 6;
Rotherham 19 Waterloo 21; London Scottish 6 Bath 31;
Sale 33 Harrogate 0; Newcastle Gosforth 12 Wasps 58;
Coventry 7 Fylde 45; Richmond 24 Tabard 16;
Harlequins 9 Saracens 5; Basingstoke 3 London Irish 18;
Sandal 5 Lydney 17; Leicester 56 Blackheath 11;
Moseley 6 Northampton 16; Bristol 41 Nottingham 10;
Exeter 9 Rugby Lions 7; Orrell 28 West Hartlepool 7

Fifth Round
Bristol 8 Leicester 16; Waterloo 13 Wasps 54;
Northampton 27 Richmond 6; Sale 55 Fylde 13; Orrell 19
Bath 25; London Irish 15 Harlequins 40; Lydney 10
Wakefield 23; Exeter 18 Aspatria 6

Quarter-finals
Sale 12 Leicester 14; Harlequins 13 Wakefield 8;
Bath 26 Northampton 6; Exeter 0, Wasps 31

Semi-finals
Leicester 22, Wasps 25; Harlequins 13, Bath 31

PILKINGTON CUP FINAL
Twickenham   May 6

Bath 36   **Wasps 16**
Tries: Hagg (2), Clarke   Tries: Dunston, D Hopley
Swift, Callard   PG: Andrew (2)
Conv: Callard (4)
PG: Callard

Bath: Callard, Swift, de Glanville*, Guscott, Adebayo,
Butland, Sanders, Yates, Adams, Ubogu (Mallett), Haag,
Redman, Robinson, Clarke, Ojomoh
Wasps: Ufton, P Hopley, D Hopley, Childs, Greenstock,
Andrew, Bates, Molloy, Dunn, Dunston, Greenwood,
Hadley, Dallaglio, Ryan*, White
This was the ninth Cup victory for Bath in 11 years.

VARSITY MATCH
Twickenham   Dec 6, 1994
Oxford University 21   Cambridge University 26
*Cambridge's victory was their 52nd in the series, Oxford
trail with 48 wins from 113 matches - there have been 13
draws since it began in 1872.*

BUSA CHAMPIONSHIP
Twickenham   Mar 22
West London Institute 31   Swansea 30

Heineken Welsh League
DIVISION 1

		P	W	D	L	PF	PA	Pts
1	**Cardiff**	22	18	0	4	672	269	36
2	Pontypridd	22	17	0	5	555	255	34
3	Treorchy	22	13	0	9	479	312	26
4	Neath	22	12	2	8	379	398	26
5	Bridgend	22	12	1	9	518	451	25
6	Swansea	22	12	0	10	475	400	24
7	Llanelli	22	10	0	12	459	409	20
8	Newport	22	9	0	13	366	433	18
9	Newbridge	22	8	0	14	302	452	16
10	Abertillery	22	8	0	14	349	604	16
11	Dunvant	22	7	1	14	333	542	15
12	Pontypool	22	4	0	18	293	655	8

DIVISION 2

		P	W	D	L	PF	PA	Pts
1	**Aberavon**	22	17	0	5	506	263	34
2	Ebbw Vale	22	16	1	5	447	283	33
3	Abercynon	22	16	1	5	380	260	33
4	SW Police	22	12	2	8	413	357	26
5	Bonymaen	22	11	1	10	370	312	23
6	Maestag	22	10	1	11	365	388	21
7	Tenby United	22	10	0	12	290	374	20
8	Llandovery	22	9	0	13	313	363	18
9	Llanharan	22	9	0	13	316	319	18
10	Cross Keys	22	8	0	14	292	438	16
11	Narbeth	22	6	2	14	299	446	14
12	Penarth	22	4	0	18	289	477	8

SWALEC CUP

Quarter Finals
Cardiff 73 Aberavon 3;
Llanelli 18 Bridgend 11;
Newbridge 11 Swansea 19;
Pontypridd 76 Mountain Ash 3

Semi Finals
Pontypridd 20 Llanelli 14
Swansea 16 Cardiff 9 *aet*

FINAL
National Stadium, Cardiff   May 6

Swansea 17   **Pontypridd 12**
Tries: Appleyard   Tries: Manley (2)
Stuart Davies   Conv: Jenkins
Conv: Williams (2)
PG: Williams

Swansea: Clement*, Harris, Boobyer, Weatherley, Simon
Davies, Williams, R Jones, Loader, Jenkins, Colclough,
Arnold, Moore, Reynolds, Stuart Davies, Appleyard
Pontypridd: Cormack, Manley, J Lewis, S Lewis, Robins
(G Jones), Jenkins, Paul John, Bezani*, Phil John,
Metcalfe, Prosser, Rowley, Lloyd (Spiller), McIntosh,
Collins

McEwan's National League
DIVISION 1

		P	W	D	L	PF	PA	Pts
1	**Stirling County**	13	11	1	1	234	162	23
2	Watsonians	13	9	0	4	296	212	18
3	Edinburgh Acads	13	7	2	4	214	141	16
4	Hawick	13	7	2	4	215	199	16
5	Boroughmuir	13	7	1	5	325	226	15
6	Heriot's FP	13	7	1	5	199	195	15
7	Gala	13	7	1	5	226	245	15
8	Melrose	13	7	0	6	308	261	14
9	Glasgow HK	13	6	1	6	228	183	13
10	Jedforest	13	6	0	7	221	256	12
11	West of Scotland	13	5	0	8	166	233	10
12	Dundee HSFP	13	3	1	9	200	264	7
13	Currie	13	3	0	10	188	280	6
14	Stewarts-Melville	13	1	0	12	158	321	2

DIVISION 2

		P	W	D	L	PF	PA	Pts
1	**Kelso**	**13**	**11**	**0**	**2**	**318**	**159**	**22**
2	Selkirk	13	10	2	1	336	184	22
3	Kirkcaldy	13	8	1	4	271	230	17
4	Biggar	13	7	2	4	180	173	16
5	Preston Lodge	13	7	1	5	269	214	15
6	Glasgow Acads	13	7	0	6	299	239	14
7	Peebles	13	7	0	6	175	204	14
8	Musselburgh	13	6	1	6	203	196	13
9	Grangemouth	13	6	0	7	223	246	12
10	Corstorphine	13	5	1	7	180	212	11
11	Edinburgh W	13	5	0	8	210	261	10
12	Wigtownshire	13	3	0	10	173	265	6
13	Gordonians	13	3	0	10	154	300	6
14	Haddington	13	2	0	11	178	277	4

Insurance Corporation All-Ireland League
DIVISION 1

		P	W	D	L	PF	PA	Pts
1	**Shannon**	**10**	**10**	**0**	**0**	**162**	**60**	**20**
2	Blackrock Coll.	10	7	0	3	228	135	14
3	St Mary's Coll.	10	7	0	3	151	134	14
4	Garryowen	10	6	0	4	160	113	12
5	Cork Constit.	10	6	0	4	148	129	12
6	Old Wesley	10	5	0	5	131	171	10
7	Lansdowne	10	3	1	6	150	225	7
8	Young Munster	10	3	0	7	115	153	6
9	Instonians	10	3	0	7	108	160	6
10	Sunday's Wells	10	2	1	7	119	165	5
11	Dungannon	10	2	0	8	114	141	4

FRENCH CLUB CHAMPIONSHIP
Final
Parc des Princes   *May 6*
Toulouse 31   **Castres 16**

Women's Rugby

International Matches

Wasps RFC	*Dec 18, 1994*
England 30	**Holland 5**
Bridgend	*Dec 18, 1994*
Wales 0	**Scotland 5**
Blackrock	*Jan 22*
Ireland 0	**Nomads 5**
Sale	*Feb 12*
England 25	**Wales 0**
Myreside	*Feb 12*
Scotland 20	**Ireland 3**
Blackrock	*Mar 5*
Ireland 10	**France 39**
Cardiff	*Mar 19*
Wales 25	**Ireland 0**
Meggetland	*Apr 30*
Scotland 10	**Italy 12**

National League

DIVISION 1

		P	W	D	L	PF	PA	Pts
1	**Richmond**	**14**	**14**	**0**	**0**	**464**	**26**	**28**
2	Saracens	14	8	2	4	196	186	18
3	Wasps	14	8	1	5	204	111	17
4	Waterloo	14	7	0	7	137	180	14
5	Clifton	14	6	1	7	122	166	13
6	Cardiff	14	6	0	8	106	215	12
7	Leeds	14	3	0	11	64	183	6
8	Blackheath*	13	3	0	10	57	247	4

* 1 match defaulted*

DIVISION 2

		P	W	D	L	PF	PA	Pts
1	O Leams	10	9	0	1	221	42	18
2	Novocastrians	10	8	0	2	253	40	16
3	Richmond II	10	7	1	2	196	59	15
4	Cheltenham	10	2	1	7	57	197	5
5	Sale	10	2	0	8	55	130	4
6	Wasps II	10	2	0	8	47	361	4

VLADIVAR CUP FINAL
Stoop, Harlequins RFC   Apr 9
Richmond 27   **Wasps 0**

International Records

WORLD CUP

1987	New Zealand	29-9
	bt France	
1991	Australia	12-6
	bt England	
1995	South Africa	15-12
	bt New Zealand *aet*	

FOUR / FIVE NATIONS CHAMPIONSHIP

1883	England
1884	England
1886	England & Scotland
1887	Scotland
1890	England & Scotland
1891	Scotland
1892	England
1893	Wales
1894	Ireland
1895	Scotland
1896	Ireland
1899	Ireland
1900	Wales
1901	Scotland
1902	Wales
1903	Scotland
1904	Scotland
1905	Wales
1906	Ireland & Wales
1907	Scotland
1908	Wales
1909	Wales
1910	England
1911	Wales
1912	England & Ireland
1913	England
1914	England
1920	England, Wales & Scotland
1921	England
1922	Wales
1923	England
1924	England
1925	Scotland
1926	Scotland & Ireland
1927	Scotland & Ireland
1928	England
1929	Scotland
1930	England
1931	Wales
1932	England, Ireland & Wales
1933	Scotland
1934	England
1935	Ireland
1936	Wales
1937	England
1938	Scotland
1939	England, Ireland & Wales
1947	Wales & England
1948	Ireland
1949	Ireland
1950	Wales
1951	Ireland
1952	Wales
1953	England
1954	England, Wales & France
1955	Wales & France
1956	Wales
1958	England
1959	France
1960	France & England
1961	France
1962	France
1963	England
1964	Scotland & Wales
1965	Wales
1966	Wales
1967	France
1968	France
1969	Wales
1970	Wales & France
1971	Wales
1973	*Five way tie*
1974	Ireland
1975	Wales
1976	Wales
1977	France
1978	Wales
1979	Wales
1980	England
1981	France
1982	Ireland
1983	France & Ireland
1984	Scotland
1985	Ireland
1986	France & Scotland
1987	France
1988	Wales & France
1989	France
1990	Scotland
1991	England
1992	England
1993	France
1994	Wales
1995	England

1885, 1888-9, 1897-8, 1972 were not completed for various reasons

BRITISH LIONS TOURS
(from 1910)

V SOUTH AFRICA

1910	Lions 10	South Africa 14
	Lions 8	South Africa 3
	Lions 5	South Africa 21
1924	Lions 3	South Africa 7
	Lions 0	South Africa 17
	Lions 3	South Africa 3
1938	Lions 12	South Africa 26
	Lions 3	South Africa 19
	Lions 21	South Africa 16
1955	Lions 23	South Africa 22
	Lions 9	South Africa 25
	Lions 9	South Africa 6
	Lions 8	South Africa 22
1962	Lions 3	South Africa 3
	Lions 0	South Africa 3
	Lions 3	South Africa 8
	Lions 14	South Africa 34
1968	Lions 20	South Africa 25
	Lions 6	South Africa 6
	Lions 6	South Africa 11
	Lions 6	South Africa 19
1974	Lions 12	South Africa 3
	Lions 28	South Africa 9
	Lions 26	South Africa 9
	Lions 13	South Africa 13
1980	Lions 22	South Africa 26
	Lions 19	South Africa 26
	Lions 10	South Africa 12
	Lions 17	South Africa 13

V NEW ZEALAND

1930	Lions 6	New Zealand 3
	Lions 10	New Zealand 13
	Lions 10	New Zealand 15
	Lions 8	New Zealand 22
1950	Lions 9	New Zealand 9
	Lions 0	New Zealand 8
	Lions 3	New Zealand 6
	Lions 8	New Zealand 11
1959	Lions 17	New Zealand 18
	Lions 8	New Zealand 11
	Lions 8	New Zealand 22
	Lions 9	New Zealand 6
1966	Lions 3	New Zealand 20
	Lions 12	New Zealand 16
	Lions 6	New Zealand 19
	Lions 11	New Zealand 24
1971	Lions 9	New Zealand 3
	Lions 12	New Zealand 22
	Lions 13	New Zealand 3
	Lions 14	New Zealand 14
1977	Lions 12	New Zealand 16
	Lions 13	New Zealand 9
	Lions 7	New Zealand 19
	Lions 9	New Zealand 10
1983	Lions 12	New Zealand 16
	Lions 0	New Zealand 9
	Lions 8	New Zealand 15
	Lions 6	New Zealand 38
1993	Lions 18	New Zealand 20
	Lions 20	New Zealand 7
	Lions 13	New Zealand 30

v AUSTRALIA

1930	Lions 5	Australia 6
1950	Lions 19	Australia 6
	Lions 24	Australia 3
1959	Lions 17	Australia 6
	Lions 24	Australia 3
1966	Lions 11	Australia 8
	Lions 31	Australia 0
1989	Lions 12	Australia 30
	Lions 19	Australia 12
	Lions 19	Australia 18

County Champions

COUNTY CHAMPIONSHIP

(the format of the competition has altered over the years)

First system
1889	**Yorkshire**
1890	**Yorkshire**

Second system
1891	**Lancashire**
1892	**Yorkshire**
1893	**Yorkshire**
1894	**Yorkshire**
1895	**Yorkshire**

Third system

	Winners	Runners-up
1896	**Yorkshire**	Surrey
1897	**Kent**	Cumberland
1898	**Northumberland**	Midlands
1899	**Devon**	Northumberland
1900	**Durham**	Devon
1901	**Devon**	Durham
1902	**Durham**	Gloucestershire
1903	**Durham**	Kent
1904	**Kent**	Durham
1905	**Durham**	Middlesex
1906	**Devon**	Durham
1907	**Devon & Durham** *(shared)*	
1908	**Cornwall**	Durham
1909	**Durham**	Cornwall
1910	**Gloucestershire**	Yorkshire
1911	**Devon**	Yorkshire
1912	**Devon**	Northumberland
1913	**Gloucestershire**	Cumberland
1914	**Midlands**	Durham
1920	**Gloucestershire**	Yorkshire

Fourth system

	Winner	Runners-up
1921	**Gloucestershire** 31	Leicestershire 4
1922	**Gloucestershire** 19	North Midlands 0
1923	**Somerset** 8	Leicestershire 6
1924	**Cumberland** 14	Kent 3
1925	**Leicestershire** 14	Gloucestershire 6
1926	**Yorkshire** 15	Hampshire 14
1927	**Kent** 22	Leicestershire 12
1928	**Yorkshire** 12	Cornwall 8
1929	**Middlesex** 9	Lancashire 8
	(after 8-8 draw)	
1930	**Gloucestershire** 13	Lancashire 7
1931	**Gloucestershire** 10	Warwickshire 9
1932	**Gloucestershire** 9	Durham 3
1933	**Hampshire** 18	Lancashire 7
1934	**East Midlands** 10	Gloucestershire 0
1935	**Lancashire** 14	Somerset 0
1936	**Hampshire** 13	Northumberland 6
1937	**Gloucestershire** 5	East Midlands 0
1938	**Lancashire** 24	Surrey 12
1939	**Warwickshire** 8	Somerset 3
1947	**Lancashire** 14	Gloucestershire 3
	(after 8-8 draw)	
1948	**Lancashire** 5	Eastern Counties 0
1949	**Lancashire** 9	Gloucestershire 3

1950	**Cheshire** 5	East Midlands 0
1951	**East Midlands** 10	Middlesex 0
1952	**Middlesex** 9	Lancashire 6
1953	**Yorkshire** 11	East Midlands 3
1954	**Middlesex** 24	Lancashire 6
1955	**Lancashire** 14	Middlesex 8
1956	**Middlesex** 13	Devon 9
1957	**Devon** 12	Yorkshire 3
1958	**Warwickshire** 16	Cornwall 8
1959	**Warwickshire** 14	Gloucestershire 9
1960	**Warwickshire** 9	Surrey 6
1961	**Cheshire** 5	Devon 3
	(after 0-0 draw)	
1962	**Warwickshire** 11	Hampshire 6
1963	**Warwickshire** 13	Yorkshire 10
1964	**Warwickshire** 8	Lancashire 6
1965	**Warwickshire** 15	Durham 9
1966	**Middlesex** 6	Lancashire 0
1967	**Surrey & Durham**	
	shared after 14-14 & 0-0 draws	
1968	**Middlesex** 9	Warwickshire 6
1969	**Lancashire** 11	Cornwall 9
1970	**Staffordshire** 11	Gloucestershire 9
1971	**Surrey** 14	Gloucestershire 3
1972	**Gloucestershire** 11	Warwickshire 6
1973	**Lancashire** 17	Gloucestershire 12
1974	**Gloucestershire** 22	Lancashire 12
1975	**Gloucestershire** 13	Eastern Counties 9
1976	**Gloucestershire** 24	Middlesex 9
1977	**Lancashire** 17	Middlesex 6
1978	**North Midlands** 10	Gloucestershire 7
1979	**Middlesex** 19	Northumberland 6
1980	**Lancashire** 21	Gloucestershire 15
1981	**Northumberland** 15	Gloucestershire 6
1982	**Lancashire** 7	North Midlands 3
1983	**Gloucestershire** 19	Yorkshire 7
1984	**Gloucestershire** 36	Somerset 18
1985	**Middlesex** 12	Notts, Lincs, Derbys 9
1986	**Warwickshire** 16	Kent 6
1987	**Yorkshire** 22	Middlesex 11
1988	**Lancashire** 23	Warwickshire 18
1989	**Durham** 13	Cornwall 9
1990	**Lancashire** 32	Middlesex 9
1991	**Cornwall** 29	Yorkshire 20
1992	**Lancashire** 9	Cornwall 6
1993	**Lancahire** 9	Yorkshire 6
1994	**Yorkshire** 26	Durham 3
1995	**Northumberland** 9	Warwickshire 15

League & Cup Winners

COURAGE LEAGUE CHAMPIONS
1987-88	**Leicester**
1988-89	**Bath**
1989-90	**Wasps**
1990-91	**Bath**
1991-92	**Bath**
1992-93	**Bath**
1993-94	**Bath**
1994-95	**Leicester**

HEINEKEN WELSH LEAGUE CHAMPIONS
1990-91	**Neath**
1991-92	**Swansea**
1992-93	**Llanelli**
1993-94	**Swansea**
1994-95	**Cardiff**

SCOTTISH LEAGUE CHAMPIONS
1973-74	**Hawick**
1974-75	**Hawick**
1975-76	**Hawick**
1976-77	**Hawick**
1977-78	**Hawick**
1978-79	**Heriots FP**
1979-80	**Gala**
1981-82	**Hawick**
1982-83	**Gala**
1983-84	**Hawick**
1984-85	**Hawick**
1985-86	**Hawick**
1986-87	**Hawick**
1987-88	**Kelso**
1988-89	**Kelso**
1989-90	**Melrose**
1990-91	**Boroughmuir**
1991-92	**Melrose**
1992-93	**Melrose**
1993-94	**Melrose**
1994-95	**Stirling County**

ALL-IRELAND LEAGUE CHAMPIONS
1990-91	**Cork Constitution**
1991-92	**Garryowen**
1992-93	**Young Munster**
1993-94	**Garryowen**
1994-95	**Shannon**

JOHN PLAYER SPECIAL/PILKINGTON CUP
	Winner	Runner-up
1972	**Gloucester** 17	Moseley 6
1973	**Coventry** 27	Bristol 15
1974	**Coventry** 26	London Scottish 6
1975	**Bedford** 28	Rosslyn Park 12
1976	**Gosforth** 23	Rosslyn Park 14
1977	**Gosforth** 27	Waterloo 11
1978	**Gloucester** 6	Leicester 3
1979	**Leicester** 15	Moseley 12
1980	**Leicester** 21	London Irish 9
1981	**Leicester** 22	Gosforth 15
1982	**Gloucester & Moseley** Shared 12-12 aet	

1983	**Bristol** 28	Leicester 22
1984	**Bath** 10	Bristol 9
1985	**Bath** 24	London Welsh 15
1986	**Bath** 25	Wasps 17
1987	**Bath** 19	Wasps 12
1988	**Harlequins** 28	Bristol 22
1989	**Bath** 10	Leicester 6
1990	**Bath** 48	Gloucester 6
1991	**Harlequins** 25	Northampton 13 aet
1992	**Bath** 15	Harlequins 12 aet
1993	**Leicester** 23	Harlequins 16
1994	**Bath** 21	Leicester 9
1995	**Bath** 36	Wasps 16

SCHWEPPES/SWALEC CUP
1972	**Neath** 15	Llanelli 9
1973	**Llanelli** 30	Cardiff 7
1974	**Llanelli** 12	Aberavon 10
1975	**Llanelli** 15	Aberavon 6
1976	**Llanelli** 15	Swansea 4
1977	**Newport** 16	Cardiff 15
1978	**Swansea** 13	Newport 9
1979	**Bridgend** 18	Pontypridd 12
1980	**Bridgend** 15	Swansea 9
1981	**Cardiff** 14	Bridgend 6
1982	**Cardiff** 12*	Bridgend 12
1983	**Pontypool** 18	Swansea 6
1984	**Cardiff** 24	Neath 19
1985	**Llanelli** 15	Cardiff 14
1986	**Cardiff** 28	Newport 21
1987	**Cardiff** 16	Swansea 15 aet
1988	**Llanelli** 28	Neath 13
1989	**Neath** 14	Llanelli 13
1990	**Neath** 16	Bridgend 10
1991	**Llanelli** 24	Pontypool 9
1992	**Llanelli** 16	Swansea 7
1993	**Llanelli** 21	Neath 18
1994	**Cardiff** 15	Llanelli 8
1995	**Swansea** 17	Pontypridd 12

* won on most tries

Shooting

Shotgun World Championships

Nicosia, Cyprus June 12-20

Men
TRAP 125
Individual

1	**Giovanni Pellielo**	**ITA**	**148.0**
2	Michael Diamond	AUS	147.5
3	Francesco Amici	SMR	147.4
15	John Grice	GBR	121.0
36	Peter Boden	GBR	119.0
76	James Brinkett-Evans	GBR	116.0

Team

1	**Italy**	**368.0**
2	Australia	366.0
3	United States	363.0
13	Great Britain	356.0

SKEET 125
Individual

1	**Abdullah Al Rashidi**	**KUW**	**148.3**
2	Valeri Timokhin	AZE	148.0
3	Hennie Dompeling	NED	147.18

Team

1	**Romania**	**362.0**
2	Italy	360.0
3	Georgia	360.0
16	Great Britain	353.0

DOUBLE TRAP 150
Individual

1	**Steve Haberman**	**AUS**	**188.0**
2	Waldemar Schanz	GER	187.0
3	Jiri Gach	CZE	185.0
47	Kevin Gill	GBR	125.0
48	Michael Rouse	GBR	125.0

Team

1	**Italy**	**420**
2	Australia	417
3	United States	413

Women
TRAP 125
Individual

	Frances Strodtman	USA	121.0
2	Deena Julin	USA	119.0
3	Satu Makela	FIN	116.1

Team

1	**United States**	**353.0**
2	Italy	342.0
3	Finland	341.0

SKEET 125
Individual

1	**Z Meftakhetdinova**	**AZE**	**118.0**
2	Connie Schiller	USA	166.6
3	Diane Igaly	HUN	116.5

Team

1	**United States**	**337.0**
2	Hungary	333.0
3	Italy	326.0

DOUBLE TRAP
Individual

1	**Deborah Gelisio**	**ITA**	**149.0**
2	Gema Usieto	ESP	141.0
3	Xu Xang	CHN	140.0
19	Lesley Goddard	GBR	96.0
30	Anita North	GBR	92.0
31	Clare Watts	GBR	91.0

Team

1	**Italy**	**323.0**
2	China	310.0
3	United States	306.0
7	Great Britain	279.0

UIT World Cup Final

Munich   *Aug 30-Sep 4*

MEN
50m Free Rifle 3x40 shots
Nemania Mirosavliev YUG
50m Free Rifle 60 shots prone
Peter Gabrielsson SWE
10m Air Rifle 60 shots standing
Wolfram Waibel AUT
50m Free Pistol 60 shots
Roberto Di Donna ITA
25m Rapid Fire Pistol 60 shots
Ralf Schumann GER
10m Air Pistol 60 shots
Wang Yifu CHN
10m Running Target 30+30 shots
Michael Jakosits GER
Trap 125 targets
Marco Venturini ITA
Skeet 125 targets
Hennie Dompeling NED
Double Trap 125 targets
Mirco Cenci ITA
WOMEN
50m Standard Rifle 3x20 shots
Renata Mauer POL
10m Air Rifle 40 shots
Carole Couesnon FRA
25m Sport Pistol 60 shots
Diana Jorgova BUL
10m Air Pistol 40 shots
Julia Siniak BLR
Double Trap 120 targets
Xu Xiang CHN

Pistol '95

Bisley   May 24-29
UIT Events Only
UIT Centrefire
1 M Cacheux   582
2 M Gault   580
3 A Lamont   579
NPA Centrefire Precision
1 M Gault   292
2 P Leatherdale 292
3 B Smith   290
UIT Standard Pistol
1 M Cacheux   563
2 A Lamont   563
3 P J Eaton   560
NPA Standard Handgun
1 M Gault   588
2 P J Flippant   581
3 A Lamont   580
UIT Women's Sport Pistol
1 C A Page   582
2 M Thomas   572
3 B Young   560
UIT Rapid Fire
1 M Jay   585
2 P J Clark   570
3 R Craven   569
NPA .22 Club Pistol
1 P Leatherdale 565
2 W E Bradnum   548
3 P Vandenhove   545
UIT Women's Air Pistol
1 C A Page   378
2 M Kausch   375
3 C A Benest   374
UIT Air Pistol
1 M Gault   575
2 P Leatherdale 571
3 A Lamont   570

NRA Imperial Meeting

Bisley   July 15-22
Queen's Prize
1	A Luckman	Sedgemoor	289.30
2	J Bellringer	O Epsomian	287.30
3	D Coleman	Surrey	286.34

Kolapore Trophy
1	Jersey	1,156.128
2	Great Britain	1,153.134
3	Canada	1,144.000

Mackinnon Cup
1	England	1,076.90
2	Canada	1,059.80
3	Scotland	1,046.52

Universities Long Range
1 Cambridge   351.29
Land Rover Discovery Challenge
1 R Clark   RAF   68.7
County Long Range
1 Surrey   444.62

Clay Pigeon

FITASC SPORTING WORLD CHAMPIONSHIPS
Burrungule Pk, Mount Gambier, Aus
Oct 29-Nov 1 1994
Men's Team
1 Great Britain   696
2 France   661
3 Spain   651
Women's Team
1 United States   440
2 France   421
3 Great Britain   419
Men's Individual
1	G Digweed	GBR	184
2	R Faulds	GBR	181
3	C Bloxham	GBR	180

Women's Individual
1	V Girardet	FRA	161
2	B Laurin	USA	160
3	C Van	USA	150

ENGLISH SPORTING WORLD CHAMPIONSHIPS
San Antonio, Texas   Mar 17-19
Men's Team
1 England
2 United States
3 Wales
Men's Individual
1	Gary Phillips	ENG
2	Brian Hebditch	ENG
3	Phil Smith	ENG

BRITISH GRAND PRIX FITASC SPORTING
Barrow Heath   Aug 26-27
1 Barry Simpson 139
2 Duane Morley   136
3 Stuart Clarke 134*

BRITISH OPEN SPORTING
Sandringham   Aug 9-13
1 George Digweed   86*
2 Richard Faulds   86*
3 Luke Riddington   85*

HOME INTERNATIONAL SKEET CHAMPIONSHIPS
Northampton SG   Sep 2
1 England   494/500
2 Scotland   486/500*
3 Wales   486/500*
Shoot-off

BRITISH OPEN SKEET
North of England CTC   July 27-30
1 Pete Dodd   100*
2 William Ford   100*
3 Martyn Moore   100*

ENGLISH OPEN OLYMPIC TRAP
Garlands SG   July 1-2
1 John Grice   192*
2 James Birkett-Evans 192*
3 Phil Newton   190

Skiing

The World Championships should have been held in the Spanish resort of Sierra Nevada in February. Around £10m was spent on the infrastructure, 3,500 temporary workers were signed up and 20 tons of sponsor's cheese was delivered, but it didn't happen. One hundred snow machines could not make up for nature's shortcoming. No snow. And a town once named Sol y Nieve (sun and snow) had to cancel. Gian-Franco Kasper, director-general of the International Ski Federation defended the lateness of the decision. "So we cancel and it snows two days before the event. They would murder us in Madrid," he said. There was consolation for Sierra Nevada, as the event was rescheduled there for 1996. A few weeks later, Europe was awash with snow.

Alberto Tomba, more than anyone, could bemoan the loss of the championship. The 28-year-old, the only man to retain an Olympic Alpine title, has yet to win a world title and he was in immaculate form. Tomba, who has had collected six World Cup titles (three each at slalom and giant slalom), has also never won a World Cup overall crown. That is largely because he does not ski the downhill or super g. However, when you win the first seven slalomsof the season it hardly matters. "Right now, he seems to be from another world," said Marc Girardelli, the five-time overall champion, as Tomba notched up his seventh win. Tomba duly won the overall crown. Now, he must hope it snows in Sierra Nevada.

Men's Downhill

VAL D'ISERE, FRANCE
Dec 16   Dist 3625m/Drop 1020m   *Snow hard*
1	**Josef Strobl**	**AUT**	**1:57.30**
45	Graham Bell	GBR	1:59.73
56	Martin Bell	GBR	2:00.88
64	Andrew Freshwater	GBR	2:03.55

Dec 17
1	**Armin Assinger**	**AUT**	**1:56.07**
41	Graham Bell	GBR	1:58.95
49	Martin Bell	GBR	1:59.45
61	Andrew Freshwater	GBR	2:02.50

KITZBÜHEL, AUSTRIA
Jan 14   Dist 2740m/Drop 680m   *Snow hard*
1	**Luc Alphand**	**FRA**	**1:40.97**
21	Graham Bell	GBR	1:42.88
42	Martin Bell	GBR	1:43.98

WENGEN, SWITZERLAND
Jan 20   Dist 4240m/Drop 1028m   *Snow hard*
1	**Kristian Ghedina**	**ITA**	**2:26.33**
32	Graham Bell	GBR	2:29.46
48	Martin Bell	GBR	2:30.34

Jan 21
1	**Kyle Rasmussen**	**USA**	**2:28.11**
32	Graham Bell	GBR	2:31.30
43	Martin Bell	GBR	2:31.96

WHISTLER, CANADA
Feb 25   Dist 3807m/Drop 1000m   *Snow packed*
1	**Kristian Ghedina**	**ITA**	**2:11.31**
51	Graham Bell	GBR	2:15.35
59	Martin Bell	GBR	2:16.30

KVITFJELL, NORWAY
Mar 11   Dist 2829/Drop 770m   *Snow hard*
1	**Kyle Rasmussen**	**USA**	**1:37.10**
40	Graham Bell	GBR	1:40.04
42	Martin Bell	GBR	1:40.16

BORMIO, ITALY
Mar 15   Dist 3270m/Drop 1010m   *Snow hard*
1	**Luc Alphand**	**FRA**	**1:53.50**

Final Downhill Standings
1	**Luc Alphand**	**FRA**	**484**
2	Kristian Ghedina	ITA	473
3	Patrick Ortlieb	AUT	426

Men's Slalom

TIGNES, FRANCE
Dec 4   Drop 185m
1	Alberto Tomba	ITA	1:41.84

SESTRIERE, ITALY
Dec 12   Drop 210m
1	Alberto Tomba	ITA	1:53.61

LECH, AUSTRIA
Dec 20   Drop 180m
1	Alberto Tomba	ITA	1:44.73

Dec 21
1	Alberto Tomba	ITA	1:43.57

GARMISCH-PARTENKIRCHEN, GERMANY
Jan 8   Drop 200m
1	Alberto Tomba	ITA	1:38.67

KITZBÜHEL, AUSTRIA
Jan 15   Drop 180m
1 Alberto Tomba   ITA   1:37.26

WENGEN, SWITZERLAND
Jan 22   Drop 155m
1 Alberto Tomba   ITA   1:33.89

FURANO, JAPAN
Feb 19   Drop 200m
1 Michael Tritscher   AUT   1:47.94

BORMIO/VALTELLINA, ITALY
Mar 19   Drop 190m
1 Ole Christian Furuseth NOR   1:40.99

Final Slalom Standings
1 Alberto Tomba   ITA   700
2 Michael Tritscher   AUT   477
3 Jure Kosir   SLO   405

- -

Men's Giant Slalom
TIGNES, FRANCE
Dec 3   Drop 440m
1 Achim Vogt   LIE   2:30.76

VAL D'ISERE, FRANCE
Dec 18   Drop 420m   Snow hard
1 Michael von Grünigen   SUI   2:25.09

ALTA-BADIA, ITALY
Dec 22   Drop 393m
1 Alberto Tomba   ITA   2:17.35

KRANJSKA GORA, SLOVENIA
Jan 6   Drop 394m
1 Alberto Tomba   ITA   2:12.01

ADELBODEN, SWITZERLAND
Feb 4   Drop 375m
1 Alberto Tomba   ITA   2:21.96

FURANO, JAPAN
Feb 20   Drop 440m
1 Mario Reiter   AUT   2:38.92

BORMIO/VALTELLINA
Mar 18   Drop 385m
1 Alberto Tomba   ITA   2:15.14

Final Giant Slalom Standings
1 Alberto Tomba   ITA   450
2 Jure Kosir   SLO   355
3 Harald Strand Nilsen   NOR   322

- -

Men's Super G
TIGNES, FRANCE
Dec 11   Dist 2623m/Drop 625m   Snow hard
1 Patrick Ortlieb   AUT   1:22.25
66 Graham Bell   GBR   1:25.72

KITZBÜHEL, AUSTRIA
Jan 16   Dist 2050m/Drop 570m   Snow hard
1 Günther Mader   AUT   1:21.52
44 Martin Bell   GBR   1:24.76

WHISTLER, CANADA
Feb 26   Dist 2449m/Drop 650m   Snow packed
1 Peter Runggaldier   ITA   1:35.84
dnf Graham Bell   GBR

KVITFJELL, NORWAY
Mar 10   Dist 2574m/Drop 641m   Snow hard
1 Werner Perathoner   ITA   1:30.47
41 Martin Bell   GBR   1:32.35

BORMIO/VALTELLINA, ITALY
Mar 16   Dist 2358m/Drop 714m   Snow hard
1 Richard Kröll   AUT   1:37.37

Final Super G Standings
1 Peter Runggaldier   ITA   332
2 Günther Mader   AUT   250
3 Werner Perathoner   ITA   237

Women's Downhill

VAIL, USA
Dec 2   Dist 2642m/Drop 667m
1 Hilary Lindh   USA   1:45.00

LAKE LOUISE, CANADA
Dec 9   Dist 2639m/Drop 707m   Snow hard
1 Picabo Street   USA   1:40.40
Dec 10
1 Hilary Lindh   USA   1:39.90

CORTINA D'AMPEZZO
Jan 20   Dist 2417m/Drop 676m   Snow hard
1 Michaela Gerg-Leitner GER   1:25.82

Jan 22
1 Picabo Street   USA   1:24.75

ARE, SWEDEN
Feb 17   Dist 1801m/Drop 515m   Snow hard
1 Picabo Street   USA   1:09.11

SAALBACH HINTERGLEMM, AUSTRIA
Mar 5   Dist 2520m/Drop 705m   Snow hard
1 Picabo Street   USA   1:37.87

LENZERHEIDE-VALBELLA, SWITZERLAND
Mar 11   Dist 3080m/Drop 780m   Snow hard
1 Picabo Street   USA   1:50.57

BORMIO, ITALY
Mar 15   Dist 2358m/Drop 714m   Snow hard
1 Picabo Street   USA   1:38.41

Final Downhill Standings
1 Picabo Street   USA   709
2 Hilary Lindh   USA   493
3 Katja Seizinger   GER   445

- -

Women's Slalom
SAAS FEE, SWITZERLAND
Cancelled due to high winds

PARK CITY, USA
Nov 27   Drop 199m   Snow hard
1 Vreni Schneider   SUI   1:39.95

SESTRIERE, ITALY
Dec 18   Drop 180m
1 Vreni Schneider   SUI   1:38.55

MERIBEL, FRANCE
Dec 30   Drop 188m
1 Urska Hrovat   SLO   1:20.15

GARMISCH-PARTENKIRCHEN, GERMANY
Jan 15   Drop 180m
1 Martina Ertl   GER   1:22.54
dnf E Carrick-Anderson   GBR

MARIBOR, SLOVENIA
Feb 26   Drop 185m
1 Vreni Schneider   SUI   1:45.26
dnf E Carrick-Anderson   GBR

PARPAN, SWITZERLAND
Mar 12   Drop 143m
1 Pernilla Wiberg   SWE   1:17.31
dnf E Carrick-Anderson   GBR

BORMIO/VALTELLINA, ITALY
Mar 19   Drop 150m
1 Vreni Schneider   SUI   1:31.69

Final Slalom Standings
1 Vreni Schneider   SUI   560
2 Pernilla Wiberg   SWE   355
3 Martina Ertl   GER   278

Women's Giant Slalom

PARK CITY, USA
Nov 26   Drop 360m
1 Heidi Zeller-Bähler   SUI   2:22.03

VAIL, USA
Dec 4   Drop 341m
1 Heidi Zeller-Bähler   SUI   2:15.08

ALTA-BADIA, ITALY
Dec 21   Drop 393m
1 Sabina Panzanini   ITA   2:21.03

HAUS-IM-ENNSTAL, AUSTRIA
Jan 8   Drop 400m
1 Deborah Compagnoni ITA   2:35.39

CORTINA D'AMPEZZO
Jan 23   Drop 400m
1 Anita Wachter   AUT   2:34.41

ARE, SWEDEN
Feb 18   Drop 325m
1 Anita Wachter   AUT   2:01.87

MARIBOR, SLOVENIA
Feb 25   Drop 335m
1 Martina Ertl   GER   2:16.88
dnf E Carrick-Anderson   GBR

BORMIO/VALTELLINA, ITALY
Mar 18   Drop 385m
1 Spela Pretnar   SLO   2:31.96

Final Giant Slalom Standings
1 Vreni Schneider   SUI   450
2 Heidi Zeller-Bähler SUI   420
3 Spela Pretnar   SLO   352

Women's Super G

VAIL, USA
Dec 3   Drop 478m/Distance 1784m   Snow hard
1 Sylvia Eder   AUT   1:21.26

LAKE LOUISE, CANADA
Dec 11   Drop 430m/Distance 1723m   Snow hard
1 Katja Seizinger   GER   1:11.58

HAUS-IM-ENNSTAL, AUSTRIA
Jan 7   Drop 516m/Distance 1930m   Snow hard
1 Anita Wachter   AUT   1:25.78

FLACHAU, AUSTRIA
Jan 10   Drop 553m   Snow hard
1 Renate Goetschl   AUT   1:21.67

GARMISCH-PARTENKIRCHEN, AUSTRIA
Jan 14   Drop 480m/Distance 1670m   Snow hard
1 Florence Masnada   FRA   1:25.92

SAALBACH HINTERGLEMM, AUSTRIA
Mar 5   Drop 483m/Distance 1515m   Snow hard
1 Heidi Zeller-Bähler   SUI   1:04.59

BORMIO/VALTELLINA, ITALY
Mar 16   Drop 546m/Distance 2030m   Snow hard
1 Katja Seizinger   GER   1:20.93

Final Super G Standings
1 Katja Seizinger   GER   446
2 Heidi Zeller-Bähler SUI   366
3 Heidi Zurbriggen   SUI   251

WORLD CUP OVERALL

Men
1 Alberto Tomba   ITA   1150
2 Günther Mader   AUT   775
3 Jure Kosir   SLO   760
4 Marc Girardelli   LUX   744
5 Kjetil Andre Aamodt NOR   708
6 Lasse Kjus   NOR   665
7 Kristian Ghedina   ITA   628
8 Luc Alphand   FRA   609
9 Michael von Grünigen SUI   578
10 Mario Reiter   AUT   559

Women
1 Vreni Schneider   SUI   1248
2 Katja Seizinger   GER   1242
3 Heidi Zeller-Bähler SUI   1044
4 Martina Ertl   GER   985
5 Picabo Street   USA   905
6 Pernilla Wiberg   SWE   816
7 Spela Pretnar   SLO   669
8 Anita Wachter   AUT   593
9 Hilary Lindh   USA   549
10 Urska Hrovat   SLO   535

British Ski Championships

Tignes
MEN
Slalom
1 **Adam Sullivan**
2 Spencer Pession
3 James Ormond
Giant Slalom
1 **Alain Baxter**
2 Martin Bell
3 James Ormond
Super G
1 **Graham Bell**
2 Martin Bell
3 Alain Baxter
Downhill
1 **Martin Bell**
2 Graham Bell
3 Dan Walker
WOMEN
Slalom
1 **Marjory Adam**
2 Sophie Ormond
3 Kirsteen McGibbon
Giant Slalom
1 **Sophie Ormond**
2 Kelly Morris
3 Kirsteen McGibbon
Super G
1 **Emma Carrick-Anderson**
2 Kelly Morris
3 Shona Robertson
Downhill
1 **Kirsteen McGibbon**
2 Kelly Morris
3 Sophie Ormand

Freestyle World Championships

La Clusaz, France   Feb 12-19
MEN
Moguls
1 E Grospiron FRA   27.15
2 J-L Brassard CAN   26.35
3 S Shupletsov RUS   26.19
Aerials
1 T Worthington USA   243.10
2 C Rijavec AUT   241.35
3 S Foucras FRA   239.39

WOMEN
Moguls
1 C Gilg FRA   25.52
2 R Monod FRA   24.89
3 T Mittermayer GER   24.62
Aerials
1 N Stone USA   176.53
2 M Lindgren SWE   169.54
3 K Marshall AUS   168.08

British Championships

MEN
Ballet
1 **Ben Benson**
2 Russel Bowes
3 Simon Gazeley
Moguls
1 **Eric Knight**
2 David Calder
3 Nathan Gardner
Aerials
Event cancelled
WOMEN
Ballet
1 **Gia Benson**
2 Zoey Gazeley
3 Vicki Simpson
Moguls
1 **Julie Gall**
2 Kim Smith
3 Angela Kerr
Aerials
1 **Zoey Gazeley**
2 Gia Benson
3 Melissa Gilliver

Nordic World Championships

Thunder Bay, Canada   Mar 9-19
MEN
10km Classic
1 **Vlad. Smirnov**   KZK   24:52.3
2 Bjørn Daehlie   NOR   25:10.1
3 Mika Myllylae   FIN   25:11.5
30km Classic
1 **Vlad. Smirnov**   KZK 1:15:52.3
2 Bjørn Daehlie   NOR 1:16:52.4
3 Alex Prokurorov   RUS 1:17:35.6
50km Freestyle
1 **Silvio Fauner**   ITA 1:56:36.0
2 Bjørn Daehlie   NOR 1:57:48.5
3 Vladimir Smirnov   KZK 1:58:10.7
Combined Pursuit
1 **Vlad. Smirnov**   KZK 1:06:19.5
2 Silvio Fauner   ITA 1:06:29.7
3 Jari Isometsae   FIN 1:06:30.0
4 x 10km Relay
1 **Norway**   1:34:27.1
2 Finland   1:35:10.5
3 Italy   1:36:28.4
K90   **Ski Jump**
1 **Takanobu Okabe JPN**   266.0
2 Hiroya Saito   JPN   256.5
3 Mika Laitinen   FIN   243.5
K120 Ski Jump
1 **Tom Ingebrigtsen NOR   272.6**
2 Andreas Goldberger AUT   259.5
3 Jens Weissflog   GER   229.9

K120 Team Ski Jump
1 **Finland**   889.0
2 Germany   882.5
3 Japan   836.9
Nordic Combined
1 **Fred Borre Lundberg NOR 0.0**
2 Jari Mantila   FIN   30.3
3 Syvain Guillaume   FRA   39.7
WOMEN
5km Classic
1 **Larissa Luzutina RUS   15:23.7**
2 Nina Gavriluk   RUS   15:47.1
3 Manuela Di Centa   ITA   15:57.8
215km Classic
1 **Larissa Lazutina RUS   41:27.5**
2 Elena Vialbe   RUS   42:39.1
3 I-H Nybraaten   NOR   43:03.2
30km Freestyle
1 **Elena Vialbe   RUS 1:16:27.3**
2 Manuela Di Centa   ITA 1:16:40.5
3 Antonina Ordina   SWE 1:16:58.6
Combined Pursuit
1 **Larissa Lazutina RUS   43:19.6**
2 Nina Gavriluk   RUS   43:45.3
3 Olga Danlova   RUS   43:56.9
4 x 5km Relay
1 **Russia**   53:47.6
2 Norway   55:18.6
3 Sweden   55:18.7

World Cup Champions

MEN'S DOWNHILL
1975	Franz Klammer AUT
1976	Franz Klammer AUT
1977	Franz Klammer AUT
1978	Franz Klammer AUT
1979	Peter Muller SUI
1980	Peter Muller SUI
1981	Harti Weirather AUT
1982	Podborski/Muller CAN/SUI
1983	Franz Klammer AUT
1984	Urs Raber SUI
1985	Helmut Hohlehner AUT
1986	Peter Wirnsberger AUT
1987	Pirmin Zurbriggen SUI
1988	Pirmin Zurbriggen SUI
1989	Marc Girardelli LUX
1990	Helmut Hohlehner AUT
1991	Franz Heinzer SUI
1992	Franz Heinzer SUI
1993	Franz Heinzer SUI
1994	Marc Girardelli LUX
1995	Luc Alphand FRA

MEN'S GIANT SLALOM
1975	Ingemar Stenmark SWE
1976	Ingemar Stenmark SWE
1977	Heini Hemmi SUI
1978	Ingemar Stenmark SWE
1979	Ingemar Stenmark SWE
1980	Ingemar Stenmark SWE
1981	Ingemar Stenmark SWE
1982	Phil Mahre USA
1983	Phil Mahre USA
1984	Ingemar Stenmark SWE
1985	Marc Girardelli LUX
1986	Joel Gaspoz SUI
1987	Pirmin Zurbriggen SUI
1988	Alberto Tomba ITA
1989	Ole Christ'n Furuseth NOR
1990	Ole Christ'n Furuseth NOR
1991	Alberto Tomba ITA
1992	Alberto Tomba ITA
1993	Kjetil Andre Aamodt NOR
1994	Christian Mayer AUT
1995	Alberto Tomba ITA

MEN'S SLALOM
1975	Ingemar Stenmark SWE
1976	Ingemar Stenmark SWE
1977	Ingemar Stenmark SWE
1978	Ingemar Stenmark SWE
1979	Ingemar Stenmark SWE
1980	Ingemar Stenmark SWE
1981	Ingemar Stenmark SWE
1982	Phil Mahre USA
1983	Ingemar Stenmark SWE
1984	Marc Girardelli LUX
1985	Marc Girardelli LUX
1986	Rok Petrovic YUG
1987	Bojan Krizaj YUG
1988	Alberto Tomba ITA
1989	Armin Bittner FRG
1990	Armin Bittner FRG
1991	Marc Girardelli LUX
1992	Alberto Tomba ITA
1993	Tomas Fogdoe SWE
1994	Alberto Tomba ITA
1995	Alberto Tomba ITA

MEN'S SUPER G
1986	Markus Wasmeier FRG
1987	Pirmin Zurbriggen SUI
1988	Pirmin Zurbriggen SUI
1989	Pirmin Zurbriggen SUI
1990	Pirmin Zurbriggen SUI
1991	Franz Heinzer SUI
1992	Paul Accola SUI
1993	Kjetil Andre Aamodt NOR
1994	Jan Einar Thorsen NOR
1995	Pater Runggaldier

WOMEN'S OVERALL
1975	A'marie Moser-Proll AUT
1976	Rosi Mittermaier FRG
1977	Lise-Marie Morerod SUI
1978	Hanni Wenzel LIE
1979	A'marie Moser-Proll AUT
1980	Hanni Wenzel LIE
1981	Marie-Therbse Nadig SUI
1982	Erika Hess SUI
1983	Tamara McKinney USA
1984	Erika Hess SUI
1985	Michela Figini SUI
1986	Maria Walliser SUI
1987	Maria Walliser SUI
1988	Michela Figini SUI
1989	Vreni Schneider SUI
1990	Petra Kronberger AUT
1991	Petra Kronberger AUT
1992	Petra Kronberger AUT
1993	Anita Wachter AUT
1994	Vreni Schneider SUI
1995	Vreni Schneider SUI

WOMEN'S DOWNHILL
1975	A'marie Moser-Proll AUT
1976	Brigite H-Totschnig AUT
1977	Brigite H-Totschnig AUT
1978	A'marie Moser-Proll AUT
1979	A'marie Moser-Proll AUT
1980	Marie-Therese Nadig SUI
1981	Marie-Therese Nadig SUI
1982	C Gros-Gaudenier FRA
1983	Doris De Agostini SUI
1984	Maria Walliser SUI
1985	Michela Figini SUI
1986	Maria Walliser SUI
1987	Michela Figini SUI
1988	Michela Figini SUI
1989	Michela Figini SUI
1990	K Gütensohn-Knopl AUT
1991	Chantal Bournissen SUI
1992	Katja Seizinger GER
1993	Katja Seizinger GER
1994	Katja Seizinger GER
1995	Picabo Street USA

WOMEN'S GIANT SLALOM
1975	A'marie Moser-Proll AUT
1976	Lise-Marie Morerod SUI
1977	Lise-Marie Morerod SUI
1978	Lise-Marie Morerod SUI
1979	Christa Kinshoffer AUT
1980	Hanni Wenzel LIE
1981	Tamara McKinney USA
1982	Irene Epple FRG
1983	Tamara McKinney USA
1984	Erika Hess SUI
1985	Michela Figini SUI &
	Marina Kiehl FRG
1986	Vreni Schneider SUI
1987	Maria Walliser SUI &
	Vreni Schneider SUI
1988	Mateja Svet YUG
1989	Vreni Schneider SUI
1990	Anita Wachter AUT
1991	Vreni Schneider SUI
1992	Carole Merle FRA
1993	Carole Merle FRA
1994	Anita Wachter AUT
1995	Vreni Schneider SUI

WOMEN'S SLALOM
1975	Lise-Marie Morerod SUI
1976	Lise-Marie Morerod SUI
1977	Lise-Marie Morerod SUI
1978	Hanni Wenzel LIE
1979	Regina Sackl AUT
1980	Perrine Pelen FRA
1981	Erika Hess SUI
1982	Erika Hess SUI
1983	Erika Hess SUI
1984	Tamara McKinney USA
1985	Erika Hess SUI
1986	Roswitha Steiner AUT
1987	C Schmidhauser SUI
1988	Roswitha Steiner AUT
1989	Vreni Schneider SUI
1990	Vreni Schneider SUI
1991	Petra Kronberger AUT
1992	Vreni Schneider SUI
1993	Vreni Schneider SUI
1994	Vreni Schneider SUI

WOMEN'S SUPER G
1986	Marina Kiehl FRG
1987	Marina Walliser SUI
1988	Michela Figini SUI
1989	Carole Merle FRA
1990	Carole Merle FRA
1991	Carole Merle FRA
1992	Carole Merle FRA
1993	Carole Merle FRA
1994	Katja Seizinger GER
1995	Katja Seizinger GER

Snooker

"Ronnie was definitely one of the favourites," said Stephen Hendry, after his 13-8 victory over O'Sullivan in the world championship quarter-final. Hendry is far too modest. There was only ever one favourite for the world title, Hendry himself. He duly collected his fifth world crown with a facile victory in the final over Nigel Bond. It was Hendry's 20th consecutive victory at The Crucible, his fourth title in a row and the sparkle on the trophy was made just that much brighter by a 147 maximum in his semi-final match against Jimmy White. Hendry scored 12 century breaks in the tournament to equal his own record and his career earnings reached £4,156,975 to make him the highest earner in the game's history.

Jimmy White must be sick to death of him, but at least this year the Londoner wasn't the losing finallist. Having filled that position for five consecutive years, White this time fell at the penultimate step. He'd already had an eventful championship, in the first round his match against Peter Francisco created as much news as Hendry's maximum, but for rather different reasons.

White beat Francisco 10-2, but an inquiry was instituted into the match following allegations of betting irregularities. What the bookies weren't too happy about was that rather a lot of people chose to bet on precisely that result. Anyone with a couple of quid on a 10-2 victory, would hardly have raised a sweat because Francisco, from the point in the match when it was two frames apiece, played like a donkey. And a beach donkey at that.

White was quickly exonerated, but the inquiry continued into Francisco's conduct. At a nine-hour meeting in Manchester, nine days after the championship finished, Francisco was banned for five years. The reason given was that the South African, "had not conducted himself during the match in a manner consistent with his status as a professional sportsman". The governing body, the WPBSA, refused to amplify the comment.

A footnote to the world championship: Raquel Welch, appearing in Sheffield in George Bernard Shaw's *The Millionairess* was much put out when she discovered all the best rooms in her hotel were occupied by snooker players. The hotel manager, deferring to her star status, knocked down a wall to make her room bigger. There's a lot of very obvious jokes here, but we're not going to make any of them.

Ronnie O'Sullivan continued his rise up the ranking ladder. He won the Benson & Hedges in February to collect the biggest cheque of his career, £120,000. The Essex boy is now ranked third behind Hendry and Davies (who won the 70th title of his career when he took the Welsh Open), yet if he looks over his shoulder another Scot is coming up on the rails. John Higgins shared the same manager as Hendry, Ian Doyle, until October 1994. Higgins was only 19 at the world championships and leapt from 51st to 11th in the season. Yet even Higgins may soon be upstaged. In June, David Gray beat Paul Hunter to win the British amateur title. Gray, 16 years and four months old, broke Jimmy White's record as the yougest ever champion. White, who won the title in 1979, was seven months older.

Gray was not born when the world championships first went to The Crucible in 1977. Dennis Taylor qualified for the last 32 in that championship and every one since - Until this year. It is an auspicious record.

Embassy World Championship ━━━━━

Crucible Theatre, Sheffield   Apr 14-30

ROUND 1		ROUND 2		Q/F		S/F	

Stephen Hendry	10						
Stefan Mazrocis	3	Stephen Hendry	13				
		Tony Drago	6				
Tony Drago	10						
Paul Cavney	2			Stephen Hendry	13		
				Ronnie O'Sullivan	8		
Ronnie O'Sullivan	10						
Dave Harold	3	Ronnie O'Sullivan	13				
		Darren Morgan	8				
Darren Morgan	10						
Anthony Davies	3					Stephen Hendry	16
						Jimmy White	12
John Parrott	10						
Brian Morgan	5	John Parrott	13				
		Joe Swail	11				
Joe Swail	10						
Nigel Gilbert	8			John Parrott	11		
				Jimmy White	13		
David Roe	10						
Billy Snaddon	6	David Roe	7				
		Jimmy White	13				
Jimmy White	10						
Peter Francisco	2						
						Stephen Hendry	**18**
Gary Wilkinson	10					Nigel Bond	9
James Wattana	8	Gary Wilkinson	13				
		Terry Griffiths	9				
Terry Griffiths	10						
Alain Robidoux	6			Gary Wilkinson	7		
				Nigel Bond	13		
Nigel Bond	10						
Stephen Lee	8	Nigel Bond	13				
		Alan McManus	10				
Alan McManus	10						
John Higgins	3					Nigel Bond	16
						Andy Hicks	11
Mark Davis	10						
Ken Doherty	7	Mark Davis	7				
		Peter Ebdon	13				
Peter Ebdon	10						
Rod Lawler	2			Peter Ebdon	8		
				Andy Hicks	13		
Willie Thorne	10						
Tai Pichit	6	Willie Thorne	7				
		Andy Hicks	13				
Andy Hicks	10						
Steve Davis	7						

Major Tournaments

Date	Tournament	Venue	Status	Final (winner bold)	S/Finalists	1st Prize
Sep 30 Oct 7	Dubai Duty Free Classic	Al Nasr Sports Hall	Ranking	**Alan McManus** Peter Ebdon	Stephen Hendry Ronnie O'Sullivan	£40,000
Oct 10 -23	New Skoda Grand Prix	Assembly Rms Derby	Ranking	**John Higgins** Dave Harold	Joe Swail Andy Hicks	£60,000
Oct 29 Nov 6	Benson & Hedges (Scotland)	Edinburgh	Ranking	**Mark Williams** Rod Lawler	Jamie Burnett Matthew Stevens	£5,000
Nov 11 -27	Royal Liver Assurance UK Championship	Guild Hall Preston	Ranking	**Stephen Hendry** Ken Doherty	Peter Ebdon James Wattana	£70,000
Dec 10 -17	Humo European Open	Sporthal Arena Antwerp	Ranking	**Stephen Hendry** John Parrott	Ronnie O'Sullivan Nigel Bond	£60,000
Jan 11 -15	Liverpool Victoria Charity Challenge		Invitation	**Stephen Hendry** Dennis Taylor	Alan McManus Terry Griffiths	
Jan 22 -29	Regal Welsh Open	Newport Centre	Ranking	**Steve Davis** John Higgins	Peter Ebdon Chris Small	£32,500
Feb 5 -12	Benson & Hedges Masters	Wembley Conf. Centre	Invitation	**Ronnie O'Sullivan** John Higgins	Peter Ebdon Jimmy White	£120,000
Feb 13 -19	International Open	Bournemouth Intern. Centre	Ranking	**John Higgins** Steve Davis	John Parrott Jimmy White	£60,000
Mar 10 -18	Kloster Thailand Open	Bangkok	Ranking	**James Wattana** Ronnie O'Sullivan	M Johnston-Allen Cliff Thorburn	£32,500
Mar 21 -26	Benson & Hedges Irish Masters	Goffs Co. Kildare	Invitation	**Peter Ebdon** Stephen Hendry	John Parrott Joe Swail	IR£70,000
Apr 1 -9	British Open	Pavilions Plymouth	Ranking	**John Higgins** Ronnie O'Sullivan	John Parrott James Wattana	£60,000
Apr 14 -30	Embassy World Championship	Crucible Sheffield	Major Ranking	**Stephen Hendry** Nigel Bond	Jimmy White Andy Hicks	£190,000

Money Winners
Top 40 1994-5

1	**Stephen Hendry**	£423,194		21	Mark J Williams	£40,885
2	John Higgins	£280,545		22	Alain Robidoux	£39,485
3	Ronnie O'Sullivan	£262,850		23	Mick Price	£38,925
4	Peter Ebdon	£199,899		24	Mike Hallett	£32,260
5	Nigel Bond	£163,260		25	Martin Clark	£30,915
6	John Parrott	£139,646		26	Jason Ferguson	£27,540
7	Jimmy White	£131,338		27	Mark Johnston-Allen	£26,805
8	Steve Davis MBE	£123,368		28	Dean Reynolds	£26,410
9	James Wattana	£118,778		29	Rod Lawler	£26,270
10	Alan McManus	£108,550		30	Brian Morgan	£25,280
11	Ken Doherty	£97,703		31	Neal Foulds	£25,260
12	Andy Hicks	£85,205		32	Anthony Hamilton	£24,930
13	Dave Harold	£81,905		33	Dene O'Kane	£24,430
14	Joe Swail	£81,231		34	Dennis Taylor	£24,310
15	Darren Morgan	£66,850		35	Billy Snaddon	£24,230
16	Terry Griffiths	£64,950		36	Drew Henry	£23,995
17	David Roe	£50,335		37	Tony Knowles	£23,100
18	Gary Wilkinson	£50,190		38	Doug Mountjoy	£22,935
19	Tony Drago	£48,635		39	Chris Small	£22,340
20	Willie Thorne	£48,500		40	Mark Bennett	£22,270

World Ranking List 1995

Rankings apply throughout the 1995/6 season

1	(1)	Stephen Hendry	50042	52	(89)	Mark A King	14305
2	(2)	Steve Davis	42395	53	(53)	Tony Chappel	14302
3	(9)	Ronnie O'Sullivan	41255	54	(84)	Mark Flowerdew	14300
4	(5)	John Parrott	38939	55	(47)	Jason Prince	13897
5	(3)	James Wattana	38904	56	(37)	Joe Johnson	13695
6	(6)	Alan McManus	36310	57	(52)	Wayne Jones	13660
7	(4)	Jimmy White	36225	58	(43)	Les Dodd	13525
8	(8)	Darren Morgan	34970	59	(65)	Mark Davis	13495
9	(7)	Ken Doherty	34507	60	(62)	Steve Newbury	13312
10	(10)	Peter Ebdon	33645	61	(91)	Terry M Murphy	13130
11	(51)	John Higgins	29962	62	(86)	Chris Small	12740
12	(11)	Nigel Bond	29394	63	(50)	Jonathan Birch	12727
13	(19)	Dave Harold	28840	64	(59)	Paul McPhillips	12697
14	(16)	Tony Drago	25944	65	(46)	Danny Fowler	12085
15	(14)	Terry Griffiths	25259	66	(55)	Paul Davies	12070
16	(13)	David Roe	24156	67	(75)	Brian Rowswell	11805
17	(33)	Andy Hicks	23775	68	(76)	Jimmy Michie	11700
18	(20)	Dene O'Kane	23654	69	(-)	Ian Brumby	11600
19	(12)	Joe Swail	23169	70	(68)	Stephen C O'Connor	11570
20	(32)	Alain Robidoux	23127	71	(56)	Jim Wych	11540
21	(27)	Mick Price	22440	72	(73)	Stefan Mazrocis	11320
22	(18)	Martin Clark	21762	73	(-)	Jamie Burnett	10790
23	(22)	Gary Wilkinson	21498	74	(85)	Steve Judd	10675
24	(21)	Tony Knowles	21455	75	(69)	Tony Meo	10640
25	(15)	Willie Thorne	21196	76	(-)	Matthew Couch	10480
26	(17)	Steve James	20699	77	(60)	Eddie Charlton	10227
27	(30)	Brian Morgan	20453	78	(67)	Karl Broughton	10145
28	(25)	Neal Foulds	20290	79	(99)	Dominic Dale	10025
29	(28)	Jason Ferguson	20183	80	(78)	Karl Payne	9700
30	(29)	Dean Reynolds	20057	81	(57)	Silvino Francisco	9697
31	(35)	Anthony S Hamilton	19670	82	(79)	Craig Edwards	9660
32	(24)	Dennis Taylor	19095	83	(80)	Sean Lanigan	9625
33	(36)	Billy Snaddon	18720	84	(-)	Lee L Richardson	9450
34	(23)	Mike Hallett	18425	85	(-)	Roger Garrett	9435
35	(39)	Drew Henry	18095	86	(-)	Chris Scanlon	9260
36	(26)	Doug Mountjoy	17569	87	(83)	Shokat Ali	9105
37	(40)	Stephen Lee	17447	88	(82)	Mark Rowing	9055
38	(42)	Fergal O'Brien	17285	89	(97)	Darren Clarke	9050
39	(58)	Mark J Williams	16815	90	(-)	Euan Henderson	9035
40	(45)	Rod Lawler	16735	91	(100)	Darryn Walker	9010
41	(54)	Cliff Thorburn	16337	92	(87)	John Read	8840
42	(31)	Mark Bennett	16091	93	(81)	Joe Grech	8625
43	(34)	Tony Jones	16075	94	(-)	Nick Walker	8555
44	(49)	Nigel Gilbert	15667	95	(70)	Ian Graham	8540
45	(64)	Anthony Davies	15577	96	(93)	Jamie Woodman	8525
46	(38)	Nick Terry	15455	97	(-)	Antony Bolsover	8345
47	(41)	Dave Finbow	15282	98	(-)	Surinder Gill	8255
48	(61)	Peter Francisco	15267	99	(71)	Eugene Hughes	8220
49	(44)	Mark Johnston-Allen	14852	100	(-)	Michael Judge	8120
50	(63)	Steve Murphy	14572	*Also*			
51	(48)	Alex Higgins	14350	191	(202)	Allison Fisher	3694

Women's Snooker

WORLD CHAMPIONSHIP
Qualifying rounds at Raunds Cue Snooker Club, May 2-4.
Final rounds at the Siri Fort Sports Complex, New Delhi   Sep 7-10
Quarter-finals
Allison Fisher bt Lisa Quick 4-1
Tessa Davidson bt Kim Shaw 4-2
Kelly Fisher bt Ann-Marie Farren 4-2
Karen Corr bt June Banks 4-0
Semi-finals
Karen Corr bt Kelly Fisher 5-2
Kim Shaw bt Allison Fisher 5-3
Final
Karen Corr bt Kim Shaw 6-3
HB: Corr 76

BERKSHIRE LADIES CLASSIC
New Berkshire Snooker Club, Windsor   Oct 23
Semi-finals
Allison Fisher bt Kelly Fisher 3-2
Kim Shaw bt Karen Corr 3-1
Final
Allison Fisher bt Kim Shaw 3-0
HB: Allison Fisher 85

REGAL MASTERS
John Spencer Snooker Club, Stirling   Nov 12-13
Semi-finals
Kelly Fisher bt Stacey Hillyard 4-3
Allison Fisher bt Karen Corr 4-2
Final
Allison Fisher bt Kelly Fisher 4-0
HB: Tessa Davidson 85

CONNIE GOUGH MEMORIAL CHAMPIONSHIP
Riley's Snooker Club, Luton   Dec 10-11
Semi-finals
Kelly Fisher bt Kim Shaw 4-2
Karen Corr bt Tessa Davidson 4-3
Final
Kelly Fisher bt Karen Corr 4-2
HB: Karen Corr 85

ACADEMY FORK LIFT LADIES CLASSIC
The Q Club, Peterborough   Jan 21-22
Semi-finals
Karen Corr bt Sarah Smith 4-1
Kelly Fisher bt Kim Shaw 4-1
Final
Kelly Fisher bt Karen Corr 4-0
HB: Kelly Fisher 116

PONTINS UK CHAMPIONSHIPS
Prestatyn   Feb 17-18
Semi-finals
Karen Corr bt Kim Shaw 4-3
Allison Fisher bt Kelly Fisher 4-1
Final
Allison Fisher bt Karen Corr 4-1
HB: Kim Shaw 92

BAILEY HOMES LADIES CLASSIC
Terry Griffiths Matchroom, Llanelli   May 27-28
Final
Allison Fisher bt Karen Corr 4-1
HB: Allison Fisher 88

REGAL WELSH CHAMPIONSHIP
Kingsway, Newport   Sep 3
Final
Allison Fisher bt Kim Shaw 4-1
HB: Sharon Dickson 66

PONTINS BRITISH CHAMPIONSHIP
Prestatyn   Sep 26-29
Final
Karen Corr bt Ann-Marie Farren 4-1
HB: Kren Corr 77

WORLD RANKING LIST
As at end of 1994/5 season
Rankings kept through 1995/96 season
Last seasons's ranking in brackets

1	(2)	**Karen Corr**	**Bourne**
2	(1)	**Allison Fisher**	**Hadlow**
3	(7)	**Kelly Fisher**	**Wisbech**
4	(6)	**Kim Shaw**	**Wisbech**
5	(4)	**Tessa Davidson**	**Bicester**
6	(5)	**Ann-Marie Ferran**	**Nottingham**
7	(14)	**June Banks**	**Llanelli**
8	(9)	**Lisa Quick**	**Weston-SM**
9	(8)	**Sara Smith**	**Sheffield**
10	(12)	**Mandy Fisher**	**Wisbech**
11	(13)	**Caroline Walch**	**Sunbury**
12	(15)	**Helen Audus**	**Leeds**
13	(17)	**Julie Kelly**	**Wexford**
14	(-)	**Julie Billings**	**Peterboro**
15	(18)	**Maria Tart**	**Hounslow**
16	(16)	**Georgina Aplin**	**Royston**
17	(-)	**Michelle Brown**	**Leeds**
18	(22)	**Teresa Carlisle**	**Mitcham**
19	(23)	**Jenny Poulter**	**Maidstone**
20	(-)	**Laura Stoddard**	**Manchester**
21	(19)	**Carla Jolly**	**Reading**
22	(21)	**Emma Bonney**	**Portsmouth**
23	(11)	**Sharon Dickson**	**Newport**
24	(10)	**Lynette Horsburgh**	**Blackpool**
25	(20)	**Julie Gillespie**	**Doune**

World Professional Champions

WORLD PROFESSIONAL CHAMPIONSHIP

World Championship took place up to 1952 when a disagreement caused the professional players to organise their own match-play tournament which ended in 1957. The world championship was not staged again until 1964 when it was revived on a challenge basis. In 1969 it adopted the knockout format.

All winners British unless otherwise stated

Year	Winner	Score	Runner-up
1927	Joe Davis	20-11	Tom Dennis
1928	Joe Davis	16-13	Fred Lawrence
1929	Joe Davis	19-14	Tom Dennis
1930	Joe Davis	25-12	Tom Dennis
1931	Joe Davis	25-21	Tom Dennis
1932	Joe Davis	30-19	Clark McConachy NZL
1933	Joe Davis	25-18	Willie Smith
1934	Joe Davis	25-23	Tom Newman
1935	Joe Davis	25-20	Willie Smith
1936	Joe Davis	34-27	Horace Lindrum AUS
1937	Joe Davis	32-29	Horace Lindrum AUS
1938	Joe Davis	37-24	Sidney Smith
1939	Joe Davis	43-30	Sidney Smith
1940	Joe Davis	37-36	Fred Davis
1946	Joe Davis	78-67	Horace Lindrum AUS
1947	Walt Donaldson	82-63	Fred Davis
1948	Fred Davis	84-61	Walter Donaldson
1949	Fred Davis	80-65	Walter Donaldson
1950	W Donaldson	51-46	Fred Davis
1951	Fred Davis	58-39	Walter Donaldson
1952	Horace Lindrum AUS	94-49	Clark McConachy NZL

Professional Match-Play Championship

Year	Winner	Score	Runner-up
1952	Fred Davis	38-35	Walter Donaldson
1953	Fred Davis	37-34	Walter Donaldson
1954	Fred Davis	39-21	Walter Donaldson
1955	Fred Davis	37-34	John Pulman
1956	Fred Davis	38-35	John Pulman
1957	John Pulman	39-34	Jackie Rea

Challenge Matches

Year	Winner	Score	Runner-up
1964	John Pulman	19-16	Fred Davis
1964	John Pulman	40-33	Rex Williams
1965	John Pulman	37-36	Fred Davis
1965	John Pulman	25-22	Rex Williams
1965	John Pulman	39-12	F van Rensburg RSA
1966	John Pulman	5-2	Fred Davis
1968	John Pulman	39-34	Eddie Charlton AUS

Knock-out

Year	Winner	Score	Runner-up
1969	John Spencer	37-34	Gary Owen
1970	Ray Reardon	37-33	John Pulman
1971*	John Spencer	37-29	Warren Simpson AUS
1972	Alex Higgins	37-32	John Spencer
1973	Ray Reardon	38-32	Eddie Charlton AUS
1974	Ray Reardon	22-12	Graham Miles
1975	Ray Reardon	31-30	Eddie Charlton AUS
1976	Ray Reardon	27-16	Alex Higgins
1977	John Spencer	25-21	Cliff Thorburn CAN
1978	Ray Reardon	25-18	Perrie Mans RSA
1979	Terry Griffiths	24-16	Dennis Taylor
1980	Cliff Thorburn CAN	18-16	Alex Higgins
1981	Steve Davis	18-12	Doug Mountjoy
1982	Alex Higgins	18-15	Ray Reardon
1983	Steve Davis	18-6	Cliff Thorburn CAN
1984	Steve Davis	18-16	Jimmy White
1985	Dennis Taylor	18-17	Steve Davis
1986	Joe Johnson	18-12	Steve Davis
1987	Steve Davis	18-14	Joe Johnson
1988	Steve Davis	18-11	Terry Griffiths
1989	Steve Davis	18-3	John Parrot
1990	Stephen Hendry	18-12	Jimmy White
1991	John Parrot	18-11	Jimmy White
1992	Stephen Hendry	18-14	Jimmy White
1993	Stephen Hendry	18-5	Jimmy White
1994	Stephen Hendry	18-17	Jimmy White
1995	Stephen Hendry	18-9	Nigel Bond

* Played November 1970

Speed Skating ▬▬▬▬▬

Long Track

World Championships - Men
Baselga di Pine, Italy Feb 11-12

500m

1	Hiroyuki Noake	JPN	**37.91**
2	Davide Carta	ITA	37.94
3	Rintje Ritsma	HOL	38.42

1500m

1	Rintje Ritsma	HOL	**1:53.31**
2	Keiji Shirahata	JPN	1:53.39
3	Neal Marshall	CAN	1:53.86

5000m

1	Frank Dittrich	GER	**6:56.66**
2	Rene Taubenrauch	GER	6:59.19
3	Takahiro Nozaki	JPN	7:01.84

10,000m

1	Rintje Ritsma	HOL	**14:09.89**
2	Keiji Shirahata	JPN	14:14.16
3	Takahiro Nozaki	JPN	14:21.80

Overall

1	Rintje Ritsma	HOL	**160.992**
2	Keiji Shirahata	JPN	161.864
3	Roberto Sighel	ITA	162.851

World Championships - Women
Savalen, Norway Mar 4-5

500m

1	Gunda Niemann	GER	**41.00**
2	Emese Hunyady	AUT	41.27
3	Moira D'Andrea	USA	41.70

1500m

1	Gunda Niemann	GER	**2:03.86**
2	Ludmila Prokasheva	KZK	2:06.15
3	Annamarie Thomas	HOL	2:06.62

3000m

1	Gunda Niemann	GER	**4:24.72**
2	Carla Zijlstra	HOL	4:25.06
3	Ludmila Prokasheva	KZK	4:26.13

5000m

1	Gunda Niemann	GER	**7:28.70**
2	Carla Zijlstra	HOL	7:37.53
3	Heike Warnicke	GER	7:39.42

Overall

1	Gunda Niemann	GER	**171.276**
2	Ludmila Prokasheva	KZK	175.201
3	Annamarie Thomas	HOL	175.548

World Sprint Championships
Milwaukee, USA Feb 18-19

MEN - Overall

1	Kim Yoon-Man	KOR	146.025
2	Hiroyasu Shimizu	JPN	146.975
3	Yasunori Miyabe	JPN	147.025

WOMEN

1	Bonnie Blair	USA	158.145
2	Oksana Ravilova	RUS	160.820
3	Franziska Schenk	GER	160.830

Short Track

World Championships
Gjorvik, Norway Mar 17-19
Only the 7 leading points scorers qualified for the 3000m event. The overall winner was determined by the points won in the four finals.

MEN

Overall

1	Chae Ji-Hoon KOR	**15 final pts**	(47 in total)
2	Marc Gagnon CAN	6 (35)	
3	Frederic Blackburn CAN	5 (37)	
10	Nicky Gooch GBR	- (19)	
30	Wilf O'Reilly GBR	- (3)	

5000m Relay

1	**Canada**	**7:09.76** *WR*
2	Italy	7:11.44
3	Japan	7:11.71

WOMEN

Overall

1	Chun Lee-Kyung KOR	**13 final pts**	(45 in total)
2	Wang Chunlu CHN	12 (48)	
3	Kim Yun-Mi KOR	6 (37)	

3000m Relay

1	**China**	**4:24.68** *WR*
2	Korea	4:24.75
3	Canada	4:26.57

World Team Championships
Zoetermeer, Holland Mar 24-26

MEN

1	**Canada**	**63 pts**
	(Blackburn/Gagnon/Gagnon/Holbech/Campbell)	
2	Korea	48
3	USA	40
6	Great Britain	21

WOMEN

1	**Korea**	**58 pts**
	(Kim/Chun/Kim/Won/An)	
2	China	51
3	Canada	41

Squash

Women's World Open Championship 1995

Hong Kong   June 25-July 2

Quarter Finals

Michelle Martin AUS bt Sue Wright ENG 9-1, 10-8, 6-9, 9-4

Cassie Jackman ENG bt Carol Owens AUS 9-7, 9-7, 7-9, 9-2

Sarah Fitz-Gerald AUS bt Liz Irving AUS 9-6, 9-6, 9-3

Fiona Geaves ENG bt Suzanne Horner ENG 9-5, 9-6, 9-1

Semi Finals

Michelle Martin bt Cassie Jackman 9-6, 7-9, 9-2, 9-3

Sarah Fitz-Gerald bt Fiona Geaves 9-6, 9-4, 9-0

Final

Michelle Martin bt Sarah Fitz-Gerald 8-10, 9-2, 9-6, 9-3

Women's World Open Championship 1994

St Peter Port, Guernsey   Oct 2-9, 1994

Second Round (selected)

Heather Wallace CAN bt Sarah Spacey ENG 9-3, 9-2, 9-3

Sue Wright ENG bt Chantal Clifton-Parks RSA 9-7, 9-6, 9-5

Suzanne Horner ENG bt Sam Langley ENG 10-8, 9-6, 9-0

Rebecca Macree ENG bt Senga MacFie SCO 4-9, 10-8, 9-0, 9-2

Jane Martin ENG bt Hugoline van Hoorn HOL 10-8, 9-3, 9-7

Carol Owens AUS bt Donia Leeves ENG 9-5, 9-2, 9-4

Cassie Jackman ENG bt Demer Holleran USA 9-7, 9-1, 9-4

Fiona Geaves ENG bt Toni Weeks AUS 4-9, 9-0, 9-2, 9-4

Linda Charman ENG bt Martine Le Moignan ENG 9-2, 5-9, 9-7, 9-6

Third Round

Michelle Martin AUS bt Heather Wallace 10-8, 9-6, 9-7

Sue Wright bt Philippa Beams NZL 9-1, 9-7, 9-1

Suzanne Horner bt Rebecca Macree 9-1, 9-1, 9-0

Sarah Fitz-Gerald bt Claire Nitch RSA 9-2, 9-4, 9-7

Carol Owens bt Jane Martin 9-3, 9-0, 9-4

Cassie Jackman bt Vicki Cardwell AUS 9-4, 9-4, 9-0

Fiona Geaves bt Sabine Schoene 9-5, 8-10, 9-5, 9-3

Liz Irving bt Linda Charman 9-0, 9-6, 5-9, 9-6

Quarter-finals

Michelle Martin bt Sue Wright 9-2, 9-7, 9-1

Suzanne Horner bt Sarah Fitz-Gerald 9-4, 10-8, 9-2

Cassie Jackman bt Carol Owens 9-6, 3-9, 9-5, 9-1

Fiona Geaves bt Liz Irving 9-7, 2-9, 9-3, 0-9, 9-7

Semi-finals

Michelle Martin bt Suzanne Horner 9-4, 9-4, 9-6

Cassie Jackman bt Fiona Geaves 9-4, 9-1, 9-2

Final

Michelle Martin bt Cassie Jackman 9-1, 9-0, 9-6

WORLD RANKINGS

As at Sept 1

Men

1	Jansher Khan	PAK	1495.625
2	Peter Marshall	ENG	836.938
3	Rodney Eyles	AUS	830.313
4	Peter Nicol	SCO	522.031
5	Brett Martin	AUS	461.667
6	Simon Parke	ENG	427.361
7	Chris Walker	ENG	423.156
8	Del Harris	ENG	382.406
9	Anthony Hill	AUS	314.389
10	Zarak Jahan Khan	PAK	244.575
11	Mark Cairns	ENG	239.417
12	Stephen Meads	ENG	237.200
13	Ross Norman	NZL	231.625
14	Sami Elopuro	FIN	227.281
15	Rodney Martin	AUS	227.250
16	Daniel Meddings	ENG	225.188
17	Tony Hands	ENG	199.225
18	Jason Nicolle	ENG	189.438
19	Philip Whitlock	ENG	164.438
20	Julien Bonetat	FRA	161.094

Women

1	Michelle Martin	AUS	1495.630
2	Sarah Fitz-Gerald	AUS	917.810
3	Liz Irving	AUS	756.250
4	Suzanne Horner	ENG	737.190
5	Cassie Jackman	ENG	575.000
6	Fiona Geaves	ENG	484.060
7	Carol Owens	AUS	463.750
8	Sue Wright	ENG	334.690
9	Sabine Schoene	GER	333.130
10	Jane Martin	ENG	323.440
11	Claire Nich	RSA	317.190
12	Vicki Cardwell	AUS	296.520
13	Rebecca Macree	ENG	288.610
14	Philippa Beams	NZL	264.690
15	Robyn Cooper	AUS	238.610
16	Meeghan Bell	AUS	218.270
17	Leilant Marsh	NZL	178.590
18	Linda Charman	ENG	175.310
19	Heather Wallace	CAN	172.500
20	Senga Macfie	SCO	167.190

Women's World Team Championships 1994

St Peter Port, Guernsey   Oct 10-15, 1994
Pool A
Australia 3 Scotland 0   Holland 1 South Africa 2
Scotland 1 South Africa 2   Australia 3 Holland 0
Australia 3 South Africa 0   Holland 2 Scotland 1
Final Standings:
1 Australia, 2 South Africa, 3 Holland, 4 Scotland

Pool B
England 3 New Zealand 0   England 3 Canada 0
England 3 Germany 0   New Zealand 2 Germany 1
New Zealand 3 Canada 0   Germany 3 Canada 0
Final Standings:
1 England, 2 New Zealand, 3 Germany, 4 Canada

Pool C
Finland 3 France 0   Finland 3 Singapore 0
Finland 3 Brazil 0   France 2 Singapore 1
France 3 Brazil 0   Singapore 2 Brazil 1
Final Standings:
1 Finland, 2 France, 3 Singapore, 4 Brazil

Pool D
USA 2 Ireland 1   USA 3 Japan 0
USA 3 Malaysia 0   Ireland 3 Malaysia 0
Ireland 3 Japan 0   Japan 2 Malaysia 1
Final Standings:
1 USA, 2 Ireland, 3 Japan, 4 Malaysia

Semi-finals
Australia 3 New Zealand 0
England 3 South Africa 0

3rd/4th Play-off
New Zealand 1 South Africa 2

Final
Australia 3 England 0
(Martin bt Horner, Irving bt Wright, Fitz-Gerald bt Jackman)

European Championships

Amsterdam, Holland   Apr 27-30
MEN
9th-10th Place
Spain 2 Ireland 2 *(Spain won 9-8 on games countback)*
7th-8th Place
Scotland 3 Netherlands 1
5th-6th Place
Wales 2 France 2 *(Wales won 10-7 on games countback)*
3rd-4th Place
Sweden 2 Germany 2 *(Sweden won 9-6 on games Countback)*

Final
England 4 Finland 0
(Walker bt Elopuro, Parke bt Raumolin, Harris bt Peltonnen, Cairns bt Pekkannen)

WOMEN
9th-10th Place
Denmark 2 Swizerland 1
7th-8th Place
Sweden 2 Ireland 1
5th-6th Place
Finland 3 France 0
3rd-4th Place
Scotland 2 Germany 1

Final
England 3 Netherlands 0
(Jackman bt Van Hoorn, Geaves bt Beumer, Wright bt Atkinson)

Leekes British Open

Cardiff   Mar 21-26
MEN
Quarter Finals
Jansher Khan PAK bt Anthony Hill AUS 15-7, 12-15, 15-6, 15-8
Rodney Eyles AUS bt Julien Bonetat FRA 15-7, 15-10, 11-15, 15-7
Brett Martin AUS bt Philip Whitlock ENG 17-14, 13-15, 15-10, 15-10
Peter Marshall ENG bt Stephen Meads ENG 15-7, 15-7, 12-15, 15-4

Semi Finals
Jansher Khan bt Rodney Eyles 12-15, 15-9, 15-12, 15-7
Peter Marshall bt Brett Martin 15-7, 15-7, 6-15, 15-12

Final
Jansher Khan bt Peter Marshall 15-4, 15-4, 15-5

WOMEN
Semi Finals
Michelle Martin AUS bt Sarah Fitz-Gerald AUS 3-9, 9-2, 3-9, 9-3, 9-2
Liz Irving AUS bt Suzanne Horner ENG 9-6, 9-3, 3-9, 9-3

Final
Michelle Martin bt Liz Irving 9-4, 9-7, 9-5

Men's Open Events

FINALS ONLY
US OPEN
Providence   Nov 3-6, 1994
Peter Nicol SCO bt Chris Walker ENG
15-13, 15-9, 13-15,12-15, 15-5

JSM SUPER SQUASH
Yokohama   Nov 9-13, 1994
Jansher Khan PAK bt Peter Marshall ENG
15-9, 17-14, 15-9

QATAR INTERNATIONAL
Doha   Nov 28-Dec 3, 1994
Jansher Khan PAK bt Rodney Eyles AUS
15-5, 15-7, 15-2

PAKISTAN OPEN
Karachi   Dec 5-9, 1994
Jansher Khan PAK bt Peter Marshall ENG
14-15, 15-14, 15-10, 9-15, 15-6

MAHINDRA CHALLENGE
Dec 8-12
Rodney Eyles AUS bt Peter Marshall ENG
15-8, 15-13, 15-7

ANDERSEN PORTUGUESE OPEN
Lisbon   Mar 7-11
Jansher Khan PAK bt Peter Marshall ENG
15-13, 15-8, 15-7

NORTH AMERICAN OPEN Final
Denver, Canada   Mar 31-Apr 3
Rodney Eyles AUS bt Mark Cairns ENG
15-7, 15-9, 6-15, 15-17, 15-12

BERMUDA OPEN
Bermuda   Apr 8-11
Zarak Jahan Khan PAK bt Brett Martin AUS
3 sets to 0

NYSC TOURNAMENT OF CHAMPIONS
Grand Central Station, New York   June 3-8
Jansher Khan PAK bt Rodney Eyles AUS
15-5, 15-8, 15-10

SINGAPORE OPEN
Singapore   Aug 15-19
Zarak Jahan Khan PAK bt Mark Chaloner ENG
15-12, 15-6, 15-7

CATHAY PACIFIC PERRIER HONG KONG OPEN
Hong Kong   Aug 29-Sep 3
Jansher Khan PAK bt Brett Martin AUS
15-12, 15-7, 15-3

JSM SUPER SQUASH
Yokohama, Japan   Sep 5-10
Jansher Khan PAK bt Brett Martin AUS 15-6, 15-4, 15-11

Women's Open Events

FINALS ONLY
GUERNSEY OPEN
Mar 1-5
Michelle Martin AUS bt Cassie Jackman ENG
9-7, 9-6, 9-1

MALAYSIAN OPEN
June 8-11
Liz Irving AUS bt Michelle Martin AUS
9-5, 9-4, 9-2

AUSTRALIAN OPEN
Aug 9-13
Michelle Martin AUS bt Sarah Fitz-Gerald AUS
9-3, 9-4, 5-9, 9-5

SINGAPORE OPEN
Aug 15-19
Michelle Martin AUS bt Sarah Fitz-Gerald AUS
2-9, 9-6, 9-5, 9-4

Domestic Events

BRITISH CHAMPIONS
Men
Stephen Meads
Women
Fiona Greaves

CLUB CHAMPIONS
Men
Colets (Surrey)
Women
Edgbaston Priory (Birmingham)

COUNTY CHAMPIONS
Men
Yorkshire
Women
Yorkshire

SUPER LEAGUE

	P	W	L	Ties W/L		Pts
Cannons	14	14	0	37	3	37
ICL Lion Herts	14	14	11	3	30	12	30
Ogmore Valley Dragons	14	10	4	26	16	26
Welsh Back Wizards	14	8	6	22	20	22
Ellis Lingfield	14	6	8	18	24	18
Walker Manchester	14	2	12	13	29	13
Jim Hall Sports Northern	14	3	11	11	31	11
Hackets	14	2	12	11	31	11

World & British Open Champions

WORLD OPEN

Men

1976 Geoff Hunt AUS
1977 Geoff Hunt AUS
1979 Geoff Hunt AUS
1980 Geoff Hunt AUS
1981 Jahangir Khan PAK
1982 Jahangir Khan PAK
1983 Jahangir Khan PAK
1984 Jahangir Khan PAK
1985 Jahangir Khan PAK
1986 Ross Norman NZL
1987 Jansher Khan PAK
1988 Jahangir Khan PAK
1989 Jansher Khan PAK
1990 Jansher Khan PAK
1991 Rodney Martin AUS
1992 Jansher Khan PAK
1993 Jansher Khan PAK
1994 Jansher Khan PAK

Women

1976 Heather McKay AUS
1979 Heather McKay AUS
1981 Rhonda Thorne AUS
1983 Vicki Cardwell AUS
1985 Susan Devoy NZL
1987 Susan Devoy NZL
1989 Martine Le Moignan GBR
1990 Susan Devoy NZL
1991 Susan Devoy NZL
1992 Susan Devoy NZL
1993 Michelle Martin AUS
1994 Michelle Martin AUS
1995 Michelle Martin AUS

WORLD AMATEUR CHAMPIONSHIP

Individual

1967 Geoff Hunt AUS
1969 Geoff Hunt AUS
1971 Geoff Hunt AUS
1973 Cameron Nancarrow AUS
1975 Kevin Shawcross AUS
1977 Maqsood Ahmed PAK
1979 Jahangir Khan PAK
1981 Steve Bowditch AUS
1983 Jahangir Khan PAK
1985 Jahangir Khan PAK

BRITISH OPEN

Men

1930 Don Butcher GBR
1931 Don Butcher GBR
1932 Abdelfattah Amr Bey EGY
1933 Abdelfattah Amr Bey EGY
1934 Abdelfattah Amr Bey EGY
1935 Abdelfattah Amr Bey EGY
1936 Abdelfattah Amr Bey EGY
1937 Abdelfattah Amr Bey EGY
1938 James Dear GBR
1946 Mahmoud Karim EGY
1947 Mahmoud Karim EGY
1948 Mahmoud Karim EGY
1949 Mahmoud Karim EGY
1950 Hashim Khan PAK
1951 Hashim Khan PAK
1952 Hashim Khan PAK
1953 Hashim Khan PAK
1954 Hashim Khan PAK
1955 Hashim Khan PAK
1956 Roshan Khan PAK
1957 Hashim Khan PAK
1958 Azam Khan PAK
1959 Azam Khan PAK
1960 Azam Khan PAK
1961 Azam Khan PAK
1962 Mohibullah Khan PAK
1963 Abdel. Abou Taleb EGY
1964 Abdelfattah Abou Taleb
1965 Abdelfattah Abou Taleb
1966 Abdelfattah AbouTaleb
1967 Jonah Barrington GBR
1968 Jonah Barrington GBR
1969 Geoff Hunt AUS
1970 Jonah Barrington GBR
1971 Jonah Bartington GBR
1972 Jonah Barrington GBR
1973 Jonah Barrington GBR
1974 Geoff Hunt AUS
1975 Qamar Zaman PAK
1976 Geoff Hunt AUS
1977 Geoff Hunt AUS
1978 Geoff Hunt AUS
1979 Geoff Hunt AUS
1980 Geoff Hunt AUS
1981 Geoff Hunt AUS
1982 Jahangir Khan PAK
1983 Jahangir Khan PAK
1984 Jahangir Khan PAK
1985 Jahangir Khan PAK
1986 Jahangir Khan PAK
1987 Jahangir Khan PAK
1988 Jahangir Khan PAK
1989 Jahangir Khan PAK
1990 Jahangir Khan PAK
1991 Jahangir Khan PAK
1992 Jansher Khan PAK
1993 Jansher Khan PAK
1994 Jansher Khan PAK
1995 Jansher Khan PAK

Women

1922 Joyce Cave GBR
1922 Sylvia Huntsman GBR
1923 Nancy Cave GBR
1924 Joyce Cave GBR
1925 Cecily Fenwick GBR
1926 Cecily Fenwick GBR
1928 Joyce Cave GBR
1929 Nancy Cave GBR
1930 Nancy Cave GBR
1931 Cecily Fenwick GBR
1932 Susan Noel GBR
1933 Susan Noel GBR
1934 Susan Noel GBR
1934 Margot Lumb GBR
1935 Margot Lumb GBR
1936 Margot Lumb GBR
1937 Margot Lumb GBR
1938 Margot Lumb GBR
1939 Margot Lumb GBR
1947 Joan Curry GBR
1948 Joan Curry GBR
1949 Joan Curry GBR
1950 Janet Morgan GBR
1951 Janet Morgan GBR
1952 Janet Morgan GBR
1953 Janet Morgan GBR
1954 Janet Morgan GBR
1955 Janet Morgan GBR
1956 Janet Morgan GBR
1957 Janet Morgan GBR
1958 Janet Morgan GBR
1959 Janet Morgan GBR
1960 Sheila Macintosh GBR
1961 Fran Marshall GBR
1962 Heather Blundell AUS
1963 Heather Blundell AUS
1964 Heather Blundell AUS
1965 Heather Blundell AUS
1966 Heather McKay (née Blundell) AUS
1967 Heather McKay AUS
1968 Heather McKay AUS
1969 Heather McKay AUS
1970 Heather McKay AUS
1971 Heather McKay AUS
1972 Heather McKay AUS
1973 Heather McKay AUS
1974 Heather McKay AUS
1975 Heather McKay AUS
1976 Heather McKay AUS
1977 Heather McKay AUS
1978 Susan Newman AUS
1979 Barbara Wall AUS
1980 Vicki Hoffman AUS
1981 Vicki Hoffman AUS
1982 Vicki Cardwell (née Hoffman) AUS
1983 Vicki Cardwell AUS
1984 Susan Devoy NZL
1985 Susan Devoy NZL
1986 Susan Devoy NZL
1987 Susan Devoy NZL
1988 Susan Devoy NZL
1989 Susan Devoy NZL
1990 Susan Devoy NZL
1991 Lisa Opie GBR
1992 Susan Devoy NZL
1993 Michelle Martin AUS
1994 Michelle Martin AUS
1995 Michelle Martin AUS

Swimming ▬▬▬▬▬▬▬▬▬▬

There is only one way to run; you put one foot after the other. It's not quite same in swimming. At the Seoul Olympics, you barely saw the backstrokers, they spent so much time underwater. Aware that spectators were paying to watch nothing but ripples on the water, officials imposed a 15 metre limit on underwater swimming. Denis Pankratov brought dolphining up-to-date at the European Championships. The 21-year-old from Volvograd broke the world record in the 100m butterfly; or the 74m butterfly as the spectators would have it. Pankratov surfaced at 26m; which was not quite as dramatic as Steven Berkoff, the backstroker who first used the technique in competition in 1988, who surfaced at 35m. You can bet your bottom rouble, though, Pankratov's dive won't be legal in Atlanta.

Pankratov's was the only world record at a championships dominated by the Russian and German teams. Franziska van Almsick was again the individual star of the Germans in the pool, but not so smart on dry land where she got in a pickle over whether she did or didn't admire Hitler. The German squad also had a tussle with their national federation, covering up sponsor's names in protest over the allocation of 400,000DM of sponsorship money. Denmark's Mette Jacobsen won five medals at three different strokes; Michelle Smith won Ireland's first-ever medal when she won the 200m IM and also won the 200m fly; and Kristina Egerszegy, still only 21, doubled up with backstroke and 400m IM.

Britain almost took gold with both Paul Palmer in the 400m free and Graeme Smith in the 1500m. Palmer missed 1994 through illness and injury, so it was an impressive comeback. Smith abandons his course at Manchester University for a year to prepare for Atlanta where they both hope for medals, though Kieren Perkins could take both golds.

Karen Pickering will have worse times than in Vienna. The 23-year-old took four bronze medals home to Ipswich, over half the British haul. A month earlier at Coventry, Pickering had equalled a 63-year-old record by winning her fifth national 200m free title.

For most of the year, the administrators at the Amateur Swimming Association were chasing the 61-year-old Australian autocrat Don Talbot to fill the post of director of coaching. They should be grateful they didn't catch him, Australian coaches are a wild bunch as Gennadi Touretski proved. The Russian-born coach to the Aussie Olympic squad, tired and emotional after the long flight from Sydney to LA, set about two passengers and two crew members. Touretski's exhuberance cost him $10,000 and 30 days in jail.

While the Talbot courtship proved embarrassing for the sport, Paul Hickson's conviction for offences against the kids he was coaching could be singularly damaging for swimming. Hickson got 17 years; it could take the sport as long to regain parents' trust.

Guy Delage would win no medals in any championship, but it's difficult to ignore the Frenchman who set off from Cape Verde last December to swim the Atlantic. The French press was almost universally scornful of the 42-year-old, who spent two-thirds of his time on his raft rather than in the water. That, they suggested, meant he floated a lot further than he swam. However, when he arrived at Barbados after 55 days and 2,500 miles at sea, even the cynics were won over. The man initially described as "a voluntary shipwreck victim" became a "poet swimmer".

European Championships ▬▬▬▬

Vienna   17-27 Aug

Men

*British results are shown when the swimmer/diver
reached the final. * denotes dead-heat*

50m Freestyle
1	Alexander Popov	RUS	22.25
2	Christophe Kalfayan	FRA	22.63
3	Torsten Spanneberg	GER	22.66
4	Mark Foster	GBR	22.76

100m Freestyle
1	Alexander Popov	RUS	49.10
2	Torsten Spanneberg	GER	49.67
3	Björn Zikarsky	GER	50.23
8	Nick Shackell	GBR	50.77

200m Freestyle
1	Jani Sievinen	FIN	1:48.98
2	Anders Holmertz	SWE	1:49.12
3	Antti Kasvio	FIN	1:49.24
6	Paul Palmer	GBR	1:49.48

400m Freestyle
1	Steffen Zesner	GER	3:50.35
2	Paul Palmer	GBR	3:50.43
3	Anders Holmertz	SWE	3:51.01

1500m Freestyle
1	Jörg Hoffmann	GER	15:11.25
2	Graeme Smith	GBR	15:11.90
3	Steffen Zesner	GER	15:20.46

100m Breaststroke
1	Fred Deburghgraeva	BEL	1:01.12
2	Karoly Güttler	HUN	1:01.38
3	Rodolfo Falcon	CUB	1:01.79

200m Breaststroke
1	Andrey Korneev	RUS	2:12.62
2	Karoly Güttler	HUN	2:12.95
3	Fred Deburghgraeva	BEL	2:14.01

100m Butterfly
1	Denis Pankratov	RUS	52.32	WR
2	Denis Silantiev	UKR	53.37	
3	Rafal Szukala	POL	53.45	

200m Butterfly
1	Denis Pankratov	RUS	1:56.34
2	Konrad Galka	POL	1:59.50
3	Chris-Carol Bremer	GER	1:59.96
7	James Hickman	GBR	2:00.79

100m Backstroke
1	Vladimir Selkov	RUS	55.48
2	Jirka Letzin	GER	56.24
3	Stefaan Maene	BEL	56.32
7	Neil Willey	GBR	56.80

200m Backstroke
1	Vladimir Selkov	RUS	1:58.48
2	Nicolae Butacu	ROM	1:59.96
3	Adam Ruckwood	GBR	2:00.16

200m Individual Medley
1	Jani Sievinen	FIN	1:58.61
2	Attila Czene	HUN	2:00.88
3	Christian Kenner	GER	2:02.24

400m Individual Medley
1	Jani Sievinen	FIN	4:14.75
2	Marcin Malinsky	POL	4:18.32
3	Luca Sacchi	ITA	4:18.82

4 x 100m Freestyle
1	Russia	3:18.84
2	Germany	3:19.76
3	Sweden	3:21.07

4 x 200m Freestyle
1	Germany	7:18.22
2	Sweden	7:19.95
3	Italy	7:20.96
5	Great Britain	7:26.13

4 x 100m Medley
1	Russia	3:38.11
2	Hungary	3:40.88
3	Germany	3:41.55

DIVING

1m Springboard
1	Edwin Jongejans	NED	420.75
2	Joakim Anderson	SWE	387.60
3	Boris Lietzow	GER	379.26

3m Springboard
1	Dmitry Sautin	RUS	670.38
2	Jan Hempel	GER	634.05
3	Roman Volodkov	UKR	615.81

10m Platform
1	Vladimir Timoshinin	RUS	673.83
2	Jan Hempel	GER	662.46
3	Dmitry Sautin	RUS	648.84

LONG DISTANCE

5 Kilometre
1	Alexey Akatiev	RUS	55:00.30
2	Christof Wandratsch	GER	56:06.80
3	Samuele Pampana	ITA	56:10.30
19	Simon Emm	GBR	1:02:34.90

25 Kilometre
1	C Wandratsch	GER	5:11:36.30
2	Alexey Akatiev	RUS	5:13:49.80
3	Stephane Lecat	FRA	5:14:16.40
10	Justin Palfrey	GBR	5:32:05.80

WATER POLO

Final
Italy 10 Hungary 8

Final Placings
1 Italy
2 Hungary
3 Germany

Women

50m Freestyle
1	Linda Olofsson	SWE	25.76
2	Franziska van Almsick	GER	25.80
3	Angela Postma	NED	25.86

100m Freestyle
1	Franziska van Almsick	GER	55.34
2	Mette Jacobsen	DEN	56.02
3	Karen Pickering	GBR	56.05

200m Freestyle
1	Kerstin Kielgass	GER	2:00.56
2	Malin Nilsson	SWE	2:01.35
3	Mette Jacobsen	DEN*	2:01.52
3	Karen Pickering	GBR*	2:01.52

400m Freestyle
1	Franziska van Almsick	GER	4:08.37
2	Carla Guerts	NED	4:10.73
3	Irene Dalby	NOR	4:13.44

800m Freestyle

1	Julia Jung	GER	8:36.08
2	Jana Henke	GER	8:36.68
3	Irene Dalby	NOR	8:38.82
7	Sarah Hardcastle	GBR	8:46.59

100m Breaststroke

1	Brigitte Becue	BEL	1:09.30
2	Svetlana Bondarenko	UKR	1:09.73
3	Agnes Kovacs	HUN	1:10.77

200m Breaststroke

1	Brigitte Becue	BEL	2:27.66
2	Svetlana Bondarenko	UKR	2:30.50
3	Alicja Peczak	POL	2:20.59
5	Marie Hardiman	GBR	2:31.16

100m Butterfly

1	Mette Jacobsen	DEN	1:00.64
2	Ilaria Tocchini	ITA	1:01.13
3	Cecile Jeanson	FRA	1:01.15

200m Butterfly

1	Michelle Smith	IRL	2:11.60
2	Mette Jacobsen	DEN	2:12.29
3	Sophie Skou	DEN	2:13.31

100m Backstroke

1	Mette Jacobsen	DEN	1:02.46
2	Cathleen Rund	GER	1:02.91
3	Nina Zhivanevskaya	RUS	1:03.06

200m Backstroke

1	Kristina Egerszegi	HUN	2:07.24
2	Brigitte Becue	BEL	2:10.60
3	Alicja Peczak	POL	2:10.96

200m Individual Medley

1	Michelle Smith	IRL	2:15.27
2	Brigitte Becue	BEL	2:16.15
3	Alicja Peczak	POL	2:17.42

400m Individual Medley

1	Kristina Egerszegy	HUN	4:40.33
2	Michelle Smith	IRL	4:42.81
3	Cathleen Rund	GER	4:46.22

4 x 100m Freestyle

1	Germany	3:43.22
2	Sweden	3:45.21
3	Great Britain	3:46.89

4 x 200m Freestyle

1	Germany	8:06.11
2	Netherlands	8:10.17
3	Great Britain	8:14.31

(Horner/Huddart/Goddard/Benett)

4 x 100m Medley

1	Germany	4:09.97
2	Hungary	4:12.00
3	Spain	4:12.52

DIVING

1m Springboard

1	Vera Ilyina	RUS	275.25
2	Dörte Lindner	GER	271.20
3	Svetlana Alekseeva	BLR	240.72

3m Springboard

1	Vera Ilyina	RUS	523.23
2	Yulia Pakalina	RUS	520.20
3	Claudia Bockner	GER	518.64
9	Victoria Stenning	GBR	414.99

10m Platform

1	Ute Wetzig	GER	444.24
2	Conny Schmalfuss	GER	435.84
3	Svetlana Timoshinina	RUS	431.55

LONG DISTANCE

5 Kilometre

1	Rita Kovacs	HUN	1:00:38.30
2	Peggy Büchse	GER	1:00:50.80
3	Valeria Casprini	ITA	1:01:07.60
10	Claire Booker	GBR	1:04:20.20

25 Kilometre

1	Peggy Büchse	GER	5:32:36.40
2	Edith van Dijk	NED	5:36:05.50
3	Yvetta Hlakova	CZE	5:38:08.30
7	Sara-Louise Ward	GBR	5:48:01.50

SYNCHRONISED

Solo

1	Olga Sedakova	RUS	99.160
2	Marianne Aeschbacher	GER	97.520
3	Christina Thalassinidou	GRE	95.360
7	Laila Vakil	GBR	92.640

Duet

1	Azarova/Kiseliova	RUS	98.880
2	Aeschbacher/Lignot	FRA	96.920
3	Burlando/Carnina	ITA	96.040
4	Geier/Thompson	GBR	92.600

Group

1	Russia	98.880
2	France	97.160
3	Italy	95.480
4	Great Britain	94.040

(Vakil/Thompson/Davenport/Wishart/Geier/Carlsen/Moreau/Whyman

WATER POLO

Final

Italy 7 Hungary 5

Final Placings

1 Italy
2 Hungary
3 Netherlands

Final Medal Table

	G	S	B
Russia	17	2	4
Germany	13	13	11
Hungary	3	7	1
Belgium	3	1	2
Finland	3	0	1
Denmark	2	2	2
Italy	2	1	6
Ireland	2	1	0
Sweden	1	5	2
Netherlands	1	3	2
France	0	4	2
Ukraine	0	3	1
Great Britain	0	2	5
Poland	0	2	3
Romania	0	1	0
Norway	0	0	2
Belarus	0	0	1
Czech Rep	0	0	1
Greece	0	0	1
Spain	0	0	1

World Cup

The World Cup comprised seven meetings; Hong Kong, Espoo, Paris, Desenzano, Malmö, Sheffield and Glesenkirchen

Final Standings

Men

Sprint Free (50m/100m/200m)
1	Mark Foster	GBR	55
2	Alexander Popov	RUS	50
3	Danyon Loader	NZL	46

Distance Free (400m/800m)
1	Steffen Zesner	GER	68
2	Jörg Hoffmann	GER	63
3	Antti Kasvio	FIN	54

Backstroke (50m/100m/200m)
1	Jirka Letzin	GER	58
2	Vladimir Selkov	RUS	57
3	Jeff Rouse	USA	54

Breaststroke (50m/100m/200m)
1	Mark Warnecke	GER	70
2	Phil Rogers	AUS	49
3	Andrey Ivanov	RUS	39

Butterfly (50m/100m/200m)
1	Chris Carol Bremer	GER	66
2	Vesa Hanski	FIN	63
3	Mark Foster	GBR	44

Individual Medley (100m/200m/400m)
1	Christian Keller	GER	80
2	Marcin Malinski	POL	67
3	Luca Sacchi	ITA	61

Women

Sprint Free (50m/100m/200m)
1	Fran. Van Almsick	GER	80
2	Rania Elwani	EGY	57
3	Martina Moravcova	SVK	51

Distance Free (400m/800m)
1	Julia Jung	GER	71
2	Sarah Hardcastle	GBR	34
3	Malin Nillson	SWE	28

Backstroke (50m/100m/200m)
1	Sandra Volker	GER	80
2	Mette Jacobsen	DEN	61
3	Antje Buschschulte	GER	52

Breaststroke (50m/100m/200m)
1	Brigitta Becue	BEL	77
2	Elin Austevoil	NOR	44
3	Manuela Nackel	GER	41

Butterfly (50m/100m/200m)
1	Michelle Smith	IRL	68
2	Mette Jacobsen	DEN	66
3	Angela Kennedy	AUS	60

Indiv. Medley (100m/200m/400m)
1	Britta Vestergaard	DEN	75
2	Daniela Hunger	GER	68
3	Anna Wilson	NZL	44

National Championships

Coventry   July 20-23

Men

50m Freestyle
1	Mark Foster	23.74
2	Alan Rapley	23.85
3	M Stevens	23.89

100m Freestyle
1	Simon Handley	52.29
2	Alan Rapley	52.32
3	M Stevens	52.40

200m Freestyle
1	Paul Palmer	1:52.74
2	Steve Mellor	1:52.75
3	M Stevens	1:54.04

400m Freestyle
1	Ian Wilson	3:59.22
2	G Hudson	4:01.56
3	Steve Mellor	4:03.40

1500m Freestyle
1	Ian Wilson	15:24.27
2	P Potter	15:57.88
3	G Hudson	16:03.30

50m Backstroke
1	Neil Willey	27.00
2	J Fitzgerald	28.02
3	L Peterson	28.35

100m Backstroke
1	Neil Willey	57.20
2	F Walker	59.24
3	C Jones	59.28

200m Backstroke
1	Adam Ruckwood	2:05.30
2	Steve Mellor	2:06.17
3	C Jones	2:06.36

50m Breaststroke
1	James Parrack	29.29
2	Peter McGinty	29.55
3	A Cooper	30.18

100m Breaststroke
1	James Parrack	1:04.22
2	Peter McGintly	1:05.21
3	R Morris	1:06.14

200m Breaststroke
1	Nick Gillingham	2:17.32
2	A Cooper	2:21.82
3	A Clapper	2:23.16

50m Butterfly
1	Mark Foster	24.77
2	Janko Gojkovic	25.58
3	D Jones	25.64

100m Butterfly
1	Andrew Clayton	55.91
2	M Watkins	56.24
3	James Hickman	56.61

200m Butterfly
1	Stephen Parry	2:03.04
2	James Hickman	2:03.66
3	R Ashcroft	2:03.74

200m Individual Medley
1	F Walker	2:07.08
2	Peter McGinty	2:08.49
3	C Jones	2:08.78

400m Individual Medley
1	J Hickman	4:30.94
2	J Harris	4:32.61
3	D Warren	4:32.97

4 x 100m Freestyle
1	City of Sheffield	3:29.85
2	City of Birmingham	3:31.45
3	City of Bristol	3:31.53

4 x 200m Freestyle
1	City of Leeds	7:43.25
2	City of Birmingham	7:43.79
3	Portsmouth Northsea	7:50.48

4 x 100m Medley
1	City of Birmingham	3:50.48
2	City of Cardiff	3:53.50
3	City of Leeds	3:55.84

Women

50m Freestyle
1	Susan Rolph	26.84
2	Karen Pickering	26.96
3	Carrie Wilmott	27.09

100m Freestyle
1	Susan Rolph	57.41
2	Karen Pickering	57.52
3	Alex Bennett	58.05

200m Freestyle
1	Karen Pickering	2:03.76
2	Sarah Hardcastle	2:03.87
3	Claire Huddart	2:04.48

400m Freestyle
1	Sarah Hardcastle	4:17.82
2	Katie Goddard	4:20.79
3	Alex Bennett	4:20.91

800m Freestyle
1	Sarah Hardcastle	8:44.19
2	Vicki Horner	8:57.21
3	Katie Goddard	8:59.14

50m Backstroke
1	H Barnes	30.63
2	Susan Rolph	30.97
3	Zöe Cray	31.10

100m Backstroke
1	Zöe Cray	1:05.32
2	Kathy Osher	1:05.36
3	Lucy Findlay	1:05.70

200m Backstroke
1	Kathy Osher	2:17.93
2	Joanne Deakins	2:19.65
3	Zöe Cray	2:20.42

50m Breaststroke
1	Karen Rake	33.63
2	Jaime King	33.66
3	Susan Rolph	34.26

100m Breaststroke
1	Karen Rake	1:11.95
2	Jaime King	1:12.16
3	L Hindmarsh	1:13.78

200m Breaststroke
1	Marie Hardiman	2:32.03
2	L Hindmarsh	2:34.53

3	Jaime King	2:36.98

50m Butterfly

1	**S Massey**	**28.88**
2	C Foot	28.95
3	Samantha Greenep	29.25

100m Butterfly

1	**C Foot**	**1:03.38**
2	Helen Jepson	1:03.78
3	A Loots	1:03.79

200m Butterfly

1	**Helen Jepson**	**2:16.84**
2	Alex Bennett	2:17.68
3	Helen Slatter	2:19.55

200m Individual Medley

1	**Susan Rolph**	**2:18.62**
2	Lucy Findley	2:19.97
3	Karen Pickering	2:21.17

400m Individual Medley

1	**Katie Goddard**	**4:58.16**
2	Lucy Findley	4:58.35
3	Vicki Horner	4:59.27

4 x 100m Freestyle

1	**City of Leeds**	**4:00.03**
2	Nova Centurion	4:02.09
3	Barnett Copthall	4:02.31

4 x 200m Freestyle

1	**Portsm'th Northsea**	**8:31.78**
2	City of Leeds	8:34.91
3	City of Bradford	8:41.09

4 x 100m Medley

1	**City of Birmingham**	**4:31.51**
2	Portsmouth Northsea	4:32.68
3	Barnett Copthall	4:34.62

British Diving Championships

Crystal Palace   *May*

Men

10m Platform

1	**Robert Morgan**	**626.30**
2	Tony Ali	559.00
3	Mark Shipman	522.30

3m Springboard

1	**Tony Ali**	**627.10**
2	Robert Morgan	558.00
3	Mark Shipman	509.80

1m Springboard

1	**Robert Morgan**	**349.90**
2	Mark Shipman	301.20
3	Tony Ali	280.30

Women

10m Platform

1	**Lesley Ward**	**439.95**
2	Hayley Allen	408.05
3	Beth Ackroyd	395.45

3m Springboard

1	**Victoria Stenning**	**449.15**
2	Jane Smith	439.75
3	Olivia Clarke	437.55

1m Springboard

1	**Olivia Clarke**	**226.50**
2	Jane Smith	213.55
3	Karen Smith	201.55

*Q*uotes

"If you ask people about Hitler, you just hear that he was evil, totally stupid and that he killed lots of people. Actually, he was quite clever. I had read *Mein Kampf* and suddenly understand how he did it" - **Franziska van Almsick, as quoted in the Austrian newspaper *Kurier*.**

"I am not a Hitler fan. I am very interested in German history and the second world war belongs to Adolf Hitler. It's not forbidden to be interested in such things" - **Van Almsick, who claimed the wrong interpretation had been put on her words by *Kurier*. Mind, if that's her defence, she'd have been better saying nothing.**

"They were more than friends. I was accepted. They were my guardians" - **Guy Delage, talking about the fish around him as he 'swam' the Atlantic.**

"(It) will put him in the record books between the world accordian champion and the man who can eat most snails" - ***Le Monde*. dismissive of Delage's venture.**

"I heard this big hollow thud and then I found myself in the water.....I just wanted to hold the blood in, or just not anybody touch it...what was going on in my mind was, 'Do I say something'. This has been an incredible guarded secret. You could throw the competition into a state of alarm. Even more so than just having hit my head on the board, I was paralysed with fear" - **Greg Louganis, in his autobiography *Breaking the surface*. In the book, Louganis aditted that he was suffering from Aids when he gashed his head on the board at the Seoul Olympics. The doctor who treated him, James Puffer, later tested negative for the virus, but stated that he never felt there was any risk.**

"I had chills through my body when I looked up and saw that I had won" - **Brooke Bennett, 15-year-old American schoolgirl, who beat Janet Evans at Alamo.**

"I should be there by November...." - **Don Talbot, who must rank as the world's most courted coach, estimating when he would take up the post of director of coaching of British swimming.**

World Champions

Men

50m Freestyle
1986 **Tom Jager** USA
1991 **Tom Jager** USA
1994 **Alexander Popov** RUS

100m Freestyle
1973 **Jim Montgomery** USA
1975 **Andrew Coan** USA
1978 **David McCagg** USA
1982 **Jorg Woithe** GDR
1986 **Matt Biondi** USA
1991 **Matt Biondi** USA
1994 **Alex'der Popov** RUS

200m Freestyle
1973 **Jim Montgomery** USA
1975 **Tim Shaw** USA
1978 **William Forrester** USA
1982 **Michael Gross** FRG
1986 **Michael Gross** FRG
1991 **Giorgio Lamberti** ITA
1994 **Antti Kasvio** FIN

400m Freestyle
1973 **Rick DeMont** USA
1975 **Tim Shaw** USA
1978 **Vladimir Salnikov** URS
1982 **Vladimir Salnikov** URS
1986 **Rainer Henkel** FRG
1991 **Jörg Hoffmann** GER
1994 **Kieren Perkins** AUS

1500m Freestyle
1973 **Steve Holland** AUS
1975 **Tim Shaw** USA
1978 **Vladimir Salnikov** URS
1982 **Vladimir Salnikov** URS
1986 **Rainer Henkel** FRG
1991 **Jörg Hoffmann** GER
1994 **Kieren Perkins** AUS

100m Backstroke
1973 **Roland Matthes** GDR
1975 **Roland Matthes** GDR
1978 **Robert Jackson** USA
1982 **Dirk Richter** GDR
1986 **Igor Polyanski** URS
1991 **Jeff Rouse** USA
1994 **Martin Zubero** ESP

200m Backstroke
1973 **Rolandd Matthes** GDR
1975 **Zoltan Verraszto** HUN
1978 **Jesse Vassallo** USA
1982 **Rick Carey** USA
1986 **Igor Polyanski** URS
1991 **Martin Zubero** ESP
1994 **Vladimir Selkov** RUS

100m Breaststroke
1973 **John Hencken** USA
1975 **David Wilkie** GBR
1978 **Walter Kusch** GDR

1982 **Steve Lundquist** USA
1986 **Victor Davis** CAN
1991 **Norbert Rosza** HUN
1994 **Norbert Rosza** HUN

200m Breaststroke
1973 **David Wilkie** GBR
1975 **David Wilkie** GBR
1978 **Nick Nevid** USA
1982 **Victor Davis** CAN
1986 **Josef Szabó** HUN
1991 **Mike Barrowman** USA
1994 **Norbert Rosza** HUN

100m Butterfly
1973 **Bruce Robertson** CAN
1975 **Greg Jagenburg** USA
1978 **Joe Bottom** USA
1982 **Matt Gribble** USA
1986 **Pablo Morales** USA
1991 **Anthony Nesty** SUR
1994 **Rafal Szukala** POL

200m Butterfly
1973 **Robin Backhaus** USA
1975 **William Forrester** USA
1978 **Mike Bruner** USA
1982 **Michael Gross** FRG
1986 **Michael Gross** FRG
1991 **Melvin Stewart** USA
1994 **Denis Pankratov** RUS

200m Individual Medley
1973 **Gunnar Larsson** SWE
1975 **András Hargitay** HUN
1978 **Graham Smith** CAN
1982 **Alexsei Sidorenko** URS
1986 **Tamás Darnyi** HUN
1991 **Tamás Darnyi** HUN
1994 **Jani Sievienen** FIN

400m Individual Medley
1973 **András Hargitay** HUN
1975 **András Hargitay** HUN
1978 **Jesse Vassallo** USA
1982 **Ricardo Prado** BRA
1986 **Tamás Darnyi** HUN
1991 **Tamás Darnyi** HUN
1994 **Tom Dolan** USA

4x100m Freestyle Relay
1973 **United States**
1975 **United States**
1978 **United States**
1982 **United States**
1986 **United States**
1991 **United States**
1994 **United States**

4x200m Freestyle Relay
1973 **United States**
1975 **West Germany**
1978 **United States**
1982 **United States**

1986 **East Germany**
1991 **Germany**
1994 **Sweden**

4x100m Medley Relay
1973 **United States**
1975 **United States**
1978 **United States**
1982 **United States**
1986 **United States**
1991 **United States**
1994 **United States**

1m Springboard Diving
1991 **Edwin Jongejans** NED
1994 **Evan Stewart** ZIM

3m Springboard Diving
1973 **Phil Boggs** USA
1975 **Phil Boggs** USA
1978 **Phil Boggs** USA
1982 **Greg Louganis** USA
1986 **Greg Louganis** USA
1991 **Kent Ferguson** USA
1994 **Zhuocheng Yu** CHN

10m Platform Diving
1973 **Klaus Dibiasi** ITA
1975 **Klaus Dibiasi** ITA
1978 **Greg Louganis** USA
1982 **Greg Louganis** USA
1986 **Greg Louganis** USA
1991 **Sun Shuwei** CHN
1994 **Dmitri Sautin** RUS

Water Polo
1973 **Hungary**
1975 **Soviet Union**
1978 **Italy**
1982 **Soviet Union**
1986 **Yugoslavia**
1991 **Yugoslavia**
1994 **Italy**

World Champions

Women

50m Freestyle
1986 **Tamara Costache** ROM
1991 **Zuang Yong** CHN
1994 **Jingyi Le** CHN

100m Freestyle
1973 **Kornelia Ender** GDR
1975 **Kornelia Ender** GDR
1978 **Barbara Krause** GDR
1982 **Birgit Meineke** GDR
1986 **Kristin Otto** GDR
1991 **Nicole Haislett** USA
1994 **Jingyi Le** CHN

200m Freestyle
1973 **Keena Rothhammer** USA
1975 **Shirley Babashoff** USA
1978 **Cynthia Woodhead** USA
1982 **Annemarie Verstappen** NED
1986 **Heike Friedrich** GDR
1991 **Hayley Lewis** AUS
1994 **F van Almsick** GER

400m Freestyle
1973 **Heather Greenwood** USA
1975 **Shirley Babashoff** USA
1978 **Tracey Wickham** AUS
1982 **Carmela Schmidt** GDR
1986 **Heike Friedrich** GDR
1991 **Janet Evans** USA
1994 **Aihua Yang** CHN

800m Freestyle
1973 **Novella Calligaris** ITA
1975 **Jenny Tunrall** AUS
1978 **Tracey Wickham** AUS
1982 **Kim Lineham** USA
1986 **Astrid Strauss** GDR
1991 **Janet Evans** USA
1994 **Janet Evans** USA

100m Backstroke
1973 **Ulrike Richter** GDR
1975 **Ulrike Richter** GDR
1978 **Linda Jezek** USA
1982 **Kristin Otto** GDR
1986 **Betsy Mitchell** USA
1991 **Kristina Egerszegi** HUN
1994 **Cihong He** CHN

200m Backstroke
1973 **Melissa Belote** USA
1975 **Birgit Treiber** GDR
1978 **Linda Jezek** USA
1982 **Cornelia Sirch** GDR
1986 **Cornelia Sirch** GDR
1991 **Kristina Egerszegi** HUN
1994 **Cihong He** CHN

100m Breaststroke
1973 **Renate Vogel** GDR
1975 **Hannelore Anke** GDR

1978 **Yulia Bogdanova** URS
1982 **Ute Geweniger** GDR
1986 **Sylvia Gerasch** GDR
1991 **Linley Frame** AUS
1994 **Samantha Riley** AUS

200m Breaststroke
1973 **Renate Vogel** GDR
1975 **Hannelore Anke** GDR
1978 **Lina Kachushite** URS
1982 **Svetlana Varganova** URS
1986 **Silke Horner** GDR
1991 **Yelena Volkova** URS
1994 **Samantha Riley** AUS

100m Butterfly
1973 **Kornelia Ender** GDR
1975 **Kornelia Ender** GDR
1978 **Mary-Joan Pennington** USA
1982 **Mary Meagher** USA
1986 **Kornelia Gressler** GDR
1991 **Qian Hong** CHN
1994 **Limin Liu** CHN

200m Butterfly
1973 **Rosemarie Kother** GDR
1975 **Rosemarie Kother** GDR
1978 **Tracy Caulkins** USA
1982 **Ines Geissler** GDR
1986 **Mary Meagher** USA
1991 **S Sanders** USA
1994 **Limin Liu** CHN

200m Individual Medley
1973 **Angela Hubner** GDR
1975 **Kathy Heddy** USA
1978 **Tracy Caulkins** USA
1982 **Petra Schneider** GDR
1986 **Kristin Otto** GDR
1991 **Lin Li** CHN
1994 **Lu Bin** CHN

400m Individual Medley
1973 **Gudrun Wegner** GDR
1975 **Ulrike Tauber** GDR
1978 **Tracy Caulkins** USA
1982 **Petra Schneider** GDR
1986 **Kathleen Nord** GDR
1991 **Lin Li** CHN
1994 **Guohong Dai** CHN

4x100m Freestyle Relay
1973 **East Germany**
1975 **East Germany**
1978 **United States**
1982 **East Germany**
1986 **East Germany**
1991 **United States**
1994 **China**

4x200m Freestyle Relay
1986 **East Germany**
1991 **Germany**
1994 **China**

4x100m Medley Relay
1973 **East Germany**
1975 **East Germany**
1978 **United States**
1982 **East Germany**
1986 **East Germany**
1991 **United States**
1994 **China**

1m Springboard Diving
1991 **Gao Min** CHN
1994 **Lixia Chen** CHN

3m Springboard Diving
1973 **Christine Kohler** GDR
1975 **Irina Kalinina** URS
1978 **Irina Kalinina** URS
1982 **Megan Neyer** USA
1986 **Gao Min** CHN
1991 **Gao Min** CHN
1994 **Shuping Tan** CHN

10m Platform Diving
1973 **Ulrike Knape** SWE
1975 **Janet Ely** USA
1978 **Irina Kalinina** URS
1982 **Wendy Wyland** USA
1986 **Lin Chen** CHN
1991 **Fu Mingxia** CHN
1994 **Fu Mingxia** CHN

Water Polo
1986 **Australia**
1991 **Netherlands**
1994 **Hungary**

Synchronised Swimming - solo
1973 **Teresa Anderson** USA
1975 **Gail Buzonas** USA
1978 **Helen Vandenburg** CAN
1982 **Tracie Ruiz** USA
1986 **Carolyn Waldo** CAN
1991 **Sylvie Frechette** CAN
1994 **Becky Dyroen Lance** USA

Synchronised Swimming - duet
1973 **Anderson/Johnson** USA
1975 **Curren/Norrish** USA
1978 **Calkins/Vandenburg** CAN
1982 **Hambrook/Kryczka** CAN
1986 **Cameron/Waldo** CAN
1991 **Josephson/Josephson** USA
1994 **Lancer/Sidduth** USA

Synchronised Swimming - team
1973 **United States**
1975 **United States**
1978 **United States**
1982 **Canada**
1986 **Canada**
1991 **United States**
1994 **United States**

Table Tennis

Small wonder that China failed in its bid to host the 2000 Olympics; give them the World Table Tennis Championships and look what happens. For only the second time since 1933, when the seventh title (women's team) was added, has a country come away with all the titles at a world championship. The only previous occasion was in 1981 at Novi Sad in Yugoslavia. The country that achieved it? Now don't be silly.

The ITTF had to face the inevitable, only once previously had the championship been held in China (1961 in Beijing), so they could hardly delay it any longer. The results sheet explains why they might have wanted to. In four of five individual finals it was China versus China. Only in the men's doubles did Primorac and Samsonov intercede.

England's men faced the steamrolling Chinese in the team competition. What did they do but wheel out the 39-year-old Desmond Douglas. What did Douglas do but win. His defeat of 19-year-old Liu Guoliang was one of the shocks of the tournament (Liu went on to the singles final), but if it was a small wave in the opposite direction, it had no effect on the tide. China won that match 3-1 and went on to defeat the Swedes for the team title.

England had another small cup of joy; three men (Douglas, Prean and Chen Xinhua) reached the third round for the first time since 1989. But table tennis is suffering from the Wimbledon syndrome; not since 1953 has a British player won a world title.

Lest we forget, this was the year that the first British champion (Fred Perry) died, it would be timely indeed for another Perry to come along.

World Championships
Tianjin, China   May 1-14
(All China unless stated)
MEN'S SINGLES
Semi-finals
Kong Linghui bt Ding Song 21-12, 21-18, 21-18
Liu Guoliang bt Wang Tao 17-21, 21-15, 21-18, 21-16
Final
Kong Linghui bt Liu Guoliang 17-21, 21-16, 15-21, 21-14, 21-10

WOMEN'S SINGLES
Semi-finals
Deng Yaping bt Liu Wei 21-12, 14-21, 21-17, 21-19
Qiao Hong bt Qiao Yunping 23-21, 21-17, 21-14
Final
Deng Yaping bt Qiao Hong 14-21, 21-17, 21-17, 14-21, 21-14

MEN'S DOUBLES
Semi-finals
Wang/Lu bt Liu/Lin 10-21, 21-14, 14-21, 21-14, 21-13
Primorac/Samsonov CRO/BLS bt Gatien/Eloi FRA 17-21, 21-15, 21-15, 21-17
Final
Wang/Lu bt Primorac/Samsonov 18-21, 21-15, 21-14, 21-17

WOMEN'S DOUBLES
Semi-finals
Liu/Qiao bt Batorfi/Toth HUN 18-21, 21-17, 21-19, 21-16
Deng/Qiao bt Wang/Wu 14-21, 20-22, 21-11, 21-18, 21-9
Final
Deng/Qiao bt Liu/Qiao 21-19, 21-17, 17-21, 21-19

MIXED DOUBLES
Semi-finals
Wang/Liu bt Lindh/Svensson SWE 21-13, 23-25, 21-9, 21-8
Kong/Deng bt Lee/Ryu KOR 21-18, 21-18, 16-21, 21-7
Final
Wang/Liu bt Kong/Deng 24-22, 21-18, 21-9

TEAM STANDINGS
Men: 1. China, 2. Sweden, 3. Korea, 13. England
Women: 1. China, 2. Korea, 3. Hong Kong, 10. England

World Team Cup 1995
Atlanta, USA   Aug 10-13
MEN
Group A
Italy 0 China 3; Brazil 1 Yugoslavia 3; China 3 Yugoslavia 0; Italy 3 Brazil 1; Italy 3 Yugoslavia 1; Brazil 0 China 3
Group B
USA 1 Sweden 3; Belgium 3 Australia 1; Belgium 2 Sweden 3; USA 3 Australia 0; Belgium 1 USA 3; Australia 0 Sweden 3
Group C
Korea 2 Austria 3; Canada 0 Japan 3; Korea 3 Japan 1; Canada 0 Austria 3; Japan 3 Austria 0; Canada 0 Korea 3

Group D
Czech Rep. 0 France 3; Nigeria 0 Germany 3; France 3
Germany 0; Czech Rep. 3 Nigeria 0; Germany 3
Czech Rep. 0; France 3 Nigeria 1
Quarter-finals
Korea 3 China 2; USA 3 France 2; Japan 3 Italy 1
Germany 3 Sweden 2
Semi-finals
USA 1 Korea 3; Germany 3 Japan 2
Final
Korea 3 *(Yoo Nam Kyu, Kim Taek Soo (2))*
Germany 2 *(Fetzner, Prause)*

WOMEN
Group A
China 3 United States 0; China 3 Germany 0;
Germany 3 United States 1
Group B
Australia 0 Korea 3; Korea 3 Hungary 0;
Hungary 3 Australia 0
Group C
Romania 3 Nigeria 1; Russian Federation 3 Romania 2;
Nigeria 0 Russian Federation 3
Group D
Sweden 3 Brazil 0; Sweden 3 Canada 2;
Canada 3 Brazil 1
Quarter-finals
Canada 0 China 3; Russian Federation 0 Hungary 3;
Romania 3 Sweden 2; Germany 0 Korea 3
Semi-finals
Hungary 0 China 3; Korea 0 Romania 3
Final
China 3 *(Deng Yaping, Qiao Hong, Yang Ying)*
Romania 0

World Team Cup 1994

Nimes, France   Oct 12-16
MEN
Group A
1. Sweden, 2. England, 3. Austria, 4. Australia
Group B
1. China, 2. Russia, 3. Japan, 4. Nigeria
Group C
1. Germany, 2. Czech Rep., 3. Italy, 4. Brazil
Group D
1. Belgium, 2. France, 3. Poland, 4. Canada

Quarter-finals
Sweden 3 Russia 0; France 3 Czech Rep. 0
Belgium 3 Germany 2; China 3 England 0
Semi-finals
Sweden 3 France 2; China 3 Belgium 2
Final
China 3 *(Lin Guo Liang, Lin Zhi Gang, Liu Guoliang)*
Sweden 1 *(Persson)*

WOMEN
Group A
1. China, 2. USA
Group B
1. Russia, 2. Chinese Taipei, 3. Australia
Group C
1. Germany, 2. Holland, 3. Brazil
Group D
1. Hungary, 2. France, 3. Japan

Quarter-finals
China 3 Chinese Taipei 0; Germany 3 France 1
Holland 3 Hungary 0; Russia 3 USA 0
Semi-finals
Russia 3 Holland 2; Germany 3 China 2
Final
Russia 3 *(Palina (2), Melnik)*
Germany 1 *(Schöpp)*

European Nations Cup (men)

Karlsruhe, Germany   Jan 13-15
Group A
Russia 3 France 2; England 3 France 1; Russia 3
England 0; England 3 Belgium 0; Russia 3 Belgium 0;
France 3 Belgium 1
Group B
Sweden 3 Germany 0; Germany 3 Hungary 1; Sweden 3
Hungary 1; Germany 3 Poland 0; Sweden 3 Poland 2;
Hungary 3 Poland 1
Semi-finals
Russia 3 Germany 2; Sweden 3 England 0
Final
Sweden 3 *(Persson (2); Waldner/Persson)*
Russia 1 *(Mazunov)*

European Team Cup (women)

Dülmen, Germany   Jan 21-22
Group A
Hungary 3 Russia 1; Hungary 3 Sweden 1;
Sweden 3 Russia 0
Group B
Romania 3 Germany 2; Romania 3 England 1;
Germany 3 England 0
Semi-finals
Germany 3 Hungary 2; Romania 3 Sweden 0
Final
Germany 3 *(Schöpp (2), Struse)*
Romania 1 *(Ciosu/Nastase-Simion)*

English Open

Cleveland   Jan 4-8

MEN'S SINGLES
Semi-finals
Damien Eloi FRA bt Thierry Cabrera BEL 21-15, 21-14,
21-11
Xiong Ke CHN bt Eric Lindh SWE 21-13, 21-12, 10-21,
14-21, 21-17
Final
Damien Eloi bt Xiong Ke 15-21, 21-14, 21-15, 21-18

WOMEN'S SINGLES
Semi-finals
Bettine Vriesekoop NED bt Asa Svensson SWE 21-18,
21-17, 21-10
Andrea Holt ENG bt Marie Svensson SWE 8-21, 21-15,
24-22, 21-18
Final
Bettine Vriesekoop bt Andrea Holt 21-6, 23-21, 21-13

MEN'S DOUBLES
Final
Christophe Legout/Eloi bt Xiong Ke/Li Jing 21-12, 21-16

WOMEN'S DOUBLES
Final
Marie Svensson/Asa Svensson bt Wang Wei/Petra Fichtinger USA/AUT 14-21, 21-14, 21-15

English National Championships
King's Lynn Mar 3-4
MEN'S SINGLES
Final
Prean (IOW) bt Xinhua (Yks) 21-12, 21-18, 21-16
WOMEN'S SINGLES
Final
Holt (Lancs) bt Gordon (Berks) 21-15, 21-13, 21-23, 14-21, 21-11
MEN'S DOUBLES
Final
Douglas/Cooke bt Mason/Andrew 21-17, 21-13
WOMEN'S DOUBLES
Final
Goodall/Holt bt Lower/Radford 21-16, 21-15
MIXED DOUBLES
Final
Holland/Radford bt Carthy/Lower 21-17, 21-16

British League

Premier

		P	W	D	L	F	A	Pts
1	BFL Grove	14	14	0	0	175	21	28
2	Team Peniel	14	11	0	3	119	77	22
3	Drumchapel Glasgow	14	9	1	4	111	85	19
4	Horsham Angels	14	8	1	5	110	86	17
5	Policy Plus St Neots	14	5	1	8	85	111	11
6	Sedgefield District	14	4	1	9	82	114	9
7	White H Launceston	14	2	2	10	68	128	6
8	Vymura International	14	0	0	14	34	162	0

Division 1 (North)

		P	W	D	L	F	A	Pts
1	BFL Grove II	14	12	0	2	88	27	24
2	R M Lincoln	14	9	3	2	71	41	21
3	Olton & W Warwicks	14	9	2	3	69	43	20
4	Vymura Int'l II	14	6	4	4	58	54	16
5	Sedgefield II	14	5	3	6	58	54	13
6	Uxbridge (Burton)	14	3	4	7	43	69	10
7	Bribar Humberside	14	3	0	11	35	77	6
8	Leicester Lions	14	0	2	12	29	83	2

Division 1 (South)

		P	W	D	L	F	A	Pts
1	BFL Grove III	14	11	1	2	79	33	23
2	L Farrow (Euston)	14	11	1	2	76	36	23
3	OLOP (Reading)	14	9	2	3	71	41	20
4	Edison (Haringey)	14	9	1	4	75	37	19
5	Horsham Angels II	14	3	4	7	43	69	10
6	BSG Brentwood	14	2	4	8	41	71	8
7	Milton Keynes	14	2	4	8	38	74	8
8	Byng Hall	14	0	1	13	25	87	1

EPSON
World Rankings
As at Sep 6
MEN

1	Wang Tao	CHN	1660
2	Kong Linghui	CHN	1645
3	Jean-Michel Saive	BEL	1631
4	Jan-Ove Waldner	SWE	1609
5	Kim Taek Soo	KOR	1607
6	Liu Guoliang	CHN	1580
7	Jean-Philippe Gatien	FRA	1575
8	Jörg Rosskopf	GER	1567
9	Zoran Primorac	CRO	1560
10	Ding Song	CHN	1558
11	Ma Wenge	CHN	1553
12	Peter Karlsson	SWE	1537
13	Johnny Huang	CAN	1516
14	Jorgen Persson	SWE	1503
15	Yoo Nam Kyu	KOR	1493
16	Vladimir Samsonov	BLR	1462
17	Wang Yonggang	CHN	1443
18	Chen Xinhua	ENG	1427
19	Andrzej Grubba	POL	1422
20	Patrick Chila	FRA	1407
30	Carl Prean	ENG	1348
52	Alan Cooke	ENG	1248
63	Desmond Douglas	ENG	1212
65	Matthew Syed	ENG	1211

WOMEN

1	Deng Yaping	CHN	1862
2	Qiao Hong	CHN	1750
3	Liu Wei	CHN	1619
4	Chai Po Wa	HKG	1615
5	Geng Lijuan	CAN	1597
6	Wang Chen	CHN	1579
7	Chen Jing	TPE	1558
8	Wang Nan	CHN	1557
9	Chire Koyama	JPN	1551
10	Chen Zihe	CHN	1547
11	Yang Ying	CHN	1528
12	Qiao Yunping	CHN	1514
13	Jie Schöpp	GER	1507
14	Jing Jun Hong	SIN	1506
15	Li Ju	CHN	1487
16	Wu Na	CHN	1486
17	Nicole Struse	GER	1481
	Bettine Vriesekoop	NED	1481
19	Otilia Badescu	ROM	1480
20	Tan Lui Chan	HKG	1470
58	Lisa Lomas	ENG	1272
60	Andrea Holt	ENG	1258

World Champions

MEN'S SINGLES
1926 Roland Jacobi HUN
1928 Zoltan Mechlovits HUN
1929 Fred Perry GBR
1930 Viktor Barna HUN
1931 Miklos Szabados HUN
1932 Viktor Barna HUN
1933 Viktor Barna HUN
1934 Viktor Barna HUN
1935 Viktor Barna HUN
1936 Stanislav Kolar TCH
1937 Richard Bergmann AUT
1938 Bohumil Vana TCH
1939 Richard Bergmann AUT
1947 Bohumil Vana TCH
1948 Richard Bergmann GBR
1949 Johnny Leach GBR
1950 Richard Bergmann GBR
1951 Johnny Leach GBR
1952 Hiroji Satoh JPN
1953 Ferenc Sidó HUN
1954 Ichiro Ogimura JPN
1955 Toshiaki Tanaka JPN
1956 Ichiro Ogimura JPN
1957 Toshiaki Tanaka JPN
1959 Jung Kuo-tuan CHN
1961 Chuang Tse-tung CHN
1963 Chuang Tse-tung CHN
1965 Chuang Tse-tung CHN
1967 Nobuhiko Hasegawa JPN
1969 Shigeo Ito JPN
1971 Stellan Bengtsson SWE
1973 Hsi En-ting CHN
1975 Istvan Jonyer HUN
1977 Mitsuru Kohno JPN
1979 Seiji Ono JPN
1981 Guo Yuehua CHN
1983 Guo Yuehua CHN
1985 Jiang Jialiang CHN
1987 Jiang Jialiang CHN
1989 Jan-Ove Waldner SWE
1991 Jorgen Persson SWE
1993 Jean-Philipe Gatien FRA
1995 Kong Linghui CHN

MEN'S TEAM *1971 on*
1971 China
1973 Sweden
1975 China
1977 China
1979 Hungary
1981 China
1983 China
1985 China
1987 China
1989 Sweden
1991 Sweden
1993 Sweden
1995 China

WOMEN'S SINGLES
1926 Maria Mednyanszky HUN
1928 Maria Mednyanszky HUN
1929 Maria Mednyanszky HUN
1930 Maria Mednyanszky HUN
1931 Maria Mednyanszky HUN
1932 Anna Sipos HUN
1933 Anna Sipos HUN
1934 Marie Kettnerova TCH
1935 Marie Kettnerova TCH
1936 Ruth Aarons USA
1937 Ruth Aarons USA and Trudi Pritzi AUT *
1938 Trudi Pritzi AUT
1939 Vlasta Depetrisova TCH
1947 Gizi Farkas HUN
1948 Gizi Farkas HUN
1949 Gizi Farkas HUN
1950 Angelica Rozeanu ROM
1951 Angelica Rozeanu ROM
1952 Angelica Rozeanu ROM
1953 Angelica Rozeanu ROM
1954 Angelica Rozeanu ROM
1955 Angelica Rozeanu ROM
1956 Tomi Okawa JPN
1957 Fujie Eguchi JPN
1959 Kimiyo Matsuzaki JPN
1961 Chiu Chunghui CHN
1963 Kimiyo Matsuzaki JPN
1965 Naoko Fukazu JPN
1967 Sachiko Morisawa JPN
1969 Toshiko Kowada JPN
1971 Lin Huiching CHN
1973 Hu Yu-lan CHN
1975 Pak Yung-sun KOR
1977 Pak Yung-sun KOR
1979 Ge Xinai CHN
1981 Tong Ling CHN
1983 Cao Yanhua CHN
1985 Cao Yanhua CHN
1987 He Zhili CHN
1989 Qiao Hong CHN
1991 Deng Yaping CHN
1993 Hyun Jung Hwa CHN
1995 Deng Yaping CHN
* Both were finalists. Title was left vacant

MEN'S TEAM *1977 on*
1977 China
1979 China
1981 China
1983 China
1985 China
1987 China
1989 China
1991 Korea
1993 China
1995 China

MEN'S DOUBLES *1965 on*
1965 Chuang/Hsu CHN
1967 Alser/Johansson SWE
1969 Alser/Johansson SWE
1971 Jonyer/Klampar HUN
1973 Bengtsson/Johansson SWE
1975 Gergely/Jonyer HUN
1977 Li/Liang CHN
1979 Surbek/Stipancic YUG
1981 Cai/Li CHN
1983 Surbeh/Kalinic YUG
1985 Applegren/Carlsson SWE
1987 Chen/Wei CHN
1989 Rosskopf/Fetzner FRG
1991 Karlsson/von Scheele SWE
1993 Wang/Lu CHN
1995 Wang/Lu CHN

WOMEN'S DOUBLES *1965 on*
1965 Cheng/Lin CHN
1967 Hirota/Morisawa JPN
1969 Grinberg/Rudnova URS
1971 Cheng/Lin CHN
1973 Alexandru ROM/ Hamada JPN
1975 Alexandru/Takashima
1977 Pak/Yang CHN
1979 Zhang/Zhang CHN
1981 Zhang/Cao CHN
1983 Shen/Dai CHN
1985 Dai/Geng CHN
1987 Yang/Hyun KOR
1989 Qiao/Deng CHN
1991 Chen/Gao CHN
1993 Liu/Qiao CHN
1995 Deng/Lui CHN

MIXED DOUBLES *1965 on*
1965 Kimura/Seki JPN
1967 Hasegawa/Yamanaka JPN
1969 Hasegawa/Kono JPN
1971 Chang/Lin CHN
1973 Liang/Li CHN
1975 Gomozkov/Ferdman URS
1977 Secretin/Bergeret FRA
1979 Liang/Ge CHN
1981 Xie/Huang CHN
1983 Guo/Ni CHN
1985 Cai/Cao CHN
1987 Hui/Geng CHN
1989 Yoo/Hyun KOR
1991 Wang/Liu CHN
1993 Wang/Liu CHN
1995 Wang/Liu CHN

Tennis

Two events dominated the tennis world in 1995; Monica Seles made a successful return to the sport after two and a quarter years out and Britain won a Davis Cup match. The prelude to Seles' return was a highly-publicised exhibition match at Atlantic City against Martina Navratilova. Seles' first serious competition came three weeks later at the Canadian Open in Toronto where, despite looking decidedly chubby, the American won not only her first match, but the title. As comebacks go, this was impressive stuff. It was even more impressive at Flushing Meadow, where Seles was just one set away from the US Open crown. Graf eventually got the upper hand in the final, which was just as well, too. For, no matter how much of the old mastery had stayed with Seles, it was an indictment of the women's game that someone so clearly short of fitness should return with such success.

As Seles put her problems firmly in the past, so Graf's rose up to meet her. Her chronic back problems limited her events, but not her achievements. She won in Paris, London and New York to make it 18 Grand Slam singles titles, moving up alongside Martina Navratilova and Chris Evert. Only Helen Wills Moody, 19, and Margaret Court, 24, have won more. Yet off-court, it was all turmoil as tax problems put her father in jail, pending trial, and threatened to engulf her too. This year, Graf took her career on-court earnings through the £10m barrier. You can probably treble (maybe quadruple) that to reach a realistic earnings figure. Old Man Graf's strongest defence would appear to be, with all that money why should we want to fiddle the taxman. But it doesn't work like that, does it?

Graf, apparently, lay in a darkened room listening to The Doors' *The End,* prior to her Wimbledon semi-final victory over Novotna. Maybe that was the secret of the British Davis Cup team in Monaco in July because they won a match and you have to go back to 1991 to find the last time that happened. David Lloyd, who made a fortune when his leisure company was bought out by Whitbread in a deal that valued the company at over £200m, was the man brought in to resurrect British fortunes. Lloyd, now richer even than Graf, certainly timed his entrance perfectly. The trough was his first match as non-playing captain, a 5-0 defeat by Bratislava; it could only get better. Two months later, Britain routed the great tennis power, Monaco. Lloyd hailed the "tremendous" team spirit, but to keep it in context: had Britain lost they would have spent 1996 playing teams like San Marino and Cyprus.

Thomas Muster had an extraordinary year. The Austrian should take pottery classes for his affinity to clay is something to behold. As well as becoming the first Austrian ever to win a Grand Slam tournament (Paris), he had won 10 other IBM/ATP Tour events by the end of September. He didn't bother to come to grassy Wimbledon, even admitting he missed it on television at Monte Carlo, because the TV broke down. In Paris, he beat Chang with the aid of just three aces - one more than Graf needed on her way to victory in the same event over Sanchez Vicario. At Wimbledon, by contrast, Sampras hit 21 aces on his way to victory over Becker, but still did not top the aces table. Goran Ivanisevic hit 213 aces during the tournament, an average of over 40 per game. If they took all the air out of the balls, he would not be bothered. The agency, UPI, were so impressed they even put out a report that the Croatian had served at 208mph. Kilometres, perhaps.

The Championships

Wimbledon   June 26-July 9

Sometimes, you might believe that Britain didn't want a champion. There we were with the fastest server in the world (137mph) switching allegiances and what does Wimbledon do? They slow the balls down. As it happened, the reduced pressure in the balls seemed to make little difference. Certainly, if you were watching the Ivanisevic/Kafelnikov match they travelled as fast ever. It didn't hamper Rusedski too much either as the converted Canadian was successful in his first three matches (which is as well as a Briton has done since 1973) before succumbing to Pete Sampras. The number one seed went on outplay Becker and collect his third successive title, which was a considerable achievement. Sampras, though, still fails to stir the imagination. Just think what it could have been like if Jeff Tarango had reached the final. The Californian completely lost his rag in his third round match against Mronz on court 13 when the umpire, Bruno Rebeuh penalised him for shouting "shut up" to the crowd. Tarango was defaulted and fined, but suffered the ultimate indignity when John McEnroe started telling him how he should have behaved. Yes, that John McEnroe.

The women's final was a cracker, with Sanchez Vicario playing her best-ever tennis on grass. Graf won, though, her 32nd victory in succession, her sixth Wimbledon and 17th Grand Slam title. Navratilova logged up her 19th Wimbledon title when she took the mixed doubles with Jonathan Stark (she was earlier rumoured to be playing with that nice Mr McEnroe), but the victory that British tennis most needed came when Martin Lee, 17, and James Trotman, 16, won the boys' doubles, the first British title since Bates and Durie in 1987.

MEN'S SINGLES
First Round selected
David Wheaton USA bt Ross Matheson GBR 3-6 7-5 7-6 6-3
Byron Black ZIM bt Barry Cowan GBR 6-4 7-5 6-1
Jacco Eltingh NED bt Michael Stich (9) GER 6-4 7-6 6-1
Mats Wilander SWE bt Mark Petchey GBR 7-6 6-1 6-2
Bryan Shelton USA bt Richard Krajicek (12) NED 7-6 6-3 6-3
Daniel Nestor CAN bt Danny Sapsford GBR 7-5 6-2 6-3
Derrick Rostagno USA bt Jeremy Bates GBR 7-6 6-4 7-5
Miles Maclagan GBR bt Renzo Furlan ITA 2-6 6-2 7-6 6-3
Chris Wilkinson GBR bt Henrik Dreekmann GER 6-3 6-4 7-5
Michael Joyce USA bt Marc Rosset (10) SUI 6-0 6-7 7-5 6-2
Guy Forget FRA bt Gary Henderson GBR 6-1 6-3 7-6
Greg Rusedski GBR bt Stephane Simian FRA 6-3 6-3 6-3
Tim Hanman GBR bt Paul Wekesa KEN 7-6 6-0 6-4

WOMEN'S SINGLES
First Round selected
Natasha Zvereva BLR bt M Miller GBR 6-2 6-3
Christina Singer GER bt E Jelfs GBR 6-4 6-3
Florencia Labat ARG bt Shirli-Ann Siddall GBR 6-2 6-3
Jo Durie GBR bt Alexia Dechaume-Ballaret FRA 6-2 7-6
Angelica Gavaldon MEX bt Iva Majoli CRO 1-6 6-3 6-1
Ann Grossman USA bt Clare Wood GBR 3-6 6-2 6-4
Lisa Raymond USA bt Julie Pullin GBR 6-0 7-6
Jana Kandarr GER bt Karen Cross GBR 6-3 6-1
Zina G Jackson USA bt Amanda Wainwright GBR 6-3 6-3

MEN'S DOUBLES
Final: Woodbridge/Woodforde AUS bt Leach/Melville US 7-5 7-6 7-6

WOMEN'S DOUBLES
Final: Novotna CZE/Sanchez Vicario ESp bt G Fernandez USA/Zvereva BLR 5-7 7-5 6-4

MIXED DOUBLES
Final: Stark/Navratilova USA bt Suk CZE/G Fernandez USA 6-4 6-4

WOMEN'S SENIOR
Over 35 Final: Turnbull AUS/Wade GBR bt Nagelson/Russell USA 6-3 7-6

MEN'S SENIOR
Over 35 Final: McNamara AUS/Shiras USA bt Bahrami IRN/Higueras ESP 7-6 7-5
Over 45 Final: Newcombe/Roche AUS bt Davidson AUS/Drysdale RSA 6-4 7-5

BOYS' SINGLES
Final: O Mutis FRA bt N Kiefer GER 6-2 6-2

BOYS' DOUBLES
Final: Lee/Trotman GBR bt Hernandez MEX/Puerta ARG 7-6 6-4

GIRLS' SINGLES
Final: A Olsza POL bt T Tanasugarn THA 7-5 7-6

GIRLS' DOUBLES
Final: Black ZIM/Olsza POL bt Musgrave/Richardson AUS 6-0 7-6

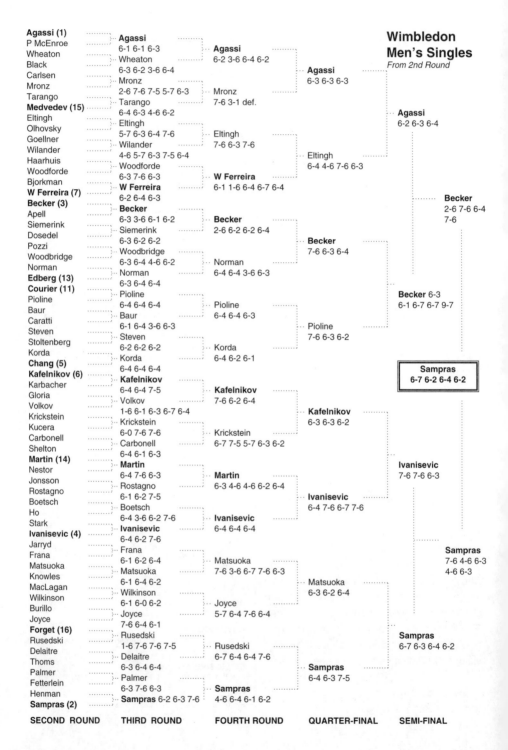

Wimbledon
Men's Singles
From 2nd Round

Agassi (1)
P McEnroe
Wheaton
Black
Carlsen
Mronz
Tarango
Medvedev (15)
Eltingh
Olhovsky
Goellner
Wilander
Haarhuis
Woodforde
Bjorkman
W Ferreira (7)
Becker (3)
Apell
Siemerink
Dosedel
Pozzi
Woodbridge
Norman
Edberg (13)
Courier (11)
Pioline
Baur
Caratti
Steven
Stoltenberg
Korda
Chang (5)
Kafelnikov (6)
Karbacher
Gloria
Volkov
Krickstein
Kucera
Carbonell
Shelton
Martin (14)
Nestor
Jonsson
Rostagno
Boetsch
Ho
Stark
Ivanisevic (4)
Jarryd
Frana
Matsuoka
Knowles
MacLagan
Wilkinson
Burillo
Joyce
Forget (16)
Rusedski
Delaitre
Thoms
Palmer
Fetterlein
Henman
Sampras (2)

Agassi
6-1 6-1 6-3
Wheaton
6-3 6-2 3-6 6-4
Mronz
2-6 7-6 7-5 5-7 6-3
Tarango
6-4 6-3 4-6 6-2
Eltingh
5-7 6-3 6-4 7-6
Wilander
4-6 5-7 6-3 7-5 6-4
Woodforde
6-3 7-6 6-3
W Ferreira
6-2 6-4 6-3
Becker
6-3 3-6 6-1 6-2
Siemerink
6-3 6-2 6-2
Woodbridge
6-3 6-4 4-6 6-2
Norman
6-3 6-4 6-4
Pioline
6-4 6-4 6-4
Baur
6-1 6-4 3-6 6-3
Steven
6-2 6-2 6-2
Korda
6-4 6-4 6-4
Kafelnikov
6-4 6-4 7-5
Volkov
1-6 6-1 6-3 6-7 6-4
Krickstein
6-0 7-6 7-6
Carbonell
6-4 6-1 6-3
Martin
6-4 7-6 6-3
Rostagno
6-1 6-2 7-5
Boetsch
6-4 3-6 6-2 7-6
Ivanisevic
6-4 6-2 7-6
Frana
6-1 6-2 6-4
Matsuoka
6-1 6-4 6-2
Wilkinson
6-1 6-0 6-2
Joyce
7-6 6-4 6-1
Rusedski
1-6 7-6 7-6 7-5
Delaitre
6-3 6-4 6-4
Palmer
6-3 7-6 6-3
Sampras 6-2 6-3 7-6

Agassi
6-2 3-6 6-4 6-2
Mronz
7-6 3-1 def.
Eltingh
7-6 6-3 7-6
W Ferreira
6-1 1-6 6-4 6-7 6-4
Becker
2-6 6-2 6-2 6-4
Norman
6-4 6-4 3-6 6-3
Pioline
6-4 6-4 6-3
Korda
6-4 6-2 6-1
Kafelnikov
7-6 6-2 6-4
Krickstein
6-7 7-5 5-7 6-3 6-2
Martin
6-3 4-6 4-6 6-2 6-4
Ivanisevic
6-4 6-4 6-4
Matsuoka
7-6 3-6 6-7 7-6 6-3
Joyce
5-7 6-4 7-6 6-4
Rusedski
6-7 6-4 6-4 7-6
Sampras
4-6 6-4 6-1 6-2

Agassi
6-3 6-3 6-3
Agassi
6-3 6-3 6-3
Becker
7-6 6-3 6-4
Becker
7-6 6-3 6-4
Kafelnikov
6-3 6-3 6-2
Ivanisevic
6-4 7-6 6-7 7-6
Matsuoka
6-3 6-2 6-4
Sampras
6-4 6-3 7-5

Agassi
6-2 6-3 6-4
Eltingh
6-4 4-6 7-6 6-3
Becker 6-3
6-1 6-7 6-7 9-7
Pioline
7-6 6-3 6-2
Ivanisevic
7-6 7-6 6-3
Sampras
6-7 6-3 6-4 6-2

Becker
2-6 7-6 6-4
7-6

| Sampras |
| 6-7 6-2 6-4 6-2 |

Sampras
7-6 4-6 6-3
4-6 6-3

SECOND ROUND   **THIRD ROUND**   **FOURTH ROUND**   **QUARTER-FINAL**   **SEMI-FINAL**

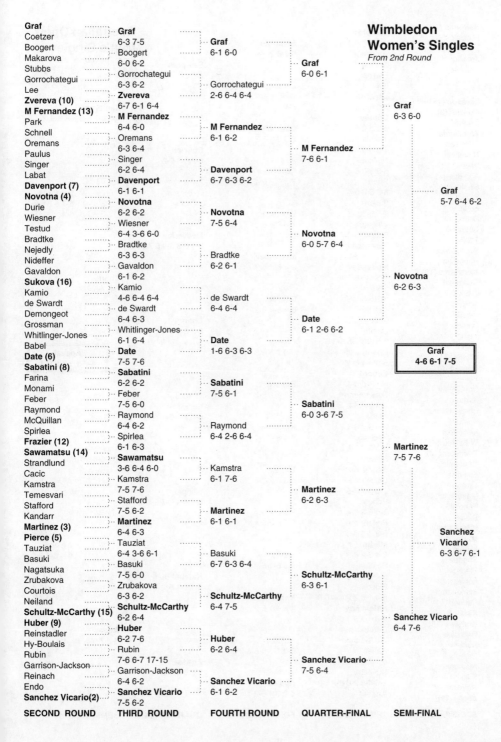

Tennis

Wimbledon
Women's Singles
From 2nd Round

Graf
4-6 6-1 7-5

SECOND ROUND THIRD ROUND FOURTH ROUND QUARTER-FINAL SEMI-FINAL

377

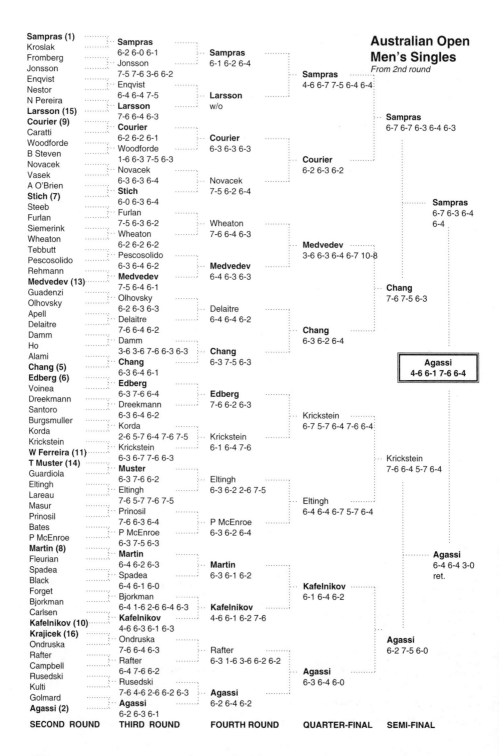

Australian Open
Men's Singles
From 2nd round

Sampras (1)
Kroslak
Fromberg
Jonsson
Enqvist
Nestor
N Pereira
Larsson (15)
Courier (9)
Caratti
Woodforde
B Steven
Novacek
Vasek
A O'Brien
Stich (7)
Steeb
Furlan
Siemerink
Wheaton
Tebbutt
Pescosolido
Rehmann
Medvedev (13)
Guadenzi
Olhovsky
Apell
Delaitre
Damm
Ho
Alami
Chang (5)
Edberg (6)
Voinea
Dreekmann
Santoro
Burgsmuller
Korda
Krickstein
W Ferreira (11)
T Muster (14)
Guardiola
Eltingh
Lareau
Masur
Prinosil
Bates
P McEnroe
Martin (8)
Fleurian
Spadea
Black
Forget
Bjorkman
Carlsen
Kafelnikov (10)
Krajicek (16)
Ondruska
Rafter
Campbell
Rusedski
Kulti
Golmard
Agassi (2)

SECOND ROUND

Sampras
6-2 6-0 6-1
Jonsson
7-5 7-6 3-6 6-2
Enqvist
6-4 6-4 7-5
Larsson
7-6 6-4 6-3
Courier
6-2 6-2 6-1
Woodforde
1-6 6-3 7-5 6-3
Novacek
6-3 6-3 6-4
Stich
6-0 6-3 6-4
Furlan
7-5 6-3 6-2
Wheaton
6-2 6-2 6-2
Pescosolido
6-3 6-4 6-2
Medvedev
7-5 6-4 6-1
Olhovsky
6-2 6-3 6-3
Delaitre
7-6 6-4 6-2
Damm
3-6 3-6 7-6 6-3 6-3
Chang
6-3 6-4 6-1
Edberg
6-3 7-6 6-4
Dreekmann
6-3 6-4 6-2
Korda
2-6 5-7 6-4 7-6 7-5
Krickstein
6-3 6-7 7-6 6-3
Muster
6-3 7-6 6-2
Eltingh
7-6 5-7 7-6 7-5
Prinosil
7-6 6-3 6-4
P McEnroe
6-3 7-5 6-3
Martin
6-4 6-2 6-3
Spadea
6-4 6-1 6-0
Bjorkman
6-4 1-6 2-6 6-4 6-3
Kafelnikov
4-6 6-3 6-1 6-3
Ondruska
7-6 6-4 6-3
Rafter
6-4 7-6 6-2
Rusedski
7-6 4-6 2-6 6-2 6-3
Agassi
6-2 6-3 6-1

THIRD ROUND

Sampras
6-1 6-2 6-4
Larsson
w/o
Courier
6-3 6-3 6-3
Novacek
7-5 6-2 6-4
Wheaton
7-6 6-4 6-3
Medvedev
6-4 6-3 6-3
Delaitre
6-4 6-4 6-2
Chang
6-3 7-5 6-3
Edberg
7-6 6-2 6-3
Krickstein
6-1 6-4 7-6
Eltingh
6-3 6-2 2-6 7-5
P McEnroe
6-3 6-2 6-4
Martin
6-3 6-1 6-2
Kafelnikov
4-6 6-1 6-2 7-6
Rafter
6-3 1-6 3-6 6-2 6-2
Agassi
6-2 6-4 6-2

FOURTH ROUND

Sampras
4-6 6-7 7-5 6-4 6-4
Courier
6-2 6-3 6-2
Medvedev
3-6 6-3 6-4 6-7 10-8
Chang
6-3 6-2 6-4
Krickstein
6-7 5-7 6-4 7-6 6-4
Eltingh
6-4 6-4 6-7 5-7 6-4
Kafelnikov
6-1 6-4 6-2
Agassi
6-3 6-4 6-0

QUARTER-FINAL

Sampras
6-7 6-7 6-3 6-4 6-3
Chang
7-6 7-5 6-3
Krickstein
7-6 6-4 5-7 6-4
Agassi
6-2 7-5 6-0

SEMI-FINAL

Sampras
6-7 6-3 6-4
6-4

Agassi
4-6 6-1 7-6 6-4

Agassi
6-4 6-4 3-0
ret.

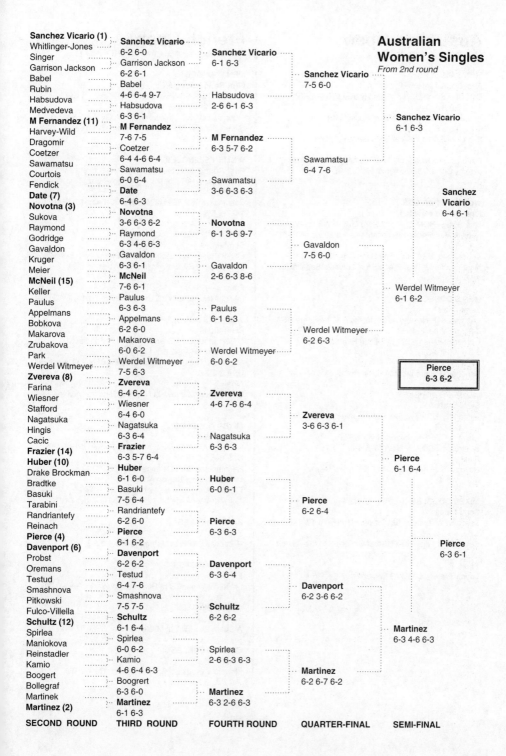

Sanchez Vicario (1)
Whitlinger-Jones
Singer
Garrison Jackson
Babel
Rubin
Habsudova
Medvedeva
M Fernandez (11)
Harvey-Wild
Dragomir
Coetzer
Sawamatsu
Courtois
Fendick
Date (7)
Novotna (3)
Sukova
Raymond
Godridge
Gavaldon
Kruger
Meier
McNeil (15)
Keller
Paulus
Appelmans
Bobkova
Makarova
Zrubakova
Park
Werdel Witmeyer
Zvereva (8)
Farina
Wiesner
Stafford
Nagatsuka
Hingis
Cacic
Frazier (14)
Huber (10)
Drake Brockman
Bradtke
Basuki
Tarabini
Randriantefy
Reinach
Pierce (4)
Davenport (6)
Probst
Oremans
Testud
Smashnova
Pitkowski
Fulco-Villella
Schultz (12)
Spirlea
Maniokova
Reinstadler
Kamio
Boogert
Bollegraf
Martinek
Martinez (2)

Australian Women's Singles
From 2nd round

SECOND ROUND

Sanchez Vicario
6-2 6-0
Garrison Jackson
6-2 6-1
Babel
4-6 6-4 9-7
Habsudova
6-3 6-1
M Fernandez
7-6 7-5
Coetzer
6-4 4-6 6-4
Sawamatsu
6-0 6-4
Date
6-4 6-3
Novotna
3-6 6-3 6-2
Raymond
6-3 4-6 6-3
Gavaldon
6-3 6-1
McNeil
7-6 6-1
Paulus
6-3 6-3
Appelmans
6-2 6-0
Makarova
6-0 6-2
Werdel Witmeyer
7-5 6-3
Zvereva
6-4 6-2
Wiesner
6-4 6-0
Nagatsuka
6-3 6-4
Frazier
6-3 5-7 6-4
Huber
6-1 6-0
Basuki
7-5 6-4
Randriantefy
6-2 6-0
Pierce
6-1 6-2
Davenport
6-2 6-2
Testud
6-4 7-6
Smashnova
7-5 7-5
Schultz
6-1 6-4
Spirlea
6-0 6-2
Kamio
4-6 6-4 6-3
Boogrert
6-3 6-0
Martinez
6-1 6-3

THIRD ROUND

Sanchez Vicario
6-1 6-3
Habsudova
2-6 6-1 6-3
M Fernandez
6-3 5-7 6-2
Sawamatsu
3-6 6-3 6-3
Novotna
6-1 3-6 9-7
Gavaldon
2-6 6-3 8-6
Paulus
6-1 6-3
Werdel Witmeyer
6-0 6-2
Zvereva
4-6 7-6 6-4
Nagatsuka
6-3 6-3
Huber
6-0 6-1
Pierce
6-3 6-3
Davenport
6-3 6-4
Schultz
6-2 6-2
Spirlea
2-6 6-3 6-3
Martinez
6-3 2-6 6-3

FOURTH ROUND

Sanchez Vicario
7-5 6-0
Sawamatsu
6-4 7-6
Gavaldon
7-5 6-0
Werdel Witmeyer
6-2 6-3
Zvereva
3-6 6-3 6-1
Pierce
6-2 6-4
Davenport
6-2 3-6 6-2
Martinez
6-2 6-7 6-2

QUARTER-FINAL

Sanchez Vicario
6-1 6-3
Werdel Witmeyer
6-1 6-2
Pierce
6-1 6-4
Martinez
6-3 4-6 6-3

SEMI-FINAL

Sanchez
Vicario
6-4 6-1
Pierce
6-3 6-1

Pierce
6-3 6-2

Australian Open
Melbourne   Jan 16-29

MEN'S SINGLES
First Round selected
Carl-Uwe Steeb GER bt Goran Ivanisevic (4) CRO
6-1 7-6 6-3
Andrea Gaudenzi ITA bt Marc Rosset (12) SUI
6-7 6-4 6-3 6-4
Patrick McEnroe USA bt Boris Becker (3) GER
6-3 6-4 7-6
Radomir Vasek CZE bt Mark Petchey GBR 6-3 6-3 7-6
Jeremy Bates GBR bt Henrik Holm SWE
6-4 6-7 3-6 7-6 6-3

WOMEN'S SINGLES
First Round selected
Irina Spirlea ROM bt Julie Halard (16) FRA 6-0 7-5
Natayla Medvedeva UKR bt Magdalena Maleeva (9) BUL
4-6 7-5 6-3
Audra Keller USA bt Sabine Hack (13) GER 75 1-6 6-0
Mariann Werdel Witmeyer USA bt Gabriela Sabatini (5)
ARG 6-4 6-4

MEN'S DOUBLES
Semi-finals
Knowles BAH/Nestor CAN bt Korda CZE/McEnroe USA
6-3 2-6 6-4 0-6 6-4
Palmer/Reneberg USA bt Eltingh/Haarhuis NED
6-3 6-4 6-7 4-6 7-5
Final
Reneberg/Palmer bt Knowles/Nestor 6-3 3-6 6-3 6-2

WOMEN'S DOUBLES
Semi-finals
Fernandez USA/Zvereva BLR bt Davenport/Raymond
USA 6-3 6-3
Novotna CZE/Sanchez Vicario ESP bt
Bollegraf NED/Neiland LAT 7-5 6-1
Final
Novotna/Sanchez Vicario bt Fernandez/Zvereva
6-3 6-7 6-4

MIXED DOUBLES
Semi-finals
Leach USA/ Zvereva BLR bt Woodbridge AUS/Sukova
CZE 4-6 6-2 7-5
Suk CZE/G Fernandez USA bt Connell CAN/Davenport
USA 6-1 7-5
Final
Leach/Zvereva bt Suk/G Fernandez 7-6 6-7 6-4

French Open
Roland Garros, Paris   May 29-June 11

MEN'S SINGLES
First Round selected
Mikael Tillstrom SWE bt Goran Ivanisevic (4) CRO
7-5 6-3 6-4
Alberto Costa ESP bt Jeremy Bates GBR 6-3 6-4 6-0
Gilbert Schaller AUT bt Pete Sampras (2) USA
7-6 4-6 6-7 6-2 6-4

WOMEN'S SINGLES
First Round selected
Paola Suarez ARG bt Mary Joe Fernandez (13) USA
6-4 6-3
Catalina Cristea ROM bt Natasha Zvereva (10) BLR
1-6 7-5 6-3

MEN'S DOUBLES
Semi-finals
Eltingh/Haarhuis NED bt Ho USA/Steven NZL 6-3 6-0
Kulti/Larsson SWE bt Hlasek SUI/Wheaton USA
3-6 6-4 6-4
Final
Eltingh/Haarhuis bt Kulti/Larsson 6-7 6-4 6-1

WOMEN'S DOUBLES
Semi-finals
G Fernandez USA/Zvereva BLR bt bt Fendick/M
Fernandez USA 6-2 6-1
Novotna CZE/Sanchez Vicario ESP bt Arendt/Davenport
USA 6-2 7-5
Final
G Fernandez/Zvereva bt Novotna/Sanchez Vicario
6-7 6-4 7-5

MIXED DOUBLES
Semi-finals
Neiland LAT/Woodforde AUS bt G Fernandez USA/Suk
CZE 6-4 4-6 12-10
Hetherington CAN/De Jager RSA bt
McQuillan/MacPherson AUS 6-4 6-1
Final
Neiland/Woodforde bt Hetherington/De Jager 7-6 7-6

BOYS' SINGLES
Final
M Zabeleta ARG bt M Puerta ARG 6-3 6-3

BOYS' DOUBLES
Final
Sluiter/Wessel NED bt Gimelstob/Wolters USA 7-6 7-5

GIRLS' SINGLES
Final
A Cocheteux FRA bt M Weingartner GER 7-5 6-4

GIRLS' DOUBLES
Final
Morariu/Varmuzova SMR bt Canepa/Casoni ITA
7-6 7-5

Quotes

"Call the supervisor, please. I have a big beef.......You are the most corrupt official in the game" - **American Jeff Tarango to umpire Bruno Rebeuh. Tarango was defaulted in his third round match at Wimbledon against Mronz.**

"I can't believe that he did that...and at Wimbledon of all places" - **John McEnroe, a man with a very selective memory, on Tarango.**

"I regret nothing. I did what I did out of love for Jeff" - **Benedict Tarango, French wife of Jeff, who clouted umpire Rebeuh.**

"I probably shouldn't have said it in front of one million people. I probably should have said it behind closed doors. I would love to have dinner with him and talk it all out" - **Tarango**

"Every time he does that union jack stuff, I sit there cringing" - **Andrew Castle, former British number one, on Greg Rusedski.**

"If they want to see slow tennis they should go to the French Open or watch women's tennis" - **Goran Ivanisevic, on moves to slow down the game. Ivanisevic, you may remember, was knocked out in the first round of the French Open by Sweden's Tillstrom - ranked 141. He was also knocked out of the first round of the US and Australian Opens.**

"I got to the stage where I knew I wanted to win the match, but couldn't always remember why" - **Chanda Rubin who beat Patricia Hy-Boulais at Wimbledon 7-6 6-7 17-15.**

"I did everything right, I wake up early and good breakfast, blah, blah, blah. I don't know" - **Conchita Martinez explaining her Australian Open defeat by Mary Pierce.**

"I don't want to know what he did. He has been known to be very fit, but on the court he almost seemed to be dying. Just 24 hours later, he is down two sets to love and is running quicker in the fifth than in the first. Either he is a good actor or something unbelievably magical happened" - **Boris Becker being cynical about Muster's performance in the Monte Carlo Open, when the Austrian defeated the German in the final.**

"When I walk through a hospital and see children in wheelchairs, children with no eyes or no arms and I'm in there for this little back problem and complaining that it hurts when I play, I realise just how small tennis is" - **Steffi Graf.**

"It doesn't matter what has happened or what is going to happen. He is my father. I will stand by him and will always see him as my father" - **Graf, in August, after he father was arrested for allegedly not paying taxes on his daughter's earnings.**

"Also, I have a doll that is me. It is wearing the same outfit that I wear on court and it has my racket and it comes in two sizes. The big one costs $2,500" - **Gabriela Sabatini.**

"It's not life or death; it's a competition that I love to do, it's the place where I can be my best and be a champion. I couldn't let him take that away from me forever. Those two years, they're gone" - **Monica Seles at the Canadian Open in Toronto. Seles won that title after an absence from the sport of 27 months.**

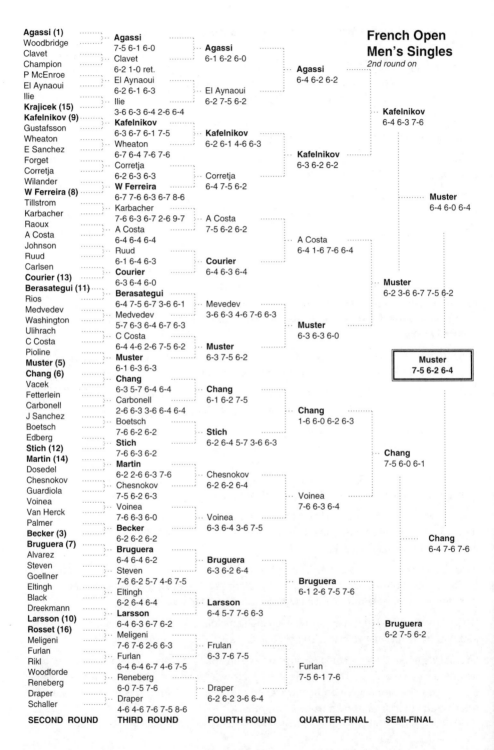

**French Open
Men's Singles**
2nd round on

Agassi (1)
Woodbridge
Clavet
Champion
P McEnroe
El Aynaoui
Ilie
Krajicek (15)
Kafelnikov (9)
Gustafsson
Wheaton
E Sanchez
Forget
Corretja
Wilander
W Ferreira (8)
Tillstrom
Karbacher
Raoux
A Costa
Johnson
Ruud
Carlsen
Courier (13)
Berasategui (11)
Rios
Medvedev
Washington
Ulihrach
C Costa
Pioline
Muster (5)
Chang (6)
Vacek
Fetterlein
Carbonell
J Sanchez
Boetsch
Edberg
Stich (12)
Martin (14)
Dosedel
Chesnokov
Guardiola
Voinea
Van Herck
Palmer
Becker (3)
Bruguera (7)
Alvarez
Steven
Goellner
Eltingh
Black
Dreekmann
Larsson (10)
Rosset (16)
Meligeni
Furlan
Rikl
Woodforde
Reneberg
Draper
Schaller

Agassi
7-5 6-1 6-0
Clavet
6-2 1-0 ret.
El Aynaoui
6-2 6-1 6-3
Ilie
3-6 6-3 6-4 2-6 6-4
Kafelnikov
6-3 6-7 6-1 7-5
Wheaton
6-7 6-4 7-6 7-6
Corretja
6-2 6-3 6-3
W Ferreira
6-7 7-6 6-3 6-7 8-6
Karbacher
7-6 6-3 6-7 2-6 9-7
A Costa
6-4 6-4 6-4
Ruud
6-1 6-4 6-3
Courier
6-3 6-4 6-0
Berasategui
6-4 7-5 6-7 3-6 6-1
Medvedev
5-7 6-3 6-4 6-7 6-3
C Costa
6-4 4-6 2-6 7-5 6-2
Muster
6-1 6-3 6-3
Chang
6-3 5-7 6-4 6-4
Carbonell
2-6 6-3 3-6 6-4 6-4
Boetsch
7-6 6-2 6-2
Stich
7-6 6-3 6-2
Martin
6-2 2-6 6-3 7-6
Chesnokov
7-5 6-2 6-3
Voinea
7-6 6-3 6-0
Becker
6-2 6-2 6-2
Bruguera
6-4 6-4 6-2
Steven
7-6 6-2 5-7 4-6 7-5
Eltingh
6-2 6-4 6-4
Larsson
6-4 6-3 6-7 6-2
Meligeni
7-6 7-6 2-6 6-3
Furlan
6-4 6-4 6-7 4-6 7-5
Reneberg
6-0 7-5 7-6
Draper
4-6 4-6 7-6 7-5 8-6

Agassi
6-1 6-2 6-0
El Aynaoui
6-2 7-5 6-2
Kafelnikov
6-2 6-1 4-6 6-3
Corretja
6-4 7-5 6-2
A Costa
7-5 6-2 6-2
Courier
6-4 6-3 6-4
Mevedev
3-6 6-3 4-6 7-6 6-3
Muster
6-3 7-5 6-2
Chang
6-1 6-2 7-5
Stich
6-2 6-4 5-7 3-6 6-3
Chesnokov
6-2 6-2 6-4
Voinea
6-3 6-4 3-6 7-5
Bruguera
6-3 6-2 6-4
Larsson
6-4 5-7 7-6 6-3
Frulan
6-3 7-6 7-5
Draper
6-2 6-2 3-6 6-4

Agassi
6-4 6-2 6-2
Kafelnikov
6-3 6-2 6-2
A Costa
6-4 1-6 7-6 6-4
Muster
6-3 6-3 6-0
Chang
1-6 6-0 6-2 6-3
Voinea
7-6 6-3 6-4
Bruguera
6-1 2-6 7-5 7-6
Furlan
7-5 6-1 7-6

Kafelnikov
6-4 6-3 7-6
Muster
6-2 3-6 6-7 7-5 6-2
Chang
7-5 6-0 6-1
Bruguera
6-2 7-5 6-2

Muster
6-4 6-0 6-4
Chang
6-4 7-6 7-6

| Muster |
| 7-5 6-2 6-4 |

SECOND ROUND   THIRD ROUND   FOURTH ROUND   QUARTER-FINAL   SEMI-FINAL

French Open
Women's Singles
From 2nd round on

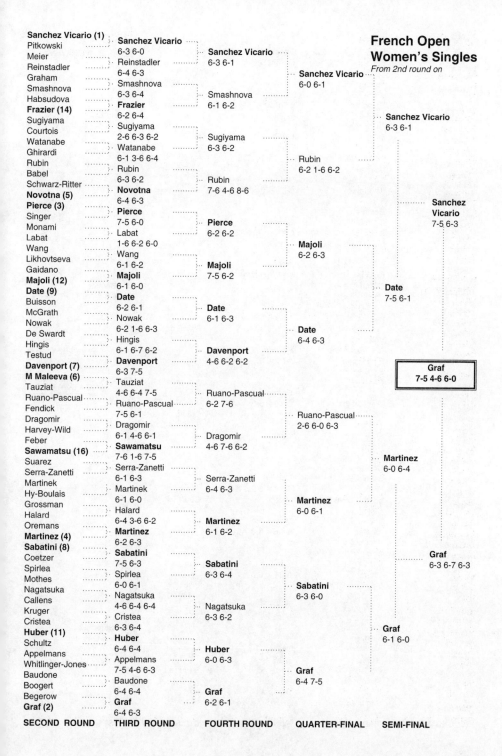

| SECOND ROUND | THIRD ROUND | FOURTH ROUND | QUARTER-FINAL | SEMI-FINAL |

Sanchez Vicario (1)
Pitkowski
Meier
Reinstadler
Graham
Smashnova
Habsudova
Frazier (14)
Sugiyama
Courtois
Watanabe
Ghirardi
Rubin
Babel
Schwarz-Ritter
Novotna (5)
Pierce (3)
Singer
Monami
Labat
Wang
Likhovtseva
Gaidano
Majoli (12)
Date (9)
Buisson
McGrath
Nowak
De Swardt
Hingis
Testud
Davenport (7)
M Maleeva (6)
Tauziat
Ruano-Pascual
Fendick
Dragomir
Harvey-Wild
Feber
Sawamatsu (16)
Suarez
Serra-Zanetti
Martinek
Hy-Boulais
Grossman
Halard
Oremans
Martinez (4)
Sabatini (8)
Coetzer
Spirlea
Mothes
Nagatsuka
Callens
Kruger
Cristea
Huber (11)
Schultz
Appelmans
Whitlinger-Jones
Baudone
Boogert
Begerow
Graf (2)

THIRD ROUND
Sanchez Vicario
6-3 6-0
Reinstadler
6-4 6-3
Smashnova
6-3 6-4
Frazier
6-2 6-4
Sugiyama
2-6 6-3 6-2
Watanabe
6-1 3-6 6-4
Rubin
6-3 6-2
Novotna
6-4 6-3
Pierce
7-5 6-0
Labat
1-6 6-2 6-0
Wang
6-1 6-2
Majoli
6-1 6-0
Date
6-2 6-1
Nowak
6-2 1-6 6-3
Hingis
6-1 6-7 6-2
Davenport
6-3 7-5
Tauziat
4-6 6-4 7-5
Ruano-Pascual
7-5 6-1
Dragomir
6-1 4-6 6-1
Sawamatsu
7-6 1-6 7-5
Serra-Zanetti
6-1 6-3
Martinek
6-1 6-0
Halard
6-4 3-6 6-2
Martinez
6-2 6-3
Sabatini
7-5 6-3
Spirlea
6-0 6-1
Nagatsuka
4-6 6-4 6-4
Cristea
6-3 6-4
Huber
6-4 6-4
Appelmans
7-5 4-6 6-3
Baudone
6-4 6-4
Graf
6-4 6-3

FOURTH ROUND
Sanchez Vicario
6-3 6-1
Smashnova
6-1 6-2
Sugiyama
6-3 6-2
Rubin
7-6 4-6 8-6
Pierce
6-2 6-2
Majoli
7-5 6-2
Date
6-1 6-3
Davenport
4-6 6-2 6-2
Ruano-Pascual
6-2 7-6
Dragomir
4-6 7-6 6-2
Serra-Zanetti
6-4 6-3
Martinez
6-1 6-2
Sabatini
6-3 6-4
Nagatsuka
6-3 6-2
Huber
6-0 6-3
Graf
6-2 6-1

QUARTER-FINAL
Sanchez Vicario
6-0 6-1
Rubin
6-2 1-6 6-2
Majoli
6-2 6-3
Date
6-4 6-3
Ruano-Pascual
2-6 6-0 6-3
Martinez
6-0 6-1
Sabatini
6-3 6-0
Graf
6-4 7-5

SEMI-FINAL
Sanchez Vicario
6-3 6-1
Date
7-5 6-1
Martinez
6-0 6-4
Graf
6-1 6-0

Sanchez Vicario
7-5 6-3

Graf
6-3 6-7 6-3

Graf
7-5 4-6 6-0

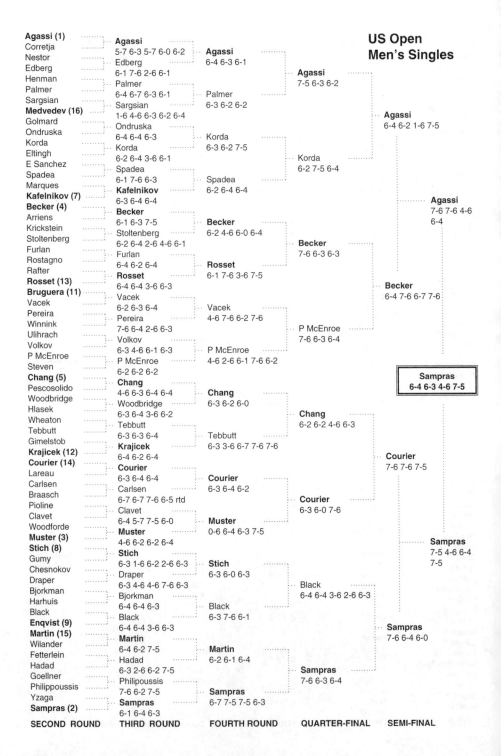

US Open
Men's Singles

Agassi (1)
Corretja
Nestor
Edberg
Henman
Palmer
Sargsian
Medvedev (16)
Golmard
Ondruska
Korda
Eltingh
E Sanchez
Spadea
Marques
Kafelnikov (7)
Becker (4)
Arriens
Krickstein
Stoltenberg
Furlan
Rostagno
Rafter
Rosset (13)
Bruguera (11)
Vacek
Pereira
Winnink
Ulihrach
Volkov
P McEnroe
Steven
Chang (5)
Pescosolido
Woodbridge
Hlasek
Wheaton
Tebbutt
Gimelstob
Krajicek (12)
Courier (14)
Lareau
Carlsen
Braasch
Pioline
Clavet
Woodforde
Muster (3)
Stich (8)
Gumy
Chesnokov
Draper
Bjorkman
Harhuis
Black
Enqvist (9)
Martin (15)
Wilander
Fetterlein
Hadad
Goellner
Philippoussis
Yzaga
Sampras (2)

Agassi
5-7 6-3 5-7 6-0 6-2
Edberg
6-1 7-6 2-6 6-1
Palmer
6-4 6-7 6-3 6-1
Sargsian
1-6 4-6 6-3 6-2 6-4
Ondruska
6-4 6-4 6-3
Korda
6-2 6-4 3-6 6-1
Spadea
6-1 7-6 6-3
Kafelnikov
6-3 6-4 6-4
Becker
6-1 6-3 7-5
Stoltenberg
6-2 6-4 2-6 4-6 6-1
Furlan
6-4 6-2 6-4
Rosset
6-4 6-4 3-6 6-3
Vacek
6-2 6-3 6-4
Pereira
7-6 6-4 2-6 6-3
Volkov
6-3 4-6 6-1 6-3
P McEnroe
6-2 6-2 6-2
Chang
4-6 6-3 6-4 6-4
Woodbridge
6-3 6-4 3-6 6-2
Tebbutt
6-3 6-3 6-4
Krajicek
6-4 6-2 6-4
Courier
6-3 6-4 6-4
Carlsen
6-7 6-7 7-6 6-5 rtd
Clavet
6-4 5-7 7-5 6-0
Muster
4-6 6-2 6-2 6-4
Stich
6-3 1-6 6-2 2-6 6-3
Draper
6-3 4-6 4-6 7-6 6-3
Bjorkman
6-4 6-4 6-3
Black
6-4 6-4 3-6 6-3
Martin
6-4 6-2 7-5
Hadad
6-3 2-6 6-2 7-5
Philipoussis
7-6 6-2 7-5
Sampras
6-1 6-4 6-3

Agassi
6-4 6-3 6-1
Palmer
6-3 6-2 6-2
Korda
6-3 6-2 7-5
Spadea
6-2 6-4 6-4
Becker
6-2 4-6 6-0 6-4
Rosset
6-1 7-6 3-6 7-5
Vacek
4-6 7-6 6-2 7-6
P McEnroe
4-6 2-6 6-1 7-6 6-2
Chang
6-3 6-2 6-0
Tebbutt
6-3 3-6 6-7 7-6 7-6
Courier
6-3 6-4 6-2
Muster
0-6 6-4 6-3 7-5
Stich
6-3 6-0 6-3
Black
6-3 7-6 6-1
Martin
6-2 6-1 6-4
Sampras
6-7 7-5 7-5 6-3

Agassi
7-5 6-3 6-2
Korda
6-2 7-5 6-4
Becker
7-6 6-3 6-3
P McEnroe
7-6 6-3 6-4
Chang
6-2 6-2 4-6 6-3
Courier
6-3 6-0 7-6
Black
6-4 6-4 3-6 2-6 6-3
Sampras
7-6 6-3 6-4

Agassi
6-4 6-2 1-6 7-5
Becker
6-4 7-6 6-7 7-6
Courier
7-6 7-6 7-5
Sampras
7-6 6-4 6-0

Agassi
7-6 7-6 4-6
6-4
Sampras
7-5 4-6 6-4
7-5

Sampras
6-4 6-3 4-6 7-5

SECOND ROUND   **THIRD ROUND**   **FOURTH ROUND**   **QUARTER-FINAL**   **SEMI-FINAL**

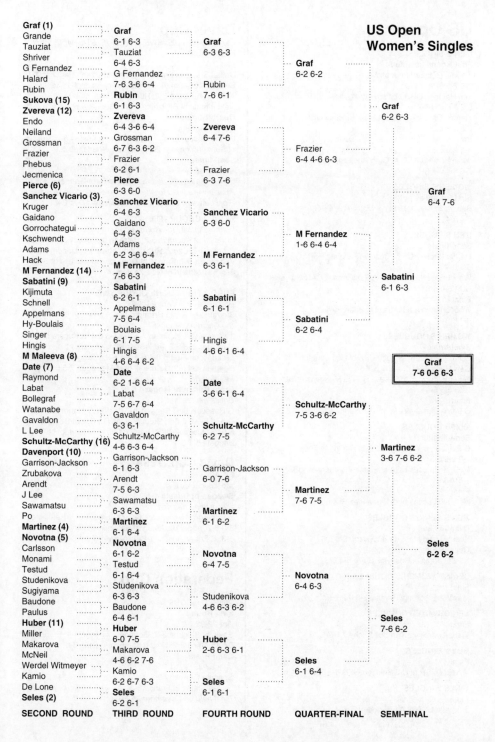

US Open
Women's Singles

Graf (1)
Grande
Tauziat
Shriver
G Fernandez
Halard
Rubin
Sukova (15)
Zvereva (12)
Endo
Neiland
Grossman
Frazier
Phebus
Jecmenica
Pierce (6)
Sanchez Vicario (3)
Kruger
Gaidano
Gorrochategui
Kschwendt
Adams
Hack
M Fernandez (14)
Sabatini (9)
Kijimuta
Schnell
Appelmans
Hy-Boulais
Singer
Hingis
M Maleeva (8)
Date (7)
Raymond
Labat
Bollegraf
Watanabe
Gavaldon
L Lee
Schultz-McCarthy (16)
Davenport (10)
Garrison-Jackson
Zrubakova
Arendt
J Lee
Sawamatsu
Po
Martinez (4)
Novotna (5)
Carlsson
Monami
Testud
Studenikova
Sugiyama
Baudone
Paulus
Huber (11)
Miller
Makarova
McNeil
Werdel Witmeyer
Kamio
De Lone
Seles (2)

SECOND ROUND

Graf
6-1 6-3
Tauziat
6-4 6-3
G Fernandez
7-6 3-6 6-4
Rubin
6-1 6-3
Zvereva
6-4 3-6 6-4
Grossman
6-7 6-3 6-2
Frazier
6-2 6-1
Pierce
6-3 6-0
Sanchez Vicario
6-4 6-3
Gaidano
6-4 6-3
Adams
6-2 3-6 6-4
M Fernandez
7-6 6-3
Sabatini
6-2 6-1
Appelmans
7-5 6-4
Boulais
6-1 7-5
Hingis
4-6 6-4 6-2
Date
6-2 1-6 6-4
Labat
7-5 6-7 6-4
Gavaldon
6-3 6-1
Schultz-McCarthy
4-6 6-3 6-4
Garrison-Jackson
6-1 6-3
Arendt
7-5 6-3
Sawamatsu
6-3 6-3
Martinez
6-1 6-4
Novotna
6-1 6-2
Testud
6-1 6-4
Studenikova
6-3 6-3
Baudone
6-4 6-1
Huber
6-0 7-5
Makarova
4-6 6-2 7-6
Kamio
6-2 6-7 6-3
Seles
6-2 6-1

THIRD ROUND

Graf
6-3 6-3
Rubin
7-6 6-1
Zvereva
6-4 7-6
Frazier
6-3 7-6
Sanchez Vicario
6-3 6-0
M Fernandez
6-3 6-1
Sabatini
6-1 6-1
Hingis
4-6 6-1 6-4
Date
3-6 6-1 6-4
Schultz-McCarthy
6-2 7-5
Garrison-Jackson
6-0 7-6
Martinez
6-1 6-2
Novotna
6-4 7-5
Studenikova
4-6 6-3 6-2
Huber
2-6 6-3 6-1
Seles
6-1 6-1

FOURTH ROUND

Graf
6-2 6-2
Frazier
6-4 4-6 6-3
M Fernandez
1-6 6-4 6-4
Sabatini
6-2 6-4
Schultz-McCarthy
7-5 3-6 6-2
Martinez
7-6 7-5
Novotna
6-4 6-3
Seles
6-1 6-4

QUARTER-FINAL

Graf
6-2 6-3
Sabatini
6-1 6-3
Martinez
3-6 7-6 6-2
Seles
7-6 6-2

SEMI-FINAL

Graf
6-4 7-6
Seles
6-2 6-2

Graf
7-6 0-6 6-3

US Open

Flushing Meadow   *Aug 28-Sep 10*
MEN'S SINGLES
First Round selected
Jerome Golmard FRA bt Wayne Ferreira (10) RSA
7-5 7-6 6-1
Tim Henman GBR bt Juan Albert Viloca ESP
6-2 4-6 6-3 6-2
Marcos Ondruska RSA bt Mark Petchey GBR
7-6 6-1 6-0
Brett Steven NZL bt Goran Ivanisevic (6) CRO
4-6 2-6 6-3 6-1
Joost Winnink NED bt Greg Rusedski GBR
7-6 6-4 6-7 6-1

WOMEN'S SINGLES
First Round selected
Babara Paulus AUT bt Iva Majoli (13) CRO
6-4 6-4

MEN'S DOUBLES
Semi-finals
O'Brien/Stolle AUS bt Casal/E Sanchez ESP
6-2 6-4
Woodbridge/Woodforde AUS bt Connell CAN/Galbraith
USA 6-0 6-2
Final
Woodbridge/Woodforde bt O'Brien/Stolle
6-3 6-3

WOMEN'S DOUBLES
Semi-finals
Schultz/McCarthy-Stubbs USA bt Hetherington
CAN/Radford AUS 4-6 7-5 7-5
G Fernandez USA/Zvereva BLR bt McNeil USA/Sukova
CZE 6-3 6-4
Final
G Fernandez/Zvereva bt S/McCarthy-Stubbs 7-5 6-3

MIXED DOUBLES
Semi-finals
G Fernandez USA/Suk CZE bt Rubin/MacPhie USA
6-3 2-6 6-3
McGrath/Lucena USA bt Pierce FRA/Jenson USA
7-5 7-6
Final
McGrath/Lucena bt G Fernandez/Suk 6-4 6-4

MEN'S SENIOR DOUBLES
Over 35 Final
Kriek/J Lloyd bt Amritraj/Wilkison 6-4 7-6
Over 45 Final
Fillol/Orantes bt Rosewall/Stolle 6-3 6-3

SENIOR WOMEN'S DOUBLES
Final
May/Wade bt King/Turnbull 3-6 6-2 7-6

SENIOR MIXED DOUBLES
Final
Wade/Orantes bt Turnbull/Roche 7-6 7-5

BOYS' SINGLES
Final
N Keifer GER bt U-J Seetzen GER 6-3 6-4

GIRLS' SINGLES
Final
T Snyder USA bt A Ellwood AUS 6-4 4-6 6-2

Davis Cup

Seeds: USA, CZE, SWE, ESP, AUS, RUS, NED, GER
First Round
Feb 3-5
United States bt France 4-1; Italy bt Czech Republic 4-1;
Sweden bt Denmark 3-2; Austria bt Spain 4-1; South
Africa bt Australia 3-2; Russia bt Belgium 4-1;
Netherlands bt Switzerland 4-1; Germany bt Croatia 4-1
Quarter-finals
Mar 31-Apr 2
United States bt Italy 5-0; Sweden bt Austria 5-0; Russia
bt South Africa 4-1; Germany bt Netherlands 4-1
Semi-finals
Sep 22-24
United States bt Sweden 4-1; Russia bt Germany 3-2
Russia were fined for the watering of courts in Moscow.
Final between Sweden and Russia held Dec 2-4.

WORLD GROUP 1996
Winners qualify for World Group
Hungary bt Australia 3-2; Belgium bt Norway 5-0; India bt
Croatia 3-2; Czech Rep bt Zimbabwe 4-1; Denmrk bt
Venezuela 3-2; France bt Morocco 5-0; Mexico bt Spain
3-2; Switzerland bt New Zealand 4-1

EURO-AFRICA ZONE GROUP TWO
Bratislava   *Apr 28-30*
Slovakia bt Great Britain 5-0
Slovakian names first
J Kroslak bt T Henman 7-5 6-3 4-6 6-4; K Kucere bt M
Maclagan 6-3 6-2 4-6 7-5; Kroslak/Krucere bt
Broad/Henman 3-6 6-4 6-4 2-6 6-2; K Kucere bt T
Henman 6-4 6-2; J Kroslak bt M Maclagan 7-5 6-2
Eastbourne   *July 14-16*
Great Britain bt Monaco 5-0
British names first
G Rusedski bt C Boggetti 6-2 6-2 7-6; T Henman bt S
Graeff 6-0 6-3 6-2; Broad/Petchey bt Graeff/Boggetti 6-4
6-0; G Rusedski bt S Graeff 6-0 6-1; T Henman bt C
Boggetti 6-1 6-4

Davis Cup, 1994
FINAL
Moscow Dec 2-4
Sweden bt Russia 4-1
Swedish names first
S Edberg t A Volkov 6-4 6-2; M Larsson bt Y Kafelnikov
6-0 6-2, Appel/Bjorkman bt Kafelnikov/Olhovsky 6-7 6-2
6-3; S Edberg lost to Y Kafelnikov 4-6 6-4 6-0; M Larsson
bt A Volkov 7-6 6-4

Federation Cup

Seeds: ESP, GER, FRA, USA
WORLD GROUP
First Round
Apr 22-23
Spain bt Bulgaria 3-2; Germany bt Japan 4-1; France bt
South Africa 3-2; United States bt Austria 5-0
Semi-finals
July 22-23
Spain bt Germany 3-2
United States bt France 3-2
Final held on November 25-26

ATP Tour 1994-95 (Men's Events) ━━━

Date	Tournament	Singles Final		Doubles Final		Prize Money
Sep 26 Oct 2	Davidoff Swiss Indoor Basle, Switzerl'd (HI)	**Ferreira** P McEnroe	4-6 6-2 7-6 6-3	**P McEnroe/Palmer** Bale/de Jager	6-3 7-6	$775,000
Sep 26 Oct 2	Trofeo Kim Top Line Palermo, Italy (CO)	**Berasategui** Corretja	2-6 7-6 6-4	**Kempers/Waite** Broad/Van Emburgh	7-6 6-4	$290,000
Sep 26 Oct 2	Salem Open Kuala Lumpur (HI)	**Eltingh** Olhovsky	7-6 2-6 6-4	**Eltingh/Haarhuis** Kulti/Wahlgren	6-0 7-5	$375,000
Oct 3 Oct 9	Australian Indoor (HI) Sydney	**Krajicek** Becker	7-6 7-6 2-6 6-3	**Eltingh/Haarhuis** Black/Stark	6-4 7-6	$895,000
Oct 3 Oct 9	GP de Toulouse (HI) Toulouse	**Larsson** Palmer	6-1 6-3	**Oosting/Vacek** P McEnroe/Palmer	7-6 6-7 6-3	$375,000
Oct 3 Oct 9	Athens Intern'l (CO) Athens	**Berasategui** Martinez	4-6 7-6 6-3	**Lobo/J Sanchez** Brandi/Mordegan	5-7 6-1 6-4	$188,750
Oct 10 Oct 16	Seiko Super Tennis Tokyo (CPI)	**Ivanisevic** Chang	6-4 6-4	**Connell/Galbraith** Black/Stark	6-3 3-6 6-4	$1,020,000
Oct 10 Oct 16	Eisenberg Open Tel Aviv (HO)	**Ferreira** Mansdorf	7-6 6-3	**Bale/de Jager** Apell/Bjorkman	6-7 6-2 7-6	$250,000
Oct 10 Oct 16	IPB Czech Indoor Ostrava (CPI)	**Washington** Boetsch	4-6 6-3 6-3	**Damm/Novacek** Muller/Norval	6-4 1-6 6-3	$290,000
Oct 17 Oct 23	Lyon GP Lyon (CPI)	**Rosset** Courier	6-4 7-6	**Hlasek/Kafelnikov** Damm/Rafter	6-7 7-6 7-6	$575,000
Oct 17 Oct 23	CA Tennis Trophy Vienna (CPI)	**Agassi** Stich	7-6 4-6 6-2 6-3	**Bauer/Rikl** Antonitsch/Rusedski	7-6 6-4	$375,000
Oct 17 Oct 23	Salem Open Bejing (CPI)	**Chang** Jarryd	7-5 7-5	**Ho/Kinnear** Adams/Olhovsky	7-6 6-3	$295,000
Oct 24 Oct 30	Stockholm Open Stockholm (CPI)	**Becker** Ivanisevic	4-6 6-4 6-3 7-6	**Woodbridge/Woodforde** Apell/Bjorkman	6-3 6-4	$1,470,000
Oct 24 Oct 30	Hellmann's Cup Santiago (CO)	**Berasategui** Clavet	6-3 6-4	**Novacek/Wilander** Carbonell/Roig	3-6 7-6 7-6	$188,750
Oct 31 Nov 6	Paris Open Paris (CPI)	**Agassi** Rosset	6-3 6-3 4-6 7-5	**Eltingh/Haarhuis** Black/Stark	3-6 7-6 7-5	$2,000,000
Oct 31 Nov 6	Topper Open Montevideo (CO)	**Berasategui** Clavet	6-4 6-0	**Filippini/Mattar** Casal/E Sanchez	7-6 6-4	$188,750
Nov 7 Nov 13	EC Championship Antwerp (CPI)	**Sampras** Larsson	7-6 6-4	**Apell/Bjorkman** Davids/Lareau	4-6 6-1 6-2	$1,100,000
Nov 7 Nov 13	Kremlin Cup Moscow (CPI)	**Volkov** C Adams	6-2 6-4	**Eltingh/Haarhuis** D Adams/Olhovsky	w/o	$1,100,000
Nov 7 Nov 13	Topper S A Open Buenos Aires (CO)	**Corretja** Frana	6-3 5-7 7-6	**Casal/E Sanchez** Carbonell/Roig	6-3 6-2	$288,750
Nov 15 Nov 20	IBM/ATP World Chps Frankfurt (C)	**Sampras** Becker	4-6 6-3 7-5 6-4			$3,000,000

Dates	Tournament	Singles	Score	Doubles	Score	Prize
Nov 23 Nov 27	World Doubles Chps Johannesburg (HO)			**Apell/Bjorkman** Woodbridge/Woodforde	6-4 4-6 4-6 7-6 7-6	$1,300,000
Jan 2 Jan 8	Qatar Open Doha (HO)	**Edberg** Larsson	7-6 6-1	**Edberg/Larsson** Olhovsky/Siemerink	7-6 6-2	$625,000
Jan 2 Jan 8	Australian Hardcourt Adelaide (HO)	**Courier** Boetsch	6-2 7-5	**Courier/Rafter** Black/Connell	7-6 6-4	$328,000
Jan 9 Jan 15	Peters NSW Open Sydney (HO)	**P McEnroe** Fromberg	6-2 7-6	**Woodbridge/Woodforde** Kronemann/MacPherson	7-6 6-4	$328,000
Jan 9 Jan 15	Danamon Indonesian Open, Jakarta (HO)	**Haarhuis** Vasek	7-5 7-5	**D Adams/Olhovsky** Agenor/Matsuoka	7-5 6-3	$328,000
Jan 9 Jan 15	Benson & Hedges Op Auckland (HO)	**Enqvist** C Adams	6-2 6-1	**Connell/Galbraith** Lobo/J Sanchez	6-4 6-3	$328,000
Jan 16 Jan 29	**Australian Open** Melbourne (HO)	**Agassi** Sampras	4-6 6-1 7-6 6-4	**Palmer/Reneberg** Knowles/Nestor	6-3 3-6 6-3 6-2	$A3,720,800
Feb 6 Feb 12	Dubai Tennis Open Dubai (HO)	**Ferreira** Gaudenzi	6-3 6-3	**Connell/Galbraith** Carbonell/Roig	6-2 4-6 6-3	$1,039,250
Feb 6 Feb 12	Open 13 Marseille (CPI)	**Becker** Vacek	6-7 6-4 7-5	**D Adams/Olhovsky** Fleurian/R Gilbert	6-1 6-4	$539,250
Feb 6 Feb 12	Sybase Open San Jose (HI)	**Agassi** Chang	6-2 1-6 6-3	**Grabb/P McEnroe** O'Brien/Stolle	3-6 7-5 6-0	$328,000
Feb 13 Feb 19	Muratti Time Indoor Milan (CI)	**Kafelnikov** Becker	7-5 5-7 7-6	**Becker/Forget** Korda/Novacek	6-2 6-4	$814,250
Feb 13 Feb 19	Kroger St Jude In't Memphis (HO)	**Martin** Haarhuis	7-6 6-4	**Palmer/Reneberg** Ho/Steven	4-6 7-6 6-1	$808,000
Feb 20 Feb 26	Eurocard Open Stuttgart (CI)	**Krajicek** Stich	7-6 6-3 6-7 1-6 6-3	**Connell/Galbraith** Suk/Vacek	6-2 6-2	$2,250,000
Feb 20 Feb 26	Comcast US Indoor Philadelphia (HI)	**Enqvist** Chang	0-6 6-4 6-0	**Grabb/Stark** Eltingh/Haarhuis	7-6 6-7 6-3	$714,250
Feb 27 Mar 5	ABN/AMRO Tour't Rotterdam (CPI)	**Krajicek** Haarhuis	7-6 6-4	**Damm/Jarryd** Carbonell/Roig	6-3 6-2	$600,000
Feb 27 Mar 5	MassMutual Champs Scottsdale (HO)	**Courier** Philippoussis	7-6 6-4	**Kronemann/MacPherson** Lobo/J Sanchez	4-6 6-3 6-4	$328,000
Feb 27 Nar 5	Mexican Open Mexico City (CL)	**Muster** Meligeni	7-6 7-5	**Frana/Lavalle** Goellner/Nargiso	7-5 6-3	$330,000
Mar 6 Mar 12	Newsweek Cup Indian Wells (HO)	**Sampras** Agassi	7-5 6-3 7-5	**Ho/Steven** Muller/Norval	6-4 7-6	$1,800,000
Mar 6 Mar 12	Copenhagen Open Copenhagen (CI)	**Sinner** Olhovsky	6-7 7-6 6-3	**Keil/Nyborg** Raoux/Rusedski	6-7 6-4 7-6	$228,000
Mar 13 Mar 19	St Petersburg Open St P'burg, Russia(CPI)	**Kafelnikov** Raoux	6-2 6-2	**Damm/Jarryd** Hlasek/Kafelnikov	6-4 6-2	$325,000
Mar 17 Mar 26	Lipton Champs Key Biscayne (HO)	**Agassi** Sampras	3-6 6-2 7-6	**Woodbridge/Woodforde** Grabb/P McEnroe	6-3 7-6	$2,500,000
Mar 20 Mar 26	GP Hassan II Casablanca (CI)	**Schaller** A Costa	6-4 6-2	**Carbonell/Roig** Couto/Cunha-Silva	6-4 6-1	$228,000

Dates	Tournament	Singles Winner	Score	Doubles Winners	Score	Prize
Apr 3 Apr 9	Estoril Open Estoril (CO)	**Muster** A Costa	6-4 6-2	Kafelnikov/Olhovsky Goellner/Nargiso	5-7 7-5 6-2	$575,000
Apr 3 Apr 9	S African Open Johannesburg (HO)	**Sinner** Raoux	6-1 6-4	R Gilbert/Raoux Sinner/Winnink	6-4 3-6 6-3	$328,000
Apr 10 Apr 16	Trofeo Conde d Godo Barcelona (Cl)	**Muster** Larsson	6-2 6-1 6-4	Kronemann/MacPherson Ivanisevic/Gaudenzi	6-2 6-4	$900,000
Apr 10 Apr 16	Japan Open Tokyo (HO)	**Courier** Agassi	6-4 6-3	Knowles/Stark Fitzgerald/Jarryd	6-3 3-6 7-6	$1,060,000
Apr 17 Apr 23	Philips Open Nice (CO)	**Rosset** Kafelnikov	6-4 6-0	Suk/Vacek L Jenson/Wheaton	3-6 7-6 7-6	$328,000
Apr 17 Apr 23	Salem Open Hong Kong (HO)	**Chang** Bjorkman	6-3 6-1	Ho/Philippoussis Fitzgerald/Jarryd	6-1 6-7 7-6	$328,000
Apr 17 Apr 23	XL Bermuda Open Bermuda (CO)	**Hadad** Frana	7-6 3-6 6-4	Connell/Martin Steven/Stoltenberg	7-6 2-6 7-5	$328,000
Apr 18 Apr 24	Volvo Monte C' Open Monte Carlo (CO)	**Muster** Becker	4-6 5-7 6-1 7-6 6-0	Eltingh/Haarhuis Lobo/J Sanchez	6-3 6-4	$1,795,000
Apr 24 Apr 30	KAL Korean Open Seoul (HO)	**Rusedski** Rehmann	6-4 3-1 ret.	Lareau/Tarango Eagle/Florent	6-3 6-2	$228,000
May 1 May 7	BMW Open Munich (CO)	**W Ferreira** Stich	7-5 7-6	Kroneman/MacPherson Lobo/J Sanchez	6-3 6-4	$425,000
May 1 May 7	AT & T Challenge Atlanta (CO)	**Chang** Agassi	6-2 6-7 6-4	Casal/E Sanchez Palmer/Reneberg	6-7 6-3 7-6	$328,000
May 8 May 14	Panasonic German Hamburg (CO)	**Medvedev** Ivanisevic	6-3 6-2 6-1	Kafelnikov/W Ferreira Black/Olhovsky	6-1 7-6	$1,795,000
May 8 May 14	US Clay Court Chps Pinehurst (CO)	**Enqvist** Frana	6-3 3-6 6-3	Woodbridge/Woodforde O'Brien/Stolle	6-2 6-4	$289,250
May 15 May 21	Italian Open-Nokia Rome (CO)	**Muster** Bruguera	3-6 7-6 6-2 6-3	Suk/Vacek Apell/Bjorkman	6-3 6-4	$2,000,000
May 15 May 21	Red Clay Champs. Coral Springs (CO)	**Woodbridge** Rusedski	6-4 6-2	Woodbridge/Woodforde Casal/E Sanchez	6-3 6-1	$255,000
May 22 May 28	Peugeot Team Chps Düsseldorf (CO)	**Sweden** Croatia	2 matches 1 match			$1,800,000
May 22 May 28	Intl di Risparmio Bologna (CO)	**Paes** Filippini	6-2 6-4	Black/Stark Pimek/Spadea	7-5 6-3	$328,000
May 29 June 11	**French Open** Paris (CO)	**Muster** Chang	7-5 6-2 6-4	Eltingh/Harrhuis Kulti/Larsson	6-7 6-4 6-1	$4,811,963
June 12 June 18	Stella Artois London (G)	**Sampras** Forget	7-6 7-6	Martin/Sampras Apell/Bjorkman	7-6 6-4	$625,000
June 12 June 18	Ordina Open Rosmalen, Holl. (G)	**Kucera** Jarryd	7-6 7-6	Krajicek/Siemerink Davids/Olhovsky	7-5 6-3	$328,000
June 12 June 18	Maia Open Oporto, Portugal	**Berasategui** C Costa	3-6 6-3 6-4	Carbonell/Roig Arrese/Corretja	6-3 7-6	$328,000
June 19 June 25	Gerry Weber Open Halle, Germany (GO)	**Rosset** Stich	3-6 7-6 7-6	Eltingh/Haarhuis Kafelnikov/Olhovsky	6-2 3-6 6-3	$725,000

Tennis

Dates	Tournament	Winner	Score	Doubles Winners	Doubles Score	Prize
June 19 June 25	Raiffeisen GP St Pölten, Austria(CO)	**Muster** Ulihrach	6-3 3-6 6-1	**Behrens/Lucena** Pimek/Talbot	7-5 6-4	$375,000
June 19 June 25	Nottingham Open Manchester (G)	**Frana** Woodbridge	7-6 6-3	**L Jensen/M Jensen** Galbraith/Visser	6-3 5-7 6-4	$328,000
June 26 July 9	**The Championships** Wimbledon (GO)	**Sampras** Becker	6-7 6-2 6-4 6-2	**Woodbridge/Woodforde** Leach/Melville	7-5 7-6 7-6	$4,455,393
July 10 July 16	Rado Swiss Open Gstaad (CO)	**Kafelnikov** Hlasek	6-3 6-4 3-6 6-3	**Lobo/J Sanchez** Boetsch/Rosset	6-7 7-6 7-6	$550,000
July 10 July 16	Swedish Open Bastad (CO)	**Meligeni** Ruud	6-4 6-4	**Apell/Bjorkman** Ireland/Kratzmann	6-3 6-0	$328,000
July 10 July 16	Hall of Fame Champs Newport, RI (GO)	**Prinosil** Wheaton	7-6 5-7 6-2	**Renzenbrink/Zoecke** Kilderry/Marques	6-1 6-2	$255,000
July 17 July 23	Mercedes Cup Stuttgart (CO)	**Muster** Apell	6-2 6-2	**Carbonell/Roig** E Ferreira/Siemerink	3-6 6-3 6-4	$1,040,000
July 17 July 23	Legg Mason Classic Washington, DC (HO)	**Agassi** Edberg	6-4 2-6 7-5	**Delaitre/Tarango** Korda/Suk	1-6 6-3 6-2	$675,000
July 24 July 30	Canadian Open Montreal (HO)	**Agassi** Sampras	3-6 6-2 6-3	**Kafelnikov/Olhovsky** McPhie/Stolle	6-2 6-2	$1,795,000
July 24 July 30	Grolsch Open Amsterdam (CO)	**Rios** Siemerink	6-4 7-5 6-4	**Rios/Schalken** Arthurs/Broad	7-6 6-2	$500,000
Jul 31 Aug 6	EA Generali Open Kitzbühel (CO)	**A Costa** Muster	4-6 6-4 7-6 2-6 6-4	**Montana/Van Emburgh** Arrese/Arthurs	6-7 6-3 7-6	$425,000
Jul 31 Aug 6	Czech Open Prague (CO)	**Ulihrach** J Sanchez	6-2 6-2	**Pimek/Talbot** Novak/Rikl	7-5 1-6 7-6	$365,000
Jul 31 Aug 6	Los Angeles Open Los Angeles (HO)	**Stich** Enqvist	6-7 7-6 6-2	**Haygarth/Kinnear** Davis/Ivanisevic	6-4 7-6	$328,000
Aug 7 Aug 13	ATP Championship Cincinnati (HO)	**Agassi** Chang	7-5 6-2	**Woodbridge/Woodforde** Knowles/Nestor	6-2 3-0 ret.	$1,795,000
Aug 7 Aug 13	San Marino Internat. San Marino	**Muster** Gaudenzi	6-2 6-0	**Arrese/Kratzmann** Albano/Mordegan	7-6 3-6 6-2	$300,00
Aug 14 Aug 24	Volvo International New Haven, Ct (HO)	**Agassi** Krajicek	3-6 7-6 6-3	**Leach/Melville** Paes/Pereira	7-6 6-4	$1,040,000
Aug 14 Aug 20	RCA Championships Indianapolis (HO)	**Enqvist** Karbacher	6-4 6-3	**Knowles/Nestor**	6-4 6-4	$1,040,000
Aug 21 Aug 27	Croatian Open Umag, Croatia	**Muster** C Costa	3-6 7-6 6-4	**Lobo/J Sanchez** Ekeret/Markovits	6-4 6-0	$400,000
Aug 21 Aug 27	The Hamlet Cup Long Island, NY	**Kafelnikov** Siemerink	7-6 6-2	**Suk/Vacek** Leach/Melville	5-7 7-6 7-6	$328,000
Aug 28 Sept 10	**US Open** Flushing M'ws (HO)	**Sampras** Agassi	6-4 6-3 4-6 7-5	**Woodbridge/Woodforde**	6-3 6-3	$4,282,400
Sept 11 Sept 17	Romanian Open Bucharest (CI)	**Muster** Schaller	6-3 6-4	**Keil/Tarango** Suk/Vacek	6-4 7-6	$1,375,000
Sept 11 Sept 17	GP Passing Shot Bordeaux (HO)	**Doumbia** Hlasek	6-4 6-4	**Hirszon/Ivanisevic** Holm/Sapsford	6-3 6-4	$400,000

Sep 11 Sep 17	Colombia Open Bogota	**Lapentti** Tobon	2-6 6-1 6-4	**Novak/Rikl** Campbell/Washington	7-6 6-2	$328,000
Sep 25 Oct 1	Davidoff Swiss Open Basel	**Courier** Siemerink	6-7 7-6 5-7 6-2 7-5	**Suk/Vacek** Keil/Nyborg	3-6 6-3 6-3	$1,000,000
Sep 25 Oct 1	Camp. Int. di Sicilia Palermo	**Clavet** Burillo	6-7 6-3 7-6	**Corretja/Santoro** Davids/Norval	6-7 6-4 6-3	$328,000

Prize Money - Year to Date
Jan 1 to Oct 10
in US dollars

1	Andre Agassi	USA	2,279,741		27	Petr Korda	CZE	449,452
2	Pete Sampras	USA	2,170,666		28	Patrick McEnroe	USA	447,623
3	Thomas Muster	AUT	2,087,129		29	Marc Rosset	SUI	439,561
4	Yevgeny Kafelnikov	RUS	1,193,061		30	Jan Apell	SWE	437,918
5	Boris Becker	GER	1,092,158		31	Andrey Olhovsky	RUS	427,379
6	Michael Chang	USA	971,140		32	Arnaud Boetsch	FRA	416,065
7	Goran Ivanisevic	CRO	943,382		33	Gilbert Schaller	AUT	408,448
8	Jim Courier	USA	807,092		34	Patrick Rafter	AUS	405,491
9	Richard Krajicek	NED	791,140		35	Alberto Berasategui	ESP	387,222
10	Michael Stich	GER	770,407		36	Brett Steven	NZL	369,834
11	Wayne Ferreira	RSA	756,535		37	Byron Black	ZIM	363,521
12	Paul Haarhuis	NED	721,982		38	Tomas Carbonell	ESP	360,235
13	Thomas Enqvist	SWE	707,546		39	Richey Reneberg	USA	355,048
14	Todd Woodbridge	AUS	679,946		40	Marcelo Rios	CHI	351,868
15	Sergi Bruguera	ESP	671,769		41	Alberto Costa	ESP	344,337
16	Jacco Eltingh	NED	659,611		42	Martin Damm	CZE	341,512
17	Magnus Larsson	SWE	652,560		43	Bernd Karbacher	GER	339,867
18	Mark Woodforde	AUS	648,581		44	Renzo Furlan	ITA	339,204
19	Andrey Medvedev	UKR	594,317		45	Carlos Costa	ESP	331,312
20	Jonas Bjorkman	SWE	589,667		46	Jared Palmer	USA	329,242
21	Stefan Edberg	SWE	585,369		47	Guy Forget	FRA	328,495
22	Daniel Vacek	CZE	542,251		48	David Wheaton	USA	325,103
23	Jan Siemerink	NED	535,958		49	Jacob Hlasek	SUI	322,450
24	Todd Martin	USA	505,703		50	Jeff Tarango	USA	319,292
25	Andrea Gaudenzi	ITA	477,817		*Also*			
26	Javier Sanchez	ESP	453,593		57	Greg Rusedski	GBR	289,038

Prize Money - Year End 1994

in US dollars

1	Pete Sampras	USA	3,607,812		13	Yevgeny Kafelnikov	RUS	1,011,583
2	Sergi Bruguera	ESP	3,031,874		14	Alberto Berasategui	ESP	939,651
3	Stefan Edberg	SWE	2,489,161		15	Paul Haarhuis	NED	930,961
4	Goran Ivanisevic	CRO	2,060,078		16	Todd Martin	USA	888,924
5	Michael Stich	GER	2,033,623		17	Mark Woodforde	AUS	885,924
6	Boris Becker	GER	2,029,756		18	Marc Rosset	SUI	768,004
7	Andre Agassi	USA	1,941,667		19	Jonas Bjorkman	SWE	756,552
8	Jim Courier	USA	1,921,584		20	Jonathan Stark	USA	689,379
9	Michael Chang	USA	1,789,495		*Also*			
10	Andrei Medvedev	UKR	1,211,134		72	Greg Rusedski	CAN	261,643
11	Wayne Ferreira	RSA	1,053,341		87	Jeremy Bates	GBR	218,434
12	Jacco Eltingh	NED	1,053,619					

Kraft/WTA Tour 1994-95 ━━━━━━━━━━

Date	Tournament	Singles Final		Doubles Final		Prize Money
Oct 3 Oct 9	European Indoors Zurich (CI)	**Mag. Maleeva** Zvereva	**7-5 3-6 6-4**	**Bollegraf/Navratilova** Fendick/McGrath	**7-6 6-1**	$750,000
Oct 10 Oct 16	Porsche Grand Prix Filderstadt (I)	**Huber** Pierce	**6-4 6-2**	**G Fernandez/Zvereva** Bollegraf/Neiland	**7-6 6-4**	$400,000
Oct 18 Oct 23	Brighton International Brighton (I)	**Novotna** Sukova	**6-7 6-3 6-4**	**Bollegraf/Neiland** M Fernandez/Novotna	**4-6 6-2 6-3**	$400,000
Oct 24 Oct 30	Nokia Grand Prix Essen (I)	**Novotna** Majoli	**6-2 6-4**	**Lindstrom/Strandlund** Maniokova/Meskhi	**6-2 6-1**	$400,000
Oct 31 Nov 6	Bank of West Classic Oakland (I)	**Sanchez Vic.** Navratilova	**1-6 7-6 7-6**	**Davenport/Sanchez Vic.** G Fernandez/Navratilova	**7-5 6-4**	$400,000
Oct 31 Nov 6	Bell Challenge Quebec City (I)	**K Maleeva** Schultz	**6-3 6-3**	**Reinach/Tauziat** Harvey-Wild/Rubin	**6-4 6-3**	$150,000
Nov 7 Nov 13	Virginia Slims Philadelphia (I)	**Huber** Pierce	**6-0 6-7 7-5**	**G Fernandez/Zvereva** Sabatini/Schultz	**4-6 6-4 6-2**	$750,000
Nov 7 Nov 13	Digital Open Surabaya, Indonesia	**Wagner** Sugiyama	**2-6 6-0 ret.**	**Basuki/Todjakuauma** Nagatsuka/Sugiyama	**Default**	$100,000
Nov 14 Nov 20	Virginia Slims New York (I)	**Sabatini** Davenport	**6-3 6-2 6-4**	**G Fernandez/Zvereva** Novotna/Sanchez-Vicario	**6-3 6-7 6-3**	$3,500,000
Nov 14 Nov 20	P&G Taiwan Open Taipei, Taiwan	**Wang** Nagatsuka	**2-6 7-5 6-3**	**Jaggard-Lai/Simpson** Feber/Fusai	**6-0 7-6**	$100,000
Jan 2 Jan 8	Danamon Indonesian Brisbane (H)	**Hack** Spirlea	**2-6 7-6 6-4**	**Porwik/Spirlea** Courtois/Feber	**6-2 6-3**	$161,250
Jan 9 Jan 15	Peters NSW Open Sydney (H)	**Sabatini** Davenport	**6-3 6-4**	**Davenport/Novotna** Fendick/M Fernandez	**7-5 2-6 6-4**	$322,500
Jan 10 Jan 15	Tasmanian Open Hobart (H)	**Meskhi** Fang	**6-2 6-3**	**Nagatsuka/Sugiyama** Bollegraf/Neiland	**2-6 6-4 6-2**	$107,500
Jan 16 Jan 29	**Australian Open** Melbourne (HO)	**Pierce** Sanchez Vicario	**6-3 6-2**	**Novotna/Sanchez Vicario** G Fernandez/Zvereva	**6-3 6-7 6-4**	$2,738,000
Jan 30 Feb 5	Amway Classic Auckland (H)	**Bradtke** Helgeson/Nielsen	**3-6 6-2 6-1**	**Hetherington/E Reinach** Golarsa/Vis	**7-6 6-2**	$107,500
Jan 31 Feb 5	Toray Pan Pacific Op. Tokyo (H)	**Date** Davenport	**6-1 6-2**	**G Fernandez/Zvereva** Davenport/Stubbs	**6-0 6-3**	$806,250
Feb 6 Feb 13	Ameritech Cup Chicago (I)	**Mag. Maleeva** Raymond	**7-5 7-6**	**Sabatini/Schultz** Whitlinger-Jones/WerdelWitmeyer	**5-7 7-6 6-4**	$430,000
Feb 13 Feb 19	IGA Tennis Classic Oklahoma, US	**Schultz** Likhovtseva	**6-1 6-2**	**Arendt/Golarsa** K Adams/Schultz	**6-4 6-3**	$161,250
Feb 14 Feb 19	Open Gaz de France Paris (I)	**Graf** Pierce	**6-2 6-2**	**McGrath/Neiland** Bollegraf/Stubbs	**6-4 6-1**	$430,000
Feb 20 Feb 26	EA-Generali Linz, Austria	**Novotna** Rittner	**6-7 6-3 6-4**	**McGrath/Tauziat** Majoli/Schwarz-Ritter	**6-1 6-2**	$161,250

Date	Tournament	Winner	Score	Doubles Winner	Score	Prize
Feb 27 Mar 5	State Farm Evert Cup Indian Wells (H)	**M Fernandez** Zvereva	6-4 6-3	Davenport/Raymond Neiland/Sanchez Vicario	2-6 6-4 6-3	$430,000
Feb 27 Mar 5	Puerto Rico Open San Juan, PR	**Kruger** Nagatsuka	7-6 6-3	Kschwendt/Simpson Golarsa/Harvey-Wild	6-2 0-6 6-4	$161,250
Mar 6 Mar 12	Delray Beach Champs Florida, US	**Graf** Martinez	6-2 6-4	M Fernandez/Novotna McNeil/Neiland	6-4 6-0	$430,000
Mar 17 Mar 26	The Lipton Champs Key Biscayne, Fla	**Graf** Date	6-1 6-4	Novotna/Sanchez Vicario G Fernandez/Zvereva	7-5 2-6 6-3	$1,550,000
Mar 27 Apr 2	Family Circle Cup Hilton Head Isl (Cl)	**Martinez** Mag. Maleeva	6-1 6-1	Arendt/Bollegraf G Fernandez/Zvereva	0-6 6-3 6-4	$806,250
Apr 3 Apr 9	Bausch & Lomb Ch. Amelia Island (Cl)	**Martinez** Sabatini	6-1 6-4	Coetzer/Gorrochategui Arendt/Bollegraf	6-2 3-6 6-2	$430,000
Apr 10 Apr 16	Houston Champs Texas, US	**Graf** Carlsson	6-1 6-1	Arendt/Bollegraf Probst/Simpson	6-4 6-2	$430,000
Apr 10 Apr 16	Japan Open Ariake Forest Park	**Frazier** Date	7-6 7-5	Saeki/Yoshida Nagatsuka/Sugiyama	6-7 6-4 7-6	$161,250
Apr 24 Apr 30	Ford Spanish Chps Barcelona (Cl)	**Sanchez Vic.** Majoli	5-7 6-0 6-2	Neiland/Sanchez Vicario de Swardt/Majoli	7-5 4-6 7-5	$430,000
Apr 24 Apr 30	Croatian Open Zagreb	**Appelmans** Meier	6-4 6-3	Paz/Simpson Golarsa/Spirlea	7-5 6-2	$161,250
May 1 May 7	Citizen Cup Hamburg (Cl)	**Martinez** Hingis	6-1 6-0	G Fernandez/Hingis Martinez/Tarabini	6-2 6-3	$430,000
May 8 May 14	Italian Open Rome	**Martinez** Sanchez Vicario	6-3 6-1	G Fernandez/Zvereva Martinez/Tarabini	3-6 7-6 6-4	$806,250
May 8 May 14	Prague Open Prague (CO)	**Halard** Richterova	6-4 6-4	Harvey-Wild/Rubin Lindstrom/Strandlund	6-7 6-3 6-2	$107,500
May 15 May 21	German Open Berlin	**Sanchez Vic.** Mag. Maleeva	6-4 6-1	Coetzer/Gorrochategui Neiland/Sabatini	4-6 7-6 6-2	$806,250
May 15 May 21	British Clay Court Bournemouth (CO)	**Richterova** Hy-Boulais	6-7 6-4 6-3	de Swardt/Dragomir Guse/Hy-Boulais	6-3 7-5	$107,500
May 22 May 28	Strasbourg Inter'nal Strasbourg (Cl)	**Davenport** Date	3-6 6-1 6-2	Davenport/M Fernandez Appelmans/Oremans	6-2 6-3	$161,250
May 24 May 27	World Doubles Cup Edinburgh			McGrath/Neiland Bollegraf/Stubbs	6-2 7-6	$188,125
May 29 June 11	**French Open** Paris (CO)	**Graf** Sanchez Vicario	7-5 4-6 6-0	G Fernandez/Zvereva Novotna/Sanchez Vicario	6-7 6-4 7-5	$3,963,100
June 12 June 18	DFS Classic Birmingham (GO)	**Garrison Jack.** McNeil	6-3 6-3	Bollegraf/Stubbs Bradtke/Radford	3-6 6-4 6-4	$161,250
June 19 June 25	Direct Line Chps Eastbourne (GO)	**Tauziat** Rubin	3-6 6-0 7-5	Novotna/Sanchez Vicario G Fernandez/Zvereva	0-6 6-3 6-4	$430,000
June 26 July 9	**The Championships** Wimbledon(GO)	**Graf** Sanchez Vicario	4-6 6-1 7-5	Novotna/Sanchez Vicario G Fernandez/Zvereva	5-7 7-5 6-4	$3,044,890
July 10 July 16	Torneo International Palermo, Sicily	**Spirlea** Hack	7-6 6-2	Bobkova/Langrova Schwarz-Ritter/Studenikova	6-4 6-1	$107,500

July 24 July 30	Styrian Open Styria, Austria	**Wiesner** Dragomir	7-6 6-3	Farina/Temesvari Fusai/Probst	6-2 6-2	$107,500
Jul 31 Aug 6	Toshibia Classic San Diego	**Martinez** Raymond	6-2 6-0	G Fernandez/Zvereva Dechaume-Balleret/Testud	6-2 6-1	$430,000
Aug 7 Aug 13	Acura Classic Manhattan Bch, Cal.	**Martinez** Rubin	4-6 6-1 6-3	G Fernandez/Zvereva Neiland/Sabatini	7-5 6-7 7-5	$430,000
Aug 15 Aug 21	Du Maurier Open Montreal	**Seles** Coetzer	6-0 6-1	Sabatini/Schultz-McCarthy 4-6 6-0 6-3 Hingis/Majoli		$806,250
Aug 28 Sep 10	**US Open** Flushing Meadow	**Graf** Seles	7-6 0-6 6-3	G Fernandez/Zvereva Schultz-McCarty/Stubbs	6-4 7-6	$4,900,000
Sep 11 Sep 17	Warsaw Cup Warsaw	**Paulus** Fusai	7-6 4-6 6-1	Cecchini/Garrone Nagyova/Szabova	5-7 6-2 6-3	$161,250
Sep 11 Sep 17	TVA Cup Nagoya, Japan	**Wild** Kleinova	6-4 6-2	Guse/Radford Park/Hiraki	6-4 6-4	$107,500
Sep 18 Sep 24	Nichirei International Tokyo	**Pierce** Sanchez Vicario	6-3 6-3	Davenport/M Fernandez Coetzer/Wild	6-3 6-2	$430,000
Sep 18 Sep 24	Moscow Open Moscow	**Mag Maleeva** Makarova	6-4 6-2	McGrath/Neiland Kournikova/Olsza	6-1 6-0	$161,250
Sep 25 Oct 1	Sparkassen Cup Leipzig, Germany	**Huber** Mag Maleeva	Walkover	McGrath/Neiland Schultz-McCarthy/Vis	6-4 6-4	$430,000
Sep 25 Oct 1	Nokia Open Beijing	**Wild** Wang	7-5 6-2	Porwik/Wild Wang/Rottier	6-1 6-0	$107,500

Prize Money
Year to Date - Jan 1 to Oct 10
in US dollars

1	Steffi Graf	GER	1,888,050		26	Zina Garrison-Jackson	USA	204,970
2	Arantxa Sanchez Vicario	ESP	1,326,256		27	Nicole Arendt	USA	181,026
3	Conchita Martinez	ESP	1,171,318		28	Manon Bollegraf	NED	179,853
4	Natasha Zvereva	RUS	658,577		29	Naoko Sawamatsu	JPN	177,332
5	Jana Novotna	CZE	655,516		30	Helena Sukova	CZE	173,092
6	Mary Pierce	FRA	653,048		31	Martina Hingis	SUI	172,557
7	Gabriela Sabatini	ARG	574,108		32	Lori McNeil	USA	170,903
8	Kimiko Date	JPN	542,113		33	Sabine Appelmans	BEL	156,452
9	Gigi Fernandez	USA	495,773		34	Rennae Stubbs	AUS	153,495
10	Iva Majoli	CRO	398,480		35	Nicole Bradtke	AUS	150,162
11	Monica Seles	USA	397,010		36	Ines Gorrochategui	ARG	145,850
12	Lindsay Davenport	USA	386,092		37	Joannette Kruger	RSA	144,136
13	Brenda Schultz-McCarthy	USA	377,504		38	Kristie Boogert	NED	143,954
14	Magdalena Maleeva	BUL	361,368		39	Julie Halard-Decugis	FRA	140,092
15	Mary Joe Fernandez	USA	352,042		40	Yayuk Basuki	INA	136,960
16	Anke Huber	GER	318,849		41	Judith Wiesner	AUT	135,075
17	Chanda Rubin	USA	316,597		42	Kyoko Nagatsuka	JPN	132,201
18	Larisa Neiland	UKR	311,825		43	Asa Carlsson	SWE	128,105
19	Nathalie Tauziat	FRA	246,726		44	Linda Wild	USA	125,586
20	Amanda Coetzer	RSA	246,586		45	Miriam Oremans	NED	122,751
21	Irina Spirlea	ROM	228,132		46	Angelica Gavaldon	USA	122,467
22	Lisa Raymond	USA	214,352		47	Mariann De Swardt	RSA	122,336
23	Meredith McGrath	USA	213,825		48	Sandrine Testud	FRA	122,013
24	Amy Frazier	USA	213,687		49	Patty Fendick	USA	117,944
25	Mariann Werdel Witmeyer	USA	208,140		50	Yone Kamio	JPN	117,701

Wimbledon Champions

Men's singles

1877 Spencer Gore GBR
1878 Frank Hadow GBR
1879 Rev. John Hartley GBR
1880 Rev. John Hartley GBR
1881 William Renshaw GBR
1882 William Renshaw GBR
1883 William Renshaw GBR
1884 William Renshaw GBR
1885 William Renshaw GBR
1886 William Renshaw GBR
1887 Herbert Lawford GBR
1888 Ernest Renshaw GBR
1889 William Renshaw GBR
1890 Willoughby Hamilton GBR
1891 Wilfred Baddeley GBR
1892 Wilfred Baddeley GBR
1893 Joshua Pim GBR
1894 Joshua Pim GBR
1895 Wilfred Baddeley GBR
1896 Harold Mahoney GBR
1897 Reginald Doherty GBR
1898 Reginald Doherty GBR
1899 Reginald Doherty GBR
1900 Reginald Doherty GBR
1901 Arthur Gore GBR
1902 Lawrence Doherty GBR
1903 Lawrence Doherty GBR
1904 Lawrence Doherty GBR
1905 Lawrence Doherty GBR.
1906 Lawrence Doherty GBR
1907 Norman Brookes AUS
1908 Arthur Gore GBR
1909 Arthur Gore GBR
1910 Tony Wilding NZL
1911 Tony Wilding NZL
1912 Tony Wilding NZL
1913 Tony Wilding NZL
1914 Norman Brookes AUS
1919 Gerald Patterson AUS
1920 Bill Tilden USA
1921 Bill Tilden USA
1922 Gerald Patterson AUS
1923 William Johnston USA
1924 Jean Borotra FRA
1925 Rene Lacoste FRA
1926 Jean Borotra FRA
1927 Henri Cochet FRA
1928 Rene Lacoste FRA
1929 Henri Cochet FRA
1930 Bill Tilden USA
1931 Sidney Wood USA
1932 Ellsworth Vines USA
1933 Jack Crawford AUS
1934 Fred Perry GBR
1935 Fred Perry GBR
1936 Fred Perry GBR
1937 Donald Budge USA
1938 Donald Budge USA
1939 Bobby Riggs USA
1946 Yvon Petra FRA

1947 Jack Kramer USA
1948 Bob Falkenburg USA
1949 Ted Schroeder USA
1950 Budge Patty USA
1951 Dick Savitt USA
1952 Frank Sedgman AUS
1953 Vic Seixas USA
1954 Jaroslav Drobny EGY
1955 Tony Trabert USA
1956 Lew Hoad AUS
1957 Lew Hoad AUS
1958 Ashley Cooper AUS
1959 Alex Olmedo USA
1960 Neale FRAser AUS
1961 Rod Laver AUS
1962 Rod Laver AUS
1963 Chuck McKinley USA
1964 Roy Emerson AUS
1965 Roy Emerson AUS
1966 Manuel Santana ESP
1967 John Newcombe AUS
1968 Rod Laver AUS
1969 Rod Laver AUS
1970 John Newcombe AUS
1971 John Newcombe AUS
1972 Stan Smith USA
1973 Jan Kodes TCH
1974 Jimmy Connors USA
1975 Arthur Ashe USA
1976 Bjorn Borg SWE
1977 Bjorn Borg SWE
1978 Bjorn Borg SWE
1979 Bjorn Borg SWE
1980 Bjorn Borg SWE
1981 John McEnroe USA
1982 Jimmy Connors USA
1983 John McEnroe USA
1984 John McEnroe USA
1985 Boris Becker FRG
1986 Boris Becker FRG
1987 Pat Cash AUS
1988 Stefan Edberg SWE
1989 Boris Becker FRG
1990 Stefan Edberg SWE
1991 Michael Stich GER
1992 Andre Agassi USA
1993 Pete Sampras USA
1994 Pete Sampras USA
1995 Pete Sampras USA

Women's Singles

1884 Maud Watson GBR
1885 Maud Watson GBR
1886 Blanche Bingley GBR
1887 Lottie Dod GBR
1888 Lottie Dod GBR
1889 Blanche Hillyard GBR
1890 Helene Rice GBR
1891 Lottie Dod GBR
1892 Lottie Dod GBR
1893 Lottie Dod GBR
1894 Blanche Hillyard GBR

1895 Charlotte Cooper GBR
1896 Charlotte Cooper GBR
1897 Blanche Hillyard GBR
1898 Charlotte Cooper GBR
1899 Blanche Hillyard GBR
1900 Blanche Hillyard GBR
1901 Charlotte Sterry GBR
1902 Muriel Robb GBR
1903 Dorothea Douglass GBR
1904 Dorothea Douglass GBR
1905 May Sutton USA
1906 Dorothea Douglass GBR
1907 May Sutton USA
1908 Charlotte Sterry GBR
1909 Dora Boothby GBR
1910 Dorothea L Chambers GBR
1911 D Lambert Chambers GBR
1912 Ethel Larcombe GBR
1913 D Lambert Chambers GBR
1914 D Lambert Chambers GBR
1919 Suzanne Lenglen FRA
1920 Suzanne Lenglen FRA
1921 Suzanne Lenglen FRA
1922 Suzanne Lenglen FRA
1923 Suzanne Lenglen FRA
1924 Kathleen McKane GBR
1925 Suzanne Lenglen FRA
1926 Kathleen Godfree GBR
1927 Helen Wills USA
1928 Helen Wills USA
1929 Helen Wills USA
1930 Helen Moody USA
1931 Cilly Aussem GER
1932 Helen Moody USA
1933 Helen Moody USA
1934 Dorothy Round GBR
1935 Helen Moody USA
1936 Helen Jacobs USA
1937 Dorothy Round GBR
1938 Helen Moody USA
1939 Alice Marble USA
1946 Pauline Betz USA
1947 Margaret Osborne USA
1948 Louise Brough USA
1949 Louise Brough USA
1950 Louise Brough USA
1951 Doris Hart USA
1952 Maureen Connolly USA
1953 Maureen Connolly USA
1954 Maureen Connolly USA
1955 Louise Brough USA
1956 Shirley Fry USA
1957 Althea Gibson USA
1958 Althea Gibson USA
1959 Maria Bueno BRA
1960 Maria Bueno BRA
1961 Angela Mortimer GBR
1962 Karen Susman USA
1963 Margaret Smith AUS
1964 Maria Bueno BRA
1965 Margaret Smith AUS

Wimbledon Champions

1966 Billie Jean King USA	1976 Gottfried/Ramirez MEX/US	1986 Navratilova/Shriver USA
1967 Billie Jean King USA	1977 Case/Masters AUS	1987 K-Kilsch/Sukova FRG/TCH
1968 Billie Jean King USA	1978 Hewitt /McMillan RSA	1988 Graf FRG/Sabatini ARG
1969 Ann Jones GBR	1979 Fleming/McEnroe USA	1989 Novotna /Sukova TCH
1970 Margaret Court AUS	1980 McNamara/McNamee AUS	1990 Novotna /Sukova TCH
1971 Evonne Goolagong AUS	1981 Fleming/McEnroe USA	1991 Savchenko/Zvereva URS
1972 Billie Jean King USA	1982 McNamara/McNamee AUS	1992 Fernandez/Zvereva US/BLR
1973 Billie Jean King USA	1983 Fleming/McEnroe USA	1993 Fernandez/Zvereva US/BLR
1974 Chris Evert USA	1984 Fleming/McEnroe USA	1994 Fernandez/Zvereva US/BLR
1975 Billy Jean King USA	1985 Gunthardt/Taróczy SUI/HUN	
1976 Chris Evert USA	1986 Nystrom/Wilander SWE	Mixed doubles *since 1946*
1977 Virginia Wade GBR	1987 Flach/Seguso USA	1946 Brown/Brough USA
1978 Martina Navratilova TCH	1988 Flach/Seguso USA	1947 Bromwich/Brough AUS/US
1979 Martina Navratilova TCH	1989 Fitzgerald/Jarryd AUS/SWE	1948 Bromwich/Brough AUS/US
1980 Evonne Cawley AUS	1990 Leach/Pugh USA	1949 Sturgess/Summers RSA
1981 Chris Evert Lloyd USA	1991 Fitzgerald AUS/Jarryd SWE	1950 Sturgess/Brough RSA/USA
1982 Martina Navratilova USA	1992 McEnroe/Stich USA/GER	1951 Sedgman/Hart AUS/USA
1983 Martina Navratilova USA	1993 Woodbridge/W'dforde AUS	1952 Sedgman/Hart AUS/USA
1984 Martina Navratilova USA	1994 Woodbridge/W'dforde AUS	1953 Seixas/Hart USA
1985 Martina Navratilova USA		1954 Seixas/Hart USA
1986 Martina Navratilova USA	Women's doubles *since 1946*	1955 Seixas/Hart USA
1987 Martina Navratilova USA	1946 Brough/Osborne USA	1956 Seixas/Fry USA
1988 Steffi Graf FRG	1947 Hart/Todd USA	1957 Rose/Hard AUS/USA
1989 Steffi Graf FRG	1948 Brough/Du Pont USA	1958 Howe/Coghlan AUS
1990 Martina Navratilova USA	1949 Brough/Du Pont USA	1959 Laver/Hard AUS/USA
1991 Steffi Graf GER	1950 Brough/Du Pont USA	1960 Laver/Hard AUS/USA
1992 Steffi Graf GER	1951 Fry/Hart USA	1961 Stolle/Turner AUS
1993 Steffi Graf GER	1952 Fry/Hart USA	1962 Fraser/Du Pont AUS/USA
1994 Conchita Martinez ESP	1953 Fry/Hart USA	1963 Fletcher/Smith AUS
1995 Steffi Graf GER	1954 Brough/Du Pont USA	1964 Stolle/Turner AUS
	1955 Mortimer/Shilcock GBR	1965 Fletcher/Smith AUS
Men's doubles *since 1946*	1956 Buxton/Gibson GBR/USA	1966 Fletcher/Smith AUS
1946 Brown/Kramer USA	1957 Gibson/Hard USA	1967 Davidson/King AUS/USA
1947 Falkenburg/Kramer USA	1958 Bueno/Gibson BRA/USA	1968 Fletcher/Court AUS
1948 Bromwich/Sedgman AUS	1959 Arth/Hard USA	1969 Stolle/ Jones AUS/GBR
1949 Gonzales/Parker USA	1960 Bueno/Hard BRA/USA	1970 Nastase/Casals ROM/USA
1950 Bromwich/Quist AUS	1961 Hantze/Moffitt USA	1971 Davidson/King AUS/USA
1951 McGregor/Sedgman AUS	1962 Moffit/Susman USA	1972 Nastase/Casals ROM/USA
1952 McGregor/Sedgman AUS	1963 Bueno/Hard BRA/USA	1973 Davidson/King AUS/USA
1953 Hoad/Rosewall AUS	1964 Smith/Turner AUS	1975 Riessen/Court US/AUS
1954 Hartwig/Rose AUS	1965 Bueno/Mofftt BRA/USA	1976 Roche/Durr AUS/FRA
1955 Hartwig/Hoad AUS	1966 Bueno/Richey BRA/USA	1977 Hewitt/Stevens RSA
1956 Hoad/Rosewall AUS	1967 Casals/King USA	1978 McMillan/Stove RSA/NED
1957 Mulloy/Patty USA	1968 Casals/King USA	1979 Hewitt/Stevens RSA
1958 Davidson/Schmidt SWE	1969 Court/Tegart AUS	1980 Austin/Austin USA
1959 Emerson/Fraser AUS	1970 Casals/King USA	1981 McMillan/Stove RSA/NED
1960 Osuna/Ralston MEX/USA	1971 Casals/King USA	1982 Curren/Smith RSA/USA
1961 Emerson/Fraser AUS	1972 King/Stove USA/NED	1983 Lloyd/Turnbull GBR/AUS
1962 Hewitt/Stolle RSA/AUS	1973 Casals/King USA	1984 Lloyd/Turnbull GBR/AUS
1963 Osuna/Palafox MEX	1974 Goolagong/Michel AUS/US	1985 McNamee/N'lova AUS/US
1964 Hewitt/Stolle RSA/AUS	1975 Kiyomura/Sawamatsu	1986 Flach/Jordan USA
1965 Newcombe/Roche AUS	USA/JPN	1987 Bates/Durie GBR
1966 Fletcher/Newcombe AUS	1976 Evert/Navratilova US/TCH	1988 Stewart/Garrison USA
1967 Hewitt /McMillan RSA	1977 Cawley/Russell AUS/USA	1989 Pugh USA/Novotna TCH
1968 Newcombe/Roche AUS	1978 Reid/Turnbull AUS	1990 Leach/Garrison USA
1969 Newcombe/Roche AUS	1979 King/Navratilova USA/TCH	1991 Fitzgerald/Smylie AUS
1970 Newcombe/Roche AUS	1980 Jordan/Smith USA	1992 Suk/Savchenko CZE/LAT
1971 Emerson/Laver AUS	1981 Navratilova /Shriver USA	1993 Woodforde/N'lova AUS/US
1972 Hewitt /McMillan RSA	1982 Navratilova /Shriver USA	1994 W'dbridge/Sukova AUS/CZ
1973 Connors/Nastase US/ROM	1983 Navratilova /Shriver USA	
1974 Newcombe/Roche AUS	1984 Navratilova /Shriver USA	
1975 Gerulaitis/Mayer USA	1985 Jordan/Smylie USA/AUS	

US & French Open Champions

US OPEN - Men's singles

Year	Champion	Country
1930	John Doeg	USA
1931	Ellsworth Vines	USA
1932	Ellsworth Vines	USA
1933	Fred Perry	GBR
1934	Fred Perry	GBR
1935	Wilmer Allison	USA
1936	Fred Perry	GBR
1937	Donald Budge	USA
1938	Donald Budge	USA
1939	Bobby Riggs	USA
1940	Donald McNeil	USA
1941	Bobby Riggs	USA
1942	Ted Schroeder	USA
1943	Joseph Hunt	USA
1944	Frank Parker	USA
1945	Frank Parker	USA
1946	Jack Kramer	USA
1947	Jack Kramer	USA
1948	Ricardo Gonzales	USA
1949	Ricardo Gonzales	USA
1950	Arthur Larsen	USA
1951	Frank Sedgman	USA
1952	Frank Sedgman	USA
1953	Tony Trabert	USA
1954	Vic Seixas	USA
1955	Tony Trabert	USA
1956	Ken Rosewall	AUS
1957	Malcolm Anderson	AUS
1958	Ashley Cooper	AUS
1959	Neale Fraser	AUS
1960	Neale Fraser	AUS
1961	Roy Emerson	AUS
1962	Rod Laver	AUS
1963	Raphael Osuna	MEX
1964	Roy Emerson	AUS
1965	Manuel Santana	ESP
1966	Fred Stolle	AUS
1967	John Newcombe	AUS
1968	Arthur Ashe	USA
Open	Arthur Ashe	USA
1969	Stan Smith	USA
Open	Rod Laver	AUS
1970	Ken Rosewall	AUS
1971	Stan Smith	USA
1972	Ilie Nastase	ROM
1973	John Newcombe	AUS
1974	Jimmy Connors	USA
1975	Manuel Orantes	ESP
1976	Jimmy Connors	USA
1977	Guillermo Vilas	ARG
1978	Jimmy Connors	USA
1979	John McEnroe	USA
1980	John McEnroe	USA
1981	John McEnroe	USA
1982	Jimmy Connors	USA
1983	Jimmy Connors	USA
1984	John McEnroe	USA
1985	Ivan Lendl	TCH
1986	Ivan Lendl	TCH
1987	Ivan Lendl	TCH
1988	Mats Wilander	SWE
1989	Boris Becker	FRG
1990	Pete Sampras	USA
1991	Stefan Edberg	SWE
1992	Stefan Edberg	SWE
1993	Pete Sampras	USA
1994	Andre Agassi	USA
1995	Pete Sampras	USA

Women's singles

Year	Champion	Country
1930	Betty Nuthall	GBR
1931	Helen Moody	USA
1932	Helen Jacobs	USA
1933	Helen Jacobs	USA
1934	Helen Jacobs	USA
1935	Helen Jacobs	USA
1936	Alice Marble	USA
1937	Anita Lizana	CHI
1938	Alice Marble	USA
1939	Alice Marble	USA
1940	Alice Marble	USA
1941	Sarah Cooke	USA
1942	Pauline Betz	USA
1943	Pauline Betz	USA
1944	Pauline Betz	USA
1945	Sarah Cooke	USA
1946	Pauline Betz	USA
1947	Louise Brough	USA
1948	Margaret Du Pont	USA
1949	Margaret Du Pont	USA
1950	Margaret Du Pont	USA
1951	Maureen Connolly	USA
1952	Maureen Connolly	USA
1953	Maureen Connolly	USA
1954	Doris Hart	USA
1955	Doris Hart	USA
1956	Shirley Fry	USA
1957	Althea Gibson	USA
1958	Althea Gibson	USA
1959	Maria Bueno	BRA
1960	Darlene Hard	USA
1961	Darlene Hard	USA
1962	Margaret Smith	AUS
1963	Maria Bueno	BRA
1964	Maria Bueno	BRA
1965	Margaret Smith	AUS
1966	Maria Bueno	BRA
1967	Billie Jean King	USA
1968	Margaret Court	AUS
Open	Virginia Wade	GBR
1969	Margaret Court	AUS
Open	Margaret Court	AUS
1970	Margaret Court	AUS
1971	Billie Jean King	USA
1972	Billie Jean King	USA
1973	Margaret Court	AUS
1974	Billie Jean King	USA
1975	Chris Evert	USA
1976	Chris Evert	USA
1977	Chris Evert	USA
1978	Chris Evert	USA
1979	Tracy Austin	USA
1980	Chris Evert Lloyd	USA
1981	Tracy Austin	USA
1982	Chris Evert Lloyd	USA
1983	Martina Navratilova	USA
1983	Martina Navratilova	USA
1985	Hanna Mandlikova	TCH
1986	Martina Navratilova	USA
1987	Martina Navratilova	USA
1988	Steffi Graf	FRG
1989	Steffi Graf	FRG
1990	Gabriela Sabatini	ARG
1991	Monica Seles	YUG
1992	Monica Seles	YUG
1993	Steffi Graf	GER
1994	Aranxta Sanchez	ESP
1995	Steffi Graf	GER

FRENCH OPEN - Men's singles

Year	Champion	Country
1930	Henri Cochet	FRA
1931	Jean Borotra	FRA
1932	Henri Cochet	FRA
1933	Jack Crawford	AUS
1934	Gottfried Von Cramm	GER
1935	Fred Perry	GBR
1936	Gottfried Von Cramm	GER
1937	Henner Henkel	GER
1938	Donald Budge	USA
1939	Donald McNeill	USA
1946	Marcel Bernard	FRA
1947	Jozsef Asboth	HUN
1948	Frank Parker	USA
1949	Frank Parker	USA
1950	Budge Patty	USA
1951	Jaroslav Drobny	EGY
1952	Jaroslav Drobny	EGY
1953	Ken Rosewall	AUS
1954	Tony Trabert	USA
1955	Tony Trabert	USA
1956	Lew Hoad	AUS
1957	Sven Davidson	SWE
1958	Mervyn Rose	AUS
1959	Nicola Pietrangeli	ITA
1960	Nicola Pietrangeli	ITA
1961	Manuel Santana	ESP
1962	Rod Laver	AUS
1963	Roy Emerson	AUS
1964	Manuel Santana	ESP
1965	Fred Stolle	AUS
1966	Tony Roche	AUS
1967	Roy Emerson	AUS
1968	Ken Rosewall	AUS
1969	Rod Laver	AUS
1970	Jan Kodes	TCH
1971	Jan Kodes	TCH
1972	Andres Gimeno	ESP
1973	Ilie Nastase	ROM
1974	Bjorn Borg	SWE
1975	Bjorn Borg	SWE
1976	Adriano Panatta	ITA
1977	Guillermo Vilas	ARG

French & Australian Open Champions

1978	Bjorn Borg SWE
1979	Bjorn Borg SWE
1980	Bjorn Borg SWE
1981	Bjorn Borg SWE
1982	Mats Wilander SWE
1983	Yannick Noah FRA
1984	Ivan Lendl TCH
1985	Mats Wilander SWE
1986	Ivan Lendl TCH
1987	Ivan Lendl TCH
1988	Mats Wilander SWE
1989	Michael Chang USA
1990	Andres Gomez ECU
1991	Jim Courier USA
1992	Jim Courier USA
1993	Sergi Bruguera ESP
1994	Sergi Bruguera ESP
1995	Thomas Muster AUT

Women's singles

1930	Helen Moody USA
1931	Cilly Aussem GER
1932	Helen Moody USA
1933	Margaret Scriven GBR
1934	Margaret Scriven GBR
1935	Hilde Sperling GER
1936	Hilde Sperling GER
1937	Hilde Sperling GER
1938	Simone Mathieu FRA
1939	Simone Mathieu FRA
1946	Margaret Osborne USA
1947	Pat Todd USA
1948	Nelly Landry FRA
1949	Margaret Du Pont USA
1950	Doris Hart USA
1951	Shirley Fry USA
1952	Doris Hart USA
1953	Maureen Connolly USA
1954	Maureen Connolly USA
1955	Angela Mortimer GBR
1956	Althea Gibson USA
1957	Shirley Bloomer GBR
1958	Zsuzsi Kormoczy HUN
1959	Christine Truman GBR
1960	Darlene Hard USA
1961	Ann Haydon GBR
1962	Margaret Smith AUS
1963	Lesley Turner AUS
1964	Margaret Smith AUS
1965	Lesley Turner AUS
1966	Ann Jones GBR
1967	Françoise Durr FRA
1968	Nancy Richey USA
1969	Margaret Court AUS
1970	Margaret Court AUS
1971	Evonne Goolagong AUS
1972	Billie Jean King USA
1973	Margaret Court AUS
1974	Chris Evert USA
1975	Chris Evert USA
1976	Sue Barker GBR
1977	Mimi Jausovec YUG

1978	Virginia Ruzici ROM
1979	Chris Evert Lloyd USA
1980	Chris Evert Lloyd USA
1981	Hana Mandlikova TCH
1982	Martina Navratilova USA
1983	Chris Evert Lloyd USA
1984	Martina Navratilova USA
1985	Chris Evert Lloyd USA
1986	Chris Evert Lloyd USA
1987	Steffi Graf FRG
1988	Steffi Graf FRG
1989	Arantxa Sanchez ESP
1990	Monica Seles YUG
1991	Monica Seles YUG
1992	Monica Seles YUG
1993	Steffi Graf GER
1994	Aranxta Sanchez ESP
1995	Steffi Graf GER

AUSTRALIAN OPEN

Men's singles

1946	John Bromwich AUS
1947	Dinny Pails AUS
1948	Adrian Quist AUS
1949	Frank Sedgman AUS
1950	Frank Sedgman AUS
1951	Dick Savitt USA
1952	Ken McGregor AUS
1953	Ken Rosewall AUS
1954	Mervyn Rose AUS
1955	Ken Rosewall AUS
1956	Lew Hoad AUS
1957	Ashley Cooper AUS
1958	Ashley Cooper AUS
1959	Alex Olmedo USA
1960	Rod Laver AUS
1961	Roy Emerson AUS
1962	Rod Laver AUS
1963	Roy Emerson AUS
1964	Roy Emerson AUS
1965	Roy Emerson AUS
1966	Roy Emerson AUS
1967	Roy Emerson AUS
1968	Bill Bowrey AUS
1969	Rod Laver AUS
1970	Arthur Ashe USA
1971	Ken Rosewall AUS
1972	Ken Rosewall AUS
1973	John Newcombe AUS
1974	Jimmy Connors USA
1975	John Newcombe AUS
1976	Mark Edmondson AUS
1977	Roscoe Tanner USA
1977	Vitas Gerulaitis USA
1978	Guillermo Vilas ARG
1979	Guillermo Vilas ARG
1980	Brian Teacher USA
1981	Johan Kriek RSA
1982	Johan Kriek RSA
1983	Mats Wilander SWE
1984	Mats Wilander SWE
1985	Stefan Edberg SWE

1987	Stefan Edberg SWE
1988	Mats Wilander SWE
1989	Ivan Lendl TCH
1990	Ivan Lendl TCH
1991	Boris Becker GER
1992	Jim Courier USA
1993	Jim Courier USA
1994	Pete Sampras USA
1995	Andre Agassi USA

Women's singles

1946	Nancye Bolton AUS
1947	Nancye Bolton AUS
1948	Nancye Bolton AUS
1949	Doris Hart USA
1950	Louise Brough USA
1951	Nancye Bolton AUS
1952	Thelma Long AUS
1953	Maureen Connolly USA
1954	Thelma Long AUS
1955	Beryl Penrose AUS
1956	Mary Carter AUS
1957	Shirley Fry USA
1958	Angela Mortimer GBR
1959	Mary Reitano AUS
1960	Margaret Smith AUS
1961	Margaret Smith AUS
1962	Margaret Smith AUS
1963	Margaret Smith AUS
1964	Margaret Smith AUS
1965	Margaret Smith AUS
1966	Margaret Smith AUS
1967	Nancy Richey USA
1968	Billie Jean King USA
1969	Margaret Court AUS
1970	Margaret Court AUS
1971	Margaret Court AUS
1972	Virginia Wade GBR
1973	Margaret Court AUS
1974	Evonne Goolagong AUS
1975	Evonne Goolagong AUS
1976	Evonne Cawley AUS
1977	Kerry Reid AUS
1977	Evonne Cawley AUS
1978	Christine O'Neill AUS
1979	Barbara Jordan USA
1980	Hana Mandlikova TCH
1981	Martina Navratilova USA
1982	Chris Evert Lloyd USA
1983	Martina Navratilova USA
1984	Chris Evert Lloyd USA
1985	Martina Navratilova USA
1987	Hana Mandlikova TCH
1988	Steffi Graf FRG
1989	Steffi Graf FRG
1990	Steffi Graf FRG
1991	Monica Seles YUG
1992	Monica Seles YUG
1993	Monica Seles YUG
1994	Steffi Graf GER
1995	Mary Pierce FRA

Tenpin Bowling ▬▬▬▬

FIQ World Championships
Reno, USA   July 9-16

MEN

Singles	Ctry	Pins	Ave
1 **Marc Doi**	**CAN**	**1364**	**227**
2 Bill Rowe	CAN	1356	226
3 Chen-Min Yang	TPE	1347	224
54 Ron Oldfield	ENG	1238	206

Doubles	Ctry	Pins	Ave
1 **Leandersson/Jansson**	**SWE**	**2702**	**224**
2 Stewart/Frawley	AUS	2627	218
3 De Faria/Carreyo	VEN	2622	218
17 Buck/Delaney	ENG	2512	209
27 Hills/Oldfield	ENG	2471	205

Trios		Ctry	Pins	
1 **Gruen/Thienpondt/Sassen**		**NED**	**3954**	**219**
2 Van Baest/Krull/Den Bosch		NED	3889	216
3 Leandersson/Johansson/Jansson		SWE	3851	213
23 Delaney/Oldfield/G Buck		GBR	3628	201
24 Hood/Hills/C Buck		GBR	3612	200

Team	Pins
1 **Netherlands**	**6282**
2 Sweden	6257
3 France	6177
11 England	6009
46 Northern Ireland	5637
47 Wales	5602
51 Scotland	5541

All-Events			
1 **M Sassen**	**NED**	**5496**	**229**

Grand masters			
1 **Chen-Min Yankg**	**TPE**	**3476**	**211**
2 Chris Barnes	USA	3447	210
3 Raymond Jansson	SWE	3445	210

WOMEN

Singles	Ctry	Pins	Ave
1 **Debby Ship**	**CAN**	**1318**	**219**
2 Elizabeth Johnson	USA	1295	215
3 Catharine Che	HKG	1288	214
10 Pauline Buck	ENG	1221	203
36 Kirsten Penny	ENG	1183	197
49 Gina Wardle	ENG	1168	194
53 C Pirie	SCO	1166	194

Doubles	Ctry	Pins	Ave
1 **Kitchatham/Kaewsuk**	**THA**	**2489**	**207**
2 Puhakko/Aalto	FIN	2450	204
3 Poh Leng/Yen Wah	SIN	2405	200
7 Penny/Burden	ENG	2366	197

Trios		Ctry	Pins	Ave
1 **Honeychurch/McLeish/Cassell**		**AUS**	**3626**	**201**
2 Zulkifli/Kwan/Chow		MAL	3606	200
3 Tseng/Tsai/Chou		TPE	3594	199
11 Penny/Burden/Buck		ENG	3508	192

Team	Pins
1 **Finland**	**5974**
2 Sweden	5914
3 France	5900
6 England	5835
25 Scotland	5468
37 Wales	4895

All-Events			
1 **Jaana Puhakka**	**FIN**	**4916**	**204**

Grand Masters			
1 **Celia Flores**	**MEX**	**3461**	**208**
2 Luz Adriana Leal	COL	3439	208
3 Asa Larsson	SWE	3419	207
5 Pauline Buck	ENG	3353	203
10 Gemma Burden	ENG	3251	198

BTBA UK Championships
May 14

Men	Pins	Hdcp	Ave
1 **Kevin Hills**	**1753**	**3558**	**219**
2 Mitch Gallant	1597	3378	199
3 Wayne Greenall	1635	3329	204
4 Graham Robson	1609	3294	201
5 Paul Delaney	1516	3243	189

Women	Pins	Hdcp	Ave
1 **Gemma Burden**	**1671**	**3545**	**208**
2 Nikki Harvery	1677	3388	209
3 Mel Isaac	1570	3219	196
4 Jo Harries	1579	3186	197
5 Lesley Martinkovic	1553	3165	194

National Championships
Rotherham   Mar 11-26

MEN

Singles	
1 **C Morris**	**724**
2 D Tovey	713
3 P Boyle	696

Doubles	
1 **Ellis/Langman**	**1291**
2 Joseph/Wood	1288
3 Gould/Cherrett	1271

Team	Pins
1 **Team Exmedia**	**3015**

WOMEN

Singles	
1 **K Michael**	**653**
2 L Woodham	649
3 H Watson	621

Doubles	
1 **Oakley/Howlett**	**1191**
2 Martinkovic/Molineux	1185
3 Walton/Michael	1183

Team	
1 **GT Pro Shops**	**2827**

Triathlon

World Olympic Distance Championships

Wellington, Nzl   Nov 27, 1994

Men

1	**Spencer Smith**	**GBR**	**1:51:04**
2	Brad Bevan	AUS	1:51:49
3	Ralf Eggert	GER	1:52:40

Women

1	**Emma Carney**	**AUS**	**2:03:18**
2	A Pederson	DEN	2:05:31
3	S Harrow	NZL	2:06:52

World Long Distance Championships

Nice, France   Sep 30

Men

1	**S Lessing**	**GBR**	**5:46:17**
2	L Van Lierde	BEL	5:48:24
3	P Reid	CAN	5:51:18

Women

1	**J Rose**	**NZL**	**6:28:06**
2	U Schafer	GER	6:39:58
3	I Estedt	GER	6:41:43

Men's Team

1	**France**	**17:40:37**
2	Belgium	15:50:50
3	Switzerland	17:55:40

Women's Team

1	**Germany**	**20:17:34**
2	France	20:33:44
3	USA	20:37:48

European Championships

Stockholm   July 30

Men

1	**R Müller**	**GER**	**1:46:24**
2	L Van Lierde	BEL	1:47:05
3	S Smith	GBR	1:47:28

Women

1	**I Mouthon-Michellys**	**FRA**	**1:59:33**
2	N Badmann	SUI	2:01.12
3	S Nielsen	DEN	2:02:22

Hawaii Iron Man

Kailua-Kona   Oct 8
Swim: 2.4 miles, Cycle: 112 miles, Run: 26.2 miles

Men

1	**M Allen**	**USA**	**8:20:34**
2	T Hellriegel	GER	8:22:59
3	R Müller	GER	8:25:23

Women

1	**K Smyers**	**USA**	**9:16:46**
2	I Mouthon-Michellys	FRA	9:29:13
3	F Keller	BRA	9:37:48

BUPA event

Bath   Sep 3

Men

1	**Simon Lessing**	**GBR**	**1:53:04**
2	Spencer Smith	GBR	1:54:22
3	Ralf Eggert	GER	1:57:45

Women

1	**Michellie Jones**	**AUS**	**2:08:29**
2	Loretta Sollars	GBR	2:16:08
3	Alison Hollington	GBR	2:19:01

British Championships

SPRINT
Market Bosworth   May 21

Men

1	**Steve Burton**	**54:54**
2	Tim Stewart	55:18
3	Colin Dixon	

Women

1	**Loretta Sollars**	**1:01:06**
2	Alison Hollington	1:02:48
3	Jessica Harrison (J)	1:03:14

OLYMPIC DISTANCE
Windsor   June 11

Men

1	**Spencer Smith**	**1:47:34**
2	Richard Allen	1:51:03
3	Steve Burton	1:52::35

Women

1	**Loretta Sollars**	**2:06:09**
2	Alison Hollington	2:08:34
3	Rachel Horn	2:09:39

MIDDLE DISTANCE
Ironbridge   July 15

Men

1	**Richard Hobson**	**4:14:32**
2	Ross Muir	4:27:07
3	Chris Meir	4:28:26

Women

1	**Annaleah Emmerson**	**4:54:15**
2	Alison Hollington	5:01:41
3	Shirley Yarde	5:22:10

RELAY
Aug 12

Men

1	**Total Fitness**	**3:03:24**
2	RN & RM	3:05:18
3	Loughborough	3:07:01

Women

1	**Total Fitness**	**3:38:55**
2	Barracuda	3:40:04
3	Southampton	3:40:43

Volleyball

National Leagues

MEN
Division 1

		P	W	L	SF	SA	Pts
1	Mizuno Lewisham	14	14	0	42	7	28
2	Newcastle Staffs	14	8	6	31	25	16
3	Wessex	14	8	6	31	26	16
4	Polonia Ealing	14	8	6	30	26	16
5	Camden Aquila	14	6	8	25	29	12
6	Reebok Liverpool City	14	5	9	21	30	10
7	Whitefield	14	4	10	20	34	8
8	Warwick Riga	14	3	11	15	38	6

Division 2

		P	W	L	SF	SA	Pts
1	KLEA Leeds	20	18	2	58	15	36
2	Shefield Wednesday	20	16	4	55	25	32
3	Solent	20	14	6	47	30	28
4	Man Utd Salford	20	11	9	44	35	22
5	Team Icarus Egham	20	11	9	43	42	22
6	Crofton Sports'house	20	11	9	40	36	22
7	Gateshead Armitage	20	10	10	40	37	20
8	Chester	20	10	10	37	37	20
9	Stockport	20	5	15	23	50	10
10	Sikh Temple (S'wick)	20	2	18	19	56	4
11	Essex Estonians	20	2	18	13	56	4

Knock-out Cup
Mizuno Malory Lewisham bt Wessex

WOMEN
Division 1

		P	W	L	SF	SA	Pts
1	London Malory	12	11	1	35	8	22
2	Britannia Music City	12	10	2	34	12	20
3	Sale	12	9	3	30	17	18
4	Ash. Guildford Spec.	12	6	6	24	22	12
5	KLEA Leeds	12	3	9	15	30	6
6	Wessex	12	3	9	11	32	6
7	Birmingham Ladies	12	0	12	8	36	0

Knock-out Cup
Sale bt Britannia Music City

European Women's Championships
Arnhem   Sep 30
Netherlands bt Croatia
15-7, 15-13, 15-2
Both teams qualified for the Olympic qualifier in Japan in November 1995

Beach Volleyball

GRAND PRIX FINAL STANDINGS
Men
1	Fairclough/Pursey	58.5
2	Dobell/Jones	54.5
3	Lucas/Roberts	30.5

Women
1	Cooper/Glover	62.5
2	Tuohey/Malone	50.5
3	Hamilton/Cowell	34.5

World Champions

	Men	Women
1949	Soviet Union	-
1952	Soviet Union	Soviet Union
1956	Czechoslovakia	Soviet Union
1960	Soviet Union	Soviet Union
1962	Soviet Union	Japan
1966	Czechoslovakia	Japan
1970	East Germany	Soviet Union
1974	Poland	Japan
1978	Soviet Union	Cuba
1982	Soviet Union	China
1986	USA	China
1990	Italy	Soviet Union
1994	Italy	Cuba

World Cup Winners

	Men	Women
1965	Soviet Union	-
1969	East Germany	-
1973	-	Soviet Union
1977	Soviet Union	Japan
1981	Soviet Union	China
1985	USA	China
1989	Cuba	Cuba
1991	Unified Team	Cuba
1993	Cuba	Italy

Water Sports

Water Skiing
World Championships
Roquebrune-sur-Argeus, Fra   Sep 17

Men's Overall

1 **P Martin**	**FRA**	**2725.3**
2 A Alessi	ITA	2642.8
3 J Llewellyn	CAN	2622.1

Slalom

1 **A Mapple**	**GBR**	
2 M Kjellander	SWE	
3 W Cox	USA	

Team

1 France	8270.1

Waterski Racing
World Championships
Belgium   Aug
Four races: Antwerp, Cheratte, Blankenberge and Viersel. The best three count.

Men

1 **Stefano Gregorio ITA**	**2976.21**	
2 Carlo Cassa	ITA	2954.52
3 Danny Van De Ven	BEL	2906.19

Women

1 **Leanne Brown**	**AUS**	**3000.00**
2 Tracey Graziano	AUS	2940.72
3 Debbie Nordblad	USA	2910.75

Nations Trophy

1 **Australia**	**13,497.63**
2 Great Britain	13,139.52
3 Belgium	11,631.35

Surfing
GB Cup
Woolacombe   June 17-18
Open: 1. Simon Tucker; 2. Randall Davies; 3. James Thomas; 4. Greg Owen; 5. Steve Winter **Bodyboard:** 1. Damien Prisk; 2. Bjorn Storey; 3. Danny Wall **Longboard:** 1. Colin Bright; 2. Lee Ryan; 3. Keith Beddoe **Kneeboard:** 1. Chris Cockett; 2. Shaun Mabey; 3. Kyle Abrahams **Women:** 1. Sarah Whiteley; 2. Charlotte Baird; 3. Robyn Davies **Women's Bodyboard:** 1. Lisa Cutts; 2. Gemma Harris; 3. Sarah Baker

Wind Surfing
World Championships
Sandown, Isle of Wight   Sep 23

Men

1 **M Bornhäuser**	**GER**	**11pts**
2 G Fridman	ISR	18.5
3 N Kaklamanakis	GRE	22.5

Women

1 **J Gardahaut**	**FRA**	**17**
2 A Francois	FRA	18
3 D De Vries	NED	22

Powerboat Racing
Formula 1 World Championship
Round 1
Porto Cerva, Sardinia   May 6-7

1 **Michael Werner**	**GER**
2 Walter Cabrini	ITA
3 Jonathan Jones	GBR

Round 2
Dunaujvaros, Hungary   May 27-28

1 **Michael Werner**	**GER**
2 Guido Cappellini	ITA
3 Danny Bertels	BEL

Round 3
Brandenburg, Germany   June 10-11

1 **Michael Werner**	**GER**
2 Guido Cappellini	ITA
3 Walter Cabrini	ITA

Round 4
Chalon-sur-Saone, France   June 24-25

1 **Guido Cappellini**	**ITA**
2 Massimo Roggierio	ITA
3 Danny Bertels	BEL

Round 5

1 **Guido Cappellini**	**ITA**
2 Michael Werner	GER
3 Jonathan Jones	GBR

Points after 5 rounds (three rounds remaining):
Werner 75, Cappellini 70, Bertels 42, Cabrini 41

FORMULA 1 WORLD CHAMPIONSHIP 1994
Final Positions
1. Guido Cappellini ITA 108; 2. Jonathan Jones GBR 97; 3. Michael Werner GER 92; 4. Danny Bertels BEL 61

Dragon Boat Racing
Hong Kong   June 11

Men

1 **Indonesia**	**2:25.64**

Women

1 **Canada**	**2:41.35**

The Dragon Boat Festival in Hong Kong is held to commemorate the memory of Chu Yuan, who drowned himself in the Milo river in Hunang to protest against government corruption 2000 years ago. The story goes that Chu's supporters sailed out to search for his body, dropping rice dumplings into the water for the fish, so the fish would eat them rather than Chu's body. Thought you'd like to know that.

Weightlifting

World Championships

Istanbul   November 18-27, 1994
Gold medals are awarded for snatch, jerk and overall in each weight. The results are given in overall order; the bold figures show which lifter won the gold medals in each discipline. Where the weights lifted are equal, the competitior with the lower body weight wins.
All weights in kilograms

MEN

54kg

			BW	Snatch	Jerk	Total
1	Mutlu Halil	TUR	53.70	**130.0**	**160.0**	**290.0**
2	Ivan Ivanov	BUL	53.76	120.0	155.0	275.0
3	S Minchev	BUL	53.94	122.5	147.5	270.0

59kg

1	Nikolai Peshalov	BUL	58.80	**135.0**	**167.5**	**302.5**
2	Hafiz Suleymanoglu	TUR	58.98	135.0	162.5	297.5
3	R Panaiotov	BUL	58.72	130.0	157.5	287.5

64kg

1	Naim Suleymanoglu	TUR	63.54	**147.5**	**182.5**	**330.0**
2	Valerios Leonidis	GRE	63.62	145.0	180.0	325.0
3	Attila Czanka	HUN	63.76	140.0	172.5	312.5
22	Ben Devonshire	GBR	63.80	105.0	135.0	240.0

70kg

1	Fedail Guler	TUR	69.52	**160.0**	**190.0**	**350.0**
2	Yoto Yotov	BUL	69.52	155.0	190.0	345.0
3	Anguel Gentchev	BUL	69.36	155.0	185.0	340.0
5	Attila Feri	HUN	69.50	145.0	**190.0**	335.0
23	S Cruikshank	GBR	70.00	120.0	150.0	270.0

76kg

1	Pablo Lara	CUB	75.84	162.5	**202.5**	**365.0**
2	Ingo Steinhöfel	GER	75.84	**165.0**	197.5	362.5
3	Ruslan Savchenko	UKR	75.70	160.0	200.0	360.0

83kg

1	Marc Huster	GER	82.54	172.5	**210.0**	**382.5**
2	Sergo Tchakoian	ARM	82.10	**175.0**	205.0	380.0
3	Sunay Bulut	TUR	82.94	165.0	210.0	375.0

91kg

1	Alexey Petrov	RUS	90.58	**185.0**	**227.5**	**412.5**
2	Kakhi Kakhiashvili	GRE	90.30	177.5	220.0	397.5
3	Y Belyatsky	BLR	90.38	172.5	207.5	380.0
17	Brian Clifton	GBR	90.96	140.0	175.0	315.0

99kg

1	Sergey Syrtsov	RUS	98.46	**192.5**	**225.0**	**417.5**
2	Viktor Tregoubov	RUS	98.50	185.0	220.0	405.0
3	S Rybalchenko	UKR	96.88	177.5	217.5	395.0

108kg

1	Timor Taimazov	UKR	107.40	**200.0**	**235.0**	**435.0**
2	Nicu Vlad	AUS	107.72	192.5	230.0	422.5
3	Artur Akoev	RUS	107.34	195.0	225.0	420.0
24	Giles Greenwood	GBR	107.24	150.0	180.0	330.0

+108kg

1	Alexander Kurlovich	BLR	136.58	**205.0**	**252.5**	**457.5**
2	Andrey Chemerkin	RUS	151.10	200.0	252.5	452.5
3	Stefan Botev	AUS	119.48	195.0	240.0	435.0

WOMEN

46kg

1	Yun Yanhong	CHN	45.44	**80.0**	**100.0**	**180.0**
2	N Kunjarani	IND	45.74	72.5	95.0	167.5
3	Tsai Huey-Woan	TPE	45.68	70.0	85.0	155.0

50kg

1	Robin Byrd	AUS	49.94	**80.0**	95.0	**175.0**
2	I Rifatova	BUL	49.72	70.0	**95.0**	165.0
3	Chen Li-Chuan	TPE	49.74	75.0	90.0	165.0

54kg

1	Karnam Maleswari	IND	54.00	87.5	**110.0**	**197.5**
2	Li Fengying	CHN	52.62	**87.5**	107.5	195.0
3	Jantea Georgieva	BUL	53.90	87.5	97.5	185.0

59kg

1	Zou Feie	CHN	58.50	**97.5**	**122.5**	**220.0**
2	Gergana Kirilova	BUL	58.58	90.0	112.5	202.5
3	K Suta	THA	58.06	85.0	112.5	197.5
9	Dianne Greenidge	GBR	58.50	75.0	95.0	170.0

64kg

1	Li Hongyun	CHN	63.70	**105.0**	**130.0**	**235.0**
2	Kuo Su-Fen	TPE	63.74	90.0	115.0	205.0
3	Erzsébet Márkus	HUN	63.60	92.5	105.0	197.5

70kg

1	Zhou Meihong	CHN	68.26	95.0	**127.5**	**222.5**
2	Qu Lihua	CHN	65.44	**97.5**	122.5	220.5
3	W Puncharkarn	THA	67.38	95.0	115.0	210.0
9	Auguste Juliana	GBR	69.76	85.0	100.0	185.0

76kg

1	P Antonopoooulou	GRE	75.50	92.5	**127.5**	**220.0**
2	Mária Takács	HUN	72.90	95.0	122.5	217.5
3	Albina Khomich	RUS	74.72	**97.5**	115.0	212.5

83kg

1	Maria Urrutia	COL	81.64	**105.0**	**132.5**	**237.5**
2	Chen Shu-Chih	TPE	82.50	105.0	130.0	235.0
3	Derya Acikgoz	TUR	77.32	100.0	120.0	220.0

+83kg

1	Karolina Lundahl	FIN	84.26	**102.5**	**127.5**	**230.0**
2	Chen Hsiao-Lien	TPE	95.14	95.0	122.5	217.5
3	Myrtle Augee	GBR	98.14	97.5	120.0	217.5

Powerlifting World Championships
Men

Johannesburg   Nov 17-19, 1994
The figures given are for squat, benchpress and deadlift. The final figure is the total weight.

52kg

1	**Andrezj Stanaszek**	**POL**	**270.0**	**177.5**	**130.0**	**577.5**
2	Hideaki Inaba	JPN	240.0	95.0	230.0	565.0
3	Hu Chun-Hsiung	TPE	225.0	105.0	230.0	560.0

56kg

1	**Hiroyuki Isagawa**	**JPN**	**205.0**	**162.5**	**225.0**	**592.5**
2	Jantry Francis	IND	195.0	115.0	225.0	535.0
3	Christian Klein	GER	175.0	115.0	170.0	460.0

60kg

1	**Wim Elyn**	**BEL**	**247.5**	**145.0**	**252.5**	**645.0**
2	Tim Taylor	USA	225.0	145.0	257.5	627.5
3	Gary Simes	GBR	242.0	145.0	235.0	620.0

67.5kg

1	**Alexei Sivokon**	**KZK**	**290.0**	**190.0**	**285.0**	**765.0**
2	Rodney Hypolite	GBR	290.0	150.0	280.0	720.0
3	Dominic Sardo	USA	260.0	170.0	257.5	687.5

75kg

1	**Dave Ricks**	**USA**	**305.0**	**192.0**	**312.5**	**807.5**
2	Per Berglund	SWE	290.0	192.5	270.0	752.5
3	Jarmo Laine	FIN	290.0	192.5	270.0	740.0

82.5kg

1	**Thomas Walter**	**USA**	**315.0**	**182.5**	**310.0**	**807.5**
2	Peter Theuser	CZE	315.0	187.5	297.5	800.0
3	Roman Szymkowiak	POL	292.5	175.0	330.0	797.5
8	Anthony Thornton	GBR	270.0	170.0	287.5	727.5

90kg

1	**Frank Schramm**	**GER**	**362.5**	**225.0**	**295.0**	**882.5**
2	Alexandr Lekomtsev	RUS	325.0	225.0	312.5	862.5
3	Janne Toivanen	FIN	310.0	190.0	335.0	835.0
11	Selvyn Calvin	GBR	272.5	150.0	305.0	727.5

100kg

1	**Ed Coan**	**USA**	**423.0**	**235.0**	**377.5**	**1035.5**
2	Vladimir Markovsky	RUS	360.0	210.0	320.0	890.0
3	Arto Rajala	FIN	342.5	207.5	310.0	860.0

110kg

1	**Kirk Karwoski**	**USA**	**412.5**	**237.5**	**330.0**	**980.0**
2	Derek Pomana	NZL	380.0	240.0	310.0	930.0
3	Ano Turtainen	FIN	340.0	217.5	342.5	900.0
7	Raymond Allison	GBR	300.0	200.0	317.5	817.5

125kg

1	**Victor Naleikin**	**UKR**	**370.0**	**230.0**	**360.0**	**960.0**
2	Scott Smith	USA	370.0	250.0	320.0	940.0
3	Sturla Davidsen	NOR	360.0	225.0	337.5	922.5

125kg+

1	**Karl Saliger**	**AUT**	**395.0**	**270.0**	**335.0**	**1000.0**
2	Miroslav Patro	SVK	385.0	217.5	362.5	965.0
3	Shane Hamman	USA	410.0	227.5	327.5	965.0

NATIONS
1. United States 66pts; 2. Finland 46; 3. Russia 44;
4. Kazakhstan 41; 5. Japan 31; 9. Great Britain 29

75kg

1	**Elena Soukhorouk**	**UKR**	**240.5**	**112.5**	**252.5**	**605.0**
2	Liz Odendaal	SUI	200.0	120.0	230.0	550.0
3	Marina Zhguleva	RUS	195.0	122.5	202.5	520.0

82.5kg

1	**N Rumyantseva**	**RUS**	**215.0**	**120.0**	**222.5**	**557.5**
2	Vicky Steenrod	USA	202.5	132.5	212.5	547.5
3	Doris Schumacher	GER	192.5	127.5	192.5	512.5

90kg

1	**Alla Korshunova**	**RUS**	**205.0**	**112.5**	**235.0**	**552.5**
2	Shelby Corson	USA	220.0	130.0	202.5	552.5
3	J Vencatachellum	FRA	222.5	115.0	215.0	552.5

90kg+

1	**Chao Chen-Yeh**	**TPE**	**235.0**	**145.0**	**210.0**	**590.0**
2	Anastasia Pavlova	RUS	230.0	140.0	210.0	580.0
3	Lee Chia-Shan	TPE	235.0	120.0	215.0	570.0
6	Sandra Mullin	GBR	170.0	75.0	150.0	395.0

NATIONS
1. Russia 63; 2. Chinese Tapei 49; 3. United States 48;
4. Japan 39; 5. France 34; 12. Great Britain 15.

Women
Chiba, Japan   May 6

44kg

1	**Raja Koskinen**	**FIN**	**156.0**	**65.0**	**145.0**	**365.0**
2	Svetlana Tesleva	RUS	137.5	67.5	150.0	355.0
3	Anna-Lisa Pinkkala	FIN	140.0	62.5	150.0	352.5

48kg

1	**Elena Yamskich**	**RUS**	**145.0**	**85.0**	**165.0**	**395.0**
2	Malou Thill	LUX	140.0	77.5	162.5	380.0
3	Vuokko Viitasaari	FIN	145.0	77.5	157.5	380.0

52kg

1	**Nadejda Mir**	**KZK**	**157.5**	**80.0**	**180.0**	**417.5**
2	Claude Coqnacq	FRA	152.5	77.5	182.5	412.5
3	Minguarti	INA	165.0	70.0	172.5	407.5

56kg

1	**Carrie Boudreau**	**USA**	**187.5**	**110.0**	**220.5**	**517.5**
2	Irina Orekhova	RUS	155.0	80.0	192.5	427.5
3	Suzanne Hagarsand	SWE	165.0	82.5	170.0	417.5
8	Jessica Kattan	GBR	137.5	80.0	170.0	387.5

60kg

1	**Eriko Himeno**	**JPN**	**170.0**	**115.0**	**190.0**	**475.0**
2	Ingeborg Marx	BEL	180.0	100.0	190.0	470.0
3	Huang Ya-Ching	TPE	165.0	87.5	170.0	422.5
4	Jackie Blasbery	GBR	150.0	77.5	175.0	402.5

67.5kg

1	**Lisa Sjöstrand**	**SWE**	**207.5**	**107.5**	**217.5**	**532.5**
2	Ekaterina Tanakova	RUS	200.0	107.5	220.0	527.5
3	Chen Hsiu-Chiung	TPE	192.5	95.0	185.0	472.5

World/Olympic Champions

Olympic champions given for 1984, 1988 and 1992. Divisions changed in 1993.

MEN

52kg
1984 Zeng Guoqiang CHN
1985 Sevdalin Marinov BUL
1986 Sevdalin Marinov BUL
1987 Sevdalin Marinov BUL
1988 Sevdalin Marinov BUL
1989 Ivan Ivanov BUL
1990 Ivan Ivanov BUL
1991 Ivan Ivanov BUL
1992 Ivan Ivanov BUL

54kg
1993 Ivan Ivanov BUL
1994 Mutlu Halil TUR

56kg
1984 Wu Shude CHN
1985 Neno Terziski BUL
1986 Mitko Grablev BUL
1987 Neno Terziski BUL
1988 Oksen Mirzoyan URS
1989 Hafis Suleimanov RUS
1990 Liu Shoubin CHN
1991 Chun Byung-Kwan KOR
1992 Chun Byung-Kwan KOR

59kg
1993 Nikolai Peshalov BUL
1994 Nikolai Peshalov BUL

60kg
1984 Chen Weiqiang CHN
1985 Neum Shalamanov BUL
1986 Neum Shalamanov BUL
1987 Stefan Topurov BUL
1988 Naim Suleymanoglu TUR
1989 Naim Suleymanoglu
1990 Nikolai Peshalov BUL
1991 Naim Suleymanoglu
1992 Naim Suleymanoglu

64kg
1993 Naim Suleymanoglu
1994 Naim Suleymanoglu

67.5kg
1984 Yao Jingyuan CHN
1985 Mikhail Petrov BUL
1986 Mikhail Petrov BUL
1987 Mikhail Petrov BUL
1988 Joachim Kunz GDR
1989 Israil Militosian URS
1990 Kim Myong-Nam PRK
1991 Yoto Yotov BUL
1992 Israil Militosian CIS

70kg
1993 Yoto Yotov BUL
1994 Fedail Guler TUR

75kg
1984 K-H Radschinsky FRG
1985 A Varbanov BUL
1986 A Varbanaov BUL
1987 Borislav Guidikov BUL
1988 Borislav Guidikov BUL
1989 A Orazdurdyev URS
1990 Fyodor Kassapu URS
1991 Pablo Lara CUB
1992 Fyodor Kassapu CIS

76kg
1993 A Orazdurdyev RUS
1994 Pablo Lara CUB

82.5kg
1984 Petre Becheru ROM
1985 Yurik Vardanyan URS
1986 Asen Zlatev BUL
1987 Laszlo Barsi HUN
1988 Israil Arsamakov URS
1989 Kiril Kounev BUL
1990 A Orazdurdyev URS
1991 Ivan Samadov URS
1992 Pyrros Dimas GRE

83kg
1993 Pyrros Dimas GRE
1994 Marc Huster GER

90kg
1984 Nicu Vlad ROM
1985 Anatoly Krapaty URS/ Viktor Solodov URS
1986 Anatoly Krapaty URS
1987 Anatoly Krapaty URS
1988 Anatoly Krapaty URS
1989 Anatoly Krapaty URS
1990 Anatoly Krapaty URS
1991 Sergey Syrtsov URS
1992 Kakhi Kakhiashvili CIS

91kg
1993 Ivan Tchakarov BUL
1994 Alexey Pertov RUS

100kg
1984 Rolf Milser FRG
1985 Sandor Szanyi HUN
1986 Nicu Vlad ROM
1987 Pavel Kuznyetsov URS
1988 Pavel Kuznyetsov URS
1989 Petar Stefanov BUL
1990 Nicu Vlad ROM
1991 Igor Sadykov URS
1992 Viktor Tregubov CIS

99kg
1993 Viktor Tregubov RUS
1994 Sergey Syrtsov RUS

110kg
1984 Norberto Oberburger ITA
1985 Yury Zakharevich URS
1986 Yury Zakharevich URS
1987 Yury Zakharevich URS
1988 Yury Zakharevich URS
1989 Stefan Botev BUL
1990 Stefan Botev BUL
1991 Artur Akoyev URS
1992 Ronny Weller GER

108kg
1993 Timor Taimazov UKR
1994 Timor Taimazov UKR

110kg+
1984 Dean Lukin AUS
1985 Antonio Krastev BUL
1986 Antonio Krastev BUL
1987 Aleksandr Kurlovich URS
1988 Aleksandr Kurlovich URS
1989 Aleksandr Kurlovich URS
1990 Leonid Taranenko URS
1991 Aleksandr Kurlovich URS
1992 Aleksandr Kurlovich CIS

108kg+
1993 Ronnie Weller GER
1994 Aleksandr Kurlovich BLR

Wrestling

World Championships

MEN'S FREESTYLE
Atlanta   Aug 10-13
Super-heavyweight (130kg)
1 Bruce Baumgartner   USA
2 Sven Thiele   GER
3 Leri Khabelov   RUS
Heavyweight (100kg)
1 Kurt Angle   USA
2 Arawat Sabeyew   GER
3 Abbas Jadidi   IRI
Light-heavyweight (90kg)
1 Rasul K Azghadi   IRI
2 Makharbek Khadartsev RUS
3 Melvin Douglas III   USA
Middleweight (82kg)
1 Kevin Jackson   USA
2 Elmadi Shabrailov   KZK
3 Ruslam Khinchagov   UZB
Welterweight (74kg)
1 Buvaisa Saityev   RUS
2 Alexander Leipold   GER
3 Alberto Rodriguez   CUB
Lightweight (68kg)
1 Arayik Gevorkian   ARM
2 Ali Akbar Fallah   IRI
3 Jesús Rodriguez   CUB
Featherweight (62kg)
1 Elbrus Tedeyev   UKR
2 Takahiro Wada   JPN
3 Magomed Azizov   RUS
Bantamweight (57kg)
1 Terry Brands   USA
2 Giya Sissaouri   CAN
3 Harun Dogán   TUR
Flyweight (52kg)
1 Valentin Jordanov   BUL
2 Gholam Mohammadi   IRI
3 Zeke Jones   USA
Light-flyweight (48kg)
1 Vugar Orudyev   RUS
2 Alexis Vila   CUB
3 Armen Mkrttchian   ARM

WOMEN'S FREESTYLE
Moscow   Sep 9-10
Heavyweight (75kg)
1 Ma Li Dongfang   CHN
2 Mitsuko Funakoshi   JPN
3 Taty. Komarniskaya   UKR
Light-heavyweight (70kg)
1 Lise Golliot   FRA
2 Yelmira Kurbanova   RUS
3 Nin Englich   GER
Middleweight (65kg)
1 Yaoyi Urano   JPN
2 Doris Blind   FRA
3 Natalya Lazarenko   RUS

Welterweight (61kg)
1 Nikola Hartmann   AUT
2 Natalya Ivanova   RUS
3 Ma Kong Yan   CHN
Lightweight (57kg)
1 Sara Eriksson   SWE
2 Lene Aanes   NOR
3 Anna Gomis   FRA
Featherweight (53kg)
1 Sophie Pluquet   FRA
2 Kozue Kimura   JPN
3 Venddy Izagvirre   VEN
Bantamweight (50kg)
1 Samira Ganatchuyeva
      RUS
2 Givla Perez   VEN
3 Yoshiko Endo   JPN
Flyweight (47kg)
1 Miyo Yamamoto   JPN
2 Ma Zhong Xiue   CHN
3 Yelena Yegoshina   RUS
Light-flyweight (44kg)
1 Shoko Yoshimura   JPN
2 Mette Barlie   NOR
3 Viekie Zummo   USA

World Cup

Freestyle
Chattanooga   Apr 7-8
1 United states   10
2 Russia   8
3 Turkey   6
Greco-roman
Kecskemét, Hun   Oct 29-30, 1994
1 Ukraine   10
2 Hungary   8
3 United States   6

European Championships

Winners only
MEN 'S FREESTYLE
Fribourg, Sui   May 11-14
Super-heavyweight (130kg)
   Mahmut Demir   TUR
Heavyweight (100kg)
   David Musulbes   RUS
Light-heavyweight (90kg)
   Makharbvek Chadrtsev   RUS
Middleweight (82kg)
   Mahammad Ibrahimov   AZE
Welterweight (74kg)
   Alexander Leipold   GER
Lightweight (68kg)
   Vadim Bogiyev   RUS

Featherweight (62kg)
   Magomed Azizov   RUS
Bantamweight (57kg)
   Aslambek Fedarov   UKR
Flyweight (52kg)
   Namik Abdullayev   AZE
Light-flyweight (48kg)
   Vugar Orudsyev   RUS

GRECO-ROMAN STYLE
Besançon, Fra   Apr 26-29
Winners and British only
Super-heavyweight (130kg)
   Aleksandr Karelin   RUS
   13th Amarjit Singh GBR
Heavyweight (100kg)
   Mikael Ljungberg   SWE
Light-heavyweight (90kg)
   Gogi Koguashvili   RUS
Middleweight (82kg)
   Sergey Tshvir   RUS
Welterweight (74kg)
   Stoyan Dobrev   BUL
Lightweight (68kg)
   Ghani Yalouz   FRA
Featherweight (62kg)
   Wlodzimierz Zawadzki   POL
   13th John Melling GBR
Bantamweight (57kg)
   Ruslan Chakimov   UKR
Flyweight (52kg)
   Arsen Nazaryan   ARM
Light-flyweight (48kg)
   Ioannis Agatzanoan   GRE

British Championships

Manchester YMCA   Apr 8
Super-heavyweight (130kg)
   Amarjit Singh (Birmingham)
Heavyweight (100kg)
   Joe Mossford (Manchester)
Light-heavyweight (90kg)
   Sergio Gnecco (Italy)
Middleweight (82kg)
   Halil Yildirim (Bristol)
Welterweight (74kg)
   Jahanghah Saidi (Bristol)
Lightweight (68kg)
   Matthias Wachter (Germany)
Featherweight (62kg)
   Kenny Devoy (Bishopbriggs)
Bantamweight (57kg)
   Adam Toole (Barton)

Yachting ━━━━━━━━━━━━━━━━━

It took 132 years before anyone could loosen the bolts that held the America's Cup to its cabinet in the New York Yacht Club. In 1983 *Australia II*, financed by Alan Bond and skippered by John Bertrand, did just that, becoming the first overseas victor since the Cup's inception in 1851. America got their trophy back again in 1987, this time under the aegis of the San Diego Yacht Club, and maybe began to believe that it would take another 132 years to budge it. However, in May, Team New Zealand, in the shape of *Black Magic I*, did not even bother to check for bolts - they made off with the cabinet and all, trouncing Dennis Conner's *Young America* in the first five races of the best-of-nine series by an average of almost three minutes a race. Even Conner bowed out gracefully. Yes, Conner.

Since 1974, Conner's name has been synonymous with the Cup. To say that he has been obsessed is kind. Conner's obsession has been such that he makes Linford Christie look like a dilletante. The Cup and winning it has been everything. This round, as ever, Conner didn't so much court publicity as wed it. Hurling abuse at the all-women crew of *MIghty Mary* just for starters, Conner then proceeded to be eliminated from the defenders' series and negotiate his way back in.

It was a delicious irony that Conner, having wiled and guiled his way back into the competition then found, with victory in his grasp, that the other two boats,*Young America & Mighty Mary,* conspired to stop him winning. Their conspiracy, mainly with weather information, proved futile and Conner not only won the defenders' series, but even persuaded John Marshall's Pact '95 team to allow him to switch to *Young America* for the defence of the Cup. Unusual? Yes. Against the rules? Probably. The only surprise though was that Conner didn't persuade Peter Blake to offer him *Black Magic I* to race in for, by this stage, it was evident that the odds favoured the New Zealand boat.

Blake and skipper Russell Coutts played a canny game. The former had won the Whitbread Round-the-World in 1993 and circumnavigated the globe in a record 74 days with Robin Knox-Johnson in 1994. To that Coutts could add an Olympic gold medal in the Finn class in 1984. Short of credits, they were not. Yet they played their chances down.

OneAustralia was the favoured challenger, but never has an America's Cup seen such an untimely exit. In its fourth race in the Louis Vuitton Cup, John Bertrand's boat split asunder and sank in little more than two minutes. The new *oneAustralia* (the first irretrievably lost) actually inflicted a 15 second defeat on *Black Magic I* six weeks later. Yet that was the New Zealand yacht's only loss. After four months racing, Coutt's crew could count 41 victories against that single defeat and a nation was in ecstasy. It was probably a good thing that the modest and resolute New Zealanders didn't win the rugby World Cup too.

America suffered another defeat when Italy won the Admiral's Cup, the Italian victory being their first in that competition. Yet if it was a gloomy year for those across the pond, it was hardly song and dance time for British yachtsmen. With the Olympics homing into sight not a single British crew placed in the world championships for Olympic events in 1995. The world ranking lists (25/9/95) paint a slightly more attractive picture; Shirley Robertson places third in the Europe class while Merrick and Walker rank second in the 470s.

America's Cup

San Diego   May 6-13
Best of nine series
Black Magic I 5 wins
(New Zealand, skipper Russell Coutts)
Young America* 0 wins
(United States, skipper Dennis Conner)
**Conners won the defenders' races (Citizen Cup) with the
yacht Stars & Stripes, but switched boats for the final.
Three boats contested the defenders' challenge: Mighty
Mary (Skipper:J J Isler), Young America (Kevin
Mahaney), Stars & Stripes (Dennis Conner).
Seven boats contested the challengers' races (the Louis
Vuitton Cup): Black Magic I (Russell Coutts),
oneAustralia (John Bertrand), Nippon 94 (John Cutler),
France 3 (Marc Pajot), NZL-39 (Chris Dickson), Rioja de
Espana (Pedro Campos), Sydney 95 (Syd Fischer)*

Admiral's Cup

Big Boat Class
1	Group 4 Seahorse	GBR
2	Pinta	GER
3	Mean Machine	Scandinavia

ILC 40 Class
1	Brava Q8	ITA
2	Pigs in Space	USA
3	Anemos	GER

Mumm 36 Class
1	Mumm a'Mia	ITA
2	Sansui Sprinter	RSA
3	Hkg	

FINAL OVERALL POSITIONS
1	**Italy**	**112.958**
2	United States	138.250
3	Germany	147.000
4	Scandinavia	191.000
5	South Africa	198.750
6	Ireland	219.750
7	Hong Kong	243.500
8	Great Britain	247.125

Mistral World Championship

(Board Sailing)
Gimil, Manitoba   Dec 8-17
Men
1	**Aaron McIntosh**	**NZL**
2	Bruce Kendall	NZL
3	Andrea Zimali	ITA
27	Dean Tomlinson	GBR
48	Matthew Wemms	GBR
59	Howard Plumb	GBR
97	Steven Ireland	GBR

Women
1	**Maud Herbert**	**FRA**
2	Ke Li	CHN
3	Natasha Sturges	AUS
11	Penny Way	GBR
31	Christine Johnston	GBR
34	Jane Claque	GBR

Finn Gold Cup

(Men's Single-handed Dinghy)
Melbourne   Jan 7-15
1	**Hans Spitzauer**	**AUT**
2	Fredrik Loof	SWE
3	Philippe Presti	FRA
20	Richard Stenhouse	GBR
45	Rob McMillan	GBR

Europe Class World Championship

(Women's Single-handed Dinghy)
North Shore City, New Zealand Jan 27-Feb 4
1	**Kristine Roug**	**DEN**
2	Margriet Matthysse	NED
3	Natalia Dufresne	ESP
13	Shirley Robertson	GBR

World Match Race Rankings
As at Aug 21

1	**Russell Coutts**	**NZL**	**12082**
2	Peter Gilmour	AUS	11443
3	Ed Baird	USA	11252
4	Bertrand Pace	FRA	10948
5	Rod Davis	AUS	10257
6	Roy Heiner	NED	10221
7	Jesper Bank	DEN	9669
8	Magnus Holmberg	SWE	9609
9	Thierry Peponnet	FRA	9545
10	Apul Cayard	USA	8986
11	Markus Wieser	GER	7696
12	Chris Law	GBR	7638
13	Neville Wittey	AUS	7498
14	Peter Holmberg	ISV	7307
15	Andy Beadsworth	GBR	6652
16	Stuart Childerly	GBR	6537
17	Luc Pillot	FRA	6447
18	Marc Bouet	FRA	6413
19	Sten Mohr	DEN	6138
20	Anders Myralf	DEN	6076
21	Morten Henriksen	DEN	5967
22	Luis Doreste	ESP	5928
23	H H Johannessen	NOR	5806
24	Henrik Lundberg	FIN	5714
25	Peter Bromby	BER	5544
26	Eddie Warden-Owen	GBR	5484
27	John Cutler	JPN	5238
28	Freddy Markelin	FIN	5118
29	Manuel Doreste	ESP	4875
30	Mitja Kosmina	SLO	4834

*Q*uotes

"We knew from the first trials that she was very fast, something special, but we wanted to keep things low-key, so we planted a few lies in the Auckland pubs where the sailors drink and watched them multiply" - **Russell Coutts, skipper of Team New Zealand boat Black Magic, on the pschology of the America's Cup.**

"Waterside gossip says the outfit is bureaucratic and the boats are slow" - *The Sunday Times* **America's Cup preview in January, estimating Team New Zealand's chances.**

"I wouldn't count that man out of any regatta unless I'd driven a stake through his heart and buried him myself" - **The late Tom Blackaller's estimation of Dennis Conner, skipper of Young America.**

"There's one thing that goes down faster than an Australian yacht - Steinlager" - **Advert for the New Zealand lager which appeared shortly after the yacht oneAustralia sank in the challengers' cup series in March. OneAustralia took just 2 minutes and 22 seconds to go down. A Steinlager usually takes longer.**

"You know what sucks about this, America? That we didn't give this bitch a proper burial when the keel fell off" - **A not-too-happy crew-member of Stars & Stripes, shortly after they had replaced a broken keel. Stars & Stripes won the race, but lost it in the jury room.**

"We haven't sped up our boat much. We're still pushing a slug around" - **Conner's navigator Jim Brady, wondering how Stars & Stripes was winning the final trials, having been outclassed at the first stage.**

"Anyone in touch with reality would not be looking forward to defending the Cup with this boat" - **Conner on Stars & Stripes, the boat with which he originally qualified (well, sort of).**

"It's the largest discrepancy in speed between two yachts I have ever seen. I don't feel I'm in a sailboat race" - **Paul Cayard, frustrated helmsman of Young America, the boat that Conner's team switched to.**

"Conner is a Goner" - **Sign outside an Auckland waterfront bar as Team New Zealand won the fifth race in a row and took the Cup.**

"It's New Zealand's proudest day since Everest" - **Dame Catherine Tizard, governor-general of New Zealand.**

"Scratch a Kiwi and you're going to find a lot of pride in physical prowess, quiet resolve, courage under adversity and a very low level of bragging or brashness" - **Graham Vaughan, professor of social psychology at Auckland University, who just happens to be an...er...New Zealander.**

"This was the impossible dream, the farthest Grail" - **Don Cameron, New Zealand sportswriter.**

470 Class World Championships
(Double-handed Dinghy)

Toronto   Aug 10-20

Men
1 **Andreas Kosmatopoulos/Kostas Trigonis GRE**
2 Matteo Ivaldi/Michele Ivaldi   ITA
3 Nir Shental/Ran Shental   ISR

Women
1 **Theresa Zabell/Begona Via Dufresne   ESP**
2 Ruslana Taran/Elena Paholchik   UKR
3 Yumiko Shige/Alicia Kinoshita   JPN
No British competitors in either category

Laser Class World Championships
(Centreboard Dinghy)

Tenerife   June 5-14
1 **Robert Scheidt**   BRA
2 Nickolas Burfoot   NZL
3 Elvin Melleby   NOR
16 Iain Percy   GBR
21 Ben Ainslie   GBR
28 Christopher Gowers   GBR
41 Richard Stenhouse   GBR
48 Gareth Kelly   GBR
66 Andrew Oddie   GBR
68 Steve Cockerill   GBR
93 Simon Dodds   GBR
97 Nicholas Harrison   GBR

Tornado Class World Championship
(Two-person Multi-hull)

Kingston, Canada   Aug 10-18
1 **Oliver Schwall/Rene Schwall   GER**
2 Andreas Hagara/Florian Schneeberger AUT
3 Fernando Leon/Jose Ballester   ESP
46 William Sunnucks/Will Crossley   GBR
57 Philip Crebbin/James Barnes   GBR

Soling World Championship
(Three-person Keelboat)

Kingston, Canada   Aug 11-18
1 **Spain**
   (Luis Doreste/Domingo Manrique/David Vera)
2 Sweden
   (Magnus Holmberg/Johan Barne/Bjorn Alm)
3 Australia
   (Matt Hayes/Barry Watson/Stephen McConagh)
No British competitors

Star Class World Championship
(Two-person Keelboat)

Laredo, Spain   Sep 6-16
1 **Reynolds/Haenel**   USA
2 Grael/Ferreira   BRA
3 Rasmussen/Harsberg   DEN
28 Smith/Mason   GBR
42 Hudson/Downer   GBR

What's in a name. Well, quite a lot it appears. The 72ft yacht Nicorette, which won three races at Cowes and the Fastnet, had the Cape Town to Rio Race on its 1996 schedule. It did until the race organisers banned it from the event on the grounds, they said, that they didn't want to embarrass their sponsors, Rothmans. Presumably because Nicorette is what you take when you want to stop taking any more Rothmans.

As well as leaving the Swedish skipper of Nicorette, Ludde Ingvall, extremely brassed off, the decision has could have ramifications in almost every other sport.

If they do succeed in keeping Nicorette out of the Cape to Rio Race (and the rustling of legal briefs cannot be far away on this one) sponsors might just look for the next available sanction.

What, after all, would happen to the Carling Premiership if Carling decided to reject all those teams supported by other brews; bye-bye Liverpool, Newcastle, Chelsea, Nottingham Forest and reigning champions Blackburn Rovers who sell the virtues of Carlsberg, Newcastle Breweries, Coors, Labatts and McEwans respectively.

For some, even that may not be enough. The failure to smoke, for example, could be seen as an implicit indictment of smoking, so all non-smokers would be inelligible for the Benson & Hedges Cup and Phillip Tufnell would lead a new county, Bensonshire, to a stunning victory at the hastily renamed ground in Manchester, Old Holborn.

In snooker, though, it would be simple. Jimmy White would win the Embassy World Championship. At Last.

British Olympic Trials

Weymouth   Aug 29-Sep 9

Mistral

Men
1 Howard Plumb
3 Barrie Edgington
3 Dean Tomlinson

Women
1 Penny Way
2 Jane Clague
3 Marie Buchanan

Finn
1 Richard Stenhouse
2 James Lyne
3 Rob McMillan

Europe
1 Shirley Robertson
2 Anne Lucas
3 Jayne Singleton

470

Men
1 John Merricks/Ian Walker
2 Jason Belben/Nick Fenwick
3 Andy Richards/Ian Park

Women
1 Bethan Raggatt/Sue Carr
2 Severine Rees Jones/Inga Leask
3 Liz Walker/Liz Mushall

Laser
1 Ben Ainslie
2 Hugh Styles
3 Mark Littlejohn

Tornado
1 David Williams/Ian Rhodes
2 Jonathan Pierce/Steve Park
3 William Sunnucks/Will Crossley

Soling
1 Andy Beadsworth/Barry Parkin/Adrian Stead
2 Eddie Warden Owen/Ossie Stewart/Rob Cruickshank
3 Chris Law/Andy Hemmings/Neal McDonald

BRITISH OLYMPIC TEAM
Mistral Men: Howard Plumb
Mistral Women: Penny Way
Finn: Richard Stenhouse
470 Men: John Merricks/Ian Walker
470 Women: Bethan Raggett/Sue Carr
Tornado: David Williams/Ian Rhodes
Soling: Andy Beadsworth/Barry Parkin/Adrian Stead

America's Cup Winners

Year	Winning boat (skipper)	Score	Challenger
1870	**Magic (**Andrew Comstock)	-	Cambria GBR
1871	**Columbia** (Nelson Comstoek)	4-1	Livonia GBR
	Sappho (Sam Greenwood)		
1876	**Madeleine** (Josephus Williams)	2-0	Countess Dufferin CAN
1881	**Mischief** (Nathaniel Clock)	2-0	Atalanta CAN
1885	**Puritan** (Aubrey Crocker)	2-0	Genesta GBR
1886	**Mayflower** (Martin Stone)	2-0	Galatea GBR
1887	**Volunteer** (Henry Haff)	2-0	Thistle GBR
1893	**Vigilant** (William Hansen)	3-0	Valkyrie II GBR
1895	**Defender** (Henry Haff)	3-0	Valkyrie lil GBR
1899	**Columbia** (James Barr)	3-0	Shamrock GBR
1901	**Columbia** (James Barr)	3-0	Shamrock II GBR
1903	**Reliance** (James Barr)	3-0	Shamrock lil GBR
1920	**Resolute** (Charles Adams)	3-2	Shamrock IV GBR
1930	**Enterprise** (Harold Vanderbilt)	4-0	Shamrock V GBR
1934	**Rainbow** (Harold Vanderbilt)	4-2	Endeavour GBR
1937	**Ranger** (Harold Vanderbilt)	4-0	Endeavour II GBR
1958	**Columbia** (Briggs Cunningham)	4-0	Sceptre GBR
1962	**Weatherly** (Emil MosbacherJr)	4-1	Gretel AUS
1964	**Constellation** (Bob Bavier Jr)	4-0	Sovereign GBR
1967	**Intrepid** (Emil Mosbacher Jr)	4-0	Dame Pattie AUS
1970	**Intrepid** (Bill Ficker)	4-1	Gretel II AUS
1974	**Courageous** (Ted Hood)	4-0	Southern Cross AUS
1977	**Courageous** (Ted Turner)	4-0	Australia AUS
1980	**Freedom** (Dennis Conner)	4-1	Australia AUS
1983	**Australia II** (John Bertrand)	4-3	Liberty USA
1987	**Stars & Stripes** (Dennis Conner)	4-0	Kookaburra lil AUS
1988	**Stars & Stripes** (Dennis Conner)	2-0	New Zealand NZL
1992	**America 3** (Bill Koch)	4-1	Il Moro di Venezia ITA
1995	**Black Magic I** (Russell Coutts)	5-0	Young America USA

Admiral's Cup Winners

1957	**Great Britain**	1977	**Great Britain**
1959	**Great Britain**	1979	**Australia**
1961	**United States**	1981	**Great Britain**
1963	**Great Britain**	1983	**West Germany**
1965	**Great Britain**	1985	**West Germany**
1967	**Australia**	1987	**New Zealand**
1969	**United States**	1989	**Great Britain**
1971	**Great Britain**	1991	**France**
1973	**West Germany**	1993	**Germany**
1975	**Great Britain**	1995	**Italy**

Extras

Aerial Sports

PARAGLIDING WORLD CHAMPIONSHIP
Kyushu, Japan   *Mar 12-26*
Open
1	**Stefan Stiegler**	**AUS**
2	Hans Bollinger	SUI
3	Jocky Sanderson	GBR

Women
1	**Judy Leden**	**GBR**
2	Miyuki Tanaka	JPN
3	Natalie Berger	FRA

BRITISH CHAMPIONSHIP
Held at three venues: Llandinium, Wales; Keswick, England; and St Andre, France.
Final Standings
1	**John Silvester**	**Edel**
2	Peter Brown	Nova
3	Bruce Goldsmith	Airwave

Australian Rules

GRAND FINAL
Sydney   *Sep 30*
Carlton 141 Geelong 80

Croquet

BRITISH OPEN CHAMPIONSHIP
Hurlingham   July 9-16
Final
Reg Bamford RSA by Robert Fulford 3-2
+24tp +26tp -26tp -26 +26tp

Greyhound Racing

**DAILY MIRROR/SPORTING LIFE
GREYHOUND DERBY**
Wimbledon June 24
1	**Moaning Lad**	**5/2**
2	Summerhill Joy	3/1
3	Curryhills Fancy	50/1
4	Pearl's Girl	2/1 Fav
5	Mustang Joe	5/1
6	Here's Seanie	5/1

Hurling

ALL-IRELAND CHAMPIONSHIP FINAL
Croke Park, Dublin   *Sep 2*
Clare 16   Offaly 14

Petanque

NATIONAL SINGLES CHAMPIONSHIP
Norwich   *Sep 4*
Semi-finals
A Jamieson (East Midlands) bt
P Watts (Eastern) 13-1
P Enoch (Eastern) bt
J Goldie (Eastern) 13-6
Final
P Enoch bt A Jamieson 13-6

Polo

FIP WORLD CHAMPIONSHIPS
St Moritz   *July 30*
Brazil bt Argentina 11-10

BRITISH OPEN
Cowdray Park   *June 24-July 16*
Ellerston White bt Black Bears 12-10
Ellerston: Hipwood/Gracida/Pieres/K Packer)
Bears: Schwarzenbach/S Merlos/P Merlos/Secunda

Speedway

WORLD OVERSEAS FINAL
Coventry   *June 11*
1	**Ryan Sullivan**	**AUS**	**14**
2	Leigh Adams	AUS	14
3	Jason Lyons	AUS	12

Sullivan won after run-off

WORLD CHAMPIONSHIP
Final Standings
1	**Hans Nielsen**	**DEN**	**103**
2	Tony Rickardsson	SWE	88
3	Sam Ermolenko	USA	83
4	Greg Hancock	USA	82
5	B Hamill	USA	80
6	Mark Loram	GBR	77

DIVISION ONE - FINAL TABLE 1994
	P	W	D	L	BP	Pts
Poole	40	30	1	9	**16**	**77**
Eastbourne	40	23	2	15	14	62
Wolverh'ton	40	20	2	18	12	54
Coventry	40	19	3	18	11	52
Kings Lynn	40	20	1	19	10	51
Ipswich	40	19	2	19	10	50
Bradford	40	18	1	21	11	48
Arena Essex	40	19	0	21	7	46
Cradley H'th	40	16	3	21	7	42
Reading	40	14	2	24	6	36
Belle Vue	40	13	1	26	5	32

Obituary ▬▬▬▬▬▬▬▬▬▬▬▬▬▬▬

Maurice Allom, cricketer   Allom took four wickets in five balls on his England debut against New Zealand in 1929. Altogether, he took 605 wickets in his playing career with Surrey. Allom was president of the MCC in 1969-70. He died, aged 89, on March 23.

Richard Baerlein, racing journalist   Baerlein was a journalist with the *Evening Standard, The Observer* and *The Guardian* and, with Alex Bird, enjoyed a spell as a professional gambler. He continued writing into his eighties and died in March, aged 84.

Marcia Anastasia Beaverbrook, the Dowager Lady, racehorse owner   Lady Beaverbrook, widow of Sir James Dunn and the 1st Lord Beaverbrook (both multi-milliionaires), became one of the countries leading racehorse owners after the latter's death in 1964. She won three classics; the St Leger with Bustino and Minster's Son, and the 2000 Guineas with Mystiko. She died in October 1994, aged 84.

Dave Bowen, footballer and football manager   Bowen achieved two landmarks in his careers; as a player he led Wales to an unexpected quarter-final place in the 1958 World Cup (where they lost to Brazil) and as a manager took Northampton Town from the Fourth to the First Division. "We went up without spending anything and, once we were up, spent nothing on ensuring we stayed up," he once recalled. Northampton sunk as quickly as they had risen. Bowen moved on from manager to director and president of the club. He died, aged 67, in September.

Alec Brown, snooker player   Brown was four times a semi-finallist in the world champion, but could never breach the dominance of Joe Davis. He earned his place in snooker history when, in a match against Tom Newman, he produced a five-inch cue from his top pocket to play a shot. The governing body immediately introduced a rule that banned cues of less than three feet in length. Brown died on September 3rd, aged 87.

Godfrey Brown, athlete   The culmination of Brown's athletic career was at the 1936 Olympics at Berlin. Brown narrowly lost the individual 400m final to American Archie Williams, but collected gold in the 4 x 400m relay when the British quartet (Fred Woolf, Godfrey Rampling, William Roberts and Brown) easily beat the Americans. Brown died on February 4, aged 79.

Vic Buckingham, footballer and manager   Though all his playing years were spent with just one club, Tottenham Hotspur, Buckingham's managerial was altogether more itinerant. He had spells at Sheffield Wednesday, Fulham and West Brom (when they won the Cup in 1954) and took charge at Barcelona, Seville and Ajax, when Cruyff was an emerging talent.

Richard Burnell, oarsman   Burnell won his Olympic gold medal on a stretch of water he was most familiar with - the Thames at Henley. In the double sculls at the 1948 London Games, he was partnered by Bert Bushnell and they won from the Danish pairing of Parsner and Larsen by four seconds. From 1946-67 Burnell was *The Times* rowing correspondent. He died on January 29, aged 77.

Johnny Carey, footballer   Carey was one of the most versatile post-war footballers, in a careeer which encompassed 306 league appearances he played in 10 positions. At Manchester United, he was part of a team that finished second in the championship four times in five years before they eventually won the title in 1952. Born in Dublin, Carey represented the Irish Republic 29 times and Northern Ireland seven times. After retiring, he managed Blackburn, Leyton Orient and Nottingham Forest. Carey died on August 23rd, aged 76.

Raich Carter, footballer   Although his prime was lost in the war years, Carter played for England 13 times and established a reputation as one of the classic inside forwards of his age. Carter won League and Cup medals with Sunderland in the immediate pre-war years, scoring 31 goals in 31 games in the year (1936) that they won the League. Carter, who had suffered strokes in the past few years, died at his home in Willerby on April 9, aged 80.

Patrick Cobbold, football club chairman   Patrick Cobbold suceeded his brother John as chairman of Ipswich Town in 1976. The family brewery, Tolly Cobbold, supplied the financial muscle for the club and Patrick Cobbold stayed in control for 14 years. He retired in 1990 and died on December 16, 1994 aged 60.

Michael Coleman, sports journalist   Coleman, a keen runner, covered a variety of sports as a journalist and acted as an agent for a number of major-city marathons. He died while out running on January 22, of a heart attack. He was 64.

Davie Cooper, fooballer   Cooper's lengthy career embraced Clydebank, Rangers and Motherwell. A skilful winger, Cooper won 22 caps for his country and three championship medals during his time at Rangers. In the evening of his career, Cooper had returned to play for his first club Clydebank though he intended to retire this year. He collapsed while filming a coaching programme and died, following a brain haemorrhage on Feb 25. He was 39.

Frank Costin, racing car designer   Costin worked with Colin Chapman, head of Lotus, and together they produced the Vanwall racing cars. Costin died on February 5, aged 74.

Ted Drake, footballer and manager   Drake won three League championships and a FA Cup winners medal with the renowned Arsenal side of the Thirties. It was for that team, in 1935, that Drake performed the remarkable feat of scoring all seven goals in a match at Aston Villa. An eighth shot hit the bar. Drake was later appointed manager of Chelsea and took them to their only League title in 1955. He died, May 30, aged 82.

Karen Ellicott, horsewoman   Ellicott, a junior horse trials competitor and earmarked for the British junior team,was trampled by a horse she was shoeing. Ellicott, 18, died in April.

Frank England, motor racing   England's name was synonymous with the success of Jaguar racing cars in the fifties. Between 1951 and 1957 Jaguar won the Le Mans 24-hour race five times. England, who went on to become chairman and chief executive of Jaguar retired in 1972. He died on May 24, aged 83.

Peter Geoffrey Foster, cricketer   Foster, who played for Kent before the was, went on to become president of the club in 1991. He died in December 1994, aged 78.

Stafford Heginbotham, football club chairman   A Bradford toymaker, Heginbotham was chairman of Bradford City in 1985 when the disastrous fire claimed 56 lives. Heginbotham, who had previously saved the club from bankruptcy, died in May following a heart transplant operation.

Richard Langhorn, rugby union player   Langhorn played second row an back row for Harlequins. In 1993, the 6ft 6in Langhorn was called into the England squad against Canada, but last season was forced into retirement through injury. He died on November 27th, 1994 when, following a back operation, he had a heart attack.

Harold Larwood, cricketer   Larwood's name will be forever associated with the 'bodyline' series of 1932-33 when the Nottinghamshire pace bowler was the most potent weapon in the captain Douglas Jardine's armoury. Jardine called the approach "leg theory" and instructed Larwood to bowl short-pitched balls to a leg-trap field. The tactic was devastatingly effective, England winning the series 4-1 and Larwood claiming 33 wickets at just 19 apiece. The series generated such outrage that, on his return home, Larwood was ordered to apologise. He refused and never played for his country again. In 1950, Larwood emigrated to Australia with his family. He lived there till his death, aged 90, on July 22. In 1994, over 60 years after the Bodyline series ended, Larwood was awarded the MBE.

Tony Lock, cricketer   Lock, a left-arm spinner, helped Surrey to seven successive championships in the fifties. Most famously paired for both county and country with Jim Laker, he took 174 Test wickets in a first-class career total of 2,844. Lock, who accumulated 800 or more catches, was no stranger to controversy and several times during his career was called for throwing. Lock, who later emigrated to Australia, died on Mar 30 of cancer, aged 65.

Jason McRoy, cyclist   McRoy was British mountain bike champion in 1992. He died folowing a collision with a lorry in August. McRoy was 24.

Leonard Martin, broadcaster   Martin became famous as the man who read the football results on BBC's *Grandstand* programme. Martin, who was Australian, held the job for 37 years, presenting the results in such a way that once you had heard the first score in a game, you always knew what the second would be. Martin died on August 21, aged 76.

P B H May, cricketer   May was considered one of the finest post-war English batsmen. He made 4,537 runs in 66 Tests at an average of 46.77 and captained England in a record 41 Tests. In a first-class career that lasted from 1948 to 1963, before his premature retirement at 32, May accumulated a total of 27,592 runs at an average of more than 51. In 1957, he partnered colin Cowdrey in a record 411 stand against the West Indies. May later returned to the cricketing fold as chairman of the selectors, but he did not find that administrative post a comfortable one. May died, aged 65, from a brain tumour.

Harry Mitchell, yachtsman   Mitchell was lost in seas off southern Chile in March, while taking part in the BOC Challenge around-the-world race. He was 70.

Peter Murray Willis, cricketer   Captain of Northamptonshire in 1946, Murray Willis's best year was in 1934 when he scored 2,565 runs. He died on January 7, aged 84.

Tom Nickalls, racing journalist   Nickalls wrote for *The Sporting Life* for 23 years from 1945-67 and *The Field* until into his eighties. He died on June 18, aged 91.

George Harvey Noble, racing driver   Noble was one of the best-known drivers at the Brooklands track in Weybridge during the thirties. He died in December 1994, aged 84.

Fred Perry, tennis player   Born in Stockport, the son of a Labour MP, Perry was the last British man to win the Wimbledon singles title, which he did three times in succession - 1934, 1935 & 1936. Perry was also the first player in the sport to win the grand slam of titles; the Australian, French, Wimbledon and US Open titles and led Britain to four successive Davis Cup victories. Perry had graduated to tennis from table tennis, at which he had been world champion in 1929. In the same year that he won his third Wimbledon title and after having defeated Donald Budge for the US Open crown, Perry turned professional. Following his retirement in the late forties, he went on to coach and commentate. Perry, who was also the founder of a major leisurewear company, died at Melbourne in February, aged 85.

Kay Petre, motor racing driver   Petre was one of an elite band of female motor racing and rally drivers in the thirties. She competed at Brooklands and in both the Alpine and Monte Carlo Rallies before her career was cut short when she was badly injured in a crash. Petre died on August 10, aged 91.

Mollie Phillips, ice skater and ice skating judge   Phillips was British pairs champion with Rodney Murdoch in 1933 and they also won a bronze in the European Championships of the same year. Phillips competed in six Olympics (her highest placing seventh) and in retirement was the first woman ever to referee a world championship. She died on December 15, 1994, aged 87.

Dr Keith Scott, rugby player   Scott played rugby for England in the post-war years and cricket for Gloucester. He died, aged 76, on June 3.

Graham Sharp, ice skater   Sharp won the world figure skating title in Budapest in 1939 when just 22. Had the war not intervened, Sharp could well have become the 1940 Olympic champion. He died, aged 77, on Jauary 2nd.

Harold Shepherdson, football trainer   Shepherdson acted as trainer for the England team for 171 games and held the post when England won the World Cup in 1966. He died in September, aged 76.

Sir John Smith, sports administrator   Smith became chairman of Liverpool in 1973, just before the resignation of Bill Shankley. The arrival of Bob Paisley heralded an arrival dominance of the English game. In the years before Smith stepped down, the club had won 10 League Championships, four European Cup and three FA Cups. Smith also had to give a lead when the tragedies at Hillsborough and Huysel engulfed the club. It was during this latter period that Smith also fulfilled the role of chairman of the Sports Council. He died on February 1, aged 74.

Dorothy Stanley-Turner, racing driver   Stanley-Turner was one of a small band of women who raced during the thirties. She died on July 8, aged 78.

Bobby Stokes, footballer   In 1976, Stokes scored the goal that gave Laurie McMenemy's Southampton team the FA Cup, the second division side beating Manchester United 1-0. Stokes, who played more than 200 games for Southampton, retired to run a harbourside café in Portsmouth. He was found unconscious at his home in May and died in hospital. Stokes was 44.

Robert Elliot Storey Wyatt, cricketer   Bob Wyatt captained England 16 times and was vice-captain to Douglas Jardine on the infamous "bodyline" tour of 1932-33. In a career that spanned 28 years, he scored almost 40,000 runs and took over 900 wickets. Wyatt died on Apr 21, just 11 days short of his 94th birthday.

OVERSEAS

François Boutin, France, racehorse trainer   Assitant to the famous French trainer Etienne Pollet, Boutin went on to match the achievements of his mentor. In 30 years, the indefatigable Boutin turned out 17 winners of French Classics, though he is perhaps best known in this country for the Classic winner he didn't get; Nureyev disqualified in the 1980 2000 guineas after finishing first past the post. Boutin died of cancer on February 1, aged 58.

Hamaed Buhaleeba, United Arab Emirates, powerboat racer   Buhaleeba was killed when his boat somersaulted during the World Class Powerboat Championships off the Isle of Wight in August.

Pierantonio Caimi, Italy, water skier   Caimi, winner of the European Formula 2 title in 1991, was killed in July when competing in the Italian Waterski Championships. The 23-year-old collided with a boat on Lake Como.

Fabio Casartelli, Italy, cyclist   Casartelli was the Olympic road race champion at Barcelona in 1992. The young Italian turned professional after the Games and was a member of the Motorola team in the 1995 Tour de France. Casartelli crashed on the 19th July during the 15th stage of the Tour, while descending a mountain in the Pyrenees. He hit his head on a concrete block and died 30 minutes after arriving at hospital. Casartelli, the third rider to die in the history of the race, was 25.

Florence Chadwick, America, swimmer   During the fifties, when swimming the English Channel was still a feat of note, Chadwick twice made the crossing. On the latter occasion, she set a record for either sex of 13 hours and 55 minutes. She died, of leukaemia on Mar 15, aged 76.

Segey Choupletsov, Russia, freestyle skier   Choupletsov, who was a silver medallist at the Lillehammer Olympics, died in July in a motorcycle accident. He was 25.

Denny Cordell-Laverack, Ireland, racehorse trainer   Cordell-Laverick's first working incarnation was as a record producer; the Moody Blues, Procul Harem and Joe Cocker were all in his sixties stable. In the seventies, Cordell-Laverick abandoned the music business and took up training and breeding in Ireland. His new stable was not quite as illustrious, although his colt Baba Karum was the highest rated 2-year-old in 1986. Cordell-Laverick died in Dublin in February. He was 51.

Howard Cosell, America, sports commentator Arguably the best-known sports commentator in the history of American broadcasting, the oft-controversial Cosell became a national instuitution for his boxing commentaries and his *Monday Night Football* programme with ABC. It was Cosell who leapt to Muhammed Ali's defence when the world champion refused to fight in Vietnam and Cosell who broadcast from the Olympic village in 1972 when arab terrorists invaded the Israeli team's quarters. At his peak, ratings revealed Cosell to be both the most popular and the most hated celebrity in America. In recent years, he suffered cancer and strokes and died in April aged 77.

Leon Day, America, baseball pitcher Day, a pitcher in the Negro Leagues was elected to the Hall of Fame just a week before his death in March, aged 78.

Noel de Mille, Canada, rower De Mille took the bronze medal in the double sculls at the Los Angeles in 1932. He was partnered by Ned Pratt. De Mille died on Mar 6, aged 85.

Manfred Donike, Germany, chemist Donike was one of the world's leading authorities on drug-testing in sport. He joined the International Olympic Committee Medical Commission in 1980 and was intrumental in closing many of the loopholes in the testing systems. In 1983, it was Donike who arrived unexpectedly at the Pan-American Games in Caracas with sophisticated testing equipment that trapped 19 athletes at the Games. Another 13 left the Games in a hurry, claiming "business reasons" for their sudden departures. Donike, a professional cyclist in his youth, died on a flight to South Africa on August 21 from a heart attack. He was 61.

Juan Manuel Fangio, Argentina, racing driver Fangio dominated the early days of grand prix motor racing. Born in the country town of Balcarce, 250 miles south of Buenos Aires, Fangio began racing in 1936, when he was 25. However, it was not until he was 38 and he arrived in Europe, that the most celebrated phase of his career began. Fangio became world champion for the first time in 1951 and by the time he retired in 1958 had added four more titles to the list. From 51 GP races, the Argentinian won 24 and on 23 occasions set lap records. Racing was far more dangerous in the fifties and 30 of Fangio's contemporaries were killed during his career. Fangio, though, was injured only once, when he arrived tired for a meeting in Monza in 1952 and broke a bone in his neck. Fangio, who won his titles for Maserati, Mercedes-Benz and Ferrari, retired with five world championship titles, a record that has still not been equalled. He died on June 24, aged 84.

Jimmy Garcia, Colombia, boxer Garcia, 23, died as a result of injuries received in his WBC super-featherweight title fight against Gabriel Ruelas on May 6. Garcia collapsed after the fight and never regained consciousness. He died on May 19.

Pancho Gonzales, America, tennis player Gonzales won two US Open titles, the French Open and a doubles title at Wimbledon in his brief amateur career. He turned professional and in 1953 won the first of eight pro titles. When the game went open Gonzales returned to the major events and in the 1969 Wimbledon championships (he was a then a 41-year-old grandfather) played his part in the longest singles match in the event's history. Gonzales beat Charlie Pasarell 22-24 1-6 16-14, 6-3 11-9 in five hours and 12 minutes. Gonzales died of cancer on July 3, aged 67.

Danny Hamel, America, motor racing   Hamel was a five-time winner of the Baja championship. He died after crashing during a race at Ensenada, Mexico in June. Hamel was 23.

Ralph Hill, America, athlete   Hill was twice impeded by the Finn Lauri Lehtinen in the final 200m of the 5000m at the LA Games of 1932.The Finn kept the Gold because Hill, beaten by inches, would not lodge a complaint. Hill died in October 1994, aged 85.

Clarence Houser, America, athlete   'Bud' Houser won both the shot and the discus at the 1924 Olympics, the last man to do that particular double. Houser retained his discus title in 1928. He died on October 1, 1994, aged 93.

Paul Kipkoech, Kenya, athlete   World 10,000m champion in 1987, Kipkoech never fully realised his considerable talent, bedevilled by malaria and alcohol problems. He died, in March, aged 33.

Falani Latoa, New Zealand, rugby league player   Latoa died on March 3 following injuries received in a game for North Harbour against Auckland Warriors.

Fred Lebow, America, marathon organiser   Lebow, a Romanian emigré, created the New York marathon in 1976, a race that became one of the world's great sporting events and inspired Chris Brasher and John Disley to set up the London equivalent in 1981. Despite treatment for a brain tumour, Lebow ran his own race in 1993. He died in October 1994, just two weeks before the marathon.

Ron Luciano, America, major league umpire   Luciano committed suicide in January, aged 57.

Stewart MacPherson, Canada, commentator   MacPherson came to England in 1937 and worked initially for the BBC as an ice hockey commentator. He went on to report on a multitude of sports and become a war correspondent. MacPherson also chaired the radio programmes *Ignorance is Bliss* and *Twenty Questions*. He died on April 16, aged 86.

Micky Mantle, America, baseball player   Throughout the fifties, Mantle was comfortably baseball's biggest star. A Switch-hitter (he batted both right and left-handed) for the New York Yankees, Mantle accumulated a total of 536 home runs in his career. In retirement, Mantle continued the heavy drinking that started during his career. In 1994, he was dignosed as having advanced cirrhosis of the liver and, though he received a new liver in May 1995, the cancer spread to his lungs and, on August 13, aged 63, Mantle died.

Gisela Mauermayer, Germany, athlete   Mauermayer was Germany's greatest pre-war female athlete. She won the Olympic discus title in 1936, her victory coming midpoint in a run of 65 successive discus victories. Her discus world record lasted 14 years, her shot putt world record lasted 12 years and she four times broke the world pentathlon record. Sadly for Mauermayer neither the shot nor the pentathlon were then Olympic events. She died on January 9, aged 81.

Carlos Monzon, Argentina, boxer   Monzon was world middleweight champion for the seven years from 1970-77 and ranked among the best-ever at his weight. When his boxing career ended he enjoyed a brief career as an actor. In 1989 he was jailed for the murder of his third wife. Monzon was driving back to prison on January 8th, after a period of parole, when he was killed in a car accident. He was 52.

Ichiro Ogimura, Japan, table tennis player and administrator   Ogimura was one of the wave of 'pen-holder' players who transformed the game in the fifties. In that decade, Ogimura held 12 world titles. In 1987 he became president of the International Table Tennis Federation and accelerated the march toward professionalism. He died on December 4, 1994, aged 62.

Karl Pallas, Estonia, triathlete   Pallas, a 15 year-old youth competitor in the European Championships at Stockholm in July died after being hit by a car during the cycling section.

Wilma Rudolph, America, athlete   Rudolph was the 20th of 22 children born to a railway porter. She had double pneumonia and scarlet fever as a child and almost died. Rudolph survived, although she had to walk with a leg brace, and in Rome, in 1960, won three Olympic gold medals in the 100m, 200m and 4 x 100m relay. It was an achievement that only Fanny Blankers-Koen had previously surpassed. Rudolph retired in 1962, while still only 22, and taught and coached before acting as a spokewoman for a variety of companies. She died on November 12, 1994 of brain cancer, aged 54.

Franz Stampfl, Austrian, athletics coach   Stampfl took athletics coaching into the modern era. In the fities, having left Austria before the 2nd World War, he applied his methods of interval training to a talented group of British runners that included Roger Bannister. The methods bore fruit on May 6th 1954, when Bannister broke the four minute mile. Stampfl, who spent his later years wheelchair bound after a car accident, died in Melbourne on Mar 19, aged 81.

Roderick Stephens, America, yacht designer   With his brother Olin, Stephens was responsible for designing three yachts that carried off the America's Cup. He died on January 10, aged 85.

Oleg Tverdokhleb, Ukraine, athlete   Tverdokhleb won the European 400m hurdles title at Helsinki in 1994. The 25-year-old Ukranian died on September 17, electrocuted while making repairs at his mother's house in Dnepropetrovsk.

Olympic Preview

The Golden Bow

In the history of the modern Olympics only three men have ever won gold medals in four or more consecutive Games; the Danish yachtsman Paul Elvström, the American discus thrower Al Oerter and the Hungarian fencer Aladar Gerevich. Elvström failed to finish his first race in the Olympics and failed to start his last, but won four Finn class titles, 1948-1960, nevertheless. Oerter won his first title in Melbourne in 1956, completed his four-timer in 1968 at Mexico City and came out of retirement, at 43, for the 1980 US Olympic trials. Oerter came fourth, missing out on selection by a single place, but the team didn't go anyway as Reagan's boycott took effect.

Gerevich had it toughest; he had won two gold medals in the team sabre and an individual bronze when war intervened. The Hungarian returned to the Olympic stage in London where he won gold in both the team and individual events. Four years later in Helsinki, Gerevich pocketed another gold and silver. By the time the remarkable Hungarian had finished, at the age of 50 in the Rome Olympics, he had accumulated six straight team golds and an individual medal of each colour.

In Atlanta, Steven Redgrave could join that illustrious company. If Redgrave and Matthew Pinsent win the coxless pairs, it will be the Marlow oarsman's fourth in a row. In Los Angeles, he shared the glory with Martin Cross, Richard Budgett, Andrew Holmes and Adrian Ellison in the coxed fours. In Seoul, he partnered Holmes to victory in the coxless pairs and, less than 24 hours later, took a bronze in the coxed pairs. Holmes later said: "We came as near to perfection as I'm sure it's possible to get. That outing (the coxless pairs)...was utterly resplendent, just totally sublime". Holmes retired after Seoul. Come Barcelona, it was a third combination and a third gold.

Redgrave had paired with Simon Berrisford in the 1989 World Championships and they had come home with silver but, when Berrisford's career was prematurely ended through a back injury, the double Olympic champion was once again in search of a partner.

Matthew Pinsent was an Old Etonian at Oxford, old school you could say. Redgrave was a Great Marlow schoolboy who played every sport going and left school at 16. When new school met old school, it worked surprisingly well. They won the trials and took bronze at the 1990 World Championships. In 1991, Jurgen Grobler arrived from East Germany and became their coach. He switched Redgrave from stroke to the bow and the combination took wing. In those seats, they haven't been beaten since the 1992 Olympics. In Tampere, they claimed their fourth successive world title and Redgrave bowed out of Henley with 15 cups, seven of them in the celebrated Silver Goblets (three with Pinsent).

Redgrave has lacked only one thing in his career so far; the limelight. He's not a natural-born song and dance man. If it wasn't for that fact that he stands 6ft 5in and weighs in at 230 pounds, he'd probably slip by unnoticed. After July 27th, though, he might just have to do a few curtain calls.

July19-Aug 4	19	20	21	22	23	24	25	26	27	28	29	30	31	1	2	3	4
Ceremonies	●																●
Archery										●	●	●	●	●	●		
Athletics								●	●	●	●		●	●	●	●	●
Badminton					●	●	●	●	●	●	●	●	●				
Baseball		●	●	●	●	●	●		●	●	●	●		●	●		
Basketball		●	●	●	●	●	●	●	●	●	●	●	●	●	●	●	●
Boxing		●	●	●	●	●	●	●	●	●		●	●	●	●	●	●
Canoeing								●	●	●		●	●	●	●	●	●
Cycling		●			●	●	●	●	●			●	●			●	
Equestrian		●	●	●	●	●	●	●	●	●		●	●			●	●
Fencing		●	●	●	●	●	●										
Football		●	●	●	●	●	●		●	●		●	●	●	●		
Gymnastics		●	●	●	●	●	●		●	●	●		●	●	●		●
Handball					●	●	●	●	●	●	●	●	●	●	●	●	●
Hockey		●	●	●	●	●	●	●	●	●	●	●	●	●	●		
Judo		●	●	●	●	●	●	●									
Modern Pent.												●					
Rowing			●	●	●	●	●	●	●	●							
Shooting		●	●	●	●	●	●	●	●	●							
Softball			●	●	●	●	●	●	●		●	●					
Swimming		●	●	●	●	●	●	●									
- Diving								●	●	●	●	●	●	●	●		
- Synchronised												●			●		
- Water Polo		●	●	●	●	●		●	●	●							
Table Tennis					●	●	●	●	●	●	●	●	●	●			
Tennis					●	●	●	●	●	●	●	●	●	●	●	●	
Beach Volleyball					●	●	●	●	●	●							
Ind. Volleyball		●	●	●	●	●	●	●	●	●	●	●	●	●	●	●	●
Weightlifting			●	●	●	●	●		●	●	●	●	●				
Wrestling			●	●	●	●						●	●	●	●		
Yachting				●	●	●	●	●	●	●	●	●	●	●			

Olympic Timetable (Finals Only) ▬▬▬

Dates given for finals or final day.
Dates subject to change.

Athletics

July 26	20km Walk (M) Shot (M)
July 27	Javelin (W) 100m (M) 100m (W)
July 28	Marathon (W) Hammer (M) High Jump (M) Triple Jump (W) 5000m (W) Heptathlon (W)
July 29	10km Walk (W) Discus (W) Triple Jump (M) 800m (W) 110mh (M) 10,000m (M)
July 31	Discus (M) 400mh (W) 400m (M) 400m (W) 800m (M)
Aug 1	800m Wheelchair (W) 1500m Wheelchair (M) Long Jump (M) 400mh (M) 200m (W) 200m (M) 100mh (W) Decathlon (M)
Aug 2	50km Walk Pole Vault (M) Shot (W) Long Jump (W) 3000msc (M) 10,000m (W)
Aug 3	High Jump (W) Javelin (M) 4x100m (W) 4x100m (M) 1500m (W) 1500m (M) 5000m (M) 4x400m (W) 4x400m (M)
Aug 4	Marathon (M)

Badminton

July 31	Men's Doubles Women's Doubles

Aug 1	Men's Singles Women's Singles Mixed Doubles

Baseball

Aug 2	Final

Basketball

Aug 3	Men's Final Women's Final

Boxing

Aug 3	Light-flyweight Bantamweight Lightweight Welterweight Middleweight Heavyweight
Aug 4	Flyweight Featherweight Light-welterweight Light-middleweight Light-heavyweight Super-heavyweight

Canoeing

July 27	K1 Slalom (W) C1 Slalom (W)
Jul 28	K1 Slalom (W) C2 Slalom (M)
Aug 3	K2 1000m (M) C1 1000m (M) K4 500m (W) K1 1000m (M) C2 1000m (M) K4 1000m (M)
Aug 4	K2 500m (M) C1 500m (M) K1 500m (W) K1 500m (M) C2 500m (M) K2 500m (W)

Cycling

July 21	Road Race (W)
July 24	1km Time Trial (M)
July 25	Individual Pursuit (M)
July 27	Sprint (W) Team Pursuit (M)
July 28	Points Race (M) Sprint (M) Points Race (W)

July 30	Cross-country (W) Cross-country (M)
July 31	Road Race (M)
Aug 3	Individual Time Trial (M) Individual Time Trial (W)

Equestrian

July 24	Three-day Team
July 26	Three-Day Individual
July 28	Team Dressage
Aug 1	Team Showjumping
Aug 3	Individual Dressage
Aug 4	Individual Jumping

Fencing

July 20	Individual Epee (M)
July 21	Individual Epee (W) Individual Sabre (M)
July 22	Individual Foil (W) Individual Foil (M)
July 23	Team Epee (M)
July 24	Team Epee (W) Team Sabre (M)
July 25	Team Foil (W) Team Foil (M)

Football

Aug 1	Women's Final
Aug 3	Men's Final

Gymnastics

July 22	Team (M)
July 23	Team (W)
July 24	All Round (M)
July 25	All Round (W)
July 28	Floor (M) Vault (W) Pommel (M) Asymmetric Bars (W) Rings (M)
July 29	Vault (M) Beam (W) Parallel Bars (M) Floor (W) Horizontal Bar (M)
Aug 2	Rhythmic Group (W)
Aug 4	Rhythmic Individual (W)

Handball

Aug 3	Women's Final
Aug 4	Men's Final

Hockey

Aug 1	Women's Final
Aug 2	Men's Final

Judo

July 20	+95kg (M) +72kg (W)
July 21	95kg (M) 72kg (W)
July 22	86kg (M) 66kg (W)
July 23	78kg (M) 61kg (W)
July 24	71kg (M) 56kg (W)
July 25	65kg (M) 52kg (W)
July 26	60kg (M) 48kg (W)

Modern Pentath.

July 30	All events

Rowing

July 27	Coxless Pairs (M) Coxless Pairs (W) Double Sculls (M) Double Sculls (W) Coxless Fours (M) Single Sculls (W) Single Sculls (M)
July 28	Ltwt Double Sculls (M) Ltwt Double Sculls (W) Ltwt Coxless Fours (M) Quad Sculls (W) Quad Sculls (M) Eights (M) Eights (W)

Shooting

July 20	10m Air Rifle (W) 10m Air Pistol (M)
July 21	10m Air Pistol (W) Trap (M)
July 22	10m Air Rifle (M)
July 23	50m Free Pistol (M) Double Trap (W)
July 24	50m Rifle 3-pos (W)

	Double Trap (M)
July 25	50m Free Rifle prone (M) 25m Rapid Fire Ptl (M)
July 26	25m Sport Pistol (W) 10m Running Target (M)
July 27	Skeet (M) 50m Free Rifle 3-pos (M)

Softball

July 30	Women's Final

Swimming

July 20	100m Free (W) 100m Breast (M) 400m IM (W) 200m Free (M)
July 21	200m Free (W) 400m IM (M) 100m Breast (W) 4x200m Free (M)
July 22	400m Free (W) 100m Free (M) 100m Back (W) 200m Fly (W) 4x100m Free (W)
July 23	400m Free (M) 200m Breast (W) 100m Back (M) 100m Fly (W) 4x100m Free (M)
July 24	200m Breast (W) 200m IM (W) 100m Fly (M) 4x100 Medley (W)
July 25	800m (W) 50m Free (M) 200m Back (W) 200m IM (M) 4x200m Free (W)
July 26	200m Fly (W) 200m Back (M) 50m Free (W) 1500m Free (M) 4x100m Medley (M)
July 27	Platform Diving (W)
July 28	Water Polo Final (M)
July 29	Springboard Diving (M)
July 31	Springboard Diving (W)
Aug 2	Platform Diving (M) Synchro Team (W)

Table Tennis

July 29	Women's Doubles
July 30	Men's Doubles

July 31	Women's Singles
Aug 1	Men's Singles

Tennis

Aug 2	Women's Singles Men's Doubles
Aug 3	Men's Singles Women's Doubles

Volleyball, Beach

July 27	Women's Final
July 28	Men's Final

Volleyball, Indoor

Aug 3	Women's Final
Aug 4	Men's Final

Weightlifting

July 20	54kg
July 21	59kg
July 22	64kg
July 23	70kg
July 24	76kg
July 26	83kg
July 27	91kg
July 28	99kg
July 29	108kg
July 30	+108kg

Wrestling

July 21	Greco-Roman: 48kg, 57kg, 68kg, 82kg, 100kg
July 23	Greco-Roman: 52kg, 62kg, 74kg, 90kg, 130kg
July 31	Freestyle: 48kg, 57kg, 68kg, 82kg, 100kg
Aug 1	Freestyle: 52kg, 62kg, 74kg, 90kg, 130kg

Yachting

July 27	Finn (M)
July 29	Mistral (M) Mistral (W) Star (Open)
July 30	Laser (Open) Europe (W) Tornado (Open)
Aug 1	Soling (Open) 470 (M), 470 (W)

Reigning Olympic Champions

Archery

MEN
Individual: **Sebastien Flute** FRA
Team: **Spain**
WOMEN
Individual: **Cho Youn-Jeong** KOR
Team: **Korea**

Athletics

MEN
100m: **Linford Christie** GBR
200m: **Mike Marsh** USA
400m: **Quincy Watts** USA
800m: **William Tanui** KEN
1500m: **Fermin Cacho** ESP
5000m: **Dieter Baumann** GER
10,000: **Khalid Skah** MAR
Marathon: **Hwang Young-jo** KOR
3000msc: **Matthew Birir** KEN
110mh: **Mark McKoy** CAN
400mh: **Kevin Young** USA
PV: **Maksim Tarasov** EUN
HJ: **Javier Sotomayor** CUB
LJ: **Carl Lewis** USA
TJ: **Mike Conley** USA
SP: **Mike Stulce** USA
DT: **Romas Ubartas** LIT
HT:**Andrey Abduvaleyiv** EUN
JT: **Jan Zelezny** TCH
Decathlon: **Robert Zmelik** TCH
20km walk: **Daniel Plaza** ESP
50km walk: **Andrey Perlov** EUN
4x100m relay: **United States**
4x400m relay: **United States**
WOMEN
100m: **Gail Devers** USA
200m: **Gwen Torrence** USA
400m: **Marie-José Pérec** FRA
800m: **Ellen van Langen** NED
1500m: **Hassiba Boulmerka** ALG
3000m: **Yelena Romanova** EUN
10,000m: **Derartu Tulu** ETH
Marat'n: **Valenina Yegorova** EUN
100mh:**P Patoulidou** GRE
400mh: **Sally Gunnell** GBR
HJ: **Heike Henkel** GER
LJ: **Heike Drechsler** GER
SP: **Svetlana Krivelyova** EUN
DT: **Maritza Marten** CUB
JT: **Silke Renk** GER
Heptathlon: **J Joyner-Kersee** USA
10km walk: **Chen Yueling** CHN
4x100m relay: **United States**
4x400m relay: **Unified Team**

Badminton

MEN
Singles: **Allan Budi Kusuma** INA
Doubles: **Kim/Park** KOR

Baseball

MEN
Team: **Cuba**

Basketball

MEN
Team: **United States**
WOMEN
Team: **Unified Team**

Boxing

48kg: **Rogelio Marcelo** CUB
51kg: **Chul Su Chol** PRK
54kg: **Joel Casamayor** CUB
57kg: **Andreas Tews** GER
60kg: **Oscar De La Hoya** USA
63.5kg: **Hector Vinent** CUB
67kg: **Michael Carruth** IRL
71kg: **JuanLemus** CUB
75kg: **Ariel Hernandez** CUB
81kg: **Torsten May** GER
91kg: **Felix Savon** CUB
+91kg: **Roberto Balado** CUB

Canoeing

MEN
K1 500m: **M Kolehmainen** FIN
K2 500m: **Bluhm/Gutsche** GER
K1 1000m: **Clint Robinson** AUS
K2 1000m: **Bluhm/Gutsche** GER
K4 1000m: **Germany**
C1 500m: **Nikolai Boukhalov** BUL
C2 500m:**Massiekov/Dovgalenok** EUN
C1 1000m: **Nikolai Boukhalov**
C2 1000m: **Papke/Spelly** GER
K1 Slalom:**Piespeole Ferrazzi** ITA
C1 Slalom: **Lukas Pollert** TCH
C2 Slalom: **Strausbaugh/Jacobi** USA
WOMEN
K1 500m: **Birgit Schmidt** GER
K2 500m:**Portwich/Von Seck**GER
K4 500m: **Hungary**
K1 Slalom: **Elisabeth Micheler** GER

Cycling

MEN
1km TT: **Jose Moreno** ESP
Sprint: **Jens Fiedler** GER
Pursuit: **Chris Boardman** GBR
Team Pursuit: **Germany**
Points Race: **G Lombardi** ITA
Road Rce: **Fabio Casartelli** ITA
Team Trial: **Germany**
WOMEN
Sprint: **Erika Salumae** EUN
Pursuit: **Petra Rossner** GER
Road Race: **Kathryn Watt** AUS

Equestrian

3-Day Event: **Matthew Ryan** AUS
3-Day Event Team: **Australia**
Dressage: **Nicole Uphoff** GER
Dressaage Team: **Germany**
Jumping: **Ludger Beerbaum** GER
Jumping Team: **Netherlands**

Fencing

MEN
Foil: **Philippe Omnes** FRA
Foil Team: **Germany**
Epee: **Eric Srecki** FRA
Epee Team: **Germany**
Sabre: **Bence Szabo** HUN
Sabre Team: **Unified Team**
WOMEN
Foil: **Tiovanna Trillini** ITA
Foil Team: **Italy**

Football

MEN
Team: **Spain**

Gymnastics

MEN
Floor: **Xiaosahuang Li** CHN
Para Bars: **Vitaly Scherbo** EUN
Pommel: **Vitaly Scherbo &
Pae Gil-Su** PRK
Rings: **Vitaly Scherbo** EUN
Vault: **Vitaly Scherbo** EUN
Horiz Bar: **Trent Dimas** USA
All Round: **Vitaly Scherbo** EUN
WOMEN
Floor: **Lavinia Milosovici** ROM
Asymm Bars: **Lu Li** CHN
Vault: **Henrietta Onodi** HUN
Beam: **Tatyana Lyssenko** EUN
All Round: **Tatyana Gutsu** EUN
Team: **Unified Team**
Rhythmic: **A Timoshenko** EUN

Handball

MEN
Team: **Unified Team**
WOMEN
Team: **South Korea**

Hockey

MEN
Team: **Germany**
WOMEN
Team: **Spain**

Reigning Olympic Champions

Judo
MEN
60kg: **Nazim Gousseinov** EUN
65kg: **Rogerio Sampaio** BRA
71kg: **Toshihiko Koga** JPN
78kg: **Hidehiko Yoshida** JPN
86kg: **Waldemar Legien** POL
95kg: **Antal Kovacs** HUN
+95kg: **D Khakhaleichvili** EUN
WOMEN
48kg: **Cecile Nowak** FRA
52kg: **Almudena Martinez** ESP
56kg: **Miriam Blasco** ESP
61kg: **Catherine Fleury** FRA
66kg: **Odalis Reve** CUB
72kg: **Kim Mi-Jung** KOR
+72kg: **Zhuang Xiaoyan** CHN

Modern Pentathlon
MEN
Individual: **A Skrzypaszek** POL
Team: **Poland**

Rowing
MEN
S'gle Sculls: **Thomas Lange** GER
D'ble Sculls: **Hawkins/Peter** AUS
Quads: **Germany**
Coxless 2: **Redgrave/Pinsent** GB
Coxed 2: **Searle/Searle/Herbert**
Coxless Fours: **Australia**
Coxed Fours: **Romania**
Eights: **Canada**
WOMEN
S'gle Sculls: **E Lipa** ROM
D'le Sculls: **Koeppen/Boron** GER
Quads: **Germany**
Coxless 2: **McBean/Heddle** CAN
Coxless Fours: **Canada**
Eights: **Canada**

Shooting
MEN
25m Rapid: **Ralf Schumann** GER
50m Free: **K Loukachik** EUN
10m Air: **Wang Yifu** CHN
10m Running: **M Jakosits** GER
10m Air: **Yuri Fedkine** EUN
50m Free(3-pos): **G Petikian** EUN
50m Free: **Lee Eun-Chui** KOR
WOMEN
25m Sport: **M Logvinenko** EUN
10m Air P: **M Logvinenko** EUN
10m Air R: **Yeo Kab-Soon** KOR
50m Rifle: **Petr Hrdlicka** TCH

Swimming
MEN
50m Free: **Alexander Popov** EUN
100m Free: **Alexander Popov**
200m Free: **Evgeny Sadovyi** EUN
400m Free: **Evgeny Sadovyi** EUN
1500m Free: **Kieren Perkins** AUS
100m Back: **M Tewkesbury** CAN
200m Back: **Martin Zubero** ESP
100m Breast: **Nelson Diebel** USA
200m Breast: **M Barrowman** USA
100m Fly: **Pablo Morales** USA
200m Fly: **Mel Stewart** USA
200m IM: **Tamas Darnyi** HUN
400m IM: **Tamas Darnyi** HUN
4x100m Free: **United States**
4x200m Free: **Unified Team**
4x100m Medley: **United States**
Platform Diving: **Shuwei Sun** CHN
S'Board Diiving: **M Lenzi** USA
Water Polo Team: **Italy**
WOMEN
50m Free: **Yang Wenyi** CHN
100m Free: **Zhuang Yong** CHN
200m Free: **Nicole Haislett** AUS
400m Free: **Dagmar Hase** GER
800m Free: **Janet Evans** USA
100m Back: **K Egerszegi** HUN
200m Back: **Kristina Egerszegi**
100m Br'st: **ERoudkovskaya** EUN
200m Br'st: **Kyonko Iwasaki** JPN
100m Fly: **Quian Hong** CHN
200m Fly: **Summer Sanders** USA
200m IM: **Li Lin** CHN
400m IM: **Kristina Egerszegi**
4x100m Free: **United States**
4x100m Medley: **United States**
Platform Diving: **Fu Mingxia** CHN
S'Board Diving: **Gao Min** CHN
Sync Solo: **K Babb-Sprague** USA
Sync D't: **Josephson/Josephson** USA

Table Tennis
MEN
Singles: **Jan-Ove Waldner** SWE
Doubles: **Lu Lin/Wang Tao** CHN
WOMEN
Singles: **Deng Yaping** CHN
Doubles: **Yaping/Qiao Hong** CHN

Tennis
MEN
Singles: **Marc Rosset** SUI
Doubles: **Becker/Stich** GER
WOMEN
Singles: **Jennifer Capriati** USA
Doubles: **Fernandez/Fernandez** USA

Volleyball
MEN
Team: **Brazil**
WOMEN
Team: **Unified Team**

Weightlifting
52kg: **Ivan Ivanov** BUI
56kg: **Chun Byung-Kwan** KOR
60kg: **Naim Suleymanoglu** TUR
67.5kg: **Israel Militossian** EUN
75kg: **Fedor Kassapu** EUN
82.5kg: **Pyrros Dimas** GRE
90kg: **Kakhi Kakhiachvilli** EUN
100kg: **Viktor Tregubov** EUN
110kg: **Ronny Weller** GER
+110kg: **Alexander Kurlovich** EUN

Wrestling
FREESTYLE
48kg: **Kim Il** KOR
52kg: **Li Hak-Son** KOR
57kg: **A Puerto** CUB
62kg: **John Smith** USA
68kg: **Arsen Fadzaev** EUN
74kg: **Jang Soon** KOR
82kg: **K Jackson** USA
90kg: **M Khardartsev** EUN
100kg: **Leri Khabelov** EUN
130kg: **Bruce Baumgartner** USA
GRECO-ROMAN
48kg: **O Koutcherenko** EUN
52kg: **Jon Ronningen** NOR
57kg: **An Han-Bong** KOR
62kg: **M Akif Pirim** TUR
68kg: **Attila Repka** HUN
74kg: **M Iskandarian** EUN
82kg: **Peter Farkas** HUN
90kg: **Malk Bullmann** GER
100kg: **Hector Millan** CUB
130kg: **Alexander Karelin** EUN

Yachting
MEN
Mistral: **Franck David** FRA
470: **Calafat/Sanchez** ESP
Finn: **J Garcia** ESP
WOMEN
Mistral: **Babara Kendall** NZL
470: **Zabel/Guerra** ESP
Europe: **Linda Anderson** NOR
OPEN
Soling: **Denmark**
Flying Dutchman: **Spain**
Star: **Reynolds/Haenal** USA
Tornado: **Loday/Henard** FRA

British Olympic Champions (& best performances)

S or B in brackets denotes a silver or Bronze medal.
All others are gold medals. Placing in events where we
have never won a medal are not shown.

Archery

York Round	William Dod	1908
National Rd	Queenie Newall	1908
Men's Team	Great Britain (B)	1988
Men's Olymp	Simon Terry (B)	1992

Athletics

MEN

100m	Harold Abrahams	1924
	Allan Wells	1980
	Linford Christie	1992
200m	Walter Rengeley (S)	1928
	Allan Wells (S)	1980
400m	Wyndham Halswelle	1908
	Eric Liddell	1924
800m	Alfred Tysoe	1900
	Albert Hill	1920
	Douglas Lowe	1924
	Douglas Lowe	1928
	Thomas Hampson	1932
	Steve Ovett	1980
1500m	Charles Bennett	1900
	Arnold Jackson	1912
	Albert Hill	1920
	Sebastian Coe	1980
	Sebastian Coe	1984
5000m	Gordon Pirie (S)	1956
10,000m	Henry Hawtrey	1906
	Emil Voigt	1908
S'chase (4k)	John Rimmer	1900
(3.2k)	Arthur Russell	1908
(3k)	Percy Hodge	1920
	Chris Brasher	1956
Marathon	Sam Ferris (S)	1932
	Ernest Harper (S)	1936
	Tom Richards	1948
	Basil Heatley	1964
110mh	Grantley Goulding (S)	1896
	Alfred Healey (S)	1906
	Don Finlay (S)	1936
	Colin Jackson (S)	1988
400mh	Lord Burghley	1928
	David Hemery	1968
4x100m	Great Britain	1912
4x400m	Great Britain	1920
	Great Britain	1936
20km walk	Ken Matthews	1964
50km walk	Thomas Green	1932
	Harold Whitlock	1936
	DonThompson	1960
High Jump	Con Lea	1906
Long jump	Lynn Davies	1964
Triple jump	Peter O'Connor	1906
	Tim Ahearne	1908
Shot	Dennis Horgan (S)	1908

Hammer	Malcolm Noakes	1924
Javelin	David Ottley (S)	1984
Decathlon	Thomas Kiely	1904
	Daley Thompson	1980
	Daley Thompson	1984

DISCONTINUED EVENTS

3000m Team	Great Britain (S)	1920
	Great Britain (S)	1924
3 miles team	Great Britain	1908
5000m team	Great Britain	1900
X-country	Great Britain (S)	1920
3550m walk	George Larner	1908
10,000m wk	Ernest Webb (S)	1912
	Gordon Goodwin (S)	1924
10 mile walk	George Larner	1908

WOMEN

100m	Dorothy Manley (S)	1948
	Dorothy Hyman (S)	1960
200m	Audrey Williamson (S)	1948
400m	Ann Packer (S)	1964
	Lillian Board (S)	1968
800m	Ann Packer	1964
3000m	Yvonne Murray (B)	1988
10,000m	Liz McColgan (S)	1988
100mh	Maureen Gardner (S)	1948
	Carol Quinton (S)	1960
	Shirley Strong (S)	1984
400mh	Sally Gunnell	1992
4x100m	Great Britain (S)	1936
	Great Britain (S)	1956
4x400m	Great Britain (B)	1980
	Great Britain (B)	1992
High jump	Dorothy Odam (S)	1936
	Dorothy Tyler (S)	1948
	Sheila Lerwill (S)	1952
	Thelma Hopkins (S)	1956
	Dorothy Shirley (S)	1960
Long jump	Mary Rand	1964
Javelin	Tessa Sanderson	1984

DISCONTINUED EVENTS

Pentathlon	Mary Peters	1972

Boxing

Light-fly	Ralph Evans (B)	1972
Flyweight	Terry Spinks	1956
Bantamwt	Henry Thomas	1908
Featherwt	Richard Gunn	1908
Lightweight	Fred Grace	1908
	Dick McTaggart	1956
Lightwelter	Tony Willis (B)	1980
Welterweight	Alexander Ireland (S)	1920
Light-middle	John McCormack (B)	1956
	William Fisher (B)	1960
	Alan Minter (B)	1972
	Richie Woodhall (B)	1988
	Robin Reid (B)	1992

British Olympic Champions (& best performances)

Middleweight	John Douglas	1908
	Henry Mallin	1920
	Henry Mallin	1924
	Chris Finnegan	1968
Light-heavy	Harry Mitchell	1924
Heavyweight	Albert Oldham	1908
	Ronald Rawson	1920
Super-heavy	Robert Wells (B)	1984

Cycling
MEN

1km TT	Herbert Crowther (S)	1906
Sprint	HC Bouffler (S)	1906
	H Thomas Johnson	1920
	Reg Harris	1948
4km P't Tm	Great Britain	1908
4km Pursuit	Chris Boardman	1992
Road Race	Frederick Grubb (S)	1912
	Frank Southall (S)	1928

DISCONTINUED EVENTS

2km tandem	Great Britain	1906
	Great Britain	1920
Rd Race Tm	Great Britain (S)	1912
	Great Britain (S)	1928
	Great Britain (S)	1948
	Great Britain (S)	1956
600yds	Victor Johnson	1908
5km Track	Benjamin Jones	1908
20km Track	William Pett	1906
	Charles Kingsbury	1908
50km Track	Cyril Alden (S)	1920
	Cyril Alden (S)	1924
100km Track	Charles Bartlett	1908
12hrs track	F Keeping (S)	1896

Canoeing
MEN

C1 Slalom	Gareth Marriott (S)	1992

Equestrian

Jumping	Marion Coates (S) *Stroller*	1968
	Ann Moore (S) *Psalm*	1972
Jumping Tm	Great Britain	1952
3-day	Richard Meade *Lauriston*	1972
3-day Team	Great Britain	1956
	Great Britain	1968
	Great Britain	1972

Fencing
MEN

Epee	Alan Jay (S)	1960
	Bill Hoskyns (S)	1964

Epee Team	Great Britain (S)	1906
	Great Britain (S)	1908
	Great Britain (S)	1912
	Great Britain (S)	1960
WOMEN		
Foil	Gillian Sheen	1956

Football
MEN

Team	Great Britain	1900
	Great Britain	1908
	Great Britain	1912

Gymnastics
MEN

All Round	S W Tysal	1908
Team	Great Britain (B)	1912
WOMEN		
Team	Great Britain (B)	1928

Hockey
MEN

Team	England	1908
	England	1920
	Great Britain	1988
WOMEN		
Team	Great Britain (B)	1992

Judo
MEN

60kg	Neil Eckersley (B)	1984
71kg	Neil Adams (S)	1980
78kg	Neil Adams (S)	1984
86kg	Brian Jacks (B)	1972
95kg	David Starbrook (S)	1972
	Ray Stevens (S)	1992
Open	Keith Remfry (S)	1976
WOMEN		
52kg	Sharon Rendle (B)	1992
56kg	Nicola Fairbrother (S)	1992
66kg	Kate Howey (B)	1992

Modern Pentathlon
MEN

Team	Great Britain	1976

Rowing
MEN

Single sculls	Harry Blackstaffe	1908
	William Kinnear	1912
	Jack Beresford	1924
D'ble sculls	Beresford/Southwood	1936
	Burnell/Bushnell	1948
Coxless prs	Fenning/Thompson	1908
	Edwards/Clive	1932
	Wilson/Laurie	1948
	Holmes/Redgrave	1988
	Holmes/Pinsent	1992

British Olympic Champions (& best performances)

Coxless frs	Great Britain	1908
	Great Britain	1924
	Great Britain	1928
	Great Britain	1932
Coxed fours	Great Britain	1984
Coxed pairs	Searle/Searle/Herbert	1992
Eights	Great Britain	1908
	Great Britain	1912

Shooting
MEN

Free Pistol	Charles Stewart (B)	1912
SB Rifle (pr)	A A Carnell	1908
SB Rifle (3-p)	Malcolm Cooper	1984
	Malcolm Cooper	1988
Olympic Trap	Gerald Merline	1906
Trap (double)	Sidney Merlin	1906
	Bob Braithwaite	1968
Moving Tgt	John Kynoch (B)	1972

DISCONTINUED EVENTS

Free rifle	Jerry Millner	1908
Military team	Great Britain (S)	1908
	Great Britain (S)	1912
SB Rfle MT	A F Fleming	1908
SB Rifle DT	William Styles	1908
SB Rifle Tm	Great Britain	1908
	Great Britain	1912
Live Pigeon	C Robinson (B)	1900
Clay P Team	Great Britain	1908
Runn'g Deer	Ted Ranken	1908
	C W Mackworth-Praed	1924
R Deer Team	Great Britain	1908
	Great Britain	1924
Team event	Great Britain	1912

Swimming
MEN

100m Free	Bobbie McGregor (S)	1964
400m Free	Henry Taylor	1906
1500m Free	John Jarvis (1k)	1900
	Henry Taylor (1m)	1906
	Henry Taylor	1908
100m Back	Herbert Haresnape (B)	1908
100m Breast	Duncan Goodhew	1980
	Adrian Moorhouse	1988
200m breast	Fredenck Holman	1908
	David Wilkie	1976
100m Fly	Andrew Jameson	1988
200m Fly	Martyn Woodruff (S)	1968
	Phil Hubble (S)	1980
200m IM	Neil Cochran	1984
4x100m Free	Great Britain	1908
4x100m Med	Great Britain (B)	1980
Platform Dvg	Harold Clarke (B)	1924
	Brian Phelps (B)	1960

WOMEN

100m Free	Jennie Fletcher (B)	1912
	Joyce Cooper (B)	1928
	Natalie Steward (B)	1960
400m Free	Sarah Hardcastle (S)	1984
800m Free	Sarah Hardcastle (B)	1984
100m Back	Judy Grinham	1956
200m breast	Lucy Morton	1924
	Anita Lonsbrough	1960
400m IM	Sharron Davis	1980
4x100m Free	Great Britain	1912
4x100m Med	Great Britain (S)	1980
Platofrm Dvg	Eileen Armstrong	1920
Springboard	Liz Ferris (B)	1960

DISCONTINUED EVENTS, MEN

200m obstacle	Peter Kemp (B)	1900
400m breast	Percy Courtman (B)	1912
4000m free	John Jarvis	1900

Water Polo

Team	Great Britain	1900
	Great Britain	1908
	Great Britain	1912
	Great Britain	1920

Weightlifting

Bantam	Julian Creus (S)	1948
Lightweight	James Halliday (B)	1948
Middle-heavy	Louis Martin (S)	1964
Heavyweight	Launceston Eliot*	1896
90kg	David Mercer	1984

* One-handed lifting

Wrestling
FREESTYLE

Bantam	William Press (S)	1908
Feather	James Slim (S)	1908
Lightweight	George de Relwyskow	1908
Middleweight	Stanley Bacon	1908
Heavyweight	George O'Keilly	1908
90kg	Noel Loban	1984

Yachting
MEN

Finn	Charles Curry (S)	1952

OPEN

Flying Dutchman		
	Pattison/Macdonald-Smith	1968
	Pattison/Davies	1972
Soling	Smith/Cuikshank/Stewart (B)	1992
Star	McIntyre/Vaile	1988
Tornado	White/Osborn	1976

No Discontinued Events listed for yachting-no space

1996 Calendar

The calendar is arranged by date within sport. All dates are subject to change.

AERIAL SPORTS
May 24-June 7
European Championships
Vaga, Norway

AMERICAN FOOTBALL
Jan 6-7
Divisional Playoffs
various, USA

Jan 14
Conference Championships
various, USA

Jan 28
Super Bowl XXX
Tempe, Arizona, USA

Feb 4
Pro Bowl
Honolulu, Hawaii

June
World Bowl '96
tbc

ANGLING
May 27-June 3
World Fly Fishing Championship
Czech Republic

Sep 7-8
World Freshwater Championships
River Mincio, Verona, Italy

ARCHERY
Feb 14-18
European Indoor Championships
Moi, Belgium

Apr 9-14
British Olympic Trials
Atlanta, USA

June 24-30
World Field Championships
Kranjska Gora, Slovenia

July 4-9
World Junior Championships
San Diego, USA

ASSOCIATION FOOTBALL
Jan 6
Tennents Scottish Cup, 2nd round
various, Scotland
FA Cup, 3rd round
various

Jan 10
Coca-Cola Cup, 5th round
various

Jan 27
Tennents Scottish Cup, 3rd round
various

Jan 27
FA Cup, 4th round
various

Feb 11
Coca-Cola , semi-final 1, 1st leg
tbc
England v Portugal, women
Portugal

Feb 14
Coca-Cola , semi-final 2, 1st leg
tbc

Feb 17
FA Cup, 5th round
various
Tennents Scottish Cup, 4th round
various

Feb 21
Coca-Cola , semi-final 1, 2nd leg
tbc

Feb 25
Coca-Cola , semi-final 2, 2nd leg
tbc

Mar 9
Tennents Scottish Cup, 5th round
various
FA Cup, 6th round
various

Mar 13
BUSA Football Final
Milton Keynes

Mar 16
England v Italy, women
Italy

Mar 24
Coca-Cola Cup Final
Wembley

Mar 31
FA Cup semi-finals
various

Apr 6
Tennents Scottish Cup, semi-finals
various

Apr 14
Auto Windscreens Shield Final
Wembley

Apr 18
England v Croatia, women
Croatia

Apr 28
FA Women's Cup Final
tbc

May 1
UEFA Cup Final, first leg
tbc

May 4
Irish Cup Final
Windsor Park, Belfast
FA Premiership, final weekend
various

May 8
European Cup Winners' Cup Final
tbc

May 11
FA Cup Final
Wembley

May 15
UEFA Cup Final, second leg
tbc

May 18
Tennents Scottish Cup Final
Hampden Park

May 19
Welsh Cup Final
National Stadium, Cardiff
England v Portugal, women
tbc

May 22
European Champion Clubs Cup Final
tbc

May 25
Third Division Play-off Final
Wembley

May 26
Second Division Play-off Final
Wembley

May 27
First Division Play-off Final
Wembley

June 8-30
European Championship
Various, England

ATHLETICS
Feb 10
International Indoor Meeting
Birmingham

Mar 8-10
European Indoor Championships
Stockholm, Sweden

Mar 23
World Cross-country Championships
Cape Town, South Africa

Apr 13
World Road Relay Championships
Copenhagen, Denmark

May 3-4
Atlanta International Meeting
Atlanta, United States

May 4
BUSA Championships
Birmingham, England

May 11
Grand Prix I Meeting
Sao Paulo, Brazil

May 19
Grand Prix I Meeting
New York, United States

May 25
Bruce Jenner Classic, GP I
San José, United States

June 5
Golden Gala GP I
Rome, Italy

June 22-23
European Cup - Super League
Madrid, Spain

July 1
Grand Prix I Meeting
Paris, France

July 3
Grand Prix I Meeting
Lausanne, Switzerland

July 5
Bislett Games GP I
Oslo, Norway

July 9
DN Galan GP I
Stockholm, Sweden

July 12
Grand Prix I Meeting
Crystal Palace

July 15
Nikaia Meeting GP I
Nice, France

Aug 10
Grand Prix I Meeting
Monte Carlo

Aug 11
IAAF Permit Meeting
Edinburgh

Aug 14
Weltklasse GP I
Zürich, Switzerland

Aug 18
Weltklasse (Cologne) GP I
Cologne, Germany

Aug 21-25
World Junior Championships
Sydney, Australia

Aug 23
Iva Van Damme Meeting GP I
Brussels, Belgium

Aug 25
IAAF Permit Meeting
Sheffield

Aug 30
ISTAF '96
Berlin, Germany

Sep 7
Grand Prix Final
tbc

Oct 5-6
World Half-marathon Champs
Palma de Mallorca, Spain

Dec 14 or 15
European Cross-country Championships
Charleroi, Belgium

BADMINTON
Mar 12-17
All England Championships
tbc

Apr 14-21
European Championships
Herning, Denmark

May 17-26
Thomas & Uber Cup Finals
Hong Kong

Nov 19-24
World Junior Championships
Silkeborg, Denmark

Dec 10-15
World Grand Prix Finals
tbc

BASEBALL
Oct 21
World Series starts
tbc, United States

BASKETBALL
Mar 21
European Cup Final, women
tbc

Mar 3
Sainsbury's National Cup Finals
Sheffield Arena

Mar 6
European Rochetti Cup Fl, 1st leg
tbc

Mar 6
European Korac Final, 1st leg
tbc

Mar 12
European Cup Final, men
Vitoria, Spain

Mar 13
European Rochetti Cup Final, 2nd leg
tbc
European Korac Cup Fl, 2nd leg
tbc

Apr 11
European Championship Final for Men's Clubs
Paris, France

Apr 25th
NBA Play-offs start
various, United States

May 4-5
Budweiser Championships Finals
Wembley

BIATHLON
Jan 11-14
World Cup (Race 3)
Antholz, Italy

Jan 18-21
World Cup (Race 4)
Osrblie, Sweden

Feb 1-4
European Championships
tbc

Feb 11-18
World Championships
Ruhpolding , Germany

Feb 25-Mar 3
Junior World Championships
Osrblie, Sweden

Mar 7-10
World Cup (Race 5)
Pokljuka, Slovenia

Mar 14-17
World Cup (Race 6)
Badgastein, Austria

BILLIARDS
Feb 27-Mar 7
Strachan UK Championships
Wigan, England

Sep 25-30
World Championships
Bombay, India

BOBSLEIGH
Jan 22-28
European Championships
St Moritz, Switzerland

Jan 29-Feb 2
British Championships
St Moritz, Switzerland

Feb 8-24
World Championships
Calgary, Canada

BOWLS
Feb 12-25
Churchill World Indoor Singles
Preston, England

Mar 4-6
**British Isles Indoor
Championships & International
Series**
Auckinlech, Scotland

Mar 18-31
World Championships
Adelaide, Australia

Apr 13-27
English Indoor Championships
Melton & District

July 1-5
British Isles Championships
tbc, Ireland

BOXING
Aug 18-30
EBA National Championships
Worthing, England

Mar 6
ABA Finals
NIA, Birmingham

Mar 28-Apr 8
European Championships
Vejle, Denmark

CANOEING
Mar 30-31
**British Olympic Slalom Trials,
race 1**
Holme Pierrepont, Nottingham

Apr 6
**British Olympic Slalom Trials,
race 2**
River Tay, Grandtuly, Perth

May 11-12
Flatwater Olympic Qualifying
Seville, Spain

June 8-9
**Flatwater National
Championships**
Holme Pierrepont, Nottingham

Aug 24-25
World Marathon Championships
Vaxholm, Sweden

CRICKET
Jan 2-6
England v South Africa, 5th Test
Cape Town, South Africa

Jan 9
**England v South Africa,
1st One-day International**
Cape Town, South Africa

Jan 11
**England v South Africa,
2nd One-day International**
Bloemfontein, South Africa

Jan 13
**England v South Africa,
3rd One-day International**
Johannesburg, South Africa

Jan 14
**England v South, 4th
One-day International**
Centurion Park, South Africa

Jan 17
**England v South Africa,
5th One-day International**
Durban, South Africa

Jan 19
**England v South Africa,
6th One-day International**
East London, South Africa

Jan 21
**England v South Africa,
7th One-day International**
Port Elizabeth, South Africa

Feb 11-Mar 17
World Cup
various, Pakistan & India

May 23
**England v India,
1st One-day International**
The Oval

May 25
**England v India,
2nd One-day International**
Headingley

May 26
**England v India,
3rd One-day International**
Old Trafford

June 6-10
England v India, 1st Test
Edgbaston

June 11
Benson & Hedges Cup Final
Lord's

June 24
BUSA Cricket Final
Luton

June 20-24
England v India, 2nd Test
Lord's

July 4-9
England v India, 3rd Test
Trent Bridge

July 25-29
England v Pakistan, 1st Test
Lord's

Aug 3-21
**Lombard World Challenge
(U-15 World Cup)**
England

Aug 8-12
England v Pakistan, 2nd Test
Headingley

Aug 22-26
England v Pakistan, 3rd Test
The Oval

Aug 29
**England v Pakistan,
1st One-day International**
Old Trafford

Aug 31
**England v Pakistan,
1st One-day International**
Edgbaston

Sep 1
**England v Pakistan,
3rd One-day International**
Trent Bridge

Sep 7
**NatWest Bank Trophy
Final**
Lord's

CROQUET
July 7-14
British Championships
Hurlingham Club, London

Nov
**International Team
Championships**
Cape Town, South Africa

CURLING
Mar 9-17
**World Junior
Championships**
Red Deer, Alta, Canada

Mar 23-31
World Championships
Hamilton, Canada

CYCLING

Jan 14
National Cyclo-cross Championships
Birmingham

Mar 23
Milan-San Remo World Cup race
Italy

Apr 7
Tour of Flanders World cup race
Belgium

Apr 14
Paris-Roubaix World Cup race
France

Apr 21
Liège-Bastogne-Liège World Cup race
Belgium

Apr 27
Amstel Gold - World Cup race
Netherlands

May 18-June 9
Giro d'Italia - Tour of Italy
Italy

June 23
British Professional Road Racing Championships
England

June 29-July 21
Tour de France
France

Aug 10
San Sebastian Classic World Cup race
Spain

Aug 18
Leeds Classic World Cup race
Leeds

Aug 25
Championship of Zürich World Cup race
Switzerland

Aug 28-Sep 7
World Track Championships
Manchester, England

Sep 7-29
Vuelta a España Tour of Spain
Spain

Sep 14-22
World Mountain Bike Championships
Cairns, Australia

Oct 3
World Championship time trial
Switzerland

Oct 6
World Championship road race
Switzerland

Oct 13
Paris-Tours - World Cup race
France

Oct 19
Tour of Lombardy World Cup race
France

Oct 27
Japan Cup - World Cup race
Japan

DARTS

Dec 27-Jan 1
WDC World Championship
Circus Tavern, Purfleet

Jan 1-7
Embassy World Championships
Lakeside CC, Frimley Green, Surrey

EQUESTRIANISM

Mar 3
Showjumping Event
Birmingham

Apr 17-21
Volvo World Cup Final
Gothenburg, Sweden

May 2-5
Badminton 3-Day Event
Badminton

May 30-June 2
Hickstead Showjumping
Hickstead, Sussex

June 6-9
Bramham 3-Day Event
Bramham

July 25-28
World Vaulting Championships
Kaposvar, Hungary

Aug 27-Sep 1
World Driving Championships
Waregem, Belgium

Sep 5-8
Burghley 3-Day Event
Burghley House, Stamford, Lincs

Sep 19-22
Blenheim 3-Day Event
Blenheim, Woodstock, Oxon

Sep 21-22
World Endurance Championships
Fort Riley, United States

Dec 18-22
Olympia International
Olympia, London

FENCING

Jan 27
British Epee Chamionships
tbc

Mar 16
British Sabre Championships
tbc

Apr 27
Ipswich Cup, women's epee
tbc

May 4
British Foil Championships
tbc

GREYHOUND RACING

June 22
Greyhound Derby Final
Wimbledon

GOLF

Mar 28-31
The PLAYERS Championship
Sawgrass, Ponte Vedra, Florida
United States

Apr 11-14
US Masters
Augusta, Georgia, United States

May 16-19
Benson & Hedges International
Open
The Oxfordshire, Thame, Oxon

May 24-27
Volvo PGA Championship
Wentworth, Surrey

May 30-June 2
Women's US Open
Southern Pines, North Carolina
United States

June 6-9
English Open
Forest of Arden, Warwicks

June 13-16
US Open
Oakland Hills, Birmingham
United States

June 19
BUSA Team Championship
Nottingham, England

July 10-13
The Scottish Open
Carnoustie, Angus

July 18-21
The Open Championship
Royal Lytham & St Annes

Aug 8-11
US PGA
Valhalla GC, Louisville, Kentucky,
United States

Aug 29-Sep 1
European Masters
Crans-sur-Sierre, Switzerland

Sep 20-22
Solheim Cup
St Pierre Hotel CC, Chepstow

Oct 24-27
THE TOUR Championship
Southern Hills CC, Tulsa,
Oklahoma, United States

Oct 24-27
Volvo Masters
Valderrama, Sotogrande, Spain

Oct 31-Nov 3
**Sarazen World Open
Championship**
Atlanta, United States

Nov 21-24
World Cup of Golf
tbc

Dec 19-22
World Championship
Montego Bay, Jamaica

GYMNASTICS
May 6-13
European Championships, men
Copenhagen, Denmark

May 16-19
**European Championships,
women**
Birmingham NEC

May 21-23
World Rhythmic Championships
Hungary

Nov 16-17
**British Championships
men**
tbc

Oct 4-6
**British Championships
women**
Guildford, Surrey

HANDBALL
May 11
British Cup Final
tbc

May 23-June 2
European Championship, men
tbc, Spain

Oct 7-8
Hummel Supercup
Nottingham

Dec 5-17
World Championship, women
tbc, Austria

HOCKEY
Jan 19-28
**Olympic Qualifying Tournament,
men**
Terrassa, Spain

Jan 26-28
**European Indoor Nations Cup
women**
Glasgow

Feb 17-18
**European Indoor Club
Championship-women**
Bratislava, Slovakia

Mar 9
Ireland v England, women
Dublin

Apr 5-8
**European Clubs Cup Winners
Cup-women**
tbc

Apr 27-28
**County Championships Finals
women**
Bournemouth

May 24-27
**European Club championship
Women**
tbc

June 13-16
**Four Nations Tournament
men & women**
Milton Keynes

HORSE RACING
Mar 12
Champion Hurdle
Cheltenham

Mar 14
Cheltenham Gold Cup
Cheltenham

Mar 30
Grand National
Aintree

Apr 27
Whitbread Gold Cup
Sandown

May 4
Madagans 2000 Guineas
Newmarket

May 5
Madagans 1000 Guineas
Newmarket

June 8
Vodafone Derby
Epsom

June 9
Vodafone Oaks
Epsom

June 18-21
Royal Ascot Meeting
Ascot

July 6
Coral-Eclipse
Sandown

July 30-Aug 1
Goodwood Meeting
Goodwood

July 27
**King George VI and Queen
Elizabeth Stakes**
Ascot

Aug 20-22
York Meeting
York

Sep 28
Queen Elizabeth II Stakes
Ascot

Oct 19
Dubai Champion Stakes
Newmarket

Nov 16
Mackeson Gold Cup
Cheltenham

Nov 30
Hennessy Gold Cup
Newbury

Dec 27
King George VI Chase
Kempton

ICE HOCKEY
Mar 30-31
British Championship
Wembley

Apr 4-14
World Championship, Pool B
tbc, Netherlands

Apr 21-May 5
World Championship, Pool A
Vienna, Austria

ICE SKATING
Jan 22-28
**European Figure Skating
Championships**
Sofia, Bulgaria

Feb 23-25
Grand Prix Final
Paris

Mar 18-24
World Figure Skating Championships
Edmonton, Canada

JUDO
Apr 13
British Open Championships
Birmingham NIA

May 9-12
European Championships
Den Haag, Netherlands

Oct 19-20
European Team Championships
St Petersburg, Russia

KARATE
Mar 11
English Championship
Crystal Palace

May 3-5
EKU '96
tbc, France

KORFBALL
Jan 6-7
European Clubs Indoor Champ.
Crystal Palace

Apr 13
National League Championship Final
Crystal Palace

LACROSSE
Apr 13
Scotland v England, women
tbc, Scotland

Apr 20
England v Wales, women
tbc, England

LUGE
Jan 8-14
European Championships
Sigulda, Latvia

Jan 29-Feb 4
World Championships
Altenberg, Germany

MODERN PENTATHLON
July 6-7
British Championships
Milton Keynes

MOTOR CYCLING
Mar 31
Malaysian GP
Shah Alam

Apr 7
Indonesian GP
Sentul

Apr 14
Le Mans 24-hour
France

Apr 21
Japanese GP
Suzuka

May 12
Spanish GP
Jerez, Spain

May 26
Italian GP
Mugello

June 9
French GP
tbc

June 29
Dutch GP
Assen, Netherlands

July 7
German GP
Nürburgring

July 21
British GP
Donington

Aug 4
Austrian GP
Österreichring

Aug 18
Czech GP
Brno

Sep 29
Brazilian GP
Jacarepagua, Rio

Sep 1
Imola GP
Italy

Sep 15
Catalunyan GP
Barcelona, Spain

Oct 6
Argentinian GP
Buenos Aires

Oct 20
Australian GP
Eastern Creek

MOTOR RACING
Mar 3
Indy Car World Series (Race 1)
Homestead Motorsports, US

Mar 17
Indy Car World Series (Race 2)
Nelson Piquet Raceway, Rio, Brazil

Mar 22-23
Vauxhall Rally of Wales
Chester

Mar 31
Indy Car World Series (Race 3)
Surfers Paradise, Queensland, Australia

Apr 8
British Touring Car Championship (rds 1/2)
Donington Pk

Apr 14
Indy Car World Series (Race 4)
Long Beach, California, United States

Apr 21
British Touring Car Championship (rds 3/4)
Brands Hatch

Apr 27-28
Pirelli Rally
Carlisle

Apr 28
Indy Car World Series (Race 5)
Nazareth Speedway, Penn, United States

May 6
British Touring Car Championship (rds 5/6)
Thruxton

May 19
British Touring Car Championship (rds 7/8)
Silverstone

May 27
British Touring Car Championship (rds 9/10)
Oulton Park England

June 2
Indy Car World Series (Race 6)
Milwaukee, Wisconsin, United States

June 9
Indy Car World Series (Race 7)
Detroit, Michigan, United States

July 14
Indy Car World Series (Race 10)
Toronto, Canada

June 16
British Touring Car Championship (rds 11/12)
Snetterton

June 23
Indy Car World Series (Race 8)
Portland International Raceway United States

June 30
British Touring Car Championship (rds 13/14)
Brands Hatch

June 30
Indy Car World Series (Race 9)
Cleveland, Ohio, United States

June 31-July 2
Perth Scottish Rally
Scotland

July 13-14
**British Touring Car
Championship (rds 15/16)**
Silverstone

July 14
British Grand Prix
Silverstone

July 28
Indy Car World Series (Race 11)
Michigan International Speedway,
United States
**British Touring Car
Championship (rds 17/18)**
Knockhill

Aug 1-3
Ulster Rally
Belfast

Aug 11
**British Touring Car
Championship (rds 19/20)**
Oulton Park

Aug 11
Indy Car World Series (Race 12)
Mid-Ohio Sports Car Course, United
States

Aug 18
Indy Car World Series (Race 13)
Road America, United States

Aug 26
**British Touring Car
Championship (rds 21/22)**
Thruxton

Sep 1
Indy Car World Series (Race 14)
Vancouver, Canada

Sep 8
Indy Car World Series (Race 15)
Laguna Seca Raceway, California,
United States
**British Touring Car
Championship (rds 23/24)**
Donington Park

Sep 12-14
Manx International Rally
Douglas, Isle of Man

Sep 22
**British Touring Car
Championship (rds 25/26)**
Brands Hatch

Nov 24-27
RAC Rally
Chester

NETBALL
Feb 24
England v Northern Ireland
tbc, England

Mar 9
England v Republic of Ireland
tbc, Ireland

Mar 23
England v Wales
tbc, England

Apr 28
National Club Final
tbc, England

OLYMPICS
July 20-Aug 4
Olympic Games
Atlanta, United States

ORIENTEERING
May 4-5
British Championships
Oban, Scotland

POLO
May 10-26
Prince of Wales' Trophy
Royal Berkshire PC

May 21-June 2
Warwickshire Cup
Cirencester

June 4-23
Queens Cup
Guards PC

June 29-July 21
The Gold Cup - British Open
Cowdray Park

July 28
International Day
Guards PC

RACKETBALL
Mar 22-24
**National Singles
Championships**
Bromley, Kent

Nov 22-24
**National Doubles
Championships**
Bromley, Kent

RACKETS
Jan 27-28
**Professional Singles
Championships**
Harrow, Middx

May 12
The Queen's Club Cup
Queen's Club, London

REAL TENNIS
Jan 5-9
**Professional Doubles
Championships**
Queen's Club, London

May 6-12
**Professional Singles
Championships**
Holyport

ROWING
Mar 30
Head of the River
River Thames, London

Apr 6
The Beefeater Boat Race
River Thames
(Putney to Mortlake)

May 17-19
Duisburg Regatta
Germany

May 31-June 2
**The Rotsee
Lucerne Regatta**
Switzerland

July 13-14
Nations Cup
Hazewinkel, Belgium

June 8-9
Hazewinkel Regatta
Belgium

June 22-23
Women's Henley
River Thames, Henley

Jul 3-7
Henley Royal Regatta
River Thames, Henley

Jul 19-21
National Championships
Holme Pierrepont
Nottingham

Aug 6-11
World Championships
Strathclyde, Scotland

RUGBY LEAGUE
Jan 13
Regal Trophy Final
tbc, England

Mar 28
Super League starts
various

Apr 27
**Silk Cut Challenge Cup
Final**
Wembley

RUGBY UNION

Jan 7
European Club
Championships Final
National Stadium, Cardiff

Jan 20
France v England, Five Nations
Parc des Princes, Paris
Ireland v Scotland, Five Nations
Lansdowne Road, Dublin

Feb 3
England v Wales, Five Nations
Twickenham
Scotland v France, Five Nations
Murrayfield, Edinburgh

Feb 17
Wales v Scotland, Five Nations
National Stadium, Cardiff
France v Ireland, Five Nations
Parc des Princes, Paris

Mar 2
Ireland v Wales, Five Nations
Lansdowne Road, Dublin
Scotland v England, Five Nations
Murrayfield, Edinburgh

Mar 16
England v Ireland, Five Nations
Twickenham
Wales v France, Five Nations
National Stadium, Cardiff

Mar 20
BUSA Rugby Final
Twickenham

Mar 30-31
Hong Kong Sevens
Hong Kong

Apr 20
Hawick Sevens
Scotland
County Championship Final
Twickenham

May 4
Swalec Cup
National Stadium, Cardiff
The Pilkington Cup Final
Twickenham

May 11
Middlesex Sevens
Twickenham
SRU Tennent's 1556
Cup Final
Murrayfield, Edinburgh

Nov 30
Ireland v Australia
Lansdowne Road
Dublin

SHOOTING

Mar 26-Apr 1
European Air Gun
Championships
Budapest, Hungary

Apr 10-16
World Cup round
Lima, Peru

Apr 18-19
World Cup round
Guatemala

Apr 22-29
World Cup round
Atlanta, United States

May 27-30
World Cup round
Munich, Germany

May 29-30
World Cup round
Plsen, Czech Republic

June 2-7
World Cup round
Milan, Italy

June 4-7
World Cup round
Lonato, Italy

June 10-16
World Cup round
Suhl, Germany

June 26-July 3
European Clay Pigeon
Championships
Tallin, Estonia

July 13-27
Queen's Prize Meeting
Bisley

SKIING, ALPINE

Jan 6-7
World Cup, men
Flachau, Austria
World Cup, women
Maribor, Slovenia

Jan 12-14
World Cup, men
Kitzbühel, Austria

Jan 13-14
World Cup, women
Garmisch Partenkirchen
Germany

Jan 16
World Cup, men
Adelboden, Switzerland

Jan 19-21
World Cup, men
Wengen, Switzerland
World Cup, women
Cortina d'Ampezzo, Italy

Jan 23
World Cup, men
Valloire, France

Jan 27
World Cup, men & women
Sestriere, Italy

Jan 28
World Cup, women
Megeve/St Gervais, France

Feb 2-3
World Cup, men & women
Garmisch Partenkirchen, Germany
World Cup, women
Crans Montana, Switzerland

Feb 10
World Cup, men & women
Hinterstode, Austria

Feb 11-25
World Championships
Sierra Nevada, Spain

Mar 2-3
World Cup, men & women
Nagano, Japan

Mar 4-10
World Cup Final, men & women
tbc

Mar 17-24
British Championships
Tignes, France

Mar 22-24
World Cup Final
Meiringen, Switzerland

SKIING, NORDIC

Mar 15-17
World Cup Final
Oslo, Norway

SNOOKER

Jan 27-Feb 3
Regal Welsh
Newport Centre, Wales

Feb 4-11
Benson & Hedges
Wembley Conference Centre

Mar 8-16
Thailand Open
Bangkok

Feb 18-24
International Open
tbc

Feb 26-Mar 3
European Open
tbc

Mar 26-31
Benson & Hedges Irish Masters
Goffs Complex, County Kildare
Ireland

Apr 1-8
British Open
Plymouth Pavilions

Apr 20-May 6
World Championship
Crucible Theatre, Sheffield

May
Women's World Championship
tbc

SPEED SKATING
Jan 5-6
British Short Track Championships
Guildford

Jan 19-21
Long Track European Championships
Heerenveen, Netherlands

Jan 20-21
European Short Track Championships
Oberstdorf, Germany

Feb 2-4
Long Track World Championships
Inzell, Germany

Mar 1-3
World Short Track Championships
The Hague, Netherlands

SPEEDWAY
Sep 8
Long Track World Championship Final
Herxheim, Germany

Sep 15
Team World Championship Final
Miskolc, Hungary

SQUASH
Jan 9-15
National Championship
tbc

Apr 10-21
British Open
tbc

May 2-5
European Team Championships
tbc, Netherlands

Oct 6-19
Women's World Championship
Guadeloupe, West Indies

SWIMMING
Jan 6-7
World Cup 1
Hong Kong

Jan 24-25
World Cup 2
Sheffield

Jan 27-28
World Cup 3
Espoo, Finland

Jan 30-31
World Cup 4
Malmo, Sweden

Feb 3-4
World Cup 5
Paris

Feb 6-11
World Cup 6
Genoa & Florence, Itlay

Mar 21-24
GB Olympic Trials
Sheffield

June 22-July 3
World Masters Championships
Sheffield

July 11-14
ASA National Championships
Leeds

July 14
Long Distance Swimming World Cup
Lausanne/Evian

Nov 2-4
National Synchronised Swimming Championships
tbc, England

Dec 12-15
ASA National Winter Championships
Sheffield

TABLE TENNIS
Jan 10-14
European Olympic Qualifying Tournament
Manchester

Jan 19-21
European Nations Cup
Bayreuth, Germany

Apr 5-8
English Open
tbc

Apr 25-May 5
European Championships
Bratislava, Slovakia

Sep 5-8
Women's World Cup
tbc

Oct 10-13
Men's World Cup
tbc

Dec 12-15
World Grand Prix Finals
tbc

TENNIS
Jan 15-28
Australian Open
Melbourne, Australia

Feb 5
Davis Cup World Group, 1st round
various

Mar 11-17
Newsweek Champions Cup (ATP Super 9)
Indian Wells, California, US

Mar 16-25
The Lipton Championships (ATP Super 9)
Key Biscayne, Florida, US

Apr 1
Davis Cup World Group, 2nd round
various

Apr 22-28
Volvo Monte Carlo Open (ATP Super 9)
Monte Carlo

Apr 22
Federation Cup World Group, 1st round
various

Apr 26-28
Davis Cup, Euro/African Zone Group 1, 1st round (Britain's group)
tbc

May 6-12
Panasonic German Open (ATP Super 9)
Hamburg, Germany

May 13-19
Nokia Italian Open (ATP Super 9)
Rome, Italy

May 27-June 9
French Open
Roland Garros, Paris

June 10-16
Stella Artois Championships
Queen's Club, London

June 17-22
Direct Line Championships
Eastbourne

June 17-23
Nottingham Open
Nottingham

June 24-July 7
The Championships
Wimbledon

July 8
Federation Cup, 2nd round
various

July 12-14
**Davis Cup, Euro/African Zone
Group 1, 2nd round (Britain's
group)**
tbc

Aug 5-11
**Thriftway ATP Championships
(ATP Super 9)**
Cincinnati, US

Aug 19-25
**Canadian Open
(ATP Super 9)**
Toronto, Canada

Aug 26-Sep 8
US Open
Flushing Meadows, New York State
United States

Sep 16
**Davis Cup World Group, 3rd
round**
various

Sep 20-22
**Davis Cup, Euro/African Zone
Group 1, 3rd round
(Britain's group)**
tbc

Sep 23
**Federation Cup,
3rd round**
various

Oct 21-27
**Eurocard Open
(ATP Super 9)**
Stuttgart, Germany

Oct 28-Nov 3
**Paris Open
(ATP Super 9)**
Paris

Nov 18-23
WTA TOUR Championships
New York

Nov 25
Davis Cup Final
tbc

TENPIN BOWLING
Sep 19-22
British Open
Nottingham Bowl

Mar 9-24
BTBA National Championships
Swindon Superbowl

TRAMPOLINING
July 6-7
English National Championships
Kettering

Aug 23-25
World Championships
Vancouver, Canada

Nov 23
Scottish National Championships
tbc

TRIATHLON
Aug 24-25
World Championships
Cleveland, Ohio

VOLLEYBALL
Mar 30
National Cup Finals
Sheffield

Apr 20-27
EVA Cup
tbc

WATER POLO
Feb 10-18
**Olympic Qualifying Tournament
(men)**
Berlin, Germany

June 29-July 7
Olympic Year Tournament
Papendal, Holland

July 13
Men's Club Finals
Sheffield

WATER SKIING
Jan 27
European Congress
Brighton, England

Aug 21-25
European Championships
Vallenbaek, Denmark

WEIGHTLIFTING
Mar 3
**British Powerlifting
Champioonships, women**
Manchester

Jun 29-30
**British Powerlifting
Championships, men**
Birmingham

WRESTLING
Mar 21-24
European Freestyle Style
Budapest, Hungary

Mar 27-30
European Greco-Roman Style
Budapest, Hungary

YACHTING
Jan 8-13
Tornado World Championship
Brisbane, Australia

Jan 13
Rothmans Rio Race
Cape Town-Rio

Jan 15-30
470 World Championship
Porto Alegre   Brazil

Mar 24-30
Soling World Championship
Punta Ala   Italy

May 4-11
Tornado European Championship
Attersee   Austria

May 8-15
Finn Gold Cup
La Rochelle, France

June 17-28
Cowes
Isle of Wight

Sep 19-27
Soling European Championship
Balaton, Hungary

Sports Federations ▬▬▬▬▬▬▬▬

AMERICAN FOOTBALL
British American Football
Association
22A Market Place, Still Lane,
Boston, Lincs PE21 6EH
Tel: 01205 363522
Fax: 01205 358139

ANGLING
National Federation of Anglers
Halliday House, Egginton Junction,
Nr Hilton, Derbyshire DE65 6GU
Tel: 01283 734735
Fax: 01283 734799

ARCHERY
Grand National Archery Society
National Agricultural Centre
Seventh Street, Stoneleigh Park
Kenilworth, Warwickshire CV8 2LG
Tel: 01203 696631
Fax: 01203 419662

ASSOCIATION FOOTBALL
The Football Association
16 Lancaster Gate, London W2
3LW
Tel: 0171 262 4542
Fax: 0171 402 0486

The Football League Ltd
319 Clifton Drive South
Lytham St Annes, Lancs FY8 1 JG
Tel: 01253 729421
Fax: 01253 724786

Football Association of Wales
3 Westgate Street, Cardiff CF1 1DD
Tel: 01222 372325
Fax: 01222 343961

Scottish Football Association
6 Park Gardens, Glasgow G3 7YF
Tel: 0141 332 6372
Fax: 0141 332 7559

Womens Football Association
9 Wyllyotts Place
Potters Bar, Herts EN6 2JD
Tel: 01707 651840
Fax: 01707 644190

ATHLETICS
British Athletic Federation
225a Bristol Road
Edgbaston
Birmingham B5 7UB
Tel: 0121 440 5000
Fax: 0121 440 0555

BADMINTON
Badminton Association of England
National Badminton Centre
Bradwell Road, Loughton Lodge
Milton Keynes MK8 9LA
Tel: 01908 568822
Fax: 01908 566922

BALLOONING
British Ballon and Airship Club
Forde Abbey Farm House
Chard, Somerset TA20 4LP
Tel: 01460 20880

BASEBALL
British Baseball Federation
66 Belvedere Road,
Hessle, North Humberside
Tel: 0482 643551
Fax: 0482 643551

BASKETBALL
English Basketball Association
48 Bradford Road, Stanningley
Leeds, W.Yorkshire LS28 6DF
Tel: 0113 236 1166
Fax: 0113 236 1022

BILLIARDS AND SNOOKER
World Ladies Billiards and Snooker
Association
3 Felsted Avenue, Wisbech
Cambs PE13 3SL
Tel: 01945 589589
Fax: 01945 589589

World Professional Billiards and
Snooker Association
27 Oakfield Road
Clifton, Bristol BS8 2AT
Tel: 0117 974 4491
Fax: 0117 974 4931

BOBSLEIGH
British Bobsleigh Association
The Chestnuts
85 High Street
Codford, Warminster
Wilts BN12 0ND
Tel: 01985 850064
Fax: 01985 850064

BOWLS
English Bowling Association
Lyndhurst Road
Worthing, W.Sussex BN11 2AZ
Tel: 01903 820222
Fax: 01903 820444

BOXING
Amateur Boxing Association
Crystal Palace National Sports
Centre
London SE19 2BB
Tel: 0181 778 0251
Fax: 0181 778 9324

British Boxing Board of Control
Jack Petersen House
52A Borough High Street, London
SE1 1XW
Tel: 071 403 5879
Fax: 071 378 6670

CANOEING
British Canoe Union
John Dudderidge House
Adbolton Lane, West Bridgford
Nottingham NG2 5AS
Tel: 0115 982 1100
Fax: 0115 982 1797

CRICKET
Test and County Cricket Board
Lord's Cricket Ground
St John's Wood
London NW8 8QN
Tel: 0171 286 4405
Fax: 0171 289 5619

Womens Cricket Association
41 St Michaels Lane
Headingley, Leeds LS6 3BR
Tel: 0532 742398

CROQUET
The Croquet Association
Hurlingham Club
Ranelagh Gardens
London SW6 3PR
Tel: 071 736 3148
Fax: 071 736 3148

CURLING
English Curling Association
Eric Hinds
Little Wethers
Sandy Lane
Northwood
Middlesex HA6 3HA
Tel: 01023 825004

CYCLING
British Cycling Federation
National Cycling Centre
Stewart Street
Manchester M11 4DQ
Tel: 0161 230 2301
Fax: 0161 231 0591

DARTS
British Darts Organisation
2 Pages Lane
Muswell Hill, London N10 1PS
Tel: 0181 883 5544
Fax: 0181 883 0109

EQUESTRIAN
British Equestrian Federation
British Equestrian Centre
Stoneleigh Park, Kenilworth
Warwickshire CV8 2LR
Terl: 0203 696697
Fax: 0203 696484

FENCING
Amateur Fencing Association
1 Barons Gate,
33 Rothschild Rd
London W4 5HT
Tel: 081 742 3032
Fax: 081 742 3033

GLIDING
British Gliding Association
Kimberley House
47 Vaughan Way,
Leicester LE1 4SE
Tel: 0116 253 1051
Fax: 0116 251 5939

GOLF
Professional Golfers' Association
Apollo House
The Belfry, Wishaw
Sutton Coldfield, W Mids B76 9PT
Tel: 01675 470333
Fax: 01675 470674

Womens Professional Golfers'
European Tour
The Tytherington Club
Dorchester Way, Tytherington
Macclesfield, Cheshire SK10 2JP
Tel: 0625 611444
Fax: 01625 610406

GREYHOUND RACING
National Greyhound Racing Club
24-28 Oval Road
London NW1 7DA
Tel: 0171 267 9256
Fax: 0171 482 1023

GYMNASTICS
British Amateur Gymnastics Assoc
Registered Office, Ford Hall
Lilleshall National Sports Centre
Newport, Salop TF10 9NB
Tel: 01952 820330
Fax: 01952 820326

HANDBALL
British Handball Association
60 Church Street
Radcliffe, Manchester M26 8SQ
Tel: 0161 7249656
Fax: 0161 7249656

HANG GLIDING
British Hang Gliding and Paragliding
Association
The Old School Room
Loughborough Road
Leicester LE4 5PJ
Tel: 0116 261 1322
Fax: 0116 261 1323

HOCKEY
All England Womens Hockey
Association
51 High Street
Shrewsbury SY1 1ST
Tel: 01743 233572
Fax: 01743 233583

The Hockey Association
Norfolk House
102 Saxon Gate West
Milton Keynes MK9 2EP
Tel: 01908 241100
Fax: 01908 241106

BRITISH HORSERACING BOARD
42 Portman Square
London W1H 0EN
Tel: 0171 396 0011
Fax: 0171 935 3626

ICE HOCKEY
British Ice Hockey Association
Second Floor Suite
517 Christchurch Road
Boscombe
Bournemouth BH1 4AG
Tel: 01202 303946
Fax: 01202 398005

JUDO
British Judo Association
7A Rutland Street
Leicester LE1 1RB
Tel: 0116 255 9669

LACROSSE
All England Womens Lacrosse Ass
4 Western Court
Bromley Street, Digbeth
Birmingham B9 4AN
Tel: 0121 773 4422
Fax: 0121 753 0042

English Lacrosse Union
Winton House, Winton Road
Bowdon, Altrincham
Cheshire WA14 2PB
Tel: 0161 928 9600

LAWN TENNIS
All England Lawn Tennis & Croquet
Club
Church Road
Wimbledon, London SW19 5AE
Tel: 0181 944 1066
Fax: 0181 947 8752

Lawn Tennis Association
The Queens Club
Barons Court, West Kensington
London W14 9EG
Tel: 0171 381 7000
Fax: 0171 381 5965

MARTIAL ARTS
British Kendo Association
Security House, LIttleton Drive
off Coxborough Lane
Huntingdon
Staffs WS12 4TS
Tel: 01543 466334
Fax: 01543 505882

English Karate Governing Body
12 Princes Avenue
Woodford Green, Essex IG8 0LN
Tel: 0181 599 0711

MODERN PENTATHLON
Modern Pentathlon Assoc. of GB
8 The Commons
Shaftesbury, Dorset SP7 8JU
Tel: 01747 855833
Fax: 01747 855593

MOTOR CYCLING
Auto-Cycle Union, ACU House
Wood Street, Rugby
Warwickshire CV21 2YX
Tel: 01788 540519
Fax: 01788 573585

MOTOR SPORTS
British Automobile Racing Club
Thruxton Racing Circuit
Thruxton, Andover
Hants SP11 8PN
Tel: 01264 772607
Fax: 01264 773794

RAC Motor Sports Association Ltd
Motor Sports House
Riverside Park, Colnbrook
Slough SL3 0HG
Tel: 01753 681736
Fax: 01753 682938

NETBALL
All England Netball Association
Netball House
9 Paynes Park
Hitchin, Herts SG5 1EH
Tel: 01462 442344
Fax: 01462 442343

ORIENTEERING
British Orienteering Federation
Riversdale, Dale Road North
Darley Dale, Matlock
Derbyshire DE4 2HX
Tel: 01629 734042
Fax: 01629 733769

POLO
Hurlingham Polo Association
Winterlake, Kirtlington
Oxford OX5 3HG
Tel: 01869 350044
Fax: 01869 350625

POOL
English Pool Association
44 Jones House
Penkridge Street, Walsall WS2 8JX
Tel: 01922 35587

RACKETS
Tennis and Rackets Association
c/o The Queens Club
Palliser Road, West Kensington
London W14 9EQ
Tel: 0171 386 3448

ROWING
Amateur Rowing Association
The Priory, 6 Lower Mall
Hammersmith, London W6 9DJ
Tel: 0181 741 5314
Fax: 0181 741 4658

RUGBY LEAGUE
The Rugby Football League
Red Hall
Red Hall Lane
Leeds LS 17 8NB
Tel: 0113 232 9111
Fax: 0113 232 3666

RUGBY UNION
The Rugby Football Union
Rugby Road
Twickenham, Middx TW1 1DZ
Tel: 0181 892 8161
Fax: 0181 892 9816

Irish Rugby Football Union
62 Lansdowne Road
Ballsbridge, Dublin
Tel: 00 3531 668 4601
Fax: 00 3531 660 5640

Scottish Rugby Union
7/9 Roseburn Street
Edinburgh EH12 5PJ
Tel: 0131 3372346

Welsh Rugby Union
PO Box 22, Cardiff CF1 1JL
Tel: 01222 390111
Fax: 01222 378472

Womens Rugby Football Union
Meadow House, Springfield Farm
Shipston-on-Stour
Warwickshire CV36 4HQ
Tel: 01703 453371 Ext. 4348

SHOOTING
National Rifle Association
Bisley Camp, Brookwood
Woking, Surrey GU24 0PB
Tel: 01483 797777
Fax: 01483 797285

SKATING
National Ice Skating Association of
UK Ltd
15-27 Gee Street,
London EC1V 3RE
Tel: 0171 2533824
Fax: 0171 4902589

SKIING
British Ski Federation
258 Main Street
East Calder, Livingston
West Lothian EH53 0EE
Tel: 01506 884343
Fax: 01506 882952

SPEEDWAY
Speedway Control Board Ltd
ACU Headquarters, Wood Street
Rugby, Warwickshire CV21 2YX
Tel: 01788 540096
Fax: 01788 552308

SQUASH
Squash Rackets Association
PO Box 1106
London W3 0TD
Tel: 0181 746 1616
Fax: 0181 746 0580

SWIMMING
Amateur Swimming Association
Harold Fern House, Derby Square
Loughborough, Leics LE11 0AL
Tel: 01509 230431
Fax: 01509 610720

TABLE TENNIS
English Table Tennis Association
Queensbury House, Havelock Road
Hastings, E.Sussex TN34 1HF
Tel: 01424 722525
Fax: 01424 422103

TENPIN BOWLING
British Tenpin Bowling Association
114 Balfour Road
Ilford, Essex IG1 4JD
Tel: 0181 478 1745
Fax: 0181 514 3665

TRAMPOLINING
British Trampoline Federation Ltd
146 College Road
Harrow, Middx HA1 1BH
Tel: 0181 863 7278

TRIATHLON
British Triathlon Association
PO Box 26
Ashby de la Zouche
Leicester LE65 2ZR
Tel: 01530 414234
Fax: 01530 560279

TUG-OF-WAR
Tug-of-War Association
57 Lynton Road
Chesham, Bucks HP5 2BT
Tel: 01494 783057
Fax: 01494 772040

VOLLEYBALL
British Volleyball Federation
27 South Road, West Bridgford
Nottingham NG2 7AG
Tel: 0115 981 6324
Fax: 0115 945 5429

WATER SKIING
British Water Ski Federation
390 City Road, London, EC1V 2QA
Tel: 0171 833 2855
Fax: 0171 837 5879

WEIGHTLIFTING
British Amateur Weight Lifters
Association
3 Iffley Turn
Oxford OX4 4DU
Tel: 01865 778319
Fax: 01865 249281

WRESTLING
British Amateur Wrestling
Association
41 Great Clowes Street, Salford
Greater Manchester M7 9RQ
Tel: 0161 832 9209
Fax: 0161 833 1120

YACHTING
Royal Yachting Association
RYA House, Romsey Road
Eastleigh, Hants SO50 9YA
Tel: 01703 629962
Fax: 01703 629924